Encyclopedia of

Women *and*

Gender

SEX SIMILARITIES AND DIFFERENCES
AND THE IMPACT OF SOCIETY ON GENDER

L–Z
VOLUME TWO

Encyclopedia of

Women and

Gender

SEX SIMILARITIES AND DIFFERENCES AND THE IMPACT OF SOCIETY ON GENDER

EDITOR-IN-CHIEF

Judith Worell

University of Kentucky, Lexington

L–Z

VOLUME TWO

ACADEMIC PRESS
A Harcourt Science and Technology Company

San Diego   San Francisco   New York   Boston   London   Sydney   Tokyo

The sponsoring editor for this encyclopedia was Nikki Levy, the senior developmental editor was Barbara Makinster, and the production managers were Joanna Dinsmore and Molly Wofford. The cover was designed by Linda Shapiro. Composition was done by ATLIS Graphics & Design, Camp Hill, PA, and the encyclopedia was printed and bound by Edwards Brothers, Ann Arbor, MI.

This book is printed on acid-free paper. ♾

Academic Press
A Harcourt Science and Technology Company
525 B Street, Suite 1900, San Diego, California 92101-4495, USA
http://www.academicpress.com

Academic Press
Harcourt Place, 32 Jamestown Road, London NW1 7BY, UK
http://www.academicpress.com

Library of Congress Catalog Card Number:

International Standard Book Number: 0-12-227245-5 (Set)
International Standard Book Number: 0-12-227246-3 (Volume 1)
International Standard Book Number: 0-12-227247-1 (Volume 2)

PRINTED IN THE UNITED STATES OF AMERICA
01 02 03 04 05 06 EB 9 8 7 6 5 4 3 2 1

CONTENTS

T

W

CONTENTS OF VOLUME ONE

A

B

C

D

E

G

F

H

I

PREFACE

When I entered the field of psychology, theory and research related to women and gender were relatively invisible. The majority of research within the social sciences was based on the assumption that data obtained mainly from the lives and perspectives of men represented the totality of human experience. The rise of a revitalized women's movement provided the impetus for scholars and researchers to challenge the absence of knowledge about the lives of girls and women. In the ensuing years, a plethora of gender-related scholarship and research produced an abundant body of literature that changed the direction of the discipline. We began asking new questions, naming new problems, confronting the limitations of traditional research paradigms, and applying the fruits of our research to issues of human welfare, public policy, and social justice. The outcome of these efforts is a revised discipline that provides a rich source of theory and research on the psychology of women and gender.

Purpose and Scope

This encyclopedia provides comprehensive coverage of the many topics that encompass current research and scholarship on the psychology of women and gender. The content of these volumes is intended to be accessible to and informative for students and scholars searcall academic disciplines, as well as interested readers in the public or corporate domains who wish to explore and expand their understanding of the factors that influence the diverse lives of women and men. Many articles will be particularly interesting and relevant to those in allied professions such as nursing, social work, medicine, and the law.

The authors include prominent and outstanding experts on gender, as well as some excellent emergent scholars. The articles cover a broad array of topics related to the psychology of gender, with additional contributions searcallied social sciences including sociology, anthropology, and communications. In contrast to earlier considerations of gender as the study of sex differences, the authors of these articles present a wide range of perspectives on the multiple meanings of sex and gender. Many authors point out that differences among women and groups of women, for example, are greater than most differences that may be found between women and men. Thus, comparisons across the diversity of women is as important as those between the two sexes. Our main focus here is on understanding girls and women in the context of their lives and experiences. In particular, the importance of context is emphasized throughout, in recognition thatcall behavior is multidetermined and assumes meaning only if understood within particular cultures, situations, and historical time frames. Across the articles attention is given to multicultural issues of diversity in human experience, including those related to nationality, economics, sexuality, and racial/ethnic variables. Our overall goal is to explore through theory and research how social and cultural influences have structured and shaped the gender-related roles, behaviors, well-being, life events, and opportunities afforded to diverse groups of women and men.

Content

The articles in this volume are comprehensive and cover topics in depth rather than in condensed formats. Each article reviews a theme that is important to the psychology of gender in human experience and includes a glossary of relevant concepts and timely references that will be invaluable for further reading. Although the content is ordered alphabetically by title, we conceptualized and developed it more broadly according to significant topical areas. A sample of these topics is summarized below.

The basis of most psychological research rests on theoretical structures that provide a framework and assumptions about human nature and experience. Several articles discuss theories of gender development from the perspectives of evolutionary psychology, biology and genetics, social construction, psychoanalysis, social roles, social learning, gender schemas, the history of gender study, and the feminist movement. Next we considered that in examining theories and questions related to women and gender, researchers depend upon a variety of quantitative and qualitative methods. Standard empirical methods of research and analysis, as well as some newer approaches to understanding people's lives, are carefully explained and evaluated. Several articles examine the characteristics of feminist research and the implications of research on sex differences for our understandings of gender. Then, since gender development is multidetermined, we present reviews of major periods and issues in women's development, including cognitive development, gender acquisition and expression in childhood and adolescence, children's play patterns, marriage, motherhood, childcare options, divorce and child custody, mid-life, menopause, and aging.

Psychologists have traditionally been interested in personality; we review the research on gender-related personal characteristics such as social identity, self-esteem, empathy, emotional expressiveness, assertiveness, anger, humor, leadership, ethical/moral judgment, personal and social power, entitlement, and aggression. Health and mental health are important to the well-being of girls and women; we cover topics on life satisfaction, health care, stress and coping, trauma, depression, eating disorders, agoraphobia, anxiety, body image, attractiveness, safer sex behaviors, reproductive technologies, abortion, substance abuse, chronic illiness, disability, psychiatric diagnosis, and recovered memories. Various approaches to psychotherapy and counseling are included to consider alternatives for women's healing and well-being. In all these articles, implications across cultures and social policy are integrated.

Moving to dyadic and community relationships, we explore research on friendship, love, intimacy, lesbian and heterosexual partnering, family, sexuality and sexual desire, and social support. Since most women are involved in heterosexual relationships at some time in their lives, we include an article on men and conceptions of masculinity. Societal or cultural contributions to gender development are reflected in articles on parenting in diverse cultures, academic and achievement options, educational settings, school climate, media influences, and participation in sports and athletics. Gender-related research on work and employment environments is covered in articles on affirmative action, mentoring, nontraditional careers, work–family balance, career achievement, women in the military, and employment-related sexual harassment.

The gender-related effects of biased experiences and minority status include articles on stereotyping, prejudice, androcentrism, test bias, self-fulfilling prophesies, ethnicity and sexual orientation, and poverty. A number of articles cover the critical research area of gender-related violence and implications for social policy. Violence in the lives of women is addressed in reviews of child physical and sexual abuse, emotional abuse, women-battering, rape, sexual misconduct with clients in therapy, hate crimes, prostitution and the sex industry, media violence, torture, and imprisonment. As an important factor in implementing social policy, we include an article on political behavior. We anticipate that the many exciting and interesting reviews in these volumes will stimulate readers to explore further in their own areas of interest.

Collaboration

An original and ambitious enterprise such as this could not have been accomplished without the collaboration of a distinguished, capable, and hardworking Executive Advisory Board. Together, we generated the topics to be covered and the names of article authors who could best contribute to the excellence of the reviews. I am grateful to these colleagues for their wisdom and perspective in selecting an outstanding group of eminent and accomplished authors. I appreciate their continuing interest and support in bringing these volumes to fruition. I am also grateful for and appreciative of the efforts of each of the superb article authors, who carved out time in their crowded schedules to help us complete this outstanding work.

Finally, I thank the staff at Academic Press for their sustained involvement and support. I thank Nikki Levy for her insight in initiating the development and production of these volumes and for her generosity in negotiating an acceptable range of ti-tles, and Barbara Makinster for her consummate patience and skills in arranging the mechanics of the production with both efficiency and grace. I am confident that these volumes will represent an outstanding and useful contribution to our understanding and appreciation of the lives of women and men in the context of the realities of contemporary society.

Judith Worell

ABOUT THE EDITOR-IN-CHIEF

JUDITH WORELL is professor emerita and past chair of the Department of Educational and Counseling Psychology at the University of Kentucky. She received her Ph.D. from the Ohio State University and is a licensed clinical psychologist. She has served as associate editor of the *Journal of Consulting and Clinical Psychology* and as editor of the *Psychology of Women Quarterly*. She served an eight-year term as member and chair of the Publications and Communications Board of the American Psychological Association and also has served on the editorial board of numerous psychology journals. She has over 100 publications and presentations, including eight books.

Dr. Worell has been highly active in both community and professional organizations on behalf of girls and women and was president of the Kentucky Psychological Association, the Southeastern Psychological Association, and the Society for the Psychology of Women, a division of the American Psychological Association. She has been named Outstanding Graduate Professor at the University of Kentucky, Lexington Woman of the Year, Distinguished Kentucky Psychologist, and Distinguished Leader for Women of the American Psychological Association. She was awarded a Presidential Citation from the American Psychological Association for her continuing work on the concerns of women, and an honorary doctorate of letters from Colby-Sawyer College. Dr. Worell's current research focuses on process and outcomes of feminist therapy with women and on a model of women's mental health that emphasizes women's empowerment and resilience.

ABOUT THE EXECUTIVE ADVISORY BOARD

JANET SHIBLEY HYDE is chair of the Department of Psychology and Helen Thompson Woolley Professor of Psychology and Women's Studies at the University of Wisconsin–Madison. She is the author of two undergraduate textbooks on the psychology of women and human sexuality. For more than a decade she has carried out a program of research using meta-analysis to synthesize the existing research on psychological gender differences. In addition, she is conducting a longitudinal study on maternity leave and how women balance work and family. She is a past president of the American Psychological Association Division 35, the Society for the Psychology of Women.

KEN POPE is in independent practice as a licensed psychologist. His practice, research, writings, and presentations specifically address the needs of people who have experienced political or governmental torture, contracted AIDS, endured racial, sexual, and other forms of discrimination or harassment, experienced physical or sexual assault, were exploited by therapists, or lacked access to traditional services. He has developed and implemented models for providing preventive, clinical, and other services in these areas. His publications include 10 books and over 100 articles and chapters in peer-reviewed scientific and professional journals and books. He is a charter fellow of the American Psychological Society (APS) and a fellow of the American Psychological Association (APA) Divisions 1, 2, 12, 29, 35, 41, 42, 44, and 51. He received the APA Division 12 Award for Distinguished Professional Contributions to Clinical Psychology, the APA Division 42 Presidential Citation "In Recognition of His Voluntary Contributions, His Generosity of Time, the Sharing of His Caring Spirit [and] His Personal Resources," and the APA Award for Distinguished Contributions to Public Service.

PAMELA TROTMAN REID is professor of psychology and education at the University of Michigan in Ann Arbor and a research scientist at the University's Institute for Research on Women and Gender. Dr. Reid earned her Ph.D. from the University of Pennsylvania and has been an educator for more than 30 years, holding faculty and administrative positions at several universities. Her research has focused on gender and ethnic issues, particularly on the intersections of gender and race as they impact African American women and children. Dr. Reid has published numerous journals articles and book chapters in this arena as well as on the socialization of girls and boys, issues of poverty, and prejudice. She is a fellow of the American Psychological Association and has been on the Board of Educational Affairs there as well as having been president of the Division of Psychology of Women. She has received a number of awards, including the Distinguished Leadership Award by the Committee on Women in Psychology and the Distinguished Publication Award from the Association of Women in Psychology. She has also been named one of 100 Distinguished Women in the Psychology of Women.

STEPHANIE RIGER   is professor of psychology and gender and women's studies at the University of Illinois at Chicago. She received her doctorate from the University of Michigan and is the recipient of the American Psychological Association's Division 27 Award for Distinguished Contributions to Research and Theory and a two-time winner of the Association for Women in Psychology's Distinguished Publication Award. Dr. Riger is the author of numerous journal articles and books on gender psychology. Her current research focuses on the impact of welfare reform on intimate violence and the evaluation of domestic violence and sexual assault services.

JANIS SANCHEZ-HUCLES   is a professor of psychology at Old Dominion University in Norfolk, Virginia, and a clinical psychologist in private practice in Virginia Beach, Virginia. She is also a faculty member of the Virginia Consortium in Clinical Psychology and a community faculty member of Eastern Virginia Medical School. Dr. Sanchez received her Ph.D. from the University of North Carolina–Chapel Hill, and she has been involved in developing and teaching courses titled The Psychology of Women, The Psychology of African Americans, and Diversity Issues in Psychodynamic Therapy. Her research has focused on clinical training, women and families of color, diversity, feminism, and issues pertaining to trauma and violence, and she is the author of numerous book chapters and journal articles and a book in this area. Dr. Sanchez is a fellow of the American Psychological Association (APA) and has served on a variety of APA committees, including an APA Presidential Task Force on Violence and the Family, task forces on the restructuring of the council of representatives and on the integration of science and practice, the APA Council of Representatives, the Committee on Structure and Function of Council, the advisory board for the APA Science Directorate, the Board of Educational Affairs, and the Executive Board for Division 35, the Society for Psychology of Women. She is also past chair of the APA's Committee on Urban Initiatives.

BRENDA TONER   is currently head of the Women's Mental Health and Addiction Research Section at the Centre for Addiction Mental Health and professor and head of the Women's Mental Health Program, Department of Psychiatry, University of Toronto. Dr. Toner received her Ph.D. from the University of Toronto, followed by a postdoctoral fellowship in eating disorders. She has published and presented on a variety of health-related problems that are disproportionately diagnosed in women, including eating disorders, anxiety, depression, chronic pelvic pain, chronic fatigue, and irritable bowel syndrome. She is particularly interested in investigating factors in the lives of women that cut across diagnoses, including violence, body dissatisfaction, poverty, discrimination, gender role conflicts, and isolation. One of her major research interests is psychosocial assessment and treatment of functional gastrointestinal disorders.

CHERYL BROWN TRAVIS   is a professor in the Department of Psychology at the University of Tennessee, specializing in gender-diversity issues and health psychology, with an emphasis on policy, planning, risk perception and communication, and decision making. She is a fellow of the American Psychological Association and a past president of the Society for the Psychology of Women. Publications by Dr. Travis include books on women's health as well as articles on medical decision making and physician practice patterns. Her professional activities have involved symposia on medical decision making and informed consent. She has participated in a briefing to members of Congress on women's health issues and has provided formal Senate testimony on authorization hearings for the Environmental Protection Agency, in which she advocated behavioral and psychological approaches to environmental health. She is currently an associate editor of *American Psychologist* and the founding editor of the *Psychology of Women* book series.

HOW TO USE THE ENCYCLOPEDIA

The *Encyclopedia of Women and Gender* is intended for use by students, research professionals, and practicing clinicians. Articles have been chosen to reflect major disciplines in women's studies and gender issues, common topics of research by professionals in this domain, and areas of public interest and concern. Each article serves as a comprehensive overview of a given area, providing both breadth of coverage for students and depth of coverage for research professionals. We have designed the encyclopedia with the following features for maximum accessibility for all readers.

Articles in the encyclopedia are arranged alphabetically by subject. Complete tables of contents appear in all volumes. The index is located in Volume 2. Because the reader's topic of interest may be listed under a broader article title, we encourage use of the Index for access to a subject area, rather than use of the Table of Contents alone. Because a topic of study is often applicable to more than one article, the Index provides a complete listing of where a subject is covered and in what context.

Each article contains an outline, a glossary, cross-references, and a suggested reading section. The outline allows a quick scan of the major areas discussed within each article. The glossary contains terms that may be unfamiliar to the reader, with each term defined *in the context of its use in that article*. Thus, a term may appear in the glossary for another article defined in a slightly different manner or with a subtle nuance specific to that article. For clarity, we have allowed these differences in definition to remain so that the terms are defined relative to the context of the particular article.

The articles have been cross-referenced to other related articles in the encyclopedia. Cross-references are found at the first or predominant mention of a subject area covered elsewhere in the encyclopedia. Cross-references will always appear at the end of a paragraph. Where multiple cross-references apply to a single paragraph, the cross-references are listed in alphabetical order. We encourage readers to use the cross-references to locate other encyclopedia articles that will provide more detailed information about a subject.

The suggested readings at the close of each article list recent secondary sources to aid the reader in locating more detailed or technical information. Review articles and research articles that are considered of primary importance to the understanding of a given subject area are also listed. This section is not intended to provide a full reference listing of all material covered in the context of a given article, but is provided as a guide to further reading.

Leadership

Virginia E. O'Leary

Elizabeth H. Flanagan

Auburn University

Glossary

Gender composition of the work environment The finding that the numbers of women and men in an organization affect the subjective states and the behavior of women in the organization.

Gender-role congruency hypothesis The idea that women are evaluated more negatively when they adopt masculine leadership styles than when they adopt feminine leadership styles.

Male managerial model The empirical finding that the concept of "manager" is more like the conception of "male" than "female."

Myths about female (in)competence The prevailing notion that women are not successful managers despite the research evidence, which suggests that there are few, if any, gender differences in the leadership effectiveness of men and women.

Social role theory A theory which posits that men and women are expected to participate in activities that are in accordance with their culturally defined gender roles.

Transformational leadership A style of leadership that involves mobilizing power to change social systems and reform institutions, and also involves raising the consciousness of followers by appealing to their higher ideals and moral values.

THE ISSUE OF GENDER AND LEADERSHIP has been an important topic in the past 30 years as women have become a stronger presence in the workforce. Meta-analyses examining differences in men's and women's leadership style, emergence, evaluation, and effectiveness have found few gender differences. Given the lack of empirical support for gender differences in leadership, the important question is, then, why are women not better represented in leadership positions? In 1974, Virginia E. O'Leary offered a model of barriers to women's leadership. The past 25 years of research have empirically supported the external barriers to women's leadership (sex-role stereotypes, myths about female competence, and the male managerial model), but not the internal barriers (low self-esteem, fear of failure, fear of success, and role conflict). Based on this research, we present a new model of barriers to women's leadership. Cultural factors affecting the number of women in leadership positions include sex role stereotypes, social roles, the male managerial model, and myths about female competence. Factors affected by both culture and individual differences are self-construal and gender schemas. The relationship between these factors and the number of women leaders is moderated by the gender composition of the environment. This model suggests that the barriers to women's leadership are socially constructed and that there is a simple solution: alter the gender composition of organizations and the number of women who lead them will also change.

I. An Overview of the Literature on Gender and Leadership

As women began leaving their homes for the workplace in the 1960s, gender and leadership emerged as a topic of interest for psychology. Early questions centered on barriers to the advancement of women into positions of status and power. In the past decade, four meta-analyses were conducted investigating whether there were gender differences in leadership style, effectiveness, evaluation, and emergence. These meta-analyses found few large gender differences, and most were small. Today, labor statistics show that gender differences in the number of men and women in higher-level positions, and wages that they receive in these positions are smaller than they have ever been before. According to the U.S. Bureau of the Census, since 1993 there has been a 29% increase in the number of women in managerial positions (compared to a 19% increase for men). Also, since 1993 the number of *Fortune* 500 companies who have at least one woman on their board has increased by 21%. Though the situation for women is better than it has ever been, it is still not what it should be. Industries with the highest proportion of female board members are "female-oriented" industries (toys, cosmetics, savings institutions, publishing, etc.), and women still earn 73 cents for every dollar a man earns.

What factors prevent women from having equal representation in the higher-level positions and earning equal wages, and how can these factors be eliminated? In an attempt to answer this question, findings from the literature on gender and leadership will be reviewed, focusing on the meta-analyses. Then, Virginia E. O'Leary's 1974 model, describing barriers to women's leadership will be presented and evaluated against the current research evidence. Finally, a new model of barriers to women's leadership will be presented.

Research on the relationship between gender and leadership is substantial. When the words *gender* and *leadership* were entered as key words into PsycINFO (done February 10, 2000), 418 entries were found. Many of the studies cited in this list were conducted by social psychologists investigating features or correlates of leadership. The focus of these studies is varied, but includes the examination of gender differences in leadership, people's perceptions of leaders (and how those perceptions are affected by gender stereotypes), methods for assessing leadership, and the relationship between leadership and self-esteem, self-concept, and self-efficacy. The settings in which these studies were conducted also varies. Many studies examine how leadership works in organizational (field) settings using correlational designs. Laboratory studies manipulate leadership behavior in college students and examine the effect. One popular publication outlet for laboratory studies is *Sex Roles*.

Some research on leadership is conducted by clinical or counseling psychologists interested in leadership and its correlates among therapists and therapy supervisors. A substantial portion of articles examining gender and leadership are dissertations (81), and the results of most of these were not published in journals. Considering the number of dissertations conducted on this topic, it is surprising that more of them were not published. Many, if not most, doctoral students in psychology do not publish their dissertations. Still, a plausible alternative explanation for the low rate of publication is the possibility that the investigators failed to support their hypotheses. Null results are likely in dissertations since they are often a researcher's first solo work. Null results are particularly likely in dissertations of the relationship between gender and leadership, since meta-analyses show that there are very few differences in the behavior of men and women leaders.

Recently, an area of leadership that had received much attention is *transformational leadership*. In 1978, James M. Burns argued that transformational leadership involves mobilizing power to change social systems and reform institutions and raising the consciousness of followers by appealing to their higher ideals and moral values. A number of researchers have speculated that there are gender differences in the use of transformational leadership though there is a notable lack of evidence for this theory. A recent study of transformational leadership found that superiors evaluated female leaders as more transformational and female leaders rated themselves as more transformational. However, on the behavior-specific level, no gender differences were found between male and female leaders.

The literature on gender and leadership has grown considerably over time. There was an explosion of publications in the 1990s in response to meta-analyses by Alice Eagly and colleagues. Most of the articles at this time further investigated findings from the meta-analyses and found results that were generally consistent. Given that recent studies in this area fail to reach new conclusions and often obtain null results, it is noteworthy that the literature is growing. A growing literature about a subject indicates that the research community is interested in that subject. A subject whose literature has a flat or negative growth rate is considered a "dying" literature and that area is seen as less important to researchers in the field.

This chapter focuses on the findings from Eagly's meta-analyses that summarize many of the studies that have been done on the relationship between gender and leadership. However, there are other issues that are not addressed in these meta-analyses, such as the interdependence of leaders and followers examined by Edwin P. Hollander in 1992. Readers looking for a broader review of the literature on gender and leadership should examine D. Anthony Butterfield and James P. Grinnell's chapter, cited in the "Suggested Reading" section.

II. Findings from the Meta-analyses

Alice Eagly and colleagues published four prominent meta-analyses on gender and leadership in the early 1990s. Together these articles offer a comprehensive review of the social psychological literature on gender and leadership, covering the topics of leadership style, emergence of leaders, evaluation of leaders, and effectiveness of leaders. Since these studies have been so influential and since they summarize much of the research conducted on gender and leadership in the past 20 years, they will be discussed in depth.

A. LEADERSHIP STYLE

In 1990, Alice Eagly and Blair Johnson published the first meta-analysis investigating the relationship between gender and leadership style. The studies used in this meta-analysis were published between 1961 and 1987 and were listed in one of six prominent databases (e.g., *Psychological Abstracts, Disserta-*

tions Abstracts International). Each study had to fulfill four criteria that ensured that a representative, normal, adult sample was used. The studies were conducted in three different settings. This meta-analysis included 162 studies and 370 comparisons of men and women.

Studies included in this meta-analysis assessed task-oriented and interpersonally oriented styles of leadership. Those who lead with the *task accomplishment* leadership style lead by having subordinates follow rules and procedures, by maintaining high standards for performance, and by making leader and subordinate roles explicit. Those who have a more *interpersonally* oriented leadership style engage in behaviors such as helping and doing favors for subordinates, looking out for their welfare, explaining procedures, and being friendly and available. Another aspect of leadership style that was investigated was the extent to which leaders were autocratic versus democratic. Autocratic leaders discourage subordinates from participating in decision making, while democratic leaders are accepting of subordinates' desires to participate in decision making. Given the gender stereotypes, it is likely that men would be more autocratic (since they are seen as more instrumental or agentic), while women would be more likely to be democratic (since they are perceived to be more expressive and interpersonal).

Based on their meta-analysis, Eagly and Johnson found that the sex differences in interpersonal and task styles of leadership were quite small, and that women were slightly more concerned than men about both maintenance of interpersonal relationships and task accomplishment. Interestingly, differences between women's and men's styles depended on the setting of the study. The effect size for laboratory studies was the largest. Thus, in laboratory settings men were more likely to evidence interpersonal styles of leadership. In organizational and assessment settings, women were more likely to evidence interpersonal leadership styles but since the effect size was so small, this difference is negligible. The meta-analysis also showed that leadership style was related to the setting of the research. Women were more task oriented in female-dominated industries and men were more task oriented in male-dominated industries. In 1999, Maria Gardiner and Marika Tiggerman further substantiated this finding.

Women and men also differed in the extent to which they used *democratic and autocratic styles of leadership*. Across all three types of studies (i.e., laboratory, organizational, assessment), the effect size of the difference between men and women was moderate, with men favoring the autocratic style. Comparing across research settings this effect size was consistent, although smaller in value. All of these effect sizes are small and indicate only a moderate difference between men and women's leadership styles. Eagly and Johnson, however, do not qualify their conclusions on account of the moderate effect sizes and state only "women tended to adopt a more democratic or participatory style and a less autocratic or directive style than did men"(p. 233). This phrase in the abstract somewhat overstates the results obtained.

B. LEADERSHIP EMERGENCE

The second meta-analysis done by Alice Eagly and Steven Karau in 1991 examined the relationship between gender and leadership emergence in initially leaderless groups. In this analysis, 54 studies were found using the same search techniques as the previous meta-analysis. These studies, which contained 74 gender comparisons, used two experimental paradigms. In lab studies, undergraduates were put into problem-solving groups. A small proportion of these studies used Edwin I. Megargee's 1969 paradigm where participants with differing levels of dominance were asked to perform a task in which one participant was to be the leader and the other was to be the follower. A second type of study used students enrolled in university courses who were working on group projects. In both paradigms, many different leadership behaviors were measured. Direct measures of leadership included task contribution, social contribution, group members' ratings of each other, and researchers' ratings of who was the leader. Leadership was also measured through amount of participation. Finally, there were indirect measures of leadership such as who chose the leader of the group, who sat at the head of the table, and who initiated a discussion.

As in the first meta-analysis on leadership style, different kinds of leadership were assessed. Task leadership was assessed through group ratings of task contributions, researchers' coding of members' task behavior, and indices of production. Social leadership was measured through group members' ratings of social contributions, researchers' coding of positive social behaviors, and indices of liking by other group members. Most of the studies were designed to assess not task or social leadership

but leadership in general, and thus used various measures.

From this meta-analysis, Eagly and Karau concluded that men emerged as leaders more frequently than women did on task leadership, general leadership, and unspecified leadership. Women emerged more frequently as leaders on social leadership. Some of the effect sizes approached the "medium" range although others were "small." The effect size for women's greater social leadership was particularly small and should be interpreted with caution.

Some of the most interesting findings were the factors that moderated whether men emerged as leaders. First, men were less likely to become leaders when the task involved more social interaction. This finding is consistent with the results of studies indicating that women have a more interactive leadership style than men. Amount of time in the group affected whether men emerged as leaders. Men were more likely to emerge as leaders if groups met for short periods of time. Men were also less likely to emerge as leaders if the task of the group was perceived as feminine. In addition, the sex distribution of the group affected whether men emerged as leaders. The tendency for males to lead was weaker in groups with a female majority or equal numbers of females and males. Group size also affected whether males emerged as leaders. Males were most likely to become leaders in dyads. Finally, Eagly and Karau found that year of publication and age of participants were related to males' leadership emergence. Males were more likely to emerge as leaders in earlier studies and among older individuals.

C. LEADERSHIP EVALUATION

The third meta-analysis, done by Alice Eagly, Mona Makhijani, and Bruce Klonsky in 1992, investigated gender and leadership evaluation. Studies in this meta-analysis were selected using the same search methods used in the previous two meta-analyses. A total of 56 studies and 147 gender comparisons were included in the analysis. In these studies, all characteristics of the leader were held constant and the sex of the leader was varied. Two types of studies were used: (1) vignette studies and (2) studies where confederates were trained to lead in a particular way. Thus, these studies did not assess participants' evaluations of men and women who occupy leadership or managerial roles in natural settings.

From the meta-analysis, Eagly and colleagues concluded that there was a small tendency to evaluate female leaders less favorably than male leaders. They reported that men were rated higher on competence, satisfaction with the leader, and potency, while women were rated as having a better leadership style. When looking at specific leadership styles, however, they argued that women were higher on both interpersonal orientation and task orientation, consistent with what Eagly and Johnson had found. Given the small magnitude of these effect sizes, it is likely that there are no meaningful differences between men and women on these dimensions.

As in the previous meta-analysis, several moderators of these findings were identified. When investigating the relationship between leadership style, gender, and evaluation, it was found that women were perceived more negatively when they adopted more masculine, autocratic leadership styles than when they led in a more participatory way. Interestingly, though, both men and women were evaluated more favorably when they led in a feminine manner. Interesting interactions were also found based on the type of role occupied. Men were viewed more favorably than women in roles typically occupied by men (e.g., doctors, CEOs, etc.). Men and women were viewed almost equally favorably in roles typically occupied by women. There was also a relationship between the sex of the rater and evaluation of male and female leaders. Male raters were more likely than their female counterparts to devalue female leaders. Surprisingly, evaluation of performance was not related to perceived competence. More bias was displayed against women in written vignettes and male leaders were evaluated more favorably in recently published studies. The latter finding is provocative since it contradicts the common assumption that the evaluation of women has improved as they have received more equal opportunities.

D. LEADERSHIP EFFECTIVENESS

The last meta-analysis, done by Alice Eagly, Steven Karau, and Mona Makhijani in 1995, concerns gender and leadership effectiveness. In this analysis, 88 studies and 76 gender comparisons were investigated. They were found using the methods outlined in the description of Eagly and Johnson's meta-analysis. There were two types of studies. A few were laboratory studies with college students, but many more were organizational studies conducted with managers in a variety of organizations. The organizational studies compared male and female managers who had the same managerial role or type of role

(i.e., middle manager). In the laboratory experiments, leaders were usually randomly appointed to lead other students in solving a few problems for one experimental session. Effectiveness was regarded as the outcomes of leaders' behavior rather than as a particular type of behavior. To assess these outcomes, multiple criteria of effectiveness were used, such as ratings of leaders' performance, ratings of subordinates satisfaction with leaders, and measures of group and organizational productivity. Reputational ratings were also used as there is some evidence that consensual perceptions of leaders are moderately accurate.

In this analysis, Eagly and colleagues concluded that female and male leaders did not differ in effectiveness. However, in the discussion section they commented that there was much inconsistency across the studies, but that there were conditions in which male or female leaders were preferred. As in the meta-analysis of leadership evaluation, effectiveness ratings were related to the gender congruence of the role. Leadership roles defined in male terms favored male leaders; roles defined in feminine terms favored female leaders. Research published since this meta-analysis has found that perceived effectiveness of the manager is affected by the gender of the rater.

Additional analysis found that males were rated as more effective when they occupied a male role and their subordinates were men. Analysis by type of organization found that only military organizations favored male leaders. Analysis by level of leadership showed that men were more effective as first-level managers, while women were more effective in middle management positions. These results are interesting in light of findings that first-level managers are more concerned with accurate task completion and findings that women were more concerned with task completion. Second-level managers are asked to do more arbitration and be more involved in social interactions. Since Alice Eagly and Wendy Wood found in 1991 that women tend to be seen as more socially skilled than men, they may be seen as better suited for middle managerial roles. Analysis by rater showed that as in the meta-analysis of gender and evaluation, the higher the proportion of men among raters, the more the effectiveness ratings favored men.

E. SUMMARY

There do seem to be a few gender differences in leadership style and evaluation, although there are no gender differences in leadership effectiveness. Eagly and colleagues have highlighted these gender differences in their meta-analytic work. Aside from the few differences mentioned here, most of the findings from the meta-analyses failed to obtain convincing evidence for gender differences in leadership. When compiled across studies, most effect sizes for gender differences between men and women were close to $d = 0$. Thus, critics have argued that the effect sizes obtained by Eagly and colleagues do not indicate overall trends. For example, in 1996, Elizabeth Aries argued that many of the effect sizes that Eagly interpreted as indicating difference were below ($d = .2$). When $d = .2$, there is a 95% overlap between the distributions of males and females. Given this degree of overlap, the differences within each sex group may be considerably more important than the differences between the two groups.

III. *A 1974 Model of Gender and Leadership*

In 1974, Virginia E. O'Leary proposed one of the first heuristic models to explain the absence of women in positions of power and prestige in management (see Figure 1). She posited two kinds of barriers to women's advancement: external and internal. External barriers included attitudes about women's competence, the male managerial model, and sex stereotypes. Among the internal factors were low self-esteem, role conflict, fear of failure and fear of success. In 1973, Aletha H. Stein and Margaret M. Bailey argued that these internal barriers were kept in place by a lack of female role models and by socialization pressures aimed at ensuring that women's achievement motivation was expressed in terms of affiliation.

IV. *Evaluation of the 1974 Model*

More than 25 years have passed since the publication of O'Leary's model and many of the internal factors proposed as significant inhibitors of women's professional success have not withstood the test of empirical investigation. In contrast, most of the external barriers have not only been substantiated by further research, they have continued to impede women's progress into the ranks of the powerful in numbers commensurate with their representation in the population.

A. EXTERNAL FACTORS

1. Sex-Role Stereotypes

Stereotypes of men and women have remained stable during the past quarter century. In 1978, Paul D. Werner and Georgina W. LaRussa found that 62% of the adjectives used to describe men and 77% of the adjectives used to describe women continued to have currency after more than two decades. In 1991, David J. Bergen and John E. Williams gave college students 300 adjectives from the adjective checklist and asked them to rate whether the adjectives are more frequently associated with men or women. In 1982, John E. Williams and Deborah L. Best found evidence that gender stereotypes are universal. In a study of 25 countries, women were described as sentimental, submissive, and superstitious, while men were described as adventurous, independent, and strong. Despite changes in both the achieved and ascribed roles of women and men, stereotypes have remained remarkably persistent. Exceptions to prevailing stereotypes are disregarded and instead the instances that coincide with the stereotype are better remembered. Because of their pervasiveness, universality, and resistance to change, sex-role stereotypes remain important barriers to women's success as leaders. [*See* GENDER STEREOTYPES.]

2. Attitudes about Women's Competence

Since Inge K. Broverman and colleagues found in 1972 that male-valued traits constitute a competency cluster assumed antithetical to femininity, studies of attitudes about women's competence have investigated reactions toward women who adopt masculine leadership styles. The results of Eagly and colleagues' meta-analysis in 1992 indicated a slight tendency to assess female leaders negatively, especially among raters who were male. This was true, despite clear evidence found by Eagly and colleagues in 1995 that female and male leaders are equally effective.

Also, in 1992, Eagly and colleagues concluded that their findings provided support for the gender-role congruency hypothesis, which states that women are viewed negatively when they adopt masculine leadership styles. Given that male-valued traits represent a competency cluster, these results appear to suggest that women are evaluated more negatively when they behave competently. However, subsequent analysis showed that successful women leaders were not rated more harshly than men, and that when the quality of the woman's performance was not known, she

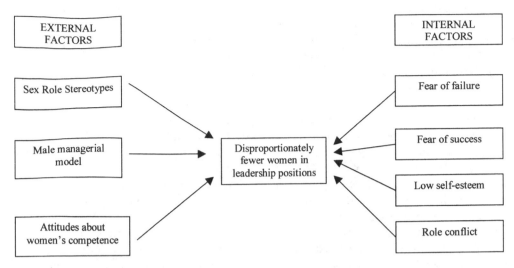

Figure I   O'Leary's (1974) model of barriers to women in leadership positions.

was not devalued. Thus, it is not competence per se that results in less favorable evaluations of women. However, when women display their leadership in a way that is perceived as masculine, they are evaluated more negatively. Interestingly, a recent study by Christine Kawakami, Judith B. White, and Ellen J. Langer in 2000 found that women who emulated a masculine leadership style in a mindful and thus genuine way were perceived by male subordinates (both college-aged and middle-aged) as effective, in contrast to women who emulated a masculine style of leadership mindlessly, who were seen as ingenuine. Mindfulness involves actively drawing novel distinctions that serve to keep one situated in the present and result in the observer's conviction that the actor's behavior is genuine.

3. The Male Managerial Model

In 1973 and 1975, Virginia E. Schein did studies which found that successful middle managers are perceived to have characteristics, attitudes, and temperaments that are more commonly attributed to males in general than females in general. A 1989 replication of this study, found that males adhered to the male managerial stereotype and indicated that successful managers would have the characteristics, attitudes, and temperaments more commonly ascribed to men. However, females viewed middle managers as having characteristics, attitudes, and temperaments that could be ascribed to both women and men. Recently, these studies have been done

cross-culturally. In a study of the United Kingdom, Germany, and the United States, Virginia E. Schein and Ruediger Mueller found in 1992 that males in all three countries responded like the males in the 1989 study: they perceived that middle managers have more male traits. For females, the pattern varied across countries. German females sex-typed the managerial position almost as much as males, U.K. females sex-typed the position less, and the U.S. females did not sex-type the position. In a 1996 study of management students in Japan and China, Virginia E. Schein, Ruediger Mueller, Terri Lituchy, and Jiang Liu found results similar to the original study. There was a strong association between male and manager for both the male and female students. From these results, Schein and colleagues concluded that "think manager think male" is a global phenomenon, especially among males. The only females who did show the sex-typing hypothesis were the U.S. females. These results suggest that the male managerial model is still an important barrier to women's success as leaders. [See CROSS-CULTURAL GENDER ROLES.]

B. INTERNAL FACTORS

1. Role Conflict

There has been much interest in the role conflict of women since these early studies. Alice Eagly's social role theory argues that women would feel conflict between their social role at work and their personal role as women. However, studies by

Rosalind C. Barnett and colleagues in 1985 and 1992 generally found that women's mental health and overall happiness ratings increase with multiple roles. n fact, in 1985, Rosalind C. Barnett and Grace K. Baruch found that women who work outside the home are in better physical and emotional health than women who are full-time homemakers. Barnett's 1992 analysis of these roles found that the quality of both men's and women's experiences in both worlds affects their distress level similarly. Work experiences did not affect men's mental health more than women's, and family experiences did not affect women's mental health more than men's. From these findings, Barnett concluded that gender is not related to role experiences and psychological distress. Instead, women's and men's distress is related to their happiness in their work and family roles.

2. Low Self-Esteem

The question of whether women have lower self-esteem has been of interest both to the popular media and psychological researchers. The opinion expressed by many in the media is that females have lower self-esteem. In psychology, two major reviews of gender differences in self-esteem done by Eleanor E. Maccoby and Carol N. Jacklin in 1974 and Ruth C. Wylie in 1979 suggested that there was no consistent gender difference. After the advent of meta analysis, a meta-analysis by Alan Feingold in 1994 and another by Judith A. Hall in 1984 found small differences in self-esteem favoring males. However, the focus on both of these studies was not gender differences in self-esteem; thus the coverage of the articles included is questionable. Differences in self-esteem have also been found as a function of race; Jacquelynne Eccles has found that African American girls have higher self-esteem than non–African American girls.

In 1999, a meta-analysis by Kristen C. Kling, Janet S. Hyde, Carolin J. Showers, and Brenda N. Buswell addressed the sole issue of gender differences in self-esteem. It improved on the methods of the previous meta-analyses through its conceptualization of self-esteem, the scope of its literature search, and its analysis of moderating variables, such as the age and ethnicity of the respondent and the self-esteem measure used. Kling and colleagues found that across studies that included 216 effect sizes, the overall effect size was $d = .21$, suggesting that males have higher self-esteem. Also, the largest effect sizes oc-

curred in late adolescence. In addition to conducting the meta-analysis, these researchers analyzed three data sets from the National Center for Education Statistics. All of the effect sizes from these data sets also suggested that males have higher self-esteem. When interpreting these results, the authors emphasize that the effects were quite consistent across studies. A total of 83% of the studies found a difference favoring males and the effect size was consistent across country, measure, and age. However, the authors also point out that that such an effect size is small by Jacob Cohen's standard and is also small in comparison with the magnitude of gender differences found in other studies. More important, the gender difference is small compared to effect sizes that have been shown to have important consequences in the laboratory. From analyzing other studies, the authors concluded that a self-esteem difference that had an effect size of $d = 1.64$ would be needed to attain significant differences in outcome measures.

An effect size less than 0.3 does not represent a great degree of difference between the two distributions. The considerable degree of overlap between the two distributions suggests that the intragender differences are likely to be more important than the intergender differences. Given the small effect size of the gender difference in self-esteem and the empirical demonstration that such an effect size would not be likely to cause significant differences in outcome, we suggest that low self-esteem is not an important deterrent to women's success as leaders. [See SELF-ESTEEM.]

3. Fear of Success

Fear of success was discussed by Matina S. Horner in 1972, who saw it as a mediating factor in whether women choose to achieve. According to Horner, success in a traditional masculine context may have a negative valence for women. Women fear that success may bring them social rejection and threaten their femininity and normality. The literature on the fear of success has had an interesting development over the past 25 years. Two studies, one by Theodore H. Wang and Carol F. Crededon in 1989 and another by Sharon Fried-Buchalter in 1997, found evidence that women had higher fear of success than men did. In 1989, Martha T. Mednick published an influential paper in the *American Psychologist* arguing that the construct of fear of success is more of a popular than intellectual construct.

Subsequent research looked at the relationship between fear of success and other constructs and concluded that the gender differences in fear of success could be due to gender role orientation, self-esteem, achievement motivation, and fear of the negative consequences of being deviant. Still other researchers have found no gender differences in fear of success. Also, the methods used to study fear of success have been criticized. In 1993, Joseph Kasof argued that age, intellectual competence, and attractiveness connotations are often confounded with fear of success in studies, thus it is difficult to know which variable is causing the effect. Because of these criticisms and because of the research findings that support other constructs, fear of success is no longer considered a barrier to women's leadership success.

4. Fear of Failure

Fear of failure is when one is motivated to avoid failure and the shame and humiliation associated with it. Researchers have argued that the tendency to avoid failure combats that to achieve success and results in lower achievement. The construct of fear of failure has been investigated extensively in the past 25 years. Some studies such as one by Alexander Minneart in 1999 have found that women have a higher fear of failure, while another study by Sharon Fried-Buchalter in 1997 found that there are no gender differences in fear of failure. A further study found that moderating variables affect the relationship between gender and fear of failure. In 1994, Herman Brutsaert and his colleague found that student well-being and low fear of failure were more related to the school environment than to the gender composition of the pupil population. Boys were negatively affected by a school environment composed largely of female teachers, while girls were not affected by the gender organization of the school. In a meta-analysis of studies in 1998 comparing gender differences in learning orientations, Sabine Severiens and Geert ten Dam found that women report more fear of failure than men. However, the gender differences varied across the studies and the effect size was small ($d = -.18$). Thus, since most studies found that gender was unrelated or only indirectly related to fear of failure, and since the meta-analysis showed that the effect size of the gender difference in the fear of failure across studies was small, we conclude that fear of failure is no longer an important barrier to the success of women leaders.

V. A 21st Century Model

Given that it has been more than 25 years since O'Leary's initial model of barriers to women's leadership was introduced and a great deal of research has been conducted on the factors comprising that model, as well as factors affecting general psychosocial health and performance of individuals, a new model of barriers to women's leadership is posited (see Figure 2). Many factors that are important to leadership (i.e., adult development, derailment, personality, leadership behaviors) do not differentially affect female and male leaders. They are not included in the model. The purpose of this model is to represent more global factors that affect the overall number of women in leadership positions.

The model includes some of the factors from the 1974 model as well as additional variables that have been found to be important to leadership in the past 25 years. The model divides the factors affecting women's leadership into two categories: cultural factors and factors affected by both individual differences and culture. Included within the umbrella of culture are different ethnicities. Both ethnicity and culture have important mediating effects on the subjective importance as well as expression of many of the factors in the model, in particular sex-role stereotypes, social roles, and self-construal.

A. CULTURAL FACTORS

The influence of culture is one of the most important topics in social psychology today. The cultural factors in O'Leary's original model that received strong empirical support (sex-role stereotypes, the male managerial model, and attitudes about women's competence) will not be discussed further, although they are included in the model. Only the role of one factor, sex-role stereotypes, is conceptualized in a new way. Sex-role stereotypes are hypothesized to affect the number of women in leadership positions through two paths: a direct path and another path through attitudes about women's competence. Of course, the subjective importance and the expression of sex-role stereotypes are also affected by culture and ethnicity.

1. Social Roles

Social roles represent a source of cultural barriers to women's leadership. Alice Eagly's social role

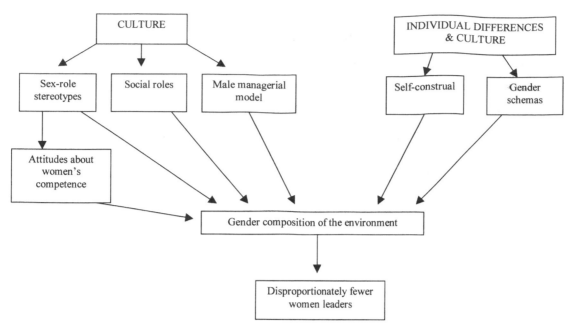

Figure 2   A 21st century model of barriers to women's leadership.

theory posits that "as a general tendency, people are expected to engage in activities that are consistent with their culturally defined gender roles" (p. 126). Domestic duties are no longer the primary role of women, but they are a prominent role. In 1999, Francine M. Deutsch argued that White, middle-class women still do more than 60% of the domestic work done in the home, while, in 1998, Rosalind C. Barnett and Carol Rivers argued that the gender distribution of domestic work is closer to equal. Daphne John, Beth Anne Shelton, and Kristen Luschen in 1995 studied multicultural families and found that African American and Hispanic men spent more time on housework than Caucasian men. They also found that there was no difference between Hispanic, African American, and Caucasian women in whether they thought the division of labor in their household was fair. However, when compared to their own husbands, African American and Caucasian women were significantly more likely to see the division of housework as unfair. [See SOCIAL ROLE THEORY OF SEX DIFFERENCES AND SIMILARITIES.]

The carryover into the workplace of gender-based expectations for behavior has been termed to be "gender-role spillover." Gender-role spillover results in different expectations for female and male managers. In a *Harvard Business Review* article in 1989, Felice N. Schwartz argued that women professionals could be categorized as those who are career ori-

ented and those who want to balance career and family. She described career-family-oriented women as being on the "Mommy-track" and suggested that they are seen by superiors as less committed to their jobs and as potential liabilities to the company. This position suggests that women's dual roles as care takers and professionals affects the perception of their capability. [See WORK–FAMILY BALANCE.]

Strong support for the social-role theory of sex differences was obtained by Sara E. Snodgrass in 1985 in studies examining the impact of sex (female versus male) and role (superior versus subordinate) on interpersonal sensitivity. She found that those in the subordinate role, regardless of sex, were more sensitive to the other's feelings than those in the superior role. Overall, women were generally more sensitive then men, regardless of what role they had been assigned, and women were less sensitive to other women then to men. Findings such as these have provided role-relevant explanations (rather than person-centered or trait-deficit explanations) for women's lower status in the marketplace compared to men's.

B. FACTORS AFFECTED BY BOTH CULTURE AND INDIVIDUAL DIFFERENCES

In addition to cultural variables, there are factors that are affected by both culture and individual differences that influence leadership.

1. Gender Schemas

In 1998, Virginia Valian, a cognitive psychologist, argued that we have gender schemas, implicit, non-conscious hypotheses about sex differences. These gender schemas alter our expectations and evaluations of women and men. These expectations and evaluations generally favor men. Over time, they accumulate and create advantage for men and disadvantage for women. Because of these gender schemas, then, men tend to be overrated and women to be underrated. Valian believes that gender schemas are learned. Parents teach these schemas through their treatment of differently gendered children and through encouraging children to engage in activities "appropriate" for their sex. She suggests that even parents who profess egalitarian beliefs act in accordance with the culture's view of what it means to be female or male. Gender schemas are also developed through the types of children's play and through the work assigned to children in the form of household chores. In 1998, Eleanor E. Maccoby reversed the differential emphasis given by Valian, arguing that same-sex play in childhood, not parental influence, is the primary shaper of cognitions about gender.

Although Valian's hypothesis provides a viable and interesting model of how men accumulate advantage and women accumulate disadvantage, one weakness of this model lies in its failure to accurately assess gender schemas. In 1974, Sandra M. Bem argued that her sex-role inventory differentiated between gender-schematic and gender-aschematic people. However, subsequent studies failed to support this claim, leading Janet T. Spence to conclude in 1993 that sex-role inventories measured only instrumental and expressive traits and were not measures of gender schemas. Despite this criticism, Bem's sex-role inventory continues to be used to assess gender schemas, and new measures of gender schemas have not been developed. Because gender schemas represent learned cognitive processes, they appear in the model as factors that are affected by both culture and individual differences.

2. Self-Construal

In 1991, Hazel R. Markus and Shinobu Kitayama argued that there are two kinds of self-construals: independent and interdependent. For those who have an independent self-construal, others are not central to their current self-definition or identity. On the other hand, for those with an interdependent self-construal, their sense of self is interdependent with the surrounding social context and others play an important part in their interpretation of their individual experiences. Markus and Kitayama argue that individuals from individualistic cultures have an independent self-construal while those from collectivist cultures have interdependent self-construals.

In 1997, Susan E. Cross and Laura Madson applied this model to the sex differences literature and concluded that observed differences in women's and men's behavior was the result of women's interdependent self-construal in contrast to the independent self-construals of men. Although this hypothesis has not been tested empirically yet, data from Eagly and Johnson's meta-analysis support it. Women's interdependent and democratic leadership style and men's independent and autocratic leadership style may be plausibly explained by differences in self-construal. It is important to note, as well, that this relationship between self-construal and leadership style may also be affected by cultural norms and norms of ethnic subcultures.

However, these findings do not deem that women will always be interdependent while men will always be independent. Eagly and Johnson found that leadership style was affected by the setting in that women were more likely to lead with an interpersonal and democratic style in more female-dominated organizations, while women's and men's leadership styles are more similar in male-dominated organizations. Perhaps the effect of self-construal is also moderated by the gender composition of the environment. Recent research has shown that self-construal and its effect on behavior is subject to environmental manipulation. In 1999, Wendi L. Gardner, Shira Gabriel, and Angela Y. Lee found that priming of independent or interdependent self-construals resulted in the participants adopting those self-construals, regardless of the type of self-constual that is typically found in that culture. Specifically, European Americans often have independent self-construals. However, when they were primed for interdependence, they shifted toward more collectivist social values. Similarly, when Hong Kong students (who typically have interdependent self-construals) were primed with independent stimuli, they adopted more individualistic values.

C. THE MODERATING VARIABLE: WORK ENVIRONMENT

Empirical research has generally shown that the gender composition of the work environment affects the subjective states of women. Specifically, studies have shown that the proportion of women in a group is related to the favorableness with which women regard the psychological environment. For instance, Eve Spangler and colleagues found that women in a law school where only a small proportion of the students were women scored significantly higher on measures of performance pressure and social isolation than did women in a school with a more balanced gender composition.

Studies have also found that the proportion of women in a workplace affects women's perceptions of their own efficacy and performance. In a study of local unions in 1995, Steven Mellor found that women in unions where only a small proportion of officers were women evaluated their own competence and ability to participate significantly lower than did women in unions with more women officers. Similarly, studies have found that women in groups with relatively few women members are less satisfied than women in more gender-balanced groups. For example, in 1992, Alison M. Konrad and colleagues found that women's social isolation increased and their job satisfaction decreased as the number of women in the organization declined. In addition, studies have demonstrated that the lower the proportion of women in a group, the more likely a woman is to consider leaving it.

Studies have found that the gender composition of the organization also affects the perception of men and women. Specifically, women are evaluated more negatively when there are fewer women in the organization. Robin J. Ely found that women in firms with few women were likely to characterize other women as "flirtatious" and "sexually involved with coworkers," while women in firms with more women were likely to characterize other women as "aggressive" and "able to promote oneself." Similarly, Ely found that women's attitudes toward male group members were most favorable when there were fewer women in the group. These attitudes became less favorable as the percentage of women in the group increased. These findings indicate that women's psychological satisfaction and positive attitudes toward women increase as the number of women in the organization increases. As women's satisfaction and the attitude toward women improves, the setting becomes more conducive for women leaders. Thus, the gender composition of the organization may represent a variable that moderates the number of women leaders likely to ascend to positions of power and authority.

VI. Summary and Conclusions

The goals of this article were to present an overview of the literature on gender and leadership, to evalu-

ate previous work addressing the absence of women in leadership positions, and to propose a new model to investigate barriers to women's leadership. According to the new model, most of the factors affecting the rise of women to leadership positions are cultural (i.e., sex-role stereotypes, social roles, and the male managerial model). Empirical studies have shown that the effect of these variables is moderated by the gender composition of the organization. These findings suggest that the solution to women's underrepresentation in the ranks of leaders is simple—change the numbers. If men's perception of women's effectiveness is preventing women from attaining leadership positions (as shown by Eagly and colleagues in their 1995 meta-analysis), changing the gender composition of the organization will make the observed sex differences disappear. If stereotypes of women leaders and the male managerial model result in fewer women emerging as leaders (as shown by Eagly and Karau's meta-analysis), changing the gender composition of the organization will change the role and stereotypic associations with that role.

The conclusion from this analysis of the literature on gender and leadership is that gender differences in leadership are not based on behavioral differences. Instead, gender differences in leadership represent a socially constructed phenomenon. The disproportionately low number of women leaders is caused by cultural stereotypes of women and by the perception of the manager role as one occupied by a male. It is held in place by organizations that have unequal gender compositions. Thus, the solution to the problem is far simpler than most people would think: changing the gender composition of organizations, especially at the highest levels, will change the number of women who lead them.

SUGGESTED READING

Aries, E. *Men and Women: An Interaction.* Harvard University Press, Cambridge, MA.

Butterfield, D. A., and Grinnell, J. P. (1999). In *Handbook of Gender and Work* (G. N. Powell, ed.). Sage, Thousand Oaks, CA.

Cleveland, J. N., Stockdale, M., and Murphy, K. R. (2000). *Women and Men in Organizations: Sex and Gender Issues at Work.* Erlbaum, Manwah, NJ.

Maccoby, E. E. (1998). *The Two Sexes: Growing up Apart, Coming Together.* Harvard University Press, Cambridge, MA.

Nieva, V. F., and Gutek, B. A. (1981). *Women and Work: A Psychological Perspective.* Praeger, New York.

Tanton, M. (ed.) (1994). *Women in Management: A Developing Presence.* Routledge, London.

Valian, V. (1998). *Why So Slow?* Massachusetts Institute of Technology, Cambridge.

Walsh, M. R. (ed.) (1997). *Women, Men, and Gender: Ongoing Debates.* Yale University Press, New Haven, CT

Lesbians, Gay Men, and Bisexuals in Relationships

Letitia Anne Peplau
Kristin P. Beals
University of California, Los Angeles

Glossary

Affirmative therapies New approaches to individual and couples' counseling that are based on knowledge about and acceptance of the life experiences of lesbians, gay men and bisexuals.

Commitment to a relationship An individual's desire to continue a relationship into the future.

Sexual identity An individual's self-definition as heterosexual, homosexual (gay man, lesbian woman), or bisexual.

Sexual orientation The extent to which an individual is emotionally and sexually attracted to other-sex partners (heterosexual), same-sex partners (homosexual), or both (bisexual).

Sexual prejudice Negative attitudes toward lesbians, gay men, bisexuals, and other members of sexual minority groups.

THE INTIMATE RELATIONSHIPS OF CONTEMPORARY LESBIANS AND GAY MEN are described and analyzed in a small but growing body of empirical research. This article reviews this literature and shows that contrary to stereotypes, these relationships do not typically mimic the gender-based roles of provider and homemaker found among heterosexual couples. Same-sex couples are often able to create satisfying, long-lasting relationships. Factors that enhance happiness and commitment in same-sex and heterosexual relationships tend to be similar. Researchers have also investigated specific types of interaction in same-sex couples, including sexuality and conflict. Therapists who counsel lesbians and gay men are increasingly aware of the special issues facing same-sex couples. Researchers are just beginning to investigate the intimate relationships of bisexual individuals.

I. Understanding Lesbian, Gay, and Bisexual Relationships

In understanding the relationships of lesbians, gay men, and bisexuals, three general issues are noteworthy. First, there are many commonalities in the nature of close romantic relationships regardless of the sexual orientation—lesbian, gay, bisexual, or heterosexual—of the partners. Human needs for intimacy, the capacity to form strong emotional attachments, and factors influencing the quality of close relationships show many similarities across all types of couples. Second, cultural conceptions of gender influence all relationships, but their impact differs for same-sex and male-female couples.

Third, as sexual minorities in our society, lesbians, gay men, and bisexuals confront unique challenges and opportunities. It is important to recognize the existence of widespread negative attitudes toward lesbians, gay men, and bisexuals, known as sexual prejudice. Although the attitudes of North Americans about civil rights for homosexuals have become more tolerant in recent years, many people continue to condemn homosexuality and discriminate against same-sex relationships. Studies have shown that hotel staff are less likely to accept a room reservation for a same-sex couple than an opposite-sex couple, and same-sex couples may confront biased service by store clerks. Many institutional policies, such as insurance regulations and hospital visitation rules, do not acknowledge gay and lesbian relationships. Moreover, lesbian and gay relationships have limited options for public recognition and legal status. We know little about how experiences of sexual prejudice affect the daily lives of gay and lesbian couples or about the strategies that same-sex couples use to cope with sexual prejudice.

Furthermore, the tendency to use heterosexual dating and marriage as standards for conceptualizing and evaluating intimate relationships has influenced not only public attitudes toward sexual minority couples, but also the questions asked by scientific researchers, and the way that therapists respond to gay and lesbian clients. At the same time, the creation of gay, lesbian, and bisexual subcultures and institutions has provided new social opportunities and sources of support for sexual minority couples. Freed from the constraints of traditional marriage, gay men, lesbians, and bisexuals have greater room for innovation in their relationships.

This article reviews major findings about the relationships of lesbians and gay men and presents preliminary information about the relationships of bisexuals. Available studies are limited in number and suffer from several methodological problems. Many homosexual and bisexual individuals are not fully open about their sexual orientation and may therefore be reluctant to volunteer for scientific research projects. Most research is based on convenience samples of younger, well-educated individuals. Relationship research often recruits only one partner from a couple. Participants' sexual identity—whether they define themselves as gay, lesbian, bisexual or heterosexual—is typically assessed by self-report. Further, lacking information from marriage records and census data, researchers studying same-sex couples are limited in their ability to obtain representative samples or to estimate population characteristics. Generalizations about lesbian and gay relationships must be made with caution.

II. Gender Roles in Gay and Lesbian Relationships

In Western society, heterosexual relationships have traditionally been structured by roles based on gender: the man is the provider and decision maker; the woman is the homemaker and follower. When both partners are of the same sex, how do couples organize their lives together? A common stereotype is that same-sex couples adopt husband-wife roles as a model for their relationships. In fact, most contemporary lesbians and gay men reject these roles.

A. PROVIDERS AND HOMEMAKERS

The provider-homemaker distinction is largely absent among lesbian and gay couples today. Most lesbians and gay men are in dual-earner relationships, so neither partner is the exclusive breadwinner and each partner is economically independent. The most common division of labor involves flexibility, with partners sharing domestic activities or dividing tasks according to personal preferences. In a 1978 study, Alan P. Bell and Martin S. Weinberg asked lesbians and gay men if one partner consistently does all the "feminine tasks" or all the "masculine tasks." Approximately 90% of lesbians and gay men said no. When asked which partner does the housework, nearly 60% of lesbians and gay men said that housework was shared equally.

In a 1993 study, Lawrence A. Kurdek looked at the division of household chores such as cooking, shopping, and cleaning in couples without children. Among heterosexual married couples, the wives typically did the bulk of the housework. In contrast, gay and lesbian couples were likely to split tasks so that each partner performed an equal number of activities. Gay men tended to arrive at equality by each partner specializing in certain tasks; lesbian partners were more likely to share tasks. Furthermore, among couples raising children, lesbian couples shared child care much more evenly than did heterosexual couples. Little is known about how gay male couples divide family work when children are present. In summary, although the equal sharing of household labor is not inevitable in same-sex couples, it is much more common than among heterosexuals.

B. POWER AND DECISION MAKING

Another area in which same-sex couples reject traditional marriage as a model concerns power and decision making. Lesbians and gay men are strong proponents of equality (equal power) in their relationships, although lesbians often endorse the value of equality even more highly than do gay men. Not all couples who strive for equality achieve this ideal. The percentage of lesbians and gay men describing their relationship as equal in power has varied across studies, but an estimate of roughly 60% is reasonable.

Researchers are beginning to identify factors that tip the balance of power away from equality. One hypothesis is that greater power accrues to the partner who has relatively greater personal resources, such as greater education, money, or social standing. Several studies have confirmed this prediction, with the clearest evidence being found for gay male couples. In their 1983 American Couples Study, Philip Blumstein and Pepper Schwartz considered several thousand gay, lesbian, and heterosexual couples. They found that income was an extremely important force in determining which partner was dominant in gay male couples. For lesbians, research findings on personal resources and power are less clear-cut. Two studies have found that partner differences in income were significantly related to power. In contrast, Blumstein and Schwartz concluded from their research that lesbians do not use income to establish dominance in their relationship but rather use it to avoid having one woman dependent on the other. Additional research on the balance of power among les-

bian couples is needed to clarify these inconsistent results.

A further aspect of power concerns the specific tactics that partners use to influence each other. In a 1980 study, Toni Falbo and Letitia A. Peplau asked lesbians, gay men, and heterosexuals to describe how they influence their romantic partner to do what they want. Analyses of responses led to two major results. First, gender affected power tactics, but only among heterosexuals. Whereas heterosexual women were more likely to withdraw or express negative emotions, heterosexual men were more likely to use bargaining or reasoning. This sex difference did *not* emerge in comparisons of lesbians and gay men influencing their same-sex partner. Second, regardless of gender or sexual orientation, individuals who perceived themselves as relatively more powerful in the relationship tended to use persuasion and bargaining. In contrast, partners low in power tended to use withdrawal and negative emotions. These results suggest that although some influence strategies have been stereotyped as masculine (e.g., bargaining) or feminine (e.g., withdrawal), their use may be understood more correctly as a reflection of power rather than gender. [*See* POWER.]

In summary, research shows that most contemporary lesbians and gay men reject "masculine" and "feminine" roles as the basis for organizing their lives together. Instead they create a more egalitarian pattern of shared responsibilities and decision making.

C. MODELS FOR SAME-SEX RELATIONSHIPS

In historical and cross-cultural perspective, men's and women's same-sex relationships are remarkable for their diversity. At least three distinctive patterns have been identified. The peer or friendship model that typifies many lesbian and gay male relationships in the United States today is not the only model for same-sex relationships. A second pattern is based on age differences between partners. In a 1984 study of gay male couples, Joseph Harry found that most partners were relatively similar in age, but a minority of couples involved a man over age 40 in a relationship with a man under 30. In such cases, the man who was older usually had greater income and tended to be more influential in couple decision making.

Finally, although not the predominant pattern in the United States today, same-sex relationships based on a model of gender roles have been described in other times and places. Many American Indian cultures permitted men to live as women, engage in traditionally feminine activities, and marry a traditionally masculine husband. Similar options existed for women. During the 1950s, working-class lesbians in parts of the United States developed a subculture in which intimate relationships were based on gendered distinctions between a masculine ("butch") and a feminine ("femme") partner. In short, same-sex intimate relationships can take many forms, depending on cultural norms and the personal preferences of partners.

III. *Satisfaction in Lesbian and Gay Relationships*

Stereotypes depict gay and lesbian relationships as unhappy. For example, heterosexual college students have described the relationships of lesbians and gay men as lower in love, less satisfying, and more prone to discord than those of heterosexuals. In contrast, empirical research refutes these misconceptions, finding no consistent differences between the quality of same-sex and heterosexual relationships.

In the past 20 years, several studies have compared satisfaction and relationship adjustment among gay male, lesbian, and heterosexual couples. For example, in a 1980 study, Letitia A. Peplau and Susan D. Cochran compared matched samples of lesbians, gay men, and heterosexuals who were all currently in a romantic/sexual relationship. Among this sample of young adults, about 60% said they were in love with their partner, and most of the rest said they were "uncertain" about whether they were in love. On standardized measures of love and liking, the lesbians and gay men generally reported very positive feelings for their partners and rated their current relationships as highly satisfying and close. No significant differences were found among lesbians, gay men, and heterosexuals on any measure of relationship quality. In a 1998 longitudinal study of married heterosexual and cohabiting homosexual couples, Lawrence A. Kurdek found similar results: the three types of couples did not differ in relationship satisfaction at initial testing. Over the five years of this study, all types of couples tended to decrease in relationship satisfaction, but no differences were found in the rate of change in satisfaction among gay, lesbian, or heterosexual couples. Several studies have replicated the finding that gay men and lesbians report as much satisfaction—or discontent—with their relationships as do heterosexuals.

Most studies of satisfaction in gay and lesbian relationships have been based predominantly on White participants. One exception is a 1997 survey of more than 700 African American lesbians and gay men in committed same-sex relationships conducted by Letitia A. Peplau, Susan D. Cochran, and Vickie M. Mays. The majority of participants—74% of women and 61% of men—indicated that they were in love with their partner. Only 10% were not in love and the rest were unsure. Respondents reported high levels of closeness in their relationship, with mean scores approaching 6 on a 7-point scale. In this sample, the partner's race was unrelated to relationship satisfaction: interracial couples were no more or less satisfied, on average, than same-race couples.

Recently, researchers have begun to investigate aspects of relationship quality that might be linked to gender. In a 1998 study, Kurdek hypothesized that due to their gender socialization, women may emphasize intimacy and men may emphasize independence in their relationships. These patterns should be strongest in relationships where both partners are of the same sex. Kurdek assessed intimacy by self-reports of the partners' spending time together, engaging in joint activities, building an identity as a couple, and thinking in terms of "we" instead of "me." As predicted, lesbians reported significantly greater intimacy than heterosexuals or gay men, although the effect size was small. Kurdek assessed independence or autonomy by self-reports of the partners' having major interests and friends outside of the relationship, maintaining a sense of being an individual, and making decisions on their own. Contrary to expectation, both lesbians and gay partners reported greater personal autonomy than did heterosexual partners.

A. CORRELATES OF SATISFACTION

What factors enhance satisfaction in same-sex relationships? Same-sex partners are happier when they perceive their relationship as providing many rewards and few costs. Satisfaction is higher when partners are equally involved in or committed to a relationship and when partners believe they share relatively equally in power and decision making.

Personality may also affect same-sex relationships. There is some evidence that the personality attribute of neuroticism may detract from the quality of gay and lesbian relationships, as it does in heterosexual couples. Although individual differences in attachment style have been studied extensively among heterosexuals, little is known about the possible attachment issues among lesbians and gay men. In a 1998 study by Stacy R. Ridge and Judith A. Feeney, lesbian and gay adults did not differ from heterosexuals in the likelihood of reporting secure versus insecure attachment. For all groups, secure attachment was significantly associated with higher relationship satisfaction.

Finally, researchers are beginning to examine how the social stigma of homosexuality may affect same-sex relationships. It has been suggested that the stress associated with concealing one's homosexuality can diminish relationship satisfaction. Some studies have found that more extensive disclosure to parents, friends, and employers is associated with greater relationship satisfaction among gay men and lesbians. In contrast, other studies have found no association between the extent of disclosure of sexual orientation and relationship satisfaction. The explanation for these contradictory findings may be that disclosure can have mixed consequences, ranging from rejection and estrangement from family and friends at one extreme to acceptance and increased social support at the other. If some gay men and lesbians suffer from disclosure but others benefit, the overall effects of disclosure may appear to be minimal. A better understanding of this issue, including studies of ethnic minority lesbians and gay men, is needed.

IV. Relationship Commitment and Stability

Several factors affect an individual's commitment to the relationship, that is, the desire to continue a relationship into the future. One factor concerns positive attractions that make individuals want to stay with a partner, such as feelings of love and satisfaction with the relationship. As noted earlier, research shows that same-sex and male-female couples typically report comparable levels of happiness (or misery) in their relationships.

Second, commitment is affected by barriers that make it difficult to leave a relationship. Barriers include anything that increases the psychological, emotional, or financial costs of ending a relationship. Heterosexual marriage can create many barriers such as the cost of divorce, investments in joint property,

concerns about children, and a wife's possible financial dependence on her husband. These obstacles may encourage married couples to work toward improving a declining relationship, rather than ending it. In contrast, gay and lesbian couples are less likely to experience comparable barriers: they cannot marry legally and are less likely to own property jointly, to have children in common, or to receive support from their families of origin. Researchers have systematically compared the attractions and barriers experienced by partners in gay, lesbian, heterosexual cohabiting, and married couples. In general, all types of couples report comparable feelings of love and satisfaction. However, married couples report significantly more barriers than either gays or lesbians, and cohabiting heterosexual couples report the fewest barriers of all.

A third important factor concerns the availability of alternatives to the current relationship, including other possible partners or the prospect of being without a partner. The lack of desirable alternatives can be a major obstacle to ending a relationship. Several studies have demonstrated that each of these three factors—attractions, barriers, and alternatives—is significantly associated with feelings of commitment to lesbian and gay relationships.

A. STAYING TOGETHER OVER TIME

How likely are lesbians and gay men to maintain enduring intimate relationships? We know relatively little about the longevity of same-sex partnerships. Several small-scale studies have documented the existence of gay and lesbian couples who have been together for 20 years or longer. The large American Couples Study conducted by Blumstein and Schwartz compared the stability of gay, lesbian, and heterosexual relationships over an 18-month period. During this time, less than 6% of couples who had already been together for at least 10 years broke up. Among couples together for only two years or less, breakups were more common: 22% for lesbian couples, 16% for gay male couples, 17% for heterosexual cohabiting couples, and 4% for married couples. Note that the biggest difference among these short-term couples was not between heterosexual and homosexual couples, but rather between legally married couples and other couples, both heterosexual and homosexual, who were not married. In a 1998 five-year longitudinal study, Kurdek found that the majority of cohabiting gay, lesbian, and married heterosexual couples stayed together. Nonetheless, breakup rates were significantly higher for gay (14%) and lesbian (16%) couples than for married heterosexuals (7%).

A few studies have investigated factors that are associated with the stability of same-sex relationships over time. One approach has been to describe the behaviors that gay and lesbian couples use to sustain a successful relationship. Many of these activities are similar to those reported previously by heterosexual couples; they include being helpful and cheerful, giving presents, being open about feelings, providing verbal assurances of commitment and love, and participating in joint activities. In addition, same-sex partners have also described activities designed to solidify their relationship in the face of a hostile social environment. One strategy is to seek gay/lesbian supportive environments in which to socialize, live, or work. Another strategy is to be "out as a couple" that is, to live openly together and participate in family and social activities as a couple.

Another research approach has been to follow couples over time to determine factors associated with staying together versus ending a relationship. In general, partners are more likely to continue their relationship if they initially experienced high levels of intimacy and commitment, reported greater equality in their relationship, perceived more barriers to ending their relationship, and used more constructive methods for solving problems.

A third approach to understanding factors that lead to breakups is to ask partners why a recent relationship ended. Many similarities have been found in the issues described by gay, lesbian, and heterosexual partners. These include a partner's frequent absence, sexual incompatibility, mental cruelty, and lack of love. Other common reasons were a partner's nonresponsiveness (e.g., poor communication or lack of support from the partner), a partner's personal problems (e.g., an alcohol problem), or sexual issues (e.g., the partner had an affair).

In summary, research finds that gay and lesbian couples can and do have committed, enduring relationships. On average, heterosexual and homosexual couples report similar levels of attraction toward their partner and satisfaction with their relationship. Where couples differ, however, is in the obstacles that make it difficult to end a relationship. Here, the legal and social context of marriage creates barriers to breaking up that do not typically exist for same-sex partners or for cohabiting heterosexuals. The relative lack of barriers may make it less likely that lesbians and gay men will be trapped in hopelessly miserable and deteriorating relationships. But weaker barriers may also allow partners to end relationships that might have improved if given more time and effort. As lesbians and gay men gain greater legal and social recognition as domestic partners, the barriers for gay and lesbian relationships may become more similar to those of heterosexuals. The impact of such trends on the stability of same-sex relationships is an important topic for further investigation.

B. REACTIONS TO THE ENDING OF A RELATIONSHIP

The dissolution of a serious romantic relationship is often difficult and emotionally upsetting. When asked to describe their emotional reactions to ending a recent relationship, lesbians and gay men have indicated a range of responses. The most common negative reactions were loneliness, confusion, anger, guilt, and helplessness. The most common positive emotions were personal growth, relief from conflict, increased happiness, and independence. It is likely that emotional reactions to the breakup differed for the partner who initiated the breakup (who may have felt guilt but also relief) and the partner who was left behind (who may have felt lonely, angry, and helpless). Former partners also reported experiencing a variety of problems after the breakup, including the nature of their continuing relationship with the ex-partner, financial stress, and difficulties in getting involved with someone else. The limited data currently available suggest that partners' reactions to the ending of same-sex and heterosexual relationships are generally similar. However, there may also be distinctive issues for lesbians and gay men. For example, because gay male and lesbian communities are often small, there may be pressure for ex-lovers to handle breakups tactfully and to remain friends.

Bereavement, the loss of a loved partner through death, can be traumatic, and the emotional aftermath of bereavement may be similar for surviving partners whatever their sexual orientation. However, the social circumstances surrounding bereavement often differ for homosexual and heterosexual partners. When a heterosexual spouse dies, a period of public grieving is common. In addition to the social support of friends and families, bereaved spouses can turn to religious institutions for comfort and may receive financial support from their partner's pension. In contrast, gay men and lesbians may encounter unique problems. They may not be eligible for survivor benefits and, without wills or other legal documents, may have no claim to the estate of a long-term partner that they contributed to building. Some researchers have speculated that the stress of bereavement may be increased if the surviving partner has concealed his or her sexual orientation so that open grieving is not possible.

During the past 20 years, the AIDS epidemic has had a devastating impact on the lives of gay men. The difficulties of bereavement are heightened when AIDS is the cause of death, both because victims tend to die at an untimely young age and because of the social stigma surrounding this disease. A few studies have investigated how losing a relationship partner to AIDS affects a surviving partner who is himself HIV-positive. It has been found that bereavement can impair the immune functioning of the surviving partner. This may be most common if the partner is unable to find positive meaning in the experience of loss. Much remains to be learned about the bereavement experiences of lesbians and gay men.

V. Sexuality

There is a small but growing body of research on sexuality in lesbian and gay relationships. On average, gay male couples have sex more often than heterosexual couples, who in turn have sex more often than lesbian couples. In Blumstein and Schwartz's American Couples Study, for example, 46% of gay male couples reported having "sexual relations" at least three times a week, as compared to 35% of married or cohabiting heterosexual couples, and 20% of lesbian couples.

This lower frequency of sex among lesbian couples has been a topic of debate among researchers. Some have speculated that this pattern reflects women's socialization to be more sexually inhibited than men. Another possibility is that available findings reflect problems about how to conceptualize and measure sexuality in relationships. Feminist researchers have observed that people tend to define sex as penile-vaginal intercourse. Indeed, in a 1999 survey of almost 600 college undergraduates conducted by Stephanie Sanders and June Reinisch, 59% did not consider oral-genital contact to be "having sex" with a partner. These heterosexual definitions of sexuality may be poorly suited for understanding same-sex couples and, in particular, lesbian relationships. We know very little about how lesbians and gay men conceptualize sexuality in their relationships.

Sexual monogamy versus openness is an issue for all intimate couples. In contrast to heterosexual and lesbian couples, gay male couples are distinctive in their likelihood of having a nonmonogamous relationship. In Blumstein and Schwartz' American Couples Study, 82% of the gay male couples reported being nonmonogamous, compared to 28% of lesbian couples, 23% of heterosexual married couples, and 31% of heterosexual cohabiting couples. Unlike gay men, most lesbians characterize their relationships as monogamous.

Many lesbians report that they prefer a sexually exclusive relationship. In contrast, gay men are more likely to view sex outside a primary relationship as acceptable and to have an agreement with their partner that it is permissible. As a result, the impact of nonmonogamy may differ for lesbian and gay male couples. Research has shown that among lesbian couples, nonmonogamy is associated with lower sexual satisfaction with the primary partner and less commitment to their relationship; for gay men, outside sex is often unrelated to satisfaction or commitment to the relationship. [*See* SEXUALITY AND SEXUAL DESIRE.]

VI. Conflict and Violence

Problems and disagreements seem to be inevitable in close relationships. Available evidence shows that lesbian, gay male, and heterosexual couples are similar in how often and how intensely they report arguing. Similar types of issues are likely to spark conflict in same-sex and heterosexual couples, with concerns about intimacy, power, and the partner's personal flaws being cited frequently. Some differences in the sources of conflict have also been found. For example, gay and lesbian couples report less conflict about money management and income than do heterosexual couples, perhaps because same-sex couples are less likely to merge their funds and more likely to have two incomes. Further, gay and lesbian couples confront special issues, such as revealing versus concealing their sexual orientation and the nature of their intimate relationship to friends or family. Decisions also arise about how actively partners want to participate in gay or lesbian communities, political organizations, and social events. These distinctive concerns can be a source of conflict between partners.

Same-sex couples may also experience unique problems based on their shared gender-role socialization. Some clinicians have speculated that because women are socialized to place a strong value on closeness and emotional connection, lesbian partners may become so close that personal boundaries are blurred, and a healthy sense of individuality is threatened. It has also been suggested that gay men may have problems establishing intimacy and closeness in a relationship. Currently, empirical support for these hypothesized male-female differences is very limited, and contradictory evidence has been reported. Indeed, there is some evidence that high levels of intimacy in lesbian couples are associated with greater satisfaction and are not dysfunctional. Similarly, there is some evidence that gay male couples are emotionally expressive and do not have problems with intimacy. Systematic research is needed to test the accuracy, prevalence, and generalizability of clinical beliefs about gender-linked problems in gay and lesbian couples. [*See* INTIMACY AND LOVE.]

How well do lesbians and gay men solve problems that arise in their relationships? Research finds no differences between same-sex and heterosexual couples in the likelihood of using positive problem-solving styles such as focusing on the problem, negotiating, or compromising. Nor have differences been found in the use of poor strategies, such as launching personal attacks or refusing to talk to the partner. As in heterosexual couples, happy lesbian and gay male couples are more likely to use constructive problem-solving approaches than are unhappy couples.

Recently, researchers have begun to investigate violence in same-sex relationships. Given problems of obtaining representative samples and participants' possible reluctance to admit socially undesirable acts of violence, it is impossible to estimate accurately the frequency of such violence in same-sex couples. In general, lesbians and gay men appear to experience similar kinds of abuse, with threats, slapping, pushing, and punching being the most common. In 1995 Michael Johnson suggested that two types of violence can occur among heterosexual couples. "Common couple violence" occurs when partners' occasionally have outbursts of violence, and men and women are equally likely to commit these acts. In contrast, "intimate terrorism" refers to cases in which men systematically use threats, physical violence, and isolation to control and subjugate a female partner; this violence often escalates over time and can lead to serious injury. Do these two types of violence occur in same-sex relationships? Research does not yet provide an answer. Additional research on the nature of abuse and its causes in same-sex relationships is needed. [*See* BATTERING IN ADULT RELATIONSHIPS.]

VII. *Couples' Counseling*

When problems arise in a relationship, individuals and couples sometimes seek the aid of a counselor or psychotherapist. Although many relationship issues, such as personal discontent, conflict, or loss of sexual interest, are common among all relationships, therapists need additional expertise to work effectively with lesbian and gay couples. In recent years, there has been growing awareness of potential anti-homosexual bias among some therapists and a corresponding effort to develop new therapies for gay and lesbian couples.

A. BIAS IN PSYCHOTHERAPY

The process of psychotherapy is inevitably influenced by the values and biases of the therapist. The American Psychological Association has taken many steps to educate both professionals and the public about scientific research showing that homosexuality is not a form of pathology nor is it associated with mental illness. In 1975, the American Psychological Association Council of Representatives adopted a resolution stating that

homosexuality per se implies no impairment in judgment, stability, reliability or general social or vocational capabilities; further, the American Psychological Association urges all professionals to take the lead in removing the stigma of mental illness that has long been associated with homosexual orientations.

Nonetheless, a subsequent survey of members of the American Psychological Association identified many ways in which therapists sometimes provide biased and inadequate care to lesbian and gay clients. Some therapists may view homosexuality as a sign of psychological disorder or demean gay and lesbian lifestyles. In other instances, therapists may be poorly informed about the experiences of lesbians and gay men or about the social context of sexual prejudice. Turning to the specific domain of relationship problems, a therapist may underestimate the importance of intimate relationships for lesbians and gay men or be misinformed about the variety of issues facing same-sex couples. In addition, a therapist may fail to suggest couples' counseling when it is more appropriate than individual psychotherapy. Therapists who are themselves gay or lesbian are not necessarily invulnerable to bias. For all these reasons, gay men and lesbians may experience greater difficulties than their heterosexual counterparts in getting adequate professional help for relationship problems.

B. AFFIRMATIVE THERAPIES FOR LESBIAN AND GAY COUPLES

Some therapists believe that clinicians should go beyond providing unbiased therapy by developing new approaches to therapy that affirm the value and legitimacy of gay and lesbian lifestyles. These approaches are called affirmative therapies. Affirmative therapists are especially sensitive to the potential impact of societal prejudice in the lives of lesbians and gay men, and to the value of therapeutic approaches that acknowledge the importance of gay and lesbian relationships. For some relationship problems, counseling a couple together may be preferable to seeing one or both partners individually.

Although many gay affirmative therapists are themselves gay or lesbian, an affirmative approach can be used by therapists regardless of their sexual orientation. The key is drawing on knowledge about the personal and relationship experiences of lesbians and gay men, being sensitive to the diversity among lesbians and gay men, and developing expertise in effective treatment approaches. On February 26, 2000, the Council of Representatives of the American Psychological Association adopted "Guidelines for Psychotherapy with Lesbian, Gay, and Bisexual Clients" designed to improve the education of mental health professionals and the services they provide to sexual-minority clients.

VIII. *The Relationships of Bisexual Women and Men*

What are relationships like for individuals who report romantic attractions toward both men and women? Scientific research on this topic is virtually nonexistent. One complication is that the term "bisexual" has been defined in widely differing ways. Some use the term to refer to a presumed innate human capacity to respond to partners of both sexes. Others characterize a person as bisexual if his or her lifetime history of sexual attractions or behavior includes partners of both sexes. We will focus on individuals who self-identify as bisexual, as we did in re-

viewing research on the relationships of men and women who self-identify as lesbian or gay.

Heterosexuals sometimes stereotype bisexuals as having poor intimate relationships. In particular, bisexuals are seen as more likely than other people to be sexually unfaithful and to give a sexually transmitted disease to a partner. Lesbians and gay men may also have negative stereotypes of bisexuals, for example, believing that bisexuals are denying their "true" sexual orientation or that bisexuals are likely to desert a same-sex partner for a heterosexual one.

Research on the relationships of bisexuals is extremely limited and largely based on White, urban, well-educated individuals. Some self-identified bisexuals do not idealize monogamy; they may indicate a preference for a primary relationship with one person and secondary sexual or romantic relationships with other partners. Often, the primary partner is of the other sex, and in some cases the partners are married. In contrast, some bisexuals prefer sexual exclusivity in a relationship with one person. Still others prefer casual dating or relationships with several partners rather than having a more committed relationship.

Research on the relationships of bisexuals has barely begun, and many important questions remain unanswered. How does the gender of a bisexual's partner affect their relationship? For example, does the relationship of a bisexual woman differ on such dimensions as power, the division of labor, sexuality, or commitment if her partner is a woman versus a man? A second research direction is to identify issues that may be unique to the relationships of bisexuals. For instance, if lesbians and gay men endorse the stereotype that bisexuals are likely to abandon their same-sex lovers, are jealousy and concerns about commitment frequent problems in the same-sex relationships of bisexuals? Future research on the relationships of bisexual men and women can take many promising directions.

SUGGESTED READING

Blumstein, P., and Schwartz, P. (1983). *American Couples: Money, Work, Sex.* Morrow, New York.

Cabaj, R. P., and Stein, T. S. (eds.) (1996). *Textbook of Homosexuality and Mental Health.* American Psychiatric Press, Washington, DC.

Firestein, B. A. (ed.) (1996). *Bisexuality: The Psychology and Politics of an Invisible Minority.* Sage, Thousand Oaks, CA.

Kurdek, L. A. (1995). Lesbian and gay couples. In *Lesbian, Gay and Bisexual Identities over the Lifespan* (R. D'Augelli and C. J. Patterson, eds.), pp. 243–261. Oxford University Press, New York.

Laird, J., and Green, R. (eds.) (1996). *Lesbians and Gays in Couples and Families*. Jossey-Bass, San Francisco.

Peplau, L. A., and Garnets, L. D. (eds.) (2000). Women's sexualities: Perspectives on sexual orientation and gender. *Journal of Social Issues* **56**(2) (entire volume).

Peplau, L. A., and Spalding, L. R. (2000). The intimate relationships of lesbians, gay men and bisexuals. In *Close Relationships: A Sourcebook* (C. Hendrick and S. S. Hendrick, eds.), pp. 111–124. Sage, Thousand Oaks, CA.

Perez, R. M., DeBord, K. A., and Bieschke, K. J. (eds.) (2000). *Handbook of Counseling and Psychotherapy with Lesbian, Gay, and Bisexual Clients*. American Psychological Association, Washington, DC.

Savin-Williams, R. C. (1996). Dating and romantic relationships among gay, lesbian and bisexual youths. In *The Lives of Lesbians, Gays, and Bisexuals* (R. C. Savin-Williams and K. M. Cohen eds.), pp. 166–180. Harcourt Brace, Orlando, FL.

Weinberg, M. S., Williams, C. J., and Pryor, D. W. (1994). *Dual Attraction: Understanding Bisexuality*. Oxford University Press, New York.

Life Satisfaction

Lorie Sousa

Sonja Lyubomirsky

University of California, Riverside

Glossary

Affect Experiences pertaining to feelings, emotion, or mood.

Cognitive The mental process of knowing, thinking, learning, and judging.

Collectivist cultures Members of collectivist cultures (e.g., Japan, China, Mexico) tend to value family, belonging, and the needs of the group.

Confounding variable A variable that is so well correlated with the variable of interest that it is difficult to determine whether differences or changes are due to the variable of interest or to the confound.

Experience sampling A method used to evaluate a participant's experience, mood, or behavior at a particular point in time. Experience sampling data are generally collected over several days and participants are asked to record their responses at the moment.

Individualist cultures Member of individualist cultures (e.g., the United States, Western Europe) tend to value individuality and independence.

Informant data Data obtained from a significant other such as a mother, father, spouse, or friend.

Internal consistency Reliability of a measure determined by the intercorrelations of the components or items of the measure.

Longitudinal design A research design in which participants are evaluated over a period of time.

Meta-analysis A technique applied to summarize the literature in a particular area and to investigate conflicting findings. This method involves gathering the results from many studies on a specific topic to determine the average comprehensive finding.

Objective Objective factors are those that are perceptible to the outside world and can be evaluated by others.

Predictor A known variable that is used to predict a change in another variable. For example, if one is interested in the extent to which exercise, weight, and smoking are related to heart disease, then one might collect information on the three predictor variables (i.e., exercise, weight, and smoking), as well as on the outcome variable (i.e., disease). Such data will presumably tell researchers something valuable about the potential influence of exercise, weight, and smoking on the rate of disease.

Social desirability bias A bias reflected by participants altering their responses based on their need for social approval. For example, a respondent who is concerned with social approval may inflate her response to the interview question, "Are you a happy person," because she does not wish to appear sad or depressed to the interviewer.

Subjective Subjective factors are those that are perceived only by the affected individual; they are not perceptible to the senses of another person.

Subjective well-being An evaluation of one's life assessed by measures of global life satisfaction, frequency of positive affect, and frequency of negative affect.

SATISFACTION is a Latin word that means to make or do enough. Satisfaction with one's life implies a contentment with or acceptance of one's life circumstances or the fulfillment of one's want and needs for one's life as a whole. In essence, life satisfaction is a subjective assessment of the quality of one's life. Because it is inherently an evaluation, judgments of life satisfaction have a large cognitive component.

I. Distinction from Related Constructs

A. LIFE SATISFACTION VERSUS SUBJECTIVE WELL-BEING

According to Ed Diener and his colleagues (1999), subjective well-being, or happiness, has both an affective (i.e., emotional) and a cognitive (i.e., judgmental) component. The affective component consists of how frequently an individual reports experiencing positive and negative affect. Life satisfaction is considered to be the cognitive component of this broader construct.

B. LIFE SATISFACTION VERSUS LIFE-DOMAIN SATISFACTION

Researchers differentiate between life-domain satisfaction and life-as-a-whole (or global) life satisfaction. Life-domain satisfaction refers to satisfaction with specific areas of an individual's life, such as work, marriage, and income, whereas judgments of global life satisfaction are much more broad, consisting of an individual's comprehensive judgment of her life.

II. Introduction

The success of a community or nation is frequently judged by objective standards. Political parties often remind citizens of the prosperity of the nation during their party's governance as a method to encourage appreciation and reelection. To persuade people that quality of life has improved under their administration, they cite such factors as low unemployment rates, greater income, lower taxes, lower crime rates, and improvements in education and health care. The quality of life of the individual, however, cannot be quantified in this manner. Indeed, objective measures of quality of life (i.e., income, education) are often weakly related to people's subjective self-reports of the extent to which they are satisfied with their lives. For example, one might predict that individuals who have suffered traumatic spinal cord injury would be significantly less satisfied with their lives than individuals who have not suffered such an injury. However, empirical research has not supported this contention—in fact, disabled individuals do not report lower levels of satisfaction than nondisabled ones. It is clear that a one-to-one relationship between observable life circumstances and subjective judgments of life satisfaction does not always exist.

A great deal of psychological research has explored the sources of people's life satisfaction. These sources include one's overall wealth, whether one is single or married, male or female, or young or old. Because most researchers investigating the predictors of life satisfaction have not specifically focused on the experiences of women, this review of the life satisfaction literature will describe research conducted with both sexes. Fortunately, however, the findings of many of these studies are directly relevant to women's lives. Life circumstances such as bearing and raising children, marriage, poverty, and inequality all influence the life satisfaction of women, despite the fact that studies of these factors have not necessarily been conducted with women participants only or been specifically analyzed for gender differences. Thus, this review focuses on life satisfaction in general but with women's lives and experiences in mind.

III. Measurement

Before delving into the literature examining the factors related to life satisfaction, it is important to discuss how life satisfaction is measured. Researchers' overwhelming choice for assessing life satisfaction is through self-report. Self-report measures require respondents to indicate the extent to which they are satisfied with their lives by selecting a symbol (i.e., a number or a facial expression) on a rating scale (e.g., from 1 to 7). Because life satisfaction is assumed to be a judgment, researchers believe that self-report is the most direct and most accurate way to measure it.

A. SINGLE-ITEM VERSUS MULTI-ITEM MEASURES OF LIFE SATISFACTION

There are many self-report measures of life satisfaction. Some measures consist of a single question, such as "How satisfied with your life are you overall?" Other measures require participants to respond to multiple items. Overall, researchers agree that multi-item scales of life satisfaction are preferable to single-item scales. Although single-item scales have adequate convergent validity (i.e., the scales correlate well with other similar measures) and satisfactory reliability (i.e., the scale measures similarly over time), only multiple-item scales allow for the assessment of internal consistency, as well as the identification of errors associated with wording and measurement. Additionally, Ed Diener (1984) has argued that multi-item scales have demonstrated greater reliability and validity overall than single-item scales. Furthermore, a meta-analysis conducted by Martin Pinquart and Silvia Sorensen (2000) found that correlations between life satisfaction and variables such as income, education, gender, and age are significantly reduced when single-item, rather than multiple-item, scales are used. Researchers speculate that single-item scales may be more susceptible to social desirability biases than multiple-item ones because the latter request a wider range of information with more specificity. Despite these concerns, however, single-item scales have tended to correlate well with the multiple-item scales, so if an abridged version is needed, single-item scales appear to be adequate. The most widely used and most well-validated measure of life satisfaction is a multi-item scale, the Satisfaction with Life Scale.

B. SATISFACTION WITH LIFE SCALE

The five-item Satisfaction with Life Scale (SWLS) was designed by Ed Diener and his colleagues (1985) to measure global life satisfaction. Because the authors consider life satisfaction as the cognitive component of subjective well-being, they constructed this scale without reference to affect. The language used for the scale items is relatively broad and nonspecific, allowing the respondents to evaluate their overall life satisfaction subjectively.

The SWLS has been administered to many different groups of participants and has been found to have high internal consistency and reliability across gender, ethnicity, and age. This measure also has high convergent validity—for example, it correlates well with clinical ratings of satisfaction, and informant reports of satisfaction, as well as with scales assessing self-esteem. The instructions for the SWLS ask participants to rate the following five statements on 7-point Likert-type scales (1 = *strongly disagree*, 4 = *neither agree nor disagree*, 7 = *strongly agree*):

_____ In most ways my life is close to my ideal.
_____ The conditions of my life are excellent.
_____ I am satisfied with my life.
_____ So far I have gotten the important things I want in life.
_____ If I could live my life over, I would change almost nothing.

C. OTHER MEASURES OF SATISFACTION

1. Hadley Cantril's (1965) Self-Anchoring Scale

This is a single-item measure of life satisfaction, which instructs participants to mark one rung on a ladder, with the top of the ladder labeled "best life for you" and the bottom of the ladder labeled "worst possible life for you," to indicate their life satisfaction judgment.

2. Frank Andrews and Stephen Withey's (1976) Delighted-Terrible Scale

This single-item scale requires participants to indicate their level of life satisfaction by selecting one of seven faces ranging from a happy face (smiling, delighted) to a sad face (frowning, terrible) in response to the question, "How do you feel about your life as a whole?"

D. POTENTIAL PROBLEMS WITH LIFE SATISFACTION MEASUREMENT

Several concerns have been raised regarding the validity of life satisfaction measures. Critics have questioned whether people (1) are aware of their levels of satisfaction, (2) inflate their responses to appear more satisfied than they actually are, (3) confuse their own perceptions with how others perceive them, and (4) interpret the questions differently depending on their gender or their culture. Fortunately, each of these concerns appears to be unfounded. First, participants rarely fail to respond to satisfaction questions and they tend to answer such questions quickly, indicating that the extent to which they are satisfied with life is something they are well aware of and think about often. Second, as most life satisfaction assessments are conducted anonymously, there is little reason to believe that social desirability effects are greatly inflating people's responses. Third, it is unlikely that respondents may confuse their own perceptions with that of others because then one would expect more affluent or better educated individuals to report much higher rates of satisfaction than others of less means or education. This has not generally been found. Finally, because the SWLS is written in very general terms—a procedure that allows each individual to define life satisfaction for herself or himself—this widely used life satisfaction scale appears to be gender and culture neutral (see also Section VI.A). For example, in a recent study, Kari Tucker and colleagues found that the SWLS measures life satisfaction similarly for females and males in two different cultures.

IV. How Do People Make Life Satisfaction Judgments?

We know that most people are fully capable of rating the level of their own life satisfaction. However, the question still remains, how exactly do people make such judgments? The conceptualizations of life satisfaction proposed by theorists in this area offer several clues. For example, Angus Campbell and his colleagues (1976) conceptualized life satisfaction as the difference between what one wants and what one has—essentially, a comparison between reality and the ideal. Thus, a woman's judgment of her life satisfaction involves drawing on her personal standards and expectations for herself and assessing the extent to which her life measures up.

Alex Michalos's multiple discrepancy theory (1986) also specifies how a woman might arrive at her personal level of satisfaction. According to this theory, satisfaction is determined by one's perceptions of "how things are" versus "how they should

be." Comparisons between how things are and what one wants, what one had, what one expected, what others have, and what one feels one deserves combine to determine life satisfaction. Small discrepancies among these areas result in greater life *satisfaction*. Large discrepancies among these areas result in greater life *dissatisfaction*. Michalos's theory was supported using a sample of nearly 700 undergraduate participants, 54% of whom were women. Both women and men in his sample appeared to derive global satisfaction in comparable ways.

Joseph Sirgy's theory (1998) similarly mentions several comparisons that women may consider before arriving at a judgment of their life satisfaction. He suggests that expectations of what one is capable of accomplishing, one's past circumstances, one's ideals, what one feels one deserves, what one minimally requires to be content, and what one ultimately believes will occur are comparisons that help determine overall life satisfaction.

Other researchers have investigated whether people determine their personal estimates of their life satisfaction through a "top-down" or a "bottom-up" approach. If a woman were to use a top-down procedure, she might reflect on the value of her life as a whole, probe her sense or intuition for how happy and satisfied she is overall, and therefore conclude that she must have a good (or not-so-good) life. Alternatively, if she were to use a bottom-up approach, she might think about the various domains of her life (e.g., marriage, children, work, friendships, income) and arrive at her life satisfaction judgment based on the average satisfaction she obtains from each of these domains. In other words, does a woman have a good life because she is satisfied or is she satisfied because she has a good life? Preliminary research suggests that the answer is both, but additional work is needed to address this question further.

V. What Determines Life Satisfaction? Environment Versus Personality

One of the principal questions that researchers are tackling is, what causes life satisfaction? That is, why are some women more satisfied than others? Most of the research in this area can be subsumed under two categories—namely, evidence implicating personality (i.e., genetics, inborn traits) and evidence implicating environment (i.e., life circumstances and life events). A great deal of work has investigated whether life satisfaction is a stable, enduring trait or whether it is a variable that is highly influenced by external events and life circumstances. For example, will the experience of discrimination or harassment, the birth of a child, a divorce, purchasing a house, obtaining an advanced degree, or the day-to-day hassles of balancing work and home life greatly influence a woman's satisfaction with her life? Alternatively, will a woman's stable characteristic patterns of responding to events determine her life satisfaction, such that she remains satisfied (or dissatisfied) despite changes in income, social relationships, employment, or other significant life events. In support of the latter view, research has shown that individuals tend to show similar levels of satisfaction across time and across many life domains. For example, women who are content with their marriages are also likely to be content with their work, their children, their financial situation, and even the daily weather. However, this finding should not be overstated, as it is certainly possible to be dissatisfied with one's partner but satisfied with one's job. In support of the alternative perspective, another study found that the proportion of positive to negative life events experienced during the previous year predicted an individual's life satisfaction during the following year. This finding suggests that life events, such as a new marriage or a new job, may indeed significantly boost or deflate one's overall life satisfaction.

Eunkook Suh and his colleagues (1996) conducted a longitudinal study that may help explain such conflicting findings. They asked recent female and male college graduates to report their significant life events and their subjective well-being, including their life satisfaction, approximately every six months over a two-year period. The results showed that the occurrence of particular life events in these students' lives was related to changes in their well-being—but these effects did not endure. Recent life events in both men and women predicted changes in well-being while distal events did not, possibly because people adapt to significant life changes over long periods of time. The results of this study suggest that "personality" or "environmental" explanations in isolation may not be sufficient to explain the source of people's life satisfaction judgments. That is, life satisfaction may have both stable, traitlike components (reflecting the effect of a personality predisposition), as well as vari-

able, statelike components (reflecting environmental influences). However, it may be impossible to entirely discriminate between these two sets of components because one's personality may influence one's life events. For example, an extroverted woman may place herself in social situations, giving herself the opportunity to have more encounters and a greater wealth of life experiences. Indeed, Robert Plomin and his colleagues (1990) provide evidence that genes do have a small influence on the actual types of life events people experience.

Supporting the argument that personality plays a role in determining life satisfaction, personality variables such as psychological resilience, assertiveness, empathy, internal locus of control, extraversion, and openness to experience have been found to be related to life satisfaction. Furthermore, Keith Magnus and his colleagues (1993) found in a longitudinal study that personality predicted life satisfaction four years subsequent to the study. This pattern of results suggests that life satisfaction may have a dispositional component or at least interacts with the environment to influence life satisfaction. Finally, as previously mentioned, satisfied individuals tend to be satisfied across several life domains. Combined, these findings suggest that life satisfaction is stable over time and consistent across situations.

Further supporting the view that life satisfaction has traitlike characteristics, several studies have also found that subjective well-being, which encompasses life satisfaction, has a substantial genetic component. For example, Auke Tellegen and his colleagues showed that identical twins (who share 100% of their genes) reared in separate environments are more alike in their levels of well-being than fraternal twins (who share 50% of their genes) reared in either separate or similar environments. Future research would benefit from studies that measure life satisfaction specifically to reach stronger conclusions about the links between personality and ife satisfaction. Currently, the literature suggests that personality plays a significant role in whether a women will judge her life to be satisfying. However, proximal environmental factors (e.g., recent life events) can influence life satisfaction judgments in the short term. In conclusion, as with many variables in the field of psychology, both nature and nurture (i.e., personality and environment) appear to be influential in determining life satisfaction, and to discount one explanation in favor of the other would not be empirically or theoretically productive.

VI. Demographic Variables as Predictors of Life Satisfaction

The vast majority of research on life satisfaction investigates the extent to which various demographic variables predict life satisfaction. However, because researchers are not able to perform true experiments by randomly assigning participants to demographic groups (e.g., gender, income, age), all of this research has necessarily been correlational. Much of the work has focused on the "objective" determinants of life satisfaction—that is, the extent to which satisfaction is related to the environment, both imposed (e.g., culture) and relatively controllable (e.g., income, occupation, education, marriage), as well as to specific aspects of persons (e.g., gender, age).

A. CULTURE

Before describing research on cultural influences, we must revisit the question of whether life satisfaction can be measured similarly across cultures. Fortunately, satisfaction appears to be a universal term, and cross-cultural researchers have not had any difficulty translating measures of life satisfaction into many different languages. People from different cultures are able to distinguish between such terms as "happiness," "satisfaction with life," "best possible life," and "worst possible life," and there does not appear to be a linguistic bias. Thus, research suggests that life satisfaction is not a uniquely Western concept. For example, nonresponse and "don't know" answers to questions about life satisfaction are no more frequent in non-Western cultures than in Western ones. In sum, such evidence for the cultural universality of the construct of life satisfaction has allowed researchers to compare life satisfaction across cultures.

Current research shows that members of individualist cultures (e.g., the United States, England, Australia) report greater satisfaction relative to members of collectivist cultures (e.g., China, Japan, India). Life satisfaction also appears to vary with other cultural dimensions. For example, citizens of wealthy, industrialized nations have very high levels of satisfaction overall, and citizens of poor, third-world nations have low levels of satisfaction overall. Research suggests that once a community of people reach a decent standard of living, however, differences in life satisfaction are less likely to be related to differences in wealth.

Once subsistence levels have been reached, recent research suggests that members of different cultures reach life satisfaction judgments in distinct ways. Eunkook Suh and colleagues (1998) conducted a large international study of 61 nations, with close to 62,500 participants. Their findings suggested that members of collectivist and individualist cultures chronically rely on different types of information when assessing their life satisfaction. That is, members of collectivist cultures appear to rely on cultural norms (i.e., "Am I expected to be satisfied?") to determine their life satisfaction judgments, whereas members of individualist cultures appear to rely on emotional experiences (i.e., "Do I frequently feel happy and content?") as their guide to life satisfaction judgments. Interestingly, participants from Hong Kong, a collectivist city, appear to rely on emotion to determine their life satisfaction judgments. The rapid Westernization and modernization of this continually changing culture may account for this surprising finding. Moreover, it serves as an example of our earlier point that personality and environment are both important determinants of life satisfaction—that is, life satisfaction judgments can be fluid and subject to the changing social environment.

Reinforcing the importance of the social climate in people's life satisfaction, researchers have also found that life satisfaction is greatest among prosperous nations characterized by gender equality, care for human rights, political freedom, and access to knowledge. Cultures that are more accepting of differences (e.g., gender, sexual orientation, age, ethnicity, religion) and those that demand equal treatment of and equal opportunity for their citizens, appear to foster greater overall satisfaction. It is not surprising that women living in patriarchal cultures in which equal opportunities are unavailable and equal value is not afforded would experience greater dissatisfaction with their lives than women living in egalitarian cultures. [See CROSS-CULTURAL GENDER ROLES.]

B. GENDER

An apparently paradoxical finding in the literature is that women show higher rates of depression than men, but also report higher levels of well-being. At the same time, the majority of studies find no gender differences in life satisfaction. These conflicting findings can be resolved by considering the range of affect that men and women typically experience. Women report experiencing affect—both positive and negative—with greater intensity and frequency than do men. That is, women tend to experience greater joy and deeper sadness—and experience these emotions more often—than do men. Hence, measures of depression and subjective well-being, which include affective components, appear to capture the extreme lows that leave women vulnerable to depression, as well as the extreme highs that allow for greater well-being. By contrast, men and women report similar rates of global life satisfaction, which is primarily a cognitive assessment. [*See* DEPRESSION.]

Despite similar levels of life satisfaction across gender, women and men appear to derive life satisfaction from different sources. For example, Ed Diener and Frank Fujita (1995) found that social resources (i.e., family, friends, access to social services) are predictive of life satisfaction for both men and women, but they are more predictive of life satisfaction for women. Perhaps women's roles as the conservators of contact with friends and family—both a blessing and a burden—lead to their relatively greater reliance on social support. By contrast, factors that may be more relevant to men's personal goals, such as athleticism, influential connections, and authority, were found to be related to life satisfaction for men but not for women.

A meta-analysis of the predictors of life satisfaction in the elderly conducted by Martin Pinquart and Silvia Sorensen (2000) found additional support for the assertion that men and women derive satisfaction from different sources. In their study, life satisfaction was more highly related to income for men than for women. The authors hypothesized that because men are more socialized to draw their sense of identity from work and income, they tend to look to income as a barometer of their success and satisfaction with their life. In addition, more women live in poverty than do men, so it may be easier for men to obtain satisfaction from their financial situation than it is for women.

Although most research on life satisfaction has not been directly focused on the experiences of women, a few studies have investigated the unique predictors of life satisfaction for women. For example, as stated previously, several studies have demonstrated that the greater the gender equality within a culture (i.e., freedom to make reproductive choices, equal pay, equal value under the law, equal opportunity to education and achievement), the greater reported life satisfaction. This finding spans both equality in the broader cultural sense and equality within a marriage. For example, Gloria Cowan and her colleagues (1998) found that women who report greater equal-

ity in their marriages tend to report greater life satisfaction than women whose marriages are relatively more traditional. That is, women seem to achieve greater satisfaction with their lives overall when they are in marriages in which their roles are not traditionally proscribed. Marital equality may manifest itself in the sharing of household chores and responsibility for childcare, as well as equal say in family decision making. However, this ideal is not often achieved. Susan Nolen-Hoeksema and her colleagues (1999) found that women carry the overwhelming burden in regard to household and parental responsibility and report feeling relatively less appreciated by their spouse. Regardless of the type of marriage, however, married women report greater life satisfaction than single, widowed, or divorced women.

In further research, Arlene Metha and her colleagues (1989) conducted a survey investigating the major regrets and priorities of women. Overall, the least satisfied women surveyed reported that their greatest regret was having failed to take risks. Possibly because of women's childcare burdens, many cultures discourage women from risk taking. However, despite their many dangers, taking risks also provides access to greater opportunities. Without the ability to take risks, a woman would not be able to start her own business, move to a new city, pursue a graduate education, or ask for a promotion. Thus, it would not be difficult to imagine that failing to take risks might translate into missed opportunities and greater dissatisfaction.

John Haworth and his colleagues (1997) found that, among their sample of North American working women, those who had an internal locus of control (i.e., who believed that control of events comes from within themselves rather than outside of themselves) were relatively more satisfied with their lives. For example, a woman who perceives her success to be due to her hard work and determination would report greater satisfaction than a woman who perceives her success to be due to luck or chance. This is not surprising, as a belief in one's own ability to effect changes and choose the course of one's life is undoubtedly more satisfying than believing that one has no control over life's outcomes.

An additional study found that women's hostility toward other women was inversely associated with life satisfaction. That is, women who harbored hostile feelings toward other women were less likely to be satisfied with their own lives. This finding appears to correspond well with the comparison theories discussed earlier. Researchers have suggested that people's perceptions of their life satisfaction are in part due to comparisons that they make between what they have, what they want, what they used to have, and what others have. Thus, hostility toward other women may be a consequence of unfavorable social comparisons. That is, the recognition that another woman is clearly better off may be related to dissatisfaction with one's own life.

C. AGE

Numerous studies have provided evidence that, contrary to common expectations, life satisfaction does not decline with age. For example, in a cross-cultural study conducted in 40 different nations and with nearly 6000 participants, Ed Diener and Eunkook Suh (1998) found that reported life satisfaction generally remained stable throughout the life span, showing just a slight increasing trend between the ages of 20 and 80 years.

The predominant explanation for this surprising lack of difference in life satisfaction levels across the life span is that people have an extraordinary capacity to adapt to significant life changes. In a study by Carol Ryff (1991), older participants reported smaller discrepancies between their realistic and their ideal selves than did younger participants. Perhaps, as women age, they revise their ideals to accommodate their current circumstances (i.e., engage in "accommodative coping"). For example, a woman who had intended to have three children may have only been able to bear two. With time, she might decide that having three is impractical financially and that having two is actually preferable. This conclusion would serve to decrease the discrepancy between her ideal and the reality of her life. Indeed, according to Jochen Brandtstaedter and Gerolf Renner (1990), accommodative coping does tend to increase with age. Alternatively, as women age, they may achieve their goals with greater frequency (i.e., a family, a career success, and financial comfort), moving closer to their ideal self.

D. SOCIAL RELATIONSHIPS

Francis Bacon (1625) said that human relationships double our joys and halve our sorrows. Many studies have supported this contention. High levels of social support have been shown to be strongly associated with high levels of life satisfaction. For example, one study found that participants who could list five or more friends were happier than participants who could not list many friends. In addition to the number of social contacts, it appears that gender is a factor in the quality of intimate relationships as well. Women tend to provide greater and more meaningful support than men. That is, both women and men report that their friendships with women are more intimate, nurturing, and supportive than their friendships with men. Perhaps this is due to the finding that conversations with women involve greater self-disclosure and empathy.

In Western nations, marriage appears to be even more predictive of life satisfaction than relationships with friends and family. Ed Diener and his colleagues (2000) found that married women do not differ in their levels of life satisfaction from married men. However, married men reported greater positive affect than did married women, as well as did single people of both genders. Thus, men appear to benefit more from marriage than do women—possibly because husbands become dependent on their wives' emotional support and household care. This study also found that cohabiting unmarried participants, especially those from collectivist cultures, reported less life satisfaction than did married participants.

Interestingly, having children does not appear to increase people's life satisfaction, although this finding is difficult to interpret given that childless individuals are different from parents in numerous ways. However, for those who have children, the quality of their relationships with their children is highly related to their level of satisfaction with their life overall. Also, several studies have suggested that parents' life satisfaction tends to correlate negatively with the number of children that they have—that is, life satisfaction decreases as the number of children increases. [*See* SOCIAL SUPPORT.]

E. INCOME

The relationship between income and life satisfaction is a complicated one. It seems that within nations, wealthier individuals are more satisfied than poorer individuals. Across nations, wealthier nations also show greater levels of life satisfaction than poorer nations; however, across-nation differences are smaller than within-nation differences. Furthermore, a robust finding in this literature concerns the distribution of wealth within a nation—the greater the economic disparities among income levels and classes in a nation, the greater the dissatisfaction expressed overall and the greater the disparity between satisfaction levels of the wealthy and the poor. Thus, women who live in poorer, less egalitarian nations tend to be less satisfied with their lives overall than women who live in wealthier nations.

Despite significant correlations between life satisfaction and wealth, longitudinal research has shown that rises in people's incomes do not necessarily coincide with related increases in life satisfaction. For example, Americans' levels of life satisfaction before and after World War II did not increase despite significant growth in income during this time period. Several explanations have been offered to account for these results. Perhaps once a certain level of wealth is obtained, life satisfaction is no longer anchored to increases in wealth and in material goods. In addition, social comparison may account for this effect—that is, comparing oneself with others as income and wealth increase may produce corresponding increases in expectations such that levels of satisfaction remain stable.

F. EMPLOYMENT

An individual's employment status, regardless of income, appears to predict life satisfaction, such that the unemployed report significantly diminished satisfaction compared with the employed. When gender is taken into account, it appears that employment (or lack thereof) is more strongly associated with life satisfaction for men than for women. This finding is not surprising, given that there is less cultural pressure on women to work outside the home. However, this pattern may change as existing gender roles broaden. At present, men's sense of self and identity is more strongly tied to their employment status than it is for women.

G. EDUCATION

Overall, researchers have found a small correlation between education and life satisfaction. However, the correlation appears to disappear when income and occupation are statistically controlled. The relationship between education and life satisfaction is probably due to the fact that higher levels of education are associated with higher incomes.

Education also appears to be more highly related to life satisfaction for individuals with lower incomes and in poor nations. Perhaps poorer persons obtain greater satisfaction from education because the achievement surpasses their expectations of what is attainable. For example, poor women in some cultures have little access to education, so when they do gain access, they may value and appreciate the experience more than those who perceive access to education as universal and easily available. Education may also provide access to greater occupational and income opportunities, which may additionally influence life satisfaction.

Despite the overall trend suggesting that education is more strongly related to life satisfaction for the poor, recent studies have found that, in wealthy nations, the most highly educated individuals seem to be slightly dissatisfied with their lives. It is possible that the educational elite have higher expectations or greater cynicism about their lives. Indeed, income appears to be a better predictor of life satisfaction than level of education.

H. GENERAL COMMENTS

While this review of the predictors of life satisfaction provides valuable information and raises some intriguing questions, we must be cautious in interpreting these findings because the possibility of selection effects may artificially bolster some of the results. For example, the observation that married individuals are more satisfied with their lives than unmarried ones may be confounded by the fact that more mentally healthy, extraverted, and stable individuals are able to find and sustain quality relationships with a spouse, and those factors are also correlated with life satisfaction. Similar selection effects may account for some of the findings regarding gender, income, employment, education, and age.

VII. *Future Directions*

The vast majority of studies investigating life satisfaction have been survey based. Although current self-report measures of life satisfaction have good reliability and validity, the field would benefit greatly from the use of alternative methodologies. For example, expanding the measurement of life satisfaction with physiological data (e.g., skin conductance, heart rate, blood pressure, neuropsychological measures), informant data, daily experience sampling, facial expressions, and cognitive procedures (e.g., reaction times) would greatly bolster the validity of self-reports and ensure that future measures of life satisfaction are completely gender neutral.

Studies of life satisfaction would also benefit from greater complexity of research design. Longitudinal studies and studies using causal modeling statistical techniques would bolster researchers' conclusions by moving beyond correlational methods that make it difficult to disentangle causal relationships among variables. For example, the finding that income seems to be more strongly related to life satisfaction for men than for women is difficult to interpret without greater statistical and methodological precision.

More sophisticated methodologies could also shed light on how interactions between women's personalities and their environment (i.e., nature and nurture) may influence their life satisfaction. Sonja Lyubomirsky (2000) has argued that three types of personality-environment interactions may be operating in this area. One type of interaction is referred to as "reactive"—that is, satisfied women may perceive and respond to the same circumstances differently from unsatisfied ones (e.g., cope better with poverty or adversity). Another type of interaction is called "evocative"—that is, satisfied women may evoke different kinds of reactions in others (e.g., may be better liked and more successful at obtaining jobs or marriage partners). The final type of interaction is called "proactive"—that is, satisfied women may find and construct different social worlds and environments (e.g., choose to leave an unfulfilling job or to move abroad). Empirical investigations of these personality-environment interactions may help shed light on some of the conflicting findings regarding the predictors of life satisfaction. For example, studies of this kind may help reconcile the findings that life satisfaction has been found to be both stable over time as well as influenced by recent life events.

VIII. Conclusions

Although much of the research described in this article has not specifically addressed the experiences of women, it nevertheless provides a great deal of information about life satisfaction in women. For example, women who live in egalitarian nations characterized by greater gender equality are relatively more satisfied with their lives than women who live in regions in which more traditional gender roles are observed. In addition, women who show an internal locus of control and less hostility toward other women, who have less traditional marriages and rel-

atively more friends, and who have relatively higher income and greater levels of education tend to be more satisfied with their lives. Because measures of life satisfaction have been shown to be gender neutral, researchers can maintain a reasonable degree of confidence in these findings. Interestingly, women and men appear to differ with respect to the sources from which they derive their life satisfaction. For example, women tend to draw on social resources (i.e., friends, family, community) to assess their satisfaction with their lives, whereas men are inclined to draw on financial and occupational status. Further research, however, is needed to specify more precisely the differences in the factors related to life satisfaction judgments for men versus women. Additionally, questions such as "Is the life satisfaction of women from diverse backgrounds (i.e., different races, cultures, ages, classes, and sexual orientations) related to a unique set of variables?" remain to be explored. Future studies focusing on the lives and experiences of women are needed to further develop and explore such questions.

SUGGESTED READING

Argyle, M. (1999). Causes and correlates of happiness. In *Well-Being: The Foundations of Hedonic Psychology* (D. Kahneman and E. Diener, eds.), pp. 353–373. Russell Sage Foundation, New York.

Diener, E., Emmons, R. A., Larsen, R. J., and Griffin, S., (1985). The satisfaction with life scale. *Journal of Personality Assessment 49*, 71–157.

Diener, E., Suh, E. M., Lucas, R. E., and Smith, H. L. (1999). Subjective well-being: Three decades of progress. *Psychological Bulletin 125*, 276–302.

Emmons, R. A., and Diener, E. (1985). Factors predicting satisfaction judgments: A comparative examination. *Social Indicators Research 16*, 157–167.

Fujita, F., Diener, E., and Sandvik, E. (1991). Gender differences in negative affect and well-being: The case for emotional intensity. *Journal of Personality and Social Psychology 61*, 427–434.

Headey, B., and Wearing, A. (1989). Personality, life events, and subjective well-being: Toward a dynamic equilibrium model. *Journal of Personality and Social Psychology 57*, 731–739.

Pinquart, M., and Sorensen, S. (2000). Influences of socioeconomic status, social network, and competence on subjective well-being in later life: A meta-analysis. *Psychology and Aging 15*, 187–224.

Veenhoven, R. (1996). Developments in satisfaction research. *Social Indicators Research 37*, 1–46.

Marriage: Still "His" and "Hers"?

Janice M. Steil
Adelphi University

*"There are two marriages . . . in every marital union, his and hers.
And his . . . is better than hers."—Bernard, 1982, p. 14.*

Glossary

Emotion work The efforts partners make to understand each other and to empathize with the other's situation and feelings.

Marital equality Involves equal participation in the responsibilities of the home, equal commitment to the responsibility to provide, equal voice in decision making, and equal commitment to, and investment in, the work of relationships. Equal relationships require that equal value is given to each partner's aspirations and abilities and work, and that the partners give equal valuing to the relationship itself.

The provider role Emerged as both a role and an identity specific to males around the 1830s as the United States transitioned from a subsistence to a market economy. The identification of the provider role as male had significant social, economic, and psychological implications including the asymmetrical distribution of power between husbands and wives.

Psychological symptomatology Symptoms of psychological distress, such as nervousness, fainting, headaches, and more severe disorders, such as depression, severe anxiety, and phobic tendencies.

Subjective well-being Men's and women's self-reported satisfaction and happiness with their marriages and their lives.

THE "HIS" AND "HER" MARRIAGE is a phrase coined in the early 1970s by Jesse Bernard. It describes her findings that there are two marriages within every marital union: "his" and "hers." Bernard found that while marriage is good for both men and women in terms of their well being, it is better for men than for women.

I. Jesse Bernard and the "His" and "Her" Marriage

In 1972, Jessie Bernard published a book in which she examined the relationship between sex (female or male), marital status (never married, married, widowed, or divorced), and a number of measures of well-being among women and men in the United States. The measures of well-being were essentially of two types. The first type measured subjective well-being, including assessments of men's and women's self-reported satisfaction and happiness with their marriages and their lives. The second type measured psychological symptomatology, including assessments of the prevalence of symptoms of psychological distress, such as nervousness, fainting, headaches, and trembling hands, and more severe disorders, such as depression and phobic tendencies.

On each of the well-being measures, Bernard compared (1) married men with married women, (2) unmarried men with unmarried women, and (3) the married with the unmarried. When she compared the well-being of married men with never-married men, she found that the married were less likely to show serious symptoms of psychological distress and were less likely to suffer mental health impairments than those who were never married. On the average, married men also lived longer, experienced greater career success, and were less likely to be involved in crime than men who were never married. Among men, then, the married fared far better than the unmarried. When Bernard compared married women with never-married women, she again found that the married generally fared better than the unmarried. Overall, then, marriage seemed to have a beneficial effect both for women and for men.

Next Bernard compared married women with married men on each of the well-being measures and found that among the married, women did not fare as well as men. Married women were more likely to have felt that they were about to have a nervous breakdown; more likely to experience psychological and physical anxiety (nervousness and insomnia, headaches, and heart palpitations); and showed more phobic reactions, more depression, and more passivity than married men. Among the married, then, women did not fare as well as men.

Bernard then compared the well-being of men and women who had never married. Among the never married, the pattern was reversed. Never-married men were more likely to show health impairments than never-married women. They were more depressed and passive, showed more anxiety and antisocial tendencies, and were more lkely to have felt they were about to have a nervous breakdown and to experience psychological anxiety. It was only among the married, then, that women showed more symptomatology than men. Marriage, it seems, is good for both women and men, but better for men.

Over the ensuing quarter of a century, Bernard's conclusions have been challenged on a number of fronts including gender differences in mate selection, gender differences in help-seeking behavior, and gender bias in the kinds of psychological symptoms and disorders that were studied. Yet with some caveats, the fundamental assertion of marriage as a relationship that benefits men more than women has been sustained. The question then became, why?

Bernard explained the well-being differences among the married in terms of the structural strains that the institution of marriage imposes on wives, particularly housewives. She offered a social roles explanation that focused particularly on the psychological costs of "housewifery" and the lack of outside sources of gratification when women are unemployed. The role of a full-time homemaker, she argued, is socially isolating, unstructured, subject to unceasing demands, and makes women ill.

II. The "His" and "Her" Marriage Today

In the 1970's, when Bernard reported her findings, nearly 60% of married women with husbands present were unemployed, with White women less likely to be employed than Black women. In the following quarter century, however, women's roles changed dramatically. By 1992, White women were just as likely to be employed as Black women; and today, 61% of married women with husbands present, nearly 64% of mothers with children under six years of age, and 77% of mothers with school-aged children are employed.

One of the most visible consequences of married women's increased labor force participation is the change in the number of dual-earner marriages. By 1998, of married couples with children under 18 years of age, 4% had employed mothers and unemployed fathers, 28.9% had employed fathers and unemployed mothers, and 64.1% had both employed mothers and employed fathers. By 1992, fewer than half (42%) of White men and only a third (33%) of Black men served as their families' main breadwinners, defined as bringing in at least 70% of the family income. Currently, approximately 25% of dual-earner wives have higher hourly wages, and 20% have higher annual earnings, than their spouses.

A. CHANGING ATTITUDES

Changing attitudes have paralleled the changing employment patterns. From 1970 to the present, attitudes regarding gendered family roles have become increasingly egalitarian. In the early 1970s, half of all women and 48% of men said that the most satisfying lifestyle was a marriage where the husband worked and the wife stayed home and took care of the house and children; and more than 70% of women said that it was more important for a wife to help her husband's career than to have a career herself. Similar attitudes continued into the 1980s when surveys showed that 50% of Americans believed that "working mothers are bad for children" and "weaken the family as an institution," beliefs that have not been supported by the empirical literature. A 1996 study found that the proportion of survey respondents agreeing that "it is better for everyone if men are the achievers and women take care of the home" and that "it is more important for a wife to help her husbands's career than to have one of her own" had decreased to a significant minority (30% and 20%, respectively). Since then, however, the rate of change has slowed significantly and support for egalitarian relationships is far from universal. Indeed, a 1997 survey found that 41% of paid workers agreed that "it is much better for everyone involved if the man earns the money and the woman takes care of the home and children." Sixty-seven percent, however, agreed that "a mother who works outside the home can have just as good a relationship with her children as a mother who does not work."

During this period, women consistently reported more egalitarian attitudes than men, and, among women, those with at least some college and those who were employed full time were the most egalitarian of all. Among men, older, less educated, married, and, among the married, men with full-time homemaker wives were less egalitarian in their views than younger, highly educated, high-status men with wives employed full-time. There are differences by race and ethnicity as well. Hispanic women are less likely to be employed and less likely to endorse egalitarian beliefs than White or Black women. The findings with regard to men are mixed. Hispanic men seem least likely to endorse egalitarian attitudes, but some studies find Black men endorsing more egalitarian attitudes than Whites, while others find the reverse.

B. UNCHANGING ASYMMETRIES

Despite changing attitudes, husbands are still more likely to work full time, to earn more, and to be in higher-status positions than their wives. Further, wives, despite their involvement in the paid labor force, still do a disproportionate share of domestic and relational work and report significantly less choice over their involvement in these activities than their husbands do.

Some, like Myra Ferree, remind us that we should not lose sight of the variability in couples' domestic work sharing. Findings from a representative sample of dual-earner households showed that while 29% of the sample, labeled "drudge wives," had full-time jobs and did more than 60% of the housework, another 38% were in "two-housekeeper" couples in which wives were employed full time and did 60% or less of the unpaid work. Similarly, Rosalind Barnett found that dual-earner husbands performed as much as 45% of household tasks. Most studies, however, find that, on average, employed wives continue to do significantly more housework than their husbands, including two-thirds of the repetitive, time-consuming and low-schedule control tasks such as cooking, cleaning, and laundry.

Fathers have increased their involvement in child care. A 1997 study found that over the past 20 years, dual-earner fathers had increased their time in child care by 30 minutes per workday. Yet wives continue to do from one quarter to two-thirds more child care than their husbands and according to Scott Coltrane, even "involved" fathers are likely to be involved primarily as "helpers" waiting to be told "what to do, when to do it, and how it should be done."

Wives also do vastly more of the emotion and interaction work that relationships require. Though empirical work in this area is limited, Pamela Fishman conducted a detailed analysis of 52 hours of taped conversations of White professional couples at home. Findings showed that wives were three times more likely than husbands to ask questions as a means of initiating and maintaining interaction. Wives used minimal responses such as "yeah" and "umm" to demonstrate interest, whereas husbands more often used these same minimal responses to display a *lack* of interest. Wives tried more often to initiate conversation but were less successful due to husbands' failure to respond. Husbands tried less often but seldom failed because wives more often did the interactional work.

Gender differences in emotion work result in wives providing better emotional support for husbands than husbands provide for wives. Studies show that more men than women say they receive affirmation and support from their spouse, and when asked to focus on the person closest to them (excluding parents and siblings), wives were twice as likely as husbands (22% versus 12%) to describe a relationship with a same-sex best friend rather than with their husband. Indeed, 64% of a sample of married heterosexual women reported being more emotionally intimate with other women, as compared to only 11% who said they were more emotionally intimate with their partners. Perhaps due to an overall paucity of research in this area, studies of the level and quality of relationship intimacy have been conducted on primarily White samples. There is some evidence, however, that gender differences in nurturance also characterize the relationships of Blacks. Among married Black women, 43% named a family member (exclusive of spouse) as the person "to whom they felt closest," 33.3% named a female friend, and only 19.6% named their spouse.

C. UNEQUAL BENEFITS

These asymmetries persist reqardless of a woman's employment status. Thus, women, whether they are full-time homemakers or employed outside the home, continue to do more of the work of the home and relationships and seem to provide better emotional support for husbands than husbands provide for them. As a result, marriage continues to benefit men more than women across a number of dimensions including the quality of their lives, their mental health, and their professional opportunities.

Findings from a number of studies show that married men have better physical and psychological health than their unmarried counterparts. Married men show lower levels of problem drinking, are less likely to be depressed, and (the longevity gap not withstanding) have lower risks of dying at any point in their lives than the unmarried. Married men report more emotional satisfaction with their sex lives than men who are either unmarried or cohabiting, occupy higher-level positions, earn more money, and are more satisfied with their careers than the unmarried, even after controlling for age.

Like men, women who were married reported more emotional satisfaction with their sex lives than those who were single or cohabiting; yet married women reported significantly less satisfaction than did married men.

The extent to which, and the conditions under which, the sex differences in the benefits of marriage extend across race and class are not fully known. Class and race are often confounded, and many groups, including Latinos and Asians, have been lit-

tle studied. Yet on some dimensions, the disparity seems to be greatest among Blacks. Twenty years ago, Elaine Carmen, Nancy Russo, and Jean Baker Miller constructed an index based on the proportional difference between the rates of illness among the married as compared to the never married and found a 71% reduction in vulnerability to mental illness for minority-race men who married, a 63% reduction for White men, but only a 28% reduction for White women and a mere 8% reduction for minority race women. These findings were supported in two subsequent studies, both of which found that marriage had little, if any, protective effect for Black women.

Others have tried to assess the extent to which the benefits of marriage are due to something unique about marriage per se, as compared to a number of underlying factors often associated with, but not exclusive to, marriage. The findings have been mixed. In 1977, Leonard Pearlin and Joyce Johnson assessed the extent to which the married might enjoy higher levels of psychological well-being simply because they are less likely to experience certain life stresses such as economic hardship and social isolation. Looking at the relationship between economic hardship, social isolation, and depression among the married and the unmarried, they found that the unmarried were doubly burdened whereas the married were doubly benefited. The unmarried were more likely to experience economic strain and social isolation. Further, the same levels of strain and isolation were more strongly associated with depression among the unmarried than the married. This finding was equally true for Blacks as well as Whites, and for the young as well as the old. The married, by contrast, were less likely to experience economic hardship and social isolation, but when they did, marriage seemed to provide some level of protection.

More recently, Catherine Ross examined the relationship between social attachment, emotional and economic support, relationship quality, and well-being among four groups: respondents who were married, respondents who were cohabiting but not married, respondents who were unmarried but with a partner outside the household, and those with no partner. Overall, the married reported the highest household incomes, the lowest levels of perceived economic hardship, and the happiest relationships. Levels of emotional support were significantly negatively associated with depression; yet in Ross's study the highest levels of emotional support were reported not by the married, but by the unmarried who lived with their partners, followed by people with partners outside the household.

Overall, findings showed that those who had partners, whether married or not, and who had the benefits of economic and emotional support, were as well off as those who were married. People in happy relationships had the lowest levels of depression. Those in unhappy relationships, however, were worse off than those with no partner at all. The extent to which these findings differed by sex was not reported.

III. The Benefits of Marital Equality

Some have suggested that the patterns of well-being among the married are closely related to the way that power is distributed between husbands and wives. Studies of decision making say are extensive. Findings consistently show that wife dominance is reported least often and is associated with the lowest levels of relationship satisfaction for men and women alike. Some studies show that husbands are equally satisfied either when they have greater say or when decision making say is equal; but most studies show that both partners are most satisfied when decision making say is equal. Other studies show that relationships in which decision making is described as equal are characterized by more mutually supportive communication; less manipulative forms of influence; more affirmation, affection, and intimacy; greater sexual and marital satisfaction for both partners; and less dysphoria for wives than relationships in which one of the partners is dominant.

Studies of influence strategy use have been conducted with both same-sex and cross-sex couples. Strategies reflecting an imbalance of power between partners are associated with dissatisfaction and less intimacy; whereas strategies associated with a more equal balance of power are associated with the highest levels of relationship satisfaction and the highest levels of relationship intimacy. [*See* POWER.]

Other studies of relationship equality have been based primarily on purposive samples of high-achieving White couples seen to represent the vanguard of change. These findings are suggestive, rather than conclusive, and there are several limits to their generalizability. Besides the obvious restrictions of race and class, the samples, for the most part, represent self-selected groups who valued and were seeking more equal relationships. With these caveats, we noted that studies comparing relationships in which women and men regard themselves as equally responsible for providing financially for the family, as compared to those who see the husband as responsible for providing, showed that husbands and wives were more satisfied with their relationships, reported a greater likelihood of confiding and showing affection, and the wives were less likely to be depressed. Finally, a recent study of men and women in egalitarian, as compared to traditional marriages, found that those who reported that housework was equally shared scored lower on measures of dysphoria than those who said the wife was primarily responsible. Similarly, men and women who said that child care was equally shared reported a greater sense of fairness, less stress at home, and more benefits from having responsibilities both in and out of the home, including feelings of competence and feeling like a well-rounded person who is able to use all one's talents.

Consistent with the findings reported earlier, data from several studies confirm the importance of emotional support to partner well-being. Women with a confiding relationship with a spouse or boyfriend are less likely to become depressed, and both women and men in relationships rated as high in intimacy are less likely to report symptoms of depression and anxiety than those in relationships rated as low in intimacy.

In sum, a number of surveys based on large national representative samples show that endorsement of somewhat more equal relationships has increased significantly over the past 25 years. Women consistently report more egalitarian attitudes than men. Hispanics consistently report less egalitarian attitudes than Blacks and Whites. Other research, based on more restricted samples, suggests that the inequality of heterosexual relationships is a factor in partner well-being that helps explain why marriage is often more beneficial for men than for women. Yet, despite some increase in husband participation in both child care and household tasks, relationships remain unequal. The question then is, why? What is it about the processes within relationships and the social context in which those relationships are set that supports and maintains gendered marriages in which roles are divided rather than shared?

IV. Why Is Equality in Marriage So Difficult to Achieve?

A. GENDERED CONTEXTS

Gender is a system of inequality that is created and recreated daily across all interactional contexts. While families are only one of the arenas of gender, they are the context within which the construction of our gendered self first begins. As part of this process, children are introduced to gender-based patterns of family labor at an early age. Studies of children as young as age six, studies of children through the school years, and studies of adolescents all show that boys are allowed to spend more time in leisure activities than girls; and girls are asked to spend more time in household tasks and child care and to contribute a greater share of family work than are boys.

These gendered family structures shape and limit girls aspirations, make wives financially vulnerable, give different meanings to the resources that husbands and wives contribute to relationships, prescribe differences in men's and women's sense of entitlement, and legitimize a gendered workforce that fails to provide adequate supports to working parents. Each of these factors also undermines a woman's ability to achieve an equal position in marriage. [*See* ENTITLEMENT.]

B. ACCESS TO RESOURCES

In the third or more of marriages in which wives are unemployed, men are responsible for the financial support of the family and are, therefore, more likely to develop concrete, universally valued resources such as earning power and job prestige. Women in such gender-defined relationships are responsible for the home, child rearing, and relationship maintenance. As a result, they develop primarily personal and relationship-specific resources such as love and affection. Thus, the gendered division of work precludes women's access to the more concrete and, often, more highly valued resources associated with paid employment, while also promoting wives economic dependence on their husbands.

But paid employment is more than access to earning power. Across both sex and class, work outside the home can be a source of independent identity, increased self-esteem, and enhanced social contacts. Thus, when a wife is unemployed, she not only loses her financial independence, but her access to limited and primarily relationship-specific resources; her absence of alternative sources of achievement, self-esteem, and affirmation; and the inevitable reduction in her bargaining power converge in ways that make it exceedingly difficult for her to interact with her spouse as an equal partner.

C. GENDERED MEANINGS, GENDERED OUTCOMES

Yet paid employment often fails to bring the same benefits to wives as it does to husbands. The gendered division of labor in families, particularly girls'

expectations of becoming the primary parent, interacts with societal structures of paid employment in ways that encourage gendered career choices from an early age. Men and women are often segregated into different occupations, industries, and jobs with those in female-dominant positions paid less than those in male-dominant positions. Yet, according to a 1999 review by Patricia Roos and Mary Gatta, the sex gap in earnings persists within both majority male and majority female occupations such that, regardless of occupational type, females earn less than comparable males, and this is particularly true for women who become mothers.

Even when wives succeed in earning as much or more than their husbands, they rarely achieve equality at home. Studies show that the more men earn relative to their partners, the greater their say in decision making, the lower their involvement in domestic work, and the better they feel about themselves as spouses. This is not the case for women. Employed wives have greater say in marital decision making than unemployed wives, but they do not achieve equal sharing of domestic tasks, and women who earn significantly more than their husbands often do not have equal say in financial matters. Moreover, studies have shown that women who earn more than their husbands do not feel better about themselves as spouses, and for some their husbands actually do less work at home.

This difference in outcomes is due to the different meanings ascribed to the paid work of wives and husbands in the context of a gendered society. Despite the changing demographics, most women and men continue to endorse the importance of the husband as the primary provider. This is true for Blacks as well as Whites and Hispanics. Because African American wives have a longer history of waged work than European American wives, a Black wife's employment is more likely to be seen by herself and her husband as an integral and normative component of her roles of wife and mother. Yet Black women seem no less likely than White women to emphasize the importance of husband as provider and to see themselves as holding primary responsibility for the home and children. When wives endorse the importance of the husband as the primary provider, they grant him significant power, irrespective of his wife's employment status and income.

In 1992, Maureen Perry Jenkins and her colleagues divided employed women into three groups: coproviders, who saw their income as important to the family and saw the provider role as equally shared; ambivalent coproviders, who admitted that the family was dependent on their incomes but were uncomfortable with the reality of shared economic responsibility; and main-secondary providers, who viewed their incomes as helpful but not vital to the family's well-being. Although none of the husbands shared the work of the home equally, husbands of both coprovider and ambivalent coprovider wives spent twice the time in household tasks as other husbands, and coprovider wives experienced less depression than any other group.

Yet even those who endorse egalitarian views struggle with their own gendered expectations. An interview study of White professional dual-career couples found that almost all men and women felt that it would be easier for the wives' careers to be less successful than the husbands' than for the reverse. Among the reasons wives gave for this disparity were (1) his work is more important to his sense of self, (2) she needed her husband to be successful, and (3) she feared that people would say his lack of success was her fault for making him help at home. Others found that when women and men assessed the importance of their own careers to themselves, both rated their careers as highly important with no differences by sex. When these same men and women were asked to respond on behalf of their spouses, however, men perceived their wives' careers as only moderately important to them, whereas women perceived their husbands' careers as being extremely important to them. Though all of the respondents endorsed equal relationships as ideal, and as important to themselves, half said that the husband's career was primary No respondent said that a wife's career was primary, even though 22% of the women earned as much or more than their husbands earned.

Others find that even when women generate all or most of the family's income, they seem to feel that supporting the family does not compensate for the household labor that their husbands perform, and eschew any attempt at staking some claim of control over money or decision making. Similarly, the question of who should remain at home with children is typically resolved along gender lines. As several authors have pointed out, couples can consider themselves equal because they jointly participated in the decision making about child care, a process that obscures the fact that a gendered outcome was almost foreordained. [*See* WORK–FAMILY BALANCE.]

D. THE PARADOX OF THE CONTENTED WIFE

Some have argued that the primary paradox of the relationship literature is women's relative lack of grievance over the inequalities of heterosexual marriage. Although wives and husbands agree that women disproportionately bear the burden of the imbalances in domestic life, the majority of both employed and unemployed wives report the division of labor as fair. Indeed, it is only when wives perform in excess of two-thirds of the work that they began to report the distribution as less than fair. Why?

E. GENDERED MEANINGS REVISITED

Some have argued that women's lack of grievance can best be understood in terms of the gendered meanings of housework and the differences in what women and men value and want from relationships. According to this perspective, the most highly valued outcomes for women are interpersonal. Women, then, do the housework in part as an expression of love and a way of caring for others. Indeed, studies have shown that feeling appreciated by their husbands for the domestic work they do is one of the best predictors of wives' perceptions of marital fairness, and husbands' provision of emotional support has a more significant positive effect on wives' perceived well-being than husbands' contributions to housework or child care. From this perspective, then, a context of support and appreciation changes the meaning of domestic tasks, and women perceive their relationships as fair when they receive the interpersonal outcomes they value.

F. JUSTICE THEORY

Others argue that women's lack of grievance with the asymmetries of married life is better explained by a failure to believe in the feasibility of change and a sense of entitlement that is lower than their husbands'. In a singularly systematic study of the predictors of a sense of unfairness, Faye Crosby showed that women are unlikely to perceive conditions as unfair until they see that other conditions are possible, want such conditions for themselves, and believe that they are entitled to them. [*See* ENTITLEMENT.]

G. SAME-SEX RELATIONSHIPS AND THE EGALITARIAN POTENTIAL

Some have suggested that same-sex couples provide a blueprint of the potential for egalitarianism for heterosexual marriage. Women in lesbian relationships hold no expectation of economic security provided by marriage and accept a lifelong responsibility to support themselves. As a result, women in lesbian relationships are more likely to be employed, more likely to be employed full time, and on average earn higher salaries than their heterosexual counterparts.

As well, same-sex couples are more likely to reject a husband–wife, masculine–feminine division of labor, to share household tasks equitably, and value equality more than heterosexual married couples. Indeed, 97% of a sample of lesbian women said that partners should have exactly equal say in relationships, and this is true even in families with children. A study of 66 lesbian mothers found that household labor, decision making, and child care were more equally shared than is usually the case in heterosexual couples, even though biological mothers were seen as doing somwhat more child care than their partners. In sum, most scholars conclude that lesbian relationships tend to be more equal, more autonomous, and more intimate than the relationships of married heterosexuals. Further, and consistent with the studies of the married, equal power is associated with partners' greater relationship satisfaction and greater liking for each other. [*See* LESBIANS, GAY MEN, AND BISEXUALS IN RELATIONSHIPS.]

H. FURTHER SOCIETAL CONSTRAINTS

On a societal level, gendered beliefs support structural barriers to women's inequality by continuing to legitimize a male-oriented workplace that fails to support parenting. In 1992, Susan Lewis and her colleagues reported a series of studies on eight industrialized countries in Europe and Asia. These studies identified a number of gendered beliefs as primary factors in determining career opportunities for women and role sharing among couples. When masculinity was defined by the provider role, when children were believed to require full-time maternal care, and when mothers allegedly worked by choice, there was little societal or partner support for women in the paid labor force. Societies that endorsed these beliefs provided little public child care, freed husbands from domestic responsibilities, and left employed mothers to work out their own support systems. According to the authors, when men are defined as breadwinners and women as homemakers, there is no restructuring of paid or domestic work to take into account women's employment. Thus, for women, equality at work means equality with men under conditions established for men without home responsibility.

I. FURTHER GENDER AND IDENTITY CONSTRAINTS

Other factors that impede the achievement of equality include the fact that relationship equality is generally perceived as something that primarily benefits women, that women disproportionately bear the burden of initiating change, and that women's role as change agent conflicts with their primary role as nurturer and relationship maintainer.

Since simply being employed often reflects some element of increased power, independence, prestige, and self-esteem, any movement in the direction of equality is often viewed as beneficial to women. For men, however, the achievement of equality is most often viewed in terms of costs: interference with their ability to meet career demands, loss of the power and privileges associated with being the sole provider, loss of the services of a nonemployed wife, increased stress, and demands to participate in family life in unfamiliar ways that conflict with masculine identity. Less attention has been paid to the *costs* of inequality for men including both excessive work involvement and loss of their nurturing, caregiving selves. Finally, even less attention has been paid to the *benefits* of relationship equality for men: relief from the achievement and performance pressures associated with their sole breadwinner role; richer, more intimate, and more satisfying relationships with their wives and childern; less relationship stress; and greater freedom to express and experience themselves more authentically.

Scott Coltrane interviewed a sample of fathers who shared parenting equally. Because many of these men were fathers in dual-earner families where the parents worked split shifts, the fathers were forced to overcome feelings of ambivalence and awkwardness and assume the role of primary caretaker in their wives' absence. Unexpectedly, it was found that as men became more sensitive parents, their marital relations improved. As a result of learning how to care for their children, fathers paid more attention to emotional cues from their wives and engaged in more reciprocal communication.

Equal relationships are widely viewed as more stressful than more traditional relationships. Yet, contrary to expectations, study findings showed exactly the opposite. When the amount of stress reported by men and women in equal, transitional, and traditional relationships was compared, it was found that those in equal relationships reported feeling stressed by the responsibilities arising from their marital relationships *least* often, and traditionals reported feeling stressed *most* often. While equal relationships require more frequent negotiation and compromise, it may be precisely the need for continued interpersonal contact and involvement that contributes to the high levels of satisfaction found among egalitarian couples. As one male study respondent noted:

Maybe you end up having certain arguments that you might not have had, arguments about whose responsibility it is to do this, that, and the other. But I think, in a way, if you don't have those arguements, you end up having arguments about other things sooner or later. The arguments you have about responsibilities are not as vicious as the ones you have later about resentment.

Perhaps because equality is viewed as primarily benefiting women, women disproportionately bear the burden of initiating change. Even among a sample of dual-career respondents among whom there were no differences in the extent to which they reported equality as important in their own relationships, 90% of wives and 55% of husbands said that the wives were more likely to raise issues of equality in their own relationships. Yet a woman's role as change agent is often in conflict with her primary role as nurturer and relationship maintainer. Women often feel that attempts to act on their own behalf, or take steps toward their own growth, are repudiations of femininity and will be viewed as attacks on men. Similarly, women often suppress their own interests to "keep the peace." But as Dana Jack has shown, women who "silence" themselves increase their risk for depression.

V. The Future of Marriage: Where from Here?

The continuing inequality in the division of labor at home has come to symbolize the psychological complexity of modern marital relationships in which both women and men struggle with issues of identity and fairness. Integrating both the justice and the gender perspectives, Ferree pointed out that the family is simultaneously a communal structure that endeavors to satisfy the needs of all members and a locus of struggle through which each member strives to satisfy independent interests. Thus, it is only through understanding the cultural framework in which familial negotiations take place that we can understand both the resistance to change and the process by which change is emerging.

Women struggle with their husbands to get them to do more work at home, and with themselves over issues of restricted entitlement and traditional notions of mothering. Men struggle with their partners over issues of privilege and fairness, and with themselves in redefining traditional notions of career and fathering. Parents, particularly mothers, struggle with the lack of societal supports, including inflexible work schedules and a paucity of affordable, quality child care.

When husbands resist wives' attempts at change, wives often defer. But they pay a heavy price, including a devaluation of themselves. According to Fran Deutsch, equality requires strong women and fair men, for it is not conflict, but rather the avoidance of conflict that signals a lack of mutual respect. To fight for equality means a wife believes her husband is fair minded and capable of being as good a parent and partner as she is.

The future is unclear. Some assert that under the present conditions of political, social, and sexual inequality, truly egalitarian marriage is not possible for the majority. Others have argued that if gender is socially constructed, then gender can be socially reconstructed, paving the way for more equal and less gendered relationships. As women's options expand, their willingness to support the continuing inequalities of relationships will continue to decline. As women increasingly enter the labor force and the gendered income gap declines, so does women's financial dependence on men. Those who marry are waiting longer to do so, and are significantly less likely to remarry if they are subsequently widowed or divorced. In 1970, the U.S. Census reported that 123 per thousand divorced women remarried. By 1990 this number had declined to 76 per thousand.

For all involved, the stakes are enormous. More equal relationships offer men the opportunity to relinquish the mantle of total economic responsibility and family dependency, to involve themselves in parenting, and to more fully express their emotional and nurturing selves. More equal relationships offer women the opportunity to develop themselves professionally, to develop a sense of self independent of their husband and their children, and to achieve economic independence and higher self-esteem. More equal relationships offer men and women together the opportunity to be part of more intimate relationships based on the mutual reliance and respect that is so important to a satisfying relationship and to both husbands' and wives' well-being. Finally, more equal relationships offer the family the potential to be the crucial first school where children develop a sense of fairness and a context in which the construction of our nongendered selves first begins.

SUGGESTED READING

Bernard, J. (1982). *The Future of Marriage, 2nd ed.* Yale University Press, New Haven, CT.

Coltrane, S. (1996). *Family Man: Fatherhood, Housework, and Gender Equality.* Oxford University Press, New York.

Deutsch, F. (1999). *Halving It All: How Equally Shared Parenting Works.* Harvard University Press, Cambridge, MA.

Ferree, M. M. (1990). Beyond separate spheres: Feminism and family research. *Journal of Marriage and the Family 52,* 866–844.

Steil, J. (1997). *Marital Equality: Its Relationship to the Well-Being of Husbands and Wives.* Sage, Thousand Oaks, CA.

Media Influences

L. Monique Ward

Allison Caruthers

University of Michigan

Glossary

Cultivation theory A theoretical perspective originally proposed by George Gerbner and his colleagues that is typically used for examining how media exposure affects viewers' attitudes and beliefs about the world. This theory proposes that television's consistent yet restricted images and portrayals construct a specific portrait of reality, and as viewers watch more and more television, they gradually come to cultivate or adopt beliefs about the world that coincide with this portrait.

Drench hypothesis A proposition offered by media researcher Bradley Greenberg that emphasizes the power of individual portrayals to affect viewers. This perspective suggests that specific critical portrayals may exert a stronger force on viewers' impressions and beliefs than might exposure to the masses of similar TV characters and behaviors regularly viewed.

Gender constancy The understanding that sex remains constant, across time and across superficial external transformations (e.g., in hair length, in dress). This realization that you cannot change your sex was originally believed to occur between ages five and seven, but is now believed to take place earlier.

Gender schema theory An information-processing approach to understanding how beliefs about gender develop and shape future perceptions and interpretations. Gender schemas are organized sets of beliefs and expectations about females and males that influence the kinds of information people attend to, encode, and remember. Schemas are used to interpret the world and to guide behavior. There is a strong tendency for new information to be made to fit the existing schema, and this desire to be gender consistent is believed to lead children to preferentially learn same-sex-typed behaviors. Individual differences are believed to exist in the depth, accessibility, and strength of people's gender schemas. A *gender schematic* person can be defined as one whose gender schema is highly accessible, readily used, and broad in coverage; a *gender aschematic* person can be defined as one who is less likely to categorize by gender and whose gender schema is less accessible, infrequently used, and less broad in coverage.

Priming theory A theoretical perspective typically used for examining short-term effects of media stimuli. This theory asserts that the presentation of a certain stimulus with a particular meaning primes or activates semantically related concepts and calls them to mind. Such priming increases the likelihood that subsequently encountered persons or events will be appraised in the context of the primed schema. This process can occur automatically and without conscious awareness.

Social learning theory A psychological perspective examining the influence of observational learning on the adoption of specific behaviors. While the theory has been expanded from its original form to acknowledge the role of cognitive processes, the basic premises emphasize the importance of influential models. Several factors are believed to determine who and what are modeled, including the cognitive skills, preconceptions, affective states, motivations, and value preferences of the observer, as well as the salience, attractiveness, complexity, and functional value of the activity modeled. For example, observers are believed to be more likely to learn and model the behavior of models who are perceived as attractive, powerful, and similar, and whose behaviors are rewarded or not punished.

MEDIA INFLUENCES are often underestimated. Although the media are typically used for entertainment, they have also become important sources for learning about the world of gender. Through their themes, storylines, characterizations, and dialogue, the media, and television in particular, provide countless examples of how women and men should look, act, and be. However, analyses of media content conducted over the past 40 years have consistently documented that these examples are frequently limited, traditional, and stereotypical, thereby raising concern about the cumulative effect of repeated exposure. Might frequent exposure encourage viewers to adopt limited and stereotypical conceptions about gender roles? In efforts to answer this question, researchers have examined the impact of several dimensions of media use on several dimensions of gender from multiple perspectives. This review presents a summary of the current findings in the field. Whereas no one study can provide all of the answers, by examining the findings produced by the literature as a whole, we can begin to grasp the full nature of the media's influence.

I. Introduction

One of the most pervasive influences on the character of American life over the past few decades has been the media. Whether watching television, going to the movies, or listening to the radio, Americans' exposure to the media has become extensive, routine, and necessary. Recent numbers indicate that American children watch three to four hours of television each day and will have spent more hours with the media than in school by the time they are 18. Given such high levels of exposure, it is no surprise that parents, researchers, and policy makers have become interested in the impact of these rituals, and of media content in particular, on American youth. Of chief concern is how media content and portrayals shape viewers' social attitudes, assumptions, schemas, and behaviors. Although the media are typically used for entertainment, they also have become important sources for learning about the world, especially about gender roles. Indeed, because virtually every media portrayal consists of male or female characters of some type, each exposure transmits important messages about society's beliefs about women and men. Every time we read a magazine, watch a television program, or glimpse a commercial, we receive messages about how women and men should look, act, and be. The models are prevalent, appealing, and unavoidable.

What messages about gender roles do these models transmit? Analyses of media content conducted over the past 40 years have documented limited portrayals of the sexes and pervasive gender stereotyping. On television, for example, males outnumber females in nearly every genre except soap operas and are typically featured in major roles two to three times more often than women. Men are portrayed as active, powerful, knowledgeable, authoritative, and important; they are the doers and the thinkers. Male characters are featured in a greater variety of roles and occupations and are seen as rational, assertive, problem-solving agents whose needs and opinions are taken seriously. Women, on the other hand, typically assume the roles of wife, mother, or love interest, whose stories are secondary and whose characters have less depth. Female characters are more often passive, dependent, emotional, deferent, youthful, and attractive. If employed outside the home, they typically hold low-status stereotypical occupations and cannot successfully manage the demands of marriage and career. In advertising and in music videos, women are frequently depicted as decorative or sexual objects whose main purpose is to look beautiful and attract attention. While there have been some improvements in these trends over the past decade, with increasing portrayals of professional women and of nurturing fathers, evidence indicates that the general patterns persist. Whether intentional or accidental, these portrayals do not reflect the reality and the depths of either women or men, but instead exaggerate a selection of real-life circumstances and assumptions. They are stereotypes.

What, then, is the cumulative effect of repeated exposure to these images? Might frequent exposure encourage viewers to adopt limited and stereotypical conceptions about gender roles? While these are important questions, the relationships they address are complex, allowing no simple or direct answers. First, both media exposure and gender roles are broad, multidimensional constructs, each commonly operationalized in different ways. Media use covers many behaviors, including regular viewing amounts, various forms of viewer involvement and identification, and even experimental exposure. A diverse array of media are involved, including television, music, films, and magazines, each of which contains multiple genres of its own. Moreover, media habits typically develop early, change throughout the life course, and are frequently influenced by both external and internal forces. "Gender roles" is an equally complex construct, encompassing conceptions, beliefs, and expectations about gender, as well as related behaviors and choices. Indeed, in their 6 × 4 matrix of gender-typing constructs and content areas, Diane Ruble and Carol Martin identified more than 24 dimensions of gender, each possessing additional subtypes. Moreover, expectations of the appropriate roles and behavior for each gender change over time, such that what was customary for most women and men in the 1940s has become less so today.

Second, the path of influence between media exposure and gender roles is complex, with many theorized mechanisms and mediators. The typical question raised is, how exactly does media content get into the minds of viewers, shaping their gender-related preferences, attitudes, schemas, and behaviors? Whereas initial speculations may have taken the "magic bullet" approach, in which content shoots directly from the television to the mind of the viewer, current theorizing acknowledges the general complexity of the dynamics involved. Viewers, even the youngest of children, are not mindless drones, soaking up and imitating all media images. Indeed, many viewers are exposed to the same stereotypical content, but their subsequent beliefs and behaviors are not always equivalent. Instead, it is now believed that viewers construct meaning from the content presented based on their existing worldviews, schemas,

and personal experiences. Consequently, any given content must be integrated with existing perspectives and with input from other sources (e.g., peers, family) and is therefore likely to mean different things to different people. Several theoretical models (e.g., priming theory, cultivation theory) have been proposed to address this complexity, some focusing on short-term effects and others on long-term effects. It is also now assumed that these relationships are bidirectional. While media content may influence viewers, it is the viewers who actively select and are drawn to specific content. Finally, there are numerous mediators involved, determining under what conditions media effects will and will not occur. To underscore the complex nature of these processes, Table I presents a compilation of many of the mediating factors believed to participate. Thus, in considering the research questions and relationships under study, we must bear in mind that the dynamics of how the media influence gender-role attitudes and behavior are neither simple nor direct, but instead involve multiple constructs, mechanisms, and mediating variables.

II. The State of the Field

Despite these complexities, dozens of researchers have attempted to answer these and related questions, resulting in a substantial literature examining the impact of the media on gender roles. Driven largely by concerns raised by the women's movement in the 1960s, research in this area began slowly at the close of that decade, flourished in the 1970s and 1980s, and declined substantially in the 1990s. Although researchers in this domain have not had the benefit of large-scale government-funded initiatives, as is the case with research on media violence, individual efforts of more than 60 different authors/writing teams have produced a sizable body of findings, which now includes more than 75 published studies. Most of these works (approximately 85%) focus on the effects of television (e.g., soap operas, commercials, cartoons), with some examination of the role of magazine advertisements, music, and films. Due largely to concerns about the media's impact on young people, approximately half of the studies focus on children, and another 17% center on adolescents. Although predominantly White samples are the norm, drawn largely from middle-class populations, recent efforts have attempted to sample more broadly.

Table I
Summary of Factors Mediating the Impact of Media Exposure

Characteristics of the content	Viewer characteristics
Medium (e.g., TV, radio, magazines)	Age
Genre (e.g., drama, comedy, commercial)	Sex
Degree of similarity between viewer and content	Socioeconomic status
Simplicity/complexity	Cognitive capabilities (e.g., IQ)
Degree of realism	Ethnic group background
Clarity of ideas/messages	Time normally spent with that medium
Level of positive reinforcement themes receive	Perceived realism of content/medium
Status/prestige of protagonists	Degree of attention given to content
Degree of active participation allowed	Identification with and attitude toward characters
Familiarity of content	Needs, interests, and motivations for exposure
Degree to which content is understandable	Arousal level/mood state
Degree of arousal content provokes	Level of active versus passive viewing
Degree of repetition of the message or theme	Knowledge about the medium
Format (e.g., animated, live action)	Nature and social context of viewing experience
Mood/tone (e.g., educational, entertainment)	Level of personal experience with the issue
Credibility of characters/spokespersons	Level of critical viewing
Vividness of messages/salience	Understanding of content
Objectivity of presentation	Cognitive preconceptions (e.g., prior attitudes)
Duration	Identity and personality characteristics (e.g., feminist, conservative,
Consistency of messages and behaviors modeled	veteran, parent)

Sources: Bandura, A. (1994). Social cognitive theory of mass communication. In *Media Effects: Advances in Theory and Research* (J. Bryant and D. Zillmann, eds.), (pp. 61–90). Erlbaum, Hillsdale, NJ; Dorr, A. (1986). *Television and Children: A Special Medium for a Special Audience.* Sage, Beverly Hills, CA; Stewart, D. and Ward, S. (1994). Media effects on advertising. In *Media Effects: Advances in Theory and Research* (J. Bryant and D. Zillmann, eds.), (pp. 315–364). Erlbaum, Hillsdale, NJ; Stroman, C. A. (1990). Television's role in the socialization of African American children and adolescents. *Journal of Negro Education* 60, 314–327.

One strength of the field is that is contains a nice blend of experimental and survey designs, each working to address a particular concern. Because they capture relationships as they naturally exist, survey designs are typically used for investigating whether regular, habitual media use is associated with gender stereotyping. When the intent is to determine if Context X causes greater gender stereotyping than does Content Not-X, experimental designs are generally employed. The experimental format is especially beneficial because it allows researchers to control the exact nature of the content and of the viewing experience. As an additional mechanism of control, a number of studies use laboratory-created stimuli. Here, researchers compose scenarios in the laboratory, videotape male and female models acting them out, and later present the scenes to experimental participants. More than one-third of the studies reviewed here used laboratory-created stimuli, ranging from simple displays of a model selecting specific toys to lab-recreated commercials.

An additional strength of the existing literature is its diversity. Researchers have examined the influence of the media on gender roles from the perspective of social learning theory, cultivation theory, priming theory, gender schema theory, and the drench hypothesis. Additionally, media use and exposure have been assessed in more than a dozen different ways, with researchers tapping average daily viewing amounts, viewing amounts for particular genres, identification with popular characters, and exposure to print advertisements. Several dimensions of gender have been examined as well, including stereotypes about activities, occupations, and traits; attitudes about the appropriate roles for males and females; career aspirations; and the imitation of same-sex models. Whereas this diversity can sometimes make it difficult to discern a coherent picture and to draw definitive conclusions, it also strengthens the validity of the findings themselves. Indeed, if different theoretical and methodological paths are taken, and each leads to the same conclusion, we gain additional assurance that the findings are valid, real, and meaningful.

It appears, then, that scholarly examination of the impact of the media on gender roles has made substantial strides in exploring a complex set of relationships. Researchers have examined the impact of several dimensions of media use on several dimensions of gender from several different perspectives. Whereas no one study is comprehensive enough to provide all of the answers, by examining the findings produced by the literature as a whole, we can begin to understand the full nature of the media's influence.

III. The Research Findings

Several attempts have been made to summarize and review the diverse findings in this area. Descriptive reviews produced by Sandra Calvert and Aletha Huston, Kevin Durkin, Barrie Gunter, Nancy Signorielli, and others have focused mainly on the contributions of television, concluding that weak to moderate links exist between television exposure and gender stereotyping. Two meta-analyses addressing this subject have reached a similar conclusion. In their 1996 meta-analysis, Jennifer Herrett-Skjellum and Mike Allen examined the strength and consistency of the association between television viewing and the acceptance of gender stereotypes. Their goal was to produce a quantitative estimate of the relationship between these phenomena by averaging effects across studies. Analysis of the findings of 11 experimental studies reported a significant, average positive correlation of $r = .207$. This result indicates that exposure to content depicting traditional gender roles tended to increase endorsement of those stereotypes. Analysis of the outcomes of 19 nonexperimental studies revealed a significant, average positive correlation of $r = .101$ between self-reported amounts of television viewing and acceptance of gender-role stereotypes. This means that acceptance of gender stereotypes was typically stronger among more frequent viewers. A similar meta-analysis reported in 1997 by Michael Morgan and J. Shanahan revealed an average effects size of .102 for 14 studies exploring correlational links between viewing amounts and gender roles.

Our goal then is to build on and extend these previous reviews by examining the impact of several media in addition to television; by including samples of children, adolescents, and adults; and by incorporating multiple dimensions of gender. In this review we examine the contributions of 76 survey and experimental studies that were published after 1970. To keep the review manageable, we examined only findings from published pieces (no dissertations or unpublished conference papers) and from pieces that examined some connection between *actual* media exposure and participants' gender-role beliefs and behaviors. Studies that analyzed only viewers' *perceptions* of specific content without assessing the content's impact on gender were not included. Also not included were pieces in which media use represented exposure to pornography or sexually explicit materials, or in which only body dissatisfaction, sexual attitudes, or sexual behaviors were examined as outcomes. Whereas these constructs often exhibit gender-specific patterns, they were not covered here. Finally, we chose not to include literature on the impact of storybook and textbook content and characters; instead, we focus on the impact of television programs and commercials, music videos, and magazines, media on which the bulk of research concentrates. Our discussion of the findings is segmented by the gender construct in question, of which there are seven.

A. HOW DO MEDIA USE AND EXPOSURE SHAPE ATTITUDES ABOUT THE APPROPRIATE ROLES AND BEHAVIORS OF WOMEN AND MEN?

One of the largest categories of findings examines the impact of media use and exposure on people's attitudes about women and men, focusing on their attitudes about the appropriate roles and behaviors of husbands and wives, the appropriateness of women's place in the domestic and work arenas, and the competencies and skills of each sex. This line of research addresses the critical question, does frequent exposure to media images, many of which are traditional and stereotypical, lead viewers to adopt similar sexist notions? In examining this question, researchers solicit participants' level of agreement with the following types of statements: "men are more rational than women," "married women should stay home and be housewives and mothers," "swearing is worse for a girl than for a boy," "there is something wrong with a woman who doesn't want to marry and raise a family," and "our society discriminates against women."

One approach has been to examine this issue via correlational surveys, which typically have compared the strength of participants' sexist attitudes with either their regular viewing amounts (e.g., "How much TV do you watch in a typical day?") or their liking of or involvement with popular television characters. Results with this approach have been somewhat mixed, with some studies reporting associations between more frequent or involved viewing and sexist attitudes, others noting links only for certain genres or for certain populations (e.g., among females only), and some reporting no effects at all. Two research teams even reported the opposite effect among some samples, with heavier media use correlating with more egalitarian attitudes. Perhaps the strongest expected outcomes were reported in 1983 by Michael Morgan and Nancy Rothschild, who examined links between eighth graders' attitudes about who should do certain chores and the students' viewing amounts and cable access. Here, Time 1 viewing amounts correlated with sexism scores at Time 1 and at Time 2 (approximately six months later) and were strongest among teens with cable access and fewer social affiliations.

More consistent findings have emerged from experimental approaches in which participants are exposed to stereotypical, neutral, or counterstereotypical media stimuli and are then surveyed concerning their own gender-role attitudes or beliefs. The expectation is not that this one exposure will cause viewers to adopt sexist attitudes permanently, but that the exposure will prime existing attitudes and will make salient and validate certain ways of viewing the world. Findings indicate that participants exposed to traditional images typically do score higher on measures of sexism than do participants exposed to neutral or more progressive stimuli. At the same time, exposure to egalitarian or progressive stimuli appears to produce lower sexism scores. These effects have emerged using several genres of media, including commercials, PBS programs, and print ads, and among child, teen, and adult participants. For example, in their 1997 study, Natalie MacKay and Katherine Covell exposed undergraduates to 10 advertisements portraying women either as sex objects or in a more progressive fashion. Participants rated each ad on four neutral dimensions (e.g., graphical design), and then completed measures assessing their acceptance of both gender-role stereotypes and feminism. Female and male students who had viewed the progressive images of women agreed less with the traditional statements about gender roles and offered greater support of feminism and the women's

movement. Thus, although null results have also been reported for some studies, samples, and viewing conditions, the bulk of the experimental evidence suggests that experimental exposure can prime traditional or nontraditional attitudes about gender, depending on the nature of the stimuli and the viewer.

How can it be that experimental exposure repeatedly appears to affect support for stereotypical attitudes, but that links between regular viewing amounts and gender role attitudes are neither strong nor consistent? These somewhat contradictory trends are a likely consequence of both the complexity of the relationships involved and the limitations of survey research. The impact of media exposure on viewers' gender-role attitudes is not likely to be uniform or absolute, but instead is likely to vary based on several internal and external factors (e.g., existing level of sexism, actual media diet). With experimental paradigms, many of these factors are controlled; yet with examinations of real-world viewing habits, there is more noise to dilute the effects. Thus, the connections in question may indeed be present, but additional work is needed to tease out which of the many viewer and content variables described in Table I strengthen and weaken them.

B. DOES MEDIA EXPOSURE CONTRIBUTE TO STEREOTYPED ASSOCIATIONS ABOUT THE SEXES?

An equally large set of studies examines the impact of the media on people's gender stereotyping and flexibility. Here the concern is whether media exposure influences people's beliefs about the activities, attributes, and occupations associated with each sex. For example, does frequent exposure to the media's stereotypical portrayals lead viewers to believe that certain occupations (e.g., medicine, law enforcement) or certain personality traits (e.g., assertiveness, sensitivity) are associated only with one sex? Studies of this kind have commonly asked participants to assign items from a list or from pictures to males, to females, or to both sexes. Stereotyping is typically defined as the number of items believed to belong only to one sex, while flexibility is typically defined as the number of items assigned to both sexes. A second approach has asked participants to estimate the numbers of real-world females and males who occupy certain roles or occupations. Does more frequent media exposure lead viewers to offer skewed estimates of the numbers of housewives or working women?

Findings from survey data indicate a number of positive connections between participants' regular media use and their stereotyping. First, frequent television viewing is associated with holding more stereotypical associations about masculine and feminine traits, activities, chores, and occupations. Second, greater exposure to specific genres is associated with viewers' assumptions about the distribution of real-world roles and occupations. More specifically, greater exposure to action/adventure programs is associated with lower estimates of the number of working and professional women; conversely, greater exposure to soap operas is associated with higher estimates of the numbers of housewives and the numbers of professional women and men. Finally, strong associations have been reported between regular exposure to educational television or to programs with nontraditional themes or characters and greater flexibility. One innovative example of the power of media exposure is seen in Mary Kimball's 1984 report of the degree of stereotyping among sixth and ninth graders living with different levels of access to television. Students living in a town with no television initially stereotyped significantly less than did students living in towns with access to one or more channels; however, the levels of stereotyping became equivalent across the towns once television access was secured for all. While minimal and conditional results (i.e., among females only) have been reported by some research teams, it does appear as if regular television exposure shapes viewers' assumptions about who the sexes are and what they typically do.

Again, even stronger results exist for experimental studies. Exposing children to images of the sexes in stereotypical roles and activities appears to strengthen children's stereotyping of the sexes, although the power of this finding has been found to vary by children's level of gender constancy. In like fashion, others report that exposure to nontraditional films and television programs reduces children's stereotyping. This finding has occurred among participants aged 3 to 10, and from laboratory exposures lasting from 30 minutes to four weeks. For example, over a four-week period, Shirley O'Bryant and Charles Corder-Bolz exposed 5-year-old through 10-year-old children to either traditional or nontraditional commercials that had been produced in the laboratory and then spliced into videotapes of network cartoons. These commercials featured women in either traditional roles (e.g., telephone operator, manicurist) or nontraditional roles (e.g., pharmacist, butcher). Posttest measures revealed that children in

the traditional group increased in their stereotyping as a result of the exposure, seeing traditionally female occupations as appropriate only for women. Conversely, children exposed to nontraditional commercials decreased in their stereotyping, accepting many traditionally male occupations as appropriate for women and men. While some studies in this area report null or contrary results, overall these findings highlight the potential of media images both to reinforce and to reduce stereotyped associations about the sexes. Because all of these studies were conducted with children, further work is needed to determine whether these trends extend to adults.

C. HOW DO MEDIA USE AND EXPOSURE AFFECT VIEWERS' EVALUATIONS OF OTHER FEMALES AND MALES?

A third group of studies examines the impact of the media's portrayals of gender on people's evaluations of others. More specifically, many have questioned whether sex affects how likable, effective, or credible a particular media persona or character is perceived to be. For example, is a report or newscast perceived similarly if delivered by a male versus a female?

To address this question, one approach has been to examine whether the sex of the commentator or spokesmodel affects her or his believability or likability. Effects of this nature have been consistently absent or minimal, with both children and adults evaluating speakers similarly regardless of their sex. A second approach has been to investigate how viewing stereotypic, neutral, or counterstereotypic material affects people's evaluations of subsequent males and females. Does watching stereotypic content prime a stereotypic gender schema, creating a specific gendered lens through which later images are viewed and evaluated? This is a provocative question because it presents the opportunity for television portrayals to affect how real-world people are perceived. Results from several studies indicate that such priming does indeed take place, with models or interactions perceived differently based on the nature of the gender-typed images that preceded them. For example, in their 1988 study, Christine and Ranald Hansen asked undergraduates to watch a few music videos and then evaluate the taped interactions of two job applicants. Whereas students who had watched three neutral music videos later perceived a man's "hitting" on a female colleague to be akin to sexual harassment, students who had viewed stereotypic music videos perceived his sexual advances as appropriate and thought less favorably of the female colleague if she rejected him. Therefore, whereas sex does not appear to affect how a spokesperson's performance is evaluated, sex-biased evaluations are possible if primed by stereotypical content.

D. DOES MEDIA EXPOSURE SHAPE VIEWERS' PREFERENCES FOR TRADITIONAL ACTIVITIES AND CAREERS?

Media exposure not only contributes to our views and assumptions about the sexes, but it also influences our own gender-related preferences and behaviors. Accordingly, one question that has frequently emerged in the literature is, could frequent viewing of women or men performing a limited range of activities shape viewers' preferences for and interest in traditional and nontraditional activities? The underlying assumption is that repeated exposure to mainstream media, which frequently feature traditional role models, will encourage preferences for traditional activities and jobs. Highlighted here is the potential of the media to establish a sense of what is possible (e.g., career-wise) and preferable.

Only a handful of studies have attempted to address these concerns, most focusing on links between children's media exposure and their toy/activity preferences and career aspirations. Among the correlational data, the trend is that frequent viewers typically verbalize stronger preferences than do lighter viewers for traditional activities and occupations, although some of the studies are flawed, and null results have been reported. When the traditionality of the viewing diet is examined, significant correlations emerge, but only among girls. Whereas these studies suggest that regular viewing amounts and diets are associated with students' activity and career preferences, more work is needed before definitive statements can be made.

Again, however, support from experimental work appears to be stronger. Experimental exposure to nontraditional models has been found to highlight the importance of achievement in female undergraduates' future aspirations, to increase girls' preferences for stereotypically masculine jobs, and to heighten children's interest in nontraditional activities and hobbies. Similarly, experimental exposure to traditional images or models has been linked with less interest in political participation among both female and male students and with girls' expressing a stronger preference for feminine toys. Additional ev-

idence was reported in 1982 by Kay Bussey and Albert Bandura, who created videotaped displays of child models playing with gender-neutral toys. After watching these videotapes, young children's own preferences for those toys varied based on the sex of the child who had modeled preferences for it. Here, stereotyped associations and subsequent viewer preferences were created to neutral objects based merely on the sex of the television model. [*See* ACHIEVEMENT.]

Thus, although null findings are sometimes reported, evidence suggests that media exposure does shape viewers' preferences for stereotypically feminine and masculine activities and occupations. Results appear stronger among girls, whose ideas about what they want to be when they grow up appear to be influenced by the range of possibilities to which they are exposed. With limited options, their own interests appear limited, but when presented with images of women pursuing and enjoying challenging careers, their options and interests expand.

E. ARE MEDIA USE AND EXPOSURE RELATED DIRECTLY TO GENDER-TYPED BEHAVIOR?

A critical concern among media researchers is not only for how the portrayals affect viewers' attitudes, stereotypes, and preferences, but also for how they influence viewers' real-world choices and behaviors. While this has been a central question in the media and violence research, it has been a marginal issue here, most likely because gender roles do not translate as easily into an obvious behavior, or translate into so many behaviors that studying this phenomenon becomes difficult. Despite these challenges, a handful of studies have attempted to investigate this important connection.

One approach for examining a link between media use and actual behavior has been to examine connections between regular amounts of television viewing and the sex-typed nature of the chores children do around the house. Are the teens who watch greater amounts of television also the ones who perform stereotypical chores? Results indicate no links between these two factors. It can be argued, however, that this may not be a true test of the contribution of television exposure to behavior because chore selection is not always within the child's control. Perhaps a more accurate test of this relation would be to examine correlations between media exposure and a set of behaviors that are generally self-selected, such as the games and activities a child plays regularly (e.g., hopscotch, kickball). Thus, further exploration of this issue is needed before firm conclusions can be drawn.

The bulk of experimental research addressing this concern has looked at it from the perspective of social learning theory, with an emphasis on behavior modeling. Here, participants (typically young children) are asked to watch specific stimuli and are then observed in their subsequent behavior. Are children more likely to imitate the behaviors of same-sex or gender-traditional models than of other-sex or gender-nontraditional models? Results are mixed, with most findings supporting this expectation, but some countering it. To begin to determine the conditions under which such modeling occurs, researchers have experimentally manipulated specific factors, testing whether it is something about the models and their actions or something about the child viewer that encourages imitation in some cases but not others. Results indicate that both factors play a role. Models are more likely to be imitated if they have social power, receive positive or no consequences for their behavior, are consistent in their gender typing, and are not perceived as outliers among their same-gender peers. Children themselves are more likely to imitate same-sex models and avoid cross-sex behavior if they have reached higher levels of gender constancy.

Overall, it appears as if young viewers are inclined to imitate traditional models and behavior more often than nontraditional ones, and that several aspects of both the model and the viewer strengthen this tendency. However, because most of the studies in this area used young children and simple, laboratory-created modeling displays, further work is needed to investigate whether these results generalize to older children or to real television programming. Indeed, on television, the behaviors and plotlines are typically much more intricate than laboratory stimuli, and the cues about the gender appropriateness of behaviors are typically more subtle.

Although television characters' behaviors are not consistently imitated, powerful experimental results have been obtained when more conceptually related behaviors were examined. In their 1980 experiment, Jennings, Geis, and Brown examined whether viewing traditional or nontraditional images of femininity affects women's subsequent self-confidence. In the first portion of the experiment, participants viewed either four commercials with males and females in traditional domestic roles or four commercials with the roles reversed (e.g., a man serving din-

ner to a woman). Later the women participated individually in two tasks designed to assess their self-confidence and self-assertion. One task assessed participants' willingness to disagree publicly with misrepresented information. A second task required participants to give a four-minute extemporaneous speech before two judges who rated the women's nonverbal behavior for signs of confidence and tentativeness. Results indicated that women who had seen the counterstereotyped commercials exhibited greater independence of judgment and more self-confidence than did women who had viewed the stereotyped commercials. Thus, viewing particular content affected viewers' subsequent behavior, not in a direct-modeling sense, but in a conceptually related arena. [*See* SOCIAL ROLE THEORY OF SEX DIFFERENCES AND SIMILARITIES.]

F. DO MEDIA USE AND EXPOSURE AFFECT VIEWERS' GENDER ORIENTATIONS AND SELF-PERCEPTIONS?

A small number of studies have examined links between media exposure and viewers' personal orientations, both to gender and to self. For example, using different measures of gender orientation, two sets of researchers have found that adults who watched more television defined themselves in more traditional/gender stereotypical ways. No such investigations have been done with children. Nevertheless, this is an interesting association, and further work is needed to establish causal links and to explore potential contributions of outside variables.

Evidence also indicates a potential link between exposure to a strong same-sex protagonist and children's self-concepts. In a 1996 study, Jan Ochman exposed children aged seven to nine to 12 videotaped stories with a competent and non-gender-role stereotyped child protagonist. Girls exposed to stories with a female protagonist were found to have a higher self-concept than girls exposed to stories with a male protagonist. The same trend occurred for boys, who reported higher self-concepts with a male protagonist than with a female protagonist. This powerful finding again highlights the potential power of same-sex models. Indeed, if seeing a lead character like oneself makes a child feel better about him or herself, this finding underscores the potential harm of the media's underrepresentation of women. It is true that stereotypical female portrayals may be harmful, but a lack of female characters may be detrimental as well.

G. DOES THE SEX OF THE CHARACTER AND/OR THE STEREOTYPICALITY OF THE ACTIONS AFFECT RECALL?

The final set of studies reviewed here does not examine the impact of the media on gender roles per se, but investigates differences in recall based on the model's sex or stereotypically of her or his behavior. Because using the media involves perceiving, analyzing, and understanding complex images and story lines, it becomes appropriate to examine if either the gender-typed nature of the material or the sex of the actor affects viewers' ability to recall it. The underlying assumption is that content remembered is more likely to have an impact, and that certain types of content may be more memorable. Debate exists, however, concerning which types of content are more memorable. According to assumptions of gender schema theory, viewers should recall media content that conforms to gender stereotypes better than they recall neutral or counterstereotypical content and may even transform content that does not match their existing schema. However, according to Greenberg's drench hypothesis, the strength of particularly salient or meaningful portrayals may override the messages of masses of others. Thus, counterstereotypical portrayals could resonate, stand out, and be remembered. [*See* GENDER DEVELOPMENT: GENDER SCHEMA THEORY.]

What does the evidence suggest? Results from the 18 studies examined for this portion of the review indicate a mixed picture, revealing that several aspects of both the content and the viewer affect recall. On the content side, some have found that children and teens recall traditional content more accurately than nontraditional content and recall more behavior of the same sex model, regardless of the stereotypically of the model's behavior. However, others report that neither the sex of the model nor the traditional nature of the model's behavior influences viewers' recall of details. Moreover, across three studies, the sex of the commentator had little impact on students' recall of general news content. Conditional results have also been reported whereby recall of the same-sex model's behavior was stronger when the same-sex character was the dominant one and when the model was highly consistent in his/her sex-typed behavior.

Several aspects of individual viewers also play a role in determining what is remembered. More specifically, recall and selective attention have been found to vary according to viewers' existing orientations to gender. Results indicate that masculine girls and boys recall more behavior of the male model than of the female model and that gender aschematic undergraduates recall more information about nontraditional plotlines than do gender schematic students. Level of gender constancy plays a role as well, with boys and girls higher in gender constancy attending more selectively to same-sex models than children lower in gender constancy.

The complexity of these dynamics is seen in one set of studies presented by Glenn Cordua, Ronald Drabman, and their colleagues. Here the researchers developed a videotaped presentation of a child's visit to the doctor, offering various permutations of the male doctor–female nurse paradigm. Thus, participants saw a male doctor with a female nurse, a female doctor with a male nurse, or both actors of the same sex. Results across several studies indicate a tendency for young students (fourth grade and under) to reverse the sexes when asked to recall portrayals that were counterstereotypical, especially concerning male nurses; older students recalled the counterstereotypical roles accurately.

Overall, it appears as if traditional content is only sometimes recalled better than nontraditional content. This does not appear to be a broad or strong phenomenon, but instead depends heavily on specific aspects of the portrayals themselves (e.g., dominance of the same-sex character) and of the viewer (i.e., age, gender-role orientation). Much more work is needed to better understand when and why results do not occur, to investigate these issues with more realistic media stimuli, and to investigate other factors that affect these processes.

In summary, there are numerous indications that media models have the power to shape viewers' conceptions of gender. Evidence indicates that greater exposure to mainstream media portrayals increases support for sexist attitudes, reinforces stereotyped associations about what the sexes do and how they act, strengthens preferences for traditional occupations and activities, and colors evaluations of women and men encountered subsequently. At the same time, exposure to counterstereotypical images encourages more flexible associations about the sexes, strengthens preferences for nontraditional roles and activities, and leads to increased self-confidence in young women. Thus, frequent or directed exposure to stereotypical images appears to strengthen traditional orientations to gender, while frequent or directed exposure to egalitarian images appears to weaken them.

Yet the results in both cases are neither as strong nor as consistent as content analyses and theoretical models would predict, with equally prominent null and conditional results emerging. Results from experimental paradigms were commonly stronger and more consistent than outcomes produced by survey data assessing regular media use. With survey data, the results typically supported expectations, but were frequently more mixed and conditional. As noted earlier, part of this noise is to be expected given the limitations of survey research and the complexity of the relationships involved. Multiple forces affect our conceptions of gender, of which media exposure is only one; additionally, as illustrated in Table I, multiple factors affect the impact of media exposure on any individual. Thus, in any one study, and across the field as a whole, there are likely to be numerous factors, apparent and hidden, that shape the course of the outcomes. The discussion that follows examines in detail a few of the variables that may have influenced when and for whom effects occurred.

IV. The Mediators

A. IMPACT OF HOW MEDIA USE/EXPOSURE WAS ASSESSED

As noted earlier, media exposure has been assessed in numerous ways. For experimental studies, some researchers employed a one-time, laboratory-created stimulus; others used real programming presented to participants over several days. Among the correlational studies, some researchers asked about total amounts of television viewing, whereas others focused on the frequency of viewing particular programs or genres. Could the manner in which media exposure was assessed have affected the strength of the results? Previous reports indicate such a connection, revealing that more precise or genre-oriented assessments of media exposure typically draw stronger results.

Accordingly, to examine the extent to which this factor played a role here, we conducted an informal analysis investigating whether some assessment approaches produced stronger effects than others. As a first step, we sorted the media exposure measures by type, resulting in 11 different categories—6 for experimental formats and 5 for survey formats. Next, a global rating system was created with which the strength of each study's findings could be evaluated. With this system, the results obtained for each dependent variable in each study were rated using the following three categories: (1) null results/minimal or no relationship between the variables; (2) moder-

ate yet conditional effects, occurring only for specific viewing conditions, variables, or samples (e.g., only among women), and (3) strong effects, in which 50% or more of the expected relationships were significant. Interesting differences in the outcomes did emerge based on the assessment technique used. Producing the highest percentage of "strong" or significant effects among the experimental formats were studies that employed a one-time exposure to a real-media video stimulus. Using a laboratory-produced stimulus or a laboratory-recreated newscast was less effectual. Producing the highest percentage of "strong" effects among the survey formats were studies in which media exposure had tapped some aspect of viewer involvement (e.g., character liking) or had assessed viewing amounts by having participants rate their frequency of viewing specific programs listed. While informative, this analysis is only tentative. It is difficult to assess the full impact of some assessment approaches because they were not employed widely. Moreover, because different assessments of media exposure were used for different gender constructs, we could not easily disentangle their contributions. Nonetheless, this analysis suggests that the different approaches taken to assess media exposure may have contributed to the mixed results in the field.

B. IMPACT OF SPECIFIC CHARACTERISTICS OF THE VIEWER/MEDIA CONSUMER

Of the many potential mediating factors noted in Table I, the viewer variable appearing to have the strongest effect on the results is gender. Significant results repeatedly occurred among female participants only, especially concerning the media's impact on gender-role attitudes and on preferences for traditional or nontraditional activities and occupations. In some cases, this pattern was even expected a priori, such that the researchers had tested only females.

There are several plausible explanations as to why girls' and women's gender roles appear to be more affected by media exposure than do men's, each of which is worthy of further study. First, this trend may be a by-product of the slant of the questions asked. In many cases, researchers focused on stereotypes and issues of more relevance to women than to men, frequently addressing stereotypes of femininity and portrayals of traditional and nontraditional women. The material may have seemed less salient or relevant to male participants, who were consequently less affected by it.

A second factor that may have contributed to this asymmetry is that women and men come to the screen from different positions. At the outset, men are generally more inclined than women to accept gender-role stereotypes and to have more traditional attitudes. Therefore, exposure to traditional stereotypes may not make men more traditional because they already endorse the stereotypes. Moreover, men have less incentive to abandon these stereotypes and leave the status quo after viewing counterstereotypical images because doing so would mean moving away from privilege and status. Indeed, research suggests that nontraditional portrayals of men are most effective if the male characters are perceived to still possess power of some sort.

Inconsistencies in the results may also have resulted from age differences in the samples. It is commonly believed that younger children are especially vulnerable to the influence of stereotypical or counterstereotypical portrayals because of both their cognitive immaturity and their limited real-world experiences. As a reflection of this belief, children are more often the subjects of this research and served as participants in over half of the studies. Were the studies that produced the expected outcomes also the ones that tested the youngest participants? Our informal analysis does indicate that the proportion of "strong" (i.e., category 3) results was higher among child than among teen and adult samples. However, it is not clear if this pattern is a consequence of age alone, because age is confounded with the gender construct addressed. Among younger samples, studies often focused on students' recall of gendered content and on behavior modeling, areas that often produced positive results. Among older participants, a common focus was the impact of the media on sexist attitudes, an area in which results were more inconsistent. Moreover, in the Herret-Skjellum and Allen meta-analysis discussed earlier, age was not a significant mediator for the correlational studies. Thus, while age may play a role in some way, the media's impact on gender is not a phenomenon reserved only for the young and impressionable.

Consideration is also warranted concerning the impact of viewers' existing orientations to gender, especially their levels of gender constancy and gender schematicity. In most cases when these constructs were examined, they did appear to differentiate who was and who was not affected by media exposure. Children higher in gender constancy appeared to attend to and model same-sex models more consistently than did children lower in gender constancy. Viewers who were less strongly gender typed recalled more nontraditional information than did viewers who were more strongly gender typed. Moreover, among males, being more traditional predicted both heavier future television viewing and a lower likelihood of being affected by experimental exposure to stereotypical portrayals. Thus, children's existing orientations to gender do appear to affect the degree to which they are influenced by exposure to specific content and also predict their regular viewing behavior.

Thus a number of factors are likely to have influenced why some studies produced strong results and others did not. Included among these factors are the particular research paradigm employed (i.e., survey versus experiment), the manner in which media exposure was assessed, the gender and gender-role orientations of individual participants, and the ages of the samples. Other factors not examined are likely to have played a role as well. As noted earlier, the research questions and relationships under study are unavoidably complex, involving multiple constructs, mechanisms, and mediating variables. No simple or direct answers are expected. Future research must continue to investigate how specific viewer and content variables mediate these processes. Indeed, there are several directions that the field can go from here in order to clarify the dynamics of these relationships, to address limitations of particular research paradigms, and to keep pace with the changing media environment. We therefore conclude our review with several suggestions for future research directions.

V. The Future: Ten Suggestions for Future Research Directions

1. *Need to move away from using non-media-like laboratory-produced stimuli.* Laboratory-produced stimuli are the foundation of psychological research on media effects (i.e., Bandura's Bobo doll experiments) and serve as an excellent way to vary and control media content. However, they are typically quite artificial and often bear little resemblance to real media. While it is true that using such stimuli often produces results, it is unclear what these results mean or if and how such effects extend to real viewing experiences. Indeed, for many people, television is more than just a random set of scenarios to respond to. With laboratory-produced stimuli, there are no familiar characters to recognize and embrace,

no story lines to become absorbed in, and no theme songs to hum in the car. Reducing "media" to a series of random images, slides, or scenarios removes much of what makes using them interesting and engaging.

A better choice might be to use clips or segments from popular network programming. Indeed, situation comedies, dramas, and soap operas are among the most heavily watched formats, but they are seldom used as experimental stimuli. If content is used that is popular among viewers, the chances increase that a real-world phenomenon is being replicated. If additional control of the image is called for, real media stimuli can be manipulated via computer wizardry.

2. *Need to expand definitions of "gender" to cover the full complexity of the construct.* Up to this point, investigations of the impact of the media on gender roles have managed to cover several important domains of gender, including preferences for traditional and nontraditional occupations, stereotyping of activities, and sexist attitudes. Yet because gender is a broad construct composed of multiple dimensions (more than 24, as noted earlier), attention is needed on other significant components of gender. For example, minimal attention has been given to the media's impact on viewers' preferences for specific feminine or masculine attributes or their definitions of femininity and masculinity. Does media exposure affect viewers' actual display of stereotypical characteristics, modes of dress, and use of language? Does it affect the importance they assign to their own and other's conforming to these stereotypes? Is there any impact of media exposure on gender affect (i.e., how good or bad one feels about her or his sex)? These and other important questions await further study.

3. *Need to use more comprehensive and age-appropriate measures to tap these dimensions.* In assessing these and other issues of gender, research needs to build on and expand current measures and assessment techniques. For example, if the concern is the media's impact on gender-role attitudes, examination is needed of attitudes other than the appropriateness of women at home versus in the workplace. Because the field's early focus was on issues of a "woman's place," less attention has been given to viewers' attitudes about men's roles or about relationship dynamics that may be particularly salient to children. If gender-related behavior is the focus, study is needed of outcomes other than direct imitation of a modeling display or of the chores children perform

at home. Attention is needed concerning the media's impact on what children and adults actually do activity- and career-wise. It would also be informative to examine viewers' intention to behave, such as participants' willingness to hire male or female applicants as baby-sitters or their comfort with cross-sex behavior.

4. *Need longitudinal research exploring if the media's impact on gender changes over time.*

5. *Need to expand the demographics of the samples tested.* Despite repeated reports that Black and Latino youth watch more television and attend more movies than their European American counterparts, research examining the impact of media use on these groups has been sparse. For example, of the studies examined here that reported demographic information about their samples, 73% used predominantly White samples, and 53% chose only participants from the middle class. Whereas these patterns mirror those of psychological research in general, they make it difficult to judge how social demographic factors affect the processes in question. As a result, it is unclear whether stereotypical portrayals may affect minority youth more because of their greater exposure levels or less because of the lack of minority representation on the screen. Additional work is needed to address this critical issue.

6. *Need to expand domains of media exposure to include other genres.* As noted earlier, the bulk of the research in this field has focused on the potential impact of television comedies and dramas, commercials, music videos, and laboratory-produced scenarios. While additional work is required to fully understand their influence, expansion into other domains is warranted as well. Study is needed concerning the impact on gender roles both of other media, such as video games, magazines, films, music, and the Internet, and other genres of television programming, such as talk shows and reality programming. Indeed, reality-based programming has expanded dramatically in recent years. Included in this group are programs such as *Cops* and *Unsolved Mysteries,* which feature reenactments of real crimes; programs such as *Ripley's Believe It or Not* and *I Dare You,* which depict unusual human feats and skills; and voyeuristic programs such as *The Real World, Big Brother,* and *Survivor,* in which the lives of everyday people are followed. With these formats come new questions concerning the effects of television content. More specifically, do viewers identify more with real-world characters than with characters from fictional dramas and comedies? Does real-

ity-based content have more impact? Indeed in a 1978 study, Suzanne Pingree reported that children were more affected by commercials when told that the characters were real people than when told that they were paid actors. A line of research examining the impact of this new reality-based programming would be of critical importance. Moreover, general study is needed of whether individual media and formats are equally influential. For example, is stereotypical content depicted in a situation comedy equally influential as similar content prescribed in a music video or Disney feature film?

7. *Need to incorporate dimensions of media use other than amount of exposure. More attention is needed concerning the contributions of viewer involvement (e.g., identification, perceived realism, parasocial interaction, active viewing, critical viewing, viewing motives).* Virtually all of the studies in this field focus strictly on the *amount* of media exposure involved, with minimal attention given to aspects of viewer involvement such as identification and perceived realism. Yet it is highly likely that media influence operates along avenues other than amount of exposure. Indeed, there is richness in our experience with television programs and characters that is not easily represented by the amount watched. A particular viewer may not watch a great deal of television, but if she is especially connected to specific portrayals, these characters may strongly affect her conceptions of gender. Accordingly, many hypothesize that viewers' identification with particular characters, the level of realism they assign to the portrayals, the degree to which they actively or passively view the content, and their particular viewing motivations (e.g., for learning, for escapism) will enhance or diminish any content effects. Because these behaviors may or may not coexist with frequent viewing, important avenues of television's influence may be overlooked if the sole focus is on viewing amounts.

8. *Need research that draws comparisons across theoretical models and across mediums.*

9. *Need to investigate the impact of underrepresentation versus misrepresentation.* Much of the research discussed thus far has focused on the influence of stereotypical versus nonstereotypical portrayals. However, several decades of content analyses indicate that women are not only misrepresented (i.e., portrayed stereotypically), but also are underrepresented in relation to their numbers in the real world. Which of these two conditions is more detrimental to women's and men's perceptions of gender? Are women perceived as less important, competent, or powerful when they are absent on television or when they are present, yet depicted negatively or stereotypically? Further experimental work is needed to explore these important questions.

10. *Need to employ more specific assessments of media exposure.* Current assessments of media exposure have been more general than specific, assuming that since most portrayals are stereotypical, tapping the general quantity of exposure to a medium is sufficient. It is assumed that the nature and intensity of the stereotypical content are not likely to differ greatly within a medium or genre. Yet as media markets continue to diversify, focusing on specific audience niches and consumer interests, this assumption may be less valid. Boys watching the World Wrestling Federation, reading *Flex*, and playing martial arts video games may be exposed to somewhat different messages about gender roles than girls reading *Seventeen*, watching *Dawson's Creek*, and listening to Faith Hill. Thus, it can no longer be assumed that investigating the number of hours participants spend consuming medium X captures the diversity of the actual messages received. Instead, as Jane Brown and Jeanne Steele have argued, research must begin to examine the content and impact of specific media diets.

Assessments of media exposure also need to begin to examine participants' histories of media use. The assumption underlying much of the thinking in this area is that, all things being equal, those exposed to more stereotypical images during their formative years (e.g., ages 3 to 15) will be more accepting of these stereotypes than those exposed to fewer such images. Yet direct assessments of media histories are seldom made. Instead, survey data typically examine links between current media use and current conceptions of gender. This information is useful in addressing the larger issue only to the extent that current media habits are representative of a person's lifetime of media use. Yet has this link been established? Media habits have been found to change throughout the life course, for example, with television viewing amounts often decreasing in adolescence, and exposure and involvement with popular music increasing. Tastes and interests are likely to change and evolve as well. Thus, assessments capturing exposure levels only at one point in time may not fully represent the nature and quantity of exposure over the years.

SUGGESTED READING

Calvert, S. L., and Huston, A. C. (1987). Television and children's gender schemata. In *New Directions for Child Development, No. 38: Children's Gender Schemata* (L. S. Liben and M. L. Signorella, eds.), (pp. 75–88). Jossey-Bass, San Francisco.

Durkin, K. (1985). Television and sex-role acquisition 2: Effects. *British Journal of Social Psychology* 24, 191–210.

Durkin, K. (1985). Television and sex-role acquisition 3: Counter-stereotyping. *British Journal of Social Psychology* 24, 211–222.

Gunter, B. (1986). *Television and Sex Role Stereotyping.* J. Libbey, London.

Herrett-Skjellum, J., and Allen, M. (1996). Television programming and sex stereotyping: A meta-analysis. In *Communication Yearbook 19* (B. Burleson, ed.), (pp. 157–185). Sage, Thousand Oaks, CA.

Signorielli, N. (1990). Children, television, and gender roles: Messages and impact. *Journal of Adolescent Health Care* 11, 50–58.

Media Stereotypes

Sandra Pacheco
California State University, Monterey Bay

Aída Hurtado
University of California, Santa Cruz

Glossary

Critical analysis The application of critical theory to the construction of knowledge and to the assessment of research produced form a noncritical perspective.

Critical theory Theory produced from a multidisciplinary perspective. The focus is on making explicit the assumptions and biases in mainstream disciplines. Critical theory takes as central to the production of all knowledge the integration of class, race, ethnicity, gender, sexuality, physical challenges simultaneously to deconstruct the belief that scientific knowledge is "objective" and not influenced by social and economic power.

Familia Family.

Symptomatology The combined symptoms that make up a disease or disorder.

Telenovelas Soap operas.

MEDIA STEREOTYPES that suggest there are expected roles for women including women as sexual objects, women as submissive and less knowledgeable, and women as housewives preoccupied with house cleaning and laundry are still prevalent in the United States. In addition to these expected roles, the media sends messages pertaining to what is physically valued in terms of beauty. The standard for a beautiful woman remains one who is White and of substantially below average weight. These messages permeate various forms of media, with the Internet fast becoming the latest avenue for sociocultural transmission of gender stereotypes.

I. Introduction

North American culture is characterized by two very distinct components: entertainment and the economics surrounding its production. Together they form a multibillion dollar industry that bombards us with social, cultural, and political messages on a daily basis. We receive these messages via print (newspapers and magazines), television, radio, film, and now via the Internet. These messages take shape not only in the venue we are attending to, but also in the advertising sponsoring its production. Advertising occupies a substantial amount of space within each of the preceding venues. Newspapers and magazines devote the majority of their space to advertising, with radio and television dedicating much less of their time to advertising during prime-time hours, but in a more intrusive manner. That is, unlike magazines and newspapers, which allow you to attend to the primary source of information without interruption, the radio and television media force advertising upon their viewing and listening audiences during the span of the program. In terms of the average television viewer alone, this translates into an average of 350,000 commercials by the time one reaches the age of 18. Combined together, they are a powerful agent of enculturation, so much so that the entertainment industry has the potential to be more influential than education on the thinking and decisions made by future citizens. According to recent census figures, the majority of these citizens are currently and will be women. Hence the representation and participation of women in the media becomes even more significant.

At the early stages of the feminist movement, Betty Friedan accused the media and various affiliated experts (doctors, sociologist, and psychiatrists) of instilling a sense of inadequacy in women who could not live up to the esteemed value of the "happy housewife heroine." She further argued that the media portrayal of women limit them to the status of sex objects whose identities do not span beyond beauty, sex, and reproduction, thereby commercializing women's images. In the 1970s, early evidence, in terms of magazine advertisement research, found that indeed women were relegated to a second-class presence. Specifically, women were portrayed in magazines in four reoccurring negative themes. These included (1) a women's place is located within the home, (2) women do not make important decisions, (3) women are dependent and need a men's attention, and (4) men regard women primarily as sex objects. These early insights provided a framework for contemporary research pertaining to women in the media. In addition to the understanding of the general portrayal of women in the media, contemporary, salient topics in the field include the relationship between body image and media representations, the analysis of media images of violence toward women, and sexual representations of women in pornographic media. Lastly, the newest of media venues, the Internet, is proving to be an emerging presence in media research as a format that rivals television, but which holds a particular curiosity as representations of gender can either be "corporate" dictated or self created. That is, the Internet can follow the same corporate format we find in existing media formats or it can now, given the accessibility of technology, be created according to the perspective of the consumer who now becomes a producer. This is most evident in the ability for anyone to produce a Web page that has the potential to reach millions of viewers.

II. General Portrayal of Women

Recent research trends have found that gender stereotyping is experienced by our youngest viewers of television in the form of advertising targeting children. Using content analysis methodology, it has been found that more boys than girls are present in advertising, with disparity increasing with age. Both boys and girls of school age appear equally; however, when the representation focuses on teenagers, males are more than twice as likely to be represented than females. This trend continues into adult representations where men still remain the dominant figure in advertising. Aside from the lack of presence, girls in relation to boys are depicted as being less knowledgeable, less active, less aggressive, and less instrumental. In terms of "authority," male voiceovers or background narration are more common overall and represent the vast majority when the product is gender neutral or targeting males. Further, advertising targeting adults and other forms of print media like magazines also support early research on the negative portrayal of women. In general, women continue to be portrayed in submissive positions to men, in unnatural poses, as sexual objects, with body parts in isolation, with sexually connotative facial expressions, and as the subject of violent imagery. Similarly, the emphasis on the body is of a particular body type, one that is substantially lower in weight than the average woman. When the body is not being emphasized, the role of women as "sanitizer" of home, clothing, and family becomes the focal point.

Research on the representation of minorities in the media has increased significantly from the early

1970s when media analysis focused primarily on White women. Research in various media (e.g., advertising, magazines, pornography) has found that aside from the typical portrayals of women and disparity in representation, African American women are more often featured in formats that are dehumanizing, suggesting animal-like qualities. This is most characteristically seen in scenarios were African American women are portrayed in clothing using animal prints with the print patterning predatory animals. Use of such animal prints suggests sexual stereotypes that have been historically associated with African American women.

III. Violence

Recent data suggest that very few cases of violence toward women in the form of rape get publicized in the news. Those that do receive print or air time have historically been incidences of unusual or sensational cases. Characteristic of the cases portrayed are those that highlight minority men in singular incidents of rape, involve strangers, and those that involve gangs—all which in reality are rare. Such emphasis on nontypical violence toward women has the effect of minimizing the daily domination and violence that women suffer. Examination of the nature of rape in the media has found that over the past 20 years, magazines covering rape portrayed the less typical stranger or gang rape the majority of the time. With the true range of rape characteristics missing, both women and men are less likely to recognize certain acts as rape, such as the more typical date and "acquaintance" rape. This has led to serious concerns because the lack of a representative portrayal of rape cases further encourages the myth that only stereotypical stranger rape is a real rape. [See RAPE.]

Related to media coverage of violence toward women is the use of violent imagery in the entertainment industry. Traditionally, research on violent imagery toward women has focused on the potential subsequent antisocial behavior of men. For example, victims of domestic abuse have often reported that their abuser used pornographic material with White women indicating a higher proportion of use by their partners than either Hispanic or African American women. However, of particular interest is the impact that viewing violence toward women has on women. Preliminary research has already suggested that when the salience of rape was increased in a woman's mind, self-esteem, trust, and a sense of self-control was negatively impacted. Further, experimental methodologies have shown that repeated exposure to both mild and explicit sexual violence imagery situations serves to desensitize women to such violence, with women tending to rate such imagery as "less degrading." In addition, women who have been exposed to a mildly sexual but graphically violent condition are less likely to be sympathetic to a victim in a simulated rape trial. Unlike men's response to violent imagery toward women, women's responses are more likely to be psychological as they incorporate views of appropriate sexual relations between men and women and shape their perceptions of themselves and other women.

IV. Body Image

Women are inundated with daily images of thin women and messages that tell them they should be thin. Images of women found on television and magazines portray women who are substantially below the average weight. Not only are the women portrayed below weight, but also messages pertaining to beauty and worth are intimately suggested. The result has been to "normalize" the thin body as the ideal, resulting in the average woman feeling dissatisfied with her body. This portrayal of unrealistic thinness has resulted in research that has examined the relationship between media representations of women and body image in general and eating disorders in particular.

Currently it is known that, in comparison to the general population, women of below average weight are overrepresented in television. Not only are they overrepresented, they also tend to receive more positive comments associated with their physical appearance as compared to their heavier counterparts. Positive comments are negatively correlated, such that the thinner the character, the more positive comments she receives. It is suggested that continuous exposure to such characters encourages women to internalize an ideal that can subsequently lead to eating disorder symptomatology and eating disorders. In particular, frequent viewers of soap operas tended to be more concerned about their body weight than viewers who watch less frequently or nonviewers. Furthermore, the more attraction viewers feel toward the characters, the greater their efforts to be similar to the character's representation by modeling their behavior. For Spanish-speaking populations in the United States, *telenovelas* (soap operas in Spanish) are also a source reinforcing the same messages of thinness, hegemonic femininity, and the privileging of whiteness. Systematic analyses of *telenovelas* show that main characters, especially the most desirable ones, are depicted as racially White. Working-class characters, and other less desirable ones, are darker and indigenous looking. *Telenovelas* reinforce the same gender and race messages as White mainstream media. Magazine representations of thinness have proven to be equally complicit in promoting eating disorder symptomatology. Undergraduate women who view fashion magazines are more likely to prefer lower body weights, be less satisfied with their bodies, feel more frustrated about their bodies, be more preoccupied with desires of "thinness," and be more concerned with weight gain than undergraduates who viewed only news magazines. This exposure to idealized thinness is found to cause an increased weight concern in most young women, save those who were satisfied with their bodies to begin with. It is suggested that young women engage in a social comparison process whereby they assess their appearance relative to the standards of society as reflected by the media.

Recent research on body image in magazines has provided evidence on how standards of society are subtly transmitted. Employing content analysis methodology on female-targeted and male-targeted magazines commonly read by either men or women, researchers found that the vast majority of women's magazine covers contained messages pertaining to physical appearance, whereas the men's magazine covers contained almost no such messages. In addition, the positioning of information pertaining to weight-related material suggested that weight loss could lead to a better life. For example, popular women's magazine covers often display headlines such as "Get the Figure You Want" next to headlines such as "Get Your Man to Really Listen." Such a juxtaposition of information can lead to the erroneous conclusion that a woman's personal relationships are a function of her physical appearance. Aside from the insinuations that thin is better, conflicting information about weight-loss strategies can be found on magazine covers—for example, messages for "thinness" are positioned next to images of high fat foods. The overall result is that women are not only being told to achieve the unrealistically thin ideal, but they are also being told that they can do so while preparing or consuming fatty food and that to succeed in doing so will result in a "better life." The impact of attempting to reach such unrealistic

ideals has the potential of leading women toward more drastic measures to control their weight. [*See* Body Image Concerns; Eating Disorders and Disordered Eating.]

V. Pornography

As mainstream media portrayals of women have shown, the use of body parts instead of whole women is prominent. The practice of fragmenting the female body into closeups of her sexual organs, whether revealed or not, reduces women to functional objects. Nowhere is this more evident than in the pornography industry. The exaggerated closeups of nude body parts are directed toward male sexual satisfaction and the encouragement of male gaze. Camera angles that position females at physically lower levels than the males on screen further enhance the image of women as powerless and submissive and objects of male desire for sexual power and domination.

Pornography is not simply an issue of gender in isolation, but one of race and gender interaction. In the case of magazines, most printed material identified the ethnicity of the person in the title. Further, women of color are portrayed in far more disparaging fashion than their White counterparts. Specifically, African American women tend to be depicted as animals, incapable of self-control, sexually depraved and unclean. Asian women, on the other hand, tend to be depicted as "sweet young innocent blossoms" or as objects of bondage to be worked into submission. White women are seen more often in general, suggesting standards of beauty and desirability. Similarly, different races express sexism within pornography differently, and racism in pornography is expressed differently by each sex. In particular African American women are the targets of more acts of aggression in general and specifically are more often "victimized" in cross-race interactions. [*See* Prostitution.]

VI. The Internet

The personal computer has given users not only a form of work assistance and entertainment, but the potential for a powerful level of influence. At present anyone with a computer and a connection to the Internet is capable of accessing millions of sites, both personal and commercial. Likewise, anyone may construct a Web site. These sites, for the most part, especially those generated by mainstream corporate America, resemble more common media portrayals of women. Aside from merely viewing numerous sites, viewers are offered various forms of interactive entertainment. Some of these sites include game rooms and chat rooms. Currently there exists no unified body to "oversee" or regulate content. Current attempts at regulation are challenging for two reasons. First, those who are charged to engage in regulation activities are typically from the prepersonal computer era and are not clear on the function and capabilities of the Internet. Second, it is unclear how to regulate material that is not contained in any one country, company, or computer server. This makes for interesting possibilities, both negative (such as the already potent pornography industry) and positive (in the form of accessibility and voice for women who might not otherwise be heard). In terms of pornography, the nature of women's representations echoes current pornographic media formats. The issue rather now becomes one of ease of accessibility, particularly where it concerns children and their gender socialization. Though some sites do require some form of age validation to enter them, they are vastly outnumbered by sites that do not. This is attributed to both the inability to currently establish regulation at a global level and the ability for anyone with access to technology to create a Web site.

Researchers are already identifying the Internet as a major site for future inquiry on gender issues. Researchers are especially interested because gender identity online is more than just a mirror of existing media formats. The more interactive form of this new medium, chat rooms, provides a person an opportunity to construct and reconstruct identities at whim. Chat room participants can experiment with different personas and representations of self. This includes the opportunity for men to present themselves as women and women to present themselves as men or for either to engage in gender-neutral representations. Because the "body" for the most part is not available in online communications, usual modes of culturally symbolic comprehension are challenged. More specifically, gender markers are not necessarily made available to "dictate" socially prescribed interactions. This is especially evident in chat rooms where a person can enter with a "handle" or alias. These aliases may be typically feminine proper names (Katie, Donna), masculine proper names (David, Mike), creative names suggesting a feminine persona (Wildkitty, Happygirl17), creative names suggesting

a masculine persona (BigDaddy, MasterDarkness), or neutral names leaving others uncertain of gender (ABC123, Loveseeker2). This anonymity provides women the ability to hide their gender and voice their opinions without fear of retribution.

Not only does online communication allow women to speak more freely, but it also allows them to do so on topics that would normally be considered more appropriate for men. These topics include mainstream topics such as politics and more marginal topics such as explicit sexuality. Such freedom of "voice" would suggest women's empowerment, a place where women are able to speak freely, providing an opportunity to be heard and to engage in various "public" forums more confidently and in higher proportions. This is especially emphasized when recalling that historically, public speaking and opinion have been male dominated. Women, on the other hand, have typically been subject to a double bind when speaking out. Women who speak out risk shame or harsh criticism. The alternative is to remain silent. Either of these proves to be a losing situation. The Internet provides a seemingly benign opportunity to ameliorate some of these historic inequities. However, it is important to note that one of the reasons women are able to speak freely online is because they have concealed their gender identity or have remained anonymous, thus reinforcing that gender in terms of the feminine is devalued and that it is still not necessarily "safe" to voice your opinions as a woman. Still, this technology does hold the potential for women as producers of online information to engage in narrative rewrites that subvert traditional discourses dictating stereotypical roles for women.

VII. Nature of Research on Gender and the Media

Literature research on gender and the media typically falls into two categories: content analyses, which compare gender images of men and women, and critical analyses, which examine a single character or show using a more contextual approach. Either way, research in the past did not clearly differentiate between the concepts of sex and gender, often treating gender as a dichotomy, as in female and male. Content analysis research typically tallies sex, the biologically based understanding of difference, and then subsequently presents results in terms of gender, a dynamic sociological term infused with social and cultural expectations of behavior. This is especially problematic when examining representations of women of color as it reduces them to mere numbers in the larger analysis of gender in the media. Critical analyses, on the other hand, while more conscientious of gender construction, still approaches gender as a categorical variable. For example, feminist theory has made outstanding efforts to critically examine representations of women in media. However, it does so from the assumption that gender can be analyzed in isolation from race and class. For example, in the case of pornography, it is important to remember that pornography did not emerge in isolation, targeting one specific group, as some feminist assumptions suggest, but rather emerged within a specific system of social and class relationships. As such, race cannot be merely "added on." Instead, critical theoretical research challenges us to understand the social construction of race and gender in the media. Research in the pornographic industry underscores how the industry has depicted African American women as an economic commodity subject to exploitation, ownership, trade, death, and consumption. Similarities can be found in the continuing gendered construction of the Native American woman in the media as princess who saves or helps the White man or as the squaw who engages indiscriminately with both White and Native American men. Ultimately, the Native American presence is defined by Whites and is continually regenerated by economic structures, such as Disney, which often resurrect the stereotypes. Even when media producers have the good intention of representing women of color in their entirety, the subjects' perspective is overlooked. For example, when Allison Anders, director of *Mi Vida Loca,* wanted to "humanize" people who have been traditionally marginalized on the screen, she chose to leave out the voice of the actual subjects. In this case, Anders did well on her details of the "homegirl" experience. However, she left out the substance, the narratives of young women detailing the intricate network of relationships, of "familia."

VIII. Conclusions

Despite strides made by women during the past four decades, media representations of gender continue to inform us that women do not matter except as submissive, less knowing, less instrumental victims and sexual objects who are preoccupied with maintaining clothes and keeping their homes clean. The incorporation of women's fragmented bodies as decorative elements in advertisements continues to be prominent, reinforcing the perception of women as objects to be "gazed" upon. Compounding the denigrating representation of women is the exclusion of women of color, thereby reinforcing the social status quo that values whiteness in terms of desirability and beauty. Efforts to ameliorate such negative images must go beyond implementing positive representations. Consequently, change requires an understanding of the systems, mainly male-dominated economies, that market women's images as commodities. This will be particularly challenging on the Internet where regulation at present is minimal.

SUGGESTED READING

Byant, J., and Zilmann, D. (eds.) (1991). *Responding to the Screen: Reception and Reaction Processes.* Erlbaum, Hillsdale, NJ.

Dines, G., Jensen, R., and Russo, A. (1998). *Pornography: The Production and Consumption of Inequality.* Routledge, New York.

Fregoso, R. L. (1993). *The Bronze Screen: Chicana and Chicano Film Culture.* University of Minnesota Press, Minneapolis.

Kern-Foxworth, M. (1994). *Aunt Jemima, Uncle Ben, and Rastus: Blacks in Advertising, Yesterday, Today, and Tomorrow.* Greenwood Press, Westport, CT.

Meyers, M. (1997). *News Coverage of Violence against Women: Engendering Blame.* Sage, Thousand Oaks, CA.

Newcomb, H. (ed.). (1994). *Television: The Critical View.* Oxford University Press, New York.

Rodriquez, C. (ed.) (1997). *Latino Looks: Images of Latinas and Latinos in the U.S. Media.* Westview Press, Boulder, CO.

Smith, M. A., and Kollock, P. (eds.) (1999). *Communities in Cyberspace.* Routledge, New York.

van Zoonen, L. (1994). *Feminist Media Studies.* Sage, London.

Wolf, N. (1991). *The Beauty Myth: How Images of Beauty Are Used against Women.* Morrow, New York.

Media Violence

Edward Donnerstein
University of California, Santa Barbara

Glossary

Critical viewing skills Curricula designed to teach individuals to recognize certain types of negative portrayals of social behavior in the media and to provide them with alternative ways of interpreting these portrayals.

Desensitization effects Reductions in physiological and emotional arousal in the face of violence.

Fear effects Learning about violence in the news and in fictional programming, which may lead to the belief that the world is generally a scary and dangerous place.

Mass communication A process in which professional communicators use media to disseminate messages.

Media violence Any overt depiction of a credible threat of physical force or the actual use of such force intended to physically harm an animate being or group of beings. Violence also includes certain depictions of physically harmful consequences against an animate being or group that occur as a result of unseen violent means.

Sexualized violence Media depictions that combine both violence and sexual content within the same violent interaction.

THE MAJOR SOCIAL FUNCTION OF THE MASS MEDIA is to influence viewers. One of the influences that has received considerable attention is that of aggressive behavior. Does the viewing of mass media violence contribute to violent behavior? A recent report from the surgeon general of the United States found strong evidence that exposure to violence in the media can increase children's "aggressive behavior" in the short term and concluded that there should be sustained efforts to curb the adverse effects of media violence on youth. This article examines this important social issue.

I. The Issue of Violence in the United States

Americans live in a violent society. As a nation, the United States ranks first among all developed countries in the world in homicides. The statistics on violence are staggering, particularly with regard to children and adolescents. What accounts for these alarming figures? There is universal agreement that many factors contribute to violent behavior in society, including gangs, drugs, guns, poverty, and racism. Many of these variables may independently or interactively affect antisocial responding. Due to the complexity of these and other contributory factors, groups such as the American Psychological Association, the American Medical Association, the National Academy of Science, and the Centers for Disease Control have examined extensively the multiple causes of violence. Cutting across all these investigations was a profound realization that the mass media also contributes to aggressive behavior in the United States.

Of course, there is no single cause to violent behavior, and media violence is not the most important contributor to antisocial actions. Furthermore, not every violent act on television or in film is of concern. Not will every child or adult act aggressively after watching a violent media portrayal. But there is clear evidence, as this article will show, that exposure to media violence contributes to aggressive behavior in viewers. This conclusion is based on careful and critical readings of more than 40 years of social scientific research. Before examining this literature, however, it is important to examine the types of violent images that are portrayed in the mass media, particular on television.

II. What Types of Violent Images Exist in the Mass Media?

With a steady viewing diet of two to three hours of television per day, how much violence are children being exposed to? Researchers have estimated that by the time a child finishes elementary school, he or she will have seen approximately 8000 murders and more than 100,000 other acts of violence on television.

Several content analyses over the past three decades have been conducted to systematically assess the prevalence of violence on television. The largest and most rigorous of these was the National Television Violence Study (NTVS), which examined longitudinally the amount and context of violence on U.S. television for three consecutive years. Of the several unique contributions NTVS has offered to the body of social science research, the first is the highly conservative definition of violence used in the study. The definition of violence was as follows:

Violence is defined as any overt depiction of a credible threat of physical force, or the actual use of such force intended to physically harm an animate being or group of beings.

The programs for NTVS were randomly sampled from 23 broadcast and cable channels over a 20-week period of time ranging from October to June during the 1994–1998 viewing seasons. Programs were selected randomly from 6 a.m. to 11 p.m. across all seven days of the week. A representative composite week was compiled for each programming source, yielding a sum of 119 hours per channel or 2500 hours of television programming assessed each year. To date, this is the largest and most representative sample of television programming in the history of social science research.

What is the prevalence of violence on U.S. television? The results from the third-year NTVS report reveal that a full 61% of programs on television contain some violence. Only 4% of all violent programs on television feature an "antiviolence" theme. Put in another way, 96% of all violent television programs use aggression as a narrative, cinematic devise for simply entertaining the audience. These prevalence findings are incredibly consistent across two randomly sampled composite weeks of television from two different years.

While the aforementioned results are interesting, they only inform us about the prevalence of violence on television. What should be of greater concern is the context or way in which violence is portrayed on television. When we look more closely at the context of violence, the results reveal that most aggression on television is glamorized. Nearly one-half (44%) of the violent interactions on television involve perpetrators who have some attractive qualities worthy of emulation. Nearly 40% of the scenes involve humor either directed at the violence or used by characters involved with violence. Furthermore, nearly 75% of all violent scenes on television feature no immediate punishment or condemnation for violence, and almost 45% of the programs feature "bad" characters who are never or rarely punished for their aggressive actions. These findings are also incredibly consistent across two composite weeks of television sampled over a two-year period.

Much of the violence on television is also sanitized. For example, over half of the violent behavioral interactions on television feature no pain (51%) and 47% feature no harm. A full 34% of the violent behavioral interactions depict harm in an unrealistic fashion with the greatest prevalence of unrealistic harm appearing in children's programming, presumably due to cartoons. Of all violent scenes on television, 86% feature *no* blood or gore. This is surprising given that nearly 40% of all interactions involve conventional weapons such as guns, knives, bombs, or other heavy weaponry! Finally, only 16% of violent programs featured the long-term, realistic consequences of violence.

The National Television Violence Study is not without limitations, however. Perhaps one of the major drawbacks of this study was the decision to sample but *not* assess violence in news programs. Empirical research indicates that much of news programming is filled with stories about crime and violence. Approximately 15% of the programs on the broadcast networks and 10% of the programs on the independent stations are news, not to mention the two CNN channels on basic cable. Given that news stories often feature violence or its harmful aftermath, the prevalence of violence on American television may be considerably higher than the NTVS findings reveal.

III. What Does the Research Community Conclude?

Over the past few decades, many governmental and professional organizations have conducted exhaustive reviews of social scientific research on the relationship between media violence and aggressive behavior. These investigations have consistently acknowledged that media violence, across various genres, may be related to aggressive behavior in many children, adolescents, and adults and may influence their perceptions and attitudes about real-world violence.

Two early, major reports from the U.S. government, the 1972 Surgeon General's Report and the 10-year follow up from the National Institute of Mental Health (NIHM), concluded that television occupied a significant role in the lives of both children and adults. Both of these reports were unanimous in their claim that many types of televised violence can influence aggressive behavior. The Surgeon General's Report concluded that there was a significant and consistent correlation between viewing television violence and aggressive behavior. This finding emerged across many different measures of aggressive behavior and across different methodological approaches (e.g., correlational investigations, experimental studies, longitudinal field studies) to studying the problem. The surgeon general's research made clear that there was a direct, casual link between exposure to television violence and subsequent aggressive behavior by the viewer.

The NIMH report added to the conclusions of the Surgeon General's Report in two significant ways. First, the age range of the effects could be extended to include preschoolers and older adolescents and were generalizable to both genders. Research had shown that both boys and girls were affected by exposure to televised violence. Second, and perhaps more important, it was established that viewers may learn more than aggressive behavior from watching television violence. They may also learn to fear becoming a victim of violence. Heavy viewing may lead to aggression, but for some individuals it will lead to fear and apprehension about being aggressed against in the real world. It is more than aggressive behavior, the report concluded, that should be of concern. [*See* AGGRESSION.]

In recent years additional reports, particularly from the Centers for Disease Control, the National Academy of Science, the American Medical Association, and the American Psychological Association, have lent further support to the contribution of the mass media to aggressive attitudes and behavior. Like previous investigations into violence, the role of the mass media was considered and the conclusions reached were similar. In summary, these reports made the following conclusions:

1. Nearly four decades of research on television viewing and other media have documented the almost universal exposure of American children to high levels of media violence.

2. There is absolutely no doubt that those who are heavy viewers of this violence demonstrate increased acceptance of aggressive attitudes and increased aggressive behavior. Furthermore, this correlation between violence viewing and aggressive behavior is fairly stable over time, place, and demographics, and also across varieties of television genres. An examination of hundreds of experimental and longitudinal studies supported the position that viewing violence in the mass media is related to aggressive behavior. More important, naturalistic field studies and cross-national studies supported the position that the viewing of televised aggression leads to increases in subsequent aggression and that such behavior can become part of a lasting behavioral pattern. Aggressive habits learned early in life form the foundation for later behavior. Aggressive children who have trouble in school and relating to peers tend to watch more television; the violence they see there, in turn, reinforces their tendency toward aggression. These effects are long-lasting. In fact,

Roewll Huesmann found a clear and significant relationship between early exposure to televised violence at age eight and adult aggressive behavior (e.g., seriousness of criminal acts) 22 years later. Aggressive habits seem to be learned early in life and, once established, are resistant to change and predictive of serious adult antisocial behavior. If a child's observation of media violence promotes the learning of aggressive habits, it can have harmful lifelong consequences. Consistent with this theory, early television habits are, in fact, correlated with adult criminality. Consequently, children's exposure to violence in the mass media, particularly at young ages, can have lifelong consequences.

3. In addition to increasing violent behaviors toward others, viewing violence on television changes attitudes and behaviors toward violence in two significant ways. First, prolonged viewing of media violence can lead to emotional desensitization toward real-world violence and the victims of violence, which can result in callous attitudes toward aggression directed at others and a decreased likelihood to take action on behalf of the victim when violence occurs. Research on desensitization to media violence has shown that although observers react initially with relatively intense physiological responses to scenes of violence, habituation can occur with prolonged or repeated exposure and this habituation can carry over to other settings. Once viewers are emotionally "comfortable" with violent content, they may also evaluate media violence more favorably in other domains (e.g., Linz, Donnerstein, and Penrod, 1988).

Second, viewing violence can increase one's fear of becoming a victim of violence, with a resultant increase in self-protective behaviors and increased mistrust of others. Research has shown that heavy viewers of media violence tend to have a perception of social reality that "matches" that which is presented in the mass media. Heavy viewers tend to see the world as more crime-ridden and dangerous and are more fearful of walking alone in their own neighborhoods. Furthermore, viewing violence increases viewers' appetites for becoming involved in violence or exposing themselves to violence.

In summary, the research literature over the past three decades as examined by the American Psychological Association and other groups has been highly consistent in recognizing that there are three major effects that occur as a result of exposure to media violence. First, there is increased violence toward others due primarily to the effect of learning

and imitation. Second, there is increased callousness toward violence among others, which has commonly been labeled the desensitization effect. Third, there is increased apprehension about becoming a victim of violence, often referred to as the fear effect. In the following section, we will overview the major theoretical explanations for each of these effects.

IV. The Special Issue of Sexualized Violence

In explicit depictions of sexual violence, primarily in R-rated films, messages about violence against women appears to affect the attitudes of adolescents about rape and violence toward women. Recent inquiries into media violence have begun to consider the implications of exposure to sexually violent materials due to the opportunities for exposure to such materials within the confines of R-rated cable or VCR viewing. Sexual violence in the media includes explicit sexualized violence against women including rape, images of torture, murder, and mutilation.

Films that depict women as willingly being raped have been shown to increase men's beliefs that women desire rape and deserve sexual abuse. Male youth who view sexualized violence or depictions of rape on television or in film are more likely to display callousness toward female victims of violence, especially rape. Laboratory studies also have shown an increase in men's aggression against women after exposure to violent sexual displays, as well as increased sexual arousal. In addition, research indicates that these attitude and arousal patterns may have some relationship to real-world aggression toward women.

Finally, we could speculate that stronger effects might be expected for younger viewers because they lack the critical viewing skills and the experience necessary to discount the myths about women and sexual violence. To a young adolescent who is searching for information about sexual relationships, sexual violence in popular films may be a potent formative influence on attitudes toward sexuality. A young teenager's first exposure to sex may come in the form of a mildly erotic, but a violent R-rated movie. This film would not be restricted because it did not carry an X rating. It could easily be rented at a video outlet or found on a late-night cable movie. [See RAPE.]

V. The Importance of Context: Not All Violence Is the Same

The research reviewed earlier indicates that media violence can have three distinct types of harmful effects on viewers and that different types of content are capable of producing different effects. However, not all violent portrayals are equal with regard to the risk they might pose. Consider, for example, a documentary about gangs that contains scenes of violence in order to inform audiences about this societal problem. The overall message about violence in such a program is likely to be quite different from that of an action-adventure movie featuring a violent hero. The documentary actually may discourage aggression whereas the action-adventure movie may seem to glamorize it. A comparison of a film like *Schindler's List* about the Holocaust with a film like *The Terminator* illustrates this difference.

Such a contrast underscores the importance of considering the context within which violence is portrayed. Several major reviews of social science research demonstrate that certain depictions are more likely than others to pose risks for viewers. There are nine contextual factors that the literature suggests are major in this regard. We will look briefly at each of these.

A. NATURE OF PERPETRATOR

When a violent event occurs in a program, typically there is a character or group of characters who can be identified as the perpetrator. The meaning of the violence is closely connected to the characteristics of the perpetrator. Character evaluations have important implications for how a viewer ultimately will respond to a particular portrayal. Research indicates that both children and adults are more likely to attend to and learn from models who are perceived as attractive.

What types of characters are perceived as attractive in entertainment programming? Studies suggest that viewers assign more positive ratings to characters who act prosocially than to characters who are cruel. Moreover, children as young as four years of age can distinguish between prototypically good and bad characters in a television program.

B. NATURE OF TARGET

Just as the nature of the perpetrator is an important contextual feature of violence, so is the nature of the target. Once again, viewers are more likely to react strongly to a target who is perceived as likable or attractive. Interestingly, the nature of the target is most likely to influence audience fear rather than learning. Research indicates that viewers feel concern for characters who are perceived as attractive and often share such characters' emotional experiences. This type of empathic response has been found with characters who are benevolent or heroic, as well as characters who are perceived to be similar to the viewer.

C. REASON FOR VIOLENCE

How we interpret an act of violence is dependent to a great extent on a character's motives or reasons for engaging in such behavior. Research establishes that television violence that is motivated by protection or retaliation, to the extent that it appears to be justified, should facilitate viewer aggression. Researchers have speculated that when violence is portrayed as morally proper or somehow beneficial, it lowers a viewer's inhibitions against aggression. The prototypical "justified" scenario is the hero who employs violence to protect society against villainous characters. In contrast, violence that is undeserved or purely malicious should decrease the risk of audience imitation or learning of aggression.

D. PRESENCE OF WEAPONS

Leonard Berkowitz has argued that certain visual cues in a film can activate or "prime" aggressive thoughts and behaviors in a viewer, and that weapons can function as such cues. In support of this idea, a recent meta-analysis of 56 published experiments found that the presence of weapons, either pictorially or in the natural environment, significantly enhanced aggression among angered as well as nonangered subjects. Weapons like guns and knives are more likely than unconventional means to instigate or prime aggression in viewers because such devices are commonly associated with previous violent events stored in memory. Thus, a television portrayal that features traditional weapons poses the greatest risk for the so-called weapons effect on audiences.

E. EXTENT AND GRAPHICNESS OF VIOLENCE

Television programs and especially movies vary widely in the extent and graphicness of the violence they contain. A violent interaction between a perpetrator and a target can last only a few seconds and be shot from a distance or it can persist for several minutes and involve many closeups on the action.

Research suggests that audiences can be influenced by the extent and explicitness of violent portrayals. Most attention has been devoted to the impact of extensive or repeated violence on viewer desensitization. For example, several early studies on adults showed that physiological arousal to prolonged scenes of brutality steadily declines over time. Even children have been shown to exhibit such physiological desensitization over time during exposure to a violent film, with the decrement being strongest for those who were heavy viewers of television violence. More recently, studies have confirmed that exposure to extensive graphic violence, either within a single program or across several programs, produces decreased arousal and sensitivity to violence.

F. REALISM OF VIOLENCE

Numerous studies indicate that realistic portrayals of violence can pose more risks for viewers than unrealistic ones. Not only adults but children too seem to respond to the realism of violence. Children who perceived the content media violence to be more realistic subsequently behaved more aggressively.

The realism of a portrayal can also enhance viewers' fear reactions to violence. Studies have demonstrated that adults are far more emotionally aroused by violent scenes that are perceived to have actually happened than if the same scenes are believed to be fictional.

G. REWARDS AND PUNISHMENTS

A critical feature of any violent portrayal concerns whether the aggressive behavior is reinforced or rewarded. In general, rewarded violence or violence that is not overtly punished fosters the learning of aggressive attitudes and behavior among viewers. In contrast, portrayals of punished violence can inhibit or reduce the learning of aggression. These conclusions are established by a strong base of direct empirical evidence as well as meta analyses (Paik and Comstock, 1994).

H. CONSEQUENCES OF VIOLENCE

Another important contextual feature of media violence concerns whether the consequences of aggressive actions are depicted. Several studies suggest that

viewers interpret violent scenes with observable harm and pain as more serious and more violent than scenes that show no such consequences. Cries of pain and other signs of suffering can affect not only interpretations but also imitation of aggression. Numerous experiments have found that adults who are exposed to overt, intense pain cues from a victim subsequently behave less aggressively than do those who see no such pain cues. The assumptions is that pain cues inhibit aggression by eliciting sympathy and reminding the viewer of social norms against violence. Children also have been shown to be influenced by the consequences of violence. In one experiment, boys who viewed a violent film clip that showed explicit injuries and blood subsequently were less aggressive than were those who saw a violent clip with no such consequences.

I. HUMOR

Portrayals of violence are sometimes cast in a humorous light. What impact does the addition of humor to a violence scene have on the viewer? Of all the contextual variables that have been examined, we know the least about humor. Nevertheless, an examination of the limited research would suggest that the presence of humor will generally contribute to the learning of aggression. However, we should underscore that our conclusion about this facilitative effect is tentative until more systematic research on the impact of a violent scene with and without different forms of humor is undertaken.

VI. *Solutions to the Problem of Media Violence*

As an alternative to regulation, which is always at the forefront of discussions, a large number of organizations concerned with the well-being of children and families have recommended that professionals take a more active role in reducing the impact of violent media (these organizations include the American Academy of Pediatrics, the American Medical Association, the American Psychological Association, the Group for the Advancement of Psychiatry, and the National Parent Teachers Association). Research on intervention programs has indicated that we can reduce some of the impact of media violence by "empowering" parents in their roles as monitors of children's television viewing.

Another strategy has been to provide child viewers themselves with the cognitive tools necessary to resist the influence of television violence. A number of programs have been designed to build "critical viewing skills" that may ameliorate the impact of television violence on younger viewers. Curricula are designed to teach students to recognize certain types of negative portrayals of social behavior and to provide them with alternative ways of interpreting these portrayals. Others have speculated that the effects of exposure to certain mass communications could be modified if a viewer has the ability to devalue the source of information, assess motivations for presenting information, and perceive the degree of reality intended.

Another educational resource is the mass media itself. Educational movies about violence that are written, designed and professionally produced to be entertaining have great potential for informing the public and, under some conditions, might even change antisocial attitudes about violence. Research evaluating the impact of antismoking television information spots, for example, has demonstrated that these messages have been successful in increasing public awareness about the negative health consequences of smoking.

As an example of entertainment programming that can influence individuals' attitudes, the National Broadcast Company (NBC) aired several made-for-television movies designed to inform, as well as entertain, viewers about the problem of acquaintance or date rape. In September of 1990, NBC aired a made-for-television movie about the trauma and aftermath of acquaintance rape. This program, titled *She Said No,* was featured during prime-time hours and attracted a large viewing audience.

An evaluation of the effectiveness of this movie was undertaken by Barbara Wilson and her colleagues. They examined whether exposure to this movie would decrease acceptance of rape myths or increase awareness of date rape as a serious social problem. The results of this study indicated that the television movie was a useful tool in educating and altering perceptions about date rape. Specifically, exposure to the movie increased awareness of date rape as a social problem across all viewers. The movie also had a prosocial effect on older females who were less likely to attribute blame to women in date rape situations after viewing the film.

VII. Conclusion

Overall, we may conclude that the mass media contributes to a number of antisocial effects in both children and adults. We must keep in mind, however, that the mass media is but one factor, which may not even be the most important, that contributes to antisocial attitudes and behaviors in individuals. Furthermore, the mass media's impact can be mitigated or controlled with reasonable insight. This article has explored a number of ways in which the media, parents, and others can be used to prevent the antisocial effects of exposure to violent mass media fare.

SUGGESTED READING

Comstock, G., and Paik, H. (1991). *Television and the American child.* Academic Press, San Diego, CA.

Donnerstein, E., Slaby, R., and Eron, L. (1994). The mass media and youth violence. In *Youth and Violence: Psychology's Response* (L. Eron and J. Gentry, eds.), Vol. 2. American Psychological Association, Washington, DC.

Hamilton, J. (ed.) (1998). *Television Violence and Public Policy.* University of Michigan, Ann Arbor, MI.

Huston, A. C., Donnerstein, E., Fairchild, H., Feshbach, N. D., Katz, P. A., Murray, J. P., Rubinstein, E. A., Wilcox, B. L., and Zuckerman, D. (1992). *Big World, Small Screen: The Role of Television in American Society.* University of Nebraska Press, Lincoln, NE.

National Television Violence Study: Volume 3 (1999). Author. Sage, Thousand Oaks, CA.

Paik, H., and Comstock, G. (1994). The effects of television violence on antisocial behavior. A meta-analysis. *Communication Research,* **21,** 516–546.

Singer, D., and Singer, J. (eds.) (2001). *Handbook of Children and the Media.* Sage, Thousand Oaks, CA.

Men and Masculinity

Ronald F. Levant
Nova Southeastern University

Glossary

Action empathy The ability to see things from another person's point of view and predict what the other person will, or should, *do*.

Destructive entitlement The unconscious belief that people in one's adult life are required to make up for what one didn't get as a child.

Discrepancy strain Results when one fails to live up to one's internalized manhood ideal, which, among contemporary adult males, is often a close approximation of the traditional code.

Dysfunction strain Results even when one fulfills the requirements of the male code, because many of the characteristics viewed as desirable in men can have negative side effects on the men themselves and on those close to them.

Emotion socialization The socialization of emotional expression in early childhood.

Gender role strain Because gender roles are socially constructed, they do not always fit individual personalities very well, resulting in gender role strain.

Masculinity ideology. Beliefs about normative behavior or roles of men in society.

Normative alexithymia An inability, common among men, to sense one's feelings and put them into words. It is a less severe variant of a clinical condition known as alexithymia, which literally means "without words for emotions."

Trauma strain Results from the ordeal of the male role socialization process, which is now recognized as inherently traumatic.

A NEW STUDY OF THE PSYCHOLOGY OF MEN AND MASCULINITY is both overdue and urgently needed. Men are disproportionately represented among many problem populations—parents estranged from their children, the homeless, substance abusers, perpetrators of family and interpersonal violence, sex addicts and sex offenders, victims of lifestyle and stress-related fatal illnesses, and victims of homicide, suicide, and fatal automobile accidents. A new psychology of men might contribute to the understanding and solution of some of these male problems, which have long impacted women, men, children, and society in negative ways.

I. Why Study the Psychology of Men?

Those not familiar with this new work sometimes ask: "Why do we need a psychology of men? Isn't all psychology the psychology of men?" Well, yes, of course, males have been the focal point of most psychological research. However, these were studies that viewed males as representative of humanity as a whole. Feminist scholars challenged this traditional viewpoint by arguing for a gender-specific approach, and in the past three decades, have developed a new psychology of women. In the same spirit, men's studies scholars over the past 15 years have begun to examine masculinity not as a standard by which to measure humanity (both males and females), but rather as a complex and problematic construct. In so doing, they have provided a framework for a psychological approach to men and masculinity that questions traditional norms of the male role, such as the emphasis on toughness, competition, status, and emotional stoicism, and views certain male problems (such as aggression and violence, devaluation of women, fear and hatred of homosexuals, neglect of health needs, and detached fathering) as unfortunate but predictable results of the male role socialization process. They have also provided a framework for creating positive new definitions of masculinity that support the optimal development of men, women, and children.

In addition, there is a "crisis of connection" between men and women resulting from major structural changes in women's roles over the past 40 years without compensatory changes in men's roles. This resulted from women's dramatically increased participation in the labor market. There has been an almost 600% rise in the employment of mothers of small children since the 1950s: 12% of mothers with children under the age of six were employed in 1950, whereas almost 70% were employed in 2000. Women have thus moved from a sole emphasis on the family, and now combine career and family concerns. In making this shift, they have integrated traditional values such as love, family, and caring for others with newer values such as independence, career, and defining themselves through their own accomplishments. Many men have yet to make equivalent and corresponding changes. Although there has been some increase in men's openness to relationships, and greater participation in the emotional and domestic arenas, most men still cling to the older definitions, and emphasize work and individual accomplishment over emotional intimacy and family involvement. As a result, the pressures on men to behave in ways that conflict with various aspects of the traditional masculinity ideology have never been greater. These new pressures—pressures to commit to relationships, to communicate one's innermost feelings, to share in housework, to nurture children, to integrate sexuality with love, and to curb aggression and violence—have shaken traditional mas-

culinity ideology to such an extent there is now a "masculinity crisis" in which many men feel bewildered and confused, and the pride associated with being a man is lower than at any time in the recent past.

II. The Masculinity Crisis

To many men, the question of what it means to be a man today is one of the most persistent unresolved issues in their lives. Raised to be like their fathers, they were mandated to become the good provider for their families and to be strong and silent. They were discouraged from expressing both vulnerable and caring emotions, and they were required to put a sharp edge around their masculinity by avoiding anything that hinted of femininity. Unlike their sisters, they received little, if any, training in nurturing others and in being sensitive to their needs and empathic with their voice. On the other hand, they received lots of training in logical thinking, problem solving, staying calm in the face of danger, risk taking, and assertion and aggression. Finally, they were required at an early age to renounce their dependence on their mothers and accept the pale substitute of their psychologically, if not physically, absent fathers.

For the past several decades, men have attempted to fulfill the requirements of the masculine mandate in the midst of criticism that has risen to a crescendo. Men feel that they are being told that what they have been trying to accomplish is irrelevant to the world of today. Since women now work and can earn their own living, there is no longer any need for "the good provider." Furthermore, society no longer seems to value or even recognize the traditional male way of demonstrating care, through *taking care* of his family and friends, by looking out for them, solving their problems, and being one who can be counted on to be there when needed. In its place, men are being asked to take on roles and show care in ways that violate the traditional male code and require skills that they do not have, such as revealing weakness, expressing their most intimate feelings, and nurturing children. The net result of this for many men is a loss of self-esteem and an unnerving sense of uncertainty about what it means to be a man.

The masculinity crisis involves the collapse of the basic pattern by which men have traditionally fulfilled the code for masculine role behavior—the good provider role. The major manifestations of the masculinity crisis, which have taken center stage in the public eye in the last decade, include, in addition to the loss of the good provider role, the failure of the good family man role to replace the good provider role, the fragility of marriage, the treatment of men in the media, the new image of the "angry White male," and the growth of large-scale men's rallies.

Men are caught in a trap both because they do not have the incentives and because they are ill-equipped to address the loss of the good provider role in a collaborative and equitable fashion with the women in their lives, and as a result react with anger and defensiveness. They do not have the incentives to address the loss of the good provider role in collaboration with their wives because of the power, prerogatives, and entitlements that accrue to them in a patriarchal society. They are not equipped to address it in this way because to do so would require a degree of comfort and fluency with emotions (particularly those emotions that make one feel vulnerable, such as sadness, fear, or shame) that is rare among men, due to the effects of the male gender role socialization process.

A. THE LOSS OF THE GOOD PROVIDER ROLE

The loss of the good provider role has been the central factor in the development of the masculinity crisis. White middle-class men are no longer the "good providers" for their families that their fathers were, and that they expected themselves to be. With the majority of adult women in the workforce, very few men are sole providers; instead, most are coproviders. This has been documented repeatedly. For example, a 1995 study found that 55% of employed women provide half or more of the household income. The loss of the good provider role brings White middle-class men closer to the experience of men of color and the lower class, who (albeit for very different reasons) have historically been impeded from being the economic providers for their family.

The good provider role has been such an important part of the definition of what it means to be a man that one would think that its loss would impel an immediate search for alternatives. Although some men are actively involved in constructing new definitions of masculinity that do not require devotion to work, many others seem caught up in denial.

B. THE GOOD FAMILY MAN ROLE

The obvious candidate to replace the good provider is the "good family man," the husband who shares child care and housework, as well as provision, with his wife. However, given the analysis so far, it should be no surprise to learn that men have not flocked to this new role. Although some think that contemporary culture has embraced the idea of the nurturing father, there really haven't been major changes in workplace and government family policies that would accommodate a large-scale involvement of men in family life. Men themselves have not fully embraced this new family man role either, judging from studies on family work that estimate that men, on the average, perform only about one-third of the total family work. Indeed, only in a rare combination of circumstances do men make a primary commitment to home and family: when the man has already achieved a sense of accomplishment in life, when the woman commands higher income, when household and child care demands are less onerous, and when there is a supportive social environment. The failure of men at large to adopt the good family man role has resulted in a "second shift" for working wives, which has intensified the crisis of connection between men and women.

C. THE FRAGILITY OF MARRIAGE AND THE REALITIES OF DIVORCE

The crisis of connection is also manifested in the increasingly fragile nature of marriage. As is well known, the divorce rate more than doubled between 1965 and 1979, fueled by changes in women's work roles and the development of "no-fault" divorce laws. The conventional wisdom has been that the divorce rate has been moderating since 1980. However, recent demographic research indicates that there was an initial decline in the rate followed by a rather dramatic increase. Varying estimates of the divorce rate indicate that from 50 to 60% percent of all marriages will end in divorce.

Findings also show that women are now twice as likely as men to initiate divorce. Comparable figures from earlier periods are not available, and thus one cannot state with confidence how much this has actually changed over time. However, it is reasonable to assume that more women are initiating divorce now as compared to earlier times, if only because of the dramatic changes in their work roles, which makes them less financially dependent on men.

When children are involved they reside with the mother 90% of the time after the divorce, and the father becomes the noncustodial, visitation parent. The reality of visitation fatherhood is dismal, judging from the fact that more than half of noncustodial fathers drop out of their children's lives. For some men, dropping out of their children's lives is the easy way out, facilitated by their privileged position as a man in a patriarchal society. Others drop out because the role is so difficult and they are so ill-equipped emotionally to deal with their feelings of loss, disempowerment, shame, humiliation, and fear. One may never see so much pain in one room as when you get together a group of six to eight recently separated or divorced dads who are trying to maintain their connections to their children. These men are clearly in crisis and in need of supportive psychoeducational services that will enable them to develop the emotional skills they need to cope with the difficult role of noncustodial father. [*See* DIVORCE AND CHILD CUSTODY; MARRIAGE.]

D. MEN IN THE MEDIA

Although media outlets do run positive stories about men, there has been a noticeable tilt toward criticism over the past decade. Some of this has been useful. For example, male abuse of power in heterosexual relationships has been exposed in the media through a long series of sensational cases, with the result that there is now greater likelihood that women will challenge these behaviors and that men will think twice before enacting them. These cases began in 1991 with Anita Hill's allegations of sexual harassment against Clarence Thomas, a candidate for the Supreme Court, during his Senate confirmation hearings. They continued on throughout the 1990s with the highly publicized rape trials of the Kennedy family scion William Kennedy Smith and the world champion heavyweight boxer Mike Tyson, the high-profile accusations of sexual harassment that drove U.S. Senator Bob Packwood from office, the sexual harassment and assault that was exposed as endemic at conventions of the U. S. Navy Tailhook Society (as well as numerous other sexual scandals in other branches of the U. S. military), the O. J. Simpson double murder trial, and the Bill Clinton sex scandals ("Monicagate" and others). However, there has also been a tendency for the media to go too far at times, such that not only are positive aspects of traditional masculinity ignored, but there has also been a wholesale trashing of men on television talk shows, magazine articles, books, and even comic strips. Some of the worst examples of this are books with titles like *No Good Men* or television "relationship experts" advising women to train men like dogs. This media bashing obviously erodes the pride associated with being a man and tends to increase male defensiveness.

E. THE IMAGE OF THE ANGRY WHITE MALE

The "angry White male" image has emerged on the scene over the past decade, reflecting a man who wants to turn the clock back and reassert his "rightful place" ahead of ethnic minorities, women, and gays. Michael Douglas portrayed the prototypic angry White male in the movie *Falling Down*. Douglas's character was a man whose life had fallen apart. Divorced, restricted from seeing his child, and unemployed, he was unable to look at himself and examine the sources of his arrogant and abusive behavior. Instead, he focused on the loss of his (imagined) picture-perfect, White, English-speaking world to urban decay, immigration, and civic corruption and began a one-day binge of violence, taking out his venom on the ethnic minority people he encountered as he attempted an uninvited and very unwelcome "homecoming" to his wife and child. Although this was only a film, and the character was admittedly psychotic, it illustrates (albeit in exaggerated form) a characteristic response of some men to the masculinity crisis. Rather than viewing the collapse of traditional masculinity as an opportunity to reexamine a code of behavior that was basically foisted on men and reinforced by shame, such men respond very defensively, seeing any erosion of male power as an attack to which they must respond aggressively.

F. THE GROWTH OF MEN'S RALLIES

Finally, there is the growth of men's rallies. It started out with gatherings of hundreds of men in the woods for mythopoetic workshops, which failed to attract masses of men because of the emphasis on emotional expression, vulnerability, and loss. Then the Promise Keepers came on the scene. The Promise Keepers have used football stadiums for their gatherings, which is not only a familiar venue for many men, but one that also evokes images of traditional masculinity in the form of the modern gladiator—the football player. Led by a former football coach, with a message of brotherhood and religious revival, and seeming to be hospitable to men of all races, this movement has attracted dramatically larger crowds than the mythopoets: 45,000 in Oakland, 50,000 in St. Petersburg, and 62,000 in Minneapolis among the 13 venues in 1995, which drew a grand total of 720,000.

The message that men who attend these gatherings receive is for the most part very regressive, supporting the inclination to cling to the code of masculinity and to react to requests for change with anger and defensiveness. The Promise Keepers are openly antigay, and despite disclaimers that the group is not antiwomen, the bible of the movement, *Seven Promises of a Promise Keeper,* urges men in no uncertain terms to "reclaim their manhood" by taking control as the "head of the family."

G. WHAT WILL HELP?

As the relative power between men and women shifts as a result of the gains of feminism and women's increasing financial independence from men, men derive less benefit from their power and become more aware of their pain. To help men take the next step and connect their pain to a critical examination and reconstruction of masculinity, we need to do two things. First of all, society must take men's experience seriously and adopt an empathic approach to their pain. Second, the masculinity crisis has resulted in a wholesale trashing of all aspects of masculinity, such that for many men the essential dilemma is that much of what they have been taught to value since childhood is under attack. To help men come to terms with the crisis and restore their lost sense of pride, society also must honor the still-valuable aspects of masculinity in order to restore the lost sense of pride associated with being a man. But before undertaking such a project of helping men reconstruct masculinity, it is important to have an in-depth understanding of the psychology of men and masculinity and of gender role strain.

III. The Gender Role Strain Paradigm

The new psychology of men views gender roles not as biological or even social "givens," but rather as psychologically and socially constructed entities that bring certain advantages and disadvantages and, most important, can change. This perspective acknowledges the biological differences between men and women, but argues that it is not the biological differences of sex that make for "masculinity" and "femininity." These notions are socially constructed from biological, psychological, and social experience to serve particular purposes. Traditional constructions of gender serve patriarchal purposes; nontraditional constructions, such as anthropologists described among the Tahitians and the Semai, serve more equalitarian purposes.

The gender role strain paradigm, originally formulated by Joseph Pleck, is the forerunner, in the new psychology of men, of social constructionism and of modern critical thinking about masculinity. It spawned a number of major research programs that have deepened our understanding of the strain men experience when they attempt to live up to the impossibility of the male role. The paradigm that had dominated the research on masculinity for 50 years (1930–1980)—the gender role identity paradigm—not only poorly accounts for the observed data, but also promotes the patriarchal bifurcation of society on the basis of stereotyped gender roles. In its place, Pleck proposed the gender role strain paradigm.

The older gender role identity paradigm assumed that people have an inner psychological need to have a gender role identity and that optimal personality development required its formation. The extent to which this "inherent" need is met is determined by how completely a person embraces one's traditional gender role. From such a perspective, the development of appropriate gender role identity is viewed as a failure-prone process; failure for men to achieve a masculine gender role identity is thought to result in negative attitudes toward women, homosexuality, or defensive hypermasculinity. This paradigm springs from the same philosophical roots as the "essentialist" view of sex roles—the notion that (in the case of men) there is a clear masculine "essence" that is historically invariant.

In contrast, the gender role strain paradigm proposes that contemporary gender roles are contradictory and inconsistent, that the proportion of persons who violate gender roles is high, that violation of gender roles leads to condemnation and negative psychological consequences, that actual or imagined violation of gender roles leads people to overconform to them, that violating gender roles results in more severe consequences for males than for females, and that certain prescribed gender role traits (such as male aggression) are often dysfunctional. In this paradigm, appropriate gender roles are determined by the prevailing gender ideology (which is operationally defined by gender role stereotypes and norms) and are imposed on the developing child by parents, teachers, and peers—the cultural transmitters who subscribe to the prevailing gender ideology.

A. MASCULINITY IDEOLOGY

Masculinity ideology is the core construct in the body of research assessing attitudes toward men and male roles. Masculinity, or gender, ideology is a different construct from the older notion of gender orientation. Gender orientation arises out of the identity paradigm, and assumes that masculinity and femininity are rooted in actual differences between men and women. This approach has attempted to assess the personality *traits* more often associated with men than women. In contrast, studies of masculinity ideology take a *normative* approach, in which masculinity is viewed as a socially constructed gender ideal for men. Whereas the masculine male in the orientation/trait approach is one who *possesses* particular personality traits, the traditional male in the ideology/normative approach is one who endorses the ideology that men *should* have sex-specific characteristics (and women should not display these characteristics). Empirical research has found that gender orientation and gender ideologies are independent constructs and have different correlates.

1. Masculinity Ideologies

The strain paradigm asserts that there is no single standard for masculinity nor is there an unvarying masculinity ideology. Rather, since masculinity is a social construction, ideals of manhood may differ for men of different social classes, races, ethnic groups, sexual orientations, life stages, and historical eras. We therefore prefer to speak of masculinity ideolog*ies*. To illustrate, consider these brief descriptions of varying male codes among four ethnic-minority groups in the contemporary United States:

African-American males have adopted distinctive actions and attitudes known as cool pose . . . *Emphasizing honor, virility, and physical strength, the Latino male adheres to a code of* machismo . . . *The American-Indian male struggles to maintain contact with a way of life and the traditions of elders while faced with economic castration and political trauma . . . Asian-American men resolve uncertainty privately in order to save face and surrender personal autonomy to family obligations and needs. (Lazur and Majors, 1995, p. 338)*

2. Traditional Masculinity Ideology

Despite the diversity in masculinity ideology in the contemporary United States, there is a *particular* constellation of standards and expectations that are commonly referred to as "traditional" masculinity ideology, since it was the dominant view in the United States prior to the deconstruction of gender that took place beginning in the 1970s.

Traditional masculinity ideology is thought to be a multidimensional construct. Brannon identified four components of traditional masculinity ideology: that men should not be feminine ("no sissy stuff"); that men should never show weakness ("the sturdy oak"); that men should strive to be respected for successful achievement ("the big wheel"); and that men should seek adventure and risk, even accepting violence if necessary ("give 'em hell"). More recently, Levant defined traditional masculinity ideology in terms of seven dimensions: the requirement to avoid all things feminine; the injunction to restrict one's emotional life; the emphasis on achieving status above all else; the injunction to be completely self-reliant; the emphasis on toughness and aggression; nonrelational, objectifying attitudes toward sexuality; and fear and hatred of homosexuals.

B. TYPES OF GENDER ROLE STRAIN

The gender role strain paradigm stimulated research on three varieties of male gender role strain: discrepancy strain, dysfunction strain, and trauma strain. Discrepancy strain results when one fails to live up to one's internalized manhood ideal, which, among contemporary adult males is often a close approximation of the traditional code. Dysfunction strain results even when one fulfills the requirements of the male code, because many of the characteristics viewed as desirable in men can have negative side effects on the men themselves and on those close to them. Trauma strain results from the ordeal of the male role socialization process, which is now recognized as inherently traumatic.

C. DISCREPANCY STRAIN

One approach to investigating discrepancy strain used a version of the self/ideal-self research method, in which participants are first asked, using adjectival rating scales, to describe the "ideal man" and then asked to describe themselves. The discrepancy between the two ratings was used as index of discrepancy strain, which was then studied in terms of its correlations with other variables such as self-esteem. This line of research has not been particularly productive. Another approach has been more fruitful, which does not ask participants whether discrepancy strain exists for them, but rather inquires as to whether they would experience particular gender discrepancies as conflictual or stressful if they did exist. Two major research programs have used this approach: O'Neil's work on male gender role conflict and Eisler's work on masculine gender role stress.

D. DYSFUNCTION STRAIN

The second type of gender role strain is dysfunction strain. The notion behind dysfunction strain is that the fulfillment of the requirements of the male code can be dysfunctional because many of the characteristics viewed as desirable in men can have negative side effects on the men themselves and on those close to them. The research that documents the existence of dysfunction strain includes studies that find negative outcomes associated with masculine gender-related personality traits on the one hand, and lack of involvement in family roles on the other hand. As examples of the latter, one study by Rosalind Barnett and colleagues found that the low quality of men's parental role, but not that of their marital role, was a significant predictor of men's physical health problems. Another by the same group found that low quality of men's marital role and of their parental role are both significant predictors of men's psychological distress.

In addition, Brooks and Silverstein have pointed out that there are significant social and public health problems that result, through one pathway or another, from adherence to traditional masculinity ideology. These problems include (1) relationship dysfunctions, including inadequate emotional partnering, nonnurturing fathering, and nonparticipative household partnering; (2) socially irresponsible behaviors, including chemical dependence, risk-seeking behavior, physical self-abuse, absent fathering, and homelessness/vagrancy; (3) sexual excess, including promiscuity, involvement with pornography, and sexual addiction, and (4) violence, including male violence against women in the family, rape and sexual assault, and sexual harassment.

E. TRAUMA STRAIN

The concept of trauma strain has been applied to certain groups of men whose experiences with gender role strain are thought to be particularly harsh. This includes war veterans (especially Vietnam-era vets), professional athletes, survivors of child abuse (including sexual abuse), men of color, and gay and bisexual men.

But above and beyond the recognition that certain classes of men may experience trauma strain, a perspective on the male role socialization process has emerged that views socialization under traditional masculinity ideology as *inherently* traumatic. Contemporary adult men grew up in an era when traditional masculinity ideology held sway. According to the tenets of the gender role strain paradigm, growing up male under these conditions was an ordeal with traumatic consequences. This perspective and male gender role socialization are best examined by first discussing emotion socialization, using the lens of social learning theory and associated empirical data, and then discussing certain associated normative developmental traumas, using the lens of a gender-strain-paradigm-informed version of psychoanalytic developmental psychology.

IV. Male Gender Role Socialization

A. THE ORDEAL OF EMOTION SOCIALIZATION

Due to what seem to be biologically based differences, males start out life more emotionally expressive than females. Data from 12 studies (11 of which were of neonates) concluded that male infants are more emotionally reactive and expressive than their female counterparts—that they startle more easily, become excited or distressed more quickly, have a lower tolerance for tension and frustration, cry sooner and more often, and fluctuate more rapidly between emotional states. Another study found that infant boys were judged to be more emotionally expressive than were infant girls, even when the judges were misinformed about the infant's actual gender, thus controlling for the effects of gender-role stereotyping on the part of judges. Finally, boys remain more emotional than girls at least until six months of age: six-month-old boys exhibited significantly more joy and anger, more fussiness, crying, and positive vocalizations, and more gestural signals directed toward the mother than girls.

Despite this initial advantage in emotional expressivity, males learn to tune out, suppress, and channel their emotions, whereas the emotion socialization of females encourages their expressivity. These effects become evident with respect to verbal expression by two years of age and facial expression by six years of age. Two-year-old girls were found to refer to feeling states more frequently than do two-year-old boys.

One investigator assessed the ability of mothers of four to six-year-old boys and girls to accurately identify their child's emotional responses to a series of slides by observing their child's facial expressions on a TV monitor. The older the boy, the less expressive his face, and the harder it was for his mother to tell what he was feeling. No such correlation was found among the girls: their mothers were able to identify their emotions no matter what their age. Hence, between the ages of four and six, boys apparently inhibit and mask their overt response to emotion to an increasing extent, while girls continue to respond relatively freely.

What are the socialization pressures that would account for this crossover in emotional expression, such that boys start out more emotional than girls and wind up much less so? Levant and Kopecky proposed that the socialization influences of mother, father, and peer group combine to result in the suppression and channeling of male emotionality and the encouragement of female emotionality. The mechanisms of emotion socialization include selective reinforcement, direct teaching, differential life experiences, and punishment.

The suppression and channeling of male emotionality by mothers, fathers, and peer groups has four major consequences: the development of a gender-specific form of empathy called "action empathy," normative alexithymia, the overdevelopment of anger, and the channeling of caring emotions into sexuality.

1. Action Empathy

Many men develop a form of empathy that I call "action empathy," which can be defined as the ability to see things from another person's point of view and predict what the other person will, or should, *do*. This is in contrast to emotional empathy—taking another person's perspective and being able to know how the other *feels*—a skill that men typically do not have in abundance. Action empathy is usually learned in the gymnasiums and on the playing fields, from gym teachers and sports coaches, who put a premium on learning an opponent's general approach, strengths, weaknesses, and body language in order to be able to figure out how the opponent might react in a given situation.

2. Normative Alexithymia

Normative alexithymia is an inability, common among men, to sense ones' feelings and put them

into words. It is a less severe variant of a clinical condition known as alexithymia, which literally means "without words for emotions." Normative alexithymia is a predictable result of the male gender role socialization process. Specifically, it is a result of boys being socialized to restrict the expression of their vulnerable and caring/connection emotions and to be emotionally stoic. This socialization process includes both the creation of skill deficits (by not teaching boys emotional skills nor allowing them to have experiences that would facilitate their learning these skills) and trauma (including prohibitions against boys' natural emotional expressivity and punishment, often in the form of making the boy feel deeply ashamed of himself for violating these prohibitions).

Men who are having an emotion that they cannot bring into awareness often experience it in one of two ways: (1) as a bodily sensation, which may be the result of the physiological components of the emotion (examples of which are tightness in the throat, constriction in the chest, clenching of the gut, antsy feeling in the legs, constriction in the face, difficulty concentrating, and gritting of teeth) and (2) as a response to external pressure (i.e., feeling "stressed out," "overloaded," "zapped," or having the need to "just veg out").

3. The Overdevelopment of Anger and Aggression

An important corollary of normative alexithymia is the overdevelopment of anger and aggression. Boys are allowed to feel and become aware of emotions in the anger and rage part of the spectrum, as prescribed in the toughness dimension of the male code. As a result, men express anger more aggressively than do women. The aggressive expression of anger is, in fact, one of the very few ways boys are encouraged to express emotion, and as a consequence the outlawed vulnerable emotions, such as hurt, disappointment, fear, and shame, get funneled into the anger channel. In truth, though, for some men the process is more active. For these men the vulnerable emotions are actively *transformed* into anger, a process learned on the playing fields, as when a boy is pushed to the ground and he knows that his job is to come back up with a fistful of gravel rather than a face full of tears.

In addition, due to the general lack of sensitivity to emotional states that characterizes alexithymia, many men do not recognize anger in its mild forms, such as irritation or annoyance, but only detect it when they are very angry. Consequently, angry outbursts often come too readily in men. Such men are victims of a "rubber band syndrome," in which men ignore their own feelings of annoyance or mild anger until these feelings build up to the point that they snap back with fury, much like a rubber band that has been pulled and stretched to its limits and is then finally released. [*See* AGGRESSION; ANGER.]

4. The Suppression and Channeling of Caring Feelings into Sexuality

Boys experience sharp limitations on the expression of caring/connection emotions. Many men recall that their first experience with these limitations occurred in the context of their relationships with their fathers, for, in the traditional postwar family, hugs and kisses between father and son typically came to an end by the time the boy was ready to enter school. Preadolescent boys also get the message from their peers that it is not socially acceptable to express affection to, or receive affection from, mothers (lest they be a "mama's boy"), girls (a peer might taunt, sing-song fashion, "Johnny loves Susie"), or boys (where anything but a cool, buddy-type relationship with another boy can give rise to the dreaded accusation of homosexuality). Socialization experiences of this type set up powerful barriers to the overt expression of caring/connection emotions, which thus get suppressed and even repressed.

Later, in adolescence, interest in sexuality suddenly accelerates due to the combined effects of hormones and culture. Boys become aware of their sexuality, experience nocturnal emissions ("wet dreams") and masturbation, and become intensely interested in the release of their sexual urges. Prevailing images of females as sex objects give boys' emerging objectification of girls a cultural imprimatur. Acting on messages from peers and the culture at large, adolescent boys also develop the need to prove themselves as men by "scoring" with girls, adding an additional layer of self-involvement. Boys' deficits in emotional empathy reinforce this self-involved objectification of girls by preventing boys from realizing how it might feel to the girls who are the object of their lust. The long-suppressed caring/connection emotions get swept along in this turbulent stream, but they are well outside of awareness. As a result, sexuality for boys becomes, at the conscious level, unconnected and nonrelational. For example, a large-scale study found that only half as many men as women reported that affection for their partner was

the reason for having sexual intercourse for the first time.

How do teenage boys learn about sex? An absence of realistic, compassionate portrayals of sexuality combined with ubiquitous fantasy images of sexy women foster the development of unconnected lust. Throughout adolescence the caring/connection emotions remain an underground, unconscious aspect of the sexual experience, reinforced in this position by fear of the shame that results from violations of the traditional code of masculinity. Later in adulthood, the caring/connection emotions begin to surface, taking the form, as described by many men, of feeling most closely connected to their wives while making love.

5. Summary

Hence, the male emotion socialization ordeal, through the combined influences of mothers, fathers, and peer groups, suppress and channel natural male emotionality to such an extent that boys grow up to be men who develop an action-oriented variant of empathy, who cannot readily sense their feelings and put them into words, and who tend to channel or transform their vulnerable feelings into anger and their caring feelings into sexuality. [*See* EMPATHY AND EMOTIONAL EXPRESSIVITY.]

B. NORMATIVE DEVELOPMENTAL TRAUMAS

Certain additional traumas are theorized to reliably occur as a part of male development to such an extent that they must be considered "normative": the early separation from the mother during the separation–individuation phase, required for the socialization of boys, and the unavailability of the father.

1. Separation from Mother

According to modern psychoanalytic theory, the gender role socialization of boys includes the requirement of an early and sharp separation from their mothers during the separation–individuation phase of early childhood. Girls, on the other hand, can prolong the symbiotic attachment with their mothers (in which there is such a high-degree of closeness that the boundaries between mother and daughter are unclear to the daughter) and avoid experiencing this emotional rupture. However, for the sake of balance it should be pointed out that this prolonged attachment may leave some females vulnerable to "enmeshment" in later relationships, a phenomenon in which people reexperience the symbiosis of early childhood relationships in their adult relationships.

At an early age, according the theory, boys are given the prize of a sense of themselves as separate individuals; in return, they are required to give up their close attachments to their mothers. Hence, as boys grow up, yearnings for maternal closeness and attachment (which never completely go away) become associated with fears of losing their sense of themselves as separate. Thus, when such yearnings for maternal closeness begin to emerge into awareness, they often bring with them terrifying fears of the loss of the sense of self. Consequently, many adult men feel much safer being alone than being close to someone. This may be experienced as a fear of engulfment, which often motivates the well-known clinical pattern of male distancing in marriage. On the other hand, those yearnings for maternal attachment also get expressed in marriages, in the form of husband's (often unconscious, certainly unacknowledged) dependence on their wives.

The early separation of boys from their mothers robs boys of the tranquility of childhood and is never acknowledged, much less mourned, leaving men vulnerable to developing destructive entitlement—the unconscious belief that people in one's adult life are required to make up for what one did not get as a child.

2. Father Absence and "The Wound"

The socialization ordeal for boys also includes the requirement that they identify with their psychologically—if not physically—absent, emotionally unavailable fathers. The stress of this ordeal is further complicated by the fact that when the father is available, he is often very demanding of his son. Paradoxically, many men feel that their lives will not be complete unless they have a son, and then when they do have a son wind up being very hard on him. Part of this has to do with the father feeling that he must take an active role in enforcing his son's compliance with gender stereotypes. Developmental research has found that fathers traditionally take an influential role in enforcing sex role stereotypes with their children, whereas mothers are more gender neutral.

The difficult father-son relationship leaves a deep impression on the man—referred to as the "father wound" in the men's studies literature—which is manifested in myriad direct and disguised forms of desperately seeking some contact, some closeness with one's father (or his surrogate), or in being furious at him for his failures. Many men are burdened with feelings that they never knew their fathers, nor how their fathers felt as men, nor if their fathers even liked them, nor if their fathers ever really approved of them.

V. *Toward the Reconstruction of Masculinity*

As noted earlier, two steps must be taken before Western society can help men engage in a critical examination and reconstruction of masculinity. First, men's experience must be taken seriously so as to adopt an empathic approach to their pain. Second, to help men come to terms with the crisis and restore their lost sense of pride, society must honor the still-valuable aspects of masculinity. In keeping with this approach, this proposed reconstruction will separate out the aspects of the traditional male code that are still quite valuable and suggest that these be celebrated, and identify those aspects that are obsolete and dysfunctional and target those for change.

Some of the positive attributes that should be celebrated are a man's willingness to set aside his own needs for the sake of his family; his tendency to take care of people and solve their problems as if they were his own; his ability to withstand hardship and pain to protect others; his way of expressing love by doing things for others; his loyalty, dedication, and commitment; his stick-to-it-iveness and will to hang in until the situation is corrected; and his abilities to rely on himself, solve problems, think logically, take risks, stay calm in the face of danger, and assert himself. These traits are natural results of the male role socialization process, attributes of the male code that are still quite valuable, but that have been lying around in the dust ever since the edifice of masculinity collapsed. Expressing a societal appreciation for these traits will allow men to regain some of the lost esteem and pride associated with being a man.

Then there are the other traits, those parts of the male role that are obsolete and dysfunctional, which include men's relative inability to experience emotional empathy, men's difficulty in being able to identify and express their own emotional states, the tendency for men's anger to flip into rage and result in violence, men's tendency to experience sexuality as separated from relationships, men's difficulties with emotional intimacy, men's difficulties in becoming full partners with their wives in maintaining a home and raising children, and men's tendencies to prefer competitiveness over cooperation and dominance over equality. These traits are results of the male-role socialization process. Rectifying them requires learning new skills and doing emotional work.

A. THE NEW MASCULINITIES

What form will the new masculinities take? Who will be the new role models? For contemporary, White middle-class men, the "strong silent" model of masculinity that suited our fathers clearly does not work. The "sensitive man," as portrayed by the actor Alan Alda in several popular films, seemed to offer an alternative. Unfortunately this image of modern masculinity has been so negatively caricatured that many men will not touch it. In addition, we have to consider what are appropriate models for different racial and ethnic groups, socioeconomic classes, and sexual orientations. The search for appropriate images of what it means to be a man is a central issue today.

Certain elements are likely to be evident in the new masculinities. The new men will posses a combination of old and new traits. They will still be strong, self-reliant, and reliable. They will show care by doing for others, looking out for them, and helping them to solve their problems. They will be logical and live by a moral code. They will be good at solving problems and in being assertive. But they will no longer be strangers to emotions. They will have a greater appreciation of their own emotional life and an ability to express their emotions in words. Their emotional lives will also be richer and more complex. Anger will retreat to an appropriate level, and they will be more comfortable with sadness and fear. They will feel less afraid of shame. They will be aware of the emotions of others and adept at reading their subtle nuances. They will have a better balance in their lives between work and love. They will be better husbands and lovers because they will be able to experience the true joys of intimacy and come to prefer that over nonrelational sex. They will be the fathers that they wanted for themselves.

ACKNOWLEDGMENTS

Sections of this article were adapted, with permission, from Levant, R. F. (1996). The new psychology of men. *Professional Psychology: Research and Practice* 27, 259–265, Copyright © 1996 by the American Psychological Association; Levant, R. F. (1992). Toward the reconstruction of masculinity. *Journal of Family Psychology* 5, 379–402, Copyright © 1992 by the American Psychological Association; Levant, R. F. (1997). The masculinity crisis. *The Journal of Men's Studies* 5, 221–231.

SUGGESTED READING

Brooks, G. R. (1995). *The Centerfold Syndrome*. Jossey-Bass, San Francisco.

Brooks, G. R. and Silverstein, L. S. (1995). Understanding the dark side of masculinity: An interactive systems model. In *A New Psychology of Men* (R. F. Levant and W. S. Pollack, eds.). Basic Books, New York.

Clatterbaugh, K (1990). *Contemporary Perspectives on Masculinity: Men, Women and Politics in Modern Society*. Westview Press, Boulder, CO.

David, D., and Brannon, R. (eds.) (1976). *The Forty-nine Percent Majority: The Male Sex Role*. Addison-Wesley, Reading, MA.

Eisler, R. M. (1995). The relationship between masculine gender role stress and men's health risk: The validation of a construct. In *A New Psychology of Men*. (R. F. Levant and W. S. Pollack, eds.). Basic Books, New York.

Gilmore, D. (1990). *Manhood in the Making: Cultural Concepts of Masculinity*. Yale University Press, New Haven, CT.

Kimmel, M. (1995). *Manhood in American: A Cultural History*. The Free Press, New York.

Lazur, R. F., and Majors, R. (1995). Men of color: Ethnocultural variations of male gender role strain. In *A New Psychology of Men* (R. F. Levant and W. S. Pollack, eds.). Basic Books, New York.

Levant, R. F., and Brooks, G. R. (1997). *Men and Sex: New Psychological Perspectives*. John Wiley & Sons, New York.

Levant, R. F., and Kopecky, G. (1995/1996). *Masculinity Reconstructed: Changing the Rules of Manhood*. Dutton/Plume, New York.

Levant, R. F., and Pollack, W. S. (1995). *A New Psychology of Men*. Basic Books, New York.

O'Neil, J. M., Good, G. E., and Holmes, S (1995). Fifteen years of theory and research on men's gender role conflict: New paradigms for empirical research. In *A New Psychology of Men* (R. F. Levant and W. S. Pollack, eds.). Basic Books, New York.

Osherson, S. (1986). Finding Our Fathers: *The Unfinished Business of Manhood*. The Free Press, New York.

Pleck, J. H. (1981). The *Myth of Masculinity*. MIT Press, Cambridge, MA.

Pollack, W. S. (1995). No man is an island: Toward a new psychoanalytic psychology of men. In *A New Psychology of Men* (R. F. Levant and W. S. Pollack, eds.). Basic Books, New York.

Promise Keepers. (1994). *Seven Promises of a Promise Keeper*. Focus on the Family Publishing, Colorado Springs, CO.

Menopause

Barbara Sommer

University of California, Davis

Glossary

Amenorrhea Absence or abnormal cessation of menstrual periods.

Androgen Primary male hormone; testosterone, androstenedione, dihydrotestosterone; also termed a *gonadal* or *reproductive hormones*.

Andropause Decline in androgen associated with aging in the male, also called *viropause*.

Anovulatory cycles Cycles in which no egg is released by the ovary.

Climacteric Process of reproductive decline in midlife.

Endometrial cancer Cancer of the uterus.

Endorphins Naturally occurring opiates.

Estradiol Most biologically active of the estrogens.

Estriol An estrogen.

Estrogen Primary female hormones (estradiol, estriol, and estrone), also termed *gonadal* or *reproductive hormones.*

Estrone An estrogen.

Follicle (ovarian) Cells surrounding the egg.

Free androgen index (FAI) Index of free testosterone, ratio of serum (blood) testosterone to SHBG, multiplied by 100.

FSH (follicle-stimulating hormone) A gonadotropin produced by the pituitary gland.

GnRH (gonadotropin-releasing hormone) Produced by the hypothalamus, stimulates the pituitary gland to secrete gonadotropins.

Gonad Organ that produces reproductive cells—eggs or sperm.

Gonadal hormones Substances produced by the gonad, called sex hormones or reproductive hormones; include estrogens, progesterone, androgen, inhibin, and activin.

Gonadotropins Secreted by the pituitary into the bloodstream, stimulate the gonads; the two types are follicle-stimulating hormone (FSH) and luteinizing hormone (LH).

Hormone replacement therapy (HRT) Substances taken to augment the declining levels of reproductive hormones produced by the ovary.

Hypothalamus Collection of nerve cells in the brain, which influences numerous bodily functions including water balance, temperature regulation, and appetite.

Hysterectomy Surgical removal of the uterus (womb).

LH (luteinizing hormone) A gonadotropin.

Menopause A period of one year without a menstrual period.

Neurotransmitters Substances that influence neural activity.

Osteoporosis Disease characterized by low bone mass.

Ovaries Female gonads, located near the womb, which produce eggs.

Ovulation Release of a mature egg by the rupturing follicle in the ovary.

Perimenopause From the first indication of menstrual irregularity to the end of menstruation, ranging from three to nine years.

Phytoestrogens Plan-based, estrogen-like substances.

Pituitary gland Pea-sized organ located beneath the hypothalamus.

Postmenopause Time after menopause.

Premature menopause Menopause before the age of 40.

Premenopause Time preceding the observable changes of menopause.

Progesterone A gonadal hormone.

Progestin Synthetic or natural progesterone, often prescribed to counter harmful effects of estrogen.

Sebaceous glands Located in the skin and genital area, produce oil.

SHBG (sex hormone binding globulin) Substance in the bloodstream that binds with androgen (testosterone).

Surgical menopause Removal of both ovaries.

Testes Male gonads, glands in the scrotum, produce sperm.

Testosterone Primary male hormone, a gonadal or reproductive hormone, also called *androgen*.

Vaginal atrophy Increasing dryness, shortening, and thinning of the walls.

Vasomotor instability Unpredictable blood vessel dilation and contraction.

Viropause Decline in androgen associated with aging in the male, also called *andropause*.

THE WORD MENOPAUSE is a combination of Greek terms for "month" and "cessation." Its occurrence is marked by a woman's last menstrual period which generally occurs between the ages of 48 and 52, with a median of 51.5 years. "Last menstrual period" technically has occurred following a year without menses—hence menopause is always defined retrospectively, a year after the fact. Other popular expressions are "change of life," "critical time," "the change," "the dangerous age," and "the dodging time."

I. The Menopausal Transition

The medical term for the overall transition from a reproductive to a nonreproductive state is climacteric (from the Greek word *klimacter,* a combination of "rung of ladder" and "critical time"). The useful distinction between event (menopause) and process (climacteric) tends to be lost as the word *menopause* is often used for both. The World Health Organization (WHO) has recommended the following categories for describing the menopausal transition:

Premenopause. The time preceding observable changes resulting from alteration in ovarian function
Perimenopause. From the first indication of menstrual irregularity to the end of menstruation, ranging from three to nine years
Postmenopause. The time after the last menstrual period.

The menopausal transition can be seen as puberty in reverse, with ovarian function declining instead of gearing up for reproduction; and like puberty, the changes occur over a number of years.

Menopause is a physical change that takes place within a larger social and cultural context. Relative to puberty and menstruation, menopause has the additional quality of occurring in a mature person with considerable life experience. Therefore, the way in which menopause is experienced by the individual reflects a multitude of physiological, psychological, sociological, and cultural features. To fully appreciate the impact of menopause, one must recognize that the physiological changes have implications that extend far beyond their physical ramifications. Bodily changes can affect one's mood. Attitude and other qualities of a psychological nature are likely to influence a woman's perception of and feelings about the physical changes of menopause. At the sociocultural level, people's expectations of and responses to menopausal and postmenopausal women are likely to be influenced by the degree to which a woman's role is defined by her reproductive capacity and by other cultural beliefs about aging and gender, and the woman herself is likely to share those expectations, perceptions, and beliefs.

II. *Physiology of Menstruation and Menopause*

For both women and men there is a complex hormonal feedback system underlying reproduction. Three key physical structures are involved: the gonads and two brain structures, the hypothalamus, and the pituitary gland.

The gonads are the primary sex organs, consisting of ovaries (egg-containing structures located near the womb) in the female and testes (glands in the scrotum) in the male. The hypothalamus is a collection of nerve cells in the brain that influences numerous bodily functions including water balance, temperature regulation, and appetite. It also produces gonadotropin-releasing hormone (GnRH), which is secreted into the bloodstream and carried to the pituitary gland. The pituitary gland is a pea-sized organ located near the hypothalamus.

Stimulated by GnRH, the pituitary gland produces its own chemical substances called gonadotropins, so termed because they stimulate the gonads. There are two gonadotropins, follicle stimulating hormone (FSH) and luteinizing hormone (LH). Traveling through the bloodstream, the gonadotropins reach the ovaries in the female and testes in the male. Their effect is to stimulate production of the gonadal hormones (also termed sex hormones or reproductive hormones). In the female, FSH stimulates the growth of follicles (structures containing eggs), which produce estrogen. After sufficient estrogen production to produce a pituitary surge of LH release at midcycle, the ovarian follicle ruptures, the egg is released, and the remaining follicular cells produce progesterone. In the male, FSH and LH stimulate the production of androgen (testosterone) in the testes.

A balance in hormone level is maintained by a negative feedback loop. The gonadal hormones (estrogen/progesterone and androgen) cause the hypothalamus to inhibit the output of GnRH. That leads to less stimulation of the pituitary gland, less FSH and LH, and subsequently less estrogen, progesterone, and androgen. These gonadal hormones also provide negative feedback to the pituitary gland to reduce gonadotropin secretion. When the levels of the gonadal hormones drop, the inhibition on the hypothalamus and the pituitary gland is removed and gonadal hormone production increases again. The feedback loop is illustrated in Figure 1.

In the mature female, the pattern of hormonal secretion is cyclic and produces the rhythmic occurrence of ovulation and menstruation, with interruption during pregnancy. The pattern for cyclic secretion may be present in the brain prior to birth. Sex differences in GnRH secretion are seen during the first two to three years of life and through puberty and adult life. Gonadotropin secretion and sex hormone release in the male do not show the marked 26- to 28-day cyclic fluctuation found in the female. [*See* MENSTRUATION.]

The cessation of menstruation is preceded by a lengthy period of decreased ovarian function. The exact cause of the ovarian decline is not clear, but is related to aging and probably lies within the ovary itself. The human female is born with 1 million immature eggs in her ovaries. By puberty, over 99% of the eggs have degenerated. A few of the remaining eggs ripen in the course of each menstrual cycle and the surrounding follicle produces estrogen and progesterone in the process. Usually, only one of the eggs reaches full development (two will result in fraternal twins if fertilization occurs). The other eggs that started to mature either regress or are reabsorbed in the body. With age, the pattern of regression on the part of the developing eggs is accentuated. The follicles seem to be less responsive to the stimulation provided by FSH and therefore produce less estrogen and progesterone.

The decline in the process of egg development is gradual. Ovulation (the release of a mature egg) becomes less frequent, with a corollary increase in anovulatory cycles (those without eggs). The result is the oft-observed irregularity in timing and menstrual flow that precedes actual menopause. The decline in ovarian hormonal output reduces the inhibition to the hypothalamus, which in turn leads to a marked increase in FSH in the bloodstream. Elevated FSH is often used as an indicator of menopausal status. However, a single occurrence of elevated FSH in the bloodstream does not necessarily indicate menopausal status.

Although the levels of reproductive hormones drop considerably after menopause, they do not cease entirely. The ovaries continue to produce some estrogens, in decreasing amounts with age, and other structures in the body (e.g., the adrenal glands and fat tissue) produce some forms of estrogen.

III. *Timing of Menopause*

Genetic factors probably play a role in determining when a woman goes through menopause. There is some evidence that on the average, African

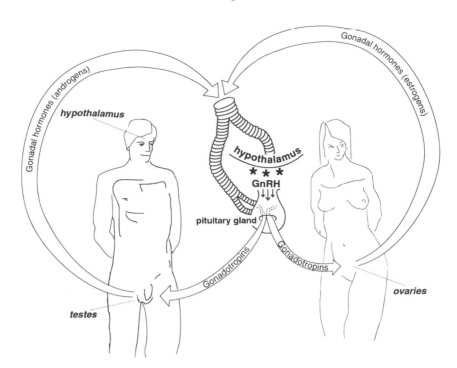

Figure I   Shematic diagram of the relationship between the hypothalamus, pituitary, and gonads.

American women have an earlier menopause than Caucasian women—a difference of about four to eight months. As African American girls reach puberty sooner, the overall length of the reproductive years is probably about the same for both groups.

A number of studies have taken into account reproductive factors (age at puberty, number of children, sexual behavior or history, the use of hormone-based oral contraceptives) and a variety of other socioeconomic and health-related variables. A mechanism proposed for their having an effect on timing is their role in reducing the number of ovulatory cycles, thereby preserving eggs longer, with the result of a later menopause. The findings with regard to these variables are not consistent, nor has it been established that more eggs leads to a later menopause. The only consistent finding is the association of smoking with earlier menopause.

Premature ovarian failure can be brought about by illness, radiation, or other sources of physical damage. Menopause is considered premature if it occurs before the age of 40. It is considered to be late when it occurs after age 54. Removal of both ovaries results in menopause (termed *surgical menopause*). One functioning ovary is sufficient to prevent premature menopause.

The situation with hysterectomy (removal of the uterus/womb) reveals the ambiguity of menopause terminology. Although the technical definition of menopause is the cessation of menstruation, what one is generally talking about is the shutdown of the ovaries. Hysterectomy alone does not result in menopause in the usual sense. The ovaries continue to produce hormones, and the negative feedback cycle with FSH and LH continues. Menstrual bleeding ceases because there is no longer a uterus in which the menstrual blood supply forms. A woman with a hysterectomy, but intact ovaries, will go through menopause in much the same way as other women (e.g., likely to experience hot flashes), except for the change in bleeding patterns that characterize the perimenopausal woman with an intact uterus.

IV. Body and Behavioral Changes

A number of the body's physical and psychological systems are affected by the changing hormonal pattern of menopause.

A. MENSTRUAL IRREGULARITY

The most consistent indicator of impending menopause is menstrual irregularity. For some women, it is the only symptom. A typical pattern is the shortening of menstrual cycle length due to declining estrogen levels. A light blood flow or just spotting around the time of one's regular period is a suggestion that ovulation has not occurred. Skipping a period also indicates anovulation (absence of ovulation), although one must also be alert to the possibility of pregnancy.

Heavier than normal menstrual flow can also be associated with the transition. The ovaries are still producing estrogen, but in the absence of ovulation there is little progesterone to counteract the effect of the estrogen in building up the endometrium (lining of the uterus). The result is heavier bleeding.

Irregular periods, intermenstrual spotting, excessive and prolonged menstruation, and episodes of amenorrhea (missed periods) are not unusual during the perimenopause. However, it is important to monitor the changes, particularly if flow or discomfort becomes excessive. After natural menopause, any bleeding is abnormal and calls for medical examination.

B. HOT FLASHES/VASOMOTOR INSTABILITY AND SOMATIC SYMPTOMS

Experiencing "hot flashes" is the most frequently reported symptom of menopause, and their occurrence may precede the cessation of menstruation. A hot flash is a sensation of body heat, generally beginning in one part of the body and spreading quickly to other areas. The hot flash is a true increase in body temperature and ranges from 0.5 to 3 degrees Celsius. A flush is an accompanying blush resulting from dilation of the blood vessels (which is a means of reducing body temperature). The hot flash may last from 30 seconds to over 12 minutes. There is considerable variability across women with regard to the frequency and patterning of hot flashes. Some women experience the flash with little flushing. Others flush and then flash. Often the hot flash is followed by sweating, particularly in the upper body. The evaporation of sweat reduces body temperature. A unique aspect of menopausal hot flashes is that they are internally produced (hence the query "Is it hot in here—or is it me?"). They are not entirely independent of the environment in that stress or excitement may precipitate a flash. A temperature increase, coffee, wine, or spicy food can trigger a hot flash. Hot flashes are sometimes accompanied by other symptoms such as increased heart rate or heart throbbing or fluttering (palpitations).

Both the frequency and the intensity of hot flashes decrease over time (a range of six months to two years is often mentioned), but some women report hot flashes for a much longer period of time. The subjective experience as rated by women varies from mild (a barely noticeable warm feeling) to severe (an extreme or unbearable discomfort that leads a woman to disrupt normal activity in search of relief, perhaps accompanied by a drenching sweat, dizziness, and feelings of suffocation).

The hot flash is attributed to vasomotor instability, an unpredictable contraction and dilation of the blood vessels. The underlying cause probably lies within the temperature-regulating neurons in the hypothalamus. Reduced gonadal hormones (estrogen and progesterone) and changes in pituitary hormones seem to be associated with a downward setting of the hypothalamic thermostat. One's skin becomes cold and clammy just before the flash. The blood flow to the arms and legs increases 4- to 30-fold and heart rate increases, with the result being the warmth of the hot flash. Flushing and sweating bring the body temperature back down to normal. The mechanism is not a simple one of presence or absence of estrogen. Prepubescent females have low levels of estrogen and do not experience hot flashes. It may be that declining levels of estrogen effect some other set of substances that influence the hypothalamus, for example, neurotransmitters (substances that influence neural activity) or endorphins (naturally occurring opiates).

A majority of women experience hot flashes at some point during the menopausal transition, and the symptoms are relieved by estrogen replacement therapy. When the therapy is stopped, the hot flashes return. Factors associated with an increased likelihood of hot flashes are early menopause, surgical menopause (removal of the ovaries), and low body fat—probably because fat tissue produces estrogen.

Suggestions for dealing with hot flashes include the keeping of a diary in order to identify trigger events or substances that subsequently can be avoided, dressing in layers, cooling with water or ice immediately at the onset of a flash, keeping one's environment cool, regular exercise, and avoidance of emotionally charged or stressful situations.

Recent studies involving large samples have found an increase in the number of women reporting somatic symptoms (e.g., joint pain, headaches, dizziness, stiffness of shoulder and neck, and sleep difficulties) during the perimenopause, the phase between the early signs of menopause and the last menstrual period.

C. UROGENITAL CHANGES

The lower vagina, bladder, and urinary tract develop from the same tissue and are composed of estrogen-sensitive tissue. Thus all are affected to some extent by a decrease in circulating estrogen. The walls of the vagina, as well as that of the bladder and urethra, become more thin. The consequences of these changes can be painful intercourse and more frequent urination, as well as occasional urine leakage. Aging leads to a reduction in subcutaneous fat and skin collagen. The result is a wrinkling of the skin. The external genitals become more thin and less sensitive to the touch. The sebaceous (oil) glands diminish their secretion, and a thinning of pubic hair is common.

Vaginal atrophy—increasing dryness, thinning of the walls, and shortening—may be associated with discomfort such as irritation, itching, and burning. The shift from an acidic to alkaline vaginal environment may produce some vaginal discharge.

With regard to sexual responsiveness, sexual arousal produces some lubrication, even in the absence of estrogen, by increasing the blood flow to the area. Although the cells lining the vagina are the primary source of secretion and lubrication, improved blood flow will keep tissues supple. Although there is documentation indicating that sexual activity declines after menopause, it is not clear how much of that is due directly to the changes of menopause and how much it has to do with other aspects of one's life—for example, increasing age of one's partner, the quality of the relationship, and a willingness to accommodate to the need for more time for arousal. [See AGING.]

D. SKELETAL/OSTEOPOROSIS

Osteoporosis is a disease characterized by low bone mass leading to structural deterioration of the skeleton. It is the most common bone disease in humans, with the majority of cases involving postmenopausal women. The physical signs are loss of height, collapsed vertebra, or "dowager's hump" (curved spine). Most women and men lose about 1 to 1.5 inches of height as they age, due to shrinking of the spine (a result of reduction in the fluid content of spongy areas between each vertebra). A loss greater than 1.5 inches may indicate osteoporosis. Back pain is another indicator. The occurrence of a fracture, in particular a broken hip, may be the first obvious indication of osteoporosis.

Bones provide a storage area in the body for calcium, and resorption is important in maintaining blood calcium levels. Calcium is essential for a number of functions such as blood coagulation, nerve conduction, muscle contraction, and maintaining the acid-base balance. These processes take precedence over the creation of new bone. Hence a shortage of calcium within the body at any age results in a loss of bone because resorption (breakdown) outpaces rebuilding.

Bone mass increases through childhood and adolescence, and peaks during the late 20s or early 30s. As both sexes move into middle age, the process of old bone removal begins to exceed that of replacement with new bone. The exact reason for the shift in balance between breakdown and construction is not clear. Calcium absorption declines with age as does manufacture of vitamin D, an essential element in bone remodeling. Thus prevention of osteoporosis involves developing a high bone mass during the first two decades and then preserving it. Women's calcium requirements increase during and after menopause as does the rate of bone loss and therefore risk of osteoporosis. At present there is no sure cure for osteoporosis. It is a preventable disease, if intervention occurs at an early age; and steps can be taken to reduce, though not reverse, subsequent bone loss.

The key factor determining bone mass is genetic. Women whose female relatives have osteoporosis are at risk, as are those with a slight build. Lifestyle factors play an important role. Bone health requires weight-bearing exercise and a balanced diet with sufficient calories, protein, calcium, and vitamin D throughout life. Physical activity contributes to bone mass development through mechanical stimulation of bone, especially at places where tendons attach. Prolonged bed rest is associated with rapid and significant bone loss, as is spending time in a gravity-free environment. Steroid hormones used to treat other diseases such as rheumatoid arthritis, hepatitis, or asthma cause bone loss. Cigarette smoking and heavy alcohol consumption increase the risk of osteoporosis. The fact that the rate of resorption (breakdown) increases after menopause and is considerably higher for women than men suggests that the drop in estrogen level plays a role. Over the lifetime, men's bone loss is about two-thirds that of women. Women undergoing early menopause, especially surgical menopause, are particularly at risk. A range of medical techniques are available for measuring bone mineral density.

E. CORONARY ARTERY/HEART DISEASE

Postmenopausal women are at increased risk for heart disease and more prone to arteriosclerosis. Although the link is probably to estrogen, its exact nature is not known but may be related to estrogen's role in promoting healthy cholesterol levels in the blood.

F. OTHER PHYSICAL CHANGES

Other physical changes include a thinning of the hair, slight increase in facial hair, loss of breast fullness and elasticity. For many women there is a redistribution of body fat, (e.g., a shift from the buttocks to the abdomen). Weight gain has been associated with menopause, but recent research suggests that the gain has more to do with behavior (e.g., lack of exercise or increased alcohol intake) than with menopause per se.

G. PSYCHOLOGICAL AND BEHAVIORAL CHANGE

A number of studies have shown that women with a history of menstrual problems are more likely to report menopausal problems. This fairly consistent finding suggests several possibilities. One is that the hormonal substrate that contributes to menstrual difficulties may also lead to problems during the menopausal transition. Another possibility is that some women are more sensitive or vulnerable to hormonal fluctuations in general, thereby being affected both by the normal fluctuation of the menstrual cycle and the disruption produced by the changes of the climacteric. A third possibility is a self-report bias—some women are more likely to reports symptoms of any type, thus producing a relationship that has more to do with reporting than the hormonal effects. For example, bloating or weight gain may be a readily-noticed effect. Other women may take little note of such changes. The reliance on self-report for assessing the severity of symptoms makes it very difficult to disentangle the relative contributions of physiological (i.e., hormonal) and psychological factors.

H. MOOD

The reporting of negative feelings and emotion, particularly tension, irritability, anxiety, and feeling depressed, is not unusual during the menopausal transition. These mood symptoms are reported far less often than hot flashes; and as with somatic symptoms, they are more likely to be associated with the perimenopause, the phase between the early signs of menopause and the last menstrual period.

There are a number of ways in which hormonal changes or fluctuations might contribute to negative mood. One possibility relates to the declining level of estrogen and suggests that changing hormonal levels which produce menstrual irregularity and hot flashes also contribute to negative mood by directly affecting the brain areas involved in emotion. However, if estrogen level alone were responsible, postmenopausal women should be the most likely to report negative mood, and that is not the case. Another possibility is that the fluctuation or instability of circulating estrogen and progesterone, rather than level alone, is responsible for the negative mood.

Hormonal instability might exert an indirect effect on feelings and emotion. The discomfort associated with hot flashes or joint pain may produce to irritability or tension. Hot flashes or pain may interfere with sleep, the lack of which further contributes to negative mood.

Psychological factors could play a role. For example, menstrual irregularity and hot flashes serve as indicators or reminders of impending menopause and aging, an association that may cause some women to feel anxious, tense, or depressed. These sets of explanations are not mutually exclusive. Physiological and psychological factors may operate in tandem to produce negative feelings.

The search for cause is further complicated by two major considerations: the sociocultural context and individual characteristics. The meaning of menopause varies across cultures and among individuals. In Western culture, with its emphasis on youth, menopause bears a clear connection with aging and its associated limitations. In other societies, menopause has had a liberating effect on women by removing many of the taboos associated with fertility. At the individual level, a woman's interpretation of menopause is likely to be influenced by her own life experience, her reproductive history (i.e., experience with menstruation, pregnancy, and birth), and her observations of other women within and outside of her family.

I. MENTAL FUNCTION

Other changes that have been associated with menopause in the popular mind are decrements in memory and concentration. It is extremely difficult to disentangle potential menopausal effects from those associated with the aging process. Perimenopausal reports of forgetfulness, distractibility, and problem-solving difficulties are not unusual. Unfortunately there is not a good body of research characterizing cognitive function through the menopausal transition. Recent suggestions that estrogen therapy slows or may prevent the development of certain types of cognitive dysfunction merit further study.

IV. Male Menopause

Is there such process as male menopause? In the strict sense of the term *menopause* the answer is no. In women the end of ovulation (and cessation of menstruation) indicates the end of reproductive capacity and occurs in every woman. In contrast, men continue to be fertile until very old age and may not experience a significant change in hormonal function. However, in the more general sense of the climacteric—a decline in the availability of gonadal hormones for stimulation of target tissues—the answer is yes. The terms used to refer to this change are *andropause* (*andro* is the Greek word for "male"), used in Europe, and *viropause* (*vir* is the Latin prefix for "man"), used in the United Kingdom.

Testosterone (androgen) is secreted in very small amounts by the testes into the bloodstream and much of it is quickly bound in a reversible manner to molecules of sex hormone binding globulin (SHBG). The bound testosterone is biologically unavailable to the target organs in the brain and body. The male androgens do not show the consistent 26- to 28-day cycle seen in the female. However, levels fluctuate rhythmically, varying three to four times per hour. There is a daily rhythm with higher levels in the morning and lower levels in the afternoon. Men show individual monthly patterns of hormone production, and there is a yearly cycle with highest levels occurring in the fall (October) and lowest levels in the spring (April).

Although overall testosterone levels do not decline much with age, the ratio of free testosterone to bound testosterone does drop, meaning that there is a statistically significant decline in testosterone available for the stimulation of target sites in the brain and body. When the levels of free testosterone decline, there is an increase in gonadotropin (LH) similar to that observed in the menopausal woman. Testicular size and the amount of free testosterone start to decline around age 40. For most men, andropause begins around age 40 to 45, although it can begin as

early as 35 or as late as 65 years of age. The following formula has been used to measure active testosterone levels:

Blood testosterone/SHBG $\times$ 100

$\qquad$ = Free Androgen Index (FAI)

When the FAI falls below 50%, symptoms of andropause are often observed. These can include nervousness, depression, impaired memory, inability to concentrate, easy fatigability, insomnia, hot flashes, sweating, and loss of libido and potency. With the exception of the last, the symptoms are those commonly associated with menopause. Erections take longer to occur and are not as firm, ejaculation is less forceful and there is less ejaculate.

Abdominal fat increases as men age. Continuing the analogy with menopause, hormonal therapy is being considered and researched for andropause. Concerns about increasing cardiovascular risk and also the linkage of testosterone with the development of prostate cancer have probably contributed to a less-enthusiastic promotion of hormone replacement therapy for men.

In a pattern analogous to that of women, the pituitary gonadotropins (LH and FSH) increase in response to the decline in testosterone. Men also show progressive bone loss with age similar to that of women. There has been less research done and it is not at all clear whether or not declining androgen (testosterone) levels are the cause. There is evidence both for and against a direct role.

There are similarities and differences between the symptoms of andropause and menopause. The similarities are weight gain, changes in fat distribution, and physical and psychological symptoms. Andropause is more gradual and less dramatic than menopause. A key difference is the maintenance of male fertility. The distinction between the sexes in this regard is attributed to natural selection. Pregnancy is a major drain on the body's energy resources. During the early evolution of the species, the survival of the human infant, with its prolonged period of dependency, required maternal care. An infant with a weakened or older mother would be less likely to survive and pass its genes on to offspring. Thus females whose fertility ended earlier would increase the likelihood of their children's reaching reproductive age. Such women would be able to invest more care in existing offspring and not have to expend energy on new arrivals. In contrast there seems little adaptive advantage for fertility to cease in males.

VI. The Social Construction of Menopause

There is no question that menopause is a biological occurrence. However, many of the meanings associated with it are social constructions. They reflect ideas and inferences that go beyond the facts of biology. In Western culture (European/American) the term *menopause* did not exist until the late 19th century, although the phenomenon is described in medical writings from the 7th century. A longer life expectancy has led to an increased interest in menopause.

At the end of the 20th century in the United States, a woman's life expectancy is about 75 years. An average age of menopause at 51 means that many women will be spending nearly a third of their lives in a postmenopausal state—underscoring the limitations of a social role that is centered around fertility, childbearing, and child rearing. The disjunction between an extended life and one that is limited by reproductive capacity is elaborated in literature—both fiction and nonfiction. It is not unusual to read about unhappy women who having lost their youth and beauty have become empty barren husks of their former selves. They may be described as meddling mothers-in-law who have no other outlet for energy previously taken up with child rearing. Some writings characterize postmenopausal women as practically invisible, no longer of value or use, idling their lives away knitting and crocheting or involving themselves in unpaid volunteer work or aimless shopping and socializing.

Perhaps as a reaction to the preceding characterizations, there have been attempts to place menopause within an evolutionary context; the underlying theme being that older women contribute to the survival of the species through their experience, wisdom, and assistance to the young. They may offer protection for younger women and children from predatory males, when the father or other male kin are unable to do so. The validity of these hypotheses remains to be seen. We use the concepts and theories with which we are most familiar in order to understand and explain our world. Such constructs may or may not be compatible with biological observations.

Within feminist circles there has been a move to celebrate menopause and aging and to emphasize their beneficial aspects—for example, freedom from menstruation and pregnancy, and an opportunity to set aside many of the prescriptions and proscriptions on behavior that are associated with the female role. In some non-Western societies (e.g., the Rajput of India and the Maya of Mexico), reaching menopause frees women from many of the restrictions that were placed on them during the reproductive years. Over the centuries in many cultures, menstruation had an aura of danger. Menopause indicates an end to that threat.

The social meanings assigned to menopause, along with other dominant cultural themes, shape the way in which individuals and social institutions respond. In Europe and North America, and increasingly in Asia, menopause has become a medical disorder, specifically a deficiency disease, and as such, needs to be treated. [*See* SOCIAL IDENTITY.]

VII. Hormone Replacement Therapy (HRT)

Hormone replacement (HRT) augments the declining levels of reproductive hormone production by the ovaries. The earliest uses of HRT involved estrogens. Estrogen is a family of three hormones: estradiol (the most active), estrone, and estriol. The substances were first isolated in a laboratory in 1923. There are both plant and animal sources of estrogen that have biological activity similar to human estrogen; a plant example is Australian red clover. The most common source in the United States for natural estrogen has been pregnant mare's urine (hence the name Premarin for one of the major commercial products). Premarin contains a horse estrogen that is not the same as human estrogen and may not have all the benefits or risks of human estrogen. It is now possible to create synthetic as well as human estrogen in the laboratory.

In 1963 a book by Robert A. Wilson titled *Feminine Forever* had a major impact on U.S. women. His message was that estrogen was the elixir of youth. Thousands of copies of the book were sold and thousands of menopausal women started taking estrogen. By the 1980s the less salubrious effects of estrogen became apparent in the marked increase of endometrial (uterine) cancer. Further, Wilson's claims were exaggerated. Although estrogen may provide some beneficial effects with regard to maintaining the secondary sexual structures (e.g., vaginal tract, breast fullness), it does not reverse the effects of aging.

The use of estrogen replacement dropped markedly. Subsequently, progestin (a synthetic progesterone) was added to the hormonal preparations to reduce the deleterious effect of estrogen on the lining of the uterus.

Today, there are several pharmaceutical products that can be taken in different forms: daily pills, skin patches, skin creams, and vaginal suppositories. These contain various forms of estrogen, and generally a progestin to ameliorate the effect of unopposed estrogen. They can be taken in cyclic fashion, which continues a pattern of menstruation, or can be taken in continuous dosage, which, for many women, eliminates bleeding.

The benefits and risks of HRT constitute a major research area. As new information is constantly being published, it is difficult to draw firm conclusions at this time. What is known is that HRT eliminates hot flashes, reduces sleep disturbances, and helps maintain the urogenital tract (vagina, urethra, and bladder). How helpful it is in retaining skin tone, hair thickness, and other youthful qualities is not obvious. Although earlier in life estrogen is associated with youthful and secondary sex characteristics (e.g., supple skin and breast fullness) the body's receptors are probably less responsive to external estrogens ingested late in life. Estrogen does not postpone the occurrence of natural menopause.

Research studies have found that HRT has been associated with a wide range of positive health outcomes including reduced risk of heart attack, stroke, and osteoporosis. It has been shown to improve mood and cognitive function, particularly in the areas of short-term memory and attention. It has not been an effective treatment for major depression. A major shortcoming of the research is that much of it has failed to take into account socioeconomic factors. Women who use HRT tend to be healthier and wealthier in the first place. Thus, it is difficult to attribute the positive association solely to the effect of HRT.

HRT has also been associated with an increased risk of uterine cancer and possibly breast cancer. The uterine cancer risk is diminished by adding a progestin to counter the effect of estrogen on the uterus.

It is not clear exactly how many women are currently using hormonal replacement therapy, but it is not a majority. Whether or not to use HRT can be a difficult decision. It certainly is one that should be made on a case-by-case basis, taking into account the individual woman's particular set of needs and characteristics.

There is an increasing body of research on the beneficial effects dietary phytoestrogens (plant-based estrogen-like substances found in soy products) and progestins (found in yams). There are also numerous herbal remedies for menopausal symptoms. Unfortunately, the effectiveness of most of these has not been documented through double-blind trials, and it is difficult to discern how much of their support comes from genuine rather than placebo effects. A very effective nonhormonal treatment for menopausal symptoms is exercise and good nutrition, both of which also help retain bone mass. The consequences of not taking HRT seems to be a period of change and adjustment followed by an eventual restoration of equilibrium in body and mood.

SUGGESTED READING

Cherry, S. H., and Runowicz, C. D. (1994). *The Menopause Book: A Guide to Health and Well-Being for Women.* Macmillan, New York.

Hill, A. M. (1993). *Viropause/Andropause, the Male Menopause: Emotional and Physical Changes Mid-life Men Experience.* New Horizon Press, Far Hills, NJ.

Love, S. M., and Lindsey, K. (1997). *Dr. Susan Love's Hormone Book: Making Informed Choices about Menopause.* Random House, New York.

Minkin, M. J., and Wright, C. V. (1996). *What Every Woman Needs to Know about Menopause: The Years Before, During, and After.* Yale University Press, New Haven, CT.

Notelovitz, M., and Tonnessen, D. (1993). *Menopause and Midlife Health.* St. Martin's Press, New York.

The North American Menopause Society (NAMS) Web site: http://www.menopause.org/

Menstruation

Nancy King Reame

University of Michigan, Ann Arbor

"I used to worry about having my period. It seemed that all my friends had gotten it already. . . . I felt left out. I began to think of it as a symbol: When I got my period, I would become a woman."

"As I entered menopause, my periods started coming much less often. After several period-free months, another period would surprise me, and back I would be scrambling for tampons and a heating pad. I'd feel, "Oh my God, isn't this finished?" At the same time I'd feel nostalgic and a little sad, like this might be the last period I'd ever have."

—Our Bodies, Ourselves, by Rome, Reame, and Sanford, 2000, Chapter 12

Glossary

Endometrium The lining of the uterus; the site of implantation of the early embryo.

Menarche The first menstrual period occurring in girls usually between the ages of 10 and 16.

Menstrual cycle Based on the functional changes in the ovary (rather than the uterus), the reproductive cycle can also be divided into the follicular phase (or pre-ovulatory phase, approximate cycle days 1–12; day 1 of the menstrual cycle is the first day of menstrual bleeding), ovulation phase (days 13–14), and the luteal phase (cycle days 15–28 when progesterone is produced by the corpus luteum).

Menstrual phase Refers to the days of actual menstrual bleeding. During menstruation, most of the endometrial lining is shed; the bottom third remains to form a new lining.

Menstruation The menstrual period, or flow, is the natural process of shedding the uterine tissue, blood vessels, and unfertilized egg when a pregnancy has not occurred. Derived from the Latin *mensis*, for "month," menstruation marks the end of one reproductive cycle and the beginning of the next.

Proliferative phase First half of the uterine cycle. Estrogen, made by the maturing follicle containing the egg that will eventually ovulate, causes endometrial glands to grow and thicken, and increases the blood supply to these glands.

Secretory phase The last half of the uterine cycle (approximately 14 days) in which progesterone, made by the ruptured follicle after the egg is released at ovulation, stimulates the glands in the endometrium to begin secreting embryo-nourishing substances.

MENSTRUATION, or the menstrual flow, serves as a social, psychologic, and cultural symbol of "being female." Depending on the culture, the menstruating woman has been feared, revered, shunned, or shielded as testiment to the power of menstrual blood in defining female role expectations and behavioral norms. In Western medicine, the neuroendocrinology of the menstrual cycle has been used to account for gender-based differences in mood disorders and rates of depression without taking into consideration the social and environmental forces that contribute to differences in men's and women's lived experiences.

I. The Cultural View of Menstruation

Menstruation, the menstrual period, or flow is the natural process of shedding the uterine tissue, blood vessels, and unfertilized egg when a pregnancy has not occurred. Derived from the Latin *mensis,* for "month," menstruation marks the end of one reproductive cycle and the beginning of the next. As such, it is the singular, biologic process unique to women during their childbearing years that serves as the physical, psychological, sociocultural, and political signal of an individual's reproductive potential and, in many cultures, her place in society. Cultural, religion, and personal attitudes about menstruation are a part of the menstrual experience and often reflect society's attitudes toward women. Certain cultures have isolated women entirely or put them in the company of other women during their periods, because people thought that menstrual blood was unclean or because they thought menstruating women had supernatural powers. These powers were sometimes seen as good, but more often they were feared to be destructive. Women themselves may have started these practices to give themselves time for meditation or to give older women a chance to pass on their knowledge to younger women. Taboos regarding menstruation that can be found in the dominant culture of the Western world today include refraining from exercise, showers, and sexual intercourse, or hiding the fact of menstruation entirely. Examining the wording in television and print advertisements for menstrual products highlights how the media reinforces this phobia.

For women, the human life cycle has traditionally been viewed by many cultures within the context of reproductive function. Menarche, or the first menstrual period, marks the transition from childhood to womanhood and childbearing. The reproductive life span extends from puberty through the childbearing years to the perimenopausal or climacteric years. Across this spectrum, fertility progressively diminishes and cycles become irregular until the time of the final menstrual period or menopause. This reproductive life span extends from approximately age 12 to about age 51 in the majority of cultures where food is plentiful. [*See* MENOPAUSE.]

For women in many cultures, the rites of passage across the life span have typically been related to these reproductive events. As pointed out by Naomi Wolfe, the first menstruation, loss of virginity, childbirth, and even menopause has been used to define female adulthood ("now you're a woman"). The view that women who are childless, either voluntarily or involuntarily, are not "real women" or are emotionally dysfunctional was a central tenant of 19th-century psychoanalytic theory (Deutsch). The term "hysterical" comes from the Greek *hyster* meaning uterus, because it was believed that depression was due to unresolved conflicts about femininity and the desire for pregnancy.

Clearly this view of women as centered around reproductive function is limiting because it assumes that women have only one biological (reproduction) and social role (child rearing). It fails to account for the important and multiple roles of women that are separate from childbearing. Some feminist writers have argued for a reframing of the life cycle of women to include their role in "social reproduction," that is, the nurturing and parenting of extended families, neighborhoods, local communities, and even national political activism.

II. The Biology of Menstruation

Menstruation is part of the process whereby the lining of the uterus (endometrium) undergoes repetitive, cyclic changes in structure and function in preparation for receiving and nourishing the developing embryo in the earliest stages of pregnancy. A series of hormonal signals originating in the ovary drives the development and transformation of the endometrium—the site of implantation of the early embryo. Estrogen, made by the maturing follicle containing the egg that will eventually ovulate, causes endometrial glands to grow and thicken and increases the blood supply to these glands in the first half of the menstrual cycle. This part of the uterine cycle is called the *proliferative* phase and can vary greatly in length, from 6 to 20 days. Progesterone, made by the ruptured follicle after the egg is released at ovulation, stimulates the glands in the endometrium to begin secreting embryo-nourishing substances (*secretory phase*), which lasts approximately 14 days. Based on the functional changes in the ovary, (rather than the uterus), the menstrual cycle can also be divided into the follicular phase (or preovulatory phase, approximately occurring on cycle days 1 to 12; day 1 of the menstrual cycle is the first day of menstrual bleeding), ovulation phase (days 13 to 14), and the luteal phase (cycle days 15 to 28 when progesterone is produced by the corpus luteum).

If conception has not occurred, the leftover follicle in the ovary (corpus luteum) will produce estrogen and progesterone for only about 12 days, with the amount gradually lessening after the first 5 to 7 days. As the estrogen and progesterone levels drop, the tiny arteries and veins in the uterus close off. The lining is no longer nourished and is shed. This is menstruation. During menstruation, most of the lining is shed; the bottom third remains to form a new lining. The *menstrual phase* refers to the days of actual menstrual bleeding. Then a new follicle starts growing and secreting estrogen, a new uterine lining grows, and the cycle begins again.

The changes at the level of the uterus occur as part of a dynamic communication system between the brain and the ovary. The hormones of the neuroreproductive axis govern the menstrual cycle through a highly synchronized interplay of negative and positive feedback systems that are sensitive to moment-to-moment fluctuations in pulsatile secretion. These hormones are gonadotropin-releasing hormone (GnRH) from the hypothalamus, the pituitary hormones, luteinizing hormone (LH), and follicle stimulating hormone (FSH) and the ovarian sex steroids, estradiol (the most potent form of estrogen), and progesterone. Under the direction of GnRH, the gonadotropins, LH, and FSH are released from the pituitary in a coordinated fashion to stimulate the ovary to produce a developing egg for potential fertilization and, in turn, increasing amounts of estrogen followed by progesterone, the sex steroids needed to transform the uterus and breast in preparation for pregnancy.

The secretory patterns in blood, urine, and saliva of the reproductive hormones across the stages of the menstrual cycle have been well characterized, allowing researchers to link various behavioral, psychological, or physiological phenomena with specific cycle phases. Further, the sequential and synergistic effects of estrogen and progesterone on the breast, reproductive tract, and body temperature are used by clinicians, researchers, and women themselves to monitor signs of fertility, pregnancy, or reproductive health problems.

A number of behavioral and cognitive phenomena, such as excessive exercise, compulsive dieting, depression, or other psychologic stress, can interfere with menstrual cycle regularity, disrupt the normal ovulatory process, and lead to states of low estrogen, amenorrhea (failure to menstruate), and, in turn, bone thinning and infertility. These environmental influences are believed to be mediated by inhibitory stimuli from higher brain centers interacting with the GnRH neurons via neuromodulators such opioids (eg endorphins), dopamine, seratonin, and norepinephrine. The hormones of the stress axis also suppress the function of the reproductive system. Thus the menstrual cycle serves as an elegant example of a complex biobehavioral phenomenon responsive to both internal and external environmental stimuli.

The term "menstruation" is from the Latin *mensis* for "month." Although the average length of the menstrual cycle is 28 days, the length of the cycle varies between women, usually ranging from 20 to 36 days. Any cycle that is more or less regular is normal. The average period or menses lasts two to eight days, with four to six days being the average. The total volume of blood discharged across the entire menstrual period is about four to six tablespoons, or two to three ounces. The menstrual fluid contains cervical mucus, vaginal secretions, mucus, cells, and endometrial particles, as well as blood (sometimes clotted), but this mixture is not obvious since the blood stains everything red or brown. The fluid usually does not smell until it makes contact with the bacteria in the air and starts to decompose. Women in different cultures employ many methods to absorb their menstrual flow, including the use of pads and tampons made from cloth rags, sponges, or commercially produced rayon and cotton blends. Toxic shock syndrome (TSS) is a rare but life-threatening blood infection, which is linked to the use of tampons, especially high-absorbancy tampons made from rayon and other synthetic ingredients.

III. *Menstruation and Mood*

There is much evidence to suggest that most women have been socialized to have negative expectations about menstruation, thus leading to self-fulfilling prophecies of negative mood and psychologic distress. Women seeking costly medical treatment for perimenstrual symptoms may have certain expectations about the origin, nature, and course of their distress. Studies suggest that approximately 50% of women who seek medical treatment for perimenstrual discomforts fail to demonstrate changes entrained to menstruation when prospectiving charting of daily symptoms is performed. Moreover, as Phyllis Mansfield discovered, when research participants are not told of the purpose of the study, the male members of married couples demonstrate more pronounced entrainment of mood and physical symptoms (eg fatigue) around their spouse's menstrual cycles than do the women themselves. Feminist scholars have challenged the practice of tracking only negative symptoms, arguing that women should also chart symptoms of health and well-being to heighten awareness of positive changes in mood and energy across the menstrual cycle.

The medicalization of women's menstrual function has predominated in biomedical research with little attention to the interaction of psychologic, sociocultural, lifestyle, and health factors. Behavioral scientists have focused on defining these influences on the range of menstrual cycle experiences, moving beyond those of gynecologic patient populations to the broader spectrum of healthy community samples. Feminist scholars in particular have called for a reframing of menstrual symptoms and illness within the greater context of a woman's lived experience. This paradigm shift has expanded the scope of explanatory models and methods for menstrual cycle research. In North America, the Society for Menstrual Cycle Research, composed of mostly women scientists, nurse–researchers, and clinicians, is committed to a better understanding of the psychosocial and cultural influences on the range and diversity of menstrual cycle health and illness. Formed in 1976, the society has been at the forefront of the movement away from a deconstructionist perspective to a more comprehensive approach to the study of women's health.

The etiology of premenstrual syndrome (PMS) has been the topic of particularly keen interest among menstrual cycle researchers. This work has helped characterize the biopsychosocial context of PMS, its impact on women's lives, and methods to distinguish it from other menstruation-related conditions. For nearly two decades, Nancy Woods, her students, and colleagues at the University of Washington School of Nursing have focused on the development of explanatory models that incorporate family, psychosocial, and cultural predictors of perimenstrual symptoms. Using a daily health diary and a symptom analysis method that have now been tested by nurse researchers in the United States and other countries, their body of work defined three types of symptom patterns in healthy menstruating women: (1) low-intensity, acyclic symptoms; (2) a PMS pattern; and (3) high intensity symptoms that increase in severity during the premenstrual week (premenstrual magnification). These symptom patterns are related to a number of psychosocial correlates, such as psychological stress level, years of education, and maternal symptom pattern, as well as age, laboratory-induced arousal, and stress responsivity. A secondary analysis of two national data sets revealed that premenstrual distress is more common among women who have been sexually assaulted, especially among those assaulted repeatedly by the same offender. Increased rates of depression among these victims did not account for this association.

In keeping with the challenge of Lentz and Woods for woman-centered research to consider the dynamic and multidimensional nature of women's health phenomena, there is a need to move away from the concept of the menstrual cycle as a static construct, employing single-occasion measures that fail to address it as an interactive process with evolving symptom patterns. To better define the complete spectrum of menstrual cycle health, future studies should examine the effects of seasonality, social rhythms, sexual preference, occupational stressors, and transition periods (e.g., divorce) in women across the reproductive life span.

SUGGESTED READING

Golding, J. M., and Taylor, D. (1996). Sexual assault and premenstrual distress in two general population samples. *Journal of Women's Health* 5(2), 143–152.

Mansfield, P. K., Hood, K., and Henderson, J. (1989). Variations in mood and arousal among women and their spouses: Biological and social factors. *Psychosomatic Medicine* 51, 66–80.

Rome, E., Reame, N., and Sanford, W. (1998). Sexual anatomy, reproduction and menstrual cycle. In *Our Bodies, Ourselves* (The Boston Women's Health Book Collective), 4th ed., pp. 269–287. Simon & Schuster, New York.

Society for Menstrual Cycle Research web site, http://www.pop.psu.edu/smcr

Taylor, D., and Woods, N. (eds.) (1991). *Menstruation, Health and Illness*. Hemisphere, New York.

Mentoring and Feminist Mentoring

Michèle Harway

Phillips Graduate Institute

Glossary

Diversified mentoring relationships Occur among mentors and mentees who differ in such things as majority/minority status, gender, and other factors associated with power in organizations in contrast to homogeneous mentoring relationships.

Feminist mentoring A mentoring relationship characterized by mutuality, respect, collaboration, awareness of power relationships and giving voice to the mentee.

Formal mentoring The result of a formal program that seeks to match available mentors with individuals who request mentoring.

Homogeneous mentoring relationships Occur when mentors and mentees are matched in terms of ethnicity, gender, and other characteristics related to power in organizations.

Informal mentoring The result of relationships that develop without intervention from an organization.

Mentees Individuals, also known as *protégés*, who benefit from a relationship with a mentor.

Mentors Senior-level individuals who have a personal interest or an emotional investment in the development of a junior-level person. Another term used to describe a similar relationship is *developmental relationship*, where one person contributes to the personal growth and professional advancement of another.

Peer mentoring Involves people who are at similar levels in the organization and where there is mutual support, encouragement, and assistance.

Role models Senior-level professionals whose characteristics are emulated by newer professionals. Role models may be unaware of the function they serve for junior-level persons.

Sponsors Those who are said to give instrumental or career help to junior professionals. This is a more limited relationship than a mentoring one as the personal investment is usually absent here.

MENTORING AND FEMINIST MENTORING are terms which describe the relationship between a mentor—a senior-level individual with a personal interest or emotional investment in the development of a junior-level person—and a mentee, usually a junior-level person. Mentoring can be part of a formal mentoring program or can occur informally. Characteristics of the individuals involved in the mentoring relationship may be diversified in terms of majority/minority status, gender, and other factors associated with power in organizations or may be homogeneous on these dimensions. Because of the scarcity of women and people of color at senior levels of employment, formal mentors are more likely to be white males. Feminist mentoring relationships focus on the reciprocal nature of the mentoring relationship and its impact on the mentor as well as the mentee. Research describes the impact of these various mentoring relationships on the mentee. Special ethical issues affect mentoring relationships.

I. Traditional Notions of Mentoring

The traditional image of a mentor is of a wise, experienced, knowledgeable professional (usually a man) who either demands or gently coaxes the most out of a willing, eager, young professional with high potential (usually also a man). As more women have entered the labor market, definitions of mentoring have become more complex. The name "mentor" comes from Ancient Greece. Mentor was Odysseus' wise and kind servant who was asked to oversee the development of young Telemachus while Odysseus traveled the world.

II. The Widespread Nature of Research on Mentoring

In the past 15 years, mentoring has been studied in many occupational settings: in the legal profession, in hospitals, in corporate environments, in psychology, with engineers, with college personnel workers, in academia, with teachers of gifted students, and with nurses. It has also been studied outside of the occupational context, for example: with single mothers, with adult students, among business students, with inner city African American students, with secondary school peer mentors and mentees, and with the gifted, to cite a few.

Studies of mentoring have examined a wide variety of issues including the potential dual roles in faculty–student mentoring relationships, the impact of mentoring on job satisfaction, other impacts of mentoring on the career of the mentee, gender differences in the outcomes of mentoring, the role of the mentee's personality in mentoring, experience of ethnic minority professionals, effects of gender, including focusing on the willingness to mentor by sex, the genders' different experiences of mentoring, differential outcomes of mentoring by gender, gender barriers to gaining a mentor, satisfaction with the mentoring relationship, differential career impacts of mentoring by gender, issues of power and equality in mentoring relationships, impact of mentoring of women by male mentors, and attraction factors in forming mentoring dyads.

Some studies have looked at the mentors specifically. Mentors have been characterized in terms of their attributes (wisdom, knowledge, experience, power, ability are some of the attributes mentioned), their roles (patron, coach, counselor, teacher, guide, sponsor) and their functions (teaching, assisting with career decisions, counseling, facilitating career moves).

It is clear that mentoring has been a much studied topic. This article details some aspects of mentoring that are documented in the rather extensive mentoring literature and examines a specific kind of mentoring that has not been much addressed in the literature, namely, feminist mentoring.

III. Cultural Need for the Development of the Mentor Role

Developing a clear definition of mentoring has been a difficult task because the concept of a mentor is a relatively new one. As Western society has developed into more of an individualistic one, young adults no longer benefit from the collective socialization provided by the group of elders. Except for certain trades, learning by apprenticeship no longer is available for most workers. Today, some limited professional socialization occurs in formal training programs, but there are few formal structures set in place to continue this socialization outside of educational environments.

It is not uncommon for much of this professional socialization to occur in mentoring relationships. However, some individuals may be particularly adept at engaging with a mentor, while others may be less skillful and may in fact never succeed in obtaining much needed mentoring. Mentoring is likely to be useful to everyone, as there is some evidence that receiving mentoring early in a career is related to later occupational success. Therefore, knowing how to engage a mentor is an important interpersonal and occupational skill. As the occupational world continues to change and many people enter new careers several times during the adult years, mentoring needs may vary even more than they do now.

IV. Mentoring Functions

While the mentor is usually described as a single individual, the functions of a mentor may be provided by a combination of individuals and institutions. Kathy Kram described the functions that mentors perform as falling into two broad categories: career development help functions and personal help functions. The career functions of mentoring may involve sponsoring a younger individual for positions, helping expose him or her professionally, introducing the mentee to prominent or powerful superiors, coaching, providing protection, and promoting for challenging assignments, all intended to enhance the mentee's professional advancement. The psychosocial functions of mentoring may include role modeling, personal validation, personal growth development, counseling and advice giving, and friendship, intended to enhance the mentee's confidence, professional and personal identity, and sense of competence, and resulting in increased professional effectiveness. [*See* ACHIEVEMENT; CAREER ACHIEVEMENT.]

V. Stages in the Mentoring Relationship

In 1983, Kathy Kram described the process of becoming involved in a mentor–mentee relationship as consisting of four phases. Initiation is the first phase of mentoring where mentor and mentee select each other and begin to learn about the other's style and habits. Cultivation, the next phase of mentoring, leads to increases in mentoring behaviors and the development of a strong relationship between mentor and mentee.

Separation is when the mentoring relationship ends, often as a result of geographic separation, and redefinition is the final phase of mentoring, where the mentoring relationship changes to more closely resemble a peer relationship.

VI. Matching Mentors and Mentees

The dilemma is that there is some evidence that people benefit the most from mentors who are most like them demographically. Demographic characteristics vary widely from those usually considered such as race and sex to those less often considered such as regional background, parental status, and many others. Most of the writing on diversified mentoring, however, has focused on race and sex. According to this perspective, women are better served by a female mentor; African Americans by an African American mentor, and so on. To the extent, however, that the glass ceiling (an invisible barrier to advancement) has prevented women and people of color from attaining positions in the upper echelons of the corporate or academic structure, the numbers of demographically matched mentors for women and ethnic minorities are limited. However, there is contradictory evidence that diversified mentoring relationships are more helpful to the professional attainment of women and people of color than are homogeneous mentoring relationships.

Many organizations recently have simplified their hierarchies and reduced the number of layers, resulting in a reduction in the number of mentors of *any* demographic type. Moreover, senior-level managers have less time for traditional developmental roles. Thus, it is the lucky mentee who is able to find a traditional mentor to provide the professional socialization that he or she is seeking.

VII. Peer Mentoring

Peer mentoring provides a solution to both the reduction of traditional mentors and the limited number of demographically matched mentors. Peer mentors may share information with each other, strategize for career advancement, network, give job-related feedback, and provide professional and personal validation, emotional support, and friendship. One important aspect of peer mentoring is mutuality between partners. The research supports the individual benefits of peer mentoring as enhancing self-confidence, improving communication skills, and, as stated earlier, providing friendship and emotional support. On the other hand, peer mentoring is limited by the relative professional inexperience of most peer mentors.

VIII. Formal Programs

By contrast to peer mentoring relationships, many organizations have developed formal mentoring programs. These organizations believe that the positive effects of mentoring on the performance of mentees warrants the formalizing of such programs. They point to the findings that individuals who experienced a mentoring relationship receive more promotions and higher salaries, are more effective and influential in their work settings, and are more satisfied with their work settings and careers than those who have not enjoyed such an experience. Data also suggest that mentees are more committed to their organizations, thus less likely to leave, and more likely to eventually assume leadership in the company. Organizations who want to retain their employees after investing money and effort into training them often develop formal mentoring programs in which they pair mentors with mentees. There is some evidence that, as with dating relationships, such matchmaking is not always successful as the factors that draw mentees to mentors (and vice versa) and create successful mentoring relationships are not always objective ones. As a consequence, formal mentoring programs may be less successful overall than informal ones. [See LEADERSHIP.]

IX. Gender, Ethnicity, and Mentoring

An unresolved issue has to do with the roles that gender and ethnicity play in mentoring. What is clear is that mentoring is essential for both women and ethnic minorities. Mentoring for these groups has been seen as a way to overcome barriers to promotion and as a way to break through the glass ceiling. Mentors are described as key to protecting these groups against discrimination. Mentors also provide information about available positions within and outside of the organization, strategies about how to negotiate around the barriers in the way of advancement, and training in the politics of the organization, all knowledge that is more typically kept within the "old boy network." Belle Ragins describes mentees as benefiting from the "reflected power" of their mentors.

Much of the research on the impact of gender on mentoring focuses on the gender of the mentee. Belle Ragins describes mentoring as taking different forms for male and female mentees because of differential gender socialization, such as differences in women's and men's willingness to admit to needing help, different comfort levels in close relationships, and the need for self-esteem enhancement for men, which may require them to manage self and other perceptions of career independence and status. But being mentored seems to provide equivalent benefits to men and women. The mentoring relationship itself may sometimes be perceived differently by male and female mentees, with male mentees perceiving more events in the mentoring relationship as conflict producing. There is no information on how gender affects the stages of mentoring described earlier.

By contrast to the information on mentee gender, there is not much research on mentor gender and outcomes. Male mentors are more likely than female mentors to report mentoring relationships and to take credit for the accomplishments of their mentees. It is speculated that doing so helps them maintain their status and superiority. Ragins reports that male mentors do seem to bring more power to the mentoring relationship than do female mentors because the former have more power in the organization. Male mentors' power is then reflected onto the mentees. Moreover, women may face more obstacles to assuming mentoring roles than men, because of their sometimes precarious positions in their organizations and the fact that many women must devote substantial time and energy to advancing their own career, leaving little left over for helping others. The greatest barriers to mentoring for prospective female mentors are at midlevel management positions where most women managers are congregated. There is mixed support for the belief that female mentors enact more psychosocial functions than male mentors.

The gender composition of the mentoring dyad may have the greatest impact of all on the mentoring relationship. Women are more likely to be in cross-gender relationships. These relationships are said to be more difficult to manage than same-sex ones because of sexual issues and the negative reactions of others. In general, cross-sex relationships are less likely to provide psychosocial and role-modeling functions than same-sex ones. There is some evidence that in same-sex relationships there is more mutuality and trust. This appears to hold as well as for same-race relationships. Findings on this issue, however are not consistent across studies. One dilemma of female mentor/female mentee pairings is that these may be threatening to others in the organization as they may be seen as planning a takeover. Male/male mentoring relationships are most common. Female mentor/male mentee relationships are relatively infrequent.

Regarding mentees' preference for same- or other-sex relationships, there are no consistent findings. There are also no clear findings about gender composition of the mentoring dyad and outcomes. Other areas about which relatively little is known regarding gender and mentoring are gender differences in the individual decision to mentor and about gender differences in the costs and benefits of mentoring to the mentor.

Relatively less information is available regarding people of color and mentoring. As with women, key issues have to do with trust and rapport. Because senior levels of management remain mostly White, this results in a lack of available mentors of color at upper levels of management. As a result, ethnic minority employees may fall through the cracks when it comes to being mentored. In educational institutions, the relative paucity of faculty of color may also result in scarcity of mentoring for students of color, other than in cross-race mentoring. Cross-race mentoring, while not much studied by mentoring researchers, seems to exhibit many of the same characteristics of cross-sex mentoring, without the sexual innuendoes. However, given the tense relationships that still exist in this country between different ethnic groups, cross-race mentoring dyads may suffer from lack of comfort and rapport. This is especially true if the mentor is of the other sex in addition to being of another race.

Virtually no information exists about mentoring within specific ethnic groups. Two exceptions are the relatively scarce literature about African Americans and mentoring and some early focus on Asian Americans.

For African American women in particular, being in the labor force is a difficult experience. These women are seen as being inferior both because of their gender and their race. Often, they are in fact invisible. Mentoring needs among African American women, thus, are great. However, their invisibility in the workplace unfortunately is reflected in the almost complete absence of mentoring research on Black women. Stacy Blake's 1999 qualitative study of Black women's mentoring experiences does provide some information. Most of the women in her study had White male mentors who provided the ca-

reer advancement functions of mentoring quite effectively. Largely missing from these mentoring relationships were the psychosocial functions of mentoring, such as emotional bonding and friendship.

Asian Americans present a particular challenge in the area of mentoring. Because Asian cultures are more often collectivistic than individualistic (as is the North American mainstream culture), Asian Americans are constantly negotiating the clash between these cultural values. Other cultural values may preclude Asian Americans from seeking out mentoring relationships: they may not wish to burden others, their expectations of mentoring are different from those of the mainstream and thus they do not seek or recognize mainstream mentoring opportunities, and they may expect more formal hierarchical relationships. There is some evidence too that mentors do not pursue Asian Americans as mentees, because they perceive this ethnic group as already successful and not needing mentoring relationships.

Given these facts, it is likely that most women and people of color, at least in the near future, will be involved in diversified mentoring relationships—those where mentors and mentees differ in their membership in one or more groups with differential access to power. A power perspective is indeed a useful one from which to view mentoring relationships, and as additional research is completed on the impact of diversified mentoring relationships we will be better able to understand their impact.

X. Feminist Mentoring

Feminist mentoring may well resolve some of the issues around mentoring and gender. Research on more traditional forms of mentoring have approached the understanding of mentoring relationships almost entirely from the perspective of the impact on the mentee. Yet mentors must get something out of being a mentor, even if nothing more than a sense of satisfaction at having helped another.

Michele Harway and Ruth Fassinger independently describe feminist mentoring relationships as focusing on the reciprocal nature of the mentoring relationship and its impact on the mentor as well as the mentee. Key aspect of the feminist mentoring relationship are both the reciprocal nature of the relationship and its construction of power. Power impacts the feminist mentoring relationship on several levels. First, feminist mentoring relationships tend to be nonhierarchical. This is reflected in the valuation of collaborative endeavors, in the desire to give voice to the mentee, and in the mutual valuation of and respect for each other's knowledge and feelings. Underlying these values are the beliefs that relational issues are key and a commitment to diversity. An analysis and understanding of the impact of power politics in the workplace, in the mentoring relationship itself, and in the surrounding cultural context is in the foreground of most feminist mentoring interactions. The sex of the mentor and mentee are irrelevant to whether mentoring is feminist or not. Some male mentors are adept at feminist mentoring. Some male mentees report involvement in feminist mentoring relationships.

Also important in feminist mentoring is the understanding that the mentor gets as much as she or he gives. Thus, especially if the mentor is isolated as a woman or a person of color paired with a mentee of like gender or ethnicity and both are functioning in a primarily White, male-dominated organization, the mentee may provide a form of colleagueship that the mentor may lack. The mentor also benefits from the assistance the mentee may provide with tasks that the mentor is unable or unwilling to do. This in turn may lead to increased productivity for the mentor through this collaboration. Mentees may also develop creative professional ideas that contribute to both the mentor and mentee's professional development. There is much to learn too from a mentee (if the mentor is open to the experience). Learnings are not necessarily directly related to the workplace but may come from areas of expertise or personal strengths that are unique to the mentee. Finally, mentoring gives the mentor an opportunity to provide support that she herself may not have received. In turn, she may benefit from the appreciation, respect, and friendship that the mentee provides.

XI. Ethical Issues and Mentoring

Because most mentoring relationships are long term, complex, multifaceted, and may be emotionally intimate, they present some unique ethical dilemmas. As in other dyadic relationships, dual relationships may present problems, for example, where the mentor is also responsible for decisions regarding the mentee's future. Other ethical problems may emerge when the interests of the individuals change, when differences

in judgment exist between mentor and mentee, or when extreme dependency builds between the dyad. In formal mentoring programs, mismatches between mentor and mentee may result in significant interpersonal difficulties. Such relationships may be characterized as dysfunctional—this occurs when the needs of one or both of the parties are not being met or when one or both parties are suffering distress because of being in the relationship. In 1998, Terry Scandura described four outcomes of dysfunctional mentoring relationships as depending on whether the person has good or bad intents toward the other and whether the relational process is inherent in the relationship pattern or emergent. The four outcomes are negative relations, difficulty, sabotage, or spoiling. Negative relations typically involve a mentor who is exploitive or abusive. Difficulty occurs when the person has good intentions toward the other, but there are problems in the way the two relate to each other. Sabotage may occur when mentors develop such a dependency on the mentees that they may subvert or delay their advancement. Spoiling occurs when a good relationship goes sour because of a perceived or actual act of betrayal.

Other problematic events in mentor–mentee relationships may include deception perpetrated by either party on the other to get compliance from the other, unresolved issues from past relationships (parent–child, romantic relationships) playing themselves out in the mentoring relationship, and more extreme problems such as sexual harassment or gender or race discrimination. As with any other interpersonal relationship, a mentoring relationship requires work to remain healthy and may require many adjustments as the two parties change and grow.

SUGGESTED READING

Johnson, W. B., and Nelson, N. (1999). Mentor-protégé relationships in graduate training: Some ethical concerns. *Ethics and Behavior* 9(3), 189–210.

Kram, K. (1985). *Mentoring at Work.* Scott, Foresman, Glenview, IL.

Murrell, A. J. , Crosby, F. J. and Ely, R. J. (1999). *Mentoring Dilemmas: Developmental Relationships in Multicultural Organizations.* Erlbaum, Mahwah, NJ.

Ragins, B. R. (1999). Gender and mentoring relationships. In *Handbook of Gender and Work* (G. N. Powell, ed.). Sage, Newbury Park, CA.

Scandura, T. A. (1998). Dysfunctional mentoring relationships and outcomes. *International Management*, 24(4), 449–467.

Methods for
Studying Gender

Ellen B. Kimmel
University of South Florida

Mary Crawford
University of Connecticut

Glossary

Critical psychology An approach to psychology in which researchers not only produce knowledge about psychological phenomena but also analyze the moral, political, and scientific claims of psychology and try to influence the direction of the field as a whole.

Feminist A person who believes that women and men are of equal value and who acts so as to make this ideal a reality.

Objectivity Traditionally, a desired attribute of both the researcher and the product of research, that it be free of personal or systematic bias. Used as a criterion for what counts as knowledge, though impossible to achieve in practice.

Reflexivity A process of disciplined reflection on how the identity and social position of the researcher influences research, and conversely, how doing research influences the self. Extends to a critical perspective on one's field of study.

HOW DO RESEARCHERS produce knowledge about gender? What methods do they use and what philosophy underlies them? Following a brief history of feminist stances on methodological issues, this article reviews a number of features or standards that characterize feminist approaches to the study of gender: these include concerns with redefining objectivity, exploring reflexivity and subjectivity, expanding psychology's diversity, attending to power relations in the research process, giving benefits to participants, fostering social change, and accepting methodological plurality. A sample of specific methods are described, and the obstacles researchers encounter when engaging in research on gender are considered. Finally, we speculate on the social context of future research on gender.

I. A Brief History of Feminist Stances on Methodological Issues

A. FIRST WAVE (ABOUT 1848–1920)

Throughout the history of psychology, many have voiced complaint about psychology's treatment of women and people of color. As early as 1876, Mary Putman Jacobi completed a Harvard dissertation questioning the notion that the menstrual cycle handicapped women mentally and physically. Jacobi pointed out that research on the supposed limitations of women, like research on the supposed inferiority of people of color, was rarely conducted by women or people of color themselves. Moreover, she argued, the privileged White men who did such research were prone to ascribe differences uncritically to "nature." Jacobi's critique is one of the first articulations of the claim that psychological knowledge is socially situated.

At the turn of the 20th century, the first cohort of North American women began to receive higher degrees in psychology. Among this cohort, several questioned the prevailing beliefs about innate sex differences in personality and ability. Helen Thompson Wooley conducted the first experimental laboratory study of sex differences in mental traits, using a variety of innovative measures. In interpreting her results, she stressed the overall similarity of the sexes and the environmental determinants of observed differences, remarking in a much-quoted 1910 *Psychological Bulletin* article that "There is perhaps no field aspiring to be scientific where flagrant personal bias, logic martyred in the cause of supporting a prejudice, unfounded assertions, and even sentimental rot and drivel, have run riot to such an extent as here." Inspired by Wooley's work, Leta Stetter Hollingworth attempted to refute the variability hypothesis, which was being used to claim that women were less likely than men to be highly creative or intelligent. These early women psychologists pioneered the use of critical empirical research to challenge unexamined assumptions about women's "natural" limitations. However, their research topics and methods were dictated by the need to oppose sexism in science. Thus, they labored to refute hypotheses that they themselves did not originate and that they did not believe could account for the inferior social position of women. Moreover, because their own ability and their very right to do research were doubted, they were able to gain credibility only insofar as they used the methods valued by the psychological establishment.

B. SECOND WAVE (ABOUT 1960–PRESENT)

In the late 1960s, the second wave of the women's movement revitalized feminist critique of psychological theory, research, and practice. Organized activism by the Association for Women in Psychology and the newly formed American Psychological Association (APA) Division 35 (then named Division of the Psychology of Women, now the Society for the Psychology of Women) led to a surge in symposia and papers on women and gender issues at APA national conferences starting around 1970. It also led to an increase in books and journal articles and the founding of new journals such as *Psychology of Women Quarterly* and *Sex Roles*. The 1970s feminist critique openly challenged psychology's choice of research topics, its theoretical constructs, and its modes of diagnosis and therapeutic intervention. Moreover it questioned psychology's most characteristic research methods and the values underlying them. Evolved into a branch of critical psychology, the new psychology of women and gender challenges the moral, political, and scientific claims of psychology and tries to influence the direction of the field as a whole. Its goal is the systematic analysis of women's psychology and of the impact of gender on human subjectivity and experience.

From this critical perspective, much of psychological knowledge is seen as androcentric, or male centered. Historically, men have been studied much more often than women, and research questions have often been formulated from gender-biased perspectives. Women's behavior has been judged against a (White, middle-class) male norm. Women's behavior, more often than men's, has been explained in biologically determinist terms, neglecting the influence of the different social contexts of women and men. Psychological adjustment for women has been conceptualized in terms of conformity to gender norms that limit women's autonomy and opportunity to demonstrate competence. Gender biases have been documented in theories of intelligence, attribution, social influence, learning, memory, thinking, identity, clinical diagnosis, and therapy, among others.

As we have noted, both first- and second-wave feminists criticized psychology for sexist biases in research methods. With the second wave, however, came a more fundamental criticism, not of flaws and biases in the use of (otherwise admirable) methods, but of the value of the discipline's most characteristic and central methods themselves. Psychology, it was charged, overrelied on experimental methods, which strip behavior from its social context and position the experimenter as an expert manipulator of the participant and situation. Second-wave feminists have also criticized what they see as the naive belief that psychology can discover universal laws of behavior.

There is today considerable variability in the methods used to study women and gender within psychology. The majority of articles published in the two leading U.S. feminist journals, *Psychology of Women Quarterly* and *Sex Roles,* as well as those published in general psychological journals, use quantitative methods such as experimental and correlational designs and meta-analysis. Only the U.K. journal *Feminism & Psychology* routinely publishes more qualitative and discursive work. However, even outside of feminist studies, psychology has a long tradition of inquiry that transcends laboratory manipulation of isolated variables: field research, observational techniques, content analysis, participant observation, and case studies are a few examples. A significant minority of feminist researchers draws on these traditions as well as newer, postmodern influenced forms of analysis. The feminist call for methodological plurality has had some effects. Special issues of *Psychology of Women Quarterly* have focused on method and theory, transforming psychology, and innovative methods for feminist research.

Regardless of the particular method to study women and gender, there is a growing agreement among feminists that the research process itself must adhere to certain rules of fair play if the results are to be considered valid and useful. The remainder of this article reviews these rules and concludes with projections for the future of the study of gender. [*See* ANDROCENTRISM; THE FEMINIST MOVEMENT; FEMINIST THEORIES; HISTORY OF THE STUDY OF GENDER PSYCHOLOGY.]

II. Redefining Objectivity

For over two decades feminist researchers have deliberated over issues of objectivity and their relationship to science and epistemology. As the "feminist branch" of critical psychology, they have challenged positivist approaches to the human sciences, including the apparent objectivity of the experimental method. Some have argued against the value of quantitative analyses in explicating the lives of girls and women and analyzing power inequalities between the sexes (and other unequal categories of humans, such as race and class). Traditional methods for studying gender and other psychological phenomena have been placed under scrutiny, all of which has led to a questioning of all scientific activity. Many in the academy argue that it is a myth that science is neutral, value free, or objective. For example, the questions that researchers ask are historically influenced. When researchers produce knowledge that supports a political position, such as one that asserts that women of all groups and men of color are inferior, they may not be able to see this fact if they do not ask themselves why they are doing what they do.

In 1988 Donna Haraway laid out three conditions feminist research must meet to approach objectivity. We say approach, because it is a given that knowledge production is a historical process embedded in the particular situations of the actors in that process (the researcher and the researched). Scientists must examine their practices, procedures, and outcomes in the context of the social, political, economic, and ideological processes of the time.

Once feminists began to do this seriously for the field of psychology in general, they recognized the limitations of their own research such that a project on gender with White middle-class girls, for instance, cannot speak for poor girls of color, immigrant girls, girls with disabilities, and so on. In other words, it is incumbent upon all researchers to own the partiality of their work. Haraway offers that feminists can redefine objectivity to describe any work as providing only a particular, limited truth. In her view feminist research should answer to three conditions: accountability, positioning, and partiality. To do this, the researchers should report who sponsors the research, who will benefit from the findings (accountability), who is the researcher, where do her or his career and research goals intersect or clash (positioning), and what are the researcher's politics, values, and beliefs (partiality).

To be accountable, any study that claims a feminist framework must not reinscribe or reinvent inequality, that is, document that women belong in an inferior status they are shown to inhabit. The accountability is not only to the research participants but also to the overall goal of feminism, equality between women and men. For example, a research report that shows that Black South African women suffer from low career aspirations must not blame the victim, but place these data in the context of a society that institutionally undermines women's prospects for career success. To meet the criterion of positioning, research reports must also describe and analyze the micropolitical processes at play during the conduct of the research. Recognizing the partiality of all knowledge, the researcher must also be explicit about the differences among participants and between the participants and the researcher. For example, a focus group study of adolescent males' attitudes toward date rape must provide detailed information about the gender, age, race, and so forth of the adolescents and about the school, neighborhood, or region of the county in which they reside. How these youths differed from the focus group facilitator is also a key to understanding the outcomes of the study, and results must be interpreted in the light of these specific facts. A young, White, middle-class woman interviewer who does not live among the participants, who are Black, male, and poor, might produce different results than if the interviewer were an older Black male who was seen as "one of them."

In sum, feminist objectivity, in Sandra Harding's term, is a strong objectivity. Rather than repressing and denying human values and perspectives in the research process, it encompasses values and contextualizes each project. Recognizing the impossibility of fully meeting the three criteria, feminists nonetheless strive to be accountable and to discern and acknowledge the positioning and partiality of their research.

III. Exploring Reflexivity and Subjectivity

Feminist methods are reflexive; they involve recognition of the social identity and involvement of the researcher. Reflexivity is a general concept that can refer to the researcher's disciplined self-reflection on how her identity or subjectivity influences her work and, in turn, how doing research influences the self. It can refer to a critical analysis of the relationships among researchers and participants. Finally, it can refer to a broader kind of systematic reflection that occurs when feminist researchers take a critical per-

spective on their academic discipline, scrutinizing how its dominant paradigms are sustained by powerful institutions. We will give examples of each kind of reflexivity in turn.

Personal reflexivity, as defined by Sue Wilkinson, is a continuing process of reflection on the part of the researcher about how her multiple identities (her positioning in terms of social class, gender, age, status, feminist stance, ethnicity, and so on) influence her work and how her work influences these and other aspects of the self. Psychology has long denied that the social identity of the researcher affects her or his choice of research topics, theories, methods, and interpretation of research results. The reflexive researcher acknowledges these connections, is willing to explore them, and recognizes that the researcher is not exempt from the psychological processes she studies in others.

Elizabeth Merrill engages in personal reflexivity when she analyzes her research process in a study of pregnant African American adolescents. Merrill writes that her first attempts at analyzing her interview data resulted in highly abstract summaries that were distant from the participants' worldviews. Reflecting on why her well-meant analysis went wrong, Merrill suggests that her own emotional reactions to the hardship and poverty of the pregnant girls' lives interfered with her ability to understand their realities. Recognizing her desire to take care of these girls, to distance herself from their difficulties, and also to persevere in her research project, she suggests that the abstraction of her data analysis was a kind of emotional withdrawal. With enhanced self-knowledge, she reimmersed herself in the interviews, learned more about her participants' worlds from other sources, and took responsibility for her own standpoint, resulting in a different, more satisfying interpretation of her data.

Reflexivity encompasses analysis, too, of the social relationships among research collaborators. Few researchers work entirely alone; most are embedded in institutional hierarchies and working in groups of people with differing levels of experience, expertise, and skill. The effects of these differences on the researchers and the research process are open for exploration by the reflexive researcher. In an article describing the group process in a feminist research group studying adult women survivors of childhood sexual abuse, Frances Grossman and her colleagues explored the researchers' own needs for intimacy and equality. These needs affected the researchers' understanding of participants' accounts, created difficulties and frustrations in working together as a team, and were implicated in the group's decision making. Too often, these crucial aspects of doing research are ignored, a result of the legacy of positivistic psychology, which assumed that human emotions and values could be separated from scientific research. Feminist research groups like Grossman's improve the research process by taking them into account and seeking to understand their impact.

Reflexivity extends to an ongoing critical stance on the discipline. As described earlier, feminist psychology is, at its best, a form of critical psychology. This disciplinary critique was exemplified by the early second-wave theorists Naomi Weisstein, Phyllis Chesler (in her *Women and Madness* book), and Carolyn Sherif. Weisstein criticized psychology for unacknowledged gender bias; Chesler analyzed the psychiatric establishment as an institution of social control; and Sherif documented the influence of the military-industrial complex on psychology's research agenda. Today, this form of reflexivity continues. Richard Walsh-Bower, for example, analyzed the underlying assumptions of the *APA Publication Manual*. Critically examining its definitions of research and the roles of those who conduct and participate in it, he discussed the *Manual*'s function in socializing students into the culture of the discipline.

IV. Expanding Diversity of Participants and Topics

Since the 1940s psychology has come to rely more and more on college student samples, creating biases of age, social class, and developmental stage. Moreover, males have been more likely to be studied than females. While the past few decades have seen an increase in research on girls and women, subtler kinds of sex bias persist. Nearly 30 percent of psychological journal articles still do not report the sex of the participants. Textual analysis has shown that, when researchers use an all-female (versus an all-male) sample, they are more likely to state it in the article's title, to discuss their reasons for a single-sex sample, and to point out that their results cannot be generalized to the other sex. While an all-female sample is recognized as limited, an all-male sample is still treated as unremarkable.

The topics of psychological research have historically been biased against issues of concern to women.

Among the significantly underresearched topics identified by Mary Crawford and Rhoda Unger in their recent survey of the field were women's sexuality and sexual desire, the psychology of childbirth, motherhood and family roles, women's health, the effects of sexism on women's psychological functioning, and gender issues in mid- and later life.

Research on ethnic minority people of both sexes is scarce except when they are seen as creating social problems. Poor and working-class women, too, have been virtually ignored. As with research on White women, the topics considered important often have been selective and biased. For example, there is abundant research on teen pregnancy among African American women but little research on their leadership, creativity, or coping skills for dealing with racism. Women's friendships across racial and ethnic divides have been virtually ignored in social research.

The Society for the Psychology of Women of APA has worked energetically to increase the diversity of women in leadership positions within the society and in the APA generally. With its encouragement, the APA reviewed its inclusion of women and minority men in the formal publication process as editors and reviewers. One of the society's task forces led to the publication of a volume dedicated to bringing cultural diversity to feminist psychology, including research practices. Its section on women of color has promoted and recognized research on and by women of color.

In summary, feminist psychology has not yet adequately encompassed the diversity of women, despite ongoing attention to this issue. Its research base and its practitioners are still largely White, middle-class, heterosexually identified, and North American. Its research topics, while expanding and becoming more sensitive to diversity, are still shaped by the priorities of institutions and funding agencies allowing limited scope for innovation.

V. Analyzing Power Relations within the Research Process

Researchers who study psychological and social issues often delve into highly sensitive and private areas of human experience, and this inquiry is usually one way: down a power hierarchy. Historically, little attention was paid to the power dynamics involved in psychological research—it usually went unremarked that White, middle-class, male researchers were given the power to query, observe, deceive, manipulate, and label other, less powerful people, in the name of science. It was second-wave feminist theorists in psychology who pointed out that psychology's most valued method, the laboratory experiment is inherently hierarchical. The inequality of the experimental situation may be particularly acute when the researcher is male and the participant is female, reflecting and reinforcing the dominance of male values and interests. Hierarchies between researcher and participants are not limited to experiments, however. They are an inevitable part of working within a hierarchical social system. When a group of psychology graduate students was asked to comment on the article by Frances Grossman described earlier, in which conflicts of intimacy and power differences were analyzed, they argued forcefully that it is naive to try to make feminist research nonhierarchical. Unequal distribution of power is a fact of life in the academy. The students believed that hierarchies can function fairly so that those with less power are not left "voiceless" in the research project. [*See* POWER.]

VI. Giving Back to Participants

Closely connected to the concern for power relations within the research process is the idea that the researcher should give something back to the participants, in addition to promoting the welfare of girls and women in general.

For the researcher, there are many inherent rewards in conducting research, such as satisfying curiosity, enhancing a career, or the feeling of being a part of an important social movement. But what do the participants gain for their time and their wisdom? Feminists must attend to assuring reciprocity if they do not wish to reproduce oppression by the researcher of the researched.

One particularly innovative example comes from the work of Glenda M. Russell and Janis S. Bohan. After the citizens of Colorado approved Amendment 2 of their constitution that removed any legal protection for lesbian, gay, and bisexual (LGB) people from discrimination based on sexual orientation, Russell used a survey to document the psychological impact of this vote. One open-ended item yielded 496 responses that were coded for themes to elucidate the meaning of this vote to the respondents. The researcher gave many talks throughout the state about the results, which was one way to benefit any who cared about the issue. The themes informed new

curricula for college courses on sexual orientation and were applied in a number of clinical and supervisory situations. The data also were included in an *amicus* brief prepared by the American Psychological Association (APA) for the Supreme Court case against Amendment 2. Most interestingly, the themes were woven into an oratorio that was performed by Harmony, Denver's LGB chorus, first in Denver and then at an international festival of LGB choruses.

Personal experience has shown that, with the use of methods that involve querying women and girls about their experiences of such things as body image dissatisfaction, loss of confidence in mathematics, feminist pedagogy, failure to persuade, feminism, or experiential learning, many if not most participants relish the opportunity to reflect and then describe to another interested person something about their lives. For example, a year after serving as a participant, one woman called with thanks for the "transformative" interview. She explained that the research caused her to think more deeply and led to some profound changes in her understanding of the phenomenon under investigation.

VII. Initiating Social Action

One of the salient characteristics of feminist research is its dedication to issues of social change. Sociologist Margaret Anderson went so far as to assert that the purpose of feminist research was not "to contribute grand theories that have no relevance to the lives of actual human beings . . . [rather the] purpose is the transformation of gender relations and the society in which we live." Feminists who study gender hold a "dual vision"—that their research will increase knowledge and contribute to the welfare of women and girls. Research can stimulate social change by raising consciousness, informing and shaping policies, and guiding interventions or practice. Thus, the fact that gender research often addresses social issues makes it practical as well as scholarly. Legislative reform, community action initiatives, and policy recommendations for private and public institutions are all examples of the impact that feminist research efforts have in improving the personal and professional lives of women.

Feminist research contributes to social action in two distinct ways. Explorations of social injustices and inequities produce an awareness, a consciousness-raising, that is essential for creating an impetus for action. Other forms of feminist research provide policy makers with important factual information that can bolster their arguments for social reform. There is no standard method for conducting social action research: among the published literature the reader will find traditional quantitative analyses as well as more innovative qualitative and blended methods.

Psychologist Gloria Levin encourages feminist researchers to direct their research to topics that will be useful to policy makers. While criticisms of bias and subjectivity are often leveled at researchers engaged in social reform efforts, Annette Kuhn celebrates this partiality as "passionate detachment." (DuBois uses the phrase "passionate scholarship.") Being passionate about one's research does not necessarily mean being unable to maintain objectivity. The passion felt for a particular issue may very well contribute to an increased dedication to thoroughness and a greater attention to meeting the criteria of strong objectivity described earlier.

Feminist activists need to pay special attention to the diverse needs of women while promoting social change. For example, efforts to help women gain stronger marital property rights should not ignore the needs of women in committed nonmarital relationships. Research into issues of sexual violence needs to address this issue for homosexual as well as heterosexual relationships at all stages of the life cycle. Without this inclusiveness, feminist researchers would be guilty of the same type of patriarchal prejudice that is typical of much positivist research. To foster this inclusiveness, alliances and collaborations with other researchers is often necessary and always beneficial.

An influential addition to the field of social action research is the establishment of centers devoted specifically to gathering and disseminating feminist studies. While such centers are few, their numbers are growing. The Institute for Women's Policy Research in Washington, D.C., is one example of a center that serves as an intermediary between individual feminist researchers and structures having the power to initiate social change on a large scale. Centers such as these have the clout to create media attention and to bring critical issues to a wide audience.

VIII. Valuing Methodological Plurality

Research on gender is characterized by the use of many, diverse methods to answer the question at hand. Unlike the more traditional psychological community that privileges the experiment above all other methods, within feminist psychology there is no one "right" way to do research. In place of methodological elitism is variety and creativity. Research methods on gender reach into all the disciplines, sometimes singly, other times in combination. In many cases feminists modify existing methods, create new ones, or use innovative combinations of familiar methods. The goals of feminist researchers often differ from those of other investigators. They range from describing women's unique experiences and gaining deeper meanings that women attach to their experiences, to exploring the situation of women within a societal discourse of gender difference and inequality, to fostering radical social change. These goals require invention above tradition, such that issues of replicability or generalizability may be given less importance. Many gender researchers accept the impossibility of "foundational" knowledge and thus do not attempt to uncover reliable "new facts." Rather, they focus on making sense of the ordinary. They accept the accusation of engaging in passionate inquiry and adhere to the dictum, "Above all else, the method must serve the question."

In many cases feminists adopt the methods of their disciplines, using the power of these methods to serve feminist goals. Feminist psychologists in particular employ this strategy. One example is the many meta-analytic studies that analyze socially constructed mediators of gender differences in cognition, personality, and social roles. However, even while expanding their repertoire of methods and using more qualitative approaches, aspiring academics are still worried about the detrimental effects to their careers of deviating from traditional ways to collect data. Still it is fair to say that one distinguishing quality of recent research on gender is researchers' refusal to be constrained by existing standards of "acceptable" methods and their willingness to implement new approaches. Experimental, meta-analytic, and survey research abounds in feminist psychology. So does the use of some less well known methods, a sample of which follows (see Suggested Reading for more). These illustrate the diversity and richness of the study of gender.

A. COLLABORATIVE METHODS

Both researchers and participants gather data when collaborative methods are employed, often in cross-cultural settings. The Community Education Team of Wilfred Laurier University used dramatic presentations with 7th through 12th graders to engage students in changing the incidence of violence against women and then evaluated the impact of their work with the students. The key was developing relationality between the researchers and the researched, so they worked as partners on the research process.

B. ETHNOGRAPHY

In this approach, researchers traditionally go "undercover" in an effort to gain perspective from the viewpoint of the subject of the research. The goal is to become "one of them" in order to collect data that are ecologically valid. More recent forms of ethnography are found in gender studies. For example, Michelle Fine and Pat MacPherson invited groups of adolescent girls to Fine's home to have dinner and "just talk." This more natural way of interviewing yields data that might not be offered in an artificial setting—places one never goes (a laboratory) and people to whom one would not ordinarily talk (adult researchers).

C. NARRATIVE INVESTIGATIONS

Here, the stories that people tell are the focus of the research. Human experiences are cognitively organized, remembered, and shared through narrative. Allowing the participant to narrate freely a particular incident or experience helps uncover the meaning that is attached to it. Feminists are rightly concerned that the interpretation of the meaning of the life that is being narrated should incorporate both the participant's and the researcher's theory and perspective. Rosario Ceballo highlights this method and its unique features and issues in the life narrative she completed with an elderly African American social worker.

D. DISCOURSE ANALYSIS

Analyzing the language of written and oral texts can provide important information about the social construction of meaning. Discourse analysis attempts to classify, codify, and deconstruct forms of writing and speaking. A study done in New Zealand by Nicola Gavey and Kathryn McPhillips provides an interesting example. The authors selected two interviews (from 14) and used discourse analysis to explore accounts of women being unable to initiate condom use despite their stated intentions not to have intercourse without a condom and having the condoms

in their possession. The researchers analyzed this passivity in the context of a societal discourse of feminine heterosexuality generally and of heterosexual romance particularly. This helps to explain why otherwise assertive women sometimes do not follow their intentions and why certain approaches to sexuality education that demand assertiveness might not be effective.

E. EXISTENTIAL PHENOMENOLOGY

Participants become "coresearchers" by contributing naive descriptions of their experiences so that the researcher can identify common themes of meaning among those who have experienced the investigated phenomenon. Rhonda Reitz began her career working in law where she interviewed women who were seeking warrants of arrest against their partners for domestic violence. Often the battered women would ask her, "Why does he do this?" She had no answer. A number of years later she entered a doctoral program at the University of Tennessee and decided to try to find that answer through her dissertation research on batterers. She used the existential phenomenological method to generate a "rich description" of the experience of battering. By extracting shared themes from the talk of the men she interviewed, she began to develop a picture of what goes on in the minds of people as they engage in this violent act against someone they say they love. Based on this deeper understanding of the phenomenon, Reitz offered a number of suggestions for treatment and intervention for this entrenched social problem.

F. FOCUS GROUPS

Market researchers and economists have used this technique for many years. Feminists employ focus groups to provide a free-form discussion about a topic in small groups and analyze the tape-recorded conversation using various qualitative methods of extracting main ideas or themes. The advantages of this method include the fact that focus groups are relatively naturalistic (as opposed to artificial), afford social contexts in which to make meaning, and shift the balance of power somewhat from the researcher to the researched.

G. Q-METHODOLOGY

Introduced in the 1950s, Q-methodology has not been used to measure attitudes extensively since.

Here, participants are asked to evaluate a large number of statements taken from narratives or interviews on a particular topic. The Q-sort classifies participant responses and provides a multidimensional profile of participants' viewpoints. Recently, Susan Snelling employed the method to identify and describe the multiple perspectives women have on feminism, which supports the feminist notion of plurality and diversity in all aspects of human experience.

H. PERFORMATIVE PSYCHOLOGY

This controversial method provides a unique way of capturing participant feelings and socialized reactions around certain topics. Through the use of art, improvisation, music, poetry, drama, or other artistic modalities, participants express emotions that they might not be able to communicate through traditional verbal or narrative methods.

We have mentioned a variety of innovative methods, and our list has been far from complete. However, this is not to say that doubts about methodological innovation and feminist perspectives, along with institutional resistance, are ancient history. In a recent compendium, a group of feminist graduate students in psychology discuss the perceived costs of innovative qualitative approaches, including their labor-intensiveness, required emotional investment, dependence on language and talk, and lack of generalizability, validity, reliability and replicability. Moreover, they discuss frankly their fears that such research would not help them get good academic jobs or tenure and that it might not foster the progress of psychological science. Echoing the values of the psychological establishment, they call on researchers who use innovative methods to convince others of the worth of these approaches.

On a final note, gender researchers are not open to everything. As critics of the status quo, researchers must continuously look out for signs of nonfeminist consciousness, from accepting uncritically the conventions of one's discipline to lauding methodological novelty for its own sake. Researchers may elect to use a method that has been criticized, such as experimental or meta-analytic designs, but they would do so as a conscious, self-reflexive choice. Likewise, researchers would choose an unusual method only after reflection on its strengths and limitations for feminist research. Ideally, those who study women and gender choose their methods with the goals of understanding the lives of girls and women, situat-

ing gender as a social construction, and impacting social policy to benefit diverse women.

IX. *The Future of Feminist Methods for Studying Gender*

We noted earlier that the second-wave focus on methods has existed for over three decades. During that time once-young researchers have grayed a bit, and many have enjoyed successful careers as academics. They are now editors of journals that publish research on gender. They write textbooks and encyclopedias, teach courses on gender that are a standard part of most colleges' curriculum, and serve in leadership roles, including APA's august Publication and Communication Board. Although they regard themselves as advocates and agents of change, they occupy gatekeeper roles typical of the insiders they have challenged throughout their careers. Is it paradoxical to be part of the establishment one is trying to change?

One benefit of becoming part of the establishment is that feminist researchers have greater power to shape the landscape of the research enterprise. In our view, this means that there will be a greater acceptance and refining of the characteristics of methods for studying gender outlined here. Innovation and methodological diversity will increase, as will the insistence on reflexivity, feminist objectivity, diversity, social action, and reciprocity with participants. Psychologists have not been as interdisciplinary as other groups, such as women's studies, in part because of the discipline's xenophobia. This might change. More certain is that there will be more research, conducted with increasingly diverse participants, and no doubt more controversy, as gender researchers struggle to deepen our knowledge and expand our global understanding of what gender means in the lives of citizens around the world.

But it would be remiss not to note the fact that women as a group are still outsiders in the male dominated, patriarchal academy, as changed as it might appear to be by the increasing presence of women students, faculty, and administrators. Overt gender discrimination is legally proscribed, but the institution of higher education, the locus of most research on gender, has hardly changed.

Women occupy a continuum of outsider status. Their work on gender often is seen as peripheral to the "real" research endeavor that academic men control. Indeed, as Jill Morawski has noted, feminist science is often caricatured as oppositional to the scientific mission altogether. The usually covert, even unconscious, denigration of politically motivated (read, not legitimate) feminist research marginalizes those who engage in it, even when they achieve the rank of full professor and win presidencies of their scientific societies. Feeling the precariousness of their position in the power system of their organizations, many women faculty avoid using their intellectual skills politically to improve women's status in fear of threatening the relations they have established with male colleagues or the wider community. Women with any sort of feminist consciousness experience a constant tension between resisting their placement as an outsider and protecting the limited acceptance they may have gained. Women researchers on gender construct their professional identities within a masculinist culture of science. The methods they use to explore and the topics they choose are embedded in the academy's gendered world of research. To support the full, unfettered exploration of gender, the future also will contain the need to change the way the academy "does gender."

ACKNOWLEDGMENT

We thank Dr. Janet Marderness for helping to develop the manuscript by searching for background materials and taking notes.

SUGGESTED READING

Bohan, J. S. (Ed.) (1992). *Seldom Seen, Rarely Heard: Women's Place in Psychology*. Westview Press, Boulder, CO.

Bhavnani, K-K. (1993). Tracing the contours: Feminist research and feminist objectivity. *Women's Studies International Forum* **16**, 95–104.

Crawford, M., and Unger, R. (2000). *Women and Gender: A Feminist Psychology*, 3rd ed. McGraw Hill, Boston.

Haraway, D. (1988). Situated knowledges: The science question in feminism and the privilege of partial perspective. *Feminist Studies* **14**, 575–599.

Kimmel, E. B., and Crawford, M. (eds.) (2000). *Innovations in Feminist Psychological Research*. Cambridge University Press, New York.

Morawski, J. (1997). The science behind feminist research methods. *Journal of Social Issues* **53**, 667–681.

Reinharz, S. (1992). *Feminist Methods in Social Research*. Oxford University Press, New York, Oxford.

Worell, J., and Johnson, N. (eds.) (1997). *Shaping the Future of Feminist Psychology: Education, Research, and Practice*. American Psychological Association, Washington, DC.

Midlife Transitions[1]

Claire A. Etaugh
Bradley University

Judith S. Bridges
University of Connecticut, Hartford

Glossary

Agency Stereotypically masculine personality characteristics reflecting a concern about accomplishing tasks, such as achievement orientation and competitiveness.

Communion Stereotypically feminine personality traits reflecting a concern about other people, such as sympathy and warmth.

Double standard of aging The view that aging women are judged more harshly than aging men.

Late midlife astonishment A sudden awareness by some women in their fifties of diminished physical/sexual attractiveness, which produces feelings of amazement and despair.

Life review An intensive self-evaluation of numerous aspects of one's life.

Postmenopausal zest A sense of increased determination, energy, and ability to gain control of one's life experienced by women who have reached menopause.

Skip-generation parents Grandparents who are raising grandchildren on their own.

THE MIDLIFE TRANSITIONS OF WOMEN are examined in this article. "Midlife" as a distinct period is a 20th-century construction made possible by the dramatic increase in the numbers of adults who enjoy healthy active lives well into older age. There is no firm consensus on when middle-age begins, although it is popularly thought to begin around age 40 and end in the mid-60's. No one biological or psychological event signals its beginning. Rather,

[1]From Claire A. Etaugh and Judith S. Bridges, *The Psychology of Women: A Lifespan Perspective*, © 2001 by Allyn & Bacon. Adapted by permission.

individuals typically experience a number of life events and role changes during these years, including those related to physical changes, sexuality, marital status, parenting, caregiving for ill family members, grandparenting, and entry into or retirement from the workforce. Historically, women have been allocated the major responsibility for child care, kin relations, and care of impaired relatives in midlife, thereby restricting their participation in the labor force. Fundamental changes in social attitudes regarding gender roles over the past several decades have begun to broaden the opportunities available to women in midlife as well as in other life stages. Important to understanding the impact of role transitions in midlife is the timing or degree of predictability of these changes. For example, having the last child leave home or becoming a grandparent are frequently expected and welcome role transitions, whereas divorce, death of a spouse, or providing care for ailing parents are often unplanned and stressful changes.

I. Health

Although midlife is generally a time of good health, the first indications of physical aging become noticeable and signs of chronic health conditions may appear. There are enormous individual differences in rates of aging and emergence of chronic illness. Genetic makeup and lifestyle choices involving good nutrition, physical activity, and not smoking all contribute to health during the middle years.

One of the most visible signs of aging is in physical appearance. Hair becomes thinner and grayer, the skin becomes drier, and the muscles, blood vessels, and other tissues begin to lose their elasticity. These changes result in sagging and wrinkling of the skin, especially on the face, neck, and hands. Lines appear on the forehead as a result of smiling, frowning, and other facial expressions repeated over time. Small, pigmented age spots appear, especially in skin that has been exposed to the sun. Fat becomes redistributed, decreasing in the face, legs, thighs, and lower arms, and increasing in the abdomen, buttocks, and upper arms. Starting at about age 40, the discs between the spinal vertebrae begin to compress, resulting in an eventual loss in height of one to two inches. [*See* AGING.]

In our youth-oriented society, the prospect of getting older generally is not relished by either sex. For women, however, the stigma of aging is greater than it is for men, a phenomenon labeled the "double standard of aging." The same gray hair and wrinkles that enhance the perceived status and attractiveness of an older man diminish the perceived attractiveness and desirability of an older woman. Some researchers account for this by noting that a woman's most socially valued qualities—her ability to provide sex and bear children—are associated with the physical beauty and fertility of youth. As she ages, she is seen as less attractive because her years of social usefulness as childbearer are behind her. Men, on the other hand, are seen as possessing qualities—competence, autonomy, and power—which are not associated with youth but rather increase with age. Given these societal views, it is not surprising that midlife women, compared with midlife men, are more dissatisfied with their bodies and use more age concealment techniques. They are more critical of the appearance of middle-aged women than are women of other age groups or men. The more a woman has based her sense of identity and self-esteem upon her youthful physical attractiveness, the greater the impact of midlife changes in her physical appearance. Some women in their fifties experience a transition labeled "late midlife astonishment," a sudden awareness of diminished physical and sexual attractiveness, which produces feelings of amazement and despair.

It may be difficult for women to feel comfortable about aging in a culture where older women do not often appear in the media, and those who do are praised for their youthful appearance and for hiding the signs of aging. Editors of women's magazines admit that signs of age are removed from photographs through computer imaging, making 60 year-old women look 45. Popular films portray "older" women (over age 35!) as more unfriendly, unintelligent, unattractive, and wicked. Attractive actresses such as Meryl Streep, Jessica Lange, and Diane Keaton are labeled "geezer babes"—and thus too old for romantic parts—while male actors many years their senior are paired with young ingenues. Women over the age of 39 have accounted for only one-quarter of all Academy Award winners for Best Actress, while men in the same age category have won two-thirds of the Best Actor awards.

The most distinct physiological change for most midlife women is menopause, the cessation of menses. In Western societies, menopause is often viewed in terms of loss of reproductive capability and decline in sexual functioning. Menopause continues to be defined in medical and psychological literature by a long list of negative symptoms and terms such as "estrogen deprivation" and "total ovarian failure." The popular press reinforces the notion of menopause as a condition of disease and deterioration that requires treatment by drugs. Most middle-aged North American women, however, minimize the significance of menopause, viewing it as only a temporary inconvenience, and feeling relief when their menstrual periods stop. Postmenopausal women have more positive attitudes toward menopause than younger midlife women, with young women holding the most negative views of all.

Women in other cultures often have menopausal experiences and attitudes very different from those reported by Western women, indicating that menopausal symptoms are at least in part socially constructed. For example, women of high social castes in India report very few negative symptoms, and hot flashes are virtually unknown among Mayan women. Similarly, Japanese women are much less likely than U.S. and Canadian women to report hot flashes. In some cultures, menopause is an eagerly anticipated event. For example, when high caste Indian women reach menopause, they are freed from menstrual taboos that restrict their full participation in society. No wonder these women experience few negative menopausal symptoms! [*See* MENOPAUSE; MENSTRUATION.]

While most midlife adults enjoy good health, the frequency of chronic illness begins to increase during this time. Men have a higher prevalence of fatal diseases (e.g., heart disease, cancer, stroke) while women have a higher incidence of nonfatal ones (e.g., arthritis, gallstones, bladder infections and varicose veins). This so-called gender paradox is summed up in the saying "Women are sicker; men die quicker." These statistics do not mean, however, that women are more likely than men to develop health problems. Women spend 64 of their years in good health and free of disability, compared with only 59 years for men. But because women live longer than men, it is women who more often live many years with chronic, often disabling, illnesses. [*See* CHRONIC ILLNESS ADJUSTMENT.]

Many factors contribute to individual and gender differences in disease and injury, including biological predispositions, lifestyle, and health habits. One biological explanation for women's greater longevity is that their second X chromosome protects them against certain lethal diseases such as hemophilia and some forms of muscular dystrophy that are more apt to occur in individuals (men) who have only one

X chromosome. Another biological reason for women's greater longevity may be their higher estrogen level, which seems to provide protection against fatal conditions such as heart disease. In addition, women have a lower rate of metabolism, which is linked to greater longevity.

For most diseases and conditions, the way we live our lives has the greatest impact on the prevention and delay of physiological decline and disease. One lifestyle factor accounting for the gender gap in mortality is that men are more likely than women to engage in potentially risky behaviors such as smoking, drinking, violence, and reckless driving. They also may be exposed to more hazardous workplace conditions. In the United States, accidents and unintentional injuries are the fourth leading cause of death of males, but the seventh leading cause for females. Cirrhosis, caused largely by excessive drinking, and homicide are the ninth and tenth most common causes of death for males, but do not appear on the "Top Ten" list for females.

Another gender difference in health habits is that women make greater use of preventive health services and are more likely to seek medical treatment when they are ill. This may help explain why women live longer than men after the diagnosis of a potentially fatal disease. Women's greater tendency to visit the doctor's office suggests that they are more health conscious than men. Women generally know more than men about health, do more to prevent illness, are more aware of symptoms, and are more likely to talk about their health concerns. Women also outlive men because of their more extensive social support networks involving family, friends, and formal organizational memberships. Involvement in social relationships is related to living longer, perhaps because social ties reduce the impact of life stresses. [*See* SOCIAL SUPPORT.]

On the other hand, midlife women are more likely than men to engage in certain deleterious health habits. More women are overweight, consume higher levels of dietary fat, and are physically inactive. These lifestyle factors contribute to a host of diseases and medical conditions including heart disease, many kinds of cancer, and stroke, the three leading causes of death for both women and men. Moreover, as women's lifestyles have become more similar to men's, so have some of their health behaviors. For example, while the frequency of men's smoking has declined, that of women's has increased. The result is that deaths from lung cancer among U.S. women nearly tripled between 1970 and 1997, whereas the increase for men was only 2%. This is one of the reasons that lung cancer has surpassed breast cancer as the leading cause of cancer deaths among women.

Although heart disease is by far the number one killer of women in middle and old age, many women are unaware of this fact. The majority of women believe that they are more likely to die of breast cancer than heart disease. They also perceive breast cancer as a greater threat to their health than lung cancer. [See HEALTH AND HEALTH CARE.]

II. Sexuality

Sexual activity and satisfaction vary among midlife women just as they do among young women. Sexual activity decreases only slightly and gradually for most women, but some experience greater declines as a result of physical or psychological changes. Furthermore, while some women report a decline in sexual interest and the capacity for orgasm during these years, others report the opposite pattern, and some women report an increased desire for nongenital sexual expression such as cuddling, hugging, and kissing.

Changes in sexual physiology and in hormone levels are some of the factors determining female sexuality in the middle years. Most women experience a number of physical changes as they enter menopause, some of which may affect sexual activity. Decline in the production of estrogen is responsible for many of these changes. The vaginal walls become less elastic, thinner, and more easily irritated, causing pain and bleeding during intercourse. Decreases in vaginal lubrication also can lead to painful intercourse. Normal acidic vaginal secretions become less acidic, increasing the likelihood of yeast infections. Signs of sexual arousal, clitoral, labial, and breast engorgement and nipple erection become less intense, and sexual arousal is slower. Most menopausal women, however, experience little or no change in *subjective* arousal. Although the number and intensity of orgasmic contractions are reduced, few women either notice or complain about these changes. Furthermore, slower arousal time for both women and men may lengthen the time of pleasurable sexual activity.

Other physical causes of declining sexual activity include various medical conditions, surgery, certain medications, and heavy drinking. Hysterectomy does not impair sexual functioning and in fact may lead to greater sexual desire, an increase in orgasms, and

a drop in painful intercourse. However, if a woman feels that her ability to enjoy sex after a hysterectomy is diminished, counseling can be helpful. Similarly, mastectomy does not interfere with sexual responsiveness, but a woman may lose her sexual desire or sense of being desired. Talking with other women who have had a mastectomy often helps. One resource is the American Cancer Society's Reach to Recovery program.

In addition to physiological factors, the sexual lives of midlife women are strongly influenced by past sexual enjoyment and experience. Women who in their earlier years found sexual expression to be fulfilling typically continue to enjoy sex in their middle years and beyond. Other women, whose sexual desires were not strong earlier, may find that their interest diminishes further during middle age.

Psychological factors also affect midlife women's sexual experiences. Many postmenopausal women find that their sexual interest and pleasure are heightened. One possible reason for this is freedom from worries about pregnancy. This factor may be especially relevant for older cohorts of women for whom highly effective birth control methods were unavailable during their childbearing years. A second possible reason is the increase in marital satisfaction, which often develops during the postparental years. On the other hand, dissatisfaction with one's partner and worries about family matters, finances, or work can negatively affect sexual experience.

Not surprisingly, sexual activity and contentment during middle age is more likely to diminish for individuals who have lost their partners. For example, a recent nationally representative study of sexuality in Americans age 45 and over found that just over half of those polled, but two-thirds of those with sexual partners, were satisfied with their sex lives. While women in their 40s and 50s are nearly as likely as men to have a sexual partner, the "partner gap" between women and men grows in the later years.

III. Midlife: Crisis or Prime of Life?

Contrary to popular literature's depiction of middle age as a time of crisis, turmoil, and self-doubt, empirical evidence shows that midlife women consider this period to be one of vibrancy and opportunity for growth. Valory Mitchell and Ravenna Helson characterize the early post-parental period as women's prime of life. Others describe midlife as a period of "post-menopausal zest," in which women have an increased determination, energy, and ability to fulfill their dreams and gain control over their lives. Freedom from reproductive concerns, a sense of accomplishment accompanying the successful launching of children, and an increase in available time enable women to focus more on their self-development and on their partner, job, and community.

An integral part of this change for many women is a decrease in gender typing; that is, a significant increase in women's agency and a lesser decrease in communion. Between early and middle adulthood, women's self-ratings of competence and self-confidence increase and their self-ratings of emotional dependence decrease. This increased balance between communion and agency among women is associated with greater well-being. According to Mitchell and Helson, the absence of children from the home enables women with partners to work on their own relationships and develop greater intimacy with one another. This greater intimacy combined with a greater sense of autonomy that emerges during middle adulthood enhances women's quality of life.

Some researchers suggest that the decrease in gender typing in midlife reflects major changes in women's parenting responsibilities during middle adulthood and new or more involved employment roles engaged in by many midlife women. As women relinquish their nurturing duties, they are able to develop previously unexpressed aspects of themselves, including more agentic qualities. Additionally, as they begin their employment roles or expand their involvement in their careers, women may develop the agentic traits associated with the work role.

An alternative explanation focuses on societal changes during the second half of the 20th century. Middle-class women who reached midlife at the end of the 20th century were exposed to two very different constructions of gender during their lifetimes. While growing up, these women were socialized into the traditional stay-at-home wife and mother roles. Shortly after assuming these roles, however, they were influenced by the women's movement of the 1960s and 1970s, which encouraged them to consider an expanded array of options and a more flexible construction of gender. Thus, it is possible that midlife women experienced an alteration in their own gender schemas that permitted development of characteristics previously viewed as male-related traits.

IV. Midlife Role Transitions: An Overview

Although few women experience a midlife crisis, many women who reached their middle adult years toward the end of the 20th century go through a process of life review, that is, an intensive self-evaluation of numerous aspects of their lives. They reexamine their family and occupational values and goals, evaluate their accomplishments, and sometimes consider new career directions. Some make transitions to different jobs during their middle adult years, and others begin their paid work role at this point in their lives. Because of the myriad societal gender role messages encountered by the current cohort of midlife women, some have followed traditional roles early in adulthood and have continued these roles at midlife while others began their adult lives committed to traditional roles but made changes in their middle adult years. Still others have deviated from traditional expectations by committing themselves to careers in early adulthood.

Given the changing societal standards about appropriate roles for women, it is not surprising that one characteristic theme in the life reviews of current midlife women has been the search for an independent identity. Ravenna Helson has noted that for many women, the need to rewrite the life story in middle age is related to the lessening of the dependence and restriction associated with marriage and motherhood as children grow up. Thus, many heterosexual women attempt to affirm their own being, independent of their family, through graduate education, beginning a career, or switching careers. Lesbian midlife women, however, generally do not experience major transitions at midlife. Many are not mothers and have not experienced the role constraints characteristic of traditional heterosexual marriages. Therefore, they are not aiming to redefine themselves as separate from significant others. Furthermore, they already have a strong sense of self due to years of defining themselves independently of others' expectations and fighting oppression against the lesbian community, and most have considered work an important part of their identity throughout their adult lives.

For many midlife women, paid work is a significant predictor of psychological well-being. Middle-aged women who are involved in either beginning or building their career are both psychologically and physically healthier than women who are maintaining or reducing their career involvement. Also, women who have attained the occupational goals they set for themselves in young adulthood have a greater sense of life purpose and are less depressed in midlife than those who fall short of their expectations. Furthermore, satisfaction with work predicts a general sense of well-being: the more satisfied women are with their jobs, the better they feel in general. [*See* WORK–FAMILY BALANCE.]

For other women, being a full-time homemaker or student can be associated with the same degree of psychological well-being as that experienced by women who are employed. Midlife homemakers whose life goal was this domestic role have a comparable sense of purpose in life to women who aspired toward and achieved an occupational role. Not surprisingly, however, women who are involuntarily out of the workforce, due to forced early retirement or layoff, are not as satisfied with midlife as women with a chosen role. Thus, there are multiple routes to well-being in midlife, and it appears that a key factor influencing midlife role evaluation is not a woman's *role* per se but fulfillment of her *preferred role*.

Although some midlife women are satisfied with traditional roles, others are disturbed about missed educational or occupational opportunities. Some middle-class women who, as young adults devoted themselves solely to marriage and motherhood, in midlife voice regrets about their earlier traditional decisions. Abigail Stewart and Elizabeth Vandewater examined regrets experienced by women who graduated in the mid-1960s from either Radcliffe College or the University of Michigan. The concerns reported by these women centered on disappointment about not pursuing a more prestigious career, marrying before establishing a career, and not returning to work after having children. Stewart and Vandewater found that the experience of regret was not necessarily associated with reduced psychological adjustment. Instead, the crucial factor appeared to be acting on these regrets to effect life changes. The women who acknowledged their regrets and made modifications based on these regrets experienced greater psychological well-being at midlife than did those who had regrets but did not use those as a basis for altering their life direction. [*See* ACADEMIC ASPIRATIONS AND DEGREE ATTAINMENT OF WOMEN; CAREER ACHIEVEMENT.]

V. Spousal Role Transitions

Experiences with marriage, divorce, widowhood, and remarriage during the middle years vary for women and men. Men in the United States are more likely than women to be married during midlife, especially during the years from 55 to 64, when 80% of men but only 68% of women are still married. Marital disruption is more common among Black women, poor women, and women with disabilities than among White, more affluent, and able-bodied women.

Following divorce or widowhood, women are less likely than men to remarry, and they do so less quickly. This is especially true for Black women. Remarriage rates are much lower for women than men because of several factors. For one thing, older women outnumber older men. In the United States for example, there are only two men for every three women by age 65, and this difference widens with age. Second, Western cultural values sanction the marriage of men to much younger women but frown on the opposite pattern, thus expanding the pool of potential mates for an older man but shrinking it for an older woman. Finally, previously married women are less inclined to remarry than previously married men, who appear to be more dependent on marriage.

Despite the increasing divorce rate, most marriages are terminated not by divorce, but by the death of a spouse. Women are much more likely to become widowed than are men, since women not only have a longer life expectancy but also tend to marry men older than themselves. As of 1998, there were 12 million widows but only 2.6 million widowers in the United States, a ratio of more than four to one. About 13% of women between the ages of 55 and 64, but fewer than 3% of men the same age, are widowed, with Black women widowed earlier than White women.

Common reactions to losing a spouse or partner include restlessness, sleep problems, feelings of depression, emptiness, anger, and guilt. While most individuals adjust to their spouse's or partner's death within two to four years, feelings of loneliness, yearning, and missing their partner remain for extended periods of time. Loss of a lesbian's partner is especially stressful if the relationship was not publicly acknowledged, but even when the relationship is open, friends may not comprehend the severity and nature of the loss. As many as 10 to 20% of widows experience long-term problems, including clinical depression, abuse of alcohol and prescription drugs, and increased susceptibility to physical illness. Such problems are more prevalent among younger women, those with a prior history of depression, those whose marriages were less satisfactory, women whose husbands' deaths followed the deaths of other close relatives and friends, those whose spouses died unexpectedly, those who depended on their husbands for most social contacts, and women with limited financial and social resources. Support from families and children, especially daughters, does much to enhance the psychological well-being of widows. Women friends who are themselves widowed can be particularly supportive. Interestingly, research has found more loneliness among women who have lived with a spouse for many years than among women who live alone.

Keep in mind that our knowledge of widows has been obtained primarily from older women, most of whom had traditional marriages. When the young women of today become widows, they will be more likely than the current population of widows to have had a different set of life experiences, including a college education and a job or career that will better prepare them for a healthy adjustment to widowhood.

VI. *Parental Role Transitions*

Although midlife women who had children during their teen years have already launched their children into young adulthood, and other midlife women are still chasing toddlers around the house, a major event for many mothers during their middle years is the departure of their children from the home. Similar to common folklore characterizing midlife as a time of crisis, this postparental period is popularly but inaccurately viewed as an unhappy "empty nest" stage of life for most women. Women generally describe the postparental years in positive rather than negative terms. Because children can be a source of tension in any marriage, women report higher marital satisfaction once their children have left home. Also, the decreased complexity of family relationships at this time enables women to develop greater intimacy with their partners. Furthermore, the departure of the last child from the home is an opportunity to begin or expand the development of a personal identity independent of family roles. For many women, as we have seen, this event marks the beginning of a midlife review period when they evaluate their lives and consider other options such as pursuing new careers, furthering their education, or providing service to their communities. However, the significant redefinition of their parenting responsibilities and the end to their identity as a child caregiver can be some-

what problematic for women whose primary identity has been that of mother. Mothers who are employed during the child-rearing years and establish an identity additional to their mother role find it easier to relinquish their child care responsibilities when their children leave home than do women who have identified primarily with their role as mother.

Of course, mothers do not stop being parents when their children move out. Instead, they redefine parenting to a less-involved phase. A new type of interpersonal relationship is created and mothers remain involved in their children's lives, although in somewhat different ways. While their contacts are generally less frequent, they continue to offer advice and encouragement and sometimes provide goal-directed help, such as financial assistance.

Because the parental bond remains strong despite the changes in day-to-day caregiving and interactions, women's psychological adjustment during the postparental period continues to be associated with their children's lives. At this stage of life, women are concerned about the type of people their children have become; they evaluate how their children have developed educationally, occupationally, interpersonally, and psychologically. Parents' perceptions of their children's personal and social adjustment, and, to a lesser extent, their educational and occupational attainment, predict their own well-being. The more well adjusted they believe their children to be, the higher their own well-being and the lower their depression. Furthermore, parents who view their children's adjustment and attainment more positively express a greater sense of responsibility for those outcomes compared to parents with negative evaluations of their children's outcomes. [*See* PARENTING.]

Although most mothers experience the departure of their children at some point during midlife, there are variations in children's age of departure, and a significant number return home for some period of time after leaving, for financial reasons or following divorce. Nearly half of middle-aged parents with children over the age of 18 have an adult child living with them. Parents' reaction to their children's return is related to the degree to which the return is characterized by a continued dependence on the parents. Parents experience greater parent–child strain the greater the children's financial dependency and the lower their educational attainment. Furthermore, parents' satisfaction with the living arrangement is positively related to their child's self-esteem, possibly because low self-esteem signals difficulty in assuming independent adult roles. These findings suggest that parents are most satisfied with the parent–child relationship and experience the highest degree of well-being when they perceive their children assuming the normative roles of adulthood.

VII. Caregiver Role Transitions

Midlife adults are often referred to as the "sandwich" or "squeeze" generation because of the responsibilities that they assume for their adolescent and young adult children on the one hand and their aging parents on the other. At the same time that middle-aged parents are providing assistance and support for the young adult children who are staying at home or returning home, they also maintain ties with and provide care for their elderly parents. The extent of assistance provided may range from no help at all (either because none is needed or because it is provided by others) to around-the-clock care, including household maintenance, transportation, cooking, grocery shopping, and personal and medical care. Typically it is the middle-aged (or even elderly) daughter or daughter-in-law who provides such services. These unpaid caregivers are the core of the long-term care system in the United States, providing three-quarters of the help needed by the frail elderly. Demographic changes in recent years are increasing the parent care responsibilities of midlife women. More parents are living well into old age, and their care-giving children themselves are becoming old. Furthermore, as the birthrate declines, there are fewer siblings to share the burden of the care. In addition, middle-aged women are increasingly likely to be employed, adding to their list of competing roles and responsibilities. For some individuals, caring for a parent and the sense of reciprocating the nurturance and care once provided by that parent can be very rewarding. For many, however, caregiving can adversely affect psychological and physical well-being. Older women caregivers with few economic resources and a limited support system are most likely to develop psychological distress.

VIII. Grandparental Role Transitions

The stereotypical portrayal of a grandmother is often an elderly white-haired woman providing treats for her young grandchildren. However, grandmothers do not fit into any one pattern. While more than 75% of Americans over age 65 are grandparents,

some people become grandparents as early as their late twenties and over half of women experience this event before the age of 54. Nowadays, many middle-aged grandmothers are in the labor force and may also have responsibilities for caring for their elderly parents. Thus, they may have less time to devote to grandparenting activities. Grandmothers tend to have warmer relationships with their grandchildren than do grandfathers. The maternal grandmother often has the most contact and the closest relationship with grandchildren, especially her granddaughters.

During their grandchild's infancy, grandmothers often provide the children's parents with considerable emotional support, information, help with infant care and household chores, and, to a lesser degree, financial support. Nearly one-half of all grandmothers in the United States provide such help on a regular basis. The grandmother's role in providing child care as well as economic, social, and emotional support for her grandchildren is more active in many ethnic minority groups than among Whites. Black grandmothers, for example, are significant figures in the stability and continuity of the family. The involvement of Black grandmothers in single-mother families facilitates the mother's participation in self-improvement activities, increases the quality of child care, and reduces the negative effects of single parenting.

For some children, grandparents are part of the family household. The number of American children living in homes with a grandparent has risen from 2.2 million in 1970 to 3.9 million in 1998, including 12.3% of Black children, 6.5% of Latin American children, and 3.7% of White children. Some of the increase results from an uncertain economy and the growing number of single mothers, which has sent young adults and their children back to the parental nest. In other cases, elderly adults are moving in with their adult children's families when they can no longer live on their own. New immigrants with a tradition of multigenerational households also have swelled the number of such living arrangements. The arrangement benefits all parties. Grandparents and their grandchildren are able to interact on a daily basis, and grandparents may assume some parenting responsibilities.

Increasing numbers of grandparents now find themselves raising their grandchildren as their own. Of the nearly 4 million children in the United States living in a household with a grandparent, about one-third are being raised by the grandparents without a parent present. These "skip-generation parents" overwhelmingly are grandmothers. Reasons that grandparents become full-time caregivers for their grandchildren include parental child abuse or neglect, substance abuse, and psychological or financial problems. Another cause is the growth of AIDS cases among heterosexuals, whose parents care for their dying children and raise the grandchildren who are left behind.

The belief that caregiving grandmothers are primarily poor women of color is a myth. Parenting grandmothers can be found across racial and socioeconomic lines. More than two-thirds of U.S. grandparents raising grandchildren are White, nearly 30% are Black, and 10% are Latin American. Black women who are raising their grandchildren, compared to White women, report feeling less burdened and more satisfied in their caregiving role, even though they are generally in poorer health, dealing with more difficult situations, and dealing with them more often alone.

Rearing a grandchild is full of both rewards and challenges. While parenting a grandchild is an emotionally fulfilling experience, there are also psychological, health, and economic costs. A grandmother raising the young child of her drug-addicted adult daughter may concurrently feel delight with her grandchild, shame for her daughter, anxiety about her own future, health, and finances, anger at the loss of retirement leisure, and guilt for feeling angry. Grandparents raising grandchildren often are stymied by existing laws that give them no legal status unless they gain custody of the grandchild or become the child's foster parents. Each of these procedures involves considerable time, effort, and expense. Yet without custody or foster parent rights, grandparents may encounter difficulties such as obtaining the child's medical records or enrolling the child in school. In most instances, grandchildren are ineligible for coverage under grandparents' medical insurance, even if the grandparents have custody. [*See* FAMILY ROLES AND PATTERNS, CONTEMPORARY TRENDS.]

IX. *Labor Force Transitions*

Labor force participation of middle-aged and older women has increased sharply over the past four decades. Two-thirds of married women and nearly 70% of unmarried women age 45 to 64 now are in the U.S. labor force. During the same 40-year period, by contrast, men have been retiring earlier. By 1998, only 84% of 45- to 64-year-old married men were in the workforce, compared to 94% in 1960. As a consequence of these changes, which hold across all ethnic groups, the proportion of paid workers 45 and over who are women is higher than ever before.

Many midlife and older women have been employed throughout adulthood. For some working-class women, women of color, and single women, economic necessity has been the driving force. But for many women, a more typical pattern has been movement in and out of the labor force in response to changing family roles and responsibilities. Some women decide to reenter the labor force after their children are grown or following divorce or the death of their spouse.

Older women work for most of the same reasons as younger women. Economic necessity is a key factor at all ages. In addition, feeling challenged and productive and meeting new coworkers and friends give women a sense of personal satisfaction and recognition outside the family. Active involvement in work and outside interests in women's middle and later years appear to promote physical and psychological well-being. Work-centered women broaden their interests as they grow older and become more satisfied with their lives. Employed older women have higher morale than women retirees, whereas women who have never been employed outside the home have the lowest.

As women get older, they also confront age discrimination in the workplace. Because many women enter or reenter the workforce when they are older, they face age discrimination at the point of hiring more often than men do. While women's complaints filed with the Equal Employment Opportunity Commission primarily concern hiring, promotion, wages, and fringe benefits, men more often file on the basis of job termination and involuntary retirement. Women also experience age discrimination at a younger age than men. This is another example of the double standard of aging, with women seen as becoming older at an earlier age than men. Western society's emphasis on youthful sexual attractiveness for women, and the stereotype of older women as powerless, weak, sick, helpless, and unproductive, create obstacles for older women who are seeking employment or who wish to remain employed.

As retirement age approaches, women and men may differ in their readiness to retire. Compared to men, women arrive at the threshold of retirement with a different work and family history, less planning for retirement, and fewer financial resources. A man who has put in several decades in the workforce may be eager to retire once he meets Social Security or pension eligibility requirements. A woman, on the other hand, may have entered the labor force later, after children entered school or were launched. In addition to still being enthusiastic about her job, she may want to continue working in order to build up her pension and Social Security benefits. A growing number of women continue to work after their husbands retire. Women who did not work when their children were young, compared to those who did, are more likely to continue working after their husbands retire. Widowed and divorced women are more apt than married women to plan for postponed retirement or no retirement at all. In addition, women who have strong work identities have more negative attitudes toward retiring than those with weaker work identities. Professional women and those who are self-employed, who presumably have strong work identities, are less likely than other women to retire early. Older professional women often do not make systematic plans for their retirement, nor do they wish to do so.

While some women delay their retirement, others retire early. Poor health is one of the major determinants of early retirement. Since aging Black women and men tend to be in poorer health than aging Whites, they are likely to retire earlier. Women's role as primary caregiver to elderly parents, spouses, or other relatives is another factor contributing to their early retirement. Elder care responsibilities often result in increased tardiness and absenteeism at work, as well as health problems for the caregiver. Most businesses do not offer work flexibility or support to workers who care for elder relatives. As a result, nearly one-quarter of women caregivers reduce their hours or take time off without pay. Of those who continue to work, some are forced to retire earlier than planned. Women whose husbands are in poor health are more likely to retire than women whose husbands enjoy good health. Some women, of course, simply want to retire, whether to spend more time with a partner, family, or friends, to start one's own business, to pursue lifelong interests, or to develop new ones.

Both women and men typically adjust well to retirement, although women may take longer to get adjusted. For example, newly retired women report lower morale and greater depression than do newly retired men. Men seem to enjoy the freedom from work pressure when they retire, whereas women appear to experience the retirement transition as a loss

of roles. Because women are not under the same socially prescribed pressures to be employed as are men, those women who do work, whether out of financial need or commitment to their job, may find it more difficult to stop working.

X. Postscript

The midlife experiences discussed here must be placed in their historical and social context. As social constructions of gender have evolved over time, women have experienced differing perceptions of their own options. Women examined in the research reported here were in their middle adult years at the end of the 20th century. Consequently, the gender-based social climate that shaped their development was different from the societal attitudes influencing the lives of future generations of midlife women. For example, today's midlife women were exposed to traditional and flexible gender role expectations at different points of their lives. Thus, it is likely that they experienced more regrets about previous traditional choices than future generations of midlife women will, and perhaps more adjustments in their work roles. Because there are greater options for young women today than there were in the 1960s and 1970s when current midlife women were making life choices, it is possible that fewer young women today will find the need to make significant revisions in their paths during middle age. Today's elderly women also have experienced different constructions of women's roles than have current midlife women. Because they were in midlife prior to the major societal role changes discussed here, they did not experience the career and role opportunities encountered by today's midlife women, and consequently were not faced with decisions about major role changes.

A second cautionary note is that most of the research on women's midlife transitions has been done with White, highly educated, middle-class Western women. The midlife experiences of women of color, less educated women, poor women, and those in non-Western cultures have been almost completely unexplored. Large variations in the options available to these different groups of women can affect their aspirations and opportunities during both early adulthood and at midlife. For example, poor women may feel so constrained by poverty that significant change and growth at midlife appears outside the realm of possibility.

SUGGESTED READING

Daniluk, J. C. (1998). *Women's Sexuality across the Life Span: Challenging Myths, Creating Meanings.* Guilford, New York.

Doress-Worters, P. B., and Siegal, D. N. (1994). *The New Ourselves, Growing Older.* Simon & Schuster, New York.

Etaugh, C. A., and Bridges, J. S. (2001). *Psychology of Women: A Life Span Perspective.* Allyn & Bacon, Boston.

Friedan, B. (1993). *The Fountain of Age.* Simon & Schuster, New York.

Goldman, M. B., and Hatch, M. C. (eds.) (2000). *Women and Health.* Academic Press, New York.

Josselson, R. (1996). *Raising Herself: The Story of Women's Identity from College to Midlife.* Oxford, New York.

Mitchell, V., and Helson, R. (1990). Women's prime of life: Is it the 50s? *Psychology of Women Quarterly* **14,** 451–470.

Stewart, A. J. and Vandewater, E. A. (1999). "If I had it to do over again": Midlife review, midcourse corrections, and women's well-being in midlife. *Journal of Personality and Social Psychology* **76,** 270–283.

Willis, S. L., and Reid, J. D. (eds.) (1999). *Life in the Middle: Psychological and Social Development in Middle Age.* Academic Press, San Diego, CA.

Military Women

Janice D. Yoder

University of Akron

Glossary

Discrimination Overt and subtle negative acts that assert one group's superiority over another.

Gender integration The processes by which occupations, and jobs within an occupation, move toward an equal balance of women and men workers.

General accounting office The investigative arm of the U.S. Congress charged to oversee federal programs and operations.

Sexual harassment A form of sexual discrimination that involves deliberate or repeated unwelcome sexual advances, requests for sexual favors, and other verbal or physical conduct of a sexual nature.

Tokenism Negative consequences that accompany proportional underrepresentation in a group (operationalized as being a member of a subgroup comprising less than 15% of the whole).

U.S. Department of Defense (DoD) A branch of the U.S. government, headed by the secretary of defense and headquartered in the Pentagon, charged to protect the nation's security.

U.S. military academies Includes the U.S. Military Academy at West Point (New York) (Army), the U.S. Naval Academy at Annapolis (Maryland), the Air Force Academy (near Colorado Springs, Colorado), and the Coast Guard Academy (New London, CT); first admitted women in 1976 in compliance with Public Law 94-106.

WOMEN IN THE U.S. MILITARY have been studied by military psychologists and by gender psychologists. Military psychology is the study and application of psychological methods and principles to a military setting. For military psychologists, interest in women becomes a special topic within the broader domains of selection, classification and assignment, human factors, environmental factors, leadership, individual and group behavior, and clinical and consultative/organizational psychology in the military. Gender psychology explores how being female or male affects the life experiences of individuals. Gender psychologists are interested in the military to the extent that it provides a unique setting in which broader gender issues can be framed and studied. The present overview draws from both literatures to understand the experiences of women in the military. It is organized around topics identified by gender psychologists as important to understanding women in the workplace, including attitudes about women's roles in nontraditional occupations, work and family issues, gender integration of male-dominated environments, discrimination against women, and women's health care.

I. History and Current Participation

Before delving into each of these topics, it is instructive to understand the military context in the United States and the history of women's inclusion in it. Beginning in the American War for Independence, women were relied on primarily to provide nursing care. This role became formalized in World War I with the creation of the U.S. Army Nurse Corps in 1901 and the U.S. Navy Nurse Corps in 1908. Although nursing was the most visible role played by women, involving 34,000 nurses in World War I and 350,000 in World War II, historians documented the more informal participation of women in active combat, in artillery units, as disguised enlisted "men," in militia units, and in frontier warfare during the early years of U.S. history and as spies and scouts during the Civil War. These non-nursing roles expanded for women during World War II; for example, a group of 1074 women pilots ferried aircraft and instructed Air Force pilots. As surgical units became more mobile and women's roles expanded, they were increasingly exposed to combat. A 1998 study estimated that 7.4% of women veterans from World War II and the Korean and Vietnam conflicts were exposed to combat, 73.5% as nurses.

A watershed for women's expanding participation in the military was the implementation of the all-volunteer force in 1973 at the end of the Vietnam conflict. In 1967 the 2% ceiling on women's enlistment was lifted, and in 1974, all occupational specialties were opened to women, except those directly related to combat. Beginning in 1975, pregnant women had the option to remain on active duty during and after a pregnancy. The service academies were open to women in 1976; the women's corps was integrated into the regular organizations with men in 1978; and effective in 1980, officer promotion lists were integrated. Throughout the 1970s and 1980s, women moved toward more equal access to health care, training, higher education through the military, and veterans' benefits. A fivefold increase in the number of active duty women occurred between 1973 and the end of the 1980s, expanding women's participation to 10.8% of the military and ranking the United States first in the world for its representation of women. Despite these gains, there also was a backlash in the 1980s against women's participation, during which the Army instituted an official "pause" in recruiting women. Twenty-three occupational specialties were reclassified as combat related and closed to women, and other specialties were made off limits to women ostensibly because of heavy physical demands. Debate about women shifted from emphasizing equal opportunity to increasingly discussing military readiness and effectiveness, which some argued were jeopardized by the inclusion of women.

In 1990, intensive news reporting gave North Americans their first highly visible glimpse of women being deployed to a war zone in the Persian Gulf. Some of these 40,782 women (7.2% of the total force) were shown performing a wide array of military jobs, carrying arms, and being exposed to the dangers of combat. Military policy requiring mothers and single fathers to formally arrange alternative care for their children in case of rapid deployment was put to the test, and the media showcased stories of parents, mostly mothers, separated from their children. Thirteen women died; two became prisoners of war.

These events renewed debate about the combat exclusion policy. In 1988, the Department of Defense's risk rule was revamped with the goals of narrowing and standardizing each service's interpretation of combat. Gradually through the early 1990s, women's exclusion was chipped away. In 1992, service in combat aircraft was open to women. In 1993, the Navy developed a legislative proposal to permit the assignment of women to combatant ships, and in 1994, the *USS Eisenhower* became the first combatant ship to carry an integrated crew. Most important, in 1994, the Department of Defense (DoD) risk rule was rescinded and was replaced by a directive from the U.S. secretary of defense that excluded only assignments to below the administratively broad brigade level with the primary mission of ground combat. Other permissible exclusions involved units and positions required to physically collocate with direct ground combat units, prohibitive costs of providing living space for women, units engaged in special operations missions, or job-related physical requirements that exclude the vast majority of women. (No jobs are currently closed for this last reason.) These changes opened up 32,699 new positions to women, mostly in the Marine Corps. All units and positions in the Army became accessible to women except direct ground support and support units physically collocated with them. Overall, women were eligible to serve in over 80% of all military jobs. In sum, the United States inched toward elimination of all combat exclusion, coming closer to joining the ranks of countries without such restrictions (Canada, Denmark, Norway, and Belgium).

As of January 31, 2000, women composed 14.4% of the U.S. military. Women served as 14.27% of all officers and 14.4% of all enlisted personnel, and they were severely underrepresented in the Marine Corps (5.9%) (see Table I). The majority of women were White (53.7%), with 31.9% African American and 7.6% Hispanic women. The United States retained its top ranking with the highest female representation in the world, followed by Canada and Israel, each with 11%, and the United Kingdom with 6%.

The preceding overview provides a rudimentary review of the history of women's roles in the U.S. military and of the present context in which military women serve. The remainder of this article focuses on five topical areas identified by gender psychologists as central to our understanding of women and work: attitudes about women's roles in nontraditional occupations, work and family issues, gender integration of male-dominated settings, discrimination against women (including promotion patterns, sexual harassment, and sexual orientation policy), and women's health care.

II. Attitudes about Military Women

Scholarly surveys of the public's attitudes about women in the military are scarce. The General Social Survey (GSS) conducted by the National Opinion Research Center, one of the most prominent surveys of U.S. attitudes now conducted biannually, last queried respondents about women's roles in the military in 1982. A less rigorous but more recent survey by the Roper organization was fielded in July 1992 to explore popular attitudes about women in combat; these findings appear below in italics.

Although majority support for all roles except ground combat (35%) indicated general public approval of military women, patterns within roles closely paralleled gender stereotypes. Public support was near universal for military women in traditional roles: typist (97%) and combat nurse (93%). Support dropped somewhat for women in nontraditional roles (mechanic, 83%, and air transport, 73%) and declined even more precipitously for high-prestige (base commander, 58%) and combat roles (fighter pilot, 62% [69%]; missile gunner, 59% [58%]; fighting ship, 57% [69%], and ground combat, 35% [38%]). These population attitudes were echoed in a 1994 report of college women's attitudes during the Persian Gulf War. Although these respondents strongly endorsed the comparable capacities and equivalent effectiveness of women and men in the military, less favorable attitudes emerged when

Table I
Active Duty Military Personnel as of January 31, 2000

	Total	Army	Navy	Marine Corps	Air Force
Total personnel	1,355,523	468,718	363,342	171,612	351,851
Women	194,605	70,269	48,989	10,167	65,180
Percent women	14.4%	15.0%	13.5%	5.9%	18.5%
Percent minority women	46.3%	57.5%	45.2%	43.1%	35.6%
Officers					
Total officers	216,533	76,928	52,993	17,879	68,733
Women	30,656	10,502	7,647	905	11,602
Percent women	14.2%	13.7%	14.4%	5.1%	16.9%
Percent minority women	25.9%	33.4%	22.3%	24.3%	21.8%
Enlisted					
Total enlisted	1,138,990	391,790	310,349	153,733	283,118
Women	163,949	59,767	41,342	9,262	53,578
Percent women	14.4%	15.3%	13.3%	6.0%	18.9%
Percent minority women	50.1%	61.7%	49.4%	44.9%	38.6%

issues of combat and women's roles as wives and mothers were considered.

Closely related to attitudes about women in combat roles are respondents' perceptions of the impact of women on military effectiveness. Data from the 1982 GSS demonstrated that most Americans felt that the inclusion of women had raised the effectiveness of the military (22.4%) or made no difference (68.7%). These favorable sentiments about military readiness were shared by military personnel themselves. In a 1999 survey reported by the General Accounting Office, the majority of military women and men attested to personal readiness, physical and training preparedness, and their willingness to deploy to a war zone. Although women's attitudes about their own preparedness and their impact were more favorable than men's attitudes about women, a majority of military men indicated that women affected military readiness in either a positive way or not at all.

In sum, attitudes about military women reflect patterns common to gender stereotypes in that the more nontraditional the role, the more dissent. However, like gender attitudes in general, overall support for military women engaged in a wide array of roles is remarkably favorable. [*See* WOMEN IN NONTRADITIONAL WORK FIELDS.]

III. Work and Family Issues

Much of the research that has focused on work and family issues for military women has concentrated on the simple access of married women and mothers to service. Unlike the civilian workplace, women were openly denied admission to military service by virtue of their family status. When the Army Nurse Corps was formed in 1901, it expressly prohibited nurses from marrying or being mothers. Barriers to marriage fell first and most completely, with married women serving in World War II and with marriage forming a basis for *voluntary* discharge through the late 1970s. Today, marriage is not a legitimate basis for separation in any of the services. In 1973, only 18% of enlisted women were married (compared to 52% of the men), but this figure jumped to 47% by 1991 (56% for men), virtually closing the gendered marriage gap.

Questions raised about the compatibility of military service with pregnancy and motherhood have been more difficult to resolve. Lawsuits chipped away at mandatory separation policies for pregnancy in the early 1970s, ultimately leading to a 1975 Department of Defense directive discontinuing involuntary discharges and instituting an optional separation policy initiated by the woman. Since then, military policy has fluctuated between guaranteed separation on request and separation only if conditions warrant and obligation are met. At present, both the Army and Air Force give discharge authority to the installation where the solider is assigned. All services involuntarily terminate women found to be pregnant during basic training.

Combining motherhood with military service affects a growing proportion of military women. Although mothers compose a small percentage of the total active duty force (about 5%), they represent a significant percentage of military women. Demographic information published about Navy personnel in 1993 revealed that 34% of Navy women were mothers whose children live with them (mean number of children, 1.6). These mothers were about equally divided as single (32%), with a civilian spouse (32%), and with a military spouse (37%), in contrast to military fathers who largely were married to a civilian spouse (91%; 6% were single and 3% were part of a dual-military family). These patterns make dual-military assignments and parental arrangements important issues for a disproportionate number of military women and a proportionally small but numerically sizable group of men.

Women-friendly policies and provisions are developing slowly and being expanded to encompass men. A landmark 1973 Supreme Court decision decreed that military women were entitled to the same benefits for their dependents as military men. Presently, most bases and posts include family-friendly support services, such as commissaries and exchanges, medical services for dependents, family housing, child development centers including infancy care, family service centers, and after-school and youth programs. Each of the services requires single and dual-military parents to file a dependent care certificate that outlines plans for the care of children in case of parental deployment. The adequacy of these plans was tested during the Gulf War when child care problems interfered with the deployment of only 4 of the more than 21,000 naval reservists called to active duty and less than 0.1% of Army personnel. Postwar policy now allows new mothers and single parents who recently acquired custody to defer service for four months.

Despite policy and provisions to facilitate the blending of military service with family demands, mothers appear to be separated more frequently than are fathers for reasons related to dependents. For example, a 1990 review of separations from the Navy showed that 0.91% of mothers and 0.05% of fathers were discharged for parenthood. This gap is likely inflated by the disproportionate involvement of military women in dual-military marriages relative to men, noted earlier, and the tendency for more women to leave the military in the face of a geographic separation from their military spouse. None of the services provides for dual-career assignments.

Two outcomes often cited as related to work–family conflict for women in the gender literature, absenteeism and retention, have been explored in military settings. First, a study of 2285 enlisted women and 3104 men on active duty in the Navy, published in 1994, concluded that the amount of time lost from the job did not differ for women and men, even when pregnancy and postpartum convalescence leave were included. Because the proportions of personnel affected by pregnancy and new motherhood were nominal at most sites, pregnancy had little impact on command effectiveness and staffing, except in designated locations that received pregnant women moved off ships.

Second, a study of retention, published in 1998 and sampling 638 women from a database containing all women who either served in the Air Force on active duty or were active members of the guard or reserve during the Gulf War, examined differences between leavers and stayers two years after the war. Several unexpected contrasts were found. Of the 81% who stayed in the military, their rate of activation was significantly higher than that of those who left. Retainees had more dependent children and reported more disruptions in their children's lives. Although deployment, even if disruptive, did not predict nonretention, child care provisions, new motherhood, and dual-military partnerships did. Attrition rates were above the norm among deployed women who left their children in the care of ex-spouses (38.5%), among women who had a baby during or since the war (31%), and among women with an active duty partner (22%).

In conclusion, there are both commonalties and differences in the family–work experiences of military and civilian women. Unlike civilian settings, the military has unabashedly considered the marital, pregnancy, and parental status of women in recruitment and retention. Also unlike much of the civilian sector, the military itself is routinely providing some family-friendly facilities. Like the civilian workplace,

issues of relocation, dual-career accommodations, and child care arrangements (although these needs can be more long-term in the military with the prospect of deployment) remain unresolved and indeed do affect women's participation. Further research in each of these areas is warranted.

IV. Gender Integration

The proportion of women involved in both the civilian and military workforces across the past 30 years has grown remarkably. However, the military has led the way in the genuine integration of women across jobs. For example, a 1986 study using data from the National Longitudinal Survey of Youth Labor Market Behavior found that 34% of women in the military, but only 3% of women in the civilian sector, held jobs in which 90% or more of civilian workers were male. Conversely, 28% of civilian and only 3% of military workers worked jobs that in the civilian sector were composed of 90% or more women. In other words, military women were more likely to do jobs stereotypically regarded as masculine and less likely to do traditionally feminine jobs than civilian women.

Looking within the military itself, women tend to cluster into traditional occupational classifications. According to a General Accounting Office (GAO) report, enlisted women in 1998 served predominantly in functional support and administration including personnel, recruiting and counseling, law, supply administration, auditing and accounting, and general administration. The second largest concentration of enlisted women was in medical and dental specialties. Over 40% of women officers worked in health care occupations, with administration taking second place. Comparing job patterns in 1990 to those in 1998, the GAO concluded that although a large percentage of women continued to cluster into more traditional jobs, women were making substantial inroads into more nontraditional fields such as aviation, surface warfare, air traffic control, and field artillery.

The GAO cited two institutional barriers that inhibited the full integration of military women. The combat exclusion policy continues to bar women from some units even though some jobs contained within them are open to women. For example, the Navy limits the number of women who can pursue medical corps training because the Navy supplies these personnel to Marine Corps units that exclude women. Similarly, the Marine Corps restricts women from serving as helicopter crew chiefs because these jobs often require assignment to Navy ships, some of which do not have facilities to accommodate women at this time. Second, use of the Armed Services Vocational Aptitude Battery to determine assignments for new recruits contains sections that measure exposure rather than aptitude and thus may disadvantage women whose typical background with traditionally male experiences is oftentimes limited. Revisions of this test are in progress.

Access to gender atypical work is just the first step toward understanding gender integration. A complete analysis calls for studies of what happens when women assume masculine jobs and research that draws on a variety of methodologies including large-scale surveys and more personalized, systematically collected ethnographies. Despite an abundance of opportunities to study jobs that have been newly open to women, the *process* of gender integration in military settings has been sorrowfully understudied. Judith Stiehm has studied gender integration involving enlisted women and women cadets at the U.S. Air Force Academy. Lois DeFleur published a brief glimpse of gender integration across four years at the Air Force Academy. Project Athena, involving Jerome Adams, Robert Priest, and others, closely monitored the first coeducational classes at the U.S. Military Academy at West Point, and the General Accounting Office (GAO) released a 1999 followup report of gender integration at West Point.

Looking across these studies, patterns emerge that fit well with Rosabeth Moss Kanter's descriptions of proportional underrepresentation ("tokenism") and its consequences. The three military academies were first open to women in 1976, and since then, each has matriculated 10 to 15% women in subsequent classes. Across these studies, there is no clear evidence of performance decrements for women. For example, the GAO's data show that women cadets at West Point in the classes of 1988 through 1992 outscored male cadets on 13 indicators of academic performance (which heavily weighted math and science), were outscored on 25 measures, and tied on 2. Gender differences were widest during the first two academic years, then closed and sometimes reversed for upperclass cadets. A similar pattern was found for military development grades, favoring women on 10 and men on 24 indicators (with a significant difference appearing in only one year). In contrast, physical education scores (scaled to accommodate physiological sex differences, which include both lower and higher requirements for women) favored women 4 to 1. These variable data hardly indite women's abilities to do the job.

Rather, clear and consistent patterns surface across these studies that paint markedly different pictures of the contexts experienced by women and men who are coexisting in the same setting. Unlike men, accounts of newly admitted women's experiences included intense and undiminished media attention, contending with men's fears that women will benefit from preferential treatment, stresses and performance pressures, social isolation, and feelings of less peer acceptance. Women struggled with overprotection and marginalization, and they grappled with the disjunction between gendered expectations and the masculinized demands of their work, such that women's leadership abilities were evaluated less favorably by others. For example, in the more recent study of West Point cadets, women were selected for top leadership positions at lower rates than men in fully seven of eight semesters. Across all studies, women's attrition rates were significantly higher than those for men.

These findings of heightened visibility, marginalization, and role deviance are consistent with what has been documented across a wide range of male-dominated civilian occupations by tokenism researchers. The convergence of Project Athena data with the more recent information about West Point collected by the GAO suggests that tokenism effects persist from initial integration through 16 years, at least when gender ratios remain stable. Although tokenism theorists advocate for increasing the representation of women as a means for reducing negative tokenism effects, research in civilian settings suggests that this strategy can open up new and different problems, such as enhanced boundary tightening and exclusion. Other approaches to confronting tokenism, such as organizational legitimatization of women and mentoring, could be tested productively in military settings by future researchers.

V. Gender Discrimination

As in the civilian sector, gender discrimination is exceedingly difficult to document, appearing more readily in the aggregate than at an individual level. Three areas of potential gender discrimination toward military women have been explored involving promotions, sexual harassment, and the blatant exclusion of lesbians.

A. PROMOTION PERCEPTIONS AND PATTERNS

In a review of research on service members' perceptions of gender inequities, the General Accounting Office concluded in 1998 that some inequities were believed to exist, especially regarding local assignment policies and practices established by unit commanders. For example, some women reported being assigned to clerical and administrative duties rather than to the nontraditional specialties for which they were trained. Some women felt that prerequisite requirements were designed illegitimately to limit the positions open to them, and both some women and some men believed that the combat exclusion policy unnecessarily limited women's opportunities for advancement.

Aggregate data on promotion patterns for 1993 through 1997 collected by the General Accounting Office did not substantiate these perceptions at the broader level of the military as a whole, but some exceptions were evident within branches. Across the services, promotion of officers is conducted by centralized boards, and enlisted personnel are advanced through examination or board recommendations. Rates for women's and men's promotion were similar in 82% of the boards and examinations reviewed, with 15% of the remainder favoring women and 3% preferring men. Only the Army exhibited more significant differences advantaging men. Looking at professional military education selection, routinely conducted by boards, comparable rates occurred 46% of the time, with 29% of the remainder favoring women and 25% preferring men. Within services, the Army and Navy tended to favor men; the Air Force and Marines, women. For key military assignments, the Marine Corps and Navy rely on centralized boards; the Army and Air Force on decentralized boards. Across all services, 53% of selections showed similar rates for women and men, with the remaining 15% preferring women and 32% favoring men. The Air Force and Navy had more significant differences that advantaged men; the Army slightly favored women; and no significant differences in assignment rates were found in the Marine Corps. In sum, the aggregated promotion data at a military-wide level did not document clear patterns and practices of gender discrimination, at least within broad categories of promotion. However, more detailed analyses might probe for promotion to the most prestigious ranks of enlisted and officer assignments. (For example, in 2000, only 12 of the Navy's 220 admirals were women.)

More consistent suggestions of gender inequities emerge from analyses of the promotion materials submitted on behalf of women and men. A series of studies, conducted by the Department of Defense throughout the 1980s and 1990s, and summarized by the General Accounting Office in 1995, questioned the gender-neutrality of performance appraisals. For example, a 1994 analysis found that women's fitness reports contained significantly more references to personality traits and that women were devalued as leaders. Two 1983 experiments presented raters with masculinized and feminized narratives and found that promotion choices favored men and masculine evaluations of women. These findings are consistent with research on hiring biases for civilian workers. Most troubling was a 1993 exploration by the Army Research Institute of the reasons why promotable women leave the Army. These researchers concluded that in addition to career opportunities, family issues, and monetary issues, promotable women identified treatment and equal opportunity issues, gender-based discrimination, and sexual harassment and the Army's response to it as reasons for their attrition.

Paralleling the civilian workforce, women's perceptions of gender inequities can be contradicted by global promotion patterns, at least using broad clusters of job categories and by avoiding the top tiers of the hierarchy. More subtle indicators of biases in promotion, as found in informal performance appraisals and exit interviews, prove more consistent with women's perceptions, suggesting that gender discrimination remains but at a more elusive, covert level. [*See* CAREER ACHIEVEMENT.]

B. SEXUAL HARASSMENT

Department of Defense policies prohibiting discrimination based on race, color, and religion first appeared in the 1940s, but sex discrimination did not make its way into these policies until 1970. Sexual harassment per se was not addressed until 1979, reflecting Equal Employment Opportunity Commission (EEOC) guidelines for civilian employees: "Sexual harassment is a form of sexual discrimination that involves deliberate or repeated unwelcome sexual advances, requests for sexual favors, and other verbal or physical conduct of a sexual nature." The first military-wide sexual harassment survey was conducted in 1988, modeling the surveys of federal workers developed by the U.S. Merit Systems Protection Board, which had identified 10 behavioral indicators of sexual harassment. Reported sexual harassment was found to be more widespread among military (64%) than federal (42%) women.

The turning point in this research area occurred in 1991 with the highly publicized coverage of the sexual abuse and harassment of 83 women by naval aviators during the Tailhook Association convention in Las Vegas. This incident sparked military interest in a followup survey to the 1988 report, resulting in a 1995 survey of 22,372 women and 5924 men. About 69% of respondents were enlisted personnel, 29% were commissioned officers, and 2% were warrant officers, proportionally representing the four service branches and the Coast Guard. The majority of the sample was non-Hispanic White (63%), and it encompassed 24% non-Hispanic Blacks, 8% Hispanics, and 5% Asian, Pacific Islander, American Indian, or Native Alaskan participants. The mean age of respondents was 32 years with approximately 10 years of military service.

The survey contained three parts: (1) a replication of the 1988 behavioral indices of sexual harassment; (2) the Sexual Experiences Questionnaire (SEQ), developed by Louise Fitzgerald and her colleagues and modified to be relevant to the military context, which includes 24 behavioral indicators and a write-in "other" item; and (3) potential correlates, including measures of physical health and psychological well-being, workplace characteristics and attitudes (job satisfaction, work productivity, and commitment to the military), and detailed questions probing an incident chosen by the respondent to represent the "situation that had the greatest effect" on her or him. Results of this survey were reported in Department of Defense publications and in a special issue of the journal *Military Psychology* edited by Fritz Drasgow.

Direct comparisons of responses from 1988 to 1995 suggested declines in overall incidence rates, from 64% to 55% of women and from 17% to 14% of men. However, such optimism is mitigated by the more comprehensive measures of sexual harassment using the SEQ. Only 24% of women and fully 64% of men reported no experiences with sexual harassment during the past 12 months of their military service. Independent research in 1991 with women cadets at the military academies estimated almost universal incidence rates of 93 to 97%. Sexual harassment clearly continues to be problematic throughout the military.

The second and third parts of the 1995 military-wide survey allowed for a more in-depth exploration of sexual harassment beyond simple incidence rates.

The SEQ assessed four types of sexual harassment: gender harassment involving sexist hostility (e.g., "Put you down or was condescending to you because of your sex"), gender harassment involving sexual hostility (e.g., "Stared, leered, or ogled you in a way that made you feel uncomfortable"), unwanted sexual attention (e.g., "Made unwanted attempts to establish a romantic sexual relationship with you despite your efforts to discourage it"), and sexual coercion (e.g., "Made you afraid you would be treated poorly if you didn't cooperate sexually"). Table II presents the types of harassment reported by women and men. Almost all incidents of sexual harassment reported by men involved the two forms of gender harassment. Gender harassment also dominated women's responses, but it combined with unwanted sexual attention for one of every four women. Sexual coercion affected more women than men and always in combination with the other three types of harassment for both sexes.

Variations in reporting rates emerged by race/ethnicity, service branch, and personnel category. Native American women reported the highest incidence across all four types of harassment, followed by Hispanic women overall and African American women for sexual coercion. Asian American women described the lowest incidence, and White women fell in between. Women Marines reported the most harassment, being tied by Army women for sexual coercion. Army women generally came in second, with Air Force and Coast Guard women reporting the least harassment. Enlisted personnel were more

Table II

Types of Sexual Harassment Identified by the Sexual Experiences Questionnaire in 1995

Types of harassment	Incidence rates	
	Women (%)	Men (%)
No experiences	24	64
Sexist hostility only	8	2
Sexual hostility only	8	18
Sexist and sexual	24	9
Unwanted sexual attention only	1	
Sexist and attention	1	
Sexual and attention	4	3
Sexist, sexual and attention	21	3
All four types	9	1

likely to check off each type of harassment than officers, with the most noteworthy difference appearing for sexual coercion (14% among enlisted; 3% among officers).

Exploring details about the incident selected as most influential by each respondent, 91.91% of the women identified a male perpetrator, 1.6% a female, and 6.49% referred to both sexes. For men, a majority (52.34%) implicated another man, 32% a woman, and 15.66% both. Men infrequently reported unwanted sexual attention and sexual coercion, and it was with these forms of harassment that they most typically implicated a female (i.e., heterosexual) offender. Men were usually victimized by both forms of gender harassment, such as exposure to sexually suggestive materials, offensive stories or jokes, and sexist remarks; the perpetrators of these offenses were more commonly men.

Repeating a pattern often found with civilian respondents, sexually harassing behaviors were not always acknowledged by their targets as harassing. Of those who checked at least one item of the SEQ and thus indicated that behaviorally they had been the target of sexual harassment, 33% of the women and fully 76% of the men reported that they had not been sexually harassed.

Finally, the 1995 survey included questions hypothesized to correlate with experiences of sexual harassment. Harassment was related to negative job attitudes, jeopardized psychological well-being, and reduced health satisfaction, even after controlling for job effects. Negative psychosocial reactions to harassment included productivity problems, unfavorable attitudes toward the military, emotional distress, and disrupted relations with family. Harassment was found to occur less frequently in gender-balanced work groups and in settings where personnel believed that the organization's upper echelons would not tolerate such behavior. Exploring this last finding in more detail, perceptions about enforcement were most important. Of the military's efforts to implement practices to respond effectively to harassment, provide resources like counseling for targets, and train its personnel about harassment, only perceived implementation was related to reduced incidence of harassment, especially for women. Additionally, a lack of perceived organizational implementation directly contributed to negative job-related outcomes for targets beyond the effects of experiencing the harassment itself. Specifically, targets who felt that the military did little to respond to charges of harassment suffered reduced commitment to the military, work dissatisfaction, and dissatisfaction with supervisors.

The military has taken the lead in systematically and comprehensively studying sexual harassment. This work has moved this research area beyond the simple behavioral indicators of 1980s studies to define harassment and explore its correlates in a nuanced, sensitive way. The resulting data clearly highlight the proactive role an organization can shoulder to minimize harassment in the workplace. Nowhere is such a top-down approach to being intolerant of harassment more likely to find a better testing ground than in the unambiguously hierarchical military. [*See* SEXUAL HARASSMENT.]

C. DISCRIMINATION AGAINST LESBIANS

The military's formal policy surrounding gays in the military is rooted in the 1919 Articles of War, which banned sodomy. When psychological screening became part of military selection in the 1940s, U.S. psychiatry's emerging views about homosexuality as pathological shifted the military's focus from homosexual acts to homosexual persons. Pressing needs for recruits during the war loosened screening procedures but these tightened again with the end of the war, resulting in the involuntary discharge and stigmatization of some veterans. Throughout the 1950s and 1960s, open acknowledgment of a gay orientation barred an individual from military service. Unsuccessful legal challenges to this policy characterized the 1970s, and considerable discretion about inclusion by local commanders produced widely divergent practices throughout the military. Desiring uniformity, a revised policy was delineated in 1982 stating that "Homosexuality is incompatible with military service. The presence in the military environment of persons who engage in homosexual conduct or who, by their statements, demonstrate a propensity to engage in homosexual conduct, seriously impairs the accomplishment of the military mission."

During the 1980s, the military discharged 16,919 women and men under the separation category of homosexuality, with White women being terminated at a disproportionately high rate. Although White women composed only 6.4% of military personnel, they accounted for fully 20.2% of those discharged for homosexuality. The Navy was the most active, accounting for only 27% of the active force but fully 51% of all discharges of women and men. Discharge rates for purported lesbianism were out of proportion in the Marine Corps where 28% of discharges involved women who composed just 5% of the corps. Also symptomatic of this decade were virulent witch-hunts. For example, the Marine Corps investigated 65 drill instructors at Parris Island. The Navy attempted to discharge 19 of the 61 women, including all eight African American women, aboard the *USS Norton Sound* (actually discharging two). At West Point, the Army discharged eight military police officers and investigated its women's softball team. The Air Force followed suit and scrutinized its women's volleyball team.

In 1993, President Clinton followed up on a campaign promise to lift the ban, which can be done by executive order, but heated debate raged in Congress resulting in the current "Don't Ask, Don't Tell" policy. The policy encompassed four components. First, it differentiated between homosexual acts and an "abstract desire" or orientation toward homosexuality. Second, it removed questions about sexual orientation from enlistment. Third, it allowed association with gays and lesbians so long as the individual did not share their propensity. Fourth, it reinstated discretion for commanding officers.

Critics argue that the military's position regarding homosexuality is inextricably linked with its policies regarding women in general. Lesbians are directly affected by it, being forced to either abandon military prospects or keep closeted. Beyond the obvious, the ban indirectly challenges the simple presence of women in the military. Most rationales against the full inclusion of gays concentrate on gay men and their presumed disruption of unit cohesiveness. Ultimately these fears boil down to concerns about the demasculinizing of the military, a fear that is fed by the inclusion of women as well as gay men. It seems as though gay men (and all women) challenge the masculinity of the military.

Discrimination against lesbians threatens all women with charges of, and ultimately dismissal for, homosexuality. This threat is not idle in practice. Although women represented only 10% of military personnel in 1992, they accounted for fully 23% of discharges for homosexuality. Beyond being a tool for gender discrimination, the continuation of the ban on being openly gay in the military sets up a dilemma for all women: be too masculine and risk being branded as lesbian; be too feminine and risk being regarded as incompetent in a male-valued world. The pressure on women to carefully strike a balance between these two extremes has been documented by Melissa Herbert. Thus, ironically, it may

be the ban itself that threatens unit effectiveness by undermining women's unfettered participation.

On March 24, 2000, the Department of Defense Inspector General's office released a survey of 71,000 service members that put these issues back in the public spotlight. More than 80% of those surveyed reported that they had heard derogatory names, jokes or remarks regarding homosexuals in the past year. Fully 85% believed that other service members as well as military leaders tolerated such offensive language. Furthermore, 37% said that they personally experienced or witnessed homophobic harassment, most frequently in the form of offensive speech (88%) and less frequently as hostile gestures (34.7%), threats or intimidation (19.8%), graffiti (15.2%), vandalism of a service member's property (7.6%), physical assault (9%), limiting or denying training or career opportunities (8.9%), and disciplinary actions or punishments (9.5%). Coworkers were identified as the most frequent sources of harassment (by 61% of those reporting exposure), followed by immediate supervisors (11.1%). Finally, 5% of all respondents surveyed felt that the chain of command tolerated such overt harassment.

As with sexual harassment, the most recent military survey regarding discrimination against gay men and lesbians challenges the chain of command to take decisive action. In all three areas of gender discrimination explored here, the military has the opportunity to assume a leadership role in moving toward positive social innovation. The inclusion of social scientists, both military and civilian, in its examination of sexual harassment reflects a productive step toward gender equity and toward further collaboration between military and gender psychologists.

VI. Women's Health Care

Interest in women's health care in the military has concentrated on utilization patterns, physical training, and substance use. Studies of physical health care utilization with civilian samples consistently find that women's usage exceeds men's, and the same pattern is confirmed in the military. For example, in a sample of women on active duty or as active members of the guard or reserve forces during the Persian Gulf War, 76% used military health care services for the treatment of gender-specific health problems. Similarly, an analysis of 20 ships' sick-call logs during June 1989 revealed that the age-adjusted visit ratio for women to men was 1.44:1; excluding female-specific visits, the ratio remained unbalanced at 1.21:1. Removing women-specific reasons, illness accounted for the gender difference in visits; there were no gender differences for injury or general health services.

Looking within naval women's data, significantly higher sick-call visits occurred for women in nontraditional as compared to traditional occupations. Much of this difference (44%) was accounted for by injury, followed by nervous and sensory organ disorders (17%), including migraines, disorders of the external ear, and inflammation of the eye or eyelid. Skin disorders (13%), mental disorders (10%) involving mostly tension headaches and psychological counseling, and neoplasms (5%) made up the remaining major contributors. Mental and physical health psychologists could add to our understanding of these patterns.

Meeting physical standards has long been a hallmark of military life. The military distinguishes between two types of physical requirements: job specific (applicable to particular tasks) and general physical fitness (with the purpose of maintaining overall health and conditioning). General fitness requirements apply to all military personnel regardless of age or duty assignment and concentrate on cardiovascular endurance, muscular strength and endurance, and maintenance of body fat within a specified range. Each of the four services designs its own programs and standards, resulting in a hodgepodge of criteria and measures.

A 1998 report by the General Accounting Office concluded that inconsistent and sometimes arbitrary standards created potential gender inequities. For example, in contrast to male standards, which routinely were calibrated with actual performance data, women's criteria were often subjectively estimated, extrapolated from male standards, or based on command judgment. Body fat measures, which ignored racial differences in bone density, have been criticized for overstating the body fat of minority personnel. Furthermore, a 1998 National Academy of Sciences report suggested that setting a high body fat limit for women selects strong women who lack endurance; alternatively, establishing a low body fat standard values endurance over strength. A 1991 study of cadets at the military academies concluded that women's fitness performances from 1977 to 1987 showed greater improvement over time both for individual women compared to individual men and across later versus earlier cohorts. In sum, the work of establishing gender-fair fitness measures and

standards as well as programs to help military women meet these standards through lifestyle changes and without disordered eating could benefit from the expertise of health psychologists.

Turning to stress and substance use, a 1995 Department of Defense survey of health behaviors of more than 16,000 military personnel disclosed that military women (5.3%) reported drinking less heavily in the past month than men (18.8%), but had similar rates of illicit drug use in the past year (5.3% for women and 6.7% for men) and cigarette smoking in the past month (26.3% for women and 32.7% for men). The amount of stress associated with being a woman in the military was predictive of both illicit drug and cigarette use. Unlike men, stress at work or in the family was not associated with substance use among women. Again, further research and interventions designed by physical and mental health professionals appear warranted.

VII. Conclusions

Research with women in the military necessarily reflects the uniqueness of the military context, yet many of the general patterns we have explored here are consistent with, and oftentimes extend, research conducted with employed women in civilian settings. Public attitudes about the work roles open to military women are congruent with general popular support for women in a myriad of male-dominated jobs and occupations. Work and family issues continue to challenge civilian and military women, men, and their employers, raising concerns about relocation, dual-career accommodations, and child care arrangements. The military, which has a long, accepted, and indeed expected history of providing benefits for the dependents of its employees, is poised to make a real difference for working mothers and fathers by expanding family-supportive facilities and policies.

Although the civilian workplace remains largely gender segregated, there are few remaining barriers to women's pioneering inclusion in jobs and occupations. As combat restrictions continue to fall and jobs held exclusively by men open up to women, the possibilities for social scientific research are invaluable to military and gender researchers alike. It is incumbent on these researchers to regard gender integration as more than simple access and to study the full, day-to-day processes of integration. The military also offers a lucrative setting for piloting interventions to facilitate women's genuine integration.

Questions have been raised in the military about the existence of gender discrimination involving promotional glass ceilings and concrete walls, sexual harassment, and the exclusion of gay men and lesbians. Nowhere is the productivity of cooperation between military and gender researchers clearer than with their joint efforts to study sexual harassment. Finally, the involvement of mental and physical health psychologists could contribute more to our understanding of health utilization, physical training, and substance use.

The present integration of research, guided by gender psychologists interested in women and work but most often conducted by military psychologists and government research bodies, was hampered by the tendencies of the two fields to work separately and to publish to different audiences. The most noteworthy exception to this general pattern involved research on sexual harassment. In this area, the expertise of gender psychologists Louise Fitzgerald and her colleagues combined with knowledge of the mil-itary context to yield data of interest to military and gender psychologists alike. Our richer understanding of the lives, goals, needs, and successes of military women would be enhanced by further collaboration along these lines.

SUGGESTED READINGS

Drasgow, F. (ed.) (1999). Sexual harassment. Special issue of *Military Psychology* **11**(3).

Hoiberg, A. (1991). Military psychology and women's role in the military. In *Handbook of Military Psychology* (R. Gal and A. D. Mangelsdorff, ed.), pp. 725–739. Wiley, New York.

Thomas, P. J., and Thomas, M. D. (1993). Mothers in uniform. In *The Military Family in Peace and War* (F. W. Kaslow, ed), pp. 25–47. Springer, New York.

Thomas, P. J., and Thomas, M. D. (1996). Integration of women in the military: Parallels to the progress of homosexuals? In *Out in Force: Sexual Orientation in the Military* (G. M. Herek, J. B. Jobe, and R. M. Carney, eds.), pp. 65–85. University of Chicago Press, Chicago.

Yoder, J. D., Adams, J., and Prince, H. T. (1983). The price of a token. *Journal of Political and Military Sociology* **11**(2), 325–337.

Motherhood: Its Changing Face

Paula J. Caplan

Brown University

Glossary

Matrophobia Fear or hatred of mothers.

Momism (1) In the mid-20th century, the notion purveyed by Philip Wylie in *Generation of Vipers* that mothers were excessively controlling of and dominating over their children. (2) Paula J. Caplan's use of the term to refer to the pervasive demeaning and oppression of mothers (see *Don't Blame Mother: Mending the Mother–Daughter Relationship*).

Some aspects of motherhood have greatly changed since the Second Wave of the women's movement in North America began in the late 1960s, but there has been little or no change in others. Changes have included increased pressures on mothers to meet a growing list of real and alleged needs that parenting "experts" say their children have while increasing numbers of mothers have no choice but to do paid work as well. Other changes have come in the greater visibility of various groups of marginalized mothers and research documenting their ability to be good parents. What has not changed has been the prevalence of the destructive practice of blaming mothers for anything that goes wrong in their children's lives.

I. A Brief, Selected, Recent History

Motherhood no doubt has always been the most-populated category of unpaid work, and it comes laden with gargantuan responsibilities and expectations for performance. However, although the specific expectations about motherwork have changed to some extent, their magnitude has only increased, and the intensity with which mothers are blamed for any of their young or adult offspring's problems has not decreased; for where mothers formerly were expected to teach their children to fit their traditional "sex-appropriate" roles, now all are expected *in addition* to show their daughters the way to balancing work and family while maintaining some of their "femininity" and to show their sons the way to being sensitive and nurturant as well as achievement oriented. Furthermore, mothers are often blamed for wider social problems, such as substance abuse and juvenile crime. In an important sense, mother-blame is like air pollution: it is so much a part of North American culture that one tends not to notice it until one moves to a location where it is absent.

Before the Second Wave, most of what was written about motherhood was prescriptive, filled with descriptions of how mothers were supposed to act, primarily in keeping with the Victorian image of the mother as the "angel in the house," the selfless provider of nurturance, support, sanctuary, and comfort. What was not prescriptive could be unashamedly vicious. Philip Wylie's venomously mother-hating book, *Generation of Vipers*, was so popular after its 1946 publication that it went through many printings. Wylie coined the term "momism," which became widely used to refer to mothers' allegedly excessive control of and domination over their offspring. Wylie alone could not have created such mother-hate but rather was welcomed by a society that already demeaned and pathologized mothers. His book remained popular during the period after World War II when there was great pressure on women to be stay-at-home mothers (many giving back to men the jobs they had held while the men were off fighting the war) and to be happy and contented while doing so. As a result, in 1963 in *The Feminine Mystique*, Betty Friedan took North America by surprise when she reported that it was extremely common for the stay-at-home mother to feel bored, frustrated, and unappreciated in her fulltime mothering work and, most poignant of all, to consider herself unfeminine, unwomanly, selfish, or even crazy for feeling that way. Friedan described this as "the problem that has no name," reflecting each such woman's fear of talking about her feelings and the consequent isolation of untold numbers of women who feared the disapproval of others if they were to speak the truth.

In her groundbreaking 1976 book, *Of Woman Born: Motherhood as Experience and Institution*, Adrienne Rich made a fundamental distinction between, on the one hand, the many loving and tender moments between mother and child that are not shaped by social expectations and, on the other hand, the restrictive and oppressive expectations placed on mothers by society. In yet another important, early book called *The Mermaid and the Minotaur: Sexual Arrangements and Human Malaise*, Dorothy Dinnerstein pointed out the way that society burdens mothers with virtually total responsibility for child rearing, including the setting of limits and enforcing of rules, which leads children of both sexes to resent their mothers. Dinnerstein made the proposal then considered radical—that fathers and mothers should share these tasks equally. But even by the beginning of the 21st century, the distribution of household and child care related tasks had hardly changed at all (see Section III, Who Can Be a Good Mother?). Phyllis Chesler's *With Child: A Diary of Motherhood*, another book written from a feminist perspective, was her first-person account of the joys and the terrors of motherhood. Judith Arcana explored the relationship between mothers and daughters in *Our Mothers' Daughters* and between mothers and sons in *Every Mother's Son: The Role of Mothers in the Making of Men*.

More controversial but widely read books were Nancy Friday's *My Mother/My Self* and Nancy Chodorow's *The Reproduction of Mothering: Psychoanalysis and the Sociology of Gender*. Friday did not present herself as a feminist, and indeed her book was regarded as mother-blaming, even mother-hating, and profoundly and unduly pessimistic about the possibilities for good relationships between mothers and daughters. Chodorow's book was important in underlining Dinnerstein's point about the ways that completely mother-raised children could easily come to resent their mothers, but Chodorow presented what appeared at times to be an infantilizing view of mothers, suggesting, for instance, that in order to be a good mother one had in some sense to return to one's infancy, essentially assuming the infant's experiences to be like one's own. In fact, the reverse seems to be the case, so that a good parent of either sex will be skilled in distinguishing the infant's needs from her or his own. Chodorow also wrote as though mothers are by definition heterosexual and paired with men. Her important 1982 paper with Susan Contratto, "The Fantasy of the Perfect Mother" (see Barrie Thorne and Marilyn Yalom, eds., *Rethinking the Family: Some Feminist Questions*), was written from a more clearly feminist perspective, focusing in part on the impossible standards mothers are expected to meet.

The widespread demeaning and devaluing of mothers is reflected in the very different kinds of images that come to most people's minds when they hear the term "Mama's boy" in contrast to the term, "Daddy's girl"; the former tends to be associated with images of an overprotective, smothering mother who spoils her son and renders him psychologically sick, whereas the latter tends to be associated with images of a fortunate daughter who is the special recipient of her male parent's valued attention. Indeed, anything associated with or regarded as similar to the characteristics or work of mothers tends to be demeaned, devalued, and pathologized. For instance, a 1998–1999 Department of Labor report reveals that two kinds of workers who must have many of the same skills and perform many of the same tasks as mothers—child care workers and home health care aides—were paid only 73% and 81%, respectively, as much as a nonsupervisory animal caretaker.

One of the most pervasive consequences of societal devaluing and scapegoating of mothers is internalized mother-blame, the belief of mothers that they themselves are unworthy of respect and are responsible for anything bad that happens to their families. The sense of unworthiness and self-blame tend to propel most mothers into trying even harder to be perfect parents and also tend to reduce the likelihood that they will try to change the distribution of work in their households or to join with other mothers to protest the ways they are treated.

A. NEWER WRITING

The end of the 20th century brought a burgeoning of research and clinical writing about mothers from new perspectives, including the emergence and strengthening of the voices of feminists and of mothers from traditionally marginalized groups. Two groundbreaking conferences were held in the mid- to late-1980s, one called "Don't Blame Mother," organized by Janet Stickney in Toronto, and the other called "Woman-Defined Motherhood: A Conference for Therapists," organized by Jane Price Knowles and Ellen Cole and held at Goddard College. In 1997, Andrea O'Reilly and Sharon Abbey in Canada began an ongoing series of annual international conferences about mothers. Together, they organized conferences about mothers and daughters and about mothers and sons, and Abbey spearheaded a conference about mothers and education. Other conferences organized by O'Reilly and various colleagues focused on topics such as mothering in the African diaspora, lesbian mothers, becoming a mother, and mothering and peace; many more are slated for the future. In 1998 O'Reilly and others founded the Association for Research on Mothering (email address: arm@yorku.ca), and its *Journal of the Association for Research on Mothering*. *Canadian Woman Studies/Les cahiers de la femme* published a special issue in 1998 called "Looking Back, Looking Forward: Mothers, Daughters, and Feminism."

Approximately twice as many articles and books related to mothers and daughters were published in the last 12 years of the 20th century as in the 12 previous years. Some of this recent work has perpetuated traditional sexist and mother-blaming assumptions and interpretations—often through the use of research designs and clinical questions and theories that are founded on the assumption that mothers are responsible for all problems—and some has been more enlightened. A major theme in some of the recent work has been how mothers from marginalized groups try to fend off the wrong, hurtful, and pathologizing assumptions that are made about them by the dominant culture, such as African American mothers dealing with the stereotype that they are "too strong and aggressive" and Asian American mothers dealing with the stereotype that they are "too passive." Another major theme is the way mothers struggle to cope with the claims of traditional researchers and therapists that anyone other than a White, able-bodied, heterosexual, married, middle-class, biological mother in just the "right" age range is likely to produce emotionally disturbed children.

These stereotypes are particularly important because of the large number of mothers who fall into the nonidealized categories. For instance, according to the 1999 *Statistical Abstracts of the United States*, in 1998 there were more than 25 million married, presumably heterosexual, couples with children in the United States but also more than 7.5 million "female householders," presumably single mothers, living with their children. Of women who had had a child within the previous year, 20% were employed, 33% were unemployed, and 35% were not in the labor force. In addition, 31% of women who had had a child during the previous year were married with "spouse present," but 22% were never married (the largest group being Blacks, the next largest Hispanics), 12% were married with spouse absent (the largest group being Hispanics, the next largest being Blacks), and 6% were widowed or divorced. Based on the same source, more than 3 million couples were classified as interracial, considering only people classified as Black, White, Hispanic, or other. According to the Stepfamily Association of America (Web site www.stepfamily.org), 23% of children in the United States live with their biological mother but not their biological father (with only 4% in the reverse situation), and 30% live in a family in which they have a legal or cohabiting stepparent, the most common such constellations being the biological mother with stepfather and the stepmother–stepfather combined families (usually with the man's biological children living with their biological mother most of the time). *Statistical Abstracts of the United States* did not contain a breakdown of mothers by sexual orientation, but the number of lesbian mothers in the United States has been estimated at, at the very least, 6 million (April Martin's *The Guide to Lesbian and Gay Parenting*).

Enlightened research in recent years has helped to combat stereotypes about marginalized mothers, revealing, for instance, that African American mothers with HIV focus on their children's needs and help to educate the wider community about the dangers of HIV, that mothers with disabilities are happy to be mothers, that mothers diagnosed as mentally retarded who have neglected their children have been able to learn child-care skills that eliminate the neglect, that children raised by lesbian women have no higher rate of emotional problems than children of heterosexual women, and that single-mother family members have more social interaction at dinner than members of married families. Furthermore, since whether a child was wanted and planned for can have significant effects on how the child is welcomed into the world and raised, it is significant that, as Jess Wells has noted ("Lesbians Raising Sons: Bringing Up a New Breed of Men," in *Mothers and Sons: Feminism, Masculinity, and the Struggle to Raise Our Sons*, Andrea O'Reilly, ed.) "nearly all children of lesbians are wanted, since we have no 'oops' method of family planning."

II. To Be or Not to Be a Mother

Changes in recent decades have included the introduction of new factors into the question of whether or not to become a mother at all. These factors include new forms and increased legal availability of birth control, as well as the women's movement's advocacy of a woman's right to choose whether and when to have children. As a result, there has been some increase in social support for women who choose not to have children at all and for women who choose the timing and spacing of their childbearing. Thus, for example, women who choose not to bear or raise children are somewhat less likely now than even 20 years ago to be regarded as selfish and unwomanly, but by no means can they be certain of receiving support from family and friends for their decision, for the long-standing stigma associated with choosing not to have a child has not been eradicated.

The advent of reproductive technologies ("repro tech") such as *in vitro* fertilization has made it possible for some women to conceive and bear children when they might not otherwise have been able to do so. On the one hand, this has given some women more options in regard to becoming mothers—although not as many as one might assume from reading media reports and interviews with the heads of fertility clinics, who tend to exaggerate the rates of

pregnancy resulting from repro tech and to minimize the number of physical procedures (surgeries, drugs), pains, and financial expenses endured by their average woman patient. On the other hand, repro tech has increased the pressure on women to give birth, because in general, women who are physically capable of giving birth are still expected to do so. When such women come from wealthy families or have life partners with paid jobs, they run a significant risk of being labeled self-absorbed and unfeminine for choosing to spend their time and energies on careers, volunteer work, or artistic/creative endeavors instead of raising children. Related to this is the still-pervasive tendency for mothers who choose to yield custody of their children to ex-spouses, other relatives, or the state—for whatever reason—to be considered selfish and uncaring. [*See* REPRODUCTIVE TECHNOLOGIES.]

Religious and economic factors continue to play major roles in the availability of options. Religious factors affect girls' and women's views about whether (and which) options, if any, they should even consider. Economic factors put some options beyond the reach of those who might wish to use them. For example, the financial cost of various forms of birth control makes them inaccessible to vast numbers of girls and women in the United States who have no insurance that covers such products and services or indeed no health insurance at all. In addition, some women seeking abortions now must cope with the prospect of confronting representatives of the hostile and even dangerous wing of the antichoice movement who harrass patients and staff entering abortion clinics and the offices of private practitioners who perform the procedures.

III. Who Can Be a Good Mother?

Historically in North America, the image of a "good mother" has been that of a married, heterosexual, White, adult woman who has no physical or mental disabilities or addictions, is a full-time mother, has a husband who provides the financial support, lives with her husband and children in a house or apartment, and is her children's biological mother. Despite the paucity of social support for mothers who do not fit this pattern—such as mothers from racialized groups, poor mothers, mothers on welfare, homeless mothers, lesbian and bisexual mothers, mothers with disabilities, mothers with substance abuse problems, adoptive mothers, and teen mothers—and despite the paucity of financial support for poor women and their families, "nonideal" mothers have been blamed for not fitting the picture and held virtually solely responsible for all of their children's problems. Furthermore, both society in general and the courts in particular have tended to assume that mothers who fail to fit that picture cannot possibly be good mothers, cannot raise happy and well-adjusted children, are likely to do harm to their children, or should be deprived of their custody. The tendency of the mental health establishment to use fluctuating, sexist, racist, and other biased definitions of mental disorder has also put mothers, especially those from marginalized groups, at great risk for being classified as mentally ill and therefore as unfit mothers.

This situation has begun to change as more lawyers and judges become enlightened, as more research is published that demonstrates that children raised by mothers who do not fit the idealized picture are no more likely than other children to have emotional problems, and as women receive support from each other and from some men in their struggles to keep and raise their children. However, the long-standing biases persist, leading many mothers from these marginalized groups to lose custody of their children. As described by Phyllis Chesler in *Mothers on Trial: The Battle for Children and Custody* and by Molly Ladd-Taylor and Lauri Umansky, editors of *"Bad" Mothers: The Politics of Blame in Twentieth-Century America,* the courts have taken children away from mothers who in any way have failed to fit the picture of a woman living in a traditional, heterosexual, married, nuclear family; from mothers who have been unable to protect their children from harm; and from mothers of children who have somehow "gone wrong."

Particularly disturbing has been the trend for the courts to take child custody from mothers who report that their children's fathers have sexually or otherwise physically abused their children, as Chesler has written. This pattern has led to the dilemma that informed mothers face when they suspect or know that their children are being abused; they realize that to report that abuse will actually *increase* the likelihood that the courts will regard them as unfit mothers, for allegedly trying to turn them against their fathers, and will accordingly take custody of the children away from them. In recent years, it has become increasingly common for the lawyer representing a father accused of sexual or other abuse of his children to claim that the mother making the allegation is mentally ill, suffering from a disorder that

makes her pretend or persuade herself that her children are being harmed. The most frequently used diagnosis is that of Munchausen Syndrome by Proxy (see David Allison and Mark Roberts, *Disordered Mothers or Disordered Diagnosis: Munchausen by Proxy Syndrome*). However, experts such as psychologist Peter Jaffe, who has worked for many years at the London, Ontario, Family Court Clinic, present a different picture. Jaffe explains that after being involved in more than 500 custody and access disputes over a 6-year period, in only two cases in which abuse was alleged had no abuse occurred, and in both of those cases the mothers genuinely believed that it had (cited in Paula J. Caplan and Mary Lou Fassel, "Women Get Blame in Incest Cases," *Globe and Mail* [Toronto], February 10, 1987).

Society's hypocritical treatment of mothers has also been starkly demonstrated in the case of pregnant women who have substance abuse problems, as Katha Pollitt wrote in her chapter, "Fetal Rights: A New Assault on Feminism," in Ladd-Taylor's and Umanski's book, *"Bad" Mothers.* Judges have often ordered that children be taken away from these women, but the same judges have rarely taken into consideration the fact that most drug treatment programs have a policy of refusing to accept pregnant women and have rarely ordered such treatment programs to change that policy. As a consequence, pregnant substance abusers seeking help and wanting to protect their fetuses and later their children are denied help and then blamed for not overcoming their addiction on their own. [*See* Substance Abuse.]

A. MOTHERS WITH PAID JOBS

Whereas working-class mothers have always been highly likely to have paid jobs, the number of middle-class mothers in the workforce was substantially higher in the year 2000 than it was in, say, the 1950s. The pressure on mothers with paid jobs to provide excellent mothering for their children as well as to perform superbly at the factory or office creates a barely tolerable or intolerable burden for many women. Most mothers in this position worry constantly that they are shortchanging their children, their workplaces, or both. This is not surprising, because they are likely to be subjected to a barrage of insinuations or outright accusations that they are not sufficiently devoted to either their children or their employers. Nor have their anxieties and shame been much alleviated by the little-publicized but excellent research showing the following, for instance:

- Day care is not damaging to children and can actually provide advantages by encouraging social interaction.
- Preteen children of single mothers who have paid jobs regard their families as more cohesive and better organized than do preteen children of mothers without paid jobs.
- Whether or not the mother is employed is unrelated to children's development, and in both cases the quality and quantity of stimulation and of parent–child interactions are the same.

Even mothers who might be aware of these kinds of research findings often remain anxious, because they worry that their children might be exceptions, and when one's children's welfare is at stake, how can one not be frightened? As Arlie Russell Hochschild pointed out in her book, *The Time Bind: When Work Becomes Home and Home Becomes Work,* whereas mothers receive few expressions of appreciation for their mothering work in the home, they are more likely in the workplace to feel appreciated, to have clear definitions of what counts as success, and to receive praise for work that is done well. One might also note that in the workplace, women receive at least some pay for their work, a sign that someone places at least some value on what they do. Historically, disproportionately large numbers of African American women have had no choice about whether they had to do paid work, often having to take the lowest-paid jobs under horrendous conditions, as Beverly Greene has described. (e.g., see Beverly Greene, "Sturdy Bridges: The Role of African-American Mothers in the Socialization of African-American Children," *Women and Therapy* **10**, 1990, 205–225, and "What Has Gone Before: The Legacy of Racism and Sexism in the Lives of Black Mothers and Daughters," *Women and Therapy* **9**, 1990, 207–230; see also Norma J. Burgess and Hayward Derrick Horton, "African American Women and Work: A Socio-historical Perspective," *Journal of Family History* **18**, 1993, 53–63). Despite research showing that they often shouldered the double load effectively and were respected by their children for doing so, they have had to struggle against the view by the dominant society that they were "too powerful."

Many of these mothers carrying a "double load" are single mothers, but even women living with men only rarely find much relief. Despite the plethora of media stories about "new men" who share these tasks equally with women, research by such scholars as Joseph Pleck, who has been a pioneer in tracking this issue, shows that fathers' "engagement time" with children is only two-fifths that of mothers. That does represent an increase from the one-third of more than a decade ago, but this distribution must be considered in light of the fact that work hours per year for the average paid worker *of either sex* have increased by an entire month in the past two decades; thus, mothers are more likely to work far more hours at paid jobs than ever before, and the slight increase in men's share of family work does not bring them up to parity. Furthermore, women's family work continues disproportionately to be composed of tasks that require daily action (such as cooking, washing dishes, and tidying up), whereas men's is more likely to be composed of such tasks as changing the oil in the car, making men less subject to daily, home-related pressures. In child care, women spend proportionally more time doing maintenance, while men do more of the playing, and women spend more time doing family tasks simultaneously than men do. At least as significant is the fact that both wives and husbands report that the wives have more *responsibility* than do their husbands for family work.

While not giving up hope that household work will become more evenly distributed, some women and men have tried to develop workplace solutions to some of these problems for mothers who do paid work. In large part, however, they have met with limited success, although in principle they seem promising. These have included on-the-job day care sites, which are sometimes good but sometimes understaffed or poorly staffed and are still unavailable in most workplaces. Furthermore, about a decade ago, psychologist Louise Silverstein ("Transforming the Debate about Childcare and Maternal Employment," *American Psychologist* **46**, 1991, 1025–1032) issued a challenge to stop focusing on the possible negative consequences of day care and maternal employment and to concentrate instead on the consequences of *not* providing high-quality, affordable day care. However, this enterprise has hardly begun. It is understandable that a society that remains pervaded by mother-blame would be reluctant to give up the former approach and afraid of what might be learned if the switch were made.

Other steps that are potentially useful for mothers with paid jobs have been the implementation of policies in some workplaces that allow for flextime or flexplace and for parental leave. Flextime refers to workers' freedom to choose *which* hours they will work, so that they can arrange schedules that take into account their household tasks. Flexplace refers to the opportunity for people to do work at home. Parental leave is paid or unpaid time off, usually taken after a new baby is born or adopted into the family. There have also been increasing discussions of the need for more part-time jobs and for jobs that are shared by two or more people who may or may not be each other's family partners. But part-time work often includes few or no benefits such as health insurance, and typically it carries little or no job security. Women who are paid to do part-time work often work far more hours than those for which they are paid, because they are trying to prove that they are good workers who deserve to be kept on. In addition, part-time workers are often socially marginalized, accorded less respect and social support than full-time workers. The latter also often resent the former, based on the assumption that part-timers are "getting away with something." A major problem with the other options is that workers who wish to avail themselves of flextime, flexplace, or parental leave usually need to ask their employers for permission to do so. In large organizations, although the top executives may endorse these policies, it is usually the middle managers who are in the position to allow workers to exercise those options. However, middle managers are the people who are most likely to be, or to fear that they will be, inconvenienced by these atypical arrangements. Furthermore, precisely because these options are so intensively associated with women, especially mothers, the options in many workplaces are devalued, regarded as the choices of employees who are not fully committed to their employers. [See CHILD CARE; FAMILY ROLES AND PATTERNS, CONTEMPORARY TRENDS; MARRIAGE; WORK-FAMILY BALANCE.]

B. MOTHER-BLAME BY THERAPISTS

According to the published writings of therapists, hardly any mother is a good one. In systematic research into the articles written by clinicians of both sexes from a wide variety of theoretical orientations, Paula Caplan and Ian Hall-McCorquodale found that in 125 articles, mothers were blamed for 72 different kinds of problems in their offspring, ranging from bed wetting to schizophrenia, from inability to deal with color blindness to aggressive behavior, from learning problems to "homicidal transsexualism" (Paula J. Caplan and Ian Hall-McCorquodale, "Mother-blaming in major clinical journals," *American Journal of Orthopsychiatry* 55, 1985, 345–353;

and Caplan and Hall-McCorquodale, "The Scapegoating of Mothers: A Call for Change," *American Journal of Orthopsychiatry* 55, 1985, 610–613). This pattern has persisted until the present day, sometimes taking the form of pathologizing mothers and their mothering behavior and other times holding mothers disproportionately responsible for their children's problems.

Two areas of literature where there has been, if anything, an upsurge in mother-blame are those about eating disorders and both sexual and nonsexual child abuse. With regard to eating disorders, in the vast majority of clinical studies and case reports published in recent years, mothers are the only possible causes of the disorders that are even studied (Paula J. Caplan, *Don't Blame Mother: Mending the Mother–Daughter Relationship*, 2000). This is true regardless of the racial categories in which those studied are placed, despite the fact that for African Americans there is some evidence that both daughters and mothers have healthier attitudes about eating and weight than do Whites. In some studies, the article's title includes the word "parents," but the only parents actually described in the text are mothers. An exception is the excellent work of Judith Rabinor, who has criticized therapists for "explaining" to eating-disordered girls and women how their mothers caused their disorders and for choosing interventions designed to "fix" the mothers. Rabinor found this particularly unconscionable because, when therapists ask mothers about their experiences, they frequently learn that the mothers' husbands and fathers mocked them about their weight, often in front of their daughters, and the mothers are often trying desperately, if misguidedly, to spare their daughters similar treatment. Rabinor suggested that a woman's appearance "is often the most obvious or the only socially condoned form of power openly afforded her," ("Mothers, Daughters, and Eating Disorders: Honoring the Mother-Daughter Relationship," in *Feminist Perspectives on Eating Disorders*, edited by Patricia Fallon, Melanie Katzman, *et al.*), and so it might be better to help the eating-disordered woman and her mother explore healthy ways to experience power than to cast blame.

Similar patterns of asking only how the mother is at fault, rather than what various factors might contribute to the problems, appear in recent articles about children on drugs, people with "borderline personality disorder," and a host of other problems. With regard to both physical abuse and sexual abuse of children, mothers continue to be considered blameworthy, sometimes even more than the perpe-trators themselves, regardless of the circumstances of the abuse and even of whether or not the mother knew about it. Some researchers on nonsexual phys-ical abuse of children have claimed that mothers are more likely than fathers to inflict such abuse, but those researchers rarely investigate how much time each parent spends with the children. Since mothers in most two-parent, heterosexual families spend more time than fathers with the children, and since the vast majority of single-parent families are headed by women, a hasty look at the data can leave one with the impression that mothers are the more abusive parents. However, for each hour spent with the chil-dren, mothers actually inflict abuse far less than fa-thers do. Another problem with the research is that simply counting frequencies and severity of physical abuse is not enough and leads to focusing on indi-vidual mothers as the sources of trouble. It is crucial also to investigate important issues that tend to in-crease the likelihood of abuse, such as mothers' lack of financial resources and lack of adequate day care and other kinds of human support. [*See* CHILD ABUSE.]

In the area of sexual abuse of children, efforts by feminists and others, especially in the 1980s, led to the demolition of the myth long purveyed in psychi-atric textbooks that the so-called incest taboo made incest extremely rare. As millions of women gained the courage to reveal that they had been sexually abused as children, the public in general became more aware of the frequency of child sexual abuse and its often devastating consequences. As a result, signs that such abuse was happening became more likely to be noticed by family members, friends, teachers, and others. But with this increase in re-porting came a tidal wave of mother-blame. Moth-ers who had not known their children were being abused were condemned for not knowing, even though perpetrators of the abuse are often fathers or other close family members whose attempts to per-suade or terrorize the child victims into silence are often profoundly effective. Furthermore, because most women have been socialized to put the most positive interpretations possible on the behavior of the men in their families, this socialization has often made women likely to miss signs that their children were being abused. But, as described earlier, when they *do* notice and report such abuse, both they and their children are often punished for that, and at the very least the mothers are likely to be criticized for

being too suspicious of the men. Mothers who have known that their children were being abused but who had reason to believe that they, their children, or both would be in mortal danger from the perpe-trator if they reported the abuse to the authorities have also been condemned for "doing nothing." So have mothers from marginalized groups who made no report of the abuse because of previously having experienced racist, classist, or other kinds of dis-criminatory or punitive behavior at the hands of the child welfare authorities to whom the report would be made. Other mothers have been so frightened by the prospect of "destroying" the nuclear family, with the risks they have been told that that will entail for their children's psychological (and often economic) welfare, that they have been reluctant to report abuse. Still other mothers, as described earlier, know that they are less likely to obtain or retain custody of their children if they report the abuse, and this places them in an impossible situation. No doubt some mothers have failed to deal appropriately with abuse for more culpable reasons, but the essential point is that most mothers try their best to cope with this frightening matter and all that it entails, and yet they are blamed almost no matter what they do.

Often, the blame that hurts mothers the most is that which comes from their children, and although under some circumstances the anger of offspring at their mothers is understandable and even warranted, that is not always so, and the child may not know all of the relevant information. Sometimes the rea-sons for a mother's way of responding to the knowl-edge that her child is being sexually abused are al-most unthinkable but very powerful. For instance, an adult woman incest survivor told her therapist that she was angry at her mother because "When I was nine years old and my father abused me, I told Mother, and she never said a single word about it." The therapist encouraged her to ask her mother about it, and reluctantly she did so. Her mother replied that she had immediately believed that her daughter was telling the truth when she first re-ported the abuse, but it was in a time and place in which abuse was rarely mentioned, and she was so frightened of mishandling the news in a way that would harm her daughter further that she did not trust herself to speak. When her daughter left for school, she contacted a psychiatrist and told him the story. His response was, "The greatest gift you could give your daughter would be never to speak of this again."

C. QUESTIONING THE STEREOTYPES

Recent years have marked an upsurge in the questioning and challenging of stereotypes about mothers, propelled in large part by the women's movement's encouragement of women to speak out about the difficulties of their lives. Negative stereotypes have been major sources of these difficulties, and some examples of these will be discussed. Daniel Patrick Moynihan's boldly racist and sexist claim that Black American families were pathological because they were headed by strong women who had paid jobs was a major stereotype, the effects of which still pervade North American culture.

Another negative stereotype about African-American mothers was the portrayal of the typical unmarried mother as a Black, probably teenage female who repeatedly became pregnant in order to collect government support monies. Associated with this image was the assignment to unmarried mothers of the pejorative label, "unwed." It is a telling commentary on the way a racist and sexist society functions that as the number of White, middle-class and wealthy women choosing to have and raise children alone has increased, the label "unwed" has often been replaced by the term "single." On the positive side, this change has the potential to lessen the stigmatization of unmarried motherhood for females of all classes and racial groups.

Rachel Josefowitz Siegel, in a landmark paper called "Antisemitism and Sexism in Stereotypes of Jewish Women" (*A Guide to Dynamics of Feminist Therapy,* Doris Howard, ed.), pointed out the virulence of stereotypes that Jewish mothers are, among other things, intrusive, overly emotional, and overcontrolling. This work, and subsequent writing on this subject, has helped reveal the dilemma of mothers who live in fear that their expressions of warmth and concern for their children will be labeled as—indeed, might even *be*—damaging. This is a concern that plagues large numbers of mothers in all groups, but for Jewish women it has been combined with the fear of feeding a contemptuous stereotype of Jewish mothers.

Similarly, adoptive mothers and stepmothers have begun to protest the common tendency for even their reasonable limit-setting for their children to be regarded as gratuitous, "wicked stepmother" or "non-biological mother" cruelty and their expressions of love and care as attempts to act *as though* they are attached to their young. The underlying assumption now being questioned is that children who are not one's blood kin cannot possibly inspire the same genuine love as biologically related ones. Increases in divorce and remarriage, as well as increases in cross-national and cross-racial adoptions, have increased the numbers of stepmothers and adoptive mothers, some of whom have challenged these negative stereotypes.

Still another category of marginalized mothers that has been negatively stereotyped is that of mothers in prison. Feminists and other social progressives have questioned the assumption that mothers in prison are not fit for contact with their children because such contact could only have harmful effects on the children. Fledgling programs in some prisons aimed at ensuring mother–child connection while the mother serves her sentence have helped not only to maintain and strengthen those relationships but also to demonstrate their value.

IV. Myths and Blame

The ways women, men, girls, and boys think about motherhood are shaped by powerful myths that pervade our society. Although some myths are more salient in some cultural groups than others within North America, few people's expectations about mothers are unaffected by the existence of these myths. Motherhood myths fall into two groups: perfect mother myths and bad mother myths (see Caplan, 2000). The perfect mother myths encourage people to set standards for mothers that are so high that no human being could possibly meet them. These myths include the following:

- *Myth 1.* The measure of a good mother is a perfect child.
- *Myth 2.* Mothers are endless founts of nurturance.
- *Myth 3.* Mothers naturally know how to raise children.
- *Myth 4.* Mothers don't get angry.

The bad mother myths work in a somewhat more complicated fashion. These myths encourage people to take anything a mother might do, be it bad, neutral, or even good, and interpret it as a sign that the mother is bad. These myths include the following:

- *Myth 5.* Mothers are inferior to fathers.
- *Myth 6.* Mothers need experts' advice to raise healthy children.

- *Myth 7.* Mothers are bottomless pits of neediness.
- *Myth 8.* Mother–daughter closeness is unhealthy.
- *Myth 9.* Mothers are dangerous when they are powerful.
- *Myth 10.* Both stay-at-home mothers and mothers with paid jobs are bad mothers.

At least two pairs of these myths are mutually exclusive: myths 2 and 7 and myths 3 and 6. It is important to recognize that these myths coexist despite the fact that they cancel each other out, which sheds light on the function served by the myths taken as a group. That function is to maintain mothers as a scapegoated group who can be blamed for a wide variety of social ills. Those people and groups who wield the greatest social, economic, and political power are in danger of losing their power if they are held responsible for various kinds of problems, so they tend to find other groups and individuals onto whom to deflect blame. Mother-blame perpetuates the unequal distribution of power between the sexes by keeping mothers down, ashamed, frightened, and insecure about their mothering. Any society is more likely to condone the choice of certain scapegoats if those scapegoats are believed to be inferior, evil, or otherwise deserving of condemnation and dismissal. Thus there is a mother myth for every occasion; no matter what a mother might do, even if it is good, one or more myths can be used to interpret that deed as further proof that she deserves scapegoating or that mothers in general do. Scapegoating of mothers is also fed by the fear of mothers' power, which is instilled in children of both sexes because mothers in most families have nearly sole responsibility for making and enforcing rules and routines.

In the personal realm, it is difficult for anyone to back away from the prism the myths create in order to see mothers realistically, to question whether any particular bit of a mother's behavior merits any interpretation other than one of the negative ones promoted by the myths. Therefore, a great deal of trouble in mother-daughter and mother-son relationships is either created or exacerbated by the existence of the myths and by the fact that they are likely to have been deeply ingrained in both mother and offspring. What many mother–offspring pairs have found to be extremely useful in seeing their relationships and each other more clearly and going beyond the myths is the mother's telling of her life story to her daughter or son (Karen G. Howe, "Daughters Discover Their Mothers through Biographies and Genograms: Educational and Clinical Parallels," in Jane Price

Knowles and Ellen Cole, eds., *Woman-Defined Motherhood* and Caplan, 2000, lists suggested questions for the daughter or son to ask). Even offspring whose mothers have died or from whom they are estranged have found it helpful to record everything they know about their mothers, interview people who knew them, and examine old letters, books their mothers read, photographs in family albums, and so on in order to try to create as full and realistic a picture of their mothers as possible. This often results in the child's being able to stop seeing the parent as just "my mother the mother," solely within the framework of her role. It enables the children to ask questions that they may never have asked their own mothers but might well have asked of strangers at a cocktail party. Acquiring a more nearly complete picture of one's mother often allows one to understand why she did things that may have been bewildering or frankly hurtful. Daughters and sons who come together with their mothers to discuss the ways that the mother myths were played out in their families often find that they can move their relationships to healthier and happier levels as they go beyond the socially ingrained mother-blame, which puts mothers on the defensive and causes shame and discomfort in the offspring who indulge in it.

Because the myths are so powerful, most mothers vigilantly monitor their own mothering behavior, wondering whether they are doing too much of one thing (e.g., being protective of their children) and not enough of another (e.g., encouraging their independence)—or the reverse. A narrow band of behavior is considered acceptable for mothers. In a clinical setting, for instance, one way this narrowness is manifested is that clinicians often interpret a mother's sitting close to her child as a sign of her intrusiveness or overinvolvement, yet they often interpret a mother's failure to sit close to her child as a sign that she is cold and rejecting. This narrowness gives rise to shame, fear, and anxiety in mothers, who know that they are likely to be blamed for any problems their children have or cause but who understandably have difficulty figuring out just what a good mother is supposed to do. The seriousness of this dilemma is reflected in the fact that therapists who disagree about many things nevertheless agree that it tends to be harmful to relationships to be plagued by shame, fear, and anxiety.

Indeed, virtually everything that is associated with mothers has tended to be demeaned and devalued in dominant North American culture. For instance, suppose that an adult daughter starting her own business moves back to live with her widowed mother. The daughter cooks for both of them and the mother does the laundry for both. The daughter's cooking for her mother is often pathologized as a sign of role reversal between mother and daughter, while the mother's cooking for the daughter is pathologized as a sign that she is infantilizing her adult offspring. In contrast, consider how this situation might be perceived if we omitted the word "mother," such as "two adults who share living space, one of whom does the cooking and the other of whom does the laundry for both." Presented this way, the relationship is likely to elicit positive descriptions such as "That's nice. They share the work."

The devaluing of feelings and behavior associated with mothers is a part of a more generally sexist tendency in dominant North American culture to devalue whatever is considered female or feminine in relation to whatever is considered male or masculine (e.g., see Mary Ann Cejka and Alice Eagly, "Gender-Stereotypic Images of Occupations Correspond to the Sex Segregation of Employment," *Personality and Social Psychology Bulletin* **25**, 1999, 413–423). For instance, concern with feelings and human relationships had long been given the demeaning label of "dependency," with its connotations of immaturity and psychopathology, until such feminist writers as Rachel Josefowitz Siegel (see "Women's 'Dependency' in a Male-Centered Value System," *Women and Therapy* **7**, 1988, 113–23) and the Stone Center group at Wellesley College including Judith Jordan, Alexandra Kaplan, Jean Baker Miller, Irene Stiver, and Janet Surrey (see Judith Jordan, Alexandra Kaplan, Jean Baker Miller, Irene Stiver, and Janet Surrey, eds., *Women's Growth in Connection: Writings from the Stone Center*) began promoting the relabeling of such behavior as "interdependent" or "relational." In the absence of this kind of relabeling, however, sons have been pressured to prove their masculinity by becoming as emotionally and physically distant from their mothers as soon as possible, and daughters have been given the double message that they are supposed to remain close to their mothers but that this closeness will be pathologized and mocked. Although much of motherwork is extremely important and promotes growth and happiness in their children, and although that work is often appreciated in principle or in the abstract (as on Mother's Day cards) it is rarely spoken of with appreciation or respect by children or partners and certainly not on a regular basis, not even with the frequency with which paid workers receive paychecks as signs that someone values their labor (Caplan, 2000). Its value is, however, noted in its absence, as when mothers are ill or too busy to do laundry or prepare meals.

V. Mother-Blame as Hate Speech

Historically, as each liberation movement takes effect, people become increasingly aware of the forms taken by prejudice and hate speech directed toward the movement's target group. With each wave of liberation, it tends to become decreasingly socially acceptable to insult and oppress the members of the target group. Of course, this does not rapidly do away with fundamental prejudices, fears, and hatred of people because of the groups to which they belong or with which they are identified. Often the forms taken by the oppression and hate speech become more subtle and therefore harder to identify, prove, and condemn. As part of this process, the women's movement has had some success in reducing or actually outlawing some forms of oppression of women, and in some social and work environments it is no longer considered socially acceptable to tell antiwoman "jokes." However, even in most of those environments, the same "jokes," the same scathing comments can be made with impunity as long as the speaker replaces the word "woman" with the word "mother" or, even safer, "mother-in-law" or "stepmother." It is arguably the case that mother-blame is the most pervasive, unrecognized form of hate speech in North America and many other places as well. Objecting to a slur against mothers or mother figures remains likely to elicit claims of "But you don't know *my* mother" and accusations that the person voicing the objection is humorless. If one imagines someone defending an antisemitic or racist remark, for instance, with the retort, "But you don't know *this* Jew" or "But you don't know *this* Black guy," the hate-speech nature of the retorts is clear. The rarity with which similar remarks about mothers are recognized as hate speech is testimony to the relative invisibility and the social acceptability of mother-blame.

VI. Conclusions

As mothers and their allies become increasingly aware of mother-blame's pervasiveness and power, and especially as researchers and other writers increasingly recognize the degree to which mothers are intolerably burdened, there is hope that the damaging myths of motherhood will be dismantled. Such a trend would bring substantial benefits to mothers, their offspring, and the relationships between them.

SUGGESTED READING[1]

Chess, S. (1982). The "blame the mother" ideology. *International Journal of Mental Health* **11**, 95–107.

Coll, C. Garcia, Surrey, J. L., and Weingarten, K. (eds.) (1998). *Mothering against the Odds: Diverse Voices of Contemporary Mothers.* Guilford, New York.

Collins, P. H. (1997). The meaning of motherhood in Black culture and Black mother/daughter relationships. In *Toward a New Psychology of Gender* (M. M. Gergen and S. H. Davis, eds.), pp. 325–340. Routledge, New York.

Dohrn, B. (1995). Bad mothers, good mothers, and the state: Children on the margins. *University of Chicago Law School Roundtable* **2**, 12.

Galinsky, E. (1999). *Ask the Children.* William Morrow, New York.

Knowles, J. Price, and Cole, E. (eds.) (1990). *Woman-Defined Motherhood.* Harrington Park Press, New York.

Ruddick, S. (1980). Maternal thinking. *Feminist Studies* **6**, 354–380.

Siegel, R. Josefowitz, Cole, E., and Steinberg-Oren, S. (eds.) (2000). *Jewish Mothers Tell Their Stories: Acts of Love and Courage.* Haworth, New York.

Sommers, E. (1995). *Voices from Within: Women Who Have Broken the Law.* University of Toronto Press, Toronto.

Tasker, F., and Golombok, S. (1995). Adults raised as children in lesbian families. *American Journal of Orthopsychiatry* **65**, 203–215.

[1]Readers are urged to read both references listed here and those mentioned in the text.

Parenting

Phyllis Bronstein

University of Vermont

Glossary

Androgynous Having both feminine and masculine characteristics, as defined within a particular culture—for example, in appearance or behavior.

Ethnography The scientific description of a culture's customs, beliefs, and normative behaviors.

Kibbutz (*pl. kibbutzim*) A collective farm or settlement in modern Israel.

Metapelet A caretaker of children, especially on *kibbutzim* in Israel.

Social construction of gender The beliefs, meanings, values, and behavioral norms within a culture that are associated with being female or male.

PARENTING in societies around the world takes many different forms. Even within the United States, parental roles and behaviors may vary widely, shaped by such factors as cultural norms and values, ethnic traditions, economic necessity, family configuration, individual history, and the relationship between the parental figures. However, one factor that helps shape parenting across *all* cultures, interwoven with each one's norms, traditions, and social structures, is gender.

Gender affects parenting in several essential ways. At the most basic level, cultural norms about gender determine who the key parental figures in a child's life are likely to be and what roles they are

destined to play. For example, in the United States, those key figures have traditionally been the biological mother and father, with the mother in the role of primary caretaker, and custodial parent should divorce occur. On a more specific level, parents' gender influences their day-to-day parenting behavior, in that mothers and fathers—often quite unawarely—incorporate the culture's norms for female and male behavior into their interactions with their children, and thus provide models of these norms for children to emulate. Finally, children's gender also influences parenting behavior. In many cultures, whether the child is a girl or a boy affects the tasks parents' assign, the resources they provide (such as toys and educational opportunities), and their daily interactions, activities, and level of involvement with the child.

I. Gender and Parental Roles

Mothers' and fathers' parenting roles to some extent have a biological basis. Historically, the fact that only women can lactate meant that they provided the primary sustenance for children during infancy and early childhood and that most mothers were nursing throughout their childbearing years. This biologically determined connection made it more feasible for mothers to take primary responsibility for child care, and as cultures developed, the responsibility often extended to encompass broader home-making tasks. The nature of this homemaking role has varied across cultures; in some, it has included mainly housekeeping and meal preparation, whereas in others, it has included such tasks as obtaining water, gathering food and fuel for cooking, and tending a vegetable garden. Fathers, on the other hand, freed from the demands of child care and household work, could devote their time to providing additional resources for their family—for example, through hunting, fishing, farming, or paid employment.

Yet it is interesting to note that many variations in parenting roles have existed throughout history, which would seem to suggest that other arrangements were possible, even given the underlying biological base. For example, mothers have often had help, and sometimes substitutes, in rearing their children. In extended families in the United States, grandmothers have often assumed a caregiver role; in Israel *kibbutzim,* children from infancy on have been put in the care of a special attendant called a *metapelet,* so that mothers could return to work; and in many countries, wealthy families have frequently turned the child rearing over to nannies. Lactation, the biological basis for mothers' traditional caregiving role, has also at times been circumvented. It was common practice up until the 20th century for well-to-do European families to farm their infants out to wet nurses, who were paid for their efforts, and in the 20th century, the manufacture of infant formula made bottle feeding a common practice in developed countries.[1] In addition, anthropological data suggest that women have not always remained close to home and children; for example, in the Tchambuli tribe of New Guinea, the women do the fishing to provide food for the family, and among the Agta foragers of the Philippine Islands, the women participate along with the men in hunting wild pig and deer. Fathers' roles have also shown wide variations, in terms of involvement with and responsibility for children. In some African societies, husbands and wives live in separate quarters, with fathers having very little contact with their children in the early years. In the United States, many fathers are absent altogether from their children's lives, yet there is

also a growing number of fathers who are primary caretakers.

These variations suggest that within each culture, parental involvement with and responsibility for children may have less to do with biology than with the ways that gender roles are defined. As a rule, gender-role definitions have tended to support societies' political and economic agendas. For example, during World War II, U.S. women were welcomed into the workforce in huge numbers to support the war effort and replace the men who had gone off to fight. Following the war, however, the doors to the workplace slammed shut. Women were now enshrined in the home and adulated for fulfilling their "natural" role, which included catering to their husbands' personal and career needs, fostering their children's optimal development, and accumulating all the material comforts their husbands' earnings would allow. This narrowed gender-role definition helped both to make room in the workplace for returning GIs and to prime the country's transition from a wartime to consumerist economy. However, as we have witnessed over the past 40 years, societal definitions of gender roles are not exclusively dictated from the top down; grassroots movements can also have a powerful effect. In particular, the women's liberation movement, which began in the United States and other industrialized countries in the 1960s, has not only brought about dramatic political, social, and economic changes in those countries, but has had an ever-widening impact in many other cultures around the world. Within the United States, the reexamination of gender roles that it generated has contributed not only to important changes in women's educational and employment opportunities, but also to changes in family configurations and dynamics and the quality and quantity of parents' involvement in their children's lives.

A. A CROSS-CULTURAL PERSPECTIVE ON GENDER AND PARENTAL ROLES

An examination of data from around the world reveals that in every sector, including industrial and nonindustrial societies, urban centers, and remote tribal villages, mothers are expected to be the primary caretakers. Although they may have help in meeting the demands of their role—for example, from cowives in polygynous societies, from adult female relatives in extended family households, from husbands in nuclear family households, or from paid child care workers such as baby-sitters, au pairs,

---

[1] The customary use of wet nurses unfortunately had dire consequences, in terms of greatly increased infant mortality. The modern-day use of baby formula as a substitute for breast-feeding has also been called into question, particularly in terms of long-term detrimental effects on child health and development, as well as its role in infant mortality in developing countries, where imported formula has often been used by uninformed caregivers under unsanitary conditions.

nursemaids, or nannies—essentially, mothers have the prime responsibility for meeting their children's physical and emotional needs, and teaching them life skills and the norms for social behavior. Yet political and economic changes, as well as changing gender-role definitions in both developed and developing countries, are altering the nature of the traditional mothering role. In many countries, women's employment outside the home has substantially increased over the past several decades. This means not only that the proximity and availability of mothers to their children can no longer be assumed, but also that children are seeing very different models of adult female behavior—ones that demonstrate women's competence as family providers and the ability to make their way in the wider world. Little is known as yet about the effects of this change on the cognitive, social, and psychological development, or the gender-role socialization of the children.

Interestingly, there seems to be more research available on the role of fathers, perhaps because there is such cross-cultural variation. Even the likelihood of fathers' presence (or absence) varies widely across cultural groups. For example, cross-cultural researchers Ruth and Robert Munroe, comparing father–child relations in Belize, Kenya, Nepal, and American Samoa, found that father absence ranged from 4 to 50%, depending on the culture. One constant about fathers, however, is that when they *are* present in the family, they spend significantly less time in child care than do mothers, with children of all ages. A review of ethnographies from 186 cultures reported that although fathers were frequently in close proximity with infants in 32% of the cultures and with young children in 52%, they had regular, close relationships with infants in only 2% of the cultures and with young children in only 5%. In some cultures, fathers may contribute financially to their children's upkeep, but may not be involved in childrearing, particularly in the early years. For example, in traditional family arrangements in Botswana, the father generally lives in a separate dwelling, while responsibility for the children falls to the mother's brother.

In keeping with traditional gender role dichotomies, which portray women (but not men) as capable of nurturance and men as instrumental and aggressive, fathers in many cultures have been cast in the role of disciplinarian. Psychologists Patrice Engle and Cynthia Breaux, in their 1998 social policy report on fathers' involvement with children in developing countries, described the traditional model of the father in West Africa, China, and Latino families in the United States and Brazil as emotionally distant figures who provide economic support and discipline. Yet they also described cultures in which fathers play a very different role. For example, among the Aka pygmies, a hunger–gatherer–trader people who live in the African tropical forest, fathers have frequently been observed to cuddle, clean, and play with infants, and Aka adolescents have reported that fathers provide as much nurturance and emotional support as mothers, with mothers likely to be more punitive than fathers. In addition, there is evidence to suggest that the traditional model of the aloof, authoritarian father is not universal for Latino families. In this author's own research in Mexico, which involved more than 20,000 observations of parent–child interaction in the home, fathers turned out to be more emotionally nurturant and more playful and companionable with their children than mothers were—although mothers showed more physical caregiving, in terms of providing food and attending to grooming, safety, and health. Thus, there is a fair amount of evidence that the amount and kind of involvement fathers have in their children's lives may be determined mainly by a culture's definitions of adult gender roles, rather than by men's biological makeup.

There seem to be a number of specific factors that influence fathers' family roles. In societies in which husband and wife spend substantial time together in cooperative activities, fathers are more likely to be involved in the care of young children. The Aka pygmies and the Batek, a foraging society in Malaysia, are examples of cultures where husband and wife work together to obtain food and where fathers also show a high rate of involvement in child care. Beatrice Whiting and Carolyn Edwards, in their 1988 book *Children of Different Worlds,* which compared child rearing in 12 communities around the world, found that across all 12 sites, children spent more time with mothers than with fathers; however, this gender difference in parental involvement was smallest in Tarong in the Philippines and in Taira in Okinawa, communities that also had the most egalitarian relations between husbands and wives. On the other hand, difference between mothers' and fathers' level of involvement with children was greatest in Juxtlahuaca in Mexico and Khalapur in northern India, cultures that stress gender-role distinctions starting in early childhood. It appears from this cross-cultural study that fathers' level of involvement with their children is affected by a culturally mandated, gender-based division of labor. In addition, as the authors noted, fathers' involvement may be influenced by the arrangement of the living space and the intimacy between husbands and wives. Specifically, in cultures where the husband and wife sleep and eat separately, as is the case in traditional sub-Saharan African societies, the man is likely to have little contact with his children in their early years; in contrast, if husband and wife share a bedroom, and particularly if there are no other adults living with them, the man is much more likely to become involved in child care. Thus, societal gender-role definitions that allow spouses to work together collaboratively (rather than assigning completely separate work domains for males and females), and allow living arrangements that foster intimacy and collaboration between the marital pair, are likely to lead to fathers' greater involvement in the daily lives of their children from infancy on.

There is also evidence to suggest that fathers' roles in many cultures are changing, in response to the broad economic and social changes that accompany technological advancement. Emmy Elisabeth Werner, in her 1979 book *Cross-Cultural Child Development: A View from the Planet Earth*, described a number of studies examining factors such as urbanization and enhanced educational and career opportunities that might affect African parental roles and behaviors. Among Yoruba communities in Nigeria, the Sisala of northern Ghana, and tribal groups from the Ivory Coast, anthropologists found that these factors were associated with more egalitarian husband–wife relations and fathers' greater involvement with children, in a manner that showed more warmth and acceptance and less restrictiveness and discipline than was customary in traditional families. To some extent, these changes may be due to shifts in living arrangements, from sex-segregated and extended family domains to nuclear households, in which spouses are more dependent on one another for companionship, emotional support, and practical help. In addition, women's greater access to education and their increasing movement into the workplace can only contribute further to the transformation of traditional parental roles. [*See* CROSS-CULTURAL GENDER ROLES.]

B. GENDER AND PARENTAL ROLES IN THE UNITED STATES

Social and economic changes within the United States have also brought about changes in traditional parental roles. Mothers in two-parent families have been entering the workforce in ever-increasing numbers; over the past four decades, the percentage of married mothers working outside the home has gone from 28 to 71%. This can be attributed both to the burgeoning of educational and career opportunities for women and to rising costs for maintaining a family, which have motivated many mothers in two-parent households to seek paid employment. As much as these changes have introduced new possibilities for women's lives, they have also produced stress and confusion about how to manage both work and family roles.

Media accounts of family-oriented men and stay-at-home dads imply that as women have moved into the workforce, men have reciprocated by taking on more responsibility for child care and household work. However, available data suggest that married mothers who are employed full time still do substantially more family work than their husbands do; a recent study found that nearly one-third of employed mothers did household work that was the equivalent of an additional full-time job. Psychologists Carolyn and Philip Cowan, in their 1992 book *When Partners Become Parents*, described their longitudinal research on couples having their first child. Exploring the dynamics of what often happens in contemporary families, they found that whereas most of the couples prior to having a baby described an ideology of more equal work and family roles than their parents had had, after the baby was born, the role arrangements involved less sharing than they had expected and more conflict and disagreement than before. Most of the new mothers struggled with questions of whether or when to return to work, and couples struggled with discrepancies between what had been expected of the fathers' participation in family work and what it actually turned out to be. Despite couples' intentions for child care to be equitably shared, for most of them, the division of labor that emerged was along traditional gender lines— even after mothers returned to work.

Many other studies of U.S. families have found that this gender-based division persists throughout infancy into middle childhood and adolescence, with mothers remaining much more available to children than fathers do. Studies from other Western cultures (e.g., Australia, Great Britain, France, and Belgium) suggest that these patterns are prevalent there as well. It appears that despite changing occupational roles and opportunities for women, and despite parents' desires for more egalitarian sharing of parenting responsibilities, traditional gender-role definitions exert a strong pull. The Cowans discuss some of the factors that keep old roles in place: that most new parents have internalized messages that women should be the primary caregivers; that they have had no models of males in nurturing roles; that fathers' initial uncertainty and mothers' perceived expertise and can lead men to feel inadequate in the caregiver role; that men may receive negative feedback from their own parents for taking an active role in infant care; and that workplace constraints (such as lower wages for women and the absence of paternity leave) as well a lack of high-quality, affordable child care can make traditional parental roles seem more beneficial for the child and more workable for the family. On the other hand, there is some research evidence to suggest that men who question the notion of maternal instincts and biologically based gender differences are more likely to be involved in caregiving with infants and young children.

It is also the case that changing economic patterns are having some effect on traditional gender-role definitions within the family. For example, there is evidence that in economic hard times, the more a woman earns relative to her husband, the more likely the husband is to take on a primary caregiver role. There is also evidence that in dual-earner, low-income families, particularly when parents' work schedules do not overlap, fathers are tending to take increasing responsibility for child care. The economic pressures that require both parents to be employed and the high cost of adequate day care have led significantly greater numbers of men to become involved in caring for their children than there were 20 years ago. There is a small amount of research that suggests what the effects such arrangements might have on gender-role socialization. Whereas an early study showed no effects on children's gender-role orientation, a followup with the same sample in adolescence found that the more the father had been involved previously in caregiving, the more the adolescents were likely to endorse nontraditional family patterns of employment and childrearing. [*See* FAMILY ROLES AND PATTERNS, CONTEMPORARY TRENDS; WORK–FAMILY BALANCE.]

1. Alternative Family Configurations

Perhaps the greatest shifts within the United States in traditional gender-based parental roles can be seen in some alternative family configurations. As a result of the rising trend for fathers to seek and be awarded custody following divorce, approximately one-sixth of U.S. single parents are men—which represents a 25% increase between 1995 and 1998. This trend suggests a greater acceptance by mothers, the courts, and society that men can parent effectively on their own. There is also research showing that social and psychological outcomes for children in father-custody families are similar to those in mother-custody families, with a few studies suggesting that children may tend to do better in the former—due perhaps to higher income, fewer children in the household, and greater continuing involvement of the noncustodial parent.

Variations in the traditional gender-based definitions of parental roles can also be seen in lesbian and gay two-parent families. In lesbian families, both parents are usually wage earners, and both usually invest equal time in household work. Researchers have found that although biological mothers tend to be more involved in child care and nonbiological mothers tend to spend more time in paid employment, nonbiological mothers tend to be significantly more involved in caregiving than are fathers in heterosexual two-parent families. There is also evidence that within lesbian families children may be better adjusted and parents more satisfied when child care is shared more equally. Similar patterns of shared household and child care responsibilities have been found for gay, two-father families, along with greater relationship satisfaction when those responsibilities are mutually shared. Although there is little research available about these families, studies of gay fathers in general suggest that they may be more nurturing, less concerned with economic providing, more consistent in limit setting, more reasoning, and more democratic in family decision making than heterosexual fathers tend to be.

Questions have been raised, particularly in custody disputes, as to the effects of parental lesbian or gay identity on children's gender-role and sexual orientation. Stereotypes of lesbians as overly masculine have led to concerns about inappropriate modeling and parenting behavior. However, in the research that has been conducted, no differences have been found between lesbian and heterosexual mothers' reports of their gender-role behavior, interest in child rearing, or warmth toward their children. Only one study, comparing African American lesbian and heterosexual mothers, found a difference relevant to gender-role development, which was that lesbian mothers were more likely to have nontraditional expectations for their daughters. [*See* LESBIANS, GAY MEN, AND BISEXUALS IN RELATIONSHIPS.]

In terms of gender-role socialization, the findings for children have been mixed. Studies comparing gender identity development as a function of mother's sexual orientation have found no differences between children of lesbian and heterosexual mothers. Studies comparing the preferences of those two groups for toys, games, television programs, television characters, and vocations have found few differences regarding sex-typed preferences; in general, the preferences of both groups were consistent with conventional gender-role norms. One study did find that daughters of lesbians were more likely than daughters of heterosexual mothers to wear less traditionally feminine clothes, play with traditionally masculine toys such as guns or trucks, engage in rough-and-tumble play, and aspire to careers in traditionally masculine professions; in addition, they found that both daughters and sons of lesbians were less likely than children of heterosexual mothers to prefer sex-typed activities at school and in their neighborhood. Another study, which found no differences in toy preferences, found that sons of lesbians rated themselves as more gentle and aware of others' feelings and daughters of lesbians rated themselves as more adventuresome and higher in leadership than did children of heterosexual mothers. Although all differences that were found were within the normal range, it appears that there may be more gender-role flexibility or psychological androgyny for children of lesbian mothers—and androgyny has been found in other research to be associated with better psychological adjustment. In terms of sexual orientation, studies of adolescent children of lesbians and gay men have found that they are no more likely to identify as lesbian or gay than are children of heterosexual parents.

2. Cultural Variations in Parental Roles

Within diverse cultural groups in the United States, parental roles frequently reflect norms that hark back to the culture of origin. For example, Latino families may show traditional gender role divisions of labor, as well as male dominance and female subordination in family decision making. However, there is also substantial evidence to suggest that marital and parenting roles in Mexican American families have become much more egalitarian, particularly as a result of women's employment outside the home, and that fathers are more involved with their children and less authoritarian in their parenting than had generally been assumed. Asian American families have tended to retain traditional roles, with women expected to be nurturing, family oriented and home centered, and men expected to be dominant, strong, stoic, and family oriented, but also worldly. Respect, order, hierar-

chical authority, and duty are key values that have been retained from the culture of origin. African American families often include extended kinship relationships, which reflect historical patterns of African tribal life; relatives and community members may play a role in child rearing, providing care, protection, guidance, and discipline. African American women have historically been wage earners, and fathers have frequently been absent from the home; in fact, 60% of African American children live in households with no father present—although in many instances, the father maintains some degree of involvement in the child's life. Clearly, the majority culture's traditional gender-based parental roles are not a typical characteristic of African American families.

II. *Gender Differences in Parenting Behavior*

As the preceding discussion demonstrates, in all societies, mothers and fathers to some extent have different family roles, and children get to see particular models of female and male parenting. To what degree this modeling affects their gender-role development is difficult to determine, although the findings of less gender-stereotypic attitudes among children from lesbian-couple and single-father families suggest that it does make a difference. Children whose fathers cook and clean or whose mothers are available only weekday evenings and weekends are likely to have different notions of appropriate gender-role behavior compared with children whose parents assume more traditional family roles. But in addition to this general avenue of influence, there is a more specific way that parental modeling may contribute to gender-role socialization, and that is in the kinds of day-to-day interactions that parents have with their children from birth on. At every stage of development, in the minutiae of daily verbal and nonverbal behaviors toward their children, mothers and fathers are providing gender-role models.

A. MOTHER–FATHER DIFFERENCES IN THE INFANCY PERIOD

Although the findings are somewhat mixed, it appears that mothers and fathers do have different ways of interacting with infants. Across many cultures, mothers not only spend much more time with infants than fathers do, but they spend a greater proportion of that time in caregiving, whereas fathers spend a greater proportion of their time in playful and sociable activities. In terms of behavioral styles, there are some similarities as well as some gender-based differences. Psychologist Ross Parke and his colleagues, observing fathers interacting with newborns in a series of studies, found that U.S. and German fathers showed the same kinds of nurturant behaviors (e.g., vocalizing, touching, kissing) that mothers did. However, they also found that fathers were more likely than mothers to hold, rock, and provide auditory and physical stimulation for their infants. Pediatrician Michael Yogman, studying parents interacting with infants from two weeks to six months of age, found that fathers were more likely than mothers to engage in tactile, arousing, unpredictable games, often involving limb movement; mothers, on the other hand, were more likely to engage in soothing, verbal games, and when they played limb-movement games, they were usually more contained and predictable ones, such as peek-a-boo and pat-a-cake. A number of other studies involving parents with infants up to 30 months of age found that fathers were more likely than mothers to engage in physically arousing play (e.g., bouncing and lifting). Additional studies have found that mothers were more verbal, sociable, and affectionate than fathers with their infants, more likely to engage in reading or toy play with them, and more responsive to the infants' cues of interest and attention—although one study of parents with older infants did not find a difference in responsiveness. Interestingly, the age of the father has proved to be an important factor. In a number of studies, the older the father was, the less likely he was to initiate vigorous physical activity with his infant, and the more likely he was to be responsive and affectionate and to engage the infant in cognitive activities.

Thus, in the first two years of life, babies in many U.S. families may be getting different messages about adult female and male behavior. They may see that mothers are more frequently there, that they take care of bodily needs, that they are attentive and responsive, and that they offer a soothing kind of play. They may also see that fathers are less often present, and that when they are, they are more unpredictable and exciting—but also less responsive to the infant's cues. These initial differences in parental behaviors provide the first steps toward gender-role socialization. However, it is important to note that differences in mothers' and fathers' interactions are themselves culturally influenced. Evidence for this can be found in research conducted in other cultures; although studies in England and India have shown patterns similar to those found in the United States, studies in Sweden and Israel have shown no clear differences between mothers' and fathers' tendencies to engage in play, or in the kinds of play initiated.

B. MOTHER–FATHER DIFFERENCES DURING THE EARLY CHILDHOOD YEARS

Only a small amount of research on parental behavior with young children has included the naturalistic observations of caregiving and spontaneous play that characterize parent–infant research. Psychologist Deborah Best and her colleagues, who studied parents interacting with young children in playground settings in three European countries, found patterns similar to those from U.S. infancy studies. Specifically, in each setting, mothers showed more caregiving behaviors than fathers did, and French and Italian fathers played more with their children than mothers did—although the opposite play pattern emerged for German parents.

In general, however, the research on parent–child interaction during the preschool years has involved more task, teaching, and structured play situations. Even so, some of the findings have been quite similar to those from infancy studies—most notably that fathers engaged children in active, physical play more than mothers did and that mothers were more likely than fathers to engage children with objects such as toys or books and to be more cooperative and emotionally supportive during joint play and problem-solving tasks. In addition, several studies found that fathers were more likely than mothers to show a kind of verbal dominance with their children, in terms of interrupting, talking simultaneously, and giving commands, directions, and rules—and also to provide more cognitive input in the form of functional information and encouragement of children's task performance. On the other hand, another study found that whereas fathers spent more of their time with toddlers and preschoolers in play activities than mothers did, mothers were the ones who gave more instructions and directions. In terms of parents' perceptions of their own behaviors, fathers more than mothers reported behaviors that encouraged their children's intellectual development, whereas mothers put more emphasis than fathers on social development. A further finding of interest is that fathers were more likely than mothers to encourage children to play with toys traditionally deemed appropriate for their sex, while discouraging play with toys seen as appropriate for the opposite sex.

It is difficult to assess the influence of this kind of everyday modeling. Evidence that parents' gender-role attitudes and behaviors help shape children's gender concepts has emerged in studies that examined young children's knowledge of gender stereotypes. Psychologist Beverly Fagot and her colleagues found that in families where fathers gave more sex-typed responses on questionnaires measuring attitudes toward women and child rearing, children showed more knowledge of gender stereotypes. They also found that in families where mothers endorsed more traditional attitudes toward women and gender roles in the family, and initiated and encouraged more sex-typed toy play, children showed greater understanding of gender labels. Furthermore, they found that children whose parents gave more emotionally charged reactions to sex-typed behaviors learned gender labels earlier and played more with sex-typed toys—and that early-labeling girls spent more time communicating with adults and showed less aggression than boys or late-labeling girls. In a similar vein, psychologist Marsha Weinraub and coinvestigators found that fathers' sex-typed personality traits, attitudes about gender roles, and reported activities in their children's presence were associated with children's knowledge of gender differences; however, this association was not found for mothers.

C. MOTHER–FATHER DIFFERENCES IN MIDDLE CHILDHOOD THROUGH ADOLESCENCE

Although there has been less research on gender differences in parenting behavior with older children and adolescents than there has been with infants and preschoolers, the findings tend to be similar. In a number of survey studies in the United States, both girls and boys from ages 6 to 18 reported experiencing more warmth, closeness, support, and affection from mothers than from fathers, which echoes findings from studies with younger children that mothers provided more emotional support. However, the older children and adolescents also reported that mothers provided more limit setting and discipline than fathers did, a finding that did not emerge in the early childhood research. Studies involving older children and adolescents also found that mothers tended to spend more time with their children than fathers did and that they were more likely to be involved in caregiving. In contrast, fathers' time with their children was more likely to be

recreational and their interactions more instrumentally focused.

Gender-related patterns of parenting, reminiscent of those found with infants and preschoolers, have also emerged in cross-cultural studies with older children. Psychologists Graeme and Alan Russell, examining Australian parent–child relationships in middle childhood, found that mothers were more involved with children in caregiving, household tasks, schoolwork, reading, playing with toys, and doing arts and crafts than fathers were. In contrast, fathers were more involved in physical and outdoor play and fixing things around the house than mothers were. Similar findings emerged in a study by this author that compared observations of parents interacting with children from 7 to 12 years of age in three samples of families—one in Mexico, and two in the United States. In the Mexican sample, mothers showed a higher level of caregiving (for example, offering food and helping with grooming) than fathers did, and in the Mexican and one U.S. sample, mothers interacted more frequently with their children than fathers did during the observation sessions. Further, in both U.S. studies, family members reported that mothers were more involved than fathers in various aspects of children's lives (for example, talking over problems and taking them to cultural or recreational activities), and mothers reported being more responsive to children's input in rule making and resolving disagreements. Fathers, on the other hand, in all three samples, engaged in more playful interaction with their children than mothers did and, in the Mexican sample, explained things more to their children.

A recent review by psychologist Campbell Leaper and colleagues examined a large number of observational studies of parents' verbal interaction with children, who ranged in age from infancy to adolescence. The fact that all the data were based on researchers' observations rather than on parents' reports meant that the findings represented what parents actually did, as opposed to what they thought they did. Leaper and colleagues found a number of differences between mothers' and fathers' behaviors across the age range. As in some of the studies mentioned earlier, they found that mothers were more talkative with their children and that they used more supportive language than fathers did. And perhaps related to the finding mentioned earlier that mothers provided more limit setting and discipline with older children and adolescents, these researchers found that mothers used more negative speech with their children than fathers did. For fathers, the pattern of findings was similar to those in studies mentioned earlier, in that fathers provided more cognitively oriented, instrumental interaction in the form of asking questions and giving information and directives.

Thus, gender-based patterns of parenting, evident during the infancy period, seem to persist throughout childhood and adolescence. The model that mothers (compared with fathers) typically present continues to involve spending more time with children, providing for their physical needs, offering emotional support and closeness, being responsive to children's wishes and opinions, and, prior to the adolescent years, engaging with them in activities such as reading and toy play. The model that fathers (compared with mothers) typically present continues to include less overall time with children and less involvement in their lives, with interactions characterized by playfulness and physical activity. In addition, the tendency fathers show with preschoolers to encourage cognitive development by providing functional information also appears with older children, in the form of explaining things, giving directions, and focusing on instrumental topics.

III. *Effects of Children's Gender on Parenting Behavior*

As discussed earlier, culturally determined adult gender roles influence how mothers and fathers typically behave toward their children. However, the child's gender is also a powerful shaping factor, based on cultural beliefs regarding the inherent nature of girls and boys and how they should be socialized. It should be noted that psychologists are by no means in agreement about this topic. An extensive review of the research literature by Eleanor Maccoby and Carol Jacklin, and another by Hugh Lytton and David Romney, concluded that across studies, there were few consistent differences in parents' treatment of girls and boys. On the other hand, Jeanne Block pointed out that few of the studies examined in Maccoby and Jacklin's review looked at fathers, who might be expected to emphasize gender roles more than mothers do, and that most of the studies focused on the early childhood period, when gender-role socialization might be less of a concern for parents than when their children were older.

In addition, the design and methodology of much of the research covered in those two reviews may have limited the extent to which parental gender-role socialization could be examined. Such studies have typically been conducted in the laboratory, or in the home under laboratory-like conditions, and have involved a one-time videotaped session of a mother or father with the child, carrying out a task specified by the researcher. Thus, it hard to know to what extent the observed interactions were representative of the daily interactions that actually occurred between parent and child in the home, around such things as meals, chores, recreation, and bedtime. Leaper and colleagues' recent review of the literature found that both overall differences in mothers' and fathers' behaviors and differences in their behaviors to girls and boys were more pronounced in studies that took place in the home rather than in the lab; thus it appears that laboratory studies may not pick up some socialization differences that do exist. Another reason the earlier reviews may have underestimated actual differences in parents' behaviors to girls and boys is that the small differences found during a single observation session cannot give the full picture of the eight or so hours a day, seven days a week, that parents and children are together, during which those differences, examined cumulatively, might prove to be substantial. Furthermore, some of the categories they used for examining parenting behavior across studies may have been too broad to pick up finer distinctions—for example, looking at parental "control" of girls and boys without examining differences in the *kinds* of controlling behaviors parents directed toward each. Even so, in the bodies of literature they reviewed, a number of important differences did emerge, and those that did not reach statistical significance were generally in the expected direction.

Studies conducted since those earlier reviews were published have continued to find differences in the ways that parents interact with children, depending on their gender. There is also evidence from other cultures to suggest that around the world and across age groups, child gender influences parenting behavior. Further, it is worthwhile to note that in the parenting literature over the past 30 years, although the extent of the differences in behaviors to girls and boys has varied somewhat depending on whether self-reports, lab-type observations, or naturalistic home observations were used, the results from these three different approaches have often converged.

A. PARENTAL RESPONSES TO GENDER IN INFANCY AND TODDLERHOOD

Even before they have interacted with their newborn infants, parents have shown preconceptions of the infants' characteristics based entirely on gender. When asked in one study to describe their newborns within 24 hours of birth, parents of daughters described them as softer, finer featured, littler, and more inattentive than did parents of sons. Fathers made larger gender distinctions than mothers did, in particular, viewing sons as more coordinated, alert, strong, and hardy—although there were no significant gender differences in size, appearance, or muscle tonicity as rated by the physicians who delivered the children. Fathers have also been found to differ more than mothers in their interactions with girls and boys in the first two years of life. With very young infants, fathers of sons tended to show more interested attention than did fathers of daughters, more frequently feeding and diapering them and also more frequently touching, looking, vocalizing, and responding to them. Similar findings have emerged in studies with older infants, in which fathers of sons watched, vocalized to, and played with their babies more than did fathers of daughters. This evidence of a greater interest in and involvement with sons is consistent with findings that fathers to a much greater degree than mothers have shown a preference for having male children. In addition, evidence of fathers' greater interest in infant sons has been found in cultures as diverse as Botswana and Israel.

As well as showing greater levels of interest in and involvement with sons, fathers have been found to interact with them in a manner that is different from the way they interact with daughters. Findings from infancy studies by psychologists Michael Lamb, Tiffany Field, and Ross Parke and his colleagues revealed that fathers of sons engaged in more physical and arousing play and interactive games, and encouraged more visual, fine-motor, and locomotor exploration than did fathers of daughters, whereas fathers of daughters encouraged more vocal behavior than did fathers of sons.

Mothers, too, have shown differences in their behaviors to girl and boy infants, although to a lesser extent than fathers have, and the findings have been less consistent across studies. Developmental psychologist Charles Super, comparing observational data from 13 societies in Africa, Latin America, Europe, and the United States, found that mothers of boys were more likely than mothers of girls to retain the primary caregiving role, rather than turning it over to someone else, that they gave more attention and physical stimulation to their infants than did mothers of girls, and that they were slightly more likely to touch or hold their babies, compared with

mothers of girls. In contrast, in a Swedish study involving nine-month-olds, mothers of girls were in more visual and physical contact with their child and were rated as more sensitive than were mothers of boys, and in a number of U.S. studies of babies and toddlers, mothers of girls were more emotionally responsive to their children than were mothers of boys.

Particularly interesting are findings that suggest that mothers may provide early gender-based messages about what emotions are "appropriate" or "inappropriate" for children to express. One study found that mothers had more contact with female than with male infants when they cried, and that this differential response increased over time; by the time the infants were three months old, mothers were still offering contact to distressed daughters, but with sons, the more the babies cried, the less contact the mothers offered. Another study found that whereas mothers responded less to negative than to positive facial expressions of emotion in three- and six-month-old infants of both sexes, they responded almost not at all to boy's expression of pain. It appears that mothers, most likely without being aware of it, may have interacted with infant sons in ways that served to extinguish crying and expressions of vulnerability—which have traditionally been regarded in this culture as undesirable behaviors in males.

Psychologist Beverly Fagot and her colleagues, who conducted a number of studies examining mothers' and fathers' interactions with girls and boys during toddlerhood, also found recurring distinctions. In general, parents were more accepting of negative, assertive behaviors and vigorous physical activity from boys than from girls. On the other hand, they showed more positive reactions to girls' than to boys' attempts to communicate, and responded more positively to girls' than to boys' requests for help. In addition, parents encouraged girls to help with tasks, but discouraged boys from doing so, and reinforced girls for staying close by—with fathers in particular encouraging their daughters' proximity. Furthermore, parents gave more instructions to girls than to boys; among parent–child dyads, mothers of girls gave the most instruction, and fathers of boys the least. In regard to toy play, parents showed more positive responses when children played with toys deemed appropriate for their gender (e.g., trucks and blocks for boys, dolls and puppets for girls), and fathers in particular responded negatively to boys' play with female-typical toys.

Thus the picture of parenting behavior that has

emerged from research on infants and toddlers shows fairly convincing indications of gender-role socialization. With daughters, parents seem to be encouraging physical and emotional closeness, communication, and the expression of feelings, which may be fostering the kind of relational and emotional orientation that characterizes the traditional female role in this culture. In addition, parents' seem to be promoting girls' dependency by being more willing to help them, encouraging them to stay close by, and giving them more instruction—which may convey the cultural message that females are not as capable as males of doing things on their own. Parents also seem to be socializing girls at this very young age to be helpful to others, which would seem to reflect the traditional gender-role expectation that women should attend to others' needs.

With sons, parents (particularly fathers) seem to be providing more interested attention than with daughters, which may enhance boys' self-confidence and sense of importance. In addition, they seem to be encouraging more physical activity and aggressiveness, while discouraging dependency and fostering autonomy—behavioral characteristics that fit well with the male gender role in Western culture. Furthermore, both fathers and mothers seem to be emotionally "toughening" their sons. Mothers, as described earlier, seem to be teaching infant boys to eschew crying and perhaps even to extinguish their awareness of discomfort or pain. Fathers, on the other hand, may be teaching their sons to suppress fear. In their play with infant and toddler boys, fathers do acrobatic and arousing things: they lift them high in the air, toss them up and catch them, and swing them around upside down by their feet. Although there are data suggesting that young boys come to enjoy such activities, there are no data on their *initial* reactions to this kind of play. It may be that those initial reactions are startle and fear—until the infant catches sight of his father's excited face and hears the enthusiastic "Whee!" which labels the activity as fun rather than danger. What this very early pattern of father–son interaction may represent is a process that teaches boys to equate fun with gross physical activity, sudden movement, a sense of risk or danger, and the translation of fear into excitement. This socialization process could help explain why, throughout childhood, boys consistently show more gross motor play activity and impulsive behavior than girls do. It may also help explain why, from toddlerhood on, many more males than females are treated in hospital emergency rooms

for accidental injury, and why the accidental death rate at all ages is much higher for males than for females.

B. PARENTAL RESPONSES TO GENDER IN THE EARLY CHILDHOOD YEARS

Parents' differential behaviors to girls and boys seem to be most pronounced during toddlerhood, with some differences apparently persisting throughout childhood and adolescence. Researchers have found relatively few distinctions during the early childhood/preschool years, the most consistent ones being that parents emphasized intellectual development for boys more than for girls and used stronger control strategies (such as prohibitions, reprimands, or punishment) with boys than with girls; this latter finding emerged both in never-divorced families and in custodial-mother families following divorce. Findings about fathers in particular, based on a very few studies, are that they interacted more positively and sociably with daughters than with sons, were more controlling and directive with sons than with daughters, and encouraged children to play with toys deemed appropriate for their gender—in particular, discouraging boys' play with female-typical toys. Thus, some of parents' gender-differentiated behaviors in the early childhood years seem consistent with those found in the infancy and toddler periods; parents still seem to be emphasizing cognitive development more for boys and social development more for girls, and encouraging children (particularly boys) to play mainly with same-sex-typical toys. However, one new difference that has emerged at this stage is that parents seem to be exerting stronger control with boys. This may be in response to boys' more active and aggressive behaviors and lower level of compliance, compared with girls, which have been found in a number of U.S. and cross-cultural studies.

C. DIFFERENCES IN PARENTAL BEHAVIORS TO GIRLS AND BOYS FROM MIDDLE CHILDHOOD THROUGH ADOLESCENCE

More extensive differences in parental gender-role socialization have been found beginning in middle childhood than in the preschool years, both in studies of particular age groups and also those involving a wide age range from childhood into adolescence. One finding of interest across the age range is in the area of nurturance. A number of studies, mainly conducted in the United States, found that mothers tended to be more talkative, supportive, and closer to daughters than to sons. However, this differential supportiveness may not be the same in all cultures. Whiting and Edwards, considering parenting with children between the ages of 2 and 10 in their book *Children of Different Worlds*, found that mothers were more nurturant toward daughters in some cultures and towards sons in others. Other studies have found that fathers, in contrast, were closer to sons than to daughters, with the relationships characterized by more interested attention, intellectual involvement, and mutual activity than were their relationships with daughters. Also of note is that several studies found that both parents interrupted girls more than boys.

Another finding from studies of older children and adolescents is that mothers were generally more directive toward girls than toward boys, whether in laboratory task performance or observations in the home. There is some evidence here of consistency across cultures. Whiting and Edwards found that mothers in most of their sample communities assigned more tasks to girls than to boys and expected more help from girls in household work and caring for younger siblings—which presumably would involve a substantial amount of maternal direction giving. Cross-cultural researchers Herbert Barry, Margaret Bacon, and Irvin Child, reviewing ethnographic reports from 110 cultures around the world, found a widespread pattern of parents fostering nurturance, obedience, and responsibility in girls, while encouraging self-reliance and achievement striving in boys. Thus, across a wide range of settings, parents were training girls to follow directions, often in the domains of housework and child care, while training boys to strive for autonomy and achievement. In a similar vein, in a U.S. study focused on domains related to academic success (such as monitoring and helping with homework), mothers granted more autonomy to boys than to girls. Although some scholars have proposed that African American girls have been socialized to be as independent and assertive as are boys, as yet insufficient data are available on the behaviors of African American parents that might foster these characteristics.

A final area of difference is parental discipline and behavioral control. In a number of U.S. studies and across cultures, parents directed commanding and disciplinary behavior more toward boys than toward girls, possibly because boys were less compliant and obedient than were girls. In one study, European American parents of elementary school children em-

phasized obedience for sons more than for daughters, and African American parents disciplined boys more than girls by withdrawing privileges. Whiting and Edwards, summing up the findings from their study of 12 cultures, concluded that boys, because of ongoing socialization, may tend to be less sensitive to the needs of others than girls are and thus less compliant to their mothers' directions—thereby eliciting stronger and more intrusive control strategies from their mothers. By late adolescence, however, the picture is less clear and appears to be influenced by cultural factors. In one study comparing three subgroups of families, African American and European American parents had fewer at-home rules for girls than for boys, whereas Latino parents exerted more at-home control over girls than over boys. On the other hand, African American parents gave more freedom to boys than to girls outside the home, whereas European American and Latino parents gave girls more outside freedom.

An overview of the findings of differential parenting behaviors to girls and boys from middle childhood through adolescence reveals several patterns. In terms of nurturance and attention, although a clear picture does not emerge for mothers, it does for fathers. As found in the research with infants, toddlers, and preschoolers, fathers of school-age children and adolescents continue to show more interested attention to sons, promote their cognitive/intellectual development more, and do more activities with them than they do with daughters. In terms of directiveness, mothers in many cultures play a clear role in socializing their daughters for obedience and responsibility, apparently preparing them for traditional female role obligations regarding homemaking and child care, while socializing their sons for the kind of independence and achievement that frequently characterize the male role. In terms of behavioral control and discipline, at least until adolescence, parents seem to be more forceful with boys than with girls. This may be mainly because boys have not been socialized for obedience, and the autonomy that parents have fostered in them may start to extend into areas over which parents feel they should have more control.

IV. Conclusions

The social construction of gender—the beliefs, meanings, values, and behavioral norms that are associated with being female or male—has a major impact on parenting. Within every culture, it defines expected roles and behaviors for adult women and men, including the work they do inside and outside of the home. In providing templates for culturally appropriate female and male parenting behavior, it mandates who will be the primary caregiver for the children and what mothering and fathering behavior should consist of. It also influences the kind of interactions parents have with female and male children as they socialize them for their expected gender roles.

Although two influential reviews of the developmental literature concluded that there was little consistent evidence of parents' involvement in gender-role socialization, a wider—and also closer—look at available data gives a very different picture. Cross-cultural studies have shown that mothers and fathers around the world do assume distinct family roles, thereby providing models for children of what are female and male domains of responsibility. Numerous studies in the United States and elsewhere have found consistent differences in mothers' and fathers' styles of interaction with their children, indicating that they also provide models of culturally expected female and male behavioral styles. In addition, there is ample evidence from both U.S. and cross-cultural research that parents treat girls and boys differently, in ways that are consistent with culturally prescribed gender roles.

In regard to gender and parental roles, it is clear that in cultures around the world, mothers much more than fathers are primary caregivers within the family and have primary responsibility for household work. This holds true even in societies in which a large percentage of mothers are in the workforce. However, data from U.S. studies of households in which the parenting figures are single fathers or gay or lesbian couples provide strong evidence that parental roles have more to do with social than biological factors. Parenting partners in gay- and lesbian-headed families have been found to share household and child care tasks to a much greater degree than do married mothers and fathers, and single fathers have been found to be nurturant and effective primary caregivers.

In regard to behavioral styles, there is ample research evidence that mothers and fathers provide distinct, ongoing gender-role models for their children in several important ways. From infancy on, mothers (compared with fathers) are generally more available to their children, more attentive to their physical needs, and more emotionally supportive and responsive. Fathers, on the other hand, when they are available, spend proportionately more time play-

ing with their children, often in physically active and arousing ways. After the infancy stage, they also tend to be more cognitively oriented, instrumental, and dominant in their interactions—asking questions, explaining, giving directives, and interrupting. In addition, fathers more than mothers encourage children (especially sons) to play with sex-typical toys. Thus, mothers are modeling for children characteristics that reflect traditional female values—specifically, a focus on creating and maintaining relationships by sharing emotions, fostering intimacy, supporting others, and putting others' needs ahead of one's own. In contrast, fathers, in the form of play and recreation, are modeling vigorous physical activity, which can be viewed as representing the traditional male values of action and adventure. In addition, in showing dominant, instrumental, cognitively oriented, and gender-restrictive behaviors, they are providing models of the cultural script that men take charge, figure things out, get things done, and avoid female-typical activities. It should be noted, however, that although it is possible to speculate about the effects of such modeling on children's gender-role development, not much has been attempted to assess such effects. There is some evidence that parents' gender-role attitudes and behaviors influence children's gender-role concepts, but further research is needed to understand the connections, if any, between specific parent and child gender-typical behaviors.

In regard to parents' differential treatment of girls and boys, there is consistent evidence of gender-role socialization both across cultures and across a wide age range. Parents not only model gender-role behaviors, but the ways they treat daughters and sons in everyday interactions also provide a kind of training in those behaviors. On the most obvious level, an analysis of ethnographies from around the world showed that parents assign tasks that foster nurturance, obedience, and responsibility in girls and self-reliance and achievement striving in boys. On a more subtle level, developmental researchers in studies at home and in the laboratory have found that from toddlerhood on, parents are likely to encourage girls' sociability, dependency, and helpfulness and boys' autonomy and assertiveness, and from the preschool years on, to encourage intellectual development more for boys and social development more for girls. Thus, both the division of labor that parents create for their children and their interactions with them in play, problem solving, and household activities seem to be steering girls and boys toward traditional adult gender roles.

Furthermore, research on parents with infants and toddlers suggests that parents may also be socializing children's emotional expressiveness according to their gender. Specifically, mothers, in not responding to boys' crying and expressions of pain, may be desensitizing them to feelings of distress, while fathers may be teaching boys to ignore or deny fear and to relabel it as excitement. In addition, in allowing boys more than girls to show negative and aggressive behaviors, parents may be signaling that anger is an appropriate emotion for boys but not girls to feel and express. This early differential training may be the first step in socializing children to conform to cultural mandates regarding which emotions are appropriate and which are not for each sex.

In conclusion, the fact that gender-role definitions can change within a given culture, influenced by such things as the international women's movement, technological advancement, urbanization, and economic necessity, only serves to demonstrate that gender, with all its attendant meanings and dictates, is a social construction rather than a biological given. Within each culture, this social construction has a powerful impact on child rearing. Parents both awarely and unawarely, directly and indirectly, foster behaviors and self-perceptions in children that are consonant with their society's gender-role norms. Despite an increased understanding within U.S. culture over the past 30 years of the detrimental effects of gender stereotyping, research on child rearing has continued to find evidence of parental behaviors that contribute to traditional gender-role socialization. It is important to understand this process, so that we can address the limitations it imposes on male as well as female development, and move toward allowing all people to maximize their individual potential.

SUGGESTED READING

Block, J. H. (1979). Another look at sex differentiation in the socialization behaviors of mothers and fathers. In *Psychology of Women: Future Directions for Research* (F. L. Denmark and J. Sherman, eds.), pp. 29–87. Psychological Dimensions, New York.

Bronstein, P. (1988). Father–child interaction: Implications for gender-role socialization. In *Fatherhood Today: Men's Changing Role in the Family* (P. Bronstein and C. P. Cowan, eds.), pp. 107–124. John Wiley & Sons, New York.

Cowan, C. P. and Cowan, P. A. (1992). *When Partners Become Parents: The Big Life Change for Couples*. Basic Books, New York.

Fagot, B. I. (1995). Parenting boys and girls. In *Handbook of Parenting* (M. H. Bornstein, ed.), pp. 163–183. Erlbaum, Mahwah, NJ.

Hrdy, S. B. (1999). *Mother Nature: A History of Mothers, Infants, and Natural Selection*. Pantheon Books, New York.

Leaper, C., Anderson, K. J., and Sanders, P. (1998). Moderators of gender effects on parents' talk to their children: A meta-analysis. *Developmental Psychology* **34**, 3–27.

Lytton, H., and Romney, D. M. (1991). Parents' differential socialization of boys and girls: A meta-analysis. *Psychological Bulletin* **109**, 267–296.

Parke, R. D. (1995). Fathers and families. In *Handbook of Parenting* (M. H. Bornstein, ed.), Vol. 3, pp. 27–63. Erlbaum, Mahwah, NJ.

Patterson, C. J. (1995). Lesbian and gay parenthood. In *Handbook of Parenting* (M. H. Bornstein, ed.), Vol. 3, pp. 255–274. Erlbaum, Mahwah, NJ.

Whiting, B. B., and Edwards, C. P. (1988). *Children of Different Worlds: The Formation of Social Behavior*. Harvard University Press, Cambridge, MA.

Play Patterns and Gender

Carolyn Pope Edwards

Lisa Knoche

Asiye Kumru

University of Nebraska, Lincoln

Glossary

Agents of socialization Individuals or groups (such as parents, peers, media, school) who help guide the younger generation to learn how to behave appropriately, live well, and succeed as members of their social community.

Gender asymmetry Difference in the reactions of one gender group versus the other, for example, a more extreme reaction by boys to male peers who act "girllike," than the reaction by girls to girls peers who act "boylike."

Gender segregation The physical separation, or drawing apart, of females and males for social interaction, work, or play. This is commonly seen in middle childhood play groups.

Gender socialization The process by which the older generation passes to the next generation the capacities to behave in ways deemed appropriate for males and females in a society.

Gender-typed Something that is associated more with one gender (female or male) than the other.

Mixed sex Involving both sexes, for example, when girls and boys join in play.

Sex-role attitudes Thoughts, beliefs, and values that people hold about their own gender group and how they think it is appropriate for males and females to think, believe, and act.

Sex-stereotypes Assumptions about behaviors and beliefs based on gender; for example, the belief that females and males differ in competent driving skill. Stereotypes are generalizations that may or may not be upheld by documented evidence from research.

PLAY is a culturally universal activity through which children explore themselves and their environment, test out and practice different social roles, and learn to interact with other children and adults. Early in life, children identify themselves as a girl or a boy, and this basic self-categorization lays a foundation for their developing beliefs about with whom, what, how, and where they will play. Children play an active role in their own and their peers' gender socialization (the process by which they come to acquire the knowledge, values, and skills needed to behave "appropriately" as a male or female in their society). However, they are greatly influenced by the adult community, as represented by the institutions of family, neighborhood, school, and the media. These agents of socialization contribute to children's understanding of gender roles and expectations, and these in turn influence the developing play patterns of children.

I. Play Companions

Play companions are important for children because they influence social interaction, activities, and toy preferences. After the age of three, girls and boys tend to play separately rather than together, particularly when they are in large single-age peer groups. The pulling apart of girls and boys into separate play groups is one of the most striking, well-documented, and culturally universal phenomena of middle childhood.

Girls tend to show the preference for same-sex interactions earlier than boys do. Ate the age of three, girls are often seen in small group activities with other girls. By the age of four, boys begin to show a preference for large group interactions with other boys and even take an active role in maintaining the boys' separation from the girls. From preschool age continuing up until adolescence, children say they like children of their own sex better and want to play with them more. However, in most cases, children do not actively dislike or want to avoid totally the other sex, but instead, simply prefer their own. Patterns of gender segregation for play and leisure, seen in middle childhood, are found throughout the world and in all subcultures that have been studied.

There are multiple reasons suggested for the segregation of the sexes in play. Eleanor Maccoby, a noted psychologist who has written a great deal about this issue, has contended that boys and girls have different styles of play that are not attractive to each other. Boys tend to monopolize play space and materials and to use a confrontational and physical style intended to secure them access to what they want. Their rough play style, as they wrestle and chase, is not so congenial to girls. Same-sex playmates appear to be more compatible in the pacing and flow of their play. Girls seek a smoothly flowing style of play and interaction. They can be observed easily taking turns and incorporating one another's words and ideas into their play, and they readily adjust the noise and activity level of their play to the context they are in. Girls also have a better command of language at an earlier age, allowing them to express their ideas relatively well and communicate their ideas to reach a common understanding. In contrast, boys seem to prefer an exciting even if more discontinuous flow of play. Boys can be seen using and responding to the more direct strategies of control, such as strong commands ("Come outside!"). They are less likely to appreciate and formulate indirect expressions, such as, "I wish we could go outside now." Boys also more frequently resort to physical forms of persuasion than do girls.

As a result of their different styles of play, Eleanor Maccoby believes that each sex comes to develop stereotypes about the other group that create separate worlds of meaning and friendship. The world of each sex is not well understood by the other. Friendship selection comes to be gender based, with girls and boys utilizing different criteria in the selection process. Boys select a peer group based primarily on shared interests and activities, such as playing soccer or riding bicycles. Girls tend to think about interests also, but in addition, consciously make their friendship selections considering liked and disliked personality characteristics.

Agents of socialization—peers, parents, and teachers—play an important part in shaping the play and friendship patterns of children. Both peers and adults tend to encourage children to play with others of the same sex, particularly once children are beyond preschool. Many parents feel it is their role to help their children form and maintain friendships, by helping them to make play dates or getting them together with family or neighborhood friends who have children deemed appropriate for their own to play with. Peers also play a role in shaping children's friendship patterns by expressing disapproval for cross-sex play. Boys do this most; they disapprove and tease other boys for being a "sissy" more than girls tease other girls for being a "tomboy." Boys may even experience the companionship and the play scenarios of girls as something "dangerous" to be avoided if they want to be accepted into the world of male peer play. Thus, from a fairly young age, children develop concerns and expectations about how peers might react to their own play and behavior by observing what children around them say and do to one another.

School structures and practices may reinforce these perceptions as well. Children separate by sex in the lunchroom, on the playground, in the hallway, and wherever they have freedom of movement. Same-sex preferences dominate children's school associations, starting about kindergarten, increasing through the middle school years, and then declining during early or late adolescence, depending on the cultural community.

On the other hand, girls and boys do play together at times. These mixed-sex play groups tend to include more than just two or a few children and may be focused around a large group game (such as a ball game) or dramatic and fantasy play. In addition, teachers often use activity settings and toys or materials to encourage children to play with a wider group of peers. For example, teachers sometimes use attractive novel toys or lessons to attract diverse children to play or work together. At other times, they assign children to activities to prevent them from gravitating to their usual same-sex friends. When teachers form mixed-sex collaborative groups, they provide girls and boys with opportunities to come close and understand each other better. As the children spend more time together, the girls and boys may develop some common play themes and learn to play together more cooperatively.

In some situations, boys can dominate mixed-sex play groups. Aggression, conflicts, and rejecting behaviors occur more frequently in mixed-sex than single-sex play groups. Perhaps these negative behaviors are simply another indication of the difficulty in merging girls' and boys' play styles and preferences. When a girl or boy does seek to join a cross-sex playgroup, that child is rarely considered a central member of the group. For example, when a girl attempts to join a male peer group, she may find herself ignored by the boys or left on the outskirts of events. When a boy tries to participate in female activities, he may fare even worse and receive negative feedback from peers, both girls and boys.

II. Toy and Activity Preferences

As they grow older, boys and girls differ not only in playmates but also in their preferred toys, games, and activities. The difference in regards to toy preference appears around the age of two and strengthens by the age of five, as children come under the socializing influences of peers, parents, and the media. Societal expectations and values can create powerful pressures for females and males to behave appropriately according to gender and cultural norms. While it is too simplistic to assume that children never like to play with toys and materials considered more appropriate for the other sex, nevertheless, there are overall patterns of preference and some commonly occurring themes specific to boys or girls. For the past 60 years, the literature on play has found distinctive patterns of gender-typed preferences in childhood toys and activities.

Girls' play tends to center on themes related to family and domestic life. In many communities, girls can often be observed playing with dolls, household objects, dress-up clothes, and related materials for creative expression. The dramatic play of young girls, even when highly imaginative, tends to be structured by goals or "scripts" with a specific sequence and outcome in mind from the onset, based on discussion and agreement. When girls start a dramatic play script in the preschool, they are upset when someone interferes and prevents them from completing the sequence of events they have agreed upon.

The play activity of boys, in contrast, may be different in form and focus from that of girls. Boys are often found playing with transportation toys, weapons, and building materials. They are often noisy in their play, shouting out the "swoosh" of the sword or the "crash" of the car. As they grow older, boys engage in much large group competitive play, such as sports. There is a certain gender asymmetry in this, in that boys from kindergarten onward tend to be more concerned with selecting toys and activities that they consider appropriate to their sex than are girls. Boys may be quite concerned with not appearing "girl-like," and they may closely monitor each other's play.

Studies have found that not only do males' gender-typed preferences emerge earlier than do girls, but also their preferences are more stable and consistent. That is, girls may play with many different types of toys, but boys more predictably turn to the masculine stereotyped play items. These toy choices may reflect a desire for peer approval and the wish to avoid negative reactions. Indeed, playmates of the same sex are more likely to approach a child when he or she is using toys that are considered gender appropriate. However, how the children label the toys as "for girls" or "for boys" is a bit flexible and influenced partially by the children's personal inclinations and experiences. For example, certain boys may consider drawing and art as fine for boys, while many girls today judge computers and vigorous sports as equally appropriate for both girls and boys. Children can change their minds as to what boys and girls "like to do" when their experiences provide them good reason to believe that what is "okay" is actually different from what they used to think.

Children's toy preferences and activities are also influenced in many ways by parents. Parents provide gender-typed environments that may be subtle ways of channeling children's preferences and their behavioral tendencies for activities and interests. Parents tend to present girls and boys with distinct social contexts. For example, even from birth, parents provide gender-typed environments by how they decorate their babies' bedrooms, using more soft colors, ruffled materials, and rounded, multicolor designs for girls and more bright colors and linear styling for boys.

Additionally, parents attempt to pass their own sex-role attitudes on to their children, along with the gender-typed environments they create. Those parents who hold particularly traditional sex-role attitudes have been found to gravitate most toward gender-stereotyped toys for their children. For example, at holidays and birthdays, they may be seen purchasing racecars and plastic guns for their sons and dolls and tea sets for their daughters. However, their reasons behind these choices may be complicated. On the one hand, parents may be buying children toys that adults consider gender appropriate and thereby guiding their children's emerging preferences. On the other hand, parents also respond to preferences that their children assert and to the requests that children declare. Thus, the direction of influence may go both ways.

Children's preferences about toys and activities are also influenced by the media and advertising. In fact, in much film and television programming, the sexes are portrayed in stereotypic ways, although lately there have been some improvements, particularly in educational television and some of the cable channels invented for young viewers. When young children gather in play groups, boys are more likely to enact fictional, superhero roles portrayed on television ("Power Rangers"), whereas girls are more likely to portray familial characters ("Rug Rats"). On the other hand, television also has the potential to soften or reverse children's gender-stereotypic attitudes. Research has found that when children receive exposure over time to nontraditional media portrayals of adult occupations, they may be influenced to realize, for example, that men can be nurses and women can be doctors or airline pilots.

The overall effect of commercial television is to promote children's preferences for gender-stereotyped toys and activities. Children not only watch many hours of cartoons and other programs, but also seem to use television heroes and animated characters as important symbolic figures to incorporate into their play. Manufacturers of toys, clothing, and food targeted for children know that children are very interested in what they see on television. They therefore take advantage of children's interests to promote gender-stereotyped toys and other products in a direct and explicit way. Children thus come to consume not only the products but also the gender stereotypes but forward by the pervasive images seen in the media. Children may take in the ideas, attitudes, and values consistent with the rather simplified and extreme versions of gender stereotypes that the commercial media promote. [See MEDIA INFLUENCES; MEDIA STEREOTYPES.]

Additionally, children's play today is increasingly coming to be influenced by video games and the Internet. Many video games are highly sexist and limiting in the styles of thinking and acting that they foster, particularly in the way that they steer boys toward fantasy violence. These new media can come to create a highly gender-stereotypic play environment for children.

However, not all video games are gender typed, just as not all television programs promote gender stereotypes. Many learning-based computer games present nonstereotyped images, and many television programs, particularly on public television, seek to present alternative and expansive views of the world. Moreover, many toys and activities are gender neutral, that is, liked by both girls and boys. Wagons, roller blades, scooters, stuffed animals, puppets, and constructive materials such as water, sand, paint, and clay tend to encourage mixed-sex play. Also, activities such as dodge ball and hide-and-seek that do not involve choosing sides also encourage mixed-sex play. At school, many teachers try to plan, organize, and structure activities so as to sometimes minimize sex differentiation in play patterns.

III. Types of Play

Sex differences are seen not only in children's play companions, toys, and activities, but also in *how* and *where* they play. Children engage in many types of play, ranging from simple symbolic (pretend) play to complex games with rules.

A. SYMBOLIC PLAY

Children use objects in play in a symbolic way more and more during the second and third years of life. They begin to substitute different meanings for the same object, for example, pretending a wooden block is a racecar or a scrap of cloth is a doll blanket. As they develop stories and roles, their simple pretend play elaborates into sociodramatic, make-believe play, which is especially prevalent during the preschool and early primary years. Sociodramatic play has three elements: props, plots, and roles. Further examination of the elements highlights differences in girls' and boys' symbolic play.

Both girls and boys engage in sociodramatic play with equal frequency, motivation, and maturity. Thus, sociodramatic play is similar across gender groups, even if its specific content and themes are different. In many cultural communities, boys pretend to be heroic characters, warriors, monsters, and men who control or manage large animals. Overall, they show higher levels of noise and physical activity in their sociodramatic play than do girls. In their play, boys explore imaginative and realistic themes that make great use of the tools and vehicles they see in use in the masculine world around them. Girls, in contrast, more typically prefer to act out scenes from familiar settings, such as the home, school, and doctor's office, where they can rehearse and create domestic roles and helping themes that involve complex coordination and cooperation. Girls are focused on enacting "real" events during pretend play, like going to the doctor's office or to school. Interrelationships and nurturance persist in girls' pretend play throughout the primary grades.

In choosing roles, children often select a part to play that is consistent with their gender. Boys prefer the roles of father, brother, husband, or a traditionally male occupation, whereas girls often choose the roles of mother, sister, wife, or what they see as a female occupation. They may act out activities based on practices at their home, choosing, for example, cleaning chores or yard work in accordance with how these tasks are assigned in their extended family.

But children do not limit themselves exclusively to real-world constraints. Cross-sex role play can easily be seen in children, particularly at younger ages. Children often incorporate many disparate elements into their play, for example, pretending to be a repairman but carrying a vacuum cleaner in the tool kit, or wearing a hardhat but carrying a purse. If they choose, boys and girls can act out and vicariously experience traditionally cross-sex roles during their play. It seems that children are interested in the play of the other sex, regardless of whether or not they participate. They also often like to watch or be drawn into others' sociodramatic play and know about play themes that are good for mixed sex play.

B. ROUGH-AND-TUMBLE PLAY

Rough-and-tumble play is more typical of boys than of girls in many cultural communities around the world. In this play style, children engage in what looks like aggression (hitting, chasing, pushing, name calling), but is in fact play. The behavior is accompanied by laughter, "play faces," and excitement that only sometimes gets out of control and escalates into hostile aggression and the intent to hurt. In rough-and-tumble play, children test out their strength and toughness and develop the capacity to compete and struggle for dominance without injury or lasting damage. Girls, too, sometimes engage in rough-and-tumble play, especially in cultural communities where girls and boys have a lot of freedom to play outside, in mixed-sex groups, away from direct supervision and the pressure to be neat, clean, and controlled.

Evidence suggests that girls are just as physically active as boys until age four or five. But girls are better able to moderate and tone down their activity levels in response to contextual cues (for example, whether they are indoors or outdoors or according to the social expectations). After the age of five, boys demonstrate more boisterous physical levels than do girls.

C. CONSTRUCTIVE/CREATIVE PLAY

Constructive play involves creating or constructing something using any of a variety of natural or synthetic materials. All around the world, both boys and girls engage in a great deal of this kind of play. Both sexes enjoy drawing, painting, puzzles, and making things of paper, clay, wire, and natural materials. Traditionally, building toys, such as plastic blocks, and scientific toys, such as magnets and motors, were marketed more for boys than girls, though today this is changing to some degree. Teachers actively promote constructive/creative play, because they believe that it is very important for children's learning and development. Therefore, they may seek to ensure that both girls and boys engage in constructive and creative activities, often side by side or in cooperation with children of the other sex.

D. GAMES

Games are a type of play based on rules and standards of performance. Competitive games, especially those involving physical testing, seem to be highly attractive to many boys beyond the preschool age.

Today, in many societies, opportunities for sports such as soccer, gymnastics, basketball, softball, volleyball, and tennis are also increasingly opening to girls of all ages. In addition, girls like games that include rhythm, whole body coordination, and chanting or singing (for example, jump rope, hopscotch, and clapping games), while boys select games involving the use of large muscles and skills of throwing and hitting targets (baseball, marbles, wrestling, archery). Boys' play is often congenial to a large group, whereas girls' games work well for smaller groups. Both girls and boys are interested in fairness issues and use conflict and argument to develop skills of negotiation and group dynamics.

IV. Play Location

Finally, sex differences can be found in *where* children play. In general, girls are more often found closer to home or indoors except when they are sent on a specific errand, such as fetching firewood or water. They spend more time in contact with supervising adults (usually mothers and other female relatives), doing responsible work or child care that they can often combine with pleasurable talk or moments of playful fun. In contrast, boys tend to play farther away from home, outdoors, away from direct adult supervision, less often involved in responsible work than girls. In cultural communities where children at a young age begin helping their families with significant chores, both girls and boys can often be seen integrating play into their work activities, for example, building a dam of mud and sticks in the stream while herding animals or combining songs, jokes, and a game of jacks with infant care.

In the school yard, where many children of a similar age and skill level are gathered, boys and girls often segregate themselves into separate play areas. Boys tend to take over a larger, more central space, leaving the girls to play along the periphery. Boys take up to 10 times the amount of space on the playground than do girls, and they often invade girls' activities. During the middle childhood years, both girls and boys often engage in a playful kind of "border work," where they tease, chase, and taunt one another, seeking the attention of the other group (and the teacher!) and exploring each other's world from the margins.

Gender segregation is most common on the school yard. It is less likely to be seen in the backyard and around the neighborhood, where children more com-

monly play in mixed-age and mixed-sex groups. Away from the school yard, ancient games prevail, such as hide and seek, tag, card games, and ball games, that easily allow children to cross sex and age lines. In the neighborhood and nearby woods, lots, and fields, children like to build forts, castles, and houses and to act out elaborate fantasy scripts. Such activities are attractive to both mixed- and single-sex groups of children ranging from preschool age to the end of middle childhood.

V. Socialization

Children are active agents in their own gender learning and socialization, but the adults and the community around them are also influential shapers of their preferences and patterns of play. Many parents promote early learning of gender distinctions by providing toys and materials that encourage single-sex play or by drawing children into activities that are strongly gender typed in their culture. Research studies have found that children learn gender labels (such as "girl," "boy," "woman," and "man," and gender pronouns) at an earlier age when their parents use more traditional practices and encourage their use of gender-stereotyped toys in free play. Additionally, by encouraging particular activities, parents may influence children's learning of cognitive and social skills. For instance, when parents give girls dollhouses and encourage them to arrange the tiny furniture and figures, they support fine motor development and aesthetic values. When they encourage boys' constructive play with building blocks and mechanical toys, they may foster their greater skill at visual-spatial and logical-mathematical tasks and thereby contribute to emerging gender differences in these areas. Furthermore, when parents provide toys and materials according to gender, they may also indirectly influence their children's interaction styles. For example, toys such as wagons, fire trucks, and tricycles tend to encourage action play with less physical proximity and less intimate verbal interaction with peers than do toys such as small figures, stuffed animals, and toy dishes and clothing.

Children themselves may influence their own gender socialization by how they segregate themselves into single-sex groups. As we have said, in these groups children practice gender-typed play with toys and learn gender-typed interaction styles. Over the long-term, girls' and boys' experiences in separate play worlds may have enduring consequences. The social norms, skills, and expectations learned in peer groups may influence children's aspirations and social achievements. Many girls may become comfortable in activities that emphasize cooperation, and boys may come to enjoy and seek out activities that emphasize overt competition.

Finally, schools and teachers perform an important and multifaceted role in gender development. Research has documented many ways in which schools and teachers subtly or otherwise direct boys and girls toward separate interests and to feel competence in different areas. On the other hand, in the school setting, children have many opportunities to observe and come close to the other sex and to engage in lessons that promote the same basic kinds of symbolic skills and interests in both girls and boys. Through school experience, children become more at ease with the other sex and are exposed to similar information about the outside world and the range of academic subjects. [*See* ACADEMIC ENVIRONMENTS.]

Teachers with more traditional gender roles tend to have teaching practices that encourage greater sex segregation in children's schoolwork and play, and that reinforce different behaviors in stereotyped ways. Instead, however, teachers can choose picture books, textbooks, and software that may incline children toward either more or less gender-typed play. They can arrange the free play environment and children's placement at work tables so as to either encourage or discourage single-sex versus mixed-sex play and interaction. They can introduce children to computer games and educational television programming that encourages more open attitudes toward gender roles and play. Finally, they can engage children's families in dialogue about how to plan play spaces, join their children's play, and help children learn skills of conflict resolution that enhance less gender-typed play learning opportunities for children.

SUGGESTED READING

Fagot, B. I., and Leinbach, M. D. (1991). Gender-role development in young children: From discrimination to labeling. *Developmental Review* **13**, 205–224.

Fromberg, D. P., and Bergen, D. (1998). *Play from Birth to Twelve and Beyond: Context, Perspectives, and Meanings.* Garland, New York and London.

Maccoby, E. (1998). *The Two Sexes: Growing up Apart, Coming Together.* Harvard University Press, Cambridge, MA.

Ruble, D. N., and Martin, C. L. (1998). Gender development. In *Handbook of Child Psychology* (W. Damon, ed.), 5th ed., vol. 3; *Social, Emotional, and Personality Development* (N. Eisenberg, vol. ed.), pp. 933–1016. Wiley, New York.

Sutton-Smith, B. (1979). The play of girls. In *Becoming Female: Perspectives on Development* (C. B. Kopp and M. Kirkpatrick, eds.), pp. 229–257. Plenum, New York.

Whiting, B. B., and Edwards, C. P. (1998). *Children of Different Worlds: The Formation of Social Behavior.* Harvard University Press, Cambridge, MA.

Political Behavior

Lauren E. Duncan
Smith College

I. History of Politics and Gender
II. Antecedents of Nonconventional Political Behavior
III. Effects of the Women's Movement on Women's Political Behavior
IV. Summary and Future Directions

Glossary

Feminist consciousness The belief that women are unjustly deprived of power and influence through systemic or structural factors.

Political behavior Characterizes efforts to affect the distribution of power and resources in a state community. It includes collective and individual acts that are motivated by political purposes or have political consequences. Conventional political behavior encompasses mainstream activities such as voting and office holding. Nonconventional political behavior includes activities such as participation in boycotts, demonstrations, consciousness-raising groups, and organizations trying to effect political change.

Political efficacy The belief that one's efforts in the political sphere can have an impact on politics.

Private versus public sphere The division of the world into two separate and complementary arenas, the private (home, family) and the public (work, politics, government), often believed to be the appropriate realms of women and men, respectively.

Relative deprivation A negative emotion experienced by individuals who feel they are unjustly deprived of something they desire relative to others.

Socialization The process whereby one learns culturally prescribed attitudes, values, and behavior, usually through direct teaching or indirect modeling.

DEFINITIONS OF POLITICAL BEHAVIOR have changed over time and in response to critiques of feminists and other scholars interested in including the behaviors of groups of people who traditionally have not held a lot of power and influence in North American society. This article briefly reviews the traditional and current definitions of political behavior, specifically examining how gender and politics have been treated by social scientists. The effects of the women's movement on women's political behavior are examined closely. Throughout this article, distinctions will be made between conventional and nonconventional political behavior, with conventional behavior being more characteristic of White men and nonconventional behavior being more characteristic of people of color and women of all races and ethnicities.

I. History of Politics and Gender

Research in political science has consistently reported that women are not as interested in or involved in mainstream political activities as men. At least until the early 1970s, studies found that women scored lower than men on political efficacy and interest in politics, and were less likely to vote and hold political office. In terms of political attitudes, women have been shown to be more compassionate than tough-minded, communal rather than individualistic, and public interested rather than self interested. These differences are evident in women's greater likelihood (relative to men) of supporting issues such as welfare, arms control, leniency on capital punishment, and social services. However, a number of feminist scholars have identified limitations and biases apparent in this research. For example, Karen Beckwith showed that gender differences in political participation have been overstated by researchers. Studies based on large, nationally representative samples have shown small (and shrinking) differences between women and men in their voter participation since 1952, and negligible differences in likelihood to contribute to political campaigns, attend political meetings, and work for political parties and organizations. M. Kent Jennings demonstrated that for political party delegates, men's and women's rates of voluntary participation have not differed much over time. However, men and women do seem to concentrate their efforts on different issues (e.g., men are more likely to work for veterans', fraternal, labor, service, and occupational organizations whereas women are more likely to work for reproductive rights, teachers', school-related, public interest, and women's organizations). Obviously, then, how one defines political behavior has a great impact on how involved researchers find women and men to be.

Roberta Sigel discussed these biases and limitations in detail, identifying three ways political scientists and the public have thought about gender since World War II that have affected research on women and men's political behavior. Immediately following the war, research in political science largely ignored women. When women were discussed at all, the emphasis was on how women differed from men and relied on essentialist arguments based on "nature," or the assumption of innate biological differences. During the second stage, differences were still emphasized but presumed to be a result of socialization, not biology, and during the third stage, the emphasis switched to considerations of how power differences (rather than sex differences) influenced political behavior.

A. ESSENTIALIST EXPLANATIONS

In the first two decades following World War II, research on the political behavior of women was largely nonexistent. Sigel argued that this was due to the belief popular with the public and scholars that women and men occupied two different and complementary spheres: women were responsible for the home, pro-

viding for the comfort of husbands and the moral education of children, and men were obligated to provide the family with material necessities and to run the economy and government. At this time politics was defined as a male domain, an impure activity that would corrupt women. There were a few women discussed as rare exceptions (such as Golda Meir and Indira Gandhi) to the rule that women were not interested in, nor particularly suited to, participation in politics. Thus, definitions of political behavior included attempts to influence the major centers of government and ignored more alternative or quasi-political activities such as attempts to influence local educational programs, which were more likely to attract women and others with less political power (such as people of color and working-class people).

Because women were not visible in mainstream public politics, they were often considered to be disinterested or ill suited to politics. For example, after women gained suffrage in 1921, they did not turn out to vote in great numbers (and they voted less frequently than men). Political scientists explained this finding using what were essentially biological explanations about how women lacked the propensity for political conflict or at least the appetite for its competitiveness and aggression. In other words, their emotional temperaments caused them to avoid politics altogether and focus on pursuits more suited to their tender natures, which tended to be private sphere concerns. Men, on the other hand, were born aggressive and enjoyed tough-minded decision making; thus, they were naturally well suited to the rough-and-tumble world of politics.

An alternative explanation offered by feminist scholars relies on the fact that at the time, there was a strong public feeling that women were not suited to politics and that voting constituted unladylike behavior. Women socialized before suffrage was gained were especially susceptible to these pressures. The fact that, over time, differences between women's and men's voting turnout have disappeared lends credence to the latter argument, that social pressures and habit played a greater role in determining political behavior than did biology.

When political scientists did consider women's political behavior, they searched for gender differences. Male political behavior was taken as the norm and women's behavior was compared to male standards. In such comparisons, women were almost always found to be lacking. For example, they were found to be less likely to hold political office than men, to express less interest in politics than men, and to display lower levels of political efficacy than men. Again, these differences were taken as support for biologically based explanations about essential differences between women's and men's natures that led women to be less suited to politics; explanations exploring women's position in the social structure were not offered. It should be noted that similar arguments have been used to explain the less frequent voting behavior and office-holding of ethnic minorities in this country.

B. SOCIALIZATION EXPLANATIONS

After about 1960, political scientists explained deficits in women's political participation in terms of socialization. In contrast to strict biological explanations, socialization arguments recognized the influence of social pressures on women's and men's behaviors. However, Sigel argued that these explanations also had their flaws. First, early writings argued that socialization into private versus public spheres was positive and necessary to maintain society. There was no acknowledgement of the fact that females were socialized into roles that involved subordination to males and emphasized less socially valued family roles. Second, these arguments overemphasized the influence of childhood political socialization, characterizing women as passive agents in their own lives, incapable of resisting this socialization or making changes as adults. We know from research on the effects of the 1960s and 1970s women's movement that women who participated often made dramatic changes in their life circumstances and personalities. In addition, any research that emphasized differences between groups— whether based on biological or socialization arguments—tended to ignore both similarities *between* groups and differences *within* groups. The history of research on sex differences in psychology is rife with this kind of bias. For example, research on gender focuses on the differences between men and women, and not on the similarities between men and women, or on the differences among men and the differences among women. In many ways, this focus on group differences has perpetuated implicit justifications for women's exclusion from mainstream politics by treating women and men as separate and complementary species.[SEE HISTORY OF THE STUDY OF GENDER PSYCHOLOGY.]

Additionally, this emphasis on group differences has led researchers to ignore very real situational pressures and constraints that help shape behavior. In other words, we are all familiar with what gender role socialization requires of conventional men and women in certain situations (e.g., in arguments men should focus on winning their point whereas women should focus on maintaining or repairing interpersonal relationships). Whether men and women comply with these pressures is dependent on complicated situational factors (e.g., status of the other person in the dyad). Thus, in some situations, there is more pressure to act in ways that are consistent with prescribed gender roles, even if in other circumstances one would tend to act quite differently. For example, female job applicants have been shown to vary their clothing, makeup, behavior, and even opinions according to how traditional their potential employer was believed to be. Finally, research on group differences tends to take one group as the norm and compare the other to it. As discussed in the previous section, men were taken as the starting point and women compared to them. This resulted in a perpetuation of traditional definitions of political behavior that tended to ignore or discount ways in which women have traditionally been politically active. As mentioned earlier, these sorts of comparisons tend to treat members of each sex as a unitary group, ignoring real differences among women and men in life experiences and socialization (e.g., the socialization of middle-class White girls might include the expectation of college and a period of unemployment devoted to child rearing, whereas the socialization of working-class girls of all races and ethnicities might include the hope of college and the expectation of an uninterrupted work life).

C. GENDER AND POWER

More recently, the notion that gender is a social construction, used to create and maintain power differences, has become central to feminist understandings of men's and women's behavior. Acknowledging the connection between power and gender also allows scholars to recognize the distinction between private and public spheres as another social construction that serves to keep women in the home and out of politics. In terms of political behavior, paying attention to issues of power means reconceptualizing women's political behavior to take into account their material positions in society. For example, studies have shown that people in relatively powerless positions tend to use different types of tactics than more powerful people to get what they want, and these tactics are usually more indirect, less confrontational, and may rely on resistance and rebellion rather than operating through conventional political channels. These insights have informed our recent understanding of the political behavior of women, as well as people of color.

Patricia Hill Collins discussed Black women's activism as encompassing two traditions. The first is a struggle for group survival, consisting of actions taken to create Black female spheres of influence. In most cases, this type of activism does not directly challenge oppressive structures because direct opposition can be extremely costly, for example, by incurring job loss or physical danger. Instead, women involved in creating female spheres of influence do so by undermining, rather than directly challenging, oppressive structures. Collins gives the examples of Black domestic workers who act as though they are grateful for clothing handouts from White employers but then discard the clothing when they get home or workers who do not disclose the fact that their children are attending college. These actions undermine an oppressive structure by giving control over self-definition to the domestic worker. That is, the oppressive structure assumes that women who have accepted their subordinate position in the social structure should be grateful for handouts instead of raises and would not encourage their children to go to college. By insisting on defining themselves regardless of stereotypes or requirements for their low-status positions, these women resist structural pressures that are eager to pigeonhole them into restrictive roles. Similarly, some contemporary feminists have argued that they are "reclaiming" ultra-feminine dress, makeup, and cultural icons such as Barbie and reworking them into feminist symbols.

The second strand of traditional Black women's activism that Collins discussed consists of the struggle for institutional transformation or the struggle to change existing oppressive structures. Participating in so-called disorderly political behavior (nonconventional or nonmainstream politics) includes participation in civil rights organizations, labor unions, feminist groups, boycotts, and revolts. These types of nonmainstream activities have traditionally been utilized by people with little access to conventional forms of political power, and at times they have been very successful in achieving their aims. One of the reasons these methods are successful is that they rely on existing neighborhood, church, or community networks. For example, in 1955, the African American community in Montgomery, Alabama, was able to mobilize, literally overnight, to participate in the famous bus boycott catalyzed by Rosa Parks's refusal to give up her seat on a bus to a White man. The Black community was able to sustain this boycott for over a year because of the cohesion of the group and the emotional support provided by their local churches and church leaders. Certainly, the tight neighborhood networks utilized during the civil rights movement illustrate a great strength of African American society. However, especially at the local level, organizers for women's rights have also been able to utilize grass-roots networks. For example, Faye Ginsburg discussed the importance of these networks to mobilizing both prochoice and prolife groups in Fargo, North Dakota, in the early 1980s in response to the establishment of an abortion clinic in the city.

To summarize, social scientific conceptualizations of gender and politics have gone through three stages in understanding women's political behavior. First, women's participation was largely ignored, as women were considered to be disinterested or ill suited to conventional party politics. These arguments were based on essentialist explanations that justified separate and complementary spheres for women and men. Later, biological explanations were rejected, and socialization arguments took their place. These explanations relied on the acknowledgement of social pressures to adhere to traditional gender roles, but were limited because they did not take into account real constraints on women's behavior. Finally, feminist reconceptualizations of political behavior have tended to recognize the interconnectedness of gender and power, acknowledging that gender role socialization is used to maintain separate spheres for women and men. These reconceptualizations have also begun defining women's political behavior by looking at women's lives and including nonconventional forms of political activity such as those formerly considered to be illustrative of private sphere concerns (e.g., activities on behalf of alcohol prohibition, schools, the community, and the church.)

Of course, social scientific research on gender and political behavior has gone beyond simple documentation of participation rates. Many researchers are interested in understanding the factors that contribute to political participation. The following section reviews the research on antecedents of political behavior, with a special emphasis on motivation for nonconventional political behavior.

II. Antecedents of Nonconventional Political Behavior

Political science research on the antecedents of conventional political participation tends to focus on childhood learning, or political socialization, as a major factor. Agents of political socialization include the family, school, peers, media, and historical events. Political socialization, in turn, is affected in various ways by social structural variables such as generation, gender, social class, race and ethnicity, and religion. Intrapersonally, variables such as political efficacy and trust influence levels of participation, as do educational attainment and employment in particular settings. These demographic variables have been well studied in political science, but do not necessarily tell us much about the psychological connections to participation. More interesting and relevant to women's lives is recent research exploring the antecedents and correlates of nonconventional political participation.

Research arising from the widespread student protests of the 1960s and 1970s showed that early participants in these movements tended to come from politically liberal backgrounds and non- or liberal religious families. Research on the child-rearing styles of the parents of student activists showed that these early activists came from relatively warm and permissive homes where discipline per se was not emphasized, where parents were likely to involve the child in family decisions, and where the environment was accepting and affirming. Finally, some studies have suggested that parents' active commitment to collective action as a "way of doing" social change encouraged children to do the same. These characteristics seem to have differentiated early movement participants from nonparticipants. By the late 1960s, when participation in student movements was more widespread, participants were more heterogeneous in terms of personality and family background characteristics.

In terms of personality, research on correlates of student activism showed that politically active students scored higher on measures of cognitive flexibility, lower on measures of impulse control, and higher on measures of autonomy. Political salience, or a tendency to attach personal meaning to the larger social world, has been found to be associated with political activism in college students and midlife women. Erik Erikson's concept of generativity, or the desire to contribute to the welfare of future generations, has been found to relate to political activism in women. In addition, Bill Peterson found that generative individuals were more likely to attach personal meaning to social and historical events, especially those concerned with dismantling oppressive social structures (e.g., the civil rights movement). Finally, some researchers have found that the combination of high political efficacy and high political trust is related to conventional political participation, while high efficacy and low trust is associated with participation in forceful and nonconventional social change.

Any discussion of variables affecting political behavior must consider *how* they affect behavior. It is not enough to say, for example, that political efficacy or autonomy increase levels of participation. Why these variables would have such an effect is a much more interesting question. Three related constructs—relative deprivation, group consciousness, and nigrescence theory—provide a much needed connection between individual-level variables and political participation.

A. RELATIVE DEPRIVATION

The notion of relative deprivation was developed by social scientists to describe the negative emotions experienced by individuals who felt they were unjustly deprived of something they desired. According to Faye Crosby's model, relative deprivation occurs when five preconditions are met: (1) one sees that another possesses X, (2) one wants X, (3) one feels deserving of X, (4) one thinks it feasible to obtain X, and (5) one lacks a sense of responsibility for failure to possess X. For example, relative deprivation can be used to describe the emotions of suffragettes working for the vote during the late 19th and early 20th centuries: they saw that White men had the vote, they wanted to vote, they felt that as contributing citizens to the country they deserved to vote, they saw that the timing might be right to obtain the vote (because there was talk of giving Black men the vote), and they did not believe it was due to individual failures that they did not have the vote. It is important to note that all five preconditions are necessary to feel relative deprivation. In fact, it is possible to reduce a group's motivation to fight for their rights if one or more of the preconditions is removed. For example, relative deprivation about the right to vote never developed for a large number of women because of the popular notion that voting was a public sphere activity and thus not appropriate or desirable for a conventional woman (interfering with precondition 2 and perhaps precondition 3). In the United States, many members of minority groups fail to develop relative deprivation in terms of employment, education, or health care because of the strength of the belief in individualistic causes and solutions to social problems (interfering with precondition 5) or perhaps because they think change is not feasible (precondition 4). Thus, it is the purpose of many social movement organizations to clarify the existence of these missing preconditions, especially preconditions 4 and 5.

Crosby reviewed a large body of empirical literature to support her model and then later expanded it to allow for deprivation felt on the behalf of members of other groups ("ideological deprivation") and also to allow for resentment over a third party's undeserved possession of goods. Jennings posited that these two extensions of relative deprivation theory might account for participation in social movements by members of groups that did not directly benefit from the achievement of the movement's goals.

Personal relative deprivation may occur at an apolitical level—for example, a basketball player who feels that she has been unjustly deprived of playing time may feel relative deprivation. However, when the group comparison occurs at a political level, or the justification for the inequity is explicitly political, the relative deprivation that develops can be a powerful motivator of political participation. Crosby also outlined the possible outcomes for the individual and society after relative deprivation. Depending on personality and environmental factors, relative deprivation can lead either to nonviolent personal or social change or to violence against the self or society.

B. GROUP CONSCIOUSNESS

Stratum or group consciousness was defined by Patricia Gurin and her colleagues as composed of four elements: (1) identification with a group, that is, recognition of shared interests among the group or a sense of common fate; (2) power discontent, or belief that one's group is deprived of power and influence relative to the dominant group; (3) withdrawal of legitimacy, or belief that disparities based on group membership are illegitimate; and (4) collective orientation, or belief that members of one's group should

pool their resources to eliminate those obstacles that affect them as a group. Identifying oneself as a member of a group is not enough to demonstrate fulfillment of element 1; for example, most women identify as women, but a much smaller number would use their sex as an important grouping mechanism with which to identify common threats or benefits (a sense of common fate). The latter three elements constitute a distinctive political ideology around the group membership, one that recognizes the group's position in a power hierarchy, rejects the dominant group's rationalization of its relative position, and embraces a collective solution to group problems.

In analyses of data from national probability samples, Gurin and her colleagues used these dimensions to describe the gender consciousness of women, age consciousness of older people, race consciousness of African Americans and Whites, and class consciousness of blue-collar and middle-class workers. In addition, they used common fate, recognition of power differentials, and rejection of legitimacy to predict collective orientation in these samples. In the political science literature, Ethel Klein described similar elements of societal feminist consciousness. Gurin and others have noted that women are less likely to develop gender consciousness than other dispossessed groups, perhaps because of the likelihood that they live in such close proximity to dominant group members, regardless of race or ethnicity.

C. NIGRESCENCE THEORY

William Cross's theory of nigrescence, introduced to explain the transformation of a nonpoliticized Black identity into a politicized one, can be adapted to describe the development of other types of group consciousness as well (e.g., based on gender, class, or sexual orientation). The five stages involved in the development of group consciousness document the process of rejecting an old, dominant group-oriented (e.g., White) ideology and adopting or developing a new, subordinate group-centered (e.g., Black) one. Cross's first stage, preencounter, described the steady-state worldview of a preidentification individual as having internalized the dominant individualistic ideology, seeing their group membership as a negative part of identity and advancement possible only through individual effort. The encounter stage of nigrescence marks the awakening of the individual to the realities of the position of her group in society, through some sort of dramatic personal experience, such as encounters with racism or sexism. The third stage, immersion/emersion, involves a total rejection of the values of the dominant culture and an uncritical acceptance of the subordinate, involving heavy reliance on the collective. Stage 4 involves internalization of the new identity, which allows individuals to reduce their reliance on the collective for self-definition, working out distinctive ways to be members of the group. Stage 5, internalization-commitment, is characterized by an active and continuing commitment to redressing injustices encountered by the group. Other theorists have adapted this model to explain the development of group consciousness in women, gays and lesbians, and other ethnic groups.

Stage models may be limited in that they are inherently hierarchical and developmental, excluding the experiences of individuals who might have taken different paths to group consciousness or who experience more than one stage simultaneously. However, even if one ignores the stage aspect, these models can be useful in their descriptions of different types of race and feminist consciousness. For example, the encounter/revelation stage is characterized by feelings of anger at how members of one's group are treated. As suggested by the stage model, this type of reaction may be common when developing group consciousness. However, individuals may experience similar feelings when they encounter new instances of oppression. In addition, these stages may not be experienced in the same order by all people. Immersion in Black culture or women's groups may lead to race or feminist consciousness by exposing the individual to an alternative ideology that serves as an "encounter."

Empirically, several studies have supported models of race and feminist consciousness. For example, Kathryn Rickard showed that college women categorized as possessing preencounter identities were more likely to belong to conservative and traditional campus organizations (right-to-life and college textiles and clothing organizations), hold traditional views about dating, and endorse negative attitudes toward working women. College women categorized as having internalized a politicized (feminist) identity were more likely to belong to the National Organization of Women and the campus gay/lesbian alliance, hold nontraditional views about dating, and feel more positively toward working women. Other research has shown that women with feminist identities are more politically active than their nonfeminist peers for a variety of causes.

D. INTEGRATION OF RELATIVE DEPRIVATION, GROUP CONSCIOUSNESS, AND NIGRESCENCE THEORIES

Table I presents the central elements of the three theories thus discussed in order to illustrate their commonalties and differences. Central to all three models is a sense of power discontent and rejection of individualistic explanations for these power differences—perhaps best summarized as feelings of relative deprivation (all elements of relative deprivation theory, elements 2 and 3 of group consciousness, and elements 2 and 3 of nigrescence theory.) A sense of identification with a disfranchised group is key to making these comparisons in the first place, for without the proper reference group, there is no feeling of relative deprivation. The three theories differ in their articulation of the connections between these feelings of deprivation or consciousness and action taken on behalf of the group. For example, group consciousness theory specifies that a collective (rather than individualistic) orientation toward action is required, whereas nigrescence theory does not specify the nature of action but simply labels it as the ultimate achievement in demonstrating an integrated identity. Crosby's relative deprivation theory, on the other hand, considers the differing implications of an individualistic versus a collectivist orientation, positing different outcomes for the self and society of each.

These theories are most useful in explaining why people might participate in nonconventional political behavior when taken in conjunction with each other. Relative deprivation theory describes a

Table I

Key Elements of Three Theories Used to Explain Participation in Nonconventional Political Behavior

Relative deprivation	Group consciousness	Nigrescence theory
1. See others with X	1. Group identification	1. Pre-encounter
2. Want X	2. Power discontent	2. Encounter
3. Deserve X	3. Rejection of legitimacy	3. Immersion/emersion
4. Feasible to get X	4. Collective orientation	4. Internalization
5. Not own fault that one does not have X		5. Internalization/commitment

negative emotional state and consequences for action of such emotions, but does not explicitly identify the sense of common fate that is necessary for experiencing such emotion at the group level. Group consciousness theory includes the collective element necessary for developing such a political ideology, but does not articulate an explicit connection to action or outline a process of how such consciousness might develop on an individual level. Nigrescence theory fills in the latter gap, providing a detailed description of one way individuals can develop relative deprivation or group consciousness. Thus, all three theories are useful for understanding why some people—above and beyond their demographic characteristics—might participate in nonconventional political behavior.

As mentioned earlier, previous research has shown that political participation can have profound effects on participants. The following section considers the effects of the women's movement on the lives, personalities, and political behavior of women.

III. Effects of the Women's Movement on Women's Political Behavior

Susan Carroll identified three major changes in the pattern of gender relations that occurred after the women's movement gained momentum in the late 1960s. First, there is greater public acceptance of women's participation in mainstream politics. Second, any gaps that had existed in women's and men's conventional political behavior have narrowed. Third, as women have become more integrated in party politics, issues previously seen as private-sphere concerns have received more attention in mainstream political venues. [See THE FEMINIST MOVEMENT.]

A. MATERIAL CHANGES

The women's movement also has had some very real material and psychological consequences for women. By increasing educational and work opportunities, the movement has contributed to later average age of first marriage for women and also allowed women to leave unsatisfying or abusive marriages. These factors have contributed to the greater autonomy of women from men. Studies have shown that autonomy or independence from men has always been related to holding profeminist attitudes, as is increased education, employment, and lack of children. In ad-

dition, women who responded to the movement were more likely than women not affected by the movement to achieve higher levels of education, income, and socioeconomic status and were more likely to work in occupations traditionally dominated by men.

Many of the women who have come of age after the height of the second wave of the women's movement grew up with the expectations that even White middle-class women should work outside the home, that household labor should not be exclusively gendered, and that girls can grow up to be doctors, presidents, and athletes. Thus, changes made in terms of social roles and expectations may have enduring effects on future generations of women and men.

B. PERSONALITY CHANGES

Psychologically, finding the women's movement personally meaningful was associated with the development of assertive and independent personality characteristics by midlife for at least one cohort of women who reached adulthood before the women's movement—graduates of the Mills College classes of 1958 and 1960. Mills graduates who identified the women's movement as an important influence on their lives increased from age 21 to age 43 on scales relating to social poise and assurance (e.g., dominance, self-acceptance, empathy). In contrast, for women just a few years younger than the Mills College graduates, society's broader acceptance of assertive and independent characteristics in women was reflected in the young adult personalities of women graduating in 1964 from Radcliffe College. The women in this cohort affected by the women's movement scored higher on social poise and assurance, but showed no greater evidence of personality change by midlife on these characteristics than their peers who were not affected. In fact, there was evidence of identity search and revision for the older Mills women affected by the movement, but not for the younger Radcliffe women. These findings are consistent with Abigail Stewart and Joseph Healy's idea that the values of social movements coinciding with young adulthood are likely to be incorporated into identity, and it is only those social movements coinciding with later life stages that necessitate identity revision to accommodate value changes.

To date there has been little research on the personality characteristics of women of the post–women's movement generation. However, although the definition of femininity has changed very little over time (including such characteristics as dependence, nurturance, and passivity), North American society today is more accepting of women who display assertive and independent characteristics. As many feminists have noted, women who take on valued masculine characteristics are more easily tolerated than men who take on feminine characteristics, perhaps in part because society is slow to embrace that which has historically been devalued. Thus, it might be hypothesized that women reaching adulthood today will continue to show the assertive and independent personality characteristics found in earlier generations of women who benefited from the movement; however, it could also be the case that the "backlash" against feminism has tempered these changes. This is clearly an area for further research.

C. CHANGES IN POLITICAL ATTITUDES AND PARTICIPATION

Research has shown that participation in political protest activities as young adults has long-term effects on political attitudes and participation. For example, research on 1960s' student activists (both liberal and conservative) found remarkable continuity in political attitudes 20 years later. In addition, both the left-wing and right-wing activists continued their political participation, often reflecting their ideology in their choice of work, volunteer activities, and mainstream politics. Research on women who participated in protest activities in the 1960s as young adults found that at midlife, they scored higher on political efficacy and collectivist orientation than did their inactive peers.

Abigail Stewart and her colleagues divided women who were young adults during the women's movement into three groups: those who were active protesters (activists), those who were engaged and interested in the movement but supported it only indirectly (engaged observers), and those who did not participate in it at all (nonactivists). They found that the three groups differed in predictable ways in levels of college activism and felt impact of the movement at later life (i.e., activists were high in both, engaged observers were only moderately active but reported strong impact of the movement, and non-activists scored low in both). In addition, relationship to the movement was associated with midlife political activities, attitudes, and self-concept. In general, the more active a participant was in the movement, the more likely she was to endorse feminist attitudes and participate in community, political, and women's issues organizations. Thus the movement

affected even women who were not directly involved in it.

IV. Summary and Future Directions

Political behavior traditionally has been defined by scholars and the public in ways that favor male activities in the public sphere. Studies defining political behavior solely in terms of voter turnout or running for local and national elected office have almost always found women to be deficient political actors. However, as feminist scholars have pointed out, these definitions of political behavior have been biased in that they ignored very real material constraints on women's lives that discouraged such public activity. Definitions of political activity were also limited. By starting with men's political lives, they were unable to account for ways in which women had been politically active, either through activities centered around private-sphere concerns (e.g., prohibition, children's welfare), through acts of resistance to oppressive structures, or through nonconventional political protest. Two of the great benefits of the women's movement were that it encouraged more women to participate in traditionally male-defined political activities (and so the gap in voter turnout and other forms of conventional political behavior have narrowed or disappeared), and the rise of feminist scholarship has redefined political behavior to include traditionally feminine ways of participating.

An intriguing question for future research to explore is what effect the increased participation in mainstream politics of North American women will have on the political process. Sidney Verba distinguished between two arguments. The first is that women as a group have a distinctive voice, regardless of ideology or party affiliation, due to their common concerns as women and their common roles. This argument implies that as more women become active in mainstream politics, the issues addressed will reflect traditional private-sphere concerns. Carroll argued that this has occurred since the height of the women's movement. On the other hand, it is quite likely that women's first inroads into conventional politics reflected private-sphere concerns by necessity; that is, women's participation in nontraditional domains has always been more acceptable to society at large when activities are related to traditional feminine domains (e.g., private-sphere concerns.) Thus, in the early 1990s, Hillary Clinton quickly refocused her attention from developing a national health care policy (seen as a male domain) to working on behalf of children (a female domain) after widespread congressional criticism and low public approval ratings. On the other hand, Elizabeth Dole has made a career out of transforming care-related interests (e.g., president of the Red Cross) into high political office (e.g., secretary of the Department of Transportation), even participating as our country's first serious female contender for president in 2000 (at least through the early Republican primaries).

The second way women's increased participation may impact mainstream politics is that as more and more women participate, a greater variety of ideologies will be represented. Just as minority "tokens" in employment settings have had to be relatively apolitical, women reaching high political office have also tended to be seen as innocuous and noncontroversial. As greater numbers participate in mainstream politics, it seems likely that women with more radical views (left and right) will be voted into political office. Clearly, this is an intriguing avenue for future research and discussion.

Another fascinating question examines women's and men's personal reactions to changes brought about by women's increased political participation. In 1985, Roberta Sigel asked 50 adults (women and men) to participate in focus groups to discuss such issues. She found that women and men used different coping strategies to deal with changing gender roles. For men, these strategies revolved around reconciling desires to maintain their material privileges as men with needing to see themselves as fair and egalitarian. On the other hand, women's strategies for dealing with changes in gender roles involved walking a fine line between attempting to attain equity in their own lives and not antagonizing the men in their lives. Similar to Patricia Gurin's research, Sigel found that the women in her study did not endorse female solidarity or collective action in great numbers; rather, they seemed to focus more on improving only their own situation. Sigel argued that by attributing greater importance to maintaining harmonious family relationships with men than to achieving complete equality, these women were being pragmatic (not passive, as they might have been defined in the past). Research on younger generations may show more tolerant reactions to women's increased political participation and efforts for gender equity.

SUGGESTED READING

Beckwith, K. (1986). *American Women and Political Participation*. Greenwood Press, New York.

Cole, E. R, and Stewart, A. J. (1996). Meanings of political participation among Black and White women: Political identity and social responsibility. *Journal of Personality and Social Psychology* **71**, 130–140.

Collins, P. H. (1991). *Black Feminist Thought*. Routledge, New York.

Cott, N. F. (ed.). (1992). *History of Women in the United States*. Vols. 17, 18, 19, and 20. K. G. Saur, London.

Duncan, L. E. (1999). Motivation for collective action: Group consciousness as mediator of personality, life experiences, and women's rights activism. *Political Psychology* **20**, 611–635.

Sigel, R. S. (ed.) (1989). *Political Learning in Adulthood*. University of Chicago Press, Chicago.

Sigel, R. S. (1996). *Ambition and Accommodation*. University of Chicago Press, Chicago.

Tilly, L. A., and Gurin, P. (eds.) (1990). *Women, Politics, and Change*. Russell Sage Foundation, New York.

Unger, R. K. (ed.) (2001). *Handbook of the Psychology of Women and Gender*. John Wiley & Sons, New York.

Posttraumatic Stress Disorder (PTSD)

Catherine Feuer

Deana Jefferson

Patricia Resick

University of Missouri, St. Louis

Glossary

Externalizing A reaction to psychological distress in which the person acts out, usually in violent or aggressive ways, against others or the environment.

Internalizing A reaction to psychological distress that takes place primarily within the person, usually in the form of depression, anxiety, or low self-esteem.

Traumatic event Experiencing, witnessing, or being confronted by an event that involves actual or threatened death or serious injury or a threat to one's own or another person's physical integrity.

POSTTRAUMATIC STRESS DISORDER (PTSD) is a syndrome that may result from experiencing a traumatic event such as an assault, abuse, domestic violence, accident, witnessing violence, natural disaster, and combat. Three hallmark symptoms characterize PTSD: reexperiencing symptoms (e.g., reliving or having disturbing memories of the trauma); avoidance symptoms (e.g., avoiding reminders of the trauma, feeling detached or numb), and arousal symptoms (e.g., feeling irritable or having difficulty sleeping).

I. Introduction

Posttraumatic stress disorder (PTSD) is a relatively new diagnosis in the *Diagnostic and Statistical Manual (DSM)*, a comprehensive listing of mental health disorders. Although PTSD has been studied extensively, relatively little of the research has explored gender differences. This article examines gender differences in PTSD across the life span by addressing the following four areas: (1) the history of the PTSD diagnosis, (2) the traumatic events experienced (3) the development and expression of PTSD and associated symptoms, and (4) responses to PTSD treatment.

II. History of Posttraumatic Stress Disorder

Over the past century and a half, our understanding of reactions to traumatic events has increased exponentially. The first mention of a trauma-related syndrome in the clinical literature was a description of "hysteria." Hysteria was discovered by the French neurologist Jean-Martin Charcot in the mid-1800s. Hysteria was characterized by symptoms such as motor paralysis, sensory loss, convulsions, and amnesia, and was thought to affect only women. While early physicians believed hysteria to be a disease originating in the uterus, later authors such as Sigmund Freud and Pierre Janet concluded that the syndrome was caused by psychological trauma. Freud became the best-known theorist on the topic of hysteria and its origins. However, he later dropped the notion that it was caused by sexual trauma, perhaps because he was troubled by the social repercussions of his hypothesis.

Male soldiers in World War I later exhibited symptoms reminiscent of hysteria. These soldiers displayed symptoms of mutism, amnesia, paralysis, tremor, blindness, and deafness. Charles Samuel Myers, a British military psychiatrist in the early 1900s, was the first to use the term "shell shock" to describe the condition supposedly brought on by exposure to exploding shells. As similar to hysteria as this syndrome seems, the medical establishment at the time believed it to be a different disorder with an organic or physical cause. Myers eventually came to believe that the cause of shell shock (later termed "war neurosis") was emotional, and he acknowledged its similarity to hysteria.

Interest in the symptoms of hysteria or shell shock resurfaced briefly during World War II, but it was not until soldiers began returning from Vietnam in the 1970s that the current notion of PTSD began to evolve. At around the same time, the feminist movement recognized similar reactions in mainly female sexual assault and domestic violence survivors. After the syndrome came to the attention of mental health professionals working with Vietnam veterans, it was included as a diagnosis in the *DSM* in 1980. Since then, the definition of PTSD has been continually refined. A concept that began as hysteria in women and reappeared years later as shell shock in men, PTSD is now seen as a disorder that affects both genders. We now recognize that PTSD can result from a wide variety of stressors, as described in this article.

We have only recently begun to understand exactly how men and women are similar and different in their reactions to trauma. This article chronicles the progress made so far in understanding gender differences in PTSD.

III. Gender Differences in Traumatic Events Experienced

The diagnosis of PTSD requires the experience of a trauma. One possible source of gender differences, both in the rates of PTSD and the symptoms experienced, may be differences in the types of trauma men and women tend to experience. In 1995, Ronald Kessler and his colleagues conducted a nationwide community survey of 5877 men and women aged 15 to 54. They assessed exposure to a variety of traumatic events and found that men were significantly more likely to report having experienced a trauma than women. The most frequently reported traumatic experiences were witnessing someone being badly injured or killed (35.6% of men and 14.5% of women); being involved in a fire, flood, or natural disaster (18.9% of men and 15.2% of women); and being involved in a life-threatening accident (25% of men and 13.8% of women). Men were significantly more likely to report each of these three, as well as physical attacks, combat experience, and being threatened with a weapon, held captive, or kidnapped. Women were significantly more likely to report experiencing rape, sexual molestation, parental neglect during childhood, and childhood physical abuse.

In a 1992 article, Fran Norris described the frequency of a variety of traumatic events in a community sample. She surveyed 1000 adults in four Southeastern cities. Although Norris studied a circumscribed geographic area, the composition of the sample was relatively diverse and included Caucasian, African American, male and female participants. She found that women were more likely to have been sexually assaulted than men. Men were more likely to have been in motor vehicle crashes, been physically assaulted, and to have experienced a violent event in general.

In 1991, Naomi Breslau and her colleagues reported on interviews with 1007 adult members of a health maintenance organization and found that 39% had experienced a traumatic event. As in Norris's community sample, men reported higher rates of traumatic events than did women. Scott Vrana and Dean Lauterbach described similar results of their 1994 study of traumatic experiences in 440 college undergraduates. They found that men experienced a greater number of events and were significantly more likely than women to be in an accident or a life-threatening situation, be in a fire, witness a death, or be in combat. Women in their sample were more likely than men to have been raped or experienced abusive relationships as adults.

Deborah Lipschitz and her colleagues found a similar gender difference in adolescents. They examined rates of traumatic events in a sample of 95 adolescent psychiatric inpatients and found that boys were significantly more likely to have experienced a physical assault, while girls were significantly more likely to endorse an episode of sexual assault. In contrast, two of the studies reviewed, both on adolescents, did not show higher rates of trauma in males. In 1995, Rose Giaconia and her colleagues (1995) found equal rates of traumatic events between male and female adolescents. In a 1998 article, Steven Cuffe and his colleagues described a study of older adolescents in which females reported experiencing more traumas than males. The methods of data collection used in these two studies were quite different from those used in the majority of the studies on rates of trauma. Both Giaconia and Cuffe reported that they used open-ended questions, asking clients whether they had ever experienced something that fit the description of a trauma. Neither study employed a checklist of the types of traumas often reported. It is possible that, when asked an open-ended question about frightening experiences, females are more likely than males to list a number of experiences. This methodological difference is significant in that it highlights the possibility that gender effects in research may be heavily influenced by the methodology of the study. [See METHODS FOR STUDYING GENDER.]

Since 1973, the National Crime Victimization Survey (NCVS) has collected data on crime victimization through yearly surveys of representative samples of 50,000 U.S. residents. These studies have consistently shown that men, the poor, Blacks, the young, single people, renters, and central city residents are at a greater risk of experiencing violent victimization. Victimization for personal crimes is about 20% higher for males than females. This difference exists despite the fact that female victims are more likely to report crimes than males. Gender differences are also apparent in specific aspects of crimes. Males are more likely to be victimized by strangers and to receive more serious physical injuries than females. While in general most violent crime is between strangers, most violent acts against females are committed by someone they know or live with or to whom they are or were married.

At this time, somewhat less is known about the crime victimization of children. This is due in part to the fact that children are unlikely to report a crime on their own without adult support. On the basis of statistics from the NCVS and Uniform Crime Report, boys appear to experience more assault, robbery, and homicide than girls, whereas girls suffer vastly more rape. In 1993, Kevin Fitzpatrick and Janet Boldizar reported that 12 to 19-year-old African American males have higher crime victimization rates than do teenagers in any other racial group. Among older teenagers, the violence is often severe, resulting in serious injury.

For young children, physical abuse within the home is a common form of trauma. In 1994, Thomas Roesler and Nancy McKenzie interviewed men and women about their experiences as children and found no significant differences between men and women in the types of physical abuse they reported experiencing at the ages of five and six. However, caretaker reports from the National Family Violence Survey show more abuse of boys after age five, rising particularly high in later adolescence.

These studies clearly indicate that the rate of sexual assault is much higher for women than for men. However, very few studies have examined the rates of sexual assault among adult men. In their 1995 national sample of 5877 men and women, Kessler and his colleagues found that 0.7 % of the men reported having been raped, as compared to 9.2% of the women. Of the men and women in their sample reporting having been raped, approximately 6% were male and 94% female. According to a 1980 article by Arthur Kaufman and his colleagues, in 1978, 10% of all rape victims were male.

A number of studies suggest that there is a tendency for violent crimes against women to be perpetrated by someone they know. This holds true for sexual assault as well, as the majority of sexual assaults against women are "acquaintance rapes." In fact, a subset of female sexual assault survivors report having been assaulted by their intimate partners. A 1990 study by Diana Russell and a 1983 study by David Finkelhor and Kersti Ylloe found that between 10 and 14% of women living with a spouse or intimate partner report having been raped by their partner.

Though the literature on sexual assault of adult males is sparse, there has been much more research on gender differences in the rates of childhood sexual abuse. In a 1990 article, David Finkelhor and his colleagues found that 16% of men and 27% of women reported having experienced child sexual abuse. As with other crimes, there is evidence that aspects of childhood sexual abuse are different for males and females. In a 1989 study, Leslie Feinauer found that 13% of sexually abused females reported being sexually abused by a natural father compared to only 4.5% of the sexually abused males. Men and women reported being sexually abused at about the same rate by other family members and by acquaintances, except that more male survivors reported being abused by a neighbor than did female survivors. Similarly, Liz Tong and her colleagues and David Finkelhor and his colleagues found boys much more likely than girls to be sexually abused by strangers, and girls more likely to be abused by family members. A 1999 report by Scott Ketring and Leslie Feinauer suggested that sexual abuse of males might involve more threat and force.

Homicide rates are very well documented compared to other crimes and are a good indicator of the rates of severe violence experienced by different demographic groups. Furthermore, the friends, family, and witnesses of homicide often experience PTSD. According to the NCVS data, 77% of all homicide victims are males. Data from the FBI's Uniform Crime Reports indicate that female victims of homicide are 1.3 times more likely than male victims to be killed by a spouse. In 1987, Angela Browne found that women who kill their partners had often endured years of severe assault and threat by those partners and had typically exhausted every option for legal action and escape before killing them. The NCVS data also indicate that rates of homicide are quite similar for younger boys and girls up to age 13, but that boys' vulnerability increases dramatically after age 13. According to the FBI's 1994 statistics for both adults and adolescents, homicides are much more likely to be committed by males, and in almost half the cases the victims knew the murderer. African Americans, particularly African American men, are at high risk for witnessing or being the victims of homicide. In 1994, Esther Jenkins and Carl Bell described the experiences of 203 African American students from public high schools in high-crime areas of Chicago. Almost two-thirds of these youths indicated that they had seen a shooting and nearly half reported that they had seen someone killed. For over one-third of the witnesses the victim was a friend, and for another third the victim was a family member. Twenty-seven percent had personally experienced severe victimization, such as shooting, stabbing, severe beating, robbery with a weapon, or rape. As in the other studies reviewed, girls were significantly more likely to be raped, and boys were more likely to report that they had been robbed, shot, or beaten.

In 1988, Richard Gelles and Murray Straus reported that domestic violence occurred in 16% of all households surveyed, and approximately 10% of both men and women reported some victimization in the past year. Other researchers believe that this 10% rate for women may be an underestimate. Jeffrey Fagan and Angela Browne's 1994 review of studies found rates from 10% to over 30%. Murray Straus, in 1993, suggested that women are as likely as men to assault an intimate partner. Domestic violence perpetrated by women against men has been documented, as have incidents of domestic violence in both lesbian and gay couples. However, the bulk of the evidence suggests that most domestic violence is perpetrated by men against women. In 1994, the U.S. Department of Justice reported that women are 10 times more likely to report victimization by male partners or ex-partners, and men are far more likely than women to be arrested for partner violence. In 2000, Patricia Tjaden and Nancy Thoennes reported that women are more likely than men to be injured in partner violence. In their 1991 article, Evan Stark and Anne Flitcraft suggested that partner violence may be the most frequent source of injury to women. According to Dean Kilpatrick in 1988, women are also more likely to be sexually victimized and emotionally abused than men.

In 1995, Janet Willer and Linda Grossman reported that among Veterans Administration (VA) outpatients, women had sharply higher rates than men of every type of traumatic event except combat. These were primarily prewar and childhood traumatic events. However, female veterans with combat experience represent only a small minority (5.2%) of the overall female veteran population. A 1999 article by Daniel King and his colleagues described a national sample of 1632 Vietnam veterans. They found that war-zone experience for many male veterans was more directly life threatening than the experience of women who served in Vietnam. In a previous study, Daniel King and his colleagues had reported that men scored significantly higher than women on all the indexes of war-zone stress they measured. Women Vietnam veterans were mostly registered nurses and did not engage in what would be called traditional combat activities. They were typically not in a position to witness or participate in the commission of atrocious or extremely violent acts. Nonetheless, women were certainly exposed to frightening and unsafe situations, both as a result of the guerrilla war in Vietnam and the threats of sexual harassment and assault that often accompany military life for women. [*See* BATTERING IN ADULT RELATIONSHIPS; CHILD ABUSE; MILITARY WOMEN; RAPE; TRAUMA ACROSS DIVERSE SETTINGS.]

IV. Gender Differences in the Development of PTSD

Studies of mixed traumatic events by Naomi Breslau and her colleagues in 1992, Fran Norris in 1992, Ronald Kessler and his colleagues in 1995, and Robert Ursano and his colleagues in 1999 have all found that women are more than twice as likely as men to suffer lifetime PTSD from any cause, and women are more likely to have chronic PTSD even after adjusting for other factors. In 1995, Rose Giaconia and her colleagues estimated that women were six times as likely as men to develop PTSD subsequent to a trauma. In 1992, William Schlenger and his colleagues found the lifetime prevalence of PTSD in the general population to be 0.3% for men and 2.5% for women. The vulnerability of male and female adolescents to the development of PTSD appears to follow the same gender pattern as found for adults. Steven Cuffe and his colleagues reported in 1998 that among 490 older adolescents, approximately 3% of female and 1% of male research participants met *DSM* criteria for PTSD. On average, females reported more symptoms of PTSD and higher stress related to the trauma. In 1993, Kevin Fitzpatrick and Janet Boldizar reported similar results for a sample of 12- to 19-year-olds: although males witnessed and were victimized more than females, those females who were victims of violence reported more PTSD symptoms. Deborah Lipschitz and her colleagues reported conflicting gender risk findings in an article published in 2000. Lipschitz and her colleagues found that among adolescent psychiatric inpatients with an average age of 16, girls endorsed significantly more symptoms of current depression, but boys and girls endorsed PTSD symptoms at equal rates. It is important to note that psychiatric inpatient adolescents are not a random sample and are likely not representative of the general population of adolescents.

While the majority of studies of adults and adolescents show women to be more vulnerable to PTSD, studies of children are more ambiguous. A number of studies of children report little or no gender variation in PTSD symptomatology. In 1992, John Richters and Pedro Martinez studied the impact of witnessing or victimization by violence in children up to grade 6 and found no differences between boys and girls in PTSD symptoms. Similarly, Pynoos and his colleagues reported no gender differences in PTSD in their 1987 article on school-aged children who were present during a sniper attack on their school playground.

Articles focusing on general trauma such as those of Fran Norris in 1992, Dean Kilpatrick and Heidi Resnick in 1992, and Naomi Breslau and her colleagues in 1991 have found both greater vulnerability of women to PTSD and coinciding high rates of sexual assault among women. Their findings suggest that sexual assault may be more likely than other crimes to cause PTSD, and thus it may partially account for the higher rates of PTSD in women. This notion was supported in the 1995 study by Ronald Kessler and his colleagues that compared the vulnerability of men and women to rape-related PTSD. They found that rape was the traumatic event most likely to cause PTSD. Among those who reported having experienced a rape, 65% of men and 45.9% of women met criteria for PTSD. This provides some evidence that the higher prevalence of PTSD in women may be related to their greater likelihood of experiencing rape.

Studies comparing men and women on vulnerability to PTSD subsequent to childhood sexual abuse are more plentiful than similar comparisons for adulthood sexual assault. In a 1994 article, Thomas Roesler and Nancy McKenzie found that males and females were similar on measures of PTSD and other symptoms. The only differences the study showed were that men were significantly less likely to report having told anyone about the abuse and were significantly more likely to report sexual dysfunction than were women. Similarly, in their 1999 article, Scott Ketring and Leslie Feinauer reported that among 419 women and 56 men who were victims of childhood sexual abuse, there were no significant differences by gender.

In a 1998 study, Kym Kilpatrick and Leanne Williams examined gender differences in PTSD among children exposed to domestic violence. Contrary to the results of several previous studies, they found that boys and girls showed similar levels of PTSD after witnessing domestic violence. They found that gender did not contribute significantly to the relationship between witnessing domestic violence and PTSD. This suggests that previously observed gender differences might reflect differing patterns of symptom expression rather than differences in the nature of the underlying disorder itself.

In 1987 and 1988, Patricia Resick and her colleagues reported the results of a study of robbery victims who had been physically victimized in some way. They found that men were less distressed than women shortly after the crime, although both exhibited some symptoms up to 18 months postcrime. This was true despite the fact that men were more likely than women to report that their assailant used a weapon during the attack.

In 1989, Arthur Lurigio and Robert Davis found men to be less fearful than women immediately after a physical assault. Expanding on that finding, David Riggs and his colleagues reported in 1995 that male victims of assault were less likely to meet criteria both at initial interview shortly after the crime and at four months after the assault.

In a 1999 study, Robert Ursano and his colleagues reported on the development of PTSD symptoms in 122 motor vehicle accident victims and 42 comparison subjects. After controlling for other demographic factors, the risk for reporting PTSD symptoms at one month after the accident was nearly five times greater for women than for men. This finding pertains only to symptoms of PTSD because the diagnosis of PTSD itself cannot be given until at least three months after the trauma. However, women were no more likely than men to develop chronic PTSD.

As is the case for other traumas, adolescents appear to show gender differences similar to those of adults following a motor vehicle accident. In 1996, C. E. Curle and C. Williams reported that among 25 adolescents with an average age of 14, girls reported higher levels of distress than boys two years after a bus accident. The authors also noted, however, that girls in this small sample were also more likely to have received lasting injuries than were boys. Anthony Spirito and his colleagues reported a conflicting result in 1988. They found no significant differences in trauma scores in adolescent male and female motor vehicle accident victims.

Robert Pynoos and his colleagues studied the reactions of 231 children (with an average age of 13) who had experienced the 1988 Armenian earthquake. There was a relatively small but significant tendency for girls to score higher than boys on total mean PTSD scores. In a 1995 study, Carol Garrison and her colleagues found that among adolescents exposed to Hurricane Andrew in Florida, females reported all but two PTSD symptoms more often and were significantly more likely to meet PTSD criteria (9.2%) than males (2.9%). The higher rate of PTSD observed among female than male adolescents is consistent with previous disaster-related PTSD findings for youths (by Kevin Fitzpatrick and Janet Boldizar in 1993 and Bonnie Green and her colleagues in 1991) and for adults (by Naomi Breslau and her colleagues in 1991 and Peter Steinglass and Ellen Gerrity in 1990).

Research on responses of women veterans to warzone experiences has revealed high rates of PTSD symptoms in women who served in Vietnam. A 1999 study by Daniel King and his colleagues supported the importance of the gender difference in Vietnam combat exposure as a factor in gender differences in PTSD. They found a link between war zone stressors and PTSD in men, but did not find such a relationship for women. However, a 1995 article by Patricia Sutker and her colleagues found no significant gender effects for PTSD subsequent to mobilization in Operation Desert Storm. Operation Desert Storm featured a much more equal gender mix of U.S. troops than had been mobilized for previous military operations, so combat exposure was more similar for male and female military personnel than it had been in previous wars.

Having examined gender differences in the probability of developing PTSD after a trauma, we now turn to the discussion of gender differences in the way PTSD and its associated symptoms are expressed. Steven Cuffe and his colleagues examined the expression of PTSD in their 1998 article. The authors found that females were more likely than males to endorse specific PTSD symptoms of distress when they are reminded of the trauma and avoidance of thoughts, feelings, and activities reminiscent of the trauma. Males in their sample showed a less consistent pattern of symptoms that differed for African American and Caucasian males. Caucasian males showed a pattern much like Caucasian women, while African American males were most likely to report physiological arousal symptoms. In her 1995 study, Carol Garrison and her colleagues found that adolescent females reported all but two PTSD symptoms more frequently than males in the aftermath of Hurricane Andrew. The two exceptions were sense of foreshortened future and diminished interest in significant activities, on which boys and girls were not significantly different.

Robert Pynoos and his colleagues found that among children who survived the 1988 earthquake in Armenia, girls were significantly more likely to endorse PTSD symptoms of physiological arousal when reminded, recurrent distressing dreams, psychological distress when reminded, and recurrent intrusive recollections. In 1988, Anthony Spirito and his colleagues reported that girls who had experienced a motor vehicle accident showed significantly more intrusive symptoms of PTSD than did boys. Considering how few studies have examined gender differences in the expression of the 17 PTSD symptoms, there is little consensus. While the majority of these studies find that females express a greater number of symptoms and meet PTSD criteria more often than males, the results in terms of specific symptoms expressed are far more ambiguous. The bulk of the literature on gender differences in post-traumatic reactions focuses on a variety of related symptoms, disorders, and behaviors, rather than specific PTSD symptoms. This "associated symptom" literature shows a somewhat clearer picture of gender differences in trauma reactions.

In 1994, Esther Jenkins and Carl Bell found that subsequent to witnessing or experiencing violence, adolescent girls reported more distress symptoms than boys, while boys reported more high-risk behaviors, such as weapon carrying, substance use, and fighting. The finding that boys tend to carry weapons subsequent to exposure to violence is particularly problematic because weapon carrying is a strong predictor of victimization for males. Thus, high-risk behaviors resulting from violence exposure may increase the likelihood of violence toward others and continued victimization.

In order for researchers to find gender differences in internalizing and externalizing symptoms and behaviors, they must have measured those constructs in their study. Traditional clinical studies often measure only the few disorders commonly thought to follow a traumatic exposure, such as PTSD and depression. Both of these disorders are composed largely of internalizing symptoms. When only those disorders are assessed, studies often find that women show more distress in general, and men show relatively little reaction. A 1980 article by Arthur Kaufman and his colleagues described the male rape survivors they interviewed as "emotionally controlled"

in comparison to the "emotionally expressive" women in the study. The majority of the men in their sample appeared "quiet, embarrassed, withdrawn, or unconcerned." The men in this study had sought treatment for their rape-related distress and so may not be representative of the population of male rape survivors, who tend to avoid traditional treatment. The lack of information on externalizing symptoms in this study makes it difficult to form a complete image of the postrape reactions of males and females.

Studies of adults molested as children, although focusing on only one type of trauma, may constitute the most comprehensive literature on gender differences in general post-traumatic reactions. Researchers consistently report that certain sexual abuse reactions of low self-esteem, low self-worth, emotional maladjustment, and a history of conflict in relationships are common to both males and females. However, John Briere and his colleagues in 1988, John Hunter in 1991, and Rodney Young and colleagues in 1994 suggested that reactions might also differ substantially by gender. In a 1996 article, Vaughn Heath and his colleagues reviewed a number of studies that examined gender differences in community samples of sexually abused children. These studies suggest that women tend to report significantly more depressive and anxiety-related symptoms (internalizing) and men report greater substance abuse and antisocial disorders (externalizing). In a 1990 survey of adult men and women, David Finkelhor and his colleagues concluded that men externalized their symptoms by using drugs or alcohol or acting out, and women internalized their symptoms through depression, fear, and anxiety.

In 1986, William Friedrich and his colleagues discovered that female children who were chronically abused by an emotionally close perpetrator exhibited high levels of internalized symptoms, whereas males with the same abuse profiles showed externalizing symptoms. In 1994, Sally Merry and Leah Andrews published a study looking at the diagnoses received by sexually abused children one year after the disclosure of recent sexual abuse. Boys were more likely to suffer from oppositional defiant disorder (a diagnosis associated with externalizing behavior problems) and functional enuresis (bed-wetting). In 1993, Richard Livingston and his colleagues reported a similar pattern of diagnoses among chronically physically or sexually abused children. They found that conduct disorder (also associated with externalizing behavior problems) was more common in abused boys than in abused girls, and that this trend increased with age.

Only one of the childhood sexual abuse studies reviewed found females to show more associated symptoms on every measure. The authors of this 1996 study, Vaughn Heath and his colleagues, suggest that this finding may have been due to their exclusive use of the subscales of the Trauma Symptom Checklist, a questionnaire assessing largely internalizing behaviors. Louise Silvern and her colleagues drew a similar conclusion in a 1995 article. The researchers found that when they measured self-esteem, depression, and trauma symptoms, female college students who had witnessed partner abuse as children appeared more distressed on all measures than their male counterparts. The authors concluded that their findings may be related to the primarily internalizing measures used, which may not have adequately tapped the externalizing symptoms that may be more common in males. [*See* ANXIETY; DEPRESSION.]

V. Gender Differences in Responses to PTSD Treatment

The 1998 study by Nicholas Tarrier and his colleagues is one of the few controlled studies to compare the outcome of PTSD treatment between male and female clients. Clients in the study had met criteria for PTSD due to a variety of crimes. Female participants responded better to treatment than male participants. At the end of treatment, men showed higher rates of severe symptoms such as psychoticism, rated treatment as less credible, were less motivated, and were more likely to miss therapy appointments. In a 2000 chapter reviewing gender differences in PTSD treatment outcome studies, Dana Cason, Anouk Grubaugh, and Patricia Resick reported that, overall, treatments appear to have a greater effect on improving women's symptoms as compared to men's. The majority of treatments that have been shown by research to alleviate the symptoms of PTSD require open expression of the fear and other strong emotions associated with the trauma. Although such expression is not easy for trauma survivors of either gender, it may feel somewhat more natural to women.

According to Gilbert (1987), women are socialized to express emotions openly, while men are socialized to repress their emotions. The emotion of anger is the exception to these socialization rules: women are

discouraged from expressing anger while it is considered natural for men to express anger. Edna Foa and her colleagues have suggested both "numbing" (or repressing emotions) and anger in the client may hinder the treatment of PTSD. Numbing and anger are thought to prevent the expression of fear necessary for successful treatment of PTSD. [*See* ANGER; EMPATHY AND EMOTIONAL EXPRESSIVITY.]

As we have discussed, types of traumas experienced tend to differ between men and women. The fact that men and women are likely to seek treatment for different types of traumas may make it difficult to tell whether a true gender difference in response to treatment exists or whether certain traumas are more difficult to treat. For example, Richard Kulka and his colleagues documented that Vietnam veterans with PTSD have high rates of concurrent substance use disorders, which may complicate treatment for PTSD.

VI. Conclusions

The literature reviewed in this article suggests that men and women are likely to experience different types of traumas at varying rates. The literature also indicates that female trauma survivors are likely to endorse more symptoms of PTSD and to meet criteria for the disorder more often than their male counterparts. Gender differences in the behaviors, symptoms, and syndromes expressed after a trauma point to a tendency for females to internalize their distress while males may tend to externalize. A number of plausible explanations for the apparent gender differences in responses to trauma have been hypothesized. These explanations include the tendency for certain traumas to be more likely to cause PTSD and to be experienced by women more often, sex-role socialization, gender differences in coping strategies, and biological differences.

The primary argument for the notion that the relationship between gender and PTSD is driven by the tendency for men and women to experience different types of traumas comes from the sexual victimization literature. A number of researchers, including Ronald Kessler and his colleagues in 1995 and Kevin Fitzpatrick and Janet Boldizar in 1993, have found sexual victimization to be the trauma most strongly associated with PTSD. According to a 1992 article by Tiffany Wind and Louise Silvern, abuse by a close family member appears to be uniquely destructive. In 1999, Scott Ketring and Leslie Feinauer supported this hypothesis with their finding that both men and women who were sexually abused by a father figure had significantly higher trauma scores than those abused by strangers. In 1998, Steven Cuffe conducted a series of analyses specifically addressing this issue and found that gender differences in traumatic reactions were accounted for by the type of trauma, in that females were much more likely to report rape or childhood sexual abuse and to report high levels of distress. While these studies provide compelling evidence for the theory that gender differences in PTSD may be caused by differential trauma rates, other studies reviewed in this article found indications of higher levels of distress in females after experiencing the same trauma as males, such as a motor vehicle accident or a natural disaster.

A second explanation for the gender difference in the development and expression of PTSD is that, from a very young age, males and females are socialized to respond differently to the world. In 1991, Laura Berk published a book detailing considerable evidence that, from infancy, boys and girls are treated differently by their parents according to prevailing gender stereotypes. For example, girls are taught to express more emotion, to cry more, and to be aware of other people's feelings. Boys are taught to suppress emotion, not to cry, to be "tough," to defend themselves, and to "fight back" when necessary. These differences could clearly impact the reactions of men and women to traumatic events. This hypothesis is supported by the tendency for gender differences in reactions to traumatic events to become more pronounced with age. Younger boys and girls are not as well socialized into their roles as adolescents and adults, so they may react in ways more similar to each other.

A number of authors have suggested that sex-role socialization may affect the apparent rates of PTSD and related reactions indirectly through willingness to report experiencing distress. An interesting finding by Kevin Fitzpatrick and Janet Boldizar in 1993 lends some support to this hypothesis. They found that among 12- to 19-year-old trauma survivors, those who lived in homes with fewer males present were more likely to report PTSD symptoms than those living in homes with more males present. The presence of males in the home may increase the importance of presenting an image fitting the male sex-role stereotype, thereby decreasing the chance that males will openly express symptoms of PTSD.

A second way in which sex-role socialization may influence gender differences in trauma reactions is through the mode of expression of distress. Quite a few of the studies reviewed in this article indicated that females may be more likely to exhibit internalizing symptoms such as depression, while men may be more likely to show externalizing behaviors such as fighting and carrying weapons. These responses to trauma are consistent with the sex-role socialization of men and women. This internalizing-externalizing socialization explanation may explain the differential rates of other mental health problems such as depression (primarily women) and antisocial behavior problems (primarily men).

In a 1989 article, Anthony Spirito and his colleagues found that boys and girls reported using different coping methods subsequent to a motor vehicle accident. Girls were more likely to use distraction, emotional expression, wishful thinking, and social withdrawal than boys, and boys were more likely to use resignation. Spirito and colleagues concluded that the coping method preferred by boys, resignation, may be a more appropriate coping strategy for helping them to accept a traumatic accident over which they had no control. The coping strategies used by the girls may be more closely associated with avoidance and denial of the trauma and therefore maintain the symptoms of PTSD and depression. These results are consistent with Susan Nolen-Hoeksema's 1987 contention that gender differences in depression are accounted for by differences in coping strategies with boys choosing more effective strategies.

Finally, it is possible that there is a biological basis for the gender differences in trauma reactions outlined in this article. Biological explanations have been explored for the gender differences found in rates of depression, but comparable work on the physiology of gender differences in PTSD is just recently being undertaken.

Any of the explanations described in this article could explain the gender differences in PTSD, and it is likely that some combination of factors is responsible. Regardless of the cause of the gender difference, the studies reviewed here indicate that we may need to broaden our understanding of trauma reactions beyond the symptoms included in the PTSD diagnosis in order to accurately capture the experience of male trauma survivors as well as we have captured the experience of females.

SUGGESTED READING

Foa, E. B., and Rothbaum, B. O. (1998). *Treating the Trauma of Rape: Cognitive-Behavioral Therapy for PTSD.* Guilford Press, New York.

Herman, J. L. (1992). *Trauma and Recovery*. Basicbooks, New York.

van der Kolk, B. A., McFarlane, A. C., and Weisaeth, L. (eds.) (1996). *Traumatic Stress: The Effects of Overwhelming Experience on Mind, Body, and Society*. Guilford Press: New York.

Wolfe, J., and Kimerling, R. (1996). Gender issues in the assessment of PTSD. In *Assessing Psychological Trauma and PTSD: A Handbook for Practitioners* (J. P. Wilson and T. M. Keane, eds.). Guilford Press, New York.

Yule, W. (ed.) (1999). *Post-Traumatic Stress Disorders: Concepts and Therapy*. John Wiley & Sons, Chichester, UK.

Poverty and Women in the United States

Karen Fraser Wyche

New York University

Glossary

Block grants Money given by the U.S. federal government to the states.

Caseload The term used to identify persons assigned to a caseworker for social welfare services.

Caseworker The job title given to a person working in programs providing social services to public assistance clients who receive money from a state if they meet the eligibility requirements.

Means tested benefits Benefits provided by government agencies based on income eligibility (e.g., food stamps or subsidized housing).

Medicaid Medical insurance for low-income persons in the United States.

Welfare reform Change made to the welfare laws in 1996 as outlined in the Personal Responsibility and Opportunity Reconciliation Act.

Workfare Job training programs mandated by U.S. welfare reform legislation.

POVERTY AND WOMEN in the United States occurs mainly in women heads of households and their children. Poverty is a complex topic for it covers both a condition of living and the resulting psychological issues that emerge for poor women and their families. In order to examine these complexities, this article reviews the ways researchers and policy makers categorized women in poverty, beliefs regarding how people become poor, and governmental definitions of poverty. Since families living in poverty are mainly supported by governmental welfare programs, these programs as they affect the lives of women recipients are evaluated. Finally homelessness as an outcome of poverty is discussed.

I. The Focus of Research and Policy Literature

The literature on poverty and women focuses primarily on either gender or racial and ethnic group comparisons. Ethnic comparisons of women are primarily between White, African American, and Latinas. Few studies include Asian American or Native American women. Distinctions among ethnic groups of women are often not addressed in governmental reports. For example, a 1999 report from the U.S. Department of Health and Human Services on trends on the well-being of America's youth reports statistics by ethnic groups only. Data are given for African American or Black, White, and Hispanic (people who may be of any race) persons. There are no subcategory distinctions to contribute to our understanding of the variability within ethnic groups. As a result, less information is known about Hispanic people who are Puerto Rican, Mexican, Cuban, or from Central or South America. Similarly, within the racial category Black, no distinction is made between African American and Caribbean people. Whites are not distinguished between heritage groups such as Italian, Irish, or Russian. Ignoring these within-group distinctions can have several consequences. Policy makers may be less effective in developing programs to eliminate poverty. Or unique problems of the economic survival of particular groups becomes lost in these homogeneous categorizations. Overall, it is not possible to the track economic progress of the specific heritage groups.

When the heterogeneity within ethnic groups is ignored, the actual trends in population growth are not monitored. While the United States still is predominately populated by Whites, this trend is slowly changing. For example, Martha Ozowa has estimated that by 2050 the U.S. population will be 52.5% White and 46.6% minorities: 22.5% Hispanic (Puerto Rican, Cuban, Mexican, and South and Central American); 14.4% Black (African American and Afro-Caribbean); 9.7% Asian (Chinese, Japanese, Filipino, and Hawaiian or part Hawaiian) and Pacific Islanders; and 0.9% American Indian, Eskimos, and Aleuts. These figures do not include mixed-race people, a growing population for whom little information is known. The federal government is beginning to recognize the importance of collecting this information as a way to increase understanding of the social conditions experienced by these groups of people. Most recently, in the 2000 census, a better effort was made to gather data about people within and between ethnic and racial group categories.

Immigration status rarely appears in data reported about gender, racial, or ethnic groups and poverty. Rather, immigration status is treated as an independent category of analysis. The lack of cross referencing of personal status variables (sex, ethnicity, or race) and immigration status is problematic to scholars who realize that women's immigration status is important in any discussion of poverty.

The level of a woman's socioeconomic status can change from what it was in her country of origin. For example, maintaining a middle-class lifestyle in the United States requires a job with a good salary. Many times women with professional jobs in their country of origin are not hired for these same jobs in the United States because of differences in training or English fluency. As a result, they can be employed in low-paying jobs that do not provide the middle-class lifestyle they enjoyed in their former country. On the other hand, many women who immigrate to the United States are poor in their home countries and come to the United States with the hope of improving their economic situation. Some of these women engage in low-wage jobs, but improve their economic situation. They remain poor economically in the United States, but have improved their financial situation.

The reasons that researchers or policy professionals often fail to discuss gender, ethnicity, race, and immigration status can only be hypothesized. One reason may be that asking about immigration status may put women at risk if they are illegal immigrants. Or researchers may avoid seeking information from women who do not speak English. Whatever the reasons, it is important that we recognize that gender, race, ethnicity, and immigration status all influence a person's economic status.

II. Beliefs about the Causes of Poverty

People hold various beliefs regarding the causes of poverty. Individualistic beliefs focus on personality attributes. These beliefs include irresponsibility, lack of discipline and effort, or lower ability and talent. Structuralistic beliefs incorporate the larger socioeconomic system such as low wages for some jobs, poor schools, prejudice, discrimination, and job availability. Fatalistic beliefs as to the reasons for a person's poverty status focus on such things as bad luck, chance, and fate.

Some researchers have been interested in how people in different racial or ethnic groups think about these issues. In a 1996 survey, Matthew Hunt compared White, African American, and Latino people's beliefs about the causes of poverty. Individualistic beliefs were expressed by individuals who had the lowest educational level of all the respondents in the survey. Those with the most education viewed poverty as an interaction of several causes. They believed that a person's educational level was an important component in determining socioeconomic status. The more education a person received, the better her or his financial situation. Compared to White people in the survey, African Americans and Latinos held both structuralistic and individualistic beliefs. They report that this duality of structuralistic and individualistic reasons for poverty were based on their own experiences as minorities in this culture. There were differences of opinion between women and men. Women were more likely than men to endorse the structuralistic beliefs.

The beliefs that a person has regarding the causes of another person's poverty leads to value judgments regarding who are the deserving and the undeserving poor. These values become attitudes expressed by individuals as behaviors. For example, you can think about your own values regarding poverty. Are you more likely to give money to a man, a woman, or a pregnant woman who is begging on the street? It is not surprising that our social policies regarding the treatment of poor in this country become shaped by these beliefs.

III. *Definitions of Poverty*

Historical factors are important in understanding the definitions of poverty. In 1955 the Department of Agriculture based the official poverty standard on a low-cost diet. With minor exceptions changes in updating the poverty threshold have been done by adjusting for changes in the overall cost of living. While the cost of food has declined, other areas needed for the survival of low-income families, such as housing, child care, and transportation have risen. As a result, Robert Hauser has argued that this current standard of poverty is not a threshold of need. He wondered, what is a useful measure of a person's economic status? Socioeconomic status is not precise because it can vary as to meaning even though it is used to characterize placement of persons, families and households, census tracts, or other aggregates with

respect to the ability to create or consume goods valued by society. Hauser suggested that occupational status is a better indicator of long-term or permanent income than socioeconomic status because occupations provide information about social standing and they are stable over time. However, occupational status is not the best indicator of economic status for women and racial and ethnic minority people. These groups experience employment discrimination, glass ceiling situations, and job segregation that can make occupational status problematic for them.

A. SUBJECTIVE MEASURES OF POVERTY

The multiple ways people define poverty are important for understanding how the condition of poverty impacts the lives of women and their families. According to Hauser, definitions of poverty have both a normative and a contextual bases. Normative definitions relate to issues regarding the acceptability of poverty, that is, a feeling that poverty is unacceptable. Contextual definitions can vary from time to time and place to place. For example, consider the context of war. During wartime poor widows as single mothers elicit sympathy. In times of relative peace, however, single teenage mothers who are poor elicit little sympathy.

Subjective measures of poverty are based on people's own perceptions of their economic situation and can be compared to standard objective measures. Social class can be viewed in this way, for it is an important marker of behaviors, beliefs, and attitudes. A Gallup/CNN *USA Today* poll conducted in 2000 indicates that 69% of Americans say they are middle class (incomes ranging from $30,829 to $49,015), but only 20% of the population have incomes in this range. This poll used both the 1997 American Housing Survey and the 1999 Current Population Survey data to divide all U.S. households into five equally sized blocks. Each block represented 20% of the population ($0 to $16,799; $16,800 to $30,828; $30,829 to $49,015; $49,016 to $76,009; and $76,010 and above). As can be seen from these figures, the perception of middle class among individuals can be very different than their actual social class level. These perceptions appear to be based on how one feels about their social class, rather than on income earned. A woman who feels she has a choice to work may define herself as middle class based on this choice, rather than on the amount of family income as a definition of social class. Conversely, a woman may feel poor not based on income. She can feel "poor" when comparing herself to a reference group. That is, her family income could be in the top 20% of households ($76,010 and above), but she could be at the lower end of that range and feel "poor" compared to her neighbors or friends who may be in the upper end of that range. Obviously, a woman in the lowest 20% of income is poor in comparison. One can feel economically deprived based on daily stress related to the family, the job, or the ecological stress of neighborhood quality. Furthermore, difficulties with financial capital, the money available to buy food, clothes, and to maintain the household, can lead to psychological stress and a feeling of being poor.

B. GOVERNMENTAL MEASURES OF POVERTY

The U.S. government is the main source of publications regarding economic trends in this country. Many different governmental departments issue this information. The usual way of categorizing this information is by racial or ethnic group, marital status, or gender comparisons. As a result, it is difficult to compare women and men within any racial or ethnic group category. Also, it is important to remember that economic data are often issued as comparisons between certain years or for a specific year.

1. The Poor

In the United States the poverty rate is calculated as the percentage of families whose before tax income falls below a certain income level. This level is based on family size. The U.S. Census Bureau began keeping track of household incomes in 1967. At that time, only two racial groups, White and Black individuals, were included. In 1972 Hispanics were added, followed by Asians in 1987. Thus, comparisons among these ethnic groups were possible only since 1987.

Household income is reported as a median figure (the amount at which 50 percent of the 120 million households have incomes above and 50 percent below) rather than as a mean. It is important to understand the reason the U.S. Census bureau reports income this way. If the mean (or arithmetic average) income of 120 million households were used, it would distort income figures in a higher direction because of the few super wealthy families in the United States. As a result the median is used as a way of avoiding this problem.

In 1999 the poverty rate was defined as a house-hold income of $17,029 for a family of four. While fewer people were in this category compared to 1998, it still represents 11.8% of the U.S. population. Certain racial and ethnic groups are overrepresented in the poverty category. That is, African Americans, Hispanics, and Native Americans have the highest rates of poverty. Within Hispanic groups, Mexican immigrant families have the highest rates of poverty followed by U.S.-born Mexicans, and Cubans. Asians and Whites have the lowest rates of poverty. However, among Asian heritage people, there is poverty among recently arrived Asian immigrant groups such as people from Southeast Asia.

2. The Nonpoor

In 1999, 2.2 million people, the overwhelming majority of whom lived in inner cities, earned incomes that put them above the poverty line. The federal government excludes from these figures the sale of stocks or property, which is more likely to effect the affluent, or benefits such as earned-income tax credit, which has assisted the working poor. For these nonpoor the median income for four persons was $40,816. This was slightly more money for this size family than in 1998. When we compare across racial and ethnic groups the following picture appears. The median income for African Americans was $27,910; for Hispanic Americans, $30,735; for non-Hispanic Whites, $40,366; and for Asians, $51,000.

Gender disparities in income continue. Women working full time still make less than men in median wages. As a group they earned a median income of $26,324 compared to men's median income of $36,376 in 1999. A report issued by the Institute for Women's Policy Research in 2000 indicates that women's earnings vary from state to state. The regional pattern is that in the Pacific West, New England, and the Middle Atlantic regions, women earn more than those in the Southeast and Mountain states. No data are available on gender and race comparisons.

3. Children

In the United States many children live in poverty. In 1990, statistics of children living in families with married parents began to be published. The 1992 Panel Study of Income Dynamics reported that among Hispanic children, Puerto Rican children were the poorest, followed by Mexican and Cuban American children. Data on child poverty indicate that the number of poor children declined slightly between 1995 to 1997 (when the economy was strong) after a steady 15-year increase, but the children who remained poor became poorer. In 1997 5.2 million children were officially counted as poor, with the highest rate (42%) of children under age six. These children were living in families with incomes 185% below the poverty line according to analyses done by Neil Bennett. The group differences were as follows: 40% African American, 38% Hispanic, and 13% of White children living in poverty. By 1999 the U.S. Department of Health and Human Services (HHS) reported data from 1998 that children living below the poverty level were as follows: White 12%; Asian 17%; Hispanic 32%, American Indian and Alaska Native 38%, and African American 40%. Thus, White and Asian children continue to be better off financially than all other groups of children.

4. Marital Status

Gender and marital status are good predictors of economic well-being. In 1993 HHS reported the poverty rate for single-mother families was 52.4% compared to 1.9% of father only families. These figures do not include income from means-tested benefits. In two-parent families, 37.1% were below poverty, and by 1995 the rate had dropped to 10%. These families were primarily biological parents rather than stepparent families.

Female-headed families can have a mother or grandmother as the head of the family. The government is unable to calculate if there are males who supply income in these families. In 1998, at or below poverty level, were female-headed families who were African American (51%), American Indian/ Alaska Native (28.7%), Hispanic (27%), White (18%), and Asian/Pacific Islander (9.8%).

Median income is another way to report economic conditions of families. While median income fails to include health benefits and other family economic resources (e.g., food stamps), it is the way the government reports family income. For 1997, mother-only families had a median income of $17,256 compared to father-only families median income of $28,668, as reported by HHS. In contrast, the median income for married-couple families in that year was $54,395, with White families having the highest incomes. Specifically White married-families median incomes were 85% higher than African American families, and 79% higher than Hispanic families. This was

due in part to the large percentage of mother-only families among Blacks (52%) and Hispanics (27%) compared to Whites (18%) in 1997.

Living in mother-only families increases the risk of living in poor neighborhoods with low-quality services and high rates of crime. In 1997, more African American children (19%), compared to Hispanic (11.3%) or White children (1.2%), lived in poor neighborhoods. Some cities provide vivid examples. For example, in New York City from 1996 to 1998, 70.7% of families living below the poverty line were households headed by women, compared to 3.6% headed by men, and 25.7% headed by husband and wife. The effects of poor neighborhoods are associated with higher rates of dropping out of high school and teen parenthood.

Divorce is another risk factor. Women who become divorced are disproportionately at risk for economic problems if they have children. They experience no or short-term alimony, inadequate child support, and divorce settlements that are not favorable economically. Child support is a very important aspect of the economic stability for these families. An Urban Institute report indicates child support reduces poverty by 5% among children with one nonresidential parent. But this same report states that only 30% of children with a child support order actually receive the full amount they are due. Additionally, in the United States meager social insurance type programs for female-headed families and child support payments are insufficient to compensate for large wage differences between men and women. These policies reflect the historical values regarding economic support for female-headed families. [*See* DIVORCE.]

When comparing group declines in poverty rates, across all ethnic and racial groups, families in which the husband and wife work are less likely to be poor than those in which the husband is the sole worker. So it is clear that two incomes in a family becomes a way out of poverty. From 1967 to 1994, families headed by a single mother had less income than those headed by a married couple at all levels of income. Women who are unmarried (the statistics are based on single versus married rather than partnered and nonmarried) increased in percentage of live births from 28% to 32.4% in that time period. These single-mother families are more likely to be or become poor, since the poverty rate is 55% for never-married mothers compared to 35% for families headed by a divorced or separated mother.

IV. Where Do the Poor Live?

Poverty rates persist in large cities despite the economic boom in the new millennium. The National Center for Children in Poverty and the Children's Defense Fund publishes analyses on problems of poor urban children based on the Census Bureau's Population Survey. In urban areas Whites and Asians are more likely to live in neighborhoods where they share the same educational level and social class status as their neighbors. In contrast, Hispanics and African Americans are more likely to be in urban centers with persons of dissimilar status, indicating that as groups they are isolated in neighborhoods. This seems to reflect the residential segregation of urban housing markets. In New York City 1.8 million are officially poor. For the New York–New Jersey metropolitan area, this represents a 24% poverty rate. Compared to other larger cities, Houston has a higher poverty rate (28.1%), with other cities slightly below: Washington (23.8%), Los Angeles (22.5%), Detroit (22.4%), Boston (22.1%), Chicago (17.3%), Dallas (17.1%), and Philadelphia (8%).

Researchers such as Neil Bennett, Dana Haynie, and Bridgett Gorman have examined differences in economic well-being between urban and rural populations. Poverty is higher in urban areas compared to suburban and rural areas. In rural areas, gender distinctions exist. Rural women are poorer than rural men. These women have less education and work less time for lower-paid work (service, technical, sales, and administrative support occupations).

Reports from the Children's Defense Fund discuss the serious material hardships experienced by poor families. These reports estimate that 50% of poor families have experienced cutoffs of electricity and phones, not enough food in the past four months, crowded housing, and no refrigerator or stove.

V. What Happens to Poor Women?

Who are the women who are officially poor in the United States? They overwhelmingly head single-mother families, with almost half having incomes below the poverty line during 1993 through 1997, years of strong economic expansion. Researcher Valerie Primis and her colleagues have written about this problem. For those who were employed during these years, single mothers and other low-income families had increased earnings, but these earnings paralleled a decline in government benefits based on income (i.e., means-tested benefits). As a result, higher earnings could not offset the loss of these benefits even with the expansion of the earned income tax credit. One example to illustrate this situation is the food stamp program. Between 1995 and 1997 the number of people receiving food stamps fell 16.6%. This situation means that more wages were needed to buy food since food stamps were not available. As a result, families in this situation have not gained economically.

A. HEALTH

Low-income and minority women are at great risk for physical and mental health problems on virtually every measure of health care (breast exams, mammography, pap test, colon cancer screening, etc.). The picture becomes even clearer when income levels are taken into account. A survey of 2850 women conducted by Louis Harris and Associates from May to November 1998 for the Commonwealth Fund indicates that when women had incomes of $16,000 and below, they were six times as likely to report fair or poor health compared to women with family incomes above $50,000. Also, these lower-income women had higher levels of depressive symptoms, anxiety, and smoking. As Debra Bell wrote, the finding of poverty and depression is a long-standing one. The Society for the Psychology of Women's Task Force on Women, Poverty, and Public Assistance issued a report in 1998 about both poor women and women on welfare. This report's review of the literature concluded that women in the lowest economic strata are diagnosed with higher levels of mental disorder than those in the highest socioeconomic status group. The overwhelming evidence is that poverty is not good for mental or physical health.

Alcohol and substance abuse is a concomitant factor in health issues for some poor women. The Legal Action Center estimates that in 1997, 16 to 20% of welfare recipients were estimated to have alcohol and drug problems. The consequences for women who use drugs is especially problematic when they are also mothers. Poor women who have a dual diagnosis of mental, substance, and or alcohol abuse problems are most at-risk since there are fewer treatment facilities for women compared to men. Also, if these women are on welfare, states impose sanctions on obtaining certain cash and in-kind benefits. [*See* SUBSTANCE ABUSE.]

Physical health is also a concern. The Center for Reproductive Law and Policy has followed the issue of health care for poor women. African American and Hispanic women have less health insurance than White women and are more likely to be uninsured. For women under age 65, 23% of African American and 42% of Hispanic women have no health insurance compared to 13% of White women. Medicaid beneficiaries who are enrolled in managed care organizations present a variety of challenges. While this provides medical care to low-income women, Medicaid managed care compared to commercial managed care differs in quality. There are difficulties in obtaining preventive care, long waits for appointments, difficulties in accessing providers in some regions of the country, and lack of employer advocacy to influence their managed care plans for more responsive service. [*See* HEALTH AND HEALTH CARE.]

VI. Welfare

Public assistance or welfare was the way in which the federal and state governments provided income and other benefits to low-income individuals and families. Financial hardship was the eligibility criteria established for various programs (financial support for families with dependent children, medical insurance, food stamps, etc.). "Means testing" is the term used to cover the various ways states and the federal government established eligibility that varied from state to state. Historically, the welfare system was complex, large, and controversial. The public perception of the undeserving poor obtaining benefits paid for by taxpayer monies was a common theme.

In 1996, welfare policies were dramatically changed in the United States. The legislation that enacted welfare reform is called the Personal Responsibility and Work Opportunity Reconciliation Act of 1996. This legislation eliminated the program known as Aid to Families with Dependent Children, a program for women and their minor children. Under the new legislation, states receive grants of money, called block grants, to carry out this reform. These block grants are known as Temporary Assistance to Needy Families (TANF). This grant allotment requires 50% of any state's welfare caseload to be employed by 2002. The majority of individuals affected by these policies are single mothers who constitute more than 90% of welfare families in which an adult is receiving assistance. Single parents eligible for the public assistance from states (e.g., money, Medicaid, or food stamps) can maintain these benefits for a minimum

of two consecutive years or a lifetime five-year limit only by fulfilling mandatory work requirements. States have the ability to cut off all benefits whether or not recipients have found employment within those time limits. The only work exemptions are for mothers with infants under one year of age. Many states dropped welfare recipients before the law went into effect, thus cutting the total number of people on their caseload. Between 1995 to 1997, 3 million or 22.2% of persons receiving welfare were no longer receiving this assistance.

States can develop their own policies by deciding the criteria of noncompliance and the resulting reduction in benefits. These penalties can range from full-family sanctions in the most extreme form—the removal of adults from Medicaid, cash benefits, or food stamps for failure to comply with TANF work requirements. Some states require no notification, while 31 states require caseworkers to warn families of their noncompliance before being terminated from benefits. The U.S. General Accounting Office reported that in 1998, 135,800 families received partial or full-family sanctions during any given month. The characteristics of these families were female heads of household, most often high school dropouts, with problems related to health, transportation, or child care. The General Accounting Office also reported that of these women, 33% returned to the workfare programs and 41% found jobs.

By August 2000, with the anniversary of the passage of welfare overhaul, President Clinton announced that the welfare rolls in 1999 were at the lowest levels in 35 years. The percentage of Americans on welfare was 2.3% of the population or about 2.2 million families. This same report indicates that the average starting hourly wage for workers hired from welfare rolls is $7.80 per hour, higher than the $5.15 per hour minimum wage. This still leaves women with a salary that is insufficient to maintain a family.

Advocacy groups such as the Children's Defense Fund have issued reports calling for an increase in the federal minimum wage so that full-time work exceeds the poverty line. Issues still remaining for poor people entering the workforce are child care, transportation, and training. A report from the Welfare to Work Partnership, sponsored by top corporate executives (United Airlines, Sprint, Citigroup, Time Warner, Bank of America, Burger King, Monsanto, United Parcel Service, and IBM), recommends that the U.S. Congress increase tax credits, child care grants, subsidized housing, and transportation costs so welfare recipients can get to work more easily. These issues continue to challenge any reform movement.

A study of Michigan recipients who experience barriers to employment show similar problems as those reported here. Sandra Danzier and her colleagues reported on 728 women who received welfare in February 1997. In addition to problems of health and mental health, child care, transportation, and lack of a high school diploma, there were other barriers. These were domestic violence, poor job skills, multiple incidences of perceived workplace discrimination, and a lack of understanding regarding workplace norms even though some women had past work experiences. However, these women were no more likely to have drug or alcohol dependence than were women in the general population.

Immigrant families are also affected by this legislation. Illegal immigrants are barred from receiving Medicaid or food stamps. In families where one child may be born in the United States, that child would be eligible for benefits, but not the parents or any other children born outside of the United States. These mixed-immigration households face a bleak economic future within in this legislation.

Employment of former welfare recipients is mainly done by states creating programs called workfare. These programs have recipients work in exchange for their benefits. Women in these programs search, and often compete, for jobs with other low-income women—jobs that pay too little to move families out of poverty. As a result, barriers remain to gaining economic security. How a state defines success in placing former recipients into jobs can have a very different meaning than that thought of by the lay public. For example, a study by Valerie Polakow and her colleagues in Michigan tracked welfare recipients' work patterns. Findings were that 11% of those in mandatory work programs were considered successfully working if they were at a job at least 20 hours per week after three months. These jobs certainly do not pay a living wage. In addition, job availability is questionable in certain areas of the country. For example, in 1997 in California, 25% of public assistance families lived in rural areas where both jobs and public transportation were scarce.

Educational advancement, the way in which women move out of poverty, is limited because college attendance is no longer paid for. The new law stipulates that being enrolled in college does not meet the definition of "work." However, vocational and job skills training is permitted while the option of postsecondary education is excluded. This policy limits a woman's educational advancement. Government reports from HHS show education protects against poverty. With a college degree workers earn higher and more livable wages. Education is related to one's ability to obtain a job and to work full time because educational skills are needed for employability. College graduates have the lowest rates of poverty (3%), compared to high school graduates (29%). For single mothers with less than a high school degree and working, poverty rates are 82% if she is working part time and 39% if she is working full time. A 2000 survey conducted by the Children's Defense Fund of 180 social service providers indicates that those most likely to earn enough income to escape poverty are workers with at least a two-year postsecondary or vocational degree. The benefits of postsecondary education for a mother also relate to her children who perform academically at higher levels than women who only have a high school diploma. [*See* ACADEMIC ASPIRATIONS AND DEGREE ATTAINMENT.]

VII. The Homeless

Homelessness can be a result of poverty. Homelessness is probably the most visible sign of poverty seen by the general public. Reasons for homelessness vary over time. Victoria Banyard and Sandra Graham-Bermann have noted that one explanation, the structural analysis of poverty, views homelessness as a result of an unequal distribution of societal resources (e.g., good jobs and housing). The individual differences explanation examines factors related to the individual such as alcohol and substance abuse or psychiatric problems that pose risk factors for homelessness. While the public perception may continue to be influenced by these conceptualizations, researchers now understand that homelessness is more complex. Researchers argue that homelessness can result from the interaction between individual resources (e.g., social supports, coping strategies, and mental well-being) and larger social and environmental factors (e.g., housing availability, shifts in housing patterns, job availability, wages paid, government policies, emergency resources, and available and affordable child care). Ellen Bussuk and her colleagues elucidated this further. A study of these risk and protective factors between homeless and low-income women in Worcester, Massachusetts, indicated that predictive factors of homelessness are several. Some predictors of future homelessness seem to begin as early as childhood, such as foster care placement and the respondent's mother's drug use. Independent risk factors were minority status, recent arrival in the community, recent eviction, mental illness, and substance abuse. Protective factors were being younger, receiving cash assistance or a housing subsidy, graduating high school, and a larger social network compared to the homeless women. Social supports as protective factors appear to be very important. Several studies have found that poor female-headed households compared to female-headed homeless families have an active and effective social support network.

It is difficult to accurately count the number of individuals who are homeless. Some homeless individuals move into shelters, others move in with family or friends on a rotation basis, while others live on the street, in parks, in abandoned buildings, or in cars. A study done by James Wright and Joel Devine of New Orleans homeless used 60-day housing histories from substance abusers. Several patterns of homelessness emerged. Recent homelessness was defined as one or more homeless episodes within the past year. Chronic homelessness was considered one episode lasting longer than one year. Episodic homelessness was defined as numerous events of homelessness. Most of the women in this sample were new homeless.

Many studies of the homeless focus on social indicators—that is, what are the social and ecological factors that predispose a person for homelessness. Studies of homeless women report childhood and adult physical abuse and sexual abuse. Lisa Goodman, Mary Ann Dutton, and Maxine Harris concluded that for mentally ill women in their study, the lifetime of major abuse was so severe that only 3 of their 99 respondents reported no experience of physical or sexual abuse in childhood or adulthood. These findings indicate that for seriously ill homeless women, there is lifetime risk for victimization. These women, diagnosed with serious mental illness, were interviewed upon discharge from a local shelter or psychiatric hospital. They were primarily African American and had a median age of 41 (ranging from 21 to 71); 50% had never been married, 25% were divorced, and 25% were separated or married; 83% were heterosexual, and 71% were mothers. While over half (58%) had worked within the past five years, 44% were, along with their psychiatric diagnosis, engaged in alcohol or other substance abuse.

Other researchers also report histories of physical violence. Angela Brown and Shari Bausch studied 436 homeless and housed poor mothers and found that almost two-thirds reported severe physical violence in childhood, 42% reported childhood sexual molestation, and 61% suffered abuse from an adult male partner. These findings clearly indicate that both homeless and poor women are at risk for severe physical assault.

In a study of 228 homeless adults in Buffalo, New York, Carolyn Roll and her colleagues interviewed homeless women with and without children. Their findings were that both groups of women had more psychological distress, were recently assaulted, and had more contact with family members than men. The men had more substance abuse histories and criminal behaviors. Other researchers (Joan Morris and her colleagues) also found that family contact is maintained, but only for homeless women with children, compared to women and men without children. This group of mothers also had higher levels of self-esteem and spent less time homeless than did the other two groups.

Children living in homeless families have been another area of research. Typically studies have been conducted on children living in shelters with their mothers, with findings that developmental delays, behavior problems, and depressive symptoms are difficulties experienced by these school-aged children. Comparisons to children in female-headed, low-income families are that these children appear to be at greater risk for stressful life events, therefore experiencing these difficulties. Other comparisons between homeless and low-income female headed families have been in the area of child-rearing practices. Findings are that low-income homeless mothers provide less cognitive and social stimulation, warmth, and affection to their children compared to low-income nonhomeless mothers. However, living in a shelter compared to one's home can greatly influence parent–child interactions.

Some researchers have examined the meaning of a homeless identity for women. Using ethnographic methods, Julia Wardhaugh found that women discussed family or partnership breakdown and leaving violent situations as common causes of homelessness. Many of the women she studied discussed that they managed to live in the male-dominated streets by disappearing from visible places to maintain safety.

VIII. Programs That Are Helping

Experiments in increasing income and decreasing poverty levels are taking place with those families affected by welfare reform. One of the most successful to date is in Minnesota, where an experimental program increased earned income by not deducting money earned on a job from the welfare grant calculation. This pilot program had 14,000 families and ran for two years (1994 to 1996). Results indicate that for single-parent families there was an increase in employment and earnings, a decrease in poverty, and a decreased reliance on welfare as the main type of support. Couples with children had higher marriage rates, marital stability, and a decrease in domestic abuse. For children ages 5 to 12 in single-parent families, problem behaviors decreased and school performance increased.

IX. Conclusion

Overall, our solutions to poverty have never been aimed at rethinking what economic well-being means for individuals and families. Instead our solutions are often training programs for low-paying jobs that will provide some income, but not adequate levels of income for all individuals to enjoy a stable standard of living. The solution to this problem is difficult, for the historical ideology of the United States is that individuals should succeed without help. In reality this is never true. Women living in poverty experience a chronicity of economic deprivation rather than variability in social class status. Our values regarding them are shaped by our attitudes and stereotypes. Women are devalued and viewed as having children without regard to their ability to do so or as lazy and unwilling to work. These are only a few examples of subjective views regarding poor women and their families.

Current welfare reform in the United States is the newest in a trail of policy changes that have been aimed at restructuring governmental income distribution. The effectiveness of this reform for elevating poverty is still to be determined. What can be said is that the problem is not solved.

SUGGESTED READING

Bennett, N. (1999, June). Young children in poverty: A statistical update. National Center for Children in Poverty. Columbia University School of Public Health, pp. 1–12. New York.

Berstein, J., McNochol, E. C., and Mishel, L. Zahradnik, R. (2000, January). Pulling apart: A state-by-state analysis of income trends. Center on Budget and Policy Priorities/Economic Policy Institute, Washington, DC.

Gardyn, R. (2000). Unmarried mothers. *American Demographics* **22**(3), 24.

IWPR Welfare Reform Network News: Institute for Women's Policy Research. Washington, DC. Available at Welfare-L@ American.edu.

Samaan, R. (2000). The influences of race, ethnicity and poverty on the mental health of children. *Journal of Health Care for the Poor and Underserved* **11**, 100–110.

Society for the Psychology of Women Task Force on Women, Poverty, and Public Assistance, APA Division of the Psychology of Women. (1998). *Making welfare to work really work*. American Psychological Association, Washington, DC. Available from http://www.apa.org/pi/wop/welftowork.html.

U.S. Department of Health and Human Services (1999). Trends in the well-being of America's children and youth. Available at http://aspe.hhs.gov/hsp/99trends/index.htm.

Wyche, K. F. (1996). Conceptualizations of social class in African American women: Congruence of client and therapist definitions. *Women and Therapy* **16**(3/4), 35–44.

Zima, B., Bussing, R., Bystritsky, M., Widawski, M., Belin, T., and Benjamin, B. (1999). Psychological stressors among sheltered homeless children: Relationship to behavior problems and depressive symptoms. *American Journal of Orthopsychiatry* **69**, 127–141.

Power
Social and Interpersonal Aspects

Hilary M. Lips
Radford University

Glossary

Bases of power Resources controlled by someone that enable that person to exert power over others (for example, the ability to reward or punish others).

Cultural power system The set of practices, including language, norms, and roles, that maintain a cultural system of dominance relations (such as the dominance of men over women).

Disempowerment A heightened sense of vulnerability or lack of control over one's own life and choices.

Empowerment A sense of having control over one's own behavior, feelings, thoughts, and development.

Feminist therapy An approach in which the therapist explicitly acknowledges the power relations between women and men and makes this power relationship a central issue in therapy.

Glass ceiling A barrier, comprised of a systematic set of hidden obstacles, that keeps women from rising past a certain point in organizations.

Glass escalator A systematic set of hidden advantages that can produce positive discrimination toward men in hiring and promotion.

Hierarchy-attenuating values Values that oppose existing hierarchies of power and emphasize the interests of oppressed groups.

Hierarchy-enhancing values Values that support existing power hierarchies and promote the interests of elite, powerful groups in society.

Influence styles The kinds of strategies an individual uses in attempting to influence someone else (for example, confrontation or withdrawal).

Legitimate power Power that a person is seen to hold because she or he is thought to have a right to make certain demands or requests.

Masculinism An ideology that includes assumptions that society should be male centered and that qualities perceived as masculine are necessary for effective leadership.

Power as a social construction The idea that power is something that exists only within relationships, as it is perceived by the participants in the relationship.

Power motive The need to feel one is having an impact on others.

Profligate impulsive behaviors Reckless, destructive behaviors such as aggression and sexual exploitation.

POWER is defined in the *American Heritage Dictionary* as the ability or capacity to perform or act effectively and in the *Cambridge International Dictionary* as the ability to control people and events. Traditionally, social scientists have emphasized the themes of effective action and control in their definitions. For example, in their work on the social psychology of groups, John Thibaut and Harold Kelley defined power as the capacity to affect another person's outcomes. In his book on the power motive, David Winter defined power as the capacity to have an impact on the behavior or feelings of another person. Jean Baker Miller, in a feminist analysis of power, emphasized the effective action aspect of the definition, arguing that power should be conceptualized as the capacity to develop one's abilities.

I. Introduction

On March 31, 2000, a group of women in suburban Westchester County were being interviewed by National Public Radio's Melissa Block about Hillary Clinton's candidacy for the United States Senate in the state of New York. These women, who Block described as mostly Democrats between 37 and 57 years of age, were commenting on a change that definitely violated their expectations about women, femininity, and power. They were called upon to comment on a first in U.S. politics, a first for women: the first time this country's First Lady has run for political office—and doing so while still in her role as First Lady. The following are a few typical comments in response to the interviewer's questions:

One of the interviewees concluded her comments with "I think she's clueless about what it takes to stay home and be a mother. So how can she possibly represent me?" This was followed by another's, "I don't understand why she can't be like Eleanor Roosevelt. Why does she have to be a senator?"

Later in response to Melissa Block's question, "Does it strike you that you're being too hard on [Hillary]? Are you setting the bar very high for her for some reason?" a long-term liberal Democrat responded, "I don't think we're setting the bar too high

for her. I think . . . being a woman, the bar is always set high for us. We cannot function like men do, and get to the same place, because we would be called 'bitches' . . . and everything else. So, yes. The bar is set higher. But I think . . . [all of us] . . . have that business. Why shouldn't she be held to the same standard we are?" When Black asked, "The same double standard?" the interviewee answered, "Absolutely!"

The remarks of these New York women reveal that the relationship between gender and power is a complex one. Furthermore, they capture something critical about that relationship: women and power mix with difficulty. To begin to understand this difficulty, it is necessary to explore several different faces and levels of power.

Dictionary definitions of power provide a beginning. They remind us that in common usage power includes "position of ascendancy," "ability to compel obedience," "capability of acting or producing an effect," "influence, prestige," and "legal authority—all of which are included in *Webster's Third New International Dictionary* under the entry for power. Most of these meanings of power are in some way reflected in the example presented earlier and have been incorporated in traditional social science definitions. Social psychologists John Thibaut and Harold Kelley, writing in 1959, defined power as the capacity to affect another's outcomes; Dorwin Cartwright and Alvin Zander later defined it as the ability to get someone to do what one wants, despite initial resistance. In 1982, Carolyn Sherif described power as control over resources and core social institutions, making possible the initiation of effective action, decision making, and imposition of sanctions.

These definitions treat power as a commodity— something that belongs to an individual or group, temporarily or permanently. Alternative approaches, such as the perspective provided by Elizabeth Janeway in her 1981 book *Powers of the Weak*, view power not as a thing that is possessed but as a process in which people engage, not as something that persons *have*, but as something that they *do*. Theorists Jeanne Maracek, Glenda Russell, and Janice Bohan have argued that power can be seen as a social construction: something that exists only within the context of a relationship and is part of the process of that relationship.

Scholars who have analyzed power have further noted that, besides the interpersonal aspects, power also includes personal meanings such as empowerment and inner strength, as well as institutionalized systems of power that transcend and shape interpersonal interactions. Belle Ragins and Eric Sundstrom argued in an influential 1989 paper that power can be analyzed at different levels: individual, interpersonal, organizational, and societal. However, as argued in Lips, *Women, Men, and Power* (1991), these levels cannot always be neatly separated and have a tendency to overlap.

II. Gender and Images of Power

Social scientists have noted that power works best when it is viewed as legitimate and have explored the mechanisms through which persons or groups using power come to be seen as having a right to wield such power. Theorists such as sociologist Jessie Bernard and anthropologist Michelle Rosaldo have noted that one of the major issues with respect to gender and power is that women's use of power is often viewed as illegitimate, whereas men's use of power is more likely to be viewed as legitimate.

The evaluation of women's use of power as illegitimate springs from and reinforces cultural notions that femininity and power are incongruous. When I have asked students in Canada and in the United States to list powerful persons, they are far more likely to list males than females. In one Australian study, reported in 1995 by Jenny Onyx, Rosemary Leonard, and Kitty Vivekananda, nearly half the male respondents used what researchers called the "iron maiden" stereotype when asked to list descriptors for unspecified powerful women, using labels such as "man hater," "unfeminine," "asexual," "cold," and "hard."

Even those who have been chagrined by women's lack of access to power have apparently been influenced by the notion that women should not hold certain kinds of power. This influence is revealed in Janeway's notion that there are two kinds of power: "a limiting power to compel and a liberating power to act," also labeled as power-over (domination) and power-to (personal empowerment) by Janice Yoder and Arnold Kahn in a 1992 article.

The reduction of power to two modes has been criticized by Joan Griscom, who argued in 1992 that the distinction leads to two common errors: the tendency to view power-over as bad and power-to as good, and the labeling of power-over as masculine and power-to as feminine. She noted that such distinctions are insupportable in real life, where, for instance, a loving parent or caretaker, often female, may use power-over to ensure the welfare of a child

or Alzheimer's patient. As she argued, "in daily life, domination and nurturance overlap in complex ways and cannot be clearly distinguished as 'bad' or 'good'."

There is limited evidence that women and men may differ, at least in terms of emphasis, in the way they view power. In a 1985 study, Lips found that, when asked to explain what power meant to one sample of Canadian university students, both women and men, in approximately equal proportions, included themes of influence over others, achievement, and self-worth in their definitions. However, certain kinds of experiences were more often listed by the men as sources of feelings of power: having material possessions, being physically strong, and participation in sports.

Theorists and researchers have examined themes in women's ideas about power. For example, in 1982, Jean Baker Miller, speaking from clinical observations and discussions with women, described the fears women confront in thinking of themselves as powerful. She identified themes of selfishness, destructiveness, and abandonment, as well as concerns about inadequacy and loss of identity in women's descriptions of power. Hildreth Grossman and Abigail Stewart later searched for these themes in the responses of a sample of women who hold power over others: psychotherapists and professors. They found evidence of all three of Miller's themes in their interviews. As well they uncovered some more positive themes in these women's descriptions of their experience of power: the rewards of power expressed as nurturance, the use of power to strive for equality and mutuality, and exhilaration in the use of power. Grossman and Stewart also noted themes of some strains and stresses associated with power: the idea that nurturance must be limited, the potential danger to relationships, and threats associated with challenges to one's authority.

Several researchers who have specifically examined women's views of power have found that women hold understandings of power that they believe to be at variance with societal or traditional definitions. Cynthia Miller and Gaye Cummins, who collected responses from 125 women ranging in age from 21 to 63 years, reported in 1992 that women tended to define power for themselves in terms of personal authority and that they reported feeling powerful when experiencing self-enhancement or self-control. On the other hand, these women believed that society defined power largely in terms of control over others and control over resources. Six years later,

Alessandra Pollock found that college women defined power in society as consistent with traditional
definitions of power, but that their definition and reported use of power as individuals was consistent
with a feminist model. A 1994 study of the meaning
and experience of power among a sample of disadvantaged women showed that these women were
more likely to describe relational than nonrelational
experiences of power, according to Kathryn Peder-
sen, Bonita Long, and Ruth Linn. The dominant
themes of power that emerged in this study were
power as legitimized by a women's role and power
as destructive when used in negative ways. About
one-third of the women in this sample linked power
in its negative forms with the men in their lives and
with men's roles in society in general.

There has also been some investigation of differences among women with respect to their understandings of power. Debbie Weekes and Terri Mac-
Dermott, in a 1995 study, explored the differing
conceptions of power used by Black and White
women when understanding themselves and others.
Their interviews revealed that Black women were less
likely than White women to link negative forms of
power primarily with men and that they were more
likely to evaluate their power according to their position in terms of race and gender relations within a
global context. The Black women these authors interviewed were aware of a racialized gendered identity that had implications for power relations, whereas
the White women focused mainly on gender differences as sources of power differences. Age has also
been shown to be related to women's experiences of
power. In samples of U.S. and Kenyan women, Judith
Todd, Ariella Friedman, and Priscilla Kariuki showed
in 1990 that higher-status women displayed a stronger
sense of interpersonal power in older (44 to 60 years)
than younger (21 to 36 years) age groups. However,
this shift in the sense of power with age did not appear among lower-status women. A similar study of
Arab women in Israel by Friedman and Ayala Pines
also showed higher levels of perceived power among
these women at midlife than at younger ages, and a
third study by Friedman and her colleagues showed
higher levels of perceived power among older than
younger Israeli women in both the city and the kibbutz. These studies suggest that dimensions of diversity such as race/ethnicity and age within socioeconomic groups account for some differences among
women in their visions of power.

Gender differences in perceptions and experiences
of power may be, to some extent, a product of child-

hood socialization. In a 1994 article, Lips argued
that research on the treatment of girls and boys by
parents, teachers, and peers suggests that girls may,
in certain ways, be "culturally prepared" for powerlessness by receiving less attention and being less
successful in their influence attempts than boys. In
addition, Eleanor Maccoby showed, in her 1998
book *The Two Sexes: Growing up Apart, Coming
Together,* that boys and girls who spend large
amounts of time in same-sex groups may socialize
one another into different interaction styles: a constricting, competitive interaction style for boys and
an enabling, facilitative interaction style for girls.
When they reach young adulthood and begin spending more time with the other sex, females who have
learned to be facilitative may find they are at a disadvantage in influencing males. Males, on the other
hand, may find themselves well rehearsed in being
insistent and persistent in getting their way, and they
may be more easily able to influence females. If this
is the case, then it is not surprising that women come
to think of power as something masculine and, perhaps, unpleasant. [*See* PLAY PATTERNS AND GENDER.]

III. *Power Motive*

Researchers have investigated possible links between
gender and the power motive: the need and desire to
have an impact on one's environment. David Winter
and Abigail Stewart, in a series of studies, have shown
that there are no gender differences in the strength
of the power motive under neutral conditions (i.e.,
when there is no special reason for the power motive
to be aroused) and that the need for power can be
aroused in both women and men by using similar
procedures. Their research also indicates that the
correlates of a high need for power are similar for
women and men in the realm of leadership behaviors: for both sexes, a high need for power is associated with the acquisition of formal social power
through leadership roles and through careers in fields
such as management, teaching, clinical psychology,
and religious ministry that involve direct, legitimate
power over others. Sharon Rae Jenkins reported in
1994 on one study in which women whose need for
power had been measured during their college years
were followed up 14 years later and asked about
their job satisfaction. Women who had scored high
in the need for power during college reported more
sources of job satisfaction and dissatisfaction that
were power-relevant than non-power-relevant than

did women who had scored low in the need for power. Furthermore, the need for power predicted career progress only for women in power-relevant careers.

David Winter, in 1988, summarized evidence that a divergence between women and men with respect to correlates of the power motive appears in the category of behaviors that has been termed *profligate impulsive*: reckless, destructive behaviors such as drinking, aggression, and sexual exploitation. He and Stewart had demonstrated 10 years earlier that, for men, a high need for power was correlated with difficulties in their relationships with women and the tendency to view such relationships in an exploitative way. Highly power-motivated men tend to have more sexual partners, to prefer their wives to be dependent and submissive, and to read pornographic magazines. David McClelland showed that such men are also more likely than lower power-motivated men to be divorced or separated. High power motivation has been linked with the tendency for male, but not female, college undergraduates to physically abuse their intimate partners, according to 1987 research by Avonne Mason and Virginia Blankenship. For women, the relationship between power motivation and relationship difficulties seems to be the reverse of that for men: Abigail Stewart showed in a 1975 study that highly power-motivated women tended to stay in one relationship, avoid extramarital affairs, and not to divorce.

Research findings suggest that socialization for responsibility is an important variable in determining how the power motive will be expressed. Furthermore, gender differences in the way one's need for power relates to profligate impulsive behaviors may be at least partly an outcome of the differences in the way females and males are socialized with respect to responsibility. David Winter found that, for both women and men, the power motive is more strongly linked to responsible leadership behaviors among those who have younger siblings or who have children of their own. In 1985, Winter and Nicole Barenbaum found that, among adults who score high on a measure of responsibility, high power motivation predicts social leadership behaviors; among adults who score low on responsibility, high power motivation predicts a variety of profligate impulsive behaviors. Cross-cultural research by Beatrice and John Whiting has shown that an orientation toward responsible nurturance is one of the major ways in which social expectations and socialization differ for females and males; this difference may set the stage

for female-male differences in the correlates of the power motive.

IV. Empowerment

Often labeled as power-to, power-for, or inner strength, empowerment refers to a sense of control over one's own behavior, feelings, thoughts, and development. The concept has its roots in the work of Jean Baker Miller. Miller focused on power as a feeling of personal effectiveness that did not involve limiting the effectiveness of others but that could be experienced in connection with others. It also draws on the work of Albert Bandura, whose focus on self-efficacy placed a similar emphasis on self-control. Research on this topic has emphasized ways in which certain interventions, such as participation in therapy, education, or political action, can have empowering effects on individuals and on groups. Discussions of the empowerment have often focused on issues of diversity and difference among women and the ways that certain groups, such as women of color or lesbians, can become empowered to seek and achieve social change.

Some work has also been done on the reverse of empowerment: disempowerment. Disempowerment refers to a heightened sense of vulnerability and lack of control over one's own life and choices that may be produced under certain circumstances. Penny Reid and Gillian Finchilescu in South Africa and Ginger Hudson and Hilary Lips in the United States have explored the disempowering impact on viewers of exposure to media depictions of interpersonal violence, finding that viewing portrayals of women as victims of violence does have a disempowering effect on women.

V. Gender and Interpersonal Power

A. RESOURCES AND INFLUENCE STYLES

One line of research on gender and interpersonal power has concentrated on the analysis of the underlying resources and influence styles that characterize the use of power between individuals. This approach draws on a 1959 paper by John French and Bertram Raven, who delineated five bases of power: reward, coercion, expertise, legitimacy, and referent power. Reward and coercion involve, respectively, the perceived capacity of an individual to produce positive or negative outcomes for another person. Expertise involves the perception that the individual has a body of knowledge at her or his command that provides superior understanding of and insight into the issue under discussion. Legitimacy means the extent to which the individual is perceived to be entitled to exert influence, because of role, position, custom, or interpersonal agreement. Referent power refers to a person's ability to influence others because of their liking, admiration, or respect for him or her. These five sources of power may be accessible to individuals to varying degrees. Thus, the potential of one individual to exert power on another is said to depend on the type and amount of access to particular bases of power that the individuals in the interaction see themselves and the other as having. This approach has implications for understanding the ways power is gendered, since women and men have, in many contexts, differential access to the various bases of power. For example, in many situations, men hold the positions of authority that underlie legitimate power, and social norms that designate men as heads of households or "natural" leaders also convey legitimacy.

The influence style used by one individual with respect to another may depend on the way power resources are perceived to be distributed between the individuals. Researchers have shown that influence styles used by women and men tend to differ under some circumstances. Paula Johnson, in 1976, delineated three dimensions of influence styles: directness-indirectness, concreteness-personalness of resources, and competence-helplessness. She argued that women's use of power tended to be less direct, concrete, and competent than men's, citing women's lower access to resources such as concrete resources, expertise, and authority. Her own research demonstrated that college student respondents associated direct, concrete, competent styles of influence with men and personal styles with women. As well, in a group task situation in the lab, she found that male leaders relied more heavily on competence-based styles of influence, while female leaders were more likely to use helplessness to influence other group members.

Other researchers have also found gender differences in the influence styles used by women and men. A 1990 meta-analysis by Alice Eagly and Blair Johnson looked at 162 studies examining gender differences in leadership style. The analysis showed that women were less directive in their leadership behaviors than men, and this gender difference appeared across laboratory and field research settings and with students and nonstudent adult samples. A 1989 self-report study by Jacquelyn White and Mary Roufail of preferred influence strategies among university students revealed that women and men agree in their rankings of such strategies, with both sexes preferring to use direct strategies where possible. For both women and men in this study, the influence strategy ranked highest in order of preference was "use reason and logic," followed by "simply state my desires," and "offer to compromise." However, despite their agreement on the ranking of preferred strategies, women and men did differ in their reports of the frequency with which they actually used certain strategies. Men reported more use of high-pressure tactics, such as arguing and yelling, threatening force, and forceful assertion as first-choice strategies; women were more likely than men to report the use of negative emotion (pleading, crying, acting cold, getting angry, and demanding) as their first choice.

It has now become clear that influence styles vary, not specifically according to gender, but according to the power held by both parties. In 1980, Toni Falbo and Anne Peplau coded power strategies on two dimensions, directness-indirectness and bilaterality-unilaterality, and found that within male-female, female-female, and male-male couples, parties who reported feeling that they had less power in the relationship were more likely to use indirect and unilateral strategies of influence: the "weak" strategies. However, in heterosexual couples, power was confounded with gender: the women were more likely than the men to report being at a power disadvantage. A similar pattern was found by Judith Howard, Phillip Blumstein, and Pepper Schwartz, whose 1986 study of adults in long-term mixed-sex and same-sex relationships revealed that seeing oneself as more dependent in a relationship, controlling fewer resources, and having a male partner were all predictive of the use of the weaker influence strategies of manipulation (indirect) and supplication (helpless) influence tactics. Yukie Aida and Toni Falbo, exploring the relationship among marital satisfaction, resources, and power strategies, later found that married couples in which both partners described themselves as equally responsible for the financial support of the family were more satisfied and used fewer power strategies than did couples in which roles were divided in traditional ways; however, there were no overall gender differences in the use of influence strategies. Irene Frieze and Maureen McHugh, who interviewed self-identified battered wives and a comparison sample of wives, also reported in 1992 that the distribution of power in relationships is an important factor in the types of influence strategies used. Women with violent husbands had less decision-making power and used more influence strategies overall than did other women.

Not only in intimate, but also in nonintimate relationships, the distribution of power appears to be more important than the sex of the influencer in determining the type of power strategy that is used. Lynda Sagrestano asked participants to respond to scenarios in which they were trying to influence a nonintimate friend. She varied the balance of power in the hypothetical dyad by instructing respondents to think of themselves as either an expert or a novice in the topic under discussion, in comparison to the respondent's friend. Her results, reported in 1992 showed that power, not sex of influencer or target, was the main determinant of the type of influence strategy used.

Whereas the balance of power in a relationship appears to be a critical variable affecting the choice of influence strategies, the sex composition of the dyad is also important. Toni Falbo, Michael Hazen, and Diane Linimon reported in 1982 that women and men who used influence strategies deemed appropriate for the other gender were less liked and judged less competent and less qualified than other influence agents. Nonetheless, individuals using gender-appropriate and gender-inappropriate strategies were equally influential. Laurie Rudman found that the impact of self-promotion of one's own competence differs for women and men. In her 1998 study, women who promoted their own competence in an interview situation did receive higher competence ratings than other women; however, they were less liked and less likely to be hired—particularly by women. If they were self-effacing, they were judged as less competent but they were liked more. For men, on the other hand, self-effacement was a costly strategy, decreasing competence and hireability ratings. Linda Carli reported in 1990 that women tended to speak more tentatively in mixed-sex than in same-sex dyads; furthermore, women who spoke tentatively were more influential with men and less influential with women. Carli also demonstrated in 1998 that participants in a discussion responded differently to a female or male confederate who disagreed with them directly during a discussion. She found that, although participants tended to match their partners in the amount they agreed or disagreed, they increased their own stated disagreement more in response to the female confederate who disagreed

than to the male confederate who disagreed. Also, they expressed more overt hostility toward the disagreeing woman than the disagreeing man. Carli argued, on the basis of these results, that people tend to respond pleasantly and agreeably to women only as long as they behave in expected (i.e., pleasant and agreeable) ways. However, women who are direct and resistant to others' ideas encounter more aggression and hostility than men behaving in similar ways. Thus, it appears that there is a context of social approval that is different for women and men: women pay a higher price for being direct and disagreeable than men do. These studies indicate that individuals are aware of this difference and may adjust their own influence styles to fit it. As Carli noted in a 1999 article, the adjustment is problematic for women: "women end up experiencing a double bind. They can either convey modesty and be appealing to others but perceived as less competent, or they can self-promote and convey competence and risk rejection."

Gender may be an important predictor of influence styles precisely *because* gender affects the amount and type of power individuals hold. Many sources of power, such as expertise and legitimacy, are primarily the result of the way an individual is perceived by others. For example, if one person is perceived to be more expert than another, that person will hold more expert power—even if, by objective standards, she or he actually is no more expert than the other person. A 1999 review of the literature by Linda Carli illustrated that, because of pervasive gender stereotypes, women are generally viewed as less competent than men, with the result that women have less access to power based on expertise. She also showed that women are less likely than men to be seen as entitled to exert influence, meaning that women hold less legitimate power than men do. On the other hand, she noted that women are generally rated as more likable than men, and that this difference gives women more access than men to referent power. These differences, she argued, make it easier in many situations for men to exert power in direct, competence-based, assertive ways, and for women to exert power in ways that depend on warmth, agreeableness, and democratic leadership.

B. THE PROCESS OF COMMUNICATION

A second line of research on interpersonal power has focused on the process of communication. Nancy Henley's 1977 book on gender and nonverbal communication illustrated that dominance is expressed, though often unrecognized, through modes of nonverbal communication such as touching and the use of space. Her work provides a good illustration of the impossibility of separating interpersonal from organizational or societal power: while power expressed nonverbally in an interaction (such as a man touching a woman more easily than she touches him) conveys that one person is more powerful and thus more free to initiate touch in a given relationship, a pattern of such differences illustrates the presence of a more general hierarchy of power, in which men express dominance over women.

Research on other aspects of nonverbal communication also shows an interaction between power and gender. One 1988 study by John Dovidio and his colleagues showed that in mixed-sex pairs, expertise was associated with visual dominance (the tendency to look at another when speaking and to look away when listening) for both women and men. However, when there was no difference in expertise, men showed greater visual dominance than women did.

Verbal communication too appears to reflect the balance of power between the sexes. North American research by Victoria DeFrancisco showed that men try harder than women do to hold the floor in conversational interactions and that they often effectively silence women by interrupting them. If a woman tries to interrupt a man, she may become a target of disapproval, evaluated as being illegitimately assertive, according to research by Marianne LaFrance. Some group differences have been observed in these gendered patterns of conversational dominance. Emily Filardo, studying African American and European American adolescents, reported in 1996 that in the European American groups, but *not* in the African American groups, a higher percentage of the young women's than the young men's utterances were interrupted and never completed. The differences associated with ethnicity did not seem to be a result of facilitative conversational behavior by African American men, but rather of African American women's stronger determination not to let themselves be interrupted.

VI. Power, Gender, and Public Leadership

A. REACTIONS TO FEMALE AND MALE POWER HOLDERS

A growing body of research shows that people react differently to women and men who hold or aspire to hold power. Respondents associate power holders with stereotypically masculine qualities and link feminine characteristics to people who hold less power. Researchers such as Madeline Heilman and her colleagues have found in the past that traditional managerial roles, probably because they require stereotypically masculine behaviors, are viewed, especially by men, as a better "fit" for men than for women. Furthermore, women who adopt the autocratic or directive style of leadership that is traditional for hierarchical organizations are more likely than men to be targets of disapproval, according to a 1992 meta-analysis by Alice Eagly, Mona Makhijani, and Bruce Klonsky. [*See* LEADERSHIP.]

It is increasingly clear, however, that the sociocultural context plays an important role in the way women experience power and leadership. There are certain contexts in which stereotypes are most likely to impede the progress of female leaders. Foremost among them are conditions in which people are not used to female leaders: male-dominated occupations or roles, roles that call for a directive "masculine" style, and settings in which most of the participants are male. Under such conditions, Eagly and her colleagues have shown that women leaders are likely to be evaluated more harshly than men.

In settings where women are expected to predominate, females are more likely to be chosen as leaders and are not so likely to face discrimination. However, women face many more difficulties with advancement in organizations that are male-dominated, where there are very few women in senior, authoritative positions. For example, a study by Theresa Siskind and Sharon Kearns showed that female faculty members at the Citadel, a military academy that admitted only male students until recently, can face a lot of silent resistance to their authority. [*See* MILITARY WOMEN.]

In a setting in which women are not expected to hold formal power, it can be extraordinarily difficult for a woman to gain acceptance as a leader. Janice Yoder, Thomas Schleicher, and Theodore McDonald recently designed a laboratory experiment in which women were placed in leadership positions with all-male groups on a masculine-stereotyped task. This procedure was meant to simulate the situation in which women find themselves when they take on leadership roles in male-dominated organizations. In all three experimental conditions, group members were told that the woman had been randomly appointed by the experimenters to lead the group. In two of the three conditions, the women leaders received pretask training to give them expertise on the group task. However, in one of these two conditions, the women were told *not* to reveal that they had been trained. In the other condition, a male experimenter informed the group that the woman who would be leading them had come in early for special training and that she had information that could be useful to the group as they made their decisions. Thus, the experiment compared the outcomes for an appointed-only leader, an appointed and trained leader, and an appointed, trained, and "legitimated as credible" leader. Results showed that only the women who had been not only appointed and trained but also legitimated as credible by the male experimenter were effective in influencing the performance of their all-male group. Women who had been simply appointed leaders but not trained or legitimated were often relegated to secretarial roles in their groups. Women who had been appointed and trained but not introduced by the experimenter as experts were continually frustrated in their attempts to share their expertise with their groups. These women, who had been trained but had not had legitimacy bestowed on them by an external authoritative source, were apparently viewed by the male group members as ineffectual and as minor contributors to the group. The researchers argued, based on these findings, that, no matter how competent they are, women in male-dominated organizations often cannot overcome the stereotype that women are not expected to be leaders unless they are empowered by an external endorsement from the organization.

Research also suggests that women and men are stereotyped in terms of their values about power and leadership. One study found that women are assumed to hold values that are hierarchy attenuating (i.e., that run counter to established hierarchies and emphasize the interests of oppressed groups), whereas men are assumed to hold values that are hierarchy enhancing (i.e., that support existing hierarchies and promote the interests of the elite, powerful groups in society). In this study, when participants were given the task of placing applicants in positions with different emphases on hierarchy enhancement or hierarchy attenuation, they favored women for the hierarchy-attenuating jobs and men for the hierarchy-enhancing jobs. This pattern held even when applicants' résumés violated the stereotypes, according to researchers Felicia Pratto, Jim Sidanius, and Bret Siers.

The stereotypes of female and male leaders do have an impact on behavior toward them. In a telling 1990 laboratory study, Dore Butler and Florence Geis trained female and male confederates to try to become the leaders in mixed-gender, four-person groups. The males and females used the same scripts, made the same suggestions, using the same words, and followed similar tactics in trying to get the other group members to follow their lead. What Butler and Geis found was that women trying to take leadership of the groups became the targets of nonverbal disapproval. People frowned at them as they talked—and the more they talked, the more the other group members frowned. When men, using the same script as the women, tried to take leadership of their assigned groups, the nonverbal reactions were much more favorable. Their suggestions (the *same* suggestions) were greeted with smiles and nods, not frowns. It appeared that group members were made uncomfortable by the idea of a woman taking charge of mixed gender group—although these research participants said, when asked, that they had nothing against female leaders, and they were not aware of their nonverbal discouragement of the female leader. The negative nonverbal reactions to would-be female leaders were displayed by both women and men. It appears that people are not always aware of their negative reactions to female leaders.

B. GENDER AND THE EXPERIENCE OF POWERFUL POSITIONS

Given the literature on reactions to female power holders, it is not surprising to find that women are more likely than men to expect that holding powerful positions will be uncomfortable. In recent studies, Lips and her colleagues have shown that young women appear less likely than young men to believe that it will be possible for them to hold powerful positions and that women in some samples of U.S. college students report more likelihood than men do that holding powerful positions will lead to relationship problems. The relationship problems that these young women anticipate include having no time for family relationships, being disliked by subordinates or colleagues, the necessity for adversarial interactions with others, difficulties in maintaining boundaries in relationships in the workplace, and being perceived as unfriendly, uninteresting, or hypocritical. Whereas similar issues were raised by respondents in samples of students in Spain and workers in India, no gender difference in concern with them was found in these groups.

Some studies have looked specifically at the experiences of women in powerful positions. Robin Ely studied female lawyers in firms that were either strongly male dominated or gender integrated. Women in the two types of firms differed in the ways they described themselves, other women, and men, and in the qualities they believed were important for advancement and success in their firms. Women in male-dominated firms tended to believe that masculine qualities were essential for success, and some tried hard to fit the masculine mold. They were very conscious of gender stereotypes and tended to see conformity to masculine-stereotyped behavior (without, however, losing their femininity) as vital for success. For women in gender-integrated firms, however, the picture Ely found was very different. These women were not so likely to categorize feminine behavior in negative terms and tended to see both traditionally feminine and traditionally masculine qualities as important for their success. They did not have such a strong notion that they must change in order to fit in; rather, they viewed the profession as changing to adopt to women. Clearly the "culture" of the law firms in which these women worked affected their experience and use of power.

Erica Apfelbaum compared the responses of Norwegian and French women in high leadership positions and found striking differences between them. The French women experienced their positions as difficult, burdensome, and filled with conflict and discomfort. The Norwegian women, on the other hand, spoke about their roles positively. Apfelbaum reported in 1993 that these differences were apparently linked to, among other things, historical context and cultural ideas about femininity and masculinity and about the role of power in intimate heterosexual relationships. Whereas the French women were holding powerful roles in a country where women's access to formal political power was fairly new and still rare, Norwegian women held their positions in a country in which female political power had deep historical roots and was accepted. Furthermore, in France, the notion of powerful women did not fit well with the prevailing "script" for intimate heterosexual relationships: a tradition based on romance, seduction, and chivalry. Thus, the French women felt they were jeopardizing their intimate relationships by holding formal powerful positions.

The contrast between the experiences of the French and Norwegian women in Apfelbaum's study and between the two groups of lawyers in Ely's study suggest that holding powerful positions is likely to be experienced as difficult and conflictual for women unless it is done in a social context where women in positions of power are not unusual and there is cultural support for gender equality.

C. GENDER AND THE DIFFICULTY OF ACHIEVING POWERFUL POSITIONS

The search for the traits that are essential to leadership has often been characterized as fruitless. However, there is one trait that, although it appears over and over again in samples of leaders, is often overlooked: most leaders are male. Although women have been inching their way into positions of political, business, and educational leadership in recent decades, they still form a distinct minority in such positions. For example, over the life of United States, less than 1.5% of the persons elected to the Senate and less than 2% of those elected to the House of Representatives have been women. In 1998, the research and consulting firm Catalyst reported that women held only 5.3% of the line corporate officer positions in *Fortune* 500 companies, only 10.6% of the total board seats, and only two of the CEO positions.

Women aspiring to powerful positions often encounter a "glass ceiling"—a barrier that keeps them from rising past a certain point, but that is virtually invisible until the person hits it. Even women who do make it past the obstacles into top executive positions apparently do not reach a place where gender equity is the norm. A recent study by Karen Lyness and Donna Thompson of executives in one multinational corporation showed that the women who had reached this level faced a *second* glass ceiling. They made the same pay and received the same bonuses as their male counterparts, but they managed fewer people, were given fewer stock options, and obtained fewer overseas assignments than the men. They had reached the same level as the men; however, they did not have the same level of status and power in the organization. When surveyed, the women reported more obstacles and less satisfaction than the men did with their future career opportunities. They believed that they had moved up as far as they could in their company—whereas the men were more likely to see new opportunities ahead.

By contrast, men who work in female-dominated occupations sometimes report encountering a "glass escalator"—a systematic set of hidden advantages, according to research by Christine Williams. These men report experiencing positive discrimination in hiring and promotion and a series of subtle pressures to "move up" in the organization.

What accounts for the differences in women's and men's access to powerful organizational positions?

One important factor is doubtless the double bind, described earlier, that women face in trying to convey competence and expertise without incurring dislike and rejection. However, there are organizational factors at play as well. Belle Ragins and Eric Sundstrom noted that "power begets power"—that each increase in power for an individual sets the stage for the acquisition of still more power in the organization. Women can find themselves at a disadvantage at each stage of the process. First, as individuals they may suffer from the stereotype that women are less competent than men. Next, the positions into which they are hired are themselves stereotyped as low-power positions. For example, in organizations, an individual's power flows partly from the power of her or his department. Women in business organizations are disproportionately employed in people-oriented departments such as personnel or public relations, rather than in more powerful production and marketing departments. Even more insidiously, a relatively powerful position may lose power when occupied by a woman; men are more likely than women are to get the full power and prestige associated with a particular position. This loss of power is likely to carry over into the next promotion, compounding the disadvantage. Thus, during a series of transitions, from initial hiring through each level of promotion, women tend to lose ground in terms of organizational power. [*See* CAREER ACHIEVEMENT; WOMEN IN NONTRADITIONAL WORK FIELDS; WORKING ENVIRONMENTS.]

VII. Cultural Power Systems

Perhaps the most difficult face of power for researchers to analyze with respect to gender is that of power as a social structure, made up of numerous practices that maintain a cultural system of dominance. This social structure transcends, in some respects, the wishes or behavior of any particular individual and has a tendency to shape decisions, interactions, and social relations to fit it. As Jeanne Maracek commented in a paper given as part of a symposium on women and power in 2000, an institution that is inside a large culture is "like Jell-O," molding itself to fit the container.

The practices that maintain a power system include methods of discourse, shared understandings about and participation in a set of values, norms, and roles. Some scholars have examined the ways in which a power structure shapes the systems and interactions within it. For example, Elizabeth Meese, concerned about the omission of women's writings from the literary canon, analyzed the ways in which the "interpretive community" decides what "counts" as literature. She noted in her 1986 book, *Crossing the Double-Cross: The Practice of Feminist Criticism,* that the people who decide what literary works are worthy of serious reading and study are not a neutral group of scholars applying a set of logical and artistic rules. Rather, the most influential members of the interpretive community are professors and critics, most often White men, who have been trained in certain traditions and share a set of assumptions that privileges their own group. Under the guise, and perhaps the illusion, of scholarly neutrality, this group maintains the power system that excludes the works of other groups from serious literary consideration. Meese described the process as "the construction of a strong insider-outsider dynamic, a gender-based literary tribalism that comes into play as a means of control" (p. 7). This larger power system, of which most participants are unconscious, shapes the choice of literary works for inclusion in university curricula, the selection and hiring of faculty, the styles of writing that are taught and rewarded.

In a wide-ranging examination of the gendered power system embedded in politics, Rita Mae Kelly and Georgia Duerst-Lahti argued in a chapter in their 1995 edited book that a masculinist ideological base permeates social understandings about politics and governance. This ideological base includes assumptions that privilege masculinity—assumptions about human nature, appropriate power arrangements, and actions. They noted that "unstated assumptions of masculinism, a metaideology that subsumes most of what we have thought of as political ideology . . . provides the givens that become universal norms for political theory, behavior, and empirical analysis. The universality of masculinism makes feminism seem radical and different."

Feminist therapy is one setting in which the cultural power system is explicitly acknowledged and discussed. Traditional mental health knowledge bases have been slow to address how societal power issues may relate to psychological distress; feminist therapy makes this a central issue. Jeanne Maracek and Diane Kravetz recently examined the ways feminist therapists talk about power. Their discourse analysis of interviews of three experienced feminist therapists, reported in 1998, revealed that they differed widely in their approaches to talking about power.

Themes emerged that included an emphasis on men's power over women, women as victims of oppression, a concern with the power that therapists hold with respect to clients, and a concern with emphasizing connection rather than separation. All of the therapists were conscious of interpersonal power issues and tried, in various ways, to make their clients more conscious of these issues.

Yet feminist therapists, though intentional in their efforts to foreground power issues in therapy, are not independent of the larger power system in which they operate. Maracek and Kravetz noted that all three therapists were aware of the antifeminism in their environment and affected by it, and these authors raised the question of how antifeminism in Western culture restricts and inhibits feminist therapists from identifying with and practicing their feminism. In a further investigation of how the pervasive power system interacts with and influences the discourse and behavior of feminist therapists, Jeanne Maracek analyzed the interviews of 50 feminist therapists. She found that these therapists used a variety of strategies to maintain a positive feminist identity in the face of an antifeminist power system and to dissociate themselves from negative cultural definitions of feminism. For example, a number of the therapists were at pains to point out that they were not "angry" feminists, describing anger as a stage that they had gone through when they were younger. They tended to accept the characterization of typical feminists as unpleasant and described themselves as exceptions in that respect. Although they resisted it, these women appeared to be significantly influenced by the discourse, prevalent in their environment, that feminism was a negative, unpleasant, and illegitimate ideology. This is an example of the impact of a gender power system on the systems within it. [See FEMINIST APPROACHES TO PSYCHOTHERAPY.]

VIII. Conclusion

Gender and power are intertwined in a myriad of complex ways. The habit of associating men with power and women with subordination leads to a confounding of the two concepts. The inseparability of gender and power can be seen at the individual level, in the way that the power motive plays out in women's and men's behavior. It can be seen at the interpersonal level, in the ways that resources are distributed and the manner in which influence and communication strategies are used. It is apparent in the pattern of findings showing that women and men, engaging in similar powerful behaviors, are judged differently by others. It is clear as well at the organizational level, where gender stereotypes and organizational habits and values work together to reduce women's access to high-power positions. Finally, it can be observed at the cultural level. Power systems imbued with traditionally masculine values shape expectations and transcend individual, interpersonal, and organizational decision making to create a "mold" into which these other levels fit. From within this mold, any impetus toward feminine power can easily be viewed, even by participants, as suspect or illegitimate. The presence of an association between gender and power at this cultural level makes it difficult for researchers to recognize and ask all appropriate questions. Perhaps more important to most of the population, it makes it difficult for individuals to be aware of and to overcome the association between power and gender in daily life.

SUGGESTED READING

Carli, L. L. (1999). Gender, interpersonal power, and social influence. *Journal of Social Issues* 55(1), 81–99.

Duerst-Lahti, G., and Kelly, R. M. (eds.) (1995). *Gender Power, Leadership, and Governance*. The University of Michigan Press, Ann Arbor.

Griscom, J. L. (1992). Women and power: Definition, dualism and difference. *Psychology of Women Quarterly* 16(4), 389–414.

Henley, N. M. (1977). *Body Politics: Power, Sex, and Nonverbal Communication*. Prentice-Hall, Englewood Cliffs, NJ.

Janeway, E. (1981). *Powers of the Weak*. Morrow, New York.

Lips, H. M. (1991). *Women, Men, and Power*. Mayfield, Mountain View, CA.

Miller, J. B. (1976). *Toward a New Psychology of Women*. Beacon Press, Boston.

Radtke, H. L., and Stam, H. J. (eds.), *Power/Gender: Social Relations in Theory and Practice*. Sage, London.

Pregnancy[1]

Carmen L. Regan

Hospital of the University of Pennsylvania

Glossary

Integrins Transmembrane proteins, which are receptors for extracellular linkers at the cell surface.

Ontogeny The process whereby the fetus ordinarily develops.

Syncytiotrophoblast Differentiated trophoblast lining the maternal villous spaces and responsible for β-human chorionic gonadotrophin hormone production in pregnancy.

Trophoblast Fundamental placental cell of epithelial origin.

PREGNANCY is made unique by the fact of maternal tolerance of the fetus, which is by definition a semiallograft. Incompletely understood, this immune tolerance is thought to be due in part to unique antigen expression by the fetal trophoblast and to altered maternal immune responses in pregnancy. Following implantation an orchestrated sequence of events occurs local to and distant from the fetoplacental unit leading to the altered physiological state of pregnancy.

I. Ovulation, Fertilization, and Implantation

Estrus in the human female is a 28-day-cycle. Ovulation characteristically occurs on day 14 and is followed by menstruation 14 days later if fertilization fails to occur. Average human gestation lasts 280 days or 40 weeks and is divided into three parts, described as trimesters. The first trimester is from conception to 12 weeks' gestation, the second from 12 weeks to 28 weeks, and the third from 28 weeks to term.

The ovum, once fertilized, commences division over a period of hours to days and becomes the morula, which is composed of a cluster of dividing cells. The morula enters the uterus on the fifth day after fertilization. During the following few days it lies free in the uterine cavity bathed by secretions from uterine glands. A fluid-filled cavity appears within the cavity of the morula which is then termed a blastocyst. Placentation in the human involves an invasive phenomenon in which embryo-derived trophoblastic cells

[1]Reprinted with permission from the *Encyclopedia of Reproduction*, Volume 3. Copyright © 1999 by Academic Press.

progressively integrate into the maternal tissues through production of extracellular matrix degrading enzymes (matrix metalloproteinases), migratory activity, and rapid cell division. The human placenta is hemochorial. The trophoblast cells at the implanting blastocyst invade into the uterus in order to establish a blood supply. During the first two weeks of development nutrients are exchanged by diffusion; thereafter, a blood supply is established by the cytotrophoblastic columns which invade the decidua blood vessels by a process of endovascular invasion. In the process of endovascular invasion the epithelial trophoblast acquires endothelial characteristics, including the expression of endothelial-specific integrins. Human chorionic gonadotrophin (hCG) is a glycoprotein secreted by the placental syncytiotrophoblast throughout gestation. Serum levels rise rapidly over the 10 days following implantation, reaching a peak in the ninth week of gestation at 100,000 mIU. Thereafter, it falls to a level of about 10,000 mIU, at which it remains for the duration of pregnancy. The hCG acts on the corpus luteum to prevent its regression and to stimulate its production of progesterone and estradiol.

Abnormal placentation can result in loss of the fetus and may cause severe complications for the mother. For example, preeclampsia or pregnancy-induced hypertension, a disease exclusive to human pregnancy, affects 7 to 10% of all pregnancies and is thought to be due to abnormal placentation. Trophoblast cells from such pregnancies fail to invade endovasculature and show the characteristic changes to an endothelial-like phenotype.

II. Organogenesis

Fetal organogenesis occurs in the first 12 weeks, although ontogeny continues throughout pregnancy, particularly within the fetal brain. The first trimester is therefore a time of rapid cell division and differentiation. It is during this critical period that drugs exert most of their teratogenic effects. The neural tube closes at 24 to 28 days after conception, often before the pregnancy is apparent. The primitive fetal heartbeat can be detected by ultrasound from as early as 6 weeks. The fetal kidney is developed at 10 weeks and fetal urine production commences early in the second trimester. By the end of the embryonic period (10 menstrual weeks) the extremity bones, joints, and musculature have differentiated into structures with relative position and form identical to those of an adult.

III. Fetal Maturation and Growth

A. RATE OF FETAL GROWTH

From about 14 or 15 weeks the fetus gains weight at a rate of 5 g per day increasing to 10 g per day at around 20 weeks of gestation. In the third trimester the average daily weight gain is 30 to 35 g per day. The mean growth rate peaks at 230 g per week; this occurs between 33 and 36 weeks. The maximum percentage growth rate occurs in the first trimester.

B. FACTORS CONTRIBUTING TO FETAL GROWTH

Forty percent of total birth weight variation is due to genetic contributions from the mother and fetus; the remainder is environmental. The parental influence on growth is limited to the contribution of a Y chromosome. Male fetuses grow faster than females and weigh 150 to 200 g more at birth.

Numerous studies show that inadequate nutrition in pregnancy can predispose to intrauterine growth restriction (IUGR). If the insult occurs early in pregnancy then the number of cells is decreased; if it occurs later in pregnancy cell size is decreased. Inadequate weight gain in pregnancy (<0.27 kg per week or <10 kg at 40 weeks) may also contribute to low birth weight. Prepregnancy nutritional status is also important, and studies from famine situations indicate that the IUGR is more profound if nutritional deprivation predates and continues through pregnancy.

Alterations is uteroplacental perfusion affect both the growth and the status of the placenta as well as the fetus. Umbilical artery flow studies indicate a reduction of umbilical blood flow in some human growth restricted fetuses. This may be due to increased resistance downstream as a result of impaired placental perfusion secondary to thrombosis and vasoconstriction. Maternal cigarette smoking decreases birth weight by 135 to 300 g. If smoking is stopped in the third trimester, this effect is not seen. The mechanism is not well established but may be due to carboxyhemoglobin concentrations in the maternal and fetal bloodstream, which displaces oxygen from circulating hemoglobin. Maternal alcohol consumption and cocaine usage are associated with low birth weight. Growth restriction in these cases is global, affecting both fetal weight and head size. In the latter case, the reduction in head circumference is more pronounced.

IV. Maternal Adaptation to Pregnancy

In order to facilitate the growth of the fetus *in utero*, the maternal physiology undergoes dramatic change. Multiple organ systems are involved but the following sections discuss the most relevant.

A. RESPIRATORY SYSTEM

Progesterone from placenta stimulates the respiratory center in the brain to produce hyperventilation. This results in a decreased alveolar CO_2 and arterial pCO_2. The hypocarbia results in a reduced plasma bicarbonate via increased renal excretion and a minimal change in pH. Thus, pregnancy is a state of compensated respiratory alkalosis.

Tidal volume increases from about 450 to 600 ml, representing a 40% increase. In addition, minute ventilation increases by 40%, thus increasing the oxygen available to the fetus and facilitating CO_2 transfer from fetus to the mother.

B. CARDIOVASCULAR CHANGES

Cardiac output increases 30 to 50% in pregnancy and reaches a maximum at 10 weeks of gestation. It remains elevated until term, when 20% of output is directed to the kidneys, 17% to the uterus, and 10% to the skin. Cardiac output is dependent on position. Supine occlusion of the inferior vena cava occurs in late pregnancy, with an 8% drop in cardiac output from decubitus lateral to back and an 18% drop from standing to lying. Most women do not become hypotensive when standing because the fall in cardiac output is accompanied by a rise in peripheral vascular resistance. Blood pressure in pregnancy is highest when seated, lower when supine, and lowest in the left lateral position. Peripheral vascular resistance falls in pregnancy due in part to the relaxing effects of progesterone on smooth muscle. Systemic arterial blood pressure falls in the first 24 weeks and increases gradually to term.

Echocardiographic studies demonstrate that, despite increases in left ventricular dimensions and volume during pregnancy, most parameters of left ventricular function are generally similar to those in the nonpregnant state. Central hemodynamics are altered in normal pregnancy. Significant increases in cardiac output and heart rate occur, and additionally significant decreases in systemic and peripheral vascular resistance occur, resulting in no net change in mean arterial pressure, pulmonary capillary wedge pressure, central venous pressure, or left ventricular work index during normal pregnancy. There is a reduction in colloid osmotic pressure which may explain the propensity to pulmonary edema in pregnant women with enhanced capillary permeability or cardiac preload.

C. PLASMA VOLUME AND RED CELL MASS

Plasma volume in normal pregnancy increases from six to eight weeks and increases progressively until 30 to 34 weeks, after which time it reaches a plateau. The mean increase is 45 to 50% and is larger in multiple gestation and in women with bigger babies. Erythrocyte mass increases from 10 weeks and rises steadily toward term. The increase is thought to be due to erythropoietin production. Red blood cell mass increases by about 18% by term in unsupplemented patients and by 30% in those given iron. Because plasma volume increases by 50% and red blood cell mass by 18 to 30% the hematocrit falls, reaching a nadir at 30 to 34 weeks. This physiological response enhances placental perfusion by decreasing viscosity.

D. IRON REQUIREMENTS

Iron requirements increase in pregnancy. Placental transfer of iron occurs in the first trimester as soon as the tertiary villi are formed. Iron is absorbed from the proximal duodenum in the ferrous stat; only 10% is absorbed in the nonpregnant state. In pregnancy 20% of oral iron is absorbed and in deficiency states up to 40% may be absorbed. The total iron requirement in pregnancy is 1000 mg. Five hundred milligrams is required for increased red cell mass, 300 mg for the fetus, and 200 mg to compensate for normal daily losses by the mother. In the third trimester the fetus takes up all the iron available to it. Iron is actively transferred to the fetus by the placenta against a high concentration gradient, and fetal levels do not correlate with maternal levels. Iron requirements increase with advancing gestation to support the increasing red cell mass and the requirements of the fetoplacental unit. Placental volume and weight has been correlated with maternal anemia, and placental hypertrophy may represent a mechanism for improving transfer and supply of oxygen to the fetus.

E. THE RENAL TRACT

Pregnancy is associated with major anatomical and functional changes in the renal tract. Kidney volume, weight, and size increase in pregnancy, with renal length increasing by 1 cm. The renal collecting system undergoes marked dilatation, seen as early as the first trimester and persisting up to four months postpartum. These effects are attributed to both mechanical and hormonal effects. The glomerular filtration rate (GFR) and effective renal plasma flow increase by 50 to 80% above the nonpregnant value. Renal 24-hour creatinine clearance increases at 4 weeks of pregnancy, rises to a maximum at 9 or 10 weeks, and remains elevated until late pregnancy. Serum creatinine and levels of blood urea nitrogen fall in pregnancy secondary to the increase in GFR. Uric acid falls and increases toward term as a result of increased tubular reabsorbtion of urate. Plasma osmolality falls in early pregnancy due to a reduction in sodium and associated anions. A diuretic response does not occur because of a lower osmoreceptor setting in pregnancy. Sodium metabolism is altered in pregnancy. Sodium loss by the kidneys is enhanced by increased glomerular filtration and the natriuretic effect of progesterone. This is balanced by enhanced renal tubular reabsorbtion of sodium as a result of increases in circulating aldosterone, estrogen, and deoxycortisone.

F. THE COAGULATION SYSTEM

Pregnancy is a hypercoagulable state. Fibrinogen I increases during pregnancy, which is also associated with elevated levels of factors VII to X. Prothrombin II and factors V and VII remain unchanged during pregnancy, whereas XI and XIII decline somewhat. The risk of thromboembolism is 1.8 times that in the nonpregnant state in pregnancy and 5.5 times that in the puerperium. The naturally occurring anticoagulants antithrombin III and proteins C and S are important in maintaining hemostasis. Protein S falls but protein C and antithrombin III remain stable. The platelet count declines progressively in pregnancy and is associated with a fall in platelet volume. This is thought to reflect increased platelet consumption and augmented production due to a shortened platelet life span.

V. *Labor and Delivery*

Term labor is defined as labor occurring after 37 weeks of completed gestation. The stimulus heralding the onset of labor is unknown but is thought to be fetal in origin. A number of mechanisms for the initiation of labor have been proposed, including a shift in the balance of estrogen/progesterone effects toward estrogen, release of oxytocin, and increased uterine synthesis of prostaglandins.

The actual mechanism is not fully understood, although there does appear to be a common biochemical end point of an increased synthesis of prostaglandins. Recently, induction of the prostaglandin endoperoxide synthase isoform, PGHS-2 (also known as cyclooxygenase-2), in maternal reproductive tissues prior to the onset of labor has been described, and this may account for increased prostaglandin biosynthesis. In addition, prostaglandin synthase inhibitors are effective in delaying preterm labor.

Following initiation of labor, oxytocin release from the posterior pituitary gland stimulates rhythmic uterine contractions. Progressive softening and connective tissue remodeling of the cervix results in effacement, a process whereby the cervix is incorporated or "taken up" into the lower uterine segment. Following complete effacement, cervical dilatation commences. The first stage of labor is that time from the initiation of labor to complete cervical dilatation and is of variable duration depending on fetal, maternal, and uterine factors. Delay in the first stage of labor is arbitrarily defined as time taken in excess of 12 hours and is termed dystocia. The second stage of labor is the time from complete cervical dilatation to delivery of the fetus. Classically, this stage involves descent of the fetal head into the maternal pelvis by a sequence of flexion, internal rotation, extension, and, following delivery, restitution. Delay in the second stage may be due to a combination of factors, including fetal size, pelvic anatomy, and inefficient uterine action. Augmentation of labor is deemed necessary when adequate progress is made in the first stage of labor as judged by cervical dilatation and in the second stage by failure of descent of the fetal presenting part. Synthetic oxytocin is given intravenously in order to stimulate uterine contractions. The rate of oxytocin infusion varies in different centers and low- and high-dose regimens have been described. A system of labor management for nulliparous women, termed the active management of labor, has been developed and practiced in Ireland, and has resulted in a reduction in prolonged labor and cesarean section rates for dystocia. The third stage of labor is the time from delivery of the fetus to delivery of the placenta. Following delivery of the fetus, the placenta separates from the uterine wall. Separation is heralded by a vaginal gush of blood, lengthening of the umbilical cord, and firming of the uterus as palpated abdominally by the examining hand. Expulsion of the placenta follows shortly thereafter.

VI. The Puerperium

The puerperium commences immediately following the delivery of the placenta and is arbitrarily defined as a period lasting six weeks. Involution of the uterus occurs immediately and within a week is 50% of its size at the end of pregnancy. After two weeks of normal involution the uterus cannot be palpated abdominally and at 6 weeks is almost its prepregnant size. The superficial layer of decidualized endometrium is sloughed off as the lochia, whereas regeneration of the underlying endometrium occurs and is complete on the 16th postpartum day. The cervix gradually returns to a nonpregnant state over a period of three or four months and the vaginal epithelium returns to its nonpregnant state over a period of 6 to 10 weeks, although varying degrees of mucosal and facial relaxation may remain. Ovulation occurs in nonlactating women at about 10 weeks after delivery and menstruation will occur at 12 weeks postpartum in 70% of cases. Following term delivery hCG disappears from the circulation by about 12 days.

The systemic changes reflecting the maternal adaptation to pregnancy return to prepregnant levels over varying degrees of time. The major circulatory changes return to baseline over a period of six weeks. Renal function returns promptly to prepregnancy levels after delivery, with renal plasma flow being substantially diminished by five days postpartum. In contrast, the anatomical changes in the urinary system, such as increased renal size and ureteral dilatation, may persist for months.

VII. Lactation

During pregnancy there is a gradual increase in serum levels of prolactin. The effects of prolactin on the breast are inhibited by high levels of estrogen which prevents lactation during pregnancy. Following delivery there is a rapid fall in the level of estrogen, and progesterone and prolactin are able to initiate lactation. Prolactin levels decline to nonpregnant values within four to six weeks in women who do not breast-feed. In breast-feeding mothers the levels remain elevated for about two or three months postpartum and thereafter decline. As lactation continues, suckling elicits progressively less prolactin release, although the amount is sufficient to maintain lactation. Initiation of lactation is via the "letdown" reflex. Impulses generated by suckling enter the spinal cord and are relayed to the hypothalamus. The neurosecretory cells in the supraoptic and paraventricular nuclei are stimulated to secrete oxytocin and prolactin via mechanisms which are imprecisely understood. Myoepithelial cells are the effector organ for oxytocin. Contraction of these cells forces milk out of the alveolar lumina. Oxytocin is released in a pulsatile fashion which is responsible for the rhythmic contraction of myoepithelial glands within the mammary gland.

Although suckling is the primary stimulus for the release of oxytocin, this reflex may be conditioned so that the sight or sound of the baby may cause the letdown of milk. Pain, embarrassment, or distraction may inhibit it. Prolactin release following suckling is not a conditioned reflex and release is dependent solely on suckling. The composition of human milk is a mixture of fat in water that is isotonic with plasma, with water being the major constituent. Colostrum, the milk secreted in the first few days of lactation, is higher in protein and lower in carbohydrate than mature breast milk. Human milk is composed of more than 100 constituents. The principal proteins are caseins, α-lactalbumin, lactoferrin, immunoglobulin A (IgA), lysozyme, and albumin. A number of peptide hormones are present in breast milk, including epidermal growth factor and transforming growth factor-α: These may play a role in the growth of the developing infant. Growth hormones have also been identified, as have naturally occurring benzodiazepines which may have sedative properties. The advantages of nursing are evident for both mother and child. Uterine involution is facilitated by the pulsatile release of oxytocin from the posterior pituitary upon suckling. Maternal weight loss is facilitated by transfer of proteins, carbohydrates, and fats to the neonate. Bonding between mother and infant is facilitated.

Nutritionally, breast milk cannot be improved upon by formula. From an immunologic standpoint, neonatal immunity to infection is boosted by the ingestion of maternal IgA antibodies which protect against respiratory and gastrointestinal pathogens; this may be the mechanism in the reduction in sudden infant death syndrome seen in breast-fed babies. Other benefits may result from the ingestion of trophic hormones and other factors in human milk. Little is known about the cause of failing lactation in humans, and a decline in milk production occurs in the first three months postpartum. A variety of drugs have effects on lactation and breast feeding, either by effects on the mammary gland or by altering prolactin secretion. Many substances may be transmitted to the neonate through human milk and only drugs necessary for the welfare of the mother should be prescribed.

In conclusion, pregnancy involves major physiological adaptations to allow normal growth and development of the fetus. These adaptations of pregnancy begin early in gestation and are associated with major changes in important organ systems. When the normal physiological response does not take place, poor fetal growth and increased maternal morbidity result.

SUGGESTED READING

Bennett, P. R., Henderson, D. J., and Moore, G. E. (1992). Changes in the expression of the human cyclooxygenase gene in human fetal membranes and placenta with labor. *American Journal of Obstetrics and Gynecology* 167(1), 212–216.

Clark, S. L., and Cotton, D. B. (1988). Clinical indications for pulmonary artery catheterisation in the patient with severe preeclampsia. *American Journal of Obstetrics and Gynecology* 158, 453–458.

Creasy, R. K., and Resnik, R. (1994). *Maternal–Fetal Medicine: Principles and Practice*, 3rd ed. Saunders, Philadelphia.

Dubin, W. H., Johnson, J. W. C., Calhoun, S., *et al.* (1980). Plasma prostaglandins in pregnant women with term and preterm deliveries. *Obstetrics and Gynecology* 203–306.

McMaster, Librach, C. L., Zhou, *et al.* (1995). Human placental HLA-G expression is restricted to differentiated cytotrophoblasts. *Journal of Immunology* 154, 3771–3778.

O'Driscoll, K., Foley, M., and MacDonald, D. (1992). Active management of labor as an alternative for cesarean section for dystocia. *Obstetrics and Gynecology* 485–490.

Williams, R. L., Creasy, R. K., Cunningham, G. C., *et al.* (1982). Fetal growth and prenatal viability in California. *Obstetrics and Gynecology* 59, 624.

Zhou, Y., Damsky, C. H., and Fisher, S. J. (1997a). Preeclampsia is associated with failure of human cytotrophoblasts to mimic a vascular adhesion phenotype. *Journal of Clin. Invest.* 99, 2152–2164.

Zhou, Y., Fisher, S. J., Janatpour, M., Genbacev, O., Dejana, E., Wheelock, M., and Damsky, C. H. (1997b). Human cytotrophoblasts adopt a vascular phenotype as they differentiate. *Journal of Clin. Invest.* 99, 2139–2151.

Prejudice

Nancy Lynn Baker
El Granada, California

I. Introduction
II. Overview
III. Sexism
IV. Conclusions

Glossary

Discrimination Overt acts of unequal treatment or evaluation based on group or identity status (e.g., gender, race or ethnicity, sexual orientation); may also include overt acts that result in unequal consequences due to identity status.

Heterosexism A form of prejudice against gay or homosexual people defined by the existence of negative attitudes and values about persons other than heterosexuals (e.g., lesbians, gay men, bisexuals); distinguished from the term "homophobia" in that it includes all nonheterosexuals and does not require, but can include, fear of or aversion to homosexuals.

Racism A form of prejudice based on the belief that race accounts for differences in human character or ability and that a particular race is superior to others.

Sexism A form of prejudice defined by the existence of negative attitudes and values about women as a group.

Stereotype A conventional, formulaic, and oversimplified conception, opinion, or image, which serves as a cognitive component of prejudice.

Stigmatize Characterize or brand as negative, defective, or bad.

PREJUDICE, as used in this article, is defined as an adverse attitude, value, or belief about some group or category of persons formed beforehand or without knowledge or examination of the facts. Prejudices have a cognitive and emotional component. They are related to cultural or societal values, ideologies, and beliefs. While prejudice as it is defined here does not explicitly include overt behaviors, behaviors that are initiated as expressions of or as a result of systemic or individual prejudice can be called acts of prejudice.

I. Introduction

This article explores prejudice in general and the specific form of prejudice called sexism. The discussion is informed by the theoretical and empirical work of contemporary psychological study. It will include a review of the history and key concepts in the study of prejudice and the perspectives of various contemporary theories about the way we understand our world.

Prejudice is alive and well in modern North American culture. One look at Internet hate sites provides graphic confirmation that the most virulent forms of prejudice are still held and promulgated by some members of our society, including some young people. The most extreme consequences of prejudice are not relegated to the distant past. Remember the Black man dragged to death in Texas, the gay college student beaten and left to die in Wyoming, the postal worker killed because he was "foreign" by a man on his way to shoot at children at a Jewish Community Center, and the male student in Canada who shot women students simply because they were women. Group examples of virulent prejudice include recent acts of genocide in Rwanda and Kosova. Less sensational acts of prejudice are also prevalent. Sexual and racial harassment in the workplace make the headlines regularly. Despite at least 30 to 40 years of efforts to address prejudice and discrimination, U.S. citizens today generally live in racially segregated communities and do work that is segregated by gender.

The fact that most people are aware of acts of prejudice does not mean that we fully understand prejudice or even agree about what it is. Discussing meanings for constructs like prejudice, as informed by contemporary theoretical and empirical work, is quite an undertaking. Concise definitions provided in a glossary make the task appear to be simple, a matter of learning a few short phrases. However, despite the existence of dictionary definitions for prejudice, stigma, sexism, racism, and homophobia, there is not agreement on the definitions for those constructs in the discourse of contemporary scholarship.

A. EXAMINING THE DEFINITION

Prejudices are not an individual's idiosyncratic beliefs. Prejudices are views about certain groups held by other groups or even the society in general. These views relate to socially shared values about the categories for dividing people, which are important in that society. Such socially shared views are often described as ideologies or the result of ideologies.

The term "prejudice" has at its core the notion of prejudging. In that meaning prejudice is using a view based on a previously formed opinion, attitude, or belief rather than evaluating the information available in the specific or current case. By that definition, a prejudice could be a preconceived positive or a preconceived negative judgment. In practice, the term "prejudice" generally refers only to negative beliefs. Similarly, the psychological study of prejudice has generally been a study of negative attitudes, *prejudice against*.

Some experts define prejudice as a negative attitude or belief with three components: cognitive, affective, and behavioral. Using that terminology, the three components of prejudice are stereotyping, emotion, and discrimination. Others, including social psychologist Susan Fiske, a leader in psychological research on negative attitudes, use the term "preju-

dice" to refer only to the emotional or affective/feeling component of negative attitudes. She has described negative attitudes as consisting of a cognitive component, which is often referred to as stereotyping, an emotional or affective component, which can be referred to as prejudice, and a behavioral component, which is generally called discrimination.

In this article, the term "prejudice" is used to describe negative attitudes or beliefs directed at devalued groups. Those negative attitudes or beliefs can be thought of as having a cognitive or information processing component and an emotional or affective component. The negative attitude or prejudice can be thought of as separate from the behavioral category of discrimination in that discrimination requires overt, observable acts while prejudice, as defined here, does not require any overt external act. This terminology is used because it more closely reflects the usage in both the law and the vernacular than does the framework often used by social psychologists.

B. SOCIALLY CONSTRUCTED CLASSIFICATION SYSTEMS

Obviously, the prejudices of racism, sexism, and heterosexism are related to the classification systems of race, sex or gender, and sexual orientation. Some theorists, generally called social constructionists, argue that they are the result of such classification systems. Dividing people into discrete, nonoverlapping categories, often using dichotomies like male–female, means that the groups are defined by what makes them different. In this process, one group becomes the standard from which others deviate, the valued category.

Social constructionist theories suggest that the meanings assigned to the words we use to talk about prejudice constrains what is possible for us to understand about prejudice. They note that the words and categories used in this discussion are not simple reflections of the natural world, but instead are constructs that we form in order to understand our world. At the same time, these constructs cause us to see or understand our world in ways that are limited by the construct's definition. The construct of race not only divides people into races, but also creates at least the possibility for racism. Yet scientists have found no genetic basis to conclude that people assigned to one racial group are biologically or genetically different from other groups in any but the most superficial of ways. During segregation in the United States, people were legally defined as Black if one of their eight great-grandparents had been defined as Black.

Social constructionists also remind us that different areas and cultures have different issues about which they form prejudices. Additionally, two cultures may share a category of prejudice (e.g., sexism), but they may have different beliefs about it. For example, in the Muslim world, the distinction between Catholics and Protestants does not carry the same emotional weight that it does in Northern Ireland. In Chinese culture a key part of the difference between women and men is men's superiority in activities like music and poetry, not exactly a critical aspect of the U.S. concept of masculinity.

Mary Crawford, a social construction theorist, pointed out that social classification systems operate at three levels: the social structural level, the interactional level, and the interpersonal level. At the structural level, classification systems are represented in the structures of society, a society's institutions and laws. At the interactional level, classification systems are represented in the actions of groups and in the demands and interests of whole groups. For example, "women in the United States earn less than men" and "childcare is a women's issue" are statements at the interactional level. Finally, at the interpersonal level, the constraints of the classification system have effects on the interactions between individuals at the interpersonal level. When we interact with another person, that interaction is influenced by the categories to which we assign that person, for example the person's ethnicity or race, gender, sexual orientation, and age.

Our current meaning for or understanding of prejudice and various specific prejudices has been informed primarily by research about what happens at the individual or interpersonal level. This raises questions about the nature and limitations of the information that research provides. What questions do we fail to ask when we focus at the individual or group levels? What are the relationships between individual prejudices or prejudiced individuals and the existence at the societal level of systems for dividing people on the basis of race, gender, or sexual orientation categories? By what process are those societal value systems or ideologies created?

From the social constructionist perspective, understanding prejudice is about understanding the manifestations and re-creation of social values and groups in the course of social interaction. The categorization systems we construct become the words and ways we have available to think and talk about our world. Although they are only words and ideas, the effects of our constructs are real and tangible.

In examining what is known about prejudice and the prejudice of sexism in particular, it is important to consider the commentary of social constructionist theory. Any research or examination takes place at a particular place in time and within the context of a particular culture's framework for understanding. At the same time, it is helpful to examine what social science research does tell us about prejudice. The understanding of social science can assist in identifying and altering the harm caused by prejudice. [*See* SOCIAL CONSTRUCTIONIST THEORY.]

II. Overview

Some of the psychological research on prejudice was done prior to World War II. This includes a classic 1934 study by R. T. LaPiere, which found only a very weak relationship between endorsement of prejudiced attitudes and certain discriminatory behaviors. However, interest in the psychology of prejudice was sparked immediately after World War II by the Holocaust and the virulent anti-Semitism associated with it. People wanted to know how so many individuals could be involved in mass murder.

A. PROBLEMS AND LIMITATIONS IN THE RESEARCH ON PREJUDICE

One limitation of the research on prejudice has been the tendency to proceed as if all specific forms of prejudice are interchangeable manifestations of the same "pure form." Thus, research only studying the attitudes of Whites toward Blacks is described as findings about prejudice rather than as findings about White racism toward Blacks. This reduces the ability to know and understand the different ways different forms of prejudice may operate at different times and with different groups of people.

Another limitation results from treating prejudices about categories like race or ethnicity, sex or gender, and sexual orientation in isolation. Little attention is paid to the fact that the categories are not mutually exclusive. In fact, every possible permutation of each category is represented among the people of any category. While the differences in the experiences of prejudices that result are not usually the focus of research or discussion, they often are significant. Consider how the attitudes and manifestations of sexism can, for example, be very different for Latinas, Asian women, Black women, and White women. In addition to limiting our understanding of prejudice, this limitation renders some people, for example women of color and lesbians, invisible.

Of course, the way these categories of prejudice are treated also ignores their relationship with other important social factors like economic status, attractiveness, and power. Race or ethnicity in this country is tremendously confounded with poverty. Men, especially White men, have more power than women in virtually every arena. Attractiveness, which has been shown to strongly influence judgments about others, is strongly associated in this culture with a Northern European standard of appearance.

Another important difference masked by the use of a generalized concept of prejudice is the difference between the contexts of interaction. People of different racial or ethnic groups generally live in families made up of one racial or ethnic group and, at least in the United States, those families live in communities largely segregated by race or ethnicity. By contrast, women and men grow up and live in families that include both men and women generally under the same roof and always in the same extended family. Similarly, while there is debate about whether sexual orientation is present from birth, the parents of lesbians and gay men knew from birth about their children's sex and race, but not their sexual orientation. These differences in the context of prejudice have important ramifications for the formation, modification, and consequences of specific prejudices.

B. INDIVIDUAL DIFFERENCES: LOOKING FOR PREJUDICED PEOPLE

Research in the 1950s focused on individuals, seeking to identify and understand what sort of person or personality could be capable of the Holocaust atrocities. The study of authoritarian personalities was an attempt, based on the work of theorists like Freud, to identify the unique characteristics of person who would think and act in highly prejudiced ways. Authoritarian personality syndrome was defined as a strict and rigid set of conventional values, hostility toward people not conforming to those values, and a tendency to blindly follow the directions of authority. Although the authoritarian personality was based on theories that have since been largely discredited or discarded, the individual differences approach and some of the ideas involved in this research have remained a significant focus.

Research looking at prejudice as a trait or quality of individuals has involved developing scales to measure general traits like submission to authority, dominance, and conventionalism as well as their relationship to specific prejudices. Other research has developed scales to measure the level of an individual's racism, sexism, or homophobia. More recently there has been an effort to identify and measure the ways in which changes in attitudes over the past 20 or 30 years have created new forms of prejudice. Scales have been developed to demonstrate and measure the new, modern manifestations of racism and sexism.

Research based on the individual differences model has resulted in some important findings. There is a strong correlation among individually measured forms of various prejudices in research with primarily White Americans. Levels of racism, sexism, and heterosexism all tend to move together. Furthermore, these attitudes and other prejudices tend to correlate with scales designed to measure how people value individualism and their levels of support for egalitarian-humanitarian values. A major weakness of this line of work is that it has generally involved White research participants, often college students.

A key feature of this "individual differences" model for studying prejudice is the assumption that prejudice is an enduring trait or at least a relatively stable aspect of the individual's character. Critics of the individual differences model note that this approach underestimates the role of social and ideological factors in establishing what ideas and behaviors are acceptable. Some question the idea that it is reasonable or possible to think about categories like gender, race, or sexual orientation as having the same meaning in different cultures and at different times in history. The identification of new expressions of racism and sexism, which 30 years of social change appears to have created, is a demonstration of this very problem.

C. COGNITION: STEREOTYPES AND INFORMATION PROCESSING

Another approach to the study of prejudice has explored the role of cognition in prejudice and the effects of prejudice on cognition. This approach is somewhat different from the individual differences approach in that it focuses on processes that are presumed to operate for all people. It is not totally incompatible with the individual differences approach in that people can obviously have more and less of something that everybody has. The focus is, however, different.

1. Stereotypes

One of the central features of the cognitive approach to prejudice is the concept of stereotypes. Walter Lippmann, a respected journalist, introduced the term "stereotype" in 1922. The term referred to a distorted preconceived idea that interfered with the accurate perceptions about members of other groups.

Psychologist Gordon Allport, writing in the 1950s, argued that stereotypes are not pathological or unusual processes, but part of normal human functioning when dealing with information. He also introduced the separation of prejudice into cognitive, emotional, and behavioral components and stressed the importance of social context. The core of his thesis is that we use categories to help us make sense of our world. The central problem with prejudice, from Allport's perspective, was that the definitions of categories included information that was either incorrect or totally irrelevant. He also theorized that part of the process of creating categories was the process of identifying or dividing groups into those one liked or disliked, those that represent "us" versus "them," or those "like me" or "different from me."

Social psychologists since Allport have produced research that supports the theory of categorization or stereotyping as a normal process. This research has primarily utilized laboratory research, usually with college students. Research has sought to document the existence of stereotypes and study the conditions that facilitate their formation, accuracy, utilization, and modification. Although some discuss issues of social context in creating and maintaining the categorization scheme, the role of society and social structures in defining the categories and stereotypes has received relatively little attention.

There have been thousands of research articles and theoretical papers on the cognitive aspects of prejudice. Not surprisingly, within those thousands of publications, there are a number of disagreements and controversies. There are, however, some generally agreed upon conclusions.

The contents of a culture's stereotypes are learned by the members of that culture. By adulthood, most members of a culture or society know the content of the society's stereotype for a given category (e.g., women) whether or not the individual expresses agreement with the stereotype. Research has demonstrated that achievement of this general agreement

occurs at different ages for different stereotypes, suggesting that what occurs is learning and not simply maturation. In other words, children may need to develop the ability to categorize; this limits the earliest age a child could know the content of the culture's stereotype, but does not determine the age by which children do learn the stereotypes.

There may be stereotypes for the more valued or dominant group (e.g., in U.S. culture, men or Whites), but those stereotypes are generally more positive and may be less restrictive. Even when the stereotypes of the dominant group restrict acceptable behaviors, the consequences are generally less negative. For example, men are thought to be more rational and emotionally strong than women. Men are discouraged from expressing emotions, especially "weak" emotions like tenderness, fear, and sadness. But our culture values strength and rationality more than emotion. Being rational qualifies a person for many more types of activities or occupations in our society than being emotional or sensitive. Virtually all activities or occupations for which emotionality is considered critical are caretaking roles, roles which our culture does not value highly.

2. Effects of Stereotyping

Research has examined not only the existence and content of stereotypes, but also the cognitive effects of stereotypes. Not all of the components of a stereotype about any given group are unambiguously negative. For example, the stereotype of woman may include kindness or an ethnic/racial group may be stereotyped as good at math. However, stereotypes have negative cognitive effects on other's perceptions of devalued groups and their individual members.

Stereotype-consistent information about individuals is easily recognized and remembered. Members of devalued groups are perceived as more homogeneous than they are. While in some circumstances stereotype-incongruent information may be more noticed, it is less likely to be recalled. This occurs at both the individual and the group level. Thus, a woman may generally be very articulate and rational at work, but the day she becomes so frustrated or upset that she cries is more likely to be remembered and overgeneralized as typical of her character than all the days of calm rationality. With groups, the stereotype-consistent members are more easily recalled. For example, retired General Colin Powell may be the only former chairman of the Joint Chiefs of Staff whose name most White U.S. residents would recognize, but his face is probably not the first image recalled when those same people are asked to think of a Black man.

There is debate about the extent to which stereotypes contain accurate information. Part of the disagreement is simply about what does accurate mean in this context. For example, part of the stereotype about Blacks in this country is that they are good athletes. A quick look at the rosters of U.S. professional sports teams suggests that this is accurate. But do the relative proportions of Black and White professional athletes on professional sports teams tell us anything about whether Blacks, in general, are good athletes or better athletes than Whites? What happens if we include tennis or golf in the mix? If there is any difference, maybe it is in greater willingness to make the sacrifices necessary to become a professional athlete and not about ability.

Even if a stereotype is generally accurate about a group, that does not make it accurate when applied to an individual. Women are stereotyped as good homemakers, better than men at cooking and sewing. But some women cannot even sew on a button and others can barely boil water.

Because of the role of stereotypes in information processing, people from devalued groups are less likely to be seen as individuals with all of their complexity and positive attributes. This same effect can result in members of more valued groups being misperceived, but the result is different. For a man, a single episode of emotional behavior is less likely to be recalled or viewed as an indication that the particular man is emotional. This is true when the episode is of tearfulness, which is likely to be noticed but not recalled. It is also true for displays of anger, which is considered masculine, and therefore may not be evaluated or remembered as evidence of being emotional. Although stereotypes of more valued groups may restrict the accuracy of judgments or memories about an individual group member, the inaccuracy is likely to result in a more favorable evaluation of that individual.

The same behaviors can be viewed or interpreted differently based on stereotypes about the group to which the actor belongs (e.g. women, Asian American, or lesbian). A forceful and loud demand to his male subordinates from a man may be evaluated as an indication of his assertiveness or determination because the behavior is included in the stereotype of how men are supposed to behave. A woman making the same forceful and loud demand on her male sub-ordinates may be described as harsh, overly aggressive, or worse.

Stereotypes also influence the information sought, which results in differences in the information available for making a judgment. When people are making judgments or evaluations, the questions they ask are often influenced by efforts to confirm stereotypes. Additionally, decisions about what questions are important to ask may be based on stereotype influenced expectations. For example, the stereotype for Black men includes aggressiveness and an increased likelihood of substance abuse. This stereotype can result in interviewers asking a Black man questions about anger management, aggression, and substance abuse, which are not asked of a White man. Even if the two individuals have identical histories, the interviewer will have obtained different information, leading to a different judgment.

In addition to influencing the cognition and behavior of observers, awareness of negative stereotypes can negatively influence the performance of individuals in stereotyped groups. Psychologist Claude Steele, in an extensive series of experiments, has demonstrated this effect, which he calls stereotype threat. Participants in his research performed less well on achievement tests when they were told that the test measured a dimension of intelligence or ability on which their group's stereotype predicts poor performance. This effect was demonstrated across a wide range of groups, including Blacks and women. Even White males performed less well than they normally would when told that they were taking a test of math ability on which Asian students generally do better than Whites.

3. Stereotyping Outside of Awareness

Research on stereotypes has demonstrated that the cognitive effects can operate not only at the conscious level but also at the nonconscious or preconscious level. Laboratory research on stereotypes has often involved people looking at words or pictures shown on a screen or monitor. The research then measures how long it takes people to perform a cognitive task, for example, determining if a group of letters is a word. If words relating to a stereotype are recognized more quickly than stereotype-irrelevant words, this suggests that the stereotype is influencing cognitive processing. The presentation of primes—items like pictures of women, men, or Blacks—has been shown to activate the relevant stereotype, allowing people to process information related to the content of the stereotype more quickly. Yet the research participants had no awareness of the difference.

In some experiments, group labels speeded cognitive processing of stereotype-consistent words even when the labels were presented on the screen too fast for the research participants to report having seen them. Under at least some conditions, the preconscious effect of increasing negative, stereotype-consistent responses operated regardless of whether the research participants scored high or low on measures of prejudice. This suggests that even people who describe themselves as not prejudiced can have their judgments of others affected by stereotypes.

The effects of nonconscious prejudices have been shown to alter interactions as well as cognitive processing. In a series of studies, individuals whose responses on the cognitive priming tasks indicated that they held prejudices toward Blacks were found to engage in negative nonverbal behaviors toward Blacks. These behaviors included reduced eye contact and postures that are associated with discomfort and disrespect. The negative nature of this nonverbal behavior was evident to the Black participants and to nonparticipant evaluators. However, the individuals exhibiting these nonverbal behaviors were unaware that their behavior indicated any hostility or negativity.

The ability of stereotypes to influence a person's judgment and behavior without the person being aware that the stereotype is having an effect is disturbing. It suggests that when the category or prejudice is brought up, even in a caution not to use race or gender bias, the opposite effect may occur. In a series of studies on the activation of race-based stereotypes, psychologist Susan Fiske demonstrated just such results.

4. Stereotypes and Attributions

Stereotypes and classification schemes affect the attributions or explanations of the causes for people's behaviors and achievements. The effect is similar to the tendency of people in our society to overestimate internal or trait-based factors in explaining the behavior of others while overestimating situational factors as explanations for their own behavior. Here the effect is overestimating the importance of situational factors in stereotype-inconsistent behaviors or outcomes while overestimating the role of internal factors in stereotype-consistent behaviors or

outcomes (e.g., a woman who does well on a project is thought of as hard working or lucky, but when she does poorly she is incompetent).

The cognitive tendency to attribute behaviors to different causes based on stereotypes makes it difficult to modify stereotypes. For example, information that a Black person holds down two jobs while maintaining an A average in school is not interpreted as typical of Black people, but as an exception. The general or abstract conclusion is stereotype consistent even though the actual behaviors were not. Furthermore, the more general conclusion is more likely to be remembered than the specific behaviors.

Interpreting the same behavior differently but remembering only the conclusion results in a similar effect. For example, a woman's angry outburst may be interpreted as her being emotional or abrasive while a man's identical angry outburst may be interpreted as his assertiveness or his strength. The man is remembered as assertive or strong and the woman as abrasive or emotional. When what is remembered or recalled is the stereotype-influenced categorical or evaluative conclusion, the actual behaviors cannot be compared. This eliminates the opportunity for people to reevaluate their stereotypes.

The language of stereotypes suggests the operation of a relatively value-free cognitive process. An alternative view suggests that the categories for which a society or culture holds stereotypes and the content of those stereotypes reflect the society's belief system and values. In that view, learning and applying stereotypes is a mechanism by which the values of a society are assimilated by and exert influence over the members of the society. Substituting the words "social beliefs" for "stereotypes" changes the discussion from one of benign cognitive processes to one of broad social influence. [See GENDER STEREOTYPES.]

D. EMOTION IN PREJUDICE

The research on the emotional or affective component of prejudice has consisted primarily of paper-and-pencil indications of feelings toward stigmatized groups or willingness to have a member of such a group marry into one's family. The focus has been on the emotional aspects of individuals' prejudices. The question of how social structures and institutions influence which groups or categories people in a society use and about which they have strong feelings has not been an important focus. Not surprisingly, it appears that the existence of strong prejudice is related to personally viewing the category (i.e., race, gender, or sexual orientation) as important. Current psychological theories concerning what creates that importance all invoke the issue of threat. In some formulations, the threat is described as blocking the goals and welfare of the threatened group. Others point to the threat of unwanted interaction. This interaction could include not only being forced to have any interaction with members of some other group but also being forced to have some unwanted form of interaction, such as a man being forced to take orders from a woman. In still other theories, the threat described is to the value structure of the threatened, prejudiced group.

The emotional or affective component of prejudice has received less study than cognitive or information processing components. However, it has generally been a better predictor of people's discriminatory behaviors than their stereotypes. This seems reasonable, especially where displaying discriminatory behaviors would be violating general social norms such as fairness or politeness. As measurement of the emotional component of prejudice has generally involved endorsement or nonendorsement of hostile statements about target groups, it is not surprising that this is more consistent with behavioral distance from those groups than merely knowing the culture's stereotype for that group.

Theorists have also suggested that strong emotional prejudice is based on negative personal contact with the target group. This seems inconsistent with, at the very least, prejudice against lesbians and gay men. People in this country have proved capable of holding and acting on strong negative views about lesbians and gay men without any personal contact. In fact, personal contact with a person known to be lesbian or gay is generally found to be a factor in reducing prejudice, although it is quite possible that this only applies to positive personal contact.

Although the emotional component of prejudice can be difficult to study, it is a significant factor in the difficulty of altering prejudice. Purely cognitive errors may take some effort to correct, as anyone knows who has ever "learned" to spell a word incorrectly and then struggled to remember which version is the correct spelling. But basically, with purely cognitive errors, sufficient repetition of correct information will eventually result in corrected learning. With emotionally based beliefs, simply providing a person with factual information about the inaccuracy of the belief with which they justify the prejudice often has a different outcome. Rather than

changing the prejudiced belief, the information results in a change of the reason given to support that belief or an excuse for why the inaccuracy represents only an exception. For example, after learning that gays and lesbians are not more likely to be child molesters than their heterosexual counterparts, the justification for heterosexism may be switched to the (equally inaccurate) argument that homosexual behavior is "unnatural." Or when confronted with the evidence that a particular Black woman is very intelligent, the racist may simply argue that she is the exception but most Blacks are stupid.

E. BEHAVIOR: DISCRIMINATION

Most research that has dealt with prejudiced behavior has focused on particular issues. For example, there has been considerable social science research on sex discrimination and sexual harassment. There has also been considerable research on race discrimination. Because of the distinction made in this article between prejudice, defined as a belief or attitude with cognitive and emotional components, and discrimination, defined as overt behaviors and policies, relatively little attention will be paid to discriminatory behaviors.

It is, nonetheless, useful to consider the more subtle behavioral aspects of prejudice. They are involved in creating prejudice's self-fulfilling prophecy effect. People treat other people differently based on how we predict or want the other to behave. People tend to behave differently with people from whom they expect hostility either by being more deferential or by being more hostile. People direct more warmth and social approval toward those whom they expect to like. In each case, the behavior of the initial actor has been shown to increase the likelihood that the other person will behave in the expected way. Obviously, stereotypes can influence those expectations.

The subtle aspects of prejudiced behavior also include what psychologist Mary Rowe has described as the minutiae of sexism, tiny but harmful events that create subtle barriers against women's participation and success in the male world. She has called these microinequities and microaggressions. They can be relatively unintentional, based in the invisibility of those who deviate from the social norm. They may also include small but intentional acts designed to needle and degrade. Sometimes it is difficult for the target to determine what represents insensitivity and what represents intentional hostility.

Microinequities and microaggressions can be directed at any devalued group. A television interviewer congratulates Olympic gold medalist Kristi Yamaguchi, a third-generation U.S. citizen, on her ability to speak English. Successful Black professionals are followed around in stores and watched by security. A gay or lesbian person known to be partnered is told that he or she is lucky not to have in-laws. The women but not the men are asked to do the office dishes. Offensive jokes and cartoons are told and posted, offensive terms are used. These acts and the literally thousands of other potential examples, whether intentional or not, are individually demeaning and hurtful but difficult to protest without appearing to be "overly sensitive."

F. STIGMA AND DEVIANCE

Prejudice not only affects the behaviors initiated by those who hold prejudices, but it also those who are its targets. Knowledge of the stereotypes and assumptions about them can affect the members of stigmatized groups (i.e., groups that are the targets of prejudice). Members of stigmatized groups can carry expectations based on that knowledge into interactions with members of the dominant group. That knowledge can also create anxiety and lower personal expectations for success, even in settings that do not involve interpersonal behavior. For example, research studies found that telling members of a stigmatized group that they were going to be taking a test on which people from their group do badly affected performance (e.g., women taking math tests). When told that the same test measured something unrelated to the stereotype for their group, average performance went up.

"Deviance" is a term used to describe behavior that does not conform to society's standards or stereotypes. In scientific or technical usage it applies to departing from the standards or norms in any direction. However, in general usage deviance connotes something devalued. Not all statistically deviant groups are considered devalued. For example, the 2% of the U.S. population who own the vast majority of wealth definitely deviate from the norm but are not generally devalued. Not all stigmatized or devalued groups are statistically deviant. For example, women are devalued in Western culture although women make up approximately 51% of the population. But women deviate from society's standard of male as the norm for human beings. Individuals can also be viewed as deviant and stigmatized when they depart from the social norms and expectations for members of their group.

People in devalued groups are in a double bind, no-win situation. To the extent that their behavior conforms to the stereotype for their group, they may be devalued and stigmatized. To the extent that their behavior deviates from the expected behavior, they may be viewed as deviant and stigmatized. This effect is particularly seen around gender-proscribed behavior. Women who dress or act in ways that are not seen as feminine are considered deviant. They may be pathologized, their behavior attributed to some psychological problem or defect. Additionally, people whose behavior is not consistent with the social norms or stereotypes for their gender may face hostility from others.

The double bind is often slightly different for people from racial or ethnic groups whose cultures and styles have been labeled as deviant by the dominant group. In this case, retaining or conforming to one's culture is stigmatized by the dominant group. Conversely, adopting the styles, traditions, and behaviors of the dominant group may result in being stigmatized by one's own cultural or ethnic group. Consider, for example, the derogatory terms like "Uncle Tom" and "Oreo" sometimes directed at Blacks who have adopted the values of the dominant culture.

III. Sexism

A. DEFINING SEXISM

Psychologists Rhoda Unger and Mary Crawford in their textbook on women and gender defined sexism as "a form of prejudice defined by the existence of negative attitudes and values about women as a group." Sexism is not synonymous with misogyny. Misogyny is a global hatred of women while sexism includes all forms of devaluation of women as compared to men. As it is used in contemporary scholarship, the concept of sexism is inextricably linked with the concepts of sex or gender roles and with stereotypes about women and men defined by those roles.

Sandra Bem, an early critic of psychology's underlying assumptions about sex differences, described sexism as the result of three social frameworks: androcentrism, gender polarization, and biological essentialism. Androcentrism is defining male as the norm from which females differ. An example of this can be found in the statement that only women can become pregnant. Without an androcentric bias it would be equally as common to say that only men are unable to become pregnant. Gender polarization means defining gender as opposite poles of various dimensions. The meaning of each is only understood in comparison to the other, often an unstated but assumed comparison. The expression "men are strong," carries with it the implicit meaning of "stronger than women" rather than, for example, the implicit meaning of "stronger than rabbits." Biological essentialism defines gender differences as being based in biology or human nature rather than questioning the role of cultural and social forces in creating gender differences. As Bem pointed out, all of these frameworks are so ubiquitous to our culture that thinking in other ways seems odd or absurd. [See ANDROCENTRISM; DEVELOPMENT OF SEX AND GENDER.]

B. SEXISM AND STEREOTYPING

In thinking about sexism, it is important to remember that all of the conclusions about prejudice and stereotyping discussed previously apply to sexism. People are not born with stereotypes about women and men, they learn the stereotypes about women and men that their culture holds. Stereotypes about men are more consistently positive and, at least in some respects, less restrictive in terms of the roles, at least in the occupational sphere, than stereotypes about women. Stereotypes of women have negative cognitive effects on both men's and women's perceptions of individual women. Women are less likely than men to be seen as individuals with all their complexity and positive attributes recognized. Men tend to be viewed more positively than their individual behaviors or attributes warrant. Women engaging in out-of-role activities will be viewed more negatively than would a man with the same attributes and performing the same behaviors. Stereotypes operate not only at the conscious level but also at the nonconscious or preconscious level; people can apply stereotypes without realizing it. Gender-based classification schemes affect our evaluation of people's behavior and our attributions or explanations about the reasons for their experiences and achievements. Women's successes will tend to be viewed as the result of situational factors more than men's, with the reverse being true for errors or failures. Finally, the cognitive tendencies to attribute in-role and out-of-role behaviors to different causes based on stereotypes and to remember the conclusion, not the specific behaviors, makes stereotypes difficult to modify.

All of those effects have been demonstrated in the research conducted on sexism over the past 30 years. There is no evidence that they have ceased to apply. However, in some cases, the content of the stereotypes and role-proscribed behaviors has changed. For example, the female stereotype no longer demands a "stay-at-home-mom," but does still incorporate a view of women as more suited than men for the task of "taking care of the kids."

Research has also demonstrated some of the important double binds that women experience, particularly around issues of leadership and group interaction. In groups that include men, women who utilize direct communications styles, who interrupt others or attempt to do so, and who make eye contact when speaking are viewed more negatively than women who are more indirect, do not interrupt, and make more eye contact while listening than speaking. Unfortunately, the assertive behaviors that result in women being devalued are also the behaviors that, when used by men, result in men being selected as group leaders. When women use these same behaviors in groups that contain men, they are evaluated quite negatively. This tendency is strongest when the women are not already established as leaders by title and power.

C. THE ROLE OF SUBSTEREOTYPES

Research and theoretical work on sexism has also focused on the role and use of substereotypes in the maintenance of gender stereotypes. Just as people develop constructs, stereotypes about the attributes of women and men in general, they also develop constructs for subtypes based on factors like race or ethnicity, occupation, sexual orientation, appearance, and physical traits or characteristics. Research efforts to define these various subtypes have encountered difficulty in identifying consistently recognized subtypes. This is not surprising given both the variety of factors that can contribute to subtypes and the variability in individuals exposure to that variety.

Research attempting to compare the various substereotypes of women and men has also been marked by problems that interfere with the interpretation of the findings. For example, some early research used substereotypes of women that varied in compliance with the general female stereotype such as homemaker, career woman, and feminist. For substereotypes of men they used only roles consistent with the general male stereotype such as businessman, athlete, or macho man, rather than including less consistent categories like accountant, ballet dancer, or hairdresser.

Despite the limitations of current research and theorizing on the creation and use of substereotypes, they remain an important factor for understanding both the maintenance of prejudice and its effects in particular situations. Substereotypes maintain general stereotypes by allowing stereotype inconsistent behavior to be interpreted not as evidence that the stereotype is wrong, but rather as proof that there are some specific subpopulations to whom it does not apply. This effect has been demonstrated in the research on stereotyping.

In addition to representing deviation from the general stereotype, substereotypes represent different specific aspects of the general stereotype (e.g., the sexually attractive woman or the nurturing mother). Such subtypes encourage expectations and evaluations based on those particular aspects of the stereotype. Thus, the cocktail waitress is expected and allowed to engage in more "sexy" behavior than the kindergarten teacher. Furthermore, physical attractiveness may be considered a more important factor in evaluating the cocktail waitress while warmth and the ability to nurture may be more important in evaluating the kindergarten teacher. Yet both characteristics could be considered part of the general female stereotype. The female substereotypes represent almost a caricature of the stereotype-defined, devalued roles for which women are presumed to be best suited.

Our understanding of substereotypes is, at this point, somewhat limited. Research findings suggest that as subtypes depart from the general group stereotype, more gender-based hostility will be attached. There is also evidence that subtypes and general stereotypes have similar effects on evaluations and behaviors. What is less clear is the degree to which subtypes are socially or idiosyncratically constructed and how or if subtypes replace, alter, or fracture the global stereotype.

D. MEASURING SEXISM: OLD AND NEW

The study of sexism has not been limited to exploring and documenting gender stereotyping with the attendant negative effects. As with other forms of prejudice, there have also been efforts to measure sexism, to identify the various dimensions and components of sexism, to identify the underlying factors that contribute to sexism, and to explore ways to reduce or modify sexism. At the same time, as with other forms of prejudice, research and theoretical work on sexism has not always included acknowledgment and exploration of the ways sexism is influenced by a woman's race or ethnicity, sexual orientation, economic status, disability status, and age.

One major focus of research and theoretical work has been the effort to describe and measure that aspect of sexism that could be called "attitudes toward women." Psychologists have developed scales to measure those attitudes. In addition to serving a possible role in identifying, understanding, and predicting the behavior of persons holding negative views about women, well-constructed measures of sexist attitudes and beliefs can help to document changing attitudes toward women.

Of course, the changes that occurred over the past 30 years create problems for measurement efforts. For example, unlike 30 years ago, women today are well represented in professions like law, medicine, and psychology. Only a small percentage of U.S. residents still hold such rigid gender-role beliefs that they say women should not practice those professions. There is less agreement among U.S. residents about women's suitability for work in construction, where women remain a tiny fraction of the workforce, or as combat soldiers, where U.S. women's participation is still prohibited. How, then, should we interpret endorsement or nonendorsement of items about women and men's equal suitability for performing work measured during the past 30 years? Additionally, even for those who believe that women are capable of performing any job, how do attitudes about the importance of mothers, but not necessarily fathers, staying home to raise young children affect the reality of women's equal participation in the workforce? Despite, or perhaps because of, these complications, work on describing and measuring attitudes toward women has been an important topic.

One of the first of such instruments was the Attitudes Toward Women Scale (AWS) developed by Janet Spense and Robert Helmrich, first published in 1972. This 55-item scale was designed to measure people's beliefs about women's rights, roles, and responsibilities. It was later shortened to a 15-item version. It has been widely used. Longitudinal administrations of the scale to college students over the past 30 years has found, on average, a steady change toward endorsement of less restrictive attitudes. At the same time, some people, mostly men, continue to endorse very negative or restrictive attitudes. Critics of the AWS have noted, among other things, that it is influenced by social standards against the expression of support for inequality.

Borrowing from scholars studying racism, scholars interested in measuring sexism have developed new measures. The theory is that contemporary expressions of prejudice are more subtle than the openly hostile rhetoric of racism and sexism in earlier decades. Measures sensitive to these more subtle, but important, prejudices were viewed as critical.

Drawing from theories concerning modern racism, Janet Swim and her colleagues developed a "modern sexism" scale. It measured denial that discrimination based on sex continues to exist and feelings that women are asking for too much. They paired this "modern sexism" scale with a scale measuring "old-fashioned sexism." Others, also borrowing from contemporary studies of White racism against Blacks, have suggested that modern sexism is a neosexism characterized by conflict between egalitarian views and negative feelings toward women. This has resulted in the development by Francine Tongas and her colleagues of a Neosexism Scale, which measures support for public policies designed to support women, such as affirmative action. Still others have developed measures based on the view that the expression of modern racism and sexism represents a tension between individualistic value orientations and humanitarian-egalitarian value orientations. The individualistic orientations are described as emphasizing the values of hard work, self-reliance, and individual achievement. By contrast, the humanitarian-egalitarian value orientations are described as valuing equality of opportunity, social justice, and a belief in societal support for the welfare of others. The scales attempt to assesss the relationship between endorsement of these value orientations and attitudes toward women. Use of the various scales has found some confirmation of these various ideas. Additionally, there is evidence that each measures different but related components of contemporary sexism.

Not surprisingly, there is also a relationship between measures of sexism, both old and new, and measures of attitudes toward lesbians and gay men. Feminist theorists have long pointed to the role that compulsory heterosexuality plays in creating polarization between what behaviors are acceptable for men and for women. Furthermore, the threat of being labeled as a lesbian has been used to enforce women's compliance with female gender roles. In fact, researchers have documented the tendency for women and men engaged in out-of-role behaviors to be labeled as lesbian or gay. This labeling can result from merely having a physical appearance inconsistent with the appropriate gender stereotype. [*See* METHODS FOR STUDYING GENDER.]

E. LESSONS FROM THE WORKPLACE

The workplace is one of the major areas where women experience the effects of sexism. In addition to all of the items already discussed, sexism in the workplace includes sexual harassment of women. This is true both for the forms of harassment directed at obtaining sexual favors from women and the forms of harassment that represent hostility toward women, especially women working in out-of-role occupations or whose mannerisms, dress, or sexual orientation violates gender norms.

Drawing primarily on explorations of sexism in the workplace, some theorists have suggested that sexism or sexist attitudes should be divided into two different components. One component, labeled hostile sexism by Susan Fiske, describes attempts to assert male superiority in reaction to women's invasion of activities, roles, and positions of authority previously reserved for men. The other component, which Fiske labels benevolent sexism, relates to the demand that women focus on their "natural" reproductive, nurturing, and caregiving roles.

Both versions, of course, restrict women and support male domination. The first describes the restrictions that result from devaluing, demeaning, and in some cases attacking any woman stepping outside her role. The second describes the restrictions of glorifying and supporting women's "natural" roles as men's sexual partners, as mothers, and as nurturers. It is the "gilded cage," barriers in the form of protection. For example, women in the U.S. military are protected whether they like it or not from the jobs that might expose them to horrors of combat, despite the fact that those jobs are critical for career advancement within the military.

Obviously there is a difference between the overt hostility of efforts to drive women out of, for example, previously male-dominated factory jobs and the experience of being pressured by one's boss to have a sexual relationship. Similarly, there is a difference between the views that women should not do certain jobs because they are too stupid or because the experience is too gruesome for women. What is less clear is whether these differences are best described as two different types of sexism or as a distinction between the proscriptive and prescriptive aspects or effects of women's assigned gender roles (e.g., what women *should not* do and what women *should* do). [*See* Women in Nontraditional Work Fields; Working Environments.]

Nonetheless, the distinction between sexism's glorifying and punishing aspects is important. How much of the difference results from individual differences in the beliefs and values held about women? How much are differences the result of different situations and social roles? These questions have not been adequately addressed.

F. SEXISM AND THE FUTURE

We live in a world where people are divided into the mutually exclusive categories of male and female with well-developed scripts prescribing and proscribing acceptable ways of being and behaving for those in each category. These categories and their attendant baggage are often presumed to be a reflection of a natural difference. They are also assumed to be relevant to any task or evaluation unless specifically identified as irrelevant. They encourage punishment of deviant behavior and glorification of role-appropriate behavior.

Under such circumstances, it is difficult to imagine an end to sexism. However, we also live in a world where efforts to create changing opportunities for women have resulted in changing the images of women's roles. Girls today can imagine themselves as U.S. senators or professional athletes. Little boys and little girls hope to play basketball as well as Cheryl Swopes or soccer as well as Mia Hamm. How these facts will be shaped by and reshape society's values and prejudices is not clear.

IV. Conclusions

Prejudice in general and sexism in particular have profound effects on people. The consequences of prejudice range from the cumulative weight of countless microinequities to overt acts of violence and the fear such acts may create for any who could have been similarly targeted. Prejudices also range from overt hostility to subtle devaluation. They influence us even without our awareness, sometimes despite our protestations to the contrary. Prejudices constrain our experiences and influence our behavior. Our prejudices can be self-fulfilling because they alter the way we interact with and evaluate those whom we devalue or stigmatize. Expecting to be treated or evaluated in a prejudiced manner can, similarly, alter the behavior of those targeted by prejudice in ways that also serve to confirm the prejudiced beliefs. Prejudices can be difficult to identify or admit and even more difficult to alter.

Prejudice may be an inevitable result of categorization schemes that define groups on any given dimension based on the presumed irrevocable or natural differences between those groups. But it is also clear that social change can result, at least, in modifications of previously held images and values. What remains unclear is the process and possibility of more basic change in the societal values and beliefs associated with specific prejudices.

SUGGESTED READING

Bem, S. L. (1993). *The Lenses of Gender.* Yale University Press, New Haven, CT.

Bohan, J. (1992). *Seldom Seen, Rarely Heard: Women's Place in Psychology.* Westview Press, Boulder, CO.

Crawford, M. (1995). *Talking Difference.* Sage, Thousand Oaks, CA.

Frieze, I. H., and McHugh, M. (eds.) (1997). Special Issue: Measuring beliefs about appropriate roles for women and men. *Psychology of Women Quarterly* **21**, 1–151.

Gilbert, D. T., Fiske, S. T., and Lindsey, G. (eds.) (1998). *The Handbook of Social Psychology,* 4th ed. Oxford University Press, New York.

Rosenblum, K. E., and Travis, T.-M. (1996). *The Meaning of Difference: American Constructions of Race, Sex and Gender, Social Class, and Sexual Orientation.* McGraw-Hill, New York.

Prostitution
The Business of Sexual Exploitation

Melissa Farley
Prostitution Research and Education, San Francisco

You become in your own mind what these people do and say with you. You wonder how you could let yourself do this and why do these people want to do this to you?

—Author's interview with a woman who escaped prostitution

Glossary

Child prostitution Prostitution of a person under the age of eighteen.

First nations General description of the many tribes of people living in Canada before and since the European invasion.

Globalization The economic interdependence of countries and multinational corporations. Promotes prostitution and trafficking by creating conditions for women to sell their own sexual exploitation at far better rates of pay than other forms of labor.

Incest Sexual assault, sexual abuse, sexual exploitation, or sexual molestation by a child's family member or caretaker.

John, trick, or date What women in prostitution call customers.

Pimp Someone who economically benefits from the earnings of a person in prostitution; may be a boyfriend or club manager or trafficker, as well as the common pimp.

Sex worker A person who is exploited (sometimes for money and often for no money) in a commercial sex business. This term sometimes is used in place of the word "prostitute," and tends to obscure the harm of prostitution; it legitimizes the commercial sexual exploitation but offers no dignity or safety to the person in prostitution.

Trafficking Transportation of a person from her home community to another city, state, or country; method of delivering women and children into prostitution. Occurs as a result of economic exploitation and inequity between countries, educational neglect, and gender-based and race-based coercion.

PROSTITUTION is many kinds of violence against women, but it is often not clearly understood as such. Because prostitution/trafficking is so profitable, the factors that propel women into sex businesses, such as sexism, racism, poverty, and child abuse, are sometimes concealed. This article reviews evidence for the extreme violence that occurs in prostitution and the physical and psychological harm that results from that violence. Needs of women escaping prostitution and legal approaches to prostitution are described.

I. Denial

Institutions such as prostitution and slavery, which have existed for thousands of years, are so deeply embedded in cultures that they become invisible. In Mauritania, for example, there are 90,000 Africans enslaved by Arabs. Human rights activists travel to Mauritania to report on slavery, but because they do not observe precisely the stereotype of what they think slavery should look like (for example, if they do not see bidding for shackled people on auction blocks), then they conclude that the Africans working in the fields in front of them are voluntary laborers who are receiving food and shelter as salary.

In a similar way, if observers do not see exactly what the stereotype of "harmful" prostitution is, for example, if they do not see a girl being trafficked at gunpoint from one state to another, or if all they see is a streetwise teenager who says, "I like this job, and besides, I'm making a lot of money," then they do not see the harm. Prostitution tourists go to the prostitution zones of Amsterdam, Atlanta, Phnom Penh, Moscow, or Havana and see smiling girls waving at them from glass cages or strip clubs. The customers decide that prostitution is a free choice.

If we describe women as "sex workers" then we are accepting conditions that in other employment would be correctly described as sexual harassment, sexual exploitation, or rape. If prostitution is transformed into "commercial sex work," then the brutal exploitation of those prostituted by pimps becomes an employer–employee relationship. And the predatory, pedophiliac purchase of a human being by the john becomes just an everyday business transaction.

The myth that prostitution is a free choice is a major obstacle to understanding the harm of prostitution. Most people in prostitution have few or no other options for obtaining the necessities of life. One woman interviewed by Ine Vanwesenbeeck in the Netherlands, described prostitution as "volunteer slavery," clearly articulating both the appearance of choice and the overwhelming coercion behind that choice. Sexual exploitation seems to happen with the "consent" of those involved. But real consent involves the option to make other choices. In prostitution, the conditions necessary for choice—physical safety, information, equal power with customers, and real alternatives—are absent. Women in prostitution tend to be the ones who have the fewest options.

The social and legal refusal to acknowledge the harm of prostitution is stunning. Normalization of prostitution by researchers, public health agencies, and the media is a significant barrier to addressing the harm of prostitution. In 1988, for example, the World Health Organization described prostitution as "dynamic and adaptive sex work, involving a transaction between seller and buyer of a sexual service." Continuing this trend a decade later, the International Labor Organization normalized prostitution as the "sex sector" of Asian economies despite citing surveys that indicated that, for example, in Indonesia, 96% of those interviewed wanted to leave prostitution if they could. Lin Lim commented, "many groups, sometimes including government officials, have an interest in maintaining the sex sector." Libertarian ideology obfuscates the harm of prostitution, defining it as a form of sex.

In the social sciences as well, the harm of prostitution becomes invisible. The psychological literature of the 1980s blamed battered women for their victimization, describing them as "masochistic," a theoretical perspective that was later rejected for lack of evidence. However, the notion that prostituted women (who are also battered women) have personality characteristics that lead to their victimization is still promoted. Karl Abraham saw prostitution as a woman's act of hostility against her father, based on an oedipal fixation. And the sexologists, from Alfred Kinsey to Havelock Ellis to Masters and Johnson, formulated their theories of human sexuality by observing johns with prostitutes, thus normalizing prostitution-like sexuality.

Since the 1980s, there has been huge growth in socially legitimized pimping in the United States: strip clubs, nude dancing, escort services, tanning salons, massage parlors, phone sex, and computer sex. Many people do not realize that these permutations of the commercial sex industry are, in fact, prostitution. The lines between prostitution and nonprostitution have become blurred. New employees may assume they are going to dance, waitress, or tend bar, but find that the real money comes from prostituting after work. Lisa Sanchez has pointed out that the amount of physical contact between dancers and customers has escalated since the 1980s, although earnings have decreased. In addition to watching a stage show, in most strip clubs, customers can buy either a table dance performance by the dancer directly in front of them or a lap dance where the dancer sits on the customer's lap while she wears few or no clothes and grinds her genitals against his. Although he is clothed, he usually expects ejaculation. Sometimes the table dance or lap dance is in front of the customer on the main floor of the club. It may also take place behind a curtain or in a private room. The more private the sexual performance, the more it costs, and the more likely that violent sexual harassment or rape will occur. Although the typical lap-dancing scenario does not involve skin-to-skin sexual contact, for a larger tip, some dancers allow customers to touch their genitals or they masturbate or fellate johns. Used condoms are often found in lap dance clubs.

Different kinds of exploitation and abuse overlap and combine to harm women. Catharine MacKinnon has pointed out that "a great many instances of sexual harassment in essence amount to solicitation for prostitution." The words used to humiliate prostituted women are the same verbal abuse used by men when they are beating up or raping nonprostituting women. Racially constructed ideas about women in sex tourism have a greater and greater effect on the ways women of color are treated at home. For example, Asian American women reported rapes after men viewed pornography of Asian women. A vast range of abuse makes up a continuum of violence in which women are first hurt in early childhood.

II. Child Abuse and Prostitution

The prostitution of children is aggressively made invisible. For example, commenting that the connection between childhood sexual abuse and prostitution has been "exaggerated," Peter Davies and Rayah Feldman described the prostituted boys they interviewed in the United Kingdom as having an average age of under 18, with 97% of them younger than the legal age of consent. In other words, their interviewees were legally minors.

Another example of this invisibility is the common belief in Taiwan that the island's 100,000 child prostitutes want to prostitute because it pays for their "expensive tastes" in clothes and jewelry. Pimps are considered the children's bodyguards. Prejudice against indigenous people in Taiwan bolsters this denial of harm to their children, who comprise most of the children in prostitution.

In many parts of the world, a younger rather than older person is a preferred commodity, for several reasons. First, the culturally advocated pedophiliac sexuality in some countries (the Netherlands, India, the United States) channels men's sexual desire to younger and younger girls. Second, children are more easily controlled than adults by pimps and are more easily coerced by johns into behaviors that adults might resist. Third, there is the widespread but mistaken belief in some locales that younger children are safer for the customer since they are believed to be less likely to have HIV (Thailand, Zambia).

Most women over the age of 18 in prostitution began prostituting when they were adolescents. Adele du Plessis, a social worker who worked with homeless and prostituted children in Johannesburg, South Africa, reported that she could not refuse her agency's services to 21-year-olds because she understood them to be grownup child prostitutes. Estimates regarding the age of recruitment into prostitution vary, but early adolescence is the most frequently reported age of entry into any type of prostitution. Researcher Debra Boyer interviewed 60 women prostituting in escort, street, strip club, phone sex, and massage parlors (brothels) in Seattle, Washington. All of them began prostituting between the ages of 12 and 14. In another study, 89% had begun prostitution before the age of 16. Of 200 adult women in prostitution interviewed by Mimi Silbert, 78% began prostituting as juveniles and 68% began when they were younger than 16.

The artificial distinction between child and adult prostitution obscures the continuity between the two. On a continuum of violence and relative powerlessness, the prostitution of a 12-year-old is more horrific than the prostitution of a 20-year-old, not because the crimes committed against her are different, but because the younger person has less power. In other respects, the experiences of sexual exploitation, rape, verbal abuse, and social contempt are the same, whether the person being prostituted is the legal age of a child or the legal age of an adult. The antecedent poverty and attempts to escape from unbearable living conditions (violence at home or the economic violence of globalization) are similar in child and adult prostitution.

One woman interviewed by Boyer said, "We've all been molested. Over and over, and raped. We were all molested and sexually abused as children, don't you know that? We ran to get away. They didn't want us in the house anymore. We were thrown out, thrown away. We've been on the street since we were 12, 13, 14."

The chronic, systematic nature of violence against girls and women may be seen more clearly when incest is understood as child prostitution. Use of a child for sex by adults, with or without payment, is prostitution of the child. When a child is incestuously assaulted, the perpetrator's objectification of the child victim and his rationalization and denial are the same as those of the john in prostitution. Incest and prostitution cause similar physical and psychological symptoms in the victim.

Child sexual abuse is a primary risk factor for prostitution. Familial sexual abuse functions as a training ground for prostitution. One young woman told Mimi Silbert and Ayala Pines, "I started turning tricks to show my father what he made me." Andrea Dworkin described sexual abuse of children as "boot camp" for prostitution. Research and clinical reports have documented the widespread occurrence of childhood sexual abuse and chronic traumatization among prostituted women. From 60% to 90% of those in prostitution were sexually assaulted in childhood.

Multiple perpetrators of sexual abuse were common, as was physical abuse in childhood. Sixty-two percent of women in prostitution reported a history of physical abuse as children. Evelina Giobbe found that 90% of prostituted women had been physically battered in childhood; 74% were sexually abused in

their families, with 50% also having been sexually abused by someone outside the family. Of 123 survivors of prostitution at the Council for Prostitution Alternatives in Portland, 85% reported a history of incest, 90% a history of physical abuse, and 98% a history of emotional abuse.

In the 1980s, Silbert and Pines published a number of groundbreaking studies that documented the role of child sexual abuse as an antecedent to prostitution. These authors and others have noted the role of pornography in the recruitment of children into prostitution and in teaching them how to act as prostitutes. Eighty percent of a group of prostituted women and girls in Vancouver, Canada, reported that while working as prostitutes, they had been upset by someone trying to coerce them into imitating pornography.

Prostituting adolescents grow up in neglectful, often violent families. Although not all sexually abused girls are recruited into prostitution, most of those in prostitution have a history of sexual abuse as children, usually by several people. For example, in a pilot study of prostituted women in Vancouver, Melissa Farley and Jackie Lynne reported that 88% of 40 women had been sexually assaulted as children, by an average of five perpetrators. This latter statistic (those assaulted by an average of five perpetrators) did not include those who responded to the question "If there was unwanted sexual touching or sexual contact between you and an adult, how many people in all?" with "tons" or "I can't count that high" or "I was too young to remember." Sixty-three percent of those whose experiences were recorded in this study were First Nations women.

Survivors directly link physical, sexual, and emotional abuse as children to later prostitution. Seventy percent of the adult women in prostitution in one study stated that their childhood sexual abuse affected their decision to become prostitutes. They described family abuse and neglect as not only causing direct physical and emotional harm, but also creating a cycle of victimization that affected their futures. For example, one woman interviewed by Joanna Phoenix stated that by the time she was 17, "all I knew was how to be raped, and how to be attacked, and how to be beaten up, and that's all I knew. So when he put me on the game [pimped her] I was too down in the dumps to do anything. All I knew was abuse."

When she is sexually abused, the child is reinforced via attention, food, and money for behaving sexually in the way the perpetrator wishes. The perpetrator's seductive manipulation of the child causes immense psychological harm. In addition, many children are threatened with violence if they do not perform sexually.

Angela Browne and David Finkelhor described traumatic sexualization as the inappropriate conditioning of the child's sexual responsiveness and the socialization of the child into faulty beliefs and assumptions about sexuality. Traumatic sexualization leaves the girl vulnerable to additional sexual exploitation and is a critical component of the grooming process for subsequent prostitution. Some of the consequences of childhood sexual abuse are behaviors that are prostitution-like; a common symptom of sexually abused children is sexualized behavior.

Sexual abuse may result in different behaviors at different stages of the child's development. Sexualized behaviors are likely to be prominent among sexually abused preschool-age children, submerge during the latency years, and then reemerge during adolescence as behavior described as promiscuity, prostitution, or sexual aggression.

Sexual abuse causes extreme damage to children's self-esteem. Frank Putnam noted that the child may incorporate the perpetrator's perspective, eventually viewing herself as good for nothing but sex, which is to say, she may adopt the perpetrator's view that she is a prostitute. According to John Briere, this constricted sense of self of the sexually abused child and the coercive refusal of the perpetrator to respect the child's physical boundaries may result in her subsequent difficulties in asserting boundaries, in impaired self-protection, and a greater likelihood of being further sexually victimized, including becoming involved in prostitution.

The powerlessness of having been sexually assaulted as a child may be related to the frequent discussions of control and power by women who are prostituting. The emotional and physical helplessness of the sexually abused child may be reenacted in the prostitution transaction, with vigilant attention to the tiniest shard of control. Payment of money for an unwanted sex act in prostitution may make the girl or woman feel more in control when compared to the same experience with no payment of money. For example, one woman said that at age 17, she felt safer and more in control turning tricks on the street than she did in her home with her stepfather who raped her.

Children commonly run away from homes in which they are being sexually abused. If there is no safe place to escape to, the child or adolescent is left extremely vulnerable to further sexual exploitation and assault. Mimi Silbert reported that 96% of the adults she interviewed had been runaway children before they began prostituting. Louie and colleagues found that more than half of 50 prostituting Asian girls aged 11 to 16 ran away because of family problems.

Children in prostitution are recruited from runaway and homeless populations. For example, John Lowman described the average Canadian prostitute as having entered prostitution between the ages of 13 and 19, usually after running away from home. Pimps exploit the vulnerability of runaway or thrown-out children in recruiting them to prostitution. In Vancouver, 46% of homeless girls had received offers of "assistance to help them work in prostitution." One 13-year old who had run away from home was given housing by a pimp, but only in exchange for prostituting.

A survey of 500 homeless youths by Barbara Lucas and Lena Hackett in Indianapolis found that at first only 14% acknowledged that they were "working as prostitutes." This survey reveals the importance of the wording of questions about prostitution. When the Indiana adolescents were later asked nonjudgmental questions about specific behaviors, they responded as follows: 32% said that they had sex to get money; 21% said they had sex for a place to stay overnight; 12% exchanged sex for food; 10% exchanged sex for drugs; and 6% exchanged sex for clothes. In other words, a total of 81%, not 14% of these 500 homeless adolescents, were prostituting. The following wordings for inquiry about prostitution are suggested: "Have you ever exchanged sex for money or clothes, food, housing, or drugs?" or "Have you ever worked in the commercial sex industry: dancing, escort, massage, prostitution, pornography, video, internet, or phone sex?"

Like heterosexual adolescent girls, gay male adolescents' prostitution behavior is likely to be a reenactment of earlier sexual abuse. Homophobia also plays a role in the prostituting of gay young men. Gay youth may have been thrown out of their homes because of their sexual orientation. Furthermore, in many cities, prostitution was the only available entry into the gay community; it was an activity where boys could "practice" being gay. Thus gay adolescent boys may develop an identity that links their sexual orientation to prostitution. [*See* CHILD ABUSE; POSTTRAUMATIC STRESS DISORDER; POWER; RAPE; SELF-ESTEEM; TRAUMA ACROSS DIVERSE SETTINGS.]

III. Socioeconomic Contribution to Entry into Prostitution

According to Julia Davidson, "Prostitution is an institution in which one person has the social and economic power to transform another human being into the living embodiment of a masturbation fantasy." In addition to gender, poverty is a precondition for prostitution. The economic vulnerability and limited career options of poor women are significant factors in their recruitment into prostitution. Of 854 people in prostitution from nine countries (Canada, Colombia, Germany, Mexico, South Africa, Thailand, Turkey, United States, and Zambia), Melissa Farley and colleagues found that 75% were currently or previously homeless. PROMISE, a California agency serving women in prostitution, reported that 67% of those requesting services were currently or formerly homeless.

Lack of education was frequently a precursor to entering prostitution. Seventy percent of West Bengal Indian women wanted to escape prostitution, but the cultural and economic factors that channeled them into prostitution prevented that: a 6% literacy rate, beatings, starvation, rape by family members, and sexual exploitation at their jobs. As reported by Molly Chattopadhyay and her colleagues, women in most jobs in West Bengal, India, were required to permit sexual exploitation in order to stay employed. The most frequent reason given by these women for leaving their last job was that prostitution would provide "better pay for what they had to do anyway."

IV. Racism and Colonialism in Prostitution

Women in prostitution are purchased for their appearance, including skin color and characteristics based on ethnic stereotyping. Throughout history, women have been enslaved and prostituted based on race and ethnicity, as well as gender and class.

Entire communities are affected by the racism that is entrenched in prostitution. For example, legal prostitution, such as strip clubs and stores that sell pornography (that is, pictures of women in prostitution) tends to be zoned into poor neighborhoods, which in many urban areas in the United States also tend to be neighborhoods of people of color. The insidious trauma of racism continually wears away at people of color and makes them vulnerable to stress disorders. Families who have been subjected to race and class discrimination may interface with street networks that normalize hustling for economic survival. Sex businesses create a hostile environment in which girls and women are continually harassed by pimps and johns. Women and girls are actively recruited by pimps and are harassed by johns driving through their neighborhoods. As Vednita Nelson pointed out, there is a sameness between the abduction into prostitution of African women by slavers and today's cruising of African American neighborhoods by johns searching for women to buy.

Compared to their numbers in the United States as a whole, women of color are overrepresented in prostitution. For example, in Minneapolis, a city that is 96% White European American, more than half of the women in strip club prostitution are women of color. Furthermore, African American women are arrested for prostitution solicitation at a higher rate than others charged with this crime.

Colonialism exploits not only natural resources, but also the people whose land contains those resources. Especially vulnerable to violence from wars or economic devastation, indigenous women are brutally exploited in prostitution (for example, Mayan women in Mexico City, Hmong women in Minneapolis, Karen women in Bangkok, and First Nations women in Vancouver).

Once in prostitution, women of color face barriers that prevent escape. Among these is an absence of culturally sensitive advocacy services. Other barriers faced by all women escaping prostitution are the lack of services that address emergency needs (for example, shelters, drug/alcohol detoxification, and treatment of acute posttraumatic stress disorder, or PTSD). There is a similar lack of services that address long-term needs, such as treatment of depression and chronic posttraumatic stress disorder (PTSD), vocational training, and long-term housing.

V. Trafficking Is International Prostitution

Prostitution always involves marketing, and trafficking is the marketing of prostitution. Women in prostitution are transported to the most lucrative market. The United Nations estimated that two million women, girls, and boys were trafficked into prostitution in 1999. Trafficking (moving girls and women across international borders) can not exist without an acceptance of prostitution in the receiving country. Many governments protect commercial sex businesses because of the massive profits (estimated at $56 billion per year). For example, the International Labor Organization called on poor countries to take economic advantage of "the sex sector," that is, prostitution and trafficking. Governments frequently have chosen to protect the demand for prostitution, rather than adopting complex solutions, which would involve prevention through community education programs and penalization of traffickers, pimps, and customers. Governments have failed to address the root cause of prostitution, which is the unequal status of women.

In 1999, Thailand, Vietnam, China, Mexico, Russia, Ukraine, and the Czech Republic were primary source countries for trafficking of women into the United States. Source countries vary according to the economic desperation of women, promotion of prostitution/trafficking by corrupt government officials who issue passports and visas, and criminal connections in both the sending and the receiving country such as gang-controlled massage parlors and the lack of laws to protect women who immigrate. The economic interdependence of countries and multinational corporations (globalization) promotes prostitution and trafficking by creating conditions for women to sell their own sexual exploitation at far better rates of pay than other forms of labor, according to Tanya Hernandez. Pimps and traffickers take advantage of the unequal status of women and girls in the source country by exploiting sexist and racist stereotypes of women as property, commodities, servants, and sexual objects.

Researcher Donna M. Hughes analyzed the ways in which economic devastation in Russia exacerbated preexisting gender inequality, promoting sex businesses including trafficking. Russian women have been scapegoated for keeping jobs that some believe they should have given up to men (the Russian Minister of Labor Melikyan stated that all women should be unemployed before a single man lost his job); domestic violence is at epidemic proportions; and sexual harassment on the job is commonplace. Under these conditions, almost any opportunity to leave Russia, even one that involves trafficking/prostitution, seems tolerable.

International prostitution includes prostitution tourism ("sex tourism"), arranged marriages with foreign women who are sexually objectified and kept in domestic servitude ("mail-order brides)," and re-cently, promotion of sexual exploitation by internet pimping and online prostitution, as described by Hughes.

The interconnectedness of racism and sexism in prostitution is vividly apparent in sex tourism. Colonialism in Asia and the Caribbean, according to Hernandez, promoted a view of women of color as natural-born sex workers, sexually promiscuous and immoral by nature. Over time, women of color came to be viewed as "exotic others," defined as inherently hypersexual on the basis of race and gender. The prostitution tourist, reading between the lines of travel brochures, denies the racist exploitation of women in "native cultures," as in Ryan Bishop and Lillian Robinson's analysis of the Thai sex business: "Indigenous Thai people are seen as Peter-Pan-like, children who are sensual and never grow up. Thus travel brochures assure sex tourists that they are simply partaking of the Thai culture, which just happens to be 'overtly sexual.'"

VI. Pervasive Violence in Prostitution

Prostitution is like rape. It's like when I was 15 years old and I was raped. I used to experience leaving my body. I mean that's what I did when that man raped me. I looked up at the ceiling and I went to the ceiling and I numbed myself . . . because I didn't want to feel what I was feeling. I was very frightened. And while I was a prostitute I used to do that all the time. I would numb my feelings. I wouldn't even feel like I was in my body. I would actually leave my body and go somewhere else with my thoughts and with my feelings until he got off and it was over with. I don't know how else to explain it except that it felt like rape. It was rape to me. (Giobbe, 1991, p. 144)

Sexual violence and physical assault are normative experiences for women in prostitution. Silbert and Pines reported that 70% of women in prostitution were raped. The Council for Prostitution Alternatives in Portland reported that prostituted women were raped an average of once a week.

According to Ine Vanwesenbeeck, in the Netherlands, 60% of prostituted women suffered physical assaults, 70% experienced verbal threats of physical assault, 40% experienced sexual violence, and 40% had been forced into prostitution and/or sexual abuse by acquaintances. Most young women in prostitution were abused or beaten by pimps as well as johns. Eighty-five percent of women interviewed by Ruth Parriott had been raped in prostitution. Of 854 people in prostitution in nine countries, 71% had experienced physical assaults in prostitution, and 62% had been raped in prostitution, according to Farley and colleagues.

According to Jody Miller, 94% of those in street prostitution had experienced sexual assault and 75% had been raped by one or more johns. In spite of these reports of extreme violence, there is a widespread belief that the concept of rape does not apply to prostitutes. Some people assume that when a prostituted woman was raped, it was part of her job and that she deserved or even asked for the rape. Nothing could be farther from the truth.

Like battering, prostitution is domestic violence. Giobbe compared pimps and batterers and found similarities in the ways they used extreme physical violence to control women, the ways they forced women into social isolation, used minimization and denial, threats, intimidation, verbal and sexual abuse, and had an attitude of ownership. The techniques of physical violence used by pimps are often the same as those used by batterers and torturers.

The level of harassment and physical abuse of women in strip club prostitution has drastically increased in the past 20 years. Touching, grabbing, pinching, and fingering of dancers removes any boundary that previously existed between dancing, stripping, and prostitution. In 1998, Kelly Holsopple summarized the verbal, physical, and sexual abuse experienced by women in strip club prostitution, which included being grabbed on the breasts, buttocks, and genitals, as well as being kicked, bitten, slapped, spit on, and penetrated vaginally and anally during lap dancing.

VII. Trauma Symptoms among Women in Prostitution

Recruitment into prostitution begins with what Kathleen Barry has called seasoning: brutal violence designed to break the victim's will. After control is established, pimping tactics shift to brainwashing and other forms of psychological control. Pimps establish emotional dependency as quickly as possible, beginning with changing a girl's name. This obliterates her identity, separates her from her past, and isolates her from her community. The purpose of pimps' violence is to convince women of their worthlessness and social invisibility, as well as physically controlling them.

Escape from prostitution becomes more and more difficult as the woman is repeatedly overwhelmed with terror. She is forced to commit acts that are sexually humiliating and that cause her to betray her own principles. The contempt and violence aimed at her are eventually internalized, resulting in a virulent self-hate that then makes it even more difficult to defend herself. Survivors report a sense of contamination, of being different from others, and self-loathing, which lasts many years after getting out of prostitution. Judith Herman and Lenore Terr have each described the complexity of repetitive behaviors found in survivors of chronic trauma. Traumatic reenactments of abuse are common, along with psychobiological dysfunction, including self-destructive thoughts and behaviors, self-contempt, feelings of shame and worthlessness, substance abuse, eating disorders, and sexual aversions or compulsions.

Dissociation is the psychological process of banishing traumatic events from consciousness. It is an emotional shutting down, which occurs during extreme stress among prisoners of war who are being tortured, among children who are being sexually assaulted, and among women who are being battered, raped, or prostituted. The emotional distancing necessary to survive rape and prostitution is the same technique used to endure familial sexual assault. Most women report that they cannot engage in prostitution unless they dissociate. Being drunk or high has been described as chemical dissociation.

One woman described the link between johns' behavior and her dissociation while she was prostituting in a strip club:

You start changing yourself to fit a fantasy role of what they think a woman should be. In the real world, these women don't exist. They're not really looking at you. You become this empty shell. You're not you. You're not even there. (Farley, unpublished interview, 1998)

People in prostitution also suffer from posttraumatic stress disorder (PTSD). Symptoms of PTSD include anxiety, depression, insomnia, irritability, flashbacks, emotional numbing, and hyperalertness. Farley and colleagues found that 68% of 854 people in prostitution from nine countries met diagnostic criteria for PTSD, suggesting that the traumatic consequences of prostitution were similar across different cultures. The following are two examples of PTSD.

Saundra Sturdevant and Brenda Stolzfus interviewed an Okinawan woman who had been purchased by U.S. military personnel during the Vietnam War. Many years later, she still became extremely agitated and had visions of sexual assault and persecution on the 15th and 30th of each month, the days that had been Army paydays. Another woman who spoke to Farley described symptoms of PTSD that were a consequence of violence in prostitution: "I wonder why I keep going to therapists and telling them I can't sleep, and I have nightmares. They pass right over the fact that I was a prostitute and I was beaten with two-by-four boards, I had my fingers and toes broken by a pimp, and I was raped more than 30 times. Why do they ignore that?"

Over time, the violence of prostitution, the constant humiliation, the social indignity, and the misogyny result in personality changes that Judith Herman has described as complex posttraumatic stress disorder (CPTSD). Symptoms of CPTSD include changes in consciousness and self-concept, changes in the ability to regulate emotions, shifts in systems of meaning, such as loss of faith, and an unremitting sense of despair. Sexual feelings are severely damaged in prostitution. Once out of prostitution, 76% of a group of women interviewed by Ruth Parriott reported that they had great difficulty with intimate relationships.

VIII. Physical Health Consequences of Prostitution

Chronic health problems result from physical abuse and neglect in childhood, sexual assault, battering, untreated health problems, and overwhelming stress. Prostituted women suffer from all of these. Many of the chronic physical symptoms of women in prostitution are similar to the physical consequences of torture. In a 1985 study by the Canadian government, the death rate of those in prostitution was found to be 40 times higher than that of the general population.

A lack of attention to pervasive physical and sexual violence has resulted in failures of the health care system for all women. Those in prostitution lacked access to social and medical services that were available to other women. Fear of arrest and social contempt made it difficult for prostituted women to seek emergency shelter or medical treatment.

Although the majority of research on prostituted women's health from 1980 to 2000 focused exclusively on HIV or other sexually transmitted diseases (STDs), some research has addressed non-HIV-related health problems. Prostituted women had an increased risk of cervical cancer and chronic hepatitis. Incidence of abnormal Pap screens was several times higher than the state average in a Minnesota study of prostituted women's health. Childhood rape was associated with increased incidence of cervical dysplasia in Ann Coker and colleagues' study of women prisoners, many of whom had been in prostitution.

Half of the women interviewed in San Francisco in 1998 by Farley and Barkan reported physical health problems, including joint pain, cardiovascular symptoms, respiratory symptoms, neurological problems, and HIV (8%). Seventeen percent stated that, if it were accessible, they would request immediate hospital admission for drug addiction or emotional problems. Many acute and chronic problems were directly related to violence. In addition to poor nutrition, gastrointestinal problems, and pneumonia, Eleanor Miller reported that women in prostitution had bruises, broken bones, cuts, and abrasions that resulted from beatings and sexual assaults. One woman said about her health:

I've had three broken arms, nose broken twice, [and] I'm partially deaf in one ear. . . . I have a small fragment of a bone floating in my head that gives me migraines. I've had a fractured skull. My legs ain't worth shit no more; my toes have been broken. My feet, bottom of my feet, have been burned; they've been whopped with a hot iron and clothes hanger . . . the hair on my pussy had been burned off at one time. . . . I have scars. I've been cut with a knife, beat with guns, two by fours. There hasn't been a place on my body that hasn't been bruised somehow, some way, some big, some small. (Giobbe, 1992, p. 126)

Frida Spiwak reported that 70% of 100 prostituted girls and women in Bogota had physical health problems. In addition to STDs, their diseases were those of poverty and despair: allergies, respiratory problems, and blindness caused by glue sniffing, migraines, symptoms of premature aging, dental problems, and complications from abortion. Adolescent girls and boys in prostitution surveyed by D. Kelly Weisberg reported STDs, hepatitis, pregnancies, sore throats, flu, and repeated suicide attempts. Women who serviced more customers in prostitution reported more severe physical symptoms. The longer women were in prostitution, the more they suffered symptoms of STDs.

Globally, the incidence of HIV seropositivity among prostituted women and children is devastating. Homeless children are at highest risk for HIV, for example, in Romania and Colombia. Peter Piot noted that half of new AIDS cases are in the under-25 age group, and that girls are likely to become infected at a much younger age than boys, in part because of the acceptance of violence against women and girls in most cultures.

IX. Needs of Women Escaping Prostitution and Trafficking

In order to offer genuine choices to women in prostitution, it is necessary to look at the vast array of social conditions in women's lives that eliminate meaningful choices. Until the unequal status of women is changed, prostitution will exist in some form. In order to understand prostitution, it is necessary to also understand (1) incest and other childhood sexual assault, (2) poverty and homelessness, (3) the ways in which racism is inextricably connected with sexism in prostitution, (4) domestic violence, including rape, (5) colonialism and its offshoot, sex tourism, (6) drug and alcohol addiction, (7) posttraumatic stress disorder, mood and dissociative disorders as sequelae of prostitution, (8) the need for culturally-relevant evaluation and treatment, (9) the fact that the global nature of sex businesses involves interstate and intercountry trafficking as necessary to its profitable operation, and (10) the ways in which diverse cultures promote and normalize prostitution, including attitudes that justify men's purchase of women in prostitution.

Ninety-two percent of 475 people in prostitution stated that they wanted to escape. When asked about their needs, 73% told the researchers that they needed a home or place of asylum; 70% needed job training; 59% needed health care, including treatment for drug or alcohol addiction. The most urgent need of girls and women escaping prostitution was housing. Both transitional and long-term housing were needed.

According to Boyer, emergency services used by women in prostitution, such as crisis lines, emergency housing, medical and psychological treatment, substance abuse treatment, and outreach programs, rarely if ever addressed the sexual trauma of women in prostitution. Often, medical and social service providers were disrespectful to women in prostitution. Training for service providers was recommended, as were peer support groups and chemical dependence treatment specifically for survivors of commercial sexual exploitation.

Although it is commonly assumed that street prostitution is the most dangerous type of prostitution, Debra Boyer observed that women in indoor prostitution, such as strip clubs, massage parlors, and pornography, had less control over the conditions of their lives and probably faced greater risks of exploitation, enslavement, and physical harm than

women who were prostituting on the street. Her report on the needs of prostituted women in the Seattle area recommended increased outreach to women in indoor prostitution. The myth that escort and strip club prostitution are different and safer than street or brothel prostitution has not been verified by research. Most women in prostitution experience several different types of prostitution. There are indications that all elements of the commercial sex business are unpredictable and dangerous for women. In a study by Farley and colleagues in 1998, there was no difference in the incidence of posttraumatic stress disorder experienced by those prostituting on the street and those prostituting in "high-class brothels." Ruth Parriott found no differences in health problems reported by women in massage parlors, escort services, strip clubs, bars, and street prostitution.

The psychological, physical, and vocational rehabilitation needs of women escaping prostitution are complex and long term. Women leaving prostitution in their 20s and 30s may have been in prostitution since they were adolescents and may never have had a job other than prostitution. Patricia Murphy noted the vocational impact of sexual exploitation and assault. She described some of the specific ways in which posttraumatic stress disorder and head injury compromise job performance. Vocational rehabilitation counselors must be expert in labor market issues and federal and state laws regarding disability, and they must be skilled at using psychiatric diagnoses in disability applications. Law professor Margaret Baldwin, barely joking, said that, for women escaping prostitution, justice and restitution would be "a million dollars and an apology." Baldwin proposed the use of public benefits such as workers' compensation or disability claims to assist women in the transition out of prostitution. Federal welfare reform, which includes such interventions as the Violence Against Women Act, might also assist women who are escaping prostitution.

The core experience of trauma is disconnectedness. Psychiatrist Judith Herman suggested that what is needed for recovery from trauma is a process of reconnection, guided by the survivor herself. Often the first connections that can be made are with other survivors of prostitution. Individual counseling must occur in a therapy relationship in which prostitution is explicitly recognized as sexual exploitation and violence. The capacity to trust is damaged in those who survive massive, deliberately inflicted trauma such as prostitution, and the process of healing is slow, with much testing of the therapist's motives. A crucial stage in the therapy of survivors of prostitution involves remembering the extent of the harm and mourning the loss of years of her life.

X. Criminal Justice Responses to Prostitution

It is commonly assumed that the greater the legal tolerance of prostitution, the easier it is to control public health. Public health in this context refers primarily to STDs in johns rather than to the psychological and physical health of prostituted women.

Legalized prostitution involves state, county, or city ordinances that regulate prostitution, for example, issuing zoning permits, requiring STD tests, and collecting taxes. In effect, the state operates as the pimp. In Nevada, state regulations determine geographic location and size of brothels, as well as activities of women outside the brothel. Prostituted women are only allowed into nearby towns from 1 to 4 p.m., are restricted to certain locations, and are even prohibited from talking to certain persons. Respondents in South Africa and Zambia were asked whether they thought they would be safer from sexual and physical assault if prostitution were legal. A significant majority (68%) said "no." The implication was that regardless of the legal status of prostitution, those in it knew that they would continue to experience violence.

The HIV epidemic has brought with it the advocacy of another legal approach to prostitution: decriminalization, or the cessation of enforcement of all laws against prostitution. Decriminalization of prostitution has been promoted by sex businesses as a way to remove the social stigma associated with prostitution. Decriminalization would normalize commercial sex, but it would not reduce the trauma and the humiliation of being prostituted. Compared to illegal prostitution, decriminalization would facilitate men's access to women and children.

Stating that "prostitution is not a desirable social phenomenon," the Swedish government in 1999 criminalized the behavior of pimps and johns but not those who were prostituting. Noting that "it is not reasonable to punish the person who sells a sexual service [because] in the majority of cases this person is a weaker partner who is exploited," the

Swedish government allocated social welfare monies to "motivate prostitutes to seek help to leave their way of life." This progressive interventionist approach reflects the Swedish interest in counteracting growth of commercial sex businesses.

In the United States, although there is legislative concern about forced trafficking, there are few legal remedies for women who enter prostitution because of educational neglect, emotional abuse, or lack of economic alternatives. Some women in prostitution do not appear to have been forced or coerced. Public policies that offer legal, financial, and social assistance only to those who can prove violent force, or who are under age eighteen, or who crossed international borders, do not address the core of violence that is present in all types of prostitution. Legal responses to prostitution are inadequate if they fail to include johns, as well as pimps and traffickers, as perpetrators.

The state of Florida passed a remarkably progressive law that addresses some of the forces propelling girls and women into prostitution. The Florida law specifically prohibits inducement into prostitution by sexual abuse, by pornography, or by exploiting the need for food, shelter, safety, or affection.

XI. Conclusion

Commercial sex businesses are a multibillion dollar global market that includes strip clubs, massage parlors, phone sex, online prostitution, internet pimping of women and children, adult and child pornography, street, brothel, and escort prostitution. One's political perspective will determine whether prostitution is viewed primarily as a public health issue, as an issue of zoning and property values (which parts of town should house strip clubs and pornography stores?), as vocational choice, as sexual liberation, as freedom of speech (does the webmaster have the right to sell internet photographs of prostituted women being raped?), as petty crime, as domestic violence, or as human rights violation.

For the vast majority of the world's prostituted women, prostitution is the experience of being hunted, dominated, harassed, assaulted, and battered. Intrinsic to prostitution are numerous violations of human rights: sexual harassment, economic servitude, educational deprivation, job discrimination, domestic violence, racism, classism, vulnerability to frequent physical and sexual assault, and being subjected to body invasions that are equivalent to torture.

Demand creates supply in prostitution. Because men want to buy sex, prostitution is assumed to be inevitable, therefore "normal." Men's ambivalence about the purchase of women, however, is reflected in the scarcity of research interviews with johns and in their desire to remain hidden. In a series of interviews with johns conducted by women prostituting in massage parlors, Elizabeth Plumridge noted that, on the one hand, the men believed that commercial sex was a mutually pleasurable exchange, and on the other hand, they asserted that payment of money removed all social and ethical obligations. A john interviewed by Neil McKeganey and Marina Barnard said: "It's like going to have your car done, you tell them what you want done, they don't ask, you tell them you want so and so done."

Programs that assist women in prostitution can not succeed in the long run unless social systems that keep women subordinate also change. Jacquelyn White and Mary Koss observed that violent behaviors against women have been associated with attitudes that promote men's beliefs that they are entitled to sexual access to women, that they are superior to women, and that they have license for sexual aggression. Prostitution myths are a component of attitudes that normalize sexual violence. Martin Monto found that johns' acceptance of commodified sexuality was strongly associated with their acceptance of rape myths, violent sex, and less frequent use of condoms with women in prostitution. A widespread acceptance among men of what has been described as nonrelational sexuality may be a contributing factor to the normalization of prostitution. According to sociologist Kathleen Barry, in today's culture we do not distinguish sex that is exploitative or coercive from sex that is positive human experience. This blurring results in what Barry has called the prostitution of human sexuality.

Prostitution must be exposed for what it really is: a particularly lethal form of male violence against women. The focus of research, prevention, and law enforcement in the next decades must be on the demand side of prostitution.

SUGGESTED READING

Abraham, K. (1953). *Selected Papers on Psychoanalysis.* Basic Books, New York.

Baldwin, M. A. (1999). A million dollars and an apology: Prostitution and public benefits claims. *Hastings Women's Law Journal,* Winter 1999, 189–224.

Barry, K. (1995). *The Prostitution of Sexuality.* New York University Press, New York.

Bishop, R., and Robinson, L. S. (1998). *Night Market: Sexual Cultures and the Thai Economic Miracle.* Routledge, New York and London.

Boyer, D., Chapman, L., and Marshall, B. K. (1993). Survival Sex in King County: Helping Women Out. *Report Submitted to King County Women's Advisory Board, March 31, 1993.* Northwest Resource Associates, Seattle.

Briere, J. (1992). *Child Abuse Trauma: Theory and Treatment of the Lasting Effects.* Newbury Park, Sage.

Browne, A., and Finklehor, D. (1986). Impact of child sexual abuse: A review of the research. *Psychological Bulletin* 99(1), 66–77.

Burkett, E. (1997). God created me to be a slave. *New York Times Magazine* 12, 56–60.

Chattopadhyay, M., Bandyopadhyay, S., and Duttagupta, C. (1994). Biosocial factors influencing women to become prostitutes in India. *Social Biology* 41(3-4), 252–259.

Coker, A., Patel, N., Krishnaswami, S., Schmidt, W., and Richter, D. (1998). Childhood forced sex and cervical dysplasia among women prison inmates. *Violence Against Women* 4(5), 595–608.

Crowell, N. A., and Burgess, A. W. (eds.) (1996). *Understanding Violence Against Women.* National Academy Press, Washington, D.C.

Davidson, J. O. (1998). *Prostitution, Power, and Freedom.* University of Michigan Press, Ann Arbor.

Davis, N. (1993). *Prostitution: An International Handbook on Trends, Problems, and Policies.* Greenwood Press, London.

Dworkin, A. (1997). *Prostitution and Male Supremacy in Life and Death.* Free Press, New York.

Farley, M., and Barkan, H. (1998). Prostitution, violence and posttraumatic stress disorder. *Women & Health* 27(3), 37–49.

Farley, M., Baral, I., Kiremire, M., and Sezgin, U. (1998). Prostitution in five countries: Violence and posttraumatic stress disorder. *Feminism & Psychology* 8(4), 415–426.

Finstad, L., and Hoigard, C. (1993). Norway. In *Prostitution: An International Handbook on Trends, Problems, and Policies* (N. Davis, ed). Greenwood Press, London.

Giobbe, E. (1993). An analysis of individual, institutional and cultural pimping. *Michigan Journal of Gender & Law* 1, 33–57.

Giobbe, E., Harrigan, M., Ryan, J., and Gamache, D. (1990). *Prostitution: A Matter of Violence against Women.* WHISPER, Minneapolis, MN.

Herman, J. L. (1992). *Trauma and Recovery.* Basic Books, New York.

Hernandez, T. K. (2001). Sexual harassment and racial disparity: The mutual construction of gender and race. *Journal of Gender, Race & Justice* 4, 183.

Hoigard, C., and Finstad, L. (1986). *Backstreets: Prostitution, Money and Love.* Pennsylvania State University Press, University Park, PA.

Holsopple, K. (1998). Stripclubs according to strippers: Exposing workplace violence. Unpublished paper.

Hughes, D. M. (2000). The "Natasha" trade: The transnational shadow market of trafficking in women. *Journal of International Affairs* 53(2), 625–651.

Hughes, Donna M. (1999). *Pimps and Predators on the Internet—Globalizing the Sexual Exploitation of Women and Children.* The Coalition Against Trafficking in Women, Kingston, Rhode Island.

Hunter, S. K. (1994). Prostitution is cruelty and abuse to women and children. *Michigan Journal of Gender and Law* 1, 1–14.

Lim, L. L., ed. (1998). *The Sex Sector: The Economic and Social Bases of Prostitution in Southeast Asia.* International Labor Organization, Geneva.

Louie, L., Joe, K., Luu, M., and Tong, B. (1991). Chinese American adolescent runaways. Paper presented at Annual Convention of the Asian American Psychological Association, San Francisco. August 1991.

Lowman, J. (1992). Canada. In *Prostitution: An International Handbook on Trends, Problems, and Policies* (N. Davis, ed.). Greenwood Press, Westport, CT.

Lucas, B., and Hackett, L. (1995). *Street Youth: On Their Own in Indianapolis.* Health Foundation of Greater Indianapolis, IN.

MacKinnon, C. A. (1993). Prostitution and civil rights. *Michigan Journal of Gender and Law* 1, 13–31.

MacKinnon, C. A., and Dworkin, A. (1997). *In Harm's Way: The Pornography Civil Rights Hearings.* Harvard University Press, Cambridge.

McKeganey, N., and Barnard, M. (1996). *Sex Work on the Streets: Prostitutes and Their Clients.* Milton Keynes Open University Press, Buckingham, Scotland.

Miller, E. M. (1986). *Street Woman.* Temple University Press, Philadelphia.

Ministry of Labour in cooperation with the Ministry of Justice and the Ministry of Health and Social Affairs, Government of Sweden. (1998). Fact Sheet. Secretariat for Information and Communication, Ministry of Labour. Tel +46-8-405 11 55, Fax +46-8-405 12 98. Artiklnr, A98.004.

Monto, M. (1999). *Prostitution and Human Commodification: A Study of Arrested Clients of Female Street Prostitutes.* American Sociological Association, Chicago.

Murphy, P. (1993). *Making the Connections: Women, Work and Abuse: Dramatic Insight into the Lives of Abuse Victims and Practical Recommendations for Their Successful Return to Work.* Paul M. Deutsch Press, Orlando, FL.

Nelson, V. (1993). Prostitution: Where racism and sexism intersect. *Michigan Journal of Gender & Law* 1, 81–89.

Parriott, R. (1994). *Health Experiences of Twin Cities Women Used In Prostitution.* Unpublished survey initiated by WHISPER, Minneapolis, MN.

Piot, P. (1999). Remarks at United Nations Commission on the Status of Women, United Nations Press Release, March 3, New York.

Plumridge, E. W., Chetwynd, J. W., Reed, A., and Gifford, S. J. (1997). Discourses of emotionality in commercial sex: The missing client voice. *Feminism & Psychology* 7(2), 165–181.

Putnam, F. (1990). Disturbances of 'self' in victims of childhood sexual abuse. In *Incest-Related Syndromes of Adult Psychopathology* (R. Kluft, ed.), pp. 113–131. American Psychiatric Press, Washington, D.C.

Root, M. (1996). Women of color and traumatic stress in 'domestic captivity': Gender and race as disempowering statuses. In *Ethnocultural Aspects of Posttraumatic Stress Disorder: Issues, Research, and Clinical Applications* (Mirsella, A. J., Friedman, M. J., Gerrity, E. T., and Scurfield, R. M., eds.). American Psychological Assn., Washington, D.C.

Sanchez, L. (1998). Boundaries of legitimacy: Sex, violence, citizenship, and community in a local sexual economy. *Law and Social Inquiry* 22, 543–580.

Silbert, M. H., and Pines, A. M. (1983). Early sexual exploitation as an influence in prostitution. *Social Work* 28, 285–289.

Silbert, M. H., and Pines, A. M. (1984). Pornography and sexual abuse of women. *Sex Roles* 10(11-12), 857–868.

Special Committee on Pornography and Prostitution. (1985). *Pornography and Prostitution in Canada* 350.

Sturdevant, S., and Stolzfus, B. (1992). *Let the Good Times Roll: Prostitution and the US Military in Asia.* The New Press, New York.

Terr, L. C. (1991). Childhood traumas: An outline and overview. *American Journal of Psychiatry* 148, 10–20.

Vanwesenbeeck, I. (1994). *Prostitutes' Well-Being and Risk.* VU Boekhandel/Uitgeverij Press, Amsterdam.

Weisberg, D. (1985). *Children of the Night: A Study of Adolescent Prostitution.* Lexington Books, Lexington, MA.

White, J. W., and Koss, M. P. (1993). Adolescent sexual aggression within heterosexual relationships: prevalence, characteristics, and causes. In *The Juvenile Sex Offender* (H. E. Barbaree, W. L. Marshall and D. R. Laws, eds.) Guilford Press, New York.

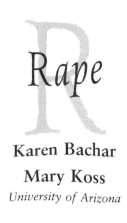

Rape

Karen Bachar

Mary Koss

University of Arizona

Glossary

Acquaintance rape Rape involving a perpetrator who is known to the victim.

Date rape Rape by an acquaintance who has some level of romantic association with a victim ranging from a first meeting to an established relationship.

Gender-based violence Gender-based violence disproportionately affects women and girls; includes sexual, physical, psychological, and economic abuse; and is due in part to women's subordinate status in society.

Psychological coercion Verbal demands and threats of bodily harm or rape used to force a woman to have sex against her will.

Rape The nonconsensual oral, anal, or vaginal penetration of the victim by the penis, fingers, or other parts of the body, or by objects, using force, threats of bodily harm, or by taking advantage of a victim incapable of giving consent.

Risk factors A combination of individual, dyadic, institutional, and societal influences that lead to perpetration.

Victim/survivor Trauma service providers frequently use the term *survivor* to signify that a victim has overcome serious injury or possible death. However, survivors still face an extended period of recovery to overcome the effects of rape on their physical, psychological, and social health.

Vulnerability factors A line of research that examines individual, dyadic, institutional, and societal-level influences thought to heighten a woman's risk for victimization. Research indicates that vulnerability is linked to earlier experiences beyond a victim's control and is not predictable.

THE DEFINITION OF RAPE varies from state to state and changes over time in response to legislative advocacy. However, most North American statutes currently define rape as the nonconsensual oral, anal, or vaginal penetration of the victim by the penis, fingers, or other parts of the body, or by objects, using force, threats of bodily harm, or by taking advantage of a victim incapable of giving consent. Penetration, however slight, constitutes rape; emission of semen is not required. In recent years, all 50 states have revised the laws defining rape. In contrast to previous definitions, the crime of rape is no longer limited to female victims, forcible situations, or to vaginal penetration exclusively. The exclusion of spouses as potential perpetrators of rape has also been eliminated. Thus current rape laws criminalize assaults by intimates, as well as assaults by strangers, and are gender neutral, suggesting that both women and men can be raped. However, it is important to note three things: First, that the rape of women is 10 times more common than the rape of men and therefore more accurately classified as gender-based violence. Next, whether the victim is male or female, perpetrators are almost always men. Perpetration by women is highly uncommon. Finally, rape is universal, that is, it occurs cross-culturally, although the prevalence rates vary among cultures.

I. Prevalence

After murder, rape is the most serious crime against a person. Because information on rape frequency comes from victims who are often reluctant to classify their experience as rape, it is also one of the most challenging crimes to count. Victims are hesitant to identify their experiences as rape both because they live in societies that blame rape victims and denigrate them as damaged goods and because survey questions often fail to clearly define their terms or ask multiple behaviorally specific questions. As a result, several important data sources on rape continue to underdetect cases and publish unrealistically low rape estimates.

Rape frequency estimates fall into two distinct categories: incidence and prevalence. Studies collecting incidence data count the occurrence of rape within a time-delimited period, usually six months to a year. When used in isolation, incidence rates can foster the misimpression that rape is an infrequent crime. Prevalence rates, on the other hand, focus on people not acts and consider the number of people (usually women) whose lives are impacted by rape over an extended period of time, up to and including their entire life span.

The United States has two federal sources of rape incidence data, the Uniform Crime Reports (UCR), a compilation of crimes reported to local authorities, and the National Crime Victimization Survey (NCVS), a nationwide, household-based crime victimization survey. According to the UCR, 96,122 crimes qualified as completed or attempted rapes in 1997. This number reflects the seventh consecutive annual decline in the crime index for rape. However, the UCR estimate fails to reflect the true scope of rape for several reasons. The UCR continues to exclude rapes that involve men, that occur when women are incapacitated or otherwise incapable of giving consent, and that involve penetration other than vaginal and with objects other than the penis. The UCR also relies exclusively on reported rapes to compile its estimate, while independent studies report between 84 and 95% of rapes are not reported to the police, depending on the group sampled. Further, although the UCR reports a decline in rape incidence, other annual studies of rape incidence such as the NCVS do not. In fact, since the NCVS was revised in 1992, it has actually shown an increase in rape incidence rates.

The second federal data set, the NCVS, attempts to discover the true incidence of both reported and unreported crimes. Using a recently revised survey, the NCVS estimates for 1994 were 432,100 rapes/sexual assaults of women 12 and older and 32,900 rapes/sexual assaults of men age 12 and older. While the rates for men remained fairly stable, the numbers for women reflected a five-fold increase over the levels detected prior to the 1992 revision. There are still strong reasons, however, to conclude that many rapes remain undetected, because the revised survey promotes the recall of violent crime over intimate crime and is administered in a manner that creates suboptimal rapport between the interviewer and the responder.

Neither UCR or NCVS estimates converge with other incidence studies. For example, the 1992 *Rape in America* report utilized equally strong samples and does not have the described measurement flaws. The study reported that 683,000 adult North American women were raped in a one-year period, or almost twice as high as the rate reported by the NCVS and more than six times that of the UCR. Because this incidence rate excludes rapes of females under the age of 18, rapes of men and boys, and rapes where the victim was unable to consent, the authors estimate that this figure still accounts for less than half of the rapes experienced by North Americans during a one-year period.

While the UCR and the NCVS focus on the incidence of rape in order to track crime trends, health professionals consider prevalence rates a more useful gauge of the true impact of rape. Thus, many of the better public health studies measure both incidence and prevalence. The *Violence Against Women Survey,* a nationally representative telephone poll of women (8000) and men (8000) was conducted between 1995 and 1996 to assess the prevalence of stalking, physical violence, and rape. The study found that 14.8% of women and 2.1% of men had sustained completed rape at some point in their lives and that 54% of the incidents occurred prior to the age of 18. The survey also noted ethnic differences in the risk of rape, and indicated that women raped prior to age 18 were significantly more likely to be raped again as adults. Another national study examined the prevalence of forced sexual intercourse and health risk behaviors among a national sample of 4609 female college students. The study found that 20% of those surveyed had been the victim of a completed rape at some point in their life. When the estimate was limited to women who had been raped since the age of 15, the authors found a prevalence rate of 15%. This estimate is virtually identical to the results of a study published in 1987, indicating that rape prevalence has stayed the same for more than a decade.

Other studies have examined the prevalence of rape and attempted rape in military populations. One such study of female U.S. Army soldiers found that 22.6% of female recruits reported having experienced a completed rape prior to enlistment. Among U.S. Navy recruits, 36.1% of female naval recruits had been raped prior to enlisting. Military recruits are an ethnically and economically diverse group who are in the same age range as youth attending college. Yet female naval recruits report victimization at rates more than twice that of college women.

Studies of rape prevalence tend to be more useful to behavioral scientists than studies of rape incidence; however, there are still methodological differences that may lead to underreporting. These differences include the representativeness of the sample, the context of the questions (questions about rape and attempted rape are frequently nested in crime, health, or sexuality surveys), the number and type of questions used to stimulate recall, the inclusion/exclusion of nonforcible rape (rape that occurs when a woman is incapable of giving consent), the use of different lower-age cutoffs for prevalence estimates (ranging from 12 to 18), and the use of the terms "sexual assault" and "sexual experiences" to assess rape prevalence. Discrepancies such as these may affect how respondents recall or classify their experiences and ultimately impact who is counted and who is excluded in studies of rape prevalence. It is a common finding that women will report that they have had intercourse against their will because a man used force, but will say no when asked if they have been raped. Behaviorally specific screening questions are a more effective strategy for detecting rape. These questions allow the interviewer to bypass individual labels the respondent may use by confining questions to specific acts and behaviors that illustrate how the investigators are defining rape. Finally, the context of the questioning, the timing and placement of the questions, as well as the gender and ethnicity of the person asking the questions are also important when interviewing rape victims.

Both the UCR and NCVS and national prevalence studies fail to adequately examine variance in rape rates for various populations such as women of color, children, men, adolescent boys, gay and lesbian populations, the homeless, the mentally ill, and patients seen in health care settings. Smaller studies have attempted to assess the frequency of rape in these populations, and have arrived at prevalence estimates that range from 2 to 97%. The latter rate was found in a study of episodically homeless and seriously mentally ill women. Their lifetime risk for physical assault and rape was so high (97%) that rape and physical battery are considered normative experiences.

Regardless of the type of study, a number of findings about rape are undisputed. The typical rape victim is young; the majority of rapes occur between the ages 12 and 24. More than 80% of rapes are committed by someone the victim knows, and most of these rapes will not be reported to the police. In one national survey, approximately one-third of stranger rapes were reported to police while only 13% of acquaintance rapes had been reported. Research has also shown that the level of violence tends to be lowest for date rape and highest for both stranger and marital rape, while the fear of being seriously injured or killed is similar regardless of the victim–offender relationship.

Researchers examining the prevalence of rape internationally face additional obstacles. They encounter difficulty in overcoming cultural norms for secrecy regarding sexual matters, they must frequently deal with the distrust of authorities and other community members, and they must develop methods to handle privacy issues in close-knit societies. Methodologically, it becomes difficult to compare studies cross-culturally because of the varying definitions of rape used by researchers and the cultural and geographic representativeness of samples of societies examined. Further, the laws of some countries including Costa Rica, Ecuador, Guatemala, Pakistan, and Sri Lanka indicate that rape is wrong only when the victim is determined to be honest and chaste. This suggests that only certain types of women deserve protection from rape. Outside the developed world, laws prohibiting marital rape are rare. International human rights organizations have documented the use of rape as a method to control women, particularly those women who attempt to better life for others, in countries including India, Pakistan, Peru, and elsewhere in Latin America. Finally, rape can be widespread under conditions of war and social disorganization.

II. Vulnerability and Risk

A number of researchers have tried to determine whether certain women are more vulnerable to rape and attempted rape than others. When examining these findings, it is important to distinguish between rape vulnerability and victim blame. Vulnerability research attempts to describe factors that may increase a woman's victimization risk without assignment of responsibility, while victim blaming is the mistaken assignment of responsibility for sexual victimization to women.

Vulnerability research can be summarized according to three overarching models. The social-psychological characteristics model focuses on personality, attitudinal schema such as adversarial beliefs (for example, gendered differences in perceived sex roles), difficulties in threat perception, psychopathology such as Post Traumatic Stress Disorder or depression, hostility, passivity, self-esteem, sexual attitudes, and the acceptance of rape myths (for example, that rape can be caused by how women choose to dress). The vulnerability-creating traumatic experiences model examines the connection between previous sexual abuse, family violence, lower socioeconomic status, and rape in adulthood. The vulnerability-enhancing situation model assesses the relationship between sexual behaviors, alcohol/drug use, and sexual violence.

Many studies have examined the link between rape and substance use. Recently a national sample of 3006 U.S. women were asked about their lifetime experience with alcohol abuse, drug use, and rape. These women were then followed for two years. Results indicated that use of drugs, but not abuse of alcohol, increased odds of new assault in the following two years. They also found that after a new assault the odds of both alcohol abuse and drug use were significantly increased, even among women with no previous use or assault history. For illicit drug use, but not alcohol use, findings supported a vicious cycle relationship in which substance use increases risk of future assault and assault increases risk of subsequent substance use. [See SUBSTANCE ABUSE.]

Like the study just cited, most research on rape vulnerability examines single factors or single levels of influence. However, Koss and Dinero examined a full range of 13 vulnerability items that correspond to the models described here. The study examined items such as adversarial sexual beliefs, rape myth acceptance, sexual behavior, alcohol use, and sexual abuse history. Using this full set of items, they were able to classify only 23% of rape survivors. They were able to predict almost as many rape survivors (19%) simply by knowing their previous sexual abuse history, and could predict 15% of rape survivors by chance alone. Thus, the 23% finding, although statistically significant, lacks practical significance. The authors interpreted their findings to indicate that rape vulnerability could not be explained by characteristics of victims. Vulnerability was linked to previous experiences that were beyond a victim's control or was not predictable. Most victims were different from women who had not been victimized primarily because they had encountered a sexually aggressive man. In sum, research on vulnerability is for the most part unproductive because no matter what researchers discover about vulnerability, women will still be susceptible to rape to the degree that men commit these acts of sexual violence.

Traditionally, risk factors for perpetrating sexual violence have been examined separately at societal, institutional, dyadic, or individual levels. Societal factors include the economic and social environment, cultural practices such as child rearing, culturally defined masculine roles, particularly those that emphasize male toughness and aggression as desirable attributes, cultural practices regarding sexual initiation, culturally defined roles for men and women in dating, and marriage. Institutional factors explore how groups such as the family, school, athletic teams, delinquent peer groups, religion, and the media stimulate gender-role stereotypes by promoting or reinforcing gender-role imbalances, minimizing the occurrence and impact of sexual aggression against women, failing to successfully promote alternatives to general or sexual aggression, and promoting impersonal sexual encounters as an ideal. Dyadic factors include the immediate context and stage of the relationship and focus on variables such as communication styles, male decision making, control of wealth, and the sexual scripts that guide the roles that each participant enacts. Individual factors include heredity, neurophysiology, physiology, traditional gender schemas, personality traits, sex and power motives, attitudes regarding rape myths, witnessing or experiencing family violence as a child, having an absent or rejecting father, and alcohol use (in terms of how alcohol interacts with other determinants). While single-factor theories add to our overall understanding of rape perpetration, they are limited because they focus on establishing correlations instead of developing or testing models that explain why men rape. In response to this limitation, researchers have begun to develop and test multifactor models that integrate classes of influence from the individual to the societal level. These models study either multiple causes of a single type of violence or examine how multiple causal factors relate to various types of violence and have some empirical support.

One of the most thoroughly researched multifactor theories constructed to explain both sexual and nonsexual aggression is called the confluence model. The model is based on the premise that it is vital to look at by-products of male physiology to understand the universality of rape. The confluence model has two components. The first is composed of a man's stance toward sexual behavior (bonded or impersonal sex); the second component examines the role of hostile masculinity in supporting sexual aggression and the tendency toward a more general orientation to human relationships. The model posits that men have a range of potentialities in expression of their sexuality, which may be shaped by their early life experiences, especially harsh formative experiences. This line of research complements other research on rape risk factors. According to the confluence model harsh childhood experiences may lead to anger and to the use of aggression to obtain sex. The use of aggression may in turn lead to sexual arousal and positive cognitions related to the use of aggression to impose one's will on another for sex. Whether a man uses aggressive/coercive tactics to gain sexual access depends on a wide range of personality characteristics, emotions, and attitudes (the acceptance of violence against women, or the belief that women ask to be raped when they engage in certain behaviors).

While no model can fully capture the variability of perpetrators, multifactor models are far ahead of earlier research based on single-factor models. Multifactor models address causal influences from the societal to the individual level and utilize a longitudinal perspective that focuses on the development of sexual and nonsexual aggression. Most important, these models emphasize risk factors related to perpetration as opposed to focusing on factors related to victimization and will be useful for developing new types of prevention education programs. It is important to note that multifactor theories are developmental (different risk factors may operate at different ages), and there are no necessary or sufficient explanations. Rather, the risk factors operate probabilistically. The more predictive factors present, the more likely sexual aggression becomes. [See AGGRESSION; ANGER.]

III. Physical and Psychological Impacts

Physical injuries following a rape frequently include bruises, abrasions, and vaginal tears. Immediate psychological responses to rape include intense fear, disorientation, shock, numbness, extreme helplessness, and disbelief. Most survivors do not seek professional help of any kind after being raped. If a rape victim does choose to seek help, she will most likely seek medical treatment from a physician who will often treat only surface physical wounds. Frequently, victims who seek health care do not disclose and are not screened for rape. Further research indicates that only 40% of victims are given information about the risk of sexually transmitted diseases and less than 50% of victims seeking treatment are advised about pregnancy testing. In order to improve services for rape victims, many communities have opted for specially trained nurses who either work at hospitals or are on call; these nurses provide both forensic exams and acute care. Such programs facilitate not only better experiences for survivors but also more complete evidence collection. Although this is a step forward in terms of services for survivors, their needs extend far beyond emergency room interventions and forensic examinations.

After a rape, many survivors experience intense feelings of guilt, shame, and self-blame, in part because they have internalized victim-blaming myths and believe that something they did or didn't do led to their rape. These negative feelings are perpetuated both by unsupportive social networks and responses from legal, medical, and mental health systems. Research suggests that institutional responses to rape often constitute secondary victimization. These responses may blame the victim, trivialize the abuse, fail to respect a victims autonomy, ignore her need for safety, violate confidentiality, and minimize the harm done. Misconceptions of a victim's role in the rape continue in spite of evidence that women's behaviors, personality, or past history play little role in differentiating women who have been raped from those who have not.

Self-blame has been shown to predict poorer adjustment and greater distress in rape victims. A rape victim's cognitive beliefs and schemas about power, safety, trust, and intimacy are also often affected by their experience. Many victims experience feelings of vulnerability and loss of predictability that stem from having faced real-world challenges to their beliefs that the world has order and meaning, that people are basically good, and that they can make good choices and protect themselves. Victims typically experience belief disruption and reconstitution in the direction of negative beliefs that people are bad, evil, and untrustworthy. Some rape victims also experience a general distrust or fear of men.

Researchers indicate that rape has long-term effects on both physical and psychological health. It has been documented that women who have a history of rape suffer disproportionately from gastrointestinal disorders and chronic pain syndromes including pelvic pain and tension headaches. By the second year after a rape, victims seek medical assistance twice as often as other women. Sexual victimization was a more powerful predictor of medical utilization among women HMO patients than other variables with well-known links to disease including smoking, drinking, life stress, age, and level of education. Recent studies have indicated that female students who had ever been raped were significantly more likely than those who had not to report a wide range of health-risk behaviors including early initiation of voluntary sexual intercourse, lowered likelihood of successful condom negotiation, smoking, alcohol use, drug use, driving after drinking alcohol, failure to use seat belts, and multiple sexual partners. Additionally, women who had been raped were more likely than those who were not to think seriously about suicide.

The most common long-term symptoms experienced by rape victims are those of fear and anxiety. Fear is often triggered by stimuli associated with the attack itself, or situations that are perceived by the victim as reminders of rape. Generalized anxiety may lead to jumpiness, sleep disruptions, or difficulty concentrating. Many survivors experience symptoms such as sleep and appetite disturbances, loss of interest in normal activities, decrease in the ability to concentrate, or feelings of alienation and loneliness. Some survivors develop major depressive disorders while others may experience some of these symp-

toms for shorter periods of time. Research indicates that almost one in five women who have been raped attempt suicide. Rape victims are also more likely than nonvictims to receive other psychiatric diagnoses including anxiety disorders, substance abuse, and alcohol dependence several years after the assault. Additionally, these women frequently experience sexual dysfunction, which may be the result of a lowered sexual self-esteem, negative feelings about men, or increased insecurities concerning sexual attractiveness due to the rape. [*See* ANXIETY.]

However, post-traumatic stress syndrome (PTSD) is the most frequent psychiatric diagnosis applied to victims of rape, as it is among survivors of other traumas that expose survivors to the threat of injury and death. Characteristic symptoms of PTSD include repeated daytime intrusive memories or nightmares that are so discomforting as to motivate patients to go to great lengths to avoid anything that reminds them of the trauma. PTSD has been diagnosed in as many as 94% of rape victims assessed immediately after an assault. Lifetime prevalence of PTSD is about 15% among victims of rape, a figure similar to that seen with male combat veterans. Because of its high prevalence combined with a high likelihood of inducing symptoms, rape victims make up the largest single group of PTSD sufferers. The primary limitation in applying PTSD to rape victims is that the diagnosis focuses on a narrow range of symptoms, while actual reactions to rape are broader. Not included in the PTSD syndrome are cognitive impacts of rape, social impacts, and sexual dysfunctions. Some mental health providers, especially in Latin America, are critical of the PTSD diagnosis because they feel it medicalizes a social problem and focuses the victim on her individual psychology rather than directing her energy toward affiliating with other targets of violence and using their cumulative energy to attack the root causes of violence within the society. [*See* POSTTRAUMATIC STRESS DISORDER; TRAUMA ACROSS DIVERSE SETTINGS.]

While all women are affected in some way by the experience of rape, it is difficult to predict the magnitude of impact and the type of response specific individuals will have. Research suggests trends for certain demographic variables of the victim, as well as certain aspects of a victim's history. For example, research has found that education and income do not appear to be related to the type or severity of symptoms, but that being married and being elderly have been associated with greater postassault distress. In addition, women with preexisting psychological distress also tend to have higher levels of postrape psychological symptoms. Prior victimization, however, creates a more complex picture. While first-time victims show more distress immediately following a rape, prior victims experience increased stress over time, show more depression, and have a longer recovery overall. Women who are raped more than once are also more likely to abuse substances and have a lifetime diagnosis of depression. Finally, having experienced other negative life stressors is also linked to greater postassault stress.

The nature of the attack has also been linked to the degree to which victims experience symptoms. First, women who have been sexually assaulted by acquaintances or family members suffer as serious psychological aftereffects as women who are assaulted by strangers. However, women raped by men they know are less likely than women raped by strangers to realize that the unwanted sexual experience meets the requirements for rape and consequently are less likely to report their victimization to police. These women have been called unacknowledged rape victims. Second, it appears that the actual violence may be less crucial in predicting response than the perceived threat, even though the number of assailants, physical threat, injury requiring medical care, and medical complications are all predictive of symptoms. Finally, research suggests that victims who were fondled and caressed tend to experience more symptoms, which may be due to later confusion with subsequent displays of affection that remind them of the attack, causing anxiety and other symptoms. Social support may moderate the impact of rape, but it appears that unsupportive behavior by significant others in particular predicts poorer social adjustment.

Culture is also an area that deserves more study. In all societies there are cultural institutions, beliefs, and practices that contribute to gender-based violence and intensify or mitigate its consequences. While there is limited research on how the impact of violence varies by culture, those that link intense, irremediable shame to rape and hold women responsible for assaults make recovery much more difficult as is the case among some Asian, Hispanic, and Middle Eastern groups.

IV. Preventive Interventions

In 1995 the National Research Council established the Panel on Research on Violence against Women.

The panel was charged with developing a comprehensive research agenda to increase both the understanding and control of gender-based violence. The panel's report, published in 1996, made several recommendations related to increasing research capacity and improving collaborative efforts between researchers and practitioners. The panel concluded that in order to significantly reduce the amount of violence against women in the United States, attention must be focused on prevention as a long-term strategy. Prevention is best viewed along a broad continuum. Primary prevention addresses those conditions that lead to rape through educational programs that help assess personal risk and vulnerability, examine personal attitudes and values, and build skills to prevent perpetration or avoid victimization. Secondary prevention deals with early identification of and intervention with existing situations so as to reduce revictimization or repeat perpetration. Tertiary prevention, which will be examined in the next section, attempts to ameliorate damage after an incident has occurred by providing support services in the areas of crisis intervention, counseling, and health, or may correspond to the treatment and rehabilitation of convicted offenders.

To date, little has been written about community-based prevention education programs. Preventive intervention efforts have largely consisted of school-based programs that focus on general violence prevention, dating violence, sexual abuse and conflict mediation, or college-based programs that attempt to challenge rape myth acceptance, decrease rape supportive attitudes, and increase knowledge. These programs vary in length, content, and theoretical basis and because the results of most prevention education programs are not published, it is difficult to know how many programs exist, what theories they use, or to whom they are offered.

Safe Dates is an example of an intervention directed at adolescent populations. Funded by the Centers for Disease Control, it is the first program to evaluate the effectiveness of a dating violence prevention program for adolescent populations using comparison group methodology. Safe Dates consists of both school- and community-based activities designed to address primary and secondary prevention. In all, 14 schools were matched according to size with one school from each pair exposed to both school-based and community-based activities (the treatment group), while students at the matched schools were only exposed to the community component of the intervention (the comparison group).

School-based activities included a theater production presented by peers, a poster contest, and a 10-session curriculum that included information on caring and abusive relationships, communication skills, anger management, rape and victim blaming, as well as how to help friends. Community activities to support adolescents included a crisis line, support groups, educational materials for parents, and training for community-based service providers. Evaluation results indicated that although there was a decrease in self-reported psychological and sexual violence perpetration, there was no corresponding decrease in self-reported victimization. Additionally, students reported that they were no more likely to seek assistance postvictimization.

In 1994 the National Association of Student Personnel Administrators mandated that college campuses receiving federal funding provide rape prevention education. As a result, rape prevention education programs seem to be increasingly common on college campuses. A recent review of research databases between 1994 and 1999 yielded fifteen university-based rape prevention education programs with published results. Eight of these programs were administered to mixed-sex audiences, four targeted men, and three were directed at women.

College-based programs directed at mixed-sex audiences utilize a number of formats including theater-based interactional dramas, audio or video presentations, interactive talk show formats, semester-long acquaintance rape education classes, and standard lecture presentations. These programs are designed to educate students about rape prevalence, rape myths/facts, communication, personal safety, alcohol use and abuse, consent, and resource availability. Some programs attempt to engender empathy for victims and male concern about rape. One semester-long program trained college students to conduct rape education for peers in campus settings. The four college-based prevention education programs that specifically targeted men attempted to change rape supportive attitudes, levels of empathy towards victims, rape myth acceptance, acceptance of sexual violence, and attraction to sexual aggression. The three college rape prevention education programs that were directed at women attempted to increase participant knowledge about rape risk, examine the connection between risk-reduction education and rape incidence for women (with and without rape histories), and explore the relationship between knowledge change and precautionary dat-

ing behaviors for women described as being at high risk for victimization.

Existing scholarship on the effectiveness of these programs provides a somewhat confusing picture. Many of the prevention efforts described here lack theoretical grounding, overemphasize content that is out of date, fail to target high-risk groups, and focus extensively on short-term outcomes. Further prevention efforts are frequently aimed at mixed-sex audiences, even though it has never been established that these programs can simultaneously provide rape prevention and rape avoidance/resistance messages without making some men defensive and polarizing program participants.

When working with women, prevention educators must consider different curricula. Programs that focus on teaching women avoidance techniques may be of questionable effectiveness since most women already have a long and sophisticated list of precautions that they take on a daily basis to minimize their risk of danger. Preventive efforts targeting women have yet to incorporate rape resistance training despite consistent evidence that the use of resistance strategies increase a woman's ability to avoid rape without increasing their chance of being injured. When included, resistance education is often inaccurate and based on rape myths rather than on empirical evidence that documents the effectiveness of verbal and physical resistance in preventing rape. Although some proportion of rapes are unavoidable, it is possible that women could better confront potential rapists if they received coaching on overcoming psychological barriers to resistance, aiding them to diagnose as soon as possible the level of danger they are facing, and giving them a series of learnable steps through which to progress from verbal to physical resistance.

The lack of programs adequately targeting male audiences results from the gap between theory development and prevention practice. Practitioners must increase the number of preventive interventions directed at men and incorporate content informed by theories that actually predict rape behavior. Since not all men are potential rapists, programs that promote positive masculinity and encourage men to act proactively when in a situation where gendered violence may occur are also needed.

Prevention practitioners must work to develop new community-based partnerships and deliver rape prevention education in new contexts. It is important to provide prevention education in areas that have traditionally been underserved such as the juvenile justice system, alternative high schools, junior colleges, job training programs, and programs for teen mothers. It is also important to link rape prevention programming with health issues like smoking, nutrition, and reproductive health, along with drug and alcohol programs.

V. Treatment Interventions

Sexual violence constitutes a continuum of attitudes and behaviors that exploit power in order to inflict harm and violate a person's sexual autonomy. Currently the majority of work with offenders revolves around cognitive behavioral-interventions that attempt to teach offenders to recognize situational and emotional states in which they are likely to reoffend and the skills to avoid or cope effectively with these states. One such long-term study utilized a cognitive-behavioral treatment strategy that was first used in the field of addictive behaviors in the late 1970s. Offenders were randomly assigned to either the treatment or control groups. The treatment group was exposed to a two-year program of intensive and highly structured behavioral, cognitive, educational, and skills training approaches designed to prevent reoffending. Additionally, offenders were provided with a number of specialty groups designed to help them deal with high risk situations. These groups were in the areas of sex education, human sexuality, relaxation, stress reduction, anger management, and social skills, as well as a prerelease preparation class. After completing the program, members of the treatment group participated in a yearlong aftercare program. Failure to participate in this program could result in a return to prison. Twenty-one percent of those randomly assigned to the treatment or control groups dropped out before the program began and 19% either dropped out or were removed for extreme disruptive behavior after treatment had begun. Results indicated that these early treatment dropouts had the highest rate of reoffending. Further, although the authors stress that it is too early to tell the overall effect of the program, preliminary results indicated that both groups had the same rate of new sexual offenses. Recent meta-analytic studies of other sex offender treatment programs that concluded these types of interventions are not promising.

In general, sex offender treatment outcome studies are rife with methodological problems, precluding any definitive conclusions. Studies of treatment effectiveness generally require random assignment in order to assure that the groups do not differ according to any important characteristics (age, type of crime, length of sentence, etc.). However, many investigators feel that it is unethical to withhold treatment from known sex offenders in an attempt to compare the recidivism rates. While it may be possible to solve this problem by placing members of the control group on a wait list to participate in the study at a later date, there are other methodological problems that pose greater difficulties in assessing programmatic outcomes. For example, it is not possible to adequately compute recidivism rates because not all reoffenders are caught. The treatments that have been studied are created for offenders who are already incarcerated. A number of these types of interventions report that participants are terminated because of disruptive behavior suggesting that those who are most likely to reoffend are too disruptive to receive treatment. Further, given the extremely low rate of conviction for men who sexually assault, this type of intervention only reaches a minority of rapists. The only way to reach the majority of offenders, who are residing undetected in the community, is through prevention education.

Rape has widespread effects on women's physical and psychological health. Because the rape was against their will and beyond their control, many rape victims resent and resist mental health services. Resolution of rape trauma on one's own is difficult even with adequate social support. These difficulties are often compounded because society holds survivors responsible (to a certain degree) for their rape. Women often try to block the rape from their minds, believing that if they don't think about what happened, they can move beyond the trauma. While there are some indications that this strategy may work for some survivors, others have more difficulty recovering from rape-related symptoms, eventually prompting them to request assistance for psychological or physical distress. Although there are a number of published studies on the efficacy of therapy for rape survivors, a growing body of research has shown that those survivors who attempt to access help from legal, medical, and mental health systems are often denied help by their communities and subjected to additional stressors that may leave them feeling revictimized. These negative experiences have been called the second rape or secondary victimization. As discussed previously, physicians are the health professionals most often approached by rape victims. Because they are the ones on the front lines, it is most important that they be trained to screen for victimization by violence, acknowledge disclosure, and direct women to appropriate resources when necessary. Even 10 years after practice guidelines were introduced, compliance with screening recommendations are low.

During the 1970s, rape crisis centers began opening as alternative responses. By 1979, there was one rape center in at least one community in every state, Puerto Rico, and the District of Columbia. These agencies have provided more care for rape victims than any other component of the response system. Crisis centers arose in response to the reality that rape victims often could not turn to their families and social networks for support or to medical service providers and community law enforcement agencies for aid. This grassroots movement provided counselors/advocates who assisted victims to process the emotional consequences of rape and advocated for better laws and services on the victim's behalf. Most current community responses to rape can be traced back to crisis center advocacy efforts. In addition to advocating for improved community response to rape and providing support groups for survivors, crisis centers often offer hospital and police accompaniment services to victims, court accompaniment programs, volunteer hot lines, self-defense training, and advocacy. They also often offer education programs for police, court, medical, and mental health professionals. They educate community and professionals about survivors and the typical responses to a rape experience to prevent incorrect diagnoses of psychopathology. Finally, centers emphasize prevention by presenting programs in schools, colleges, and the community to educate young people about rape, particularly in the context of intimate relationships.

Unfortunately, these agencies rely on grant funding, which has become more and more difficult to obtain. The result is that most centers cannot adequately staff their programs or offer all of their community services. Several agencies have had to limit their efforts to crisis intervention services, many centers have merged with other social service agencies, and some have closed altogether. Reinvesting in these community centers is vitally important in order to continue providing prevention education, continued help for survivors, and efforts to change the current societal response to rape. Adequate funding is necessary to maintain current programs, to retain qualified staff, and to extend service out to jails, detention centers, prisons, substance-abuse programs, health maintenance organizations, and other settings where a large proportion of women are rape survivors. These agencies and their communities also need to develop strategies to link rape centers with the medical, mental health, and justice systems.

Little data on the effectiveness of crisis intervention services exist. Current evaluation studies have a small number of participants who are treated by a few therapists in relatively uncomplicated cases. It is important to note that little data exists on specific treatments for adolescents, even though research has shown that adolescents are the largest population of rape victims. In addition, more study is needed on the specific treatment concerns of different ethnic groups. Finally, research needs to document that treatments focusing on processing the rape event itself are more effective than more traditional approaches that focus on symptoms of depression, anxiety, or sexual dysfunction.

Survivors choosing to seek mental health treatment have numerous group and individual therapy options. Group psychotherapeutic treatment for rape survivors has become the intervention of choice of clinicians. Group process helps empower survivors by encouraging a sense of community and feelings of activism. Group therapy also offers individual support by peers who validate the feelings, share grief, and counteract feelings of self-blame. Group therapy is widely used both in community-based programs and within the formal mental health system. Although most evaluations of therapeutic interventions focus on individual treatment, most survivors receive group interventions. The few studies that exist have suggested promising results.

Research on individual psychotherapy has focused on behavioral and cognitive behavioral techniques for rape victims. Prolonged exposure (PE) and stress inoculation training (SIT) are two widely used approaches. In PE treatments, therapists assist clients to relive memories of the traumatic event and confront events that were previously avoided because they triggered distressing memories and thoughts. In anxiety-management programs, such as SIT, clients are taught various coping strategies to manage trauma-related anxiety (i.e., thought stopping, positive self-statements, relaxation training, and cognitive restructuring). Additionally prolonged exposure and anxiety management approaches have been combined. Results of these treatments are mixed. One study that evaluated PE, SIT and combined PE-SIT interventions indicated that at one year posttreatment the prolonged exposure approach appeared to be the most effective (although this might have been due to a lower dropout rate for that treatment condition). Further the hypothesis that the combination treatment would be superior to either treatment alone was not supported. It should be noted that all of these techniques are somewhat aversive for the victim and may result in high dropout rates or reactivation of chemical abuse and suicidal attempts unless practiced by a qualified specialist.

Between 20 and 30% of those survivors who enter into individual therapeutic treatment programs drop out before completing them. Individual therapy for rape victims has been criticized as an inappropriate approach because it reduces rape from a social or political issue to an individual issue. These individualistic treatments, it is argued, encourage women to adjust to living in a rape-supportive society by focusing energy on their own recovery rather than a group process that can enhance feelings of empowerment and foster political action that could ultimately prevent rape.

While no one therapeutic modality has proven to be more effective than another, all efficacious treatments share common features. These features include the avoidance of blaming the victim; a supportive, nonstigmatizing view of rape as a criminal victimization; an environment to overcome cognitive and behavioral avoidance; provision of information about traumatic reaction; and the expectation that symptoms will improve. For rape survivors to feel more comfortable accessing mental health services, they need to know that their specific concerns will be addressed.

VI. Conclusions

In the mid 1970s rape was commonly thought to be perpetrated by men at the edge of society who were seeking social and economic control of women. As we enter the 21st century, we know better. Researchers have documented that rape is one of the most underreported crimes in the United States, and that the majority of rapes and attempted rapes are committed by someone known to the victim. Research has also shown that vulnerability factors shed little light on the occurrence of rape. Gender is still the most powerful predictor of rape—rape is predominantly a crime against women that is perpetrated by men. Rape impacts health outcomes far beyond the emergency room. The range of health problems linked to sexual violence is extensive, affecting both physical and mental health for many years past the victimization. The majority of current prevention efforts target potential victims and fail to include information on physical resistance, despite evidence that it may help women to avoid rape without increasing injury. Prevention education must focus on potential perpetrators and utilize current scholarship on risk factors. Programs that encourage positive masculinity and teach men appropriate ways to respond in situations where gendered violence may occur are also needed. These programs must be directed at both youth and adult populations and must be part of a long-term, comprehensive strategy. Treatment programs for sexual offenders have not lived up to expectations, and the majority of treatment services for victims are provided through grassroots agencies. Even in the formal mental health system, outcomes do not return survivors to their previctimization level. Based on these findings, the most viable policy to reduce the amount of violence against women in the United States is to focus on primary prevention education efforts.

SUGGESTED READING

Bachar, K. J., and Koss, M. P. (2001). From prevalence to prevention: Closing the gap between what we know about rape and what we do. In *Sourcebook on Violence against Women* (C. M. Renzetti, J. L. Edelson, and R. K. Bergen, eds.), Sage, Thousand Oaks, CA.

Breitenbecher, K. H., and Scarce, M. (1999). A longitudinal evaluation of the effectiveness of a sexual assault education program. *Journal of Interpersonal Violence* 14(5), 459–478.

Crowell, N. A., and Burgess, A. W. (eds.) (1996). *Understanding Violence against Women*. National Academy Press, Washington, DC.

Heise, L., Ellsbury, M., and Gottemoeller, M. (1999). Ending violence against women. *Population Reports*, Series L, No. 11, 1–43.

Koss, M. P., and Dinero, T. E. (1989). Discriminate analysis of risk factors for sexual victimization among a national sample of college women. *Journal of Consulting & Clinical Psychology* 57, 242–250.

Koss, M. P., and Goodman, L. (1994). *No Safe Haven: Male Violence against Women at Home, at Work, and in the Community*. American Psychological Association, Washington, DC.

Malamuth, N. M. (1998). The confluence model as an organizing framework for research on sexually aggressive men: Risk moderators, imagined aggression, and pornography consumption. In *Human Aggression: Theories, Research, and Implications for Social Policy* (R. G. Geen and E. Donnerstein, eds.), pp. 229–245. Academic Press, San Diego, CA.

National Victims Center. (1992, April 23). *Rape in America: A Report to the Nation*. Author, Arlington, VA.

Recovered Memories

Linda Stoler

Kat Quina
University of Rhode Island

Anne P. DePrince

Jennifer J. Freyd
University of Oregon

Glossary

Betrayal trauma theory A theory that predicts that the degree to which a traumatic event involves social betrayal by a trusted caregiver will influence the way in which that event is processed and remembered.

Dissociation A psychological state involving alterations in the integration of thoughts, feelings, and experiences into the stream of consciousness.

False memory A memory for an event that did not occur.

Hysteria A psychological disorder first documented in ancient Greece, with symptoms resembling posttraumatic stress disorder.

Memory accuracy The degree to which a memory is historically true.

Memory persistence The degree to which a memory has remained available over time.

Posttraumatic stress disorder Symptoms following exposure to a traumatic event, including intense thoughts, emotions, and bodily sensations.

Prospective trauma studies A research methodology in which participants who have been identified as having a documented traumatic experience are assessed over time following the event.

Psychogenic amnesia The report of forgetting experiences, usually traumatic in nature, due to psychological rather than physiological factors.

Rape trauma syndrome A pattern of psychological reactions observed in women and children who have been sexually assaulted.

Recovered memory The recollection of a memory that the individual reports had been unavailable for some period of time.

Repression An intentional forcing of distressing material from consciousness due to internal conflict.

Retrospective trauma studies A research methodology in which participants (often adults) are asked about traumatic events that occurred in the past.

MEMORY ALTERATIONS AND RECOVERED MEMORIES for traumatic events are among the many outcomes associated with trauma examined by researchers and clinicians. This article considers the history of studying memory for trauma, including recent controversy, as well as theory and empirical evidence for memory impairment associated with trauma. This article examines the relations between gender, trauma, and memory, as well as the contributions of feminist analyses to understanding recovered memory issues.

I. Introduction

The past 30 years have produced painful public and private awareness of the extent of childhood trauma. Revelations of sexual and domestic abuse, first spurred by the feminist movement of the 1970s, led children and adults of all ages to begin to tell their stories. Powerful sensory and affective memories of the horror of child abuse were recounted in shocking numbers. At the same time, pioneering studies in the prevalence of rape and childhood sexual abuse confirmed the picture emerging from the stories: sexual violence was not an uncommon experience for women and children in the United States. Furthermore, a wide array of emotional, psychosocial, and behavioral effects could be linked to childhood trauma, extending well into adulthood. Another picture also emerged from these stories: as people described their memories and the effects of rape and childhood abuse, the similarity between them and survivors of other types of trauma became clear.

One of the more perplexing sequelae of trauma is the apparent loss, and then recovery, of conscious awareness of the traumatic experience. Many lay people and professionals have erroneously assumed that a horrible experience will be vividly etched forever in the mind; in fact, the phenomenon of selectively forgetting and then recovering conscious memory for a traumatic event has been discussed in the psychological literature for over a century. The failure of memory across time has been documented in survivors of the full range of traumatic human experiences, including childhood sexual abuse.

As public awareness of childhood sexual abuse grew, so did the number of people (predominantly women) who sought assistance for dealing with recollections of childhood abuse of which they had been previously unaware. Some of these were well-known public figures, including Marilyn van Durber, a for-

mer Miss America, whose two sisters corroborated her memories with their own continuous memories of abuse at the hands of their father. Others sparked widespread outrage. For example, after Frank Fitzpatrick recovered memories of abuse by Father James Porter, dozens of other survivors stepped forward, most of whom had continuously recalled the abuse but had been silenced by social pressure not to speak ill of priests. Several won major court victories after recovering and obtaining corroboration for their memories.

Currently, more than 70 studies, using clinical and nonclinical samples, reporting retrospectively and prospectively, have found evidence of delayed memories for childhood trauma. Among adults reporting childhood abuse, as many as one-third also report some period during which they had no memory for the abuse. The existence of recovered memories of trauma has been recognized in the most recent edition of the American Psychiatric Association's *Diagnostic and Statistical Manual of Mental Disorders*, which defines dissociative amnesia as follows:

[A]n inability to recall important personal information, usually of a traumatic or stressful nature too extensive to be explained by normal forgetfulness. This disorder involves a reversible memory impairment in which memories of personal experience cannot be retrieved in a verbal form (or, if temporarily retrieved, cannot be wholly retained in consciousness).

Recovered memories have also been recognized by the American Psychological Association's Working Group on Investigation of Memories for Childhood Abuse.

Feminist analyses of recovered memories, and the response to them, reveal important gender dynamics. Studies of the family and cultural dynamics that place children in sexual danger—most often from older males—have offered vivid evidence that women and children are vulnerable not only because of their smaller size and strength, but also because patriarchal social roles deprive children of the power to refuse and mothers of the power to protect. In a patriarchal society, sexual abuse is rarely spoken about, unspeakable horrors are severely underreported, and abusers are rarely prosecuted. The patriarchal dynamics that have silenced victims also silences their memories, and the patriarchal attitudes that have allowed abusers to go unpunished reappear as efforts to undermine adult survivors' reports of their memories.

In spite of innumerable anecdotal reports, a long history of clinical observations, and the flurry of recent research concerning recovered memories, an explanation of how traumatic memories are lost and then recovered and how to best help those coping with the experience of recovering traumatic memories remains elusive. This article discusses a historical and a conceptual framework for understanding abuse memories, reviews the data and theories that inform our understanding of recovered memories, and offers currently accepted approaches for working with clients with traumatic memory issues. In doing so, we will suggest the unique contributions of gender to the phenomenon of recovered memories and to the status of sexual abuse survivors who have recovered memories.

II. Historical Context

In the late 19th century, the French neurologist Jean-Martin Charcot conducted the first systematic research into the disorder known as "hysteria." Hysteria had been accepted as a disorder afflicting women (its name was derived from the Greek word for the uterus, in which it was believed to be located) for hundreds of years. Charcot's careful observation and classification of the symptoms of hysteria inspired Sigmund Freud and Joseph Breuer of Vienna and Pierre Janet of France to set out to discover its cause. After extensive interviewing of patients, they independently reached the conclusion that hysteria was caused by unbearable emotional reactions to traumatic events, most often incest or other sexual trauma. The somatic symptoms of hysteria were disguised representations of intensely distressing events that had been exiled from memory and could be treated by a "talking cure" that would help patients recover, relive, and assimilate their memories of trauma.

Freud's famous paper, "The Aetiology of Hysteria," was met with an icy reception from colleagues, and unlike most other presentations of the time it received very little newspaper coverage. Freud felt that he was being shunned by the medical and scientific community; within a year, he recanted his thesis concerning hysteria. Freud's correspondence from this time makes frequent references to his growing concern about the social implications of his theory: if it was correct, then by implication, sexual abuse of children was widespread, not only in French lower classes but in respectable upper- and middle-class families of Vienna. This idea was simply not credible to Freud and many others of his day. There has

been much speculation, but many believe that Freud succumbed to the pressure of the German medical establishment, which offered no scientific criticism of Freud's thesis, only disavowal and disgust.

A contemporary of Freud's, Pierre Janet, introduced the term "dissociation" in late 19th century France to capture the fragmentation of memory that he observed in his traumatized patients, mostly women. Janet suggested that people with hysteria were unable to integrate traumatic memories, leaving the traumatic memory as a fixed idea set apart from normal memory processes. During Janet's career, the study of dissociation reached a pinnacle; shortly thereafter, research and clinical attention to dissociation and traumatic memory severely declined until the First World War. [See GENDER DEVELOPMENT: PSYCHOANALYTIC PERSPECTIVES.]

The First and Second World Wars once again led psychiatrists to note the link between traumatic experiences and memory disruptions in soldiers (mostly men) suffering from "shell shock." World War II brought about a strong interest in efficacious treatment for shell shock, which, like earlier work on hysteria, focused on the recovery and cathartic reliving of traumatic memories of combat, along with all the attendant emotions of terror, rage, and grief. In an attempt to speed the recovery of shell-shocked soldiers, hypnosis and drugs such as sodium amytal were used to aid in the recovery of traumatic memories. However, the psychiatrists who pioneered these techniques noted that retrieval of the memories did not by itself constitute effective treatment, but rather that the memories and their attendant emotions must be integrated into consciousness.

Trauma and its effect on memory once again received scrutiny as returning veterans of the Vietnam War began to speak out about their experiences. In response, the Veterans Administration commissioned comprehensive studies on the impact of war experiences on veterans. As a result of these studies, the American Psychiatric Association included the diagnosis of posttraumatic stress disorder (PTSD) in its official manual of mental disorders. Thus, formal recognition of the effects of psychological trauma entered the diagnostic nomenclature in 1980. Alterations in memory were included in the PTSD criteria as an inability to recall aspects of the traumatic event. [See POSTTRAUMATIC STRESS DISORDER; TRAUMA ACROSS DIVERSE SETTINGS.]

In the early 1970s Ann Burgess and Lynda Holmstrom began studying the psychological effects of rape, observing a set of reactions they called "rape trauma syndrome" and noting that some rape victim's symptoms resembled those of combat veterans. By the early 1980s it was recognized that victims of rape and child abuse often suffered from the same type of memory losses after sexual trauma that had been identified in war veterans and accident, crime and disaster survivors.

For a decade or so, documentation and information about recovered memories were accepted, and new avenues of treatment for survivors were explored. Public acknowledgment of child sexual abuse grew by leaps and bounds as the popular press provided previously unheard of coverage and first-person accounts of child sexual abuse. The early 1990s saw the advent of what many authors have called a backlash against feminism; in this context a backlash against recovered memories arose in the form of the "false memory" controversy. The fundamental characteristic of a backlash is that those who have drawn awareness to disturbing issues are the very ones who are responsible for creating or fabricating these issues. A primary accusation of this backlash, then, was that recovered memories of childhood sexual abuse are false, usually implanted in vulnerable women by their therapists or self-help books. The False Memory Syndrome Foundation (FMSF) was founded in 1992 to promote this view, primarily in the media and in court settings. The FMSF directed most of its efforts at undermining the credibility of women reporting recovered memories and their therapists, underscoring the stereotypical view of women as passive, suggestible, and unwilling to take responsibility for self-imposed problems.

III. Recovered Memories: Data, Theory, and Mechanisms

The effort to describe and explain the phenomenon of traumatic memory loss and the mechanisms behind such a loss has caused considerable confusion and debate. Various ways of characterizing such a memory loss include amnesia, repressed memories, recovered memories, delayed memories, discovered memories, betrayal blindness, fragmentation, and forgetting. Regardless of the term applied, there is evidence for various complex forms of memory loss: general amnesia for the childhood period during which abuse occurred; amnesia for part but not all of a childhood trauma (e.g., a person remembers being physically but not sexually abused or remembers

one incident while forgetting others); amnesia for previous memory of a traumatic abuse (e.g., a person discloses abuse during childhood or as an adult and then later fails to remember the abuse or the disclosure); and amnesia for all abuse, including inaccurately recalling childhood in unrealistically positive ways.

A. EMPIRICAL DESCRIPTIONS OF RECOVERED MEMORY

There are often empirical limitations on studying memory: for the most part, it is retrospective, and researchers must often rely on self-report without external corroboration. Nevertheless, an impressive body of theory and research has developed on normal and traumatic memory processes, in some cases using prospective cases—that is, people with traumatic experiences, such as children identified through medical documentation and witnesses as being abused, are followed into adulthood.

Recovered memories are not like continuous memories, in a number of ways. Most first appear in the form of a flashback, a bodily sensation, a sensory impression or memory, an intense affective response such as a panic attack, or even a dream. These sorts of memories have been referred as implicit, behavioral memories—"remembered" in the body and senses. They might be described as snapshots, often without context or sequential ordering, but are vivid in some details and laden with intense emotion. In contrast, survivors describing their continuous memories of childhood abuse, including those who have forgotten some part of the abuse, describe their experiences in a narrative form, with a fairly detailed visual description and connected to time, place, and context. Only a small proportion of people discussing their recovered memories ever comfortably describe them as narrative memories, even with post-recovery therapy; any narrative form of the memory usually emerges over a long period of time.

Individuals often cannot make coherent sense of the memories, not describe them adequately, yet they can be quite consistent and strong through multiple repetitions. Over time more pieces of the memory, including additional events, may emerge and the individual can begin to place the experience in context, forming a narrative about the experience. This process often involves a construction of the most likely scenario, which is subject to all the influences and distortions of normal memory, but tends to maintain its experiential core. People report less confidence in the accuracy of these recovered memories, even when they are corroborated, and often never get a satisfactorily complete narrative of what happened to them.

These memories are often originally triggered by some external event in the environment, a personal experience, or an event. For example, one woman reported that she first began to recall being sexually abused by her father when she was involved in an auto accident: while she was trapped in the car, a paramedic tried to soothe her by stroking her hair in a way reminiscent of her father. Other triggers are more commonplace, such as first becoming sexual with a chosen partner, having a child, and watching a television show or movie. It is not uncommon to be unaware of exactly what triggered the memory.

It is difficult to study these fragmentary memories in laboratory memory research; memories created under controlled conditions do not undergo this sort of fragmentation, and subjects are not stressed enough to produce dissociative responses. Thus, little research has been done on the memory quality. However, in one of the best prospective observational studies of the qualities of abuse memories among severely abused children, Ann Burgess and her colleagues identified both implicit behavioral abuse memories—which showed up as flashbacks, physical complaints such as unexplained pain, and reenactments of the physical movements involved in the abuse—and explicit, narrative abuse memories—describing the events verbally. As older children, some of these survivors could not produce the explicit narratives of their abuse, but continued with the implicit behavioral responses even 10 years later.

At least 30 peer-reviewed published retrospective studies of adult survivors of child sexual abuse have documented forgetting and the later recalling some or all of the abuse in between 19 and 59% of subjects. In a large-scale survey, assessing multiple types of trauma, Diane Russell found that 32% of those with trauma history indicated that they have experienced delayed recall of the traumatic event.

In Linda Meyers Williams's prospective study of adults whose childhood sexual abuse had been documented through hospital records, approximately 38% did not recall being sexually abused. An additional 16% who did recall the documented abuse reported having forgotten about the abuse for some period of time. Regardless of the sample, or whether the study was retrospective or prospective, abuse-specific amnesia has been a robust finding, with every

known study assessing amnesia for abuse having found it in at least some portion of subjects.

Two factors—younger age at time of abuse and more severe, violent abuse—have been associated with delayed recall of abuse in the literature. These variables often overlap, however, with another factor that has also been associated with delayed recall: abuse perpetrated by a caretaker. Indeed, abuse (physical and sexual) by a caretaker has been shown to be associated with memory impairment even when age at time of abuse and duration of abuse are controlled for. In addition, survivors who recover memories also describe a strong attachment to their abusers, with positive or mixed feelings about them except for their abusive behavior and a failure of other family members to believe the child or to end the abuse. Furthermore, sexual abuse is two times more likely to be forgotten than either physical or emotional abuse. [*See* CHILD ABUSE.]

B. THEORETICAL EXPLANATIONS FOR RECOVERED MEMORY

Betrayal trauma theory, proposed by Jennifer Freyd, addresses why traumatic experiences might be forgotten. The theory proposes that amnesia for childhood abuse exists not for the reduction of suffering, but for survival in the face of that suffering. From a logical analysis of developmental and cognitive research, she has argued that under certain conditions—such as sexual abuse by a parent—blocking cognitive information can be expected.

Betrayal trauma theory starts with the presumption that children rely on a caregiver for survival. If that caregiver is also causing harm, or is enabling harm to occur, the child is at great risk from two kinds of trauma. One kind of trauma is physical harm: threats to one's life or acts that can cause bodily harm and often do. This kind of trauma leads to terror, the extremely fearful emotional state required in the definition of traumatic response. However, often overlooked is the other kind of trauma: social harm. When a caregiver is causing the trauma, another dimension is triggered: betrayal of trust, along with threats to the maintenance of social relationships necessary for survival. Some traumas are high on both these dimensions. For instance, sadistic abuse by a caregiver, the Holocaust, some combat experiences, and many childhood sexual abuse situations including trusted authorities such as religious figures are both terrorizing and involving a betrayal of a relationship. While the anxiety responses found in PTSD have been linked to the terror dimension, betrayal trauma theory suggests that amnesia for traumatic events involving social relationships are linked to betrayal.

Betrayal trauma theory has been supported by research on the factors that make amnesia most probable. In accordance with the theory, childhood abuse is more likely to be forgotten if it is perpetrated by a parent or other trusted caregiver, particularly when it involves a social attachment and the caregiver–perpetrator also fills other survival needs. Betrayal trauma theory notes that if the child processed such a betrayal in the normal way, he or she would be motivated to stop interacting with the betrayer. In order to continue interacting with the abuser, to preserve the important attachment, the child blocks or disconnects information about the abuse from other mental mechanisms, notably those that control attachment and attachment behavior.

To support the notion that amnesia will be more likely when the victim is dependent on the perpetrator, several sets of extant data demonstrate higher rates of amnesia for parental or incestuous abuse than for nonparental or nonincestuous abuse. Further, Freyd and her students have collected survey data questioning individuals' memory for a wide array of specific situations of physical, emotional, and sexual abuse in childhood. The preliminary results support the prediction that the greater the victim's dependence on the perpetrator, the less persistent are memories of abuse. Together, these data sets suggest that social dependence may play an important role in memory for traumatic events.

How is a child to manage blocking out abuse information on a long-term and sometimes nearly daily basis? How is the child to succeed at maintaining this necessary relationship when a natural response is to withdraw from the source of the pain? Betrayal trauma theory proposes that the child blocks the pain of the abuse and betrayal by isolating knowledge of the abuse/betrayal from awareness and memory. There are various avenues for achieving this isolation, including conscious memories without affect and the isolation of knowledge of the event itself from awareness. Most likely, there are multiple ways for the abused child to disrupt knowledge integration and awareness of the abuse, while facilitating the important and crucial relationship. Further, there are multiple ways for the adult survivor of childhood abuse to recover these memories, and these different ways will depend in part on how the memories were isolated in the first place.

These memory processes are likely enhanced by characteristics of many of the sexual abuses perpetrated by family members: they occur at night when that normal processing is already fuzzy and when the child may interpret (or be told by abusive parents to interpret) the experience as a dream or nightmare. Another possibility is that the child is confused by an alternate reality, when denial or suggestion by an abusive parent overtakes the child's (and perhaps the abuser's own) beliefs about what must have happened. In keeping with this idea, Linda Stoler found forgetting more likely in women whose abuse was a family secret, likely happening to other related children, but who could not get any adult to believe them or to intervene.

Data from confessed child sexual abusers also supports betrayal trauma theory. In interviews, these men indicated that they actively selected and groomed certain children for betrayal. In particular, they sought out targets who were not likely to not speak up or who would not be believed if they did. The main characteristic they sought was a lack of confidence, but is also helped if the children were young, small, had family problems, and were alone. The abusers then actively isolated children further, turning family members against them or keeping them away from friends; made the children feel special, creating a strong bond of mutual attachment; developed a public persona and a relationship with the children's families as an exceptionally good person; desensitized the child to their advances; created an alternative reality such as that the sexual contact was the children's fault or idea; and promoted self-blame, including threats to family if the children did tell. These abusers had learned that children who felt shame and guilt and who had some loyalty to the abuser and to their family were well groomed for silence.

Furthermore, it has been widely reported that currently abused children often cling to a view of their abuser as good, talking about how they love and miss them, and physically clinging to them. These observations suggest that attachment to an abuser can be complex, including suppression of negative information about an attachment figure even while abuse is ongoing.

The plausibility of amnesia with mechanisms already recognized by cognitive psychology does not negate the potential for false memories to occur. Indeed, the cognitive mechanisms that support knowledge isolation and subsequent recovery may be in part the same mechanisms that may support memory errors. Furthermore, although the betrayal trauma theory has considerable potential, the current evidence in support of it is largely preliminary and exclusively correlational in nature. Although a relationship has tentatively been observed between reported memory persistence and the relationship of the victim to the alleged perpetrator, it does not necessarily follow that the cause of this relationship is betrayal trauma processes. In principle a variety of other potential factors could account for these correlations including age at the time of the event, differences in the interpretations of abuse associated with caretaker versus stranger abuse, and differences in the likelihood of talking about the two types of abuse or differences the likelihood that the memories of the two types of abuse may be fabricated. Freyd and her colleagues are measuring some of these potentially confounding variables and will be able to evaluate statistically the contribution of these covarying factors in predicting memory impairment. Preliminary analyses indicate that one factor, age at the time of the event, cannot itself account for memory persistence over time. Some issues will require specialized populations. For instance, to evaluate the possibility that there is a difference in the likelihood that memories of types of abuse are fabricated, it will be necessary to use a prospective methodology with documented abuse samples. In correlational research there is always the possibility of unmeasured confounds; because we cannot ethically vary many of the factors of interest related to real abuse, the best we can currently do is systematically evaluate the contribution of covarying factors that we identify as possibly accounting for differences in rates of reported forgetting.

Betrayal trauma theory has important implications for any analysis of recovered memories that considers gender. Betrayal trauma theory highlights the importance of the victim–perpetrator relationship, drawing particular attention to abuse perpetrated by trusted caregivers. In terms of sexual abuse, girls and boys appear to experience different patterns of abuse. Specifically, girls tend to report more sexual abuse by family members that begins at a younger age and continues for a longer duration than boys do. Boys, on the other hand, tend to report more sexual abuse by people outside of the family. This abuse tends to be shorter in duration and to occur at older ages compared to girls. This pattern in childhood sexual abuse suggests that girls may be experiencing more betrayal traumas, in terms of sexual abuse, than boys do. In turn, this might lead girls to experience higher degrees of memory impairment than boys, though this has yet to be established empirically.

C. MECHANISMS UNDERLYING RECOVERED MEMORIES

Many mechanisms have been proposed to explain the phenomenon of recovered traumatic memories.

1. Automatic/Unconscious Mechanisms

In general, extreme emotional arousal interferes with normal processes of integrating the event into memory. Two mechanisms have been proposed: repression and dissociation. Freud defined repression as a defense mechanism of the ego that forces disturbing material in the unconscious, where it is relatively inaccessible to conscious awareness. Affect associated with the memory is discharged in other ways, and the experience becomes completely absent from conscious memory under normal conditions. Freud further believed that the affect associated with a repressed event was deemed by the person to be unacceptable or impossible to express and resulted in a symptom that could be cured by the recall of the repressed event and consequent venting of unexpressed affect.

Dissociation, rather than repression, was emphasized by Pierre Janet. Janet believed that when an event was too terrifying, bizarre, or overwhelming the experience was compartmentalized and split from consciousness rather than integrated into a unitary whole, remaining disconnected from the person's awareness and thus preventing the person from being able to speak of it.

More than a hundred years later, disagreements about whether the explanatory mechanism of psychogenic amnesia is repression or dissociation still persist. While some authors appear to use the terms interchangeably, amnesia for child sexual abuse is most typically conceptualized in recent literature as dissociation. Some authors have argued that "dissociation" is a more accurate term when referring to memory loss associated with child sexual abuse because the amnesia is induced by an external trauma and not by an internal conflict as Freud suggested; moreover, the concept of dissociation allows for a continuum of coping processes. Other authors argue that dissociation more accurately describes the extensive alterations of consciousness that can result from prolonged abuse and maintain that repression is a more common experience while dissociation emerges only when the more usual defenses such as repression are insufficient.

Currently dissociation appears to be the concept that best describes the available empirical data and

clinically observed symptomotology concerning amnesia for childhood sexual abuse. The American Psychiatric Association uses the descriptive term "dissociation," rather than the more theory-laden
"repression." Dissociation, as assessed by the well-
validated Dissociative Experiences Scale, is greater
among survivors of childhood sexual abuse and in
particular is predicted by early abuse onset, multiple
forms of abuse, and chronic childhood trauma.

2. Neurobiological Mechanisms

Studies in animals have demonstrated that stress
can impair memory function, through stress hormones, brain chemicals that affect the way memories
are laid down, and lasting changes in the structure
and function of brain areas involved in memory.
Some of these findings have been replicated in humans, particularly stress responses in people who
have PTSD. Using brain imaging techniques in humans, researchers have found evidence that flashbacks or traumatic memories in individuals who have
been diagnosed with PTSD result in very different
brain activation patterns than neutral memories. In
such studies, traumatic memories were associated
with decreased activity in the brain's language production center (Broca's area). In addition, traumatic
memories were also associated with increased right
hemispheric and decreased left hemispheric activity.
Taken together, these findings illustrate changes in
brain activity for traumatic memories compared to
neutral memories. Further, the pattern of findings
suggests that some traumatic memories may be literally unspeakable in terms the patterns of brain activation (i.e., decreased activity in Broca's area and left
hemisphere). Other brain structures implicated in recovered memories are the amygdala, which is involved in the evaluation of the emotional meaning of
incoming stimuli, and the medial prefrontal cortex,
which is considered responsible for social and emotional regulation, including inhibition of fear responses to normal stimuli.

Neurochemical reactions, notably cortisol and norepinephrine levels, which normally increase during
stress, show heightened sensitivity in animals exposed to chronic early stress. Low levels of cortisol
and elevated levels of norepinephrine have been observed in adults with PTSD, even years after the
trauma. This dysregulation may maintain the high
level of emotional content attached to the original
event, while interfering with long-term storage. [See
STRESS AND COPING.]

3. Information Processing Mechanisms

Several mental mechanisms observed in normal
cognitive processing may be applied to memory loss
and recovery, the ability to process different kinds of
information in parallel, selective attention, whether
or not the information is or can be shared with others, and the length of time required to process complex information. Each of these could isolate knowledge of the abuse by interrupting the extended
processing of the event.

Memory appears to be processed in two ways,
with a dual representation of information. The most
common form is autobiographical memory, encoded
linguistically and verbally accessible in narrative
form; but there is also a lower-level perceptually
based representation of the event, encoded as bodily
sensations and emotions. If a child does not have adequate linguistic capability to comprehend or encode
an event, or if the perpetrator confuses the child by
using language that distorts the original trauma, only
sensory and emotional forms may be "remembered."

Individuals may be able to utilize more conscious
mechanisms to invoke selective forgetting of traumatic events. Through selective attention, thoughts
may be inhibited and competing thoughts may be facilitated in concert. These processes may occur at the
point of encoding a memory, when an individual
avoids the narrative rehearsals needed for normal
memory storage, or at the point of retrieval, when
an individual may learn "how to forget" already encoded unpleasant events, thus preventing their normal recall. In a cleverly designed set of studies,
Michael Anderson demonstrated that subjects who
are asked to try not to think about some part of the
material they had previously learned do indeed forget that part when asked to recall everything they
had learned. While thus far only neutral word
stimuli have been used, this cognitive suppression deserves further examination as a mechanism that might account for what others have termed
"repression."

Another way in which a narrative is assigned to a
memory is through sharing it with others. If not
shared, the information is likely to remain dynamic
and sensory in nature, less accessible for retrieval.
Sexual abuse is low in shareability—not something
we readily talk about with others—and intrafamilial
or intimate violence is perhaps uniquely nonshare-
able. Furthermore, parents may support an alternative reality in statements like "that never happened,"
"don't ever tell anyone," or "forget about it," which
may erase or change the child's memory.

Another approach suggests that traumatic events may be stored correctly, but the individual may choose not to allow the memory into "meta-awareness." Jonathan Schooler proposed that some people "discover" memories through a new awareness of what those memories mean—for example, realizing that an event was abusive—which may then be confused with memory for the event itself. Others may have been prevented from explicit description or discussion of the event or unable to self-reflect because of extreme stress or dissociation, so the memory is not available to meta-awareness. Focusing on this aspect of awareness allows one to examine confusing cases where, for example, an individual claims to have no memory of an event, but had reported it to others during the time they believed themselves to be amnestic.

These mechanisms may overlap within an individual, and different mechanisms may be operating for different people. Additional research is needed to further explicate these issues.

IV. The False Memory Controversy

Issues of sexual abuse have been a hotbed of debate and concern throughout history. Current controversies center on the extent of abuse in our culture, whether abuse leaves aftereffects in "normal" individuals, whether children can be believed, whether women "invite" rape by their dress and behavior, and whether therapy is helpful or harmful. These attacks sometimes explicitly name the feminist movement as a negative force; other attacks come from within the feminist movement, labeling those who work with survivors "victim feminists." Terms such as "hysteria," "feminist plot," and "anti-male" are used to combat reports of child sexual abuse, and a few have claimed that the opposition to adult–child sexual contact lies with "radical feminists." Accusations of sexual abuse are attributed to rageful feminist therapists who have turned their own abuse histories into fanaticism.

These debates have been particularly intense with respect to recovered memories, igniting questions about belief (did an event really happen?), narrative (how, when, and to whom can someone speak about trauma?), and power (who has the authority to determine truth and voice?). In feminist analyses of patriarchal systems, these mirror the ways in which women and children are silenced: disbelieved, denied a voice, or given no authority even over their own truths.

The plausibility of amnesia with mechanisms already recognized by cognitive psychology does not negate the potential for false memories to occur. Indeed, the cognitive mechanisms that support knowledge isolation and subsequent recovery may be in part the same mechanisms that may support memory errors.

In fact, studies report corroboration of the core experience in between 47 and 86% of recovered memories, through reports of others who were abused by same perpetrator, reports of relatives, medical and legal record, diaries, and even perpetrator acknowledgments. Studies comparing recovered and continuous memories of abuse show no difference in rates of corroboration; indeed, a review of the literature concludes that there is no scientifically valid evidence to suggest that recovered memories are more or less likely to be inaccurate than continuous memories. The exception is reports of extreme ritual abuse, where corroboration has not often been found. However, even there, the core abuse may have been experienced, with misremembering of the situation or events as they actually occurred.

While it is likely that very few memories of any sort are wholly accurate, some have viewed any error in a memory as evidence of their overall falsehood, and any recovered memory as by definition false. In such positions, the question of whether real memories can be lost and then reliably recovered has not been separated from the question of the extent to which false memories can be implanted through suggestion. This conflagration of ideas is perhaps best represented by the introduction of the term "false memory syndrome" (which has not been accepted as a genuine syndrome by any psychological or psychiatric association) by the FMSF. The letterhead of this advocacy group formed in the early 1990s for parents accused of sexual abuse identified the problem as adult daughters whose therapists had implanted their memories of sexual abuse. Joined by psychologists (urging lawsuits against fellow practitioners) and defense lawyers, members of the FMSF have fueled a national debate and actively attempted to silence voices of survivors. Tactics have included intense media campaigns, distortion and selective presentation of data and court cases, ethical complaints and lawsuits against therapists and scholars, and even picketing of homes and offices of those who study and write about traumatic memory recovery.

This strategy may be an example of what Jennifer Freyd called "DARVO": denial, attack, and reverse victim and offender. In indignant and self-righteous ways, abusers threaten, bully, and make a nightmare for anyone who holds them accountable or asks them to change their abusive behavior. This attack is intended to chill and terrify those who would speak out, through threats of lawsuits, overt and covert attacks on the whistle-blower's credibility, ridiculing the person who attempts to hold an offender accountable, and so on. The DARVO offender meanwhile portrays himself as a victim of the dangerous (woman) child.

Unilateral disbelief in the existence of recovered memories is similar in appearance to the ways in which women's accounts of oppression have been denied throughout history—there are periods of time when the medical and psychological literature have ignored or denied abuse and related issues. This is not to say that all recovered memories are true; rather, that the claim that all memories are false fits into a societal pattern of denying women's and children's experiences. For example, in the late 1980s and early 1990s, epidemiological research suggested that approximately one in four college women experienced rape or attempted rape. This finding was initially met with a great deal of media attention and concern. By the mid-1990s, a backlash had begun in which the research was attacked and women's experiences of rape were denied. On the heels of the date rape backlash, similar attacks on feminism were seen, including accusations that feminists who brought attention to violence against women had moved toward "victim feminism." Similar ebbs and flows of awareness of oppression can be seen in other areas, such as sexual harassment. As in the cases of date rape and sexual harassment, recovered memories and sexual abuse were brought to public attention as issues affecting mainly women. [See RAPE.]

Reports of large numbers of cases of false memories are from self-reports of parents who claim to have been falsely accused. In fact, the number appears to be small and not typical of most clients or most who recover memories. Three studies of retractors—individuals claiming to have false memories implanted by a therapist—have identified from 63 to 300 cases. One study found that 5% of people who reported recovered memories subsequently considered those memories to be inaccurate. Allan Scheflin and Daniel Brown reviewed 30 court cases involving women who had been in therapy as sexual abuse survivors and were subsequently suing a therapist, claiming the therapist had "implanted false memories" of sexual abuse. They observed that over-

all these women had a number of psychiatric diagnoses (5 to 7 each), had in about a third of the cases demonstrated clinically significant factitious behavior (distorting truth) while in therapy, had often disclosed abuse to previous therapists, and in every case had been exposed to a significant post-therapy suggestion that they were victims of their therapist rather than a sexual abuser. In a rather complicated twist, then, some of these retractors may have been demonstrating both an attention-seeking factitious disorder and the impact of implantation of the false belief that they were not abused.

Elizabeth Loftus has reported successful attempts to implant memories of childhood events such as being lost in a shopping mall in almost a quarter of her subjects. This paradigm relies on plausible events and on an older, trusted family member to suggest to the subject that the event occurred. She and others have generalized these results to memories first reported in therapy, claiming they too are implanted through suggestion. However, newer studies that control for demand characteristics and other biases find that the percentage in whom misinformation can be implanted is much smaller, under 5%, particularly when negative, bizarre, or improbable events are suggested. To the extent that abusers may seek to shape a child's alternate reality, this paradigm would suggest that an insistent parent might convince a more impressionable child that a more positive scenario, involving no abuse, describes their childhood years. However, without research on real-life abuse memories, these questions remain unanswerable.

Perhaps most telling are data from survivors who report recovered memories. Few of them report that a therapist first suggested that they had been abused. While about half of them report they were undergoing therapy when they recovered the memory (although they were not necessarily in a therapy session at the time), they are clear that they had entered therapy for more general symptoms and that the memories emerged as they gained more insight into these symptoms. Some clinicians have suggested that the generalized problems for which the individual sought therapy were signs that memories were about to emerge in any case.

Most laboratory studies of inaccurate remembering have involved memory for lists of words in a classic memory research paradigm. The subject is shown a list of related words and then asked to select them out of a long list of words. For over a century, researchers have shown that the subject is likely to remember an item that was not in the original list, but was related in content. For example, the subject may have been shown "toe" and "heel," but also recall seeing "foot." While these inaccurate memories can be labeled "false," this research fails to include trauma-related stimuli (e.g., remembering "penis") and cannot be generalized to more complex real-world memories. More helpful are recent studies that try to sort out the factors that enhance memory fallibility or to identify characteristics of individuals who may be particularly susceptible to suggestions of prior experiences.

One interesting aspect of this controversy has been the use of the mantle "scientist" to claim a version of truth about what are ultimately individual lives. Any data obtained from nonlaboratory sources is viewed as unbelievable, asserting that "science" (defined as empirical laboratory data) takes precedence over women's stories. Ironically, this approach seems only to hold for those who report recovered memories. Loftus and Ketcham dedicated their 1994 book, *The Myth of Repressed Memory*, to the principles of science, with its rigors of proof; yet they present personal anecdotes of denial by alleged perpetrators, including one secondhand denial by a widow, as a demonstration that recovered memories are false, without any corroborative evidence. Others have suggested that this and other examples of logical errors can only arise in a patriarchal system which supposes that science is a greater authority than an individual experience, that information labeled "science" has been generated without bias, and that any emotional content must be outside the realm of scientific accuracy.

In a related vein, attacks against recovered memory have not been confined to a specific type of therapy or to unethical or "bad" therapy. Therapy in general has come under attack, with some taking a pseudo-feminist approach that therapy automatically takes away women's power and thus harms women. Parallel attacks have become popular in courtrooms, accusing divorcing mothers of implanting beliefs in children that they were abused by fathers in order to gain custody. Sweeping claims that children cannot tell truth from fiction have been asserted in the courtroom and the media. Assertions that sexual abuse does not usually upset children or lead to adult harm have been coupled with attacks on feminist zeal. Feminist analyses have suggested these seemingly diverse lines of assault on the truth of individuals are very much related. In each case, the rationales and the solutions suggested place the adult daughter in a weaker, childlike position—ruled by a therapist, a father, or scientific (laboratory) data, which all take an authoritative stance that her own experiences are not valid. Those in power use their authority to infantilize the alleged victims, to regain the power already taken back by survivors and to silence future victims so abuse can continue unabated.

V. Approaches to Treatment

Psychotherapy, as noted earlier, has been cited as the process through which false memories of sexual abuse are created. One study of 350 licensed psychologists found that 25% of participants appeared to focus strongly on "recovered memory" techniques. However, the use of the label "recovered memory therapy" is questionable. It is not a formal or widely recognized therapeutic orientation. Nevertheless, several controversial techniques have been associated with treatment of clients who struggle with memory issues: hypnosis, dream interpretation, guided imagery, and interpretation of physical symptoms. While there is no direct evidence that these techniques can produce false memories when sensibly and responsibly applied, laboratory research suggests the possibility and therefore, clinicians have been advised to be extremely cautious and judicious in their use.

There is also a body of research and clinical experience that therapists can draw on to create therapeutic guidelines that will minimize the possibility of wholly false memories. The reality is that many clinicians will be faced with the task of treating people who present for treatment with suspicions that they have been abused, or with a host of symptoms usually associated with some history of trauma, and it is wise for therapists to prepare themselves.

Because therapy that deals with historical abuse issues usually causes clients, at least initially, to experience increased depression and decreased levels of functioning, some authors have suggested that it should not be practiced. A study of victims of Father James Porter found that indeed, those who had not recalled the abuse continuously had functioned better in their daily lives up to the point of recall, after which functioning declined and distress increased. However, most research has found that as the abuse is resolved, survivors report functioning again increases and distress decreases. Furthermore, there is evidence that the abuse might still have caused devastating consequences even without memory recovery: among Linda Stoler's survivors who had recovered memories, 93% had suicidal ideation before memory recovery, and 80% had sought therapy for unspecified emotional distress.

Kenneth Pope and Laura Brown noted that therapists need to provide a therapeutic climate in which ambiguity and uncertainty are tolerated. This necessitates finding ways to support clients without jumping to premature conclusions or closure. In addition, they strongly admonish therapists to avoid being polarized in their attitudes toward childhood sexual abuse, that is, neither to regard it as the primary cause of all distress nor to dismiss it as being of little current importance. Based on laboratory research, Daniel Brown also noted that explicit warnings that not all of what is remembered is accurate reduces misinformation suggestibility; highly suggestible clients may be especially vulnerable to distortions of memory in response to therapy; less authoritarian, more egalitarian therapists are less likely to induce memory confabulation; and memory distortions are least likely to occur when a free-recall strategy is employed in contrast to structured inquiry or leading questions.

Cognitive-behavioral, psychoanalytic, feminist, and other theoretical approaches to treatment can be found in the literature. However, in spite of different terminology, most seem to be in agreement on the primary therapeutic tasks that face therapists and clients: creating safety and stabilization through the management/reduction of intrusive symptoms such as flashbacks, nightmares, or extreme affective distress; exploring and voicing memories of the trauma as they are integrated into the client's view of self and the world; dealing with the often overwhelming affect that accompanies not only the memories but the process of integration; and, finally, establishing a new self–world view and relationships that are not determined (although may be informed) by traumatic experience. Art and other expressive therapies may be beneficial, either alone or in conjunction with psychotherapy. Eye movement desensitization and reprocessing (EMDR) is a treatment for victims of trauma that involves the use of therapist directed eye movements. Although current knowledge of neurobiology does not provide a definitive explanation for how or why EMDR works, a significant body of empirical data supporting its efficacy has been collected over the past decade.

The following are practical recommendations made by experienced therapists treating this population. During the initial stage of memory recovery the client may feel in crisis and needs to have an accessible therapist. As a result, it is helpful to all if the therapist is clear about availability, setting criteria for what constitutes a crisis for which she or he should be contacted, and if the therapist encourages the client to generate self-soothing strategies to try before calling. This not only addresses practical issues but is empowering to the client as it helps restore a sense of control over symptoms and is likely to decrease fear. Therapists should also be familiar with standard protocols for assessing suicidality and dangerousness, help clients to develop a cognitive framework for understanding the intensity of attachment they may feel to the therapist, assess client's current safety and identify any possible current environmental triggers of distress, and help client identify and use resources other than therapy that may be helpful both during crisis and the process of recovery. Finally, therapists with personal histories of sexual abuse must be especially careful to monitor countertransference reactions, that is, their own thoughts, feelings, attitudes, and behavior toward clients who report childhood sexual abuse or the suspicion of it.

It is imperative to gather information about, and be responsive to, potential ways in which the client's race, culture, social class, ethnicity, disability, sexual orientation, and gender may influence the long-term sequelae of trauma, the ability to receive help at the time of the abuse, the responses of others to the abuse history, and the most comfortable route to personal growth. Writings by feminist and multicultural therapists can be particularly helpful in this regard.

VI. Conclusions

As researchers and clinicians have examined memory for trauma, including recovered memories, approaches that capture the complexity of memory have emerged. Researchers have increasingly recognized that accurate, partially accurate, and inaccurate memories occur, perhaps in the same person about the same event. In turn, the field as a whole appears less likely to accept research and thinking that consider only absolutes—that is, claims that all recovered memories are necessarily true or false are increasingly viewed as too limited. Further, the field has also moved toward achieving an important balance between science and human experience. Researchers are increasingly grappling with the tension between excitement over research and the meaning of scientific data to competing theories with a recognition of the negativity that trauma represents for the individual, as well as the meaning of the abuse experience to the individual.

Future directions for research must include interdisciplinary approaches to questions about mechanisms. Empirical and theoretic work has yet to untangle important questions, such as whether traumatic memories are processed in an ordinary way or by different systems. An interdisciplinary approach that draws on cognitive, developmental, and clinical knowledge is needed to address such questions that capture the complex nature of memory. Beyond research into memory mechanisms, the field also needs to continue to examine important questions that relate to clinical interventions. Systematic study of the ways in which treatment approaches can minimize inaccurate memories, as well as harm when memories are recovered, is needed.

Gender issues in recovered memories and trauma have important implications for women and children. The focus on false positive reports that has resulted from the false memory controversy has led too many people to ignore true reports of abuse and to miss false negative reports (e.g., women who do not say they were abused when they were). The focus on false positives and failure to focus on false negatives has ramifications at multiple levels, including research, clinical work, and policy. The strong emotion spurred by allegations of sexual abuse has also seriously affected the social environment for children. As a society, there is a need to repair damage done both by those who have expressed disbelief in the overall veracity of children's reports and by those who, through their zeal, have inappropriately applied suggestive techniques that have likely increased errors in reporting abuse.

As empirical and clinical work that considers recovered memories moves forward, there is an urgent need for feminist analyses to continue to examine the politics and social forces that influence the field. Serious threats to individual scientists (e.g., lawsuits) and therapists (e.g., picketing, lawsuits, ethics complaints) and to victim/survivors must be closely examined. Threats in the social environment have the capacity to deeply affect research studies and interpretation of data. There remains a need to be vigilant and to examine carefully the data, as well as the politics behind the data, before interpreting research findings.

SUGGESTED READING

Freyd, J. J. (1996). *Betrayal Trauma: The Logic of Forgetting Childhood Abuse.* Harvard University Press, Cambridge, MA.

Freyd, J. J., and DePrince, A. P. (eds.) (in press). *Trauma and Cognitive Science: A Meeting of Minds, Science, and Human Experience.* Haworth Press, Binghampton, NY.

Herman, J. L. (1997). *Trauma and Recovery.* Basic Books, New York.

Pezdek, K., and Banks, W. P. (eds.) (1996). *The Recovered Memory/False Memory Debate.* Academic Press, San Diego, CA.

Pope, K. S., and Brown, L. S. (1996). *Recovered Memories of Abuse: Assessment, Therapy, Forensics.* American Psychological Association, Washington, DC.

Putnam, F. (1997). *Dissociation in Children and Adolescents: A Developmental Perspective.* Guilford, New York.

Rivera, M. (ed.) *Fragment by Fragment: Feminist Perspectives on Memory and Child Sexual Abuse.* Gynergy Books, Charlottetown, PEI, Canada.

Singer, J. L. (ed.) (1990). *Repression and Dissociation.* University of Chicago Press, Chicago.

Reproductive Technologies

Diane Scott-Jones
Boston College

Glossary

Artificial insemination The insemination (introduction of sperm into the uterus) of a woman with a partner's or donor's sperm.

Cloning Asexual reproduction, that is, reproduction of a somatic cell without the combining of sperm and ovum, resulting in offspring genetically identical to the parent. Cloning of a somatic cell requires an ovum and a woman's uterus for gestation.

Contraception Prevention of conception or prevention of implantation of the fertilized ovum.

Genetic engineering Micromanipulations of the reproductive process at the level of the cell and the genes within cells.

Infertility The failure to conceive after 12 months of regular unprotected intercourse or more than two consecutive spontaneous abortions or stillbirths.

In vitro fertilization Conception outside the woman's body, which involves the inducement of hyperovulation, the retrieval of ova from the woman's body, the insemination of the ova with sperm, and the reimplantation or freezing of selected high-quality embryos.

Menarche The first occurrence of menstruation.

Menopause The cessation of menstruation, usually occurring between 45 and 50 years of age.

Surrogate mother A woman who enters into a contract for the gestation of her own or another woman's fertilized ovum and for the relinquishing of her parental rights to the newborn baby.

REPRODUCTIVE TECHNOLOGIES refer to procedures and devices that allow control over reproduction. Technologies have been developed to prevent pregnancy and childbearing and also to assist conception, gestation, and birth. This article presents an overview of reproductive technologies, with a focus on their impact on human development in a historical and social context.

I. Control of Reproduction

Contemporary women can exert an enormous amount of control over reproductive processes. Current technologies allow women to prevent unplanned pregnancies and births. Technologies also are available to assist planned pregnancies and births in women who have difficulty conceiving and carrying a baby to term. Medical professionals have the technology both to limit reproduction and to assist it. Campaigns to limit reproduction are directed mainly toward developing nations and the poor within developed countries. In contrast, resources to facilitate conception, gestation, and birth in women who have difficulties are available mainly in developed countries and are accessible to the affluent within those countries. The increased involvement of medical technologies may ultimately limit women's reproductive freedom instead of allowing women generally to exercise greater control over their own reproduction.

Until the mid-1800s, midwives were the most typical assistants for childbirth. Around that time, physicians began to dominate childbirth. Midwifery gradually declined as the process of childbirth became more technological and controlled by medical professionals.

Until the recent past, bearing a child was understood to involve chance, unknown factors. In sexual reproduction, conception occurs when a sperm penetrates an ovum. When the sperm and ovum fuse, each provides one half of the 46 chromosomes of the cell formed. Each chromosome contains thousands of genes. The man and woman cannot control which of their genes and chromosomes are passed on to their offspring at conception. This lack of control in conception has been called a "genetic lottery."

Although a woman and man cannot control the genes they contribute in the process of conception, they can, with the assistance of medical technology and medical professionals, control many aspects of reproduction. These mechanisms of control are described here, beginning with techniques to prevent conception and concluding with cloning, a technique that would allow control over the genetic configuration of offspring by replicating a cell of a single person instead of combining germ cells of two persons. The expectation of control is increasing so that notions of a "normal" pregnancy and "normal" baby may be changing. Despite the extraordinary level of control over reproduction that is possible, it should be noted that many women still have unplanned pregnancies. Research indicates that the majority of pregnant women did not intend to become pregnant and the percentage of pregnant adolescents who did not intend to become pregnant is greater than the percentage for older pregnant women.

II. *Contraception and Suppression of Menstruation*

Compared to contemporary women, women in the past experienced less time during which conception was possible, because menarche began later and women breastfed their babies. The average age of menarche, or first menstrual period, was 16.5 to 17 years in the mid-19th century in European populations. In contrast, in the United States currently, the average age of menarche is 12.5 years and the lower limit of the normal range is 9 years. The current early age of menarche is due to high-calorie diets and relatively sedentary lifestyles, which lead to a high proportion of body fat, which, in turn, is the trigger for menarche. Obese persons have high concentrations of leptin, which may stimulate breast development, and insulin, which may stimulate production of sex hormones. Other factors that might play a role in early development are chemicals in the environment (from pesticides and plastics) and growth hormones in meat and milk. Few systematic data are available on the appearance of secondary sex characteristics; consequently, little is known about how different the current early appearance of secondary sex characteristics (eight years and younger) is from girls' experiences in earlier historical eras. Boys experience sexual maturation later than girls and there are few reliable data on the course of puberty in boys. Menopause occurs usually between 45 and 50 years of age; the typical age of menopause has remained relatively stable over time. After menopause, the woman no longer ovulates. [*See* MENOPAUSE; MENSTRUATION.]

In addition, fewer women breast-feed their newborns than in the past and those who do breast-feed do so for shorter periods of time. During the time of breast-feeding, a woman is less likely to conceive (lactational ammennorhea). Thus, a contemporary woman has more time during which pregnancy is possible. The biological conditions that, in the past, limited conception and childbearing during a woman's lifetime have been replaced by medical interventions that allow a woman to control conception and childbearing.

Women historically also experienced fewer menstrual periods during their lifetimes than is true for women today. Because of the later age of menarche, earlier and more frequent pregnancies, and lactational ammennorhea, women in the past did not have as many menstrual cycles. Some medical professionals question whether contemporary women's large number of menstrual cycles, with the frequent ovulation and bleeding, is healthy. New medication is now being tested that would allow women to have only four menstrual periods in one year. Women using this form of contraception would have 84 days on the contraceptive pill and one week off the pill. Some medical professionals, however, believe the shedding of the lining of the uterus during menstruation is necessary to prevent uterine or endometrial cancer. Still other medical professionals believe menstruation should be a woman's choice and are working on medication that would suppress ovulation and menstruation for most of a woman's life. These medical professionals believe that women who are now free from the burden of constant childbearing and lactating also want to eliminate frequent menstrual cycles and should be able to do so.

Contraceptive technologies, by definition, prevent conception. Some of these techniques also prevent implantation, if conception occurs. Women have used oral contraceptives since the early 1960s. Oral contraceptives ("the pill") typically combine estrogens and progesterones. Estrogens block ovulation, speed the passage of the ovum through the reproductive tract, alter the uterine environment to prevent implantation, and aid destruction of the corpus luteum. Progesterone inhibits the movement of sperm, slows the passage of the ovum, inhibits the sperm's penetration of the ovum, and prevents implantation. Women take oral contraceptives for 21 days, beginning on day 7 of the menstrual cycle. The woman then stops taking the oral contraceptive for 7 days, which simulates the average menstrual cycle of 28 days. The use of oral contraceptives is associated with some relatively mild side effects and other more serious but less frequent side effects. Initially, oral contraceptives contained high dosages of estrogen, which put women at risk for cardiovascular disease and some cancers, but the early versions were replaced with pills with lower amounts of estrogen or with estrogen-progesterone combinations.

Progesterone can be injected at three-month intervals (medroxyprogesterone or Depo Provera) or implanted surgically under a woman's skin (Norplant) for five years of contraception. Depo Provera and Norplant reduce the memory burden of taking pills on a schedule and are separated in time from sexual intercourse. A combination of estrogen and progesterone can be taken following intercourse ("morning-after pill") to reduce the likelihood of pregnancy.

Barrier methods of contraception include condoms, spermicides, diaphragms, and intrauterine devices. Condoms also prevent sexually transmitted diseases such as HIV and herpes. Condoms have few side effects but have a somewhat higher failure rate, approximately 2%, than oral contraceptives and injected/implanted contraceptives. Effectiveness of condoms depends on proper use. "Female condoms" are available, which are inserted into the vagina in contrast to those that are pulled over the penis. Chemical barriers, or spermicides, also prevent pregnancy by preventing sperm from entering the uterus. Spermicides have a relatively high failure rate unless combined with a barrier method.

A diaphragm is a rubber dome that covers the cervix and holds a spermicide at the opening to the uterus. The cervical cap and the single-use sponge are similar to the diaphragm.

The intrauterine device (IUD) is inserted into the uterus and it likely inhibits sperm and prevents implantation, although the mechanism by which the IUD works is not known. IUDs are painful to insert but are inexpensive because they can remain in place for several years. IUDs were associated with increased infection in the 1970s, causing many manufacturers to stop selling them in the United States and to market them instead in developing countries.

Many persons consider the rhythm method and coitus interruptus to be "natural" contraceptives because these do not involve a drug or device. If the woman's menstrual cycle is regular, it is possible to predict, from body temperature or cervical mucus, when ovulation will occur and to begin to abstain from sexual intercourse 4 days prior to and 3 days after ovulation. For example, if ovulation occurs on the 15th day of the cycle, abstaining from the 11th to the 18th day of the cycle should prevent conception. Coitus interruptus, the withdrawal of the penis before ejaculation, is used as a contraceptive method but has a high failure rate of 20%.

Most contraceptive techniques have focused on the woman's role in reproduction and not on the male role. Researchers are studying possible male contraceptives such as thermal methods and ultrasound that would inhibit production of sperm or damage sperm but none of these methods is in use.

An issue related to contraceptive use is whether adolescents should have access to contraceptives. Some concerns are related to the health and safety of adolescents, who may not know of their family medical history, which should be considered in prescribing contraceptives. Other concerns are related to the possibility that access to contraception may signal approval of adolescent sexual activity.

As effective contraception became widely available and widely used, many women delayed childbearing and some women delayed until they were close to the end of their reproductive years. Of the women who delayed childbearing, many found they needed the assistance of medical professionals to conceive and carry a child to term. Extraordinary technologies have been developed to assist reproduction.

III. *Pregnancy Monitoring*

Technology allows medical professionals to monitor the development of the fetus in the mother's uterus. The value of this monitoring or prenatal screening has been questioned. Parents, however, have a great deal of information about the developing child and often know information such as whether the child will be a boy or girl. Typically, prenatal testing through amniocentesis and chorionic villus sampling has been restricted to older women at risk for Down syndrome and to women whose offspring are at risk, because of family or personal history, for some specific genetic condition that can be diagnosed. In industrialized countries, the most common reason for pregnancy monitoring and screening is maternal age over 35 years. Ultrasound, in contrast, has become a routine component of prenatal medical care.

Because technological advances allow the diagnosis of severe disorders, parents are sometimes faced with the dilemma of choosing whether to abort the abnormal fetus, attempt some medical intervention *in utero,* or give birth to the fetus with the disorder. The decision is so difficult that some hospitals require the parents to talk with ethicists before choosing risky in utero surgery. Fetal monitoring has advanced from diagnosis to the possibility of treatment for the unborn child. Fetal surgery remains so risky that critics label it experimentation; there is little hard scientific evidence that fetal surgery will help in specific cases. Traditional experiments raise other difficult issues; one-half of parents participating would need to agree to the possibility of remaining in a control group and foregoing surgery that might save or dramatically improve their children's lives.

Amniocentesis is a technique in which a needle is inserted through the mother's abdomen to the amniotic sac and is used to withdraw amniotic fluid. It was first used in the late 1920s, to identify Rh blood type incompatibility between mother and fetus so the newborn could be given a complete blood transfusion immediately after birth. For this purpose, doctors conducted amniocentesis in the last trimester of pregnancy. Presently, doctors can use fetal cells from amniotic fluid to diagnose genetic or chromosomal abnormalities. For these purposes, doctors perform amniocentesis in the second trimester.

Ultrasound is doctors' use of low-frequency sound waves to create visual images, or sonograms, of the fetus and the placenta. This technique allows the identification of twins, the identification of the sex of the fetus, and the identification of malformations.

Chorionic villus sampling is a technique in which a needle is inserted through the mother's abdomen or cervix to the point at which the fetus is implanted into the wall of the uterus. Tissue is removed from the chorion, which is the outer membrane of the embryo and is attached to the wall of the uterus by villi. The placenta is formed from the chorion. The tissue that is removed can be used for genetic and chromosomal tests. Chorionic villus sampling can occur in the seventh week of pregnancy, which is prior to the formation of the amniotic fluid required for amniocentesis. Chorionic villus sampling results in fetal blood cells entering the mother's bloodstream. Chorionic villus sampling involves risks to the fetus, especially in older mothers, greater than for amniocentesis.

In some states, expectant mothers routinely get a maternal serum alpha-fetoprotein analysis. This technique involves the withdrawal of a blood sample from the mother, which is analyzed for the presence of alpha-fetoprotein. This test is used as a screening for mothers whose offspring have a high risk for Down syndrome or neural tube defects.

A screening technology under development is BABI—blastocyst analysis before implantation. This technique, which is already used in connection with infertility treatment, involves removing the very early embryo from the mother, testing the embryo, and reimplanting the embryo if it is normal.

Because knowledge of the sex of a child prior to birth is common, one can consider whether sex preference will be exercised in a manner that places girls at risk. In the past, a preference for males and the elimination of unwanted females has been a problem in many countries. With selective abortion following genetic screening, parents can choose whether to have a girl or boy. Notions of "family completion" (e.g., having one girl and one boy) may lead parents to choose to abort the undesired sex.

Some have argued that prenatal testing decreases,

rather than increases, a woman's control over reproduction and shifts control to medical professionals. Genetic screening is seen by others as a responsibility of parents. With prenatal screening, decisions about which children will be born can be based on genetic, physical, or chromosomal analyses. An element of eugenics may be implicit in the pregnancy monitoring techniques that are used and that are being developed. Prenatal testing may promote not just healthy children, but an unattainable goal of perfect children. The emphasis on the genetic bases of disease, and on the individual woman's responsibility to prevent the birth of children with disorders, shifts attention from the social and economic bases of children's problems. Inequities in access to health care, and the unequal distribution of wealth underlying it, are more likely than genetic disorders to diminish children's life chances.

IV. Infertility Treatments

Infertility treatment is relatively recent. The cause of infertility is not known in most cases. Environmental pollutants and toxins may contribute to infertility. Women who delay childbearing until near the end of the reproductive years have more problems with fertility than do younger women. The treatment of infertility, however, is usually aimed toward the individual case, with less attention to remedying possible environmental causes and almost no attention to mechanisms (e.g., parental leave and child care) that might help women with childbearing and childrearing earlier in their reproductive lives.

Approximately 16% of couples seek medical help for infertility. In approximately 25 to 40% of couples reporting difficulties conceiving a child, the problem is due to a condition of the male. In the past, females were assumed to be responsible for infertility. The most common infertility problem in men is low sperm count (oligospermia) and in women is failure to ovulate. Medical professionals now believe that high sperm count alone is not an indication of normal fertilizing capacity. Unless the sperm count is extremely diminished, it is not a good indicator of infertility. When there is low sperm count, doctors can use artificial insemination of the sperm or sperm injection. With these techniques, the male will still be the biological father of the child. Male infertility can be treated by laboratory procedures that involve the concentration of sperm followed by insemination. Other laboratory techniques include removing white blood cells or other substances from the semen or techniques to enhance the motility of the sperm.

A man and woman can time intercourse to maximize the likelihood of conception. Body temperature and cervical mucus are associated with ovulation. Conception is most likely to occur if sperm, which can remain viable for two to three days, are in the reproductive tract when ovulation occurs. The ovum remains viable for approximately 24 hours. [*See* PREGNANCY.]

Fertility drugs are used to increase ovulation in women. The increased ovulation, or hyperovulation, increases the likelihood of multiple births because the number of ova that develop cannot be controlled. Without fertility drugs, the incidence of multiple pregnancy is less than 2%; with fertility drugs to stimulate ovulation, the multiple pregnancy rate is 8 to 43%. Multiple births may be premature births; consequently, infertility treatment is associated with a high rate of perinatal mortality (2 to 3 times the expected rate) and neurological disorders. Multiple births lead to greater demands on parents' financial, social, and personal resources. Further, some studies have found a relationship between fertility drugs and increased incidence of ovarian and breast cancer.

V. Artificial Insemination

Artificial insemination is the insemination of a woman with sperm from a partner or donor. The technology of artificial insemination began quite simply. The sperm of the male partner, husband, or donor was placed in the uterus at the time of a fertile woman's ovulation. A woman could inseminate herself without medical supervision. Couples could collect the sperm themselves and place it in the woman's uterus on the day she ovulated. Artificial insemination has developed to include hyperovulation, from hyperstimulation of the ovaries with fertility drugs, as a preliminary procedure and microimplantation of the sperm into the ovum.

Artificial insemination raises many issues such as the sense of shame that may accompany male fertility problems, the responsibilities and rights of the male donor, and the rights of children created through donor insemination to know their genetic father. In the case of donor insemination, typically the donor's identity is not known and the donor is not held legally responsible for the offspring. In the past, this anonymity was considered desirable. Now, as adopted children seek to know their biological parents, it is more difficult to justify the secrecy regarding sperm donors. Donor insemination raises many more difficult issues regarding family relations than does insemination with a husband's or partner's sperm. Although the social father is not biologically related to the child created through donor insemination, the social father appears to develop father–child relationships in the same manner as biological fathers. Another issue is whether the donor's wife (if the donor is married) accepts the possibility that her husband may be the biological father of children that will not be known to her and raised by others who will not be known to her and her husband.

Today, sperm donors are tested for HIV and screened for genetic problems. The donated sperm is frozen for six months before use. Many donors are rejected by sperm banks. What criteria do physicians use to select donors and pair them with recipients? Eugenics may affect these criteria. Sperm donors are sometimes medical students or members of the doctors' personal networks. In some countries, such as France, sperm donors cannot accept payment, so that sperm donation can be thought of as altruistic. Studies in the United States find that two-thirds of sperm donors would not have donated without a payment. Efforts are made to maintain records on donors to prevent the overuse or inappropriate use of a donor.

Artificial insemination with a donor's sperm is used when the woman's partner has an untreatable fertility problem or has had a vasectomy. Donor insemination is also used for women who wish to become pregnant but do not have male partners. This use of donor insemination is not treatment for infertility but is a social arrangement. The woman who bears the child and her partner who helps to raise the child may know little or nothing about the identity of the child's biological father. The child may not know about the donor insemination and may mistakenly think the nurturing father, if there is one, is also the biological father. If the child does know donor insemination occurred, the child may know little or nothing of the identity of the biological father. The donor may never know if he has biological children, how many, or where the children are. This uncertainty about biological relationships is somewhat like that in adoption.

Another use of artificial insemination, which also amounts to a social arrangement and not a treatment for infertility, occurs when the sperm of a dead or dying man are frozen or cryopreserved so his wife or partner can produce his baby after his death.

Women are sometimes motivated to create a child in this manner when the man dies accidentally or from disease. In one California case, a man contemplating suicide left his sperm in a sperm bank to be used by his partner of five years. After his suicide, the sperm bank refused to give the sperm to the partner because they had not received the proper document prior to the death. The dead man's will left his estate, including his stored sperm, to his partner but the will was contested by two adult children from the dead man's previous marriage. In his suicide note to his partner and to his adult children, the dead man said of his "posthumous offspring. . . . I have loved you in my dreams, even though I never got to see you born." This case raised the unresolved issues of whether sperm can be treated as property, to be willed to heirs, and whether it is ethical for a person to attempt to create a child after death.

In addition to artificial insemination involving donor sperm, the procedure has been used in which a woman is donating ova and providing her uterus for gestation—so-called surrogate mothers. A woman may enter a contract to be inseminated with the sperm of a man to whom she has no social relationship, to carry the baby to term, and to relinquish the baby at birth to the "commissioning" parent. The multiple relationships that are possible with artificial insemination involving donor ova or donor sperm have resulted in cases of contested parenthood—a surrogate mother wants to keep the child or a semen donor claims parental rights. The male role in donating sperm is less involved than is the role of the woman who provides her uterus for the nine-month gestation period and must give the baby away immediately after birth. In contested surrogate cases, a legal determination is made regarding maternal rights, as in the "Baby M" case. In the United States, Mary Beth Whitehead agreed to artificial insemination by William Stern and carried to term in 1987 a baby who became known as "Baby M." Despite her contractual arrangement to give Baby M to Stern, Whitehead decided to keep the baby and a legal fight ensued. Custody of Baby M was granted to Stern, the commissioning father, who was also the biological father, and the decision was upheld on appeal. In their decisions, judges claimed to be acting in the best interests of the child, Baby M. Judges compared Whitehead and her husband, who were working class, financially insecure, and had little education, to Stern and his wife, who were middle class, affluent, and well educated. Judges believed the Sterns, and not the Whiteheads, were well suited to be parents, despite Elizabeth Stern's multiple sclerosis, which had led her to decide not to become pregnant. Whitehead was granted visitation rights, but not custody. Because the surrogate mother will in most instances be less affluent and less powerful than the commissioning parent, comparisons such as those that were the foundation for the judges' decisions will favor the commissioning parent.

In another case, neither the surrogate mother nor the commissioning parents wanted a baby born with microcephaly. Ultimately, the surrogate mother and her husband accepted the baby, after it was demonstrated that the husband, and not the commissioning father, was actually the biological father.

Some have argued, in the United States and other countries, that surrogacy contracts are and should be unenforceable because current laws prohibit baby selling. In many states in the United States, the birth mother is, by law, the legal mother of the child. A genetic mother who is not also the birth mother must then adopt the child.

The first report of pregnancy resulting from the insertion of ova and sperm directly into the woman's uterus, through the cervix, was reported in 1982 in the British journal *Lancet*. This technique of assisted conception involved *in vivo* fertilization and was more acceptable to those who believed *in vitro* fertilization was morally wrong. In a technique called gamete intrafallopian transfer (GIFT), semen and ova are taken from the man and woman and returned together to the woman's fallopian tubes. The sperm and ova are kept separate in the catheter used to return them to the fallopian tubes, so that *in vitro* fertilization cannot occur. *In vivo* fertilization thus can occur with the GIFT procedure. Dangers of this procedure include the possibility of ectopic pregnancies, or pregnancies outside the woman's uterus, and of multiple pregnancies. The GIFT procedure, as the acronym suggests, can be used with donor sperm, donor ova, or both.

VI. *In Vitro* Fertilization

Louise Joy Brown, born in 1978, was the first "testtube" baby—born from *in vitro* fertilization or conception outside a woman's body. Robert Edwards, a geneticist, and Patrick Steptoe, an obstetrician and gynecologist, worked on procedures for *in vitro* fertilization for 10 years before their procedures resulted in the birth of Louise Brown. The background research on the maturation of human ova was conducted with ova retrieved from women following hysterectomies or the surgical removal of ovaries. Research on other species also provided data on the maturation of ova.

Currently, *in vitro* fertilization involves the inducement of hyperovulation, the retrieval of ova from the woman's body, the insemination of the ova with sperm, and the implantation (or freezing, which is also called cryopreservation) of selected highquality embryos back into the woman's uterus. Instead of relying on naturally occurring ovulation (an ovum released each month), medical professionals use drugs to stimulate the production of ova so that more ova are retrieved and fertilized and more embryos are implanted. With hyperovulation instead of natural ovulation, the pregnancy rate is higher with a single attempt at *in vitro* fertilization.

To retrieve the ova from the woman's body, doctors use a needle, guided by ultrasound and attached to a suction apparatus, to extract fluid from the ovarian follicles. The fluid contains ova. The retrieved ova, now outside the woman's body, are placed in a culture with sperm. The fertilization rate is approximately 70%. After fertilization occurs, two pronuclei are present in the fertilized ovum. Of the fertilized ova, 85% will undergo cell division. The *in vitro* growth rate is the same as it is for *in vivo* fertilization—one division every day after fertilization for approximately six days. The rate of cell division and the regularity of morphology of the embryo are criteria used to select embryos for implantation (or freezing). Multiple embryos are returned to the mother's uterus, which increases the incidence of multiple births in addition to increasing the pregnancy rate. The embryos typically are returned to the mother's uterus at the two- to four-cell stage, which is approximately four days after the retrieval of the ova. In some instances, the embryos are returned earlier or later. Pregnancy is confirmed by the use of ultrasound to obtain a visual image of the embryo.

In vitro fertilization can be used to assist couples or individuals who cannot conceive a child through sexual intercourse. For male infertility, the sperm that do not result in fertilization through sexual intercourse can be enhanced *in vitro* so the sperm can fertilize ova *in vitro*. Some enhancement techniques involve refrigeration in solutions. In addition, sperm that are viable but immobile can be injected directly into the ova (intracytoplasmic sperm injection).

Women who are older and near menopause have difficulty with *in vitro* fertilization. As women age, the quality of ova and the functioning of the uterus decline. Ova appear not to be successfully cryopreserved, or frozen, although sperm and embryos are routinely frozen and used for *in vitro* fertilization. Ova may be donated from one woman to another. The first birth of a child from a donated ovum occurred in Australia in 1984.

With *in vitro* fertilization, genetic diagnoses can be conducted prior to implantation ("reprogenetics," the combination of reproductive and genetic technologies). The sex of the child can be known, and the possibility exists that parents will show a preference for male children over female children. Selecting the child's sex prior to implantation may be more acceptable than selectively aborting female children. Although prospective parents may simply wish to balance the number of girls and boys in their own families, historically societies have favored male offspring over female offspring when there was a preference. Proponents of limiting family size may claim that allowing parents to choose whether to have a girl or boy would prevent parents from having more children in hopes of having a child of the desired sex. In addition, females who might pass on sex-linked disorders to male children might want to choose to implant only female embryos.

In addition to the possibility of an overall preference for male children in decisions regarding which embryos are implanted, there is also the possibility of eugenics in the genetic diagnoses that precede implantation. With *in vitro* fertilization, doctors can use genetic tests to allow parents to select embryos free of genes for diseases the parents have or carry. Medical professionals can prevent the implantation of embryos known to carry genes for a specific disease or might be able to alter genes to prevent the disease. With preimplantation genetic diagnosis, women who are not affected by infertility problems use *in vitro* fertilization to "improve" the offspring they produce. The safety and efficacy of preimplantation genetic diagnosis has not been demonstrated.

This use of genetic technology for the prevention of disease may be a "backdoor" to the acceptance of programs of eugenics, in which medical professionals attempt to determine the genetic characteristics of children. Issues of access to the technology arise as well as concern for future generations if there are unanticipated effects of genetically eliminating particular characteristics from the population. The findings of behavioral genetics studies might be misused in efforts to eliminate aggression or to enhance intelligence. Currently, genetic manipulation of somatic or body cells is more acceptable than genetic manipulations that would affect the germline and subsequent generations.

Some of the issues raised by genetic diagnosis prior to implantation are the same as the issues that accompany the prenatal diagnosis made possible by amniocentesis and chorionic villus sampling. Some of the issues specific to the preimplantation diagnosis that can be used with *in vitro* fertilization are that 25 to 50% of the four- to eight-cell zygotes will not survive the procedure. This can present a problem if only a small number of embryos is available. The tests occur outside the woman's body, and so are not as invasive to the woman as are the prenatal tests she would experience. The long-term effects on children born after preimplantation diagnosis are not known. Also, the diagnoses are not very accurate and result in a relatively high number of false negatives. The diagnoses are not of the complete genetic makeup of the developing organism but are limited to disorders such as the chromosomal abnormality leading to Down syndrome and the genetic defects linked to cystic fibrosis and Tay-Sachs syndrome. The sex of the child can be determined so that female embryos can be selected for implantation, if there is the possibility of sex-linked disorders that affect males. Some other diagnoses are not possible until later in prenatal development, after the embryo has been implanted, so the woman would still need to undergo the other, typical tests such as amniocentesis. Issues of consent can arise when there are sperm donors, ova donors, or surrogate gestational mothers, in addition to "nurturing" or "commissioning" parents.

Parents can use *in vitro* fertilization to create children whose characteristics will meet the medical needs of their other children. Genetic tests allow parents to select babies with specific characteristics to serve as tissue donors. Parents of a six-year-old with a blood disease (Fanconi anemia, which often leads to leukemia) created several embryos via *in vitro* fertilization. Doctors allowed the embryos to grow to the eight-cell stage and conducted preimplantation genetic tests. Tests indicated that the tissues of only one embryo matched that of the sick six-year-old. The embryo with the matching tissue was implanted in the mother's uterus, carried to term, and was born in August 2000. Blood cells from the new baby's umbilical cord and placenta, which would have been discarded, were used to give the sick sister a transfusion. The umbilical cord blood contains stem cells and should create a new supply of blood. If the sister later needs additional stem cells, doctors plan to take them from the newborn's bone marrow. Although ethicists question whether babies should be conceived for another's medical needs, some ethicists point out that our society does not assess and rule out the reasons any parent chooses to have children. Cases have occurred in which parents of a child who had an unmet medical need (e.g., bone marrow) conceived another child, without assisted reproduction, to meet that need, even though they acknowledged that they did not want another child except for the needs of the existing child. The difference is that *in vitro* fertilization allows some precision in selecting the characteristics of the child to be born.

With new technologies, women's roles in reproduction can be as uncertain as men's roles. In the past, only men had any uncertainty regarding whether they actually were the parent of a particular child. Now, with various technologies, a woman may bear a child yet not be certain that she is the genetic mother of the child. Embryos can be mixed up when doctors implant the embryos in the woman's uterus.

Further, with new reproductive technologies, the everyday understanding of parenting and family relationships changes. The woman's role in reproduction can be divided into three kinds of "mothers": the genetic mother, the gestational (or carrying) mother, and the nurturing mother. The man's role can be divided into the genetic father and the nurturing father. The "surrogate" mother can be a genetic surrogate when she provides the ovum or a gestational surrogate when she carries the embryo to term for the commissioning parents. The ovum donor faces the invasive procedures of hyperovulation and retrieval of the ova. These divisions in the contributions of "mothers" and "fathers" also challenge the legal definitions of mother and father. Who is the legal mother, with legal rights and legal responsibilities to the child? Who is the legal father of the child? In some countries, the birth mother is the legal mother, regardless of the source of the ovum or embryo.

Other questions can be raised regarding the motivation of persons seeking *in vitro* fertilization. Should persons seeking parenthood through this and other techniques of assisted reproduction be subject to screening criteria not applied to persons who conceive children through sexual intercourse? The decisions made in the United States and other countries may reflect ideologies of "normal" or even "ideal" family life.

A woman who participates in *in vitro* fertilization may feel anxious or depressed, even when she is not the cause of the infertility. Couples also may experience negative emotions, especially when the *in vitro* fertilization attempt is not successful. Couples may need to make difficult decisions such as how long to continue to try *in vitro* fertilization, how much money to spend on the procedures, whether to turn to adoption instead of trying to create offspring who have biological ties to the parents.

Techniques are available to allow postmenopausal women to bear children. Women who delay pregnancy during their reproductive years may bear genetically unrelated children created through *in vitro* fertilization from donor ova. Hormonal treatment is necessary to enable implantation and gestation in the uterus of postmenopausal women. It is not known at what age a woman's uterus can no longer provide the environment to support embryo implantation. From the successes so far, it is clear that women who no longer ovulate can still provide the gestation of the embryo. Studies suggest that the aging of ova, not the age of the uterus, interferes with fertility. Some researchers have suggested that implantation occurs more easily in postmenopausal women than in younger women undergoing *in vitro* fertilization. The oldest reported mother is an Italian woman said to be 62 years of age when she gave birth to a son. The average life span of women has increased in developed countries in the recent past, although the average age of menopause has remained fairly constant. Although an older mother may live to see her child reach adulthood, she is likely to experience chronic illnesses, especially after age 50 years. The average life span of men is shorter than that of women; therefore, older fathers, on average, are less likely than older mothers to see their offspring reach adulthood. Because of the likelihood that they may become ill, lack the stamina to be active parents during the child's adolescence, or die before the child reaches adulthood, postmenopausal childbearing raises more concerns for births to 60-year-old parents than those to 45- to 50-year-old parents. With older parents, childrearing help from extended family and paid caregivers may be necessary. In France, postmenopausal pregnancies are prohibited in fertility clinics and, in other developed countries, many fertility clinics decline to provide *in vitro* fertilization for older mothers. Preventing multiple pregnancies, which will reduce the likelihood of premature birth, is one way physicians can reduce the physical risks to offspring and postmenopausal mothers.

Little is known about the impact on children of

the new reproductive technologies. Infertility procedures have been available since 1978 and have a low success rate (90 to 95% of women undergoing *in vitro* fertilization are not successful in having babies), so there may be relatively few children born in this manner. The few studies to date suggest that children conceived through *in vitro* fertilization experience as good or better physical development, compared to other children, and do not have a higher rate of birth defects. Because of the high percentage of multiple births, infants are likely to be low-birth-weight and to be born prematurely. Studies suggest children born from *in vitro* fertilization have more behavioral and emotional problems than other children. Cognitive development is at least normal. Some of the outcomes in children born from *in vitro* fertilization may be associated with the high socioeconomic status of the parents or the parents' strong desire to have a child. Although some models of counseling focus on individuals or couples in addressing infertility, others emphasize social relationships such as those with future offspring and with extended family members. Some argue for a strong emphasis on social policy because of the social consequences of conceiving and giving birth to children whose needs and rights society must protect.

Many children and extended family members do not know the details of the use of assisted reproductive techniques. Many questions can be raised regarding children's rights to know their origins. Should children know the details of the assisted reproduction techniques that resulted in their birth? Should children know the identity of donors of ova and sperm? Should children have full information about their genetic origins, for their own sense of identity and for medical purposes? Does the donor have a right to privacy that supersedes the right of the child to information about his or her origins? In most countries, donor identity is protected. In England, the child can be given nonidentifying information about the donor. In the Netherlands, recommendations have been made that would allow donors to consent to be identified in the future. As these children become adults, they may press for more information about themselves.

Other family members also may be affected. What are the impacts on siblings? What happens to a "surrogate" mother's children, who may be aware that their mother is giving the newborn in their family to another mother and father? The siblings may worry that they themselves might be "sold" or given to another set of parents. Further, what happens to

children if they learn they were created through assisted reproduction and that they, but not their potential siblings, were allowed to live? Little research is available to guide discussion of these important issues.

The multiple relationships that are possible with *in vitro* fertilization have resulted in cases of contested parenthood—a surrogate mother wants to keep the child or a semen donor claims parental rights. The male role in donating sperm is less involved than is the role of the woman who provides her uterus for the nine-month gestation period and must give the baby away immediately after birth. In contested surrogate cases, a legal determination is made regarding maternal rights. In addition to the Baby M case described in an earlier section, other instances of legal difficulties have occurred with surrogate arrangements. In the United States, a three-party custody battle occurred when a surrogate mother wanted to keep the baby after she learned that the commissioning father, who was also the biological father, was divorcing his wife.

Although in most states, the birth mother is the legal mother, in specific cases, judges may ignore existing law and rule in favor of genetic parents and against the gestational or birth mothers. In a 1990 California case, judges ruled against an African American surrogate mother, who was on welfare and wanted to keep the child she bore for a Caucasian couple, and did not grant her any custody or visitation rights. The judges granted custody to the genetic parents—the man and woman who provided the ovum and sperm.

With surrogate mothers, the possibility exists for the exploitation of women who assume the risks of pregnancy and childbirth for other women who have the resources to hire surrogates. A U.S. survey conducted in the late 1980s indicated that most surrogate mothers were Caucasian with low education levels and low incomes. In some cases, however, the surrogate mother is a relative of the woman who intends to be the nurturing mother; a sister or mother performs the surrogate role and the distress at relinquishing the child may be less because of the expectation that the surrogate will continue to have a relationship with the child.

The creation of more embryos than needed for one birth leads to a surplus of embryos that could be made available, not just for infertility treatment, but for genetic research and genetic engineering. With new techniques that may allow the freezing or cryopreservation of immature ova and the maturation of ova *in vitro*, scientists may bypass the ethical concerns of conducting research on human embryos.

In vitro maturation could be used on ova retrieved from aborted fetuses and from cadavers. This raises the possibility of children whose "mother" would be a dead female or a female that was never born. Who should consent to the donation of the fetal tissue or tissue from a cadaver to researchers or clinicians? Should women undergoing abortion be permitted to donate or sell the fetal ovarian tissue? Women might be encouraged to delay abortion until later in their pregnancy, so as to produce the most useful fetal tissue. Should the genetic father of the fetus consent to the use of the ovaries of a fetus? Difficult issues arise regarding circumstances under which women or girls should be permitted to donate their ova, such as the ethics of paying for ova and the ethics of parental consent for girls' donation of ova while they are living or in the case of death.

Another possible application of the cryopreservation of immature ova and subsequent *in vitro* maturation is that women could delay childbearing until after menopause, using their own preserved ova to produce a child. With the current trend toward delayed childbearing among affluent, well-educated women, the social timetable for childbearing may be retirement following a career—a time when previously women would have become grandmothers.

In 1990, the World Health Organization held a meeting on *in vitro* fertilization. Among the recommendations from that meeting were that governments should consider limiting the number of treatments per woman, the conditions indicating a need for *in vitro* fertilization, and the age (40 years or less) at which a woman could undergo *in vitro* fertilization. Governments were also urged to gather data on and monitor the equity and ethical aspects, as well as the effectiveness and costs, of fertility clinics, and to make the data public. The report recommended that fertility clinics be required to distinguish clearly between research activities and treatment geared to the individual client.

VII. Human Cloning

Reproduction is said to be the only body function for which the person carries only half of what is necessary and must seek the other half. With nuclear transfer cloning, this statement may no longer be true.

The type of cloning that has been used with humans is performed by splitting an embryo. This form of cloning was first used with human embryos in 1993, by Jerry Hall and Robert Stillman. Embryos at the two- to eight-cell stage were split into two identical cell masses, which created "twins." One possible application of creating an identical twin or clone of an embryo would be to perform tests on the cloned embryo that might damage the original embryo to be implanted.

Ian Wilmut of Scotland was first to clone an adult mammal (a female sheep), through nuclear transfer, which was reported in 1997 in the journal *Nature*. In this procedure, the researcher removes the nucleus from an unfertilized ovum and replaces it with the nucleus from a somatic (body) cell of the adult that will be cloned. A small electrical impulse is used to fuse the enucleated ovum and the somatic cell, and the fused cell begins to develop in the same manner as a fertilized ovum. In the research that produced the first cloned sheep, 277 fused cells were created. Of these fusions, 29 developed to the early-embryo stage and only one live birth resulted. The purpose of cloning sheep was to develop procedures for producing pharmaceuticals such as insulin to treat human diseases. Through genetic engineering, scientists plan to clone sheep carrying a human gene for insulin engineered to be expressed in mammary glands and to create sheep whose milk would contain human insulin. Nuclear transfer cloning holds the prospect of studying and treating other diseases in addition to diabetes.

Clones might be thought of as "delayed twins." Twins would be more like each other than would clones because twins, unlike clones, share the prenatal environment and often are raised in the same family environment. In addition, a clone would have mitochondria from the donor egg and not from the donor nucleus of the original organism.

Will there be interest in cloning humans? Some discussion has centered around the possibility of cloning an ill child to provide donor organs for transplant. Objections have been raised regarding the possibility of treating children as mere commodities. Other objections are that the cloned child might feel less an individual. This possibility, it seems, would be at least as likely, if not more likely, for twins. Twins are the same age and a cloned child would differ in age from the original child. Still other questions have been raised about parents' and cloned siblings expectations of one another. Because cloning falls far outside our ordinary notions of kinship, problems would occur in designating kinship labels such as "mother," "father," "brother," and "sister." Currently, the strongest objection to human cloning is safety. Cloning is not known to be a safe procedure for human reproduction.

Cloning is asexual reproduction. The male of the species is not necessary. A male could not clone himself without acquiring an egg and the use of a uterus from a woman. Some biologists believe that ectogenesis, gestation outside a woman's uterus, will be possible in the future. That belief is based on the current technology of *in vitro* fertilization and on the successful care of premature babies. The need for ectogenesis is claimed to be the treatment of infertility without engaging a surrogate mother and the saving of aborted fetuses. The projected cost of ectogenesis would be enormous—comparable to the costs of intensive care for premature newborns.

England recently legalized research on human cloning. Some proponents of human cloning predict that cloning will become as common as *in vitro* fertilization.

Given advances in knowledge about the human genome, would parents be motivated to manipulate genes to create a child with special characteristics? Will parents in the future be able to choose the genetic makeup of their children? Will there be "standard" children who will be cloned and raised by genetically unrelated parents? Will parents and society in general prefer that children's genetic makeup be selected instead of left to the chance outcomes of ordinary reproduction? At least part of the objection to human cloning is the concern that genetic engineering might precede cloning. In addition, because cloning can occur with only one donor cell, persons might be cloned without their knowledge.

The amount of control envisioned with human cloning may be exaggerated. The cloned child would still grow up from infancy in a particular environment that would not be identical to the environment of the adult who contributed the cells from cloning. Thus, the environment, including the prenatal environment, would lead to some differences between the cloned child and the parent.

VIII. *Conclusions*

Advances in reproductive technologies to assist conception are available to affluent individuals in developed countries. These technologies are not available in developing countries or to the poor in developed countries. The techniques are expensive and insurance coverage is not available because the "treatment" is provided to healthy individuals who do not have a recognized illness. New technologies have not improved overall health of mothers and offspring in developed countries. Countries that provide basic prenatal care to all, without advanced technologies, have lower maternal and infant mortality rates than the United States, where advanced reproductive technologies to assist conception and childbirth are available to some. Ultimately, advanced reproductive technologies may disadvantage low-income women, who may provide reproductive services to more affluent women.

An unanswered question is whether reproductive technologies actually result in women having more control over their reproductive lives and related aspects of their lives. With the involvement of medical technologies, the process of conceiving and bearing a child may require a woman to surrender her independence to the doctors. Further, the risk of assisted conception techniques is born by women, even when men have infertility problems; the techniques to assist conception almost always involve some manipulation or invasion of the female's body. Some techniques are so new that they might be considered clinical experimentation instead of treatment. Women also may bear a disproportionate share of the psychological or psychosocial problems that accompany infertility. The new techniques for assisted reproduction may result in more stress for individuals and couples who have difficulty conceiving a child.

An additional concern is the combining of new developments in genetics with the assisted reproduction technologies. Medical professionals can assess and manipulate the genetic material of the embryo in ways that were not possible before *in vitro* fertilization. A creeping acceptance of eugenics may accompany the widespread use of assisted reproduction. Genetic engineering may be defined as in the public interest and the boundaries of science may be expanded to support political decisions about the worth of individuals or categories of individuals.

The relationship of assisted reproduction techniques to adoption should be considered. Some couples may pursue adoption simultaneously with their seeking medical help with infertility. The desire to raise and nurture children might be met through adoption, if there were less emphasis on the pursuit of a genetic relationship to children and more emphasis on the importance of the parents' contribution to the child's rearing environment. Given the high cost of assisted reproduction, the question must be raised whether market forces are creating the desire for these reproductive services among the wealthy. Further, long-term effects of assisted reproduction techniques on the children are not known.

Clearly, sexual intercourse, conception, gestation and birth, and childrearing can be completely separate and independent parts of reproduction. The laws surrounding such issues are not clear-cut and may be conflicting. The most relevant bodies of law are laws that prohibit baby selling, laws that govern adoption, and general contract laws.

Despite the novelty of and interest in techniques to assist conception and gestation, it can be argued that the more pressing needs in reproductive technologies for women around the world are the prevention of unplanned pregnancies and effective prenatal care when pregnancies occur. Related social needs are child care, parental leave, and other resources that would help a wide range of women and men to raise children successfully.

SUGGESTED READING

Alpern, K. D. (ed.) (1992). *The Ethics of Reproductive Technology.* Oxford University Press, Oxford/New York.

Blank, R., and Merrick, J. C. (1995). *Human Reproduction, Emerging Technologies, and Conflicting Rights.* Congressional Quarterly Press, Washington, DC.

Burfoot, A. (ed.) (1999). *Encyclopedia of Reproductive Technologies.* Westview Press, Boulder, CO.

Duster, T. (1990). *Backdoor to Eugenics.* Routledge, New York.

Edwards, R., and Steptoe, P. (1980). *A Matter of Life.* Hutchinson, London.

Harris, J., and Holm, S. (1998). *The Future of Human Reproduction: Ethics, Choice, and Regulation.* Oxford University Press, Oxford/New York.

Hartouni, V. (1997). *Cultural Conceptions: On Reproductive Technologies and the Remaking of Life.* University of Minnesota Press, Minneapolis.

Junker-Kenny, M. (1999). *Designing Life? Genetics, Procreation, and Ethics.* Ashgate, Brookfield, VT.

Murray, T. H. (1996). *The Worth of a Child.* University of California Press, Berkeley.

National Bioethics Advisory Commission. (1997). *Cloning Human Beings.* U.S. Government Printing Office, Washington, DC.

Shenfield, F., and Sureau, C. (eds.) (1997). *Ethical Dilemmas in Assisted Reproduction.* Parthenon, New York.

Safer Sex Behaviors

Jeffrey A. Kelly
Medical College of Wisconsin

Glossary

AIDS Acquired immune deficiency syndrome, the constellation of diseases and opportunistic infections associated with advanced immune system decline due to HIV infection.

HIV Human immunodeficiency virus, the infection that causes immune system decline and, in later illness stages, AIDS-related diseases.

HIV serostatus A designation of whether or not an individual has HIV-infection (HIV-positive serostatus), does not have HIV infection (HIV-negative serostatus), or does not know (unknown HIV serostatus).

Safer sex Modifications in sexual practices that reduce risk for contracting HIV infection, such as use of condoms, other barrier protections, and nonpenetrative sexual activities.

Risk reduction intervention Programs intended to assist persons in making behavior changes to lessen the possibility of contracting or transmitting HIV infection.

SAFER SEX BEHAVIORS refer to practices intended to reduce risk for contracting sexually transmitted diseases, including HIV infection. Examples of safer sex include the use of latex condoms during intercourse and the adoption of other practices that min-

imize the likelihood of contracting HIV infection or transmitting it to others. Individuals sexually active outside of a monogamous relationship with an exclusive partner known to be HIV-negative can reduce their own risk through the consistent adoption of safer sex practices.

I. AIDS and HIV Infection

The first cases of AIDS were identified in 1981 among a small number of gay and bisexual men in New York City, San Francisco, and Los Angeles. Since that time, HIV/AIDS has emerged as the most serious infectious disease epidemic of modern times. By late 2000, approximately 900,000 persons in the United States had been diagnosed with HIV infection or AIDS, and 50,000 Americans contract new HIV infections each year. However, the HIV epidemic is global in scope, and 95% of the world's cases have occurred outside of North America. According to World Health Organization estimates, more than 36 million persons worldwide have contracted HIV, and infection prevalence is extremely high in Subsaharan Africa, much of Asia, and developing countries in other world areas.

During the first few years after AIDS was identified, most cases were diagnosed among gay or bisexual men and among injection drug users (IDUs).

In fact, one of the earliest names given to the syndrome was "gay-related infectious disease" (GRID). The early concentration of AIDS cases among men who have sex with men (MSMs) in large American cities was due to initial introduction of HIV into this population, rapid proliferation of infections among men who had large numbers of sexual partners, and the high efficiency of viral transmission during unprotected anal intercourse with an infected partner. In some large cities, up to 40% of gay or bisexual men contracted HIV infection—many before the threat of AIDS even was known—and HIV prevalence still remains very high among MSM. As a result, the likelihood that a sexually active gay or bisexual man will encounter an HIV-positive partner is very high.

Although AIDS was stereotyped early in the United States as a disease associated with homosexuality and injection drug use, this stereotype proved wrong. Women—especially inner-city, impoverished, and ethnic minority women—have also been harshly affected by HIV/AIDS. In the epidemic's early years, most women with AIDS were IDUs who contracted HIV due to their sharing of infected needles with other IDUs. However, this pattern quickly changed, and most women now living with HIV contracted their infection as a result of sexual intercourse with an HIV-positive male partner.

It has now become clear that there are multiple HIV epidemics in the United States. In some regions, HIV/AIDS is still a disease that primarily affects gay or bisexual men. In other areas, it is an epidemic primarily of IDUs. In still different regions, HIV/AIDS is now a disease that chiefly affects women. However, cutting across these patterns, several other trends are now clear. Persons are contracting HIV at a younger age than ever before, the epidemic is increasingly affecting ethnic minority communities of color, and those at greatest risk are more socially and economically disadvantaged than in the past.

The global picture of HIV epidemiology also shows regional differences. In countries of Western Europe, profiles of HIV risk are similar to the United States, with a mixed epidemic affecting MSMs, IDUs, and women. In developing countries—including Africa, where AIDS has taken a heavier toll than anywhere else on earth—HIV is almost entirely a heterosexually transmitted infection spread during unprotected vaginal intercourse from men to women and from women to men in the same manner as syphilis, gonorrhea, or any other sexually transmitted disease (STD). In both rural and urban areas of some sub-Saharan countries, 20 to 30% of all adolescents and adults have HIV infection. Average life expectancies in Africa are projected to decline substantially due to the impact of HIV/AIDS, and many millions of children have orphaned because of the disease.

HIV is a virus that affects the body's immune system by invading and killing cells (lymphocytes) that normally activate immune responses. When enough lymphocytes have been destroyed, individuals become susceptible to a wide range of opportunistic infections and—in the absence of medical intervention—eventually die of these illnesses. Throughout the first 15 years of the HIV epidemic, treatments were available to delay some of the opportunistic illnesses associated with AIDS, but none could durably reduce the quantity of HIV virus (termed "viral load") in the infected person. This is primarily because HIV mutates rapidly and becomes resistant to most antiretroviral medications. In the mid-1990s, potent new drug combinations became available, and these drugs can greatly reduce HIV's reproduction rate in the body. Termed "protease inhibitor combination therapies" or "highly-active antiretroviral therapy" (HAART), these medications have helped many persons with HIV to live longer and healthier lives, and the rate of deaths due to AIDS has declined in the United States because of lower AIDS-related mortality. However, the drug regiments are very complex and adherence is difficult, the medications sometimes lose their effectiveness even when properly taken, and some patients cannot tolerate side effects of the medications. They are also extremely expensive and are not presently available or affordable in most of the world, especially in developing countries hardest hit by AIDS.

II. Risk Behaviors and Safer Sex Practices

HIV is concentrated in the blood, semen, vaginal secretions, and certain other fluids of an infected individual. Sexual HIV transmission can occur when fluids that contain HIV enter and are absorbed into the body of the uninfected person. The likelihood that this will occur depends on a variety of factors. One is the sexual practice involved. Anal intercourse is a highly efficient vector for HIV transmission, probably because microscopic rectal tears often occur and HIV is absorbed readily through rectal mucosa. Vaginal intercourse is also an efficient route for HIV transmission, both from an infected male to an un-infected female and vice versa. Male-to-female transmission is more likely on a "per act" basis during vaginal intercourse. For reasons not fully understood, HIV transmission efficiency is significantly lower during oral sex than during either anal or vaginal intercourse. However, cases of HIV transmission have been documented as a result of both heterosexual and homosexual oral sex activities with infected partners.

Risk for HIV transmission may also be influenced by the infectivity of the HIV-positive partner. During the period immediately following the point when an individual contracts HIV infection, and again at later stages of HIV disease, viral load often reaches very high levels. With much a greater "quantity" of circulating virus, the likelihood of infecting partners is also much higher. HAART medication regimens that suppress HIV viral load may reduce infectivity, although this has not been clearly established. Finally, idiosyncratic factors and perhaps random chance influence HIV transmission efficiency. There have been cases of persons contracting HIV following one episode of unprotected sex with an infected partner, or of an infected individual transmitting HIV to multiple sexual partners during a single act of unprotected sex with each. There have also been cases of individuals who repeatedly have unprotected sex with an infected partner but who do not contract HIV. Finally, the presence of other STDs such as syphilis or herpes increases the likelihood that HIV infection will be transmitted between sexual partners because the skin lesions and genital tract irritations caused by STDs makes it easier for HIV to be exchanged.

Although it is commonplace to speak about sexual activities as being risky or safer, HIV risk is conferred only when sexual activity occurs with an infected partner. Among sexual partners who are uninfected, who are and remain sexually exclusive, and who do not engage in other risk activities such as injection drug use, any sex is—in theory—safe sex. However, relationship circumstances that confer safety cannot always be assured. For persons who have been sexually active in the past with other partners, formation of a new exclusive relationship does not automatically afford protection because one's new partner might be infected. Individuals who have outside or extra-relationship partners "bring home" the threat of HIV to their primary partners, particularly if the outside relationship involved unprotected intercourse. For this reason, HIV vulnerability can occur not only when an individual has multiple or high-risk partners, but also when the individual is sexually exclusive with a partner who engages in extra-relationship sex. This threat is especially great for women. Research has shown that a higher proportion of inner-city women report that their exclusive male partners have other sexual partners than the proportion who themselves say that they have outside partners.

Persons can learn their HIV serostatus and the serostatus of a sexual partner by having a test that detects the presence of HIV antibodies. Under most circumstances, professionally performed HIV antibody tests are quite reliable. However, persons who have very recently contracted HIV infection do not immediately develop antibodies detectable by these tests. It may require a period ranging from several weeks to several months following exposure for an HIV test to provide valid results. For that reason, it is usually recommended that persons who have recently been exposed repeat their testing following this window period for antibody development.

To reduce risk for HIV, persons with new, casual, or high-risk partners—or those with regular partners whose HIV status or extra-relationship abstinence is not conclusively known—can adopt safer sex practices. Safer sex refers to modifications in one's sexual practices that lessen risk for contracting (or transmitting) HIV infection and many other STDs. Since HIV is present in sexual fluids and is chiefly transmitted during anal or vaginal intercourse, the two most reliable forms of safer sex are intercourse protected by condoms and nonpenetrative sexual activities.

Latex condoms used by men, with a water-based lubricant if needed, afford considerable protection for both partners from sexually transmitted HIV infection. "Natural skin" condoms made from animal intestines are porous enough to allow HIV particles to pass through and are not an effective protection from HIV. The type of lubricant used with latex condoms is extremely important. Oil-based lubricants such as Vaseline, petroleum-based products, and most hand lotions weaken latex and can cause condoms to quickly deteriorate and break during intercourse. Water-based lubricants do not have this effect. For condoms to fully protect against HIV, they must be used correctly, consistently, and through the full duration of intercourse. Consumer guides periodically rate the reliability of different brands of latex condoms, and condoms are available in a range of sizes, textures, colors, and with or without lubrication. Condoms can be used during vaginal, anal, and oral intercourse.

One of the main limitations of male condoms is that their use is controlled by the man. If a man is unwilling to use condoms, his female sexual partner has historically lacked independent HIV prevention methods; female-controlled pregnancy prevention steps such as the use of contraceptive pills, intrauterine devices, and other methods prevent pregnancy but not HIV/STDs. In the late 1980s, a female condom became commercially available. Made of polyurethane, the device is vaginally inserted by the woman and its use is controlled by her. However, the female condom is noticeable in its appearance and sound, is more difficult to use correctly, and still requires the male partner's cooperation. Female condoms are considerably more expensive than male condoms, appear to afford slightly less HIV protection than male condoms (perhaps because a higher possibility of incorrect use), but are a desirable alternative for sexually active women whose partners will not use male condoms.

Sexual practices that do not involve penetration create little or no risk for HIV transmission. Mutual masturbation, external rubbing to orgasm without penetration ("frottage" or "outercourse"), and similar activities are very unlikely to result in HIV transmission although they do not necessarily protect against other more infectious STDs. There is controversy in the field concerning the HIV risk associated with oral sex. Some authorities argue that it carries potential risk and cannot be considered as safer sex. Others note that HIV transmission efficiency during oral sex is much more slight than during vaginal or anal intercourse, especially when sexual fluids are not exchanged. Barrier protections such as condoms or latex sheets ("dental dams") are sometimes used during oral sex.

For many years, researchers have been searching for HIV-protective gels, liquids, and lubricants that can be self-applied before intercourse and can reduce infection risk even if condoms are not also used. Vaginal microbicides effective against HIV and that are female-controlled would be of extraordinary importance in preventing HIV among women, and rectal microbicides would have similar benefits for men who have sex with men. Although many anti-HIV microbicides are in development and are undergoing evaluation for safety and efficacy in early-stage clinical trials, their effectiveness has not been demonstrated and they remain a hope for the future rather than a current reality. [*See* REPRODUCTIVE TECHNOLOGIES; SEXUALLY TRANSMITTED INFECTIONS AND THEIR CONSEQUENCES.]

III. Factors Associated with High-Risk and Safer Sex Behavior

Because HIV is transmitted in only a few ways, protection from sexually transmitted HIV requires change in only a few behaviors: (1) refraining from unprotected intercourse except in a relationship where partners know one another's HIV serostatus and (2) following safer practices if sexually active in any other relationship. However, while the steps needed to protect oneself from HIV infection are few in number and are easy to specify, they involve issues related to sexuality, relationships, love, gender and cultural roles, and self-identity. These are among the strongest and most psychologically significant human motivations, and they create a unique context surrounding risk behaviors for HIV infection and for efforts to change sexual risk behaviors.

A large number of studies have explored psychological, social, and relationship factors associated with high-risk sexual behavior and with the successful adoption of safer sex practices. Across different groups—including gay men, women, and adolescents—a very consistent set of psychological factors has been shown to differentiate between persons who frequently engage in risky practices (such as unprotected intercourse with nonexclusive partners) and those who remain safer in their behavior (such as by refraining from unprotected sex or consistently using condoms). Factors related to the adoption of safer sex behaviors include (1) correct knowledge about HIV transmission and risk reduction steps, (2) positive attitudes toward condom use and safer sex, (3) strong intentions to practice safer sex in one's own personal relationships, (4) high self-efficacy or confidence that one can successfully enact safer sex practices, and (5) perceptions that condom use and safer sex are accepted norms within one's peer group and among one's own sexual partners. The absence of these factors has been shown in many studies to predict patterns of frequent unsafe sex.

While psychological attitudes, beliefs, and knowledge are associated with sexual safety or risk, a number of social, cultural, relationship, and situational factors also influence success in the adoption of safer sex behaviors. Alcohol and other drug use have been shown to predict the occurrence of unsafe sex; persons who use drugs or also drink to excess are more likely to also engage in high-risk behavior with their partners. Lack of the behavioral skills needed to successfully act on one's safer sex intentions is associated with risk activities. These include "technical" skills such as how to properly use condoms, but also social skills like those involved in sexual communication and sexual assertiveness, as well as cognitive skills for problem solving how to implement safer sex practices in personal relationships. Coercive pressure from sexual partners, feelings of hopelessness and fatalism, psychological distress, and sexual boredom have been related to patterns of risk behaviors in some studies. Among gay men, HIV risk behavior levels and rates of new HIV infections remain very high among those who are young and among ethnic minority MSMs.

One of the most important determinants of safer sex adoption is the type of relationship that exists between sexual partners. As a result of AIDS education, most persons are aware of the importance of safer sex practices with new, casual, commercial, or other transient partners. Survey studies of gay men, adolescents, and heterosexual adult men and women have shown gradual increases in levels of condom use with casual partners. However, safer sex practices decline markedly in the context of affectionate relationships, relationships with partners who are "known" and who are liked or loved, or who are regular partners, even when the other person may be in the high-risk category. This is probably because condoms are often viewed as a disease protection needed with casual partners but not believed to be needed with affectionate, known, or steady partners, and because safer sex is perceived to connote lack of trust, imply infidelity, or to question the health of the partner.

Finally, adoption of safer sex is most easily accomplished in relationships where both partners carry equal power and equal roles in sexual decision making. Not all relationships are power balanced. Women, particularly disadvantaged women economically dependent on their partners and women living in cultures with strong traditional gender-role stereotypes, may be able to exert little influence over safer sex practices in their sexual relationships. This is especially true because condom use is a male controlled process and—with men resistant to condom use—insistence by a woman on safer sex raises the threat of relationship conflict, loss of needed survival resources, and violence.

IV. HIV *Prevention Interventions*

A number of studies have examined the effectiveness of individual counseling, small-group programs, and community-level interventions to encourage the adoption of safer sex among persons vulnerable to HIV/AIDS. These include programs that have been undertaken in clinics, schools, and social service settings, as well as interventions carried out in community venues and interventions targeting entire communities. Many of these research-based interventions have shown positive effects on behavior change and some have reduced incidence of STDs among participants attending them.

Individual counseling and small-group risk reduction interventions for gay men, adolescents, women, and specialized at-risk clients such as STD clinic patients that have proven successful all share certain common elements. All have provided HIV risk education and corrected participants' misconceptions about personal risk, and all have directed attention to promoting positive attitudes and intentions concerning safer sex. These interventions have also employed role play and rehearsal exercises to allow participants to practice and refine behavioral skills for using condoms, negotiating safer sex with potential partners, and assertively resisting sexual coercive pressures. The interventions found effective in the research literature have often employed other behavior-change techniques such as risk reduction problem solving; training in how to self-manage personal "triggers" for unsafe sex including substance abuse, loneliness, and negative mood status; establishing goals for behavior change; group member discussion of risk issues faced; and facilitator reinforcement of participants' behavior change efforts. For the most part, these interventions are relatively intensive, with clients attending multiple group or individual sessions, and with later session content building on the content of earlier sessions.

Such intensive skills-building and cognitive-behavioral programs, when tailored to meet the risk issues and situations of the client populations served, have produced significant changes in such outcomes as frequency of unprotected intercourse, percentage of intercourse occasions when condoms are used, and psychosocial risk-related characteristics including AIDS risk knowledge, condom attitudes, and behavior change intentions. While the basic conceptual and procedural framework of these successful interventions are similar, their content has been adapted to the needs of the client group involved. For example, interventions for gay or bisexual men must often address social and psychological issues such as homophobia, creating supports for stable same-sex relationships when few are provided by existing social and legal structures, and personal pride and responsibility. Because of the very high prevalence of HIV infection in the gay community, HIV prevention interventions for MSMs, operate in the context of very little "room for error" in consistency of safer sex adherence. Interventions for women must be tailored to address gender-role stereotypes that may inhibit assertive expression in matters involving sexuality, male reluctance to use condoms, relationship dynamics, and the possible negative consequences of behavior change especially in power-imbalanced relationships with men.

Although face-to-face counseling and group programs play an important role in HIV prevention, broader community-level interventions are also needed to curtail an HIV infection epidemic that occurs in communities. School-based programs for youth have been carried out and—when sufficiently intensive and extending beyond risk education alone— have sometimes produced positive outcomes. However, controversies concerning the content of school-based programs (specifically policy restrictions in many jurisdictions that limit programs to focus only on abstinence and that prohibit discussion of condoms, homosexuality, and other topics) have limited the capacity of some school-based interventions to effectively address the prevention needs of high-risk youth.

Because peer norms exert a strong influence on HIV risk behavior and on the adoption of protective steps, some community-level HIV prevention interventions have focused specifically on strengthening social norms for safer sex. One line of work that has proven very successful involves the identification of "popular opinion leaders" within microcommunities, and then training these peer influence leaders to disseminate safer sex endorsement conversational messages to their friends and acquaintances. In this approach, cadres of opinion leaders are taught characteristics of effective health promotion messages, practice delivering the messages, and then commit themselves to carry out outreach conversations with others in their day-to-day interactions with them. This intervention approach, in a large-scale study undertaken in gay bars, brought about substantial reductions in the prevalence of high-risk sexual practices and increases in safer sex adoption among the populations of men patronizing the clubs. It shows that key popular social leaders can redefine social norms and change the behavioral practices of populations in which they are influential.

A similar intervention approach at the community level has been studied and shown effective with inner-city women living in neighborhoods with high levels of poverty, drug use, and STDs. Undertaken in nine low-income housing developments, the intervention first invited women to attend small-group HIV prevention workshops led by other women. The workshops provided AIDS education, taught risk reduction skills, and encouraged women's discussion of the threat of AIDS to themselves, their families, and their communities. The program's second component was the recruitment and training of women who were identified by peers as popular opinion leaders to serve as AIDS educators and risk reduction endorsers for other women living in the same housing developments. The final program component involved the conduct of community events (such as family days, dinners, and picnics), which were organized by the opinion leader women and which always included AIDS awareness themes and safer sex promotion. Surveys of all women living in the nine intervention housing developments, relative to nine control group developments, revealed reductions in rates of unprotected sex, higher levels of condom use, and more frequent discussions between women and their male partners concerning AIDS and safer sex. [*See* SEXUALITY EDUCATION.]

V. Conclusions and Future Directions

The appearance of HIV/AIDS has brought about increased awareness of the threat of sexually transmitted infections and introduced the term "safer sex" into the public vernacular. While safer sex protects against HIV, condom use also decreases the risk of many other non-HIV STDs that also pose significant threats to a person's health, especially to the reproductive health of women.

Advances have been made in our understanding of factors related to safer sex adoption, and behavioral interventions have proven useful in reducing levels of high-risk behavior in some vulnerable populations. At the same time, much remains to be done. The number of new HIV infections occurring annually in the United States is unacceptably great, and the global HIV epidemic remains out of control and takes many millions of lives. While HIV prevention interventions for women have been undertaken, much less attention has been directed toward changing the condom use attitudes of high-risk heterosexual men. In cultures where male resistance to condom use is high, it is critical to improve heterosexual male attitudes toward safer sex. Female-controlled HIV protective methods remain urgently needed. Because persons contracting HIV are younger than ever before, improved primary prevention efforts for adolescents are essential. Finally, gay or bisexual men continue to account for a disproportionately high number of new HIV infections in the United States and in most Western countries. As new generations of young MSMs grow up and become sexually active, ongoing HIV prevention efforts to reach them remain urgently needed.

SUGGESTED READING

DeVita, V. T., Hellman, S., and Rosenberg, S. A. (1997). *AIDS: Etiology, Diagnosis, Treatment, and Prevention,* 4th ed. Lippincott-Raven, Philadelphia.

Kalichman, S. C. (1998). *Understanding AIDS: Advances in Research and Treatment.* American Psychological Association Press, Washington, DC.

Kelly, J. A. (1995). *Changing HIV Risk Behavior: Practical Strategies.* Guilford Press, New York.

Kelly, J. A., Murphy, D. A., Sikkema, K. J., McAuliffe, T. L., Roffman, R. A., Solomon, L. J., Winett, R. A., Kalichman, S. C., and the Community HIV prevention Research Collaborative. (1997). Randomized, controlled, community-level HIV prevention intervention for sexual risk behavior among homosexual men in U.S. cities. *The Lancet* 350, 1500–1505.

Kelly, J. A., Murphy, D. A., Washington, C. D., Wilson, T. S., Koob, J. J., Davis, D. R., Ledezma, G., and Davantes, B. (1994). The effects of HIV/AIDS intervention groups for high-risk women in urban clinics. *American Journal of Public Health* 84, 1918–1922.

O'Leary, A., and Jemmott, L. S. (1995). *Women at Risk: Issues in the Primary Prevention of AIDS.* Plenum Press, New York.

Peterson, J. L., and DiClemente, R. J. (2000). *Handbook of HIV Prevention.* Kluwer Academic/Plenum, New York.

Sikkema, K. J., Kelly, J. A., Winett, R. A., Solomon, L. J., Cargill, V. A., Roffman, R. A., McAuliffe, T. L., Heckman, T. G., Anderson, E. A., Wagstaff, D. A., Norman, A. D., Perry, M. J., Crumble, D. A., and Mercer, M. B. (2000). Outcomes of a randomized, community-level HIV prevention intervention for women living in 18 low-income housing developments. *American Journal of Public Health* 90, 57–63.

Self-Esteem

Kristen C. Kling

St. Cloud State University

Janet Shibley Hyde

University of Wisconsin, Madison

Glossary

Effect size An index of the distance between the means of two normal distributions in standard deviation units.

Mcta-analysis A collection of statistical techniques that provide an empirical summary of a body of literature.

Self-esteem An evaluation of the self that ranges from positive to negative.

THE CONCEPT OF SELF-ESTEEM has captured the imagination of both researchers and the popular press. Self-esteem is measured as an important outcome in thousands of research papers, and the bookshelves of contemporary bookstores contain many books regarding how to raise one's own self-esteem, as well as the self-esteem of one's children and intimate partner. Some of these self-help books are targeted at women and girls, who are generally believed to have lower self-esteem than men and boys. Despite society's acceptance of the belief in lower female self-esteem, an empirical approach to thc question of gender differences in self-esteem is necessary to counterbalance the relatively unchallenged view that is presented in the popular press. To examine the question of gender differences in self-esteem, it is important to consider how self-esteem is defined and assessed. This article briefly reviews thc literature, which demonstrates the psychological importance of self-esteem. The article then considers early examinations and media coverage of gender differences in self-esteem. A description of more recent attempts to examine the question of gender and self-esteem can be found in the section on recent meta-analytic reviews of gender differences in self-esteem. The discussion concludes with suggestions for further research.

I. How Self-Esteem Is Defined and Assessed

Self-esteem can be defined as an evaluation of the self that ranges from positive to negative. A self-esteem evaluation can be made for the self as a whole, or for more specific aspects of the self. When thc target is the self as a whole, the term "global self-esteem" is used to describe the evaluation. In contrast to global self-esteem, domain-specific measures of self-esteem assess beliefs about particular aspects of the self. For example, researchers interested in body image may create a measure to assess "body self-esteem," other researchers interested in sexuality may create a measure to assess "sexual self-esteem," and researchers interested in studying Internet usage may create a measure to assess "computer self-esteem." The range of possible domain-specific self-esteem measures is quite large and has yet to be organized in a systematic fashion that cuts across the multiple measures. Consequently, many researchers who are interested in self-evaluations focus on global self-esteem.

A distinction between self-esteem and self-concept can also be made, although researchers in the field often are not precise in maintaining this distinction. While self-esteem captures evaluations of the self, self-concept refers to how one thinks about various aspects of the self and which of these are most important. Global self-esteem is captured by "I am a worthwhile human being," whereas the self-concept is captured by statements such as "I am an athlete," "I am a mother," "I am a professor," or "I am a religious person." Our focus here, though, is on self-esteem.

The most commonly used measure of global self-esteem was developed by Morris Rosenberg in 1979. The 10-item Rosenberg Self-Esteem Scale represents an excellent example of how to assess self-esteem. To complete the scale, respondents indicate their level of agreement or disagreement with items such as, "On the whole, I am satisfied with myself," "I feel I am a person of worth, on an equal plane with others," and "I take a positive attitude toward myself." Note that these items are context-free—that is, they assess beliefs about the self without reference to specific domains of self-knowledge. Rosenberg's measure is still used today and is generally regarded as the gold standard for the assessment of global self-esteem. Other examples of self-esteem measures include the General Self Subscale from Herbert Marsh's Self-Description Inventory and the Global Self-Worth Subscale from Susan Harter's Self-Perception Profile for Children.

II. The Psychological Importance of Self-Esteem

The construct of global self-esteem has been the focus of numerous studies that demonstrate the importance of having a positive evaluation of the self. For example, individuals who report high levels of self-esteem also report high levels of positive affect and low levels of negative affect and depressive symptoms. High self-esteem has also been associated with the presence of the self-serving bias, a self-protective attributional pattern in which individuals take credit for their own success and deny blame for failures. In addition, self-esteem has been shown to predict better adjustment outcomes as individuals confront a variety of life's challenges. Because self-esteem influences such a broad array of psychological processes, any group differences in self-esteem could have important consequences.

III. Early Examinations and Media Coverage of Gender Differences in Self-Esteem

One of the earliest scientific reviews of gender differences in self-esteem was published in 1974 by Maccoby and Jacklin, in their book *The Psychology of Sex Differences*. Maccoby and Jacklin located 29 studies of participants ranging in age from three to early adulthood that were published between 1955 and 1973. Many of the studies showed no significant gender differences in self-esteem, and those that showed a difference were about equally split between those showing that girls and women scored higher and those showing that boys and men scored higher. Maccoby and Jacklin concluded that there was a remarkable similarity between the sexes in self-esteem through the college years and that there were too few studies of adults to reach firm conclusions for that age group.

During the 1980s, self-esteem, particularly gender differences in self-esteem, became a popular subject in self-help books and the popular media. The American Association of University Women (AAUW) conducted a national survey of self-esteem in which they compared the self-esteem of girls and boys in different age groups. The AAUW concluded that girls experience plummeting self-esteem at the beginning of adolescence. The drop was most extreme for White girls, and it did not occur for Black girls, whose self-esteem was positive in both elementary school and high school. Hispanic girls showed a pattern similar to White girls. The AAUW argued that gender inequity in the schools was a major factor in girls' declining self-esteem. The AAUW report was supplemented in 1994 by the book, *School Girls: Young Women, Self-Esteem, and the Confidence Gap*, in which journalist Peggy Ornstein reported on observations she made in the schools that confirmed the sexism suspected in the AAUW report. On the *New York Times* paperback bestseller list for more than 135 weeks, Mary Pipher's *Reviving Ophelia*, also published in 1994, made the case that adolescent girls develop in a sexist and sex-saturated world that destroys their self-esteem. By the mid-1990s, the self-esteem problems of girls and women seemed etched in the national consciousness. [*See* MEDIA INFLUENCES.]

IV. Recent Meta-analytic Reviews of Gender Differences in Self-Esteem

Critiques of the narrative review process that was used by Maccoby and Jacklin have led to the development of statistical techniques that provide an empirical summary of a body of literature. Collectively, these techniques are called meta-analysis. The first step in a meta-analysis is to identify as many studies as possible that provide data about the gender comparison of interest. Next, the data from each study are converted to a statistic called an effect size, which is an index of the distance between the male and female means in standard deviation units. For example, an effect size of 0.5 would indicate that the male and female means in the sample were half of a standard deviation apart from one another. By convention, an effect size of 0.2 is considered small, an effect size of 0.5 is considered medium, and an effect size of 0.8 is considered large. Once each gender comparison has been converted to an effect size, it is possible to combine results across different studies, even if the studies used different measures of the construct of interest. The combination of effect sizes takes sample size into effect by weighting the larger samples more heavily, and yields a single number that summarizes an entire body of literature.

Meta-analysis has been used to evaluate gender differences in global self-esteem. One such meta-analytic review was presented in 1999 by Kristen Kling, Janet Hyde, and colleagues. This analysis examined data from two different sources. The first source was articles that were published between 1987 and 1995. The second source of data was the National Center for Education Statistics, an organiza-tion that has conducted numerous large-scale studies of young people in the United States.

The first analysis began with the identification of 184 articles that included an assessment of self-esteem in both females and males. The resulting gender comparisons summarized the testing of 97,121 people. The majority of the studies took place in the United States, and the respondents ranged in age from elementary school to late adulthood. When the results for all of the respondents were statistically combined using meta-analytic techniques, the overall effect size was 0.21, a small difference favoring males. Stated in another way, males, as a group, score approximately one-fifth of a standard deviation higher than females on self-esteem measures. The magnitude of the effect size varied with age, such that the effect was largest during late adolescence ($d = 0.33$) and was not significantly different from zero in samples over the age of 60.

The second analysis focused on data from the National Center for Education Statistics (NCES). The NCES focuses on adolescents in the United States and has been tracking their psychological adjustment since 1972. Four cohorts, each composed of more than 19,000 adolescents, have been assessed. Each cohort has completed a shortened Rosenberg self-esteem scale, which contained 4 of the original 10 items: "I take a positive attitude toward myself," "I feel I am a person of worth, on an equal plane with others," "I am able to do things as well as most other people," and "On the whole, I'm satisfied with myself." This four-item scale yielded acceptable reliabilities, ranging from 0.68 to 0.73 across the four samples. Each NCES cohort was assessed multiple times. This longitudinal design provides an excellent opportunity to examine age trends in self-esteem. Contrary to the results of the AAUW, which document "plummeting" self-esteem in adolescent girls, the NCES data show that across the teenage and young adult years, self-esteem for both boys and girls remains relatively stable and even shows signs of a gradual increase. Because the NCES data track changes in individuals over time, rather than comparing individuals of different age groups, they provide a stronger test of any age trends.

In addition to examining age trends, the NCES data provide an opportunity to examine whether gender differences in self-esteem have changed in the past two decades. This analysis focused on the assessment waves that took place when the students in each cohort were 17 years old. Across time and across samples, the gender effect size has been consistently small, favoring males ($d = 0.04$ in 1972, $d = 0.12$ in 1980, $d = 0.09$ in 1982, and $d = 0.16$ in 1992). The important strengths of the NCES studies are the large samples sizes and the repeated assessments of self-esteem using the same four items over time.

Another study that used meta-analytic techniques to examine gender differences in self-esteem was presented in 1999 by Brenda Major and colleagues. Their analysis yielded an overall effect size of 0.14, a small difference favoring males, a result quite similar to that of Kling and colleagues. This effect size summarizes the responses of 82,569 respondents and spans the years of 1982 to 1992. An analysis of moderator variables indicated that the effect size favoring males was larger in White samples when compared with Black samples and that the gender difference was more pronounced in samples with lower socioeconomic status.

V. Conclusion

Despite the widespread belief that males have much higher self-esteem than females, the best available research indicates that the difference between males and females is small. The analyses reviewed thus far, however, focus only on mean levels of self-esteem. Other questions remain. For example, do women and men derive their self-esteem from the same sources? Although a number of researchers have examined this question, the pattern of findings is not clear at this point, and further inquiry is warranted. If the sources of self-esteem differ by gender, it may have important implications for how self-esteem functions for men and women and may suggest gender-specific interventions for people with low self-esteem.

SUGGESTED READING

Baumeister, R. F. (1998). The self. In *Handbook of Social Psychology* (D. T. Gilbert, S. T. Fiske, and G. Lindzey, eds.) 4th ed., pp. 680–740. McGraw-Hill, New York.

Kling, K. C., Hyde, J. S., Showers, C. J., and Buswell, B. N. (1999). Gender differences in self-esteem: A meta-analysis. *Psychological Bulletin* 125, 470–500.

Maccoby, E. E., and Jacklin, C. N. (1974). *The Psychology of Sex Differences*. Stanford University Press, Stanford, CA.

Major, B., Barr, L., Zubek, J., and Babey, S. H. (1999). Gender and self-esteem: A meta-analysis. In *Sexism and Stereotypes in Modern Society: The Gender Science of Janet Taylor Spence* (W. B. Swann, Jr., J. H. Langlois, and L. A. Gilbert, eds.), pp. 223–253. American Psychological Association, Washington, DC.

Rosenberg, M. (1979). *Conceiving the Self*. Basic Books, New York.

Self-Fulfilling Prophecies

Mark Snyder

Clifton M. Oyamot, Jr.

University of Minnesota

Glossary

Behavioral confirmation An outcome of social interaction in which the behaviors of one person (the "target") confirms the preconceived beliefs of another person (the "perceiver"). This outcome is a result of the perceiver acting on beliefs in ways that elicit the expected behaviors from the target.

Dyadic interaction A social interaction involving only two people.

Expectation Any preconceived belief about the personality of another person or the ways in which the other person will behave in a given interpersonal encounter.

Perceiver Any person who enters a social interaction holding preconceived beliefs about the person with whom one is to interact.

Perceptual confirmation An outcome of social interaction in which a person holding preconceived beliefs about another person comes to perceive that their initial beliefs have been verified by the other person, even in the absence of any actual behavioral evidence.

Self-fulfilling prophecy An interpersonal phenomenon whereby individuals act on their expectations in ways that make them come true.

Target Any person in a social interaction about whom preconceived beliefs are held.

SELF-FULFILLING PROPHECIES are interpersonal phenomena whereby individuals act on their expectations in ways that make them come true. People often enter social interactions holding preconceived beliefs and expectations about others with whom they are to interact. When people use these beliefs as guides for their own behavior, they may actually induce their interaction partners to behave in ways that confirm these initial beliefs. In this way, beliefs can operate to produce social reality. Key elements that determine if a self-fulfilling prophecy will occur include the expectations held by a perceiver, the motivations and interaction goals of perceivers and targets, and the power structure between perceivers and targets.

I. The Phenomenon: Confirmation of Expectations in Social Interaction

Social interaction is a dynamic interpersonal process that intertwines a myriad of psychological factors. Among the most important of these are the expectations and beliefs that individuals hold about the person with whom they are interacting. These a priori expectations may be idiosyncratic and specific to the interaction partner, being based on past experiences or information gleaned from third parties. Oftentimes, however, the initial expectations one person holds may be rooted in characteristics thought to be associated with more general features of the interaction partner, such as his or her sex, age, or ethnicity. Once activated, these expectations can serve as powerful guides for action, consciously or unconsciously, in the interpersonal exchange. One potential outcome of the exchange is that these actions actually prompt behaviors from the interaction partner that are consistent with the original beliefs. This sequence of events—where previously held expectations guide the actions and behaviors of one person, which in turn elicit behaviors from the interaction partner that are consistent with the initially held beliefs—is the essence of the self-fulfilling prophecy. Thus, the phenomenon of the self-fulfilling prophecy—also referred to in the research literature as behavioral confirmation or expectancy confirmation—is a subtle yet potentially powerful interpersonal process through which individuals' beliefs and expectations, accurate or erroneous, are translated into social reality.

Initially documented in field studies examining the effects of teacher expectations on student performance, the existence of self-fulfilling prophecies has been verified by researchers in diverse experimental laboratory settings and for a wide variety of beliefs and expectations, including beliefs about the typical characteristics associated with women and men, beliefs about racial differences, age-related expectations, hypotheses and beliefs about the likely personalities of an interaction partner, expectations of being liked or disliked by someone, beliefs associated with physical appearance, and beliefs about the abilities and competence of an interaction partner. Recent studies have examined both the social and psychological mechanisms that bring about a self-fulfilling prophecy as well as the limits of the phenomenon. Finally, the theoretical and practical implications of beliefs initiating self-fulfilling consequences have been explored.

The literature on self-fulfilling prophecies is extensive. This article sketches out the mechanisms and boundaries of the phenomenon of self-fulfilling beliefs, paying special attention to the gender-relevant aspects of social interactions and their consequences.

A. THEORETICAL AND EXPERIMENTAL FRAMEWORK FOR STUDYING BEHAVIORAL CONFIRMATION

Empirical investigations of the self-fulfilling prophecy parse social interaction into a sequence of steps. First, one person (the perceiver) adopts beliefs about another person (the target). Second, the perceiver then acts as if his or her beliefs and expectations are true and treat the target accordingly. Finally, guided and constrained by the actions of the perceiver, the target behaves in ways that appear to confirm the perceiver's initial beliefs. Two consequences may follow from this sequence of events: (1) *perceptual confirmation* occurs when the perceiver's initial beliefs remain intact at the conclusion of the interaction, even in the absence of target behaviors that are explicitly confirming (the perceiver sees what he or she expects to see); and/or (2) *behavioral confirmation*, in which the target actually comes to behave in accord with the perceiver's expectations. Experimental studies, which permit precise control over specific parameters of a social interaction, have examined the fundamental features associated with each step in perceptual and behavioral confirmation sequences. This article focuses on behavioral confirmation outcomes.

Researchers have employed a general paradigm for investigating the self-fulfilling effects of beliefs and expectations in the laboratory. Typically, two people are brought into the laboratory and asked to engage in some form of interpersonal exchange. One member of the dyad is assigned to be the perceiver, and it is this person who is led to expect certain traits or behaviors from their interaction partner, the target. At the conclusion of the interaction, both target and perceiver are asked a number of questions about the interaction and about their impressions of their partner. Based on the perceiver's impression of the target, one can determine if perceptual confirmation has occurred. In addition to these impressions, objective third party judges, who are unaware of the perceiver's expectations, are asked to listen to recordings of the interaction and assess the behaviors exhibited by targets. Behavioral confirmation is said to have occurred to the extent that the judges deem that targets who were expected (by the perceiver) to exhibit certain behaviors or traits actually behave in those ways.

B. BEHAVIORAL CONFIRMATION AND GENDER STEREOTYPES: A PROTOTYPIC EXAMPLE

A variant on this basic paradigm was reported in 1982 by Berna Skrypnek and Mark Snyder in an experiment designed to explore self-fulfilling prophecies in cross-sex interactions and will serve as an illustrative demonstration of how experimental research is conducted in this area. For this study, male and female pairs were brought into the laboratory ostensibly to investigate decision-making processes and task negotiation in a minimal interaction setting. The participants in each pair, ushered into separate rooms, had no opportunity to meet each other face to face. The crucial manipulation involved informing the male perceivers that their female partner was either male or female.

In the first phase of the study, the perceiver and target attempted to negotiate a division of tasks, some of which were stereotypically feminine and others that were stereotypically masculine in nature, by simultaneously indicating their preferences via an electronic signaling board. In the event of conflict, participants were allowed two attempts to successfully negotiate the task division, with the perceivers having the advantage of stating their preferences first and the targets relegated to reacting to the perceiver's actions. Behavioral confirmation was evident in this scenario, with targets labeled "male" choosing tasks that were stereotypically more masculine and targets labeled "female" subsequently choosing tasks that were stereotypically more feminine.

In the second phase of the study, the interaction partners again attempted to negotiate the division of tasks (from a different list); however, this time the target was given the opportunity to control the negotiation by responding first. Despite having fewer constraints on their behavior, the targets continued to act in ways consistent with their initial label: targets who were thought to be male by the perceiver continued to choose more masculine tasks and those thought to be female continued to chose more feminine tasks. Coupled with findings from the first phase, this study demonstrates how the consequences of behavioral confirmation may extend beyond a first encounter to guide behaviors of both perceivers *and* targets in subsequent interaction, thus maintaining and perpetuating gender stereotypes.

The Skrypnek and Snyder study contains all of the basic elements typically included in laboratory studies of self-fulfilling beliefs. The gender labeling of the target is one way in which beliefs and expectations are conveyed to the perceiver in laboratory studies. Other methods include providing other types of demographic information about the target, carefully constructed personality portfolios, or supposed photographs of the target.

In this study, as in most studies of behavioral confirmation, the target was kept unaware of the expectations the perceiver had of her. In many respects, this feature of the general paradigm mimics real life interactions where people are not necessarily privy to the expectations held by their partners. Of course, this is not always the case. A number of studies have examined the effects that target knowledge has on the behavioral confirmation process, revealing circumstances in which targets can and do disconfirm expectations held by a perceiver, especially negative and stigmatizing expectations, using a variety of self-presentational tactics. However, other features of a social interaction, in particular the power relationship between target and perceiver, may make such disconfirmation difficult even for a motivated target.

One distinguishing feature of the Skrypnek and Snyder study was that the participants engaged in two interactions in the course of the experiment. Incorporating multiple social interactions between perceivers and targets is not yet a common feature of most behavioral confirmation studies conducted in the laboratory, partly because most demonstrations attempt to model first encounters between strangers and partly because of the logistic difficulties involved. Nevertheless, some research has been done in this vein. As in the Skrypnek and Snyder study, studies that do investigate the consequences of multiple interactions in the laboratory, such as a 1997 study conducted by Dylan M. Smith, Steven L. Neuberg, Nicole T. Judice, and Jeremy C. Biesanz, have found that confirmatory behaviors on the part of targets tend to persist from one interaction to the next, even when their interaction partner changes and is led to hold different expectations of them. In this study, the targets were first interviewed by perceivers who were led to believe that the target possessed personality traits that were either appropriate (extraverted) or inappropriate (introverted) for a particular job. The targets then participated in a second interview with a new perceiver who was given the opposite expectation. It was demonstrated that targets instructed to be deferential exhibited confirmatory behavior (i.e., either being extraverted or introverted depending on the perceiver's expectation) in the first interview, and continued to behave in the same fashion during the second interview, even though the new perceiver held different beliefs about the target. Other research has found that the *mere possibility* of future encounters actually results in greater behavioral confirmation in the interaction relative to situations in which the perceivers are told that they are unlikely to meet the target again, as demonstrated in a 1995 study by Julie A. Haugen and Mark Snyder.

II. Elements of the Behavioral Confirmation Process and Their Links to Gender

The Skrypnek and Snyder study contains the basic features that are typical of investigations of the self-fulfilling consequences of beliefs and expectations. The next few sections review those elements fundamentally involved in behavioral confirmation sequences and their link to gender-related research. These factors include the expectations brought to bear in an interaction, the motivations and goals of the interaction partners, and the role of status and power.

A. EXPECTATIONS

Preconceived expectations and beliefs about other people is the fulcrum upon which behavioral confirmation rests; indeed, by definition, without prior expectations there can be no behavioral confirmation of those beliefs. As noted earlier, a wide array of expectations have been shown to initiate a behavioral confirmation sequence. This diversity of manipulated expectations attests to the generality of the self-fulfilling prophecy.

1. Gender-Related Expectations

Among the most powerful expectations that people hold are those associated with gender. As researchers in social cognition have discovered, gender functions as a primary cognitive category and organizing framework in interpersonal perceptions. The stereotypes of males and females are well articulated, relatively nonoverlapping, and learned at a very early age. In addition to the typical personality traits that are ascribed to men and women, some theorists have argued that gender stereotypes may also contain a *prescriptive* element. That is, gender stereotypes contain beliefs both about how men and women *are* and about how they *should* behave. Furthermore, it has been established that gender-related beliefs come to mind very quickly and even automatically in the presence of appropriate cues. Finally, research by Patricia Devine and others has demonstrated that even when a person does not endorse a stereotype, it is still possible for mere knowledge of stereotypes to influence the way we judge and act toward others. For example, all the participants in the Devine study were aware of the culturally shared stereotypes associated with African Americans, even if they did not personally endorse them. However, when this knowledge of the stereotype was activated outside of their conscious awareness, it affected what kinds of impressions they formed of another person regardless of whether they endorsed the stereotype or not. In particular, subliminally activating the African American stereotype led the study participants to form more unfavorable impressions of a person, relative to those whose stereotypes were not activated. [*See* GENDER STEREOTYPES.]

In most social interactions, the sex of one's interaction partner is among the first things people notice. This is especially true in cross-sex interactions because, as research has shown, that type of group composition makes gender especially salient. The salience of gender in interpersonal encounters, coupled with the particular aspects of gender stereotypes mentioned earlier, may facilitate gender-based self-fulfilling prophecies. The Skrypnek and Snyder study, which showed that simply labeling someone as male or female resulted in gender stereotypic behaviors by targets, is one example of this process. A study by Mark Snyder, Elizabeth D. Tanke, and Ellen Berscheid reported in 1977 found that female targets who were thought by male perceivers to be physically attractive were more friendly and sociable during a telephone conversation than women who were thought to be unattractive. Another relevant example of the influence of gender-related expectations is a 1975 study by Mark Zanna and Susan J. Pack, which found that women's characterization of themselves varied as a function of the desirability of their proposed male interaction partner (no interaction really took place in this study) and the supposed gender expectations of the partner. When a "desirable" male partner (described as physically appealing, smart, interested in meeting women, and a car owner) was said to hold traditional gender role beliefs, women presented themselves in a more gender-typed manner and performed poorly on an anagram task, relative to women who were paired with a desirable partner who held nontraditional views about gender. In the latter condition, women characterized themselves as more nontraditional and performed very well on the anagrams. Women paired with undesirable male partners showed no behavioral convergence to the partner's expectations. This study illustrates the potential complexities inherent in the self-fulfilling interaction sequence as it relates to cross-sex encounters, a point to which we will return shortly.

B. MOTIVATIONS

Preconceived expectations of an interaction partner set the stage for a potential self-fulfilling prophecy, but they are not the only factor that influences the course and consequences of a social interaction. In recent years, research has begun to probe the role of target and perceiver motivations—the goals and needs pursued in a given interaction—in behavioral confirmation and disconfirmation sequences. Several different lines of research have pursued the motivational bases underlying behavioral confirmation, including the research programs of John Darley, Steven Neuberg, and Mark Snyder, among others.

Several types of interaction goals and motivations have been found to facilitate behavioral confirmation. For perceivers, one facilitating motivation is the adoption of an "*action set,*" wherein a perceiver is more concerned with working on a specific task with his or her partner rather than explicitly forming an impression of him or her. However, simply instructing a perceiver to form an impression of his or her partner is no guarantee that confirmatory outcomes can be avoided. Perceivers motivated to "get to know" targets more readily elicit confirmation, especially when they are attempting to acquire a stable and predictable understanding of their partners. For targets, the desire to facilitate a smooth interaction and to "get along" with their partner makes confirmation more likely, as does a *deferential* interaction style.

Researchers have also explored the motivations and interaction goals that derail the confirmation process. For example, perceivers are less likely to elicit confirmation of their initial beliefs when they are trying to gain an accurate impression of a target (as opposed to seeking stable, predictable impressions of the target), when they adopt a "get along" strategy in the interaction, or if they are attempting to get the target to like them. In addition, targets who take an active part in trying to understand and gain knowledge about their perceiver partner, or who assume a nondeferential stance in the interaction, are more likely to disconfirm the perceiver's initial beliefs.

Thus, behavioral confirmation is not an inevitable consequence of social interactions in which perceivers enter the situation with preconceived expectations. The motivations and interaction goals that both perceivers and targets bring into the encounter affect the outcomes, sometimes making confirmation more likely. Furthermore, implicit in this set of findings is that certain combinations of perceiver and target motivations may be particularly potent in initiating a self-fulfilling sequence. For example, behavioral confirmation may be a particularly likely outcome when perceivers who are preoccupied with trying to acquire and to some extent verify knowledge of their partner, are paired with targets who are trying to create a smooth and pleasant interpersonal encounter.

1. Gender and Interaction Style

Studies that reveal gender differences in interaction and communication style are relevant to the motivational aspects of self-fulfilling interactions. As noted in several reviews of the gender literature, a general finding is that women tend to adopt interaction styles that are more accommodating of their interaction partner than men, apparently in the interest of facilitating interpersonal exchanges or seeking connection with those around them. Women often use more passive language than men, as well as exhibit more submissive nonverbal behaviors (e.g., smiling, adopting less expansive body positions), but they also demonstrate greater empathy and social sensitivity. In contrast, men tend to seek verification of their beliefs and attitudes in interactions, adopt a more competitive orientation of one-ups-manship, and are more goal oriented in their interactions. Studies have found that men tend to use more direct language than women and exhibit more willingness to interrupt women who are speaking.

These differing interaction styles bear some resemblance to those found to moderate the behavioral confirmation outcomes of social interactions. To the extent that these gender differences are reliable, men tend to adopt motivations and interaction goals that would facilitate behavioral confirmation in a target, such as being more concerned with verification of their beliefs as opposed to accuracy, as well as being more goal oriented in their communications and interactions. Women as perceivers may be less likely to induce behavioral confirmation in a partner, especially if their typical response is to ensure a smooth interaction. However, these same motivations may make women more likely to engage in confirmatory behavior when they are the targets.

Support for the preceding analysis is somewhat sparse, in part because most early studies of gender and the self-fulfilling prophecy assigned males to the perceiver role and females to the target role. A notable exception is a 1982 study by Dana Christensen and Robert Rosenthal that varied both the gender composition of the interaction dyads as well as the gender of the target and perceiver. These researchers found that male perceivers' behaviors, relative to female perceivers' behaviors, were more influenced by their preinteraction expectations; as well, male perceivers tended to elicit greater behavioral confirmation from targets relative to female perceivers. Furthermore, female targets exhibited greater assimilation to their partner's expectations, thereby producing greater behavioral confirmation, than did male targets. A 1995 field study, conducted by Taly Dvir, Dov Eden, and Michal Lang Banjo, investigated gender effects in behavioral confirmation during training sessions for the Israeli Defense Force. In this study, male and female leaders' performance expectations of male and female officer cadets were manipulated. Confirmation of performance expectations was found for groups with male leaders, but not by female-led trainee groups.

Although tempting, the conclusion that men are more likely to elicit behavioral confirmation and women are more likely to conform to expectations should be made with caution. Other studies of self-fulfilling beliefs that vary the gender of perceiver and target have had mixed results. A 1981 study by Susan Andersen and Sandra Bem, investigating responses to perceived physical attractiveness, found that gender composition per se did little to predict behavioral outcomes. Instead, an additional factor, the degree to which the participants endorsed traditional gender roles versus being androgynous in orientation, played an important role in interaction outcomes. A few other inquiries in this vein also cast doubt on a straightforward interpretation of the role that gender plays in self-fulfilling beliefs. A recent example of this ambiguity would be in the 2000 study by Lori J. Nelson and Kristin Klutas, which found behavioral confirmation only in female-female dyads (cross-sex dyads were not included in this study). Researchers Judith A. Hall and Nancy J. Briton attempted to quantitatively assess the ways in which gender composition of dyads may influence behavioral confirmation outcomes through a statistical analysis of self-fulfilling prophecy studies that included gender as a variable and in which expectations were experimentally manipulated. Their analysis was hampered by the small number of stud-

ies available that met the proper criteria, but they tentatively conclude that gender composition, in and of itself, is not a determining factor in self-fulfilling outcomes.

Considering motivations and gender composition of dyads and groups is one way to examine the role that gender may play in eliciting self-fulfilling beliefs. In addition, gender theorists have proposed an alternative perspective on gender interactions that have important implications for understanding the prevalence and likelihood of confirmation in cross-sex interactions, namely the role of power and status.

C. POWER DYNAMICS

Various lines of programmatic research investigating the situational contingencies that lead to self-fulfilling prophecies have recently turned their attention to the power dynamics inherent in social interactions. Many theorists have noted that the experimental paradigm used to investigate self-fulfilling prophecies implicitly places the perceiver in a position of greater power relative to his or her target partner; perceivers are the ones who hold the expectations, and they are often given greater opportunity to act on those beliefs and to direct the interaction. Targets, on the other hand, are often placed in a position where they are reacting to the situation as defined by the perceiver's actions and overtures. In addition, targets enter these situations at an informational disadvantage, since they are usually told little about their interaction partner. Recognition of these implicit inequities has begun to lead researchers to more concerted efforts to understand the role of power and status in social interactions generally and the impact this factor has on self-fulfilling outcomes.

A recent study by John Copeland incorporated a new twist in the general experimental paradigm by explicitly manipulating the degree to which perceivers and targets had the power to control their partner's outcomes. Behavioral confirmation only occurred when targets were placed in a relatively powerless position. When targets were able to control perceivers' outcomes, a behavioral confirmation outcome was averted. Another important and suggestive finding from this study was that the power conferred on target and perceiver appeared to influence the motivations implicitly adopted by interactants. Powerful participants, regardless of their perceiver or target designation, tended to seek to "get to know" their interaction partners. In contrast, powerless participants adopted a "get along" strategy. These motivations, as we have already noted, exert some influence on the outcomes of interpersonal interactions.

Beyond understanding the generic situational contingencies and mechanisms that govern behavioral confirmation sequences, considerations of power and status take on an added dimension of significance when one realizes that those groups of people who are most often the targets of social stereotyping and discrimination are the same groups that have less access to resources—tangible or otherwise—in our society. Implications of this perspective for cross-sex interactions are considered next. [*See* LEADERSHIP; POWER.]

1. Gender and the Power Dynamics of Social Interactions

A number of gender theorists have postulated that apparent differences in gendered behavior may be traced to differences in power and status allocated to women and men. It has been argued that power and status differences are embedded in gender and gender roles, with men enjoying more privileged status and power than women. From this perspective, these power differentials may be the core consideration in understanding the relation between gender and social behavior. Laboratory experiments on behavioral confirmation often place women in the target role, thus artificially enhancing the likelihood of drawing the conclusion that women are more susceptible to conforming to perceiver expectations. However, as described earlier, reversals in power in these simulated interactions lead to less clear-cut results. In addition, although many studies include both male and female participants, the interaction groups are often restricted to same-sex compositions. This makes sense if gender-related questions are not core considerations in a particular study because it avoids the complications potentially inherent in cross-sex interactions, but it limits the kinds of gender-related conclusions we can draw based on these studies.

Through the lens of power and status, it is possible to reinterpret existing studies on self-fulfilling prophecies and gender. In some instances, gender as a cue for judging a person may be overridden by the person's role or status when this information is provided. This finding suggests that gender expectations may be suppressed in situations in which a woman is known to have high status. Other work has found that women will exhibit typically "male" behaviors when placed in a position of power or authority,

supporting the idea that the behavioral repertoires of men and women are considerably flexible and malleable. Juxtaposing this perspective with the emerging understanding of the role that power plays in behavioral confirmation further suggests that gender per se does not make confirmatory or disconfirmatory behaviors more likely. Rather, it is possible that power differentials have an important impact on the motivations and interaction goals that men and women adopt in any given interpersonal encounter. That is, when a woman has some sort of power or status relative to her interaction partner, we might expect that she would adopt an interaction style that is likely to result in behavioral confirmation of her expectations.

III. Practical Applications

Many of the elements that lead to the fulfillment of preexisting beliefs in social interactions have been examined in experimental studies. The strengths of an experimental approach are that it allows researchers to have a great deal of control to manipulate crucial variables, such as expectations or motivations inherent in the interaction, and to establish what factors can actually cause behavioral confirmation. Clearly, these studies demonstrate that self-fulfilling prophecies can occur in discrete interpersonal encounters. In addition, researchers have attempted to assess the actual prevalence and power of the self-fulfilling prophecy in real-life situations, as well as the implications that this phenomenon can have for people who find themselves in the role of perceivers and targets. A number of contexts have been explored, and we briefly review how behavioral confirmation may emerge and affect peoples' lives in ongoing social situations in the context of gender and gender-related beliefs.

A. EDUCATIONAL DOMAINS

Beginning with Robert Rosenthal's demonstration that teacher expectations of students' abilities affected those students' actual academic performance, educational settings have been one of the most thoroughly explored domains in which self-fulfilling prophecies may operate. One question that has been explored is the degree to which gender stereotypes about academic ability and competence (e.g., girls as being mathematically challenged) may initiate self-fulfilling prophecies in the classroom and beyond. A recent analytic review by Lee Jussim, Jacquelynne Eccles, and Stephanie Madon found that teacher expectations had a greater impact for some student populations than others, in particular on girls' performance. When teacher expectations were low, girls' grades were lower and, when they were high, grades were also higher; boys' eventual grades were unaffected by teachers' expectations. The extent to which these effects can accumulate over time and seriously influence a child's educational career or occupational aspirations is currently unknown, though some theories posit disidentification with an academic domain as one potential consequence of this type of self-fulfilling prophecy. [*See* ACADEMIC ENVIRONMENTS; CLASSROOM AND SCHOOL CLIMATE.]

B. OCCUPATIONAL DOMAINS

Self-fulfilling prophecies may also manifest themselves in the domain of work. For example, one early experiment by Carl L. von Baeyer, Debbie L. Sherk, and Mark Zanna demonstrated that women who expected to be interviewed by a male who held traditional gender role beliefs presented themselves in a more traditionally feminine fashion, as measured by the types of clothing, accessories, and makeup worn to the mock interview. Also of relevance is the Dvir, Eden, and Banjo study mentioned earlier, in which leaders' expectations led to greater performance by a group, depending on the sex of the leader. However, the military setting of this study makes it difficult to generalize their results to civilian organizations, and more work in this area of leadership, gender, and the self-fulfilling prophecy is certainly warranted.

A recent study by Robert D. Ridge and Jeffrey S. Reber documents another way in which gender-based expectancies may manifest themselves in the workplace. In their study, male interviewers who were led to believe that their female interviewee was attracted to them behaved in a particularly flirtatious manner. Furthermore, in these circumstances, the male interviewer's expectations were confirmed by the female interviewees: objective raters judged these women to be more flirtatious, in response to the males' subtle overtures, than women whose interactions lacked the expectation. Of additional interest, the male interviewers saw their own behavior as professional and appropriate for the situation, even while acknowledging their playful behavior; as well, women in this study seemed not to realize that they were behaving in ways that confirmed their interviewer's ex-

pectations. This study may have important implications for gender relations in the workplace. The authors speculate that this sequence of events—males in a position of power eliciting flirtatious behavior from females unbeknownst to the female, which confirms the male's initial beliefs—may be one route to sexual harassment. [*See* SEXUAL HARASSMENT; WORKING ENVIRONMENTS.]

C. INTERPERSONAL RELATIONSHIPS

Finally, some work in the area of close relationships has documented self-fulfilling prophecies at work in both experimental and naturalistic settings. Geraldine Downey, Antonio L. Freitas, Benjamin Michaelis, and Hala Khouri, in a 1998 study using a diary methodology that captures to some extent ongoing relationships, found that women who were sensitive to rejection elicited a self-fulfilling sequence with their partners. These relationship expectations were activated specifically during interpersonal conflicts, and led to partners engaging in more rejecting behaviors. This process and outcome was not found for rejection-sensitive men or people who were low in rejection sensitivity. These studies illustrate the conditions under which gender and relationship beliefs can jointly impact peoples' lives via self-fulfilling prophecies.

IV. *Summary*

Although not the inevitable outcome of all social interactions, there is abundant evidence that behavioral confirmation can and does occur in laboratory and field settings. When preexisting beliefs of a perceiver are confirmed by a target in social interactions, it serves to preserve and perpetuate those beliefs, whether they apply to the understanding of a particular person or to the stereotypes of a social group. Experimental studies have parsed social interactions into a sequence of steps that result in the confirmation of expectations. Key elements include the expectations held by a perceiver, how those expectations influence a perceiver's behaviors toward a target, the motivations and interaction goals of perceivers and targets, and the power structure between perceivers and targets. All these elements interact in dynamic fashion to produce or to inhibit the confirmation of preexisting beliefs.

Self-fulfilling prophecies have been demonstrated to occur in a diversity of settings and with a host of expectations; thus, models of behavioral confirmation sequences can be considered a general framework. This generic formulation can be augmented to gain some understanding of the role that gender may play in either encouraging or discouraging confirmatory outcomes. Because gender is such a strong, salient, and central cognitive category, the gender composition of a social interaction can have an important impact on behavioral confirmation by activating gender-based expectations. Differing interaction styles between men and women may make men particularly prone to eliciting confirmation and women prone to accommodating a perceiver's overtures. A particularly potent elicitor of behavioral confirmation may be cross-sex interactions where a relatively powerful male perceiver interacts with a relatively powerless female target. The power conferred to each interaction participant may actually determine what interaction style is adopted. Thus, outcomes of a social interaction may have less to do with gender per se, but instead primarily with the covariation of power and gender.

Empirical research reveals a mixed set of findings regarding gender and behavioral confirmation. Some studies clearly find that women as targets readily assimilate their behavior to perceiver expectations, and that women as perceivers are less likely to elicit behavioral confirmation from a target. In contrast, men in these studies exhibit the opposite pattern. Other studies suggest that the dynamics of cross-sex interpersonal encounters are more complicated than this straight-forward interpretation. Extrapolating from work in this area is further complicated because studies using cross-sex interactions tend to adhere to a procedural standard where women and men are typically assigned to the target and perceiver role, respectively.

Experimental studies show that self-fulfilling prophecies can occur, and field studies attempt to assess the prevalence of the phenomenon in actual life situations. We briefly presented some of the ways in which gender and gender-related beliefs can potentially elicit confirmation in educational, occupational, and close interpersonal relationship contexts. The phenomenon is a general one, and, given the right set of situational contingencies, can potentially affect interaction outcomes in many life domains. The power of the self-fulfilling prophecy is that it may be a subtle, yet pervasive, phenomenon through which beliefs and expectations—accurate or erroneous—are translated into social reality.

SUGGESTED READING

Copeland, J. T. (1994). Prophecies of power: Motivational implications of social power for behavioral confirmation. *Journal of Personality and Social Psychology* **67**, 264–277.

Deaux, K., and LaFrance, M. (1998). Gender. In *The Handbook of Social Psychology* (D. T. Gilbert, S. T. Fiske, and G. Lindzey, eds.), 4th ed., Vol. 1., pp. 788–827). McGraw-Hill, Boston.

Geis, F. L. (1993). Self-fulfilling prophecies: A social psychological view of gender. In *The Psychology of Gender* (A. E. Beall and R. J. Sternberg, eds.), Ch. 2, pp. 9–54. Guilford Press, New York.

Hall, J. A., and Briton, N. J. (1993). Gender, nonverbal behavior, and expectations. In *Interpersonal Expectations: Theory, Research, and Applications* (P. D. Blanck, ed.), Ch. 14, pp. 276–295). Cambridge University Press, New York.

Jussim, L., Eccles, J., and Madon, S. (1996). Social perception, social stereotypes, and teacher expectations: Accuracy and the quest for the powerful self-fulfilling prophecy. In *Advances in Experimental Social Psychology* (M. P. Zanna, ed.), Vol. 28, pp. 281–388. Academic Press, Orlando, FL.

Snyder, M., and Stukas, A. A., Jr. (1999). Interpersonal Processes: The interplay of cognitive, motivational, and behavioral activities in social interaction. In *Annual Review of Psychology*, Vol. 50., pp. 273–03. Annual Reviews, Stanford, CA.

Sex between Therapists and Clients

Ken Pope

Norwalk, Connecticut

I. The Problem and Its History
II. Harmful Effects
III. Gender Differences
IV. Conclusion

Glossary

Ambivalence Conflicting impulses, feelings, attitudes, or desires experienced either simultaneously or in relatively rapid alteration.

Cognitive dysfunction A disruption in the thought processes, sometimes involving problems with attention, memory, and concentration; may include unbidden thoughts, intrusive images, or flashbacks.

Emotional lability Relatively rapid and sometimes unpredictable changes in emotion.

Role reversal In the context of therapist–client sexual involvement, the therapist takes on the role of the patient and the experience, moods, wants, and needs of the therapist become the focus of the sessions, and the client's role is helping the therapist.

Therapist–patient privilege This privilege, which has been recognized by the U.S. Supreme Court in *Jaffee* v. *Redmond,* legally protects confidential communications between patient and therapist.

SEX BETWEEN THERAPISTS AND CLIENTS has emerged as a significant phenomenon, one that the profession has not adequately acknowledged or addressed. Extensive research has led to a recognition of the extensive harm that therapist–client sex can produce. Nevertheless, perpetrators account for about 4.4% of therapists (7% of male therapists; 1.5% of female therapists) when data from national studies are pooled. This article looks at the history of this problem, the harm it can cause, gender patterns, the possibility that the rate of therapists sexually abusing their clients is declining, and the mental health professions' urgent, unfinished business in this area.

I. The Problem and Its History

When people are hurting, unhappy, frightened, or confused, they may seek help from a therapist. They may be depressed, perhaps thinking of killing themselves. They may be unhappy in their work or relationships and not know how to bring about change. They may be suffering trauma from rape, incest, or domestic violence. They may be binging and purging, abusing drugs and alcohol, or engaging in other behaviors that can destroy health and sometimes be fatal.

The therapeutic relationship is a special one, characterized by exceptional vulnerability and trust. People may talk to their therapists about thoughts, feelings, events, and behaviors that they would never disclose to anyone else. Every state in the United States has recognized the special nature of the therapeutic relationship and the special responsibilities that therapists have in relation to their clients by requiring special training and licensure for therapists and by recognizing a therapist–patient privilege, which safeguards the privacy of what patients talk about to their therapist.

A relatively small minority of therapists take advantage of the client's trust and vulnerability and of the power inherent in the therapist's role by sexually exploiting the client. Each state has prohibited this abuse of trust, vulnerability, and power through licensing regulations. Therapist–patient sex is also subject to civil law as a tort (i.e., offenders may be sued for malpractice), and some states have criminalized the offense. The ethics codes of all major mental health professionals prohibit the offense.

The health care professionals at their earliest beginnings recognized the harm that could result from sexual involvement with patients. The Hippocratic oath, named after the physician who practiced around the 5th century BC, prohibits sex with patients as does the code of the Nigerian Healing Arts, which was created prior to the life of Hippocrates. Freud, a pioneer of the "talking cure," emphasized the prohibition in his writings. The historical consensus among health care professionals that sex with patients is prohibited as destructive continued into the modern age. In the landmark 1976 case of *Roy v. Hartogs* (which marked one of the first times a woman successfully brought suit against her therapist on these grounds), the court held: "Thus from [Freud] to the modern practitioner we have common agreement of the harmful effects of sensual intimacies between patient and therapist."

II. Harmful Effects

What are the "harmful effects" the court referred to? While the scientific and professional literature had contained carefully documented individual case studies and theoretical papers describing the harm that therapist–patient sex could cause, larger-scale studies began to emerge in the 1960s and 1970s. William Masters and Virginia Johnson, for example, gathered data from many research participants for their 1966 report "Human Sexual Response" and the 1970 report "Human Sexual Inadequacy." They were surprised at the number of participants in their samples who had engaged in sex with therapists. The extensive data that Masters and Johnson collected on each participant allowed them to compare the consequences of sex with a therapist to the consequences of other events such as consensual sexual relationships with a spouse or life partner, consensual sex occurring outside long-term relationships, and various forms of rape, incest, and abuse. So striking were the harmful consequences associated with therapist–patient sex that Masters and Johnson wrote: "We feel that when sexual seduction of patients can be firmly established by due legal process, regardless of whether the seduction was initiated by the patient or the therapist, the therapist should be sued for rape rather than malpractice, i.e., the legal process should be criminal rather than civil."

Psychologist Phyllis Chesler, in her landmark 1972 study "Women and Madness," included a section on therapist–patient sex. She reported consequences among the sample of women whom she studied including severe depression and suicide.

Pope and Vetter published a national study of 958 patients who had been sexually involved with a therapist. The findings suggest that about 90% of patients are harmed by sex with a therapist; 80% are harmed when the sexual involvement begins *only* after termination of therapy. About 11% required hospitalization, 14% attempted suicide, and 1% committed suicide. About 10% had experienced rape prior to sexual involvement with the therapist, and about a third had experienced incest or other child sex abuse. About 5% of these patients were minors at the time of the sexual involvement with the therapist. Of those harmed, only 17% recovered fully.

The three studies mentioned earlier represent only a few of the diverse sampling procedures used to study the harm that can result from therapist–patient sex. Diverse studies have gathered samples of patients who never again sought mental health services as well as those who later entered into therapy again with a new therapist. Patients who have experienced therapist–patient sex have been compared to carefully matched control groups of patients who have experienced sex with their treating physicians who were not therapists and of patients who have been in psychotherapy but who have not experienced therapist–patient sex. The effects of therapist–patient sex have been assessed by independent clinicians, by subsequent therapists of the patients, and by the patients themselves. Data have been collected using structured behavioral observation, standardized tests and other psychometric instruments, clinical interview, and other methods.

What follows is a brief description of 10 of the most common reactions that are frequently associated with therapist–patient sex. These reactions are (1) ambivalence, (2) cognitive dysfunction, (3) emotional lability, (4) emptiness and isolation, (5) guilt, (6) impaired ability to trust, (7) increased suicide risk, (8) role reversal and boundary confusion, (9) sexual confusion, and (10) suppressed anger. While common, these reactions do *not* characterize all patients who have been sexually involved with a therapist.

A. AMBIVALENCE

Extreme ambivalence can be one of the most debilitating consequences of sexual involvement with a therapist. Caught between two sets of conflicting impulses, those suffering this consequence may find themselves psychologically paralyzed, unable to make much progress in either direction. On one hand, they may want to escape from the abusive therapist, from the destructive relationship, and from the continuing effects of the abuse. They may wish to break the taboo of silence that the therapist has imposed, to speak out truthfully about what has happened to them. They may seek justice and restitution in the courts. They may try to prevent the therapist from abusing other patients by filing formal complaints with professional ethics committees, the hospital or clinic (if any) employing the therapist, and licensing agencies, in part to see if to what degree these organizations are serious about protecting patients from abuse. They may try to make sense of and work through their experience of abuse so that they can move on with their lives.

But on the other hand, they may believe that they need to protect the abusive therapist at all costs. Abusive therapists are often exceptionally adept at creating and nurturing these dynamics. Exploited patients may learn from the therapist that the most important thing is to keep the sexual relationship secret so as not to harm the therapist's career. They may have been led to believe that the sexual relationship was an act of great self-sacrifice on the part of the therapist, a moral and ethical act that was the only way that the therapist could "cure" whatever was wrong with the patient.

Ambivalence of this kind is often found among those who have experienced other forms of abuse. Incest survivors, for example, may experience contradictory impulses to flee the abusive parent, and yet also to cling to and protect that same parent. Similarly, some battered women will desperately want to escape to safety but also feel an overwhelming impulse to submit to the batterer, to take all blame upon themselves, and to keep the battering secret from all others. [*See* BATTERING IN ADULT RELATIONSHIPS; CHILD ABUSE.]

B. COGNITIVE DYSFUNCTION

Many people who have been sexually involved with a therapist, whether the sex started before or after termination, will experience intense forms of cognitive dysfunction. There may be interference with attention, memory, and concentration. The flow of experience will often be interrupted by unbidden thoughts, intrusive images, flashbacks, memory fragments, or nightmares. These cognitive impairments may interfere significantly with the person's ability to work, to participate in social activities, and sometimes even to carry out the most routine aspects of self-care. Sometimes the pattern of consequences may fit the model of posttraumatic stress disorder.

C. EMOTIONAL LABILITY

Emotional lability reflects the severe disruption of the person's characteristic ways of feeling in a way that is similar to cognitive dysfunction reflecting the severe disruption of the person's characteristic ways of thinking. Intense emotions may erupt suddenly and without seeming cause, as if they were completely unrelated to the current situation. The emotional disconnect can be profound: a person can describe a wrenchingly sad event and burst out laughing, or talk about something funny or wonderful and begin sobbing.

Emotions begin to feel alien and threatening, as if they were unwanted intruders into the inner life. Cognitive dysfunction can involve interrupting the flow of experience with unbidden thoughts, intrusive images, and so on; emotion lability can involve interrupting the flow of experience with extreme, unpredictable, rapidly shifting feelings. The person begins to feel helpless, as if the emotions were completely out of control, as if he or she were at the mercy of a powerful, intrusive enemy, an occupying force.

D. EMPTINESS AND ISOLATION

People who have been sexually involved with a therapist may experience a subsequent sense of emptiness, as if their sense of self had been hollowed out, permanently taken away from them. The sense of emptiness is often accompanied by a sense of isolation, as if they were no longer members of society, cut off forever from feeling a social bond with other people.

The sense of emptiness and aloneness can feel overwhelming and horrifying, as Elma Pálos described clearly. Pálos had been the therapy patient and sexual partner of Sándor Ferenczi. Pálos's mother had also been the therapy patient and sexual partner of Ferenczi. She wrote in 1912: "This being alone that now awaits me will be stronger than I; I feel almost as if everything will freeze inside me. . . . If I am alone, I will cease to exist."

E. GUILT

People who become sexually involved with a therapist may become flooded with persistent, irrational guilt. The guilt is irrational because it is in all instances the therapist's responsibility to avoid sexually abusing a patient. It is the therapist who has been taught, from the earliest days of training, that engaging in sex with patients is prohibited, no matter what the rationale. It is the therapist whose ethics code clearly classifies sexual involvement with patients as a violation of ethical behavior. It is the therapist who is licensed by the state in recognition of the need to protect patients from unethical, unscrupulous, and harmful practices, and it is the licensing boards and regulations that clearly charge therapists with refraining from this form of behavior that can place patients at risk for pervasive harm.

As the research summarized in subsequent sections will show, gender effects in this area are significant. It is possible that gender may be associated with the ways in which this irrational guilt develops and is sustained. Psychiatrists Melanie Carr and Gail Robinson wrote "[W]omen are often programmed to take responsibility for and feel guilty about relationships and their problems. The almost universal expression of guilt and shame expressed by women who have been sexually involved with their therapists is a testament to the power of this conditioning" (p. 126). Psychiatrist Virginia Davidson, analyzing the similarities between therapist–patient sex and rape, wrote:

Women victims in both instances experience considerable guilt, risk loss of love and self-esteem, and often feel that they may have done something to "cause" the seduction. As with rape victims, women patients can expect to be blamed for the event and will have difficulty finding a sympathetic audience for their complaint. Added to these difficulties is the reality that each woman has consulted a therapist, thereby giving some evidence of psychological disequilibrium prior to the seduction. How the therapist may use this information after the woman decides to discuss the situation with someone else can surely dissuade many women from revealing these experiences.

F. IMPAIRED ABILITY TO TRUST

When therapists intentionally and knowingly violate their patients' trust, as they do when they decide to become sexually involved with them, the effects on the patients' ability to trust can be profound and lasting. Therapy may rest on a foundation of exceptional trust. People may walk into the offices of complete strangers and, if the stranger is a therapist, begin talking about thoughts, feelings, and impulses that they would reveal literally to no one else. Every state, appreciating the exceptionally sensitive nature of the "secrets" that patients may entrust to their therapists, have established in their laws a formal therapist–patient privilege. The ethics codes of all major mental health professions recognize the therapist's responsibility to maintain confidentiality when patients trust the therapist to the extent that they disclose personal information in therapy.

Beyond investing therapists with trust regarding their own privacy, confidentiality, and secrets, patients trust therapists to act in a way consistent with patient welfare and to avoid intentionally engaging in any behavior that not only is unethical and prohibited by law but also places the patient at so needless a risk for harm. In some ways, therapy is similar to surgery. Patients agreeing to surgery allow themselves to be opened up physically because they have been led to believe that the process has some reasonable prospects of leading to improvement. They allow a professional to do to them (i.e., cut into them) what they would not let anyone else do. They trust that the professional will not take advantage of them or abuse them, sexually or otherwise, during this process. Therapy patients submit themselves to a process in which they open up psychologically because they also have been led to believe that this process is likely to yield improvement. They trust therapists to avoid any exploitation or abuse during the process.

It was Freud who first noted this similarity. He wrote that "talking therapy" was "comparable to a surgical operation." Like the surgeon, the therapist worked with "a dangerous instrument. . . . [I]f a knife will not cut, neither will it serve a surgeon." According to Freud, the responsible therapist always honestly acknowledged the potential for enormous destruction:

[I]t is grossly to undervalue both the origins and the practical significance of the psychoneuroses to suppose that these disorders are to be removed by pottering about with a few harmless remedies. . . . [P]sychoanalysis . . . is

not afraid to handle the most dangerous forces in the mind and set them to work for the benefit of the patient."

G. INCREASED SUICIDE RISK

As a group, patients who have been sexually involved with a therapist have significantly increased risk of both suicide attempts and completed suicides when compared with the general population and other groups of patients. The research published in peer-reviewed journals suggests that about 14% will make at least one attempt at suicide and that about one in every hundred patients who have been sexually involved with a therapist commit suicide.

H. ROLE REVERSAL AND BOUNDARY CONFUSION

Therapists who sexually exploit their patients tend to violate both roles and boundaries in therapy. The focus of sessions shifts from the clinical needs of the patient to the personal desires of the therapist. The therapist brings about a reversal of roles: the sessions and the relationship are no longer about the therapist being of use to the patient in service of the patient's welfare but rather the patient being of use to the therapist in service of the therapist's sexual gratification. The fundamental clinical, ethical, and legal boundary that would prevent a therapist from turning patients into sources for the therapist of sexual pleasure, experimentation, relief, variety, or control is violated.

In a legitimate therapy, the therapeutic process, effectiveness, and improvements that therapist and patient work on during each sessions is expected to continue between sessions and, ultimately, after termination. Entering psychotherapy to become less depressed, to overcome stage fright, or to resolve conflicts with a partner would make little long-term sense if the depression, stage fright, and conflict resumed immediately after termination. Unfortunately, the harm as well as the benefits that therapy brings about can be long term. The negative effects of the therapist's violation of boundaries and reversal of roles can generalize beyond the therapy and persist long after the termination of the therapy and the sexual relationship. The roles and boundaries that people use to define, mediate, and protect the self may become not only useless for the patient but also self-defeating and self-destructive.

I. SEXUAL CONFUSION

It is perhaps not surprising that many patients who have been sexually exploited by a therapist wind up deeply confused about their own sexuality. Psychologist Janet Sonne served as one of the group therapists in 1982 and 1983 for some of the patients who participated in the UCLA Post Therapy Support Program, the first university-based program offering services to the patients who had been sexually involved with their therapists, conducting research in this area, and providing training to graduate students. She wrote that female patients who had been sexually involved with a prior therapist

expressed a cautiousness or even disgust with their sexual impulses and behavior as a result of sexual involvement with their previous therapists. For some female clients who identified themselves as heterosexual before they were involved sexually with female therapists, there tended to be significant confusion over their "true" sexual orientation.

The experience of sex with a therapist leaves some patients believing that their only worth as human beings is to provide sexual gratification to others. Some engage in sex with others on an almost obsessional basis as re-enactment of the sexual relationship with the therapist. Especially when the patient is experiencing feelings of emptiness and isolation, the specific sexual activities previously experienced with the exploitive therapist—often re-enacted in the midst of flashbacks—may represent an attempt to fill up the self and break through the isolation. For still other patients, sex becomes associated with feelings of irrational guilt. They may engage in demeaning, degrading, joyless, painful, harmful, or dangerous sexual activities that seem to express the conviction: "I am guilty, worthless, and deserve this." Some may become so confused about sexuality that they begin labeling a variety of feelings and impulses as "sexual." They may, for example, say that they are sexually aroused whenever they are feeling intensely angry, depressed, anxious, or afraid.

J. SUPPRESSED ANGER

Many patients who have been sexually abused by a therapist are justifiably angry, but it may be difficult for them to experience the anger directly. Some may feel only numbness in situations that, according to them, would have previously evoked anger. Some may turn the anger inward, becoming enraged at themselves. The anger directed inward may lead to self-loathing, self-punishment, and self-destructive behaviors including suicide.

Offending therapists are often skilled at manipulating patients into suppressing their anger. Some may use intimidation, coercion, or even force and violence to ensure that a patient will suppress anger rather than feel and express it directly. One therapist would yell at a patient, who had a history of having been sexually abused, whenever she started to become angry at him for touching her sexually during the sessions. She became terrified of her own anger and of the possibility that anyone else might become angry at her. During her subsequent therapy sessions she would sit in silence for long periods of time, terrified to say anything, finally whispering something along the lines of, "You're angry at me, aren't you." Psychologist Janet Sonne, describing the findings of the UCLA Post Therapy Support Group, wrote: "Although the patient may occasionally acknowledge her intense rage, she will more often suppress her anger for fear of being overwhelmed by it, or of harming its object (the therapist) or others." [*See* Anger.]

III. Gender Differences

Exceptional gender differences have emerged from the diverse research models investigating therapist–client sexual involvement. Data from each research approach suggest that offending therapists are overwhelmingly (though not exclusively) male, while exploited clients are overwhelmingly (though not exclusively) female. Each method of study has strengths and weaknesses, but in each, the number of male offenders exceeds the number of female offenders and the number of female victims exceeds the number of male victims, even after the overall proportions of male and female therapists and of male and female clients have been taken into account. The extreme gender differences led UCLA professor Jean Holroyd, principal investigator of the first national study of therapist–patient sex, to write that "sexual contact between therapist and patient is perhaps the quintessence of sex-biased therapeutic practice": female clients do not have equal access to nonabusive therapy. The following section reviews peer-reviewed findings representing four of the major methods of study.

One approach to gathering data in this area is to obtain anonymous reports from current and former therapy clients about whether they were or were not sexually involved with their therapist. The published data from this approach show that clients who report having been sexually involved with a therapist are overwhelmingly more likely to be female than male.

A second approach is to obtain anonymous reports from therapists about whether they have or have not been sexually involved with clients. The book *Sexual Involvement with Therapists: Patient Assessment, Subsequent Therapy, Forensics* summarizes and statistically analyzes the national self-report studies of therapists that have been published in peer-reviewed journals (for summary data about these national studies, please see http://kspope.com/8studies.shtml). The base rate of the behavior (i.e., engaging in sex with a client) is relatively low and thus the statistical differences are not always significant. In one of the studies the percentage of male offenders is nine times as large as the percentage of female offenders. When the data from all eight national studies are pooled, overall about 4.4% of the therapists report having engaged in sex with at least one client. Offenders are about four times more likely to be male than female: overall about 7% of the male therapists reported engaging in sex with one or more clients; about 1.5% of the female therapists reported engaging in therapist–client sex.

A third approach examines actuarial data from licensing boards, ethics committees, and other agencies that adjudicate complaints against therapists. A study of licensing board disciplinary actions in regard to therapist–client sexual involvement, for example, found that in 86% of the cases, the disciplined therapist was male and the client was female.

A fourth approach gathers data from subsequent treating therapists. Anonymous surveys have asked large samples of therapists whether they have encountered in their clinical work any clients who had been sexually involved with a prior therapist. The largest of such studies that gathered data on both the gender of the client and the gender of the offending therapist found that in about 88 to 92% of the cases, the sexually exploited clients were female and the offending therapists were male.

It is worth noting that although the clients who have been sexually exploited by a therapist are often spoken of as if they were adult men and women, in a significant number of cases, the clients are minors. In the Pope and Vetter study, for example, one out of every 20 clients who was sexually involved with a therapist was a minor. One national study of therapist–client sex involving minors found that the majority were female. The average age of a minor female client who had been sexually involved with a therapist was 7. They ranged in age from 3 to 17

Table I
Characteristics of Clients to Whom Psychotherapists Are Attracted[a]

	Social workers	Psychologists
Physical attractiveness	175	296
Positive mental/cognitive traits or abilities	84	124
Positive overall character/ personality	58	84
Vulnerabilities	52	85
Sexual	40	88
Other specific personality characteristics	27	14
Miscellaneous	23	15
"Good patient"	21	31
Resemblance to someone in therapist's life	14	12
Pathological characteristics	13	8
Same interests/philosophy/ background to therapist	10	0
Fills therapist's needs	8	46
Long-term client	7	7
Kind	6	66
Successful	6	33
Independent	5	23
Client's attraction	3	30
Availability (client unattached)	0	9
Sociability (sociable, extroverted, etc.)	0	6

[a]The responses from social workers in column 1 are from the study by Bernsen, A., Tabachnick, B., and Pope, K. (1994), National survey of social workers' sexual attraction to their clients: Results, implications, and comparison to psychologists, *Ethics & Behavior* 4, 369–388. The responses from the psychologists in column 2 are from the study by Pope, K. S., Keith-Spiegel, P., and Tabachnick, B. (1986), Sexual attraction to patients: The human therapist and the (sometimes) inhuman training system, *American Psychologist* 41, 147–158. There were 444 participants in the social work study (providing 552 descriptive terms) and 585 participants in the psychology study (providing 997 descriptive terms).

years old. The average age of a minor male client who had been sexually involved with a therapist was 12. The boys in this study ranged in age from 7 to 16 years old.

Gender differences also occur in a related area of research: sexual attraction to clients. Table I summarizes some of the findings from two studies of sexual attraction. In these studies, over 80% of the psychologists (in the 1986 study) and social workers (in the 1994 study) reported feeling sexually attracted to at least one client. About 92 to 95% of the male participants compared with about 70 to 76% of the female participants in these two studies reported feeling sexually attracted to at least one client. Table I presents the results when participants were asked to try to identify the most attractive characteristic of the client to whom they were attracted. The hundreds of characteristics were sorted into about 20 major categories. With the following two fascinating exceptions, there were no significant gender differences between the male and female therapists in mentioning the various characteristics. However, female therapists were overwhelmingly more likely than male therapists to mention "successful" as a sexually attractive quality. On the other hand, male therapists were overwhelmingly more likely than female therapists to mention "physical attractiveness."

The findings of these and subsequent studies suggest that a significant proportion of therapists carry in their imagination sexualized thoughts, images, or fantasies of their clients and focus on them when the client is not physically present. For example, in the two studies summarized in Table I, 27 to 30% of male therapists, compared with 13 to 14% of female therapists, reported that while they themselves were engaging in sexual activity with someone else (i.e., not the client), they engaged in sexual fantasies about the client.

IV. Conclusion

Although the prohibition against sex with patients reaches back beyond Freud, beyond the Hippocratic oath, and at least as far as the code of the Nigerian Healing Arts, it was only with systematic research that began in the 1950s that the profession began to understand the depth, pervasiveness, and persistence of the harm that can result when therapists abuse their license, role, power, and trust. Partly as a result of this increasing understanding of the consequent harm, it came to be recognized as more than a violation of professional or clinical ethics, of licensing laws, and of the civil laws (i.e., patients can sue offending therapists for malpractice in the civil courts). An increasing number of states have criminalized therapist–client sex, some classifying it as a felony. As one court held in reviewing the constitutionality of criminalizing therapist–client sex concluded:

[T]he state has a legitimate interest not only in protecting persons undergoing psychotherapy from being sexually exploited by the treating therapist but also in regulating and maintaining the integrity of the mental health profession.

It is equally obvious to us that the legislative decision to criminally proscribe a psychotherapist's knowing infliction of sexual penetration on a psychotherapy client is reasonably related to these legitimate governmental interests. . . . [It] therefore comports with due process of law.

Whether because of increasing recognition of ways in which sex with a therapist can harm a client, increasing legal penalties, or other factors, studies suggest that fewer and fewer therapists are sexually abusing their patients. The eight national studies published in peer-reviewed journals that were discussed earlier draw on anonymous self-reports from 5148 therapists. Psychiatry, psychology, and social work each provide data in at least two independent studies conducted in separate years, allowing statistical analysis of possible trends. When all factors are taken into account in statistical analysis, there is a significant gender effect, which was discussed in a previous section. Interestingly, there are *no* significant differences among psychiatrists, psychologists, and social workers in self-reports of engaging in sex with clients.[1] There effect due to the year of the study is statistically significant: there is about a 10% drop in the self-reports of therapist–client sex each year. (This does not, of course, mean that there will be no self-reports of therapist–client sex after 10 years; each year the drop is only 10% of the prior year's level.)

Research suggesting that the rate of therapists sexually abusing their clients may be declining is encouraging but it is far from enough. The mental health professions have made a modest beginning in overcoming the self-protective guild orientation, the

[1]The apparent professional differences among the eight studies are, the statistical analysis suggests, the result of a confounding correlation between two variables: "profession" and "year of study." A statistical analysis incorporating the data and variables of all studies allowed comparative evaluation of how much predictive power each variable (i.e., profession and year of study) had after the variance accounted for by the other variable was subtracted. Year of study possessed significantly more predictive power after effects due to profession had been accounted for than the predictive power of profession after effects due to year had been taken into account. When the predictive power of year of study is accounted for, there are no significant differences among the professions.

vulnerability to self-idealization, the difficulty acknowledging and taking responsibility for reprehensible behavior, the conspiracy of silence, the tendency to disbelieve or blame clients who appear to have suffered harm because of a therapist's unethical behavior, the habit of seeing causes and sources of problems as external to the profession, and other less-than-perfect traits of therapists that have made it hard to address issues of therapist–client sex effectively. The time is overdue for the mental health professions to put an end to the "quintessence of sex-biased practice," in the words of Jean Holroyd, that puts female clients, both minor and adult, at far greater risk than male clients for damaging sexual exploitation by a therapist. Adults and children who are hurting, confused, vulnerable, and sometimes desperate, who come for help and place their trust in therapists, deserve more than to be used to gratify therapists' sexual impulses. To help others who come to them with their problems, the mental health professions must first take care of their own problem of sexually exploitive therapists.

SUGGESTED READING

Abstracts & Articles: Therapy Research & Therapist Resources. Web site at http://kspope.com
Bates, C. M., and Brodsky, A. M. (1989). *Sex in the Therapy Hour: A Case of Professional Incest.* Guilford Press, New York.
Gabbard, G. O. (ed.) (1989). *Sexual Exploitation in Professional Relationships.* American Psychiatric Press, Washington, DC.
Noel, B., and Watterson, K. (1992). *You Must Be Dreaming.* Poseidon, New York.
Pope, K. S. (1994). *Sexual Involvement with Therapists: Patient Assessment, Subsequent Therapy, Forensics.* American Psychological Association, Washington, DC.
Pope, K. S. (2000). Therapists' sexual feelings and behaviors: Research, trends, and quandaries. In *Psychological Perspectives on Human Sexuality* (L. Szuchman and F. Muscarella, eds.), pp. 603–658. John Wiley & Sons, New York.
Pope, K. S., Sonne, J. L., and Holroyd, J. (1993). *Sexual Feelings in Psychotherapy: Explorations for Therapists and Therapists-in-Training.* American Psychological Association, Washington, DC.
Pope, K. S., and Vetter, V. A. (1991). Prior therapist–patient sexual involvement among patients seen by psychologists. *Psychotherapy* 28, 429–438.

Sex Difference Research
Cognitive Abilities

Diane F. Halpern
California State University, San Bernardino

Glossary

Psychobiosocial model An alternative model to the nature-nurture controversy. It is a model of multiple, sequentially interacting variables that influence each other.

Stereotype threat When negative stereotypes about one's group are made salient in a setting where the stereotype is relevant to performance, the stereotype may act to depress performance. Data in support of this concept remain mixed.

Steroidal hormones Chemicals secreted directly into the bloodstream so that they can affect organs that are distant from the site of their secretion. They act on the central nervous system.

Visuospatial working memory A limited capacity stage in memory that is involved in imaging a figure while mentally transforming it in some way.

THERE ARE NO SEX DIFFERENCES in general intelligence, but differences are usually found on selected tests of cognitive abilities. The size of the differences varies depending on the nature of the specific test and age of the participants. Some of the sex differences are small; others are very large. Sex differences in cognitive abilities are multiply determined. Recent research has highlighted the role of stereotypes and steroidal hormones. A psychobiosocial model that recognizes the reciprocal effects of nature and nurture is advanced as an explanatory concept. Readers are reminded that humans vary along multiple dimensions, and we do not have to be the same to be equal.

I. The Meaning of Differences

The many questions and unstated assumptions about the ways in which females and males differ with regard to their cognitive abilities raise a large number of ethical and empirical dilemmas. A common concern among those who are opposed to any research on questions about sex differences in comparisons of women and men is that the results will be used in ways that support a misogynist agenda. These fears are understandable given that women still earn considerably less than men, even after controlling for variables like level of education and years on the job.

The social inequalities between women and men in many countries throughout the world include separate laws that restrict basic rights like voting and access to an education, so concerns about the misuse of experimental studies on sex differences are justified. While recognizing the legitimate concerns about the misuse of experimental findings on sex differences, there are important reasons why such research is essential. Research is the only way to distinguish between beliefs about women and men that have a basis in fact and those that are not supported with data. Inequalities and prejudice flourish in the absence of valid data. Research is always conducted in a sociopolitical context that guides the type of research questions that are asked, the way data are collected, and most critically, the way data are interpreted. Even though science is always embedded in a system of values, it is the best method for reaching valid conclusions, especially when the topic being investigated is politically volatile.

The many questions concerning similarities and differences between females and males have been a consuming interest for researchers in a wide variety of disciplines and for the general public as well. Although everyone acknowledges that men and women are both similar and different, research tends to center on differences, in part because most of the commonly used research methods are designed to provide conclusions about differences, but not similarities. Most statistical techniques allow for the rejection of the hypothesis that two or more groups are similar, but cannot reject the hypothesis that they are different. It may seem that this is a bias in the research process that leads psychologists and others to overemphasize the way the sexes differ while ignoring the many similarities, but in fact it is not possible to study differences without also studying similarities and vice versa. When multiple studies fail to find evidence of sex differences, researchers can aggregate these findings using a statistical method known as meta-analysis to determine if, where, and by how much females and males differ, and by extension, if, where, and when they are similar. Thus, it is only because of studies of sex differences that we can now conclude that sex differences are minimal or essentially nonexistent in some areas that psychologists study, such as short-term verbal memory and influenceability.

In thinking about the meaning of sex differences, it is useful to think of the many ways that individuals differ. The data presented in this article show that there are both differences and similarities in the cognitive abilities of women and men, but there is no data-based rationale to support the idea that either

is the smarter or superior sex. Variation is a basic principle of biology that we can choose to value. People do not have to be the same to be equal. [*See* METHODS FOR STUDYING GENDER.]

II. Tasks and Tests That Usually Show Sex Differences

Are there sex differences in general intelligence? This is one of the easiest questions to answer because there are many reasons for concluding that, on average, there are no differences between females and males in general intelligence. All of the major tests that are commonly used to assess intelligence, such as the Wechsler Intelligence Scale for Children (WISC), Wechsler Adult Intelligence Scale (WAIS), and the Stanford-Binet Intelligence Test were written so that there would be no overall difference in total scores for males and females. Questions that favored one sex were either eliminated during the test development phase or balanced with another question that favored the other sex. Thus, we cannot turn to the usual measures of intelligence to provide an answer to the question of sex differences in overall intelligence. Despite this fact, there have been some very vocal advocates for the idea that women are less intelligent than men. These claims are made using intelligence tests that were developed and standardized so that they do not yield higher overall scores to either females or males. Thus, there is a critical flaw in any argument that uses intelligence tests that were designed and standardized to show no sex differences to then advance the idea that females or males are the more intelligent sex. Any claim for the superiority of one sex or the other based on measures that were standardized to eliminate any possible sex difference is specious and may be more reflective of a particular political agenda than carefully executed research or critical thought.

The question of sex differences in intelligence was recently addressed by Arthur Jensen, a psychologist who became well known in the late 1960s for his controversial work on race differences in intelligence. In his 1998 book, Jensen analyzed data from a large number of cognitive tests that had *not* been standardized in ways that would eliminate sex differences, thus making it more likely that he would find evidence of sex differences in intelligence, if they exist. He found that, across tests, there are no sex differences in general intelligence. He did, however, find sex differences on some of the tests that he examined, with results sometimes showing a higher average score for females and sometimes for males. Similarly, the tests used to measure intelligence show sex differences on the subscores that are used in computing the overall intelligence score. Thus, it seems that females and males differ, on average, on some measures of cognitive abilities, but not in general (overall) intelligence.

A summary of tests and tasks that usually show sex differences in cognitive abilities is shown in Table I where tasks and tests have been grouped by the cognitive process that is involved. This cognitive process taxonomy is congruent with our most recent understanding of brain processes and mechanisms, which tend to be specialized by cognitive process.

A. COGNITIVE TESTS AND TASKS THAT USUALLY FAVOR WOMEN

1. Rapid Access to and Use of Phonological, Semantic, and Episodic Information in Long-Term Memory

Large effects favoring females are found with verbal fluency tasks (e.g., name as many words as you can that start with the letter "t") and synonym generation tasks (e.g., what are some synonyms for the word "good"), with the effect size somewhere between $d = 0.5$ and 1.2 (standard deviation units—the 0.5 to 1.2 range is generally thought of as a large effect). Females also perform better than males on verbal learning tasks and many kinds of memory tasks, especially episodic memory, which is memory for personal events that include the time and place information that the event occurred.

2. Production and Comprehension of Complex Prose

In general, females also excel at reading, especially when the material tends to be complex. The female advantage in reading is supported by the fact that many more males than females are diagnosed with dyslexia and other reading disabilities. Males, however, have the advantage on tests of verbal analogies, which are a type of verbal task that may also require the transformation of information in short-term working memory.

There is also some evidence that girls may talk about one month earlier than boys and produce longer utterances than boys. There are significant sex differences in the rate of vocabulary growth during the toddler years. In a study that was published in 1991, Janelten Huttenlocher and colleagues reported that, on average, there is a 13-word difference in vocabulary size between girls and boys at 16 months of age, which grows to a 51-word difference at 20 months and a 115 word difference at 24 months. These researchers found that the differential rate in vocabulary growth was unrelated to how much mothers spoke to their children—mothers spoke as much to their boy babies as to their girl babies. They concluded that "gender differences in early vocabulary growth seem to reflect early capacity differences" (p. 245).

Standardized tests also show that females are better at spelling, and females are consistently and substantially better, on average, on college achievement tests in literature, English composition, and Spanish. A writing test was recently added to the Preliminary Scholastic Achievement Test (PSAT), a test taken by more than 1 million high school students usually in 11th grade, because females score higher on writing tests. The ability to write well is an important skill that should be predictive of success in college. The addition of a test of writing to the PSAT has already increased the number of females who will be receiving prestigious merit scholarships to pay for college. Psychologists who have argued that the female advantage on verbal abilities is small usually have not

Table I
Tasks and Tests That Usually Show Sex Differences in Cognitive Abilities

Higher average scores for females	Higher average scores for males
Rapid access to and use of phonological, semantic, and episodic information in long-term memory	Tasks that require transformation in visuospatial working memory
Production and comprehension of complex prose	Making judgments about objects that are in motion
Execution of fine motor tasks	Motor tasks that require aiming
Speech articulation (tongue twisters and rapid naming)	Fluid reasoning (especially in science and mathematics)
Perceptual speed	Standardized tests of mathematics used for admissions to college and graduate schools

included those abilities where females show the largest advantages—writing, retrieval from long-term memory, and verbal articulation tasks.

3. Fine Motor Tasks

The ability to execute fine motor tasks is usually assessed with timed tasks that require fine motor movements such as moving pegs in a peg board (although at least one researcher believes that the advantage comes from the smaller fingers that women have). Timed tests that require rapid performance are, at least in part, also tapping other noncognitive variables such as the extent to which individuals are motivated to achieve high test scores. Depending on one's political positions, these findings could be used to argue that women are naturally better at tasks like typing and sewing or tasks like neural surgery or small motor repair. Thus, as shown in this example, it is important to distinguish between research results and the interpretation of research results.

4. Speech Articulation

Another indication of the female advantage in some verbal skills is the fact that stuttering, a disability in the production of fluent speech, is many times more prevalent among males. Females also score higher on verbal articulation tasks such as reciting tongue twisters and rapidly naming objects.

5. Perceptual Thresholds

Females are generally more sensitive than males, that is, they have a lower threshold for detection of odors, sounds, and touch. Some sensitivities, particularly the perception of pain, vary clinically over the menstrual cycle. The perceptual advantages seen in females appear early in infancy with fluency differences developing in the toddler years. Girls mature earlier than boys up through adolescence, so girls frequently achieve cognitive milestones at a younger age than boys.

6. Perceptual Speed

Other tests that consistently favor women are "Finding A's," which requires the rapid scanning of rows of words to find and cross out the A's (a measure of perceptual speed or rapid access to word knowledge in long-term memory), "Identical Pictures," which involves visual matches of static dis-

plays (this is only one of several tests that show a sizable female advantage for object memory), "Coding," which requires the rapid matching of geometric symbols with numbers, and memory for location, which can be considered a spatial task.

B. COGNITIVE TESTS AND TASKS THAT USUALLY FAVOR MEN

1. Tasks That Require Transformations in Visuospatial Working Memory

One of the largest between-sex differences favoring males is reliably found on those visuospatial tasks that require transformations in visuospatial working memory. These tasks include mental rotation, which involves the imagined motion of stationary figures (e.g., what would a figure look like if it were rotated in space). Sex differences on tasks like these are found by age 4—probably the youngest age at which they can be measured reliably. In a meta-analysis of mental rotation in 1993, Masters and Sanders computed the effect size to be $d = .9$ (almost a standard deviation—a large effect size) and found that it has remained unchanged at this value for more than 18 years. This effect size is so large that many statisticians maintain that tests of statistical significance are not needed. It is among the largest effect sizes that psychologists study.

2. Tasks That Involve Judgments about Objects That Are Moving (Spatiotemporal Judgments)

The ability to make accurate judgments about moving objects is assessed with a variety of experimental paradigms. Two examples are "time of arrival" judgments where participants press a computer key to indicate when a moving ball that disappears behind a screen would hit another object that is visible on the screen or tracking a moving object through three-dimensional space. The effect size on this task is also large, but it does not have the same large number of studies or long history as mental rotation tasks, so reliable estimates of the size of this effect are not yet available.

3. Motor Tasks That Require Aiming

Males also excel at spatial-motor tasks such as throwing a ball, dart, or other object at a moving or stationary target or intercepting a moving object. Of course, one difficulty is assessing sex differences in ability with aiming tasks is the fact that most males have much more experience with aiming tasks than females.

4. Fluid Reasoning Tasks (Especially in Math and Science)

Some, but not all, quantitative tasks also show large and consistent sex differences. Consistent with a cognitive processes model, research findings are easier to interpret if readers think about the nature of the task rather than the fact that numbers are used. Females have a clear advantage at quantitative tasks in the early elementary school years when math tasks involve learning math facts and arithmetic calculations, probably reflecting rapid learning and retrieval processes. Sometime before the start of puberty, when the nature of the mathematical tasks changes and becomes more spatial (e.g., geometry, trigonometry, calculus), the advantage shifts to males who maintain their superior performance into old age. Thus, the size and direction of the effect depends on developmental stage and type of quantitative task with retrieval of math information from memory favoring females and transformations of representations favoring males.

5. Standardized Tests of Mathematics Used for Admissions to College and Graduate Schools

One of the largest differences occurs on the mathematics portion of the Scholastic Aptitude Test (SAT-M), a test used by almost every college and university in North American and many other places in the world, which shows a substantial advantage for males. Sex differences favoring males are even larger on the quantitative portion of the test used for admissions to graduate schools, the Graduate Record Examination (GRE-Q). Disproportionately more males than females score in the very highest ranges of the SAT-M and GRE-Q, where the differences are most pronounced. Large sex differences on these tests have important social policy implications because they are used in determining college and graduate school admissions.

C. UNDERSTANDING THESE DATA

In thinking about these differences, there are several important points to keep in mind. First, the largest differences are found in the tails of the distributions: males are overrepresented among the retarded and gifted, with some types of mental retardation overwhelmingly male. The sex differences in the middle of the abilities range, where most of people are, are generally smaller. It is also important to remember that data on sex differences are based on group averages, and no one is average. Many of these tests are taken by volunteer participants and other special groups (e.g., only those who need to take standardized tests as an entry requirement for college), and thus are probably not representative of all females or all males. Data like those presented here cannot be used to justify or explain the performance of any individual, despite the ubiquitous tendency to relate experimental findings to individual experiences and performance.

III. Analytic and Creative Abilities

There are multiple ways of thinking about cognitive abilities. One way of categorizing abilities is to think about tasks that require making judgments about information that is given—these are tasks that require analysis—and tasks that require coming up with new ideas—creative tasks. When cognitive abilities are seen from the dual perspective of analytic and creative, the tasks that are listed in Table I generally fall into the analytic category. The creative ability to recognize when a problem exists or to solve a problem in a novel way is an important cognitive dimension. A creative idea or solution is one that is both novel and good. It is extremely difficult to devise valid measures of creativity because novel ideas may not be recognized as good ideas during one's lifetime. There are also many different ways to be creative. Most people think of creativity in terms of the arts or sciences, but it is possible to be creative in almost any domain. Some people are creative in how they get their budgets to stretch to cover their expenses or in cooking or handling life's everyday problems. If one were to look at inventions and other events that have been recorded in history, it seems that most are attributable to men, but the excess of men in historical records may be due to the fact that women were traditionally excluded from those domains that were recorded as history such as battles, government leadership, and the sciences. In fact, there are no good data to support the idea that either males or females are the more creative sex.

IV. A Psychobiosocial Model

Knowing the ways in which males and females differ on average is theoretically less interesting than understanding why these differences occur. Researchers often attempt to determine the proportion of the variance in cognitive sex differences that can be attributed to nature or biological influences and the proportion that can be attributed to nurture or socialization influences. Unfortunately, attempts to partition variance into the two categories of nature and nurture are destined to fail because the question of how much is nature and how much is nurture is the wrong question. It is not as if there is some "true" percentage attributable to nature or nurture that exists in the world for researchers to discover.

Even simple distinctions like dividing variables into biological and environmental categories are impossible. Consider, for example, the fact that there are differences in female and male brains. The differences in brain structures could have been caused, enhanced, or decreased by environmental stimuli. Nutrition, for example, is an environmental factor with biological and behavioral consequences; a diet deficient in protein, especially in first year of life, will substantially reduce overall intellectual levels and affect development of brain structures, thus blurring the distinction between biology and environment. Brain size and structures remain plastic throughout life. Leslie Ungerleider and other psychologists and neuroscientists have used brain imaging techniques to show changes in cortical representations that occurred after specific experiences. What an individual learns influences structures like dendritic branching and cell size; brain architectures, in turn, support certain skills and abilities, which may lead us to select additional experiences. The interface between experience and biology is seamless. Biology and environment are inseparable.

The nature-nurture dichotomy is, and always has been, false. Learning is both a biological and environmental phenomenon, and we are predisposed by our biology to learn some skills more readily than others. Similarly, many stereotypes reflect real group differences and by learning and endorsing them, we may be selecting environments that increase or decrease these differences. A schematic diagram of the psychobiosocial model is shown in Figure 1. The psychobiosocial model replaces a continuum anchored by nature and nurture with a continuous feedback loop where environmental and biological variables affect each other so that it is not possible

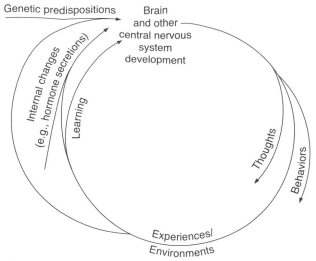

Figure 1 The psychobiosocial model, in which biological and environmental variables are conceptualized as continuously exerting reciprocal effects on each other so that the brain and other parts of the central nervous system change in response to environmental stimuli and individuals alter the environment to reflect the neural architecture of cognition. Reproduced from Halpern, D. F. (2000). *Sex Differences in Cognitive Abilities*, 3rd ed. Lawrence Erlbaum Associates, Inc., Publishers, Mahwah, NJ. Reproduced with permission.

to distinguish between these types of influences. [*See* DEVELOPMENT OF SEX AND GENDER.]

V. How Stereotypes Affect Performance on Cognitive Tasks

An exciting area of recent research has shown the importance of the unconscious effects of sex stereotypes on thought and performance. Advocates of this view have shown that categorization is a fundamental property of information processing, and stereotypes are one example of basic categorization processes. In a clever set of experiments by Mahzarin Banaji and her colleagues, participants are required to answer questions about males and females and sex-stereotyped topics like mathematics and literature. She found that stereotypes often operate unconsciously and automatically with even individuals who claim to "have no stereotypes" taking longer to process information that is incompatible with common stereotypes than information that is congruent with common stereotypes.

Claude Steele and his colleagues have shown that

negative stereotypes can decrease performance on cognitive tests when group membership is made salient (e.g., participants are asked to indicate their sex), the stereotype about one's group is negative (e.g., females are less able in math than males), performance on the test is important to the individual (e.g., scores will be used to determine college admissions), and the test is difficult. These are important studies, but this area of research, known as stereotype threat, is still new and there have been some statistically powerful studies in ecologically valid settings that have failed to find an effect for negative stereotypes. Thus, it is not possible to make any strong conclusions about the way stereotype threat affects performance on tests of cognitive abilities until additional studies are published and psychologists have a better understanding of the way in which stereotype threat operates.

VI. The Role of Steroidal Hormones on Cognition

Humans are both social and biological animals, and as explained in the psychobiosocial model, both forces operate simultaneously within a system of influences. The genetically coded information that makes each individual female or male also affects other developing systems including the brain. In normal humans, the genetic code determines whether the undifferentiated gonads will become ovaries or testes. If development is in the male direction, then approximately 7 weeks after conception the newly formed testes will secrete androgens, primarily testosterone and dihydrotestosterone. If ovaries are formed, they will develop at approximately 12 weeks following conception and secrete estrogens (e.g., estradiol) and progestins (e.g., progesterone). Although these hormones are commonly referred to as "male" and "female" hormones, all three are found in both females and males. These sex hormones are more commonly known as steroidal hormones because of their chemical structure. As these hormones circulate through the bloodstream, they are converted by enzymes into chemical structures that are important in the formation of the brain and internal and external sex organs.

Although it has long been known that prenatal hormones are important in brain development and subsequent cognition, it is only within the past 10 to 15 years that we have come to realize that normal fluctuations in adult hormone levels cause small, but measurable variations in performance on some cognitive tasks. One of the most fascinating areas of recent research has shown that testosterone and estrogen continue to play critical roles in sex-typical cognitive abilities throughout the life span in normal populations. Highly publicized studies have shown that women's cognitive abilities and fine motor skills fluctuate in a reciprocal fashion across the menstrual cycle. Several researchers have suggested that there may be an "optimal" level of some of these hormones for certain spatial abilities. Women perform better on spatial tests when they are in the menstrual phase of their menstrual cycle, a phase in which estrogen is low, than when they are in the midluteal or follicular phase, a phase in which estrogen is much higher. Performance on verbal and fine manual skills is also higher when women are in the high-estrogen phases of their cycle.

A parallel finding that never attracted the same attention in the media is that males also show cyclical patterns of hormone concentrations and the correlated rise and fall of specific cognitive abilities. The spatial skills performance of normal males fluctuates in concert with daily variations in testosterone (higher testosterone concentrations in early morning than later in the day and seasonal variations; in North America, testosterone levels are higher in autumn than in spring). Furthermore, normal aging men improved on spatial tasks and declined on verbal fluency when they were given high doses of testosterone. It seems that steroidal hormones influence performance on tests of cognitive abilities throughout the adult years and well into old age.

Further support for this conclusion comes from studies that have found that female-to-male transsexuals improved on spatial tasks and declined on verbal fluency when given high doses of testosterone. Followup studies have shown that the gain in visual-spatial skills and loss in verbal fluency was maintained over several years following the initial treatment with cross-sex hormones. Some of the most exciting work in this area has shown that women with Alzheimer's disease improved on some cognitive measures when they were given estrogen replacement therapy, although there is still much we do not know about the cognitive effects of estrogen replacement in old age. Some retrospective studies have shown an inverse relationship between dose and duration of estrogen replacement therapy and incidence of Alzheimer's disease. This suggests that estrogen plays a role in the prevention and treatment of neurodegenerative diseases, but much more research is needed before anyone can assert that estrogen is effective in the treatment or prevention of Alzheimer's disease.

The data on hormone replacement therapy do not support a definitive conclusion at this time, but there is ample reason to be optimistic. In one recent study, psychologists and others computed lifetime exposure to estrogen for a sample of healthy older women and found that those women who had had greater exposure to estrogen (for example early age of menarche and late menopause) had higher scores on a battery of cognitive tasks than women with shorter exposures to estrogen. Thus, there are multiple types of findings that provide converging evidence for the importance of estrogen and other steroidal hormones for adult cognition.

A. BRAIN STRUCTURES

Ultimately, sex differences in cognitive abilities are mediated by the brain structures and processes that underlie cognitive performance. There are multiple brain structures, unrelated to reproductive behavior, that vary by sex. For example, the corpus callosum, the thick band of neural fibers that connect the two hemispheres of the brain, is somewhat larger and more bulbous in women than in men—a conclusion that some researchers are still debating. Sex differences in the corpus callosum is an important finding because it supports the theory that female brains are more bilaterally organized in their representation of cognitive functions. The difference in the shape of the corpus callosum, which is the largest fiber track in the brain, implies better connectivity between the two cerebral hemispheres, on average, for females. Exciting advances in brain imagery have shown that there are also different patterns of activity in male and female brains when they are engaged in some cognitive tasks such as reading and navigation through space.

B. RESEARCH LINKING SEX HORMONES, BRAIN STRUCTURES, AND COGNITION

Causal links between steroidal hormones and sex differences in brain structures and organization have been determined in several different ways. Some of the strongest data to establish the fact that hormone levels cause alterations in brain structures and cognition have involved experimental manipulations with nonhuman mammals (e.g., administering testosterone or estrogens prenatally and perinatally and removing naturally occurring hormones from the prenatal and perinatal environment). For example, when female rats have their ovaries removed, they show learning and memory deficits that are reversed when estrogen is administered. Differences in brain activity are correlated with these changes (decrease in activity in hippocampus and frontal cortex when estrogen is withheld). By using an animal population, researchers are able to further explore the causal hypotheses in the relationship of estrogen-deprived states and the cognitive function.

Based on animal models, Bruce McEwen and colleagues, in 1997, hypothesized that there are essentially three effects of estrogen and progestin that are especially relevant to memory processes. (1) Estrogens and progestin regulate new excitatory synapses (synaptogenesis) in the CA1 region of the hippocampus. In addition, short-term verbal memory in humans and working memory in rats are enhanced by estrogen-induced synaptic formation. (2) There are developmentally programmed sex differences in the hippocampal structure that may help explain the differing strategies used by male and female rats in solving spatial navigation problems. The researchers assume that these principles apply to humans as well. (3) Ovarian steroids have effects throughout the entire brain, including effects on the brainstem and midbrain. There are estrogen receptors scattered throughout the brain that support this hypothesis.

Of course, experimental manipulations of hormones cannot be done with humans. To study these effects in humans, researchers examine individuals with various diseases that cause over- or underproduction of gonadal hormones either prenatally or later in life that show cognitive patterns that are in the direction predicted by the data from normal individuals. For example, girls exposed to high levels of prenatal androgens (congenital adrenal hyperplasia) are raised as girls from birth and have normal female hormones starting at birth, yet they tend to show male-typical cognitive patterns and other male typical behaviors such as preferences for "boys toys," rough play, and an increased incidence of sexual orientation toward females. Data like these from humans support the generalizations that are made from nonhuman mammals.

VII. Conclusions and Caveats

The studies presented in this article show that an understanding of cognitive sex differences and similarities requires a much better understanding of the role of sex hormones on performance on cognitive tasks and that stereotypes and steroids need to be studied together because they both play an important role in human cognitive abilities.

Beyond the call for research using multiple perspectives, what conclusion can be made from these and other data? Psychologists who favor evolutionary explanations for contemporary social behaviors look for cross-cultural similarities to support the idea that sex differences reflect evolutionary pressures. Data from many different countries support the idea that men, on average, score higher on some tests of visuospatial working memory and women score higher on some tests of encoding and retrieval from long-term memory. Evolutionary psychologists posit that these differences reflect the division of labor in hunter–gatherer societies where men traveled long distances and presumably developed a neuroarchitecture that supported spatial navigation. Women, on the other hand, gathered food and would have developed brains that supported memory for location of plant-based foods, which would change seasonally. Yet researchers who are opposed to evolutionary interpretations could also use cross-cultural data to show large differences among cultures. For example, there are disproportionately more females among the highest achieving mathematicians in some Asian countries than in the West, and students in the United States routinely score well below those in many other industrialized countries in the world, showing that culture is a critical factor.

Researchers who prefer sociocultural explanations can point to the growing body of work on stereotype threat and conclude that beliefs about the performance of one's own group affect performance in ways that we do not yet understand. Those who are opposed to sociocultural explanations can counter with the finding that stereotypes tend to be relatively accurate and when they depart from values that are found in studies of sex differences, they underestimate actual group differences.

Finally, neuroscientists find support in the data showing that hormones affect brain and cognition throughout life. The psychobiosocial model allows all of these perspectives to be, at least to some extent, correct. Hormones operate within a system of other hormones that respond to the environment and people work more diligently at tasks when they expect to be successful than when they do not expect to be successful. Behaviors and abilities undoubtedly reflect evolutionary pressures, but there is no way to falsify evolutionary explanations, and if they can explain any possible finding, they are not useful explanatory concepts. Thus, there does not have to be a single explanation for a topic that is as complex as sex and cognitive abilities.

Regardless of one's preferred explanatory framework, it is important to keep in mind the broader questions about the societal effect of the growing database of knowledge on the topic of sex and cognition. There are great many ethical questions that emerge as scientists uncover new truths about how we think and how this knowledge radically changes our view of human nature. As we gain a better understanding of the role of hormones in cognitive development, there will be increased pressures to use hormonal treatments. The use of hormone replacement therapies in aging adults is already gaining popularity, but no one can predict the long-term effects, especially because these are the same hormones that underlie many of secondary sex characteristics. The possibilities for misuse of this knowledge loom large, making it the responsibility of educated women and men to prevent the misuse of this knowledge for any political agenda—whether it is biological politics, political correctness, or any variant or alternative to these positions.

SUGGESTED READING

Banaji, M. R., and Hardin, C. D. (1996). Automatic stereotyping (2001). *Psychological Science* **7**, 136–141.

Halpern, D. F. (2000). *Sex Differences in Cognitive Abilities*, 3rd ed. Erlbaum, Mahwah, NJ.

Huttenlocher, J., Haight, W., Byrk, A., Seltzer, M., and Lkyons, T. (1991). Early vocabulary growth: Relation to language input and gender. *Developmental Psychology* **27**, 236–248.

McGillicuddy-De Lisi, A., and De Lisi, R. (eds.) (2001). *Biology, Society, and Behavior: The Development of Sex Differences in Cognition*. Ablex, Stamford, CT.

Steele, C. M. (1997). A threat in the air: How stereotypes shape intellectual identity and performance. *American Psychologist* **52**, 613–629.

Willingham, W. W., and Cole, N. (1997). *Gender and Fair Assessment*. Erlbaum, Mahwah, NJ.

Sex-Related Difference Research

Personality

Mykol C. Hamilton

Centre College

Glossary

Aggression Behavior directed toward another with the intent to harm, physically or psychologically.

Empathy Sensitivity and responsiveness to others' feelings, or feeling the emotions another is feeling.

Helping Altruism, or coming to the aid of others who are in need due to an unselfish concern for their well-being.

Influenceability The tendency to be persuaded by others, believe others, or conform to others.

Meta-analysis A statistical technique for the analysis of the combined data from many studies, resulting in an index describing the average size of a difference between group means.

Nurturance Readiness to respond to and care for others.

PERSONALITY has been defined as the relatively stable set of characteristics, traits, and behavioral tendencies one carries through life, and for the most part, the sexes possess similar personality characteristics. This article addresses the following questions: On what personality characteristics are the sexes similar or different? How are the varied results of studies on sex-related differences in personality traits best reconciled? Do the traits on which the sexes are similar outnumber the traits on which they differ? Do all women or girls score higher or lower than do all men or boys on any of these personality characteristics? What might be the causes of any existing sex-related differences—socialization, biology, or current situational factors? Should researchers study sex-related differences at all? The article first explores some of the methodological problems and philosophical underpinnings relating to the study of personality sex-related differences, then reviews the findings concerning several of the most often researched sex-related differences in personality traits.

Encyclopedia of Women and Gender, Volume Two

I. Methodological Issues in the Study of Sex-Related Personality Differences

In order to compare the sexes on personality characteristics, one must know what results would lead to a conclusion that the sexes are different or similar on a given characteristic. Making this evaluation is not as straightforward as it might first appear. Usually the sexes' mean scores on a variable are compared and an inferential statistic such as a t-test is used to decide whether the difference is statistically significant. But even a statistically significant difference can be trivially small. Furthermore, although a difference may be statistically significant and large, the overlap between the sexes is usually much greater than the average difference between the sexes. Therefore, on any personality characteristic, knowing a person's sex is a very poor predictor of how much the person possesses that characteristic.

In addition, if scores are normally distributed (that is, most scores fall in the midrange, with fewer and fewer scores falling toward the two extremes) and tightly clustered about the arithmetic average, or mean, then the mean is a good representation of the average person's possession of the personality characteristic. But distributions are often widely dispersed around the mean, skewed negatively or positively (clustered at one extreme or the other), or multimodal (having two or more very frequent scores), in which case using means to characterize the sexes on traits is not very accurate. Last, it is never the case that all females possess more or less of a personality trait than do all males, although statements such as "Women are more _____ than men" or "Men are more _____ than women," while usually intended as shorthand to communicate that one sex, on average, has more of the trait than the other, are often interpreted as implying that all members of one sex possess more of a trait than does anyone of the other sex.

In fact, out of the dozens of personality characteristics that have been studied extensively, very few show large or even reliable but small sex-related differences. For example, the sexes are, on average, similar on conscientiousness and honesty. Yet articles and book chapters that discuss sex comparisons on personality or other psychological variables, though often mentioning that sex-related similarities are overlooked in the literature, devote much space to

the research on differences and little to no space to the discussion of variables on which sex-related differences have not been found. In an informal survey of seven recent psychology of women textbooks, this author found that although most discussed the problem of overlooking sex-related similarities, four made no mention at all of particular variables on which sex-related differences have not been found, one briefly explored a few such variables in the narrative, and two simply listed several such variables in tables. In contrast, the number of pages devoted to the discussion of personality *differences* ranged from 3 to 26, with a mean of 13 pages. (In the present article on sex-related differences, once again personality traits on which the sexes are similar go virtually unexplored.)

Relatedly, because of the nature of inferential statistics, when a researcher finds a similarity (or rather the lack of a significant difference) between groups on a psychological variable, it is unclear whether no difference was found because there truly is no difference or because of problems in the design or execution of the study. For example, the instrument used to measure the psychological variable may have been insensitive, participants may not have understood the instructions or taken the study seriously, there may not have been enough participants—the possibilities are actually infinite. If the null result is the main focus of the study, then the research is unlikely to be published or presented at all, and if the result is only secondary to some significant findings, and the research is indeed disseminated, the null result is unlikely to receive much emphasis in the writeup or presentation.

The questions researchers attempt to answer and how the questions are asked affect the answers they uncover. For example, for decades, psychologists searched for answers to the questions "Why are men more intelligent than women?" and "Where does the maternal instinct come from?" Clearly, with questions framed thus, researchers are highly unlikely to find answers to the more objective questions "Are women and men similar or different in various forms of intelligence and, if so, why?" and "Are there differences in women's and men's abilities to nurture and, if so, where do they come from?" How a scientist asks a research question and what questions she or he asks reveal that person's underlying assumptions. It is vital to examine such assumptions when designing one's own research and when interpreting the research of others.

Which population of women and men or boys and

girls one wants to generalize to and how one chooses a sample to represent those groups can also affect one's results. Generalizing to all people when the sample is comprised largely of White, middle-class college students is not legitimate, for example. Yet researchers routinely sample narrowly defined groups then either explicitly or implicitly generalize their results more widely. Sometimes the limited sampling is done out of convenience, sometimes out of ignorance, and sometimes it is done because of the difficulty of working with groups to which the researcher does not belong—poor inner-city women may not wish to participate in experiments or interviews run by researchers of a different class, sex, or education level or of a different race, for example. Even if one does succeed in obtaining a representative group of one sex, sometimes it is difficult to obtain a comparable group of the other sex. To compare women's and men's achievement motivation in young adulthood, if the researcher chose to study men in their mid-20s it would seem at first blush to be reasonable to compare them directly to women in their mid-20s, but age comparability is no guarantee that the two sexes are at the same developmental stage. Differences in average age of marriage, childbearing, and child-rearing responsibilities, educational attainments, and so forth may render the achievement orientations of the two sexes noncomparable despite their matched ages. In addition, assuming the researcher succeeds in choosing comparable samples of males and females, aspects of the study not intended to be interpreted differently by participants of the two sexes, relating to such issues as personal skills, perceived risk, sex of experimenter, and research context, may indeed be interpreted differently. If, for instance, women's and men's helping behavior were compared by examining who is more likely to rescue an apparently drowning swimmer, the researcher would need to know that men and women are equally adept at swimming and lifesaving and that they assess the risks of intervening equally. Or if men's versus women's persuasibility were compared by testing how much a male experimenter was able to sway opinions about a political candidate's hawkishness, one would need to consider whether persuasion efforts by a male experimenter rather than a female experimenter might bias the results and whether the sexes were equally interested in and conversant with politician's views on war.

When sex-related differences are found, interpreting them as favoring one sex when they are in fact neutral is also a potential pitfall. In particular, the tendency to interpret differences as favoring men and limiting women has been a danger historically. For instance, sex-related differences in people's tendency to attend to the background or foreground of stimuli have been seen as evidence for men's greater field independence rather than for women's superior sensitivity to context, and studies showing a female advantage in nurturance are used to justify steering women into nursing and teaching jobs rather than into higher-paying and more prestigious jobs that also involve caring for people, such as medicine or psychiatry.

In the absence of any direct evidence about the causes of a sex-related difference, researchers often speculate about possible causes. That is perfectly reasonable, of course, but it is not good scientific practice simply to assume a particular type of cause. Unfortunately, often researchers who have discovered personality sex-related differences have assumed that if they could not see or imagine any differences in the sexes' backgrounds, training, or reinforcement histories relating to a given personality trait, then the difference on that trait must be due to biology; in reality it might not be any easier to see or imagine a specific biological cause for the difference than it was to pinpoint a socialization cause. Assuming that a sex-related difference has a biological cause poses the danger that the difference, because it is now viewed as "natural," will be used as evidence that the sexes are suited for only certain careers or roles and that it will be seen as one that should be enhanced rather than ignored or minimized. [*See* DEVELOPMENT OF SEX AND GENDER.]

The problems discussed so far concerning research on sex-related differences relate primarily to how individual studies are designed, executed, and interpreted. A broader question revolves around how one should interpret the results of multiple studies on a single topic. It is extremely unusual for all the experiments on a given personality trait to generate the same or even similar results. Instead, the typical pattern is that several studies find a sex-related difference in favor of one sex, some find no difference, and perhaps a few even find a difference in the reverse direction. How is one to make sense of such disparate results, especially knowing that the studies utilize different methods, samples, settings, and manifestations of variables? In past decades, a technique called narrative review was used to interpret multiple studies. This approach involves searching out all the literature on a given personality characteristic, summarizing the various findings, tallying how many of the studies reveal a female advantage, a male advantage, or no difference, then making general conclusions about how similar or different the sexes are overall on that characteristic.

But narrative review has limitations, one of which is that it does not take into account effect size, or the size of the sex-related difference. For about the past 25 years, researchers have been using meta-analysis to analyze the results of multiple studies. This method begins, as does narrative review, with the gathering of the relevant research, but the next step is to convert the results of the studies to a standard measurement so that the overall effect size can be taken into account in the individual studies and calculated overall. Individual studies can also be grouped according to their methodologies, so that it is possible to ascertain whether, for example, only studies in which the experimenter was male result in a male advantage. Meta-analysis constitutes a great improvement over researchers' earlier ability to consolidate the results of multiple studies, but it is not perfect. It does not guarantee that all studies are of high quality, it still relies on the interpretive abilities and objectivity of the reviewer, and it does not reveal the causes of any differences.

Finally, for a number of reasons, some feminist psychologists question whether it is reasonable to compare the sexes on psychological variables at all—they would rather the study of sex-related differences be dropped. Why, they wonder, when women's experiences are so rich and varied due to class, race, religion, sexual orientation, geographical location, and so on, should we classify all women together, draw up profiles of their average scores on personality or other variables, then attempts to contrast them to the other sex, whose experiences are also extremely diverse? In addition, conclusions based on sex-related differences research are often faulty, due to the fact that the study of sex-related differences is fraught with the dangers just described—confusion in defining differences, the overlooking of similarities, bias in what questions are asked and how they are posed, operationalizations that bias a study toward better performance by one sex or the other, generalizing from poor samples, assuming causes of differences are biological and therefore natural, and seeing differences in all or none terms. [See FEMINIST THEORIES.]

For better or worse, however, sex-related differences in the personality traits discussed here have been studied extensively. This article examines the research on these traits, explores the nature and size of any differences, critiques the research, and discusses possible causes for the differences.

II. Empathy and Related Emotional Variables

According to the common gender stereotype, women and men differ in several characteristics related to emotion—women are more emotional than men are and they are more aware of the feelings of others, more sympathetic, and more empathic. A highly empathic person might experience sadness when hearing a friend tell about a sad event that happened to her or him or feel happy when the friend relates a success experience. In other words, the person vicariously experiences someone else's emotions.

Research on empathy, a stereotypically female ability, has not been as extensive as research on the inversely related trait of aggression, stereotypically a male trait, perhaps because whereas aggression is a social problem, empathy is not. However, empathy is an important positive personality trait in its own right, in addition to being a possible cushion against aggression, and therefore, many claim, it deserves more attention.

To excel at empathy, one needs to be good at understanding others' emotions, because a prerequisite to feeling what another is feeling is having insight into what the other person's emotions are. There is some evidence that women and girls, on average, do better than men at decoding others' nonverbal cues, such as tone of voice and facial expressions. For example, females have been shown to be superior to males in discerning what a person portrayed in a photograph is feeling and at recognizing emotion by tone of voice. In contrast to the results for most emotions, however, anger is, on average, detected more accurately by males than by females, perhaps because parents tend to reinforce anger expression in girls less than in boys. In addition, the sex-related differences in detection of emotions do not hold for people in certain occupations—for instance, men in occupations in which interpersonal sensitivity is highly valued are not worse than women at decoding nonverbally expressed emotions. Status is another predictor of the ability to interpret nonverbal emotional cues, perhaps because low-status individuals must focus on the emotional states of high-status individuals more than the reverse. Women's ability to decode emotions may be linked to the fact that women's status is generally lower than men's, as may African Americans' possible superiority over Whites in the ability to decode nonverbal cues.

What about empathy itself? Does the research on sex-related differences support the stereotype? In fact, it shows mixed results. Differences tend to favor women, but the size of the difference depends on the methodology, which emotion is being studied, and the degree of demand characteristics present in the study.

When physiological measures such as pulse, heart rate, and blood pressure are compared, no sex-related differences or very small ones are found. Nonverbal indicators of empathy, such as facial expressions, vocal cues, and gestures in response to, for example, a crying infant, also show small sex-related differences. Self-report measures tend to show larger differences than do physiological or nonverbal measures. Even so, self-report measures involving reactions to actual stimuli, simulated in the laboratory or shown on videotape, result in only moderate sex-related differences. Typically, study participants are asked how concerned they are for the story's characters and are asked to indicate how much they are experiencing whatever emotions the protagonist or other characters are feeling.

Self-report studies using questionnaire responses to hypothetical situations tend to find the largest and most consistent sex-related differences in empathy. When study participants are asked, for example, whether they become upset upon seeing someone cry or whether they tend to get involved with a friend's problems, females are considerably more likely to respond in the affirmative than are males.

Why is methodology so crucial in predicting the findings of studies on sex-related differences in empathy? Perhaps it is because the more aware the participant is of the nature of the dependent variable and the more the display of empathy is under the control of the participant, the larger the contribution of self-presentation and demand characteristics. Women and men know that women are "supposed to be" more empathic than men, so if study participants are asked obvious questions about their past or current feelings of empathy, they may respond in a sex-stereotyped manner both because they feel they should fulfill the stereotypes and because they feel that by doing so they will be of help to the researcher. [*See* EMPATHY AND EMOTIONAL EXPRESSIVITY.]

III. Nurturance

Nurturance follows from empathy—empathy is necessary for nurturance, because one nurtures when one knows nurturance needed. Traditionally, psychological definitions of nurturance have been narrow, which has meant the definitions favor women. At its narrowest, nurturance has been seen as a readiness to respond to and care for children and infants. Broader definitions allow inclusion of the readiness to care for other needy individuals such as the sick or the weak. What has not usually been included in the definition is the readiness to care for healthy, strong adults, though common sense tells us that we can be nurtured throughout our lives and whatever our circumstances. The narrower the definition, the more the stereotype favors women, and reality mirrors the stereotype to a great degree, at least behaviorally—whether or not they actually have a greater readiness to nurture, women in cultures around the world are more involved in caring for others, especially babies, children, and invalids.

There may be biological sex-related differences in the readiness to nurture—in other words, in the ease with which nurturance as a personality characteristic is acquired. But there would not need to be a biological difference to explain most or all of the differences we see in the sexes—cultures seem to work very hard at training nurturant behaviors into girls and women and training those behaviors out of boys and men. Little boys and girls are equally interested in interacting with and being affectionate toward an infant, but by age 5, girls' behavior hasn't changed whereas boys would rather play with a puppy or a kitten than a baby. The sex-related difference is exaggerated further if the children are asked to pretend they are the father or mother of the child. It seems more likely that this developmental sex-related difference is due to gender socialization, such as young girls' being encouraged to play with dolls and help with infant siblings and the active discouragement of boys' doing the same, than to a biological difference.

As with all of the personality differences discussed here, results depend substantially on the method used to study the characteristic. Self-report measures of nurturance show large sex-related differences, but only a tiny fraction of studies find adult females more responsive than adult males in play with infants, children, or animals, or as having a greater physiological reaction to them—nearly 9 in 10 studies show women and men to be equally behaviorally responsive or physiologically reactive. Men certainly do not appear to be biologically incapable of interest in and nurturing of babies. In hospital and laboratory studies of reactions to newborns, men show high nurturance levels.

Further evidence for the role of social expectations in nurturance is found in the fact that in cultures where children of both sexes contribute substantially to child care, adult sex-related differences are very small. But, of course, biology may contribute as well, perhaps by making the learning of nurturant behaviors by females easier and quicker, rather than by creating a "maternal instinct." Research cited as evidence for a human maternal instinct has been criticized on many grounds. For example, though studies on androgenized girls, who have had higher than usual levels of prenatal androgens, show they have lower interest in dolls than do other girls, there are major problems with this research as evidence for a maternal instinct—the nurturance levels were reported by mothers, mothers knew whether their daughters had been androgenized, and so on.

IV. Helping

Given the stereotypes of women as more emotional and caring than men, one would expect research to reveal that women are the more helpful sex. But again, which sex is found to exhibit more of the characteristic depends to a great extent on how the characteristic is measured.

Some early research seemed to indicate that men were more altruistic than women overall. In experiments that took place in the 1970s, involving, for example, hitchikers soliciting rides, motorists on the side of the road needing help to change flat tires, or men collapsing in public settings, men were much more likely to come to a person's aid than were women. Most other early research, however, resulted in small to moderate differences favoring men or no sex-related differences at all, and in a few studies, women were somewhat more helpful than men.

Feminist researchers in the area of altruism began to see correspondences between the situations and contexts in which the helping behavior experiments took place and the results of the studies. Which sex helped more, if either, and the sizes of the differences depended on the operationalizations of help. Men tended to help more than did women, on average, when the task involved physical strength (e.g., help-ing a person who had collapsed, intervening in a fight, changing a tire), when it involved competency in realms traditionally thought of as masculine (intervening in a fight, changing a tire), when the help was short-term (all three studies mentioned so far), when there were onlookers (all three), when help was not requested directly (all three), or when physical risk was involved (all three). If helping is defined in a gender-neutral way, few sex-related differences emerge. When a stamped letter is "forgotten" in a telephone booth, men and women are equally likely to deposit it in a mailbox. If the help involves some combination of the following factors—long-term commitment, direct request, does not favor men's or women's expertise, takes little strength, and minimal physical risk is required—sex-related differences are likely to disappear or even reverse.

In fact, these descriptors usually match fairly well the sorts of help women are stereotypically believed to excel at, but which psychologists seldom define as help. For example, caring for friends or relatives most often involves the person asking for help, rarely takes much physical strength or involves physical risk, is often long term, and frequently involves specific tasks that are more female than male related. Perhaps one reason that the type of help men excel at—the more chivalrous or heroic type of help—has more often been defined as help is simply because it is easier to study physically challenging helping behaviors that involve a quick encounter with a stranger, often with onlookers present, rather than studying more ordinary, realistic forms of help, at which women may excel. But psychologists' very definition of help, as it blurs into definitions of nurturant behavior, may also be partially responsible for the findings. That is, it might be asserted that on one end of a continuum there is short-term, physically risky aid to strangers in emergency situations (traditionally defined by psychologists as helping behavior, with results more often favoring men than women) and at the other end is long-term, non-physically-risky aid to relatives and friends (traditionally defined as nurturance, with results tending to favor women). But if behaviors nearer the center of the continuum are studied, whether the research is published as a report on "helping behavior" or "nurturance" depends on where the researcher draws the line between the two variables. Methodological techniques and definitions of terms, then, go far in explaining why much helping behavior research led to the counterintuitive conclusion that men are more helpful than women.

V. Aggression and Anger

Aggression involves inflicting either physical or psychological harm. Psychological aggression can be either direct, as in verbal abuse in the presence of the victim, or indirect, for example, spreading rumors about someone. Indirect aggression may protect the aggressor from retaliation by preventing the victim from knowing the source of the aggression.

Sex-related differences in aggression have probably been studied more than any other sex-related personality difference. The stereotype is that women are less aggressive than men. In fact, research has shown that men and boys do tend to behave more aggressively than women and girls, but the size of the difference seems to depend on the research setting, the ages of those being studied, and the way in which aggression is defined and measured. Cross-cultural research indicates that, especially in Westernized cultures, boys and men are moderately more aggressive than girls and women, and that the sex-related difference may be greater at younger ages. Sex-related differences tend to be in the predicted direction but small for psychological aggression between strangers, moderate for physical aggression between strangers, and larger in laboratory than field studies. Also, girls and women may exhibit more indirect than direct aggression, though perhaps because indirect aggression requires more social skills than does direct aggression, this distinction does not appear until late childhood.

It may be the case that the two sexes are equally motivated to engage in aggressive behavior, experiencing anger, a precursor to aggression, equally, but that women inhibit their urge to aggress more than men do, because they realistically must be more fearful of reprisal, they are more concerned that aggressive behavior on their part will violate people's expectations, and they are more likely to feel guilty and anxious about behaving aggressively. The fact that sex-related differences are greater in the laboratory than the field supports this reasoning, in that participants in laboratory research are aware that their behavior is being studied, whereas in most field studies they are not. Real-life aggression differences between the sexes, as reflected in statistics on violence rates in the community, tend to be greater than research differences, which could also be due to sex-role expectations. In addition, in studies designed to reduce inhibitions to aggression—for example, studies in which the aggressor is in another room and is therefore unidentifiable—women often aggress at the same rate as men do. Further evidence for the idea that women's anger and desire to aggress are as strong as men's but that they are loathe to act on the desire is provided by research showing that sex-related differences in aggression are reduced in settings in which participants are provoked into aggression through insults, frustration, or physical attack. Given the right circumstances, women do seem quite capable of aggressive behavior.

Childhood socialization may lead females to inhibit their aggressive urges more than males do. Mothers tend to accept more aggression from boys than from girls, according to research, and children's expectations of adult reactions to assertive behaviors depend on their sex. Modeling operates at the level of media portrayals of aggression. Protagonists (or antagonists) who demonstrate that aggression can be a viable response to frustration or provocation are much more likely to be male than female. Children of both sexes tend to enjoy violent video games more than nonviolent ones, but boys are more likely to prefer games that portray violence between "humans," whereas girls seem to like less realistic characters and situations. Girls may begin inhibiting their aggressive responses early in the same way that boys inhibit their interest in babies—in a 1980 study by Eron, the effects of television aggression were the same for the sexes among three-year-olds, but later in childhood girls tended to be less aggressive than boys in response to television violence.

Of all the possible personality sex-related differences, many believe that the difference in aggression is the one most likely caused by biological factors. But this opinion is not universal—others argue that though there is evidence that biology plays an important role in sex-related differences in aggression among other species, it is as yet unclear what the biological contribution might be in humans, if in fact there is even a sex-related difference in aggression once the methodological and situational factors are accounted for. For example, testosterone seems to relate to aggression fairly directly in some species, but in humans the relationship is extremely complex and not well understood. First, the cause-effect relationship between the behavior and the hormone is unclear; second, estrogen may also be related to aggressive behavior. In humans, within-sex differences and cross-cultural differences seem to be greater than between-sex differences, pointing to a bigger role for nurture than for nature. [See AGGRESSION AND GENDER; ANGER.]

VI. Influenceability

Influenceability is stereotypically believed to be a trait more typical of women than of men. Typical influenceability experiments involve subjecting a participant to the presence of a group or individual who hold a particular opinion or who are behaving in a certain way. The confederate or confederates may or may not exert direct pressure on the participant to modify his or her opinion or behavior. Some research shows small average differences in influenceability between the sexes in the stereotypical direction, but once again, how the research is done has a major influence on the results. For example, sex-related differences tend to be larger when the study concerns group pressure rather than individual pressure, and there is no difference when pressure to conform is lacking or the participants are not being observed. Because the differences are, for the most part, only found under conditions of observation and explicit pressure, and because it is difficult to ascertain a baseline level of influenceability, it is hard to know whether even the limited differences are evidence for women being highly conforming or for men being nonconforming.

One possible reason for women's somewhat greater conformity under pressure and observation is that women and girls are socialized more than boys and men to preserve group harmony. However, meta-analysis does not seem to support this explanation. Perhaps it is just that women are socialized more than men to believe that giving in is the right thing to do, so that a combination of past socialization and current social expectations lead to the observed sex-related differences, especially under conditions likely to bring out stereotyped behaviors. In support of this idea, people of both sexes who are high in instrumentality (stereotypically masculine personality characteristics) conform less than those who are high in expressiveness (stereotypically feminine personality characteristics). Men and highly instrumental individuals resist pressure and try to appear independent and strong, especially if they are behaving publicly; women and highly expressive individuals may want to appear nonconfrontational and avoid upsetting the social balance.

Other major factors in influenceability findings for men versus women are the sex of the experimenter and the nature of the topic being discussed or acted on. Male experimenters are considerably more likely than female experimenters to find sex-related differ-ences, and research that involves typically male topics, such as the military or sports, is also more likely to result in differences.

The small sex-related differences found in earlier research on influenceability may largely be accounted for by such factors as those discussed earlier. Newer research, which involves attempts to take into account such variables as experimenter sex, gender-relatedness of topic, and whether the behaviors are done in public or private, tends to find differences only some of the time, these differences are usually very small, and there is some evidence that the differences may have to do with relative power or status (as manipulated by race, for example) at least as much as with sex.

VII. Conclusions

In looking at sex-related differences and similarities on the preceding personality variables, we see some important consistencies in the moderator variables that predict whether differences or similarities are found. In all cases, how the experimental settings and dependent measures are operationalized is crucial. For example, when demand characteristics and self-presentation cues are low because participants are not being observed (in helping behavior, aggression, and influenceability studies) or pressured (in influenceability studies), differences are small or are not obtained at all. When dependent measures involve more realistic or direct techniques (e.g., physiological measures versus questionnaires), differences tend to diminish or disappear (empathy, nurturance). When operational definitions of dependent variables are less stereotyped (helping behavior, nurturance) or the content or setting is less stereotyped (helping behavior, aggression, influenceability), differences shrink or disappear. Relatedly, for all the variables presented in this article, evidence is abundant that gender expectations in experimental settings affect the size and direction of differences, and in all five cases, past socialization has undoubtedly primed people to respond with familiarity to those gender expectations. Evidence, in contrast, for biological causes for the differences is weak or nonexistent.

Feminist researchers and statisticians have improved our knowledge about how the sexes are similar or different on personality characteristics and have righted many of the faults with early research on sex-related differences in personality. The question still remains, though: Does research on sex-related differences serve a useful purpose? Even feminist researchers cannot agree on the answer.

SUGGESTED READING

Berman, P. W. (1980). Are women more responsive than men to the young? A review of developmental and situational variables. *Psychological Bulletin* 88, 668–695.

Eagly, A. H. (1995). The science and politics of comparing women and men. *American Psychologist* 50, 145–158.

Eagly, A. H., and Crowley, M. (1986). Gender and helping behavior: A meta-analytic review of the social psychological literature. *Psychological Bulletin* 100, 203–220.

Eagly, A. H., and Steffen, V. J. (1986). Gender and aggressive behavior: A meta-analytic review of the social psychological literature. *Psychological Bulletin* 100, 309–330.

Eagly, A. H., and Wood, W. (1985). Gender and influenceability: Stereotype versus behavior. In *Women, Gender, and Social Psychology* (V. O'Leary, R. Unger, and B. Wallston, eds.), pp. 225–256. Erlbaum, Hillsdale, NJ.

Eisenberg, N., and Lennon, R. (1983). Sex differences in empathy and related capacities. *Psychological Bulletin* 94, 100–131.

Hare-Mustin, R. T., and Maracek, J. (Eds.) (1990). *Making a Difference: Psychology and the Construction of Gender.* Yale University Press, New Haven, CT.

Hyde, J. S. (1994). Should psychologists study gender differences? Yes, with some guidelines. *Feminism & Psychology* 4, 507–512.

McHugh, M. C., Koeske, R. D., and Frieze, I. H. (1986). Issues to consider in conducting non-sexist psychological research: A guide for researchers. *American Psychologist* 41, 879–889.

Sex Segregation in Education

Cynthia Fuchs Epstein

Deborah Gambs

Graduate Center, City University of New York

I. History of Coeducation in Primary and Secondary Education
II. History of Sex Segregation in Postsecondary Education
III. Debating Single-Sex Education
IV. Sex "Distinctions" and Sex Segregation
V. Legal Issues
VI. Conclusions

Glossary

Gender Distinctive qualities of men and women (or masculinity and femininity) that are culturally constructed.
Sex Attributes of men and women created by their biological characteristics.
Title IX The 1972 amendment to the Civil Rights Act of 1964, which prohibits sex discrimination in schools receiving federal funds.

SEX SEGREGATION IN EDUCATION including the issue of single-sex institutions, may be seen as one element in a much larger and extremely important issue—the question of women's and men's equal access to opportunity and equal position in society. Sex-segregated education is associated with beliefs about sex differentiation and the division of labor in societal institutions such as the family and the workplace. Educational institutions not only prepare youth to learn the skills that will serve them as citizens and workers in modern society, but they provide the settings in which young people develop relationships with others who will become their friends and associates in the work world later in life. There-

fore, whether female and male students are educated together or separately has some consequence for their adult roles and relationships.

I. History of Coeducation in Primary and Secondary Education

Unlike the educational systems of most other contemporary societies, the United States has a tradition of coeducation. The research of Stanford University scholars David Tyack and Elizabeth Hansot shows that the practice of educating girls and boys together was a gradual process that became the norm. In colonial days, formal education was available only to boys, with girls being educated at parents' discretion informally in the home. Prior to the 20th century scientists and laypersons held views that women and girls were innately inferior to men. There were even suggestions that they would become physically masculinized and lose their reproductive capacities if they exercised their mental faculties. However, regardless of attitudes regarding female "nature," girls began to be integrated in elementary or "common" schools, and by the mid-19th century almost as many girls as boys were attending them. Since that time coeducation has been part of the tradition of American public education at the primary and secondary school level. The "exceptional" nature of coeducation in the United States is attributed to the country's commitment to universal education. In 1912 a federal law mandated universal compulsory education. It came about because of practical considerations and because of the absence of religious and secular ideologies that support sex segregation in other societies.

Because of the rural character of much of the United States in the past, parallel public educational institutions were impractical. It was less expensive and more efficient to educate boys and girls in the same buildings, typically a one-room schoolhouse. However, among upper-class families in the South, single-sex primary and secondary school education in private seminaries for women and in parochial schools was common. In urban areas, coeducation was the model for public schools. Furthermore, educational philosophy stipulated that females as well as males should be educated and learn from the same curriculum. Even during the late 1700s, when the educational system of the United States was being crafted, although few girls were educated outside the home, it was advocated that girls be educated because the nation needed a new type of mother, one who was educated and equipped to raise "virtuous and informed citizens." Horace Mann, the influential educational reformer, argued in the *Duties of Woman* that the proper instruction of children was the political, religious, and domestic duty of the well-educated citizen.

Sex differentiation in schools, however, in spite of coeducation, created different tracks for girls and boys until the 1970s. In 1972, the education system was affected by the passage of the Title IX amendment of the Civil Rights Act of 1964, which mandated equal opportunity in education. It established affirmative action guidelines by the Office of Civil Rights, prohibited school districts from discriminating against students on the basis of sex, and set legal limits to single-sex education. Founded on the premises of equal opportunity, equal access, and full integration, it focused on providing complete access to participation in all functions of schooling, regardless of gender. For example, prior to this point, girls and boys were directed into different vocational courses based on sex. During the 1970s and 1980s, denial of access lessened as courses of study such as auto mechanics and home economics admitted both boys and girls. Title IX required that equitable, if not equal, education be accessible to girls and boys. [See AFFIRMATIVE ACTION.]

In the 1990s there was some dispute as to whether equal access is sufficient to provide women the same educational opportunities in subjects such as math and science. Some advocates of single-sex education have argued that girls-only schools can better educate female students in nontraditional areas. However, others have claimed that separate education would only perpetuate injustices of the past. These debates will be discussed later in this article. Private separate sex schools continue to attract students, although many formally sex-segregated schools have been integrated. The public sector is another matter. Title IX does not explicitly regulate admissions policies for K–12 public schools, except for vocational schools. At the level of primary school education, two privately supported public schools for girls were founded in New York City and Chicago.

One, the Young Women's Leadership School of East Harlem (YWLS) was created with generous private support and small classes. As yet there have been no legal challenges to it, although there have been questions about the legality of the restrictions on male students.

Public debates have also been held by advocates of separate institutions for African American boys who argue that they would perform better in sex-segregated schools. In 1991 the Detroit school district attempted to establish three schools for boys, with mentors, counseling, uniforms, an Afrocentric curriculum, and Saturday school. In this case, the judge ruled that the current urban educational environment was not failing boys because of the fact that girls were attending school with them, and thus the school district was required to allow girls to attend as well. An after-school program in Brooklyn, New York, was also required to accept girls, and schools for boys in Milwaukee have been allowed to continue by allowing girls to enroll.

II. History of Sex Segregation in Postsecondary Education

Sex-segregated education was common until the 1980s at institutions of higher education at elite private colleges and universities. The philosophy attached to higher education was somewhat different than in elementary and secondary education. Seen as a training ground, higher education was geared to educating and nurturing the sons of elites who would become governing leaders in society—roles not considered suitable or possible for their daughters. Therefore, elite colleges and universities located in the northeast United States such as Princeton, Columbia, Yale, and Harvard only admitted men. However, in response to exclusion, a number of elite colleges were founded in the 1800s to provide comparable education for women, such as Wellesley (1875), Vassar (1861), Smith (1875) and Bryn Mawr (1880). Well into the 18th century, segregation was uncommon in large state universities. Women had been admitted earlier to state universities in Maine, Michigan, Wisconsin, and Iowa, among others. This may have been because these universities had only a limited orientation to training national political and government leaders and because they were under public scrutiny to provide equal education to all citizens. Primarily they were oriented to educating the young to assume practical roles as businessmen and teachers. Thus educated in the same institutions, male and female students often chose different courses of study that confirmed with conventional views about suitable work for women and men. It was common for women to receive bachelor's degrees in education, fine arts, foreign languages, and home economics but not in business, engineering, and the physical sciences. However, the growth of women's interest in "male" fields has grown substantially in the past two decades. [*See* WOMEN IN NONTRADITIONAL WORK FIELDS.]

In the past, as well, professional schools located in public universities practiced de facto if not de jure constraints on the admission of women, and in schools of nursing and primary school teaching, social convention essentially limited the inclusion of male students. Thus informal restrictions, tied to expectations about men's and women's future occupational and social roles, created sex divisions in education that were not formalized. However, discrepancies in men's and women's overall educational attainments were reduced through the 20th century. Furthermore until the mid 1970s, women's academic attainments were greater than men's because of women's greater rate of high school completion. [*See* ACADEMIC ASPIRATIONS AND DEGREE ATTAINMENT OF WOMEN.]

The civil rights, feminist, and other social movements of the 1960s created pressure for women and students of color to be admitted to schools and workplaces heretofore closed to them through tradition and practice. Schools that excluded students of color or women as part of their official admission policies met court challenges and social pressures that struck down such practices—for African Americans in the 1950s and for women beginning in the 1970s and continuing today. [*See* THE FEMINIST MOVEMENT.]

Through the next 20 years the trend was toward sex desegregation in most institutions of higher learning—public and private. Only a small number, particularly those with religious affiliations, maintained the practice of separate-sex education.

In the 1970s most elite private colleges began to admit students of both sexes (e.g., Yale, Columbia, Amherst, Princeton, Sarah Lawrence, and Vassar), as the ideology of the women's movement specifying equal access became generally accepted in the society and norms began to change. School administrators recognized that it would be beneficial to their institutions to include women to keep their standards high. Furthermore, many institutions of higher learning found it was to their economic advantage to admit both men and women.

Interest in creating segregated educational institutions surfaced in the 1990s over a few highly publicized issues. At the level of higher education, the last two remaining publicly supported male-only colleges—The Virginia Military Institute (VMI) in Virginia and the Citadel in South Carolina—were challenged in the courts by women seeking admission. As discussed in the previous section, advocates (with the financial backing of certain foundations) interested in changing the public school system supported several sex-segregated elementary schools.

At the higher education level, the Supreme Court, in its June 26, 1996, decision on *United States v. Virginia et al.,* held that denying women admission to VMI was unconstitutional, thereby rendering the Citadel case moot and setting a standard of intermediate scrutiny with regard to assessing whether segregation by sex constitutes a violation of equality. According to Title IX standards, an alternative leadership training program at a women's school—Mary Baldwin College—was not considered equal to VMI's program. As a result of the decision, women are now admitted to both schools.

However, the decision did not affect private colleges and a number of women's private colleges have continued to exclude men, advocating that they can provide a better learning experience for women, particularly in nontraditional fields such as mathematics and science, than can coeducational institutions.

III. Debating Single-Sex Education

There continue to be debates about the negative and positive consequences of single-sex education by advocates on both sides of the issue in the popular media and in the scientific community. They include those who advocate women's equality and those who do not. This section presents some of the issues in these debates and the studies that have been referred to in the debates.

Those who advocate separate-sex education for girls and boys defend their positions by claiming that mixed-sex education accounts for deficits in performance of either girls or boys. The belief is that girls would do better in math, science, and leadership without competition from boys, and that boys would be less disruptive without reference to girls in their classrooms. These defenders of single-sex education often hold the view that the sexes have different educational requirements.

Some of those who argue for segregated education refer to the discriminatory treatment of women in mixed-sex environments. They assert that girls and women take on leadership roles in all-female settings that they otherwise would not have access to. These arguments assume that discrimination cannot be remedied in the mixed-sex setting. Researchers do not support the idea that deep-rooted male and female natures require separate education or that segregated education can provide members of each sex with the same opportunities and development of skills.

The justifications offered for the maintenance of sex-segregated institutions include the view that they are necessary because of physiological and psychological differences between men and women, they place an emphasis on assumed differences in self-esteem, they benefit women by allowing them to learn in an all-female environment, they eliminate the complications of sexual attraction between males and females in mixed-sex institutions, and finally the existence of a few sex-segregated schools means that the state can provide a diversity of educational experiences for those who wish it.

A. PHYSIOLOGICAL AND PSYCHOLOGICAL DIFFERENCES

Are there "real" differences between males and females that should be addressed in discussions of sex-segregation in schools? Recent studies and assessments of the body of scholarly literature on cognitive differences between males and females with regard to math and verbal abilities show virtually no differences between the sexes. The psychologists Janet Shibley Hyde and Elizabeth Ashby Plant noted that 25% of studies measuring gender difference found a difference that was close to zero. They pointed out

that if there has been a slant in the interpretation of test results, it has resulted from the glamorization and overemphasis on findings of gender difference; studies finding no differences have been paid scant attention. It is difficult to compare the benefits of co-education and single-sex programs for several reasons: how a program's success or failure is measured affects the outcome of studies, success and failure are defined differently from study to study, and due to selection bias researchers need to control for background variables such as socioeconomic status. Most single-sex schools are private, so that when students are reported doing well in them it may only reflect their educational and economic privileges. [*See* Gender Difference Research: Issues and Critique; Sex Difference Research: Cognitive Abilities.]

Even if there were considerable sex differences in populations of males and females in the various areas of abilities measured by psychologists, they are distributions rather than descriptions of mutually exclusive categories. Indeed, statistically significant differences may be found on the basis of a difference of only a few percentage points, but these differences are not socially significant. That is, they do not have consequences for women's or men's ability to function in society. The differences reported at the ends of distributions do not negate the fact that most males and females usually test the same. Furthermore, any differences reflected within a gender breakdown of each sex may be explained by varied experiences or individual backgrounds. Tests and experiments are snapshots at one point in time. Both males and females may change their capacities over the course of a lifetime, or even because of a change in circumstances. In addition, researchers believe that treating members of each sex differently—for example, by encouraging girls to succeed in math—would result in different test scores. Academic abilities can be fostered in a facilitating environment and diminished in others. [*See* Test Bias.]

Many supporters of sex-segregated institutions, however, claim that females and males achieve more when they attend single-sex schools. In their view, sex-segregation contributes to young men's and women's learning and assumption of leadership roles. Those who focus on males argue that males might be distracted by females and become competitive with each other in an attempt to attract female approval, thereby diminishing the male-bonding possibilities. There does not seem to be research support for this perspective.

Those who are most concerned with women's achievement argue that teachers regard male students more highly than female students and favor them by, among other things, calling on them more in class. They also argue that males are more aggressive in seeking attention and attaining leadership positions. Advocates for segregated schools seem to assume that the poor treatment female students suffer in mixed-sex situations is difficult to rectify. They do not believe there could be improvement in the way in which female students are treated by their teachers and peers and think the removal of female students from hostile environments would be the appropriate remedy. Or, as in the cases of VMI and the Citadel, the focus is directed toward the threat females in the classroom pose to the culture of symbolic "hypermasculinity." Many of the views regarding female and male interests and reactions are based on stereotypes and do not account for the wide variation between members of the same sex. For example, many boys are not aggressive in school, do not demand attention, and are not interested in math and science. Similarly, many girls do demand attention, strive for leadership roles by running for student government and writing for school newspapers, and are interested in business subjects and science. Furthermore, little or no consideration is given to the possible negative effects on students of the single-sex educational culture or to preparing men and women to live and work in a world that is increasingly integrated by sex. [*See* LEADERSHIP.]

B. SELF-ESTEEM

Proponents of single-sex schools argue that while male students enter all male institutions with high self-esteem that leads to individualism that must be undercut to permit later bonding with classmates, women tend to have lower self-esteem and they must be built up. The claim is that all-female institutions accomplish this. The research on self-esteem, however, is quite contradictory. There are numerous studies measuring self-esteem according to a number of variables, such as body image, various personality dimensions, ratings on indices of masculinity and femininity, agentic and communal behavior traits, and other factors. Some show similar rates of self-esteem between men and women; others show some differences. Many that show differences according to sex are mitigated by other factors, such as whether women are employed.

Even if young women were to have lower average self-esteem scores than young men, it does not necessarily follow that they would do worse in school

or later in life. In fact, the findings in the "fear of success" studies of college students done by Matina Horner in the 1970s showing that women had a greater fear of success than men have not been consistent, nor do they predict lack of success in careers. Similarly, research by Albert Bandura of Stanford University finds that "self-esteem affects neither personal goals nor performance."

The focus on self-esteem or efficacy as an important variable, therefore, is problematic. It is entirely possible that self-esteem can come from having an adoring mother, a car in a car culture, or the right brand of sneakers. High self-esteem may give a person confidence, but unless one has access to an open opportunity track, connections with mentors, and the ability to acquire special skills, success is not necessarily guaranteed. [*See* SELF-ESTEEM.]

C. IMPACT ON FUTURE SUCCESS

Advocates of segregated education for women have suggested that a greater proportion of women who have attended sex-segregated colleges, as compared with the proportion of those who have attended co-educational institutions, become heads of organizations or top managers or go on to medical schools. Yet because of the way in which these studies were conducted, and because of the historical period in which they occurred, the data do not support the conclusion that sex-segregated education today would produce success for women in the professions. There are several reasons why this data do not inform the present situation. First, many more women attended women's colleges in the past. As late as 1960, there were about 300 women's colleges in the United States; in 1995 there were only 84, in 2000 there were 74. Of those, 35 were religiously affiliated. Second, the criteria used to define success are suspect. In studies conducted by Elizabeth Tidball and her associates, which are regarded as the basic source for establishing a relationship between success and attendance at women's colleges, success was measured by being named in *Who's Who of American Women*, not *Who's Who*, as is commonly thought. The number of women who became top officials, managers, political leaders, and business executives was so small at the time of those studies (the early 1970s) that it is impossible to make any generalizations about their career routes. In addition, at the time of the Tidball study, women were excluded from the undergraduate institutions at most Ivy League schools, so there were few comparable coeducational institutions with which to compare the single-sex educational experience.

For the tiny number of women from single-sex colleges who did succeed in public life, some educated guesses can be ventured about the possible "causes" of their success. These might include such factors as the strength of the networks among the graduates of elite women's colleges, their social class or background, and the power of their fathers or husbands. For example, before the 1980s, female senators and governors were often the widows or daughters of men who had previously held those offices.

Small, selective, coeducational institutions, where teaching is placed at a premium, are known to achieve the same or better results for women as single-sex women's colleges. Recent research suggests that coeducational schools today are as likely to produce female scientists as are women's colleges. The psychologist Faye Crosby has noted that the National Center for Education Statistics for 1985 showed that coeducational colleges actually had a slight advantage over women's colleges in the percentage of bachelor's degrees awarded to women in engineering, mathematics, and the physical sciences. The percentage of all graduating women with these degrees was five, while the percentage of women graduating from women's colleges was four.

Similarly, recent research by the sociologists Gwen Moore and Deborah White, using a national sample of elite women in business and politics, showed that women who are business executives or who have been elected to office have had a variety of educational experiences. The majority, however, were graduates of coeducational undergraduate institutions. Moore and White suggested that "[t]he few women who achieved top positions may be those who are comfortable in informal male-centered network." The women in high-level government posts, compared to the general population, were "older, more highly educated, and from more privileged social origins."

Even if there were meaningful statistics showing that a disproportionate number of female "achievers" came from women's colleges, there is no reason to assume the sexual composition of the school was the key to their success. Single-factor explanations are suspect due to confounding variables. In the past, educated women rarely ran for office or became top executives, doctors, or lawyers, but this is not to say that they did not form a pool of intelligent, educated, and well-situated women who were available to take advantage when the doors of opportunity were finally thrown open to them. For example, most female attorneys practicing in the United States today received their law degrees after 1975, when law schools finally began to admit women. [*See* CAREER ACHIEVEMENT.]

D. SEXUALITY

Female sexuality has historically been used to justify limiting the participation of women in all aspects of public life. Women and men are believed to distract each other because of sexuality and therefore should not be in mixed settings. Yet men do not regard women as sexual distractions when they are in subordinate roles and welcome them, for example, as secretaries and nurses.

In any case, removing the person of the other sex does not mean that an environment becomes desexualized. In single-sex institutions as in coeducational institutions, same-sex dating relationships exist. Further, studies show that at single-sex institutions sexist references to the other sex tend toward the stereotypical and disparaging.

In the American Association of University Women's 1998 report *Separated By Sex: A Critical Look at Single-Sex Education for Girls,* the compilation of papers concludes that although some studies have shown that girls in single-sex institutions perform better on some measures than girls in coed institutions, overviews about these situations indicate that not all single-sex schools have benefits, and that rather, a small student body, strong emphasis on the academic program, and commitment to the school's mission and values are the important variables that contribute to success.

IV. Sex "Distinctions" and Sex Segregation

Those who argue against sex segregation in school regard sex differences as "socially constructed" and regard segregated schools in reinforcing symbols and practices that maintain unequal access to opportunities in society.

They claim that sex distinctions are common in most societies and form the basis for the division of labor both in public and private life. Assignment of jobs to women or men is called "sex labeling." Most societies assign social tasks such as child care and housework to women, although there is some variation regarding overlap, and most societies assign military roles to men. More broadly, men tend to cluster in high-prestige occupations and public roles of leadership as well as jobs in skilled work and manual labor. Women who work outside the home usually cluster in occupations associated with caretaking duties such as nursing and support services such as clerical occupations. On the whole, universally, women's jobs are lower paid and carry lower prestige than men's jobs. However, there are national differences in the sex labeling of jobs. For example, in the former Soviet Union, it was common for women to be physicians while it was unusual for women to choose this occupation in the United States until the 1980s. Sex labeling of jobs is related to access to education and training. For example, formal and informal quotas limiting or excluding girls and women from educational programs have resulted in their low percentage in military, professional, and technical careers. Similarly, men's limited education in nursing, home economics, and elementary school education has restricted their access and choice of careers in those fields. With a lowering of sex-related barriers to education, we have seen greater participation of women and men in careers historically regarded as nontraditional for their sex. [*See* SOCIAL CONSTRUCTIONIST THEORY.]

Education has not only provided the intellectual capital that has become increasingly important in a world in which skills determine life position, but, as referred to earlier, education also provides the opportunity to enter into networks of association with those similarly trained and positioned. Access to higher education, particularly to the specialized and elite education that is part of the tracking system leading to prestigious and highly remunerative positions, is a measure of equality. It has been argued that segregated schooling of women limits their access to the same educational and associational opportunities men have and that arguments supporting segregation are based on unsound criteria. Further, it has been argued that whatever the intent or ideological underpinning of such arguments, they ultimately have a negative outcome for women's equality in society.

The arguments offered in support of all-male or all-female educational institutions mask the larger issue of segregation as a means used to prevent women from controlling their lives and accessing formal and informal channels to equality. The power of these arguments is enhanced not only by support from those who wish to perpetuate men's advantages in society, but also by many people who claim to be devoted to women's equality.

There is a relationship between an individual's inherited class and social position and his or her access to specialized and elite education, although even women of privilege historically have faced institutionalized barriers to their admission to elite institutions through both custom and law. The gap between those who have access to elite education and those who do not, however, has closed in modern times. Changes in law and changes in societal norms have made it possible for men and women of diverse social backgrounds to prepare for careers in business, sciences, the arts, and the professions to a greater extent than ever before. Both formal and informal barriers restricting the access of women have been lifted. As a result, the most elite educational institutions in the United States have increased greatly the enrollment numbers of these individuals who formerly constituted a small minority or were entirely absent. To further increase female enrollment, many institutions of higher learning specializing in the sciences and engineering, like Purdue University and Virginia Polytechnic Institute, in which women had been virtually invisible, sought ways of encouraging the recruitment and retention of female students. The outcome of these changes in education is reflected in the proportion of women who have entered business, the professions, and the sciences and have established careers within these fields.

Typically, sex labeling of education and careers has often been justified as an outcome of "natural" propensities of males and females. Belief in the cognitive and emotional differences between males and females is widespread. Current studies have even found both ideological and methodological biases in the sciences. Some of these are linked to the ways in which scientific findings are reported. For example, the tendency to report differences between the sexes and not similarities, and to report small or insignificant differences between the sexes as if they were representative of the entire category. Furthermore, there is also a tendency to assume that correlations between sex status and some other attribute imply causality. For example, if it is found that 3 or 4% more girls than boys test higher on tests of verbal ability, it does not mean that girls are necessarily better, as a group, than boys. Actually, a student's class position, family background, or exposure to skilled teachers may account for the differences. Furthermore, changes over time in certain kinds of performance show that performance may change significantly for particular categories of people.

V. Legal Issues

Single-sex public education is considerably constrained by law. Restricting enrollment in a public school program to either sex may discriminate on the basis of sex and thus is contrary to Title IX. It may also violate the equal protection clauses of the U.S. Constitution and state constitutions. However, Title IX does not preclude a school district from having single-sex schools. It prohibits separate-sex classrooms in integrated schools except for certain sports activities and classes in human sexuality or as a remedy for past discrimination.

VI. Conclusions

Although single-sex educational settings may help avoid gender bias and the distractions of coeducational classrooms under certain circumstances, experts question whether they are a remedy for more basic educational goals. They express concern about the risks of separate and unequal allotment of educational resources and the reinforcement of stereotypes that certain groups are low achievers and need special help. Smaller classes, more individual attention, and teacher training in diversity and equity can solve the problems as they are identified now.

Rebutting myriad stereotypes and assumptions regarding the cause-and-effect relationships between single-sex education and the development of civic virtues and cognitive abilities could extend to the entire range of sex and gender scholarship. It is important to address the cultural assumptions and expectations created by segregation.

Sex segregation in any social institution has negative consequences for women. It reinforces the disadvantages women face when they attempt to gain access to the opportunities and networks of association that are available for men. In other institutions, actual or symbolic segregation leads to invidious distinctions and to the subordination of women. Society and subgroups within society invest heavily in the maintenance of distinctions between men and women, probably because the practice supports the status quo.

Far from relying on what are claimed to be the natural and obvious differences between the sexes, society employs laws, rules, and social codes to create sexually divided educational, political, and social spheres. Women who are persuaded that they are different may think less highly of themselves and may not aspire to a life of accomplishment. Stereotyping sometimes leads to a self-fulfilling prophecy. In segregated settings, there is the danger that women may think more highly of men without the reality check of seeing men in natural surroundings. Without regular contact in early schooling, men and women may easily categorize and stereotype each other and be ill prepared for the public life in which they will need to interact. The few advantages women receive from the social assignments that confine, isolate, and shelter them are no consolation for the overwhelming disadvantages they suffer from being designated second-class citizens.

The issue of single-sex education also has ramifications for other types of segregated schooling such as the movement for schools for young African American men in inner cities and alternative schools for gay and lesbian youth. Arguments have been made in favor of and opposing these types of chosen segregation as well. Most of the people involved in these debates all hope for the same thing, a quality education for all in order to ensure an equal opportunity future for young people. The divide occurs when it comes time to implement practical solutions to reach that goal. Recent empirical studies overwhelmingly support the notion that small classrooms, individualized attention, and adequate resources are the most effective elements in a quality education. It is erroneous to suggest that this can only be achieved through segregated classrooms and schools. Instead, the underlying social, structural, and cultural issues that maintain sexism, racism, classism, and homophobia should be considered.

SUGGESTED READING

American Association of University Women Educational Foundation. (1998). *Separated by Sex: A Critical Look at Single-Sex Education for Girls.* Washington, DC.

Epstein, C. F. (1997). The myths and justifications of sex segregation in higher education: VMI and the Citadel. *Duke Journal of Gender Law & Policy* **4**(1), pp. 101–118.

Epstein, C. F. (1988). *Deceptive Distinctions: Sex, Gender, and the Social Order.* Yale University Press, The Russell Sage Foundation, New Haven and London.

Hyde, J. S., and Plant, E. A. (1995). Magnitude of psychological gender differences: Another side to the story. *American Psychologist* V(50), 159–161.

Moore, G., and White, D. (1995). *Pathways to the Top For Women and Men Business Leaders,* paper presented at the Eastern Sociological Society (April 1, 1995).

Tidball, M. E. (1973). Perspective on academic women and affirmative action. *Educational Record* **54**(2), 130–135.

Tyack, D., and Hansot, E. (1990). *Learning Together: A History of Coeducation in American Schools.* Yale University Press, The Russell Sage Foundation, New Haven and London.

Sexual Harassment

Louise F. Fitzgerald

Linda L. Collinsworth

Melanie S. Harned

University of Illinois

Glossary

Gender harassment Sexually inappropriate behavior that consists of crude, offensive, and derogatory sex-related behavior (e.g., obscene jokes, sex-related insults) serving to convey offensive or insulting attitudes about women.

Hostile environment A legal cause of action in sexual harassment litigation in which an individual is subjected to unwelcome sex-based conduct sufficiently severe or pervasive to affect the terms and conditions of her or his employment.

Quid pro quo A legal cause of action in sexual harassment litigation in which an employee is coerced to provide sexual cooperation to secure advancement or avoid job detriment.

Sexual coercion Implicit or explicit attempts to extort sexual cooperation by the promise of rewards or threats of punishment.

Unwanted sexual attention Uninvited, unwanted, and nonreciprocal sexual attention and behavior that, although unwelcome to the recipient, is not tied to any particular condition or reward.

THE TERM "SEXUAL HARASSMENT" refers to uninvited sex-related behavior (i.e., sexist or sexual hostility, unwanted sexual attention, sexual coercion) that is unwanted by and offensive to its target. Although usually discussed in terms of its presence and effects in the workplace, sexual harassment is not limited to organizational settings and also occurs

Encyclopedia of Women and Gender, Volume Two
Copyright © 2001 by Academic Press. All rights of reproduction in any form reserved.

in educational institutions, public housing, and other venues.

I. Introduction and Overview

A reality in the lives of working women for decades, sexual harassment has only recently become a topic of legal and social scientific discourse. Although a small number of researchers had begun exploring the topic, it was the Senate confirmation hearings of Supreme Court Justice Clarence Thomas that brought the issue to the public consciousness. Since that time, research has expanded rapidly, examining a broad range of topics related to the perceptions, definitions, antecedents, and consequences of sexual harassment. Although many questions remain unanswered, this research has provided convergent data to support the conclusion that sexual harassment is a common experience for women in the workplace, that it is damaging to those who experience it, and that organizations can exert some control over its occurrence and ultimate consequences. This article summarizes the current state of scientific research in this area with the goal of providing a broad, yet comprehensive examination of the major issues.

II. A Brief Word about the Law

Although the term "sexual harassment" is by now familiar to most, confusion remains concerning the distinction between statutory and legal guidelines, on the one hand, and actual behavior on the other. From a legal perspective, individuals may encounter any number of offensive sex-related experiences that for various reasons (e.g., frequency, severity) would not qualify as illegal sex discrimination. When social scientists speak of sexual harassment, on the other hand, they are referring to behavior, not a legal finding of fact; legal determinations turn on a number of considerations (e.g., standards of proof, statutes of limitations, organizational liability) that research can inform but not assess in any particular case. Although in-depth discussion of the legal parameters of sexual harassment is beyond the scope of this article, the following overview is provided to frame the subsequent discussion. For a more thorough review, readers are referred to the resources present at the end of the article.

In brief, sexual harassment in the workplace[1] is a violation of the federal Civil Rights Act, and is also prohibited under most state and many municipal statutes. Although the legal framework continues to evolve, it is generally accepted that to prevail in a harassment claim, the plaintiff must prove that the offensive conduct was based on sex, that it was unwelcome, that it affected the victim's employment, and that the organization was responsible in that it knew or should have known of the situation but took no effective action. As case law has developed in this area, it has become clear that "based on sex" includes not only transparently sexualized conduct (e.g., sexual advances) but also sex-based hostility or animosity directed at the plaintiff that would not have occurred but for her sex.

Harassment can affect employment not only when it causes the employee some tangible job detriment, but also when it is so severe or pervasive that it essentially alters the conditions of her employment, making it more difficult for her to do her job. Legal analysis has traditionally distinguished two general categories of harassment: allegations that (1) the plaintiff was pressured to provide sexual cooperation to secure advancement or avoid job detriment (*quid pro quo*); or (2) she[2] was subjected by supervisors or coworkers to other forms of unwelcome sex-based conduct, that thus created a hostile environment.

Not surprisingly, the area most hotly contested has to do with the conditions under which an organization can be held liable for harassment perpetrated by its employees, thus triggering financial liability. The Supreme Court has recently clarified a number of issues having to do with employer liability (see *Farragher* v. *Boca Raton* and *Ellerth* v. *Burlington Industries*), indicating that an organization is directly liable when the plaintiff suffers a tangible job detriment because of the actions of the harasser, whether or not it was aware of the situation; lacking tangible harm, the plaintiff must prove that the employer knew or should have known of the situation and failed to take any remedial action. Federal law provides the right to a jury trial, as well as various levels of damage awards, depending on the size of the defendant organization.

---

[1]Although federal law also prohibits harassment in education and housing, this article focuses on the workplace, given that the great majority of research has taken place in that setting.

[2]Targets of sexual harassment are traditionally referred to in the female gender; this is not to deny that men can also be harassed.

III. The Nature, Measurement, and Prevalence of Sexual Harassment in the United States

A. THE NATURE OF SEXUAL HARASSMENT

Research on sexual harassment is not limited to legal concepts but rather focuses on the entire spectrum of offensive sex-related behavior; this body of work typically recognizes three general categories of offensive sex-related behaviors: *gender harassment, unwanted sexual attention,* and *sexual coercion.* Gender harassment is not sexual in the usual sense of erotic invitations but rather consists of crude, offensive, and derogatory sex-related behavior (e.g., obscene jokes, sex-related insults) that serves to convey offensive or insulting attitudes about women. Such behavior is not complimentary, romantic, or amusing, but rather sends a hostile message to female employees that they are not welcome and do not belong in a particular work setting.

Some studies have shown that it is possible to distinguish between two slightly differing forms of gender harassment: (1) straightforwardly sexist behavior, such as comments that women do not belong in certain jobs (*sexist hostility*), and (2) more sexualized animosity, such as referring to women by degraded names for female body parts (*sexual hostility*). The common denominator of these types of situations is reflected in the derogatory nature of both categories of behavior. Such hostility is directed at women simply because they are women and is by far the most widespread form of harassment found in work organizations; nearly half of all women who experience offensive sex-related behavior in the workplace describe experiences of gender harassment.

In contrast to gender harassment, *unwanted sexual attention* is just that; it consists of uninvited, unwanted, and nonreciprocal sexual attention and behavior that, although unwelcome to the recipient, is not tied to a job consideration or reward. *Sexual coercion* refers to implicit or explicit attempts to extort sexual cooperation by the promise of rewards or threats of punishment. Although this is a scientific, rather than a legal classification, there is a general relationship between these categories and legal concepts. As Figure 1 illustrates, sexual coercion parallels, from a behavioral perspective, the legal category referred to as *quid pro quo,* whereas gender harassment and unwanted sexual attention represent the

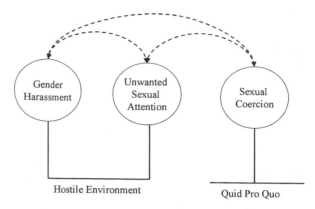

Figure 1   Model of sexually harassing behavior depicting relationship of behavioral categories to legal concepts.

behavioral components of a hostile environment. Although portrayed as distinct for purposes of simplicity, in reality these categories often overlap considerably.

B. FREQUENCY OF SEXUAL HARASSMENT

It has traditionally been difficult to reliably determine the prevalence of sexual harassment because researchers have employed differing operational definitions and no national statistics are currently maintained. The Equal Employment Opportunity Commission maintains records of the number of complaints filed each year with the federal government, but such estimates tap only the most serious cases; research reveals that very few individuals ever report their experiences to anyone, much less take legal action. Although there are numerous reports based on organizationally specific samples, it is mainly a handful of large-scale data collections, most conducted by the federal government, that provides the most reliable general estimates.

The United States Merit Protection Board conducted large-scale surveys of federal employees in 1980, 1987, and 1994 to assess the frequency of sexually harassing behavior in the nonmilitary federal workplace. In each of these studies, approximately one-third of female employees reported being the target of unwelcome sexual remarks and suggestive looks, and one-fourth reported physical touching by a coworker or supervisor. One in six reported being pressured for dates, and one in ten for sexual favors. One percent had experienced attempted or completed rape by coworkers.

The Crime Victims Research and Treatment Center collected data from a national probability sample of approximately 3000 adult women who had been employed at some point in their lives. The researchers counted as harassment only incidents that were (1) perpetrated by supervisors, (2) labeled by the respondent as sexual harassment, and (3) the respondent believed or was told by the offender that complaining or failure to comply would result in negative job consequences *or* the harassment interfered with the respondent's ability to do her job. This procedure produced a prevalence rate of 11.5%, a figure that must be regarded as a considerable underestimate; not only is most harassment perpetrated by coworkers, but the interview questions focused almost entirely on unwanted sexual attention and sexual coercion and did not inquire about gender harassment.

Finally, the Department of Defense conducted two large-scale surveys of the U.S. armed forces, one in 1988 and another in 1995. The most recent of these surveys indicated that 78% of female military personnel had experienced at least one instance of offensive sex-related behavior in the previous 12 months. Sixty-nine percent reported some type of sex discrimination, 63% reported sexual hostility, 42% reported unwanted sexual attention, and 13% had experienced some form of sexual coercion. The researchers counted as harassed all individuals who had experienced even one incident of offensive sex-related behavior by a superior or a coworker during the previous 12 months. Although likely to some degree an overestimate, such figures are consistent with other studies showing that women in male-dominated occupations are at greater risk of sexual harassment than their counterparts in more gender-balanced workplaces.

A number of researchers have included male participants in their samples and attempted to determine the degree to which men are sexually harassed. Most of these efforts suffer from a variety of methodological problems, not least of which is that it is unclear whether survey questions based on women's experiences measure the same phenomenon for men. For example, some evidence suggests that men are more likely to be harassed not by women but by other men, and that such harassment takes the form of attempts to enforce the traditional male gender role (e.g., derisive taunts about the target's masculinity, sexuality, and the like). Also, when men are sexually approached by women, they often find it flattering rather than offensive or threatening. This is not to deny that men can be sexually harassed, by both women and other men, or that such harassment

can be damaging to them. It is the case, however, that most attempts to investigate this area are hampered by lack of careful attention to theoretical and measurement issues.

IV. *Perceptions and Attitudes toward Sexual Harassment*

Because the topic of sexual harassment was originally both ambiguous and controversial, considerable attention has been devoted to examining attitudes, perceptions, and definitions of this concept. Indeed, research on perceptions of harassment constitutes one of the largest and most heterogeneous bodies of inquiry in this field. The following section provides a brief summary of the main areas, including gender differences, perceptions of severity, causality, and labeling. Readers are referred to the list of suggested reading for more detailed discussions of these topics.

A. GENDER DIFFERENCES IN PERCEPTIONS OF SEXUAL HARASSMENT

Perhaps the most consistent finding is that women and men differ in their perceptions and definitions of sexual harassment, with women being overall more likely to label a particular situation as sexual harassment than men. Women have been shown to hold more inclusive definitions of sexual harassment in numerous samples across age groups, occupations, and settings; for example, women are significantly more likely than men to define various actions as harassment, including letters, phone calls, materials of a sexual nature; touching, leaning over, cornering, or pinching; sexually suggestive looks or gestures; pressure for dates; and sexual teasing, jokes, remarks, or questions. Differences are most pronounced when the situation is depicted ambiguously (i.e., neither clearly innocuous nor unusually severe); when it is portrayed as clearly benign or particularly egregious, the perceptual gap narrows considerably.

Gender differences are also influenced by the sex of the individuals involved (e.g., one study found the gender gap was not significant in male on female situations, but male raters were less likely to perceive a situation as harassment if it was described as female on male); the physical attractiveness of the perpetrator and the victim (e.g., men made more lenient judgments when either participant was described as attractive); the status of the perpetrator (the higher the status, the less gender difference); the response of the target (e.g., a female target was judged more harshly by women if she reacted in a friendly manner); and the degree to which the rater endorses feminist views (e.g., more feminist raters are more likely to perceive a situation as sexual harassment).

Some commentators have argued that the issue of gender differences in perceptions has been overblown, that existing differences are small, and that the views of men and women are more similar than different. Although there is some merit to this view, it is still the case that, everything else being equal, women are understandably more sensitive to this topic than men.

B. SEVERITY, CAUSALITY, AND LABELING

1. Severity

Conventional wisdom generally interprets the severity of sexual harassment in terms of the characteristics of the behavior; for example, touching is usually thought to be more severe than verbal comments. Such judgments are over simplified however, as they fail to consider the context in which the behaviors occur, their nature and frequency, or the relevant characteristics of the target. For example, frequent offensive verbal behavior (e.g., sexist or sexual comments) has been shown to have as much psychological impact on targets as sexual coercion.

In addition to the characteristics of the behavior itself, other severity factors that have been examined include ratings of the stress thought to be associated with a particular behavior (e.g., unwanted touching compared to verbal sexual comments), status of perpetrator, contextual factors (e.g., the perpetrator's account of his behavior, the harasser–target relationship, the setting, the target response, negative job consequences); and individual target and rater factors. Many of these variables are discussed elsewhere in this article.

2. Causality

Causality in sexual harassment research is typically framed as the locus of responsibility for the situation; simply put, "Was it his fault or hers?" Such research tends to parallel the severity studies, examining variables such as the type of situation (e.g., the more physical the behavior, the more sympathy is demonstrated for the target) and its frequency (e.g., the more frequent the behavior, the more the perpetrator is held responsible). Other studies have identified career com-

petition (e.g., the target is more likely to be seen as responsible if the rater believes there are occupational benefits to be gained by complaining), the target–harasser relationship (e.g., the perpetrator is generally held less culpable if a previous romantic relationship existed), target response (e.g., she is viewed less sympathetically if she fails to complain), and other target characteristics (e.g., she is viewed as more responsible if she wore "provocative" clothing or heavy makeup) as significant variables in causality determinations. The parallels with rape myth research are striking.

3. Self-Labeling

Research on self-labeling of sexual harassment has lagged somewhat behind other areas of perceptions research. What can be said with some certainty is that relatively few individuals (less than 25%) who indicate having had a potentially harassing experience label it as such. Variables that have been studied in this area include age (the older the target the more likely she is to label; however, caution is needed here as age is confounded with work experience) and gender (women are more likely to label; however, their experiences tend to be more frequent and severe; thus the independent influence of gender is unclear). It is important to note, however, that the impact of offensive sexual behavior is the same whether the target labels it as harassment or not.

C. SUMMARY

Although the research on perceptions of sexual harassment has been quite extensive, it is unclear how well its findings generalize to the real world. Virtually all studies are analogue[3] in nature, many of them fairly weak and most depending on the perceptions and attitudes of captive samples of college students. Although such research is by its nature largely confined to the laboratory, the consistent combination of brief vignettes, "paper people," (i.e., pencil-and-paper scenarios) and student samples results in findings with limited external reliability. A carefully designed mock trial study, with participants drawn from actual jury rolls, could likely tell us a good bit about the generality of these results. Until then, we

[3]Analogue studies represent a type of experimental methodology in which participants are presented with an artificial situation (i.e., an analogue) representing as closely as possible the actual variables of interest—in this case, potentially harassing experiences; typically, different conditions are manipulated depending on the research question. Participants are frequently asked to respond to questions "as if" the event had happened to them.

are limited to statements such as "everything else being equal," while acknowledging that it rarely is.

V. Characteristics of Victims and Perpetrators

A. VICTIM CHARACTERISTICS

As with other forms of sexual victimization, a number of investigators have examined characteristics of victims in an attempt to establish a profile of high-risk individuals. Factors that yield some correlation with victim status are age and marital status; for example, younger, unmarried women are somewhat more likely to be harassed. Although some have taken this as support for a biological or evolutionary model of sexual harassment (discussed later), it is at least equally likely that such women are more vulnerable to predatory behavior because of employment in entry-level, transient, or other low-power occupations. It is also clearly true that harassment is in no way limited to younger women; indeed, women in all age and status groups have reported experiencing harassment.

There has also been considerable speculation in the literature that race or ethnic minority status might increase the risk of being harassed. Although intuitively reasonable (if only because minority status often correlates with economic vulnerability), this assumption has not been clearly supported by empirical data. Studies have so far yielded negative, mixed, or ambiguous findings and it is not possible to conclude at this point that minority status does or does not contribute uniquely to the risk of sexual harassment.

A major problem with this line of research is that researchers have typically not examined what sorts of behavior are experienced by which groups of women; for example, gender harassment (the most common form) is likely less correlated with age than other forms of harassment (e.g., unwanted sexual attention). Given the frequency of offensive sex-related behavior in the workplace, it is unlikely that any identifiable demographic group is exempt; thus, the search for the "typical victim" is probably a futile one. The one thing that can be said with any certainty is that the best individual predictor of sexual harassment is, quite simply, being female.

B. PERPETRATOR CHARACTERISTICS

Although many believe that sexual harassment is an aberration, perpetrated by deviant individuals who have some sort of psychological problem, this is clearly not the case. Although researchers have attempted to identify a pattern of easily recognizable demographic or interpersonal characteristics that characterize the "typical" harasser, such attempts have been largely unsuccessful. As with victims, perpetrators of sexually harassing behavior have been found in all occupations and social groups and appear to come from all ages and marital statuses; indeed, it is not possible to identify any particular observable characteristic that is associated with harasser status aside from the simple fact of being male.

Although popular belief, as well as a number of postmodern commentators, sometimes suggests that harassment is an "equal opportunity phenomenon," in which women are equally likely to harass men, this is simply not the case. The occasional counterexample not withstanding, both scientific and "softer" evidence make clear that the overwhelming majority of harassers are men. Indeed, as noted earlier, even when men themselves are harassed, it is typically by other men. Nor should it be surprising that this is so, given that it is also the case with other forms of gendered violence (e.g., sexual assault, childhood sexual abuse, battering). Commentators such as legal scholar Kathryn Franke have noted that harassment is essentially a "technology of sexism" that preserves the primacy of traditional masculinity and heterosexual privilege. It is thus not surprising that the great majority of perpetrators of harassment are men.

It should also be emphasized, however, that this does not imply that all of even most men are harassers; although a demographic profile of the typical harasser is not easy to come by, it is certainly true that some men are much more likely to harass than others. John Pryor and his colleagues have shown that it is possible to identify such propensities, which are grounded in attitudes, beliefs, and cognitive processes rather than social markers easily apparent to the naked eye. Men high in the likelihood to sexually harass (LSH) appear to be characterized by misogynistic attitudes and hostility toward women, adversarial sexual beliefs, and commitment to the traditional role arrangement between the sexes. Recently, this research has demonstrated the existence of a cognitive connection between power and sexuality such that being in a position of power over a woman is sexually arousing. Given the necessary opportunity, such men are likely to act out their attraction; however, it is important to note that appropriate environmental conditions and norms can exert a powerful "brake" on these actions, even among men who are otherwise likely to do so.

It is by now well established that environmental conditions rather than individual characteristics are the most powerful predictors of sexual harassment. Organizations characterized by a *masculinized job gender context*, that is, a skewed gender ratio (i.e., most employees are male, and women are relatively few) as well as job duties and tasks that are historically masculine in nature, and *organizational tolerance of offensive behavior* (i.e., employees believe that the issue of harassment is not taken seriously, that it is risky to complain, and that perpetrators will not be sanctioned) have far greater problems with sexual harassment. Organizational tolerance (sometimes known as organizational climate) appears to be the single most powerful factor in determining whether sexual harassment will occur and will be damaging when it does. Studies have shown that strict behavioral norms and an organizational climate that does not tolerate offensive behavior can inhibit harassment even by those with a propensity to do so. [*See* Working Environments.]

VI. *Individual Responses to Sexual Harassment and Their Prevalence*

Despite the widespread nature of sexual harassment and the seriousness of its consequences, it is by now well established that most targets do not report it and, in fact, the modal response of women who are harassed is simply to endure the situation and hope that it will somehow "go away." Although rigorous examination of women's responses to sexual harassment is only a decade old, it is already clear that a notable discrepancy exists between (1) how people believe that they themselves would respond if they were exposed to harassment and (2) how targets actually *do* respond. Research demonstrates that the majority of women *say* they would respond assertively; however, the overwhelming majority of victims clearly *do not* respond in this manner. When individuals are asked what they would do if they were harassed, most assert that they would speak up and tell the offender to stop; research also indicates that many believe that it is the woman's responsibility to do so. Despite such beliefs, it is clear that actual victims behave quite differently. Government studies report that the majority of victims either ignore the behavior or do nothing, and other studies confirm their findings. In 1982, James Gruber and Lars Bjorn found that 23% of the victims in their study said they simply ignored the behavior or put up with it,

and results are similar in virtually all studies so far. If few individuals actually confront their harasser, even fewer take action such as reporting to management. Filing formal complaints is less likely still, with estimates ranging from 2 to 12%, depending on the sample studied. In 1991, the Women's Legal Defense Fund estimated that only 1 to 7% of victims file formal complaints or seek legal help.

Despite such figures, it would be incorrect to assume that targets are passive in the face of harassment; although reporting and the factors that influence it have dominated organizational and policy-focused studies, more basic theoretical research reveals that victims employ a wide variety of strategies to manage their psychological reactions and the realities of their situation. Responses to harassment can be classified as either *internally focused* (endurance or extinction, denial, detachment, reattribution, and illusory control) or *externally focused* (avoidance, appeasement, assertion, seeking institutional relief, and seeking social support). Internal strategies are characterized by attempts to manage the thoughts and emotions associated with the experience (e.g., "I just tried to forget about it"; "I told myself it didn't matter") whereas externally focused strategies are more problem solving in nature (e.g., "I told him to leave me alone"; "I stayed away from him as much as possible"; "I reported him").

A. INTERNALLY FOCUSED RESPONSES

One of the most frequent responses to harassment is simply to ignore the situation and do nothing (*endurance/extinction*); although such a response may reflect the target's belief that the behavior is irrelevant or nonthreatening, that she has no effective alternatives, or that it is in her best interest to do nothing, a number of victims report that "doing nothing" is actually an effective practical strategy, in that resistance is often met with amusement and increased attention from the harasser. Studies show, however, that the advice "just ignore him and he'll go away" is generally ill founded, in that the behavior typically continues or escalates in the face of perceived indifference. A closely related reaction is to behave as if the situation is not happening, that it does not matter or has no effect (*denial*). Such responses are extremely common.

Little is formally known concerning the prevalence of other internally focused strategies that have been identified (*detachment, illusory control, reattribution*). Gruber and Bjorn found that a number of the victims they studied used reattribution as a coping strategy—that is, reinterpreting the situation in such a way that it was less threatening, such as rationalizing that there were extenuating circumstances explaining the offender's behavior (he was lonely, drunk, etc.) or attempting to interpret his intentions as benign. Self-blame, which we label illusory control, is rarely formally studied, although clinical observation as well as some research indicates that it appears to be common. In 1982, Inger Jensen and Barbara Gutek found that a substantial number of female victims attributed the problem in some way to their own behavior, an attribution that inhibited both reporting and seeking social support.

B. EXTERNALLY FOCUSED RESPONSES

The most common overt problem-solving strategy appears to be avoidance; the literature suggests that large numbers of victims actively attempt to cope in this way. Also common is appeasement, an attempt to "put off" the harasser without direct confrontation (humor, excuses, delaying, etc.), a response also labeled as *masking*. Studies indicate that many victims use delaying tactics hoping the harasser will "take the hint" that they are not interested.

Not surprisingly, a substantial number of individuals seeks social support; government studies report that many targets discuss the experience with a coworker or talk about it with friends or family, although the little research that exists on the reactions of third parties suggests they are less than uniformly supportive. Targets also employ a variety of assertive responses to communicate that harassment is unwelcome, most commonly, a direct request that the offender stop his behavior and leave the target alone. By far the most infrequent response is to seek some form of institutional relief (i.e., bring a formal complaint, file a lawsuit); such strategies appear to represent a last resort when all others efforts have failed. Not surprisingly, the least confrontational responses are the most common; victims in the workplace are more likely to talk with a supervisor than file a formal complaint, and legal claims are by far the least common response.

C. OUTCOMES OF RESPONSE STRATEGIES

The issue most commonly raised concerning such responses is "Why didn't she just report him?" Faced with this question, targets give a variety of answers. Most do not know where to go or what to do; others believe that nothing can or will be done, and

many are reluctant to cause problems for the offender. The most common reason, however, is fear—fear of retaliation, of not being believed, of damaging one's situation, or being shamed and humiliated. Unfortunately, such beliefs are often well founded.

Contrary to conventional wisdom, a number of studies have documented that assertive responses such as confronting the harasser or filing a complaint are not only frequently ineffective, but often actually make things worse. For example, assertive responding has been shown to be associated with more negative outcomes of every type (including psychological and health related) even after severity of harassment was controlled. Furthermore, use of confrontive responses tends to amplify associations between harassment pervasiveness and consequences; in other words, the effects of frequent harassment are more damaging when the target confronts the problem directly. In sum, despite pervasive public belief that victims should respond assertively, confront the perpetrator immediately, and report him to the appropriate authorities, reactions to such responses are generally not favorable for those who actually "blow the whistle." In 1982, Joy Livingston remarked, "Given the immense psychological and economic costs to individuals who use formal action, in contrast to the potentially meager gains, it is not surprising that so few victims choose this response."

VII. *Consequences of Sexual Harassment and Risk Factors for Harm*

Numerous studies document that experiencing offensive sex-related behavior has serious consequences, from embarrassment, anxiety, and lowered self-esteem to full-fledged psychological disorders such as major depressive disorder and posttraumatic stress disorder. In one of the first large-scale studies of its kind, in 1981 the United States Merit Systems Protection Board reported that literally thousands of female employees experienced deterioration in their emotional or physical condition as a result of experiencing unwanted sex-related behavior at work; these researchers replicated their findings in two additional studies, published in 1988 and 1995.

Barbara Gutek and Mary Koss reviewed the data on the outcomes of sexual harassment up to 1993; they reported findings of stress-related physical symptoms, including gastrointestinal disturbances, jaw tightness, teeth grinding, nervousness, binge eating, headaches, inability to sleep, tiredness, nausea, loss of appetite, weight loss, and crying spells. Emotional reactions included anger, fear, depression, anxiety, irritability, lowered self-esteem, feelings of humiliation, alienation, and a sense of helplessness and vulnerability. To this list can be added disruption of sexual adjustment (e.g., loss of desire, flashbacks during intercourse) and difficulties with partners, families, and significant others.

Although early studies can be criticized as based largely on reports of self-identified victims, a number of rigorous investigations have since confirmed that sexually harassing experiences can lead to lower levels of job satisfaction and organizational commitment, greater role ambiguity, role conflict, and job stress. Harassment is also associated with substantial emotional damage, even when less serious and intense than that typically required to trigger statutory relief. In 1997, Kim Schneider and her colleagues studied women employed in two different organizations; they examined the consequences of harassment on a variety of reliable measures of psychological status, carefully controlled for the effects of other stressors or confounding influences. Their results demonstrated that the experience of sexual harassment exerted significant and substantial impact; women who had been harassed had significantly lower levels of general psychological adjustment as well as significantly elevated symptoms of posttraumatic stress disorder (PTSD). The impact of harassment remained significant even after controlling for other potential explanations; as the authors observed, "This study presents evidence that sexual harassment, even at relatively, low frequencies, exerts significant negative impact on women's psychological well-being."

The first author and her colleagues provided an even more stringent test of the relationship between harassing behavior and emotional distress. Employing sophisticated statistical procedures, they documented a strong link between harassment and negative outcomes in a large sample of employed women. As they noted, "(O)ur results support the contention that sexual harassment is costly in both organizational and human terms. Women who were harassed not only experienced more psychological problems but also reported [more negative job outcomes]." Harassment significantly affected every aspect of these woman's lives, from job satisfaction to physical health, providing strong evidence for the assertion that harassment causes significant emotional distress, even at levels far less serious than those that typically find their way to court. These results have subsequently been replicated in large studies of the five military services, utilizing scientifically selected stratified random samples combining more than 28,000 individuals. This research confirms that harassment exerts significant negative influence on psychological status (e.g., anxiety and depression) and physical health, even after controlling for other factors; these effects "kick in" at relatively low levels of exposure.

Some of the most compelling evidence in this area arises from studies linking sexual harassment not only to psychological distress (i.e., symptoms) but also to actual diagnosable psychological disorder (e.g., major depressive disorder, post-traumatic stress disorder). Based on data from the National Women's Study, Bonnie Dansky and Dean Kilpatrick reported in 1997 that women who had experienced sexual harassment were significantly more likely to suffer from posttraumatic stress disorder and major depressive disorder than other women. Based on a large, nationally representative random sample and state-of-the-art diagnostic techniques, this study can be considered the "gold standard" in terms of scientific knowledge concerning the effects of sexual harassment on employed women. Finally, Fitzgerald and her colleagues examined 50 plaintiffs in sexual harassment litigation; consistent with Dansky and Kilpatrick, they found that the most common diagnoses in this group were major depressive disorder and posttraumatic stress disorder. [See DEPRESSION; POSTTRAUMATIC STRESS DISORDER.]

In sum, a large body of scientific data confirms that experiencing sexual harassment, even at low levels of frequency and intensity, can lead to decrements in psychological well-being and elevations in psychological distress, up to and including major emotional disorders. Although not every individual who is exposed to such experiences will develop symptoms of emotional distress, such reactions are more common than not—indeed, they appear to be the normative response.

Given the strong evidence associating sexual harassment with emotional damage, research has begun to examine models of vulnerability and harm, outlining factors that influence the severity of outcomes. These can be classified as *stimulus factors* (i.e., aspects of the behavior itself), *contextual factors* (i.e., the context in which it takes place), or *individual factors*, that is, the vulnerability of the individual target.

A. STIMULUS FACTORS

Stimulus factors refer to objectively defined aspects of the harassing behavior; for example, was it public or private, isolated or repetitive, verbal, physical, or both. Such elements can be classified into three general categories: *frequency, intensity,* and *duration.* Frequency refers simply to the number of incidents, whereas duration refers to the length of time during which the woman was subjected to the stressful situation. Intensity refers to what is generally thought of as the magnitude of the stressor. Seven aspects of intensity have so far been identified:

1. A powerful perpetrator
2. Multiple perpetrators
3. Behavior that is physical as opposed to verbal
4. Behavior that is frightening, as opposed to annoying
5. Behavior that is directly focused on the target
6. Restricted possibilities for escape
7. Multiple types of harassing behavior

A number of these factors have so far received empirical support. For example, the negative impact of frequency on target well-being has been supported in a number of studies, and in 1997, John Pryor found that targets who experience multiple types of harassment have worse outcomes than those who do not. Harassment by someone in a position of authority and control is virtually always experienced as more severe, and an empirical link has recently been demonstrated between perpetrator power and negative outcomes.

B. CONTEXTUAL FACTORS

The main finding here is that harassment is more common and targets have worse outcomes in settings tolerant of such behavior—tolerance being defined as employee perception that the issue is not taken seriously, that there is high risk for complaining, and that there is little chance that perpetrators will be sanctioned. In other words, tolerance of harassment can be defined as the general perception that there is little that can or will be done to prevent or remediate it, combined with elevated levels of risk to victims for complaining. Other aspects of tolerance include the lack of strong policies and clear procedures for dealing with sexual harassment, normative behavior that appears to tolerate harassment, and simply being in an environment where other women are being harassed (such a situation is known to social scientists as ambient harassment, or "bystander stress"). Recent studies demonstrate that ambient harassment and a tolerant climate produce psychological distress equivalent to that of being directly harassed.

C. INDIVIDUAL VULNERABILITY FACTORS

Examining individual factors shifts the lens of attention from the harassment itself and the context in which it occurs to the individuals who are its target. It is well accepted that certain personal characteristics can exacerbate or buffer the effects of a stressor, leading to more or less severe outcomes than would otherwise be the case. This concept is known as *victim vulnerability*; researchers have identified five aspects of vulnerability that may affect outcomes:

1. Victimization history
2. Personal resources
3. Attributions
4. Attitudes
5. Control

Considerable research has demonstrated that previous victimization increases not only the risk of subsequent abuse, but also its consequences. In other words, women who have been previously assaulted, sexually abused, or raped have been found to experience more psychological damage in response to subsequent experiences; however, it has recently been shown that sexual harassment contributes to the risk of major depressive disorder and posttraumatic stress disorder even after the effects of previous sexual assaults had been taken into account.

Not surprisingly, individuals with few personal resources (financial, vocational, educational, etc.) have been shown to be more vulnerable in the face of stressful life events. It is both intuitively and empirically the case that those with few options and resources are likely to be more damaged than other individuals, given an objectively equivalent injury. Finally, lack of control of an aversive situation has been both theoretically and empirically linked to subsequent psychological distress, specifically depression.

VIII. Theoretical Models

Accompanying the expansion of empirical research in sexual harassment has been the development of a number of theoretical models attempting to explain its occurrence. These models are relatively diverse, varying from macroexplanations cast in biological or evolutionary terms to those framed purely at the individual level. Although a fully developed framework of analysis has yet to be articulated, a number of more narrowly targeted models have proven heuristic. For the purposes of this article, we discuss four different levels of theoretical analysis and review a number of examples.

A. MACROLEVEL THEORIES

1. Natural/Biological Theories

One proposed explanation of sexual harassment asserts that harassing behavior is actually natural and possibly inevitable. Men have stronger sex drives, so the theory goes, and are therefore biologically motivated to engage in sexual pursuit of women; harassment is thus a natural byproduct of this situation. Although this hormonal theory is not generally afforded much credence, it is linked to a more fully developed model of evolutionary adaptation. The proponents of this approach assert that to ensure genetic survival, the ideal reproductive strategy for men is to pursue and impregnate as many women as possible. Women, on the other hand, are better served reproductively by selecting the best mate (as opposed to the most mates); they are therefore "naturally" more reticent in sociosexual situations and more offended by unsolicited sexual interest. The sexes thus have conflicting interests in sexual encounters, a conflict that leads to sexual harassment.

This biological/evolutionary approach has been criticized on a number of grounds; most important, because it can support conflicting predictions, it is not falsifiable and thus not scientific in the accepted sense of the word. In any event, the framework has had little influence on mainstream thinking about sexual harassment.

2. Power Theories

Another explanation of sexual harassment derives from the analysis of power differentials in organizations. This perspective emphasizes that the structure of organizational hierarchy invests power in certain individuals over others, power that can, in and of itself, lead to abuse. Further, it is historically the case that men have traditionally held the organizational power inherent in management and supervisory positions, whereas women have been more likely to be employed in subordinate positions. It is this imbalance of power that leads to sexual imposition on women; in other words, men harass women because

they have the opportunity and means to do so. According to this position, as women gain organizational power, the "gender gap" in harassment will begin to disappear.

An expansion of this approach attempts to account for the fact that harassment is generally perpetrated by peers (as opposed to supervisors); by including nonorganizational sources of power that nonetheless operate within the organization, the theory gains considerable explanatory force. For example, numerous studies document women's reduced access to informal means of mentoring and influence, as well as their diminished authority compared to men holding similar organizational positions. Power theory holds that these formal and informal structures engender sexually harassing behaviors and other forms of sex discrimination in the workplace and academia. A logical extension of this position would be also to incorporate the influence of men's more general social and physical power as well, thus generalizing the framework beyond organizational variables.

Power theory, although difficult to test directly, is consistent with the empirical data and accounts fairly convincingly for the means and (some) facilitating conditions of harassment; this is particularly the case if motivational factors (e.g., preservation of masculine dominance and male heterosexual privilege) are incorporated. What is missing here is any explanation of the explicitly sexual nature of harassment, a consideration at the heart of the original feminist writings on this topic. [*See* POWER.]

3. Social/Cultural Theories

Social/cultural theories assert that women's lesser status in the larger society is reflected in the workplace structures and culture; consequently, male dominance continues to be the rule. Men are naturally reluctant to relinquish this superior position of privilege. Furthermore, men are socialized into roles of sexual assertion, leadership, and persistence, whereas women are socialized to be passive, submissive, and sexual gatekeepers. These social/cultural roles are played out in the workplace, and sexual harassment is the result.

B. ORGANIZATIONAL THEORIES

1. Sex-Role Spillover

In 1982, Barbara Gutek proposed the notion of sex-role spillover—that is, the proposition that individuals bring to the workplace irrelevant gender-based expectations. Because gender identity is more salient than work identity, men rely on these gender-based expectations when interacting with women, responding to them as women, rather than employees or coworkers. Such expectations are experienced and acted out differently, depending on factors such as the gender ratio of the workgroup, the gendered nature of job duties and tasks, and so forth. Sex-role spillover theory predicts that nontraditionally employed women with mostly male coworkers will report that they are treated differently by their male coworkers, that their organization contains high levels of sociosexual behaviors, and that sexual harassment is a problem in their workplace. In contrast, women employed in traditionally female jobs will not report higher levels of sexual inappropriate behavior, possibly because they are complying with gender expectations or possibly because when they encounter sexual behavior, they may attribute it to the nature of their job (i.e., the jobs and tasks resemble the traditional female role, for example, nurturing, supporting, serving). Gutek further hypothesized that men are more likely to sexualize their experiences, including work experiences, and are therefore more likely to make sexual remarks or engage in sexualized behavior, thus accounting for the fact that women experience more sexual harassment than men.

2. The Illinois Model

Fitzgerald and her colleagues at the University of Illinois developed an organizationally based model designed to explain the antecedents (i.e., causes), consequences, and moderators of sexual harassment. They conceptualize the antecedents of harassment as (1) a masculinized job gender context and (2) an organizational climate that tolerates offensive sexual behavior. Job gender context is defined as a combination of the gender ratio of the individual's work group, the degree to which job duties and tasks are traditionally masculine, and sex of the supervisor. The concept of organizational tolerance, derived from classic theories of organizational climate, is operationalized as the degree of shared employee perceptions that sexual harassment is not taken seriously by the organization, that it is risky to complain, and that there are few meaningful sanctions for perpetrators. Sexual harassment, in turn, is predicted to have negative job-related, psychological, and health-related consequences for its targets, consequences that are moderated by the target's vulnerability and her response. The model has been supported in a number of large-scale studies in public and private-

sector organizations, and across various ethnic and racial groups. Although not attempting a motivational analysis, it appears to provide a good description of the organizational conditions under which sexual harassment will occur.

C. INTERACTIONAL THEORIES

1. Person X Situation Theory

A weakness of the models discussed so far is their inability to explain why it is that most men do not harass and those who do, do not do so under all circumstances. Building on classical social psychological theories of person-environment interaction, John Pryor has posited that some men possess a stable propensity to sexually harass women, a propensity that is either facilitated or inhibited by the relevant organizational conditions. He developed a brief inventory capable of identifying men relatively high in this propensity and conducted a number of well-controlled laboratory studies of their behavior, these investigations demonstrated that such men, when presented with the opportunity, tended to be more sexually exploitive than their colleagues. In further studies, Pryor and his colleagues have shown that (1) harassing role models facilitate harassing behavior on the part of high Likelihood to Sexually Harass (LSH) men (but not other men) and (2) that strong management norms can inhibit such behavior on the part of men who would otherwise do so. This latter finding, similar to those of the Illinois group, has considerable practical importance in that it provides empirical direction to organizations seeking to inhibit harassment in their workplace.

2. Ambivalent Sexism Model

The most innovative model of the etiology and nature of sexual harassment, developed by Susan Fiske and Peter Glick, proposes that workplace harassment arises from the interplay of (1) men's ambivalent motives toward women and (2) the complex gender stereotypes of both women and occupations. Because many men are deeply ambivalent about women, desiring intimacy with them on the one hand, and domination on the other, harassment is often marked not only by a desire for sexual interaction but also by hostility, antagonism, and contempt. The nature and contours of any particular harassing interaction thus depends on the motivational profile of the offender, a proposition that can account for the counterintuitive empirical finding that gender harassment and unwanted sexual attention frequently co-occur.

Glick and Fiske go on to observe that the gendered stereotypes of women and occupations are also heterogeneous; for example, women are frequently seen as traditional, nontraditional, sexy, or some combination, whereas female occupations are typically classified as pink (traditional), blue (nontraditional), or white (professional) collar. They propose that various combinations of gender and occupational stereotyping prime different aspects of male motivation (e.g., desire, benevolence, paternalism, hostility), placing women at more or less risk of sexual harassment and further influencing the types of harassment that occur. Based on the tenets of the theory, they propose a number of organizational interventions, most of which attempt to alter stereotypic expectations in some way (e.g., changing a masculinized job culture, moving toward a more balanced job gender ratio, providing information about employee qualifications to counter stereotypic expectations). They also emphasize the importance of reducing power asymmetries between men and women in the workplace and increasing accountability for behavior. Such interventions are consistent with those that flow from sex-role spillover theory, the Person X Situation framework, and the Illinois organizational climate model.

IX. *Generalizability of Research Results*

Almost unknown only a decade ago, sexual harassment research is by now a well-established field within social, organizational, and clinical psychology; indeed, more than 350 articles have been published in peer-reviewed journals in the past five years alone. Major governmental agencies (e.g., the National Institute of Mental Health (NIMH), the Department of Defense) routinely commission large-scale studies of workplace harassment, and studies have also been conducted in educational institutions at all levels and have included nationally representative samples of women from all backgrounds and income levels. Research is currently underway examining the impact of sexual harassment in other settings (e.g., housing) and preliminary results indicate that findings are similar to those reviewed earlier.

The degree to which research findings can be generalized beyond their original focus is an important issue. Such generalization, what social scientists label *external validity*, is the goal of all research; if such generalization were not possible, no study would have anything to contribute beyond knowledge gained concerning the specific individuals who participated in the study. Generalizability is thus the *sine qua non* of scientific activity.

The findings from sexual harassment research have proven to be quite robust. For example, studies using different samples (in different parts of the country as well as other cultures) and applying different methods provide remarkably consistent results: that is, unwanted and offensive sex-related behavior is widespread in every environment so far studied, and such experiences are emotionally distressing, anxiety producing, and psychologically disturbing to those who experience them. Although women are by far the most common recipients of sexual harassment, men are also harassed, usually by other men, and when they are, the psychological effects are similar to those found among harassed women.

These findings also generalize across ethnic, racial, and national boundaries. Although minor differences appear (e.g., traditional Hispanic women appear to experience somewhat more distress, probably because of cultural norms concerning female purity), once again the results are remarkably consistent. The structure of harassment (i.e., gender harassment, unwanted sexual attention, and sexual coercion) has been confirmed across a number of cultures, and studies from other nations (e.g., Israel, Canada, Pakistan) reveal that the phenomenon is widespread in all cultures so far examined. Another important area of consistency has to do with coping responses. Literally every study ever conducted has concluded that women rarely report sexual harassment, even when it is very serious. This finding has generalized across organizations, institutions, and the general population, as well as ethnicities, nationalities, and the two sexes.

Finally, there is considerable consistency across empirical findings concerning the workplace conditions associated with higher levels of sexual harassment. Organizations numerically dominated by men, in which job duties and tasks are traditionally masculine and that communicate a lack of interest or seriousness with respect to this problem, have far greater problems with sexual harassment. In short, it appears that one can have confidence that the findings reviewed here possess considerable external validity (i.e., generalizability).

X. Conclusion

Sexual harassment has a long past but a short history. Although a reality in women's lives at least since the advent of the Industrial Revolution, harassment was until recently invisible; as Catharine MacKinnon has remarked, lacking a name it was virtually unspeakable. This state of affairs has changed dramatically in only two short decades, and research on this topic is now entering its second generation. This research has demonstrated the extraordinarily widespread nature of harassment, the organizational factors that facilitate its occurrence, and the negative impact it has on women in terms of their work, their health, and their psychological well-being.

SUGGESTED READING

Basic and Applied Social Psychology 17, Whole No. 4, 1995.

Fitzgerald, L. F., Drasgow, F., Hulin, C. L., and Gelfand, M. J. (1997). Antecedents and consequences of sexual harassment in organizations: A test of an integrated model. *Journal of Applied Psychology* 82, 578–589.

Journal of Social Issues 51, Whole No. 1, 1995.

Journal of Vocational Behavior 42, Whole No. 1, 1993.

Lindemann, B., and Kadue, D. D. (1992). *Sexual Harassment in Employment Law.* The Bureau of National Affairs, Washington, DC.

Livingston, J. A. (1982). Responses to sexual harassment on the job: Legal, organizational, and individual actions. *Journal of Social Issues* 38(4), 5–22.

Military Psychology 11, Whole No. 3, 1999.

O'Donohue, W. (ed.) (1997). *Sexual Harassment: Theory, Research, and Treatment.* Allyn & Bacon, Boston.

Psychology, Public Policy, and Law 5, Whole No. 3, 1999.

Schneider, K. T., Swan, S., and Fitzgerald, L. F. (1997). Job-related and psychological effects of sexual harassment in the workplace: Empirical evidence from two organizations. *Journal of Applied Psychology* 82, 401–415.

Shrier, D. K. (Ed.) (1996). *Sexual Harassment in the Workplace and Academia: Psychiatric Issues.* American Psychiatric Press, Washington, DC.

Stockdale, M. S., *et al.* (ed.) (1996). *Sexual Harassment in the Workplace: Perspectives, Frontiers, and Response Strategies.* Women and work: A Research Policy Series, Vol. 5, Sage, Thousand Oaks, CA.

Sexuality and Sexual Desire

Deborah L. Tolman

Wellesley College Center for Research on Women

Lisa Diamond

University of Utah

Glossary

Androgens A class of hormones produced by the sex organs, including testosterone and other steroid hormones, that are produced in substantially greater quantities in males than in females, which play a significant role in fetal sex differentiation.

Clitoridectomy The surgical removal of the clitoris; in developing countries, the procedure is often performed without anesthesia; one of the practices referred to as female genital mutilation.

Deployment The use by authorities of concepts that are intended to be understood as fact but are actually the products of particular ideologies.

Nymphomania A medical term signifying female sexual insatiability.

Medicalization Rendering a process, procedure, or experience a medical problem or issue.

Phenomenological research Studies that collect data on people's experiences, most often in the participants' own words, in order to gain an in-depth understanding of human phenomena.

Sexual dysfunction Disturbances in sexual desire and in the psychophysiological processes associated with the sexual response cycle.

Sexual orientation An individual's general predisposition to experience sexual attractions for persons of the same sex, the other sex, or both sexes.

Sexual subjectivity The sense of oneself as a sexual person who has sexual desire, agency, and a sense of entitlement to express oneself sexually.

Token resistance Saying or implying "no" to sexual interactions when one is actually thinking "yes" or at least "maybe."

SEXUALITY AND SEXUAL DESIRE are related constructs that elude straightforward definition; that sexual desire is necessarily a component of sexuality is generally agreed upon. The sociopolitical contexts of sexuality, which produce specific discourses about sexuality that are understood to constitute it, is especially evident regarding sexual desire. Questions of "normality" underpin much of the theory and science of sexuality, though this quest is rarely acknowledged as a political process. An integrative perspective on sexuality emphasizes the interplay between biological and cultural factors.

I. *Conceptualizing Sexuality and Sexual Desire*

Defining sexuality is never an easy task; there is a cornucopia of conceptions from which to choose. More narrow conceptions tend to view sexuality as the sum total of individuals' sexual feelings, beliefs, attitudes, fantasies, and behaviors. Broader conceptions incorporate issues of body image, sexual violence and abuse, emotional affection, gender identity, gender roles, sexual fetishes, and reproductive health. Although scholars and laypeople continue to debate which of these diverse components "belong" in our conceptualizations of sexuality, practically everybody agrees that sexual desire plays a central role. Nonetheless, few agree (or even attempt to delineate) just what sexual desire is. Academic research on sexuality typically skirts the issue altogether, focusing on the prevalence of certain behaviors in different groups to the exclusion of determining the meaning and subjective quality of specific sexual experiences for different individuals.

When sexual desire receives attention, a heterosexual male conceptualization is typically adopted as the default. According to this default view, the only desires worth mentioning are discrete, easily identifiable experiences of lust directed toward other-sex partners, and the only interesting questions to ask about such desires are how often they are spontaneously experienced and how strong they are. Because men tend to (though do not always) come out ahead on such measures, many sex researchers have presumed that the single compelling question to ask about gender and sexuality is why women have "weaker" libidos or sex drives than men. Thus, just as research on sexual behavior has tended to focus on counting and classifying sexual acts without exploring their meaning and context, discussions of sexual desire have historically counted and classified sexual thoughts and fantasies—most frequently as "normal" or "deviant"—without deeper questioning about their subjective, culturally informed experience, for neither men nor women.

This reductionistic view of gender and sexual desire hampers attempts to design comprehensive educational programs and social services regarding sexuality. Yet perhaps even more important, it obscures the sociopolitical context of sexuality that each of us unconsciously negotiates on a regular basis. The very fact that some individuals' sexual experiences are deemed "normal," investigated, tabulated, and worried about, while other individuals' experiences are altogether ignored or considered "deviant," lays bare the inherently political nature of questions about sexuality and highlights the extent to which such questions can only be fully understood by attending to their specific social and historical context. This is particularly true for questions about sexual desire. Debates about the basic nature of sexual desire and about the forms of desire that should be considered normal, healthy, or moral have raged throughout history and have always been infused with sociopolitical undercurrents.

Some have attempted to avoid these messy sociopolitical factors by focusing exclusively on the biology of desire, but such attempts are ill fated and, ultimately, uninformative. At the same time, investigations of sexual desire that altogether ignore the role of bodies and biology are similarly unsatisfying. Our aim in this article is to propose a modern reappraisal of gender and sexual desire that takes into account the biological, sociocultural, and political factors that interact to shape subjective sexual experiences. Toward this end, we first review what have constituted the two highly dichotomized and polarized perspectives on sexuality that have heretofore dominated both empirical and theoretical investigations of this topic—essentialism and social constructionism—and then advance the point of view that a synthesis recognizing both the socially constructed character of sexuality and the fact that sexuality is embodied provides a way toward a more productive approach.

II. Essentialism versus Social Constructionism

Sexuality has historically been viewed by physicians, biomedical researchers, clinical psychologists, and everyday folk as the product of an innate, fixed, biologically determined drive located deep within the body. Until recently, while this conception of sexual drive had been differentially repressed, "sublimated," celebrated, and stigmatized in different cultures and historical periods, its basic operation had been presumed to be a fundamentally biological rather than sociocultural phenomenon. Sexual desire had been described and circumscribed as the product of gonadal hormones, particularly androgens such as testosterone. As such, sexual desire was understood to be a biological essence that differed in women versus men owing to well-documented sex differences in androgen levels. Specifically, men have uniformly higher levels of circulating testosterone than do women, and biomedical research has found that testosterone levels are reliably associated with self-reported sexual desire. Many have therefore concluded that testosterone is one of the most important and influential causes of differences between women's and men's self-reported experiences and physiological indices of sexual desire. This perspective has come to be known as an "essentialist" understanding of gender differences in sexuality. Its fundamental premise is that although different cultures and societies might dress up or dress down gender differences in sexuality, the underpinnings of these differences are biological, immutable, and universal. Although the average physician or biomedical sex researcher might not think of himself or herself as an essentialist, these disciplines have historically been—and continue to be—anchored in this biological weltanschauung. [*See* DEVELOPMENT OF SEX AND GENDER.]

This perspective was profoundly challenged—in fact, brought to light as a perspective—by the work of philosopher Michel Foucault, who argued that sexuality and sexual desire are cultural products that are both crafted and "deployed" by those with social authority and power as a form of social control. This perspective illuminates how cultural and historical factors do more than just heighten or dampen the biologically given contours of sexual experience: They actually co-constitute sexual experience at a more basic level. For many, this social constructionist position displaces a conceptualization of sexual desire as biological and static with a conceptualization of sexual desire as cultural and variable. That is, our beliefs and our actual subjective experiences regarding sexual desire, regarding our bodies, are, in fact, produced by the historically and culturally specific belief systems in which we are embedded. Thus, social construction makes visible how the accepted view of sexual desire as a bodily "essence" seizes on one particular difference between female and male sexual desire, renders it most salient, and posits this difference as a biological inevitability, making the case for, while at the same time relying on the assumption that, anatomy is destiny. Psychological theories of sexual socialization that emphasize the social transmission of culturally approved norms and behaviors, such as social learning theory and scripting theory, are grounded in a social constructionist perspective. [*See* GENDER DEVELOPMENT: SOCIAL LEARNING; SOCIAL CONSTRUCTIONIST THEORY.]

According to this view, there is no true or basic form of sexual desire that can be disentangled from cultural and historical variation. Rather, sexuality is a kind of "story" that we come to live, most often without conscious awareness that we are doing so. Although we might believe in a basic or "natural" form of desire, this is only because the process by which social forces shape our subjective experiences of sexuality are largely invisible to us. Much of this process involves the internalization of culturally and historically specific discourses, that is, highly organized systems of communication, about sexuality. These discourses define and legitimate specific conceptualizations of sexuality at particular sociocultural and historical moments. Thus, the significance of this conceptualization of sexuality is that it lays bare not only the historical and cultural dimensions of sexuality but also the political ones.

This perspective poses a powerful challenge to long-held assumptions about the causes of subjective sexual experiences and the bases for differences between the subjective experiences of women and men, particularly in reference to sexual desire. Rather than attributing gender differences in sexuality to biological differences between women's and men's bodies, social constructionism emphasizes the psychological processes by which men and women learn fundamentally different social and sexual scripts prescribing appropriate sexual feelings and behaviors. It also uncovers the political context of such scripts by highlighting the degree of human agency involved (at the level of systematic social forces rather than acts of individual will) in creating and reproducing specific conceptualizations of sexuality. Thus, the larger sociocultural aims served by particular notions of gender differences in sexuality at particular cultural and historical moments are explicitly analyzed.

III. Toward a New Integration

When it comes to feminist, sociocultural studies of sexuality, there is no point in measuring the popularity of essentialist models of sexuality against that of social constructionist models. Social constructionism is the undisputed winner, and as a result it is now commonplace to find sociologists, psychologists, historians, anthropologists, and cultural theorists discussing sexuality as if bodies never existed. This is problematic, however, for investigations into the psychology of subjective sexual experience. Accounts of sexual desire that altogether ignore the contribution of bodies and biology cannot elucidate the mechanisms and parameters constraining and potentiating the relationship between social scripts and subjective sexual experiences. In other words, by virtue of its wholesale rejection of biological contributors to human experience, the most extreme form of social constructionism sacrifices precision for coverage. Despite its power as a macroanalytic tool for modeling historical changes in particular groups' experiences of sexuality, it is less effective at specifying how these changes are subjectively experienced within the life courses of particular men and women or addressing how sexual desire "works" in individual bodies, that is, the embodied processes involved in sexuality.

In light of these observations, an integrative perspective on sexuality that emphasizes the interplay between biological and cultural factors can be a useful paradigm for understanding gender differences in what we come to know, experience, and describe as sexual desire. This approach acknowledges that genes, hormones and biological processes make critical contributions to subjective sexual experiences but that their role cannot be understood without analyzing the sociopolitical (and even interpersonal) contexts in which subjective sexual experiences are fundamentally produced. We are certainly not the first authors to advocate such an integrative approach, but in general it is more typical for scholars of sexuality to reproduce and reinforce the essentialism/social constructionism dichotomy than to challenge it, sometimes consciously, but more often inadvertently.

In this regard, sexuality researchers have much to learn from feminist philosophers such as Diana Fuss, who argued in her influential 1989 book, *Essentially Speaking*, that the entrenched feminist war against essentialism was largely myopic. She argued that this often vociferous antagonism had given rise to a counterproductive disdain for the notion that there were any essential underpinnings to these experiences. She suggested that this dismissal of any biological contributions had stopped and stunted feminist theorizing or understanding of the relationship between the biological and the social before the question had a chance to be posed.

This is nowhere more evident than in the domain of sexuality, with its obvious and overdetermined battle between the relative importance of hormones and the relative importance of social structure and cultural ideology. In the past five years, this battle has begun to shed its mantle of intolerance and thus has become less extreme than we have portrayed it here for explanatory purposes. Most social constructionists acknowledge some role for biological factors in sexuality, just as most essentialists acknowledge a role for culture. The devil, of course, is in the details. Practically everybody can agree on some bland form of biosocial interactionism, but the terms of this interaction remain hotly debated. Those who privilege the biological body, for example, would argue that although sociocultural and historical influences on sexuality are far from trivial, they nonetheless come into play *after* biology has already established the ground rules. Biological essences, then, define the parameters within which culture is allowed to operate. Social constructionists reject this formulation, arguing instead that the very idea of fixed biological parameters is itself a culturally derived notion.

Feminist scholars wrestling with these questions in the sexual domain have, on the whole, erred on the side of giving more weight to the social rather than the biological side. There is nothing to suggest that this approach is inherently wrong—after all, there are multiple ways to envision interactions between biological and cultural factors—but it has had the unfortunate effect of circumscribing feminism's influence on sexual scholarship. In short, it has prevented feminist scholars from using their critical analytic tools to reimagine and reframe biological as well as cultural understandings of sexual experience. In this article, we take the plunge into this project.

Before proceeding, however, several caveats are in order. First and most important, we do not attempt to formulate a singular, grand reconciliation of biological and cultural perspectives on sexuality. Rather, we would argue that there are multiple such reconciliations, and the jury is still out (rather, it has not even started deliberating) on which are the most successful and the most generative. Thus, our aim is not to present a unified front in favor of one particular biocultural calculus, but to highlight some of the most provocative possibilities and tensions. For this reason, we have elected not to whitewash the tensions in our own ongoing conversation regarding these questions. Specifically, one of the authors leans more toward the cultural end of the balance, while the other leans more toward the biological. By allowing the push and pull between these differing emphases to ebb and flow throughout this article, rather than trying to hammer out a patently uncontroversial (and probably uninteresting) middle position, we hope to cast light on the heretofore shadowy possibility that there are multiple answers to the question of how biology and culture may braid together to shape women's and men's subjective sexual experiences.

We begin, then, by demonstrating the power and importance of a social constructionist perspective on female sexuality. Several historical and cross-cultural examples will highlight what we gain when we stop thinking about sexuality as simply a "natural function" and start thinking about it as a cultural production. We will then shift gears to give biological factors their due, demonstrating how a feminist perspective on the biological underpinnings of sexual ideation and behavior can productively inform and expand the traditional social constructionist perspective. By sometimes piecing, sometimes weaving together strands of argument and evidence from both perspectives, we conclude with both cautionary and encouraging remarks about the potential for developing a more comprehensive understanding of sexuality and sexual desire through a more interactionist project.

IV. Historical and Cross-Cultural Perspectives on Female and Male Sexual Desire

Prior to the Enlightenment, the existence and necessity of female sexual pleasure for successful reproduction was a common conception in Western thought. This perspective was grounded in the belief that women's bodies were simply a variation on the male template, such that women had the same reproductive organs as men, only on the inside rather than the outside of their bodies. It was believed that both women and men had to be sexually aroused and had to experience sexual pleasure in order for conception to occur. Thomas Laquer, in his 1990

history of sexuality, cites one author writing in the 17th century who recommended preparing women for "successful" sexual intercourse with lascivious words, wanton behavior, "all kinde of dalliance," and "handl[ing]" of her secret parts and dugs, that she may take fire and be enflamed in venery." Women's sexual desire was understood not only as normal and necessary but as the very counterpoint to the pain of childbirth that kept the human race going.

However, with the Enlightenment came a reconstruction of male and female biology and of male and female sexuality not as hierarchical, with female bodies and sexuality understood as derivative of male, but as fundamentally different, distinct, and incommensurable. By the 19th century, female orgasm was no longer seen as necessary for conception. In fact, the search for anatomical and physiological differences between the sexes led to arguments about whether or not "normal" female sexual passion even existed. At the same time, a shift in the sociopolitical landscape rendered women's reproductive organs and capacities, and their roles as wives and mothers, the defining features of women's lives and identities. Within this context, nymphomania came to be defined as a specific type of disease to which women were particularly vulnerable and whose symptoms included adultery, flirting, divorce, and the desire for more sex with one's husband than the husband himself wanted. That is, any behavior that defied social norms of feminine modesty could be defined and medically "treated" (sometimes with surgical removal of the clitoris, called clitoridectomy) as nymphomania.

Yet the underlying belief that normal women were not "plagued" with sexual desire did not apply to all women. Rather, this view pertained only to White, middle-class women, who were viewed as more "evolved," civilized, moral, and restrained; thus, cultural fictions about the "nature" of White, middle-class women came to define a standard against which African American women, poor women, and immigrants could be judged by authorities and, not surprisingly, always found lacking. These groups were relegated to subnormal status and conceptualized as "naturally" more promiscuous, animalistic, and unrestrained, thus necessitating—and justifying—greater social controls. Vestiges of these beliefs still remain in contemporary Western ideologies about White and ethnic-minority women's (and also men's) bodies and sexual natures.

Conceptions of sexuality vary across cultures as well as over time. For instance, Muslim concepts of female sexuality bear little resemblance to Western beliefs about women's sexual nature. The current assumption that (normal) female sexuality is passive does not exist in Muslim societies; in fact, precisely the opposite view prevails. A quote from the founder of the Shiite sect of Islam, Ali ibn Abu Taleb, husband of Muhammed's daughter Fatima, conveys succinctly the profoundly different belief about the very nature of women's—and men's—sexuality than is held in current Western thought: "Almighty God created sexual desire in ten parts; then he gave nine parts to women and one to men." These societies maintain that women's sexuality is active and intense and that their powerful desires demand satiation. Within Islam, married women enjoy the (theoretical at least) privilege of demanding sexual satisfaction as a condition of marriage. Furthermore, whereas sexual intercourse is the primary focus of male-female sexual interaction in Western society and religion, Mohammed encouraged men to linger in sexual foreplay for the purposes of stimulating and satisfying women, a goal considered requisite for maintaining social order. [*See* CROSS-CULTURAL SEXUAL PRACTICES.]

Of course, this seemingly liberated conceptualization of women's sexuality has been used to justify women's oppression; many Islamic cultures prescribe clitoridectomy and other forms of genital mutilation as necessary means of controlling women's dangerously powerful desires. In her 1987 book, *Beyond the Veil: Male and Female Dynamics in Muslim Societies*, Fatima Mernissi observed that the different concepts of female sexuality observed in Western and Muslim societies are related to different strategies for regulating women vis à vis their sexuality. Western societies, with their emphasis on women's sexual passivity, rely on internalized sanctions against premarital sex and adultery. Muslin culture, with its view of female sexuality as active and assertive, uses more external and explicit forms of control such as veiling, constant surveillance, and the administration of severe punishments (including death) for actual or suspected violations of feminine modesty. Thus, whereas Western culture has overtly condemned sexuality, Muslim culture overtly condemns women.

V. Social Constructionism and Political Power

One of the most powerful effects of social constructionism is the skepticism it casts on modern Western notions of objective truth or reality, particularly on the notion that "natural orders" of different social groups reflect natural differences between different types of individuals. For this reason, social constructionism poses a serious threat to the social status quo by taking away the argument that things are the way they are because they are "supposed" to be that way and by revealing how privileged groups produce social institutions and cultural stories that reinforce and reproduce their power at the expense of those deemed different. For this reason, social constructionism has proved a liberating and empowering tool in the hands of those who have been historically marginalized and oppressed. For instance, in 1990 Patricia Hill Collins revealed how contemporary "controlling images" of Black women are anchored in historical myths about Black women's sexuality, exemplified by stereotypes such as the asexual "mammy," the "welfare queen," the "seductive Jezebel," or the "sexually predatory" woman. Her analysis demonstrated the way in which dominant cultural stories about Black women have been used to control their sexuality, and she posited this control as central to their oppression.

Social constructionism has also highlighted the way in which historical beliefs about homosexuality and heterosexuality have served specific sociopolitical ends. Prior to the 20th century, there was no Western conception of a homosexual—or heterosexual—identity; rather, specific sexual acts were labeled homosexual, regardless of who performed them. Over time, the desire for such acts came to be viewed as a specific form of psychopathology with a set of associated causes, symptoms, and probable outcomes. In the modern era, as political movements (such as those for civil rights and women's rights) crystallized around particular social identities, the notion of "homosexual" as a diseased state came to be replaced by the notion of "lesbian/gay" as a social identity. This shift produced in the 1970s and 1980s a "liberal humanistic" conception of lesbians and gay men as healthy, well-adjusted individuals indistinguishable from heterosexuals save for the gender of their sexual partners. Thus, whereas 19th-century physicians maintained that one "had" the disease of homosexuality or one did not, contemporary social scientists largely maintain that one either "is" gay/lesbian/bisexual or one is not. As articulated by sex researcher John Money, same-sex sexuality is no longer considered a "sin" or a "sickness" by theorists, researchers, practitioners, and many (though not all) sexual minorities, but a "status."

Although this change in conceptualization was associated with a lessening of the traditional stigma associated with same-sex sexuality, many social constructionists (most notably, British social psychologist Celia Kitzinger) argued that the liberal humanistic conception of lesbians and gay men served many of the same sociopolitical goals as the pathology conceptualization, albeit in a more palatable guise. Specifically, she maintained that the liberal humanistic conception retained the essentialist view of lesbians and gay men as distinct types of people, but effectively deflated their potential political power by portraying them as "just like the rest of us," except for their desires. Whereas the very existence of same-sex desire had previously posed an inherent threat to historical notions of the "naturalness" of heterosexuality, the liberal humanistic construction of lesbians and gay men neutralized this threat by offering them the quiet acceptance (or at least tolerance) they had long sought from mainstream society, predicated on their disavowal of any attitudes, beliefs, and behaviors that challenged the prevailing heterosexist social order. [*See* LESBIANS, GAY MEN, AND BISEXUALS IN RELATIONSHIPS.]

In many ways, the liberal humanistic view of same-sex sexuality can be understood as a response to the more radical conceptualization of same-sex sexuality articulated by Adrienne Rich in 1979. She challenged the very notion of discrete sexual categories, arguing that any close relationships among women, even purely emotional bonds, might be considered potentially lesbian, breaking down the essentialist distinction between homosexuality and heterosexuality that allowed sexual minorities to be effectively contained and controlled. She used the term "compulsory heterosexuality" to identify the invisible but powerful system of social control that grants privileges to women on the basis of their adherence to a social and sexual order that meets the needs and desires of White, economically privileged men. Rich's conceptualization posited that all women are socialized into heterosexuality through various means of persuasion and coercion, and explicit sexual ties between women were simply the most visible and salient form of resistance to this socialization. Contrary to the liberal humanistic view of sexual orientation, this view implies that lesbians and gay men are not, in fact, safe and harmless "types" of people with slightly different sexual desires, but potentially galvanizing forces for resistance against the hegemony of "natural heterosexuality," emphasizing the political contours of both heterosexuality and homosexuality.

The tension between essentialist and social constructionist conceptualizations of sexual orientation—and the debates over which standpoint offers a more positive and progressive view of sexual minorities—continues to this day. Contemporarily, essentialist conceptualizations continue to predominate, bolstered by research suggesting that at least in some individuals, sexual orientation is partly determined by genes. This evidence has been seized by some gay and lesbian activists as proof that sexual orientation is a natural form of human variation that should not be subject to social stigma or prejudice. Others, however, argue that genetic conceptualizations of sexual orientation bear an uneasy resemblance to the old pathology models, with their attendant implications for possible medical "treatment" in the service of normalization. Radical social constructionists continue to maintain that it is necessary to deconstruct any and all sexual typologies—safe, natural, and otherwise—and thus to highlight the social construction of all sexual subjectivity. The current debate is anything but new: similar arguments fractured feminist scholars and activists into antithetical liberal and radical positions on female sexual desire during the "sex wars" of the 1980s. Some feminists continue to maintain that female sexual desire is whatever women say they feel, including desire for sadomasochistic expressions of their sexuality, and that women's desire emerges as a response to their personal and social experiences. Other feminists maintain that there is a "natural" form of sexual desire for women that is more spiritual, more relational, and less aggressive than conventional male sexual desire, and that women have lost touch with these desires as a result of heterosexual oppression. Given these widely divergent perspectives, some feminists now speak of "female sexualities" rather than "female sexuality" in order to recognize and signify the variety of women's experiences and perspectives in the domain of sexuality.

VI. Bringing Biology Back

It is within the context of these historical debates that we envision a new role for bodies and biology in feminist conceptualizations of female sexuality. Surely the main contribution of feminist critical analysis to sexual scholarship is not entirely limited to a deeper appreciation of cultural influences—and surely we have already won this war. The more difficult challenge is to bring biology back in, now that we have a more sophisticated notion of the multiple cultural forces that construct, offer up, and deny, various forms and meanings of sexuality and sexual desires. This view is not held by the most radical social constructionists, who argue that there is no place for, and in fact no such thing as, a "biological" understanding of human sexuality. Yet one of the benefits of an integrative approach is that it moves research, education, public policy, and treatment of sexuality beyond the tired set of questions that has long spurred vociferous debates between essentialist and social constructionist scholars (i.e., "Do women have weaker libidos, and if so, why?") toward more complicated questions regarding how biology and culture intersect in men's and women's experiences of lust and love at different stages of life. Such questions presume that there are naturally occurring variations between and among women and men in both the biological and cultural components of sexual experiences, while at the same time not presuming that biology predates cultural constructions. It is the sophisticated interplay among such variations that deserves systematic study.

There are already several compelling examples of how this interplay can be productively theorized. One example comes from feminist biologist Anne Fausto-Sterling, who became well known for her controversial 1993 argument that there are actually five sexes rather than two, a claim she based on the (little-known) prevalence of hermaphrodism among humans. Fausto-Sterling observed that in addition to conventional males and females, there are three different types of hermaphrodites that are common and distinct enough to qualify as additional "sexes": those whose genitalia is more male than female, those whose genitalia is more female than male, and those whose genitalia is equally male and female.

Fausto-Sterling took a social constructionist stance in arguing that our conventional assumptions regarding the existence of two and only two sexes is a culturally derived notion rather than a biologically preordained fact, and she straightforwardly addressed how contemporary social practices and ideologies regarding gender and sexuality would be radically transformed if we were to acknowledge the existence of five rather than two sexes. Yet she in no way discounts the importance of biology—rather, her "five sexes" argument is based not on a wholesale rejection of restrictive biological definitions of sex and gender, but on a critical reevaluation of the extant biological data. Her analysis therefore demonstrates that some of the most profound and radical

critiques of restrictive, essentialist claims regarding "femaleness" and "maleness" can be launched from within the biological disciplines that traditionally gave rise to these essentialist notions. When wedded to a social-constructionist understanding of the way in which human experience is always and everywhere funneled through the prism of culture, these critiques can yield powerful and potentially liberating reimaginings of gender and sexuality.

Another example of such a reimagining has to do with the neurochemical substrates of sexual desire itself. As noted earlier, extensive attention has been devoted to differences between the relative strength of male and female libido, and the possibility that such differences are attributable to differences in circulating levels of testosterone. The conventional essentialist position on this question is "But of course," while the conventional social constructionist position is "Hogwash!" Our contribution to this long-standing debate is to ask an altogether new question: "Why should *testosterone* get all the attention?" There are a number of other neurochemicals that have shown demonstrable links to sexual desire, activity, and even orgasm, many of which appear to function differently in women than in men. Examples include estrogen, adrenal hormones, and the neuropeptide oxytocin, which has received increasing attention in recent years because of the critical and simultaneous roles it has been found to play in mammalian childbirth, infant care, affectional bonding, and sexual activity.

Oxytocin is most well known for stimulating the contractions of labor and facilitating milk let-down in nursing mothers, but it is also involved in multiple processes of mammalian attachment and affiliation over the life course. Studies of animals (typically rats) have identified direct effects of oxytocin on maternal feeding behavior, maternal/infant bonding, and kin recognition, but it is also associated with female sexual interest and receptivity. The scant amount of human research on oxytocin also suggests a role for this neuropeptide in human sexuality. For example, a 1994 study by Marie Carmichael and her colleagues found that oxytocin is implicated in the experience of orgasm and the feeling of satiety that follows sexual activity. Perhaps most interestingly, they found that blood levels of oxytocin were higher in females than in males during sexual activity and were associated with subjective reports of orgasm intensity among multiorgasmic females.

Yet we are not simply suggesting that researchers start measuring plasma levels of oxytocin instead of (or in addition to) plasma levels of testosterone. Rather, the complexity of neurochemicals such as oxytocin calls for a fundamentally different approach to studying biological substrates of subjective sexual experience. As noted earlier, oxytocin is also powerfully related to social and relational processes, and a 1999 study by Rebecca Turner and her colleagues found that some women showed increases and decreases in plasma oxytocin levels in response to, respectively, positive and negative emotional imagery. Clearly, the complex role of oxytocin in multiple domains of sexual and interpersonal functioning cannot be investigated with the straightforward "more chemical = more desire" approach that has characterized research on androgens. Rather, research in this emerging area will have to attend to bidirectional interactions between biological substrates and their situational and interpersonal contexts, representing a promising direction for biosocial research on sexuality.

Along the same lines, consideration of a more diverse range of biological contributors to human sexual experience invites more complex conceptualizations of gender differences in subjective sexual desire. Rather than focusing on who has more or less sexual desire, researchers can consider more sophisticated questions about the quality of women's and men's sexual desires, the contexts in which these desires are experienced, both between and within groups, and how such variations might reflect different types of biological and social or relational interactions. For example, some research suggests that we might profit by attending more closely to the distinction between an individual's urge to initiate sexual activity and his or her arousability, or capacity to become interested in sex given certain learned cues. Interestingly, these two forms of sexual desire may be differentially influenced by biological factors.

As reviewed by Kim Wallen in 1995, variability in spontaneous sexual urges (which is, notably, the form of variability that has been most frequently assessed by historically male sex researchers) appears directly linked to variability in testosterone levels. Yet variability in arousability is independent of testosterone—even hypogonadal men with castrate levels of testosterone become readily aroused to erotic stimuli. Furthermore, Wallen reviewed research on female and male primates suggesting that arousability may play a greater role in structuring female desire and sexual activity than male desire and activity, and he suggested on this basis that perhaps instead of conceptualizing female libido as "weaker" than male

libido, we might conceptualize it as more periodic and environmentally dependent.

One of the most promising aspects of such a reconceptualization in biological approaches to sexuality and sexual desire is that it explores the significant role of culturally and situationally specific factors in the experience of sexual desire at a basic, fundamental level. In other words, the constellation of social forces and ideologies that structure (and often constrain possibilities for) women's desires are not extra layers wrapped around a "real," testosterone-mediated biological core, but are part of the core itself. We do not suggest that this model of sexuality is necessarily "the right one"—Wallen's research focuses on primates, and thus the extent to which his model generalizes to humans remains to be seen—but it is a useful example of how alternative, integrative models of sexuality might prompt us to reexamine the very definition of sexual desire on which the essentialist/social constructionist debates have been premised. Rather than arguing yet again over whether testosterone matters more or less than culture, we might instead ask whether different forms of sexual desire depend on different interactions between biological and contextual factors and whether the nature of these interactions varies culturally, historically, and over the life course.

Now that our deconstruction of the dichotomy between essentialism and social constructionism is more clearly laid out, we address two of the most pressing questions about female sexuality—questions about its development and about standards of normalcy—in an effort to demonstrate the value of integrative approaches to investigations of these questions.

VII. Developmental Perspectives on Sexuality: Revelations about "Normality"

When it comes to sexuality, there have long been concerted efforts on the part of social science to identify what is "normal," and these efforts have been most strident when it comes to adolescents. The stakes of identifying "normal" and "natural" patterns of sexual development are particularly high in contemporary North America, given society's concern about sexually transmitted diseases and teen pregnancy, to the exclusion of other dimensions of sexual health. Thus, to the extent that social scientists have adopted an impoverished approach to adult sexuality that tabulates acts instead of eliciting their meanings and contexts, when adolescent sexuality and sexual development are under scrutiny, this tendency is even more exaggerated. This focus has produced a particularly limited range of information about adolescent sexuality that fails to tell us about the subjective quality of young women's and men's sexual feelings and experiences as they move through childhood and adolescence in particular cultural and historical locations. This notable oversight reveals volumes about our society's anxieties regarding childhood and adolescent sexuality and its resulting surveillance of adolescents and their behavior.

For example, although (as noted earlier) everybody seems to agree that sexual desire is a critical component of sexuality, adolescent sexual development is typically studied as if desire had nothing to do with it; instead, physical maturation receives primary emphasis. The age of menarche, breast development, and growth spurts have been dutifully charted in multiple countries across multiple generations, as have the implications of these changes for a youth's social status and attractiveness. In fact, questions regarding which developmental processes produce mature sexual desire, the mechanisms through which they do so, and the ways in which these sexual feelings build on or diverge from childhood sexuality remain open. In addition, this concern with accurately charting the precise development of reproductive maturity tends to crowd out and even dismiss efforts to understand the experiential aspects of these processes. [See Adolescent Gender Development.]

The same is true of investigations into adolescent sexual behavior. Most researchers are far more interested in finding out how often adolescents are having sex, and with whom, than in investigating the subjective quality of these experiences, such as how and why they are exploring sexuality and what it means to them. Much of this research tends to simplistically reproduce dominant ideologies about differences between male and female sexuality, as well as differences between the sexuality of ethnic-minority and White teenagers, and it rarely identifies or questions the sociopolitical context of these differences and our own attempts to assess them. Unlike virtually all other arenas of the study of adolescent development, the vast majority of research on adolescent sexuality has focused on girls, with an undue emphasis on poor girls and girls of color. This is particularly true of research on sexual decision making, contraception usage, and prevention of sexually transmitted diseases (STDs), reflecting the common expectation that girls should be the gatekeepers of adolescent heterosexuality and that boys cannot control their "more powerful" libidos.

The generally unstated rationale for such studies is the prediction and prevention of risky sexual behaviors rather than the promotion and nurturance of healthy forms of adolescent sexual expression. In part, this focus on risk reflects the pressures on researchers and educators, from both funding agencies and policy makers, to identify predictors of sexual intercourse, contraceptive use, and STD prevention—for example, studies of the prevalence and prevention of teen pregnancy and childbearing have grown into a virtual industry of "sexuality" research. The end result is a research and sex-education paradigm that focuses disproportionately on teaching adolescents skills for saying "no" to sexual intercourse rather than on trying to help them to understand the interpersonal and cultural contexts of their sexual and romantic feelings and experiences.

Prominent sexuality researcher Anke Erhardt noted in a 1996 editorial in the *American Journal of Public Health* that this approach offers an impoverished understanding of adolescent sexuality. She and others have called for a shift in focus in both research and education toward normalizing adolescents' sexual feelings, giving them the safety to consider multiple ways of expressing those feelings (including celibacy), and emphasizing sexual responsibility. Some researchers do conduct more sensitive and nuanced assessments of adolescents' desires, thoughts, and fantasies, including same-sex as well as other-sex desires, that are by necessity on a smaller scale, yet such research often receives far less attention than large-scale surveys of sexual activity and contraceptive use. A qualitative approach to adolescent sexuality strives to interpret the meaning of demographic characteristics such as gender, race, ethnicity, social class, and cultural community for adolescents' experiences of their sexuality, rather than simply determining whether these factors "predict" specific behaviors. There is a wealth of existing data suggesting powerful interplays between the physical dimensions of adolescent sexuality and the social contexts in which young women make meaning of, respond to, and deal with their changing bodies. At this point in time, there is in fact little data about these aspects of male adolescent sexuality, primarily due to assumptions that have been made about boys' experiences.

VIII. Early Experiences of Desire

Interactions between the biological and cultural contexts of adolescent sexuality become salient the moment we first ask, "When do boys and girls begin to have sexual desires?" Very young children, indeed infants, touch their genitals and masturbate: Does this involve sexual desire? We know very little about the sexual experiences of prepubertal children because we assume (and wish) that they do not feel sexual. The conventional biological explanation supporting this assumption is that children's low, prepubertal levels of testosterone and estrogen make them incapable of authentic sexual fantasies and desires, and that only after pubertal gonadal maturation (termed *gonadarche*) does mature sexuality emerge.

We now know that this convention is not biologically accurate, but our cultural privileging of puberty as the "onset" of sexuality has prevented this fact from seeping into contemporary consciousness. As Martha McClintock and Gilbert Herdt noted in their 1996 critique of the gonadarche model, this model posited the pubertal transition of 12 to 14 years of age as a momentous hormonal "switch" instantaneously transforming asexual children into sexual protoadults. Yet they reviewed newer data suggesting that it is the maturation of the adrenal glands and secretion of adrenal hormones around age 10 that appears to be associated with the development of nascent sexual attractions, cognitions, and emotions, which children subsequently begin to link up with their cultures' conceptualizations of sexuality. As they argued,

[Data on the emergence of sexual attractions around age 10] provide a key for understanding sexuality as a process of development, rather than thinking of it as a discrete event. . . . [T]he new data suggest a longer series of intertwined erotic and gender formations that differentiate beginning in middle childhood. . . . No longer can the brain at puberty be treated as a black box, which is suddenly able to process sexual stimuli de novo at the time of gonadal change.

It is particularly interesting to recognize that McClintock is a biologist, whereas Herdt is a cultural anthropologist. Thus, their collaborative critique of the gonadarche model of sexual maturation provides a useful example of the way in which creative efforts to consider interplays between biological and cultural contributors to sexual development can powerfully challenge the restrictive yet persistent essentialist models on which most prior research has been based.

IX. The Social Context of Maturation

Of course, sexual maturation involves far more than hormones. As sociologist Janice Irvine has argued, the signature changes of puberty, such as menstruation, breast development, nocturnal ejaculation, and hair growth, are given meaning by the cultures in which adolescents live. From this perspective, a full understanding of sexual maturation demands an analysis of adolescents' social contexts and the cultural stories that contour their experiences. As their bodies are changing, adolescent girls and boys are receiving multiple, powerful cultural cues about how they should express, experience, and manage sexual feelings. Feminist scholars have highlighted how romance novels, magazines, television, movies, and now the Internet provide ever-present templates of "normal" heterosexual desire, often reinforcing historical conceptions of women as "naturally" sexually passive and males as "naturally" relentless and uncontrollable.

As a result, many girls experience intense cultural pressure to "enact" compulsory heterosexuality through the internalization of their position as sexual objects rather than exploring and discovering their own sexual subjectivity and agency. Boys, meanwhile, may feel compelled to live up to the popularized image of masculinity as a form of sexual predation. Reflecting these ideas about male and female sexuality in our society, some of the most interesting and provocative research integrating biological and social perspectives on sexual maturation has found that social pressures appear to have a more significant influence on the sexual behavior of young women than young men. Yet the limitations that these beliefs confer on even the most interesting research are evident as well.

In 1987, Richard Udry and John O.G. Billy sampled 1400 adolescent "virgins" and examined the role of hormonal and social variables in predicting which of the adolescents initiated sexual activity within a two-year period. In addition to a battery of hormonal assessments, they collected data on a wide array of social factors, such as same-sex and opposite-sex friends' participation in sexual activity, popularity with the opposite sex, grades, deviance, religiosity, sexual permissiveness, future orientation, parents' education, and locus of control. They found that free testosterone level was directly and power-fully related to initiation of coitus for White males, to the exclusion of all social variables save for a male youth's popularity among female friends. The pattern of results was entirely the opposite among White girls: Hormones had no direct effect on first coitus in White females (although they were significantly related to variables assessing sexual thoughts and fantasies), but every social variable significantly influenced a White girl's initiation of first intercourse, and most of these factors operated independently of one another.

Why might sociocultural factors exert stronger effects on young White women than on young White men? Udry and his colleagues have suggested that it has to do with the fact that White adolescent men face a uniformly positive normative environment with regard to their sexual feelings and behaviors, whereas White adolescent women face an inconstant, highly differentiated normative environment. Unlike boys, girls confront conflicting combinations of positive and negative messages regarding their sexuality, combined with conflicting combinations of opportunities and constraints. When the researchers examined racial differences, they discovered that the same social factors that predicted White girls' initiation of sexual intercourse were not explanatory for Black girls. Rather, the strongest predictor of Black girls' sexual behavior was their observable level of pubertal maturation—in other words, whether they "looked mature" to their peers.

While this research provides strong evidence of variability in how the interplay between hormonal processes and social constructions shape girls' and boys' sexuality, many questions about how adolescents experience and make sense of these social constraints or supports remain to be asked and answered. It is also important to note that this research is a good representation not only of how society constructs male and female adolescent sexuality differently, but also the long-standing preoccupation with race as a key variable of interest—a preoccupation that cannot be taken lightly given the historical constructions of Black versus White sexuality that continue to circumscribe the types of questions we ask and assumptions we make about Black and White youths' sexual behavior. Udry and his colleagues described their findings of no social effects on Black girls' initiation of intercourse as "puzzling" and acknowledged that the differences may be due to factors that were not represented in their conceptual models. In truth, our current notions of what vari-

ables matter when it comes to sexuality are themselves sharply constrained by our own social and cultural locations, and we are too often blinded to the full range of factors that might shape sexual experiences for diverse youths across diverse environments. While the search for interactive effects between physiological processes and social factors can yield important new information about adolescent sexuality, the success of these efforts rests on researchers' ability to identify those variables that are most meaningful in the cultural constructions of populations under study.

X. The Importance of Experiential Questions and Answers

In order to accurately model how contemporary adolescents make sense of these physical, social, and emotional transitions, we need methodologies other than the larger-scale survey methods that have predominated in conventional social scientific research on adolescent sexuality. Specifically, such modeling requires phenomenological or experiential data collected with methods that enable and elicit youths' own perspectives. In-depth interviews with smaller, meaningfully selected samples provide one example. Research of this sort has begun to reveal important subtleties regarding contemporary young women's sexual feelings and self-concepts.

For example, in 1988, Michelle Fine conducted a year-long ethnography in an urban public school, which she intertwined with analyses of public policy and sexuality education efforts. She described a "missing discourse of desire" regarding adolescent girls, noting that discourses of victimization, morality, and disease permeated how adults spoke to and about adolescent girls. She highlighted the way in which these discourses reflected and reproduced norms of heterosexuality that rendered boys sexually irresponsible, tarnished the reputations of girls who were actively sexual, and generally associated girls' sexuality with harm. She also observed girls' efforts to challenge these discourses by straightforwardly acknowledging their own desire or pleasure, while also acknowledging the conflict and ambivalence they wrestled with as a result of wading through simultaneously negative and seductive messages about female sexuality. She argued that the reality of both the pleasure and danger involved in adolescent girls' sexuality must be recognized in order to give girls a chance to make active, safe, and responsible sexual decisions as subjects of their own sexuality rather than solely as objects of boy's desire.

Fine's research challenged the notion that girls do not feel powerful sexual feelings and opened the door for new questions about adolescent sexuality. In 1990 Sharon Thompson continued in this direction by collecting in-depth, qualitative information from adolescent girls on an event that is frequently tabulated, but rarely investigated at the level of subjective experience: first sexual intercourse. In collecting girls' descriptions of their first intercourse experiences, she learned that most of the girls found it painful and unpleasant, and were disappointed to discover that it did not meet their expectations as a gateway to deeper love and commitment. Nonetheless, a small group of girls offered more positive stories. These "pleasure narrators" noted that their mothers had talked to them about their sexuality in positive ways, had encouraged them to take their own feelings into account, and had socialized them to expect, even demand, satisfying sexual experiences. This kind of research enables an articulation of sociocultural and interpersonal factors that promote or hinder adolescents' positive, healthy sexual self-concepts. [*See* SEXUALITY EDUCATION.]

We must also remain mindful of the diversity of young women's experiences. Despite the hundreds of studies that have been done to identify predictors of adolescent girls' sexual decision making, there have been none that investigated whether girls' own sexual desire might be a factor. This oversight of girls' sexual desire is undergoing a correction. In the early 1990s, Deborah Tolman conducted an in-depth interview study of 30 urban and suburban girls in which they were asked to describe their embodied experiences of their own sexual desire. She found notable differences, as well as strong similarities, in how urban and suburban girls spoke of the "dilemmas of desire" that they experienced. This study was premised on the physiological, embodied phenomenon of sexual desire as it becomes meaningful through cultural constructions of sexuality in an attempt to circumvent the essentialist–social constructionist split in approaching sexual desire.

For instance, 90% of these girls spoke in an "erotic voice," that is, described powerful sexual feelings in their bodies that they distinguished from their romantic wish to be in a relationship, though a number of these girls conveyed that these desires were intertwined. The urban girls' narratives about their own desire embedded caution, fear of physical dangers, and concern about social consequences as fundamental features of how they responded to their own bodily feelings. The suburban girls described a tension between curiosity and conflict about their identities as "good" girls and concern about how others might think of them rather than how they might be treated. Across the urban-suburban divide, psychological typologies emerged in how girls dealt with their desire. Some described "silent bodies," that is, reporting they did not feel desire, while others were confused about whether their embodied feelings signified sexual desire or something else, such as anxiety or fear. Some girls told stories about resisting their desires, trying literally to talk their bodies out of desire, as in one girl's recollection that "my body says yes, yes, yes, yes and my mind says no, no, no." Other girls spoke about hiding their sexual feelings, taking them into the "underground" of their own private awareness but out of public sight, in order to protect themselves from perceived harm and negative consequences, for instance, drinking in public in order to "blame it on the alcohol." A few girls described a politicized resistance, where they were aware of the sanctions against their desire and refused to comply with the notion that girls are not supposed to have sexual feelings. These girls describe having sexual experiences on their own terms, as well as finding these experiences pleasurable. Not all of them had chosen to have sexual intercourse, and some of them had managed to elude attempts at sexual violation, because they were so sure of what they did and did not want to do.

Adding quantitative analytic techniques to her qualitative analyses, in 1999 Tolman and her colleague Laura Szalacha found that the context of reported sexual violations, including childhood sexual abuse or molestation, sexual attacks, and rape, emerged as an important factor for the suburban girls' experiences of their own desire as pleasurable or involving feelings of vulnerability, but not for the urban girls. This finding challenged conventional assumptions that it is urban girls (and, in most contemporary stereotypes, urban girls of color) whose sexual behavior occurs in the context of violence and victimization. It also underscored the complexity, both for young women and for researchers, of trying to understand girls' own sexual feelings in a context that either demonizes or entirely denies them, within a society that is permeated by the constant threat and reality of sexual violence. [*See* CHILD ABUSE.]

By elucidating these complexities, this type of qualitative research productively complicates our notions of the diversity in the development of girls' sexuality. For instance, it draws attention to the complexity of young women's negotiation of primarily, though not exclusively, heterosexual experiences. In 1998, Charlene Muehlenhard and Carie Rodgers noted that, in general, over a third of college women surveyed in several studies reported that they had engaged in "token resistance" to sexual intercourse they intended to have. However, when they asked 129 college women and men to write narratives about their experiences with token resistance, allowing for a more detailed assessment of how young men and women view and interpret such situations, they found that the majority had a different understanding of the concept than the researchers did. The results of the qualitative research cast doubts on both the stereotypes and the survey findings that women— and only women—tend to engage in token resistance. Based on this more nuanced and phenomenological information about token resistance, Muehlenhard and Rodgers concluded that when men and women say no to sexual intercourse, they do indeed mean it.

Similarly, qualitative longitudinal research on the desires and behaviors of young sexual-minority women has alerted us to the diversity of their developmental trajectories, challenging not only the historical presumption that all adolescents are heterosexual, but restrictive conceptualizations of same-sex sexuality. Whereas the traditional essentialist model of sexual orientation portrays it as a uniformly stable, early-appearing trait, there is extensive qualitative and quantitative data suggesting that this is not always the case, particularly among women. Sexual-minority women are more likely than sexual-minority men to experience non-exclusive sexual and romantic attractions, to experience changes in attractions and behavior, and to ascribe a role for circumstance and conscious choice in their same-sex orientation.

Such findings are inconvenient (to say the least) from a pure essentialist perspective, which can only accommodate conflicting or discontinuous attractions by attributing them to misperception, internalized homophobia, or social constraint. For example, if a lesbian who is exclusively attracted to women recalls strong attractions to men in the past, pure essentialism offers only two possible explanations: either she was never authentically attracted to men (and only believed so due to social pressure and denial of her true sexual orientation) or she is actually bisexual rather than lesbian (in spite of her current claim of exclusive same-sex attractions). Because sex-

ual orientation is theoretically fixed over the life course, one's resulting propensity to experience same-sex and opposite-sex attractions becomes similarly fixed.

Yet research increasingly challenges this framework. Sexuality in general—and female sexuality in particular—is more fluid than many have previously thought. In a recent longitudinal interview study of 89 young sexual-minority women's development, Lisa Diamond found that more than half of them changed their sexual identity labels at least once after first "coming out" as nonheterosexual. Some of these women changed identity labels because they found themselves in unexpected relationships that contradicted their perceptions of "typical" lesbian or bisexual behavior. For example, a number of lesbian women ended up having sexual contact with men as the years went by, and some felt that even if these experiences were "exceptions" to their general pattern of attraction and behavior, they could no longer comfortably claim a lesbian label. Perhaps most interesting, a surprisingly large number of women traded in their lesbian or bisexual label for an "unlabeled" identity. Many of these young women indicated that over time, they became increasingly aware of the way in which sexual identity categories failed to represent the vast diversity of sexual and romantic feelings they were capable of experiencing for female and male partners under different circumstances. As one woman said, "I'm really attracted to the person and not the gender, and there's no category for that, not even 'bisexual.'" Such data demonstrate how much we lose by shoehorning women's (and men's) complex, highly contextualized experiences of same-sex and other-sex sexuality into cookie-cutter molds of "gay," "straight," and (only recently) "bisexual."

Importantly, fluidity in sexual attractions, behavior, and identity does not necessarily tell us anything about the origins of sexual orientation. Many have assumed that if sexual orientation has any sort of genetic basis, same-sex desires should be inherently stable over the life course and impervious to sociocultural context, reflecting an essentialist paradigm. However, changes in individuals' interpersonal relationships, social environments, and even personal ideologies may render same-sex and other-sex attractions differentially salient at different stages of life, regardless of how long a particular individual has experienced these attractions, how exclusive they are, and whether or not they are "coded in the genes."

Research has only recently begun to explore instances of sexual fluidity over the life course systematically. As critiqued by Andrew Boxer and Bertram Cohler in 1989, most research on same-sex sexuality has focused disproportionately on identifying continuities between childhood and adulthood indicators of sexual orientation, while neglecting the role of change and discontinuity within the sexual minority life course. They noted that this overemphasis on continuity, exacerbated by a reliance on retrospective rather than longitudinal data, has impoverished our basic understanding of normative sexual development among heterosexual and sexual-minority youths, in both adolescence and in later adulthood. Such a basic understanding proves increasingly important in light of efforts by psychologists, clinicians, and policy makers to design research programs, therapeutic interventions, and sex education curricula addressing the concerns of sexual-minority adolescents. As a result of these efforts, many adolescent women encounter lesbian/gay/bisexual–affirmative messages at school and in community centers. At the current time, however, many such messages presume a typical sexual-minority developmental trajectory—specifying early and continuous awareness of stable, exclusive same-sex attractions—that may rarely typify the experiences of young sexual-minority women.

Thus, while gay and bisexual male youths may be successfully assured that their feelings and experiences are normal, some female youths may feel doubly deviant, their developmental trajectories reflecting neither heterosexual nor lesbian/bisexual norms. In assuming that sexual minorities represent a consistent "kind" of person whose most pressing developmental tasks are simply the recognition and disclosure of their sexual orientation, psychologists have historically neglected women whose changing desires create a similarly changing set of developmental hurdles at subsequent points along the life course. The prevailing impression that these women are few in number and exceptional in nature may be an artifact of a reliance on a restrictive set of assumptions concerning the stability and internal coherence of sexual orientation. More extensive qualitative research to chart the full diversity of women's sexual desires will prove useful not only to scientists investigating the nature of sexuality, but also to adolescents and adults secretly hungering for reassurance that their experiences are normal.

But will we be enabled—or even allowed—to conduct such studies? Researchers attempting to conduct more detailed studies about young women's and men's sexual experiences face increasing obstacles from a culture that is perfectly happy to prevent sexual risk but is ambivalent about the prospect of promoting sexual health. For example, in 1992 Richard Udry and his colleagues were awarded a grant from the National Institutes of Health to conduct a nationally representative study of many different forms of adolescent sexuality (again, in the name of preventing risk and enhancing safety rather than as an effort to understand normative features of adolescent sexuality). Objective reviewers approved the study based on its scientific merit, as is common practice in the scientific community. Yet Congress subsequently passed legislation aimed at stopping the research, making it the first federally sponsored scientific enterprise to have its funding canceled on overtly political rather than scientific grounds. We have little hope of deepening and diversifying our conceptualizations of adolescent sexuality while cultural phobias about this topic stymie scientific research.

XI. Deviance Becomes "Normality": Conceptions of Adult Sexuality

In 1966, William Masters and Virginia Johnson stunned the world by documenting what they asserted was the physiology of the human sexual response. Literally garbed in the white lab coats associated with objectivity and medical authority, the scientific presentation of these data lent credence to their claim of having discovered the "normal" sequence of events in human sexual response. This research is an excellent example of how a wholly essentialist view of human sexuality is both compelling and questionable. For instance, the impact of studying sexual physiology in a laboratory setting, apart from the more common relational context of sexual experience, laced with layers of power dynamics and differentials, was neither questioned nor assessed. Research on the quality of sexual experience has been a marginalized, often feminist, query ever since Shere Hite's infamous 1976 publication of a study reporting what women said about their sexual experiences, pleasures, desires, fears, and frustrations, in particular, that fewer than 30% of respondents reported having orgasm during heterosexual intercourse. Hite's lack of credentials seemed to justify much of the controversy about—and intense scrutiny and dismissal of—this study, in particular the reliability of the sample, which was made up of several thousand women readers of magazines and members of community groups. It is a notable contrast to the ease with which the findings of Masters and Johnson, cloaked in scientific "objectivity," were accepted as the truth of human sexuality.

Unveiling the vicissitudes and complexities of sexual subjectivity among adolescents clearly challenges and expands our society's conceptions of sexual desire and development, simultaneously acknowledging and contesting the restrictive conceptualizations of these topics reproduced by contemporary culture. The same approach needs to be applied to the study of sexuality across the life span. As it stands, sexuality research tends to ignore changes in sexual feelings and experiences that occur during the 20 to 60 years following sexual maturation, as if sexual subjectivity becomes permanently frozen once gonadal hormone levels stabilize.

When adult sexuality does receive attention, it is in the form of sexual dysfunction, a topic that has been widely publicized since the publication in 1999 of an article by Edward Laumann and his colleagues in the *Journal of the American Medical Association.* The findings of this nationally representative survey of adult sexuality revealed that sexual dissatisfaction and dysfunction among adults in the United States is far more widespread than commonly assumed. Specifically, over 30% of women over the age of 18 reported difficulties with sexual arousal and sexual desire, while over 30% of men over the age of 18 experienced premature ejaculation. Of course, the politics inherent in definitions and determinations of "sexual dysfunction" deserve close scrutiny, especially in light of increasing efforts by pharmaceutical companies to sell prescription medications aimed at alleviating whatever ails us, sexually speaking. As Leonore Tiefer argued in 1996, the encroaching "medicalization" of sexual dysfunction casts sexual problems as inherently biological, obscuring sociocultural phenomena. They are not even relational phenomena according to this framework—although doctors and sex therapists might acknowledge that both partners in a sexual relationship are affected by sexual dysfunction, they still frequently view such problems as "belonging" to one partner's body rather than the other. Accordingly, treatment proceeds by fixing the body that is determined to be broken—prescribing medication, performing surgery, alleviating problems with "hydraulics"—rather than examining how individuals' and couples' sexual experiences are shaped by their social and interpersonal environments. The search for a female Viagra and the recent establishment of a professional group of urologists dedicated to eliminating the disease of "female sexual dysfunction" are only the most recent examples of medicalized, essentialist perspectives on sexual dysfunction that downplay the potential sociocultural underpinnings of sexual problems.

Interestingly, the medical article that started the current flurry of attention to sexual dysfunction contains voluminous evidence of the social and interpersonal dimensions of the problem, yet somehow this information has been lost in the hype over just how prevalent sexual dysfunction seems to be. Specifically, Laumann and his colleagues found that sexual problems are significantly more likely to be reported by men and women with low social status (indexed by low levels of education and falling household income). They explained this association by noting that sexual dysfunction at all stages of life is positively associated with emotional and stress-related difficulties. They posited that individuals with low social status may experience more sexual problems than those with high social status, because they are under more chronic stress as a result of their social position. This finding lays an important foundation for exploring how larger sociocultural and economic conditions trickle down to construct individuals' most private subjective experiences. Yet such complexities are certainly not part of the take-home message from the mainstream media coverage of the study—and certainly pharmaceutical companies have little interest in (and little to gain from) this type of analysis.

Of course, this is not to say that there is no such thing as sexual dysfunction or that it has no biological determinants. In fact, many feminists have applauded the fact that physicians have stopped telling women that their sexual problems are all in their heads and have started taking their complaints seriously as indications of possible medical problems, giving them a new choice between pharmaceutical and talking cures (or some combination thereof). At the same time, feminists have also offered important critical perspectives on the range of possible explanations for and responses to what Janice Irvine called "desire disorders." For instance, a woman's low level of sexual interest might stem from changes in menopausal hormone levels, but on the other hand it might stem from a history of sexual abuse, psychological stress brought about by economic hardship, or underlying interpersonal tensions brought about by power differentials in her primary romantic relationship. These different possibilities demand a thorough investigation of both potential physiological *and* nonphysiological explanations and remedies for sexual problems that take the full cultural and interpersonal context of a woman's sexual subjectivity into account. Overall, however, biomedical investigations, explanations, and treatments of problems such as low or diminished sexual desire are too rarely combined with more complex, culturally specific, highly contextualized analyses (such as those often highlighted by feminist psychotherapeutic practice) of what individuals and couples want and expect in their lives and relationships and how these desires and expectations change across different environments and different stages of life. In the past, as Tiefer observed, researchers have avoided inquiring too closely into how eroticism is connected to deeply personal longings for affirmation, to the avoidance of inner doubt, to the need for power, and to a secure sense of identity. It is certainly easier to discuss sexual desire, arousal, and activity as if they are universal, standardized functions, such that any individual experience can be neatly categorized as "too little," "too much," or "just right." Yet this perspective tells us little about the real texture and meaning of sexual ecstasy, confusion, passion, and disappointment in men's and women's lives.

XII. Concluding Remarks

The obvious explanatory power of a historically grounded social constructionist account of sexuality can and should not be underestimated. However, it behooves us not to let the momentum of this pendulum swing over too far. Just as an exclusive focus on the biological underpinnings of sexual desire can inadvertently lead to a dangerously naturalized hierarchy of "normal" and "deviant" desires, an exclusive focus on the socially constructed origins of sexual desire can inadvertently lead to an untenable denial of the role of bodies and biology in human sexual experience. Both of these extreme perspectives misrepresent men's and women's actual experiences. Anatomy is not destiny, but neither is it completely irrelevant. Arguing that a woman's lust has

nothing whatsoever to do with genes, hormones, and neurotransmitters makes as little sense as arguing that it has nothing whatsoever to do with her social context.

Neither a purely biological nor a purely social perspective provides satisfying explanations for variability in adolescents' and adults' sexual desires and self-concepts, particularly gender differences in sexual subjectivity. As noted earlier, extreme essentialist perspectives explain gender differences in sexuality solely as a function of biological sex differences. Extreme social constructionist perspectives imply that any inquiries into biological differences (such as hormone levels) are ill advised and uninformative. This article demonstrates how feminist reconceptualizations of the interplay between bodies and culture can lead to more diverse, nuanced sets of questions that will provide more provocative and perceptive answers regarding sexuality and subjective sexual desires.

SUGGESTED READING

Jackson, S., and Scott, S. (eds.) (1996). *Feminism and Sexuality: A Reader.* Columbia University Press, New York.
Kitzinger, C., and Wilkinson, S. (eds.) (1993). *Heterosexuality: A Feminism and Psychology Reader.* Sage, London.
Laquer, T. (1990). *Making Sex: Body and Gender from the Greeks to Freud.* Harvard University Press, Cambridge, MA.
Laumann, E., Gagnon, J., Michael, R., and Michaels, S. (1994). *The Social Organization of Sexuality.* University of Chicago Press, Chicago.
McClintock, M., and Herdt, G. (1996). Rethinking puberty: The development of sexual attractions. *Current Directions in Psychological Science* 5, 178–183.
Paikoff, R., and Brooks-Gunn, J. (1994). Psychosexual Development across the Lifespan. In *Development through Life: A Handbook for Clinicians* (M. Rutter and D. Hays, eds), (pp. 558–582). Blackwell Scientific Press, Oxford.
Peplau, L. A., and Garnets, L. D. (eds.) (2000). Women's sexualities: New perspectives on sexual orientation and gender. Special issue of the *Journal of Social Issues* 56.
Tiefer, L. (1996). The medicalization of sexuality: Conceptual, normative, and professional issues. *Annual Review of Sex Research* 7, 252–230.
Tolman, D. (1999). Female Adolescent Sexuality in Relational Context: Beyond Sexual Decision-Making. In *Beyond Appearance: A New Look at Adolescent Girls* (N. Johnson, M. Roberts, and J. Worell, eds.), pp. 227–246. American Psychological Association, Washington, DC.
Vance, C. (1984/1992). *Pleasure and Danger: Exploring Female Sexuality.* Pandora Press, London.

Sexuality Education
What Is It, Who Gets It, and Does It Work?

Judith C. Daniluk

Kristina Towill

University of British Columbia, Vancouver

Glossary

Health Defined by the World Health Organization as "a state of complete physical, mental and social well-being, and not merely the absence of disease or injury."

Health education Learning experiences focused on facilitating thoughts and behaviors conducive to health. These may include information gathering, skill development, consciousness raising, and decision making.

Sexual health The integration of the physical, intellectual, emotional and social aspects of being sexual, in ways that are positively enriching and that enhance the individual, her or his relationships, and society.

Sexual health education A broadly based, community-supported effort focused on helping individuals make informed and responsible decisions about their sexual behaviors and expression, based on their personal, family, religious, and societal values.

Sexual health promotion The provision of formal and informal educational and structural supports for acting in ways that promote sexual health.

Sexuality A fundamental aspect of the personality of all people, encompassing the physical, psychological, social, emotional, spiritual, cultural, and ethical dimensions of the human experience.

SEXUALITY EDUCATION, commonly referred to as sexual health education, broadly describes educational initiatives that focus on the enhancement of positive sexual self perceptions and on the prevention of sexual health problems such as unintended pregnancies, sexually transmitted diseases, AIDS, and sexual exploitation and abuse. Current models of sexuality education differ in their emphasis on abstinence, their provision of information on safer sexual practices, and the extent to which they provide a comprehensive and inclusive emphasis on the development of positive, health-promoting sexual attitudes, behaviors, and self-perceptions.

I. Introduction

This article defines sexuality education and briefly describes the two most common approaches to sexuality education in the United States: abstinence models and safer-sex programs. The article then explores the characteristics of more comprehensive sexuality education, as outlined in *The Guidelines for Comprehensive Sexuality Education, Kindergarten—12th Grade* promoted by the Sexuality Information and Education Council of the United States. This is followed by a discussion of the current impetus and support for the promotion of sexuality education in the United States, the extent to which American youth receive sexuality education, and the factors that often interfere with the widespread implementation of sexuality programs in the schools. Research on the effectiveness of the various sexuality education programs is briefly reviewed and critiqued, with attention being paid to the implications of not including sexual health education in the schools.

II. Sexuality Education: What Is It?

Sexual health education, as it is most commonly referred to, broadly describes educational initiatives that focus on the enhancement of positive sexual self perceptions and behaviors and on the prevention of sexual health problems such as unintended pregnancies, sexually transmitted diseases, AIDS, and sexual exploitation and abuse. Sexuality education programs are most frequently found in formal educational institutions, including secondary schools, colleges, universities, and, to a lesser degree, elementary schools. In states and cities that support the inclusion of sexuality education in the public school curriculum, these programs are characteristically included as part of the general health and physical education curriculum. The two most prevalent models of sexuality education include abstinence models and approaches that also include information on safer sexual practices. Of these, abstinence models are the most prevalent.

Abstinence models of sexuality education are predicated on the belief that premarital abstinence from sexual intercourse is a realistic and appropriate goal for all adolescents and young adults. These models promote abstinence as the only safe and moral sexual choice for adolescents. Family values and abstinence skills—for example, how to recognize and cope with peer and media pressures—constitute the primary instructional focus of these programs. Postponing sexual involvement (PSI) is one of the most widely implemented of these abstinence programs. Aimed at early adolescents, this curriculum supports

adolescents in delaying sexual activity by addressing social and peer pressures and "by teaching teenagers skills that will enable them to set limits, resist peer pressure, be assertive in saying 'no' to sex and develop nonsexual ways to express their feelings" according to Kirby and colleagues in a 1997 report.

Safer-sex models of sexuality education are becoming increasingly more prevalent. Sometimes referred to as HIV/AIDS education, these approaches place emphasis on equipping participants with knowledge and skills in contraception and condom use to protect against unintended pregnancy, sexually transmitted disease infection (STD), and HIV-AIDS. These programs are heavily based on instilling knowledge about anatomy and physiology of the reproductive system, pregnancy and childbirth, and the prevention of STDs and HIV/AIDS. With their emphasis on reducing adolescents' sexual risk-taking behaviors, instruction is aimed at teaching participants how to protect themselves from potentially deleterious sexual interactions by delaying sexual activity, responding to peer and partner pressure, and consistently employing safe sexual practices if engaging in sexual behavior. [See SAFER SEX BEHAVIORS.]

Comprehensive sexuality education is another, less widely adopted approach to facilitating sexual health and development. Based on the perceived need for all children and adults to have access to accurate information regarding sexual health, in 1991 a task force of health, education, and sexuality professionals developed *The Guidelines for Comprehensive Sexuality Education, Kindergarten—12th Grade*. These guidelines were published by the Sexuality Information and Education Council of the United States (SIECUS) and were revised in 1996. They have been endorsed by a number of groups including Planned Parenthood Federation of America, the Association of Reproductive Health Professionals, the National Lesbian and Gay Health Foundation, the American Association of Sex Educators, Counselors and Therapists, the YWCA of the USA, the National School Boards Association, and the Religious Coalition for Reproductive Choice. Although not widely accepted or implemented, they are recommended as a foundational basis on which educators and educational institutions can build a broad-based and developmentally appropriate sexual health curriculum.

The SIECUS guidelines are based on the belief that sexuality education must be comprehensive, age and developmentally appropriate, and inclusive of differences based on sexual orientation, ethnicity, and culture. These guidelines propose that a comprehensive program includes a biopsychosocial and spiritual emphasis on the cognitive, affective, and behavioral dimensions of sexuality. This requires attention to the provision of accurate information; exploration and clarification of personal values, attitudes, and feelings; and a focus on informed decision making and the development of the communication skills necessary to successfully act upon healthy sexual choices. Ideally, with the appropriate sexuality education, young people will have the information, knowledge, and skills necessary to make personally and socially responsible sexual decisions. They will be accepting of their own diverse sexualities and will develop positive, health-promoting sexual attitudes and behaviors.

Six key concepts are covered in the SIECUS guidelines, which are meant to form the foundational structure for a comprehensive sexuality education program. These include human development, relationships, personal skills, sexual behavior, sexual health, and society and culture. Under the heading of *human development* attention is paid to providing age-appropriate information on basic reproductive anatomy and physiology, reproduction, physical changes during puberty, changes in body image during puberty and adolescence, and issues related to sexual identity development and sexual orientation. The second concept of relationships includes attention to family roles, responsibilities, and diverse family configurations; the importance of friendships across the life span; loving relationships and behaviors; dating and courtship attitudes and behaviors; and the rewards and responsibilities of having and raising children. The third component of the guidelines focuses on the development and use of personal and interpersonal skills specific to the promotion and maintenance of sexual health. This includes an emphasis on clarifying personal values and beliefs while being respectful of the diverse values and beliefs of others; learning how to make responsible and informed sexual decisions; learning how to communicate effectively with others relative to sexual and relationship issues and choices; learning how to assert one's needs and rights and negotiate with others regarding their sexual needs, desires, and responsibilities; and the development of appropriate sexual help-seeking behaviors.

While the first three components involve information and skills essential to effective development in many areas of life, the fourth focuses more specifically on *sexual behavior*. The content of this section of the guidelines is on a life-span perspective of sexual development and health; the physiology of the human sexual response with some attention to common impairments to sexual pleasure and functioning; the appropriate expression and enjoyment of sexuality within intimate relationships and with one's own body (masturbation), with particular emphasis on personal readiness; the role of sexual fantasy in sexual pleasure and expression; and abstinence from intercourse as a sexual health-promoting choice.

Also more specific to sexual behavior, the fifth component of the guidelines focuses on sexual health including contraceptive methods, decision making, and effective usage; the physical, emotional, and legal realities of abortion; the prevention of sexually transmitted diseases including HIV; naming, stopping, and preventing sexual abuse; and the importance of genital hygiene and healthy reproductive behaviors. The sixth component of the guidelines takes a metaperspective in focusing more broadly on society and culture, in terms of the ways these environmental influences shape individuals' sexual self-perceptions and their expression of, and knowledge and beliefs about, appropriate sexuality. This section addresses such topics as the developmental messages communicated within religious and cultural groups regarding what constitutes appropriate sexual expression and what it means to be a woman or a man. Emphasis is also placed more broadly on the laws governing sexual and reproductive rights and choices, sexual discrimination, the portrayal of sexuality in the arts, and the often contradictory and unrealistic portrayal of sexuality in the popular media.

III. *Sexuality Education: Who Gets It?*

Sexuality education has been widely promoted as an important educational responsibility in the United States since the 1960s, although there have been documented educational efforts to promote "sexual hygiene" for more than a hundred years. Emphasis on the importance of sexuality education has increased significantly in recent years, however, based on concerns about the rising incidence of sexually transmitted diseases among adolescents, the earlier age of onset for sexual activity, a steady increase in the number of unplanned pregnancies among teens since the 1980s, and the increasing incidence of HIV infection through heterosexual contact.

Specifically, adolescents and young adults exhibit some of the highest rates of STDs of any age group.

According to Miller, Forehand, and Kotchick, national data indicate that 15- to 19-year-olds have the highest rates of gonorrhea, syphilis, and chlamydia in the United States. In data published by the Centers for Disease Control in 1992, between 40 and 50% of 10th-grade students reported that they were sexually active or had been in the past. This figure rose to over 65% for U.S. teens by the time they graduated from high school. The United States has one of the highest rates of teenage pregnancy in Western industrialized countries, perhaps reflecting the apparent reluctance of sexually active adolescents to consistently use contraception. Even more alarming is that fact that in their 1995 report on HIV and AIDS, the Centers for Disease Control and Prevention identified 13- to 24-year-olds engaging in heterosexual sex as representing the most rapidly increasing subpopulation of AIDS cases in the United States, with the proportion of women who contracted HIV from male sexual partners increasing from 11% in 1984 to 37% in 1993. [*See* Sexually Transmitted Infections and Their Consequences.]

A number of recent medical advancements and concerns, as well as societal changes, have also highlighted the need to ensure that issues related to sexual safety and health are adequately addressed so that American youth can make more informed and responsible sexual decisions. These include advancements in contraceptive options and reproductive technologies, increasing awareness of the incidence of sexual harassment in the workplace, greater access to a proliferation of online computer programs and services, and wider public acknowledgment of the rights of lesbians and gay men.

Given these factors, it is not surprising that many U.S. parents believe that there is a need for sexuality or AIDS education, and that this should be a shared responsibility of parents, teachers, and health professionals. Even among rural parents, Welshimer and Harris found that 87% approved of sexuality education for high school students and 63% approved of sexuality education for grades K through 12. In reference to comprehensive sexuality education, SIECUS states that "almost 9 in 10 parents want their children to have it. Twenty-three states require it and 13 others encourage its teaching. Over 90 national organizations believe that all children and youth should have it. Yet only 5% of children in America receive it."

Although many educators and parents agree that young people need guidance, information, and support in making informed and responsible sexual choices, there does not appear to be consensus as to what information should be included in school-based sexuality education. There is some disagreement on whether programs should exclusively promote sexual abstinence or also provide contraceptive and safer sex information. Some parents fear that open discussions of sexual issues will constitute implicit endorsement of sexual activity, leading young women and men to engage in even earlier sexual experimentation. Some express concern about the inclusion of homosexuality as a topic in sexual health curriculums and the normalization of what some believe are aberrant and immoral behaviors. Parents also disagree about which moral perspectives toward human sexuality should be promoted. In particular, many parents consider abortion to be an inappropriate topic for inclusion in school-based sexual health education. Other primary areas of contention include conflicts over religious teachings and values, and firmly-held beliefs among a minority of parents that the provision of sexuality education for their children is their exclusive responsibility.

This helps to explain the significant differences between sexuality education programs throughout the country in terms of their comprehensive coverage of the broad range of sexual health issues promoted in the SIECUS guidelines. Although SIECUS and other sex educators underscore the importance of comprehensive, age-appropriate sexuality education throughout childhood and adolescence, the greatest public support is for the provision of sex education programs during adolescence. As such, while some schools include sexual health as part of the curriculum in the later grades of elementary school, the majority of programs are offered in junior high and high school.

In terms of the content of these programs, and in spite of considerable evidence supporting the fact that teaching adolescents about contraception and condoms does not lead to earlier or more frequent sexual activity, several states and school boards specifically avoid the inclusion of more controversial issues such as sexual orientation, contraception, and masturbation in their sex education curricula. Instead the majority of programs still focus almost exclusively on the promotion of sexual abstinence as a solution to unintended pregnancy and sexually transmitted disease infection.

It should be noted that significant variability exists in the focus and content of these programs. Although most include instruction on abstinence, contraception, pregnancy, STDs, and HIV-AIDS, programs differ in the relative importance subscribed to abstinence versus safer sexual practices and in the effectiveness of instruction in changing teens' attitudes and sexual behavior. Their overarching goal is the same however, in terms of the prevention of sexual problems rather than the provision of broadly based and inclusive sexuality education aimed at sexual health enhancement. This emphasis on abstinence and prevention of disease and unintended pregnancy led SIECUS in 1996 to lament the fact that "as we approach the end of this century, young people are still not receiving the sexuality education they need and deserve to become sexually healthy adults."

IV. Sexuality Education: Does It Work?

The amount of research that has been undertaken evaluating the effectiveness of the various sexuality programs across the country has grown considerably in recent years. However, before discussing these findings it is important to acknowledge the range of methodological problems that are common to much of the available research, which make it difficult to draw firm conclusions about the efficacy of school-based sexuality education programs. In addition to problems common to evaluative research—for example, small sample sizes and inconsistent reporting of significance levels—research on the effectiveness of sexuality education programs is marred by six specific limitations.

First, many studies on the effectiveness of sexuality education employ heterogeneous comparison groups—for example, students of different ethnicity, socioeconomic status, sex, or developmental level. Differences between students within and between comparison groups may influence receptivity to sexuality education, and the impact thereof, making it difficult to isolate the effects of sexuality education programs. Second, many evaluative studies also fail to measure actual sexual behavior before and after implementation of these sexuality education programs. Rather, most studies rely on measures of sexual knowledge and attitudes to index change, despite the often reported incongruity between knowledge and values, and sexual behavior.

Third, short time intervals between program completions and posttest measures are also problematic. Concluding that sexuality education programs increase condom use and decrease intercourse with multiple partners at six weeks post-intervention, for example, may or may not be an important finding, depending on how well such changes are maintained over time and on what particular factors support sustained change.

Fourth, pragmatic and ethical concerns often result in sampling biases, as participants typically are self-selected rather than being representative, making it difficult to disentangle the influence of sample characteristics and the impact of particular programs. Most problematic in evaluating sexuality education programs is that students may self-select to take a sexuality program based on prior sexual experience and sexual-risk level. In this case, preintervention differences, such as previous sexual knowledge and experience, may confound the impact of sexuality education at posttest.

Fifth, another shortcoming of research on the effectiveness of sexuality education programs is the difficulty in accounting for differences between various curricula and the nature of instruction they offer. More specifically, few studies provide detailed information on the actual nature of the curriculum implemented, whether instruction is integrated into other course content or presented as a separate curriculum, and the extent of instructors' training and competence. Such differences in content and delivery make program evaluation and comparison especially difficult and complex.

A final methodological insufficiency concerns the confounding of extraneous and multiple sources of sexuality education with school-based programs. Parents, media figures, advertisements, music, and peers all serve as salient influences on children's and teens' sexual development. Although most studies include some questions about other sexual influences, few comprehensively examine the relative contribution and possible interaction of the array of sexual influences in teens' lives. In evaluating the effectiveness of school-based programs, then, it is difficult to ascertain what other influences support or supplant this instruction.

With these limitations in mind, what do we know about the effectiveness of sexuality education programs? For the sake of brevity, we divide our review of the effectiveness of sexuality education into the two primary approaches that represent the foci of the majority of current programs: abstinence models and safer-sex programs. We discuss general conclusions that can be drawn from the research and, where appropriate, review in more detail particular noteworthy studies. For comprehensive reviews of sexuality education programs, see Grunseit *et al.* and Kirby *et al.* (1994).

A. ABSTINENCE MODELS

Few studies have systematically examined the effectiveness of the most prevalent model of sexuality education—the abstinence model. Of those that have been conducted, none have shown these programs to have a consistent or significant impact in delaying the initiation of intercourse or in reducing sexual activity. Among the handful of studies that have examined the effectiveness of abstinence programs, none have found these programs effective in reducing pregnancy, abortion, and birthrates among participants. Specific to the postponing sexual involvement (PSI) curriculum, in a large-scale, randomized, controlled study of 10,600 seventh and eighth graders from schools and community-based organizations in California, Kirby and colleagues found that significant changes in sexual behaviors, attitudes, and intentions at the three-month followup were not sustained at 17 months, and at neither point were there "significant positive changes in sexual behavior."

These findings are especially troubling given the fact that in many areas of the United States, abstinence models are the only sexuality education that young people receive. This limited focus on "just saying no" leaves many young women and men ill prepared to cope with their normal sexual feelings, to seek information and support regarding their sexual choices, and to make informed and responsible sexual decisions.

Particularly problematic is the incongruity between the content and objectives of abstinence models and the reality of adolescents' sexual experiences and behavior. While significant variability exists between abstinence models of sexuality education, the programs are similar in their emphasis on encouraging participants to delay the initiation of intercourse until marriage. Given that over 65% of North American teens are sexually experienced by the time they finish high school, abstinence is arguably an unrealistic educational objective. For girls and young women in particular who still bear the primary responsibility for contraceptive and condom usage, the abstinence objective runs the risk of reinforcing current gender stereotypes that "good girls say no," and that it is their responsibility to do so.

Underscoring the belief that all sexual activity leads inevitably to intercourse, these models also implicitly reinforce intercourse as the sin qua non of sexual activity. They ignore the wide range of behaviors and activities that constitute safe and developmentally appropriate sexual feelings and behaviors. In their explicit avoidance of any discussion of healthy sexual curiosity and expression, young people are faced with the task of understanding and sublimating their normal desires, rather than being taught how to accept and manage these in ways that reinforce self-respect, safety, and respect for the needs of others.

Furthermore, the "just say no" message implicit in all abstinence models does not acknowledge the real pressures and choices with which young women are faced. Girls and young women more readily bear the adverse, and potentially life-altering, consequences of unprotected sexual activity, whether through unplanned pregnancy or contracting sexually transmitted diseases or HIV/AIDS infections. Abstinence models do not equip those girls and young women who chose to be sexually active with the knowledge and skills in safe sexual practices needed to make personally fulfilling and responsible sexual choices. With their emphasis on convincing young women to resist the efforts of young men and abstain from intercourse until marriage, they have been criticized for failing to provide adolescents with the skills needed to support this decision, or other safe and health enhancing sexual choices.

These programs are also very problematic in that they privilege and normalize heterosexual attractions and relationships and focus exclusively on sexual risk taking relative to intercourse. Such a focus ignores and implicitly pathologizes the needs and sexual desires of lesbians, gays, and bisexual women and men—at the stage in life when sexual identity issues are salient. With their focus on refraining from intercourse and all behaviors that might lead to this activity, many of these programs do not provide the necessary information many young people need if they are to make responsible and safe sexual choices as they explore their diverse sexualities.

Finally, from a psychological perspective, to set intercourse up as the goal of sexual activity and pleasure—indeed as the hallmark of having reached adulthood—and then to admonish young people to sublimate their natural desires to engage in this highly pleasurable "adult" activity, is akin to putting a child in a candy store and then announcing that she or he cannot have any candy. Similar to the biblical notion of "the forbidden fruit," such an emphasis on delaying the pleasures of adult sexual activity may well make that activity becoming all the more desirable and therefore even more difficult for young people to refrain from engaging in.

B. SAFER-SEX PROGRAMS

As noted earlier, safer-sex programs and those that focus on HIV/AIDS prevention also generally include attention to delaying sexual activity. In terms of program effectiveness, the variability in course content, duration, and instructional methods make it difficult to draw meaningful comparisons between studies. These programs range quite significantly in their approach to sexual risk prevention, but overall they appear to have a positive impact on sexual attitudes and knowledge and to a degree on sexual behavior. In evaluating sexuality and HIV education programs, the National Campaign to Prevent Teen Pregnancy concluded that these programs *can* delay the onset of intercourse, reduce the number of sexual partners, and reduce the frequency of intercourse. Similarly, in their evaluation of sexuality education and STD/HIV interventions, Grunseit and colleagues concluded that in some cases these programs not only delayed the onset of sexual activity and reduced the number of sexual partners, but they also reduced unplanned pregnancy and STD rates. In their review of program effectiveness, SIECUS concluded that "recent evaluations demonstrate the effectiveness of skill-based programs that promote abstinence *and* [emphasis added] contraceptive and condom use."

Interestingly, certain program characteristics seem to be associated with greater reductions in high-risk sexual behaviors among program participants. These include the provision of specific and accurate information; skill-building experiences; modeling and practice of communication, negotiation, and refusal skills; age-, experience-, and culturally appropriate materials and teaching methods; and opportunities to personalize the information being taught.

Based on a comprehensive review of 23 school-based programs designed to reduce adolescents' sexual risk behaviors, Kirby and his colleagues identified the following six characteristics of sex education programs that are effective in delaying the onset of intercourse and reducing sexual risk taking through the use of condoms and reliable contraception:

(a) theoretical grounding in social learning or social influence theories, (b) a narrow focus on reducing specific sexual risk-taking behaviors, (c) experiential activities to convey the information on the risks of unprotected sex and how to avoid those risks and to personalize that information, (d) instruction on social influences and pressures, (e) reinforcement of individual values and group norms against unprotected sex, (f) age and experience appropriate, and (g) opportunities to increase relevant skills and confidence in using these. (pp. 358–359)

While the routine inclusion of these characteristics would seem fruitful in future program development, with the methodological shortcomings of individual studies, conclusions on the effectiveness of sexuality education programs focused on promoting safer sexual practices and HIV/AIDS prevention should be treated as preliminary.

Speaking generally, some of these programs appear to equip young women and men with preventive practices and skills to make safer sexual choices that will reduce the adverse and long-term physical, psychological, and social consequences of unprotected sexual activity. However, although safer-sex programs appear to incorporate the concepts promoted by SIECUS more comprehensively than do abstinence models, the focus and desired outcomes of these programs remains primarily on the prevention of pregnancy and STD infection. In focusing on pregnancy prevention and contraceptive methods, they also run the risk of perpetuating gender stereotypes that hold girls and women accountable for their sexual choices and behaviors as well as those of their partners.

Certainly, pregnancy and other consequences of unprotected adolescent sexual intercourse have long-term, potentially life-threatening consequences for adolescent girls and young women. Early parenting frequently jeopardizes educational aspirations and achievement and concomitantly restricts young mothers' employment opportunities and increases their dependency on welfare and social assistance. Although researchers consistently find greater evidence of sexual risk taking among young men than young women, based on their physiology women are more likely than men to contract a sexually transmitted disease during intercourse and are less likely to be diagnosed early. As a consequence, long-term complications from an STD are more common in women. The impact of infection can range from minor to life threatening and include impaired fertility and increased risk of cervical cancer. The incidence rate of AIDS among adolescent women has increased significantly in the past two decades, with AIDS now ranking among the leading causes of death for young people between the ages of 15 and 24.

While these facts are significant in reinforcing the importance of sexuality education, an emphasis on the negative consequences of sexual activities for young women can inadvertently place the onus of responsibility on females to ensure that they do not suffer the consequences of risky sexual behavior. Also, by emphasizing condom usage as one method of contraception as well as a necessary prerequisite for the prevention of HIV and other sexually transmitted disease infections, the burden of responsibility may again fall on young women to ensure the sexual activities they participate in are "safe" rather than the responsibility being shared equally by their sexual partners.

C. COMPREHENSIVE SEXUALITY PROGRAMS

In terms of more comprehensive sexual health education programs, the very limited available research is promising. For example, in 1987 Vincent, Clearie, and Schluchter examined the effectiveness of a comprehensive community- and school-based sexuality education program instituted in the southeastern United States. The program involved education for adult leaders (for example, parents and religious leaders), school-based sexuality education for children in grades K through 12, media promotion, and integration of sexuality education into health programs.

At two to three years following the program implementation, the intervention area experienced a significant 3.5% reduction in pregnancy rates for adolescent females. Matched control areas that had not received the intervention experienced statistically significant increases in pregnancy rates over the same period. As with other studies, program effectiveness was indexed by behavioral outcome measures.

In a nonrandomized control trial Turner, Korpita, Mohn, and Hill also reported changes in sexual behavior for 341 college students following a comprehensive sexual health education seminar. Specifically, men in the seminar reported increased rates of sexual abstinence at baseline and after three months, while women in the seminar reported increases in the consistent use of condoms. Women in the control group reported never using condoms far more frequently than the women who had received the intervention.

Less tangible outcomes—for example, improved sexual self-concept or increased tolerance for sexual diversity—constitute important objectives of sexuality education, but these factors were not measured in either of these studies. However, these findings do underscore the significant impact that more comprehensive public sexuality education can have in reducing risky sexual behavior.

V. Conclusions

As noted earlier, the majority of sexuality education programs focus on abstinence from intercourse or the reduction of sexual risk-taking behaviors. While some appear to be effective in delaying sexual initiation and reducing sexual risk-taking behaviors, most are limited in scope and impact. They do not address many of the components of comprehensive sexuality education necessary to meet the broad objectives of promoting and enhancing sexual health (i.e., the integration of the physical, intellectual, emotional, and social aspects of being sexual that are positively enriching and that enhance the individual, her or his relationships, and society). While some attention to sexual health is arguably better than none, programs need to be more comprehensive if they are to adequately equip children and young people from an early age with the developmentally appropriate knowledge and skills to develop positive relationships with their bodies, healthy sexual identities and esteem, and personally and socially responsible sexual decisions, now and in the future.

Despite growing public support, and the strong urging of SIECUS and other health educators for comprehensive, developmentally appropriate sexuality education, the sexuality education programs currently being provided continue to focus primarily on abstinence and preventive sexual practices to the exclusion of a more broadly based, health-enhancing curriculum. Indeed, as we head into the next century, significant gaps continue to exist between the guidelines set forth by SIECUS for comprehensive sexuality education and the current levels of sexuality education program delivery in U.S. schools. Without this education, how are young women and men to learn about what constitutes healthy sexual feelings, attitudes, and behaviors? Is the task of educating young people about sexuality to be left to the popular media? Will the internet become the primary source of sexuality information for young people? This may well be the case unless more school boards are willing to mandate developmentally appropriate and comprehensive sexuality education as an essential component of the curriculum throughout elementary and secondary school. As well, teachers need to be equipped with the requisite skills and resources to help children and young adults accept their sexuality as a normal and healthy aspect of their identities and to guide them on how to become sexually healthy and responsible human beings.

SUGGESTED READING

Baldwin, J., Whiteley, S., and Baldwin, J. (1990). Changing AIDS- and fertility-related behavior: The effectiveness of sexual education. *The Journal of Sex Research* 27, 245–262.

Center for Disease Control (CDC). (1992). *Sexual Behavior among High School Students—United States* 40, 885–888.

Centers for Disease Control and Prevention (CDC). (1995). *HIV and AIDS Surveillance Report* 7(2), 1–38.

Grunseit, A., Kippax, S., Aggleton, P., Baldo, M., and Slutkin, G. (1997). Sexuality education and young people's sexual behavior: A review of studies. *Journal of Adolescent Research* 12, 421–453.

Jorgensen, S. R., Potts, V., and Camp, B. (1993). Project taking charge: Six-month follow-up of a pregnancy prevention program for early adolescents. *Family Relations* 42, 401–406.

Kirby, D., Korpi, M., Barth, R., and Cagampang, H. (1997). The impact of the postponing sexual involvement curriculum among youths in California. *Family Planning Perspectives* 29, 100–109.

Kirby, D., Short, L., Collins, J., Rugg, D., Kolbe, L., Howard, M., Miller, B., Sonenstein, F., and Zabin, L. (1994). School-based programs to reduce sexual risk behaviors: A review of effectiveness. *Public Health Reports* 109, 339–360.

Maddock, J. W. (1989). Healthy family sexuality: Positive principles for educators and clinicians. *Family Relations* 38, 130–136.

Miller, K. S., Forehand, R., and Kotchick, B. A. (1999). Adolescent sexual behavior in two ethnic minority samples: The role of family variables. *Journal of Marriage and the Family* 61, 85–98.

Roosa, M., and Christopher, S. (1990). Evaluation of an abstinence-only adolescent pregnancy prevention program: A replication. *Family Relations* 39, 363–367.

Sexuality Information and Education Council of the United States (SIECUS). (1996). *Guidelines for Comprehensive Sexuality Education,* (2nd ed). Minnesota: 3M Education Press. <SIECUS@siecus.org> http://www.siecus.org

Turner, J., Korpita, E., Mohn, L., and Hill, W. (1993). Reduction in sexual risk behaviors among college students following a comprehensive health education intervention. *Journal of American College Health* 41, 187–193.

Welshimer, K., and Harris, S. (1994). A survey of rural parents' attitudes toward sexuality education. *Journal of School Health* 64, 347–352.

Vincent, M., Clearie, A., and Schluchter, M. (1987). Reducing adolescent pregnancy through school and community-based education. *Journal of the American Medical Association* 257, 3382–3386.

Sexually Transmitted Infections and Their Consequences

Rosemary A. Jadack

University of Wisconsin, Eau Claire

Glossary

Asymptomatic Without signs and symptoms of disease or illness.

Centers for Disease Control and Prevention (CDC) The federal public health agency that is the center for preventing, tracking, and investigating the epidemiology of sexually transmitted infections.

Cervix The narrow neck of the uterus that extends into the vagina.

Chancre The initial sore or lesion of primary syphilis.

Chlamydia The most common sexually transmitted infection that infects the reproductive system.

Direct transmission A manner of transmitting disease organisms in which the infectious agent moves immediately from the infected person to the susceptible person.

Epidemiology The study of the frequency and distribution of health-related events in specified populations.

Exposure The act or condition of coming in contact with, but not necessarily being infected by, a pathogenic agent.

Genital ulcer disease Ulcerative lesions on the genitals, usually caused by a sexually transmitted condition such as herpes or syphilis. The presence of genital ulcers may increase the risk of transmitting or acquiring an HIV infection.

Herpes simplex virus (HSV 1 and HSV 2) HSV 1 typically results in cold sores, most often on the mouth or around the eyes; HSV 2 typically causes painful sores on the genitals or anus. However, both HSV 1 and HSV 2 can be sexually transmitted and cause genital infections.

High risk behavior Activities that increase the risk of acquiring or transmitting sexually transmitted infection. Activities include unprotected (no condom) anal, vaginal, or oral sex, injection drug use, the use of mind-altering drugs, including alcohol, and multiple sexual partners.

Human papillomavirus (HPV) A contagious virus that causes genital warts. HPV has been associated with cervical cancer in women, as well as rectal cancer in either sex.

Pap smear A microscopic examination of the surface cells of the cervix, usually conducted on scrapings from the opening of the cervix, used to detect changes in cervical cells that could be forerunners of cancer.

Pelvic inflammatory disease (PID) Inflammation of the female pelvic organs; often the result of gonococcal or chlamydial infection.

Perinatal transmission Transmission of a pathogen from mother to baby during birth.

Resistance Reduction in a pathogen's sensitivity to a particular drug.

Safer sex Sexual activities and measures that are taken to avoid exposure to sexually transmitted infections. Included are use of latex barriers (e.g., condoms, dental dams) to prevent contact with body fluids, limiting the number of sex partners, knowledge of the sexual history of sex partners, and abstinence.

Trichomonas vaginalis The causative agent of trichomonas.

Virus Disease-causing parasites much smaller than bacteria.

SEXUALLY TRANSMITTED INFECTIONS (STIs) are public health problems that lack easy solutions because they are rooted in human behavior and fundamental societal problems. The United States has the highest rate of STIs in the industrialized world, adding billions of dollars yearly to the nation's health care expenditures. As this article will show, STIs present critical challenges to the public health system due to the tremendous impact on the health and well-being of targeted populations such as women, infants, adolescents, young adults, and people of low socioeconomic status.

I. Sexually Transmitted Infections (STIs): The Basics

The Centers for Disease control estimate that more than 65 million people are currently living with an incurable sexually transmitted infection (STI), with an additional 15 million people becoming infected with one or more STIs each year. Despite these numbers, STIs remain one of the most underrecognized health threats in the country today. Although STIs are widespread, cross all economic and geographical barriers, and have severe and sometimes deadly consequences, most Americans remain unaware of the scope and dangers of STI.

Incurable, viral STIs are prevalent in epidemic proportions worldwide. In 1997, the World Health Organization estimated that at least 30.6 million people worldwide were living with HIV/AIDS. In the United States, it is estimated that 650,000 to 900,000 Americans are living with HIV, and of these, roughly one in three do not know they are infected. Furthermore, up to half of all new infections in the United States are among those under age 25, with women representing one of the fastest growing groups of people acquiring HIV. Other viral sexually transmitted infections, including human papilloma virus (HPV) and genital herpes, contribute to potentially serious health outcomes including infertility, perinatal complications, and cancers.

There are important gender considerations related to the acquisition, transmission, and long-term consequences related to STI. The majority of STIs are asymptomatic in women, leading to longer wait times prior to seeking treatment and more time to develop dangerous complications such as pelvic inflammatory disease, ectoptic pregnancy, and sepsis. Biologically, women are more likely than men to acquire STI in the presence of a pathogen. This is particularly true for adolescent and young adult women. Finally, women are disproportionately more likely to bear the long-term consequences of STIs including infertility and pelvic pain.

STIs are transmitted through intimate, sexual contact. Sexual contact includes more than sexual intercourse. Sexual intercourse is clinically defined as sexual contact, including vaginal intercourse, oral intercourse (e.g., fellatio, cunnilingus), and rectal intercourse. Other forms of sexual contact that can lead to the transmission of STI include kissing, especially deep kissing, and any other type of genital contact where unprotected genital surfaces touch and come in contact with each other. STIs can be transmitted between heterosexual or homosexual partners. Some types of sexual activity may result in increased risks. For example, receptive rectal intercourse and vaginal intercourse carry the highest risks of STI transmission.

STIs are dependent on behavioral factors for transmission. Abstinent individuals will not contract an STI. The risk of STI increases with numbers of partners and frequency of unprotected sexual activity. Acquisition of STIs is also dependent on the probability of contact with an STI-infected partner, the susceptibility of the host, and how efficiently the organism is transmitted through sexual intercourse.

The likelihood of acquiring STI is related to the number of sexual partners an individual has. Not only is the absolute number of sexual partners important, but the type of sexual partner contributes to potential infection risk. Individuals with partners who are more likely to be infected with STIs (e.g., commercial sex workers, those who use drugs) are much more likely to contract an STI than individuals who do not have high-risk sexual partners. Similarly, persons with serial partners (but only one sexual partner at a time) are less likely to spread STIs than persons who have multiple concurrent sex partners.

II. STI Covariates

Several social and behavioral covariates are associated with increased incidence of STIs. Areas where there has been a decrease in available health services and poverty leading to lack of health care access and preventive health services have been associated with increased incidence of STIs. Individuals in these areas often wait longer to seek care for STI-related symptoms, leading to increased risk of transmission to others.

While STIs are present across all economic and racial categories, minority groups are disproportionately represented among persons with STI. Although STIs like chlamydia, HPV, and herpes are widespread across racial and ethnic groups, STI rates tend to be higher among African Americans than White Americans. This disparity is due, in part, to the fact that African Americans are more likely to seek care in public clinics that report STIs more completely than private providers. However, this reporting bias does not fully explain the differences. Other important factors include the distribution of poverty, access to quality health care, health-seeking behaviors, the level of drug use, and sexual networks with high STI prevalence.

The use of alcohol and other drugs is particularly associated with high-risk sexual activity. The role of alcohol and drug use in promoting sexual risk behavior has been explained as a result of their disinhibiting properties on STI-preventive sexual practices, such as condom use. Researchers have documented that substance use is associated with higher levels of STI risk behavior. They have also found that increased frequency of alcohol consumption is associated with multiple sex partners, exchanging drugs for sex, and casual partners. Studies in university settings have also found that alcohol use, especially "binge" drinking, is associated with increased rates of unintended sexual intercourse and lower rates of condom and contraceptive use. [*See* SUBSTANCE ABUSE.]

III. Clinical Aspects of Common STIs

This section examines clinical aspects of the most commonly occurring STIs. In both women and men, the most commonly occurring STIs include gonorrhea, chlamydia, syphilis, genital herpes, and human papilloma virus (see Table I). Next, trichomonas and bacterial vaginosis, two STIs that often manifest as vaginal infections in women, are addressed. Finally, pelvic inflammatory disease, a common consequence of STIs in women is discussed.

A. GONORRHEA

Gonorrhea is caused by *N. gonorrhoeae*, a gram-negative, kidney-shaped bacterium. In men, urethritis is the most common syndrome, characterized by urethral discharge or painful urination. Symptoms usually appear within one week of exposure, although as many as 5 to 10% of patients never have signs or symptoms. In women, gonorrhea affects the cervix and is often asymptomatic. Gonorrhea without symptoms is common in women and leads to the increased possibility of dangerous complications including pelvic inflammatory disease and infertility.

Table I
Major STIs

Disease (Cause)
Genital ulcer diseases
Syphilis (*T. pallidum*)
Granuloma inguinale (*Calymmatobacterium granulomatis*)
Lymphogranuloma venereum (*C. trachomatis LGV serovars*)
Chancroid (*H. ducreyi*)
Genital herpes (HSV-1, HSV-2)
HPV infection
Exudative diseases
Gonorrhea (*N. gonorrhoeae*)
Chlamydia (*C. trachomatis*)
Trichomonas (*T. vaginalis*)
Systemic diseases
HIV infection
Hepatitis B virus infection
Cytomegalovirus infection
Infestations
Scabies
Pediculosis

Asymptomatic STI is always worrisome in that persons can continue to engage in unprotected sex while infectious.

Gonorrhea can be transmitted in several ways. In addition to vaginal-penile intercourse, anorectal gonorrhea is possible in persons with a history of receptive rectal intercourse. Symptoms can include rectal pain, discharge, and constipation. Infection of the throat (gonococcal pharyngitis) is also possible. It occurs in men or women after oral sexual exposure, especially fellatio, and can either by asymptomatic or result in symptoms of a sore throat.

Gonorrhea is easily treated with antibiotics. However, resistance to antibiotics is becoming increasingly common. Dual therapy, where two antibiotics are given to treat possible co-infections with chlamydia, is often recommended. Both men and women must be advised to complete the whole course of antibiotic treatment to prevent reinfections and potential complications. In addition, partners of infected individuals need to be informed, examined, and treated. Persons with STIs often find informing sexual partners embarassing and difficult. However, it is crucial that partners be informed of exposure to STI in order to prevent further transmission and potentially serious complications.

B. CHLAMYDIA

Chlamydia infections are the most common STI in the United States, with an estimated 3 million cases annually. The clinical picture for chlamydial infection is similar to that seen in gonorrhea. The symptoms are often less severe than with gonorrhea. Because of this, chlamydia is one of the most dangerous STIs among women because it often goes undetected. Although the disease is easily cured with antibiotics, the Centers for Disease Control report that left untreated, up to 40% of women infected with chlamydia will develop pelvic inflammatory disease (PID), and 20% will become infertile. When symptoms do occur, they may manifest as vaginal discharge or abdominal or lower abdominal pain. Chlamydia, as well as gonorrhea, can also cause significant problems in newborn infants of infected mothers, including prematurity, eye disease, and pneumonia. In men, chlamydia causes urethritis. Signs and symptoms are similar to gonorrhea and include purulent discharge and painful urination.

C. SYPHILIS

Syphilis is a STI caused by the *Treponema pallidum* organism. The reported levels of syphilis are rela-

tively low in the United States. There are cyclic increases in syphilis rates approximately every 10 years, the last peak occurring in several major metropolitan areas in the early 1990s. Research implicates crack cocaine, injection drug use, and high-risk behaviors as possible factors explaining increases in recent syphilis incidence rates.

Although this bacterial infection can be diagnosed through a blood test and treated with antibiotics, syphilis can lead to severe consequences if left untreated. Syphilis is transmitted through direct contact of the mucous membrane or broken skin with an infectious lesion. Congenital syphilis is the result of the passage of the organism across the placenta. Congenital syphilis causes fetal or perinatal death in over 40% of infants affected.

Untreated syphilis progresses in stages, separated by periods of latency. A painless sore, or chancre, characterizes the first stage, referred to as primary syphilis. The chancre usually manifests one to three weeks after exposure. The chancre can appear anywhere on the body and will disappear without any medication in one to eight weeks. The primary stage is most infectious.

A rash characterizes the secondary stage of syphilis. At this stage, syphilis infects virtually every organ and tissue of the body. Rashes that appear on the palms of the hand or soles of the feet are a common symptom of this stage. Persons may also have a fever, aches, poor appetite, sore throat, or headache. The rash and flulike symptoms typically last two to six weeks, but can last for more than a year.

The third stage of syphilis is called latent syphilis. At this stage, there are no symptoms. This stage can last years. If syphilis remains untreated, up to one-third of infected persons will develop complications associated with the last stage, called tertiary syphilis. Manifestations of this most destructive stage include lesions in the central nervous and cardiovascular system.

D. GENITAL HERPES INFECTION

Lifelong infection, latency, and recurrences characterize herpes simplex virus (HSV) infections. The disease can be transmitted between sex partners and from mothers to newborns, and it can increase a person's risk of becoming infected with HIV.

Primary genital herpes is the first and usually most painful and severe outbreak. It is diagnosed when there are symptoms but an absence of antibodies to serum culture. Initial genital herpes is diagnosed by the presence of herpes simplex virus (HSV) antibodies in a serum culture. In both primary and initial infections, there may be multiple painful genital and extragenital lesions present, which may last 7 to 21 days and be distressing and debilitating.

Persons with recurrent genital herpes have had at least one previous outbreak and have tested positive for serum antibodies. Lesions during recurrences typically last from 4 to 10 days and can cause significant social and emotional disruption in people's lives. Although the severity of recurrences varies, data indicate that most individuals will face some type of recurrence; the average for recurrences is seven times per year. A variety of psychological, physical, and biochemical stressors such as menses, emotional or physical stress, infectious disease, coital friction, overexertion, and fatigue may precipitate recurrences. While there are effective medications to help speed recurrent lesion healing or prevent lesions, there is no cure for genital herpes. Therefore, herpes often represents the first chronic disease that many young adults acquire.

Transmission of the herpes virus occurs mainly by direct contact with lesions during sexual activity. Recurrent cervical lesions in women may go unnoticed but can still be easily transmitted to a sexual partner during unprotected sexual intercourse. Therefore, it is recommended that unprotected sexual activity be avoided when lesions are present. It is also important to remember that transmission can occur via oral-genital contact. As a result, persons with oral herpes virus lesions can transmit herpes to a sexual partner's genitalia.

Shedding of the virus can also occur when lesions are not present. Asymptomatic shedding of herpes virus can lead to disease transmission. In women, asymptomatic shedding of the virus occurs most frequently from the cervix and vulva. Asymptomatic shedding is more difficult to identify in men. Asymptomatic shedding is particularly stressful for many women and men because there is no clear, discernable time when unprotected sex is safe related to transmission of genital herpes.

E. HUMAN PAPILLOMA VIRUS

Human papilloma virus (HPV) causes genital warts, one of the most common STIs in the United States. Genital HPV infection is strongly associated with cervical cancer in women. This form of cancer kills more than 4,500 women each year in the United States. Experts report that more than 35% of all abnormal pap tests show evidence of HPV infection. These infections are also associated with vaginal, penile, and anal cancers.

Genital warts are usually transmitted by direct contact. HPV lesions can occur anywhere on the external genitalia, anus, rectum, cervix, and, in men, inside the urethra. Some HPV lesions are raised and visible. Other HPV lesions are flat, and cannot be detected by touch or sight. In women, when lesions are located on the cervix or vaginal wall, they often remain undetected.

Treatment for genital warts is based on surgical excision or tissue destruction. Methods of treating genital warts include freezing with liquid nitrogen, chemicals (e.g., podophyllin, trichloroacetic acid), and laser surgery. Eradication of HPV is extremely difficult because normal appearing tissues may be infected with HPV. Therefore the treatment of genital wart lesions due to HPV leads to substantial recurrence rates.

F. VAGINAL INFECTIONS: TRICHOMONAS AND BACTERIAL VAGINOSIS

Often, STIs manifest as vaginal infections in women. There is little national data on trichomonas, bacterial vaginosis, and other vaginal infections. However, these infections are commonly found in women at health care settings.

It is estimated that trichomonas infection occurs in approximately 5 million persons annually; of these, 3 million are women. It is caused by *Trichomonas vaginalis,* a flagellated protozoan. Signs and symptoms include a watery vaginal discharge, tissue irritation, and occasional cervicitis occurring in response to the vaginal infection. Men typically have fewer symptoms than women; symptoms can include urethritis (inflammation of the urethra). Trichomonas is easily treated. However, trichomonas drug resistance is increasingly a problem. Lack of effective treatment alternatives is leading to a reliance on higher doses and more prolonged courses of existing therapies.

Bacterial vaginosis (BV) develops when there is a disturbance of the normal vaginal flora. The normal vaginal flora consists predominantly of lactobacilli, which creates a naturally occurring acidic environment with a pH of <4.5. In bacterial vaginosis, alteration of the vaginal flora occurs, with the population of lactobacilli replaced by gram-negative and anerobic organisms.

Bacterial vaginosis occurs commonly as a secondary disorder due to cervical infection and inflammation (such as gonorrhea or chlamydial infection), alterations of vaginal flora as the result of antibiotic use, or use of vaginal douches. Douching is particularly associated with the development of bacterial vaginosis. Clinical recommendations include specific recommendations not to douche. However, many women have a long cultural history of douching and are reluctant to stop, viewing douching as way in which to maintain personal hygiene and cleanliness.

G. PELVIC INFLAMMATORY DISEASE

Pelvic inflammatory disease (PID) is inflammation of the upper genital tract and can include endometritis (inflammation of the uterine endometrial wall), oophoritis (inflammation of the ovaries), and pelvic peritonitis. PID usually follows an untreated lower genital tract infection, such as gonorrhea or chlamydia. The pathophysiological progression of PID is hypothesized to be a sexually transmitted lower tract (cervical) infection causing breakdown of the normal defense mechanisms followed by ascent of bacteria into the uterus, fallopian tube, and ovarian areas, causing inflammation.

Age is directly related to PID sequelae. Sexually experienced teenage women are three times more likely to be diagnosed as having PID than are women 25 years or older. There are biologic as well as behavioral characteristics that may account for this. In the female, organisms such as gonorrhea and chlamydia easily infect columnar epithelial cells of the cervix. Columnar epithelial cells in fully developed women are inside the cervical os, or in the endocervix. In young women and adolescent girls, the columnal epithelial cells are more exposed on the outside of the cervix, or exocervix, and are thereby more vulnerable to infection.

Behaviorally, several factors have also been associated with PID. These include young age at first intercourse, multiple sex partners, greater frequency of sexual intercourse, and increased rates of acquiring new partners. All of these behaviors lead to increased cervical exposure to potential pathogens.

Inflammation caused by PID often results in tubal scarring, which may cause later tubal infertility, chronic abdominal pain, and increased risk of ectopic pregnancy. An ectopic pregnancy is a pregnancy that develops outside of the uterus, usually in one of the fallopian tubes. Clinical diagnosis of PID is difficult, because many women exhibit no signs or symptoms of PID until significant damage has been done. Symptoms are broad and can include lower abdominal tenderness, fever, abnormal cervical, or vaginal discharge. Treatment requires aggressive antibiotic therapy. Hospitalization is not uncommon if oral antibiotic therapy is unsuccessful, if the woman is pregnant, or if the woman is immunocompromised.

IV. *Gender Considerations and* STI

A. GENDER COMPARISONS IN TRANSMISSION OF STI

Different patterns in transmission of STIs between men and women have been identified. Transmission of STIs that are present in genital secretions (e.g., gonorrhea, chlamydia, trichomonas, HIV) is more efficient from male to female than from female to male. Transmission from male to female may be easier due to longer mucosal contact with pathogens after sexual exposure. This is because infected semen from the male is retained in the vagina after intercourse. In contrast, in heterosexual contact, if the female partner is infected, the male's exposure is largely limited to the duration of intercourse. Conversely, transmission of STIs that cause genital ulcers or lesions (e.g., herpes simplex virus, syphilis, etc.) appears to be equally likely between the sexes. STIs that result in ulcers and lesions typically infect the host via small cuts and breaks in the genital mucosa that can occur during vigorous sex, which both women and men are equally likely to experience.

B. GENDER DIFFERENCES IN DETECTION OF STI

Detection of STIs is frequently more difficult in women than in men. Signs, symptoms, and testing may be less reliable in women. Abnormal discharge and painless genital lesions are more likely to go unnoticed in women than in men, especially if lesions are inside of the vagina. Therefore, women often wait longer before seeking STI-related treatment than men, putting them at greater risk for dangerous STI-related complications such as PID, which can result in ectopic pregnancy, infertility, and chronic pelvic pain.

C. GENDER AND THE CONSEQUENCES OF STI

Unfortunately, women and infants bear the major burden of complications and serious consequences related to STI. While infection rates of most STIs are relatively similar between men and women, the consequences of STI differ markedly.

There is a strong link between STIs and adverse pregnancy outcomes, including congenital infections, preterm birth, and low birth weight. Screening and treating women during pregnancy for bacterial vaginosis, gonorrhea, and chlamydia may help to prevent thousands of these adverse pregnancy outcomes.

Cervical cancer, caused by sexually transmitted HPV, presents a significant women's health issue. Untreated HPV has been linked to cervical dysplasia and cervical cancers. Women who are sexually active should have frequent and regular pap tests. A common misconception is that the pap test screens for STI. Pap tests only screen for cervical dysplasia or abnormal cervical cell growth. It is not a screening test for STI. Therefore, women are well advised to ask for STI testing at the time of their regular pap screening.

D. GENDER COMPARISONS IN HEALTH-CARE-SEEKING BEHAVIORS

It has long been established that women are more likely than men to seek health care. However, seeking care for STIs appears to be an important exception for several reasons. Women infected with STIs are more likely than men to be asymptomatic. When symptoms of STIs do occur, they are often less attributable to STIs in women than in men. Furthermore, when infected women do worry about symptoms, they may wait or delay treatment because of the fear and stigma often associated with STI clinics.

V. Prevention Issues Specific to Women and Men

STIs do not discriminate. Anyone, regardless of educational background, economic level, age, or race can acquire them by engaging in a sexual relationship or high-risk behaviors. Despite this fact, STIs have long been viewed as "dirty" diseases linked to promiscuity and illicit sex, and they are considered by many people to be a punishment for engaging in immoral behavior. STIs have been perceived as afflictions restricted to prostitutes, the urban poor, and with the the advent of HIV, drug users and men who have sex with men. Improvements in sexual health education and outreach in recent years may have lessened the stigma associated with STIs, but they have not eliminated it.

Educational campaigns must continue to fight the stereotypes associated with STIs. As long as this stigma exists, those who are uninfected may be inclined to deny their own susceptibility, and thus not be sufficiently motivated to adopt preventive behaviors. Behavior change is universally difficult, and the interpersonal nature of sexual decision making compounds this problem. Several strategies are effective in preventing transmission of STIs (see Table II).

Table II

STI Prevention Strategies

Reduce number of sex partners

Recognize trigger situations for intercourse with new partners (e.g., alcohol use, drug use)

Encourage frank, honest discussion of past sexual history and STI prevention with partners before sexual activity occurs

Eliminate or reduce contact with commercial sex workers

Use barrier methods of contraception (condoms, female condoms, diaphragms, cervical caps)

Use barrier methods for oral sexual activities and female-to-female sexual activity
- Consider use of dental dams (square pieces of latex) and latex gloves for female-to-female sex
- Consider use of dental dams for any oral-to-genital and/or rectal sexual activity

Use condoms 100% of the time
- Use a new condom for each act of sexual intercourse
- Read condom labels carefully to ensure that condom has not exceeded expiration date and that condom is effective against both pregnancy *and* STI
- Have condoms available in situations where sexual activity is most likely to occur
- Ensure that condom is being applied and used correctly (condom is applied during erection but prior to ejaculation, air is squeezed out of tip of condom during application, withdrawing penis and condom after orgasm while penis is still erect)

Use spermicide in addition to barrier methods
- Choose spermicides that contain Nonoxynol-9 (most common)

Consider non-penetrative sexual activity (e.g., mutual masturbation)

Abstinence

A. CONDOM USE

Since the onset of the HIV epidemic, the importance of condom use in preventing the spread of STIs has received increased attention. When used consistently and correctly, condoms are effective in preventing many STIs, including HIV infection. It is important to remember that condoms do not cover all exposed areas. Therefore, condoms only protect what they cover, and they do a better job preventing transmission between mucosal surfaces than in the prevention of infections transmitted by skin-to-skin contact. Research shows that many people do not consistently use condoms to prevent the spread of STI. Reasons for inconsistent use is broad, varied, and differs by gender. Men often report that condoms are uncomfortable, are ill fitting, reduce sexual sensation, and are inconvenient. Women report reluctance in asking partners to use condoms. Many men and women report that they do not use condoms because they trust their partners. In lesbian sexual relationships, some women report feeling that they are not susceptible to STIs and therefore do not take advantage of preventive barrier methods like gloves and dental dams during sexual activity.

Female condoms are one approach to the prevention problem, and they have been approved in the United States since 1993. The female condom is essentially a double-ring latex pouch, with one ring fitting adjacent to the cervix and the other fitting over the vaginal opening and labia. It is inserted prior to intercourse. Evaluations of the device have been mixed. Cost is the major barrier to its increased use, with the per-device cost ranging three to five times that of a condom.

B. VAGINAL SPERMICIDES

Vaginal spermicides used alone without condoms reduces the risk of cervical gonorrhea and chlamydia. Used with condoms or diaphrams, they are even more effective in protecting against cervical infections. For some women, vaginal spermicides are irritating to genital tissue. The ideal compound would be lethal to bacterial and viral pathogens while being nontoxic to the host epithelium. The role of spermicides, sponges, and diaphragms for preventing STDs in men is not yet known.

C. HEALTH PROMOTION AND STI

Several concepts related to STI prevention are based on common sense and are equally important for sex-ually active people regardless of gender, age, and sexual orientation. Individuals must be open and honest with their partners about their sexual history and abstain from sexual activity with those whose sexual histories are unknown or uncertain. Research shows, unfortunately, that people often do not fully disclose their history. This is interesting given recent data that show that the most common reason that people give for not using condoms is trust in their partners.

Men and women should not have sexual contact with persons who have unusual fluids coming from their genital area. However, many may have difficulty with the idea of examining their partners prior to sexual contact. In U.S. society, individuals receive mixed messages related to sexuality. On one hand, media sources (television, films, magazines, books, the Internet) provide a barrage of sexually related images. Most of these images of sexuality and intimacy are not accompanied with corresponding responsible, safer sexual behaviors. Yet most young persons are still socialized not to discuss sexuality openly and may therefore find it difficult to discuss safer sexual behaviors with partners.

Women and men should limit the number of partners with whom they have sexual contact. There is a direct relationship between number of partners and incidence of STI. Furthermore, adolescents should delay initiation of sexuality if possible. Delay is favorable for several reasons. In the long run, delay results in fewer partners. Delay of first intercourse is also advantageous for adolescent girls who cervical epithelial cells are particularly vulnerable to STI.

Finally, men and women must consider correlate behaviors that put persons at increased risk for STI. STIs are strongly linked to illegal drug use and sexual activity in exchange for drugs. However, STIs are also linked to drinking behaviors. The disinhibitory effects of drugs and alcohol limit an individual's ability to make sound decisions related to sexuality. Alcohol abuse, especially on college campuses, is becoming an increasingly grave problem that is leading to increased STI, date rape, crime, and other serious problems. [See SAFER SEX BEHAVIORS.]

VI. Summary

In sum, STIs are more prevalent than ever before. This is attributable to many factors. The improper and indiscriminate use of antibiotics has produced a number of resistant organisms. Unsafe sexual behaviors, especially among adolescents and young adults, have increased. Many STIs are asymptomatic and go undetected. The economic cost of STIs increases as the number of cases increases. There is an ever-increasing responsibility for both men and women in the prevention, early detection, and treatment of these diseases.

SUGGESTED READING

Aral, S. O., Holmes, K. K., Padian, N. S., and Cates, W. (1996). Overview: Individual and population approaches to the epidemiology and prevention of sexually transmitted diseases and human immunodeficiency virus infection. *Journal of Infectious Diseases* 174, S127–S133.

Cates, W. (1999). Estimates of the incidence and prevalence of sexually transmitted diseases in the United States. American Social Health Association Panel. *Sexually Transmitted Diseases* 26, S2–S7.

Cates, W., Rolfs, R. T., and Aral, S. O. (1990). Sexually transmitted diseases, pelvic inflammatory disease, and infertility: An epidemiologic update. *Epidemiologic Reviews* 12, 199–220.

Centers for Disease Control. (2000). *Tracking the Hidden Epidemic: Trends in STDs in the United States 2000.* Author, Atlanta, GA.

Centers for Disease Control and Prevention. (2000). *HIV/AIDS Surveillance Report, 12.* Author. Atlanta, GA.

Corey, L., and Handsfield, H. H. (2000). Genital herpes and public health: Addressing a global problem. *JAMA* 283, 791–794.

Division of STD Prevention. (2000). *Sexually Transmitted Disease Surveillance, 1999.* Centers for Disease Control and Prevention (CDC), Atlanta, GA.

Edlin, B. R., Irwin, K. L., Faruque, S., McCoy, C. B., Word, C., Serrano, Y., Inciardi, J. A., Bowser, B. P., Schilling, R. F., and Holmberg, S. D. (1994). Intersecting epidemics: Crack cocaine use and HIV infection among inner-city young adults. *New England Journal of Medicine* 331, 1422–1427.

Eng, T. R., and Butler, W. T. (eds.). (1997). *The Hidden Epidemic: Confronting Sexually Transmitted Diseases.* National Academy Press, Washington, DC.

Fleming, D. T., McQuillan, G. M., Johnson, R. E., Nahmias, A. J., Aral, S. O., Lee, F. K., and St. Louis, M. E. (1997). Herpes simplex virus type 2 in the United States, 1976 to 1994. *New England Journal of Medicine* 337, 1105–1111.

Fortenberry, J. D. (1995). Adolescent substance use and sexually transmitted diseases risk: A review. *Journal of Adolescent Health* 16, 304–408.

Harrison, H. R., Costin, M., Meder, J. B., Bownds, L. M., Sim, D. A., Lewis, M., and Alexander, E. R. (1985). Cervical chlamydia trachomatic infection in university women: Relationship to history, contraception, ectopy, and cervicitis. *American Journal of Obstetrics and Gynecology* 153, 244–251.

Hook, E. W., and Handsfield, H. H. (1999). Gonococcal infections in the adult. In *Sexually Transmitted Diseases* (K. K. Holmes, P. F. Sparling, and P. A. Mardh, eds.), 3rd ed. McGraw-Hill, New York.

Morrison, T. C., DiClemente, R. J., Wingwood, G. M., and Collins, C. (1998). Frequency of alcohol use and its association with STD/HIV-related risk practices, attitudes and knowledge among an African-American community-recruited sample. *International Journal of STD and AIDS* 9, 608–612.

Rosenberg, M. D., Gurvey, J. E., Adler, N., Dunlop, M. B., and Ellen, J. M. (1999). Concurrent sex partners and risk for sexually transmitted diseases among adolescents. *Sexually Transmitted Diseases* 26, 208–212.

Wasserheit, J. N., and Aral, S. O. (1996). The dynamic topology of sexually transmitted disease epidemics: Implications for prevention strategies. *Journal of Infectious Diseases* 174, S201–S213.

Wechsler, H., Davenport, A., Dowdall, G., Moeykens, B., and Castillo, S. (1994). Health and behavioral consequences of binge drinking in college: A national survey of students at 140 campuses. *JAMA* 272, 1672–1677.

Wolner-Hanssen, P., Eschenbach, D. A., Paavonen, J., Stevens, C. E., Kiviat, N. B., Critchlow, C., DeRouen, T., Koutsky, L., and Holmes, K. K. (1990). Association between vaginal douching and acute pelvic inflammatory disease. *JAMA* 263, 1936–1941.

Social Constructionist Theory

Mary Gergen

Penn State University, Delaware County

Glossary

Critical realism An approach to knowledge that emphasizes the impact of external structures of reality on the production of knowledge within language communities.

Discourse analysis Forms of research designed to investigate how various language strategies influence relationships and notions of reality.

Epistemology The branch of philosophy concerned with the study of knowledge, including questions such as what is it, how it is acquired, and how do we validate it?

Essentialism The claim that certain features of the world are inherent aspects of that entity and are influential in directing its course of activity, for example, biological sex differences.

Feminist standpoint position A perspective that emphasizes the truthful nature of personal narratives of experience. Generally the position elevates women's experiences as closer to a standard of truth than men's.

Foundationalism The view that certain principles, beliefs, and values are prelinguistically determined. Foundations do not depend on social groups to be created, but merely to be realized.

Narrative studies Forms of research that investigate how story forms within a culture function to produce its reality, for example, the heroic story of masculine achievement, sometimes called the monomyth.

Postmodernism A label for a diversity of intellectual and aesthetic positions that reject aspects of modernism, including claims to objectivity, value neutrality, and universal truths. Postmodern art, literature, and philosophy emphasize multiple perspectives, blendings of traditions and genres, and relativism with regard to truth and reality claims.

Relational theory The viewpoint that emphasizes that it is in relationships with others that reality is created and sustained and all meaning is produced. This view is in opposition to the view that individual agents are autonomous creators of meaningfulness. Relational theory may be applied to all forms of social life, and it is generative of various approaches to therapy, social services, education, legal processes, and organizational change, among others.

Social constructionism An approach to understanding forms of knowledge that emphasizes the significance of language communities in creating and sustaining ways of sense-making.

Social constructivism An approach to knowledge that emphasizes the importance of individuals' cognitive processing in sense-making. These processes are regarded as, in part, socially produced.

SOCIAL CONSTRUCTIONIST THEORY is an approach to understanding forms of knowledge that emphasizes the significance of language communities in creating and sustaining ways of sense-making. This article presents the emergence of social constructionist theory within the context of postmodern criticisms of modernism. Also explored is the relationship of constructionism to symbolic interactionism, social constructivism, and critical realism. Additionally, social construction theory is explored in relationship to gender studies. Methods of inquiry and two content areas, "gender identity and sex differences" and "sexuality," are included in order to exemplify this approach.

I. What Is Social Constructionism?

Social constructionism is a metatheoretical position that describes how our sense of reality—as we know it—is achieved. Two central tenets of social constructionism are that (1) the ways in which the world is understood are produced through relations among persons, and most focally through forms of language, and (2) through our communicative practices we originate, sustain, transform, and undermine reality claims. Thus, the world, as we understand it, is constructed socially. Knowledge, as an integral part of language communities, is always situated within particular spans of space and time, that is, it is historically and culturally specific. Because knowledge is situated, there can be no universal knowledge. The social constructionist perspective is applicable to all fields of knowledge and to all ways of comprehending the world—from the natural sciences, everyday common sense, and self-knowledge to religious experience and aesthetic appreciation.

It is also important to state that although all realities are socially constructed, they are not easily discarded, relativized, or altered. There are powerful social forces for maintaining our "facts" about the world. Biological sex, for example, is one of these seemingly obdurant facts, which under closer examination can be shown to be socially constructed. Although there is a broadly shared meaning extant, one can also locate alternative definitions of sex. For example, during a recent Olympic Games competition, a self-identified woman athlete was declared a male by the Olympic committee on the basis of the chromosomal criteria for determining sex. An extensive discussion of the "sexing" of Olympic athletes is found in *Paradoxes of Gender* by Judith Lorber. Yet alternative constructions of sex scarcely challenge the powerful commonsense cultural beliefs that one is either a male or a female. Sexual orientation and race are other categorical systems, created through social agreements, that serve as powerful constraints on people's notions of identity, social behavior, and relations with others. Despite these forces for stability in society, social constructionists reject essentialism, that is the view that certain things are prelinguistically determined, internal, and influential in causing behavior. [*See* DEVELOPMENT OF SEX AND GENDER.]

Social constructionism is less a theory about the world than it is a theory about theories. As a metatheory, it does not favor one form of reality construction over another, nor does it assert that all forms of describing the world are equal. The moon is not equally and indeterminately rock or green cheese! Whether it is rock or green cheese depends on whether one is talking with a community of geologists or poets. Because the metatheory is indeterminant about which constructions are best, in and of themselves, there is no means within social constructionism for claiming that some ways of describing the world are true and others are false. Truth and falsehood reside within a language community's constructions, not beyond it. Thus, there are no truths independent of the communal constructions of meaning from which they are produced. Also controversial but implicit in the viewpoint is the notion that no linguistic form of moral or ethical principles exists beyond communal constructions. Such entities are productions of particular groups over time, and while there may be highly similar formulations (for example, respect for human life), they are not timeless, inalienable, or universal.

It follows that a social constructionist position does not advance one school of psychology over another; each "paradigm" or way of doing psychology is a form of "language game" or symbolic system, with its own theoretical constructions, forms of empirical investigations, and preferred means of representing results. To make an evaluation of a system of meaning, such as a school of psychology, a particular perspective on the "language game" is required; the criteria by which judgments are made are selected for particular purposes. For a feminist, there are important evaluative criteria to be considered; for a Marxist, there may be others; for a free-market capitalist, other criteria may be central. There are no ultimate foundations on which to base one's judgments as to which criteria are the best. These decisions are made by those who are involved in the evaluations and in some cases by those affected by them. Here the political ramifications of scientific work become evident.

To illustrate, feminist scholars have criticized the ways in which women, as compared to men, have been more frequently labeled as mentally ill by the psychiatric profession. Women have been diagnosed as hysterical, as sexually promiscuous, and as irrational due to premenstrual tensions, categories that would not be applied to men, who might manifest similar "symptoms." As many feminists, such as Rachel Hare-Mustin, have proposed, psychiatric practice is the result of evaluative systems that have preferenced a patriarchal system of values, while simultaneously making claims to scientific neutrality. As Rhoda Unger and Mary Crawford stated in *Women and Gender: A Feminist Psychology* in 1996, "Because the values of dominant groups in a society are normative, they are not always recognized as values. When others—women and minorities, for example—question the assumptions of the dominant group, the underlying values are made more visible." [See ANDROCENTRISM.]

Social constructionism itself is a form of construction. It is a way of organizing and structuring ways of "truth making" and is itself neither true nor false. It is not a foundational position.

II. Social Constructionism and Modernism: Ideological, Literary, and Social Critiques

Social constructionist theory in the past two decades has been highly influenced by the development of postmodern thought. Of special concern to psychologists has been its critique of modernist notions of progress, and so-called Grand Narratives of history. Postmodernism itself is situated at the confluence of several intellectual strands, primarily European, and involves the pursuit of evolving and emergent versions of intellectual activity. It is also characterized by its rejection, qualification, or hyperawareness of the modernist perspectives on epistemology and the potentials of scientific inquiry, which have dominated Western philosophical thought since the Enlightenment. The emergence of postmodernist thought at the end of the 20th century might be viewed as the outcome of several diverse critiques—ideological, literary, and social—of the modernist metatheory.

A. IDEOLOGICAL CRITIQUE

The focus of ideological critique is trained on the queen of intellectual endeavors: science. In particular this critique attacks the major tenet of modern science—that its practices and ways of creating knowledge are objective. The major line of argument is that all theories, regardless of claims to value neutrality, help to sustain some forms of life and to obliterate or devalue others. Each word that is selected for description and explanation carries with it the values of the community from which it issues. Thus, every scientific term is "loaded" with implicit implications. Even the use of seemingly objective methods—statistical equations and numerical signs—can carry evaluative significance. The notion that objectivity is a desired and an obtainable goal has been severely contested by diverse critics. The Frankfurt School, in particular, with the commentaries of Adorno, Horkheimer, and Habermas, argued against the notion of value-free rationality. Feminist critics have also taken up the case against science as value-free and have used issues of gender as a central example of value-laden scientific activity. In *Feminist Philosophers*, Jean Crimshaw illustrated the ways in which a theoretical field in psychology, in this case behaviorism, demonstrated value preferencing.

A theory like behaviorism, for example, implies that human beings and human behavior can be thought of as material to be "modified," and the term "behavior modification" is often given to programmes which offer to apply behaviorist theory in order to effect changes in human behavior. Such programmes . . . imply a sharp distinction between "controllers" and "controlled" and are intrinsically and profoundly antidemocratic.

Anthropologist Emily Martin has demonstrated in her work on medical textbooks the evaluative loadings of seemingly objective scientific explanations of reproductive system processes. In particular, biological processes conform to gender stereotypes, such that certain activities, when related to women, are seen as passive and weak, while others, in men, are described as active and assertive. Highlighting a textbook description of the menstruation process, in which the woman's body is compared metaphorically to a failing factory, she wrote, "This text captures very well . . . a catastrophic disintegration: 'ceasing,' 'dying,' 'losing,' 'denuding,' and 'expelling.' On the other hand, massive productions of sperm, which are never involved in fertilization, are never seen as waste products, but are referred to in unabashedly positive terms, as a great masculine achievement."

Many other feminist writers, such as Carolyn Sherif in her classic work, "Bias in Psychology," written in 1979 for *The Prisms of Sex: Essays in the Sociology of Knowledge,* and Rhoda Unger's "Through the Looking Glass: No Wonderland Yet! (The Reciprocal Relationship between Methodology and Models of Reality)" in *Psychology of Women Quarterly* in 1983, have been critical of the scientific standard of objectivity. In "Towards a Feminist Methodology" from *Feminist Thought and the Structure of Knowledge,* the author of this article also criticized psychology for disregarding (1) the effects of relationships that exist between researcher and subjects in scientific activities, regardless of claims that these relationships are neutral; (2) the hierarchical relationship of the researcher over others involved in a scientific study; and (3) the manner in which researchers bring into focus certain features of the central event that serve their own purposes, while suppressing others that are not favorable to their accounts. In addition, other critics have made claims regarding modes of representation, such as forms of writing and speaking, that seem to be objective, but are situated and self-interested. They serve to project certain points of view over others, as the following literary critique indicates.

B. LITERARY CRITIQUE

The literary critique of scientific work has taken many forms, but perhaps its most significant challenge has been to the assumption that language can mirror or map the world—that is, to reflect the truth. Traditionally, there was little concern with the relationship between word and world, so long as the conventional language of objectivity was used. Mathematical formulations and "plain descriptive language" summarizing data were thought to unproblematically represent the world in a more or less transparent fashion, while fanciful, metaphorical, or "poetic" language forms were to be avoided. The attack on this simple and useful world/language relationship rose from several quarters. The beginning of the onslaught came with the rise of the structuralist and then poststructuralist linguistic theories in France.

Perhaps most influential has been the work of Jacques Derrida, who created a strong argument concerning the ways in which words within a text are to be understood. In his famous use of the word pun *differance,* which can be defined in French as both "difference" and "deferral," he demonstrated how much our understanding of any given word is dependent on linguistic context. But because all words are dependent on their linguistic context, with no foundational base from which to begin, the meanings of words cannot be fixed. To hear someone say, "I love the big [Apple/apple/Apel] might mean that someone loves New York City, loves a fruit, or loves a painting of the famous Dutch artist. The meaning of "love" itself is framed by the surrounding words. It is not the same to say, "I love New York!" and "I love my newborn baby." Derrida's famous expression, *"Il n'y a pas dehors le texte"* signified there is nothing outside of the text. Meaning is determined within the textual world. The representational link between the world (the unspoken version of it) and the word is broken.

Ludwig Wittgenstein, the great Austrian philosopher, is also recognized as playing an important part in problematizing how words relate to the world. One of his most catalytic ideas was that of the "language game," a phrase that has had a strong impact on social constructionism. The language game is constituted by the linguistic exchanges among persons, exchanges that have a gamelike quality in their *reka-nen* or informal (or formal) rules. To play a language game of geology is to use different vocabulary with different rules from that characterizing poetry. Language games are parts of "life forms," another Wittgenstein expression. The game of cricket is an example of a life form. Its field, wickets, balls, bats, rules of play, uniforms, player actions, tea breaks, scoring systems, lines, umpires, linguistic expressions, audience behaviors, and the conversations among the participants all make up the life form. It is a world within itself, which has meaning, purpose, rules, regulations, activities, rewards, and punishments; it is an ontology that relates to all who agree to participate in the cricket game. (To most Americans who do not participate, cricket approximates nonsensical activity, as does American football to many in the United Kingdom).

Michael Foucault's notion of an episteme, or a system of organized knowledge that comes to be recognized as a form of truth, is similar to the Wittgensteinian idea, but with a more dire cast to it. For Foucault, the episteme is not only an organizing system, but it also has normative properties—that is, there are certain expectations of how one must behave with regard to the episteme. It is not a casual elective system of truth, but a discipline to which one learns to conform. Foucault's analysis of sexual orientation expresses this idea. The culture comes to dictate that there are a certain number of sexual orientations and ways of performing sexual acts, and one must capitulate to one of these orientations, and be forever subjected to its rules and regulations, or risk one's social standing and mental health. The body becomes disciplined to these forms, as they become unquestioned and unquestionable. Clearly language games involve actions as well as words and gestures, as this example of sexual orientation indicates. It is no trivial matter to describe oneself as "straight" or "gay."

C. SOCIAL CRITIQUE

The social critique moves away from the power of the text in the shaping of reality and into the ways in which groups of people create, sustain, modify, and obliterate these realities. One of the most powerful critiques of science came from Thomas Kuhn, who dismantled the notion that science was controlled by the precepts of the "scientific method" of objectivity and linguistic transparency. His classic *The Structure of Scientific Revolutions*, which first appeared in 1962 and then in a second edition in 1970, created a great stir in the sciences, both natural and social, as well as in philosophy. Kuhn's notion of the paradigm quickly became established in

the cultural vernacular as a means to describe a way of doing science that was created by the scientists, similar to a life form in Wittgenstein's sense. A paradigm encompassed the ways in which control by gatekeepers extended to all aspects of scientific activity: proper research methods, types of equipment, laboratory organization, results interpretations, writing forms, oral presentations, topics, research questions, journals, review processes, professional organizations, conferences, prizes, grants, honors, ethical standards, and disciplinary actions for violations of the codes of conduct. Later, many sociologists of science, among them Bruno Latour and Steve Woolgar, Ivan Mitroff, Karin Knorr-Cetina, and Michael Mulkay, documented the powerful ways in which the social life in the laboratory created the characteristics of scientific knowledge.

Of special interest to feminist critics of science has been the assumptions within the laboratory that scientists dominate one another, with the senior scientist taking the top position, and underlings falling into line below, and that the scientists dominate the subject matter. Following Francis Bacon's early view that the secrets of nature must be forced from her, most scientific work has assumed a hierarchical relationship of man over nature. Of special interest to feminists has been the work of Evelyn Fox Keller, a philosopher of science, who studied the scientific activity of Nobel Prize winner Barbara McClintock. Fox Keller examined McClintock's approach to her inquiry, one that violated the assumptions of dominance over subject matter, which alienated her from many colleagues. Fox Keller described McClintock as taking a relational approach in her efforts to understand how corn grows. By becoming closely involved with the corn's activities and by trying to relate in a nondominating manner, McClintock was able to construct a new scientific theory, which greatly enhanced the nature of her discipline.

Feminist psychologists have been at the forefront of arguing that male-dominated psychology (sometimes jokingly referred to as the "male-stream") has continued this hierarchical arrangement, one that has preferred men as subjects as well as researchers, while ignoring women. Early critiques in the 1970s emphasized the gender ratio discrepancies in favor of male subjects within research that claimed generality to all people. Others noted that certain topics were gender exclusive; for example, aggression studies involved men and affiliation studies involved women. More recently, with greater gender balance in the profession, the major question raised by feminist psychologists revolves around the notion of difference. Are the sexes always and everywhere opposites? Or to what extent has the view that the sexes are opposite been taken too much on principle? Have gender stereotypes been too pervasively assumed to be a basis on which psychological studies have been done? With the advent of social constructionist influences in psychology, feminists have begun to question many assumptions that have been propagated in diverse areas of psychology, for example, the view in the literature of evolutionary psychology that women and men have opposing strategies for mate selection based on different genetic drives. [*See* GENDER DEVELOPMENT: EVOLUTIONARY PERSPECTIVES.]

III. Social Constructionism: Relationships with Symbolic Interactionism, Social Constructivism, and Critical Realism

A. SYMBOLIC INTERACTIONISM

A more complete understanding of social constructionism may be achieved by comparing it with other theoretical orientations from which it draws, but from which it is distinct. One related area is that of symbolic interactionism, and the early work of sociological theorists George Herbert Mead and Charles Cooley in particular. For Mead and Cooley, an individual's reality is dependent on the social group that surrounds the person. Cooley spoke of the "looking glass self," which referred to the ways in which individuals learned to know themselves through the reflection others shed on them.

Other more recent views, which also attended to the manner in which social life is understood as communally constructed realities, includes the work of microsociologists Harold Garfinkel and Erving Goffman. In ethnomethodology, a field of study focused on how laypeople make sense together of everyday life, for example, Garfinkel examined how the community of pathologists and medical examiners produce a label of "suicide" when a death occurs. He strove to illustrate that the social world is fragilely held together by the social agreements among people, and a suicide is not a suicide until someone declares it as such. The work of Erving Goffman, who

wrote extensively about the dramaturgical approach to social life, also explored the ways in which social life is theatrically produced by an ensemble of players working on a crowded, multileveled stage, and thus, through their acting, construct reality. For Goffman, as for Shakespeare, "All the world's a stage," and the actors are the people who take on their roles and learn to play them. To the extent that these theorists emphasized the social creation of reality, they could be called social constructionists.

B. SOCIAL CONSTRUCTIVISM

Social constructivists emphasize the creation of social meaning through individual cognitive processes. Among the primary figures in this field was George Kelly, who attracted many followers with the framework expressed in his 1955 volume *Personal Construct Theory*. Kelly emphasized the importance of cognitive construal, that is tracing the internal organizing processes used by people as they recreated their experiences of the world cognitively. Today, the constructivist movement remains robust, with diverse tributaries stemming from Kelly's project, as well as from others. Among them is constructivist therapy, an International Association of Social Constructivism, and the journal of *Constructivist Psychology*. These constructivists, including Robert and Greg Neimeyer in the United States and Donald Bannister in the United Kingdom, have emphasized the social context that instigates cognitive processes. A related enterprise, with roots in phenomenology, was developed by Peter Berger and Thomas Luckmann, who, in 1966, wrote the classic text *The Social Construction of Reality*. Despite the title, there is very little attention to the social interactions that precede internal cognitive activity, nor evoke or sustain it. In the area of gender studies, *The Social Construction of Gender*, written in 1978 by Suzanne Kessler and Wendy McKenna, has become a classic in this tradition, as well. Its importance in the study of gender identity is described next.

Cognitive psychology today is perhaps the dominant field of inquiry, with those identified with this area far outnumbering behaviorists or humanists. The relationship between this research area and social constructionism tends to be antagonistic. In social psychology, as well, the research domain of social cognition dominates the major journals. Here the integration of social processes with internal cognitive processes in order to explain individual behaviors creates a somewhat more congenial relationship with social constructionism. In the area of gender studies, Sandra Bem's *Lenses of Gender* illustrates this approach. For Bem, as well as others, the gender schema is a way of filtering the world, such that girls and women position themselves vis-à-vis the world in a "feminine" manner, which has opportunity gains and losses attendent upon it, while boys and men take a "masculine" stance, which also contains losses and gains. The original impetus for much work on gender schema theory was that of Lawrence Kohlberg, whose work is often featured in gender studies textbooks. These psychologists have emphasized the importance of the social world in the production of individual forms of meaning making. What distinguishes social constructivists from social constructionists, primarily, is that the former focus on invisible entities within the brain/mind, where the organizing of schemas, concepts, constructs, and other posited cognitive mechanisms and processes function. Social constructionists, on the other hand, while granting the necessity of embodied functions to operate successfully in the world, do not focus on mental life, but rather on the social interaction from which meaning is derived. [*See* GENDER DEVELOPMENT: GENDER SCHEMA THEORY.]

C. CRITICAL REALISM

Some theorists have attempted to meld a social constructionist and a realist position in order to integrate ideas about a socially produced reality with a realist ontology. For them it is important to recognize that features of the external world can have a formative impact on the ways in which people understand and thus construct their worlds. One such view that has been developed most extensively by philosopher Roy Bhaskar is called critical realism. A complex elaboration, critical realism shares with social constructionism the view that there are different means or conceptual systems to organize "the real," that groups of people are able to have very different notions of the real, that there are historical dimensions to language of the real, and that values are a part of statements of truth and reality. On the other hand, contrary to a social constructionist perspective, critical realism makes claims concerning the possibility of discovering real structures and mechanisms that underly social agreements and the possibility of finding ethically preferred systems of relating, for example, socialism over capitalism. This position is particularly appealing to socialist feminists, such as Erika Burman, who support the necessity of a structural analysis of social inequality, as well as those who are skeptical of modes of understanding that might undermine claims of violence, oppression, or abuse of women or minority groups. Critical realism is very well known as an intellectual position in British academic circles, but it has not as yet attracted major attention in the United States.

While sharing a critical perspective, many social constructionists remains skeptical of the attempt to add a realist ontology. The realists' categories of the real seem no less constructed than any others.

IV. Social Constructionism and Gender Studies

Social constructionism has been slowly and partially absorbed into gender studies over the past two decades. Among the first to connect a constructionist epistemology to feminism in the United States was philosopher Sandra Harding in her well-known books *The Science Question in Feminism* in 1986 and *Whose Science, Whose Knowledge? Thinking from Women's Lives* in 1991, which distinguished among three feminisms, based on their different epistemological assumptions. She called these different approaches the empiricist, the feminist standpoint position, and the postmodern. While Harding did not specifically discuss psychology, her analysis adequately describes the divisions found within feminist psychology today. For empiricist psychologists, the dominant group, the scientific method of doing objective science is accepted without much critical reflection. The goal of these feminists is to correct the biases and imperfections in current research practices—that is, to make "bad science" good. The second group of feminist standpoint theorists rely on the experiential reports of women to attain knowledge. For them knowledge is situated, and women are in a social position to be excellent sources of the truth, despite having been silenced and marginalized by the dominant male group. The two major varieties of feminist standpoint work are the socialist feminists, including Rosemary Tong, Nancy Hartsock, and Iris Young, and relational theorists, whose work is derived primarily from object relations theory. The most well-known of these in psychology are the Wellesley research group, inspired by Jean Baker Miller, and those associated with Carol Gilligan at the Harvard School of Education. The postmodernism movement encompasses a broad set of dialogues about the nature of culture, language, and hermeneutics. Postmodernist epistemology is aligned with social constructionism and is characterized by an emphasis on the discursive aspects of producing knowledge. According to Harding, representatives of this position included three French feminists, Julie Kristeva, Luce Irigaray, and Helene Cixous, all of whom were at that time scholars and critics of Lacanian psychoanalysis, which was strongly involved with issues of textuality and gender. While Harding was a harbinger of a new mode of understanding in feminist circles, she included no American exemplars in her early writings. Today forms of work that can be classified as postmodern can be found in all academic circles, although many scholars might not classify themselves as either postmodernists or social constructionists. Their topical interests and philosophical concerns may lead them to oppose any form of label whatsoever. Jane Flax, for example, as a feminist theorist, has written two important postmodern/ social constructionist books, *Thinking Fragments* and *Disputed Subjects,* but she is also a practicing psychoanalyst who strongly values this particular way of organizing reality.

V. Social Constructionism in Contemporary Gender Psychology

In gender psychology, as in other social sciences, social constructionism has been both integrated into the mainstream of its work and simultaneously held in reserve. To paraphrase one prominent feminist psychologist, Sandra Farganis, "I have one foot in social constructionism, but my other foot lags behind." On the positive side, social constructionism draws attention to the ways in which the conditions of women and men are delimited by the social categories that hold them in their places. For some, the emphasis is on the ways in which patriarchal structures have maintained power and control over other conventions of language and the action patterns that follow conventionally from these. For example, the notion of "maternal instinct" has been used to enforce a relationship of mother to child that is not required of fathers. Certain kinds of social practices, such as custody grants and maternity leaves, are conventionally associated with this view of mother–child connections. Whether or not maternal caring is treated as an instinctual matter is open to contention, with some feminists supporting this framework and

others not. However, the societal implications are strong regardless of the position one takes.

For many feminist social constructionists, this orientation offers potentials for combatting existing conditions of oppression. Especially exciting is the possibility of inviting new forms of language, which may result in more equitable lives for all. For example, new theories might define bearing and caring for children as national economic resources needed to preserve an essential aspect of the culture. Such departures from traditional language defining child care could generate more equitable treatment for women and better child care. As Rachel Hare-Mustin and Jeanne Marecek suggest in *Making a Difference: Psychology and the Construction of Gender,* when privileged members of society have the major control over meaning-making, representations of reality serve their interests. Only when gender, as a category that preferences men, is disrupted can other marginalized meanings emerge.

These new discourses can also lead to generative forms of action, related to practical, political, and social endeavors. In 1990, the prominent African American feminist bell hooks argued in *Yearning: Peace, Gender and Cultural Politics* in favor of being critical of the descriptive language associated with race and of looking for new forms of language: "We have too long had imposed on us from both the outside and the inside a narrow, constricting notion of blackness. Postmodern critiques . . . can open up new possibilities for the construction of self and the notion of agency." For hooks, the potentials of a social constructionist approach for creating new images far outweigh the loss of foundational certainty, which is often proclaimed by other viewpoints as a limit to social constructionist theory.

Other features associated with social constructionist work in the area of gender include the following:

1. *A willingness to be reflexive in terms of one's own position or use of language.* A classic study by M. Brinton Lykes, "Dialogue with Guatemalan Indian Women: Critical Perspectives on Constructing Collaborative Research," reflects on the nature of consent forms, which are taken as written proof of respect for participants in the United States, but were seen by the village women with whom she worked in Guatemala as a sign of a lack of trust and mutuality. Reflexivity allows researchers to actively question their activities from other standpoints than the dominant version. The scientist does not see herself as an invisible, neutral observer who can objectively

assess the nature of things. Feminist psychologists often review gender studies with attention to important humanistic values, which may be in conflict with scientific ones.

2. *A willingness to be open to diverse constructions and to avoid claims that one has "empirical truth" or the final truth.* If all knowledge is situated, then there are many possible knowledge bases. To be open to change, to recognize the cultural and historical embeddedness of one's own position, is a given for a social constructionist; that tomorrow, or in another place, other ways of constructing reality might better serve is an integral part of constructionism. Social constructionist feminist scholars consider when the emphasis on gender difference is a pertinent concern and when gender similarities should be advanced.

3. *An awareness that relationships between oneself and the group from which one comes, as well as the people with whom one works, have an impact on the nature of the outcomes of research.* One's emotional ties, prior commitments, preferences, values, and beliefs are all integrated into the outcomes of work.

4. *An awareness that the potential impact of one's work on others is a significant measure of the research's value.* The researcher tries to envision how the results of the work will have an impact on diverse audiences. Ethical considerations are very important; for example, if harm might come to participants, even indirectly, as a result of the research, then it should not be done. The researcher asks for whom the work is done and whether or not it is worth doing. For a social constructionist, there is an understanding that all formulations have societal consequences, great or small. Some ways of stating one's findings might be generative in supporting a group of people, while others may be detrimental. A feminist social constructionist may also ask what voices have been silenced, overlooked, or suppressed by one's work. Answers to these questions are never finalized or certain.

VI. Challenges to Social Constructionism: Deconstruction, Science, and Moral Relativism

A. DECONSTRUCTION AND ESSENTIALIST CLAIMS

The most controversial aspect of social constructionism for many feminist psychologists is the undermining of the fundamental warranting of terms that have defined the feminist movement. The de-

constructionist move is in opposition to the essentialist assumption that distinguishable objects, events, and processes exist prior to their naming and are a basic component of nature. Especially resisted is the deconstruction of essentialist categories such as *woman, oppression,* and *liberation;* the constructionist position is that these terms are within and not beyond "language games." Some feminists are indeed skeptical of the deconstructive move and believe that losing these terms as foundational hurts the feminist cause. Thus, while many feminists consider themselves as doing social constructionist work, they resist a complete and radical identification with the term. Some even see the constructionist or postmodern move as a patriarchal strategy designed to disable feminism and other less powerful groups. As Margo Culley suggested in 1991:

Most feminists and Black Studies scholars are cautious about the extreme skepticism of post-modernist thought. For it is more than ironic that just as the female and/or ethnic subject has emerged as a strong voice in the academy and on the streets that the concepts of subject and agency themselves have come under attack.

Social constructionist feminists respond to these misgivings by arguing that the move away from essentialism is not necessarily negative. There are several benefits as well. First, essentialism tends to assume that there are distinctive qualities associated with any category. These categories are stable, complete, and inevitable. Because of this fixedness, the essentialist position deprives many voices that do not properly fit the prevailing categories of sex and gender from being heard. In this sense, essentialism has failed to address issues of diversity within social categories. Many minority-group researchers, including Beverly Greene, Karen Wyche, Lillian Comas-Diaz, and Aida Hurtado, have expressed limitations to the view that feminism's essential voice has represented only the voice of the middle-class, middle-age, White, able-bodied, heterosexual woman. In contrast, the social constructionist position takes seriously the construed categories of social differences and assumes that arbitrary distinctions are always being created. The tentativeness of social constructionism in the application of categories has been beneficial to silenced voices in this regard. There is space for them to be heard.

For many social constructionists, for whom sex and gender are not foundational categories but forms of construal, gendered relations are seen as producing gender differences, and it is through diverse social arrangements and exchanges that the specific gendered nature of individuals is produced. Thus, gender identity is created through gendered performances, rather than the reverse. This form of argument undermines the possibility that any representation of feminism is totalizing; other claims can be made without destroying the possibilities of a politics of feminism.

B. SCIENTIFIC STANDARDS AND FEMINIST PSYCHOLOGY

For some feminist psychologists, there has been some reluctance in becoming associated with the constructionist position because it is critical of many of the assumptions of traditional scientific methods. Constructionism is resisted by some in order to maintain the possibility of attaining scientific recognition within the existing parameters of empirical study. Those who hold this view work to satisfy the criteria of psychology's gatekeepers in order to correct gender biases in psychology, to create a permanent repository of knowledge concerning gender issues within the existing literature, and to have an impact on the field in general. The outcomes of this strategy have not been highly successful. As Michelle Fine and Susan Gordon, among others, have shown, little of feminist psychology has been absorbed into other areas of psychology; the literature in the field of gender psychology tends to be circulated primarily within a narrow preexisting sphere. While not eschewing the potentials for engaging in traditional empirical work, social constructionists hold that a multiplicity of methods and forms of presenting research should be explored, without limitations by strictures of past scientific traditions.

Of particular concern for feminists is the imposition of the notion of a value neutrality within the practice of science. Empiricist feminists, in particular, have had to maintain a stance of value neutrality in their research practices, leaving their feminist value orientation outside the door of scientific investigations. A constructionist position allows for the integration of highly visible value positions within the scientific enterprise. As a social constructionist, one may do scientific work while claiming a value investment. In this respect, all feminist positions in psychology are in agreement. The question of difference between them concerns forms of certainty, not value commitments. The distinction made here is that the social constructionist will presume that their findings are situated, partial, historically defined, and open to alternative interpretations.

C. MORAL RELATIVISM

One of the strongest critiques of social constructionism is that it is a stance without moral conviction; constructionists seem to support the view that one claim to morality is as good as another. Social constructionism is challenged for its moral relativism—that is, for not agreeing that there are unassailable, universal moral values. Social constructionists argue that moral principles and ethical standards are created within social groups, and they do not necessarily carry over from one group to another. Thus, moral goods are negotiated, controversial, and dependent on the social group that invokes them. This position is extremely threatening to some feminists; supporting a moral relativism is thought to be an immoral stance in itself. As some have argued, moral relativism can undermine political commitment. It is difficult to claim that sexism is unjust, for example, if justice claims are in contention. While social constructionists may agree that it is more difficult to demand social justice from this position, it is also more appropriate to acknowledge that moral and ethical arguments are based in historical circumstances and that no one position has any claims to foundational truth. At the same time, this does not prevent anyone from taking a moral stance. Indeed, from a constructionist perspective, it is very difficult to claim that one's positions do not have moral, ethical, and social implications. Constructionism is not antithetical to moral investments, then, but to supplying these investments with the kinds of foundation that would allow them to eliminate all those who disagree. As Alexa Hepburn argued in "On the Alleged Incompatibility between Relativism and Feminist Psychology," published in *Feminism & Psychology* in 2000, a coherent relativist feminist psychology is a strong and vibrant alternative.

VII. Social Constructionism and Methods of Inquiry

First, and very importantly, a social constructionist position considers all methods of conducting research as acceptable discursive and behavioral systems, which produce forms of knowledge. No methods of inquiry are thus eradicated. At the same time, all methods are also open to various intellectual and ethical reflections.

With this said, however, social constructionist researchers are often engaged in research designed to explore the manner in which reality is socially constructed. For example, discourse analysis, narrative analysis, social communication patterns, and microsocial exchanges are often featured. Feminist social constructionist research is also characterized by a sensitivity to researcher-researched relations, the context in which research is done, the rhetorical forms that are used for presentations of results, and value-related issues. The following discussion will illustrate this more fully.

A. DISCOURSE ANALYSIS

There are many forms of discourse analysis, with different approaches favored by different schools of thought. The purpose of much discourse analysis is to investigate how language itself produces reality. Researchers focus on such topics as how various rhetorical forms are used in conversation, how people negotiate the nature of the real, and how various groups are advantaged and disadvantaged through various linguistic conventions. Much work on discourse analysis in gender psychology has taken place in Great Britain and the Commonwealth countries. Of particular interest to feminist psychologists is work that analyzes how gender categories are used to encourage sexism, even if done so accidentally. A source of criticism is the propagation of assessment measures that classify people according to some presumed stable, internal state, such as their masculinity or femininity. Prototypical questionnaires related to women and men, such as the Bem Sex Role Inventory (BSRI), are built on established stereotypes of femininity and masculinity. As Margaret Wetherell has shown in her analysis of the BSRI, the traits used to define femininity are drawn from the stereotype of housewife; if people describe a career women, athlete, clubwoman, or cocktail waitress, an entirely different spectrum of descriptors are produced. Wetherell has argued that we should not try to unproblematically define what is femininity or masculinity (or any other trait), but to accept the multiple interpretive possibilities of being and of interpreting within a given situation.

In other feminist discourse analysis, attention has focused on everyday forms of talk, of public writings, such as the newspaper, and in other media in order to assess women's status and place in society. For example, Dale Spender has provided evidence that masculine traits tend to be upgraded and feminine traits downgraded when evaluative aspects are integrated into psychological descriptions. For ex-

ample, in conversations, the use of tag questions, that is, adding a phrase such as "Don't you agree?" or "Right?" on the end of a statement, is interpreted as a strong controlling activity when men do it, but as an insecure, dependent request when women do it. Other discourse analysis has looked at the ideological frameworks that surround or are implicit in the ways that language is structured. Nicola Gavey, for example, in "Feminist Poststructuralism and Discourse Analysis: Contributions to Feminist Psychology," published in *Psychology of Women Quarterly* in 1989, has examined the discursive means by which women agree to have sexual intercourse with a man to avoid seeming "frigid" or "old-fashioned," or to stop his pleading and begging. This extension of the meaning of "coercive sex" blurs the linguistic boundaries between rape and consensual sexual activity.

Discourse analysis also may include nonlinguistic aspects of discourse, such as matters of style, tone, and voice. Discourse analysis can also explore the gaps, silences, and stunted language that are the results of people being excluded from a dialogue. Differences among social groups can be compared. Researchers can investigate the kinds of descriptions groups give of themselves. Minority group members are allowed certain forms of self-descriptions that are not available to majority group members. Women can talk of sexual oppression, sexual harassment, and rape much more easily than men can, and be taken seriously. This voice belongs to them. A focus on the nature of language and other symbolic systems to create and recreate the social world is a forceful methodology for interpreting gender relations.

B. NARRATIVE STUDIES

Narrative studies are forms of research that investigate how the ways in which stories within a culture function to produce forms of reality. Inquiry into the effects of narrative forms on the construction of reality has existed for almost a century. Originating with the work of the Russian folklorist Vladimir Propp and later with anthropologist Joseph Campbell in the United States, among others, the power of the tragedy, comedy, and melodrama to shape notions of the real have been extensively examined. In the past two decades, feminists have been drawn to this work, as the narrative form has provided a means for expanding understanding of questions related to life history pursuits. Some have made inquiries into issues such as what narratives are available for women, to what extent have their lives been affected by the narrow range of narrative forms, and how can new stories of lives be created. The Personal Narrative Group, composed of feminist scholars who wrote *Interpreting Women's Lives,* has used narrative-oriented research to enlarge the scope of possibility in interpreting women's emotional responses to critical events in their lives. Their question becomes, not "What did you feel?" but "What cultural influences created a feeling within you as a girl?" This author's own work on autobiography, described in *Feminist Reconstructions in Psychology,* looks at the ways famous women and men tell their life stories and suggests that men are more narrowly focused on heroic narratives than are women who are more involved with relationships. Other researchers, such as Carol Gilligan and her coauthors, have focused on the development and change of narratives over the life span. Lyn Brown and Carol Gilligan, for example, in *Meeting at the Crossroads,* have looked at ways that girls entering adolescence seem to change in their narrative styles, becoming less certain of themselves and their visions of the future. For the social constructionist researchers, the story lines available create the limits of one's world. Enriching cultural repertoires of narratives expands the possibilities of new lives and new choices.

C. ETHNOGRAPHY

The borderline between ethnographic and psychological research is becoming blurred. Traditionally ethnographers describe the customs, beliefs, and social arrangements of peoples little known to the home culture. However, as ethnographers have become involved in constructionist dialogues they have realized that there is no means of reporting on others without reflecting oneself. One result of this concern is a new range of ethnographic experiments in which the researcher makes her or his own desires, values, and beliefs clear. Some ethnographers reveal their own experiences as a means of describing others. Some, indeed, treat themselves as their research objects. In 1996 Carolyn Ellis and Art Bochner edited *Composing Ethnography,* a volume that explores the new methodological terrain. For example, there is a personal journal on being bulemic; a confession of living as the daughter of a mentally retarded mother; an elicited dialogue among a child abuser, an adult victim, and the researcher (also an abuse victim) who interviewed them; and a narrative poem about the researcher/writer's experiences with an African American family. Here ethnography and the clinical case study converge.

As constructionist ethnographers would advise, however, there are no unconstructed descriptions of patients or clients. The researcher and researched are complexly enmeshed, and "findings" should be subject to reflection from multiple standpoints.

D. INTERVIEWING

Social constructionists regard interviewing as a form of relational interchange in which the interviewer and respondent co-construct the outcomes. While standardized interviewing has often been used by psychologists to reduce interviewer bias, this effort is regarded as misleading by social constructionists. Instead, they recognize the interview as an interpersonal event, in which the interviewer's questions establish the discursive space into which the interviewee must speak. Clearly, various types of questions, framed in different languages, from multiple interviewers, in different settings and times, affect what the "other" says. In addition, the ways in which the vast amounts of material gathered from an interview are reconstructed after the fact by the researcher to address the interests of the research community add another lamination of construction. Inappropriately, the professional audience then attributes responsibility for the account to the respondent. For social constructionists interview data must be interpreted carefully and tentatively, with a willingness to reflect on the possible contributions of the researcher and the research community to the outcomes.

Some social constructionists, especially those with a commitment to social justice based on structural change, are leery of overinvolvements with interview materials and personal narratives that highlight accounts of individual experiences. Such research turns problems concerning the need for structural reform of economic and social inequities into personal adjustment issues. For example, stories about the "personal problems" women have balancing family and career obligations deflects attention from questions about how capitalist economic systems control workers' lives. This tension between individual and the social structure analyses leads to the realization that every type of method carries with it valuational implications that favor certain ways of understanding the world over others.

E. EXPERIMENTS IN REPRESENTATION

In realizing the way in which language constructs the world, constructionists are encouraged to experiment with nontraditional languages of description. Technical language, it is argued, is a language that distances the investigator from the subject matter and audience and is designed to eliminate voices other than its own. New modes of writing not only facilitate a fuller range of expression, but also reveal the fact that they are constructions. For example a social psychology textbook called *Textuality and Tectonics,* written by a committee that takes the pseudonym Beryl Curt (after Cyril Burt), uses different voices to present diverse and controversial materials. Sometimes the voices argue and make derogatory comments to one another. They gossip and avoid topics. They behave like one might behind a closed door, but they are in front of it. In another illustration, Patti Lather and Chris Smithies orchestrated *Troubling with Angels* in 1997 with the cooperation and inclusion of a group of women in an HIV-AIDS support group. The book is organized such that the women telling their stories can have the greater share of the page, while the editors each give their reflections on the stories at the bottom of the page. Additional inserts carry conventional scientific data about the disease.

If constructions create realities, then one is also encouraged to explore the diversity of ways to construct reality, including artistic and dramatic productions. In this vein, psychologists are echoing a move made by performance artists in the humanities and the arts. Gender psychologists interested in expanding their range of expression have created videos, theatrical productions, poetry, pantomines, multimedia collections, and interactive participatory engagements. From 1995 to 1999, performative symposia have been presented at the American Psychological Association meetings. In Colorado, Janis Bohan and Glenda Russell commissioned an oratorio and created a video for national public television based on their research. For social constructionists, there is no necessary limit on what rhetorical strategies are most appropriate for generating interest and understanding.

VIII. Social Constructionism and Special Topics of Inquiry

In order to flesh out the social constructionist approach, it is useful to include a brief overview of two areas of special concern to the psychology of gender: gender identity and sex differences, and sexuality.

A. GENDER IDENTITY AND SEX DIFFERENCES

The distinction made between *sex* and *gender* as psychological variables has been highly influential for the past three decades. *Sex* is defined as the biological basis of one's body, given at birth. *Gender* has been defined as the socially constructed pattern of behaviors, attitudes, and emotions associated with one's sex, which gives one a gender identity as a woman or a man. Many psychologists are involved in the study of the social construction of gender; often-asked research questions regard the extent and nature of gender differences, and if these differences are the result of nature, nurture, or some interaction between sex and gender. Social constructionist work on gender emphasizes the communal support for producing similarities and differences in the patterns of feminine and masculine behaviors. There are potentials for great flexibility and multiple roles, if the cultural norms permit. Discursive modes reflect and control the social norms of gendered activity.

While the psychology of women has been strong for the past half-century, the past two decades has seen a dramatic increase in interest in the social construction of men and masculinity. Feminist psychologists have long argued that men have been taken as the "standard human"—with women as the deviant, or the "Other," as French feminist Simone de Beauvoir called women. In part the importance of object relations theory among feminist standpoint researchers, such as the theorists influenced by the work of Jean Baker Miller and her colleagues at the Wellesley Centers for Women at Wellesley College, has led to a focus on men and boys within gender psychology. Social constructionists have been drawn into this new area of male studies, in which questions similar to those raised about the social production of femininity are applied to masculinity. Many of these studies have linked the defining characteristics of masculinity with the rejection of homosexuality, the protection of patriarchal priviledge, and the necessity of relegating women to a second-class status. A well-known article, "Masculinity as Homophobia" by Michael Kimmel, illustrates these relationships. Work on masculinity from a social constructionist perspective continues to expand rapidly. [See MEN AND MASCULINITY.]

Within gender studies, in general, socializing patterns are seen as producing gendered people. The results tend to be stable identities, especially with regard to gender. A more unconventional influence on social constructionist views of gender identity formation has been the performative perspective of philosopher Judith Butler. Among others, she has made the claim that identity is produced in the performance of social roles, such that one becomes a woman through the enactment of womanly deeds, rather than the reverse. At the same time, taking on the womanly role influences the nature of the fulfillment of the activities. Within the reciprocality of the performance and the identity, social stability and flexibility are both encompassed. From this viewpoint, gender is an enacted state that is supported through social activities, and thus, is transient to a degree. Of importance to a social constructionist, however, is the view that others with whom we interact are important solidifiers of our performances, and that we cannot simply do anything we wish without regard for the performances of others. [See GENDER DEVELOPMENT: SOCIAL LEARNING.]

While studies of gender have been unproblematically seen as the provence of social constructionism, the sex variable has been taken as an essential one. However, within a social constructionist metatheory, every linguistic formation is a communal construction. Thus, the sex variable, as Mary Crawford in *Talking Difference* has said, "is the product of social negotiation; it is culturally produced. And it is produced in the context of a pre-existing system of meanings in which difference is polarized." The first work to challenge the foundational nature of biological sex in gender psychology was that of Suzanne Kessler and Wendy McKenna. From their original contribution in 1978 on the social construction of femininity to the recent revival published in *Feminism & Psychology* in 2000, the socially constructed nature of biological sex is posited as well. The power of naming a newborn *female* or *male* is granted to the medical establishment, which defines what the necessary characteristics must be; the ambiguously defined human is an unacceptable form of life within American society, and great efforts are made to rectify "mistakes" in nature. Kessler and McKenna have been at the forefront of challenging the notion that sex is an essential given in our human world. Indeed, biology does not speak nature into the world, but the world speaks biology into nature.

B. SEXUALITY

Studies of sexual orientation in psychology are highly controversial, with many conflicting theoretical positions represented, ranging from evolutionary to social learning theories. From a social constructionist perspective, all theories of sexuality, whether favoring biology or social learning, are by-products of particular systems of meaning. Thus, there is no ultimate means of ruling between them on the basis of factual support. Both positions, as well as others, have certain advantages and disadvantages and support certain ethical and moral principles at the cost of others. Sexual orientation is itself a label that has cultural and historical significance. Various cultures throughout history have engaged in practices that today would be called homosexual, but were not considered so then. Today, bisexuality is a contested category, as some claim that it is not a useful category, and others suggest that it is a major category for understanding human sexuality. As critics lament, heterosexuality has been presumed to be the normative category, invisible in its preeminence. In one demonstration of this perspective, Sue Wilkinson and Celia Kitzinger edited *Heterosexualities*, in which they challenged a group of feminist psychologists, asking them "How does your heterosexuality contribute to your feminist politics?" Many were unable to give a satisfactory answer, even to themselves. This study demonstrated how "taken for granted" the label is and how difficult it is for those who are called heterosexuals to define their sexual orientation development. This difficulty points to the importance of a cultural narrative that could explain why one has a heterosexual orientation. This lack in the fabric of social explanation leaves the majority of the population virtually "speechless" concerning the way to answer this potentially significant, but scarcely asked, question. The silence supports the social constructionist view that the nature of reality is dependent on communities of speakers to create it.

Constructionist challenges to traditional delineations of sex preferences are also echoed in inquiry into sexual pleasure. In particular, constructionists question the traditional biological view. As Leonore Tiefer has suggested in her writings, sexual activity is as intensely regulated by social expectations as any other facet of social life. Tiefer's social constructionist view is that sexual activity is not a biological given, nor a force beyond one's control, but a form of activity more akin to a hobby or a habit than an instinctual drive. Tiefer has also written a strong critique of Masters and Johnson's definition of the four stages of the sexual act for women and men. Tiefer's analysis points out the extent to which the researchers selected out for study only those people who already defined sex as the researchers did; she also noted how the researchers essentialized their constructs in order to claim that their findings were inductively derived. Thus, women who did not have clitoral orgasms that were detectable by physiological measures were declared as nonorgasmic women, regardless of their own claims to the contrary.

Michelle Fine has written on the ways female sexual desire has been defined in the culture. Through her studies of high school sex education classes with girls, she learned how the topic of female desire has no place in the ways sexuality is constructed. In the main, girls are taught that their job is to control the sexual desires of boys; the dangers of sex (especially disease) are the appropriate concerns of girls. Other researchers as well have noted the absence of pleasure language in the sex education of girls and women. Rather, the cultural imperatives to be careful, suspicious, and negative toward sexual activity continue to be enforced in the society. [*See* SEXUALITY AND SEXUAL DESIRE.]

IX. Concluding Remarks: The Future of Social Constructionist Work in Gender Psychology

Interest in social constructionism is growing within the field of gender psychology. The acceptance of gender as a socially constructed concept, in particular, has led to a strong affinity between constructionism and gender researchers. Yet resistance does remain. The most unproductive form of relationship is that of a conflict between the metatheoretical positions that have directed traditional forms of psychology and social constructionism. The undermining of notions of universal truths, objectivity, and progress has been discrediting for many empirical psychologists who have had to see their mission as scientists challenged by the linguistic turn in social constructionist work. One feminist psychologist of note, Naomi Weisstein, typified this rejection in her comment within *Feminism & Psychology*, in 1993, "Sometimes I think that, when the fashion passes, we will find many bodies, drowned in their own wordy words, like the Druids in the bogs." Other psychologists who hope to find definative truths about gender in order to change the system in some fashion are resistant to a form of study that cannot promise certainty.

Despite differences, there are many opportunities for collaboration. Today gender psychology might be characterized as moving into this zone of mutuality. Researchers use traditional empirical methods to test their hypotheses, while using interview and observational data to give a more diverse and holistic feeling to their writings. As fieldwork continues to flourish and as communities look more askance at intrusions into their privacy, work that is interpretive, observational, and nonintrusive is valued more highly. Researchers interested in working with people in their own communities are also more willing to forego laboratory-based requirements and to find ways of using social constructionist–oriented methods to fulfill their investigative goals.

For a still small minority, the potentials of constructionism to enhance and alter gender psychology is highly attractive. One of the most enticing challenges of social constructionist ideas is that of systematically and consciously working to create new forms of discourse and practice. Within traditional research forms, psychologists are not expected to go beyond the languages and practices of their communities of participation. The challenge of constructionism is to produce new languages that in effect create new worlds of practice. Of particular interest to gender psychologists is the opportunity to help in filling in the missing voices, the silences, the secrets that have prevented women and girls from attaining their ambitions. From a constructionist position, if new words are produced, new opportunities can be created. The psychologist is not alone in this enterprise, however, but works within relationships, both professional and personal, to achieve these ends. A prime example of the fruitfulness of this approach is the development of relational theory in gender psychology. Relational theory emphasizes that it is in relationships with others that reality is created. No single individual is able to create reality alone. Knowledge is an emergent of group processes. Followed out to its applicability, relational theory undermines individualism and provides a place for connected forms of creating life. It is a radical point of departure that is attracting attention from many involved in gender studies. While still in its infancy as a theoretical approach, it offers feminist psychologists an opportunity to be on the forefront of an exciting new avenue for understanding gender relations.

SUGGESTED READING

Bohan, J., and Russell, G. M. (1999). *Conversations about Psychology and Sexual Orientation.* New York University Press, New York.

Crawford, M., and Kimmel, E. (eds.) (1999). Special issue of innovative methods. *Psychology of Women Quarterly* 23(1, 2).

Denzin, N., and Lincoln, Y. (eds.) (2000). *Handbook of Qualitative Methods,* 2nd ed. Sage, Thousand Oaks, CA.

Ellis, C., and Bochner, A. P. (eds.). (1996). *Composing Ethnography: Alternative Forms of Qualitative Writing.* AltaMira, Walnut Creek, CA.

Franz, C. E., and Stewart, A. (eds.). (1994). *Women Creating Lives: Identities, Resilience, and Resistance.* Westview Press, Boulder, CO.

Gergen, K. J. (1999). *Invitation to Social Construction.* Sage, London, Thousand Oaks, CA.

Gergen, M. (2001). *Feminist Reconstructions of Psychology: Narrative, Gender, and Performance.* Sage, Thousand Oaks, CA.

Gergen, M., and Davis, S. N. (eds.) (1997). *Toward a New Psychology of Gender.* Routledge, New York.

Potter, J. (1996). *Representing Reality: Discourse, Rhetoric and Social Construction.* Sage, London, Thousand Oaks, CA.

Tiefer, L. (1995). *Sex Is Not a Natural Act, and Other Essays.* Westview, Boulder, CO.

Travis, C. B., and White, J. W. (eds.) (2000). *Sexuality, Society, and Feminism.* American Psychological Association, Washington, DC.

Weedon, C. (1987). *Feminist Practice and Post-Structuralist Theory.* Basil Blackwell, Oxford.

Wilkinson, S., and Kitzinger, C. (eds.) (1995). *Feminism and Discourse: Psychological Perspectives.* Sage, London, Thousand Oaks, CA.

JOURNALS WITH SOCIAL CONSTRUCTIONIST CONTRIBUTIONS IN PSYCHOLOGY:

Feminism & Psychology
Narrative Inquiry
Qualitative Inquiry
Feminist Theory
Theory & Psychology

BOOK SERIES SPECIALIZING IN SOCIAL CONSTRUCTIONIST CONTRIBUTIONS IN PSYCHOLOGY

Inquiries in Social Construction (K. J. Gergen and J. Shotter, eds.). Sage, London, Thousand Oaks, CA.

The Narrative Study of Lives (R. Josselson, A. Lieblich, and D. McAdams, eds.). American Psychological Association Press (formerly published by Sage), Washington, DC.

Social Identity

Kay Deaux
City University of New York

I. Conceptions and Definitions
II. Types of Social Identity
III. Multiplicity and Intersectionality
IV. Aspects of Social Identity
V. Assessing Social Identity
VI. Development and Change
VII. Negotiating Social Identities

Glossary

Intersectionality The condition in which a person simultaneously belongs to two or more social categories or social statuses and the unique consequences that result from that combination.

Minimal group paradigm An experimental procedure for creating social identity conditions in which participants are arbitrarily assigned to one group or another.

Social representations Commonly shared and collectively elaborated beliefs about social reality held by members of a culture or subculture.

Stereotypes Organized, consensual beliefs and opinions about specific categories or groups of people.

SOCIAL IDENTIFICATION is the process by which we define ourselves in terms and categories that we share with other people. In contrast to characterizations of personal identity, which may be highly idiosyncratic, social identities assume some commonalities with others. This chapter introduces several key issues surrounding social identity, including form and content, assessment, development and change, and identity negotiation.

I. Conceptions and Definitions

"Identity" is a term that is widely used and, as a consequence, can mean many different things to different people. Identity is sometimes used to refer to a sense of integration of the self, in which different aspects come together in a unified whole. This intrapsychic emphasis is often associated with Erik Erikson, who introduced the term "identity crisis" as part of his stage model of psychological development. Another common use of the term, particularly in contemporary times, is identity politics, where the reference is typically to different political positions that are staked out by members of ethnic and nationality groups.

In this article, the term "social identity" refers specifically to those aspects of a person that are defined in terms of his or her group memberships. Although most people are members of many different groups, only some of those groups are meaningful in terms of how we define ourselves. In these cases, our self-definition is shared with other people who also claim that categorical membership, for example, as a woman, as a Muslim, as a marathon runner, or as a Democrat.

To share a social identity with others does not necessarily mean that we know or interact with every

Encyclopedia of Women and Gender, Volume Two

other member of the designated category. It does mean, however, that we believe that we share numerous features with other members of the category and that, to some degree, events that are relevant to the group as a whole also have significance for the individual member. As an example, a person who defines herself as a feminist is more likely to be aware of legislation regulating abortion, more likely to have read books by Betty Friedan or bell hooks, and more likely to be aware of salary discrepancies between women and men than is a person who does not identify as a feminist.

II. Types of Social Identity

Many forms of social identity exist, reflecting the many ways in which people connect to other groups and social categories. In our own work, we have pointed to five distinct types of social identification: ethnic and religious identities, political identities, vocations and avocations, personal relationships, and stigmatized groups (see Table I). Each of these types of social identification has some unique characteristics that make it somewhat different from another type. Relationship identities, in particular, have some special features. To be a mother, for example, can imply a sense of shared experience with other people who are mothers. Sometimes particular aspects of these experiences can be defined even more finely, as in Mothers Against Drunk Drivers (MADD). At the same time, the identity of mother implies a specific role relationship with another person, a relationship that is unique and grounded in one's own personal experience with that other person.

Other social identities can be defined more generally, tied not to any individual but to a generic group. Thus to identify as a doctor, for example, implies a shared definition with countless others, many of whom you may not know anything in particular about. Another defining characteristic of occupational identities is that they are chosen by the person (what is sometimes called an achieved status). In contrast, social identities such as ethnicity or gender are ascribed categories, given to one at birth. Social identities also differ in the status or value that is attached to them. In Table I, for example, the stigmatized identities stand apart from the other types of social identity, all of which are typically regarded more positively.

In the original study that defined the categories presented in Table I, gender was clustered together with other relationship identities in the final statisti-

Table I
Types of Social Identity

Ethnicity and religion
Asian American
Jewish
Southerner
West Indian
Political affiliation
Feminist
Republican
Environmentalist
Vocations and avocations
Psychologist
Artist
Athlete
Military veteran
Relationships
Mother
Parent
Teenager
Widow
Stigmatized identities
Person with AIDS
Homeless person
Fat person
Alcoholic

cal solution. Certainly it is true that many relationships are gendered in their definition and implications (as are many occupations as well). However, because of the importance and centrality of gender in our lives, it is often considered as a category in itself. Similarly, sexual orientation can be classified as one form of a relationship identity, but it often has greater prominence than other relationship identities. To understand more about the nature of social identity, let us consider three identities in more detail: gender, ethnicity and nationality, and sexual orientation.

A. GENDER IDENTITY

One's gender—most typically as a man or woman—is one of the most frequently mentioned identities when people are asked to describe themselves, and it is also one of the categories most often used by others to describe us. Similarly, the development of gender identity (see Section VI) has been a central topic for developmental psychologists. Because gender is such a fundamental category, it is perhaps not surprising that a great many meanings and implications are associated with gender. Personality traits (e.g., being competitive or being aware of the feelings of others), role behaviors (e.g., taking care of children or assuming leadership roles), physical characteristics (e.g., having broad shoulders or a soft voice), and a host of other associations can be linked to gender categories. [*See* SOCIAL ROLE THEORY OF SEX DIFFERENCES AND SIMILARITIES.]

At the same time, many investigators believe that it is not useful to think of gender as a single social category. Rather, many have argued for a concept of *gendered identities,* which recognizes the multiple social identities that may be influenced by one's gender. As noted earlier, both occupations (e.g., nurse) and relationships (e.g., wife) often have gender implications. Similarly, a person's identity as a woman may differ radically depending on whether she views herself as a feminist or as a more traditional type of woman. Thus, in adopting a perspective of gendered identities, one acknowledges that multiple identities are shaped by one's gender, and that social identities can intersect and overlap with one another.

B. ETHNIC AND NATIONAL IDENTITIES

For many people, ethnicity is a central element of self-definition and becomes an important social identity. In the past, social scientists categorized human beings in terms of basic racial categories, such as Asian, Caucasian, and Negroid. With increasing awareness of the arbitrary nature of the social construction of race, these categories are less frequently used. More common today is categorization on the basis of ethnicity, defined in terms of culture, language, and country of origin. Works by theorists such as William Cross on African American identity exemplify the approach to this form of categorization and identification.

Nationality can be closely linked to ethnic identity, but it often represents a distinct way of identifying oneself. In Finland, for example, being ethnically Finnish and being a citizen of Finland are highly overlapping bases of identification. In contrast, in the United States one can have an identity as an American and at the same time hold an identity (often hyphenated) as an African American, an Asian American, a Latino, or a West Indian. Like most identities, national identities are flexible and subjectively defined. People choose both whether to have an ethnic identity at all, and, if so, what identity to claim. Often second-generation immigrants, for example, feel a pressure to choose between maintaining an identity with their country of origin and developing a new identification with the host country. These two bases of identification can have quite different meanings for friendship networks, social and cultural activities, and even marriage and family. Yet at the same time, it is increasingly recognized that people are not necessarily required to choose between one of two mutually exclusive identities, but may instead maintain dual identification or may use the two sources of identity as the basis for a new emergent form of social identification, for example, as a bicultural person. Like gender, the analysis of ethnic and national identity is more complex than it sometimes first seems.

C. SEXUAL ORIENTATION

Many people use sexual orientation as a central category of social identification. As is often the case, members of the minority group—in this case, gays and lesbians—are more likely to give prominence to this social identification than are members of the dominant majority group—in this case, heterosexuals. Many analyses of gay and lesbian identification have posited stage models of development, describing the processes by which people come to recognize and then to endorse their sexual orientation. These models take into account the evidence that many individuals do not become aware of their sexual preferences until adolescence or later. At the same time, stage models are often criticized, both for assuming invariant sequences in the development of the gay/lesbian identity, as well as for assuming that the process works in the same way for gays and for lesbians. Far less work has been done in defining a heterosexual identity, in part because it is less frequently referred to by those who might see themselves that way (although heterosexuality per se has certainly been studied widely).

A critical aspect of the gay and lesbian identity is that it is, in some segments of society, a highly stigmatized identity, a characteristic that is shared with some ethnic and religious identities. The experience of prejudice and discrimination that gays and lesbians face makes the process of social identification a particularly difficult one at times, as the positive values that one typically associates with one's own group are not shared by the society at large. Identification in terms of sexual orientation also illustrates well the overlapping nature of identity categories, particularly with gender.

III. Multiplicity and Intersectionality

It is easy to talk in terms of multiple identities, for example, having separate identities as a woman, a lawyer, a spouse, a mother, a roller blader, and so on. In fact, several theoretical traditions within psychology and sociology, including role theory and symbolic interaction, encourage us to think in terms of these distinct groups. In contrast, theories emanating from personality psychology, such as that of Erik Erikson, focus on the possibilities for integrating multiple identities into a single identity. Indeed, within that particular tradition, the successful resolution of potential conflicts among identities is seen as a criterion of the healthy personality.

Each of these positions involves its own conceptual challenges. For those who favor the position that there are a set of distinct identities, one must consider how and when these identities relate to one another. Are there points of overlap among identities? Can identities be represented in some form of hierarchy, with more important or more encompassing identities at the top and other less central or more specific identities at the bottom? For those who favor the integrative position, the questions concern how integration is achieved and whether a single identity, defined as the integrated sum of various component identities, can be predictive of more domain-specific behaviors.

Another perspective on this issue is to consider the intersectionality among various social identities. "Intersectionality" is a term introduced by critical legal theorists to refer to the specific conditions that exist when one holds two or more social statuses. Often discussion has focused on the intersections of race and gender, exploring what it means, for example, to be a Black female as opposed to being a Black male or a White female. Gender, it is argued, does not necessarily carry the same meanings for members of different ethnic groups. Similarly, ethnicity may be experienced differently for women as compared to men. At the same time, proponents of intersectionality suggest that it is not possible to clearly distinguish between experience that is related to race and experience that is related to gender. Rather, the conditions are inextricably bound together in the individual's life.

Many investigations have shown the importance of considering different configurations of social categories. Often, the particular configurations and the importance of one versus another identity may change over time as well, reminding us that identity is a dynamic rather than static process. Taken to the extreme, of course, the notion of intersectionality could be problematic if all possible intersections needed to be considered at all times. More likely, however, there are a limited number of key identity categories whose influence is sufficiently strong to combine with others and it is those intersections that investigators will want to study most closely.

IV. Aspects of Social Identity

A social identity is first of all a label or a category, a way of grouping a number of people together on the basis of some shared features. Beyond the labeling, however, social identity has many more implications, both for the persons who claim the social identity and for others who see them as members of particular categories. Thus the category label can in a sense be considered the frame for a painting that is rich in cognitive beliefs, emotional associations, and behavioral consequences.

A. COGNITIVE ASPECTS

The cognitive aspects of a social identity can be extensive and varied, including personality traits, social and political attitudes, and memories for identity-related events. Because social identities are developed and defined within a social world, many of these cognitions are shared. Indeed, some investigators talk in terms of self-stereotyping, suggesting that when one views the self in terms of a particular social category, one takes on the stereotypes by which society has defined that category. Another way of talking about these shared definitions is to refer to the social representations of salient categories. Groups defined by gender, age, ethnicity, and nationality are all represented in the culture at large. There is often a consensus as to what best characterizes boys and girls, for example, or people from Australia or Turkey or Senegal.

Consider the stereotype of woman, for example. Traits typically associated with the category of woman include being emotional, kind, understanding, and helpful to others. More specifically defined types of women, such as a businesswoman, a feminist, or a housewife, carry other associations. These societally shared beliefs about a category can become part of one's own social identification with the category. However, people do not necessarily take on the whole set of associations that consensually define a category. From the general set of societal representations, people may adopt some aspects as relevant while not accepting others. In addition, people often create their own idiosyncratic definitions of what it means to be a particular type of person. Thus, the cognitive contents of a social identity are best conceived as a combination of socially shared beliefs and other attributes based on personal experience. [*See* GENDER STEREOTYPES.]

B. EMOTIONAL AND MOTIVATIONAL ASPECTS

In many cases, social identities include not only "cool" cognitions, but "hot" emotions as well. Thus to be a feminist or an environmentalist, for example, may entail strong, affectively based feelings about social equality or the preservation of the environment. Similarly, ethnic and national identities often carry deep emotional meanings. Consider the recent conflicts in the former Yugoslavia, among Serbs, Croatians, and Muslims; or the killings in Africa of Hutus and Tutsis; the troubles between Catholics and Protestants in Northern Ireland; and the continuing conflicts in the Middle East between Palestinians and Israeli Jews. In each case, identification with the ethnic group has a strong affective element that underlies the cognitive meanings associated with the identity.

Eva Hoffman, a Polish writer who emigrated to Canada, conveys the intensity of affect that can characterize an ethnic identity in the following passage:

The country of my childhood lives within me with a primacy that is a form of love . . . All we have to draw on is that first potent furnace, the uncompromising, ignorant love, the original heat and hunger for the forms of the world. (Lost in Translation: A Life in a New Language, 1990, pp. 74–75)

The recognition that identification has an emotional as well as a cognitive basis has a long history in psychology. Sigmund Freud, for example, described identification in terms of the emotional ties one has, first with a parent and later with members of groups (and especially with the group leader). Subsequently, social psychologists such as Henri Tajfel included the emotional significance of membership as part of social identification.

Social identities also have a motivational basis. Particularly in the case of identities that people choose or achieve, specific functions are believed to be satisfied by the choice of identification. Although the variety of functions served by social identities are numerous, it is possible to think about a few general types. First, social identity may serve as a means of self-definition or self-esteem, making the person feel better about the self. Second, social identification may be a means of interacting with others who share one's values and goals, providing reference group orientation and shared activity. A third function that social identification can serve is as a way of defining oneself in contrast to others who are members of another group, a way of positioning oneself in the larger community. This functional basis of identification can both serve as the impetus for joining a group, as well as become a defining agenda for group activity.

C. BEHAVIORAL ASPECTS

One reason why social identification is a topic of such high interest is because categorizations have implications for behavior. To the extent that one defines oneself in terms of a particular group, it affects the behaviors one enacts for oneself and the way one interacts with others who may be members of different groups. Early research on social identity by Tajfel and his colleagues emphasized the intergroup aspects of social identification. His research, which used a paradigm known as the minimal group, showed that it takes very little to create a sense of identification with one group and a consequent disfavoring of another group. In these simple experiments, people were assigned to be in a specified group on the basis of a preference for one painter over another, or on a bogus distinction between preference for green or blue, or even just an arbitrary assignment as an X or a Y. With even this minimal and highly artificial basis for group identification, people will allocate rewards in such a way as to favor their own group and to disadvantage the other.

But the behavioral implications of social identification go far beyond these simple experimental demonstrations. An increasing body of research shows that group identification has important motivational consequences, and that the identifications that one is assigned or chooses lead to relevant actions in a variety of domains, from volunteering for an organization to participating in social protest to choosing a mate. Not surprisingly, people who are more strongly identified with a particular group are more likely to carry out actions that are supportive of that group. [*See* INDIVIDUALISM AND COLLECTIVISM.]

V. Assessing Social Identity

Given the complexity and multifaceted nature of social identity, the question of how one assesses a social identity is important. Perhaps not surprisingly, given the ingenuity of social scientists, many different methods have been developed over the years. Disputes have also developed as to which approach is the best.

Probably the simplest way to designate a social identity is to assign it arbitrarily, as is typically done in the minimal group experiments. Almost as simple is an approach in which group membership per se is the basis for assuming social identification. Thus, if one can determine that a person is a woman, a professor, or an Asian American, it is possible to assume that the social identity is present. A problem for this assumption, however, is that social identity is more appropriately viewed as a subjective, rather than objective, state. Thus, while every student at a university can reasonably be called a student, it is not necessarily true that every student feels strongly identified with that category. Knowing how important or central an identity is to the person is necessary in order to predict how much the identity will influence the person's beliefs, emotions, and actions. To deal with this potential problem, many measures of identification have been developed in which the respondent is asked to indicate how important or unimportant a particular identity is.

Social identity involves more than just categorization, however. As suggested earlier, key features of social identification include sets of beliefs, emotional associations, and motivational considerations. Some investigators have developed more extensive questionnaires to tap a variety of aspects of social identification. One issue in developing such measures is how generic versus how identity-specific they should be. A generic measure is one that can be used to assess any social identification, and thus it allows investigators to make comparisons between different social identities in terms of their strength or centrality. An item on this type of generic scale could be the following (this one taken from the Collective Self-Esteem Scale developed by Luhtanen and Crocker): "Being a member of a social group is an important reflection of who I am." In this case, any specific social identity group could be substituted for the general term "social group."

A somewhat more specific form of identity assessment is the measure of ethnic identity developed by Jean Phinney. In this case, the scale was designed specifically to assess ethnic identity, as evidenced by items such as the following: "I have a lot of pride in my ethnic group and its accomplishments" and "I participate in cultural practices of my own group, such as special food, music, or customs." Phinney suggests that this measure can be used to assess any ethnic identification; thus it would be equally appropriate for an African American, a Cuban American, or a Vietnamese American.

General measures such as these have the advantage of allowing the investigator to make comparisons between groups, using a common metric. At the same time, these all-purpose measures have been criticized because they do not get at the specific features of a specific identification. Within the area of ethnic identification, for example, the beliefs and experiences associated with being a Black American are probably different from those associated with being a Latino (or, more specifically, a Mexican American, a Cuban American, a Puerto Rican, etc.). To capture these more unique aspects of social identification, some investigators have developed measures that are specific to a particular group. As one example, Robert Sellers and his colleagues created a measure of African American racial identity that includes both general measures of centrality and salience, as well as specific questions about racial ideology that are based on the African American experience (expressed in ideological philosophies of nationalism, oppression, assimilation, and humanism).

Other quantitative measures of identity reflect different theoretical traditions. From the perspective of Eriksonian models, for example, identity is assessed in terms of the attainment of integration among identities. Other theories, such as those that assume continuing multiplicity, suggest assessment techniques that speak to the structure and relationship among various identities. Seymour Rosenberg and Paul de Boeck have developed procedures that yield a visual representation of identity structure, showing how a person's identities are positioned relative to one another. Figure 1 illustrates such a structure. In this particular method, people are asked to list both the identities that are important to them and the attributes that they associate with each identity. Based on the degree to which identities are characterized by common attributes (and attributes are similarly ap-

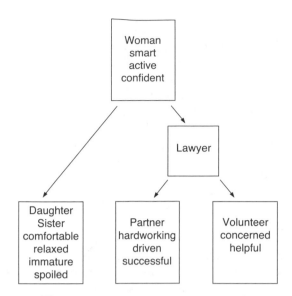

Figure 1 Example of an identity structure.

plied to identities), a structure is determined in which some identities are more encompassing or superordinate (such as woman in this example) and others are more distinctive and limited (such as daughter or volunteer in this example). Daughter and sister appear together in this figure because they are described by the same traits, i.e., comfortable, relaxed, etc. Other identities are described in other ways, as the figure shows. This method of identity assessment uses sophisticated quantitative methods, but at the same time yields very individualized portraits.

A quite different approach to assessing identity relies not on quantitative measures, but rather on various qualitative forms of data analysis, including narratives and open-ended interview material. In this approach, the investigator is more willing to let the person herself define the domains in which identity is relevant and the dimensions by which it is characterized. Qualitative methods are generally more successful than strictly quantitative methods in providing a context for identity, allowing the respondent to relate themes of self to the historical and social events in which they developed and are played out.

Qualitative assessment of identity has been particularly successful in exploring and highlighting conditions of intersectionality. By turning to the participant's own narrative, the investigator is better able to appreciate the complex ways in which various identities may combine and overlap, as well as gain a sense of the ways in which those combinations

may shift over time and place. Qualitative approaches are also a particularly useful way to enter worlds that may not be recognized and represented in more traditional approaches, which are often based on implicit norms that do not generalize.

VI. Development and Change

The sense of oneself as belonging to a particular category of people, or of being characterized by particular labels, begins quite early in life. In terms of gender identity, most investigators believe that between the age of two and three years children have a sense of their gender. Gender identity is often defined as a "fundamental, existential sense of one's maleness or femaleness." Some assume this fundamental sense of gender is biologically determined and unchangeable; others suggest that cultural norms may allow for greater or lesser variations in people's gendered definition.

Certainly the forces of socialization act on the individual to define gender. Studies have shown, for example, that parents describe their newborn children differently as a function of gender—daughters are seen as more delicate and sons as better coordinated. Similarly, teachers as early as preschool engage in behaviors that shape the behaviors of boys and girls in different ways, such as more often asking girls to be quiet or to speak softly. Thus, gender identity develops not in a vacuum, but in a social context in which representations and beliefs about gender are well established and actively fostered. [*See* GENDER DEVELOPMENT.]

In thinking about gender identity, it is important to recognize that the concept entails more than a simple label of female or male. Gender identity casts a net far wider than the biological features, including activities and interests, personal and social attributes, social relationships, communications styles, and values. Thus, a girl's gender identity might encompass playing with dolls, being encouraged to care for younger children, and smiling frequently; a boy's gender identity might emphasize sports, an emphasis on self-reliance, and a reluctance to cry. Certainly not all girls and boys adopt these or any other gender-linked characteristics. In fact, individual repertoires of gender-related behaviors can vary widely from person to person. Yet most people do maintain some sense of what it means to be a man or a woman, and what they share with others who are in that same identity category.

Racial and ethnic identity is also learned quite early. Like gender identity, racial identity is heavily influenced by the stereotypes and belief systems prevalent in the society. Early studies by Kenneth and Mamie Clark argued that segregated schools were one environment that shaped the self-images of African American children, placing a greater value on White than on Black. William Cross and others have suggested that the development of African American identity can be conceptualized as a series of stages, beginning with what is termed *preencounter,* when people do not believe race is an important aspect of their overall identity, to later stages of internalization and commitment, when racial identity is both central to self-definition and a source of positive regard.

Not everyone agrees that the development of either racial or gender identity can be characterized by a set of invariant stages, leading to a single end point. On the one hand, there are often predictable events that shape the course of identity development. In the case of gender, for example, puberty acts as an important marker and makes sexuality more salient. At the same time, educational systems often channel the experiences of boys and girls in predictable ways. On the other hand, people take various paths within these broadly defined settings and may, over the life course, negotiate and renegotiate what it means to be a particular gender or race. People who engage in sex change operations later in life serve as a dramatic example of the potential flexibility in identity definition, but there are many less vivid examples of shift and change as well. When one becomes a parent, for example, the new identity of mother or father is added to one's self-definition. Similarly, beginning a career typically involves the acquisition of a new and often very important social identity.

Long-term development of social identities can take a number of forms. In the examples provided here, identity change involves the addition of a new identity or the deletion of a previously held identity. In the case of a sex change operation, as perhaps the most dramatic example, the previous gender identity is abandoned and the other gender identity is assumed. In the examples of parenthood and occupation, the change is primarily one of adding on a new identity. One can also conceive of instances within these same domains when an identity could be dropped: when one divorces a spouse, for example, or retires from an occupation.

Other forms of identity development and change are more subtle. Change in the meaning of an identity, for example, involves shifts in the attributes and behaviors associated with an identity, while the claim to the identity continues unchanged. An attorney, for example, might shift areas of responsibility or type of legal practice, continuing to define herself or himself as a lawyer but seeing the implications of that identity differently.

Still another form of identity change is a shift in the importance or centrality of an identity. Thus, one might persist in defining oneself as an attorney over several decades, but the importance of that identity, relative to other identities and interests, might shift to become more or less central to self-definition. The importance of ethnic identity can change over time, as Kathleen Ethier and Kay Deaux showed in a study of Hispanic students who entered university and were followed through the course of the first year. Their findings showed that ethnic identity increased in importance for some students, while others gradually decreased their identification with their Hispanic heritage. Studies of immigrants show similar patterns, as the new arrivals deal with the meaning of their national identity of origin while often taking on a new identity as a resident of the country in which they now live.

In thinking about patterns of identity development and change, it is important to recognize that changes are more than intrapsychic. In other words, shifts in identity require changes in the relationship to one's social and physical environment as well. Some people have used the term "ecological self" to refer to this grounded aspect of identity. Others talk about "place identity" as a way of relating to a particular physical environment that holds meaning. These concepts recognize that *where* an identity is enacted is important. Although a social identity is rarely totally dependent on a particular physical setting, it is easy to think of examples in which identity and location are linked, such as occupational identities or athletic identities.

Equally important to the maintenance and development of a social identity is the social environment. By definition, social identities are ways in which we relate to a group or aggregate, and these social connections are critically important for defining and sustaining the identity. When a person relocates, for example when a student moves from home to university, it becomes important that social supports be developed in the new location to replace those supports that are no longer part of the immediate environment. This process of grounding an identity in a new social environment has been termed "remooring." As an example, when people who hold a strong ethnic identity change their environment, as in the case of immigration, they will often establish connections with neighborhoods, stores, and organizations in the new country that reflect and promote the ethnic identity of origin. [*See* SOCIAL SUPPORT SYSTEMS.]

VII. Negotiating Social Identities

In addition to the long-term shifts in social identities, which develop over time and often change quite slowly, the expression of social identities can fluctuate considerably. If we assume that people have multiple social identities, each of which may be characterized by distinct attributes and behaviors, then we need to consider the ways in which people may shift from one identity to another. Such fluctuations in identity, rather than evidence of instability or whimsy, provide evidence of the ways in which people respond to their environment and can make choices that seem most appropriate to that setting.

Identity negotiation is influenced by a variety of factors: the repertoire and importance of social identities that a person has, the setting in which one is located, and the actions and influence of other people in those settings. Something as simple as the number of like people in a room can affect gender identity—not only the salience that gender has, but also the beliefs and experiences that come to mind. Being the only woman in a group of men, for example, will make gender identity more salient. Similarly, being the only Caucasian in a group of African Americans will make race and ethnicity more salient. As these contexts shift, so it is likely that one's awareness of a particular social identity will shift as well (though the stable repertoire of identities is likely to remain the same).

It is also easy to imagine how specific situational cues can bring a particular social identity to the foreground. Comments by others, for example, that convey their perceptions can make an identity salient, as when an observer comments directly on one's gender, age, or ethnicity. Physically being at a university may make identities as professor or student salient for those who hold those identities. Although such environmental cues are not, in any rigid sense, determinants of one's identity, they have the ability to influence salience in a temporary sense. At the same time, it is important to recognize that people often choose their environments. The self-defined bookworm will find a library and the political activist will find a rally, thus selecting environments in which a favored social identity can best operate.

Although the optimal strategy might be to find a niche in which one's favored identities can best be enacted, circumstances sometimes create less desirable environments. Thus, for the person whose social category is to some degree stigmatized, threats to identity may be posed that require the development of strategies to cope with those threats. Sometimes this may mean negating the identity or temporarily diminishing its importance. In other cases, threat may lead to a more active search for environments in which the identity will be more favorably regarded, as when people engage in civil rights actions to promote the legitimacy and entitlement of their group.

Looking more broadly, one can see how different cultures influence the definition and choice of a social identity. The category of feminist, for example, was unrecognized in some countries until very recently. Some people have argued that even the notion of identity itself is historically bound, a product of the Renaissance period. Similarly, ideas of multiplicity, or what Robert Lifton has called the "protean self," may reflect a set of historical conditions characteristic of post-industrial societies. In short, social identity is, as the term suggests, an inherently *social* phenomenon that must be understood as a product of both individual and contextual-historical forces.

SUGGESTED READING

Capozza, D., and Brown, R. (eds.) (2000). *Social Identity Processes: Trends in Theory and Research*. Sage, London.
Deaux, K. (1996). Social identification. In *Social Psychology: Handbook of Basic Principles* (E. T. Higgins and A. K. Kruglanski, eds.). Guilford, New York.
Deaux, K., and Stewart, A. J. (2001). Framing gendered identities. In *Handbook of the Psychology of Women and Gender* (R. K. Unger, ed.). Wiley, New York.
Hogg, M. A., and Abrams, D. (1988). *Social Identifications*. Routledge and Kegan Paul, London and New York.
Ruble, D. N., and Martin, C. L. (1998). Gender development. In *Handbook of Child Psychology* (W. Damon, ed.), 5th ed., Vol. 3: Social, Emotional and Personality Development, N. Eisenberg, ed., (pp. 788–827). New York: John Wiley.
Skevington, S., and Baker, D. (eds.) (1989). *The Social Identity of Women*. Sage, London.
Stryker, S., Owens, T. J., and White, R. W. (eds.) (2000). *Self, Identity, and Social Movements*. University of Minnesota Press, Minneapolis.
Waters, M. C. (1990). *Ethnic Options: Choosing Identities in America*. University of California Press, Berkeley.

Social Role Theory of Sex Differences and Similarities

Alice H. Eagly
Northwestern University

I. Origins of Division of Labor and Gender Hierarchy
II. Gender Roles and Stereotypes
III. Relation of Gender Roles to the Social Positions of Women and Men
IV. Influence of Gender Roles on Behavior
V. Sex Differences and Similarities in Psychological Research
VI. Multiple Roles: Gender Roles and Specific Roles
VII. Changes in Gender Roles and Sex Differences over Time

Glossary

Correspondence bias The tendency of perceivers to assume that people's inner dispositions correspond to their observed behavior.

Descriptive norms Expectations about behavior derived from observations of what people do.

Gender role Shared expectations about behavior that apply to people on the basis of their socially identified sex.

Injunctive norms Expectations about the behavior that people should engage in.

Meta-analysis A review that uses quantitative methods to aggregate and integrate the findings of studies that have tested a particular hypothesis.

Social role Shared expectations about behavior that apply to people who occupy a certain social position or are members of a particular social category.

ACCORDING TO SOCIAL ROLE THEORY, sex differences in social behavior arise from the distrib-ution of men and women into social roles within a society. In current industrial and postindustrial economies, these roles are organized so that women are more likely than men to assume domestic roles of homemaker and to be primary caretakers of children, whereas men are more likely than women to assume roles in the paid economy and to be primary family providers. The distribution of men and women into social roles is in turn a product of (1) the variable factors represented by the social, economic, technological, and ecological forces present in a society and (2) inherent sex differences represented by each sex's physical attributes and related behaviors, especially women's childbearing and nursing of infants and men's greater size, speed, and upper-body strength. These physical sex differences, in interaction with social and ecological conditions, influence the roles held by men and women because certain activities are more efficiently accomplished by one sex. The benefits of this greater efficiency emerge because women and men are allied in societies and engage in a division of labor. The different positions of men

Encyclopedia of Women and Gender, Volume Two

and women in the social structure that result from this division of labor yield sex-differentiated behavior through a variety of proximal, mediating processes. One such process is the formation of gender roles, by which people of each sex are expected to have characteristics that equip them for the tasks that they typically carry out. Gender roles, along with the specific roles occupied by men and women (e.g., occupational roles), then guide social behavior. This guidance is mediated by sex-typed socialization practices as well as by processes detailed in social psychological theory and research (e.g., expectancy confirmation, self-regulatory processes). In brief, social role theory argues that sex differences in behavior are a function of gender roles and other proximal causes, which in turn arise from the distal causes that define the positions of women and men in the social structure.

I. Origins of Division of Labor and Gender Hierarchy

To provide a convincing general theory of sex differences and similarities, social role theory must explain why men and women are differently positioned in the social structure—that is, why there is sexual division of labor and often gender hierarchy. Answering this question is facilitated by studying the sex-typed social roles in a wide range of societies. Wendy Wood and Alice Eagly's review of this cross-cultural evidence that has been produced by anthropologists concluded that all known societies established a division of labor according to sex. In fact, as George Murdock and Caterina Provost demonstrated in their analysis of the division of labor in 185 societies, the majority of productive activities are carried out solely or typically by one sex within individual societies, and many activities are consistently performed by men or women across societies (e.g., men smelt ores and work metals and women cook and prepare foods from plant sources).

In addition to the existence of a division of labor, another cross-cultural commonality is that the status and power differences that exist within societies typically favor men, although the dimensions of status that are linked to sex appear to vary across societies and to be relatively independent of one another in cross-cultural analyses. Yet sex differences on these dimensions are typically in the direction of women possessing fewer resources than men, of less value being placed on women's lives, and of greater con-

trol of women's marital and sexual behavior. [See CROSS-CULTURAL GENDER ROLES.]

Most anthropologists account for the division of labor and gender hierarchy by arguments that physical sex differences, particularly women's capacity for reproduction and men's size and strength, interact with the demands of socioeconomic systems. Physical sex differences, especially women's reproductive activities of pregnancy and lactation, are critical to the division of labor because reproduction affects role occupancy directly as well as indirectly through facilitating or limiting other types of behaviors. Women's roles are directly impacted because women have responsibility for gestating, nursing, and caring for highly dependent infants. These activities in turn limit women's ability to perform tasks that require speed, uninterrupted periods of activity, or long-distance travel away from home. Therefore, women generally eschew tasks such as hunting large animals, plowing, and warfare in favor of activities that can be more easily performed simultaneously with child care. Such consequences of reproduction are less pervasive in societies with low birthrates, less reliance on lactation for feeding infants, and more nonmaternal care of young children—all of which are features that have become common in postindustrial societies.

Another determinant of the distribution of the sexes into social roles is men's greater size and strength. To the extent that productive tasks within a society are highly demanding of speed and of physical strength, especially brief bursts of force and upper-body strength, men, on average, are more likely than women to be successful at task performance. In foraging, horticultural, and agricultural societies, the activities especially likely to be facilitated by men's physical attributes include hunting large animals, plowing, and warfare. These considerations of men's greater size and strength are less important in societies in which few occupational roles demand these attributes, such as postindustrial societies in particular.

In general, physical sex differences, in interaction with demands of the economy, technology, and local ecology, influence the roles held by men and women. The resulting division of labor does not necessarily produce patriarchy. In fact, relatively egalitarian relations between the sexes are often found in decentralized, nonhierarchial societies with limited technology, especially in simple economies that derive subsistence from foraging. Yet in more complex societies, the physical attributes of the sexes generally interact with economic and technological developments to enhance men's power and status. For example, men's greater upper-body strength and speed generally give them preference over women in performance of activities, such as warfare, that can yield decision-making power, authority, and access to resources. Also, women's reproductive activity makes it difficult for them to perform other types of activities that yield status and power in the broader society, particularly activities that require intensive training and skill acquisition and that are performed outside of the household.

In summary, sex-typed social roles involving gender hierarchies and a division of labor emerge from a complex set of factors that include the physical sex differences inherent in female reproductive activity and male size and strength. Because these biological factors interact with the ecological, economic, social structural, and cultural attributes of societies, social role theory is especially attuned to understanding cross-cultural variation in gender roles and sex differences in behavior. Although physical sex differences are in general less consequential in postindustrial societies, even these societies retain some degree of male–female division of labor and aspects of patriarchal relations between the sexes. These sex-typed social roles in turn produce differences in the social behavior of women and men.

II. *Gender Roles and Stereotypes*

Because, as the subsequent sections of this article explain, gender roles emerge from the social roles occupied by men and women and foster sex-typed behavior, it is important to understand that gender roles are shared expectations about behavior that apply to people on the basis of their socially identified sex. People thus hold expectations about the behaviors that are appropriate to an individual on the basis of that person being male or female. The idea that these expectations are shared implies that they are consensual in society.

This definition of gender roles derives from the general concept of social role, which refers to the shared expectations that apply to people who occupy a certain social position or are members of a particular social category. At an individual level, roles exist as schemas, understood as abstract knowledge about a particular entity—in this case, about a group of people. Because role schemas tend to be consensual, they are important structures at the societal level as well as the individual level.

According to the role construct, people who have the same social position within a social structure such as an organization or family (e.g., middle man-

agers, fathers) or who are classified in the same general societal category (e.g., women, Native Americans) experience common situational constraints that tend to maintain their characteristic patterns of behavior. These constraints arise from the shared role schemas that people in their society hold. For example, people who have a particular paid occupation (e.g., as high school teachers or truck drivers) are subjected to a set of expectations concerning the work they should do and the style in which they should do it. If they deviate from these expectations by behaving in ways that are perceived as atypical and regarded as inappropriate for people in their occupation, negative sanctions follow.

In contrast to specific roles based on occupations, family relationships, and memberships in other groups and organizations, gender roles are rather diffuse because they apply to people who have membership in the extremely general social categories of male and female. Gender roles thus pertain to virtually all people. These roles, like other diffuse roles based on qualities such as age, race, and social class, have great scope or generality because they are applicable to all portions of one's daily life. In contrast, more specific roles based on factors such as family relationships (e.g., mother, son) and occupation (e.g., bank teller, firefighter) are mainly relevant to one's behavior in a particular group or organizational context—at work, for example, in the case of occupational roles. Gender roles coexist with specific roles and are relevant to most social interactions, including encounters that are also structured by these specific roles. This general applicability of gender roles means that they continue to have impact on behavior, even though specific roles also constrain behavior. For example, because gender roles are relevant in the workplace, people have somewhat different expectations for female and male occupants of the same workplace role.

Evidence for the existence of gender roles follows in part from research on gender stereotypes, which has consistently documented that people have differing beliefs about the typical behavior of men and women. For example, studies of gender stereotypes have shown that the content of many of these beliefs can be summarized in terms of differences on two dimensions, which are frequently given David Bakan's labels of communal and agentic. Women, more than men, are thought to behave in a manner that can be described as communal—that is, friendly, unselfish, concerned with others, and expressive. Men, more than women, are thought to behave in a manner that can be described as agentic—that is, independent, masterful, assertive, and instrumentally competent. Gender stereotypes also encompass beliefs about many other aspects of individuals, including their physical characteristics, cognitive abilities, typical roles, specific skills, and emotional dispositions. Nonetheless, such beliefs about the typical characteristics of women and men are not sufficient to demonstrate the existence of gender roles, because roles are built not merely from expectations about how people typically behave, but also from expectations about how they should behave. Thus, most research on gender stereotypes describes descriptive norms, which are expectations derived from observations of what people do. In addition, social roles encompass injunctive norms, which are expectations about what people should do. [*See* GENDER STEREOTYPES.]

Demonstrations of the existence of injunctive norms about men and women are found in research showing that stereotypic ways of behaving are perceived as generally desirable for people of each sex, at least insofar as researchers examine the evaluatively positive aspects of gender stereotypes. Other stereotype researchers have investigated people's beliefs about the ideal woman and man. These beliefs about ideal behavior tend to parallel beliefs about the typical behavior of women or men. In short, people tend to think that women and men ought to differ in many of the ways that they are perceived to differ. This oughtness transforms gender stereotypes into gender roles.

The distinction between descriptive and injunctive norms informs analyses of how gender roles influence behavior. In general, observations of deviations from descriptive norms produce surprise, whereas observations of deviations from injunctive norms produce social disapproval and efforts to induce compliance. Because descriptive norms describe what is normal or typical, they can provide guidance concerning what behaviors are likely to be effective in a situation. People thus refer to others of their own sex to find out what sorts of behaviors are usual for people of their own sex in a situation. They tend to imitate these sex-typical behaviors, especially if a situation is ambiguous or confusing and they therefore turn to others for guidance. In contrast, because injunctive norms describe what is desirable and admirable, these norms provide guidance concerning what behaviors are likely to elicit approval from others. People thus refer to what is desirable for persons of their sex when they endeavor to satisfy their motives to build and maintain social relationships. In summary, the power of gender roles to induce role-consistent behavior de-

rives from these role descriptions of what is typical of men and women and what is desirable for them.

The idea that expectations about appropriate male and female behavior are shared implies that a social consensus exists about typical and appropriate behaviors and that people are aware of this consensus. This relative consensus about perceived sex differences and the desirability of these differences has been shown repeatedly in stereotype research. Despite some individual differences in gender stereotype data, researchers have found that largely similar beliefs are held by men and women, students and older adults, and people who differ in social class and income. Moreover, social cognitive researchers such as Patricia Devine have argued that virtually everyone has acquired the stereotypic beliefs that are associated with important social categories such as sex, race, and age. In addition, people are aware that gender-stereotypic beliefs are consensual in society. This awareness has been demonstrated very directly by John Williams and Deborah Best, who asked research participants to indicate the extent to which various characteristics were generally said to be associated with each sex in their culture. These participants readily reported these stereotypes.

Gender roles form an important part of the culture and social structure of every society. In a cross-cultural project, Williams and Best examined gender stereotypes among university students in 25 nations. This research produced considerable cross-cultural commonality in beliefs about the characteristics of men and women, such that men were generally viewed as more agentic than women and women as more communal than men. Despite the generality of these themes across the nations, the research also found some evidence for cross-cultural variability. In particular, the tendency for men to be perceived as more agentic than women was less pronounced in nations that were more economically developed and in which literacy and the percentage of women attending universities were high. These findings suggest that in countries in which the division of labor between the sexes is less sex typed and the sexes have greater social and political equality, gender stereotypes and roles become less traditional.

In summary, the power of gender roles to influence behavior derives not only from their description of typical and desirable behavior, but also from their tendency to be relatively consensual and for people to be aware of this consensus. The ability of gender roles, like other social roles, to produce role-consistent behavior follows from the overall validity of the assumption that most other people hold these expectations. People thus believe that the typical other person would react approvingly to role-consistent behavior and disapprovingly to inconsistent behavior. Consequently, an individual does not have to inquire of a particular other person what he or she thinks would be appropriate male and female behavior. Instead, a person is generally correct in assuming that others endorse some version of the consensual gender roles. Therefore, to the extent that gender roles are a major influence in a situation, the most likely route to social approval and a smoothly functioning social interaction is to behave consistently with one's gender role or at least to avoid strongly deviating from this role.

III. Relation of Gender Roles to the Social Positions of Women and Men

Understanding how gender roles emerge from the typical social roles of women and men requires understanding how social perceivers use their observations of behavior to infer people's qualities. Perceivers infer that there is correspondence between the types of actions people engage in and their inner dispositions. This cognitive process constitutes a basic principle of social psychology that has been labeled correspondence bias. For example, people who behave aggressively are ordinarily assumed to have aggressive personalities. Supporting this point about correspondent inference, research has demonstrated that people fail to give much weight to the constraints of social roles in inferring role players' dispositions. Thus, perceivers who ascribe nurturance to women as a personality trait may be engaging in correspondent inference that gives little weight to role requirements by which women more frequently perform nurturant behavior in carrying out the child care aspects of the domestic role.

Reflecting this logic of correspondence bias, Curt Hoffman and Nancy Hurst argued that gender stereotypes can function as rationalizations for role distributions and that these stereotypes can develop even in the absence of any true intrinsic differences between the sexes. These researchers provided a creative experimental demonstration of this viewpoint by giving their research participants descriptions of fictitious groups of city workers and child raisers. Despite the fact that they indicated that these two

groups did not differ in their agentic and communal traits, research participants ascribed role-consistent agentic traits to city workers and communal traits to child raisers.

Underlying the principle that gender stereotypes follow from the distribution of the sexes into social roles are the insights that (1) the roles typically performed by men versus women have somewhat different requirements and demands and (2) perceivers make correspondent inferences from role behavior to the dispositions of role occupants. Perceivers' knowledge about the attributes of the sexes thus emerges from their observations of the activities of men and women in their social roles. Typical male and female activities differ because of the family division of labor and considerable sex segregation in employment, and therefore the traits ascribed to women and men differ. Gender stereotypes thus follow from observations of people in sex-typical social roles.

Research has substantiated the grounding of gender roles in a society's division of labor between the sexes. The typical male–female division of labor, which has become less extreme in postindustrial nations, assigns a disproportionate share of domestic activities to women and of other types of activities to men. Mainly women occupy the domestic role, and somewhat more men than women occupy the employee role. Although most women are employed in the paid labor force in the United States and many other industrialized nations, women are more likely than men to be employed part time or part year and tend to be employed in different occupations than men.

The link between gender roles and the specific family and employment roles of the sexes follows from the principle that social perceivers infer that men and women have attributes that equip them for their sex-typical roles. As research on gender stereotypes has shown, perceivers assume that people accommodate to their family and employment roles by acquiring role-related skills, such as women learning domestic skills and men learning skills that are useful in paid occupations, particularly male-dominated occupations. Also, women's association with the domestic role and female-dominated occupations lends the female role its pattern of interpersonally facilitative behaviors that can be termed communal. In particular, the assignment of the majority of child-rearing activities to women leads people to expect communal tendencies in women, including nurturant behaviors that facilitate care for children and other dependent individuals. The importance of close relationships to women's nurturing role favors inferences that women possess superior interpersonal skills and the ability to communicate nonverbally. In contrast, men's association with the employment role, especially male-dominated occupations, produces expectations of assertive and independent behaviors that can be termed agentic. This argument is not to deny that paid occupations show wide variation in the extent to which they favor more masculine or feminine qualities. Suggesting that expectations about the personal qualities of each sex may be shaped by their paid occupations are demonstrations that to the extent that occupations are male-dominated, success in them is perceived to follow from agentic personal qualities, whereas to the extent that occupations are female-dominated, success in them is perceived to follow from communal personal qualities.

Differences in the power and status of the typical roles of men and women lead to divergent expectations for dominant and submissive behavior. In general, men occupy roles that offer the greatest amount of power and status. Because people in more powerful roles are expected to behave in a more dominant style than people in less powerful roles, gender roles take on these prescriptions as well. Men are expected to be more dominant and women to be more subordinate. In particular, dominant behavior is controlling, assertive, and relatively directive and autocratic, and subordinate behavior is more compliant to social influence, less overtly aggressive, and more cooperative and conciliatory. Reflecting the societal tendency for women to have less power and status than men, gender roles thus encompass expectations about these dominant and subordinate aspects of behavior. [*See* POWER.]

In summary, research suggests that the stereotypic beliefs that women are especially communal and men are especially agentic have their roots in three features of social structure: (1) the division of labor between providers versus homemakers, (2) the distribution of the sexes into different paid occupations, and (3) the gender hierarchy by which men are more likely than women to occupy high-status roles.

IV. *Influence of Gender Roles on Behavior*

After correspondent inference has shaped perceivers' ideas about the dispositions of men and women and these ideas are shared to become aspects of culture, these ideas influence the self-concepts and behavior of both sexes. Because communal qualities are important for good performance of domestic activities, especially child rearing, and agentic qualities are important for

good performance of behaviors enacted in the specific roles more often occupied by men, each sex accommodates by becoming appropriately specialized by sex. More generally, each sex accommodates to its unpaid and paid specific roles. This personal participation in roles dominated by one's own sex throughout the life cycle is critical to the socialization and maintenance of sex differences. Women and men thereby learn different skills and ways of behaving and acquire different attitudes, insofar as they occupy such roles. However, social role theory goes beyond the simple statement that people who are in particular social roles generally perform in role-appropriate ways. In addition, the theory maintains that the differing histories of women and men in sex-typical social roles in a society and the embodiment of these histories in the culture in the form of consensual gender roles foster general behavioral tendencies that differ in women and men. The mechanisms that are especially important in instilling these tendencies are the behavioral confirmation of others' gender-stereotypic expectancies and the self-regulation of behavior based on gender-stereotypic self-construals.

A key assumption of a gender role analysis is that both women and men are penalized by other people for deviating from their gender roles. Behavior inconsistent with gender roles is often negatively sanctioned and tends to disrupt social interaction. The sanctions for role-inconsistent behavior may be overt (e.g., losing a job) or subtle (e.g., being ignored, disapproving looks).

Evidence abounds for negative reactions to deviations from gender roles. For example, in a review of 61 studies of evaluations of male and female leaders, Alice Eagly, Mona Makhijani, and Bruce Klonsky showed that women who adopted a male-stereotypic assertive and directive leadership style were evaluated more negatively than men who adopted this style, whereas women and men who adopted more democratic and participative styles were evaluated equivalently. Also, in small group interaction, women's competent, task-oriented contributions are more likely to be ignored and to elicit negative reactions than comparable contributions from men. Moreover, Linda Carli has shown that in task-oriented groups women tend to lose likability and influence over others when they behave in a dominant style by expressing clear-cut disagreement with another person, using direct rather than tentative speech, and behaving in an extremely competent manner. There is also some evidence than men can be penalized for behaving passively and unassertively. Such research has detailed some of the processes involved in the norm sending mechanism that helps regulate behavior in groups. Group members thus elicit conformity to gender-role norms by dispensing rewards such as liking and cooperation in return for conformity to these norms and dispensing social punishments such as rejection and neglect in return for nonconformity. [*See* LEADERSHIP.]

In general, social psychological research has established that one mechanism by which gender roles regulate social interaction derives from people's tendency to judge the value and appropriateness of others' behavior according to its conformity with gender roles. Because people often sanction behavior that is inconsistent with gender roles, these roles have a conservative impact on men and women by exacting costs from people who deviate from norms concerning male and female behavior. Weighing these negative outcomes in a cost-benefit analysis, people would not engage in nonconformity with their gender role unless it produced benefits that would outweigh these costs. Part of these perceived benefits for women, as members of a subordinate group in society, may be having some chance to gain access to rewards and opportunities formerly reserved for men.

Gender roles can produce sex differences in behavior not only by affecting the rewards and punishments received from others but also by affecting the self-concepts of women and men. Research showing that people's self-concepts tend to be gender stereotypic suggests that gender roles influence people's ideas about themselves. Consistent with social role theory's emphasis on stereotypic communal and agentic qualities is Susan Cross and Laura Madson's claim that women's construals of themselves are oriented toward interdependence in the sense that representations of others are treated as part of the self. In contrast, men's construals of themselves are oriented toward independence, separation, and dominance in the sense that representations of others are separate from the self. However, Roy Baumeister and Kristen Sommer maintained that men's seemingly independent self-construals are oriented to connections with larger social groups rather than the dyads and intimate groups favored by women and are especially directed toward competition for status and power. Research by Shirra Gabriel and Wendi Gardner has supported the principle that women focus more on the relational aspects of interdependence and men on the collective aspects of interdependence. This male emphasis on competition for power and status in larger collectives is compatible with social role theory, which argues that the male gender role follows in part from men's greater access to status and power in society. As a consequence, men's self-concepts should be marked by their striving for advantaged positions in social hierarchies. In general, because self-definitions are important in regulating behavior, sex-typed selves can underlie sex-differentiated behavior.

The internalization of gender-stereotypic qualities results in people adopting sex-typed norms as personal standards for judging their own behavior. They tend to evaluate themselves favorably to the extent that they conform to these personal standards and to evaluate themselves unfavorably to the extent that they deviate from these standards. In a demonstration of such processes, Wendy Wood, Niels Christensen, Michelle Hebl, and Hank Rothgerber investigated normative beliefs that men are powerful, dominant, and self-assertive and that women are caring, intimate with others, and emotionally expressive. They found that to the extent that these gender-role norms were personally relevant to participants, experiences that were congruent with gender norms (i.e., involving dominance for men and communion for women) yielded positive feelings about the self and brought participants' actual self-concepts closer to the standards represented by their ideal or morally desirable selves. This evidence suggests that one of the processes by which gender roles affect behavior is that they are incorporated into people's self-concepts and then operate as personal standards.

The link between gender roles and people's self-construals helps explain why there are substantial individual differences in the extent to which women and men engage in behavior consistent with the gender roles of their culture. People raised in culturally atypical environments may not internalize conventional gender-role norms and thus may have self-construals that are not typical of their gender. Consistent with research showing substantial relationships between sex-typed behaviors and self-reported masculinity and femininity, people who have self-concepts that differ from those that are typical of people of their sex are less likely to show traditionally sex-typed behavior.

V. Sex Differences and Similarities in Psychological Research

Social role theory predicts that, as general tendencies, the sex differences manifested in behavior conform to gender roles and stereotypes. As these differences are assessed by psychologists, they are behavioral tendencies that are manifested on measures of abilities, traits, and attitudes as well as enacted in laboratory settings and occasionally in field settings. To the extent that men and women actually behave stereotypically, these sex differences would act back to strengthen gender roles and stereotypes and to channel men and women into different social roles. Thus, the forward causal sequence of social role theory—from division of labor and gender hierarchy to gender roles to behavior—allows for a backward sequence as well. Moreover, to the extent that causes of sex differences not treated by social role theory (e.g., direct impact of sex hormones on behavior) have some influence, their impact would also flow backward onto gender roles and role distributions.

What have research psychologists found when they compared men and women? Increasingly, psychologists have drawn their conclusions by taking many studies into account. Faced with very large research literatures composed of multiple studies (e.g., the hundreds of studies that have compared the self-esteem or leadership style of men and women), psychologists have turned to the methods known as quantitative synthesis or meta-analysis, which provide statistically justified methods for synthesizing research. Meta-analysts typically represent the comparison between male and female behavior for each relevant study in terms of its effect size (or d), which expresses the sex difference in units of the study's standard deviation. Calculating effect sizes places each study's sex difference on a continuum that ranges from no difference to large differences. With each finding represented by an effect size, multiple studies are collectively represented by taking an average of their effect sizes. This central tendency of effect sizes is also located along this quantitative continuum and thus does not provide a simple yes or no answer to the question of whether the sexes differed in general in the available studies. Also, because findings generally differ from one study to the other, this variability illuminates the conditions under which sex differences are larger, smaller, and sometimes reversed from their typical direction.

Using these sophisticated scientific methods for integrating research findings, psychologists have shown that differences between the sexes appear in research data as distributions that overlap to a greater or lesser extent. Some sex differences are relatively large, compared with other psychological findings—for example, some cognitive performances (e.g., on tests of the ability to mentally rotate objects), some social behaviors (e.g., facial expressiveness, frequency of filled pauses in speech), some sexual behaviors (e.g., incidence of masturbation), and one class of personality traits (tender minded and nurturant tendencies). However, most aggregated sex-difference findings are in the small-to-

moderate range that appears to be more typical of research findings in psychology. Nonetheless, even small differences are not necessarily inconsequential in everyday life. When small differences cumulate over time and individuals, they can produce substantial effects.

Research comparing gender stereotypes to the meta-analyzed results of research on sex differences has shown that, for the most part, gender stereotypes match research findings on sex differences. It thus appears that people are in general competent to correctly discern the typical or average behaviors of men and women in everyday life. For example, in a study examining 77 meta-analyzed traits, abilities, and behaviors, Judith Hall and Jason Carter found a correlation of .70 between the mean of student judges' estimates of sex differences and meta-analytic effect sizes in the 77 areas. These judges displayed understanding of the relative magnitude of differences in addition to their male or female direction. However, as Hall and Carter showed, some people perceive sex differences more accurately than other people do; and, as other researchers have demonstrated, there are some systematic biases that affect the accuracy of perceptions of men and women. Nonetheless, one way of describing the sex differences established by scientific research is that they generally conform to people's ideas about men and women.

This research showing the fairly close agreement between the sex differences obtained in psychological research and perceivers' beliefs about the sexes is consistent with social role theory. However, accuracy at the level of differences between groups does not imply that predictions of individual behavior that are guided by these stereotypes are accurate. Instead, the categorization of people into groups tends to produce somewhat homogeneous perceptions of group members and thus results in some bias at the level of predicting individual behavior. [*See* METHODS FOR STUDYING GENDER.]

VI. *Multiple Roles: Gender Roles and Specific Roles*

Gender roles, viewed as shared expectations that apply to individuals on the basis of their socially identified sex, coexist with specific roles based on factors such as family relationships (e.g., mother, son) and occupation (e.g., secretary, firefighter). In workplace settings, for example, a manager occupies a role defined by occupation but is simultaneously a man or women and thus to some extent functions under the constraints of his or her gender role. Similarly, in a community organization, an individual who has the role of volunteer is simultaneously categorized as female or male and is thus perceived in terms of the expectations that are applied to people of that sex. According to social role theory, because specific social roles are typically very constraining, gender roles become relatively less important determinants of behavior in their presence.

Because specific roles have more direct implications for task performance in many natural settings, they may often be generally more important than gender roles. This conclusion was foreshadowed by experimental demonstrations that stereotypic sex differences can be eliminated by providing information that specifically counters gender-based expectations. For example, Wendy Wood and Stephen Karten manipulated competency-based status in mixed-sex groups through false feedback that described participants as low or high in competence. Controlling status in this manner eliminated the usual sex differences in interaction style by which men, compared with women, showed more active task behavior and less positive social behavior. Also suggesting an erosion of sex differences by experimental manipulation of status are Sara Snodgrass's experiments investigating the interpersonal sensitivity shown by people who interacted in higher and lower status roles that were assigned in a laboratory task. When these experiments assigned participants to teacher or learner roles or to boss or employee roles, status differences in interpersonal sensitivity were found but not the stereotypic sex differences that are typically present in research findings.

A field study by Deborah Moskowitz, Eun Jung Suh, and Julie Desaulniers used behavioral measures to examine the simultaneous influence of gender roles and organizational roles with a sample of adults who held a wide range of jobs in a variety of organizational settings. This study used an experience-sampling method by which participants monitored their interpersonal behavior for 20 days, using an event-sampling strategy. With the status of the participants' interaction partners represented in terms of the social roles of supervisor, coworker, or supervisee, the effects of participants' sex were examined. In general, agentic behavior was controlled by the relative status of the interaction partners, with participants behaving most agentically with a supervisee and least agentically with a boss. Yet communal behaviors were influenced by sex of participants, with women behaving more communally, especially in interactions with other women. Similarly, research

on physicians by Judith Hall, Debra Roter, and their collaborators has also demonstrated women's more communal behavior, even in the presence of a constraining occupational role. Female physicians, compared with male physicians, thus engaged in more partnership building with the patient, more asking of questions, more emotionally focused talk, more positive talk, and more giving of psychosocial information (e.g., concerning personal habits, impact on family).

Although research concerning the joint impact of gender roles and other roles is sparse and mainly centers on occupational roles, some tentative generalizations are suggested about the leveling of sex differences by the demands of other roles. It is thus likely that employment roles provide relatively clear-cut rules about the performance of particular tasks. For example, regardless of whether a physician is male or female, he or she must obtain information about symptoms from a patient, provide a diagnosis, and design treatment that is intended to alleviate the patient's symptoms. Within the task rules that regulate physician–patient interactions, there is still room for some variation in behavioral styles. Physicians may behave in a warm, caring manner that focuses on producing a positive relationship or in a more remote and less personally responsive style that focuses more exclusively on information exchange and problem solving. The female gender role may foster the caring, communal behavior that has been observed especially in female physicians as well as the participative style of decision making that has been observed especially in female managers. Thus, occupational roles no doubt have primary influence on how people accomplish the specific tasks required by their jobs, which would therefore be similarly accomplished by male and female role occupants. In contrast, gender roles may have their primary influence on the discretionary behaviors that are not required by the occupational role, which may sometimes be behaviors in the communal repertoire but other times be other types of behaviors. Gender roles are thus still an important factor, even through they become a secondary, background influence in settings in which specific roles are of primary importance.

VII. *Changes in Gender Roles and Sex Differences over Time*

Social role theory is a dynamic theory that accounts for change in gender roles and in the tendencies for behaviors to be differentiated by sex. The view that gender roles are rooted in the division of labor and gender hierarchy implies that these roles change if these features of social structure change. Reflecting declines in the birthrate and shifts in the occupational structure (e.g., the increasing rarity of occupations that favor male size and strength), the employment of women in the paid labor force has increased rapidly in the United States and many other nations in recent decades. Women's greatly increased education has qualified them for jobs with more status and income than the jobs that women typically held in the past. Even though the tendency for men to increase their responsibility for child care and other domestic work is modest, these changes in the division of labor, especially women's entry into paid employment, have resulted in decreasing acceptance of the traditional gender roles and a redefinition of the patterns of behavior that are most appropriate to women and men.

From the perspective of social role theory, convergent male and female secular trends should be observed most clearly in research areas that reflect masculine, but not feminine, personal dispositions. This convergence should be accounted for mainly by change in women because women's roles have changed more than men's roles. Consistent with this idea, analyses of sex differences across time periods suggest that the social behavior of women has changed to accommodate their entry into formerly male-dominated roles. For example, a meta-analytic synthesis of reports of job attribute preferences examined whether the magnitude of the sex differences varied across a period in which historical changes occurred in the employment of men and women in U.S. society. In particular, job attributes such as freedom, challenge, leadership, prestige, and power became relatively more important to women, in comparison to men, from the 1970s to the 1980s and 1990s. As the gender barriers to opportunity declined during this period, women's aspirations rose to obtain jobs with these attributes. Similarly, the career plans of male and female university students showed a marked convergence from the 1960s to the 1990s that is accounted for mainly by changes in women's career aspirations. Also, meta-analyses found decreases over time in the tendencies of men to engage in riskier behavior that women and to emerge more than women as leaders in small groups. In addition, a meta-analysis of self-report measures of masculine and feminine traits found that women's masculinity increased linearly with the studies' year of publication. Demonstrating longer-term relations between shifts in women's roles and their self-reports of assertiveness and dominance, a meta-analysis by Jean Twenge found that women increased in these tendencies from 1931 to 1945, decreased from 1946 to 1967, and increased again from 1968 to 1993, whereas men's self-reports were relatively invariant across these time periods. Such findings suggest some convergence in the psychological attributes of women and men in recent decades in traditionally masculine domains, consistent with women's increasing labor force participation and lessening concentration on child care and other domestic activities.

Not only does scientific evidence suggest some convergence of the sexes on masculine attributes, but also people believe that men and women are becoming more similar in these respects. These beliefs have been demonstrated by Amanda Diekman and Alice Eagly, who showed that people believe that women and men have converged in their personality, cognitive, and physical characteristics during the past 50 years and will continue to converge during the next 50 years. This perceived convergence mainly took the form of women increasing in the qualities typically associated with men. The studies by Diekman and Eagly also showed that perceivers function like implicit role theorists by assuming that because the roles of women and men have become more similar, their attributes converge. The demise of most sex differences with increasing gender equality, a proposition that thus fits popular beliefs about the characteristics of women and men, is a prediction of social role theory that will be more adequately tested as more societies produce conditions of equality or near equality.

SUGGESTED READING

Deaux, K., and LaFrance, M. (1998). Gender. In *The Handbook of Social Psychology* (D. T. Gilbert, S. T. Fiske, and G. Lindzey, eds.), 4th ed., Vol. 1, pp. 788–827. McGraw-Hill, Boston.

Eagly, A. H. (1987). *Sex Differences in Social Behavior: A Social-Role Interpretation.* Erlbaum, Hillsdale, NJ.

Eagly, A. H., Wood, W., and Diekman, A. (2000). Social role theory of sex differences and similarities: A current appraisal. In *The Developmental Social Psychology of Gender* (T. Eckes and H. M. Trautner, eds.), pp. 123–174. Erlbaum, Mahwah, NJ.

Johnson, B. T., and Eagly, A. H. (2000). Quantitative synthesis of social psychological research. In *Handbook of Research Methods in Social and Personality Psychology* (H. T. Reis and C. M. Judd, eds.), pp. 496–528. Cambridge University Press, New York.

Ruble, D. N., and Martin, C. L. (1998). Gender development. In *Handbook of Child Psychology* (W. Damon and N. Eisenberg, eds.), 5th ed., Vol. 3, pp. 933–1016. Wiley, New York.

Williams, J. E., and Best, D. L. (1990). *Measuring Sex Stereotypes: A Multination Study,* rev. ed. Sage, Newbury Park, CA.

Social Support

Karen S. Rook

University of California, Irvine

Glossary

Buffering effect of social support Evidence that social support is beneficial primarily for people who are experiencing life stress.

Functional aspects of social support Extent to which social network members provide various types of support, such as emotional support, appraisal support, informational support, or instrumental support.

Main effect of social support Evidence that social support is beneficial for all people, regardless of the level of life stress they are experiencing.

Perceived social support Extent to which social support is perceived to be available when needed from social network members.

Received social support Amount of social support received from social network members in a specific period of time.

Structural aspects of social support Objective characteristics of the social network members who provide support, such as the number, role relationships, or frequency of contact with these network members.

SOCIAL SUPPORT refers to the diverse forms of aid and affirmation that are provided by informal members of social networks. Social support has been found to contribute to human health and well-being in a variety of life contexts and circumstances. This article discusses the origins of scientific interest in social support, alternative conceptualizations of social support, theoretical models of the effects and processes of support, the role of gender as a central feature of the social contexts in which support transactions occur, and strategies for intervening to strengthen social support.

I. History of Scientific Interest in Social Support

The idea that close friends and family members serve vitally important roles in our lives has a very long history, as reflected in the observations of early philosophers and writers. The Roman statesman Cicero observed, for example, "Friendship makes prosperity more brilliant, and lightens adversity by dividing and sharing it." Sophocles warned in 430 B.C., "To throw away an honest friend is, as it were, to throw your life away." In the same spirit, the 17th-century Spanish writer Baltasar Gracian commented, "Friendship multiplies the good of life and divides the evil. Tis the sole remedy against misfortune, the very ventilation of the soul."

Scientific interest in the adaptive significance of informal social relationships may be traced to the 19th century, with the pioneering work of French sociologist Émile Durkheim. Durkheim observed that rates of suicide varied among different social groups, with higher rates among individuals with relatively few social ties. He inferred that less socially integrated individuals were at greater risk for suicide and other forms of behavioral disorder because they lacked the sense of meaning or purpose in life that close relationships provide and also because they lacked ties with others who could monitor their behavior and seek to discourage health-damaging behavior. In the early 20th century, this interest in the health-related effects of the social environment was reflected in research that sought to investigate whether urbanization and immigration disrupted cohesive social networks, thereby contributing to maladaptive behavior and health problems. This research generally demonstrated that the disorganization or disintegration of social ties was associated with higher rates of behavioral disorder, although the direction of causation was unclear in this early work.

Several different streams of research in the 1960s and 1970s added converging evidence of the links between close social ties and health outcomes. This work stimulated a tremendous flourishing of interest in social support that continues into the present. One important impetus to the burgeoning of interest in social support came from the field of medicine, with medical researchers such as Cassel and Cobb seeking to understand why some people fall ill when they experience significant life stress whereas others remain healthy. In influential papers published in 1976, they independently hypothesized that psychosocial resources—including access to support in the immediate social environment—provide some degree of protection from the pathogenic effects of life stress. Sparse but provocative evidence available at the time appeared to be consistent with this idea. These papers laid the foundation for several decades of research on the hypothesized health-protective effects of social support.

At roughly the same time in the 1960s to 1970s, community psychologists became keenly interested in the potential role of informal social support networks in helping to meet the needs of individuals with mental illness. This was a time when institutional care of mentally ill individuals was being abandoned in favor of community-based models of care, in which informal support networks were expected to figure prominently. Given this trend, it became important to learn more about the support networks of mentally ill individuals and how they could be strengthened or, if none existed, how they could be cultivated. Interest in the potential of informal social networks to augment traditional reliance on trained professionals for meeting the mental health needs of the nation was bolstered by evidence from the first national surveys that examined how North Americans sought to deal with personal problems, including emotional problems. These surveys indicated that North Americans overwhelmingly preferred to turn to friends and family members, rather than professionals, for help with their personal problems.

These different streams of research converged in suggesting that supportive social bonds make important contributions to physical and emotional health. They offered the hope, as well, that interventions could be designed to strengthen or cultivate supportive social ties for individuals whose existing social ties did not provide adequate social support. This early work thus gave rise both to basic and applied lines of research on social support, with the former directed at testing theoretical propositions about the health related effects of social support and the processes that account for these effects, and the latter directed at finding ways to augment or strengthen social support for people whose existing support resources are limited.

Subsequent research on social support would not have flourished to the extent it has without the emergence of early but compelling empirical evidence of the substantial impact of support on human health and well-being. Particularly striking were studies that linked social support not only to enhanced emotional and physical health but also to longevity. Two examples from this early body of work are presented here, one from the basic tradition of research and one from the applied tradition.

The influential Alameda County study, published in 1979 by Lisa Berkman and Leonard Syme, illustrated that lower levels of social integration (as measured by a summary index reflecting ties with a spouse, close friend and relatives, and participation in church and other types of groups) were associated with increased rates of mortality from all causes, especially from heart disease. This study was influential for several reasons. It was among the first to examine the health-related implications of social support (or, more specifically, social integration) prospectively, rather than concurrently or retrospectively, and in relation to a profoundly important and unambiguous outcome—mortality. The study was based on a large, representative sample of adults, and it included statistical controls for baseline health status, health risk behaviors, socioeconomic status, and other factors that could have accounted for the association between social relationships and mortality risk. Finally, the study examined several possible mechanisms by which low social integration might have contributed to the increased risk of mortality. Although the researchers were unable to pinpoint these explanatory mechanisms, they inspired others to undertake investigations of such mechanisms.

An early study from the more applied, intervention-oriented tradition of research also aroused considerable interest by illustrating the potential of support programs to enhance health. In a study conducted by David Spiegel and his colleagues, women with metastatic breast cancer were assigned either to a discussion group or to a control group. The discussion group met for approximately 90 minutes each week for one year, with discussions focused on problems the women were experiencing as a result of their breast cancer and ways of addressing some of these problems. The discussion group did not differ from the control group on indicators of psychological adjustment at 4- and 8-month followup assessments, but did exhibit significantly less psychological distress at a 12-month followup. Of particular interest was a finding from a followup study indicating that the discussion group participants had a significantly higher rate of survival in the next 10 years. Some researchers have questioned whether the discussion group, which was facilitated by a trained professional and lasted for a full year, should be viewed as a social support intervention; they argue, instead, that it represented a form of group psychotherapy. Despite this ambiguity, the study was influential in calling attention to the potential emotional- and physical-health benefits of supportive exchanges among individuals who share a common life stressor, such as a life-threatening illness.

Subsequent research has linked social support to a variety of important health outcomes, as summarized in an influential review published in 1988 by James House, Debra Umberson, and Kurt Landis. Social support has been related to emotional health; acute and chronic physical health problems; cardiovascular, immune, and neuroendocrine functioning; treatment compliance and rehabilitation outcomes; and adaptation to a variety of serious life stressors. The strength of these associations is impressive, as evidenced by the fact that interpersonal variables predict mortality and morbidity nearly as well as do more conventional risk factors, such as smoking. In

addition, neither social selection nor reverse causation appear to account fully for these effects.

Although a considerable consensus exists regarding the importance of social ties for health, less consensus exists regarding the best way to conceptualize or assess these ties. The next section discusses the various ways that researchers have conceptualized social support.

II. *Conceptualizations of Social Support*

Conceptualizations of social support vary considerably, reflecting different levels of analysis and different research objectives. No single definition of social support has won universal acceptance, but researchers tend to agree that important dimensions along which social support can be conceptualized include (1) the number and kinds of ties that exist with social network members, (2) the supportive functions performed by network members, and (3) the perceived adequacy of the support provided by network members.

A. EXISTENCE OF INFORMAL SOCIAL NETWORK TIES

Early approaches to social support tended to emphasize the first of these dimensions, the degree to which people belong to a network of informal social ties, represented by relatively objective aspects of a person's involvement in informal social networks, such as marital status, number of kin and nonkin ties, the frequency of contact with others, and the presence or absence of a confidant in the social network. Such approaches have sometimes been termed structural approaches, because they emphasize the structure of a person's ties to an informal network of family members, friends, neighbors, and others. Composite measures constructed from objective indicators of social network involvement have often yielded impressive associations with significant health outcomes in carefully controlled prospective studies, but they have been criticized as uninformative with regard to the kinds of interpersonal exchanges or underlying processes that account for the health-enhancing effects of informal social network involvement. Moreover, approaches that simply emphasize the existence of social network ties overlook the possibility that some such ties may not function as sources of social support and may even function as sources of conflict or tension. For example, some researchers who have assessed both marital status and the availability of a confidant have found that married individuals whose spouses do not function as confidants report more psychological distress than do unmarried individuals. Thus, the existence of a particular kind of social tie does not mean that it necessarily functions as a source of support.

B. SUPPORT FUNCTIONS PERFORMED BY SOCIAL NETWORK MEMBERS

An alternative approach to conceptualizing social support, often termed the functional approach, emphasizes the particular kinds of supportive behaviors performed by members of an informal social network. Because much of the scientific interest in social support grew out of the desire to understand how support might reduce the adverse effects of serious life stress, many researchers have emphasized forms of assistance from social network members that might help people respond effectively to stressful events and circumstances. A variety of different taxonomies of support functions have been proposed, but most have included emotional support (empathy, reassurance, and expressions of liking and respect), appraisal support (feedback regarding one's evaluation of, and responses to, a stressful situation), informational support (problem-solving advice and information), and instrumental support (services and other forms of tangible aid). Emotional support (especially when construed in terms of intimacy and affirmation) is believed by some researchers to be singularly important for health and well-being, both because many stressful experiences create needs for reassurance of self-worth and because intimacy appears to represent a basic human need. Some researchers, such as Thomas Wills, have offered an expanded conceptualization of support functions that includes companionship (participation in social and leisure activities). Other researchers, such as Karen Rook, have argued that it is more useful to distinguish companionship from social support and to delimit the meaning of social support to the various forms of aid and assistance provided through social network ties.

These support functions have often been assessed by asking people whether they have received various kinds of aid from others in the recent past (enacted or received support) or whether they believe that they would receive such aid if they should need it at

some future point (available support). Subscales that tap the receipt or availability of different kinds of social support are derived from such questions, allowing researchers to investigate which kinds of support are most valuable for particular kinds of life stress and at different phases of the stress-adaptation process. The support needs of someone who has lost a child may differ considerably from the support needs of someone who has lost a job. Similarly, support needs change over time, with recent widows, for example, needing different types of aid and social contact than long-term widows. These ideas about the situation-specific effects of different kinds of social support have come to be termed optimal matching theories of social support. Carolyn Cutrona and her colleagues were among the first to offer a formal matching theory of social support. Matching theories suggest that the form of support that most closely matches the needs aroused by particular stressors, at different stages in the adaptation process, will yield the greatest health benefits. Some researchers further argue that particular kinds of network members are best suited to offer particular forms of support. For example, research suggests that family members are often preferred, and best able to function, as sources of instrumental support, whereas friends are often preferred as sources of companionship and emotional support. Departures from normative or preferred patterns of support provision may dilute the impact of the support itself. This idea that particular kinds of social support are most effective when derived from particular kinds of relationships represents an extension of matching theories of social support.

Researchers have encountered some challenges, however, in their efforts to investigate hypotheses about the situation- or source-specific effects of social support. High intercorrelations have often been found among conceptually distinct forms of support, making it difficult to examine their distinctive effects. Similarly, factor analyses of items believed to represent multiple types of support have often yielded evidence of substantially fewer factors. These findings may reflect the fact that people in close relationships often exchange multiple forms of social support and, among socially integrated individuals, the multiple support functions performed by one member of their network are often replicated by other network members. This bundling of support functions within a given relationship and the duplication across relationships make it difficult to tease apart the distinctive effects of different support functions. In response to this problem, some researchers have made use of analytic methods that permit examination of a higher-order, global support factor as well as specific, intercorrelated support factors.

C. PERCEIVED ADEQUACY OF THE SUPPORT PROVIDED BY NETWORK MEMBERS

Some theorists have argued for the existence of such a general social support factor that transcends specific relationship functions, and they have suggested, further, that support is a perceptual factor—that the benefits of social support derive, in large part, from people's global evaluations of their social network members as supportive and caring. Influential proponents of this view include Brian Lakey, Irwin Sarason, and Barbara Sarason. Such perceptions are believed to emerge from experiences early in life that shape how favorably or unfavorably one's social surround is viewed. As such, they are traitlike and may exhibit only modest associations with indicators of the actual support provided by the social environment.

Evidence suggests, in fact, that measures of the perceived availability of social support tend to correlate weakly with measures of the amount of support received in a particular period. Additionally, studies suggest that perceived social support more reliably buffers the adverse effects of life stress on psychological health than does received support. Measures of perceived social support have also been found to exhibit impressive stability over time, which should not be the case if such perceptions derive from dynamic, changing transactions with social network members.

Researchers disagree, however, over the interpretation of these empirical findings, and some—such as James Coyne, Kenneth Heller, and Morton Lieberman—reject the inference that received support is less consequential for health than is perceived support. Measures of received support may correlate weakly with measures of perceived support if they are examined without regard to current levels of life stress or other conditions that create needs for support. People probably rarely seek to access the full range of support perceived to be available through their social networks in the absence of a compelling reason to do so, such as the need to cope with a disruptive life event. Moreover, even in the context of a stressful situation, people may not seek to mobilize an entire network to assist with their coping efforts; rather, they may seek help selectively from a subset of their network ties, expanding their help-seeking efforts over time only as needed. Evidence for just such a hierarchical model of support seeking has emerged in research on older adults. From this perspective, measures of perceived support and received support would be expected to correlate rather weakly in many life contexts. Similarly, greater evidence of the stress-buffering effects of received support has emerged in studies in which large samples have been disaggregated to identify subsamples of people experiencing relatively homogeneous stressors; such studies indicate that received support does buffer certain, though not all, categories of stressors. It may be most useful to regard perceived support and received support as complementary, rather than competing, constructs that describe different facets of the relationship between social support and well-being.

III. *Support Effects and Processes*

Much of the early empirical work on social support was concerned with describing and documenting the health-related effects of support and with evaluating alternative explanations for the effects of support. As this body of empirical work increased in size and sophistication, researchers gained confidence that the effects of social support on health were both real and substantial. This confidence, in turn, has allowed researchers to direct their attentions to questions regarding the underlying mechanisms or processes that account for the beneficial effects of social support.

A. MODELS OF THE HEALTH-RELATED EFFECTS OF SOCIAL SUPPORT

The effects of social support on health have most often been hypothesized as occurring in one of two forms: main (direct) effects or buffering (indirect) effects. A main effect of social support would be evident when individuals who have more support exhibit consistently greater health and well-being than do individuals who have less support, irrespective of the level of life stress they may be experiencing. Such a pattern would suggest that social support confers health-related benefits for most people, regardless of their life circumstances. A buffering effect of social support would be evident, in contrast, when people who are experiencing life stress exhibit few symptoms of illness or psychological distress if they have access to support, but exhibit more symptoms if they lack support; among people who are not experiencing life stress, levels of social support would be unrelated to well-being. Thus, social support buffers, or moderates, the effects of life stress on emotional and physical health, and this is evidenced by a statistical interaction between levels of stress and support. Excellent overviews of these and alternative theoretical models have been provided by Manuel Barrera, Nan Lin, Blair Wheaton, and Alan Vaux, among others.

A great deal of evidence has been amassed that is consistent with these two models, although the findings have varied as a function of the manner in which social support is conceptualized and assessed. In an influential review of empirical work on social support published in 1981, Sheldon Cohen and Thomas Wills concluded that main effects are found more often in studies that examine structural measures of support, whereas buffering effects are found more often in studies that examine functional measures of support. Structural measures tap the existence of important social network ties and, in the view of Cohen and Wills, reflect the extent to which a basic need to belong is satisfied. Because the need to feel a sense of belonging is presumably experienced by most people, its fulfillment would be evident in the form of main effects of structural measures of support. Functional measures, in contrast, capture the extent to which particular kinds of needed support are available and, accordingly, should be linked with health when stressful life circumstances tax a person's own coping resources and create needs for aid from others.

Most research on the effects of social support has used correlational methods to investigate the association between naturally occurring support and health-related outcomes under varying conditions of stress. In such work, researchers have often included statistical controls for factors that might be confounded with social support and health, thereby accounting for the associations observed. For example, greater socioeconomic status might contribute to both greater support and greater health, causing the observed association between support and health to be spurious rather than meaningful. Given this possibility, it is important to note that in many studies the health-related effects of social support have survived controls for a variety of demographic characteristics, personality characteristics, social skills, and other potential confounds. Carefully controlled longitudinal investigations of social support have also been conducted to shed further light on the direction of the associations between support and health-related outcomes. In many of these longitudinal stud-

ies, greater social support has been found to be associated with better health outcomes over time, controlling for initial health status.

Experimental studies of support have also been conducted, as they provide the most convincing evidence of a causal association between support and health. A typical approach in such studies involves first experimentally manipulating stress in a laboratory setting, for example, by assigning some study participants to work on insoluble problems or to prepare for a stressful task such as giving a speech. The presence or absence of support is then manipulated, for example, by having a confederate of the researcher offer to assist half of the participants with the task while other participants work alone. Subjective distress is subsequently assessed, often accompanied by assessments of physiological functioning (e.g., heart rate, blood pressure) or task performance (e.g., quality of speech presented). A common finding in these studies is that participants in the high-support condition exhibit reduced distress and enhanced functioning, relative to participants in the low-support condition.

Findings such as these, from nonexperimental and experimental studies, should not be interpreted as indicating that more social support is always associated with better health outcomes. Support researchers have long posited the existence of threshold effects, or a specific level of support beyond which further increases do little to enhance health and well-being. For example, with respect to having access to others with whom one can discuss personal worries and concerns, a single confidant may be all that is needed. That is, the greatest benefits of emotional support may be evident when one compares individuals who have no confidants with individuals who have one confidant, with diminishing benefits evident as the number of confidants increases. Similar threshold levels may characterize the effects of other forms of social support, although support researchers have not yet devoted much attention to exploration of such nonlinear patterns in their data.

Other reasons to be cautious about concluding that more support is necessarily beneficial stem from work indicating that support transactions sometimes go awry, leaving support recipients feeling worse, rather than better. People who experience life events that members of their social networks have not personally experienced appear to be particularly vulnerable to well-intentioned, but ineffective, gestures of support from others. Camille Wortman and her colleagues were among the first to document this, in studies of cancer patients, bereaved parents, and others who experienced life disruptions that were not shared by most of their network members. This led network members to make comments that were sometimes more harmful than helpful, such as suggesting to recently bereaved parents that they could "replace" the deceased child by having another child. Subsequent research revealed that network members' clumsy or awkward attempts at providing social support did not reflect a lack of understanding about what constitutes effective support, as might have been expected given their lack of firsthand experience with the stressful event; rather, their misguided comments appeared to stem from anxiety that interfered with their ability to respond effectively in their interactions with the support recipient.

Social support has been cited as having the potential to backfire in other contexts, as well, such as when a chronic illness or disabling health condition requires people to rely on spouses, family members, and others for very extensive care and support. Such long-term support provision can drain caregivers' own emotional (and sometimes material) resources, sewing the seeds for resentment, guilt, and depression. Women more often assume the responsibilities of long-term caregiving for family members and friends than do men, and although caregiving can yield rewards, it can take a toll on the emotional and physical health of those involved. This can be particularly problematic for low-income women who are often called on to provide support to others who have even fewer resources, as illustrated in the work of Deborah Belle and John Eckenrode.

Evidence of support deterioration has been documented in studies of adaptation to chronic illness, natural disasters, and other stressors that create long-term needs for support. Support can decline in quantity and quality, as support providers become depleted and tend to express resentment toward or withdraw from the individual(s) in need of support. For support recipients, the psychological costs of receiving support in such circumstance sometimes exceed the benefits. Researchers who have analyzed the dilemmas that sometimes surround transactions between support providers and recipients, especially in the context of long-term support, include James Coyne, Jeffrey Fisher, Krzysztof Kaniasty, and Renee Lyons, among others.

These examples suggest that it is important not to overstate the potential benefits of support or to ignore the contexts in which support transactions become complicated and even problematic. Despite these qualifications, evidence suggests that, on balance, social support contributes to health and well-being for many kinds of outcomes and at many points in the life course. This has led researchers to become keenly interested in the specific mechanisms, or underlying processes, that account for the beneficial effects of social support.

B. PROCESSES THAT ACCOUNT FOR THE HEALTH-RELATED EFFECTS OF SUPPORT

Analyses of the processes that underlie the effects of social support on health have emphasized explanations that involve effects of support on (1) neuroendocrine, immune, or cardiovascular functioning, (2) health behaviors, (3) coping responses and resources, and (4) affect states. Excellent reviews of empirical evidence on these underlying processes have been provided by John Cacioppo, Sheldon Cohen, Janice Kiecolt-Glaser, Harry Reis, Bert Uchino, and their colleagues.

Interaction with supportive individuals appears to soothe the neuroendocrine system and to reduce cardiovascular stress reactivity. Lack of social support during periods of acute or chronic stress has been found to be associated with worse immune functioning, as have conflictual interactions, such as arguments between spouses. These associations have been observed in laboratory and naturalistic studies, and they appear to be of sufficient magnitude to account for increased susceptibility to illness and disease over time.

Social network ties may also influence health by encouraging health-enhancing behaviors (e.g., exercise, sound nutritional practices) and discouraging health-compromising behaviors (e.g., smoking, excessive alcohol consumption). Some researchers have questioned, however, whether efforts by network members to induce change in the health behavior of significant others should be conceptualized as a form of social support, particularly since such influence attempts are often unwanted and may entail communications that are not affirming. In a recent study by Megan Lewis and Karen Rook, for example, social network members' explicit attempts to change another person's health behavior were related to greater behavioral compliance but also to psychological distress in the target person.

The support and companionship available through close relationships may promote sound health behaviors less ambiguously by contributing to life satisfaction and a sense of purpose, thereby motivating appropriate self-care. Consistent with these ideas, married individuals have been found to engage in fewer risk behaviors than do unmarried individuals. A similar pattern has been found among the unmarried who live with others, as compared with those who live alone.

Social support may also contribute to health by fostering more effective coping in the context of life stress. Social network members may help to encourage sustained coping efforts in the context of persistent stressors, may offer advice about coping responses, or may supplement coping resources by assisting with tasks that need to be completed or providing material aid.

Finally, assistance with the regulation of emotion represents another important pathway by which supportive social ties may enhance health and well-being. Contact with supportive network members reduces negative affect and appears to have a calming effect on the neuroendocrine and cardiovascular systems. Companionship provides opportunities for relaxation and restorative experiences that counter the effects of stress and that help to kindle positive affect. Positive experiences and affect states, in turn, appear to promote beneficial neuroendocrine responses. Deficient support and companionship, as reflected in social isolation or involvement in relationships characterized by conflict, have been linked to diminished immune functioning. Chronic negative affect that accompanies persistent social isolation or conflict may increase stress reactivity and subsequent vulnerability to heart disease.

In seeking to understand what accounts for the effects of social support on health, researchers have cautioned that studies are likely to be uninformative if the temporal dimensions of the support construct studied do not mesh with the temporal course of the illness or disease under investigation. Cardiovascular disease, for example, typically develops slowly over a period of many decades, making assessment of support experienced in the past week or month unlikely to shed light on the role of support in the onset or progression of this disease. An illness like influenza or the common cold, in contrast, develops in a much shorter period of time, making it more plausible that recent levels of social support could have played a role in illness susceptibility. The role of support in the onset or progression of disease, such as heart disease, may also differ from the role of support in treatment or rehabilitation, such as encouraging health-behavior change and emotional adjustment following a myocardial infarction or bypass surgery. Sheldon Cohen has provided a detailed treatment of

temporal issues such as these that must be considered in seeking to understand the links between social support and physical disease.

Some psychological disorders, similarly, follow distinctive trajectories of onset, exacerbation, remission, and possible recurrence. Researchers may miss these variations, and derive mistaken conclusions about the role of support, if they use research designs that indiscriminately mix together newly symptomatic and consistently symptomatic individuals. A given score on a measure of psychological health could potentially indicate, for different people, any of several qualitatively different states. A score of 16 or greater on the widely used Center for Epidemiological Studies Depression Scale is often viewed as suggesting the presence of clinical depression, but it is impossible to know from such a score alone whether it represents the first onset of disorder, a recurrence of disorder, or an improving or worsening trajectory in an already established disorder. Different kinds of social support may be differentially important in the onset versus maintenance of clinical disorders, but determining this requires systematic attention to the temporal dimensions of particular disorders. Scott Monroe and his colleagues have been prominent proponents of the need to take such temporal variations into account.

IV. Relationship Contexts of Social Support: The Role of Gender

The relationship contexts in which support transactions occur have important implications for the nature and effects of these transactions. Among the most important of these contextual factors is gender, and research has identified several fairly consistent gender differences in social support.

Women's social relationships have reliably been found to be characterized by greater intimacy and emotional disclosure than are those of men. Moreover, women are more likely to seek support from others when they are experiencing stress. This gender difference is especially pronounced when emotional support, rather than instrumental support, is sought. Early experimental studies indicated that women are more inclined than men to affiliate with strangers (particularly other women) under conditions of laboratory-induced stress. Given these tendencies, it is perhaps not surprising that women report more sources of support in their social networks than do men. This difference is particularly evident in studies of the social support of married individuals. Men have been found to rely on their spouses for social support to a greater extent than do women, and women report more sources of support outside of the marriage, such as friends and family members. Consistent with this, some evidence suggests that men derive greater mental- and physical-health benefits from marriage than do women. Married individuals generally enjoy better health, greater longevity, and greater life satisfaction than do unmarried individuals, but these differences are greater for men than for women. In a related vein, men appear to experience a greater risk of mortality than do women when they become widowed. [*See* MARRIAGE.]

Evidence suggests that women may be more effective than men as support providers, both in terms of the quality and quantity of support they provide. Social support provided by women appears to be more effective than does support provided by men in mitigating the adverse effects of stress. In laboratory studies, for example, support provided by women has been found to be associated with reduced cardiovascular reactivity to a stressful task, whereas a comparable benefit has not been documented for support provided by men. This pattern of effects has been observed for both male and female support recipients.

Women also tend to provide more support to others. Some research suggests that women experience greater empathy in response to others' problems, and this explains their greater willingness to respond supportively. Ironically, women's more extensive support networks and their greater tendency to experience empathy can be a potential source of strain, increasing the probability that women will learn about difficulties experienced by their network members, will react with concern, and will volunteer or be called on to provide support. Researchers such as Ronald Kessler, Elaine Wethington, and others have argued that the resulting burden of support provision that women tend to experience increases their own vulnerability to psychological distress and partly accounts for the elevated levels of depression that have been documented among women.

Explanations for women's greater involvement in networks of mutual care have most often emphasized sociocultural factors. Women are socialized to assume socioemotional roles (to do "emotion work"), and greater societal tolerance also appears to exist for support seeking among women.

A recent theoretical analysis by Shelley Taylor and her colleagues traces some of these gender differences in support seeking and affiliation to biobehavioral mechanisms. Specifically, they argue that women's greater tendencies to affiliate under conditions of threat and to engage in mutually supportive behavior have been selected through evolution because they conferred survival advantages for women. Taylor and her colleagues have challenged the widespread belief that the fight-or-flight response represents the prototypic human response to threatening situations. They have drawn on evidence from laboratory studies of animals and field observations of nonhuman primates to argue that the fight-or-flight response to threat may be prototypic for males only and that a tend-and-befriend response is more common and often more adaptive, among females. The formation of intimate ties to a social group that is organized around the provision of mutual care, often with other females, may have afforded survival advantages, particularly when the demands of caring for offspring limited the viability of a fight-or-flight response. Gender-specific neuroendocrine responses to affiliation may have played a role in reinforcing and maintaining this adaptive tend-and-befriend tendency among females. If this theoretical analysis is borne out by further empirical work, it suggests that women's greater affiliation and participation in supportive exchanges may have a biological basis, as well as a substantial sociocultural basis.

V. Social Support Interventions

An important impetus to the development of an extensive literature on social support has been the hope that insights derived from this work would provide guidelines for the design and evaluation of support interventions. In actual practice, effective translation has sometimes proven difficult because naturally occurring social support, and the benefits it affords, differ in fundamental respects from the social support that is created or strengthened through interventions. Vicki Helgeson and Sheldon Cohen described many of these differences in 1996 in a paper that sought to explain why the results of correlational, experimental, and intervention studies of social support often differ. Basic researchers have not yet addressed, moreover, many of the specific questions that arise in planning interventions, such as whether, or on what basis, to match prospective intervention participants; whether group, dyadic, or other formats are optimal for providing support; how much support should be provided or for how long; to what extent boundaries should be established between the existing support network and new sources of support that may be created through the intervention; and how support interventions can be terminated or made self-sustaining without causing harm. Despite these limitations, the literature includes many examples of support interventions that have been found to be effective, as well as some that have been found to be ineffective but that offer lessons for the planning of future interventions.

Support interventions generally have been conducted with one of two objectives in mind—introducing new sources of support or strengthening existing sources of support—as described by Benjamin Gottlieb in an extensive body of work on support interventions. Efforts to create new social network ties, or sources of support, are seen as appropriate when the existing social network is limited in scope or depleted by a host of chronic problems, when the existing network reinforces undesirable behaviors, or when the network lacks needed kinds of knowledge or expertise. Examples include the creation of support groups (for people experiencing the same stressful life experience), home visitation programs, and mentor programs.

Other interventions seek not to create new sources of support but, rather, to improve or strengthen support transactions within the existing network. This strategy is seen as appropriate when a network member plays a pivotal role in an individual's efforts to change an important health behavior (such as a spouse who can either aid or seriously undermine a partner's efforts to stop smoking), when support providers' emotional and practical resources need to be bolstered so that they can continue to provide care, and when either the stigma associated with a particular problem or cultural differences make it unlikely that individuals outside of the social network can be called on to provide support. Examples of interventions that seek to strengthen the existing network as a source of support include training social network members to become aware of their unsupportive behavior and to increase their supportive behavior, providing support programs and respite for long-term caregivers, and developing culturally sensitive support programs.

A number of important challenges exist in designing and implementing social support interventions. Two examples are considered here, to illustrate the complexity of the issues involved and the kinds of focused research that will be needed to build a knowledge base that will be useful in mounting support in-

terventions. Intervention planners often must make judgments about what constitutes the best "dosage" of support in designing their interventions, but the literature offers relatively little guidance on this point. Moreover, varied meanings of "dosage" exist—it could refer to the number of people providing support, the frequency with which support is provided, the duration of support provision over time, or the intensity with which support is provided. Intervention planning is further complicated by the fact that different dosages and different forms of social support are likely to be optimal at different points in the course of a particular intervention. In addition, planned dosages do not always correspond to delivered dosages because of variations in the rates of attendance and attrition among intervention participants. This underscores the importance of carefully monitoring individual participation in order to evaluate dose-response relationships.

A reverse version of the dosage question becomes important when time-limited interventions must be terminated: How can the support program be phased out or the interim support provider (e.g., mentor) withdrawn without doing harm? The very real possibility that terminating a support intervention might cause harm was highlighted in an early and widely cited experimental evaluation of a friendly visiting program for older adults conducted by Richard Schulz and Barbara Hanusa in 1979. Elderly residents of a retirement home who received these visits initially fared better on indicators of health and well-being than did residents who did not receive visits, but a followup assessment conducted two years later, after the program had concluded, revealed that the residents who had been visited exhibited substantially worse health than did residents who had not been visited. These declines in health were attributed to the withdrawal of the program. Thus, great care must be taken in phasing out support in interventions that create time-limited support structures. This is an especially important challenge in interventions that involve peer support groups, network enhancement, or home visitations, since evidence suggests that these interventions tend to have more beneficial effects when they are of longer duration.

VI. Conclusion

Supportive social relationships appear to represent an important source of psychological well-being and a significant contributor to physical health. Most people are strongly motivated to form close social bonds, and they care deeply about the quality of their personal relationships. In studies that have asked people what gives their lives the greatest sense of meaning, most respond with references to their personal relationships; far fewer cite work or other life domains as a centrally important source of meaning. Research on subjective well-being has confirmed that the caliber of people's personal relationships is a particularly powerful predictor of their happiness and life satisfaction. An impressive body of research has documented the role played by supportive relationships in helping to limit the toll that stressful life events can take on emotional and physical health. Studies of loneliness provide compelling evidence of the despair and self-doubts experienced by people who lack close relationships. In addition, well-controlled epidemiological studies indicate that people who lack supportive social ties experience an increased risk of morbidity and mortality, and this increased risk cannot be attributed to potentially confounded factors, such as socioeconomic status, health-risk behaviors, use of health services, or prior health status.

Recognition of the significance of close relationships in the lives of most people, and of the consequences for those who lack such relationships, provides a valuable backdrop for efforts to build a broader base of knowledge regarding the causes, mechanisms, and effects of social support. It should also help to provide motivation for the labor-intensive, but very important, task of developing a more complete understanding of how to design effective social support interventions. Ideally, greater links will be forged between the basic and applied traditions of research on social support. This will allow support interventions to be more firmly grounded in the scientific literature and will allow scientific hypotheses about support processes and effects to be tested in intervention studies.

SUGGESTED READING

Cohen, S. (1988). Psychosocial models of the role of social support in the etiology of physical disease. *Health Psychology* 7, 269–297.

Cohen, S., and Wills, T. A. (1985). Stress, social support, and the buffering hypothesis. *Psychological Bulletin* 98, 310–357.

Gottlieb, B. H. (2000). Selecting and planning support interventions. In *Social Support Measurement and Interventions: A Guide for Health and Social Scientists* (S. Cohen, L. G. Underwood, and B. H. Gottlieb, eds.), pp 195–220. Oxford University Press, New York.

Helgeson, V., and Cohen, S. (1996). Social support and adjustment to cancer: Reconciling descriptive, correlational, and intervention research. *Health Psychology* 15, 135–148.

House, J. S., Umberson, D., and Landis, K. (1988). Structures and processes of social support. *Annual Review of Sociology* 14, 293–318.

Rook, K. S., and Underwood, L. G. (2000). Social support measurement and interventions: Comments and future directions. In *Social Support Measurement and Interventions: A Guide for Health and Social Scientists* (S. Cohen, B. H. Gottlieb, and L. G. Underwood, eds.), pp. 311–334. Oxford University Press, New York.

Sarason, B. R., Sarason, I. G., and Gurung, R. A. R. (2000). Close personal relationships and health outcomes: A key to the role of social support. In *Personal Relationships: Implications for Clinical and Community Psychology*, (B. R. Sarason and S. W. Duck, eds.), pp. 15–41. Wiley, New York.

Shumaker, S. A., and Hill, D. R. (1991). Gender differences in social support and physical health. *Health Psychology* 10, 102–111.

Spiegel, D., Bloom, J. R., Kraemer, H. S., and Gottheil, E. (1989). Effects of psychosocial treatment on survival of patients with metastatic breast cancer. *Lancet* 2, 888–891.

Uchino, B. N., Cacioppo, J. T., and Kiecolt-Glaser, J. K. (1996). The relationship between social support and physiological processes: A review with emphasis on underlying mechanisms and implications for health. *Psychological Bulletin* 119, 488–531.

Vaux, A. (1988). *Social support: Theory, Research, and Intervention*. Praeger, New York.

Sport and Athletics

Diane L. Gill

University of North Carolina at Greensboro

Glossary

Gender Social and psychological characteristics and behaviors associated with females and males.

Sex differences Biologically based differences between males and females.

Title IX The education amendments to the Civil Rights Act, passed by the U.S. Congress in 1972. Title IX of Public Law 92-318 states, "No person in the United States shall, on the basis of sex, be excluded from participation in, be denied the benefits of, or be subjected to discrimination under any education program or activity receiving federal financial assistance."

THE ISSUE OF GENDER IN SPORT AND ATHLETICS is a complex one. Despite the high visibility of women athletes, women and men do not share the same sport world. Women began to enter sport and athletics in significant numbers only with the social changes of the 1970s. Because gender makes a difference in the sport world, women and men have different histories, experiences, and opportunities. Gender is pervasive and affects all sport behaviors and relations.

I. The Gendered Context of Sport

Girls and women are active participants in sport and athletics. Today, ten-year-old girls play in soccer leagues alongside 10-year-old boys, universities field intercollegiate basketball teams for women and men, and both men and women in all age categories finish triathlons. Just as clearly, gender makes a difference in sport. Gender influences our reactions to 10-year-old soccer players, female and male intercollegiate athletes face different pressures, and gender influences our options for exercise time, place, attire, and activities. Despite the pervasiveness and power of gender in sport, sport psychology research on gender is limited, and we are just beginning to understand the complexities of gender in sport and athletics. In some ways, gender in sport reflects gender in society and the larger gender scholarship. In other ways, gender in sport reflects the unique place of women in the sport world.

From the late 1800s until the 1970s, athlete meant male athlete, and those male athletes were anything but culturally diverse. Certainly some women engaged in physical activity much earlier, but females in the United States entered the modern athletic world in significant numbers only with the passage of Title

IX and the related social changes of the early 1970s. Given the short history of women's sport participation, we would not be surprised to find that the history of gender scholarship in sport is short. This lack of gender scholarship is particularly striking when even a moment's reflection, or a glance at the popular media, reveals many gender issues. The Billie Jean King–Bobby Riggs "Battle of the sexes" tennis match captured public attention in the early 1970s. Women athletes gained prominence through Olympic coverage in the 1970s, 1980s, and 1990s. The National Collegiate Athletic Association (NCAA) continues to grapple with the issue of "gender equity." As we move into millennium 2000, women world cup soccer team members and Women's National Basketball Association (WNBA) players are featured prominently in the popular media and advertisements, bringing women athletes and gender issues to the attention of the general public.

Sport psychology focuses on individual behavior, thoughts, and feelings. But we cannot fully understand the individual without considering the larger world—social context. No behavior takes place in isolation, and social context is critical for gender. Although gender clearly has a biological dimension, the biological markers and correlates are not the keys to the behaviors of interest in sport and athletics.

The theme of this article is that gender in sport is much like gender in other domains, and social context is the key. Individuals cannot be isolated from their gender. *Gender makes a difference,* and we must consider people in context to understand their behavior.

This article first reviews the historical context of today's gendered sport world by focusing on the U.S. context, which is somewhat unique in its athletic structure but which clearly carries gender connotations found around the world. The focus then shifts to gender scholarship in sport psychology, which has progressed from research on sex differences and gender roles to more current models that emphasize social processes and context.

Before considering the scholarship on gender and sport, let's see if gender does make a difference in sport. Consider how gender affects your interpretations and reactions to a soccer player who lacks control and is prone to angry outbursts on the field, and explains by stating, "I really get 'up' for the game, and sometimes I just lose it."

Does gender influence your responses? Did you identify the athlete as male or female? Do you think a coach, sport psychology consultant, trainer, or parent would behave the same with a female and male ath-

lete? If you try to be nonsexist, treat everyone the same, and assume that gender does not matter, you will have difficulty. Gender does matter. Trying to treat everyone the same does a disservice to the athletes.

Female athletic participation has exploded in recent generations, but the numbers of female and male participants are not equal. More important, female athletes are not the same as male athletes. We must look beyond numbers, biological sex, dichotomous sex differences and individual differences to the powerful, gendered, social context to understand gender and sport.

Sport is a *physical* activity. We call attention to the physical and biological. *Citius, Altius, Fortius*—the Olympic motto—translates as swifter, higher, stronger, clearly highlighting the physical. That motto—swift*er*, high*er*, strong*er*—also implies that sport is *competitive* and hierarchical (clearly not feminist). Sport seems a likely place to emphasize sex differences, and in some ways, gender in sport differs from gender in other domains. But gender is different in sport not because of the physical emphasis, but because the social-historical context is different. The average male may be higher, faster and stronger than the average female, but sport does not have to be higher, faster, stronger–sport might be *fun, flair, and friendship*.

Sport is gendered; gender is part of social context, and gender influences social processes in sport. Biological sex is related to gender, but biology does not explain gendered sport. All the meanings, social roles, expectations, standards of appropriate behavior, beauty, power, and status are constructed in the sport culture. We are not born to wear high heels or high-top sneakers.

As many articles in this encyclopedia point out, our world is shaped by gender from the time we are born. Our parents, teachers, peers, and coaches react to us as girls or boys. Gender is such a pervasive influence in society that it's impossible to pinpoint that influence. Sport is no exception, but sport does have unique characteristics.

II. The Historical Context of Gender and Sport

The history of women in sport reflects the role of women in society, but with some unique twists. In most areas, we find women pioneers facing discriminatory practices and attitudes but persisting to make a place in the world. In sport, we find a legacy of strong women leaders who developed *women's* physical education as an alternative, separate from men's physical education programs.

Women not only had a place in the early days of physical education, women had a highly visible presence. Women's colleges, which offered academic homes to pioneering women psychologists, typically promoted physical activity as part of women's education and development. Moreover, physical education for women was separated from men's physical training, and women specialists were needed to plan and conduct such programs. Women's physical education provided a women-oriented environment long before the women's movement of the 1970s began to encourage such programs.

The legacy of the early women physical educators presents both models and conflicts. No doubt the active, successful women leaders served as role models, and the professional writings of early women leaders are familiar to physical education and sport science professionals. But early women physical educators focused more on philosophical issues and professional practice than on the science of sport and exercise, and many women had difficulty maintaining a place in the field with the research emphasis in the 1960s.

One other aspect of early women's physical education that seems at odds with today's sport world is the approach to competition and athletics. Both men's and women's physical education began in the late 1800s with an emphasis on physical training as part of healthy development and education. As men's programs turned more to competitive athletics, women's physical education turned in other directions. A 1923 conference of key physical education leaders of the day is a benchmark for this anticompetition movement. The guidelines developed by this conference included putting athletes first, preventing exploitation, downplaying competition while emphasizing enjoyment and sportsmanship, promoting activity for all rather than an elite few, and women as leaders for girls and women's sports. In a 1930 clarifying statement, the Women's Division of the National Amateur Athletic Federation stated that it did believe in competition, but disapproved of highly intense, specialized competition. The evil in competition was the emphasis on winning rather than participation, and that statement concluded with the classic, "A game for every girl and every girl in a game."

The sentiments of the 1923 conference dominated women's physical education and sports programs through the social movements of the 1960s and 1970s. Today women find a vastly different athletic arena. In 1967 Kathy Switzer created a stir when she defied the rules barring women to sneak into the Boston marathon; today (after much prodding) we have an Olympic marathon for women. I grew up as an avid backyard baseball player, but was left with few options when my male teammates moved into Little League; today girls are the star players on youth sport teams. The landmark beginning for this turnaround in women's sports was the 1972 passage of Title IX of the Educational Amendments Act.

Title IX, which emerged from the civil rights and women's movements, is a broad ban on sex discrimination in all educational programs, including educational sports programs. Discrimination persists and Title IX challenges continue today, but women and girls have taken giant steps into the sport world. The number of girls in interscholastic athletics and women in intercollegiate athletic programs has increased about 6- to 10-fold from pre–Title IX days.

Women now constitute about one-third of the high school, college, and Olympic athletes in the United States. But one-third is not one-half, and in other ways women have lost a place. The world of competitive sport is hierarchical, and women are clustered at the bottom. The glass ceiling covers the sport world, and women have not become coaches, administrators, sports writers, or sports medicine personnel in significant numbers. Before Title IX nearly all (over 90%) women's athletic teams were coached by women and had a woman athletic director. Today fewer than half of the women's teams are coached by women, and few have a woman director. A review of conferences, journals, and organizations suggests that males (definitely White males) dominate research and professional practice in sport and exercise psychology as well as competitive athletics. Sport remains male-dominated with a clear hierarchical structure that is widely accepted and communicated in so many ways that we seldom notice. For example, coaches are typically seen as father figures, big-time collegiate football coaches are revered like royalty, and when a female breaks the pattern (e.g., as athletic trainer with a football team or by announcing sports) she draws attention.

III. Gender Scholarship in Sport Psychology

Gender scholarship in sport and exercise psychology largely follows gender scholarship within psychology, and that literature is well covered in other articles.

Generally, that psychology scholarship has progressed from sex differences (males and females are opposites) to an emphasis on gender role as personality (males = females, if treated alike), to more current social psychology models that emphasize social context and processes.

Today we view gender as a psychological and cultural term, and gender role expectations vary among societies as well as with ethnicity, social class, and sexual orientation. Notably, the athletic arena seems to elicit more gender stereotypes than other social settings, and sport psychologists should be particularly aware of the power of gender roles and expectations. Moreover, cultural stereotypes of masculinity and femininity are most salient at the adolescent years, and much of our sport activity involves adolescents.

A. SEX DIFFERENCES

Although current gender terminology and scholarship have moved beyond sex differences, that work dominated the scholarly literature for some time and still captures public attention. The study of sex differences has a long and colorful history, often with social-political overtones. For our purposes, we will focus on the psychology research, exemplified by Eleanor Maccoby and Carol Jacklin's 1974 review. Their main finding, which often is ignored, was that few conclusions could be drawn. They did note (and this was definitely not ignored) possible sex differences in four areas: math ability, visual-spatial ability, verbal ability, and aggressive behavior. Subsequent research, particularly meta-analyses, casts doubt even on these differences. The sex difference perspective, which continues to be prominent in media reports and some scholarship, assumed dichotomous biology-based psychological differences—male and female are opposites. In practice, dichotomous sex differences typically are translated to mean that we should treat males one way and females the other way. Today, consensus holds that psychological characteristics associated with females and males are neither dichotomous nor biology based.

Most current scholars, including Maccoby and Jacklin, advocate abandoning sex differences approaches for more multifaceted and social approaches. Most biological factors are not dichotomously divided, but normally distributed within both females and males. For example, the average male basketball center is taller than the average female center, but the average female center is taller than most men. For social psychological characteristics such as aggressiveness or confidence, even average differences are elusive, and the evidence does not support biological dichotomous sex-linked connections. With criticisms of the sex differences approach, and its failure to shed light on gender-related behavior, psychologists turned to personality and gender roles. [*See* Development of Sex and Gender; Gender Difference Research.]

B. PERSONALITY AND GENDER ROLE ORIENTATION

Psychologists and sport psychologists focused on gender role orientation and specifically on gender role constructs from Sandra Bem's 1970s work and Bem Sex Role Inventory (BSRI). According to Bem, personality is *not* a function of biology. Instead, both males and females can have stereotyped masculine or feminine traits. In contrast to earlier approaches, Bem conceived of masculinity and femininity as independent, desirable sets of characteristics rather than opposite extremes of a single dimension. When she developed the BSRI, Bem was interested in assessing androgyny, which is indicated by high scores on both masculinity and femininity. Advocates of androgyny argue that practitioners should treat everyone the same and encourage both masculine and feminine personalities. More recently, the masculine and feminine categories and measures have been widely criticized, and even Bem progressed to a more encompassing gender perspective in the 1990s. Still, most sport psychology gender research is based on her early work. [*See* Sex-Related Difference Research.]

Robert Helmreich and Janet Spence, who developed their own gender role model and measure of instrumental (masculine) and expressive (feminine) characteristics, sampled intercollegiate athletes and reported that most female athletes were either androgynous or masculine, in contrast to their nonathlete college female samples, who were most often classified as feminine. Several sport scholars conducted subsequent studies with female athletes with similar findings.

Overall, this research suggests that female athletes possess more masculine personality characteristics than do female nonathletes. This is not particularly enlightening, and both the methodology and underlying assumptions of this research have been widely criticized. Sport and physical activity, especially competitive athletics, demands instrumental, assertive (certainly competitive) behaviors. Gender role measures include "competitive" as a masculine item, and the higher masculine scores of female athletes probably reflect an overlap with competitiveness. Competitive orientation can be measured directly, and we do not need to invoke more indirect, controversial measures that do not add any information.

More important, athlete/nonathlete status is an indirect and nonspecific measure of behavior. If instrumental and expressive personality characteristics predict instrumental and expressive behaviors, we should examine those instrumental *and* expressive behaviors. Even within highly competitive sports, expressive behaviors may be advantageous. Creative, expressive actions may be the key to success for a gymnast; supportive behaviors of teammates may be critical on a soccer team; and sensitivity to others may help an Olympic coach communicate with each athlete. Today, most psychologists recognize the limits of earlier sex differences and gender role approaches, and look beyond the male-female and masculine-feminine dichotomies to social development and social cognitive models for explanations.

In a series of studies on competitive sport orientation, Gill and colleagues developed a measure of multidimensional competitive achievement and used that measure with several samples of athletes. Competitiveness is the overall achievement orientation, or the desire to compete and to strive for success in competitive sport. Gill and colleagues identified two additional dimesions: win orientation, which is the tendency to focus on competitive outcomes, and goal orientation, which is the tendency to focus on performance and mastery. Across several samples, Gill and colleagues found that males typically score higher than females do on competitiveness and win orientation, whereas females typically score slightly higher than males do on goal orientation, and males also reported more competitive sport activity and experience. However, females were just as high as males, and sometimes higher, on goal orientation and general achievement. Also, females were just as likely as males to participate in noncompetitive sport and nonsport achievement activities.

Later, working with varied athlete samples, Gill and colleagues found differences among athlete groups on competitive orientations, especially in win/goal orientation. Moreover, the variation was not simply a gender difference, but related to sport demands. With a sample of international and university athletes and nonathletes from Taiwan, Gill and colleagues found strong differences between athletes and nonathletes, but minimal gender differences. With one unique sample of ultramarathoners

(those who run 100-mile races) competing in a selective event, Gill and colleagues found low win orientations, but very high goal orientations, and no gender differences.

Generally, males are more competitive than females, but overlap and similarity is the rule. Moreover, differences between athletes and nonathletes, and within athlete samples, typically are stronger than gender differences.

Overall, gender differences in competitiveness are limited, and do not seem to reflect either general achievement orientation or interest in sport and exercise activities per se. Instead, competitiveness seems to reflect opportunity and experience in competitive sport, and gender is related to an emphasis on social comparison and winning within sport. That is, boys are given opportunities and encouraged to participate in sport more than girls, even today. Moreover, boys' activities are more likely to involve competition and social comparison, and we tend to see boys sports as training grounds for the highly competitive, win-oriented professional sport leagues.

Other researchers report similar gender influences on reactions to competitive sport. For example, in 1986 Joan Duda reported both gender and cultural influences on competitiveness with Anglo and Navajo children in the southwestern United States. Male Anglo children were the most win-oriented and placed the most emphasis on athletic ability. Although several lines of research suggest gender influences on competitive sport achievement, the research does not point to any unique gender-related personality construct as an explanation. Instead, most investigators are turning to socialization, societal influences, and social cognitive models for explanations.

Jacquelynne Eccles' model incorporates such socio-cultural factors, and Eccles recognizes that both expectations and value determine achievement choices and behaviors (see Eccles' chapter for more information). Eccles provides evidence showing that her model holds for sport as well as academic achievement, that gender influences children's sport achievement perceptions and behaviors at a very young age, and that these gender differences seem to be the product of gender role socialization.

C. PHYSICAL ACTIVITY AND SELF-PERCEPTIONS

Before moving away from personality let's consider self-perceptions, particularly body image and self-esteem. As research, popular media, and our observations suggest, females often lack confidence in their sport and exercise capabilities. Eccles has conducted considerable research on the development of expectations, competence and self-esteem, and she noted that gender differences in self-perceptions are usually much larger than one would expect given objective measures of actual performance and competence. Eccles is one of the few developmental psychologists to include sport competence in her work, and she consistently finds larger gender differences in perceptions of sport competence than in other domains. Moreover, even in sport, the gender differences in perceptions are much larger than the gender differences in actual sport-related skills.

With the gender differences in perceived sport competence, sport has a tremendous potential to enhance women's sense of competence and control. Sport offers the opportunity to develop physical strength and confidence, to strive for excellence, to accomplish a goal through effort and training, and to test oneself in competition. Diana Nyad, the marathon swimmer, expressed it this way:

When asked why, I say that marathon swimming is the most difficult physical, intellectual, and emotional battleground I have encountered, and each time I win, each time I reach the other shore, I feel worthy of any other challenge life has to offer.

Many women who begin activity programs report enhanced self-esteem and a sense of physical competence that often carries over into other aspects of their lives, and a few studies add some support to these testimonials.

In one provocative 1996 report, Sumru Erkut and her colleagues described their study of experiences (including sport experiences) that influence diverse urban girls. Girls from across the United States representing five ethnic backgrounds (Native American, African American, Anglo-European American, Asian Pacific Islander, Latino) were asked what activities make you "feel good about yourself?" Athletics was the most common response, mentioned by nearly half of the girls. When asked what about the activity made them feel good, the most common response was related to mastery or competence (e.g., I'm good at it), followed by enjoyment.

Self-perceptions related to body image are particularly connected to gender and of concern within sport and exercise settings. Our images of the ideal body, and particularly the ideal female body, have changed through history and across social contexts. Certainly today's ideal is a slender, lean female body. Just as clearly, most women recognize and strive for that ideal, which is not ideal for physical and mental health. Boys and men also have concerns about body image, but the literature indicates that girls and women are much more negative about their bodies. Moreover, body concerns are gender-related. Girls are particularly concerned with physical beauty and maintaining the ideal thin shape, whereas boys are more concerned with size, strength, and power. Society shapes body image, and this societal pressure for a body image that is not particularly healthy nor attainable for many women likely has a negative influence on self-esteem and psychological well-being, as well as on physical health and well-being.

Concerns about body image affect all women, and athletes are just as susceptible as other women to societal pressures toward unrealistic, unhealthy thinness and eating disorders. Such pressures are of particular concern in the "thin body" sports, such as gymnastics, dance, and running. Pressuring an athlete, who already has tremendous societal pressure to lose weight, is ill advised. Most enlightened coaches and instructors follow nutritional guidelines and emphasize healthy eating and exercise behaviors rather than weight standards. [*See* BODY IMAGE CONCERNS; SELF-ESTEEM.]

D. SOCIAL PERSPECTIVES

In the 1980s gender research moved away from the sex differences and personality approaches to a more social approach, emphasizing gender beliefs and stereotypes. How people *think* males and females differ is more important than how they actually differ. Although actual differences between females and males on characteristics such as independence or competitiveness are small and inconsistent, we maintain our stereotypes. These gender stereotypes are pervasive. We exaggerate minimal differences into larger perceived differences through social processes. These perceptions exert a strong influence that may elicit further gender differences. This cycle reflects the feminist position that gender is socially constructed.

Gender stereotypes and gender bias in evaluations certainly exist within sport. Eleanor Metheny identified gender stereotypes in her classic 1965 analysis of the social acceptability of various sports. Metheny concluded that it is *not appropriate* for women to engage in contests in which any one of the following applies:

- The resistance of the opponent is overcome by bodily contact.

- The resistance of a heavy object is overcome by direct application of bodily force.
- The body is projected into or through space over long distances or for extended periods of time.

According to Metheny, acceptable sports for women (e.g., gymnastics, swimming, tennis) emphasize aesthetic qualities and often are individual activities in contrast to direct competition and team sports. Although Metheny offered her analysis more than 30 years ago, our gender stereotypes have not faded away with the implementation of Title IX. Gender stereotypes persist, and they seem more persistent in sport than in other social contexts.

One prominent source of differential treatment for sport is the media. Investigations of television, newspaper, and popular magazine coverage of female and male athletes reveals clear gender bias. First, female athletes receive little coverage (less than 10%), whether considering TV air time, newspaper space, feature articles, or photographs. Moreover, females and males receive *different* coverage that reflects gender hierarchy. Generally, athletic ability and accomplishments are emphasized for men, but femininity and physical attractiveness are emphasized for female athletes. In one graphic example, the 1987–1988 Northwest Louisiana State women's basketball media guide cover showed the team members in Playboy bunny ears and tails captioned, "These girls can Play, boy!" Gender bias in the sport media usually occurs in more subtle ways.

Many colleges have sexist nicknames or symbols (e.g., adding "elle," "ette," or "Lady") that gender mark the women athletes as different from and less than the men athletes. Gender marking may be appropriate when it's symmetrical or similar for women and men, as it is for most pro tennis coverage, but asymmetrical marking labels females as "other." For example, consider that we have the WNBA, but we don't have the MNBA; what are the gender messages and implications? Gendered language also appears in sport media coverage. Comments about strength and weakness typically are ambivalent for women, but clearly about strength for men, and emotional reasons for failure (e.g., nerves, lack of confidence) are cited more often for women. Michael Messner and his colleagues noted that "dominants" in society typically are referred to by last names and subordinates by first names. They found first names used over 50% of the time to refer to females but only 10% of the time to refer to males. Also, the few male athletes referred to by first names were black male basketball players. No race differences were observed for females, and gender seemed to be the more powerful feature.

Observations of recent Olympic and NCAA tournaments suggests improvement with less stereotyping and trivialization of female athletes, but institutional change is slow and, overall, gendered beliefs seem alive and well in the sport world. Overt discrimination is unlikely, and participants may not recognize the influence of gendered beliefs in themselves or others. For example, many sport administrators and participants fail to recognize gender beliefs operating when athletic programs developed by and for men, stressing male-linked values and characteristics, are opened to girls and women. We continue to use the same equipment, facilities, rules, and "accessories" (e.g., cheerleaders, mascots, decorations) without considering alternatives.

The social aspect of gender is more than perceptions and stereotypes; it's the whole context. In her 1981 book, *The Female World,* Jesse Bernard proposed that the social worlds for females and males are different, even when they appear similar. In earlier times we created actual separate worlds for females and males with segregated physical education and sport programs. Although we now have coed activities, the separate worlds have not disappeared. The social world differs for female and male university basketball players, for male and female joggers, and for the girl and boy in a youth soccer game. The men and women basketball players do not receive the same resources, media coverage, or public acclaim; women cannot jog as safely and confidently as men can; and spectators do not look at the girl and boy on opposing soccer teams in the same way.

Stereotypes are of concern because we act on them; we exaggerate minimal gender differences and restrict opportunities for both females and males. Gender beliefs keep many women out of sport, and gender beliefs restrict the behaviors of both men and women in sport. Both girls and boys can participate in youth gymnastics or baseball, and at early ages physical capabilities are similar. Yet children see female gymnasts and male baseball players as role models, peers gravitate to sex-segregated activities, and most parents, teachers, and coaches support gender-stereotyped activities of children.

To illustrate the role of social context, consider confidence. Considerable earlier research suggested females display lower confidence than males across varied settings. In 1977, Ellen Lenney concluded that the social situation was the primary source of gender differences. Specifically, gender differences emerged with masculine-stereotyped tasks, in competitive settings, when clear, unambiguous feedback was missing. Several sport psychology studies confirmed Lenney's propositions, but these were experimental studies in controlled lab settings that purposely strip away social context. We cannot ignore social context in the real world. Sport tasks are typically seen as masculine, competition is the norm, and males and females develop their confidence along with their physical skills through radically different experiences and opportunities. [*See* GENDER STEREOTYPES; MEDIA INFLUENCES; SOCIAL ROLE THEORY OF SEX DIFFERENCES AND SIMILARITIES.]

IV. Gender Relations: Promising Directions

Feminist and social-cultural perspectives call for consideration of gender within the wider context of social diversity. Sport is not only male, but White, young, middle-class, heterosexual male. And gender affects men as well as women in sport. Sport psychology has progressed from the limited sex differences and gender role approaches, but it has not incorporated diversity or adopted relational analyses that might lead to the development of a useful gender scholarship. Ann Hall, one of the most insightful and inspiring feminist sport scholars, noted that sport psychologists rely on categorical analyses, focus on differences, and fail to analyze the powerful ways in which gender and race relations are socially and historically constructed.

A. GENDER AND SEXUALITY

Although sport is stereotypically masculine, scholars recognize that gender relations affect men. Michael Messner described sport as a powerful force that socializes boys and men into a restricted masculine identity. Messner cited the major forces in sport as follows:

- Competitive hierarchical structure with conditional self-worth that enforces the "must win" style.
- Homophobia.

Messner stated that pervasive homophobia (the irrational fear or intolerance of homosexuality) in sport

leads all boys and men (gay or straight) to conform to a narrow definition of masculinity. Real men compete and, above all, avoid anything feminine that might lead one to be branded a sissy. One successful elite athlete interviewed by Messner noted that he was interested in dance as a child, but instead threw himself into athletics as a football and track jock. He reflected that he probably would have been a dancer but wanted the macho image of the athlete. Messner ties this masculine identity to sport violence because using violence to achieve a goal is acceptable and encouraged within this identity. Notably, female athletes are less comfortable with aggression in sport. Messner further noted that homophobia in athletics is closely linked with misogyny (disparaging anything female); sport bonds men together as superior to women.

Messner's linking of homophobia and misogyny reflects Helen Lenskyj's analysis citing compulsory heterosexuality (the only acceptable sexual identity is heterosexual and all must conform) as the root of sexist sport practices and Sandra Bem's contention that sexism, heterosexism, and homophobia are all related consequences of the same gender lenses in society. We expect to see men dominate women, and we are uncomfortable with bigger, stronger women who take active, dominant roles expected of athletes.

Homophobia in sport has been discussed most often as a problem for lesbians, with good reason. Not surprisingly, those involved with women's athletics often go out of the way to avoid any appearance of lesbianism. Pat Griffin, who has written and conducted workshops on homophobia in sport and physical education, has described this state as "tip-toeing around a lavender elephant in the locker room and pretending that it's just not there." As Griffin noted, lesbians are not the problem; homophobia is the problem. Homophobia manifests itself in women's sports as

- Silence
- Denial
- Apology
- Promotion of a heterosexy (conventional heterosexual attractivenesss) image
- Attacks on lesbians
- Preference for male coaches

We stereotypically assume that sport attracts lesbians (of course not gay men), but there is no inherent relationship between sexual orientation and sport (no gay gene will turn you into a softball player or figure skater). No doubt, homophobia has kept more heterosexual women than lesbians out of sports, and homophobia restricts the behavior of all women in sport. Moreover, as Messner's analysis suggests, homophobia probably restricts men in sport even more than it restricts women.

B. SEXUAL HARASSMENT

Sexual harassment is an issue with clear gender connotations, an issue that's prevalent and likely to emerge in practice and an issue that's been neglected in sport. Recent research, particularly the work of Mary Koss, has demonstrated the prevalence of sexual harassment and assault. Although sport psychology research is lacking, the issues have been raised. For example, women cannot run any time, any place. Helen Lenskyj discussed sexual harassment in sport in a 1992 article, drawing ties to power relations and ideology of male sports. Lenskyj noted that sexual harassment raises some unique concerns for female athletes, in addition to the concerns of all women: sport (as a nonfeminine activity) may elicit derisive comments, clothes are revealing, male coaches are often fit and conventionally attractive, female athletes may have spent much time training and less in general social activity, coaches are authoritarian and rule much of athletes' lives, and for some sports merit is equated with heterosexual attractiveness. [*See* SEXUAL HARASSMENT.]

Overwhelmingly sexual harassment is males harassing females, even in less gender-structured settings than sport. As Lenskyj noted, and earlier discussion of homophobia suggest, lesbians and gay men are more likely to be the targets than perpetrators of sexual harassment. Still, allegations of lesbianism may deter female athletes (regardless of sexual orientation) from rejecting male advances or complaining about harassment. Often female coaches are so worried about charges of lesbianism that they refrain from complaining about harassment or seeking equity for their programs. Sexual harassment (heterosexual or homophobic harassment) intimidates women and maintains traditional power structures.

Sexual harassment and assault have recently been brought to public attention as a concern for male athletes, as well as female athletes. Some accounts suggest that male athletes are particularly prone to sexual assault, and more theoretical work of Lenskyj and Messner suggests that male bonding, the privileged status of athletes, and the macho image of sport are contributing factors.

So the literature does not support dichotomous sex differences; males and females are not opposites. But women and men are not the same and we cannot ignore gender. Gender is part of a complex, dynamic, ever-changing social context, and a particularly salient, powerful part within sport and exercise settings. Consideration of gender relations and recognition of diversity is critical to effective sport practice.

V. *Feminist Sport Practice*

Translating gender scholarship into sport practice is a challenge, but the expanding literature on feminist practice provides some guidance. To translate gender scholarship into feminist practice we must first avoid sexist assumptions, standards, and practices. Then we might follow the lead of psychologists who have moved beyond nonsexist practices to more actively feminist approaches. Feminist practice, as described by Judith Worell and Pam Remer, incorporates gender scholarship, emphasizes neglected women's experiences (e.g., sexual harassment), and takes a more nonhierarchical, empowering, process-oriented approach that shifts emphasis from personal change to social change.

An aggressive soccer player could be male or female, but a male soccer player is more likely to grow up in a world that reinforces aggressive behavior, and a male athlete is more likely to continue to have such behaviors reinforced. The less aggressive, more tentative approach is more typical of female athletes. Even talented, competitive female athletes are socialized to keep quiet, be good, and let others take the lead. Moreover, most female athletes have a male coach, trainer, athletic director, and professors, and deal with males in most other power positions.

Overly aggressive, uncontrolled behavior is not exclusively male, nor tentative styles exclusively female. Still, we will work more effectively with both female and male athletes if we recognize gender influences in the athlete's background and situation. Anger control or confidence building has a different context and likely requires different strategies for females and males. Behavior is not just within the athlete, but within a particular sport context and within a larger social context. Both the immediate situation and larger context are gender related. Moreover, gender relations are mixed with race, class, and other power relations of the athlete's context and background.

Recent discussion on ways to optimize the educational experiences of girls and women, along with the scholarship on feminist practice, can enhance professional practice in the sport world. Recently calls for feminist practice have been broadened to include all areas of research, education, and practice in psychology. In the preface to the collective outcome of a 1993 National Conference, Judith Worell and Norine Johnson noted that feminist practice is widely defined to include activities related to all areas of psychology: research, teaching, clinical practice and supervision, scholarly writing, leadership, and any other activities in which psychologists participate. The articles in this volume provide guidelines for sport psychologists who wish to be more inclusive, empowering, and effective in their research and practice. Some common themes of feminist practice that are particularly relevant for sport include promoting social change, embracing diversity, promoting empowerment, and promoting collaboration.

The common themes of feminist psychologists reflect many of the calls for relational analyses and attention to power relations by the feminist sport studies scholars. But the psychologists also retain concern for the individual. Although the combined focus on the individual and social relations may seem paradoxical, that combination is the essence of a useful sport psychology. Our goal is to understand behavior and help individuals optimize sport experiences, and then move from the sport setting to enhanced life experiences in the real world. Social context and relations are far more powerful in the real world than in the lab or any research setting.

Gender makes a difference; and human diversity characterizes all of us in all we do. Gender relations are dynamic and vary with the individual, situation, and time. We are just beginning to consider gender relations in our research and practice. We can continue to move on to the greater challenge of shaping a sport world that incorporates gender relations and values diversity in all forms of practice to enhance sport for all.

SUGGESTED READING

Eccles, J. S., and Harold, R. D. (1991). Gender differences in sport involvement: Applying the Eccles expectancy-value model. *Journal of Applied Sport Psychology* 3, 7–35.

Gill, D. L. (1995). Gender issues: A social-educational perspective. In *Sport Psychology Interventions* (S. M. Murphy ed.), pp. 205–234. Human Kinetics, Champaign, IL.

Hall, M. A. (1996). *Feminism and Sporting Bodies*. Human Kinetics, Champaign, IL.

Lenskyj, H. (1991). Combating homophobia in sport and physical education. *Sociology of Sport Journal* 8, 61–69.

Melpomene Institute (1990). *The Bodywise Woman*. Human Kinetics, Champaign, IL.

Messner, M. A. (1992). *Power at Play: Sports and the Problem of Masculinity*. Beacon Press, Boston.

Messner, M. A., Duncan, M. C., and Jensen, K. (1993). Separating the men from the girls: The gendered language of televised sports. In *Sport in Contemporary Society: An Anthology* 4th ed. (D. S. Eitzen ed.), pp. 219–233. St. Martin's Press, New York.

Nelson, M. B. (1991). *Are We Winning Yet: How Women Are Changing Sports and Sports Are Changing Women*. Random House, New York.

Worell, J., and Johnson, N. G. (eds). (1997). *Shaping the Future of Feminist Psychology*. American Psychological Association, Washington, D.C.

Stress and Coping

Sandra A. Graham-Bermann

Julie A. Eastin

Eric A. Bermann

University of Michigan

Glossary

Coping Actions taken to deal with or to manage stress, including appraisal of the stressful situation or consideration of strategies based on one's available resources. Coping also can be explained at the family or group level where different responses are made to external threats with the goal of promoting a good fit between the family or group and the environment.

Coping in context Occurs when the environmental or situational demands of the stressful circumstance influence the particular coping strategy that is used by an individual. The person is thought to possess a repertoire of coping responses that can be applied appropriately to meet the circumstances of a particular demand or threat.

Posttraumatic stress disorder Persistent symptoms following exposure to a traumatic event or situation. Dysfunction in four areas including unwanted remembering or flashbacks, avoidance of circumstances resembling the traumatic event, an inability to recall important aspects of the event, and symptoms showing increased sensitivity and arousal (such as difficulty falling asleep, hypervigilance, or exaggerated startle response).

Psychopathology The study of human behavior that is atypical, abnormal, maladaptive, disorganized, or detrimental. Such behaviors range from mild and transient disturbances to severe and permanent conditions. Objectionable deviant behavior is a social and cultural construct, such that the behaviors identified and used to define psychopathology can vary from culture to culture.

Resilience Variously defined as the ability to adapt despite exposure to stressful and high-risk environments, the ability to function adequately or to recover from trauma and have a capacity for self-repair, or the capacity to survive adversity.

Stress Variously defined as (1) often overwhelming common burdens, such as everyday hassles or role strain and overload, (2) incidents of major adversity and expectable life events, including confusing changes, and (3) adverse and catastrophic events, such as experiencing a threat to life, exposure to trauma, or severe violence.

STRESS AND COPING have been studied by psychologists and sociologists who seek to determine whether certain episodes or circumstances are stressful, for whom they are stressful, how they cause distress, and what contributes to or delimits the outcome of stress exposure. This article reviews three different conceptualizations of the construct of stress and how they are typically measured. How one copes with or manages stress positively or negatively affects the outcome of an individual's exposure to stress, ranging from adjustment to psychopathology. This article describes coping behaviors and styles in terms of whether coping is an individual, dispositional trait, or whether coping influences the develpment of personality, as well as whether coping is specific to given situations. Studies that focus on the intersection of coping with stress and gender fall into two categories: those that show gender differences and those that model how gender is used in the process of moderating stress. Examples of both approaches are illustrated here. Finally, this article raises a number of methodological issues and concerns arising from the review of current studies. The various topics and research studies described here were selected to illustrate some of the current issues in the field of stress and coping study.

I. *Defining Stress*

Stress was originally studied, as early as 1945, in terms of combat stress and its role in the development of individual psychopathology. Here, not only the threat to life, but the lack of sleep, physical exhaustion, hunger, separation from loved ones, injuries, and witnessing devastating events were all considered to be stressful. The dominant reaction among soldiers was one of heightened anxiety and acute fear. Some soldiers reacted by becoming withdrawn and depressed. When the exposure to violence and stress was extreme, transient symptoms or temporary reactions ranged from emotional shock, to psychosomatic disorders, to dissociation and psychosis. At that time, negative outcomes were presumed to be a result of some flaw in the individual rather than caused by the exposure to traumatic stress. Yet the stress response clearly varied among individuals and depended, only in part, on the nature of the individual's early family experience. Indeed, stress was studied primarily in terms of catastrophe and was related to outcomes of individual psychopathology.

A. WHAT CONSTITUTES A STRESSFUL EVENT?

Today, stress is much more broadly defined. Definitions range from stress as an everyday life strain, stress caused by life change or adverse events, as well as stress caused by catastrophic events, such as threats to life experienced during war. Life strains are the hassles involved in daily living. These include, for example, taking the bus to work, living in a city, exposure to loud noises, a friend betraying you, as well as working and raising children. It is the accumulation of life strains, or the aggregation of a number of such challenging and difficult events that is considered to be stressful to the individual.

A second type of stress concerns the kinds of events that, taken individually, are thought to be upsetting or disagreeable by most people. Examples of typical adverse events are the death of a close family member, divorce, personal illness, and incidents of overt racism, unemployment, and retirement. These are unique events, any one of which can be distressing and difficult to manage. However, some life events are stressful and cause tension even though most people would agree that they are positive in nature. This kind of euphoric stress is labeled eustress, as opposed to the distress just cited. The birth of a child, getting married, receiving a promotion, and buying a new house, are examples of positive yet stressful events.

A third kind of stress is that resulting from catastrophic or traumatic events. These are unexpected, random, dangerous, or threatening occurrences, such as being involved in a plane crash, witnessing a serious accident, or being the victim of devastating acts of nature. Worldwide, the most common kinds of disasters are floods, accidents, and storms. In addition, there are traumas that emanate from war and violence. Violence is defined as planned, purposeful acts of aggression that seek to cause harm, injury, or threats to life (e.g., being assaulted, raped, or kidnapped). Traumatic events such as these can be experienced as threatening or disastrous and therefore stressful, whether one is eyewitness to, or the direct victim of, the dire happening. When the catastrophic event occurs to someone loved or needed by the observer, the level of distress increases.

B. WHAT MAKES AN EVENT STRESSFUL?

Life strains or changes can be either expected or unexpected. Those changes that are characterized as expected may refer to moving to a new house, becoming an adolescent, or having an aged parent die. Unexpected changes are generally considered to be more disruptive and thus more stressful because one has no opportunity to buffer them through preparation. These may include suddenly losing a job, unanticipated pregnancy, or divorce. Further, some stressors are transient and occur only once, while other stressors are chronic and persist. While it is difficult to compare stressful events, those that appear to be beyond one's control and those that occur though natural causes (such as a flood) are sometimes thought to be less disturbing than events that involve human decisions. Negative events that are caused by human actions (e.g., war), those that are externally imposed (being fired by the boss), or those that result from human error (breaking a leg when climbing a mountain) are experienced as more difficult to adjust to than are random, but equally stressful events. Clearly, stress that is severe, chronic, and persistent is more detrimental than stress that comes with advanced warning and over which one has some degree of control.

Yet there is little agreement as to what constitutes a stressful event, as what is considered to be stressful by one person may be experienced as acceptable or even joyful by another. On the surface, it seems that most people would agree that dire and threatening events are, by definition, inherently stressful. For example, most people would agree that witnessing someone die or being seriously ill are clearly stressful events. There is more disagreement when trying to define everyday life strains and life changes as stressful events. To give a common example, riding on the bus can be a welcome relief for one person and a daily hassle for another. Thus, not all stressful events are perceived as distressing by everyone, and the characteristics of the event itself can contribute to the extent of the resulting distress. Researchers have found it difficult to capture all of these various, but important, elements when measuring exposure to stress.

C. CAN STRESS BE MEASURED THE SAME WAY FOR EVERYONE?

Until recently, stressful events were all measured in a similar way. That is, early research efforts aimed at assessing perceived stress relied on lists of stressful events named by the psychological or sociological researcher. Research participants were asked to indicate whether each stressful event either did or did not happen to them during a specified time (e.g., during the previous year). There were studies of recently occurring life events (e.g., within the previous month, six months, or a year) and lifetime tallies of stressful events (events that occurred at any time during the participant's lifetime). These lists of stressful life events included marriage, birth of a child,

death of a parent, illness, and divorce, among many others. Often, there was no way of measuring the extent to which an event was stressful to the participant, as it was the researcher who assigned weights, or points, to designate which event on the list was more stressful than another event. The respondent's job simply was to endorse whether an event had occurred. However, these approaches not only presumed given events had the same valence for all respondents, but they left out the context of the individual and the culture in which the events and the interpreter were embedded.

Further, most of the early studies relied primarily on middle-class, Caucasian participants. The experiences and evaluations of people in minority groups largely went unreported. Some researchers have argued that in order to understand the salience or valence of a particular event to a particular person, much more information is needed—namely, the meaning of the event to the individual and the context in which the event occurred. We now know that a broader representation of the culture and context in which any given event occurs is required before a meaningful (proper) evaluation of the stressful nature of an event can be made. Understanding differences between and within cultural groups begins with the recognition that culture constitutes an important part of the context for interpreting events. Thus, the more information gathered by empathic interviewers, who can learn about the culture and the life story of the participant, the more likely it is that the individual's response to events can be adequately represented and understood. Only then can we be said to truly give value to an event perceived as stressful to a particular person. Clearly, it is the meaning of events, as defined by the individual within the context of her or his culture, that ultimately determines whether and how much stress is attached to certain events.

II. Coping with Stress

Reactions taken in response to extreme environmental threat originally were thought to take the form of either fighting back or fleeing the situation. This is called the fight or flight response. Studies have shown that, under conditions of duress, when the alarm is sounded, the brain is flooded with stress hormones that take over the rational thought processes. This is thought to occur so that the person can quickly mobilize a response in order to avoid danger or extinction. In general, the more traumatic the prior history, the more quickly the stress response system becomes activated. So for some individuals, this fighting back or fleeing represents the first coping response to stressful events. Yet the many ways an individual can adapt to stress are contingent on a number of factors, including the history of trauma exposure, the nature of the threat, as well as characteristics of both the individual and the environment.

A. IS COPING A PROCESS OR A TRAIT?

Coping is traditionally defined as thought or action undertaken by an individual to manage a stressful situation or event. The thought and action that affect the well-being of the individual can be either positively or negatively toned. In their early studies of coping behavior, Suzanne Folkman and Richard Lazarus identified three essential features of coping: behavioral coping, emotion-based coping, and avoidance coping. Behavioral coping was defined as those activities undertaken following or in response to stress in order to reduce, to manage, or to eliminate the stress. Examples of behavioral coping are challenging the stressor, getting help, seeking information, and working directly to stop and to eliminate the stress. Emotion-based coping includes expressing feelings in response to the stress, such as crying, showing fear, becoming focused on the emotional reaction to the event, or numbing one's affect or expressed emotion. Avoidance coping involves moving away from the stressor, deciding to postpone managing the stressor, biding one's time, or denying aspects of the stress in order to reduce its potency or threat.

One of the ongoing debates in the field of stress and coping studies is whether coping responses are predetermined and fixed parts of personality or whether coping behaviors mold or change a person's behavioral repertoire. The first view of coping stems from some personality theorists who claim that coping is always determined by the basic character structure of the individual, regardless of the situational context of the stressor. Here, the personality is predetermined by a number of immutable elements such as temperament or genetics. In this position, coping behaviors are predetermined and constrained by the individual's personality profile. For example, the coping response to stress will be constrained by whether the person is characteristically an optimist or a pessimist. An optimist may try to solve a certain problem whereas a pessimist may characteristically avoid or deny the same problem. Thus, the range of possible coping options is considered to be narrow and delimited by personality.

Other personality theorists suggest that a person's repeated use of certain coping behaviors and coping mechanisms help to form the substrate of the personality of the individual over time. In this way, coping and personality are thought to be interactive or transactional, where repeated behaviors become part of the individual's repertoire or style, which, in turn, acts to constrain coping options in future situations. Thus, a person who was fearful and withdrew from challenges as a child may develop into an adult who actively avoids all or most anxiety-provoking or threatening situations. Personality psychologists assess such coping dispositions with standardized tests that provide profiles of coping styles. Unfortunately, a number of studies have shown that dispositional coping styles are not always good predictors of an individual's actual coping behavior.

B. WHAT IS COPING IN CONTEXT?

The personality or dispositional view of coping presented here contrasts with the view that all coping is situational and specific. For some theorists, coping is considered to be a process, rather than a personality trait, as it may vary across situations or contexts for any individual. In this conceptualization, individuals possess a variety of coping strategies to call upon depending on the situation, the stressor, and the person's history or experience in coping. For example, a woman may respond to the threat of an assault by a stranger by running away. The same woman may respond to the threat of an assault by a family member with confrontation or retaliation. Then again, the same woman may elect to bide her time, to gather information, or to consult with experts when presented with the threat of a possible severe illness. In short, the individual possesses a repertoire of responses from among which he or she can choose depending on the circumstances or the context of the threat.

Here, coping is thought to be specific to the environmental circumstances of the stress. When assessing coping responses, the social context or environment must always be taken into account and measured. Thus, studies of situational coping ask individuals what they would do in hypothetical situations or what they actually did in response to a particular event. A number of researchers have noted that our knowledge base of coping studies is incomplete. Studies of coping in the contexts of race, gender, and social class are, as yet, pretty much missing in the available literature. For example, in order to study African American women's coping, it is important to study the context of race. Considerations of the historical or chronological context of social forces such as racism and slavery may be necessary to interpreting coping in the present day.

Similarly, the coping style used by low-income women is constrained by what the environment allows, as well as, or in combination with, what the woman finds desirable and possible. It is not reasonable to evaluate someone negatively for the compromises that result in lack of opportunity or institutional biases. Thus, studies of the coping style of a low-income woman should surely include an evaluation of the institutional and economic forces against which she struggles while attempting to resolve a particular stressful situation.

Finally, coping contexts that reflect differences in power should also be taken into account. Power differentials include age differences, hierarchical position or role differences, family role differences, and relationship inequities that can delimit the coping options of an individual. For example, a battered woman may refuse the help of the police after a domestic assault against her in an effort to keep her child safe. This strategy may appear dubious until it is understood that women in her state are subject to arrest if their children are exposed to domestic violence. It can be understood in another way if she is African American and does not want to bring the police and court system into her family for this reason. Thus, her actions can be interpreted as ineffective and harmful to the child without understanding the context—that is, the power of the police to rein over her child. [*See* POWER.]

This recitation of studies of coping and stress has primarily focused on the individual as the unit of analysis. However, there are excellent examples of people working together to influence a negative event or to diminish the negative effects of a stressor or perceived threat. Examples of group, collective, or grassroots community coping include Martin Luther King's urging peaceful protest response to racism, Ghandi's calls for passive resistance to the threat of domination by the British colonials, and neighborhoods organizing to take back their streets and neighborhoods from violent gangs and drug dealers. This collective approach is particularly effective for those in disenfranchised positions where the views or actions of any one person are not likely to be influential without the actions of the larger group. Here the community takes precedence over the individual as a venue for change.

Thus, for studies of group or collective coping, the units of analysis are the meaning of the stressor to the group or culture at large, the range of coping options and resources available to the group, and the actions and outcomes associated with the overall community effort. It is not necessarily more difficult to measure change related to group activity, but it requires different sorts of measures and constructs. Change in stress or adaptation resulting from a group's coping behaviors is also usually documented over a longer time frame.

C. IS COPING WITH TRAUMA DIFFERENT?

Another area of coping research reflects coping as a response to very severe threat. Trauma theorists have studied coping responses to dangerous and threatening events. The traumatizing events are characterized as being overwhelming, sudden, and out of the range of normal and expected experience. People exposed to disastrous and catastrophic events may develop problems in adjustment, including symptoms of posttraumatic stress. The core symptoms of posttraumatic stress include being in a state of hypervigiliance or physiological arousal; having unwanted, intrusive memories of the traumatic event; and emotional numbing or dissociation from the intense feelings associated with having witnessed a traumatic event. Fear and anxiety are hypothesized to occur when the individual is newly unable to accurately and effectively appraise and respond to such events, leaving the person feeling unprotected and highly vulnerable and endangered. Psychiatrists have determined that a combination of these trauma symptoms qualifies the individual for a diagnosis of posttraumatic stress disorder. [*See* POSTTRAUMATIC STRESS DISORDER.]

Trauma exposure can be a one-time event, such as witnessing a shooting, or it can be chronic in the life of the individual, such as repeated acts of victimization or child abuse. Short- and long-term effects of traumatic exposure have been identified. For example, in work with battered women and their children, trauma effects can be seen in virtually all of the abused women but also in most of their children as well. Here, symptoms vary depending on the length of trauma exposure and the type of violence. Many children who witness the abuse of their mothers have intrusive thoughts, repetitive reenactment play aimed at mastery, and avoidance of people and places that remind them of events. Such child witnesses to their parents' victimization can become emotionally withdrawn.

Chronic and severe trauma contributes to some of the most profound changes and negative effects on development. Some of these consequences are just beginning to be identified. Long-term outcomes may include the loss of sense of self, viewing the world as unsafe, and having a restricted range of emotional expression. Physiologically, some long-term effects include cognitive deficits and changes in neurochemistry that are thought to permanently alter and affect the development of normal brain pathways during childhood. [*See* Trauma across Diverse Settings.]

D. WHAT IS RESILIENT COPING?

For more than 20 years, researchers have studied resilience, primarily in children thought to be at risk for developing problems in adjustment. By studying children raised in poverty, those in divorced families, those whose mothers were homeless, and children who were abused or living in foster care, researchers hoped to identify a range of their responses to these stressful situations. Early definitions of resilience focused on children who showed no problems at all following exposure to stress. These children were thought to be impervious to negative outcomes or resistant to stress. However, today we know that children exhibit a range of responses to trauma and adversity, from those who have significant trouble adjusting to stress, to those who appear to be unaffected by negative events.

Further, it is difficult to characterize a person as resilient, even though he or she may appear to be coping well following stress, given that negative outcomes might develop later in life. For example, a child who seems to cope well during or immediately following divorce may have problems in relationships with others as a teenager. Similarly, a woman who has been raped may not appear to experience nightmares or anxiety related the assault until years after the event. These so-called sleeper effects make it difficult to define resilience over time. Even so, the definition of resilience should include the ability to adequately develop over time following exposure to stressful events.

Currently, researchers are attempting to define their expectations of what are competent outcomes and their definitions of the quality of adaptation and positive development following stress. Several studies have tried to capture the additive effects of multiple trauma exposures in assessing resilience. There are studies of both risk factors, or those features of the individual or the environment that put the person at greater risk for negative outcomes, and studies of protective factors, or those elements that serve to reduce negative outcomes following stress expo-

sure. Specific risk factors that are thought to impede successful adaptation to stress include poverty, young age, lack of education, being depressed or anxious, living in high-crime areas, and, in some cases, gender. Examples of typical protective factors are positive parenting, superior intellectual functioning, having a friend or source of positive social support, and adequate neighborhood and community resources. Nonetheless, until more longitudinal studies have been completed, caution is required because it remains difficult to relate specific negative outcomes to specific risk factors, or specific areas of adjustment to particular protective features of the environment. Thus, resilient coping can stem from a multilayered combination of the balance of risks and protective factors for the person exposed to stress.

III. *Gender and Coping with Stress*

Studies that focus on gender and coping with stress generally can be divided into two main areas. First are those studies that distinguish between the kinds of stress more often experienced by men or by women. In the second area, theoretical models are proposed and tested to explain the ways in which gender influences either the stress itself or the coping context. Thus, recent studies have described gender more broadly and in transaction with the environment. These studies include the assessment of a wider range of gender roles, gender expectations, and gender stereotypes in their operationalization of the gender construct.

A. DOES COPING WITH STRESS DIFFER BY GENDER?

Gender is often cited as one among many factors that put a person at risk for exposure to negative life experiences. Here, gender is often reduced to indicate a unitary trait, describing a person's biological sex. In that vein, a number of studies of sex differences in stress exposure and coping have been undertaken. Research has shown gender differences in stress as related to daily hassles, sexist discrimination, age-specific stress, and stress in relationship with others, such as caregiving and intimate partner relationships. Researchers also have identified gender differences in health-related stress, such as alcoholism and physical and mental health.

Historically, men have often been studied in terms of their work roles and intellectual contributions, whereas women have been studied in terms of family relationships and domestic roles. While there are notable differences in the kinds of events that are considered to be stressful for men and for women, the range of potential stressful venues has been restricted in the extent to which stress is studied in these gender-stereotyped ways. Nonetheless, we find that women are disproportionately represented in some categories of stress exposure. Further, many of the gender and coping studies make prescriptive generalizations, in that one sex is evaluated as "doing better" and "being more successful" in coping than the other.

1. Coping and Gender Differences

In 1980, Folkman and Lazarus compared the coping strategies of men and women and found that men used more problem-focused coping than did women in their response to stress. The authors attributed this finding to differences in disposition, wherein men were thought to persevere in thinking about the problem and women were thought to give up or to more quickly decide that nothing can be done. These explanations were purely speculative, as no measures designed to identify motives were used in the study. Nonetheless, these attributions of gender difference suggested that men's coping was effective and indicative of high functioning whereas women's coping was belittled as deficient and inadequate. It was suggested that women's coping was not only less effective than men's coping but that how women chose to cope resulted in exacerbated, rather than lessened, stress.

A number of risks associated with problematic coping with stress are found to differ by gender. For example, men are at increased risk of heart disease and substance abuse. Women are more likely to become depressed when stressed, whereas men are likely to have greater alcohol involvement following stress. Still, it is difficult to determine whether the higher rates of men's or women's physical and mental illness can be attributed to maladaptive coping or whether the presence of such illnesses put them at greater risk of experiencing stress, or both.

2. Differences in Stress Exposure

Gender differences in daily stressors have largely been accounted for by men's and women's greater exposure to certain daily activities and responsibilities. For example, studies of married heterosexual couples have shown that wives have more daily stressors and may be more emotionally reactive to those stressors than are husbands. Further, in a number of studies women reported experiencing more days of moderate to high-level stress than men. In other studies there is an intersection of age, gender, and daily stressors. For example, adolescent girls reported experiencing more stressful events during the previous year, as well as overall, than did adolescent boys.

A sizeable body of evidence shows that women rate their family roles to be more stressful than do men. Over the decades, even though the numbers are shifting somewhat, women consistently have been found to have primary responsibility for housework, for child care, and for maintaining the social and emotional health of the family. Whether they also work outside of the home or not, women are disproportionately burdened with child care and home responsibilities. In studies of time equity, while men perceive that their contributions to household tasks are about equal to that of women, in fact, they are likely to inflate their contributions. It is no surprise that women find their family roles to be more stressful than do men. While conditions seem to be changing over the past few decades, such that in more recent studies men are found to spend more of their time at home engaged in housework and caring for their children than was the case in the past, the disparities between men and women's domestic contributions remain considerable.

As women's rates of participation in the workforce outside the home approaches that of men, women report more work-related stress. However, the kinds of stress men and women experience at work is, in a number of ways, quite different. Work is still characterized by a number of stressful gender disparities for women, such as lower pay for the same work, glass ceiling restrictions on promotion in certain jobs, and the loss of equity and position due to family responsibilities and childbirth. Generally, working women with partners have been found to be disproportionately responsible for, and therefore stressed by, the demands of caring for sick children and having to make arrangements for school vacations, children's days off, and family vacations.

Conversely, men report being burdened and therefore stressed by social roles that demand they make most of the money for the family. Along with the perks of more money, better promotion, and higher-status jobs, men's work-role stress is related to longer working hours and spending less time with children. Both men and women have decried the lack of time they can spend with children due to work demands. Better psychological well-being for women has been associated with the salience or centrality of the roles of parent care provider, mother, wife, and employee. Role stress has been associated with decreased life satisfaction and depressive symptoms for women whose central roles were as wife and employee, whereas women whose central role was as mother were buffered from the negative effects of role stress. [*See* Social Role Theory of Sex Differences and Similarities.]

3. Gender Discrimination

A number of studies have shown that women who experienced frequent sexism have significantly more symptoms of depression, anxiety, and bodily complaints than men in similar circumstances or than women who did not experience sexism. Similarly, sexist discrimination has now been linked to well-known gender differences in psychiatric symptoms for women. Conversely, in more recent times, men's groups have made complaints of gender discrimination in judges' granting of custody following divorce. These men argue that gender stereotypes render them much less likely to be granted custody of their children.

The impact of stress associated with sexual harassment in the workplace also has been examined. Younger and middle-aged women report the highest frequencies of sexual harassment experiences. Gender harassment and unwanted sexual attention by peers has been associated with higher levels of perceived stress. Gender harassment of professional women by men in higher positions also has been related to increased stress, negative mood, and decreased satisfaction with workplace supervision, among other outcomes. [*See* Anxiety; Depression; Sexual Harassment.]

B. WHAT THEORETICAL MODELS EXPLAIN COPING BEHAVIOR?

Recent studies have described gender more broadly and in transaction with the environment. These studies include the assessment of a wider range of gender roles, gender expectations, and gender stereotypes in their operationalization of the gender construct. In other words, it is no longer assumed that just being a male or a female determines exposure to stress, or the extent to which a stressor affects coping; rather, it is how the individual perceives and experiences the stressor and his or her options

that count. A number of such gender-based models of stress and coping have been identified in the research literature. These theoretical models seek to explain the ways in which gender interacts with stress to influence coping choices. Some researchers have argued that it is the way men and women make sense of the stress, how they think about the stress, and how they give meaning to the event(s) that influences the coping response. In this light, gender is considered to be a moderator of stress that serves to either enhance or amplify the negative effects of stress on the individual.

1. Gender, Stress, and Social Support

Social support has been identified as a powerful protective factor that can reduce negative outcomes in the aftermath of exposure to stress. The issue of whether social support reduces or enhances stress for men and for women is currently being debated. In some studies, women perceived social support from their children as most positive, while men viewed their wives as providing the most positive support. This result is unsurprising in that one of the most consistent findings in gender research is that men invest most heavily in their wives as support providers whereas women most often turn to women friends and family for support.

Many studies have shown that women's but not men's physical problems following stress were significantly reduced by the presence of social support, broadly defined. Here gender served to moderate the effects of stress on physical health. More specifically, gender differences were found in whether social support reduced the effects of stress on a person's physical symptoms and illnesses.

Interestingly, this same relationship with friends is not always a source of stress reduction for women. There is growing evidence that despite the higher value placed on social reciprocity by women, more intimate support networks may actually increase vulnerability to the adverse effects of such stress rather than buffering the negative effects of life stress. It may be that the need for support within a woman's social network (including the demands of both friends and family) can become too emotionally or physically draining and lead to even greater levels of stress. [*See* Friendship Styles; Social Support.]

The relationship between gender and the ability of single parents to manage work outside the home and family responsibilities also has been examined. Here, both men and women often report equivalent perceptions of success at managing family and work responsibilities. However, gender differences can be found in the use of supportive, financial, and organizational resources and how each parent adapts to the demands of completing occupational and caregiving roles.

2. Gender and the Perception of Stress

Gender differences have been identified in how men and women exposed to the same everyday stressful events perceive or evaluate those events. One researcher studied this question and found that women had a greater propensity to think about or to ruminate over stressful events than did men. Men either did not perceive the same events as stressful or did not spend as much time thinking about the stressful nature of the event. These findings support the gender-role perspectives theory of stress, where men and women have different expectations for their roles that, in turn, prescribe how they should evaluate and manage stress. But the research also showed that men tended to rely on alcohol to cope with negative situations while women tended to ruminate. These coping responses were, in part, dictated by social norms that allowed men to drink in response to stress (whereas such activity would be frowned upon for women) and for women to ruminate (whereas men who ruminate may be met with negative social sanctions from other men). Thus, the understanding of expected gender roles appears to be a powerful schema or internal model that motivates men's and women's coping options. Furthermore, men who reported experiencing masculine gender-role stress were at risk for experiencing alcohol-related problems in other studies. [See SUBSTANCE ABUSE.]

Several researchers have found that men who believed in traditional male role attitudes were at risk for experiencing alcohol-related problems. Women who believed more in the traditional, dominant role of men also suffered from more alcohol-related difficulties. Thus, all of those who had a higher level of stereotypes, regardless of gender, also scored higher on alcohol abuse measures.

The stressful nature of male gender-role stereotypes has been measured in a number of studies that rely on samples of college-age men and inpatient populations. Here, male stereotypes included such factors as feeling physically inadequate, being unable to express emotions adequately, being dominated or outperformed by women, and feeling intellectually inferior and a failure in either work performance or sexual performance. Further, men's strong adherence to rigid sex-role stereotypes has been associated with factors beyond substance abuse, such as anger, anxiety, and interpersonal violence.

3. Gender and the Perception of Coping

Another way of conceptualizing gender differences in response to stress is to consider the panoply of coping resources specifically available to men and to women. A number of studies have been undertaken in response to the early findings of sex difference that characterize women's coping as emotion based and men's coping as problem focused. Here, women's apparent lack of action in response to stress has been reframed as taking a more patient and thoughtful response. For example, when asked about their coping responses, women report that they use reflection, forbearance, negotiation, and social support to help them cope. In studies of battered women, some women report electing to bide their time or to wait to respond until they have acquired enough resources to move out. Women's coping resources vary a great deal and include education, income, family size, and responsibility for children. These categories have not been taken into account in most coping inventories used to assess and evaluate coping styles (such as those noted earlier).

Another model, called the tend-and-befriend response, seems to fit the description of being a female version of the fight-or-flight response that has been the predominant model in stress response patterns. The model proposes that females first engage in nurturing and protective behaviors then seek alliances with others when faced with stressful situations. The model's creators suggest that this was an evolutionarily adaptive strategy since females are the primary caretakers of the young. The following evidence for the biological basis for this model was offered: researchers have found that females with higher levels of oxytocin in their systems (a hormone seen more often at higher levels in females than males) are likely to act in nurturing and social ways. This finding appears to support the evidence that women seek out others when stressed, whereas men usually prefer to be alone.

4. Gender and the Cultural Context of Stress

The cultural context in which the stress take place may be one feature that differentiates the experiences of men and women, and thus, delimits their coping options and responses. A good illustration is found in a survey with extensive observational data of police officers. This study examined the strategies police officers used to cope with stress caused by difficulties in the workplace. Results indicated that the characteristics of gender, number of years in law enforcement, and rank were significantly related to their perceived stress level. Interestingly, the odds of belonging to a high-stress group nearly doubled when the officer was female. The authors suggest that this phenomenon is a product of the special problems and pressures for women within police organizations.

Coping strategies also differed by gender and by ethnicity. Women reported that they coped with stress by keeping written records or escaping (through alcohol or drug use) more often than did men. African-Americans relied on bonds with other minority group members, whereas Caucasian officers coped by relying on camaraderie with coworkers, expressing their feelings, and trying to make social connections with others.

The role of spirituality has been identified as central to minority women's coping in other studies. Traditionally, the church has played a central role in the life of African American families. Thus, by asking minority women to describe their typical coping strategies, a greater array of ways of coping has been identified than is found in most coping inventories. Researchers have shown that some minority women take a more pensive approach to problems, in that they elect to ponder their options before taking action, to pray, or to find ways to bide their time by patiently waiting for alternatives to develop. Again, these behaviors can be interpreted in both the present racial context of stress experiences and in the traditional ways of coping found in African American families.

IV. Methodological Issues

The method used to assess stress and coping both directs and constrains the kinds of responses that are given and hence influences conclusions that can be drawn about men's and women's coping. Issues such as who frames the questions, who decides on the outcomes that are to be evaluated, and who disseminates the knowledge are currently being debated among those who study stress and coping. Thus, it is important to consider the kinds of research methods that are available and the values and limitations inherent in each approach.

Hypothesis-testing research is that which takes a top-down approach to addressing the research question—that is, the study begins with questions or hypotheses framed and posed by the researcher. Here, it is the researcher who finds a way to measure and to test ideas of importance in the study. The research participant is asked to answer specific questions about coping. He or she is not asked to interpret the situation that is posed or to generate a range of potential responses to the stressful situation proposed. This approach relies primarily on the self-report of the respondent. It is particularly useful in gathering data quickly from a large number of respondents. However, some feminists maintain that this approach disempowers research participants, and is especially deleterious to women. Still, many researchers opt for a combination of methods to best capture the range of issues and perspectives involved.

The goal of the grounded theory approach is to develop ideas by using research that begins in concert with the individual and develops in dialogue between the researcher and the respondent. The crucial questions emerge from this transactional conversation where each party learns of the perspective and language of the other. Together they forge a better understanding of the issue than either one could bring to the project alone. Thus, the grounded theory evolves from the individual's perspective as understood by the researcher and that is reflected in framing the questions and interpreting the results. This approach assures that the research participant can name the issues of importance and that the research includes the meaning of events to the individual. Clearly, the meaning of the stressful event and the meaning of the individual's coping behavior are taken into account with this ecological approach.

Using this approach, coping behavior is defined as the end result of a process of perceiving, understanding, and making a decision about a stressful situation or circumstance. For example, a woman who elects to stay with an abusive husband may be waiting until she has acquired enough money to rent an apartment or go back to school. This strategy may be based on a past experience of leaving an abusive relationship only to have to return in need of financial support. By now the woman has weighed the circumstances and decided that her best long-range strategy is to bide her time while gathering documents, locating housing, joining a battered women's support group, and reading about her options. Without an extensive conversation about her history, the meaning of the threat, and her plans for the future, it would be easy to mischaracterize her coping as passive or avoidant. Further, this approach allows the presentation of a much more complex description of coping processes that includes a number of strategies that are employed over time, rather than relying on a single style or behavior that is then evaluated as either effective or not. Clearly, a full understanding of the situation in the context of the stressor is essential to evaluating the coping response.

V. Summary

As this review of the history of stress and coping research makes clear, the construct of stress has evolved from one viewed as primarily biological to one that encompasses mild, transient, chronic, and severe or traumatizing events. Further, the categories of stress have grown from a list of items preselected by researchers and thought to be stressful for many people to those that are unique to specific circumstances and groups of people. Similarly, ideas about the ways in which people cope with stress have evolved beyond descriptions of coping as a purely individual disposition to coping that occurs in response to and in transaction with the demands of the setting or context. As the field of stress and coping studies matures, it can be expected that researchers will continue to develop methods, to refine the definitions of central constructs, and to further delineate the kinds of event-specific coping methods that promote optimal mental and physical health.

SUGGESTED READING

American Psychiatric Association. (1994). *Diagnostic and Statistical Manual of Mental Disorders,* 4th ed. Author, Washington, DC.

Azar, B. (2000). A new stress paradigm for women. *Monitor on Psychology* **31**.

Banyard, V. L., and Graham-Bermann, S. A. (1993). Can women cope? A gender analysis of coping with stress. *Psychology of Women Quarterly* **17**, 303–318.

Graham-Bermann, S. A., and Edleson, J. L. (Eds.) (2001). *Domestic Violence in the Lives of Children: The Future of Research, Intervention, and Social Policy.* American Psychological Association Books, Washington, DC.

Herman, J. (1992). *Trauma and Recovery.* Basic Books, New York.

Janoff-Bulman, R. (1992). *Shattered Assumption: Towards a New Psychology of Trauma.* The Free Press, New York.

Lazarus, R. S., and Folkman, S. (1984). *Stress, Appraisal, and Coping.* Springer, New York.

Nolen-Hoeksema, S. (1991). Responses to depression and their effects on the duration of depressive episodes. *Journal of Abnormal Psychology* **100**, 569–582.

Substance Abuse

M. Marlyne Kilbey
Diane Burgermeister
Wayne State University

Glossary

Comorbidity The co-occurrence of one mental disorder with another. The time frame is generally lifetime unless otherwise specified.

Diagnostic classification of substance use Substance-related disorders are classified as mental disorders in the *Diagnostic and Statistical Manual of Mental Disorders,* published by The American Psychiatric Association and commonly referred to as the *DSM.* The classification applies to licit and illicit drugs provided the criteria outlined below are met (*DSM-IV-TR,* 2000).

Substance-related disorders Disorders classified in the *DSM-IV-TR* and related to the taking of a drug of abuse (including alcohol), to the side effects of a medication, or to toxin exposure. Substances are grouped into eleven classes: (1) alcohol, (2) amphetamine or similarly acting sympathomimetics, (3) caffeine, (4) cannabis, (5) cocaine, (6) hallucinogens, (7) inhalants, (8) nicotine, (9) opioids, (10) phencyclidine (PCP) or similarly acting arylcyclohexylamines, and (11) sedatives, hypnotics, or anxiolytics. Polysubstance (multiple substance) dependence and unknown substance-related disorders (usually related to medications or toxins) are included also.

Substance-related disorders are divided into substance use disorders (substance dependence and substance abuse) and substance-induced disorders (substance intoxication, substance withdrawal, etc.)

Substance use disorder, substance abuse A maladaptive pattern of substance use leading to clinically significant impairment or distress, manifested by one or more of the following during a 12-month period: (1) recurrent substance use resulting in failure to fulfill major role obligations at school, work, or home; (2) recurrent substance use in situations in which it is physically hazardous (e.g., driving or operating machinery); (3) recurrent substance-related legal problems; or (4) continued substance use despite having persistent or recurrent social or interpersonal problems caused or exacerbated by the effects of the substance (e.g., arguments with spouse about consequences of intoxication or physical fights).

Substance use disorder, substance dependence A maladaptive pattern of substance use, leading to clinically significant impairment or distress, as manifested by three or more of the following occurring at any time in the same 12-month period: (1) tolerance defined as either a need for markedly increased amounts of the substance to achieve intoxication or desired effect, or markedly diminished effect with the continued use of the same amount of the substance; (2) withdrawal, as manifested by the characteristic withdrawal syndrome for the substance or by the practice of taking the same substance to relieve or avoid withdrawal symptoms; (3) the substance is often taken in larger amounts or over a longer period than was intended; (4) there is persistent desire or unsuccessful efforts to cut down or control substance use; (5) a great deal of time is spent in activities necessary to obtain the substance (e.g., visiting multiple doctors or driving long distances), use the substance (e.g., chain smoking), or recover from its effects; (6) important social, occupational, or recreational activities are given up or reduced because of substance use; and (7) the substance use is continued despite knowledge of having a persistent or recurrent physical or psychological problem that is likely to have been caused or exacerbated by the substance (e.g., current cocaine use despite recognition of cocaine-induced depression or continued drinking despite recognition that an ulcer was made worse by alcohol consumption).

Substance withdrawal A maladaptive behavioral change, with physiological and cognitive concomitants, that occurs when blood or tissue concentrations of a substance decline in an individual who had maintained prolonged heavy use of the substance. After developing unpleasant withdrawal symptoms, the person is likely to take the substance to relieve or avoid those symptoms, typically using the substance throughout the day beginning soon after awakening. Withdrawal symptoms vary according to the substance used, with most symptoms being the opposite of those observed in intoxication with the same substance. The criteria for substance withdrawal consist of the following: (1) the development of a substance-specific syndrome due to the cessation of (or reduction in) substance use that has been heavy and prolonged; (2) the substance-specific syndrome causes clinically significant distress or impairment in social, occupational, or other important areas of functioning; or (3) the symptoms are not due to a general medical condition or better accounted for by another mental disorder.

HUMANS HAVE USED DRUGS for their psychoactive effects since the beginning of recorded history. Most drug use is experimental or controlled by socialization processes and without adverse health or social consequences. Problematic drug use is considered to result from biopsychosocial processes and, when certain conditions are met, is considered a mental disorder. This article concentrates on the known risk factors for substance use disorders, paying special attention to the impact of gender in this context.

I. Overview of Biological, Psychological, and Social Processes

The use of substances to alter one's sensation, perception, or mood—that is, for their psychoactive effects—is at least as old as recorded history. The current scientific perspective is to view drug use as resulting from a biopsychosocial process. Availability, however, is a prerequisite as only those drugs to which one has access can be used. Biological factors, such as the genetically controlled enzyme systems that metabolize drugs and those processes that determine the efficiency of neuronal responses to drugs, shape drug use. Psychological factors, such as attitudes toward, expectations of, and beliefs about drug use, sensation seeking, ability to postpone reward, and other psychological characteristics, also shape drug use, as do social factors such as peer, family, cultural, economic, and legal practices. Biological, psychological, and social processes are thought to play a role at all stages of drug use (initiation, repeated use, and dependence) as well as in cessation of use or abstinence from use. The relative contribution of each of the three processes is thought to vary at different times in the natural history of drug use. Social processes may be paramount in determining initial use, while biological and psychological processes may dominate in the development of dependence. For example, drinking alcohol with celebratory meals is a socially sanctioned behavior in many, but not all, cultures. In these cultures individuals initiate drinking as a function of normal socialization processes that also function to limit the extent of use. On the other hand, the intravenous administration of heroin is not sanctioned by any culture and is acquired by a small minority of persons who may share common biological and psychological risk factors regardless of acculturation. This article reviews work that has looked at gender as a variable in drug use, abuse, or dependence. We will pay special attention to the known risk factors for substance use disorders, which while affecting just a minority of those who ever use a drug nevertheless result in the most chronic and serious problems associated with drug use. These studies mainly address biological and psychological risk factors for drug abuse or dependence.

II. *Substance-Seeking Behavior*

Most, if not all, drugs of abuse activate the brain's dopamine neurotransmitter circuitry in structures that form the brain's "reward" system. The reward system evolved to guarantee survival of the species by making sure that behaviors necessary for its continuation (e.g., eating, drinking, and procreation) are pleasurable and thus likely to be repeated. Drugs activate these neural circuits, initiate pleasurable feelings, and increase the likelihood that the drug will be readministered. Repeated drug use is also determined by psychological factors (sensation seeking, personality, academic performance and aspiration, future orientation, etc.) and social factors (role models, social sanctions, economic and legal factors) that mediate initial use. In addition, learning processes play a major role in continued use. Objects in the environment become associated with drug outcomes, and reexposure to them motivates continued use. For example, when a person smokes while drinking, smoking can become a conditioned stimulus for drinking so that when one has a cigarette one "wants" a drink. Environmental stimuli associated with drug use also come to serve as signals for drug use. For example, the sight of a flashing neon sign may motivate drink-seeking behavior. People also learn social myths about drug use outcomes (smoking controls your appetite and keeps you thin, drinking facilities social interaction, etc.) and share in drug-taking rituals (cocktail parties, needle sharing, etc.) that emphasize these outcomes and motivate continued drug use. While the neurobiology of the cognitive factors underlying this increased motivation for substance abuse is not fully understood, it is of interest because of the important role of the learning in drug seeking.

As use continues, a subset of users develop drug dependence. As physiological dependence develops, the user needs increased amount of the drug to achieve a given drug effect (i.e., tolerance develops), and this motivates escalated drug use as a person seeks to recapture the initial drug effect. In addition, tolerant persons may use drugs to relieve or postpone adverse effects that occur with drug abstinence (i.e., drug withdrawal). Psychological factors such as the expectation that drug use reduces anxiety or dysphoria also predict the development and continuation of dependence.

III. *Use and Abuse of Substances*

Three fundamental characteristics of drug use include its prevalence, its frequency, and how it is regarded by society. Historically in U.S. society, the use of most drugs was defined as either an inconsequential or a problematic behavior. Drug use was considered inconsequential if it did not impair performance or judgment and if there were no known long-term health consequences. When drug use resulted in adverse consequences, it was viewed as problematic resulting from bad habits or moral failure. Drug use has always been viewed differently according to the age, sex, and social class of the user, and historically any use by women, the young, and the lower classes was judged more harshly. Between 1860 and 1940, as a result of social factors as well as increased knowledge about adverse effects of drug use, production, distribution and possession of many drugs became regulated by government, and use, except when prescribed, became illegal. For a brief period, the government regulated the use of alcohol. While the public will to maintain the prohibition of alcohol use was lacking, it has continued to support criminal statues prohibiting the nonprescribed use of drugs other than alcohol and tobacco. Since the inception of these laws, the use of drugs, except tobacco and alcohol, has been defined as "abuse" and considered a social problem. This includes the nonmedical use of prescribed drugs. The term "abuse," when used in this sense, should not be confused with abuse as a type of substance use disorder (see the glossary).

A. PREVALENCE OF THE USE OF MAJOR CLASSES OF DRUGS

The extent of the use of illegal drugs has been tracked over the years by annual surveys carried out by federal agencies such as the Substance Abuse and Mental Health Services Administration (SAMHSA) and the National Institute on Drug Abuse (NIDA). In recent years, such surveys have also recorded the use of alcohol, tobacco, and the nonmedical use of psychoactive therapeutic drugs. Table I shows the prevalence of lifetime and past 30-day use of the major

Table I

Percentage of Women and Men Aged 12 and Up Reporting Any Use in Lifetime and Past 30 Days of Illicit and Licit Drugs

Drug	Lifetime		Past month	
	Women	Men	Women	Men
Any illicit drug	30.3	41.6	4.5	8.1
Marijuana	27.9	38.5	3.5	6.7
Cocaine	8.2	13.1	0.5	1.1
Hallucinogens	7.4	12.6	0.6	0.8
Inhalants	3.7	7.9	0.2	0.5
Any psychotherapeutic	7.6	11.1	0.9	1.4
Alcohol	77.6	85.2	45.1	58.7
Cigarettes	64.7	75.1	25.7	29.7

Source: Substance Abuse and Mental Health Services Administration (SAMSHA). (1999). *National Household Survey on Drug Abuse: Population Estimates 1998.* Department of Health and Human Services. No (SMA) 99-3327, Rockville, MD.

categories of drugs in 1998. Use of LSD, PCP, and heroin occurs at lower rates, and for this reason rates are provided for lifetime and past year use only. These data are shown in Table II.

The data in Tables I and II clearly show that many more people try and continue to use licit substances than illicit substances. For example, the percentage of people (women and men combined) who ever use any of the illicit drugs (38.5%) is less than half that of those who report ever using alcohol (81.3%) and far lower than the percentage who report ever using cigarettes (69.7%). Furthermore, persons who used alcohol in the preceding 30 days outnumber those

Table II

Percentage of Men and Women Aged 12 and Up Reporting Any Use in Lifetime and Past Year of Three Illicit Drugs

Drug	Lifetime		Past year	
	Women	Men	Women	Men
LSD	5.8	10.2	0.7	0.9
PCP	2.7	4.4	0.1	0.1
Heroin	0.8	1.3	0.1	0.1

Source: Substance Abuse and Mental Health Services Administration (SAMSHA). (1999). *National Household Survey on Drug Abuse: Population Estimates 1998.* Department of Health and Human Services. No (SMA) 99-3327, Rockville, MD.

who have used any illicit substance in that time span by more than 8 to 1 (51.7% versus 6.2%). Thus, it is immediately apparent that legal restrictions on drug production, advertising, sale, possession, and use are associated with a lower rate of use of such drugs. Users of illicit drugs compared to users of licit drugs are less likely to continue use. Current use as a percentage of lifetime use for any illicit drug is 14.8% for women and 19.4% for men versus 58.1% of men and 68.8% of women for alcohol and 40% of both men and women for tobacco. Compared to licit drugs, these lower rates of use of illicit drugs result in less morbidity and mortality and less economic loss associated with them. While not the topic of this review, it should be noted that legal restrictions breed their own set of problems ranging from crimes associated with transporting and selling illegal drugs to crimes associated with getting money to pay for drug purchases. In addition, legal restrictions appear to place a disproportionate burden on those people who are already disadvantaged in our society as the poor, the young, and minorities are the most vulnerable to recruitment into high-paying criminal activities related to the drug trade. Moreover, compared to Caucasians, racial minorities are also more likely to be arrested, found guilty, and to serve time for drug-related crimes. Another conclusion to be drawn from Tables I and II is that women are less likely than men to use drugs regardless of whether the drug is legal or illegal.

B. DRUG DEPENDENCE

Researchers have long recognized that, regardless of the drug, some people who initiate drug use are unable to regulate its use and feel a physical or psychological need for continued use in order to function. While in the older literature, this process was often referred to as addiction, in recent years it has been termed "dependence" and defined as a mental disorder. Dependence is associated with many more problems than are associated with occasional use or abuse and is a barrier to achieving abstinence. For these reasons and possibly others, over the past decade research has begun to focus on drug dependence.

The first major expression of dependence as an issue in substance use behavior emerged from a volunteer, grassroots treatment effort for problem drinkers. In the early 20th century, Alcoholics Anonymous, a mutual support group for men with problems related to excessive drinking, was founded. It defined excessive drinking in terms of chronic disease. As a disease conceptualization of problems related to excessive drinking took hold among the general population, the way in which alcohol use was considered by health professionals began to change also. One can gain a sense of how the disease concept of drug addiction gained acceptance in the health professions by examining the various editions of the *Diagnostic and Statistical Manual (DSM)* published by the American Psychiatric Association (APA). [*See* DIAGNOSIS OF PSYCHOLOGICAL DISORDERS.]

1. History of Classification

In 1952 the first edition of the manual *(DSM I)* contained two mental disorders related to alcohol: acute brain syndrome (alcohol intoxication) and chronic brain syndrome (associated with intoxication that included syndromes such as Korsakoff's psychosis). At this time, alcohol-related mental disorders were constrained to acute states that most drinkers would experience and irreversible conditions that only a small portion of drinkers would experience. *DSM II* (1968) adopted a broader view of alcohol-associated mental disorders. It listed 11 alcohol-related psychoses under the heading of Organic Brain Syndromes, which ranged from alcoholic deterioration to delirium tremens. In both these editions, uncontrolled use of alcohol and dependence were not considered alcohol-related disorders but were identified as subtypes of sociopathic personality disorder. Behaviors ranging from episodic, excessive drinking to alcohol addiction were included in this category. By the time *DSM III* was published in 1980, research had shown that organic brain syndromes were the possible consequences of the use of all types of licit and illicit drugs including caffeine. In a departure from the earlier practice of subsuming alcohol and drug abuse and dependence under personality disorders, *DSM III* established a separate category of mental disorder for abuse of and dependence on various drugs. With the adoption of *DSM-III-R* in 1987, dependence, regardless of drug, was defined using the same criterion symptoms. These criteria were retained in the nosology of *DSM IV* (1994), and dependence was defined by the presence of three or more symptoms, from among those listed in the glossary, coexisting within the past year. The DSM criteria no longer required the presence of physiological symptoms, although the dependence diagnosis could be further specified as including physiologic dependence when physiological symptoms were present. The current *DSM-IV-TR* (2000) maintains

the *DSM-IV* criteria for substance use disorders classified as substance dependence and substance abuse. The current edition reflects new information supported by empirical studies conducted since the initial data for the *DSM-IV* (1994) were gathered in 1992. For example, the features section for substance dependence has been updated to indicate that varied degrees of tolerance may develop to the different central nervous system effects of a substance, and that a past history of tolerance or withdrawal is associated with a worse clinical course.

Theoretical differences of opinion exist on how to classify psychiatric disorders, including substance use disorders. For example Widiger and Sankis (2000) pointed out that because of the recent, rapid advancement in technology (brain imaging, gene deletion preparations, etc.), neurophysiological models of psychopathology have taken precedence over others. Neurophysiological models of mental disorders may not prove to be useful, especially if environmental factors are found to be paramount determinants of which genetic potentials are expressed. Even if these models are useful, current nosology with its focus on symptoms may not allow researchers to distinguish neurophysiological features of the various disorders. Nevertheless, for many purposes, including those as diverse as research and reimbursement for treatment, the definitions provided by the current *Diagnostic and Statistical Manual*, incorporating biological, psychological, and social dimensions of mental disorders, have become the gold standard.

C. PREVALENCE OF SUBSTANCE USE DISORDERS

Our understanding of the frequency of substance use disorders, as well as of their psychiatric comorbidities, was facilitated by adaptations of *DSM* criteria to research instruments such as the National Institute of Mental Health—Diagnostic Interview Schedule (NIMH-DIS) and the Composite International Diagnostic Interview (CIDI) developed by Robins and her coworkers in the late 1980s. The NIMH-DIS was used in a series of studies, known as the Environmental Catchment Area studies, that provided, in the mid-1980s, the first population estimates of rates of various mental disorders. An adaptation of it was used in the National Comorbidity Study, under the direction of Ronald Kessler, to survey a nationally representative household sample to determine the prevalence of mental disorders and their comorbidity. Data from this survey provide the best available description of the extent of substance use disorders (see Table III) as well as the disorders that co-occur with them (see Table IV) in men and women. In addition, the national comorbidity studies have provided evidence supporting the conceptualization of substance use disorder as a progressive disorder in that they have found that the earliest occurring symptoms of impaired performance and hazardous use are followed by symptoms of tolerance and impaired control or symptoms of withdrawal and forgoing other activities in order to use drugs. Articles from the national comorbidity study are available on line at www.hcp.med.harvard.edu/ncs.

Table III reinforces the point made by the earlier data from the National Household Survey. The proportion of persons of both sexes who use licit substances (tobacco and alcohol) is much greater than it is for those who use illicit substances, and, in general, rates of use are higher in men than in women. However, these data go beyond use criteria and provide an idea of the percentage of users who become dependent on the various drugs. In terms of the proportion of users who become dependent on a substance, a sharp distinction between licit and illicit substances is not seen. Thus, we must posit that the

factors that protect women from use of illicit substances do not protect them from dependence. For both men and women, tobacco is the drug associated with the highest proportion of people who become dependent. For 7 of the 10 drugs shown on Table III, dependence rates are higher in men. Overall, rates of dependence correlate significantly with rates of use, but that correlation is weaker for women than men.

1. Gender Differences in Dependence

As stated earlier, in general, men have higher rates of dependence, but there are some interesting exceptions in these data. The proportion of women compared to men who become dependent is higher for those who use stimulants, anxiolytics, and analgesics, even though women's rates of use are lower than men's. For women, the top three drugs in terms of rate of dependence are all stimulants (i.e., tobacco, cocaine, and other stimulants). For men, the top three drugs in terms of dependence are tobacco, heroin, and alcohol, and the latter two are depressants. The data suggest that women may be especially vulnerable to dependence on stimulant drugs. Table III does not take into account amount of use,

Table III

Estimated[a] Prevalence Proportion (P) of Extramedical Use and Lifetime Dependence by Sex

Drug	Men		Women	
	P with history of use	P of users with history of dependence	P with history of use	P of users with history of dependence
Tobacco[b]	78.3	32.7	73.1	30.9
Alcohol	93.5	21.4	89.6	9.2
Cannabis	51.7	12.0	41.0	5.5
Cocaine	19.5	18.0	12.9	14.9
Stimulants	18.4	9.7	12.2	13.3
Anxiolytics[c]	14.0	6.6	11.5	12.3
Analgesics	11.6	6.7	7.9	8.6
Psychedelics	14.1	5.0	7.2	4.7
Heroin	2.2	22.3	0.9	12.9
Inhalants	9.4	4.1	4.3	2.7

[a]Weighted estimates from the National Comorbidity Study, data 1990–1992.
[b]Tobacco use estimates, 1991 National Household Survey on Drug Use.
[c]Anxiolytics, sedatives, and hypnotic drugs grouped.
Source: Anthony, J. C., Warner, L. A., and Kessler, R. C. (1994). Comparative epidemiology of dependence on tobacco, alcohol, controlled substances and inhalants: Basic findings from the National Comorbidity Survey. *Exponential Clinical Psychopharmacology* 2, 244–268.

Table IV
Odds Ratio of Comorbidity of Substance Use Disorder and Other Psychiatric Disorders

Disorder	Alcohol dependence[a]		Nicotine dependence[b]	
	Men	Women	Men	Women
Any anxiety disorder	2.22	3.08	2.2	2.6
GAD[a][d]	3.86	3.01		
Agoraphobia	1.82	2.53		
PTSD[e]	2.22	3.08		
Any affective disorder	3.16	4.36		
Dysthymia	3.81	3.63		
Depression	2.95	4.05	3.8	3.1
Mania	12.03	5.30		
Any drug dependence disorder	9.81	15.75	6.6[c]	4.0[c]
Alcohol dependence			1.9[c]	2.6[c]

[a]Kessler, R. C., Crum, R. M., Warner, L. A., et al. (1997). Lifetime co-occurrence of DSM-IIl0-R alcohol abuse and dependence with other psychiatric disorders in the national comorbidity survey. *Archives of General Psychiatry* **54**, 313–321.

[b]Breslau, N. (1995). Psychiatric comorbidity of smoking and nicotine dependence. *Behavior Genetics* **25**, 95–101.

[c]includes both abuse and dependence disorders.

[d]Generalized anxiety disorder.

[e]Posttraumatic stress disorder.

which is an important variable when considering dependence. For example, dependence rates in smokers increase linearly when one smokes up to about a half of a pack of cigarettes per day. Whites are more likely to be dependent than Blacks because of heavier smoking, and women are more likely to be dependent than men because they experience more symptoms at similar levels of consumption (see Kandel and Chen, 2000, for further discussion of this point). It should be noted that as women are, on average, smaller than men, so less consumption on their part may, in fact, result in similar body levels of nicotine as those experienced by men who smoke more cigarettes per day. To resolve the question of how dependence relates to drug consumption, data would be needed that measured nicotine metabolites in large groups of people with varying smoking patterns, and such data are not currently available.

D. COMORBIDITY OF SUBSTANCE USE DISORDERS AND OTHER MENTAL DISORDERS

A critical step for understanding the etiology of substance use disorders is the identification of the biological, psychological, and social risk factors associated with these conditions. However, an understanding of the etiology of drug abuse and dependence is complicated by high lifetime or current rates of other mental diseases or other substance use disorders in persons with substance use disorders.

Recent research has clearly shown that both alcohol and nicotine dependence co-occur with anxiety disorders, mood disorders, and other substance use disorders in many individuals. This is illustrated in Table IV. Table IV presents the odds ratios of having a lifetime history of another disorder if one has a lifetime history of alcohol or nicotine dependence. If the risk of having a second disorder were not increased by having the first disorder, the odds ratio would be one. Table IV plainly shows that lifetime alcohol or nicotine dependence is associated with at least a twofold increase in risk for lifetime presence of other mental disorders. With few exceptions, the increased risk of having a second disorder given a first one is not strikingly different for men or women. The exceptions include the association between alcohol dependence and mania, where the odds ratio for mania, given alcohol dependence, is increased 12-fold for men versus 5-fold for women. Another is the association between alcohol dependence and any other drug dependence where the odds ratio for any other drug dependence disorder, given alcohol dependence, is increased 10-fold for men versus 15-fold for women.

1. Age of Onset of Disorders

The tabled data do not take into account the order in which the disorders develop, and looking at that question is a focus of much current research. For example, in a retrospective study, Ronald Kessler and coworkers looked at the age of onset of symptoms for alcohol dependence and mental disorders. They found that alcohol disorder occurred more often in men as a primary disorder. Women generally reported that the onset of alcohol dependence disorder occurred in the same year, or later, as another psychiatric disorder. In this work, Kessler and his colleagues did not gather information about nicotine dependence. Thus, they were not able to take into account the effects of any preexisting dependence on nicotine, a drug that is commonly used at an early age, on the development of alcohol dependence or other mental disorders. There is, however, some evidence that indicates heavy smoking (a pack or more per day) during adolescence is associated with increased risk for anxiety disorders during early adulthood. In a longitudinal study of primarily White families, J. G. Johnson and his coworkers measured smoking and anxiety disorders in youth when they were 16 years old and again at age 22 years. When age, sex, difficult childhood temperament, alcohol or drug use, anxiety and depressive disorders during adolescence, parental smoking, education, and psychopathology were controlled, adolescents who had smoked 20 cigarettes or more per day had a significantly elevated risk for agoraphobia, generalized anxiety disorders (GADs), or panic disorder during early adulthood. [*See* AGORAPHOBIA; ANXIETY.]

IV. Influence of Risk Factors

We now briefly review some recent evidence bearing on risk factors for substance use disorders. Only a small percentage of these studies have looked at women and men separately. On the other hand, many studies have looked at risk factors for a specific type of substance use disorder (alcohol, nicotine, marijuana, etc.). At this time, it is not clear whether or not all substance use disorders should be considered to result from the same biological, psychological, and social risk factors or whether some risk factors are associated with certain drugs and not others. The factors listed in Table V have been consistently identified as risks for substance use disorders. In the older literature, these associations were noted as correlations between the variables under study and substance use behaviors in cross-sectional studies. The more recent literature includes numerous longitudinal studies of drug use behaviors, and, in addition, some genetic and environmental risk variables, and their interactions, have been studied in twin samples. We will begin our discussion of risk factors by discussing work that has looked at some of these risk factors in women.

A. PREDICTORS OF POLYDRUG USE PROBLEMS IN WOMEN

Sensation seeking, social conformity, depression, academic aspirations, polydrug use, polydrug use problems, parents' drug problems, and parental support

Table V
Risk Factors for Substance Use Disorders

Genetic Risk Factors
Parents' drug use, parents' antisocial personality
Individual Risk Factors
Childhood conduct disorder
Childhood aggression
Sensation seeking
Neuroticism
Low social conformity
Low educational aspirations/achievement
Coexisting mental disorders:
  Other substance use disorders
  Major depressive disorder
  Anxiety disorder(s)
  Attention deficit hyperactivity disorder
Early drug use
Environmental Risk Factors
Peer drug use
Poor parenting skills
Lack of parental monitoring
Childhood sexual abuse

were examined as predictors of adult drug problems by A. W. Stacy and Michael Newcomb who followed a cohort of adolescent girls for 13 years. They found that adolescent drug use significantly predicted adult polydrug problems. In addition, high sensation seeking and low social conformity in adolescence were risk factors for drug problems as adults. At the neurobiological level, high sensation seeking is associated with low levels of serotonin, a brain neurotransmitter. Since serotonin is thought to inhibit dopamine's activation effects on the brain's reward system, high sensation seeking might be associated with enhanced reinforcement from drug use due to excessive dopamine activity in the presence of low serotonin levels.

B. GENETIC AND ENVIRONMENTAL RISK

Modern studies of genetic influences of substance use, abuse, and dependence began with studies of alcohol in the 1970s and have been extended to other substances, including tobacco, in recent years. The most commonly studied risk factors are parents' drug use and parents' antisocial personality disorder. Using designs that contrast presence and absence of drug use, abuse, and dependence in the biological parents of twins, recent work has shown clearly that these complex behaviors are not under the control of a single gene. Genetic risk for substance use, abuse, and dependence appears to be polygenic and probabilistic and appears to be expressed interactively with environmental factors. Furthermore, there is evidence suggesting that both genetic and environmental factors may be expressed differently in men and women. A weakness of twin studies is that they have primarily been carried out in Caucasian populations, and thus the findings may not generalize to other racial groups.

Remi Cadoret and his colleagues provided an exemplary set of studies in twins adopted away at birth by looking at genetic and environmental risks for substance use, abuse, and dependence in women and men. These researchers looked at factors predicting symptoms of alcohol or drug use in twins as a function of genetic variables (alcohol use problems, drug use problems, antisocial personality disorder in biological parents) and environmental variables (adverse conditions in the adoptive family including alcohol and drug problems, depression, other psychiatric problems, legal and marital problems, and divorce). The findings are discussed next.

1. Female Adoptees

In adopted women, genetic and environmental factors affected drug abuse measures but not alcohol abuse measures. For women, neither genetic factors nor environmental factors directly or indirectly predicted alcohol use disorder symptoms. Drug use disorder symptoms were indirectly predicted by both birth parent antisocial personality and adverse adoptive environment that contributed to increased aggression symptoms and increased child conduct disorder in the female adoptees. In turn, there was a significant pathway from child conduct disorder symptoms to drug use disorder symptoms in the adult female adoptees.

2. Male Adoptees

For male adoptees, genetic and environmental factors affected alcohol and drug abuse measures similarly. Birth parent alcohol problems and antisocial personality disorder predicted adoptee alcohol and drug use symptoms, aggression symptoms, and child conduct disorder symptoms. When the interaction of

genetic factors with adverse adoptive environment was considered, they were found to indirectly influence alcohol and drug use symptoms in two ways. Birth parent antisocial personality disorder increased adoptees' aggression symptoms, and these were positively associated with symptoms of child conduct disorder. Secondly, adverse adoptive environment factors were positively associated with child conduct disorder symptoms. Child conduct disorder symptoms, in turn, directly affected alcohol and drug use disorder symptoms. This work indicates that aggression and conduct disorders are more predictive of alcohol use problems in men than in women, while conduct disorders appear to be predictive of drug use disorders in both women and men.

3. Interaction between Genetic and Environmental Risk Factors

How might an adverse adoptive home environment influence the adoptees' use of drugs? Several lines of work have addressed this. K. J. Conger has suggested that psychiatrically impaired parents make inadequate responses to a child's antisocial behavior. Parental alcoholism and lack of parental skill has been linked to children's early drug use in work by Lauri Chassin and colleagues and Howard Chilcoat and colleagues. Robert Anda and his coworkers have shown that both early initiation of smoking and current smoking in adults are related to adverse events in childhood. In a recent retrospective study of participants in a large health maintenance organization, people who reported experiencing five or more adverse childhood experiences in any of eight categories (emotional, physical, and sexual abuse; a battered mother; parental separation or divorce, and growing up with a substance-abusing, mentally ill, or incarcerated household member), were five times more at risk for early smoking initiation and about three times more at risk for ever smoking, current smoking, and heavy smoking than those who reported fewer adverse childhood experiences. Reports of having experienced five or more adverse incidents were twice as common in women as men (7.5% vs. 3.7%), but the relationship between adverse experience and smoking behaviors was found for the total sample when gender was controlled statistically.

X. Ge and colleagues investigated possible ways by which the genetic factors related to antisocial personality and alcohol use might interact with adoptive home factors to result in drug use in adoptees. This work indicated that the warmth of the marital relationship had a direct effect on the adoptive mother's child disciplinary practices. But genetic and environmental factors also indirectly affected them. In terms of genetic factors, birth parents' psychiatric disorders directly influenced adoptee's antisocial/hostile behaviors, which, in turn, influenced the adoptive mother's disciplinary practices. These disciplinary practices, in turn, further influenced the adoptee's antisocial/hostile behaviors. This work suggests that environmental interventions aimed at modifying parenting practices could decrease alcohol and drug use problems. Remi Cadoret and coworkers suggested that these interventions might be more effective for females because their work has shown that the genetic risk for conduct disorders is not expressed in women in the absence of adverse adoptive home environments. Another consideration suggested by this work is that differential parenting of girls and boys may underlie some of the differences seen in rates of use, abuse, and dependence between women and men. However, we were unable to find work in which differences between levels of nurturing/involved parenting in girls and boys was studied in relation to substance use, abuse, and dependence to address this point.

4. Genetic Influences on Smoking

Genetic influences on smoking behaviors have also been examined in twins, although in contrast to the work reviewed earlier in this article, these twins were reared in the same environment. Andrew Heath and N. G. Martin looked at genetic effects on smoking initiation and persistence in two cohorts of twin pairs (i.e., those pairs aged 30 or younger and those over 30). For both cohorts, monozygotic twins had higher concordance for smoking initiation and persistence than dizygotic twins, indicating a genetic contribution to these behaviors. Overall genetic factors accounted for 49 to 56% of the variance in initiation and 53% of the variance in persistence. The genetic factors for initiation were independent of those for persistence. Evidence for the contribution of sex-linked environmental influences to the behaviors came from the finding that concordance rates for unlike-sex pairs of dizygotic twins were lower than those of same-sex pairs. Identification of specific sex-lined environmental factors in the initiation and persistence of smoking is an important task that remains to be done. When the researchers compared the percentage of ex-smokers in younger and older cohorts, the percentage of ex-smokers in the older

group rose substantially for men, but not for women. More than half of the women ex-smokers in the young cohort had low liability on the genetic smoking initiation dimension. While women who have lower genetic liability to initiate smoking are more likely to quit should they begin, the identification of other factors that influence quitting remains an important unfinished task.

Kenneth Kendler and his colleagues examined regular tobacco use in 778 Swedish twin pairs. Regular tobacco use was contrasted in male and female monozygotic and dizygotic twins reared together and apart. Using a biometric model, they estimated that in males genetic factors accounted for 60% of the variance and shared environmental factors and individual-specific environmental factors each accounted for 20% of the variance in risk for regular tobacco use. For women, heritability was cohort dependent. For women born after 1940, genetic factors accounted for 63% of the variance in risk for regular tobacco use.

C. NICOTINE DEPENDENCE

Naomi Breslau and her coworkers provided the first in-depth examination of the relationship between smoking and nicotine dependence. In a study of 1007 young adults in a metropolitan area, they found that the lifetime prevalence of smoking daily for a month or more was 39.1%, and the prevalence of nicotine dependence among daily smokers was 50%. Smoking cessation, defined as abstinence for one year or more, was reported by 26% of those who had ever smoked daily and was unrelated to sex, race, or education, while it was significantly more common in nondependent smokers than dependent smokers. The symptoms of nicotine dependence may be thought of as falling into three groups: those related to loss of control over use, those related to physical tolerance and withdrawal, and those related to activities lost to smoking. Loss-of-control symptoms were most common, affecting between 72 and 94% of dependent smokers. Symptoms related to physical dependence and tolerance affected between 46 and 59%, while lost activities were noted by only 13% of nicotine-dependent smokers. Rates of smoking and nicotine dependence were higher for Caucasians than for African Americans and were inversely related to level of education. However, there were no differences between men and women. Daily smoking was related to increased risk of other substance use disorders. Daily smokers, as well as dependent smokers, had significantly increased rates of other substance use disorders (i.e., alcohol, cannabis, and cocaine), but, in addition, dependent smokers were significantly more likely to experience major depressive disorder (MDD). Rates of MDD were significantly higher in nicotine-dependent persons, even when the effects of sex and other substance dependence that are related to MDD were controlled. [*See* DEPRESSION.]

1. Nicotine Dependence, Life Events, and Neuroticism

In a second study, Breslau and coworkers evaluated the effects of several life events and personality factors on nicotine dependence. Divorce was associated with smoking daily (57.% of separated/divorced persons smoked daily versus 42.4% of married persons and 34.3% of those never married), but nicotine dependence among these smokers was essentially equal for all three groups (51.6%, 52.9%, and 49.4%, respectively).

Levels of neuroticism were significantly higher in nicotine-dependent smokers than in nondependent smokers and nonsmokers. When correlates of nicotine dependence (age, sex, race, education, marital status, and personality factors) were examined in a multiple logistic regression, odds for nicotine dependence were significantly related to being Caucasian and having an increased neuroticism score.

2. Nicotine Dependence and Major Depressive Disorder

In a prospective study, Breslau and her coworkers showed that a history of MDD increased the risk for nicotine dependence, while a history of nicotine dependence increased the risk for first incidence MDD. They suggested that the relationship between nicotine dependence and MDD probably reflected the effects of a common factor that predisposed persons to both disorders. They also suggested that neuroticism might be such a common predisposing factor.

3. Nicotine Dependence, Serotonin Mechanisms, Dopamine Activity, and Neuroticism

Recent biological evidence has lent support to Breslau's hypothesis. To understand this evidence one must keep in mind that the brain's dopamine circuits are activated when an organism is engaged in rewarding behavior and that a similar activation occurs when psychoactive drugs are taken. One of the neurotransmitters that modulates dopamine's activity is serotonin (5-HT). When 5-HT is released as a function of neural activity, it remains active until it is taken back up into the neuron. The proteins that carry 5-HT back into the neuron are termed transporters, and in humans there are two forms, a short and a long form, with the long form being the more efficient form. The 5-HT transporter is encoded on chromosome 17Q12. S. Hu and his coworkers have found that in persons with the short form of the 5-HT transporter, neuroticism was positively correlated with current smoking and negatively correlated with smoking cessation. These findings were replicated by C. Lerman and coworkers, who found that high levels of neuroticism in persons with the short form of the 5-HT transporter were associated with nicotine intake, nicotine dependence, and smoking to reduce negative mood and smoking for stimulation. If less efficient reuptake of serotonin over time results in less of the neurotransmitter being available, these findings are compatible with those discussed earlier (see Section IV.A)—that less serotonergic inhibition of dopamine activity may enhance the reinforcing effects of drugs.

D. DEPRESSION

A history of major depressive disorder increases the risk for nicotine dependence for both men and women; however, women are twice as likely as men to experience a lifetime episode of major depression. Data from the National Comorbidity Study also indicate that although there are no differences in rates of initial incidence of major depression between girls and boys during childhood, by 15 years of age there is a 2:1 ratio of females to males who experience depression, and the disorder continues to predominate in women throughout the life span. Thus, smoking to regulate negative affect may be more important to women than men.

1. Affect Regulation

Affect regulation appears to be an important motivator of smoking. According to S. M. Santi and colleagues, some adolescents smoke to regulate affect as they believe that cigarettes help them to control negative affect. These researchers hypothesized that two stages of smoking are related to negative affect. In the initial stages of smoking adolescents may use smoking to regulate negative affective states and only continue when they felt that smoking helped them with these states. In the second stage, positive affect is perceived as dependent on continual smoking behaviors. It is difficult, however, to know just how effective nicotine use is in the regulation of affect. While numerous studies relate aspects of smoking to expectations of positive affect or reduction of negative affect, the controlled laboratory studies of nicotine's effect on affect is harder to interpret. David Gilbert has provided an excellent summary of the controlled laboratory studies in this area. While there is strong evidence that smoking alleviates negative affect (anxiety or depression/dysphoria) experienced in withdrawal from cigarettes, the data for smoking effects on affect in a nonwithdrawal state are weak and may be summarized by saying that several studies show a moderation of aggression by nicotine, some work shows an antianxiety effect of nicotine or smoking, and there is no evidence of an antidepressant effect.

E. ATTENTION DEFICIT HYPERACTIVITY DISORDER AND SUBSTANCE USE DISORDER

Nadine Lambert and Carolyn Hartsough described the natural history of smoking among persons diagnosed in 1974 with attention deficit hyperactivity disorder (ADHD), the majority of whom had received medication, and control participants. The investigators were able to contact 77% of the original group with ADHD and 86% of the group without ADHD as adults to determine their substance use histories. While age of smoking initiation did not differ between the groups, 46% of the group with ADHD versus 24% of the control group had begun smoking regularly by age 17. Lifetime rates of nicotine dependence differed significantly for the groups as 40% of persons with ADHD experienced nicotine dependence versus 19% of persons without ADHD. Persons with a history of ADHD were also significantly more likely to be current daily smokers compared to those without such a history (35% versus 16%). Cocaine dependence was more frequent in the group with ADHD (21%) than in the group without ADHD (10%). No significant differences between the sexes were found relative to rates of initiation of smoking, regular use of cigarettes, and adult smoking. Most work on ADHD finds higher rates of the disorder in males. Nevertheless, these data indicate that the increased risk for stimulant use seen in persons with childhood diagnoses of ADHD does not differ between women and men. This raises the prospect that the factors that account for the differ-

ence in rates of ADHD between the sexes, which are not known at present, may be independent of those factors that place a person with ADHD, regardless of sex, at risk for stimulant use and abuse. These latter factors are also not known at present.

F. SEXUAL ABUSE

Several recent studies have suggested that childhood sexual abuse is a risk factor for substance use disorder in male and female adolescents and adult women. In a longitudinal (birth to age 18) study of more than 1000 New Zealand youths, D. M. Fergusson and his coworkers found that retrospective reports of childhood sexual abuse (prior to age 16) obtained at age 18 were associated with alcohol and drug use disorders also measured at age 18. Rates of disorders increased in relation to the severity of the childhood sexual abuse with the highest rates being found for attempted or completed intercourse. Increased rates of alcohol and drug use disorders remained significant even after the potentially confounding effects of significant covariates (gender, maternal age, childhood adversity, parental attachment, and parental offense history) were considered. The authors estimated that substance use disorders in this population of young women and men would have been reduced by 10% if none of them had been exposed to sexual abuse during childhood.

While most studies, including the one just mentioned, of the relationship between childhood sexual abuse and substance use disorders cannot rule confounding effects due to recall bias, a study of the Virginia twin registry by Kenneth Kendler and his colleagues was able to look at this question in a way that offered some control of this factor. They studied a population-based sample of 1411 White, female adult twins and identified three levels of childhood sexual abuse: nongenital, genital, and intercourse. Childhood was defined as before age 16. Self-report and reports of the cotwin to a mailed questionnaire established sexual abuse, while family background and psychiatric and substance dependence disorders were established in interviews with twins and their parents. Sexual abuse was common, with 30.4% reporting any sexual abuse and 8.4% reporting intercourse. There was some discrepancy between the extent to which psychiatric disorders including substance use disorders were increased in adult women depending on who was reporting the abuse. By self-report, intercourse was associated with significantly increased odds ratios that reflected 2.5

to almost sixfold increases in major depressive disorder, GAD, panic disorder, bulimia nervosa, alcohol dependence, and drug dependence. When cotwin report was used to establish childhood intercourse, risks for GAD, panic disorder, and drug dependence were not significantly increased due to the fact that the lower rates of abuse reported by cotwins resulted in less power in the statistical analysis to detect relationships between childhood sexual abuse and psychiatric disorders. Nevertheless, even with a less powerful analysis, a significant increase in risk for major depressive disorder, bulimia nervosa and alcohol dependence was found to result from childhood sexual abuse. The lower rate of sexual abuse reported by cotwins is not surprising considering that close to 40% of abused twins reported telling no one about the abuse. The authors report that their data indicate that nongenital and genital childhood sexual abuse accounts for 6% of the variance and intercourse accounts for 12% of the variance in liability for the six psychiatric disorders measured. Perhaps the strongest evidence these researchers gathered was that obtained from 22 pairs of twins discordant for sexual abuse in which 19 of the abused twins met criteria for a psychiatric disorder. There is no similar study of childhood sexual abuse in male twins with which to compare these findings. [*See* CHILD ABUSE.]

V. Summary

The proportion of persons of both sexes who use licit substances (tobacco and alcohol) is much greater than it is for those who use illicit substances, and, in general, rates of use are higher in men than in women. Greater social conformity in women compared to men protects them from use of drugs, and research is needed to identify other factors that similarly protect women because there may be ways to emphasize these factors in the experience of boys and men and thereby lower their drug use. In general, there is no difference between licit and illicit drugs in terms of the proportion of users who become dependent on them. Thus, we must posit that the factors that protect women from use of illicit substances do not protect them from dependence given use. Overall, rates of dependence correlate significantly with rates of use, but that correlation is weaker for women than men. When one examines those drugs for which women and men have the highest rates of dependence, we see that the top three drugs for dependence in women are all stimulants (tobacco, cocaine,

and other stimulants) while for men they are tobacco followed by two depressants (heroin and alcohol). Thus, it seems as if women may be especially vulnerable to dependence on stimulant drugs. This vulnerability could result from congruity between the pharmacological effects of stimulants and gendered behavioral expectations, or it might reflect sex differences in pharmacological effects of stimulants, or, finally, it could reflect some combination of both factors. At this time, there seems to be no research on this important question.

Recent investigations of risk factors for substance use, abuse, and dependence falls into three broad categories: genetic risk factors, individual risk factors, and environmental risk factors. Evidence from genetic studies indicates that parental drug use and parental antisocial personality are risk factors for substance use for both men and women. There is some evidence of sex-specific risk factors for initiation and persistence of smoking, but what these specific risks may be is not known at present. Genetic risk for substance abuse and dependence appears to be expressed interactively with environmental factors. Research shows that conduct disorders are predictive of drug use disorders in both women and men, but that in the absence of adverse home environments among adopted children, a genetic liability for conduct disorders does not put women at risk for substance use disorders. This work suggests that social factors such as parenting practices may be especially critical for females in the prevention of future drug use problems. Longitudinal studies are needed to identify risk factors and their trajectory throughout a woman's life span. When social conditions prevail for women, such as those between 1890 and 1925 that resulted in very low smoking prevalence, genetic factors were negligible predictors of which women smoked. Heritability became an important risk factor as smoking rates increased presumably as a response to changing social conditions. Recently evidence from twin studies has shown that exposure to childhood sexual abuse is a strong environmental risk factor for substance use disorders and other psychiatric disorders in women. While cross-sectional work has suggested that the same may be true for men, critical twin studies have not yet been done in men.

Substance use disorders are associated with other types of mental disorders. A central theoretical question that remains to be answered concerns whether or not comorbid conditions result from risk factors fundamental to the comorbid conditions, or whether they are best thought of as a primary disorder and a secondary disorder. For example, does a person have a history of anxiety disorder and nicotine dependence because of having a vulnerability common to both disorders? Or is the nicotine dependence an adaptation to anxiety disorder or vice versa? A third alternative would view the comorbid conditions as arising from separate independent risk factors. Likewise, studies of comorbidities have shown that having one substance use disorder places one at risk for another substance use disorder. At this time, we do not know if substance use comorbidities, like comorbid substance use disorders and mental disorders, should be considered as resulting from common risk factors for both, an instance of a primary and a secondary disorder, or independent disorders. Investigation of these important questions should be a fruitful area of substance use research in the future.

A relation between early use of drugs and dependence is often found, and it points out the critical need to study drug use among children and adolescents. Very little is known about risk factors for the transition from experimental to regular use. For example, individual differences in responses to initial or early drug use may predict continuation of drug use, but if one does not investigate drug use until it becomes regular use or until problems have developed in later adolescence or early adulthood, any individual differences in drug response may have disappeared or be undetectable in the drug-tolerant person. Level of education is generally found to be inversely related to use of drugs, except alcohol, and dependence. It may be that educational achievement or even low educational aspirations are proxy variables for psychological risk factors for drug use, abuse, and dependence. One might ask, for example, if educational aspiration and achievement is related to sensation seeking or ability to postpone gratification; characteristics that some studies have shown convey a degree of risk for drug use, abuse, and dependence. However, there appears to be little to no research in this area.

A large number of empirical studies of nicotine dependence in the past decade have focused on the role of major depressive disorder. Since this disorder is more common in women than men, much of the work has focused on women. However, a history of major depressive disorder is associated with increased risk for nicotine dependence in both women and men. On the other hand, nicotine dependence increases the risk for initial episodes of major depressive disorder for both men and women. One factor that has been identified as a possible common basis for both nicotine dependence and major depressive disorder is high levels of neuroticism, which may itself be related to altered serotonergic neurotransmission. Thus, while recent work has increased our knowledge of both environmental and genetic risk factors, as well as their interaction, for substance use disorders, much remains to be discovered through future work.

SUGGESTED READING

American Psychiatric Association. (2000). *Diagnostic and Statistical Manual of Mental Disorders*, IV-TR ed. Author, Washington, DC.

Anda, R. F., Croft, J. B., Felitti, V. J., et al. (1999). Adverse childhood experiences and smoking during adolescence and adulthood. *Journal of the American Medical Association* **282**, 1652–1658.

Bown, S. A., Goldman, M. S., Inn, A., and Anderson, L. R. (1980). Expectations of reinforcement from alcohol: Their domain and relation to drinking patterns. *Journal of Consulting and Clinical Psychology* **48**, 419–426.

Breslau, N. (1995). Psychiatric comorbidity of smoking and nicotine dependence. *Behavior Genetics* **25**, 95–101.

Breslau, N., Kilbey, M. M., and Andreski, P. (1993). Nicotine dependence and major depression: New evidence from a prospective investigation. *Archives of General Psychiatry* **50**, 32–35.

Breslau, N., Kilbey, M. M., and Andreski, P. (1994). DSM-III-R nicotine dependence in young adults: Prevalence, correlates and associated psychiatric disorders. *Addiction* **89**, 743–754.

Cadoret, R. J., Riggings-Caspers, K., Yates, W. R., et al. (2000). Gender effects in gene-environment interactions in substance abuse. In *Gender and Its Effects on Psychopathology* (E. Frank, ed.), pp. 253–279. American Psychiatric Press, Washington, DC.

Chilcoat, H. D., Dishion, T. J., and Anthony, J. C. (1995). Parent monitoring and the incidence of drug sampling in urban elementary school children. *American Journal Epidemiology* **141**, 25–31.

Conger, K. J., Conger, R. D., Elder, G. H., et al., (1992). A family process model of economic hardship and adjustment of early adolescent boys. *Child Development* **63**, 526–541.

Chassin, L., Pillow, D. R., Curran, P. J., et al. (1993). Relation of parental alcoholism to early adolescent substance use: A test of three mediating mechanisms. *Journal Abnormal Psychology* **102**, 3–19.

Fergusson, D. M., Horwood, L. J., and Lynskey, M. T. (1996). Childhood sexual abuse and psychiatric disorder in young adulthood: II, Psychiatric outcomes of childhood sexual abuse. *Journal of the Academy of Child and Adolescent Psychiatry* **34**, 1365–1374.

Ge, X., Conger, R. D., Cadoret, R. J., et al. (1996). The developmental interface between nature and nuture: A mutual influence model of child antisocial behavior and parent behaviors. *Developmental Psychology* **32**, 574–589.

Gilbert, D. G. (1995). *Smoking: Individual Differences, Psychopathology, and Emotion*. Taylor & Francis, Washington, DC.

Hu, S., Brody, C. L., Fisher, C., *et al.* (2000). Interaction between the Serotonin transporter gene and neuroticism in cigarette smoking behavior. *Molecular Psychiatry* **5**, 181–188.

Johnson, J. G., Cohen, P., Pine, D. S., *et al.* (2000). Association between cigarette smoking and anxiety disorders during adolescence and early adulthood. *Journal of the American Medical Association* **284**, 2348–2351.

Kandel, D. B., and Chen, K. (2000). Extent of smoking and nicotine dependence in the United States: 1991–1993. *Nicotine and Tobacco Research* **2**, 263–274.

Kendler, K. S., Bulk, C. M., Spielberg, J., Hetaera, J. M., *et al.* (2000). Childhood sexual abuse and adult psychiatric and substance use disorders in women. *Archives of General Psychiatry* **57**, 953–959.

Lambert, N. M., and Hartsough, C. S. (1998). Prospective study of tobacco smoking and substance dependencies among samples of ADHD and non-ADHD participants. *Journal of Learning Disabilities* **31**, 533–544.

Lerman, C., Caporals, N. E., Adrian, J., *et al.* (2000). Interacting effects of the Serotonin transporter gene and neuroticism in smoking practices and nicotine dependence. *Molecular Psychiatry* **5**, 189–192.

Roberts, S. B., and Kendler, K. S. (1999). Neuroticism and self-esteem as indices of the vulnerability to major depression in women. *Psychological Medicine* **29**, 1101–1109.

Stacy, A. W., and Newcomb, M. D. (1999). Adolescent drug use and adult drug problems in women: Direct, interactive, and mediational effects. *Experimental and Clinical Psychopharmacology* **7**, 160–173.

Widiger, T. A., and Sankis, L. M. (2000). Adult psychopathology: Issues and controversies. *Annual Review of Psychology* **51**, 377–404.

Test Bias

Marcia C. Linn

Cathy Kessel

University of California, Berkeley

Glossary

Affirmative action Programs initiated to remedy past discrimination including discrimination based on use of biased tests. These programs include diligence in selection decisions, provision of specialized educational opportunities, and advice or coaching to individuals from groups that have suffered discrimination in the past. The latter are often social or cultural groups (e.g., women, girls, and racial, ethnic, or low-income groups).

Criterion-referenced test A test in which success or failure is determined according to standards concerning the content of the test rather than with reference to the scores of a given population, as do norm-referenced tests. In contrast with norm-referenced tests, the design and scoring of criterion-referenced tests allow the possibility that every test taker receives the highest possible score.

Educationally valid An educationally valid measure (1) is sensitive to the program for which it is used, (2) assesses test takers' abilities to monitor their own performances, and (3) promotes lifelong learning. Educationally valid measures draw on a mixture of performances. Their validity is determined by corroborating longitudinal studies rather than internal consistency.

High-stakes assessments Assessments that are traditionally used for decisions that have major conse-
quences for the test takers or for others involved with the test takers such as teachers, principals, or superintendents. Assessments are only high stakes if they result in important consequences for the participants. For example, university entrance examinations are often considered high-stakes assessments, but some universities do not use scores from these examinations in admissions decisions.

Norm-referenced test A test that is normed on representative test takers and periodically recalibrated in order to maintain a normal distribution of scores, in which half of the test takers receive scores that are below average.

Question or item context An item or question may have a setting intended to be independent of the ability to be assessed. The "cover stories" given by word problems in mathematics are a common example. These settings are known as item or question contexts.

Reliable measure A measure is reliable if it consistently yields the same score for the same individual independent of variation in time of day, context, or other irrelevant factors.

Social context The context involving other people in which most testing activities and interpretations occur. Social context is important because it often creates expectations and influences reactions in the test takers, scorers, and score users.

Standardized test A test that is administered under established conditions, scored consistently, and shown to yield reliable performance across time. Often, but not always, these tests use a multiple-choice format.

Stereotype threat Groups are sometimes stereotyped as lacking or deficient in particular abilities. A stereotype threat situation—for example, the announcement that an exam tends to show gender or race differences in average scores—triggers consciousness of that stereotype.

Test A collection of questions or tasks designed to measure abilities and skills. Testing professionals also include in this definition the stipulation that responses be scored and evaluated in a standardized way. Oral examinations are one example of an evaluative device that often does not satisfy the latter stipulation.

Test bias Tests are biased when irrelevant or systematic factors skew performance or scores for all or some of the test takers. Bias can result from numerous factors including the social context, question or item context, and setting of test administration.

University entrance examinations Tests such as the GRE, SAT, and ACT that are used in admissions decisions for undergraduate and graduate programs.

TEST BIAS occurs when individuals earn scores influenced by irrelevant factors and when test scores are used for invalid purposes. Biased scores can result when the social context, question or item context, or setting of a test impacts performance on the test but is not relevant to the construct that the test is intended to measure. For example, test questions intended to measure logic yet set in the context of baseball could be biased measures if they instead measured knowledge of baseball. Invalid use of a test occurs when the test does not align with the interpretation of the results. For example, to measure response to instruction in genetics a test of music appreciation would be biased. Establishing that a test is unbiased may require empirical investigations designed by the various stakeholders including such groups as instructional designers, classroom teachers, administrators, policy makers, and test designers.

I. Introduction

- "Don't ask me anything, I can't do science."
- "Don't believe my test score. I can't do tests. Look at my grades, my recommendations, or my science fair project."
- "How could I succeed on that test—it didn't measure anything that was taught in our school."
- "Our school spends more on testing than on curriculum. Instead of buying materials for science experiments, we buy more tests."
- "All the poor children failed—the test measures income, not achievement at our school."
- "I can't teach science with projects any more—there are too many topics to cover for the test."
- "Reading tests determine the school budget. I am not encouraged to teach science."
- "The tests give you the answers—all you have to do is select among the options; our students think memorizing is the best way to learn."

Individuals often question their own test scores, regularly explaining that a test does not accurately capture their true abilities, that their performance was unfairly influenced by external conditions, or that the test itself is a poor indicator of potential. Few argue that a test has underestimated their performance. For example, a growing proportion of individuals have been labeled learning disabled, dyslexic, or attention impaired to exempt them from typical testing constraints. At the same time, more and more people call for high-stakes tests to determine everything from individual student promotion, to teacher salaries, to statewide school budgets. Although teachers complain that tests are frequently insensitive to instructional innovation and poorly aligned with curriculum, policy makers rightfully argue that performance is too low and individuals are poorly prepared for today's workplace. Paradoxically, many complain that tests do not accurately measure their ability, saying "I'm a poor test taker" and "This test doesn't show what I can do," while still endorsing the use of tests for practically everyone else.

Historically, ability tests have added a dimension of objectivity to decisions that were often made behind closed doors and based on favoritism, patronage, or stereotype. Tests have played a positive role in increasing access of women to medical school, law school, and higher education. The United States was among the first countries to promote extensive public education. Standardized testing began in an attempt to monitor the quality of this education. Tests were also used to sort children by "aptitude" (measured by IQ tests) and "ability" (measured by achievement tests).

Increasing reliance on tests raises very complex issues about the systemic, organic, convoluted institution of education. The effectiveness and bias of a test depends on its role in the educational system. Performance on tests reflects at least the quality of instruction, the opportunity to learn, the validity of the test, and the context of assessment. Much rhetoric touts a "deficit model" to explain why one group, such as men or boys, outperforms another, such as women or girls, on any assessment. Followers of this model argue that unsuccessful groups lack a particular ability, skill, or capability that should either be remediated or accepted. An alternative explanation looks more carefully at tests and performance, stresses that there are "multiple paths" to success in a given area, checks to see if the instruction can improve performance of all students, and seeks to ensure that all students have the opportunity to learn.

A. EDUCATIONAL VALIDITY

Rather than focusing on tests irrespective of use, we consider what we call educationally valid uses of tests. Evaluating the bias of a test, or its educational validity, requires examining all the factors contributing to student success or to decisions about individuals and groups, rather than looking solely at the test. Thus, tests are only as valid as the uses to which they are put. Using a measure of height to determine presidential candidate success, for example, has historically proven to be accurate, but has no validity in terms of either instruction or prediction of success as a president. Tests that inadvertently draw, for example, on ability to compute baseball statistics might be valid for individuals in a culture where everybody follows baseball, but ineffective when individuals who lack this opportunity are included among test takers. Even the aspects of learning that tests measure may vary by social or cultural context. For example, Ann Gallagher studied students who received high SAT scores. She found that females often used more time-consuming school-taught techniques to answer SAT items while males tended to use short-cuts.

Today, increased enthusiasm for high-stakes tests in the United States has heightened the importance of making the uses of these tests educationally valid and of ensuring that programs designed to improve performance can succeed for the diverse learners in our schools. The eagerness of policy makers to use tests for high-stakes decisions including promotion, tracking, and graduation intensifies the importance of careful research and analysis of the impact of tests. Recent reports from the National Research Council on high-stakes testing reveal the complexities and difficulties of these issues. A particular concern has been the instructional sensitivity of tests and the effectiveness of programs for ameliorating difficulties revealed by tests. For example, longitudinal studies suggest that students from lower income families compared to students from higher income families are more negatively impacted by elementary school teach-to-test methods and more advantaged by developmentally appropriate programs.

Ideally, all tests would be concurrently designed with the programs they evaluate to ensure alignment between instruction and assessment. This means researching the alignment to ensure that tests are sensitive to variations in instruction and that students gain capabilities that will serve them well in the future. Programs that reward individuals, teachers, or schools for successful performance on tests need to demonstrate that improved instruction leads to improved performance both immediately and cumulatively. All too often, students are assessed on performances they have no opportunity to acquire or on dimensions that poorly predict future success.

The costs in lost opportunities and unintended consequences of denying promotion, censoring teachers, and discontinuing programs must be carefully analyzed. How can we decide whether students at a low-performing school should drill on basics or read rich, culturally sensitive accounts of individuals who have overcome unbelievable odds to succeed? What benefits arise from retaining middle school students in classes that have already failed them, especially when they drop out of school after 9th grade instead of 10th grade? Can we be sure that students assigned to remedial programs based on test scores will succeed, or must we conclude they cannot understand the topic—or cannot learn at all?

We must carefully weigh the strengths of the tests that we use for instructional, personnel, and admissions decisions and look at the tradeoffs between individual success and group progress. Many acknowledge this dilemma by calling for the use of multiple indicators, yet this is only a first step toward solving an extremely complex problem. We certainly need multiple indicators, but we also need to develop wisdom about their use. For example, multiple indicators can be misused, as Barbara Bergman, in her book *In Defense of Affirmative Action,* has pointed out. Selection committees get around affirmative action constraints by utilizing different indicators depending on which candidate they wish to remove from a pool. Individual candidates might be rejected piecemeal by the use of a particular criterion for each. However, the successful candidate could conceivably not satisfy all of these criteria. [See AFFIRMATIVE ACTION.]

B. TEST BIAS

Test bias results when indicators intended to improve the selection of individuals or the evaluation of programs are perturbed by irrelevant or inappropriate factors that result in flawed decisions. Such factors may occur in the design, administration, or use of a test. For example, the design of admissions tests may inadvertently advantage individuals who have grown up in a particular culture and be biased against members of other cultures. One famous example concerns a vocabulary item from the Scholastic Aptitude Test that required students to know the meaning of "regatta"—a term more likely to be encountered among upper-middle-class European Americans than other groups.

When tests determine the fate of programs intended to give students a head start or ameliorate injustices, bias in measurement may result in denial of services to those most in need of the treatment. For example, reading programs that teach students to use contextual cues cannot be properly evaluated by tests with items about the meanings of isolated words.

A poorly designed test may also fail to detect undesirable teaching methods. The "key word" approach for solving elementary mathematics word problems illustrates the point. In this instructional approach, students learn to translate words into operations. These students learn, for example, to perform subtraction when they encounter the word "left" in the problem statement. Such strategies may lead to short-term success on problems written following the rules, but they may fail when students compute the campaign expenses for "left-wing" causes. We invite the reader to create items that detect the flaws in the key word approach to solving word problems.

Tests may give factors indicative of success too much weight in decisions. For example, rapid computation may be a valuable mathematical skill, but college and graduate school admissions tests that reward only speed and accuracy in solving 25 to 35 problems in 30 minutes may neglect the sustained problem solving essential for long-term success in college and in careers. Consistent with this, studies have found that for a given college major, SAT scores tend to underpredict women's grades relative to those of men.

Tests may also mislead test takers about the capabilities and skills necessary for performing in settings like graduate school and the workplace. Tests can reinforce beliefs that success is dependent on a single inherent ability rather than comprised of an assortment of complex capabilities that can be learned as they are required. Complex tasks such as researching and writing a dissertation, administering a school, or running a medical practice require a broad range of skills and the ability to learn new technologies, policies, and whole fields such as electronic commerce. Recent research by Robert Sternberg and Howard Gardner on the constellation of abilities held by successful individuals underscores this view.

Often biased tests reinforce stereotypes about which groups can succeed in a given endeavor. College admissions tests in mathematics resonate with material in the popular press. Numerous slice-of-life advertisements, situation comedies, and even children's programming depict women as unable to balance checkbooks or do arithmetic. News accounts often reinforce these stereotypes and have even convinced some young women to avoid mathematics courses, in spite of the well-established finding that, on average, women earn higher grades in all mathematics courses. Blatant, subtle, and ubiquitous cultural expectations can have widespread impact on all—including test takers and test users.

Assessments that rely on a single indicator may inadvertently be biased against individuals who are capable of counteracting weaknesses and utilizing their array of talents effectively for achieving a goal. This is another reason for judicious use of a repertoire of indicators for educational and workplace decisions. Combining mathematics scores and mathematics grades, for example, helps to reduce bias in selection decisions. Understanding the biases of individual indicators and having a sense of the multiple paths that lead to success will help decision makers create repertoires of measures that at the same time encourage lifelong learning and more accurately predict success.

In summary, test bias refers to the systematic over- or underprediction of success in a given educational context. Bias arises when tests measure irrelevant, counterproductive, or unsystematic factors. The costs of test bias to individuals, programs, populations, and society as a whole can be substantial, devastating, and even life threatening (for example, consider the selection of medical school candidates or prospective engineers). Determining bias requires our understanding of the goals of education and the programs likely to promote success. We turn to a framework for educational validity and then analyze test design from this framework.

II. A Framework for Educational Validity

In a given instructional context, tests are educationally valid if they are consistent with the goals of instruction, assess learners' abilities to monitor their own performances, and promote lifelong learning. These tests draw on a mix of performances to tap the multiple paths to success, rather than relying on only the ideal or typical path. Their validity rests on longitudinal studies rather than solely on internal consistency.

Lifelong learning is of particular importance because today's learners face an uncertain future in which they are likely to change jobs and even fields regularly. The demands of the workplace ensure that individuals will need to learn how to use new technological tools like personal computers, master new communication skills such as video conferencing, understand new, complex issues such as genetic engineering or space exploration, and flexibly adapt to as yet unanticipated conditions.

Cognitive scientists have begun to characterize lifelong learning and to question prior assumptions that lifelong learning capabilities were rooted in the learning of subjects such as Latin or computer science. Research suggests that preparing individuals to master a new complex topic in depth requires that they experience mastering similar topics in depth, learn to conceptualize projects and identify useful resources, develop the ability to monitor and evaluate their own progress, and become adept at designing opportunities to learn from others when their progress falters.

Educational programs that promote lifelong learning engage students in sustained reasoning about a topic from their discipline while at the same time providing opportunities to learn contemporary skills such as searching for information on the Internet or negotiating with a health care provider. Individuals also need understanding of fundamental ideas that permeate our culture such as electronic communication, social justice, and environmental stewardship. Research shows that students gain this kind of understanding from courses and advanced programs that require extended projects, iterative refinement of solutions to complex problems, and negotiation about these solutions with others. Courses with projects, analysis of cases, and research investigations prepare students for handling complex problems in future programs and the workplace.

Designing tests to measure this kind of understanding means addressing a number of complex issues. Too often tests encourage superficial understanding rather than linked and connected ideas combined with the ability to guide one's own learning suggested by the goal of becoming a lifelong learner. Tests serve as a model for course activities and have the potential of reinforcing instruction. We need lifelong-learning assessments aligned with instruction that promotes lifelong learning. Recall and vocabulary tests not only fail to encourage lifelong learning, they frustrate teachers and students.

Marcia Linn and Sherry Hsi, in their book *Computers, Teachers, Peers—Science Learning Partners*, use case studies, classroom tests, and class projects to illustrate instruction for lifelong learning. Students in the semester-long Computer as Learning Partner course continue to build up their understanding of thermodynamics as they progress from middle school to high school. No such evidence of lifelong learning was shown by a comparison group in the traditional vocabulary-driven curriculum.

The performance of students from the Computer as Learning Partner curriculum in 12th grade demonstrates the importance of assessments that stress lifelong learning rather than requiring superficial multiple choice answers. In interviews asking about complex problems, students who initially seemed confused talked about the various alternative interpretations of a problem, compared several potential responses, and eventually created a coherent explanation based on multiple ideas. For example, Linn and Hsi described four students who attempted to explain a conundrum: Why do metal objects feel colder than wooden objects at room temperature but, when tested, measure the same temperature? In 10th grade one of these students relied on the result of the test and offered no explanation, saying they measure the same temperature. In 12th grade this student elaborated to explain the conundrum, gave a somewhat confused answer, but made some promising connections that bode well for future learning.

Using a traditional multiple choice test could mask this progress and might also reinforce superficial thinking. An essay asking for an explanation would award the 10th grade answer minimal credit and give the 12th grade answer a higher score because the student combined ideas and sought to resolve the conundrum. The multiple-choice approach could discourage lifelong learning and reinforce student reliance on memorization, while the essay question has the potential of encouraging coherent understanding. The essay question is more sensitive to instruction that promotes lifelong learning, while multiple-choice exams have a potential bias against lifelong learning.

Tests that seem to require superficial understanding of topics have the potential of reinforcing instructional programs emphasizing superficial knowledge. Teaching superficial understanding is clearly more straightforward than attempting to help students understand complex, nuanced, and uncertain phenomena. Many science texts, for example, pay no attention to current scientific controversies and instead emphasize "established" findings. Students respond to these texts by memorizing information about science. Under good instructional conditions, students remember the material they memorized at least until they take the test. However, research shows that this form of instruction results in rapid forgetting. As a result, U.S. students perform relatively poorly on national assessments and particularly poorly in areas where cumulative understanding is crucial.

The Third International Mathematics and Science Study (TIMSS) results for students in high school physics and calculus, for example, shocked leaders in science and mathematics by revealing that U.S. students were performing in the lower third of countries when only elite students were compared. These results suggest that somehow the U.S. educational system is failing to instill the cumulative understanding of these topics characteristic of instruction in other countries. Laudably, the TIMSS test included complex problem solving and short essays as well as multiple choice items. U.S. students performed poorly on all aspects of these topics, but were particularly disadvantaged in the more complex accomplishments.

A. BIAS IN DESIGN

Test designers often make seemingly innocuous decisions that result in biased scores for some test takers. For example, test designers often ask respondents to provide demographic information prior to starting the test. The most intriguing finding concerning the impact this may have comes from the psychological experiments of Claude Steele and his collaborators. Steele's research program demonstrates that simply reminding students that they belong to a cultural group stereotyped as unlikely to succeed on a high-stakes speeded, standardized assessment like the Graduate Record Examination (GRE) can dampen their performance on tests.

Steele has identified "stereotype threat" to explain why individuals aware that their cultural group is often less successful in a given endeavor are likely to perform less well. Several mechanisms have been put forth to account for this situation. Under one scenario, individuals reminded of stereotype threat become more anxious and perform less well due to debilitating anxiety. Under another model, individuals informed of stereotype threat lose motivation and try less hard because they assume the outcome of their effort. A third possible mechanism concerns playing it safe or taking fewer risks as a result of stereotype threat. Individuals choosing a safe approach might revert back to more algorithmic and less creative problem solutions or check their work extra times, thus perhaps performing less well on tests where efficiency and speed are rewarded.

Decisions about test format may advantage students with more experience, for example, in taking timed tests or using scoring sheets with bubbles. Redesign of the Graduate Record Examination as a computer-adaptive test revealed previously unstudied aspects of the test.

The computer adaptive version of the GRE revealed that many respondents were unable to finish the test, especially the analysis section, in the allotted amount of time. The computer administration allowed collection of response latencies by item and showed that for some items responses were given in less time than necessary to read the item. Previous work masked this finding because the paper-and-pencil version does not penalize test takers for guessing. Converting to a computer-adaptive format required reducing or eliminating guessing since the response to each item determines the difficulty of the next item administered. This meant that students responded to fewer items, increasing the possibility that the test would yield an unreliable score. In addition, the computer format was unfamiliar to some test takers, introducing another potential influence on performance.

In one well-publicized case, an individual received very different scores on the two versions of the test. Amy Cuddy took the computer version of the Graduate Record Examination in October 1998 and was surprised to receive scores considerably lower than her practice exam scores. She took the test again in paper-and-pencil format and her scores increased: on the analytic section of the exam, her scores for computer and paper-and-pencil formats were 300 and 690. Eventually, her lower scores were invalidated.

Research in the United States, Australia, and Europe shows that question format influences who succeeds. On average, women are more successful than men on essay questions and in large projects, and men are more successful than women on multiple-choice questions and, often, in oral exams. Caroline Gipps and Patricia Murphy demonstrate that British mathematics performance varies by test format. For example, females outperform males on advanced mathematics tests requiring projects but not on multiple-choice assessments.

Question context design decisions have been shown to advantage groups familiar with the content. Males tend to be advantaged by questions involving contexts typed as male: for example, in the SAT-V males are advantaged by reading comprehension questions concerning science articles. However, question context may play a more subtle role: for example, a study done by the Educational Testing Service found that females responding to a GRE-M item were advantaged if the item was set in a business context while males were advantaged if the item was set in a physics context (see Figure 1). Research on the GRE demonstrated that students, in general, have an advantage on reading comprehension questions in their broad major field.

B. BIAS IN SCORING

Scoring methods may incorporate biases. For example, when examinations are scored in an unstandardized way, the scorers' biases may prevail. Psychological experiments have established that raters assign different scores to identical performances on written work depending on the gender of the performer or supposed author of the work.

Research suggests that when scorers of complex accomplishments such as essays are aware of the gender of the authors, their scoring decisions are impacted. In general, knowledge that the author is a female results in a lower score than knowledge that the author is a male. This bias arises even when scorers are reading exactly the same response. Because females tend to outperform males on essay questions, this bias suggests that females may perform even more successfully than their scores reveal. This gender bias creates special problems in oral exams. For example, a female graduate student we will call Carole failed her oral qualifying examination because she did not answer enough questions in the time allotted. However, Carole was aware that a male student in her department also had not answered "enough" questions on his oral qualifying examination and was given additional time. She ap-

pealed the decision, and, after several months, the decision was overturned.

C. BIAS IN SCORE USE AND INTERPRETATION

Studies of entrance examinations like the SAT and GRE raise several concerns about score use. The SAT was designed for use in undergraduate admissions and validated by showing that it adequately predicts first-year college grades. The correlation of SAT score with overall undergraduate grades, however, varies considerably with college major. SAT scores tend to underpredict women's grades relative to those of men. The GRE is designed for use in graduate school admissions and has been validated by showing adequate correlations with first-year graduate school grades. The GRE scores of older graduate students, however, tend to underpredict their grades.

Individuals tend to interpret scores according to their preconceptions. Because mathematics is often viewed as a male domain, male success tends to be interpreted as due to ability and female success as due to effort. Researcher Meredith Kimball noted that this process occurred in reports from the Study for Mathematically Precocious Youth (SMPY). Students who volunteer to take the SAT-M in grades 7 and 8 and receive scores above a certain cutoff point qualify for SMPY. Among qualifiers there are a few girls, but the girls receive substantially higher grades in the SMPY program. Rather than question the selection process, SMPY researchers viewed SAT-M scores as determining mathematical ability and girls' higher grades as reflecting the girls' better "conduct and demeanor," rather than their mathematical ability.

D. DESIGNING THE SOCIAL CONTEXT

By defining educational validity in terms of lifelong learning, we emphasize the need for courses to promote substantial reasoning and instructions that provide feedback on progress. For males and females this may mean the social context of instruction may be as important a predictor of success as grades or admissions scores. Research suggests that some contexts are more productive for females than others. Mathematics faculty at colleges where women students predominate report, for example, that they counsel their most talented undergraduates to select from graduate programs where women have succeeded in the past. Graduate programs in mathematics vary dramatically with regard to the number of females that they admit, and even more dramatically with regard to the

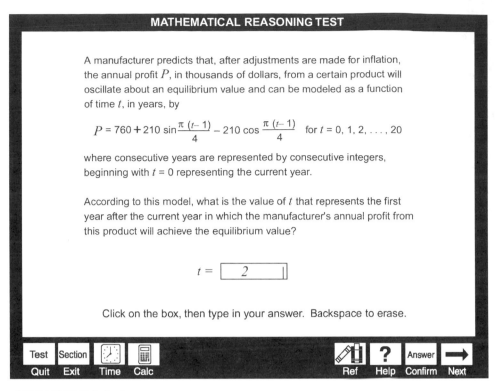

APPENDIX A.1

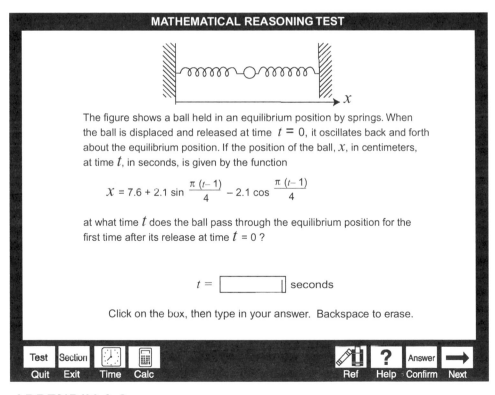

APPENDIX A.3

Figure 1 Two items that appear to assess the same ability. Reprinted by permission of Educational Testing Service, the copyright owner. All rights reserved.

likelihood that females will complete the mathematics program. Informed mathematics faculty from a number of all-female undergraduate institutions report encouraging their students to attend certain graduate programs and discouraging them from considering others. They frequently encourage their most talented undergraduates to contact alumnae in graduate school in order to get a sense of the social context for learning in different graduate programs. These counselors report excellent consistency between the program selected and the ultimate success of their graduates, finding this factor to be far more consequential than student performance during the undergraduate years.

Assessing the potential bias in tests associated with education raises special issues for gender equity as well as more general issues where gender equity is an interactive factor. As these examples suggest, attending to gender equity will enable more effective assessment of the educational validity of tests used in consequential decision making.

E. DESIGNING FOR LIFELONG LEARNING

Tests are proxies for more complex behaviors and predictions of future complex behaviors. Designing tests to measure lifelong learning that are valid and reliable, and lack unintended negative consequences, has proven difficult.

Concurrent design of instruction and assessment can increase alignment between what is taught and what is measured on tests. Today, alignment is frequently neglected. Some states and countries decree frameworks for instruction but leave testing and curriculum design open. In the United States, curriculum design and test design are often disconnected. This lack of linkage between instruction and assessment means that frequently students and teachers are held accountable on tests that have little connection to their textbooks and curriculum materials.

Often the problem is even more severe because the high-stakes tests suggest a form of teaching and learning incompatible with deep understanding and lifelong learning. For example, multiple-choice questions, which are inexpensively and easily scored, can take a scattershot approach to curriculum topics in order to have appeal to groups with diverse curricula, for example, different states with different curriculum frameworks. When teachers look at these tests they may alter instruction to eliminate emphasis on lifelong learning and focus instead on short-term and superficial understanding, including drill on vocabulary. Sim-

ilarly, students, expecting multiple choice tests, may choose a superficial approach to learning material that seems to be directly represented in the test. Even when test questions require more complex performances, research has shown that instructors can teach to the test in very specific ways, pointing out pitfalls in format and scoring that bypass the understanding the test is intended to measure. For example, in 1988 Alan Schoenfeld studied the classroom of a teacher who was very successful in having students pass the New York Regents Exam. Students focused on memorizing geometric constructions and drawing them accurately, rather than understanding connections between the constructions and proof.

Much recent research to create measures of complex understanding has investigated innovative test formats such as portfolio assessments, performance assessments, group assessments, and projects. Psychometricians analyzing these innovative formats have noted a number of threats to test reliability. Frequently, such formats concern a particular content area and either penalize students unfamiliar with that area or challenge those developing scoring methods to equate performances involving different topics. The problem is further compounded when individual scores are required for group projects and where conditions of work are rich and varied, meaning that some students may receive more assistance in performing the task than others. Tradeoffs between validity and reliability may result. Many see reliability as the more valuable goal and prefer tests that have high reliability because they fairly reproduce scores from one interval to another. Others see deep understanding of the topic as the highest goal and prefer tests that measure whether students have gained a kind of understanding necessary for lifelong learning.

This problem of varied item formats is confounded by the underlying factors that contribute to the reliability of multiple-choice tests. Researchers have shown that the similarity in performance from one test to another frequently relies far more on knowledge of vocabulary than understanding of the subject matter. Students with a more varied vocabulary may perform well on assessments in mathematics, science, social studies, and English, even though their actual grades and complex performances in these topics vary considerably. Reliance on high-stakes multiple-choice tests that are heavily influenced by vocabulary has motivated parents and representatives of dyslexic and learning-disabled students to complain that these tests unduly burden slow readers who may have less extensive vocabularies, but are fully capable of performing as well or better than their peers as long as the test measures their ability to solve a complex problem in the domain, rather than their ability to quickly define esoteric vocabulary words in a multiple-choice question.

The use of innovative formats and the assessment of complex understanding are further exacerbated by the likelihood that achieving deep understanding and the ability to engage in lifelong learning may occur along a number of different paths. One student may gain understanding by reading extensively, while another may gain it by conducting empirical tests and reflecting on the results, and still another student may learn by working in a collaborative group.

Designing assessments that honor these diverse paths to success while at the same time measuring the complex kinds of understanding necessary to become a lifelong learner requires research in classrooms. For example, in science learning, some students draw on technology concepts as well as literacy skills to read, interpret, and critique scientific information. Other students may find ways to achieve deep understanding of a topic without the associated technology or communication skills. Test designers need to pinpoint the relevant aspects of performance and tease out the irrelevant influences of question format and disciplinary focus to ensure that individuals who followed diverse paths to success are not penalized.

Many hope that tests, especially high-stakes tests, will drive educational reform. However, designing tests disconnected from opportunity to learn may neglect educationally valid accomplishments in favor of material that is difficult to learn. Biographies of successful entrepreneurs frequently point out that these individuals failed science classes and math classes, dropped out of school, and even today lack understanding of some of the topics that test developers consider essential. Ensuring that tests measure accomplishments we would like citizens to have and we know citizens can achieve is essential for achieving educational validity. Ultimately, tests should encourage students to develop capabilities that will serve them well in the future. Already the crowded curriculum in most disciplines discourages personal reflection and connections across topics. We need a more frugal curriculum and a more determined reliance on lifelong learning to prepare students for our uncertain future.

F. DESIGNING INSTRUCTIONALLY SENSITIVE TESTS

Ideally, concurrent design of assessment and instruction will result in continuous improvement of both the assessment and the instruction. This means that we will design curriculum materials that bend to the needs and demands of teachers and students, but do not break under alternative instructional conditions. It means designing assessments that provide valid and useful information for teachers and students that will allow them to make improvements in the instructional program or their own understanding.

Aligning instruction, assessment, and the social context of learning has the potential of adequately preparing lifelong learners but is difficult and costly in time and materials. Ideally programs of instruction will permit customization by teachers to the context of learning. Thus, if students are studying water quality, an ideal customization would be to tailor instruction to the specific water quality issues in their community. Similarly, if students are studying 18th-century literature, they might read works by authors from their geographical area that evoke the life and environment characteristic of their community in the past. Designing curriculum materials that are aligned with high-stakes assessments while, at the same time, are sensitive to differences in student backgrounds and student learning context remains an active area of research that has potentially great benefit for promoting lifelong learning.

Lifelong learning is best promoted if students have the opportunity to revisit the ideas that they learn in school after they complete their courses. There is never enough time in the curriculum to enable students to learn all the material they need to know. Rather, successful educational programs motivate students to continue to learn about a topic long after they have completed instruction.

Modifying the curriculum to emphasize contemporary issues in mathematics and science and to encourage learners to revisit their ideas has the potential of improving the lifelong learning outcomes of instruction. In order to align such a curriculum with valid tests, we need research programs that emphasize concurrent design of instruction and assessment. We need to identify successful ways to equate responses from students in different geographical areas who have experienced specific customizations of instruction.

In summary, assessment that promotes effective curriculum design and continuous refinement will enable teachers to use results to improve their curriculum and enable students to monitor their own progress. Such instruction will also incorporate generative and effective uses of modern technologies and valid aspects of language literacy. At the same time, these programs and assessments will be sensitive to the varied paths that students take to achieve lifelong learning and that offer mechanisms for assessing students who follow unique paths to success.

G. USING TEST FORMAT TO PROMOTE LEARNING

Concurrent design of instruction and assessment in the context of a particular school and classroom will enable teachers to contribute as much as possible to the success of their students. Ideally, assessment measures will require students to produce portfolios or engage in projects and thereby reinforce the kind of instruction most likely to lead to lifelong learning.

Some teachers not only teach to the content of a test, but also spend considerable time helping their students become familiar with test format. A large body of research demonstrates that students benefit from practice on tests because they have the opportunity to learn how to respond to new formats. An extreme implication of this finding arises when visitors to elementary school classrooms discover that teachers are devoting up to an hour a day to helping students learn how to "bubble in" responses on answer sheets. Research has clearly demonstrated the benefit of this kind of instruction, but it raises serious problems in regard to tradeoffs between logistic and intellectual activities in classrooms.

Conversely, when tests require essays, students' learning may benefit from practice with the test format. For example, regularly writing reflective essays about their books or investigations has the potential to promote students' understanding of the topic. This instruction can also instill standards of coherence and encourage lifelong interest in connecting ideas.

Several states are currently experimenting with the option for teachers to customize instruction to specific topics and to administer tests that are similarly customized. In Michigan, teachers can select one topic from a list for in-depth specialization. Students spend more time on this topic and the assessment for their performance emphasizes the topic proportionally.

III. Recommendations

Designing instruction, assessment, and opportunities for teachers and students to customize their learning so that these activities are aligned has considerable promise for reducing test bias and increasing educational validity. Because education is a complex and intricately connected field, such activities are inevitably complex. To achieve the desired forms of alignment it is clearly essential that teachers, administrators, and

innovators work in partnership, respect each other's expertise, and regularly refine educational programs. Building in methodologies for continuous improvement for both assessment and instruction will greatly enhance the effectiveness of new policies. It makes little sense to change tests and assume that students and teachers will suddenly develop the ability to respond to them, just as it makes little sense to assume that individuals can become lifelong learners by neglecting cumulative understanding.

A particular danger of increased reliance on high-stakes tests is that the deficit model of performance will be reified and reinforce stereotypic views of who can succeed in particular fields, endangering opportunities for all learners to achieve the ability to learn throughout their lives. By reinforcing such stereotypes, we discourage students viewed as having deficits from persisting. Identifying strategies that enable a more generative and productive view of disparities in performance across all groups inevitably will advantage everyone.

We have seen recently, as political groups promote legislation to end affirmative action, that many businesses and industries respond with advertising campaigns to retain these programs because they have found that by enhancing the diversity of their workforce, they also enhance the quality of their product. We are going one step further to suggest that we need to mend affirmative action in important ways, rather than ending it. We need to modify programs so they enable diverse individuals to participate in fields where they have been traditionally underrepresented without continuing to label these individuals as in need of remediation.

Lifelong learning involves a complex set of skills, concepts, capabilities, and content knowledge across varied fields. Inevitably, assessments are much narrower than the accomplishments that they are intended to measure. Unintended consequences of narrowing assessment need diligent attention, since they can lead to bias and to serious inequality of opportunity. Decisions about question format, question content, and the alignment of instruction with assessment have far-reaching impact for the opportunities of success among different groups. The complexity of the educational system makes it impossible to anticipate all the consequences of innovation and change in testing and instruction. Rather, what we need are mechanisms for monitoring these impacts and continuously improving all aspects of education.

Test bias is both a product and a concern of the whole system of education in any culture or nation. A test might be biased for one group and not for another. Tests that predict success for one group might not predict success for another. Educational programs may ameliorate weaknesses for one group but not for another. As a result, we need to look at the question of test bias by examining the full educational program.

At the same time, the recognition that test bias is a product of a complex system must not stymie us in our efforts to ensure equity and fairness for individuals. When individuals take advantage of the complexity of the educational system in order to promote the opportunities for some and demote the opportunities for others, serious consequences of a societal nature result. As this article has illustrated, for example, individuals might use a multitude of indicators to make decisions, yet apply one indicator for one group of individuals and another for a different group, in order to deselect those not desired in the final pool. Furthermore, a single indicator that advantages one group over another—for example, essay questions or multiple-choice questions—might be used to support a deficit model or reinforce stereotypes. Designing educational policies to take test bias into consideration and to make effective testing and prediction decisions requires a careful understanding and analysis of potential sources of bias, as well as willingness to cut through the complexity and look specifically at those factors likely to lead to the most effective solutions to educational problems.

Inevitably, policy makers and observers disagree when tests reveal inequalities. When particular groups fall behind, some argue this is because the educational system is failing them, and others argue that this is a natural and desired outcome for the group. Most commonly, both of these are somewhat true. However, unless we can ensure that particular groups are underrepresented for good reason, it is imperative that we demonstrate evidence that they are not underrepresented because of stereotype or bias.

ACKNOWLEDGMENTS

This material is based on research supported by the National Science Foundation under grant REC 98-73160 and REC 98-05420. Any opinions, findings, and conclusions or recommendations expressed in this publication are those of the authors and do not necessarily reflect the views of the National Science Foundation.

The authors appreciate the help and encouragement of the Science Controversies On-line: Partnerships in Education (SCOPE) and Web-based Integrated Science Environment (WISE) project research groups. Special thanks are due to Jacquie Madhok and Ann Shannon for extensive, detailed review.

Preparation of this manuscript was made possible with help from Lisa Safley, David Crowell, and Lisa Bigelow.

SUGGESTED READING

AAUW Educational Foundation Commission on Technology, Gender, and Teacher Education. (2000). *Tech-Savvy: Educating Girls in the New Computer Age.* American Association of University Women, Washington, DC.

American Educational Research Association, American Psychological Association, National Council on Measurement in Education. (1999). *Standards for Educational and Psychological Testing.* American Educational Research Association, Washington, DC.

Bergmann, B. R. (1996). *In Defense of Affirmative Action.* Basic Books, New York.

Bransford, J. D., Brown, A. L., and Cocking, R. R. (eds.) (1999). *How People Learn: Brain, Mind, Experience, and School.* National Academy Press, Washington, DC.

Caplan, P., Crawford, M., Hyde, J. S., and Richardson, J. T. E. (1997). *Gender Differences in Human Cognition.* Oxford University Press, New York.

Gould, S. J. (1981). *The Mismeasure of Man.* W. W. Norton & Company, New York.

Heubert, J. P., and Hauser, R. M. (eds.) (1999). *High Stakes: Testing for Tracking, Promotion, and Graduation.* National Academy Press, Washington, DC.

Linn, M. C., and Hsi, S. (2000). *Computers, Teachers, Peers: Science Learning Partners.* Erlbaum, Mahwah, NJ.

Linn, M. C., and Kessel, C. (1996). Success in Mathematics: Increasing Talent and Gender Diversity. In *Research in Collegiate Mathematics Education II* (A. Schoenfeld, E. Dubinsky, and J. Kaput, eds.), pp. 101–144. American Mathematical Society, Providence, RI.

Steele, C. (1997). A threat in the air: How stereotypes shape intellectual identity and performance. *American Psychologist* 52(6), 613–629.

Sternberg, R. (2000). The holey grail of general intelligence. *Science* 289, 399, 401.

U.S. Congress, Office of Technology Assessment. (1992). *Testing in American Schools: Asking the Right Questions,* OTA-SET-519. U.S. Government Printing Office, Washington, DC.

Valian, V. (1998). *Why So Slow? The Advancement of Women.* MIT Press, Cambridge, MA.

Willingham, W. W., and Cole, N. S., in collaboration with B. Bridgeman. (1997). *Gender and Fair Assessment.* Erlbaum, Mahwah, NJ.

Torture

Ken Pope
Norwalk, Connecticut

I. The Nature and Scope of Torture
II. Torture Directed at Women
III. Strategies to Accommodate, Accept, or Justify Torture
IV. Conclusion

Glossary

Amnesty International An organization of around 1 million members in more than 160 countries and territories working to promote the human rights that are set forth in the Universal Declaration of Human Rights.

Bell (*campana*) A method of torture leaving no external marks in which the person's head is placed within a pail or other metal container, which is then struck repeatedly, causing sudden loud sounds and reverberations.

Buzzer (*chicharra*) A method of torture in which the person is repeatedly shocked through wires or other conducting objects that are attached to parts of the body (e.g., ears, eyes, eyelids, genitals, gums, soles of feet).

Carry on A method of communal torture in which a group of guards use batons, pick handles, and other weapons to beat prisoners.

Chepuwal A method of torture in which the person's thighs are tightly bound with bamboo or similar materials.

Falanga A method of torture in which the soles of the feet are repeatedly struck with either hard (e.g., canes) or pliable (e.g., wires) objects.

Helicopter trip A method of torture in which the person is hung upright or upside down from one of the large blades of a ceiling fan and is struck repeatedly as the blade revolves.

Necklacing A method of torture in which a tire, filled with gasoline or similar flammable liquid, is placed around the person's neck and set afire; also, a method of psychological torture in which a landmine, grenade, or similar explosive is tied around the person's neck in a way that it is difficult or impossible to remove without detonation.

Telephone (*telefono*) A method of torture in which both ears are clapped or otherwise struck.

Torment of the sticks (*supplice de baguettes*) A method of torture in which two sticks are placed through a wire encircling the person's head and are slowly turned, tightening the wire.

Torture Intentionally inflicting severe physical or psychological pain or suffering.

TORTURE, although prohibited by international law and widely recognized as inhumane, is nevertheless relatively widespread. This article notes the most typical forms that torture can take, examines torture directed at women, and considers the cognitive and other strategies by which individuals, groups, and governments enable torture to be viewed as justified or even necessary.

Encyclopedia of Women and Gender, Volume Two

I. *The Nature and Scope of Torture*

In 1975 the United Nations (UN) General Assembly unanimously approved the "Declaration on the Protection of All Persons from Being Subjected to Torture and Other Cruel, Inhuman or Degrading Treatment or Punishment." Member nations agreed to eliminate torture. As Article 3 made clear, "No State may permit or tolerate torture or other cruel, inhuman or degrading treatment or punishment." The states assumed active responsibility to eliminate torture. Exceptional events, situations, or factors would not provide an exception to the prohibition against torture. Article 3 continued, "Exceptional circumstances such as a state of war or a threat of war, internal political instability or any other public emergency may not be invoked as a justification of torture or other cruel, inhuman or degrading treatment or punishment."

Member nations assumed the responsibility to take preventive measures to ensure that no one be allowed to engage in torture. Article 4 stated, "Each State shall in accordance with the provisions of this Declaration, take effective measures to prevent torture and other cruel, inhuman or degrading treatment or punishment from being practised within its jurisdiction." Previously, the UN had stated the principle on which member nations now committed themselves to act. Article 5 of the UN's 1948 "Universal Declaration of Human Rights" stated, "No one shall be subjected to torture or to cruel, inhuman or degrading treatment or punishment."

Yet as this article is written a quarter of a century later, torture is practiced in an astonishing array of countries. Amnesty International's (AI) *Report 2000* presents reports of instances involving security forces, police, or other state authorities in 132 countries. Although many studies focus on torture practiced by the police, military, and other branches of government, torture also can occur—especially when women and children are targeted—within families and other domestic contexts.

Torture is also practiced in an astonishing array of forms. Physical torture may involve beating, burning, cutting, starving, hanging (e.g., by the thumbs or feet), kicking, mutilating, forcing body parts into icy or boiling water, blinding, puncturing ear drums, removing body parts, applying acid or electric shocks, administering drugs or noxious materials, holding the person under water or otherwise preventing access to air, breaking bones, denying adequate shelter from extremely hot or cold weather, and so on. Some

methods have become so common that they are given their own names such as "bell," "buzzer," "carry on," "*chepuwa*," "*falanga*," "helicopter trip," "necklacing," and "telephone" (see the glossary).

Although all forms of physical torture are likely to have psychological aspects and consequences, some forms of torture are primarily psychological in nature. For example, people may be forced to watch family or friends being tortured, may be given false reports about the torture, death, or betrayal of loved ones, or may be told that they are about to be executed (sometimes followed by a fake execution, in which, e.g., an unloaded gun is held to the person's head and the trigger pulled). Victims of torture may be told that no one remembers them or cares, and that if they survive, no one will believe them. The psychological aspects of torture may range from the seeming inevitability of a fixed routine (e.g., the dread of interrogation and physical torture at set times each day) to an inability to anticipate what will happen next. Jacobo Timerman, editor and publisher of the Argentinean newspaper *La Opinion* until his arrest by the military, emphasized the agonizing unpredictability of his years in prison in his book *Prisoner Without a Name, Cell Without a Number*.

[W]henever someone was being prepared for transfer, his eyes blindfolded, his hands tied behind him, thrown on the ground in the back of a car and covered with a blanket, he would have preferred to remain in the clandestine prison. You never knew whether you were being led to an interrogation, torture, death, or another prison.

Some of the cruelest techniques of psychological torture are those that appear to make the person an active participant. The person may be told to choose which of two family members, friends, or other fellow prisoners should be tortured or put to death. The person may be directed to undress and use the torture devices on him- or herself. The person may be commanded to reveal the names or locations of individuals whom the torturers want to capture; failure to reveal the information will result in the torture and death of fellow prisoners. The person may be forced to participate actively in the torture of others. The person may be asked what form of torture he or she prefers, or where on his or her body the torture should begin, or which piece of the body the person can most easily do without. The person may be lead to make false and damaging statements in writing or while being videotaped.

The literature on torture tends to focus on adult victims, but children too serve as the targets of torture. In all areas of the world, children have been subjected to forms of physical, psychological, and sexual torture. AI has documented the prevalence of child torture and referred to it as "a hidden scandal" because it receives so little attention. For many groups and individuals engaging in torture, children may make especially inviting targets because of their relative lack of size and strength, their tendency—especially when very young—to be dependent on adult authority, and the belief that children are most likely to be dismissed as unreliable witnesses whose accounts of torture will not be believed.

II. Torture Directed at Women

A major shift in awareness over the past decade or two has been the growing recognition of the ways in which the torture directed at women has tended to be minimized or overlooked, especially in the area of sexual torture. Historically, rape and other acts of sexual violence that are primarily (though not exclusively) perpetrated by men and primarily (though not exclusively) directed at women have often been ignored (as extremely rare events, unworthy of book-length discussion), discounted (e.g., as of little importance or consequence), or dismissed (e.g., as false memories created by women who, by nature, secretly long to be raped). It is difficult to find any book devoted exclusively to the topic of rape prior to the 1970s. The 1970 edition of Wigmore's *Evidence in Trials at Common Law,* cited as the authoritative text in many court opinions, reveals the extent to which the law, the mental health professions, and society more generally believed that almost all charges of sexual violence reflected an inherent female tendency to make false accusations based on believed-in but imaginary memories of having been sexually abused. The text concludes that

No judge should ever let a sex offense go to the jury unless the female complainant's social history and mental makeup have been examined and testified to by a qualified physician. . . . The reason I think that rape in particular belongs in this category is one well known to psychologists, namely, that fantasies of being raped are exceedingly common in women, indeed one may almost say that they are probably universal.

The raping of prisoners of war, of people in police custody or jail, and of those who have been abducted or "disappeared" has often tended to be dismissed using rationales similar to those in the Wigmore text

on legal evidence. Even when it has been officially established and acknowledged that soldiers, the police, or other officials raped someone in their custody, it has, until relatively recently, tended to be viewed as a private matter. A landmark in the shift from this view was AI's 1991 publication of *Rape and Sexual Abuse: Torture and the Ill-Treatment of Women in Detention,* documenting the nature and scope of sexual violence inflicted on women held against their will. Of exceptional influence was AI's clear statement: "When a policeman or soldier rapes a woman in his custody, that rape is no longer an act of private violence, but an act of torture or ill-treatment for which the state bears responsibility." One year later the United Nation's Special Rapportur on Torture stated to the UN Commission on Human Rights that because "rape or other forms of sexual assault against women in detention were a particularly ignominious violation of the inherent dignity and the right to physical integrity of the human being, they accordingly constituted an act of torture."

This growing awareness of rape as a form of sexual torture has been met with a backlash. Police, military officers, and other security personnel in some countries now conduct what they term *virginity testing.* Women are taken into custody and either threatened with or administered a supposed test to determine whether they are virgins. The formal rationale—which has no validity—given for the test is that if it can be established that certain women are not virgins, the conclusion must be drawn that they are sexually active and therefore cannot reasonably claim to be raped while detained. In actuality, the "findings" from the test can be used to inflict suffering on women. If the test supposedly shows that women are not virgins, officials may threaten to make this information public. The loss of virginity may be viewed by many in the society as a loss of honor and of any prospects for marriage. In some societies ostracism and more severe penalties may be imposed by families, communities, and the state. However, if the test supposedly shows that women are virgins, officials may threaten to rape them. The awareness that any woman can be detained at any time and administered a virginity test can constitute an exceptional form of oppression, injustice, and intimidation. [*See* RAPE.]

Torture in the form of sexual violence is relatively widespread. In one study of refugees seeking help from a center for victims of torture, four out of five women and slightly over half of the men had been subjected to sexual torture. In addition to the pain, disfigurement, and psychological harm, the effects of sexual torture can, depending on the circumstances, include sexually transmitted diseases such as HIV, sexual dysfunction, conception, and infertility or sterility.

Women seeking asylum as refugees may face special risks and hardships. They may find themselves lacking food, clothing, shelter, or other resources (for themselves and in many cases for their children) and unfamiliar with the country's language, customs, and laws. These circumstances may make them exceptionally vulnerable to sexual demands (in exchange for survival) and attack. They may be rounded up and placed in detention centers as undocumented aliens, effectively prevented—regardless of national or international law—from making claims for political asylum. The detention center's leadership and staff, as well as the male detainees, may subject them to rape and other forms of sexual torture. They may encounter threats to harm their children if they attempt to resist rape, file a complaint, or inform anyone else.

Current United States law requires those petitioning for asylum to demonstrate that to return home would subject them to persecution because of at least one of five factors: membership in a social group, nationality, political opinion, race, or religion. What constitutes a social group facing persecution in various countries has been the focus of much litigation and constant evolution. In 1994, gays and lesbians were first recognized as meeting this criterion, as were members of certain clans (e.g., Somalis). As this article is written, the U.S. Justice Department submitted a proposal that battered wives and other victims of domestic violence be considered a "social group" under this law.

Fauziya Kasinga brought about a landmark change in U.S. immigration law. When she was young and growing up in Togo, her father resisted the custom of female genital mutilation (FGM), and protected her from it. After he passed away, the family entered into an agreement that Fauziya Kasinga be married. One of the conditions was that she undergo FGM. Right before the operation, while those who had come to perform the operation were meeting in the kitchen, she escaped with the aid of her mother and sister. She fled to the United States but was held in custody for two years as an undocumented alien and subjected to severe conditions.

Various groups, such as Equality Now and Amnesty International USA, worked to help gain both her freedom and her safety from being forced to return to Togo. Her petition for asylum was rejected. Others, however, helped bring an appeal. In a ruling with far-reaching implications, the Board of Immigration Appeals, U.S. Department of Justice, decided in her favor on June 13, 1996. It held

The applicant has a well-founded fear of persecution in the form of FGM if returned to Togo. The persecution she fears is on account of her membership in a particular social group consisting of young women of the Tchamba-Kunsuntu Tribe who have not had FGM, as practiced by that tribe, and who oppose the practice. . . . [W]e grant her asylum.

Although both men and women may be tortured, targeted, or threatened because of their words or acts (e.g., speaking out against a repressive regime or trying to rescue those who are being tortured), women may also be harmed or endangered because of the words or acts of their husbands, male blood relatives, or other relationships. They may be tortured as a reprisal for what their brothers, husbands, or other male associates have done, or to intimidate the men into silence and inaction. In order to force a male suspect to confess to crimes or provide information, torturers may rape and otherwise torture his wife, sister, or other female relatives while he watches. However, when these women flee to other countries and petition for political asylum, they may be turned away because they themselves are not—or are not viewed as—politically active or targeted for their own political stances.

Women who have experienced torture or threats of torture may—because of strong cultural and other factors—find it virtually impossible to speak of these matters to anyone else, particularly in a formal setting. Asked if they have been raped or subjected to other sexual torture, they may find themselves unable to speak aloud about such matters. Many women will not disclose their experiences of torture with a male interviewer, even if the interviewer is empathetic, well trained, and conducting the interview in the context of providing medical, clinical, or other services. Many will not disclose their experiences of torture, especially sexual torture, while in the presence of family members, whether male or female. Many will not testify in public about such matters, even if it means they will be returned to the country from which they have just fled and face almost certain death. In summary, the growing recognition of the diverse ways that women are targeted for torture and that the torturing of women has tended to be denied or discounted has been accompanied by an increasing awareness of the many risks and costs—some of them fatal—to women seeking asylum from or speaking out about their experience of torture.

III. *Strategies to Accommodate, Accept, or Justify Torture*

The prohibitions against torture, the extent to which torture is currently inflicted on so many, and torture's heinous nature, including the special ways that women are targeted lead, when considered together, to a particularly difficult but pressing set of questions. How do we as human beings allow torture to occur in our midst? How is such a cruel and inhumane activity that has been so widely condemned allowed to persist? How do the citizens of a state accommodate themselves to the presence of torture within the state? How do we—as individuals, groups, governments, and cultures—come to accept and even support it? How do we justify its occurrence?

The extensive literature in this area has attempted to identify some factors that help answer these questions. The most common strategies of accommodation, acceptance, or justification include relying on state authority and formal orders, using abstraction and other linguistic transformations, dehumanizing victims, sanctioning revenge, preventing destruction, making the torturer the victim, obtaining essential information, denying relationship or responsibility, and denying the existence of torture. A brief discussion of each follows.

A. TORTURE LEGITIMIZED BY THE STATE AND FORMAL ORDERS

The citizens of a state, including those who engage in torture, may claim that the state is the source of legitimacy and whatever procedures the state initiates must by definition be considered legitimate. In authoritarian states, the ruler's authority may seem to bestow its own inherent legitimacy. Citizens who engage in torture ordered by the state may argue that their role is to act in obedience to and on behalf of the state, regardless of their personal views. Citizens who are not direct participants in the torture may argue that such matters are none of their business, that they are not expected to understand or even be aware of state procedures and rationales. For all citizens in authoritarian states, questioning the authority of the state may be viewed as contrary to the interests of the state and the role of the citizen. In many authoritarian states, questioning the state's authority may be punished severely, sometimes by execution without trial.

In democratic states, on the other hand, the fundamental principle may be seen as "government by law," conferring legitimacy to the actions the law requires or permits. Individuals may be expected to conform their actions to a law, however much they may disagree with it. They may work to change a law viewed as wrong or unjust but, pending that change, may be expected to obey. Within this narrow framework (which does not embrace civil disobedience or other ways of challenging laws believed to be unjust), citizens may believe that no one is "above the law," that no one can simply pick and chose which laws to obey and which to ignore. Those acting under legal authority as members of the state or local police, of the military, of the government's internal or external intelligence or security forces, and so on may argue that their role is to follow orders from their legally appointed supervisors. Combat soldiers, for example, may point out that a normal part of their work involves inflicting wounds or death on enemy soldiers and that they are in no position to question assignments that they find repugnant.

The claim that a state's authority, laws, or orders can legitimize torture focused the world's attention during the Nuremberg and similar trials after World War II. Those who participated in the inhumane medical experiments and other forms of torture that were a part of the Nazi atrocities defended their acts by saying that they were just doing what the state required them to do. They were "just following orders." The war crimes courts, however, held that this was not a valid defense for engaging in torture and other war crimes.

After the rulings of the war crimes courts following World War II, other organizations began to emphasize explicitly that individuals could not evade responsibility for inflicting or condoning torture and that torture itself could not be legitimized through "orders." *The Convention against Torture and Other Cruel, Inhuman, or Degrading Treatment or Punishment,* for example, stated clearly: "An order from a superior officer or a public authority may not be invoked as a justification of torture."

B. ABSTRACTION AND OTHER LINGUISTIC TRANSFORMATIONS

The horrors of torture can be obscured by achieving a sufficient level of abstraction, euphemism, and other forms of linguistic transformation. Repeatedly in the Nuremberg trials, the most heinous forms of torture carried out by Nazi doctors, concentration camp guards, soldiers, and others were characterized dismissively by the defendants as "medical matters." Institutions in which those with views unacceptable to the state are tortured until they renounce the views and pledge loyalty to the state may be termed "Education Camps" or "Re-education Academies." Inflicting pain, disfigurement, and ultimately death in order to obtain information may go by such names as "depth interrogation," "directed probing," or "motivated debriefing." Many of the names for torture that are listed in the glossary fail to communicate any of the horrors involved, some of them sounding almost like children's games. Analyzing in 1946 the ways that language can hide or blur atrocities, George Orwell provided the following examples:

Defenceless villages are bombarded from the air, the inhabitants driven out into the countryside, the cattle machine-gunned, the huts set on fire with incendiary bullets; this is called pacification. *Millions of peasants are robbed of their farms and sent trudging along the road with no more than they can carry; this is called* transfer of population *or* rectification of frontiers.

C. "THEY DON'T COUNT"

Governmental leaders, torturers, and the other citizens may justify torture by regarding those who are being tortured as of little importance. Racial, ethnic, national, religious, gender-related, and other stereotypes, labels, and slurs are used to characterize those targeted for torture. The torture victims are categorized as inferior, inhuman, unnecessary, unwanted, and "different" in ways that preclude recognition of their humanity and right to humane treatment. Just as the prior strategy used abstraction to create the illusion that torture was not torture, the "They Don't Count" strategy creates the illusion that the people targeted for torture are not actually people but rather genetic or cultural "trash," of no inherent importance.

The system of laws may echo this strategy. Certain groups of citizens within a country may receive less protection under the law, making them more vulnerable to torture. Even when a country accords full rights to all citizens, the law may not affirm those rights for those who are not citizens (e.g., refugees).

Similarly, those charged with enforcing the law may treat some within a country as if they do not count. The police and the courts may provide differential treatment to members of certain groups. Whatever ideal the system of laws has set forth to protect individuals from torture, the day-to-day practice of law enforcement may create conditions in which torture is allowed or even encouraged for members of certain groups that fall below the law's protection.

D. "THEY DESERVE IT BECAUSE OF WHAT THEY HAVE DONE"

Certain acts may cause such destruction, pain, and outrage that torture is set forth as the only fitting punishment. Justice is possible, according to this view, only when those who have caused great suffering are made to endure great suffering. Torture is seen as righteous and well-deserved revenge.

In some instances, this is portrayed as an "eye for an eye" philosophy. If someone has gouged out another's eye, then that person's own eye must be gouged out. If someone has crushed the hand of another, then that person's own hand must be crushed. If someone has caused the slow, agonizing death of another, the perpetrator must suffer a slow, agonizing death.

The torture may target those who, while causing no harm themselves, had some direct relationship to those who originally caused harm. If terrorists inflicted pain and abuse on the children of others, their own children may be tortured as a consequence.

The torture may also extend to those who, having caused no harm themselves, had some indirect relationship to those who caused harm. If soldiers massacred civilians, those acting on behalf of the massacred civilians might torture other soldiers from the same army, citizens of the country from which the soldiers came, or, depending on the circumstances, virtually anyone matching the soldiers' race, ethnicity, religion, and so on.

Those condoning torture in this way may sometimes perform a sort of moral calculus, weighing what is being done by each side. They may acknowledge engaging in torture in the context of the following claim: "Yes, we have had to resort to extreme methods, but what the other side has done is much worse and what we are doing is as nothing compared to what they continue to do." The weighing may also focus on the temporal sequence of events: "Yes, we acted, but only after they initiated the atrocities. *They* started it!"

E. "THEY ARE THREATS"

Under this justification, torture is appropriate not because of what people have done but because of what they will, might, or can do. Certain citizens may be seen as internal threats, putting at risk the safety and stability of the state. Various foreign individuals or groups may be seen as external threats, able and willing to inflict severe damage on the country and its citizens. Some may be identified as terrorists whose capabilities are unknown but whose intentions—either stated explicitly by the group itself or inferred by others—is to inflict maximum destruction, distress, and destabilization. One of the goals of such groups is often to provoke, through rhetoric and behavior, an overreaction by the country it is attacking. The country under such attack may suspend civil liberties and violate citizen's rights, engage in preemptive atrocities such as torture, and create martyrs.

Those who accommodate, accept, or justify torture on the basis that the victims constitute threats often claim that the horrendous nature of torture may not only deter those who are tortured but also frighten other people who are threats to the state. Under this rationale, it matters little whether the victims of torture were correctly identified as threats: They stand as vivid examples of what can happen to anyone who is perceived as a threat. The more reckless, impulsive, and almost arbitrary the torturers are in choosing victims, the greater the intimidation. People may avoid any speech or behavior that might, rightly or wrongly, lead to being tortured.

F. SWITCHING ROLES: TORTURER AS VICTIM

One of the most creative strategies is switching roles. Torturers portray themselves and are portrayed by those who accommodate, accept, or justify the torture as the actual victims and as legitimate objects of sympathy for what they have suffered. One of the most famous claims to this status was made by Adolf Eichman during his trial in the early 1960s. A Nazi leader, Eichman had served as chief of the Gestapo's Jewish Office and as SS lieutenant-colonel. He was subsequently convicted of crimes against humanity and crimes against the Jewish people, and executed. During his trial, Eichman testified: "I am not the monster I am made out to be. I am the victim."

Torturers are only one of many groups of those who are more powerful and who victimize others and yet may be seen by themselves and others as victims. Male therapists who sexually abuse their female clients often claim to have been victimized. Adults, particularly men, who sexually attack children, particularly girls, often attribute the power, the knowledge, and the responsibility to the child while

portraying themselves as virtually helpless. In some instances, the courts have accepted this justification. One judge discounted a man's responsibility for sexually assaulting a five-year-old girl, holding that the girl, whom the judge described as "an unusually sexually promiscuous young lady," was responsible because she allegedly initiated the sexual contact. Another judge declined to confine a man who had pleaded no contest to sexually assaulting a young girl, holding that the man had been victimized by her "provocative clothing." The provocative clothing in this case consisted of blue jeans, a blouse over a turtleneck sweater, and tennis shoes. The judge held that the man was helpless because rape is a "normal" reaction to such "provocative clothing." Yet another judge refused to convict two adult defendants of raping an eight-year-old girl because of the judge's opinion that she was "a willing participant." [*See* CHILD ABUSE.]

In what sense may torturers be viewed as victims? Many emphasize the horrific nature of what they do. In order to torture others, they themselves must inflict and witness intense human suffering. Many emphasize the guilt they must endure. Many talk of being victimized by those whom they tortured: those whom they tortured provoked the torture, caused the torture, bear responsibility for the torture, left the torturer no alternatives. Often they will speak of being victims of fate or circumstances, led helplessly by events to the role they played. Sometimes they will speak of being victimized by their leaders, colleagues, family, and friends, who convinced them that using torture was the right thing to do. All such constructions portray torturers as the relatively helpless victims of external forces beyond their control.

G. "WE MUST HAVE THE INFORMATION THEY HAVE"

One of the most common rationales for engaging in torture is to obtain information that supposedly could not be gathered by other means. Assume hypothetically that a small group of terrorists has stolen documents providing the identities and locations of every undercover agent—as well as of the agents' families—working for the country, the launch codes for all weapons including those with nuclear warheads, or other information likely to be put to use promptly to kill many people. Assume that the authorities have a week or less to prevent mass casualties. One of the terrorists is captured, but refuses to talk. Some may argue that torturing the terrorist to obtain the information to save lives is not only permissible but a moral necessity. Torturers and those who condone their methods in these circumstances see a stark choice of conflicting rights: either recognize the individual's right to avoid torture, thus seeming to ensure the impending deaths of hundreds, thousands, or more, or engage in physical and psychological torture to save lives.

If the impending loss of a great many lives outweighs an individual's right to be free of torture, the justification of torture may apply to a wide variety of individuals. If the terrorist in the previous scenario is to be tortured to yield the information quickly (within a week), it seems impossible to allow adequate preparation for a criminal trial, the trial itself, the possibility of appeals, and so forth. Therefore, torture may be inflicted on someone who is a suspect. In a crisis, law enforcement, the military, or counterterrorist intelligence groups may identify a number of suspects. If the suspected terrorist is not yet in custody, would torturing his or her child, parent, spouse or partner, close friends, or neighbors yield information about the suspect's current location, habits, resources, or other information to help enable capture? Would torturing those who have been a member of, affiliated with, or supportive of the terrorist group yield information to identify the terrorists? In each case those supporting torture may claim that subjecting an individual to a relatively brief experience of torture may be necessary for a greater good: preventing the loss of a great many lives.

H. "THIS IS NO CONCERN OF MINE"

Those who are aware of torture may come to accept its presence in their community or state by viewing it as something that is none of their business. In many cases it is as if they compartmentalized their awareness and placed the phenomenon of torture in a compartment to which they pay virtually no attention, habituating to it so that they no longer notice it. For some, this process of attention directed away from torture seems to occur quickly and with little or no effort. The process itself seems to happen out of their awareness. For others, it seems a much more active process in which the person must consciously push the thoughts of torture out of consciousness again and again.

Reminders that torture is occurring may be inescapable. Some people may hear screams from a building in their neighborhood or from the darkened streets at night. They may see neighbors and others with signs of burning, cutting, and other mutilations. They may hear reports of torture. But somehow it is viewed as none of their concern, as something that has no reality, importance, or implications for their own lives. It is not something to devote time, thought, or action to. It is an unrelated aspect of life.

There are also many who recognize the reality of torture in their community or state but accommodate themselves to it—take no action—and become passive bystanders. The tendency of bystanders to do nothing in the face of even the most horrendous acts as they are suffered by others became a focus of research after the slow murder of Catherine Genovese in New York City on the morning of March 13, 1964. As she was returning home from work, she began walking from her car to her apartment building. A man began chasing her, caught her, and began stabbing her. She screamed. The lights began to go on in the windows of the buildings on each side of the street. The man ran but then, when nothing happened, returned to her and began stabbing her again. His attack continued and it took 45 minutes for her to die. Thirty-eight people watched this happen from their windows. Not one went outside to help. Not one called the police. No one took any action to stop the attack, to help her, or to summon aid.

One ironic finding of the subsequent research is that the *more* people who are present, the *less* likely any of them are to take action to help. When more people are present, each individual may feel less responsible for taking action. There may be less sense of personal responsibility because it is easier to assume that, with so many people present, someone else is likely to respond or has more information about the situation, more knowledge about what to do, or more resources and ability. When there are others around who can act in such situations, it may seem better to refrain from "becoming involved." Not acting may seem easier and safer. The responsibility may seem to lie with others or—in a blurred and diffuse way—with the group as a whole, but not with the individual.

I. "THIS IS A LIE, AN EXAGGERATION, OR A MISTAKE"

One of the bluntest ways that people can accommodate torture in their midst is to deny that it exists, usually by dismissing any signs, reports, or evidence of torture as lies, exaggerations, or mistakes. The reality of torture may be so overwhelming that individuals act quickly to convince themselves that it is not, would not, could not be occurring in their midst. If they can accept the premise that the torture is not occurring, then there is no need to confront the reality of torture, no need to seek additional information and take action. They face neither the fears and risks of acting to stop the torture nor the shame and guilt of doing nothing to stop the infliction of pain and suffering on their fellow human beings. They are free to go about their lives as if the torture were not happening for they have convinced themselves that the torture is *not* happening.

Although many people seem to engage in forms of this denial on their own, those who order and inflict torture may foster this approach. They may flatly, vigorously, and convincingly state that no torture is occurring. They may spread false information and manufacture bogus evidence to support their claims. They may provide arguments and evidence that anyone who reports torture is lying, exaggerating, or mistaken.

The arsenal that torturers and their immediate supporters have to discredit reports and evidence of torture is impressive. Imagine a country that subjects countless citizens to torture. What evidence can there be that the torture is actually occurring? There may be people who report that it is occurring but reports may be dismissed as lies, exaggerations, or mistakes. There may be claims by those who say they have been tortured, but such claims, if they are not characterized as intentional lies, may be dismissed as sincerely believed false memories. If those claiming to have been tortured show scars and mutilation, such visible signs of torture may be dismissed as self-inflicted or the result of an accident. There may be eye-witness accounts from disinterested parties, but there is extensive research that has been used to dismiss eye-witness testimony as unreliable, subject to a variety of perceptual and cognitive errors, postevent influences, and other distorting factors undermining its validity. There may be confessions from those who ordered or carried out the torture, but there is also an extensive literature on the potential invalidity of confessions based on an array of such factors as coercion, suggestion, the dynamics of interrogation, psychological needs for attention or punishment, and so on. There may be photographs or videotapes or torture sessions, perhaps taken by hidden cameras, but such images can be dismissed as fakes (i.e., the popular movies *Jurassic Park* and *The Lost World*, with their seemingly realistic images of dinosaurs, are *not* evidence that such creatures currently roam the earth). There may be sworn testimony but testimony can be dismissed as perjured or sincerely believed but based on false memories; if the testimony appears in a court transcript or other document, the document itself can be dismissed as fake or significantly altered, not representing the actual testimony.

If only a few raise the issue of torture, they can be dismissed as a small band of troubled people or trouble makers. Their motivation can be subjected to rumor and innuendo: they are out for profit, for fame, for revenge. They are enemies of the state, lacking in patriotism and loyalty, seeking to harm their country by spreading false accounts of torture. If many are raising the issue of torture, they can be dismissed as victims of mass hysteria, suggestible people who have been intentionally mislead or caught up in the contagion of a rumor. They may be dismissed as a danger to the state, evil people out on a witch-hunt.

A variant of this strategy is to concede that there may actually have been one or more instances of torture but that it has been greatly exaggerated. It was not nearly as extreme nor as widespread as claimed. It was not authorized but carried out only by one or two officials, soldiers, or others who were acting on their own. It was simply an isolated incident, an anomalous event that has been dealt with and is unlikely to happen again. Further, whatever torture may have happened, happened in the past. It is over, it is history. To bring it up now is to wallow in the past, ignoring the pressing concerns of the present.

IV. Conclusion

Understanding and preventing torture requires countering effectively the strategies of acceptance, accommodation, and justification. But the strategies may carry special appeal in the context of inertia, noninvolvement, and the costs of recognizing torture's realities. Harvard psychiatrist Judith Herman wrote:

It is very tempting to take the side of the perpetrator. All the perpetrator asks is that the bystander do nothing. He appeals to the universal desire to see, hear, and speak no evil. The victim, on the contrary, asks the bystander to share the burden of pain. The victim demands action, engagement, and remembering.

It may be exceptionally difficult to acknowledge not only many people's willingness and ability to inflict horrendous physical and psychological torture on fellow human beings but also torture victims' personal experiences of being cut, burned, beaten, drugged, mutilated, and the other forms of suffering to which people are subjected on a daily basis. Perhaps one way to alter the context in which the strategies of acceptance, accommodation, and justification carry a special appeal may be to ensure it includes a focus on two questions: What are we doing to understand and prevent torture and help its victims? If we are not doing all we can, why?

SUGGESTED READING

Abstracts and Articles: Therapy Research and Therapist Resources Web site at http://kspope.com

Amnesty International Online Web site at http://www.amnesty.org

Amnesty International USA Web site at http://www.amnesty-usa.org

Center for Victims of Torture Web site at http://www.cvt.org

Conroy, J. (2000). *Unspeakable Acts, Ordinary People: The Dynamics of torture.* Knopf, New York.

Duner, B. (1998). *An End to Torture: Strategies for Its Eradication.* Zed, London.

Innes, B. (ed.) (1998). *History of Torture.* St. Martin's Press, New York.

International Human Rights Instruments Web site at http://www.unhchr.ch/html/intlinst.htm

Pope, K. S., and Garcia-Peltoniemi, R. (1990). Responding to victims of torture: Clinical issues, professional responsibilities, and useful resources. *Professional Psychology: Research and Practice* **22**, 269–276.

Trauma across Diverse Settings

Janis Sanchez-Hucles

Patrick Hudgins

Old Dominion University and The Virginia Consortium Program in Clinical Psychology

Glossary

Child abuse and maltreatment Physical or mental injury, negligent treatment, or maltreatment of a child by a person responsible for the child's welfare.

Child sexual abuse Sexual activities with a child that can damage, harm, or threaten the child's welfare.

Disaster A severe disruption that overtaxes a community's capacity to cope.

Rape Nonconsensual sexual penetration obtained by threat of harm or physical force or when the victim is unable to give consent.

Sexual harassment Unwanted, deliberate, and repeated comments, gestures, and physical contacts of a sexual nature.

Spousal or partner abuse Violence or assaultive behavior in the context of an intimate, sexual, and usually cohabiting relationship.

Torture Any mental or physical act that involves the intentional infliction of severe pain or suffering with the purpose of securing information or a confession, punishing an individual for suspected or actual behavior, or intimidating an individual or a third party.

A TRAUMA is a possible result when an individual experiences, witnesses, or is confronted with an event or events that involve actual or threatened death or serious injury or a threat to the physical integrity of the self and others and the person responds with intense fear, helplessness, or horror. Although it was once commonly believed that traumatic events were rare, it is now clear that 70% of women experience a traumatic event across the diverse settings of their lives. Although trauma affects both women and men, there is a significant gender component to trauma due to patriarchal structures, and women are more likely than men to be exposed to trauma that is sustained, repeated, and more damaging in type and severity. The sociopolitical forces that have subordinated women historically continue to pose difficulties in allowing women to validate and recognize the trauma they suffer in accepted diagnostic classifications. As women gain more power in society, they have been able to expand the classification systems and definitions of trauma to be more representative of women's lives. Progress is being made in adopting holistic approaches to examining the trauma in the lives of women that avoid revictimizing and blaming victims and that strive to minimize and decrease the impact of trauma in all its varied forms.

I. Introduction

It is ironic that the term "trauma" is used very commonly but actually has a complex history and myriad meanings. It was once thought that traumatic events rarely happened and were experienced by only a few individuals. Susan Solomon and Jonathan Davidson, in a 1997 review of prevalence studies on trauma, reported that from 60 to 74% of individuals in the United States report at least one traumatic event in their lives. Approximately 70% of women experience at least one traumatic event, and from a third to a half of individuals who experience one trauma will experience another. With a greater recognition of how widespread trauma actually is, the American Psychiatric Association (APA) in its *Diagnostic and Statistical Manuel of Mental Disorders IV* (*DSM*) defines trauma as a possible result when an individual experiences, witnesses, or is confronted with an event or events that involve actual or threatened death or serious injury or a threat to the physical integrity of the self and others and the person responds with intense fear, helplessness, or horror.

The work of Solomon and Davidson indicates that the most common traumatic events include witnessing someone who is badly injured or killed; experiencing a fire, flood, hurricane or other natural disaster; and being involved in a life-threatening accident. The next most frequently occurring type of trauma are life-threatening events, such as robbery, or the sudden death or injury to a close friend or relative. The least common but perhaps the most devastating events are molestation, physical attack, rape, combat, and physical abuse. Men are more prone to experience combat trauma, physical attacks, being threatened with a weapon, or kidnapped. Women

are most likely to be exposed to rape, sexual molestation, and neglect and physical abuse in childhood.

Although trauma affects both men and women, there is a significant gender component to trauma. Patriarchal social structures have supported the legal subordination of females in the wider society and in the home. As a result, males have been given implicit if not explicit support to control women through intimidation, threats, physical beatings, and rape and sexual violence. It is not accidental that a traditional sign of domination in war is to use the rape of women as a form of aggression and power indicating victory over other men.

Increasingly there is a wider recognition that perhaps the higher rates of women seeking medical and mental health services are related to the traumas associated with gender. Studies have shown that almost half of women in psychiatric hospitals were exposed to physical or sexual abuse. Women are more likely than men to endure sustained abuse, and while men react to abuse with aggression, women are more likely to evidence self-destructive behaviors like mutilation or suicidal attempts. It appears that women are disproportionately exposed to forms of trauma that are more damaging in type and severity.

Youth also are exposed to various types of trauma. They are exposed to sexual and physical maltreatment as well as individual and community violence. Erwin Parson, in a 1997 study, reported on several national studies in the United States that revealed that 23% of high school students were the victims of gun violence, 42% had witnessed a shooting or a stabbing, and 22% had seen a person killed.

When trauma is applied to events that are deemed to be "acts of nature" such as volcanoes or hurricanes, there has long been a consensus that affected individuals may demonstrate physical or psychological effects that may be serious and long lasting. In contrast, public opinion has been slow to agree on what comprises trauma with respect to acts of harm by humans toward each other. Events are not deemed traumatic until political movements legitimize the use of this term.

It was not until a questioning of the legitimacy of wars and combat developed that the term "post-traumatic stress disorder" was applied to individuals' exposure to war and its aftereffects. The feminist movement created a sociopolitical environment that labeled the long-existing sexual, physical, emotional, and psychological abuse of women and children as trauma. Currently, many individuals believe that concepts of trauma need to be expanded to include the effects of racism, sexism, classism, homophobia, disability, religious persecution, and secondary trauma, which occurs after witnessing, aiding, or simply being exposed to those who have experienced trauma first hand.

It is difficult to expand conceptions of trauma because the individuals with the most power to inflict trauma on others are also the gatekeepers to control and influence those who develop the criteria and definitions for what should be considered traumatic. As a result, women and people of color have had to fight long and hard to force recognition of the trauma in their lives.

Individuals who experience trauma need to have their realities validated. Society, however, often retraumatizes victims in its attempts to minimize, distort, deny, or dismiss these realities in order to avoid dealing with horrific events and having to acknowledge the culpability of victimizers. As a result, it is only when persistent public opinion supports those in society who are devalued as victims that new definitions of trauma are developed.

This article reviews the historical origins of trauma and current classification issues. An overview of various types of trauma will be conducted using the 1993 classification system of the International Federation of Red Cross and Red Crescent Societies (IFRC). Most diagnostic categories discuss trauma as being either due to natural or human-made disasters. The IFRC classification system organizes trauma victims into (1) victims of natural and industrial disasters; (2) war veterans, victims of terrorism, and refugeeism; and (3) victims of violence, rape, and sexual assault. Newer conceptions of trauma will also be explored that include secondary trauma, complex trauma, and trauma related to race, ethnicity, sexual orientation, religion, and ability status.

II. History of Trauma

Historical and literary references to trauma have existed for more than 4000 years. It was not until 1980 however that the American Psychiatric Association introduced the category of posttraumatic stress disorder (PTSD). This category was designed to systematize conceptual understandings and symptoms of the survivors of traumatic and catastrophic stress.

In summarizing the history of the concept of trauma, trauma expert and feminist psychiatrist Judith Herman has identified three significant eras.

These periods related to applying the concept of trauma to "hysterical" women in the latter part of the 19th century, to individuals who suffered from shell shock or combat neurosis from the first World War through the Vietnam War, and finally to the victims of sexual and domestic violence in the latter part of the 20th century.

A. THE TRAUMA OF "HYSTERICAL" WOMEN

French neurologist Jean-Martin Charcot investigated the disorder of hysteria, which had been long believed to be a strange disease that affected women and consisted of a wide range of physical and psychological symptoms such as paralysis, sensory loss, convulsions, and amnesia. Many of the women that Charcot studied had been exposed to violence, exploitation, and rape, but prior to his legitimizing the study of hysteria, these women were seen as malingerers and not worthy of serious attention and medical treatment. It was Pierre Janet, Joseph Breuer, and Sigmund Freud who concluded that the cause of the extreme emotional reactions and dissociation seen in hysteria was due to psychological trauma. It was theorized that the somatic symptoms of hysteria represented attempts to forget memories of extremely distressing events. Therapists noticed that hysterical symptoms could be alleviated if traumatic memories and feelings could be recovered and put into words. This discovery provided the stimulus to a "talking cure," otherwise known as psychoanalysis.

Freud initially believed that major causes of hysteria in women were early experiences of sexual assault, abuse, and incest. Freud repudiated this connection between hysteria and sexual abuse when he realized that if he were correct in his original theory, given the large numbers of women suffering from hysteria, there must have been widespread abuse of these women not just in the lower socioeconomic classes but also in the middle and upper echelons. He and his colleagues found the possibility that perverted acts against children could be so widespread to be unacceptable and beyond credibility. As a consequence, interest in connecting trauma to the violence and abuse of women and children was eradicated until almost a century later.

B. WAR TRAUMA

The study of hysterical symptoms reemerged with World War I. There were widespread reports of military personnel in combat showing symptoms of crying, screaming, muteness, unresponsivity, amnesia, dissociation, and mental breakdown. Initially the origin of these symptoms was believed to be physical and due to nervous exhaustion caused by the concussive effects of exploding weaponry. Hence, this disorder was first called "shell shock." With the recognition that individuals showed shell shock symptoms even when not exposed to combat, military personnel concluded that the emotional distress of sustained exposure to the violence of war was due to psychological trauma. This syndrome of "combat neurosis" produced symptoms in men that looked very similar to the symptoms of hysteria that had previously been documented in women. Although initially it was believed that men who succumbed to the traumatic stress of war were cowardly, malingerers, or somehow inferior, it was eventually determined that combat neurosis was a legitimate psychiatric disorder that could occur in even the best of soldiers.

Treatment of war trauma was often minimized and it was believed that removing a person with symptoms for a week would then allow the person to return to combat without any significant harm. However, the organized protests of Vietnam veterans made the medical and mental health community acknowledge that the effects of war trauma could be pervasive and long term and required significant and sustained treatment interventions.

C. TRAUMA IN THE LIVES OF WOMEN AND CHILDREN

With the recognition and acceptance of the trauma of war for men in the 1970s, the women's liberation movement created the climate that allowed professionals and the public to understand that the most common posttraumatic disorders occur in women as a result of sexual abuse and domestic violence. Research by sociologist Diane Russell documented an incidence rate in women of one in four having been raped and one in three having been the victim of sexual abuse as a child. Ann Burgess and Lynda Holmstrom described a pattern of psychological reactions that they called "rape trauma syndrome" in 1972. They highlighted the fact that rape was not a crime of sex but was a life-threatening event of power and control in which females were fearful of death and mutilation. The aftereffects for rape survivors included symptoms of insomnia, nausea, hypervigilance and startle responses, nightmares, and dissociative disorders and numbness that were similar to the responses of veterans of combat.

Susan Brownmiller's groundbreaking work on rape asserted that rape has historically been used by men as a weapon of intimidation that allows men to keep women in a state of fear. This public debate on rape allowed a deeper exploration of the violence toward women in society and resulted in the recognition of rape in marriage, acquaintance rape, and date rape as well as domestic violence involving women (termed "battered women syndrome" by Lenore Walker) or children ("battered child syndrome"), sexual harassment, sexual abuse, and incest. Herman noted that the symptoms of incest survivors that she interviewed were essentially the same as those observed in women in the late 19th century who were diagnosed with hysteria due to sexual abuse and incest.

III. *Posttraumatic Stress Disorder*

Although research by Solomon and Davis had indicated that approximately 70% of individuals in the United States have sustained some type of traumatic event, only about a quarter of these individuals develop all the symptoms of the PTSD diagnosis with rape correlated with the highest rates of PTSD. Hence, it is important to understand that trauma exposure is a necessary but not sufficient criterion for producing PTSD.

A. DIAGNOSTIC CRITERIA

In 1952 the American Psychiatric Association published its first *Diagnostic and Statistical Manual*. Under the category of transient situational personality disorders was a category named "gross stress reaction," which referred to acute reactions to unusual stress as a result of combat or some civilian catastrophe. It was believed that symptoms of stress would recede as the trauma abated. Any longer-term symptoms or disturbance were attributed to preexisting and long-term psychopathology. [*See* DIAGNOSIS OF PSYCHOLOGICAL DISORDERS.]

In 1968, *DSM-II* was released containing the category of "adjustment reaction of adult life" and listing three examples including a woman going through an unwanted pregnancy, a frightened soldier in combat, and a prisoner facing execution in a death penalty case. In retrospect, theorists have wondered why these examples are so simplistic and inadequate in illuminating the array of trauma, the effects on psychological functioning both immediately and over time, and the accompanying clinical features. It is not clear why an unwanted pregnancy was listed without also including the trauma of infertility or a miscarriage. Many scholars also found it remarkable that the *DSM-II* ignored the impact of such traumatic events as the Korean, Middle Eastern, and Vietnam Wars, civil violence in Northern Ireland and England, major natural disasters, and a growing recognition of the high prevalence of childhood, sexual, and domestic violence.

In the 1980 *DSM-III*, a separate diagnostic category was created among the anxiety disorders and was titled "posttraumatic stress disorder" (PTSD). PTSD was classified among the anxiety disorders because it was believed that trauma produced anxiety, emotional distress, and disequilibrium. It is interesting to note that finally in this version of the *DSM* there is a recognition that trauma can have system wide impact on emotional expressiveness, cognition, motivation, interpersonal relationships, and physiological functioning. *DSM-III* also addressed important symptomatology missing in previous versions, such as dissociative processing and flashbacks, and the acknowledgment was made that the primary diagnostic criteria was the existence of a stressor that would likely evoke significant symptoms of distress in almost anyone.

With this new diagnostic category of PTSD, the argument was made that PTSD is a normal reaction to abnormally stressful events. It was also asserted that many of the symptoms of trauma are expectable, normal, and predictable. Psychopathology is not apparent unless symptoms persist and interfere with the adaptive functioning of individuals and both environmental and preexisting individual factors mediate the severity and chronicity of PTSD symptom expression.

In discussing the history of PTSD, John Wilson has summarized the impact of this initially controversial term. First, this classification clearly indicates that after the injury of trauma, some individuals may show difficulty in their usual way of functioning and show specific reaction patterns and symptoms. Many medical and legal scholars were initially resistant to recognizing PTSD as a category distinct from other diagnoses. But additional research into this area has actually helped to validate and legitimize those exposed to trauma and to lead to better diagnoses and treatment. Because PTSD became a distinct diagnostic classification, it could then be used in legal deliberations involving compensation and disability payments and could be presented as a legal defense. Finally, the greater attention paid to trauma and its

consequences and antecedents has led to more refinement in understanding the complexity of diverse types of trauma, new diagnoses, and additional research and collaboration that resulted in more expanded versions of PTSD.

DSM-III-R in 1987 used research and clinical work to revise the criteria for PTSD. An attempt was made to clarify the language, meaning, and specificity of trauma reactions. The total number of diagnostic symptoms was increased to 17, and individuals had to demonstrate evidence of the following symptoms that could not have been present before the trauma: avoidance, numbing reactions, and physiological arousal. These symptoms had to last for at least a month and the stressors that triggered trauma reactions were deemed to be external events that were outside of the range of usual experiences but that would be distressing to almost everyone. It was believed that the stressors that produced PTSD were generally extreme and that the more severe and life threatening a trauma was, the higher the possibility that PTSD would result.

As research on PTSD has proliferated, it became increasingly clear that the *DSM-III* and *DSM-III-R*'s characterization of traumatic events as "outside the range of usual human experience" was not accurate. Epidemiological studies and clinical practice confirmed repeatedly that, unfortunately, exposure to trauma and possible PTSD development is *not* uncommon. As a consequence, the 1994 *DSM-IV* has eliminated the idea that a traumatic stressor is deemed outside the range of usual human experience.

The *DSM-IV* has six criteria that must be met for a diagnosis of PTSD. Criterion A requires that an individual has been exposed to a traumatic event in which the person experienced, witnessed, or was confronted with an event involving actual or threatened death or serious injury, or a threat to the physical integrity of self or others. Bonnie Green has grouped eight generic types of trauma:

1. Threat to life and limb
2. Severe physical harm or injury
3. Receipt of intentional injury/harm
4. Exposure to the grotesque
5. Violent/sudden death of a loved one
6. Witnessing or learning of violence to a loved one
7. Learning of exposure to a noxious agent
8. Causing death or severe harm to another

In addition to experiencing one of the above-mentioned types of trauma, the individual's response must show intense fear, helplessness, or horror or, in the case of children, disorganized or agitated behavior. This second component of the first criterion introduces a new and subjective element to what a specific individual finds traumatic.

There has been considerable debate with respect to how to determine when some of the common challenges of daily life such as relationship endings, serious illness, failure, or rejection become traumatic events. Individuals differ in their threshold for and appraisal of trauma. Some individuals appear well insulated and others are more prone to develop clinical symptoms following exposure to trauma. Historical, psychological, social, political, and ethnocultural factors may therefore mediate an emotional response to a stressor. Many feminists have also expressed concern over the fact that in *DSM-IV*, there is a greater emphasis on threat and life threatening trauma, which minimizes the trauma of events such as date rape.

The second criterion represents the hallmark signs of trauma by focusing on the characteristic intrusive memories. Criterion B requires that the traumatic event is reexperienced in one or more of the following manners: (1) recurrent and intrusive distressing recollections such as images, thoughts, perceptions or repetitive play in children; (2) recurrent distressing dreams; (3) acting or feeling as if the traumatic events were recurring including illusions, hallucinations, disassociation, flashbacks, or (in children) reenactment; (4) intense distress at exposure to internal or external cues that symbolize or resemble some aspect of the traumatic event; or (5) physiological reactivity on exposure to cues that symbolize or resemble an aspect of the traumatic event. These intrusive symptoms are often the first to fade in PTSD.

Symptoms of avoidance and numbing constitute criterion C. These symptoms demonstrate the emotional, behavioral, and cognitive tactics that individuals use to minimize their exposure or the intensity of their responses to stimuli that trigger trauma. Individuals may use behavioral strategies to avoid situations in which they risk being exposed to any cues that remind them of their trauma. At its most extreme form, individuals may appear to be agoraphobic, that is, afraid to leave the safety of home lest they are exposed to a reminder of their trauma.

In the numbing side of this criterion, individuals attempt to distance themselves from overwhelming emotions related to the trauma by separating the affective elements from the cognitive and only focusing on the cognitive. This process has been termed psychic numbing and is also linked to disassociative

and amnesic responses to trauma. Theorists have noted that psychic numbing has been observed in survivors of bomb attacks and in combat veterans. This splitting of emotions from thoughts also makes it challenging for individuals with PTSD to have effective interpersonal relationships.

Panic and anxiety symptoms characterize criterion D, which hallmarks signs of physiological hyperarousal and includes anxiety, panic, hypervigilance, and startle responses. In some cases, startle, anxiety, and panic responses may lead an individual to appear to be highly paranoid. The symptoms of avoidance and hyperarousal are among the most longlasting symptoms of PTSD.

Criterion E specifies that PTSD symptoms must persist for at least one month. If the symptoms persist for less than three months, the PTSD episode is considered acute; if they last for longer than three months, the PTSD episode is deemed chronic. It is also important to note that PTSD does not have to appear within a certain time span following an exposure to trauma. In some situations, individuals do not show symptoms for months or years following a traumatic event. Finally, criterion F posits that PTSD must cause clinically significant distress or impairment in social, occupational, or other areas of functioning.

A third diagnostic category for stress in *DSM-IV* is partial PTSD. This is an abbreviated version of PTSD whereby individuals must meet criterion A with respect to a stressor and criterion E by showing symptoms for at least one month; the individual only has to show five rather than the six symptoms for PTSD in criteria B, C, and D. [*See* Anxiety; Posttraumatic Stress Disorder.]

IV. Additional Stress and Trauma Diagnoses

Individuals present with a variety of posttraumatic reactions. Some of these syndromes have been categorized as part of the *DSM-IV* disorders, while other reactions do not yet conform to existing diagnoses. Certainly, the concept of trauma is broader than the PTSD syndrome. Clinicians and researchers have long recognized that individuals exposed to trauma may self-medicate with alcohol or drugs. In addition, affective disorders, anxiety disorders, eating disorders, dissociative disorders, somatoform disorders, conversion disorders, features of the borderline personality, and psychotic behaviors have all been related to trauma.

Because people suffer in such idiosyncratic ways from exposure to trauma, it is important to recognize the validity of posttraumatic responses that may not fit neatly into a *DSM* diagnosis. In fact, some theorists believe that problems with the reliability of PTSD diagnoses argue for the use of terms such as trauma "symptoms" or "reactions" rather than rigid use of the term "diagnoses." The following section explores some of the additional trauma and stress syndromes and diagnoses.

An acute stress disorder (ASD) involves the development of characteristic anxiety, disassociation, and other symptoms that occur within one month after an extreme traumatic stressor. The symptoms must last at least two days but must not exceed four weeks. This disorder is similar to PTSD but it lasts for a briefer period and typically involves more disassociation. Prominent features include psychic numbing and detachment, depersonalization, derealization, difficulties in cognitive processing, and physiological hyperarousal. ASD often serves as a precursor to a diagnosis of PTSD. Although it is normal to show physical and psychological responses to stress, the severity of some individual's reactions and the impairment to social and occupational functioning has led to the inclusion of this category.

Brief psychotic disorder with marked stressors (BPDMS) refers to a disorder characterized by psychoses triggered by a precipitating trauma. The event is similar to PTSD or ASD, but it initiates a vivid and abrupt breakdown. This diagnosis requires that at least one of the following four symptoms are present, although in many cases there are multiple symptoms: delusions, hallucinations, disorganized speech, and grossly disorganized or catatonic behavior. Individuals with this diagnosis also typically show extreme agitation, emotional distress, and confusion. Symptoms last from one day to less than one month, and if they persist, schizophreniform disorder, mood disorder with psychotic features, or some other chronic psychotic condition may be diagnosed. [*See* STRESS AND COPING.]

V. Disorders Associated with Traumatic Experiences

Trauma may also lead individuals to demonstrate symptomatology that is consistent with other *DSM-IV* diagnostic categories. These disorders include dissociative disorders, conversion disorders, somatization disorders, and borderline personality disorder.

The dissociative disorders are believed to result from some trauma-inducing event. The symptoms of these disorders function to reduce physical and psychological responses to high levels of stress and/or conflict. Dissociative disorders help individuals to minimize conscious awareness of memories, feelings, thoughts, actions, and associations with a traumatic event. *DSM-IV* identifies dissociative disorders as representing a disruption in the usually integrated functions of consciousness, memory, identity, or perception of the environment. Some of the trauma that have been related to dissociative disorders include child, physical, and sexual abuse, combat, torture, imprisonment, and natural disasters. Amnesia, fugue, identity disorder, depersonalization, and dissociative disorder not otherwise specified comprise this category. [*See* RECOVERED MEMORIES.]

In dissociative amnesia, individuals are unable to recall important personal information following exposure to a trauma or stressor. This disorder has been specifically linked with combat stress, internment in concentration camps, sexual and physical assaults and rapes.

Dissociative fugue involves sudden and unexpected travel away from a home location with a corresponding inability to recall all or some of the past. This diagnosis often is linked to individuals exposed to war and natural disasters that have produced disruption and dislocation.

Dissociative identity disorder was previously known as multiple personality disorder and is regarded to be the most colorful and controversial dissociative disorder. Characteristic of this diagnosis is the presence of two or more distinct identities that periodically take control of the person's behavior and that cause memory lapses that are too extensive to be considered ordinary forgetfulness. This disorder has been highly associated with severe childhood sexual, ritualistic, or physical abuse, witnessing a murder, or the death or loss of a loved one.

In depersonalization disorder, individuals report feelings of detachment and estrangement from one's self, feeling unreal, a sense of distortion about one's body parts, lack of control over the body, and sensory anesthesia. Because of these frightening symptoms, panic and anxiety are often present as well. This disorder has been related to life-threatening dangers such as accidents, natural disasters, being taken hostage, and the death of a child.

The last category under dissociative disorders is dissociative disorder not otherwise specified. This diagnosis is used when there is evidence of some dissociative symptoms, but the pattern does not correspond to any of the aforementioned categories. This category is often used because exposure to trauma causes a broad variety of reactions that do not always fit *DSM* diagnoses.

Conversion disorders are believed to result from a major stressor or extreme psychological conflict. Typical stressors that can precipitate a conversion disorder include combat, the death of a loved one, or child abuse. The symptoms of this disorder include a malfunction in the voluntary motor or sensory system and include seizures, paralysis, blindness, deafness, anesthesia, inability to speak, and hallucinations. What is striking is that these symptoms do not appear to be related to any physical cause and in fact do not conform to the typical medical understandings of these disorders with respect to etiology and course. It is believed that these symptoms are triggered by trauma or stress and serve a psychological function for the individual.

Similarly, somatization disorders consist of a broad array of exaggerated physical symptoms that cannot be related to an organic cause. Symptoms include headaches, backaches, nausea, vomiting, sexual dysfunction, paralysis, and amnesia. Somatization disorders have been found to develop following the traumas of childhood maltreatment, sexual abuse, war, disasters, and assault. Both conversion and somatization disorders may function to allow individuals to communicate their hurt and distress following a trauma in which they believe that more direct communications would be harmful, invalidated, or otherwise unacceptable.

According to *DSM-IV*, borderline personality disorder reflects a pervasive pattern of instability in interpersonal relationships, self-image, and affect, and marked impulsivity beginning by adulthood and apparent in a variety of contexts. Individuals with this diagnosis fear abandonment; they also express intense and unstable relationships, problems with a stable sense of identity, impulsivity in sex, substance abuse, reckless driving or binge eating, recurrent suicidal and or self-mutilating behaviors, affective instability, chronic feelings of emptiness, inappropriate and intense anger, and transient paranoid or dissociative ideology. Research has shown relationships between childhood traumas, such as severe childhood sexual or physical abuse and neglect, and the development of borderline personality disorder in adulthood.

It is important to note that many feminist scholars have recognized that all too often, women who have experienced different forms of trauma such as abuse are presented with a *DSM* diagnosis like borderline personality disorder that pathologizes the individual rather than the trauma. It is essential that therapists be aware that symptoms of substance abuse, eating disorders, somatic complaints and even psychotic disorders may indicate that individual is reacting to some type of trauma. The focus must remain on supporting and understanding the origin of symptoms rather than on distancing and blaming women for the trauma that they have sustained.

A. TYPE I AND II TRAUMA

In 1991, Lenore Terr made a distinction between short-term Type I trauma and prolonged Type II traumatic events. Type I traumas are typically unexpected, short term, and include sudden, devastating events of a limited duration with a better prognosis than is found in Type II events. Examples include natural disasters, car accidents, and a rape. In contrast, Type II traumas tend to involve repeated or chronic exposure to stressors such as long-term incest or abuse. The trauma is so severe, repetitive, or long lasting that it takes a greater toll on the individual and engenders dissociation, detachment, and emotional and interpersonal difficulties. Individuals in this Type II category have a poorer prognosis than do individuals experiencing Type I trauma.

B. COMPLEX PTSD AND DESNOS

Although not formally recognized as a part of *DSM-IV*, complex PTSD, as proposed by Herman in 1992, has generated a great deal of interest and investigation. This diagnosis has also been called disorders of extreme stress not otherwise specified (DESNOS). DESNOS and complex PTSD refer to Type II trauma disorders and arise from severe, prolonged, and repeated trauma that is typically of an interpersonal nature. Herman and other theorists and clinicians have recognized that much of the trauma that women in particular must contend with is sustained and repetitive.

Both Lenore Walker and Laura Brown directed attention to the repetitive nature of the abuse of women when they developed the term "abuse and oppression artifact disorder." This term reflects the ongoing nature of abuse and distinguishes abuse from interpersonal agents such as partners, strangers, and acquaintances versus cultural and environmental stressors that increase the risk of abuse like racism or homophobia. Examples can include torture, captivity in a concentration camp or as a prisoner of war, extended child abuse, chronic spouse abuse, and exposure to cumulative and sustained discrimination based on race, gender, ethnicity, sexual orientation, disability, and religion.

What is very significant in complex PTSD is the recognition that many individuals suffer repeated trauma rather than exposure to a single catastrophic event. Bessel van der Kolk has renamed this category "disorders of extreme stress" (DES) and investigated this diagnosis with clinical populations. Van der Kolk, like Herman and others, believed that the PTSD diagnosis did not adequately explain the effects of repeated and sustained trauma. Based on the findings of clinical trials, Van der Kolk has combined PTSD and DES into a DES scale that is a supplement to PTSD diagnoses. The DES scale entails disregulation of affective arousal, dissociation and amnesia, somatization, disruption in perception of self and others, and alteration in symptoms of meaning.

C. INSIDIOUS TRAUMA

Maria Root has used another term that is analogous to complex PTSD and DES that she calls "insidious trauma." Insidious trauma also is used to describe repetitive and cumulative experiences of trauma. These acts are aimed at individuals who are considered disempowered on some dimension in society and are perpetrated by those with power and resources. Insidious trauma includes repeated acts of violence, oppression, genocide, and femicide.

Insidious trauma shapes the reality of those who experience trauma such that they are compelled to pass on to other possible victims stories about what they have experienced. As a result, the original victims of this trauma as well as those who hear about it can become reactive, sensitive, or avoidant of situations that might lead to trauma.

Insidious trauma leads individuals to discard any theories about how life works in fair ways for all individuals. Ronnie Janoff-Bulman believes that what is often shattered for victims of trauma are their assumptions that the world is benevolent, events are meaningful, and the self is positive and worthy. Janoff-Bulman has asserted that most individuals believe that events make sense and follow predictable social laws.

Theorists have pointed out that those persons who repeatedly experience bias and discrimination do not enjoy the luxury of believing in a benevolent world. Many individuals come to believe that oppression can flourish, their rights are not protected, they are not in control of their safety, and their lives have less

value than the lives of other individuals. Insidious trauma provides a useful framework for understanding the long-term consequences of many types of institutionalized racism, oppression, and bias. The "driving while Black or Brown" syndrome, in which people of color believe that racial profiling by the police leads to unfair traffic stops, offers another example of insidious trauma.

Root added that insidious trauma can lead to negative self-evaluation, a malevolent view of the world, and difficulty in trusting one's self and others. In the case of girls and women, they come to understand that their gender conveys a lack of protection from danger. They are at disproportionately higher risk than men and boys for rape, sexual abuse, child physical abuse, and domestic violence.

D. DOMESTIC CAPTIVITY

Root has asserted that the repeated and historical patterns of violence that women endure at the hands of male intimates subjects them to what she has called "domestic captivity." This domestic captivity extends beyond the confines of the home, for women are also the victims of random sexual aggression. As a result, women must constantly be vigilant about their daily behaviors. They are fearful of being out at night, walking to their cars, or living in housing that is not highly secure. While all women can suffer from this domestic captivity, those with less privilege—who are not racial majority members, heterosexual, financially secure, and able bodied—are at higher risk to be objectified and attacked.

Studies have shown that children and adults with disabilities are at increased risk for neglect and sexual and physical abuse. In addition, half of all gay, lesbian, bisexual, and transgendered individuals report that they have been discriminated against because of their sexual orientation and between 10 and 20% report incidents of physical violence. This violence is part of an escalation in hate crimes in general and may relate to AIDS. Some individuals have blamed gay, lesbian, bisexual, and transgendered individuals for the spread of the AIDS virus and have launched violent attacks on these individuals. [*See* HATE CRIMES.]

E. POSTCOLONIAL SYNDROME

Many clinicians and theorists of color have developed the term "postcolonial syndrome" to describe the long-lasting effects of institutionalized practices of racism and genocide. Across race and ethnicity, populations that have been colonized by another group seem to sustain what Native American writers call a "soul wound" that leaves them at higher risk for a variety of social, psychological, and physical problems. Colonized groups have often been murdered, raped, tortured, displaced from their homes and land, and endured disruption of their family units. They have also been put under extreme pressure to assimilate to the conquering culture and to abandon their own language, traditions, worldviews, and values. Because colonization and genocidal practices are sanctioned by governments, society blames the victims for any of their problems and victims react with despair, powerlessness, internalized racism, and self-hatred that can lead to harmful and self-defeating behaviors toward the self or others.

Intense exploration of the Holocaust and the genocidal practices aimed at Jewish individuals has helped clarify the postcolonial syndrome in the United States that has been aimed at Native Americans and African Americans. Holocaust survivors and their families suffered extreme PTSD symptoms and the effects were often transgenerational. One of the major differences between the Holocaust survivors and Native and African Americans is that the holocaust has been widely acknowledged and validated with such developments as the creation of a new country and legal accountability through the courts, while the validation of the harm to Native Americans and African Americans is much weaker.

Researchers are unsure of how many millions of individuals of African descent died during the transatlantic passage and while enslaved. There is a growing realization, however, that the Native American population was at 10 million at the beginning of the colonization movement and is currently at about 1 million. Many scholars believe that the systematic and institutionalized practices of racism and discrimination have created painful legacies in these two communities.

Both Native Americans and African Americans have disproportionately high rates of imprisonment and violence within their communities, including homicide, domestic violence, and suicide for Native Americans. Research has shown that because of the devaluation of women of color, they are often the targets of the rage, impotence, and frustration that men of color feel from society but redirect against them. Both groups are most likely to direct violence to members of their own group, and Native Americans must also contend with disproportionately high rates of substance abuse.

Clinicians and scholars believe that it is important that society recognize postcolonial syndrome in communities of color and understand that it is a pervasive manifestation of trauma that is passed across generations. It is also important to move away from limited Western and majority cultural thinking about what can cause and cure the PTSD-like consequences of postcolonial syndrome. Therapists are beginning to show positive results from including cultural traditions and healing rituals in treatment protocols for ethnic populations.

VI. Culture-Bound Stress Disorders

Researchers and clinicians have noted that it is important to consider ethnocultural variations in trauma. Individual and societal perceptions of what is deemed traumatic vary within and across cultural and subcultural groups. In a response to this thinking, culture-bound stress disorders appear in the appendix of *DSM-IV*. These disorders reflect a growing appreciation for the fact that current *DSM* diagnoses of PTSD are integrally linked to North American Caucasian culture. Many of the culture-bound syndromes involve high levels of anxiety, disassociation, and somatization. The three syndromes that are described relate to Hispanic populations although it is acknowledged that culture-bound syndromes can be found in cultural groups around the world. The three classifications in the appendix of *DSM-IV* are attaques de nervios, nervios, and susto.

Attaques de nervios is most prevalent among Puerto Ricans but is also found in other Latin populations. Symptoms include heart palpitations, sobbing, agitation, intense heat spreading from the chest to the head, amnesia, shouting, convulsions, physical aggression, and possible loss of consciousness. Stressors that can precipitate these attacks include automobile accidents, arguments, death of a loved one, and natural disasters.

Nervios involves a tendency to respond to stress with anxiety and somatatization. Typically the symptoms of nervios are less extreme than those for attaques de nervios and the stressors tend to be more diffuse, more chronic, and less severe. Symptoms are triggered by a stressor and include headaches, stomachaches, sleep disorders, dizziness, emotional distress, and agitation.

Susto is caused by an intense and life-threatening event that is thought to cause the soul to leave the body. States of agitation, anxiety, and hyperarousal produce appetite loss, sleep problems, startle reactions, worrying, depression, and multiple somatic symptoms such as headaches, muscle aches, and gastrointestinal distress.

VII. Risk Factors for Trauma

In general, research on risk factors has found that the best predictor for the development of PTSD is the intensity of the trauma rather than individual psychological factors. The issue remains, however, that all individuals who are exposed to trauma do not show the same effects and individuals exposed to the same trauma vary in their responses. Theorists have noted that understanding the impact of trauma requires specific knowledge of the individual affected, an individual's subjective response, an understanding of cultural context, characteristics of the stressor, and the response of others in the immediate environment.

Matthew Friedman and Anthony Marsella have offered a summary of risk factors based on the empirical literature. First of all, having access to help, a positive environment, support, and someone to confide in within the first 24 to 72 hours following exposure to a traumatic event appear to decrease adverse responses to trauma.

The severity of a trauma continues to be significant in posttraumatic distress. Rape victims who know their abuser or who were threatened with death, wounded veterans, and observers or participants in violence, atrocities, and abuse have all been related to more negative prognoses.

A variety of studies have indicated that all of the following factors are significant risk factors for PTSD: psychiatric illness among close relatives, poverty, childhood violence and abuse, marital disruptions in children's lives before the age of 10, being female, low self-esteem before the age of 15, psychiatric disturbances, and high levels of life stress before and after the trauma.

John Briere has pointed out that some variables are not only risk factors for a worse prognosis following a diagnosis of PTSD but also put individuals at greater risk to be exposed to trauma in the first place. For instance, females, people of color, people who live in poverty, people who are homeless, and individuals who have been previously traumatized all are at high risk for both trauma and a more negative prognosis for PTSD. What we see happening is that those individuals who face systematic and institutionalized oppression are at greatest risk for being

victims of trauma and in having difficulty in their recovery. Many individuals suffer from double or multiple traumas, as in the case where a woman who was sexually abused as a child may suffer a date rape in her adolescence.

Another risk for trauma victims is "secondary victimization." This refers to the negative responses victims may receive from family, friends, and agencies that attempt to silence, minimize, deny, blame, or stigmatize the victim and his or her message. Many therapists have expressed support for the idea that society could minimize the experience of multiple traumatization or victimization through better education and prevention efforts. It is particularly important, for instance, to minimize the revictimization of individuals who seek legal action against their abusers in the court system.

Because of the complexity of factors that determine the posttraumatic responses of individuals, it is not easy to come up with many hard and fast rules about the effect of trauma across situations and individuals. Despite the harm of sexual abuse to young children, research has found that older people tend to fare even worse than do children following this abuse. Correspondingly, men show a greater likelihood of developing PTSD following domestic violence or sexual abuse, although women are the more frequent targets.

Donald Meichenbaum has cataloged significant gender effects that are associated with trauma. First, because women are victims of such a broad array of traumas, such as rape, physical and sexual violence and assault, and criminal and noncriminal trauma, the majority of women in the United States (69%) have sustained at least one traumatic event in their lives. The highest rates of PTSD are associated with a completed rape. There is also research that suggests that women and men may cope differently with trauma. Women show higher levels of anxiety and depression while men show higher levels of substance use and antisocial personality disorder.

The pattern of exposure to trauma varies by gender. Men are exposed to more traumatic events such as combat, assaults, and vehicular accidents. Women are exposed to fewer events but show more severe reactions due to the nature of the trauma and are more likely to develop PTSD. Females are at higher risk for rape and childhood sexual abuse and abusive and violent relationships. Because of gender socialization, women seem to make themselves more available to assist others who are in stress and therefore risk more secondary trauma. Males are less likely than females to self-disclose and consequently less able to benefit from being heard, validated, and supported. Both male and female homosexuals and bisexuals are at risk for victimization due to sexual orientation.

John Fairbank, William Schlenger, P. A. Saigh, and John Davidson have found evidence of resiliency factors that protect individuals from PTSD. These factors include stable families, safe environments, community support, little or no substance use, and belonging to a cultural group that is open to discussion of trauma and that values survivors but does not stigmatize victims of PTSD. [*See* SOCIAL SUPPORT.]

Although some individuals exposed to trauma develop PTSD or other psychiatric diagnoses, the majority of individuals exposed to trauma do not. Individuals are idiosyncratic and diverse with respect to their responses to trauma and to their symptoms of PTSD.

Robert Ursano has noted that exposure to trama can also have benefits. Survivors often report a heightened appreciation of their coping skills, a better appreciation of what is important in life, and a sense of cohesion and communality with other survivors.

VIII. Overview of Diverse Traumas

Researchers, theorists, and clinicians have gradually come to classify trama into three categories: natural and industrial disasters; victims of war, terrorism, and refugeeism; and victims of violence, rape, and sexual assault.

A. NATURAL AND INDUSTRIAL DISASTERS

The term "disaster" has been variously defined as a severe disruption that overtaxes a community's capacity to cope. Disasters are typically perceived to be catastrophic events and usually associated with natural phenomena such as hurricanes, volcanoes, avalanches, floods, tornadoes, and earthquakes. According to the World Health Organization's research in 1992, there were 8000 natural disasters reported worldwide between 1967 and 1991. These disasters resulted in the deaths of 3 million people, had a negative impact on 800 million individuals, and caused $23 billion of damage. The majority of these disasters and fatalities occurred in developing countries that were already struggling with high rates of poverty.

Data from the International Federation of the Red Cross for the period 1967–1991 indicated that the most frequent disasters were floods, followed by accidents and storms. The highest mortality rates were related to civil strife and droughts.

But other events, such as nuclear or industrial accidents, explosions, or chemical spills, can also be classified as disasters. Charles Fritz has defined disasters as concentrated in time and space and posing severe danger and loss to society to the extent that there is such disruption to individual members and the physical environment that the normal functioning of society cannot continue.

Allen Barton has advanced the view that the impact of the trauma on a community can be determined by understanding how many people or how large a geographic area is affected, the suddenness of the impact, how long the disaster lasted, and the degree of preparedness a community had with respect to emergency resources and personnel.

Although Barton's formula for calculating the impact of a disaster may appear straightforward, the reality is more complex. For instance, civil strife can also affect the economic functioning of an entire society and thus impact more people than were directly involved in the civil strife. The initial reaction to natural disasters tends to be symptoms of shock and bewilderment that last from minutes to hours. Many trauma symptoms improve after six weeks and by three months, half of those affected by PTSD symptoms will have recovered. Often it is the initial response to a trauma that best predicts future adjustment.

B. TECHNOLOGICAL DISASTERS

Technological disasters pose unique threats because victims must cope with both immediate problems as well as possible future problems due to exposure to toxic materials. Affected individuals worry about heightened susceptibility to cancer, birth defects, and other diseases in themselves and in their children. Studies of the Three Mile Island nuclear accident, the radioactive leak in Fernald, Ohio, and the nuclear accident in Chernobyl suggest that symptoms may not reach the PTSD criteria but may include anxiety, depression, alienation, reduced trust, apathy, and hopelessness.

C. TRANSPORTATION ACCIDENTS

This category of disasters can involve accidents with airplanes, trains, ski lifts, cars, and sea-bearing vessels. Typically these situations involve high fatality and injury rates and affect a large number of people both directly and indirectly. Individuals involved in these accidents respond with depression, anxiety, and PTSD. In addition, trauma can occur in more individualized ways with auto and other vehicle accidents (boats, motorcycles, and recreational vehicles). These accidents can involve injury to self or to a partner, child, or loved one. Both victims and other survivors and family members can show symptoms of PTSD and ASD.

D. TRAUMA ASSOCIATED WITH WAR, TORTURE, TERRORISM, AND REFUGEE STATUS

War represents the most enduring example of large-scale, human-made violence. Since World War II, there have been 150 wars and an estimated fatality rate of 21 to 40 million. War must be understood to include conflicts, skirmishes, and military and police violence that, while not formally called a war, have the same impact on victims. Wars inflict a variety of trauma including feared and actual death, injury, disfigurement, injuring, or killing others, and witnessing or being a participant in rape, torture, capture, deprivation, or confinement.

Historically, male combatants were the central focus of war and trauma, but increasingly civilians, women, and children are involved on the front lines as participants and casualties of war. For example, 90% of the deaths recorded are civilians for conflicts in Somalia, the former Yugoslavia, and Lebanon. Theorists are also beginning to highlight that men and women experience the trauma of war differently. While men do counts of win-loss battle records and those who are injured, missing, or killed, violence toward women in war is designed to weaken the morale and resolve of men. Hence, women often face daily atrocities that are often ignored. The majority of wars are in developing countries.

War exposure produces a variety of symptoms including dissociation, depression, anxiety, substance abuse, guilt, aggression, and suicidal feelings and attempts. Most of the data available on trauma and war focus on the Vietnam War. Research indicates that currently 15% of men and 9% of women are currently suffering from PTSD following the Vietnam War, with a lifetime prevalence of 31% for men and 27% for women.

PTSD in women was a largely ignored phenomenon until the mid-1980s. Gradually, caregivers began to recognize the impact of the Vietnam War on women. Most of these female military staff members served in hospitals. They were exposed to military

attacks and rigorous schedules of duty, and they faced trauma from a variety of sources. Like males they had to contend with observing sudden injury, dismemberment, and death. In addition, due in part to the scarcity of women, female veterans were frequent victims of unwanted attention, sexual harassment, and rape.

These women also had to deal with uncomfortable and abrupt transitions from the war and home. Some of these women were stereotyped as promiscuous or lesbian by virtue of being a numerical scarcity among men in the military. They also had to contend with the same lack of societal support that returning men had to face. In addition to dealing with primary trauma, the nature of their jobs as medical caregivers also put them at high risk for secondary trauma.

The United Nations has indicated that due to war and political terrorism, it provides services to an expanding group of refugees. In the mid 1970s, services were provided to 2.5 million, and by the mid 1990s, services were provided to approximately 19 million. It has been estimated that by the early 1990s, refugees and internally displaced people account for 43 million individuals. Mothers and children account for 50 to 70% of the world refugee population.

The United Nations has defined torture as any mental or physical act that involves the intentional infliction of severe pain or suffering with the purpose of securing information or a confession, or to punish an individual for suspected or actual behavior, or to intimidate an individual or a third party. Although this is a general definition, John Briere has noted that it fails to subsume the variety of inhumane acts that individuals may be subject to by military forces, the abduction, rape, and torture of women and children, and torture that may be a part of domestic violence.

Torture can be either psychological or physical and can also be a combination of both. Psychological techniques involve threats, mock executions, sleep and sensory deprivation, humiliation, sexual exposure, and blaming individuals for the harm or death of others. Physical torture includes beatings, electric shocks, sexual abuse and assault, breaking bones and joints, and exposure to chemicals or extreme temperatures.

Unfortunately many countries either allow torture or sanction its use. The experience of torture can be so horrific that it is difficult to gain accurate data about the prevalence of torture and its victims. It is likely, however, that refugees are frequent targets of torture. The consequences of torture vary across individuals based on the actual experiences of the type and context of the torture. Frequently noted consequences include suicidal behavior, somatic illnesses, anxiety, depression, sleep and sexual disorders, and nervous breakdowns. [See TORTURE.]

Immigrants migrate for a variety of reasons including better economic opportunities, political freedom, escape from political oppression and torture, and possible reunion with other family members. These individuals have also often faced the trauma of racism, colonialization, and warfare. Individuals who choose to immigrate face the loss of family, friends, culture, and identity. Immigrants often face torture, political prosecution and or imprisonment, abduction of family members, and flight without adequate preparation for food, shelter, medical care, and safety.

The death rates for refugees are estimated to be from 5 to 25 times the rates in their home countries. Women are exposed to the additional trauma of sexual atrocities that include rape and sexual torture. Women are threatened that their children will be harmed or killed if they do not comply with their torturers and women are often abused as a way to torture men. Sexual violations are often perceived to be particularly insidious in countries that value and extol female virginity and chastity. Refugees are also at times subjected to secondary trauma by being forced to endure the threats or the reality of witnessing the arrest, torture, or execution of loved ones.

The actual course of immigrating is fraught with trauma, as is the period of resettlement. Individuals who have immigrated show increased violence, cultural losses, and disorganization of traditional family ties and values. Men often reenact the violence they have experienced and direct this violence toward women. They also control women by using intimidation and threats to harm or kill the woman's children or to have her children deported.

E. RAPE AND SEXUAL ASSAULT

Mary Koss has explained rape as a nonconsensual sexual penetration that is obtained by threat of harm or by physical force when the victim is unable to give consent. Sexual assault is now understood to include fondling, unwanted touching, and oral, vaginal, or anal penetration. This category of rape includes date rape, sexual harassment, and sex between a client and a professional caregiver.

The categories of rape, sexual harassment, and sexual assault are different with respect to how much violence may be shown but are similar in that they typically involve men using their greater physical and societal power against women. The greater valuing of men in society encourages some men to believe that they have the right to touch, intimidate, rape, or batter women. As a consequence, women who experience one or more of these types of abuse are made to feel violated and powerless. Secondary victimization occurs when rape victims are accused of provocative behavior that invited the attack, when sexual harassment is minimized as positive attention, when women are labeled as just "too sensitive," or when an abused woman is blamed for provoking her husband and ridiculed for not leaving him and ending the abuse.

Women who encounter sexual and physical assaults also struggle to name the violence that they have suffered, because it has only been in the last 20 years that society has developed the terms to identify male violence toward women and children. Women themselves have been socialized to minimize and deny their own experiences of abuse, which contributes to their sense of confusion, blame, and trauma.

It is difficult to gain accurate prevalence rates for the rape of men and women because the shame, secrecy, and stigma of this type of assault make it difficult for both women and men victims to come forward. Individuals fear the embarrassment, invasiveness, and humiliation of dealing with medical, police, and legal personnel. Hence, these acts of violence often flourish in the silence and invisibility of women's lives.

Only recently has there been societal acceptance of the idea that men could be rape victims. Typically, men are the most at risk for being raped in prison where homosexual rape is common. There are also rare cases where women rape men. The prevalence rate is estimated at about 20% for women and 10% for men. In 1987, Mary Koss completed a survey revealing that one in four women were the victims of rape or a rape attack, 84% knew their attacker, and 57% of the attacks occurred on dates.

The aftereffects of rape can include fear, anxiety, depression, dissociation, reduced self-esteem and interpersonal functioning, sexual difficulties, substance abuse, PTSD, and physical symptoms. Research suggests that about 32% of rape victims fit the diagnostic criteria for PTSD. Physical symptoms can include menstrual bleeding, pelvic pain, gastric disturbances, weight and eating disorders, and neurological problems. The onset of symptoms tends to occur shortly after the rape but symptoms often last weeks, months, and even years. The aftereffects of rape, assault, and harassment often depend on factors such as whether the victim knew the assailant, the nature of the attack, the perception of danger and fear, and age. Individuals vary in their behavioral responses. While some women show anxiety, tension, fear, and crying, other women mask their feelings with an outward demonstration of calm. Most women report feeling devalued, hopeless, guilty, and at blame for being raped. They no longer feel safe and invulnerable and may have difficulty in trusting others. In addition to psychological difficulties, women are often in pain and bruised and must be concerned about whether they have to worry about pregnancy, AIDS, or a sexually transmitted disease. For women who are married, they must determine the next steps in their relationship. Although 10 to 15% of women are raped by their spouses or ex-husbands, women who want to prosecute these men must also worry about financial, psychological, or physical retaliation from them.

The issue of pursuing legal redress is complex for all rape victims. The experience of women in the courts has been so negative historically that women are often fearful and pessimistic about legal avenues. They rightfully feel that they will be harassed, blamed, or might risk retaliation from their assailant. Unfortunately, women can be further traumatized or "doubly victimized" by family and friends as well if these individuals blame the woman for the rape and are not forthcoming with validation, help, and support. While some women have long-term negative consequences following a rape, other women have become stronger and more resilient as a result of their trauma. Research has shown that men, older adults, and people with traditional gender-role stereotypes are most likely to blame women for rape.

Sexual harassment usually does not involve violence but refers to unwanted, deliberate and repeated comments, gestures, and physical contacts of a sexual nature. The two general categories involve threats by an individual with more power to someone with less power that sexual advances must be accepted or a negative consequence will ensue. The other type of sexual harassment involves a hostile work environment where a work or school setting is so offensive that it impacts negatively on the performance of the student or employee.

Although women can harass men and same-sex harassment exists, most instances of sexual harassment involve males who use their greater power, resources, and societal prerogative to sexually objectify women. Reported rates of sexual harassment are high. In academic settings, from 20 to 40% of undergraduates report harassment, and these rates are higher in graduate and professional schools, especially in schools that provide training for male-dominant professions like medicine. Similarly, 90% of women in the military and in blue-collar professions report harassment.

The consequences of harassment are often traumatic to women. Harassment can lead to the woman quitting or being terminated in school or at work, negative evaluations, demotions, pay cuts, and limited options for mobility. Women often respond to single or repeated episodes of harassment with anger, depression, anxiety, decreased confidence, and somatic, sleep, and eating disorders. If a woman speaks out, individuals who defend her abuser—and increase her sense of marginalization, helplessness, and powerlessness—typically retraumatize her. The psychological and financial costs of either speaking out or remaining silent are very high for women who are harassed. [*See* RAPE; SEXUAL HARASSMENT.]

F. SPOUSE OR PARTNER ABUSE

Spouse or partner abuse involves violence or assaultive behavior in the context of an intimate, sexual, and usually cohabiting relationship. Some theorists prefer the term "abuse of women" to domestic violence. The argument can be correctly made that women can be abused even when they are not cohabiting with a partner and the abuse can be psychological and sexual in addition to being physical. Other theorists, recognizing that most of this abuse is by men toward women, focus on abuse as an expression of men's hostility toward women that exists in addition to more institutionalized aggression toward women. This abuse exists across all cultures and demographic groups, although individuals with access to money and power are typically more successful in hiding their abuse by seeking services from private rather than public caregivers (who routinely report the incidence of this abuse).

Physical abuse can include but is not restricted to strangling, hitting, punching, kicking, shoving, burning, and using weapons as threats. Psychological and emotional abuse can include silent treatments, humiliation, intimidation, insults, and withholding resources such as money or the car.

Although society often focuses on the abuse of men by women, research consistently demonstrates that women account for the majority of abuse victims and the abuse of women is much more severe, repeated, and long term than the abuse of men. Women are at much greater risk to sustain injuries and hospital visits, and are at greatest risk to be killed by their male partner than by all other victimizers. In 1989, Angela Browne reported that male partners killed 52% of women murdered from 1980 to 1985.

Collecting accurate data on the incidence of abuse is difficult since private violence is stigmatized and hidden. Many studies suggest that physical battering is the most common cause of female injury brought to medical attention, although women will often attribute their injuries to accidents rather than abuse. Research has estimated that about 25 to 30% of women in the United States will experience abuse, with experts like Lenore Walker indicating that 50% is a more accurate figure. A disturbing risk factor for abuse is pregnancy, with 17% of these individuals reporting abuse. Even in dating relationships, some research has shown 47% of these women have experienced some type of physical violence and 65% have endured some type of psychological or emotional abuse.

Less is known about abuse among intimate partners who are gay and lesbian. There have been estimates that partner abuse in same-sex couples may be as high as 40%. Partner abuse among same-sex couples does not illustrate the same gender dynamics between males and females that are used to control and coerce women in general. However, power dynamics can exist in same sex relationships. It is often difficult for same-sex partners to come forward to seek services and risk subtle or overt harassment and insensitivity.

Women go to great lengths to avoid abuse, which leads to hypervigilant behaviors in order to prepare for and possibly prevent their abuse. Typical consequences of abuse include fear, depression, anxiety, sleep and eating disorders, physical injuries, disability, scars, wounds, miscarriages, harm to a fetus *in utero,* and suicidal behaviors. The consequences of battering have a major impact on children who witness and or know about the battering. Children may learn from this modeling that male domination of women through physical means is acceptable. Children, like their mothers, can show symptoms of psychological shock as well as chronic patterns of symptoms. These children are also at high risk for the violence to be directed toward them. [*See* EMOTIONAL ABUSE OF WOMEN.]

G. CHILD SEXUAL ABUSE

Child sexual abuse refers to sexual activities with a child that can damage, harm, or threaten the child's welfare. Typically the victim is under the age of 18 and the perpetrator is at least 5 years older. Individuals who are close to the child and are responsible for their care, protection, and well-being typically perpetrate the abuse. It is difficult to determine accurate rates of prevalence, and recorded figures are likely to be underestimates of the true scope of this problem. Most sexual victimization involves adult males assaulting young females with much fewer cases of adult males or females victimizing male children. Researchers report about 20 to 25% of girls have experienced sexual abuse by the time they are 18, and it is estimated that about half as many boys are abused sexually. This abuse can occur in the home, in school, and religious settings, in health care settings, and in the provision of child day care and baby-sitting. With respect to sexual abuse by relatives, or incest, research has suggested that relatives victimized 46% of female rape victims under the age of 12. Mary Koss reported in 1990 that family members were responsible for 90% of the physical and sexual assaults reported by psychiatric patients.

Because children are actively engaged in the developmental process both psychologically and physically, rape can have a major impact. Symptoms can include fear, guilt, anxiety, depression, nightmares, and sleep disorders. Long-term aftereffects can include problems with trust and interpersonal relationships, eating disorders, sexual dysfunction including poor decision making, and physical problems with the reproductive system. Children like adults also risk secondary victimization with regard to receiving support and validation from their family. It is extremely difficult for most of these abused children to find the words and concepts to explain this violation to someone else. Should they be brave enough to confide in someone, they risk problems with having others deny, minimize, or distort what they say or even blame or find them responsible. It is often particularly true in communities of color that children and adults are afraid to report the sexual misconduct of an adult, and adults are fearful of trusting or using legal systems of prosecution. Another potential source of trauma is the issue of recovered memories. When children repress the memory of something horrifying and report it at a later time, many experts have cataloged these memories as false and invalidated the individual's experiences. [*See* CHILD ABUSE.]

H. CHILD ABUSE AND MALTREATMENT

Child abuse and maltreatment refers to physical or mental injury, negligent treatment, or maltreatment of a child by a person responsible for the child's welfare. This category encompasses emotional child abuse and neglect as well as various forms of maltreatment. Child abuse and maltreatment can occur regardless of ethnicity, religion, age, and sexual orientation. Those who are at high risk include children who are unwanted or who remind the abusers of someone that is disliked, children who are living in poverty or whose families have limited resources, and children who live in families that are socially isolated. Symptoms that are associated with this trauma include psychosomatic illnesses and physical complaints that cannot be confirmed. Children may respond with running away, school truancy, rebellious and acting out behaviors, interpersonal difficulties, sleep and eating problems, or more internalized symptoms such as anxiety and depression. Physical violence toward these children can produce long-term physical, mental, and psychological disabilities. Risk factors for the parents or parental figures who are abusive or neglectful include problems with alcoholism and/or substance abuse, rigid and unrealistic expectations about parenting, and wife abuse.

I. SECONDARY TRAUMATIC STRESS

Secondary traumatic stress (STS) is a syndrome with a variety of other names. It has also been called compassion fatigue disorder, vicarious traumatization, secondary victimization, emotional contagion, covictimization, and secondary survivor disorder. These terms refer to the finding that family, friends, and professional caregivers who associated with or work with traumatized individuals are susceptible to "catching" or manifesting the same stress symptomatology as the victims. Noted traumatologist Charles Figley has defined secondary stress as the natural behavioral and emotional consequences that accrue from knowing about, helping, or wanting to help a traumatized or suffering person.

Both *DSM-III* and *DSM-IV* under criterion A1 provide for the understanding that trauma symptoms can result indirectly from learning about trauma in family members or close associates. Hence, Figley has argued that PTSD should really stand for *primary* traumatic stress disorder because all stress reactions are inherently *post*, and this distinction would better recognize how family, friends, and caregivers can be vulnerable to secondary stress from those exposed to primary stress.

The list of individuals who are at risk to suffer secondary trauma is extensive and in addition to friends and family includes crisis, rescue, and emergency workers; medical personnel; law enforcement workers; therapists; and those individuals who must identify deceased victims. Because women in many societies are socialized to be good listeners and to be supportive and helpful, they are at high risk for STS. Correspondingly, it is exactly those characteristics that might make a caregiver effective that are most likely to increase the vulnerability to be affected by STS. These factors include being empathic, having personal experience of trauma and unresolved trauma that can be reactivated, and finally having to deal with the heart-rending pain of child victims.

In her work in STS, B. Hudnall Stamm advised individuals who work with trauma victims to not work alone and to gain support and monitoring of one's work through consultations and supervision with trusted friends and colleagues. Susan McCammon also warned that faculty and students can also suffer STS because they are involved in courses and clinical training in which trauma related material is reviewed. Overall, experts in the field of STS advocate not just providing caregivers with the technical skills to help traumatized individuals but also teaching self-care, how to marshal social support and societal responsibility for others, and how to promote resiliency and interventions that foster positive coping.

In addition to the caregivers, family and friends are highly susceptible to experiencing STS. The two populations that have received the most attention are Holocaust survivors and their families and combat veterans and their families. Although there is a paucity of rigorous research on the families of Holocaust survivors, the fact that these survivors appear to suffer some form of long-lasting PTSD raises the issue that it appears possible in some cases that partners and children of survivors may show evidence of some impairment as a result of their exposure.

Research on combat veterans has suggested that the PTSD of the veteran can directly impact children and partner of the veteran. In some situations, the severity of the PTSD in the parent is highly related to PTSD symptoms in children.

J. CRIMINAL VICTIMIZATION

Although crime victimization is not routinely found in international classifications of trauma, its high prevalence in the United States warrants its inclusion. Research by Robert Finkelhor in 1994 revealed that for children aged 12 to 19, 58% experienced an assault, 12% experienced robbery, and almost 1% were exposed to homicide. Approximately 83% of individuals in the United States will experience a violent crime, and 99% will be exposed to theft. Children and youth are at increasing risk from either witnessing or being the victims of gun violence, and homicide is the leading cause of death for African American males aged 15 to 44.

Inner city youth are at such high risk for neglect, violence, and criminal victimization that the term "urban violence traumatic stress response syndrome" has been proposed. Primary and secondary exposure to the trauma of crime and violence produces symptoms of depression, anxiety, somatization, hostility, and fear. PTSD symptoms are highly correlated with the severity of crimes. Long-term consequences involve the secondary trauma that family and friends experience when they learn of a crime. The impact of violence and homicide is often devastating to survivors, particularly in the case of parents who are anguished over their inability to protect their children and other loved ones. Another long-term consequence is a sustained fear of future victimization that all too often becomes a reality.

IX. Treatment Approaches for Trauma

Despite the high prevalence of trauma, there are few studies using carefully randomized therapeutic methodology. There are numerous studies that support the effectiveness of cognitive behavioral, psychodynamic, pharmacological, and group treatments for traumatized individuals. Many therapists rely on the principles of treatment developed by Herman: establishing a safe environment, stabilization and trust, helping the patient to tell the trauma story and thereby promote reintegration of intrusive memories, thoughts and feelings, and finally helping to develop the coping skills that will allow the integration of the trauma and a reconnection to self, family, and society.

Increasingly, therapists understand the importance of culture and demographic features that mediate the healing process. Individuals need to reconstruct a sense of meaning, rebuild hope, and gain a sense of empowerment. But this healing must take place in the context of families and communities and not just within the individual. Treatment cannot be effective without holistic approaches that address immediate survival issues and the ongoing trauma of sexism, racism, and economic, educational, and political disenfranchisement.

X. Conclusions

It is essential that we take a holistic approach in order to avoid pathologizing and revictimizing individuals with trauma. While we are limited in what we can do about natural disasters, there is much that we can do to decrease and minimize the impact of human-made trauma. To prevent the effects of trauma, society must initiate human rights initiatives and constructive political changes.

SUGGESTED READING

Briere, J. (1997). *Psychological Assessment of Adult Posttraumatic States.* American Psychological Association, Washington, DC.

Everly, G. S., and Lating, J. M. (eds.) (1995). *Psychotraumatology: Key Papers and Core Concepts in Post-Traumatic Stress.* Plenum Press, New York.

Figley, C. (1985). *Trauma and Its Wake: The Study of and Treatment of Posttraumatic Stress Disorder.* Brunner/Mazel, New York.

Foy, D. (ed.) (1992). *Treating PTSD: Procedure for Combat Veterans, Battered Women, Adult and Child Sexual Assaults.* Guilford Press, New York.

Herman, J. (1997). *Trauma and Recovery.* Basic Books, New York.

Marsella, A. J., Friedman, M. J., Gerrity, E. T., and Scurfield, R. M. (eds.) (1996). *Ethnocultural Aspects of Posttraumatic Stress Disorder: Issues, Research and Clinical Applications.* American Psychological Association, Washington, DC.

Stamm, B. H. (1999). *Secondary Traumatic Stress: Self-Care Issues for Clinicians, Researchers and Educators.* The Sidran Press, Lutherville, MD.

Waites, E. A. (1993). *Trauma and Survival: Post-traumatic and Dissociative Disorders in Women.* W.W. Norton & Company, New York.

Walker, L. (1994). *Abused Women and Survivor Therapy: A Practical Guide for the Psychotherapist.* American Psychological Association, Washington, DC.

Women in Nontraditional Occupational Fields

Ruth E. Fassinger
University of Maryland at College Park

I. Overview of Women in Nontraditional Fields
II. Importance of Mathematics, Science, Technology, and Engineering
III. Barriers to Women's Participation in Nontraditional Fields

Glossary

Barriers Factors that prevent women from entering, achieving, and advancing within, or deriving satisfaction from, particular occupational fields.

External/contextual barriers (also termed **structural factors**) Features of the environmental context—specific organizations and workplaces, the educational system, society at large—that serve to limit access to or opportunities within those environments. Contextual barriers exist outside the individual, and although they can be expressed by individual persons, they are rooted in societal structures such as institutions, norms, policies, and practices. Examples include occupational stereotyping, educational discrimination, and discriminatory practices in compensation and advancement.

Gender-stereotypic Another term used for fields in which one sex or the other tends to dominate, and **gender minority** is sometimes used to characterize persons who are in fields dominated by the other sex (i.e., women are a gender minority in the field of physics, which is gender-stereotypic for men).

Individual/internal barriers (also termed **cultural factors**) Beliefs and attitudes common to members of particular groups that inhibit optimal vocational development. Often these beliefs have been inculcated by society (e.g., ideas about appropriate roles for women), but become translated into internalized, self-perpetuating representations of the self. Examples of internal barriers include underestimation of capabilities, restrictive gender-role socialization, and multiple role conflict.

MSTE fields An abbreviation for mathematics, science, technology, and engineering, these fields include: mathematics; physical, chemical, and biological sciences; social and behavioral sciences; various branches of engineering (e.g., chemical, nuclear, civil); and applied technological fields such as information technology, electronics, aeronautics, biotechnology, and medicine.

Nontraditional (also termed **male-dominated**) **occupational fields** Those where the proportionate representation of women is low; such fields include business, law, skilled trades, the military, mathematics, the sciences, engineering, and technological fields

Traditional (also termed **female-dominated**) **occupational fields** Those where the representation of women in proportion to men is high; such fields include nursing, teaching, secretarial work, and social services.

WOMEN ARE UNDERREPRESENTED IN A WIDE RANGE OF OCCUPATIONAL FIELDS dominated by men. This article outlines the scope of the problem and discusses both external and internal barriers to women's participation in nontraditional occupations.

I. Overview of Women in Nontraditional Fields

The history of women in the workplace is a complex amalgam of factors rooted in social, political, historical, economic, and religious conditions, and it differs for women in diverse demographic locations (e.g., the conditions for upper-class European women in the 17th century who wished to pursue education or work were very different from those of Black women who worked as slaves on plantations in the 19th century United States). However, a common thread that runs through many centuries of change is the persistent difficulty for women of entering into work environments dominated and controlled by men, the notable absence of women in many occupational fields, and the consistent segregation of women into a narrow range of work roles characterized by less compensation and opportunity for advancement than roles afforded to men.

Unfortunately, despite seemingly radical social change during the past several decades, these conditions remain the reality for most women in the United States today. By the mid-1990s, White men made up only 33% of the population but were represented disproportionately in society's highest professional ranks: they comprised 85% of tenured professors; 80% of the U.S. House of Representatives; 90% of the U.S. Senate; 85% of partners in law firms; 95% of *Fortune* 500 CEOs; 99.9% of athletic team owners; and 100% of U.S. Presidents. Blue-collar occupations are considerably more gender-segregated than the professions, with less than 9% of employees in skilled crafts, repair, and precision production being women. Even in fields traditional for women, such as education, men predominate at the top ranks. In 1995, women held 40% of the administrative posts in higher education, but most at lower levels: At Harvard University, women held only 40% of managerial posts with salaries greater than $55,000; at Duke, the number was 32%; at Brown, 26%; and at Dartmouth and MIT, 13%. Only 6 women but 94 men were presidents of private Ph.D.-granting uni-

versities, while 25 women and 75 men were presidents at less prestigious two-year colleges. Approximately 97% of school superintendents in the mid-1990s were men.

Certainly, there has been dramatic change in women's entry into nontraditional careers in recent decades. In 1970, women earned only 0.9% of dentistry degrees, 8.4% of medical degrees, and 5.4% of law degrees; by 1992, these percentages had risen to 32.3%, 35.7%, and 42.7%, respectively, and continued to climb through the 1990s. Unprecedented numbers of women attend college at present, and in some historically male-dominated fields, such as psychology, the percentage of women has surpassed that of men.

However, even in fields such as medicine, where the influx of women is obvious (currently representing 44% of those admitted to medical school), the top ranks remain male-dominated. In 1996, 40% of medical students and 20% of practicing physicians were women, but only 3% of medical school deans and 5% of department chairs were women. There were fewer than 16 female full professors per medical school (as compared to 155 men), and the majority of schools still did not have even one female full professor in the specialties of obstetrics/gynecology, surgery, anesthesiology, and family practice. The proportion of women faculty at the rank of professor remained below 10% in 1996 (the same as it was in 1980), and recent cohort studies reveal that after a mean of 11 years (for both sexes) on a medical school faculty, 23% of a national sample of men but only 5% of women had achieved the rank of full professor. Moreover, even when research productivity is held constant, women in academic medicine receive less compensation and are promoted less frequently than men. For practicing physicians with six to nine years of experience, women earn 96% of men's income after adjusting for specialty (which, in turn, relates to number of hours worked); for those with more than 10 years of experience, women's income is 85% that of men.

The military is another example of the difficulties facing women in entering nontraditional fields. Recent changes in legislation and policy have opened up 90% of the armed services' career fields to women, resulting in fairly dramatic increases. For example, from 1993 to 1998, the number of female Marine Corps officers who were pilots or naval flight officers increased from 0 to 62, representing 7% of all female Marine Corps officers; 2% of women were general/flag officers or executives in 1998, as compared to none in 1992; and 8% of female officers served in surface warfare occupations in 1998, as compared to less than 3% in 1990. However, large percentages of women in the military remain clustered in the areas of health care (40% of female officers are in this sector), administration, supply occupations, and personnel. In addition, policies barring women from some units dictate limitations for women entering occupations officially open to them within those units (e.g., the U.S. Navy limits the number of women in its nuclear training program because women cannot serve on submarines), suggesting mixed messages to women regarding opportunities in the military. [*See* MILITARY WOMEN.]

In the business sector, of the top 150 Silicon Valley companies, only 28 of the 755 senior executives are women. In 1990, only 6.3% of White women and 3.6% of women of color who were full-time salaried managers earned incomes in the top 20% of their fields. A recent report indicated that of the 100 best-compensated Silicon Valley executives, only two were women; the average compensation package (including salary, bonuses, options) for men was $1.4 million as compared to $829,922 for women, suggesting that women fare worse than men at even the highest salary levels.

Similar salary differences exist in mathematics, science, technology, and engineering (MSTE) fields. In 1997, the median annual salary for women scientists and engineers was about 20% less than the median salary for men; for those holding their degrees less than five years, women's salaries were 83% those of men. Salary patterns for women of color in MSTE fields are similar to those of White women, except for Asian American women, who fare slightly better. Salaries tend to be correlated directly with the percentage of males in a field, resulting in the irony of wider salary gaps in MSTE fields where women are beginning to have more presence. In 1997, for example, women's salaries were 12% less than men's in computer and mathematical science occupations (where men predominate), whereas there was a 24% salary difference (favoring males) in the social and behavioral sciences, fields in which the percentages of women are now equal to or slightly greater than those of men. In addition to salary gaps, there are gender differences in the amount of debt incurred in obtaining an education—the MSTE field with the highest percentages and levels of educational debt is psychology, which accounts for about 30% of female MSTE doctorates, compared to 10% of males.

Despite intransigent gaps in opportunity, advancement, and compensation, there is growing consensus that workforce diversity is good for society and a concomitant push to move women into fields once closed to them. Research indicates that organizations with diverse groups of people are more open to innovative ideas, and that women bring unique strengths to the workplace. For example, women physicians are more likely than men to work in clinics serving the indigent, talk and listen to their patients more, and place greater value on the psychosocial aspects of medicine (versus the technical and legal aspects favored by men). A 1994 study found that the 7.7 million women-owned businesses in the United States employed 15.5 million people— 35% more than all *Fortune* 500 companies combined. These kinds of examples underscore the benefits to society of a more inclusive workforce.

II. *Inportance of Mathematics, Science, Technology, and Engineering*

MSTE fields are considered crucial to U. S. economic growth, they are expanding rapidly (e.g., the need for computer specialists will double between 1996 and 2006), they tend to be well-compensated and conducive to advancement opportunities, unemployment is half that of the overall workforce, and it is believed that future demand for workers in these fields will far outstrip supply—indeed, some claim that worker shortages already are limiting U. S. economic progress and creating pressure for larger immigrant quotas to fill needed positions. Since demographic trends indicate that women and minorities represent the greatest increases in workforce participation in the present and future, it is reasonable to expect that many future MSTE workers will be women. However, the paucity of women in MSTE fields is well documented, as are efforts to significantly increase the participation of girls and women in math and science activities, courses, and careers.

The overall pattern of female workforce participation in MSTE fields over the past several decades demonstrates increasing numbers of women (including minority women) entering these fields, but continuing severe underrepresentation continues in all MSTE fields except the life and social sciences, with recent leveling off and even decreases in some fields. The number of women with doctorates in MSTE fields has increased dramatically (more than five-fold) over the past quarter century. Women constituted

9% of the doctoral academic MSTE workforce in 1973, compared to approximately 25% in 1997. In 1995, minority women represented 19% of all females in the MSTE labor force and 4% of all scientists and engineers in the overall labor force (by ethnic category, Black women represented 1.3%, Hispanic women 0.6%, Asian American women 2.2%, and American Indian women .1%).

However, MSTE fields remain overwhelmingly populated by men. In 1997, White men constituted 36% of the population, but 65% of the MSTE labor force; by comparison, women made up slightly more than one-fifth (23%) of the MSTE labor force, but close to half (46%) of the overall U.S. labor force. The intransigence of this problem can be seen within the field of academic chemistry. In 1980, several of the top chemistry departments in the United States (Harvard, Stanford, MIT, University of Chicago, Columbia) contained either no female faculty or one woman; in 1997, after almost 20 years of public focus on recruiting women, these same departments all had one female faculty member, suggesting that very little actual progress had been made. Although private institutions tend to lag behind public institutions in recruiting and retaining women in MSTE fields, it should be noted that even public institutions are not progressing well—in the top 40 Ph.D.-granting departments of chemistry, the average percentage of women faculty is 8.9%, with a range of 0 to 25%.

Moreover, although women earn about the same proportion of bachelor's and advanced degrees in non-MSTE fields (59% of bachelor's and 53% of doctoral degrees in 1995), the percentage of advanced degrees is lower in MSTE fields—in 1996, women earned almost half (47%) of the MSTE bachelor's degrees, but only 38% of the master's degrees and 32% of the doctorates. In addition, women remain segregated in pockets of the MSTE workforce. Increases in the life and social sciences by women have been dramatic (in 1997, 84% of MSTE doctorates earned by women were in these areas), but this growth skews statistics and obscures the lack of progress into other MSTE fields. Of the 32% of MSTE doctorates earned by women in 1996, 51% were in the social and behavioral sciences, 42% in biological sciences, but only 12% in engineering, 15% in computer sciences, and 21% in mathematics. Only 9% of women held degrees in the physical and environmental sciences in 1997, representing a decline of 14% in these fields since 1973, and the engineering percentages represent an increase of less than 1% since 1966. From 1993 to 1995, women's enrollment decreased in the physical sciences (by 1%), mathematics (6%), computer science (4%), and in aerospace (2%), electrical (3%), and mechanical engineering (6%). The patterns of MSTE field location are similar for White and minority women, except that the proportion of Asian American women in the social sciences remains quite low.

Field segregation and decreasing representation of women with advanced degrees indicate a well-documented "pipeline" problem for women in MSTE fields—the further along in education, occupational entry, and career advancement, the fewer the numbers of women. Recent research suggests that women are entering some MSTE fields in numbers similar to men. However, even when academic preparation of women is equal or superior to that of men, women show a greater tendency than men to abandon MSTE majors in college. In addition, women with MSTE bachelor's degrees, in comparison to men, more often report financial reasons for not entering graduate study in MSTE fields (53% versus 38%), more men than women in chemistry and biology report plans to complete postdoctoral training, and more women than men attend graduate school part time. These latter findings are supported by the fact that men are more likely to report having a research assistantship than women (35% versus 27%) and much less likely to report self-support as their primary resource for advanced education and training (22% versus 33%); these differences are due, in part, to women's tendency to locate into MSTE fields where resources are not as abundant (e.g., social sciences). Financial support is critically important, because it leads to higher completion rates and shorter time to degree for students; inadequate resources for education clearly place women at a disadvantage in pursuing advanced MSTE degrees.

The pipeline problem persists for MSTE faculty, where the percentage of men increases while the percentage of women decreases in moving up the academic ranks from instructors and junior faculty to full professors; in 1997, 12% of women were full professors, 25% were associate professors, and 37% were assistant professors and instructors. Moreover, this academic pipeline pattern is particularly salient for minority women. In grant support (critical for tenure and promotion in academic science), twice as many men as women applied for National Institutes of Health (NIH) first awards from 1988 to 1997. Although women were as successful as men in receiving first grants and competitive renewals from NIH, the overall percentage of NIH awards earned by women increased only slightly over the decade (18.3% in 1988 to 22.3% in 1997). Regarding peer recognition for achievements, fewer than 100 women are included in the membership of more than 1600 in the prestigious National Academy of Sciences, most of them concentrated in the biological sciences and very few in chemistry, physics, or engineering. Using one year as an example, in 1994 only one of the eight recipients of the National Medal of Science was a woman.

In terms of overall employment, male scientists and engineers are more likely to be employed full time in their field of highest degree, while women are more likely to be unemployed, employed part time, and employed in fields outside their degree (Black and Asian American women, however, are more likely than other women to be employed full time in a field related to their degree). Men are more likely to be employed in business and industry and women are more likely to be employed in educational institutions, particularly elementary or secondary schools (11% women versus 4% men) and two-year colleges (12% women versus 9% men). Overall, the education and employment patterns for women and men in MSTE occupations suggest pervasive gender effects, related to well-documented barriers to women's participation in nontraditional fields.

III. *Barriers to Women's Participation in Nontraditional Fields*

A. EXTERNAL/CONTEXTUAL BARRIERS

1. Occupational Stereotyping

Occupational stereotyping involves pervasive beliefs about the appropriateness or suitability of particular jobs for one sex or the other based on gender-role stereotypes (e.g., beliefs that women are too vulnerable to be in military combat roles or incapable of the complex thinking required in mathematics). Such stereotypes not only limit females' perceptions of acceptable occupational choices, but also function through employer attitudes and workplace climate to restrict actual entry into certain jobs (e.g., men being hired over equally qualified women) or opportunities to advance once in the organization (e.g., women being skipped over for deserved promotions or clientele requesting male professionals). Research indicates that occupational stereotypes are formed early, remain evident in secondary and college years, and are reinforced powerfully by the me-

dia. Research also demonstrates that males engage in more gender stereotyping than do females, and negative consequences for gender-role deviant behavior by females (such as academic or vocational success) are well documented.

In regard to MSTE fields, a large body of research has attempted to explain gender differences in mathematics and science attitudes, participation, and achievement. Overall, for females, this literature demonstrates a pattern of performance, participation, and positive attitudes similar or superior to those of males during the elementary grades, but then steadily decreasing throughout middle school and high school. Although recent research suggests a narrowing of the gender gap in standardized tests of advanced mathematics skills, large gaps favoring males persist in terms of participation in mathematics and science courses and activities throughout adolescence. Attitudinal patterns suggest that science and mathematics come to be viewed as male domains by both females and males, but particularly strongly by males. Many of the factors discussed later, such as test bias, gender-role socialization, and discriminatory educational practices, have been implicated in explaining these kinds of patterns, as well as the image of the science "nerd"— isolated, unattractive, asexual, with thick eyeglasses and a pocket protector—which is thought to dampen the aspirations of young women regarding MSTE fields. Moreover, despite some progress regarding the inclusion of women in mathematics and science textbooks, many of these learning tools remain steeped in stereotypic depictions of women and men.

Research suggests that purposeful exposure to models and cognitive training in the form of increased information about actual job activity reduces gender stereotyping of occupations, but it is unclear whether such changes lead to real expansion of vocational options. Moreover, there is evidence that rising numbers of women in male-dominated occupations make those careers more appealing to women but not necessarily more attractive to men, suggesting relatively intractable ideologies on the part of men about women in particular career fields. [*See* CAREER ACHIEVEMENT.]

2. Educational Discrimination

Pervasive bias against women in education is well documented. Problems for female students include classroom interaction and communication patterns that exclude or marginalize (e.g., sexist jokes, use of examples and analogies familiar to males); faculty behavior that ignores or belittles (e.g., excessive attention to males, low expectations of female performance); faculty and peer harassment that frightens and intimidates (e.g., sexual harassment); curriculum content and practices that alienate (e.g., greater opportunity for males to use manipulative equipment, excessive focus on rote learning, lack of interpersonal contact with faculty or peers, textbooks that marginalize or stereotype women); extracurricular activities and organizations that exclude (e.g., women excluded from field trips considered too "rough"); and the absence of women in positions of power and influence to serve as role models, mentors, and advocates for female students. These problems are exacerbated for racial/ethnic and sexual minority students, who face additional discrimination related to their minority status. Socioeconomic background also is an important factor in educational achievement; one recent study found that academically successful women from disadvantaged backgrounds attributed their success to the fact that they did not disclose their background to faculty, suggesting that they perceived classist attitudes in professional educators.

It should be noted that women's colleges and historically Black institutions have excellent records of producing high-achieving women. Women's colleges have graduated a disproportionate number of female physicians, college presidents, members of Congress, rising stars of *Fortune* 500 companies, and research Ph.D.s, while historically Black institutions are largely responsible for the number of Black women pursuing advanced degrees in MSTE fields. Although selection standards likely play an important role in these kinds of patterns, it also seems clear that an environment in which females are taken seriously can result in positive educational outcomes for young women.

Unfortunately, the blatant educational discrimination of the past often is replaced by benign tolerance on the part of faculty, offering no support or encouragement and leaving young women even more confused and self-blaming when goals are thwarted or fail to materialize; for example, a professor might point out to a female chemistry student that her weak math background is likely to bar her from desirable jobs, but then offer no suggestions for improving her skills. Recent research on retention of students in MSTE majors supports the importance of faculty relationships for women students. Not only were female students about twice as likely as males to have chosen these majors through the active influence of someone important to them (e.g., a teacher)

and to arrive at college with greater expectations of having personal relationships with faculty, but they also were more affected by faculty attitudes and behaviors (e.g., praise, criticism) than males and were less able to separate their feelings about faculty from their own performance in classes. Perhaps due to female gender socialization, which teaches women to perform for and measure their success by the opinions of others, female students tend to be more dependent on teachers for performance evaluation and academic support than are men. This represents a serious handicap for women students, whose self-confidence is seriously compromised by the large impersonal classes and lack of feedback that characterize undergraduate education in most research universities. An educational environment that is not particularly encouraging of students is termed a "null environment," and it is thought to be especially harmful (i.e., discriminatory) toward female students in its failure to take into account (and therefore proactively address) the vastly different circumstances from which male and female students come in terms of support for academic and career pursuits. [*See* Academic Aspirations and Degree Attainment of Women; Classroom and School Climate.]

3. Compensation Discrimination

Research indicates that men in virtually every occupation advance faster, further, and with greater compensation than do their female peers, and differential salary patterns have remained quite consistent over time (women now earn $0.72 for every dollar earned by men, up from $0.63 20 years ago but down from its high of $0.76 in the mid-1990s). Several examples of salary gaps were presented earlier in this article, and it is important to note that various documented compensation differences persist even when factors such as age, education, experience, and performance are controlled. Occupational status appears to be related to earning differentials, with female-dominated occupations compensated much more poorly than male-dominated occupations requiring comparable training and skill. Moreover, the literature makes clear that the high levels of occupational gender stratification occurring in the workforce stem from discrimination, not merely from career "choices" made by women.

Gender-role attitudes have been strongly implicated in earnings differentials. For example, a depressed-entitlement effect has been documented, in which women in simulated work tasks pay themselves less than men for the same amount and quality of work. Similarly, marriage and parenthood are associated with higher salaries for men but lower salaries for women, and evidence also indicates that women often are not viewed as coproviders in dual-career families even when they earn as much or more than their husbands. Such findings buttress the argument that women in the workplace are not taken as seriously as men, particularly when their family roles are made salient.

4. Discrimination in Advancement and Achievement

Research documents pervasive sex differences in patterns of occupational advancement and achievement (often termed the "glass ceiling"), with women consistently disadvantaged despite education, qualifications, tenure, and occupational attitudes comparable to or surpassing those of men. A recent study of female workers found that 55 to 62% of the variance in career success was attributable to sex discrimination, and studies document perceptions of work environments as significantly more hostile to women than men. Such perceptions have critical implications for job satisfaction and turnover; for both men and women, the friendlier they perceive the work environment to be, the longer they plan to stay in the organization. Job satisfaction also is strongly linked to family attitudes and behaviors (e.g., spousal support), internal conflict regarding multiple roles, mentoring, social support, income, and occupational rank and type, all areas in which women typically are disadvantaged relative to men.

Workplace discrimination against women ranges from blatant to subtle, with recent scholarly emphasis on "cumulative disadvantage"—the occurrence of microinequities that seem insignificant in isolation but accumulate over time to produce tangible unfairness and harm to women. Computer simulation research has demonstrated the usefulness of this concept in understanding sex differences in status attainment. One study of promotion practices in a hypothetical corporation demonstrated that small-scale gender bias—bias accounting for only 1% of the variability in promotion—resulted in 65% males at the top of an eight-level hierarchy after repeated promotions.

Specific barriers to women's status attainment center around the decision-making power in most organizations (especially those in male-dominated fields) being in the hands of "old boys," senior-level men who often are uncomfortable with women's movement into their ranks, and typically promote other men. This leads to job segregation, tracking women into a narrow band of less desirable positions and assignments, with decreased opportunity to demonstrate abilities and receive recognition for achievements. Added to job segregation is the tendency for women to be burdened with "shadow jobs"—responsibility for organizational tasks that impede advancement; in academe, for example, women faculty often have excessive administrative, teaching, advising, and mentoring demands, which are expected of them as women but not rewarded in tenure and promotion. Such patterns affect evaluations of job performance, which tend to be poorer for women than men, especially when women are present in low numbers; research suggests that women are judged more positively when their percentages in the organization reach one-third (or, in hiring, when they comprise at least 30% of an applicant pool). An irony of job performance for women is the mixed message they often receive—gender-role stereotypes lead to decreased expectations for women's success, yet women consistently report having to surpass men in achievements in order to obtain even minimal recognition for their work. [*See* POWER.]

Double standards for male and female behavior present an additional barrier to women's advancement. Research indicates that there is greater expectation and acceptance for displaying leadership behavior (e.g., being assertive, firm, aggressive, self-promoting) in men than women, and even successful female leaders are perceived as having less leadership ability than men. Any behaviors viewed as aggressive or self-serving are especially negatively judged in women leaders and managers—suggesting a double bind for women in that good leadership/management practices are largely incompatible with acceptable female behavior. Other well-documented barriers to women's advancement include sexist attitudes and behaviors of superiors and coworkers, the prevalence of sexual harassment and rape on the job, lack of institutional resources for advancement, and juggling of work and family.

As an example, a recent study of faculty at 24 U.S. medical schools found that women were less productive and less satisfied with their career progress than were their male peers, publishing an average of 18 journal articles to men's 29; lack of institutional support (e.g., secretarial help, grant support) as well as greater responsibility for children were implicated in this gender gap. A large study of hospital-affiliated internists found that 67% of women reported gender discrimination by patients themselves, 56% by peer physicians, and 48% by senior physicians. Two much-publicized recent studies in MSTE fields—the Project Access study of elite scientists and a study of female science faculty at MIT—documented widespread institutional and individual discrimination. Eminent female scientists in another study cited as barriers to advancement the unfair or inaccurate assessment of women by men, lack of institutional financial support during the critical early years of their careers, lack of inclusion in old-boy networks, lack of mentors, and persistent negative societal attitudes. Studies of attorneys reveal that women are more likely than men to be questioned about their credentials and professional status, receive compliments about their appearance rather than accomplishments, and experience sexist jokes and sexual harassment (especially those with high career aspirations); both male and female clients show greater deference to male lawyers than females; male attorneys are given more attention and credibility than female attorneys by judges; and preference is given to male lawyers in partnership decisions.

The effects of workplace discrimination may be especially high for women in blue-collar occupations or low-level positions, and for those who are members of other oppressed groups (e.g., racial/ethnic and sexual minorities). A recent study of female firefighters found that they experienced more sexist events, more job stress, and lower perceived valuation by coworkers than did women in more traditional careers. Tradeswomen report particularly high levels of isolation, harassment, discrimination, and impediments to advancement; because skills in these fields are acquired in apprenticeships or on the job, lack of support by coworkers and superiors is especially damaging to their careers. Research indicates that sexist discrimination contributes far more to women's psychiatric and physical symptoms (such as depressive and somatic complaints) than do more generic stressors, suggesting that occupational discrimination exacts a high price in women's mental health.

Evidence also suggests that standing out as a male in a female-dominated field is advantageous to men, while the reverse is not true for women. The latter is perhaps due to the double bind of tokenism for women—excessive demands and expectations based on being one of only a few women, yet lack of credibility and widespread dismissal of one's efforts and accomplishments as a woman. Increased visibility results in greater scrutiny, performance pressure, attention to non-job-related characteristics (e.g., appearance), and tests of loyalty to the dominant group, but not greater support. Tokenism also interacts with the tendency for people to believe in a just world, so that the visibility of a few highly placed women results in the widespread misperception that vocational meritocracy functions adequately and fairly for women.

5. Climate of Science

In MSTE fields, there is growing recognition that the "chilly climate" in science is an additional force that discourages women from pursuing and remaining in those fields. Implicated in an inhospitable climate are a male model of career success in science that emphasizes excessive competitiveness, combativeness, aggression, self-promotion, and the use of ordeals in grooming young scientists; alienating linguistic patterns (e.g., use of "dirty" jokes, masculine images) that permeate laboratories and classrooms; narrow views of scientific investigation and scholarship, with emphasis on quantity rather than quality of output; a dispassionate attitude of detachment, objectivity, and focus on incontrovertible answers; teaching methods that emphasize memorization and rapid problem-solving rather than discussion and exploring fundamental concepts; the exclusion of females from both formal and informal networks; resource allocation favoring men and excluding women; and institutional policies that disadvantage women (e.g., academic tenure, which coincides with women's childbearing years, forcing them to choose between career and family). Some scholars have suggested that the large influx of foreign-born men into U.S. science, many of whom hold cultural beliefs in the inherent inferiority of women, may exacerbate these problems. Moreover, it has been suggested that many academic women in MSTE fields choose small liberal arts colleges rather than large research universities in pursuing their careers to avoid more negative workplace climates.

6. Mentoring

While much of the difficulty for women of negotiating male-dominated work environments stems from lack of male support, the absence of other women also constitutes a barrier to their participation in nontraditional fields. Professional isolation virtually guarantees that women will not gain access to knowledge critical to their success. In fact, research demonstrates that more women than men lack information about what is required for career advancement; since women also tend to be excluded from informal networks, they receive little feedback regarding their performance and are less able than men to take corrective action and position themselves for desirable outcomes. The presence of women in positions of power in organizations and institutions helps to legitimize other women and provides models of status attainment with which women can identify. In addition, many women seek role models and mentors who can help them manage the home-work interface, and women may be more capable than senior men of providing this modeling.

Although research indicates that having mentors has positive effects on women's career advancement, it is exceedingly difficult to obtain mentors due to the lack of women (particularly racial/ethnic and sexual minorities) in the upper ranks of most workplaces. Studies indicate that individuals receive more support for advancement from same-sex workers and also that men tend to support other men while women support both women and men; simple math applied to these findings suggests that men are far more likely to be in mentoring relationships than women. This workplace reality is supported by reports from female scientists, who indicate that exclusion from information-rich old-boy networks constitutes a critical impediment to their success, compounded by the general lack of women in science to serve as role models and supporters and to help counteract persistent negative social attitudes. Further support comes from studies of the career success of women of color, who consistently report difficulties in finding mentors similar to themselves and assert the critical importance of mentoring to career achievement. [*See* MENTORING AND FEMINIST MENTORING.]

7. Bias in Counseling and Testing

Bias in counseling and testing is an especially pernicious problem in the early years of learning about, choosing, and entering careers. For example, the widely-used SAT underpredicts women's college grades, placing them at a disadvantage in admissions decisions. The Armed Services Vocational Aptitude Battery (ASVAB), an aptitude test used extensively in the military to match enlisted personnel to occupations, contains sections based on exposure to activities (e.g., automotive mechanics) rather than aptitude, thereby restricting women's placements. Another example is the presumed hexagonal structure of occupational interests (realistic, investigative, artistic, social, enterprising, and conventional), which underlies several widely used interest inventories as well as the organization of many career centers, occupational resource materials, and commercial resources; research suggests that this structure may not fit female interest patterns, thus rendering these resources inadequate in assisting women with career decisions.

There is a voluminous literature in gender-related issues in psychological testing; suffice it to say here that many of the assessment devices commonly used in career counseling have been criticized for their inaccuracy or lack of applicability to women (including racial/ethnic and sexual minorities), and much research has explored test modifications and assessment alternatives that better serve diverse populations. Unfortunately, this psychometric work does not always filter down into the training of counselors and psychologists, who often harbor their own biases, resulting in counseling that is unhelpful at best and harmful at worst. Research indicates that many counseling and clinical graduate training programs do not prepare trainees adequately in the areas of gender, sexual orientation, and race/ethnicity, suggesting that individual clients may or may not get skilled, sensitive help with their vocational concerns. Indeed, a recent review of several decades of literature in women's career development indicates that many existing assessment tools and interventions used in counseling continue to restrict occupational options considered by women. [*See* TEST BIAS.]

8. Workplace Structure and the Home-Work Interface

Women's difficulties in managing the home-work interface constitute one of the most formidable barriers to their career development, and the structure of the workplace bears the blame for much of this problem. Generally, workplaces have not provided accessible child care, flexible working arrangements (e.g., flextime, job sharing), viable alternative paths to success (e.g., longer or more circuitous tenure tracks), and liberal parental leave policies. A recent study by the Families and Work Institute indicated that of the 1057 employers surveyed, only 9% offered onsite child care, a mere 5% helped workers pay for child care, and only 36% provided information for locating child care. It is important to note the tangible benefits to companies offering child care—a cost-benefit analysis by a large banking firm of its policy of providing 20 days of backup child care in emergency situations showed that the policy saved the company $825,000 in reduced absenteeism in one year, suggesting the fiscal wisdom in providing such services. Interestingly, companies with women in top positions were six times more likely to provide child care than male-dominated companies (19% versus 3%), and retail trade (characterized by female workers in lower echelons and males in positions of authority) was the least likely to offer child care.

Research indicates that many women entering the workforce today plan to combine career and family; for example, 80% of married female medical school faculty have at least one child. In addition, patterns of caretaking suggest that even women without partners or children are likely to be caring for family members or friends. The lack of workplace structural supports for multiple roles places women at risk for internalizing blame when the home-work interface becomes difficult to manage. This is but one example of the interaction between external and internal barriers to women's vocational pursuits. [*See* CHILD CARE; MOTHERHOOD; WORK–FAMILY BALANCE.]

B. INTERNAL/INDIVIDUAL BARRIERS

1. Multiple Role Conflict

One of the most persistent barriers to women's participation in nontraditional (particularly MSTE) fields is the widespread perception (among both women and men) that these fields are incompatible with child rearing. Although ample evidence has accumulated pointing to the beneficial aspects of multiple roles (especially work roles) for women, there is consensus in the literature that many face additional challenges in their career planning and implementation due to combining work and family roles. Indeed, the presence of marriage and children traditionally has been the most salient factor in women's career direction and achievement, and the impact of parenting on career trajectories continues to be experienced far more strongly by women than men. Although shifts in women's employment patterns in recent decades reflect greater workforce participation, higher levels of employment, and smaller families started later in life, women's level of involvement in housework and childcare is still far greater than that of men—that is, women (even working) continue to shoulder most of

the family burden. Recent findings indicate that women spend more than 15 hours per week on housework alone (vs. 9 hours for men), women average 15 hours per week more than men on both housework and child care, and medical school faculty mothers devoted 22 hours weekly to child care as compared to 14 hours for faculty fathers.

These patterns are related to continued societal endorsement of the "motherhood mandate"—the traditional expectation that women's primary fulfillment and responsibility will reside in bearing and caring for children. However, since family roles for women often include caring for aging parents, extended family, close friends, and even community members, multiple role difficulties are likely to affect most women, even those without children. Studies indicate that women feel more comfortable and confident about managing multiple roles if they are pursuing careers in traditional rather than nontraditional fields (perhaps due to perceptions of greater flexibility in traditional jobs), suggesting that women's plans to combine work and family may contribute to occupational segregation.

Although many women plan to combine work and family roles, research indicates that they expect and want their partners to participate equitably in housework and child care, and marital satisfaction is strongly linked to perceptions of cooperation regarding domestic tasks. Other variables that influence the well-being of women in multiple roles are the spouse's views of her employment, gender-role attitudes of spouses and other family members, family climate regarding work outside the home, and aspects of the work environment such as occupational rank and congruence of employment status with personal preferences. Unfortunately, men's expectations regarding their participation in household labor and child care exhibit wide discrepancies from those of women, and their actual performance of domestic tasks is far less than that of their female partners, even in couples who view their relationships as egalitarian. For example, eminent female scientists with children, many of whom are married to scientists (who presumably understand the rigors of a scientific career), have reported that they shoulder most of the responsibility for child care. Thus, it is not simply the combining of multiple roles that creates stress and compromises women's well-being, but rather the lack of concrete support in the workplace and family, forcing women into personal responsibility for impediments to role management that are beyond their control.

2. Self-Concept Issues

One of the most pervasive and intractable attitudinal barriers to women's career success is their lack of confidence and underestimation of competencies, talents, and capabilities. Research suggests that the erosion of girls' self-confidence occurs steadily throughout secondary school and is most obvious in early adulthood, the age at which critical career decisions are being made. Self-concept has been operationalized in many forms in the literature, perhaps most effectively as self-efficacy,—that is, the expectation or belief that one can successfully perform a given task or behavior. Self-efficacy is thought to affect both the types of behaviors attempted and persistence of behaviors when difficulties are encountered. The linking of self-efficacy to career development has resulted in a large body of findings in the vocational literature. Much of this research demonstrates how various sources of self-efficacy (e.g., successful performance, vicarious learning through observation and modeling, persuasive messages) are compromised by female gender-role socialization such that self-efficacy for many vocationally related behaviors is low for women. In particular, weak self-efficacy expectations have been found in girls regarding math performance and study (e.g., boys see themselves as better at math than girls, even when girls' performance outstrips that of boys), as well as the successful completion of male-dominated (e.g., MSTE) majors and careers.

Much scholarly attention during the past two decades has been devoted to demonstrating the debilitating effects of low self-efficacy on pursuit of and persistence in both vocationally relevant tasks and particular career fields. In addition, relationships have been found between self-efficacy and other career variables such as outcome expectations, vocational aspirations, academic success, career barriers, vocational interests, social support, and occupational fit in terms of individual abilities. The literature indicates that females continue to exhibit lower self-efficacy in regard to traditionally male activities and occupations (especially math and science); self-efficacy is a stronger predictor of career choice than past performance or achievement; instrumental behavioral characteristics (e.g., assertiveness, independence) are related to greater self-efficacy in completing career search tasks and in women's choices of nontraditional careers; perceptions of academic gender bias by women are associated with lower career self-efficacy expectations; self-efficacy in combination with other career variables (e.g., ability, support, barriers) predicts persistence in engineering; and prevalent patterns of career self-efficacy favoring males apply to ethnic minority samples as well. Interestingly, self-efficacy differences between males and females characterize college samples but are less pronounced for employed adults, indicating that women successfully engaged in an occupation are about as confident as men and suggesting that self-efficacy expectations can be altered by actual experiences of workplace achievement.

3. Gender Role Socialization

Many attitudinal career barriers in women stem from gender socialization. Despite obvious social change in gender roles and attitudes over the past several decades, research indicates that females still are likely to be taught to be passive, emotional, nurturing, and dependent, while males are more likely to have learned independence, assertiveness, and self-sufficiency. Females frequently are socialized to downplay their competence and intelligence (especially around males), derive their sense of self-worth from their physical attractiveness and appeal to males, base their self-judgments on the opinions of others, expect to marry and bear children, eschew competition in favor of cooperation and pleasantness, be selfless and focus on others' needs, and avoid gender-non-stereotypic activities and interests. Given these socialization patterns, it is hardly surprising that many women may lack career decision-making skills and confidence; perceive insurmountable occupational barriers and hold low expectations for successful outcomes; be sensitive to others' criticisms; and experience guilt, self-doubt, and self-denigration.

Research demonstrates the relationship between perceptions of external occupational barriers (e.g., workplace discrimination) and low outcome expectations regarding careers; females perceive greater career barriers and poorer outcome expectations than males, and racial/ethnic and sexual minority women perceive additional barriers related to those statuses. Evidence also suggests that females are far more likely than males to perceive role conflicts, which may further illuminate women's decisional difficulties. Moreover, women tend to demonstrate lower career aspirations than comparably-talented males, attribute their successes to external factors rather than personal effort or ability, are less self-promoting and more modest than men about their accomplishments, and are less apt to see themselves as qualified for top positions, even when their credentials are equal or superior to those of men.

Even the elite female scientists in the Project Access study reported less self-confidence and clarity about their career aspirations than did males.

Socialized habits of caretaking and self-denial render women susceptible to excessive worry about the judgment of others and guilt about nonparenting pursuits, a difficult problem in a society fueled by media images of women's fulfillment at hearth and home and the lonely heartache of singlehood (regardless of vocational success). Indeed, research indicates that home-work conflicts for women may be due in part to the simultaneous endorsement of conflicting ideologies, holding liberal attitudes about work and careers but more traditional expectations regarding family responsibilities. Moreover, self-doubt leaves women particularly vulnerable to internalizing negative aspects of the environment (e.g., discrimination, denigrating remarks about being single) in a cycle of self-blame that prevents effective action from being taken. An example of this phenomenon is a lesbian worker who is discriminated against in a job evaluation, but blames herself for not being more careful in protecting her hidden identity rather than challenging the discrimination, personally or legally.

4. Gender Effects in "Doing" Science

A final note regarding women in nontraditional occupations is the growing consensus that women in MSTE fields may "do" science differently from men. For example, there is evidence that women follow a niche approach, creating their own area of expertise rather than competing with other researchers in more popular fields. In addition, research suggests that women publish fewer papers than their male counterparts because they take longer on a project, are more thorough and perfectionistic, and take on broader, more comprehensive projects; this emphasis on quality rather than quantity is supported by some evidence that women's articles tend to receive more citations than men's. Differential publication rates for men and women also have been linked to greater resources and more institutional support held by men (e.g., larger labs and more assistants), higher levels of aggressiveness and self-promotion by men, and more involvement in teaching, mentoring, and administrative activities by women.

Many scholars argue that until a "critical mass" of women in an organization or field is reached (estimates of necessary critical mass range from 15% to 38%), no changes will occur in the way that occupation is conceived and practiced. Moreover, pervasive isolation and occupational fragmentation suggest that even when small percentages of women are present, opportunities for interaction and mutual support may be rare. In addition, it is likely that many of the current senior women in male-dominated fields have succeeded by adapting to masculine workplace norms; they may have little investment in changing the culture or encouraging other women to do so. Thus, influxes of women may be required across several generations before changes in workplace culture occur. Results from the Project Access study additionally suggest that only when the percentages of women and men approach equality do barriers to women in those environments really begin to dissipate—a clarion call for continued attention to programs and interventions targeting the increased representation of women in nontraditional occupational fields.

SUGGESTED READING

Ambrose, S. A., Dunkle, K. L., Lazarus, B. B., Nair, I., and Harkus, D. A. (1997). _Journeys of Women in Science and Engineering: No Universal Constants._ Temple University Press, Philadelphia.

Davis, C., Ginorio, A. B., Hollenshead, C. S., Lazarus, B. B., and Rayman, P. M. (1996). _The Equity Equation: Fostering the Advancement of Women in the Sciences, Mathematics, and Engineering._ Jossey-Bass, San Francisco.

Seymour, E., and Hewitt, N. M. (1997). _Talking about Leaving: Why Undergraduates Leave the Sciences._ Westview Press, Boulder, CO.

Sonnert, G., and Holton, G. (1995). _Gender Differences in Science Careers: The Project Access Study._ Rutgers University Press, New Brunswick, NJ.

Tidball, M. E., Smith, G. E., Tidball, C. S., and Wolf-Wendel, L. E. (1999). _Taking Women Seriously: Lessons and Legacies for Educating the Majority._ American Council on Education and Oryx Press, Phoenix, AZ.

Valian, V. (1998). _Why So Slow? The Advancement of Women._ MIT Press, Cambridge, MA.

Work–Family Balance

Rosalind Chait Barnett
Brandeis University and Harvard University

I. History
II. Assumptions, Demographics, and Attitudinal Shifts
III. New Directions

Glossary

Enhancement model Social roles confer benefits to incumbent, such that the more roles one occupies, the more benefits are likely to accrue.

Family Social networks involving caring commitments that will be met regardless of monetary recompense.

Work–family balance To give equal weight to the work and nonwork aspects of one's life.

Work–nonwork integration To redesign work so that it enables employees to meet workplace demands while fulfilling nonwork demands.

Scarcity model Social roles deplete energy reserves, such that the more roles one occupies, the fewer are one's energy reserves, increasing the likelihood of negative outcomes.

THE PHRASE "WORK–FAMILY BALANCE" is relatively new to the research and corporate-policy lexicons and reflects issues raised by changes in workforce demographics, family patterns, women's employment, attitudes toward work and family, and changes in the traditional employee–employer contract. In contrast to most other areas of empirical research in the social sciences, this area is distinguished by having two major sources of research—basic, academic research and practice-driven applied research—each operating within different and often conflicting theoretical paradigms. The *basic* research

question concerns the costs and benefits of combining work and family roles. The dominant (but certainly not the only) theoretical perspective is that human energy is expansive (i.e., the expansion hypothesis) and multiple roles are, therefore, beneficial, conferring both mental- and physical-health benefits to those who occupy more rather than fewer roles. The *practice-driven* applied research question concerns the policies and practices that permit employees to combine work and family roles most successfully from their perspective as well as that of the employing organization. The dominant theoretical perspective is that human energy is limited (i.e., the scarcity hypothesis) and each additional role, therefore, drains energy from a fixed supply. Thus, expending energy in one arena by necessity diminishes the energy available to other arenas, hence multiple-role occupancy leads inevitably to role conflict and to increased likelihood of negative mental- and physical-health outcomes. Although the existence of two such different hypotheses might be expected to generate a wealth of studies evaluating their relative predictive power, few such studies have been done. In contrast, researchers within the basic and applied domains tend to work separately and in parallel, reporting their results in different journals reaching different audiences: academic researchers and practitioners. Although recent efforts at bridging these approaches are beginning to appear, their relative isolation has contributed to a conceptual divide, limiting needed cross-fertilization and theoretical advances.

This article traces the history of this research area, highlighting the major assumptions underlying these two research traditions, research findings, policy developments, and methodological advances.

I. History

The growth of work–family research (sometimes referred to as work–life or work–nonwork) tracks the rise in married women's labor-force participation. Although their employment had been increasing steadily since before and during World War II, it declined in the postwar years of the 1950s and 1960s before experiencing a major resurgence beginning in the 1970s and continuing to the present. Indeed, the massive movement of women into the labor force has been described as one of the most significant social and economic trends in modern U.S. history.

It is currently estimated that 75% of married women are in the labor force. The recent increase is primarily among married women with young children. For example, between 1970 and 1990, among married women with preschool children in the home, the proportion in the labor force nearly doubled, jumping from 30% to 50%. Between 1976 and 1996, the participation rate for mothers whose youngest child was school age (6 to 17 years) rose 22% to 77%, and the rate for mothers of preschoolers posted a 24-point gain, rising to 62%. Moreover, by 1996, 55.4% of women 18 to 44 years old who had given birth within the last 12 months were in the labor force. Only 14 years earlier, in 1976, the proportion of women with children under age one who were in the labor force was only 31%. Moreover, the vast majority of women return to work within three months of giving birth and most stay employed full time. Interestingly, there are more women who change from part-time work during pregnancy to full-time work after childbirth than vice versa.

There is general agreement that the marked growth in women's labor force participation is due to greater opportunities for women in the labor market, increased educational attainment among women, decreased family size, stagnant or declining wages for men, the increased cost of maintaining a middle-class life style, the lengthening life span, and the liberalization of attitudes concerning women's and men's proper roles within the family. In contrast, there is far less agreement about women's ability to function well in the two demanding arenas of work and family. Men's ability to succeed at the same bal-

ancing feat has been taken for granted because, historically, successful fulfillment of the worker role was synonymous with successful fulfillment of the husband/father role. In practice, by focusing heavily on women, work–family research has reflected the assumption that work–family issues are women's issues—an assumption increasingly called into question.

In addition, the overwhelming focus on cross-sectional research, typically with young-to-middle-aged employees, paints a static picture of the nature of work–family issues. Life-course analyses, in contrast, track changes in the way individuals and couples experience and negotiate these issues at various points in their lives. These studies paint a dynamic picture, suggesting that some periods of life are more vulnerable to certain work–family stressors than others and that family systems are dynamic and fluid in their ability to respond to changing internal and external circumstances.

With the growing presence of women in the labor force and with more and more women remaining at work during their child-bearing years, issues of balancing work and family are more pressing than ever. As of 1998, women constituted 48% of the labor force and their labor-force pattern closely mirrored that of their male counterparts (i.e., full time, full year). Moreover, downsizing and increased globalization have created expectations for longer and longer work hours. As of 1997, large minorities of highly educated male and female employees (43.6% of males and 24.6% of females) were working very long hours (i.e., more than 50 hours per week). When you add an average of approximately 4 hours per week in commuting time, many employees are away from their families about 54 hours per week, making any type of balancing very difficult for both women and men.

The picture is complicated by the fact that many employees are in two-earner couples, and among highly educated employees, their spouses are also likely to be highly educated professionals or managers. Thus, often both partners in full-time employed dual-earner couples are faced with expectations for extremely long work hours and do not have the flexibility to support one another or handle nonwork situations. The ascendance of the full-time employed dual-earner couple as the modal North American family creates both challenges for employers and rich opportunities for researchers to study the effect of gender on work–family issues.

In the past, when gender roles were more highly specialized, this line of inquiry was limited by the fact that few males were seriously involved in "family" roles and few women were seriously engaged in "work" roles. Now that at least some women are in jobs that men occupy and some men are heavily engaged in household and child care tasks, it is possible to assess the effects of gender on the linkages between these two roles and such outcomes as job satisfaction, quality of life, and stress-related health problems. Evidence from studies of such couples suggests few gender differences in the magnitude of the relationship between work and family experiences and mental- and physical-health outcomes. A good job is as closely related to women's as to men's mental health, and good family relationships are as critical to men's as to women's psychological well-being. Moreover, having good family relationships is more predictive of men's stress-related physical-health problems than are problems on the job, and having positive family roles buffers men from the distress they would otherwise experience when their jobs are problematic.

Thus, at least within the basic research arena, the original focus on women employees within work-family research is now broadening to include males. Similarly, practice-driven research is beginning to consider the effects of workplace family policies on men. This interest coincided with the current tight labor market in which employers are increasingly anxious to retain their valued employees—male as well as female. Moreover, several surveys indicate that male as well as female employees are highly dissatisfied with the long work hours they are putting in and are willing to forgo future pay raises and promotions for increased nonwork time. Indeed, high turnover rates among professionals and managers have prompted internal scrutiny and consideration of new policies in particular industries (e.g., service industries) and employers (e.g., large private employers). Further evidence suggests that desirable highly educated employees are increasingly attracted to employers who offer family-friendly policies. However, even with all this pressure, most employers offer only a meager array of such policies, which are often undermined by the reluctance of supervisory personnel to implement them.

Concern about the impact of work-family issues on men, especially men in dual-earner couples, also coincided with the demise of the traditional employee–employer contract. The 1980s and 1990s were marked by rampant cost containment efforts that brought to corporate America a rush of mergers, acquisitions, downsizings, and reengineerings. Lifelong employment for the loyal employee—once a hallmark of the U.S. labor force—was eradicated. The workaholic—long esteemed as the prototypic ideal worker—was just as likely as her or his more easygoing counterpart to receive a pink slip. In this climate, employees had to question the "work always comes first" ethic. Employees had to think ahead, constantly positioning themselves to minimize the risk of being downsized out. At the same time, corporations had to think of ways of attracting and retaining good employees, an increasing number of whom are in two-earner families.

Moreover, as elder care issues begin to grab headlines, it is increasingly apparent that employed men as well as women will be called on to provide care to their parents. Indeed, among companies that offer such policies, men and women are equally likely to use them and to spend equal amounts of time per week in providing such care.

Finally, evidence is mounting that work-family issues impact children. Whereas children's ratings of their mothers' and fathers' parenting skills are quite positive and unrelated to whether their parents work or not, they perceive their working parents as tired and stressed. Moreover, the nature of parents' jobs (i.e., mother's and father's) impact children's developmental outcomes. For example, mothers whose jobs do not fully utilize their abilities are more likely than mothers whose jobs are challenging to have children with verbal, emotional, and behavioral deficits. Further, distress is relational; when one member of a family is distressed, so too are the other members. Thus, work–family is neither a woman's nor a man's issue—it is a family-systems issue.

Yet, as noted earlier, few new family-friendly initiatives have been designed, so that the policies provided today are remarkably similar to those offered 25 years ago, when the workforce and its needs were dramatically different than they are today. This stagnation is due to well-entrenched but out-of-date assumptions about men and women, work and family. These highly gendered assumptions also help explain why so often employees, especially those not covered by union contracts, are reluctant to take advantage of the family-friendly policies that are available.

II. Assumptions, Demographics, and Attitudinal Shifts

The publication in 1987 of "Workforce 2000" was a wakeup call to industry. The report predicted that the workforce of the 21st century would be less male, less White, and older than the previous workforce. Employers would need to attract and retain these new employees if their businesses were to succeed. The development of family-friendly benefits became one arena in which some corporations believed they could achieve competitive advantage. Prevalent attitudes shaped these early benefits in ways that are unfortunate and hard to reverse. That is, the underlying models about gender, work, and family roles have changed over time, but corporate work–family policies have not for the most part reflected these changes.

A. SEPARATE-SPHERES ASSUMPTIONS

The prevailing gender-role attitudes in the 1970s were far more traditional than they are today. Briefly, there was general consensus that a woman's primary social role was wife and mother, whereas a man's primary role was breadwinner. Moreover, there was widespread agreement that the mother–child bond is special and unique and that fathers are not suited for child care or housework. There were also pervasive beliefs, growing directly out of the scarcity hypothesis, that multiple roles were "bad" for women; married women with children who took on the added role of employee were inevitably exhausted, highly vulnerable to stress-related problems, and unable to manage adequately the various demands of their complicated and energy-depleting lives. As a result, employed married women with children were less resilient employees than their male counterparts and, therefore, at higher risk for stress-related illnesses such as depression and anxiety. Furthermore, they were shortchanging their children and husbands or partners and putting them at risk for emotional problems. These traditional gender-role attitudes—prevalent in the 1950s, 1960s, and 1970s—are still rampant despite strong evidence that undermines their validity.

Stated differently, the dominant assumption was that the worlds of work and family constituted "separate spheres," each having its own pressing demands. Trying to manage both sets of demands would lead inevitably to conflict. Moreover, this conflict was unique to women (especially to women with young children) and was exacerbated by women's inability to keep family matters from intruding into the workplace. It was (and often still is) assumed that discord and tension would arise as married women with young children entered the workforce

and attempted this difficult balancing act. These assumptions gave rise to the original descriptor for this line of research, namely, "work–family conflict."

Within the organizational domain, the focus was on the interface between the separate spheres. Difficulties due to conflict between work and home were thought to reflect women's inadequate boundaries and inappropriate priorities. Little thought was given to the corporations' role in creating policies and practices that heightened this interrole conflict. For example, early morning, late afternoon, and weekend meetings, short-notice travel plans, limited flexibility of work hours, and, most importantly, the then (and still) dominant management fixation on "face time" as a reflection of employee commitment and productivity add to the difficulty of combining work and family.

Against this attitudinal and demographic background, corporations crafted specific work–family aims and policies. The primary aim initially was to help women employees better manage the *boundary* between work and family (i.e., young children) so that they could be more productive workers. The primary specific policies were parental leave, flextime, onsite child care, and child care referral services. [*See* CHILD CARE.]

Many corporations have such policies on their books, but in practice, asking for these benefits is often taken as an admission of inadequacy—a sign that women are unable to manage their work and family demands. Moreover, many women felt, accurately, that these benefits came with strings attached—women who took advantage of them were seen as less committed and less desirable. Their opportunities at the workplace were often curtailed and their long-term career plans jeopardized. Thus, the informal corporate culture was often more critical in shaping employee behavior than the formal policies. Importantly, such "corporate-convenient" policies took employers off the hook; they were able to claim that they were addressing work–family issues without having to rework the nuts and bolts of their operations. By discouraging innovative workplace practices, policies aimed at the work–family interface maintained gender stereotypes and the status quo.

Although these policies and practices did alleviate certain kinds of stress, they did not and could not address the fundamental problems because the underlying assumptions were wrong. Research on multiple roles and stress has provided ample evidence that challenges these old assumptions. For example, we now know that (1) men, not just women, need and want to respond to nonwork obligations; (2) for men and women, combining roles is often energizing, not depleting, especially when the roles are experienced as more rewarding than problematic; (3) the nature of the job itself, not the interface, is often the major source of stress; and (4) work and family are *not* separate spheres—what happens in one affects what happens in the other. For example, positive experiences at work spill over into the family domain, such that women with young children at home who have rewarding (i.e., challenging) jobs are better able to manage the stresses associated with child care without experiencing psychological distress.

B. DEMOGRAPHIC AND ATTITUDINAL SHIFTS

Although single-earner married families still constitute a sizable minority of families, the era of the sole-breadwinner dad and the stay-at-home mom has given way to the era of the two-earner couple. While numerically a relatively small group, families headed by a single parent have experienced a rapid increase, especially those headed by a single father. Indeed, in the past 20 years, the demographics of the workforce have undergone a massive change and have spurred new views of work–family balance. These trends are shown in Figure 1.

Seven trends are especially noteworthy: (1) the continuing increase of dual-earner couples, (2) the increase in the percentage of mothers with young children in the workforce, (3) the growing similarity in the labor force patterns of women and men, (4) the proliferation of new family forms, (5) the high percentage of married men and women, especially well-educated, professional employees, who would like to reduce their work hours and spend more time with their families, (6) the sharp decline in the number of children couples are having, and (7) the lengthening life span, which means that more and more workers are thinking beyond their work lives and making commitments to nonwork activities that are rewarding today and that may some day be their central concern. In this new era, the workaholic credo holds little appeal for most workers who have to harmonize their work and nonwork needs with the demands of at least two workplaces.

These demographic shifts are mirrored in a recently documented major shift in gender-role attitudes—a shift toward a more egalitarian view of male and female roles. For example, increasingly large numbers of adult males and females 18 years and older now disagree with such statements as "it is always better for men to be the breadwinners and for women to be at home with the children." These attitudes, which have enormous implications for work-family life policies, coincide with greater sharing of household and child care tasks within the family. Recent data indicate the following:

• *Men and women have equal responsibility for maintaining the home.* Men in dual-earner couples do roughly 45% of the housework, as assessed by their own and their wives' reports. The decreasing gap between the time women and men spend in household and child care tasks is due mostly to large increases in time spent by men.
• *Women and men have equal responsibility for breadwinning.* With respect to hourly earnings, a

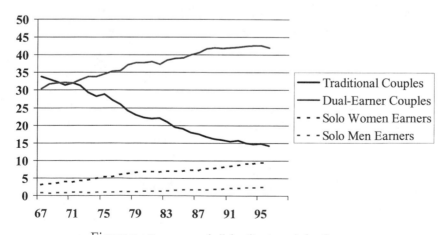

Figure I Percentage of all families in each family type.

growing percentage of wives earn as much as or more than their husbands. In 1996, this "role reversal" was present in 29% of all two-earner couples and in 39% of couples in which the wife was college-educated. In a sample of full-time employed dual-earner couples, the corresponding figure was 31.5%. Also note that the quality of work experiences is as strongly associated with women's well-being as with men's.

- *The mother–child bond is no more special than the father–child bond.* The quality of family experiences—marriage and parenting—is as strongly tied to men's well-being as to women's. In addition, men and women experience equally high levels of separation anxiety when their children are in day care.

- *Fathers can and should play a major role in child care.* Men's relationships with their children are central to men's physical and psychological well-being. When those relationships are troubled, men experience high levels of stress-related health problems. Also, men who do less child care relative to their wives experience high distress, and their wives feel more dissatisfied about their marriages.

These new demographic and attitudinal shifts have led to the realization that there is a strong interdependence between work and family—the separate spheres model is no longer applicable. Moreover, the single-minded focus on conflict and problems (e.g., work–family conflict) that was associated with the separate spheres model has given way to an appreciation of the positive effects of operating simultaneously in two (or more) spheres. For example, substantial empirical evidence indicates that men and women who are seriously engaged in work and family roles enjoy better mental, physical, and relationship health than their counterparts who are involved in fewer roles or who are less involved in the same number of roles.

With the realization that the boundaries between work and family overlap, the tendency for researchers to focus solely on interface issues has diminished. More attention is now being paid to the ways in which work is organized both at the workplace and in the home. These changes are reflected in the term "work–family balance," conveying the idea that we need to understand the ways in which work and family (nonwork) can be redesigned so that workers can give equal weight to these two central life domains. [See FAMILY ROLES AND PATTERNS, CONTEMPORARY TRENDS.]

C. OVERLAPPING-SPHERES ASSUMPTIONS

The assumptions underlying this model are vastly different from those associated with the separate-spheres model. In particular, (1) work and nonwork life are two spheres that overlap considerably, (2) what happens in one sphere has a major effect on what happens in the other, (3) there is no implicit conflict between the demands made in the two spheres, (4) positive outcomes are often possible as a consequence of functioning simultaneously in the work and family spheres, and (5) both men and women have to balance these two aspects of their lives.

As more and more men and women share the breadwinning and nurturing aspects of their lives, they look to their employers to recognize and facilitate these new and complex needs. From the employer's perspective, it is increasingly necessary to attract both partners in order to keep one. Yet for the most part, corporate work–family policies have not responded to this need. The work–family polices and practices associated with this model were the same as those associated with the earlier separate-spheres model: parental leave, flextime, onsite child care, and child care referral services.

Whereas many employees who have family-friendly options take advantage of them, many employers, unfortunately, do not offer them, again underscoring the gap between rhetoric and policies. Even when companies do offer these options, there is still widespread concern about such possible unintended negative consequences as being passed over for promotions or denied challenging work opportunities. These concerns are heightened at times of downsizings, mergers, and layoffs. Thus, despite high levels of perceived conflict between work, personal, and family life, considerable displeasure with the demands of long work hours, and a strong preference among men and women for substantially reducing their time on the job, many employees are reluctant to take advantage of these work–family options.

When the considerable attitudinal and demographic changes are compared with the predominant work–family polices and practices, the most striking conclusion is that everything has changed and nothing has changed.

D. DUAL-EARNER ASSUMPTIONS

Research on dual-earner families indicates clearly that the unit of analysis in work–family studies has to be the family, not the individual employee. For example, each partner's job affects the other partner's level of distress. In other words, a good job benefits both the employee and the spouse, and a bad job impairs the functioning of not only one but two workers. Thus, every employer benefits if all employers institute effective work–family policies that support dual-earner couples.

The realization that most workers are partnered and that the needs and wishes of the partner also have to be considered is beginning to affect corporate policies. Now the expressed aim of some corporate programs is to help women *and* men better integrate their work and nonwork lives. These programs are thought to attract and retain outstanding workers and to optimize their productivity. This aim also reflects the growing realization that men as well as women and parents as well as nonparents are multidimensional beings, and men as well as women thrive when they are engaged in several roles. Thus corporate policies are needed to aid *all* employees in integrating the various aspects of their lives.

What new corporate policies have been instituted to reflect this new aim? Unfortunately, there have been almost no new policy initiatives within corporations. Currently, the most widely available work-family policies are parental leave, flextime, onsite child care, child care referral services, and elder care referral services. Thus, these massive changes in the nature of the workforce, in gender-role attitudes, and in underlying assumptions are not adequately reflected in corporate or workplace policies. With the exception of elder care referral services, we have the same policies that marked the separate-spheres era. Once again we see a disconnect between findings from basic research and corporate practice.

Moreover, although there is general consensus about the worthiness of this small subset of policies and programs, surprisingly few of even large, progressive companies make this package available to their employees. In a recent survey, which will be discussed in greater detail, of the top 10 "family friendly" companies as assessed by their employees, all 10 had elder care programs, 9 out of 10 had flextime and job sharing as well as unpaid family leave beyond that mandated by the Family and Medical Leave Act (FMLA), but only 3 out of 10 had onsite or near-site child care and subsidies, allowances, or vouchers for child care. Moreover, these benefits are much more prevalent in the large companies that were overrepresented in the survey.

Furthermore, there is no evidence that employees are less fearful of the consequences of using these ben-

efits. Many employees report "high immediate and long-term costs" of opting for family-friendly policies. In a large-scale study funded by the National Institute of Mental Health, 63% of the men reported that they did not take parental leave when their babies were born because their supervisors would not like it and 43% said that they feared negative repercussions from coworkers. Corporate cultures can create obstacles that block positive outcomes that might accrue to corporations if employees felt free to take advantage of available family-friendly policies (e.g., employees who take advantage of available family-friendly policies are generally more loyal to their employers and have lower turnover and fewer unplanned absences). Thus, utilization of these policies has direct benefits for the employers as well as the employees.

Given the seismic shifts we discussed earlier, it is clear that policies developed for a simpler time and a different attitudinal climate are no longer adequate. A new vision is required.

E. WORK-LIFE INTEGRATION

Work–family policies were addressed to employees with specific needs (e.g., child care), which were seen as unrelated to decisions about how the work itself should be organized. In contrast, the new focus on work-life integration reflects the belief that every aspect of work affects all employees' ability to have meaningful nonwork lives and that an effective workforce is one that is not compelled to choose between meeting the demands of the workplace and those of the home. Understanding the intertwined nature of work and nonwork raises up for review a host of workplace practices that might be redesigned to better accommodate nonwork needs. Here the focus shifts from benefits directed at certain employees to workplace practices that affect the way work gets done by all employees.

In the present climate, record low unemployment means that desirable employees are likely to have choices about where to work and will be better able to maximize their work-life strategies. Thus, businesses with more innovative and responsive workplace practices will be increasingly attractive to those very employees they most want to recruit and retain. To develop such practices, businesses need a new model, one that challenges stereotypic views of men and women and takes into account the complex lives today's employees lead.

This model differs from its predecessors in that (1) the operative unit is the worker's work-life system, *not* the individual worker; (2) the work-life system is conceptualized as including persons (whether traditionally defined as "family" or not), organizations, or activities to which the employee has responsibilities; (3) the employee's well-being is seen as dependent on the quality of her or his work and nonwork (i.e., life) experiences; (4) work-life decisions are no longer seen as pitting one person's needs against another's; and (5) such decisions are made to optimize the well-being of the system. This new systems perspective is referred to as the "work-life integration" model.

To implement this work-life integration model, businesses will have to introduce a range of new policies. Importantly, these policies would not be seen as benefits for which only certain employees could apply, but rather as basic entitlements open to all employees. For example, except in times of crisis, employers could eliminate all before- and after-hours meetings as well as all last-minute travel. Under such circumstances, employees could arrange their child care schedules and make family or other nonwork commitments free of the anxiety that last-minute disruptions might result in their failure to fulfill these obligations.

In addition, if performance were evaluated more on output than visible input (i.e., face time), then workers would have more control over when they did their work. These policies would increase workers' control over critical aspects of their lives, leading, in turn, to decreased distress and heightened well-being. Such an approach has been tried on an experimental basis at several large employers. For example, recent research at Xerox and Fleet Bank suggests that changes in the way work gets done (e.g., job redesign) and changes in informal corporate culture (e.g., training for supervisors) may have such positive indirect effects on work life as reducing work-family conflict and improving productivity on the job.

Thus, fully implementing this perspective requires a paradigm shift; merely reworking current policies will no longer suffice. The following two recommendations reflect such a shift: (1) developing work-life impact assessments as tools for corporate decision makers and (2) focusing on the importance of how work gets done. Businesses need to factor work-life issues into their core decisions; they need to consider how these decisions will affect the ability of employees and their families to manage their work and nonwork lives. By taking the needs of workers and their families into account and preparing "family (nonwork) impact statements" that analyze the costs to employees' work-life systems of business decisions *before* they are implemented, businesses could avoid unnecessary costs—psychological and monetary—and show their commitment to helping all employees integrate the various aspects of their lives.

This approach would reflect a new focus on the way work gets done rather than on boundary issues. Although problems at the work–family interface persist, they have already received a disproportionate share of attention compared to other problems that may, in fact, be of greater concern to today's employees. Indeed, numerous studies indicate that boundary issues are *not* the primary concern of working parents. As pointed out previously, continued attention to these issues may reflect a "corporate-convenient" strategy rather than "employee-centered" strategy. Stated differently, it is relatively painless for companies to adjust workers' hours and provide day care. Other changes, for example, changes in how the work actually gets organized, are far more difficult to implement.

Changing structural aspects of the workplace (e.g., limiting before- and after-hours meetings) is crucial for workers' ability to reconcile their work, family, and personal lives and ultimately for their own physical and mental health. Such changes provide predictability and, in combination with flexibility of scheduling to meet family/nonwork demands, can significantly reduce work-life conflict with beneficial results for workplace productivity and nonwork place satisfaction. Many employees not only desire these job conditions but are even willing to change their jobs to get them. In a recent analysis, on average, about 25% of workers who did not have flexible schedules indicated that they would be willing to change jobs to get flexibility. Among professional women and men with children under six, the comparable figure was about 30%. The importance of being able to take time off for family reasons was echoed recently in a first-ever survey conducted by *Business Week* magazine and Boston College. Employees of a small group of large (i.e., at least 100 employees) and progressive companies were asked about the family-friendly policies at their places of work. Employees were most critical about the need to work long hours and the inability to take time off for family reasons. Fully 62% of employees at the top 10 companies agreed that their organization asked too much of them—at the expense of their family time.

It is thought that the double whammy of employee dissatisfaction with the status quo and positive effects on the bottom line associated with the kinds of cultural and structural changes described thus far will over time create a new workplace. To the extent that this view is implemented, formal policies and informal corporate culture, which have often been at odds, will come together, thereby alleviating a major source of frustration and anxiety for employees. As of now, too little information is available to determine whether this new perspective will take hold.

The challenges ahead in integrating work and family may be increased as a result of several new workplace trends. Two are particularly worrisome—the movement toward a 24-hour, 7-day-a-week workforce and the rise of contingent workers.

With globalization, there is increased need for workers in many sectors (e.g., financial services, information services, retail) to be available around the clock. At present we know that working nonstandard shifts poses problems for couples with children and may, under certain circumstances, increase the likelihood of marital disruption.

The contingent workforce (i.e., workers who are hired on short-term contracts, usually with few if any benefits and with no long-term career possibilities) is growing rapidly. Currently, women outnumber men in this segment of the labor force, although this pattern may change. As of now, we have no systematic data on the long-term effects on the employees, their partners, their relationship, or their children of living with chronic job insecurity and with the constant pressure of having to adjust to new work situations. Moreover, this trend will lead inevitably to periods of under- or unemployment, both of which are associated with heightened distress. As men and women are brought into this labor market, partners in two-earner couples will have to cope with switching roles in accordance with the vicissitudes of their employment status.

III. New Directions

Increasingly more sophisticated and textured models of work-family issues are needed that focus on the various costs and benefits of integrating work and nonwork roles. Such models have to take into account the corporate climate (formal and informal), changing employment patterns, each partner's job situation and job conditions, the needs of the children, and, increasingly, the needs of elderly dependents. Data need to be collected from both members of dual-earner couples and measurement tools and analytic strategies have to be employed that can assess each partner's evaluation of the differing positive and negative aspects of integrating work and nonwork pursuits. Additionally, longitudinal studies need to be conducted to assess the effects over time of various corporate policies and work arrangements on employees' capacity to integrate their work and nonwork lives. Moreover, technological advances such as telecommuting and teleconferencing are changing how and where work gets done. For employees, these changes often mean increased autonomy but could also lead to more intrusion of work into nonwork time. Collectively these changes will impact corporate polices, management strategies, and both formal and informal corporate culture. There is also a need for research to examine which policies, practices, and work arrangements affect which employees in which ways. In other words, we have to ask new questions, such as the following: (1) Does the age of the working couple affect their capacity to integrate their work and nonwork lives? (2) Do different child care arrangements mitigate or exacerbate work-life integration?

Finally, we have to be more inventive and look beyond corporations to provide answers to work-family integration. Local, state, or national leaders may have to play a role. For example, when public transportation stops running regularly after rush hour and doctors will only schedule appointments during regular work hours, no number of corporate policies are going to alleviate work-family integration problems. Governmental leaders need to realize that the modal U.S. family is the two-earner family and that existing local, state, and national institutions and policies are not family-work friendly. With that realization, they may become more responsive to their constituents and, in partnership with corporations, make changes that would reduce stresses on dual-earner couples, thereby facilitating work-life integration to the betterment of all involved.

SUGGESTED READING

Bailyn, L. (1993). *Breaking the Mold: Women, Men and Time in the New Corporate World.* The Free Press, New York.

Barnett, R. C., and Rivers, C. (1998). *She Works/He Works: How Two-Income Families Are Happy, Healthy, and Thriving.* Harvard University Press, Cambridge, MA.

Boston Bar Association Task Force on Professional Challenges and Family Needs. (1999). *Facing the Grail: Confronting the Cost of Work-Family Imbalance.* Boston Bar Association, Boston.

Coontz, S. (1997). *The Way We Never Were: American Families and the Nostalgia Trap.* Basic Books, New York.

Galinsky, E. (1999). *Ask the Children.* Morrow, New York.

Harrington, M. (1999). *Care and Equality.* Knopf, New York.

Kanter, R. M. (1977). *Men and Women of the Corporation.* Basic Books, New York.

Moen, P. (1996). Gender, age and the life course. In *Handbook of Aging and the Social Sciences* (R. H. Binstock and L. K. George, eds.), Vol. 3, pp. 171–187. Academic Press, San Diego, CA.

Rapoport, R., and Bailyn, L. (1996). *Relinking Life and Work: Toward a Better Future: A Report to the Ford Foundation Based on a Research Project in Collaboration with Xerox Corporation, Tandem Computers, Inc., and Corning Inc.* The Ford Foundation, New York.

Williams, J. (2000). *Unbending Gender: Why Family and Work Conflict and What to Do about It.* Oxford University Press, New York.

Working Environments

Barbara A. Gutek

University of Arizona

Glossary

Glass ceiling A term used to describe the fact that a very small percentage (under 5%) of executive and other high-level positions are held by women.

Hostile work environment A legal term referring to situations where unwelcome sexual conduct is sufficiently severe and pervasive to create a hostile, intimidating, or offensive work environment.

Nontraditional job For women, a job in which most of the workers are men. For men, a job in which most of the workers are women.

Sex segregation, horizontal A condition in which men and women tend to work in different jobs.

Sex segregation, vertical A condition in which men and women tend to work at different levels in the organizational hierarchy, with men at the higher levels and women at the lower levels.

Token status The situation of being different from most of the other people in a group.

WORKING ENVIRONMENTS are the physical and psychological features of the job context that affect workers' experiences. Here, the term "working environments" refers to the various features of the context in which women work that affect women's equal opportunity in the workplace. Work environments are typically sex-segregated—that is, men tend to work with other men, women with other women. The women who work mostly with men face problems in their work environment that other women do not (i.e., there are problems resulting from token status). In virtually all work environments, women's earnings are, on average, less than men's. Some work environments are unfriendly to women, and some women may feel they do not fit in well. A "hostile work environment" is a legal term referring to situations where unwanted sexual conduct is severe and pervasive enough to affect women's equal opportunity at work. Some might contend that if women's work environments are different from men's it is because women have different job preferences, although existing comprehensive reviews of that literature suggest otherwise. Finally, various human resource practices have developed in an effort to ensure that women receive equal opportunity in work environments.

I. Introduction

In 1970, about 38% of adult women were in the labor force in the United States; the proportion of management positions held by women at that time was about 16%. By 1990, the proportion of women employed was about 57.5%; women held 39% of management jobs. These percentages represent major changes over 20 years. While there is evidence that the rate of change has slowed considerably since 1990, it is instructive to examine the factors that have influenced that change. This article concentrates on one such influence, the environments in which women work. In the past, men and women tended to work almost exclusively in different occupations and different jobs, even when they worked in the same or similar fields: men were doctors, women, nurses; men were scientists, women science teachers; men were managers, women were secretaries and administrative assistants. Want ads in the newspaper listed jobs by sex; there were job openings for men and job openings for women. Women were not allowed into many universities and their numbers were limited in many programs and areas of study. Even where women and men were doing the same tasks, they might have different job titles. Both sexes could expect to encounter problems if they sought a job in the "other sex's" territory. Women who wanted to be scientists or managers were considered to be lacking in femininity; men who wanted to be nurses had their sexual orientation questioned. In short, sex segregation of work was unquestioned and viewed by many as a normal and natural outgrowth of differences between the sexes.

Not everyone agreed, of course. Furthermore, for women, the sex segregation of work was associated with a number of negative outcomes. For example, relative to the great number of occupations and jobs held by people, a very small percentage of those were considered women's jobs. Furthermore, there was not a single "woman's job" that led to high levels of remuneration. In general, women's jobs required a fair amount of literacy and other skills but were paid poorly and tended to have few fringe benefits. Researchers talked about women being "crowded" into a few fields, creating substantial competition among women for those jobs, and thereby holding down wages in women's jobs.

Things began to change with the passage of the Civil Rights Act of 1964, which made it illegal for an employer to "discriminate with respect to compensation, terms, conditions, or privileges of employment because of such individual's race, color, gender, religion or national origin." A key reason for the passage of the Civil Rights Act was to "level the playing field," to provide everyone with an equal opportunity in the workplace. One effect of the Civil Rights Act of 1964 and its successor was to pressure organizations to remove barriers and to create more opportunities for previously excluded groups of people, including women.

Under the umbrella of "working environments," this article covers several features of the context in which women work that affect women's equal opportunity in the workplace. Chief among them is the sex-segregated nature of work. What are the dimensions of sex-segregated work and how does it affect women's opportunities and wages in the workplace? To what extent are work environments hostile to women, and which ones are more likely to be hostile? To what extent has the law and organizational practice changed work environments to make them friendlier to women?

II. Sex-Segregated Work Environments

Sex-segregation of jobs is an enduring feature of most work environments. That is, men and women work in different jobs, and often do so in different organizations. Whether a job tends to be done by women or by men defines the subsequent choices for women and men. The fact that women tend to be concentrated in low-paying jobs with other women contributes to the earnings gap between women and men, as will be discussed later.

Sex segregation can be divided into two types: horizontal segregation and vertical segregation. Horizontal segregation refers to the segregation of men and women across fields and jobs, like physician, elementary schoolteacher, baker, or real estate agent. Vertical segregation refers to the separation of men and women within hierarchies. For example, senior executives, high-level government officials, and high-ranking professional positions tend to be held more often by men than by women, whereas women tend to hold positions at lower levels in governmental and private-sector organizations.

A. HORIZONTAL SEX SEGREGATION

There are at least three distinct features of the horizontal sex segregation of work, and there are specific statistics that measure all three of these types of sex segregation. One dimension of segregation is the extent to which women and men are distributed across fields. This indicates the extent to which women and men go into each field and it determines whether a job is considered a "man's job" or a "woman's job." The extent to which a job is sex segregated is indicated by the percentage of one sex that would have to change jobs in order for each job to be held equally often by men and by women. From 1970 to 1990, the index of dissimilarity used to measure this feature of sex segregation has been going down. Based on detailed occupational classifications, in 1997 about half of all women would have to change jobs in order for men and women to be equally distributed across jobs.

A second feature of sex segregation is the crowding of women into a relatively small number of occupations. Crowding is important for two reasons: (1) it is an indication of the amount of opportunity for women, and (2) the financial potential of a field is influenced by supply and demand. If women are crowded into a relatively few jobs, the supply of (female) labor will meet or exceed the demand, holding down wages in these jobs. In contrast, since there are many more jobs that are considered "men's jobs," the demand for (male) labor in many of these jobs will not be met by the supply available, leading to high wages in those jobs where supply cannot meet demand.

A third feature of sex segregation is the chance that women and men share an occupation. This feature determines the amount of contact between the sexes. To take an extreme case, if a job is held only by men, then the men in that job will not come into contact with any women holding that job. If one woman enters that job, all of her contact with others in that job will be with men, whereas each man may still have almost no contact with women because all but one of the people in their job is a man. There are many more jobs in which men predominate than there are jobs in which women predominate. Thus, the average employed woman has a fair chance of working with men in the same field (because even if only a few women work in each male-dominated job, there will be quite a few women working with men in one of the many jobs held mostly by men). In contrast, the average employed man has a much smaller chance of working with women in the same field (because very few men will be working with women in one of the few jobs into which women are crowded).

It is worth noting that the indicators of sex segregation are sensitive to the units of analysis. When broad categories of occupations are used (like managers, professionals, clerical workers), the percentage of women who would have to change jobs so that women were distributed across these broad categories the same as men is about 33%. When more detailed occupations are used (like lawyers, carpenters, sociologists, or bakers), more sex segregation is revealed. One study showed that when jobs consisted of the job titles of people in organizations, in the 1970s, many organizations' jobs were completely sex segregated (i.e., there were no job titles held by both sexes).

A key finding, however, is that sex segregation has declined considerably. Since the early 1970s, the various indicators of horizontal sex segregation have shown that the amount of sex segregation has declined and it has declined most rapidly in the professions and in management. It has declined much less in fields typically held by people who are high school graduates. Nevertheless, the amount of sex segregation is still substantial and the declines were much less impressive (or nonexistent) in the 1990s relative to the preceding two decades.

The main reason for declines in the sex segregation of work is the entry of women into many predominantly male jobs, including many of the professions and various managerial jobs. These jobs have become available to women as a result of federal legislation starting with the Civil Rights Act of 1964. The jobs that were considered "women's jobs" in the 1970s and earlier have not, however, been particularly attractive to men. For the most part, they have remained highly sex segregated. The net effect is that there is now less crowding as women have moved into a variety of jobs held formerly by men alone. This reduction in crowding should benefit women in traditional and nontraditional jobs. As women move into more nontraditional jobs, there should be less competition among women for traditionally female jobs, thus forcing wages to rise in order to attract highly qualified women to those jobs. (Unfortunately, sometimes something else happens other than raising wages, for example, restructuring or automating the job, moving it "off shore" to another country where wages are less, or hiring more foreign workers to increase competition for the job.) [*See* WOMEN IN NON-TRADITIONAL WORK FIELDS.]

B. VERTICAL SEX SEGREGATION

The amount of vertical sex segregation is determined by examining where women and men work in the organizational hierarchy. Vertical segregation exists when the men who work in the organization tend to hold jobs at the higher levels and women work at the lower levels. Some organizations, especially government civil service jobs, have grade classifications, such as grades 1 through 10. Analyses of such grade classifications typically show that the majority of the people in the higher grade levels are men, and women tend to be in the lower grade classifications. In fact, it is almost universally true that the higher up one goes in rank (whether in an organization or within a job classification), the proportion of workers who are women goes down. For example, the proportion of psychology majors who are women is larger than the proportion of psychology Ph.D. students who are women, which is larger than the proportion of psychology junior faculty who are women, which is larger than the proportion of psychology full professors who are women. The same story is replayed in virtually every field, in female-dominated jobs and in male-dominated jobs.

This virtually universal trend has been noted by many scholars. Despite the fact that women have increased their labor force participation substantially since 1970, women occupy a paltry number of executive-level positions in business, government, and other fields. The proportion of female executive in large U.S. corporations was 0.5% in 1979 and 2.9% in 1989. In 1986, the proportion of female executives in Fortune 500 corporations was 1.7%. A United Nations report on *The World's Women: 1970–1990* revealed that at the end of 1990, only 3.8% (6) of the 159 United Nations member states were headed by a woman. In addition, only 3.5% of the world's cabinet ministers were female; women held no ministerial positions in 93 countries, and women consisted of more than 15% of parliamentary representation in fewer than 25 of the 159 countries.

Although there are few universal "laws" in the social sciences, it appears to be a universal phenomenon that in not a single field open to both sexes do women occupy as high a percentage of managerial or executive level positions as worker positions—in any country in the world. This has led some to postulate the existence of a "glass ceiling," a term first used by the *Wall Street Journal,* and some to postulate the existence of a "sticky floor."

The glass ceiling refers to the fact that it seems very difficult for women to penetrate the higher levels of organizations, as if "a glass ceiling" existed that one cannot see but is nonetheless effective in keeping women out of the executive suite. Studies of women who have risen above the glass ceiling reveal a number of problems they face. They often report

that they have had a difficult time finding a mentor and they are excluded from informal networks. To overcome these problems, they use a number of tactics. Whereas executive men generally claim they are successful because of their talent and hard work, women typically claim they need more than just a good track record, although that is important. For example, some suggest the importance of obtaining appropriate academic credentials, such as an MBA from an elite business school, and maintaining and using the network of contacts gained through their educational programs. Also they may try to be similar to their male peers or point out similarities that already exist. If talking sports, politics, and what is in today's *Wall Street Journal* is what is required, that is what many do.

Others have suggested the existence of "sticky floors" in women's jobs, meaning that many women's jobs have a short "career ladder." They do not lead to promotions, but are dead-end jobs. Research has shown that by-and-large, jobs in which women predominate tend to have short career ladders. That is, many of the jobs held by women are not viewed as preparation for higher level jobs. Many clerical and production jobs held by women fit this pattern. Women may hold production jobs, but first-level managers may be (mostly male) college graduates hired from the outside. Some grocery stores tended to promote workers from the produce department (mostly men) but not workers from the bakery (mostly women). Other jobs have longer career ladders, but they provide little opportunity outside that job area. Take the job of secretary, for example. Historically, when most secretaries were men, the position did offer an opportunity to move into management, but that changed when women became secretaries. Starting 80 years or so ago, working as a secretary did not prepare one to become a manager. One may rise in the secretarial ranks, but it was virtually impossible to move from the secretarial ladder to the managerial ladder. In the past few decades, some organizational leaders have come to realize that the secretaries in their company were a possible source of managerial talent.

Why does vertical sex segregation exist? Some of it may be a holdover from the pre-equal-opportunity days. Some say it is a "pipeline problem." There simply are not enough women in the pipeline for promotion. If women do not get Ph.D.s in psychology, they cannot be full professors in psychology. There will be more women full professors when there are more women getting Ph.D.s. Similarly, there will be more female chief executive officers (CEOs) when more women get MBAs. In general, the pipeline model does not seem to adequately explain the current situation, as women have been in the pipeline in many fields for quite a while with few of them penetrating the glass ceiling. Some suggest that a better model is a "leaky pipeline" with women falling by the wayside (or leaking out of the pipeline) at a higher rate than men all along the pipeline. The leaky pipeline might be caused by discriminatory, unsupportive, or hostile work environments, or it could be caused by family obligations, women's socialization, gender roles, or something else. Or it could be caused by a combination of all of these factors—and more.

Like horizontal sex segregation, vertical sex segregation has a number of consequences for women. The few women who pierce the glass ceiling are "tokens," and they have all the problems characteristic of tokens, a topic covered in the next section. Lack of women at the top also means that most women work in places with few women at the top. An interesting question is: Does having women in high-level positions have any effect on women at other lower levels? Interesting research by Robin Ely suggests that it does. She compared women attorneys who worked in firms with a small proportion of female partners (fewer than 15% of partners were women) with women who worked in firms in which there were relatively more female partners (more than 15% of partners were women). Female attorneys who worked in firms with a few or no female partners were, compared to other female attorneys, less likely to perceive relationships with same-sex peers as supportive, and they were also less likely to perceive women partners as suitable role models. In addition, women in firms with fewer women partners were more likely to characterize women as flirtatious and "sexually involved with coworkers" compared with women in firms with a greater number of women partners. Women in the latter firms were more likely to characterize women partners as "aggressive" and "able to promote oneself." The women in firms with few women partners tended to see their male associates as having the traits required to succeed as attorneys whereas the women who worked in firms with more female partners were more favorable in their evaluation of women having the characteristics necessary to succeed. It is also likely that women who work in firms with more women in senior or executive positions may be less likely to judge their own work environment as hostile (discussed later), relative to those women who work in firms with few or no senior women.

III. Token Status

One of the effects of sex-segregated work is the creation of solos and tokens. A solo is a person who is different from others in the same work unit or organization. A woman engineer in a department where all the other engineers are men is a solo. When there is one or two or a very small percentage of one kind of person, say fewer than 15%, the numerical minority are called tokens. A few researchers reserve the term "token" for a solo who is viewed as being hired because of pressure to hire previously underrepresented groups. Unless otherwise specified, solo and token refer to a numerical minority in this article.

In 1977, Rosabeth Kanter investigated what has become known as "token dynamics," or how having skewed sex ratios (one or a few women and many men, for example) affects both the token (the persons in the numerical minority) and those people who are in the numerical majority in the group. Kanter claimed that token dynamics is a general process that applies across social categories (like race, gender, age, or religion) and applies equally regardless of which sex or race, for example, is in the minority. A solo man working with all women should encounter the same token dynamics as a solo women working with all men.

Kanter identified three "token dynamics:" visibility that leads to performance pressures, contrast effects that lead to social isolation of the token, and role encapsulation or stereotyping of the token. Because the token is different, where that difference is highly visible (as is sex and race, for example), the token will get extra attention. He or she is noticeable and noticed. Because the token is unusual in that position, attention is likely to be focused on whether or not the token can perform as well as the numerical majority, the people who have traditionally held that job. That means that a solo woman engineer, for example, will find that her work will be scrutinized in more detail than the work of her male colleagues. The pressure to perform is exacerbated by the fact that the solo may be expected to represent all members of her group. In short, each of the male engineers can fail without his failure affecting others' judgments of men's ability to be engineers, but if the solo woman fails, her failure is likely to affect others' judgments of women's ability to be engineers.

A second token dynamic is contrast, that is, the majority tends to focus on differences between themselves and the tokens, leading to increased solidarity among the majority group members and social isolation of the tokens. They may start to identify themselves as men, for example, instead of simply as engineers, once a token woman engineer shows up, or notice characteristics they may have in common that the token lacks, such as experience in the military or team sports. The third token dynamic is stereotyping. In particular, Kanter identified four "familiar roles" that token women may be expected to enact (depending on which seems most suitable): mother, pet, sex object, and, for the woman who rejects those roles, militant or iron maiden (or simply, bitch).

Token dynamics have been studied extensively leading to both limitations and extensions of Kanter's original work. One conclusion of the body of research that developed in the 1980s and 1990s is that token dynamics does not apply equally to all groups. In particular, it seems to apply to tokens who are in low-status groups more so than it does for tokens in high-status groups. Thus, it applies to women, but not men. For example, there is no evidence that token men (for example, male nurses) experience social isolation or performance pressures the way token women do (for example, female lawyers or medical students).

There is research showing that tokenism is associated with some negative outcomes for women. For example, women who work in groups with relatively few women sometimes experience less satisfaction with their pay and their job than those women who have more female colleagues. Women who are tokens may question their own competence and ability more than women who are part of the majority in their work group. They may also be subject to more sexual harassment, blocked mobility, and wage inequities. Women attorneys who worked in law firms with few female partners are likely to perceive greater differences between the attributes of successful lawyers and their own attributes than women attorneys who work in law firms with relatively more women partners (say, more than 15% of the partners are women.) Other studies have shown that women's grades tend to be higher where there are relatively more women in their course, that female union officers felt more constrained to conform to traditional gender roles when there were few women union officers than when women constituted a higher percentage of union officers, and the few women who have reached the highest corporate or political positions are less integrated into informal networks and are outside the most influential group of high-level position holders.

Women typically have a more difficult time than men finding a mentor and token women are especially likely to be in that position. In addition, token women who are executives may have a difficult time being seen as a mentor. Promising junior men and some women may avoid a female mentor if they think a woman will not be able to help them as much as a man who, unlike the female executive, may not be outside the inner circle of power. In short, in a wide variety of situations, being a token creates problems for women, problems having to do with performance pressure, social isolation, and stereotyping. Although there are fewer studies of men who are tokens, these studies generally fail to find results consistent with the view that for men, token status is fraught with problems. In fact, the solo man in a work group of women may be the supervisor of the work unit, a situation that is highly unlikely for the solo woman.

If token status is problematic for women, then why do women persist in token positions? Some do not. Research by Jerry Jacobs shows that most women who take nontraditional (male-dominated) jobs tend to move to more traditional jobs when they change jobs; in fact, for every 11 women who work in nontraditional jobs, about 10 will eventually move to a female-dominated job. These findings suggest that nontraditional work environments are neither comfortable nor supportive for token women. Nevertheless, nontraditional jobs are attractive to women because many of the most interesting, challenging, lucrative jobs and those with the most opportunity to lead to other even more interesting, challenging and lucrative jobs are nontraditional, male-dominated jobs.

IV. *Gendered Work Environments*

There is a long-standing tradition that organizations and the managers within them need to serve two different functions or roles: they need to be oriented toward tasks and task completion and they need to be oriented toward people and their participation and cooperation in getting work done. These two functions have a variety of different names: task versus socioemotional orientation, initiating structure versus consideration, instrumental versus expressive. Although it is no doubt a simplification of reality, sometimes the task function is considered masculine and the people function, feminine. Furthermore, according to some, most work environments are "masculine," in that they tend to emphasize the importance of the task activities over the people activities. For example, although one person may fill task and socioemotional functions, when they are filled by two different people in a work group, the task-oriented person is the one most likely to be identified as the leader of the group. The socioemotional "leader" is less likely to be considered the leader by observers.

Beyond the functions that need to be filled in organizations, organizations vary in their "culture," the practices and norms that permeate one organization and that distinguish it from other organizations. Organizational culture is a broad concept including such diverse elements as informal dress codes, norms about punctuality and working hours (how many and at what times), and work attitudes. One may argue further that work cultures vary in the extent to which they are gendered. They are masculine to the extent that their cultures embody norms and metaphors that are associated with men and masculinity. For example, an organization that emphasizes competition and winning is "masculinist" and may be compared with an organization that emphasizes collaboration and compromise. An emphasis on hierarchy and individualism may be considered masculinist in comparison to egalitarianism and community. Or giving priority to career advancement might be masculine, whereas active balancing of life activities and relationships might be considered feminine.

It is important to note that there is no strong consensus about the extent to which these differences in organizational culture are really gendered, that is, whether they really apply to differences between women and men. It is clear that women in nontraditional jobs, including executive and other high-level administrative jobs, commonly report that they do not fit in all that well and that the culture is less than friendly. Nevertheless, some oppose characterizing work environments as masculine or feminine because that seems to support the notion of "essentialism." Essentialism is the belief that there are essential elements that make up masculinity and other essential elements of femininity. Essentialism tends to pigeonhole men and women and it minimizes differences among women and among men while focusing on supposed "essential" differences between women and men. Essentialism makes it easy to conclude that there is a "woman's way" and a "man's way" of doing, seeing, feeling, or thinking despite a lack of research evidence for consistent differences. Nevertheless, it is likely that organizations do differ in ways

that might be considered more or less masculine and that some of the features of those organizations are uncomfortable to a lot of women (and perhaps to a lot of men, as well).

One might argue then that a masculinist working environment discriminates against women because it promulgates norms that are uncomfortable or unusual for more women than men. Some conscious attempts to avoid a masculinist culture have been made. For example, when *Ms.* magazine was developing in the 1970s, everyone had offices of the same size emphasizing egalitarianism and community. The founders of the feminist magazine decided deliberately to be nonhierarchical as much as possible. More recently an analysis by Joanne Martin, Kathleen Knopoff, and Christine Beckman about The Body Shop International, a publicly owned multinational cosmetics firm, concluded that when an organization has a lot of women, including at the top levels, it may establish norms that are unusual in large organizations. In the case of The Body Shop, Anita Roddick, founder and chief executive officer until 1993, actively rejected a number of traditional bureaucratic controls. In this company, Martin and her colleagues discovered that the norm of impersonality found in so many large firms did not exist; instead they found that at The Body Shop, there was a norm of "bounded emotionality." Bounded emotionality is a norm that encourages a certain amount and kind of emotional expression at work for the purpose of encouraging community building and personal well-being in the work environment. Martin and her colleagues reported that it was not necessarily easy for The Body Shop to enact bounded emotionality consistently, and it is not clear that bounded emotionality is necessarily better than impersonality, but it is different and it works for The Body Shop. Whether women fare better or are happier in organizations that actively reject some of the features of organizations that might be considered masculinist remains to be seen. It is clear that The Body Shop provides an alternative to the standard bureaucracy.

V. Wage Inequalities

The United States first began tracking the earnings ratio between women and men in 1955. The direction of the results is always the same: women's earnings are less than men's and that statement is true no matter how one defines earnings (annual versus weekly pay, mean earnings versus median earnings). Women earn less in all ethnic groups, across all educational categories, across the life cycle, within detailed occupational categories, across male-dominated and female-dominated occupations, and across cultures. The earnings gender gap is as close as one gets to a social fact. It is not likely to go away soon.

From 1955 to 1981, the earnings ratio showed a slight decline. The median annual earnings of women who worked year-round, full time was 64% that of comparable men in 1955 and 59% in 1981. After 1981, the earnings ratio rose steadily from 59% in 1981 to 71% in 1995. Although it is too early to tell for sure, it appears that since 1995 the earnings ratio has been flat or has even shown a slight decline. Because more women than men work part-time, when part-time workers are taken into account, the earnings ratio is, as one might expect, lower. In general, the earnings ratio is highest among young workers and women's earnings relative to men's decline with age and experience (until after age 55 when the ratio improves slightly). It is important to note that the earnings gap exists no matter how occupations and jobs are considered. For example, if one compares the wages of women and men in a very specific job category like electrical and electrical equipment assemblers or hotel clerks, men's average wages invariably are higher than women's. The earnings gap in the United States is larger than it is in some other countries, including Sweden (where women earn 90% of male earnings on average), Denmark (85%), Norway (83%), and Australia (83%).

Specific information on wage differences has at various times garnered a lot of attention. For a while, many women sported buttons that simply said "$.59" in an effort to rally support for wage equality. Another widely disseminated and dramatic condition is a comparison of the average female college graduate's income with that of a male high school dropout. In 1990, a college-educated woman earned, on average, only $5,000 more than a male high school dropout and she made the same amount as a male high school graduate (about $25,000). Increasing the education of women does increase their wages, but does not affect the female-to-male earnings ratio and certainly does not eradicate the wage gap.

Differences in earnings do not automatically imply discrimination against women. In fact, some economists argue that wage discrimination cannot exist because if one employer paid more for men, that employer should not be competitive with another employer who hired women (for less money). Eventually the firm employing the less expensive women should drive out of business the firm employing the more expensive men, assuming that the women and men are equally productive (and the two organizations are otherwise equivalent).

Despite this appealing theory, it makes assumptions that are not warranted, it is too simplistic, and it does not fit the facts. For example, there is no evidence that competition is so intense that wage discrimination will put an organization out of business or that organizations are so efficient that they pay workers exactly what the market will bear. They may overpay some workers whom they believe most likely to stay with the firm (mostly men) so that they will stay with the firm (and keep down the cost of replacing workers). Furthermore, if everyone pays men more, then no firm is disadvantaged relative to other firms. In addition, when highly qualified women first brought into a job are treated like tokens, then they are likely to be less productive than they could be in a more supportive work environment. It is also possible that some men may be less productive if they find themselves in a work environment that is counter to long-standing norms and traditions, for example, having a female boss. Employers have traditionally avoided this situation by sex segregation of jobs, where women's jobs lead to few opportunities for promotion so that it is highly unlikely that any man would ever have a female boss. Indeed, it is the case that when women are supervisors and managers, they mostly manage other women.

One way researchers typically examine the extent to which the wage gap might be an indication of sex discrimination is to try to predict wages in a field including as many reasonable explanations for gender differences as possible. These include the number of hours worked, tenure, occupation, industry, whether one works with money, things, or people, and the like. These factors tend to diminish but do not eliminate the significant gender gap in earnings. Women's greater family responsibilities also affect their wages and engagement in household activities is associated with lower wages; the more housework and child care one does, the lower one's wages, on average. In using this approach, researchers have been able to narrow the gender gap in income but never fully account for it. Some argue that the residual wage gap is the result of discrimination whereas others claim that it is a function of legitimate but unmeasured factors (whatever they might be) or measurement error. Those who believe that discrimination does factor into the difference between men's and women's wages point out that some of the explanatory factors, like negative effects on wages for those who work with people (rather than things or money), do more housework and child care, and work predominantly with women, may themselves be indicators of discrimination.

There are also some psychological factors that may help explain women's lower earnings. For example, because women have earned less than men since such statistics have been kept (and most likely before that, too), women expect lower wages. Many studies show that men feel entitled to more and women expect less. Many women may be satisfied with wages that would not be satisfactory to many men. It is simply unrealistic for women to assume that their compensation will be extraordinary when the vast majority of the very highly compensated are men. Observers tend to agree. In general, what observers think is good pay "for a woman" is less than what they consider good pay "for a man."

One reason many women may be satisfied with relatively less is because they compare themselves to other women when they assess their situation. Faye Crosby has examined the concept of relative deprivation as it applies to working women. Because most women tend to work with other women, they compare themselves and their level of rewards with other women. In short, secretaries do not compare their wages to the wages of managers; instead, they compare themselves to other secretaries. The result is that, in general, many women do not feel underpaid because they compare themselves to other (underpaid) women, all of whom are in the same job.

VI. Hostile Work Environments

In 1979, legal scholar, Catharine MacKinnon wrote an influential book, *The Sexual Harassment of Working Women,* which provided a legal framework for dealing with sexual harassment. MacKinnon argued that sexual harassment was a form of sex discrimination and therefore Title VII of the 1964 Civil Rights Act, which forbade discrimination on the basis of sex, should apply. A year after her book was published, the Equal Employment Opportunity Commission (EEOC) established influential guidelines on sexual harassment as behavior that was prohibited by Title VII.

One type of sexual harassment is "hostile work environment" harassment. It occurs when "unwelcome sexual advances, requests for sexual favors, and other verbal or physical conduct of a sexual nature" create an intimidating or hostile work environment. In order to be illegal, these unwelcome behaviors must be severe or pervasive enough to meet a reasonable person's and the complainant's standard of a hostile work environment. In other words, sexual harassment must meet a "subjective" criterion (i.e., the recipient must find it to be severe or pervasive) and an "objective" criterion (i.e., a reasonable person would find the behavior sufficiently severe or pervasive to meet a legal definition). This latter requirement is necessary, according to the law, to prevent frivolous lawsuits by hypersensitive plaintiffs who see sexual harassment in otherwise innocent or harmless behavior.

Despite some concern about what are the appropriate limits of legal (or illegal) behavior, the law now acknowledges that there are circumstances in which the working environment can be hostile and where that hostility is based on a person's sex, the working environment is discriminatory. That is, a woman in a sexually hostile work environment does not have an equal opportunity with men to succeed in that environment. It is also the case that many women may work in environments that they perceive as at least somewhat hostile, but the level of hostility does not rise to meet a legal standard.

What do these hostile work environments look like and why do they exist? Research on sexual harassment shows that a variety of "social-sexual behaviors," behavior with a sexual content that is not work-related and invokes a potentially inappropriate infusion of sex, sex roles, gender, or sexuality into the workplace, are quite common. These behaviors can include sexual jokes and comments; visual material like sexual pinups, posters, pictures, or cartoons that are sexual in nature or derogatory to women; unwelcome sexual touching including grabbing, fondling, or stroking; repeated unwelcome requests for dates or sexual favors; repeated staring, ogling, leering; and the like. When they are severe or pervasive, they can be illegal. But even if they are not illegal, they may affect a woman's views of her work, herself, her coworkers and supervisors, and her organization. A hostile work environment is likely to be stressful and it may encourage her to change jobs or affect her job satisfaction, commitment to her employer, and commitment to her occupation.

Hostile work environments are more likely to occur under several conditions: when the organization tolerates sexual harassment and when the work environment is sexualized. It is sexualized when sexual jokes and sexual material are common; where women workers may be expected to serve as sex objects (through their dress, either uniforms or general dress codes), behavior, or words; workers or supervisors discuss their sexual behavior with coworkers and encourage their coworkers to divulge details of their own sexual activity; or workers are addressed in sexual terms. When these activities are common, women are likely to experience the work environment as hostile. Some observers have noted that women are most likely to be sexually harassed when a man who is likely to sexually harass works in an environment where sexual harassment is tolerated. Although we do not know how many men are likely to sexually harass, research to date suggests the number is quite small. Unfortunately, each would-be harasser can harass many different women and there is some evidence to suggest that many of them do.

Hostile work environments are also more common when there are relatively few women in the work environment or relatively few or no women in higher-level positions in the organization. Thus, there seems to be more hostile work environment harassment when there is either horizontal or vertical sex segregation, or both. When there are many men in the work environment, women are more likely to come into contact with a man or a group of men who sexually harass. In the case of horizontal sex segregation, a high percentage of one sex in the job is likely to lead to the spillover from the sex role of that sex to the work role. Barbara Gutek and her colleagues defined sex-role spillover as the carryover of gender-based expectations to the workplace. If the work environment is male dominated, then people in that role are likely to be expected to behave "like men," however that is defined in that particular place. The female token is likely to be seen as different and may be rejected by her male coworkers and supervisors. One way to do so is through sexual hostility, that is, sexually derogatory jokes, comments, printed and posted material, sexual epithets, and the like. One possible outcome of such rejection is for the woman to quit her job and seek a new job in a more traditional field where more of her coworkers are female.

If the work environment is female dominated, the job itself takes on aspects of the female sex role (i.e., the activities associated with being a member of the female sex). The work role overlaps substantially with the sex role. Different traditionally female jobs emphasize different aspects of the female sex role. For example, jobs in which women interact primarily with children, the sick, the aged, the handicapped, or the poor are likely to emphasize the nurturing aspect of the female sex role. When women are expected to be sex objects—cocktail waitresses, some receptionists or personal assistants, actresses, and the like—they may receive unwelcome sexual attention, such as comments and overtures from male customers or other men they work with. Where women are expected to act as sex objects, even where the sex object role is not as blatant as it is at a place like Hooters restaurants, women may also be targets for the other kind of sexual harassment, called *quid pro quo* harassment. *Quid pro quo* harassment occurs when workers are expected to engage in sexual activity as a condition of employment or a condition of work. In a work environment where women are behaving as sex objects, it would not be surprising to see some men offer to exchange work-related benefits for sexual favors. In sum, sex-role spillover may facilitate the sexual harassment of women who work mostly with men in male-dominated jobs or who work in female-dominated jobs where they are expected to be sex objects. [*See* SEXUAL HARASSMENT.]

VII. Sex Differences and Similarities in Preferences for Job Attributes

If men and women, on average, have different values or preferences for jobs, and if preferences affect the kinds of jobs that people get, then most women would work with other women and men with other men. Job attributes preferences are "the extent to which people desire a variety of specific qualities and outcomes from their job." (Konrad *et al.*, 2000, p. 593). Examples include performing tasks that are challenging, getting paid a lot of money, or having the opportunity to travel as part of one's job. Not surprisingly, having different preferences is often given as one of the reasons why jobs are sex segregated.

Women and men might have different preferences about their working environments for at least two reasons. Sex roles might encourage women and men to prefer different job attributes. Women, for example, are often assumed to want to work fewer hours in order to accommodate family responsibilities whereas men are assumed to be willing to work more hours and expect fringe benefits if they are considered the family's main financial provider. Different preferences may also arise from personality differences between men and women. For example, if men are more dominant than women, on average, they are more likely to seek jobs that allow them to be dominant (as managers or consultants). If women are more nurturing than men on average, they are more likely to seek jobs that allow them to work with people, especially children (as elementary school teachers, nurses, or pediatricians, for example).

Until recently, the body of research on job attributes was not very coherent, in part because various researchers used different terms for job attributes (for example, work values) and in part because there were no systematic and thorough reviews of the literature. Both of those flaws were remedied by two major meta-analytic reviews (quantitative reviews) of the literature by Alison Konrad and her colleagues and students. They analyzed 242 samples consisting of more than 600,000 women and men and girls and boys (as young as elementary school) in which they classified and analyzed 40 job attributes for sex differences in preference. In general, sex differences were found in 33 of the 40 job attributes, but in 26 of them the difference was quite small.

The reviews of Konrad and associates allow us to make fairly definite statements about gender differences in job preferences with a degree of confidence not possible even a few years ago. In general, men and women, on average, do exhibit some differences in preferences for job characteristics. Most of the differences are small and consistent with gender roles and stereotypes. Men, more than women, valued high earnings, promotions, freedom, challenge, leadership, and power. Women especially valued good hours, an easy commute, interpersonal relationships, helping others, and a number of intrinsic job characteristics. Intrinsic job characteristics refer to characteristics of the job itself, such as providing challenge, creativeness, cultural and aesthetic accomplishment, continued development in one's job, intellectual stimulation, and the like. In general, women rated intrinsic job attributes higher than men did with a few exceptions: women did not rate freedom and challenge higher.

Men tended to value what are considered "extrinsic aspects" of the job more than women, namely pay, fringe benefits, job security, and the opportunity for promotion. These modest sex differences in intrinsic (preferred slightly by women and girls) and extrinsic (preferred slightly by men and boys) features of jobs are interesting because prior to these reviews, some scholars predicted that men valued both intrinsic and extrinsic features more than women whereas others argued that men preferred extrinsic characteristics whereas women preferred intrinsic characteristics more than men. Men should value the

extrinsic aspects of jobs (like earnings and status) if they are more instrumental in their approach to life than women; women should value the intrinsic aspects of jobs if they are more expressive, that is, they should enjoy jobs that are enjoyable and have meaning to them. On the other hand, because paid work is a more central life interest to men than women (who are supposed to be oriented to family roles of wife and mother), some contend that men should value both intrinsic and extrinsic aspects of work more than women (for whom work is presumably a secondary activity). The review by Konrad and associates did not support the contention that men prefer intrinsic job attributes more than women.

When only managers and business students are considered, men rated earnings and responsibility as more important than women did, but by the 1980s, the difference between men and women in wanting responsibility disappeared. Women considered prestige, challenge, task significance, variety, growth, job security, good coworkers, a good supervisor, and a good physical work environment to be more important than men did. These differences were generally very small. Typically the difference in preference was slightly larger for business students than for managers and changes from the 1970s to 1980s to 1990s showed that women increased their ratings of the importance of four job attributes relative to men. The changes over time suggest that women's aspirations have risen, as they valued challenge more than men in the 1980s and 1990s but not in the 1970s. In the 1970s, men valued opportunities to use their abilities and intrinsic values more than women but in the 1980s and 1990s women managers and business students valued them more than men.

What can we conclude about the preferences of women and men and the role of these preferences in the working environments of women and men? In general, women and men do not differ in their preference for a number of job attributes like the importance of feedback or the number of job openings. Many differences are very small. Overall, it is important to keep in mind that there is generally more variation within sex (that is, among women or among men) than there is between the sexes (that is, differences between men as a group and women as a group) in preferences for various attributes of jobs. In general, the research results suggest that women have been responsive to the greater opportunities in the workplace that they enjoyed in the 1990s relative to the 1970s. Greater opportunities have resulted in higher aspirations among women. The research results further suggest that it is unlikely that sex differences in preference for job attributes adequately explain existing sex segregation of jobs or women's lower status in management relative to men's. [*See* CAREER ACHIEVEMENT.]

VIII. The Effects of Organizational Practices on Women's Work Environments

The Civil Rights Act of 1964 represents the beginning of a series of executive orders, laws, and judicial decisions that have affected working environments in the direction of more equal opportunities for women. One of the broadest and most controversial government programs is affirmative action (AA). Employing organizations that adopt affirmative action establish goals for increasing the numbers of underrepresented groups, including women, and set up policies and procedures for achieving their goals, usually within a given timetable.

As a result of affirmative action, employers have developed many human resource management mechanisms to ensure that equal opportunity occurs. More than 100 different mechanisms have been identified that might assist organizations in reaching affirmative action goals. These different mechanisms can be divided into two types: identity-blind activities and identity-conscious activities. Identity-blind activities include activities such as formal mentoring programs, flextime work schedules, employee assistance programs, and posting of jobs that become available in the firm. These programs are designed to help ensure that people are evaluated and rewarded on the basis of merit under a "veil of ignorance" about one's sex or race.

Identity-conscious activities include those activities that, in addition to other factors, consider one's sex or race. The rationale underlying identity-conscious mechanisms is that gender, race, and national origin should play a part in human resource decisions and may do so for at least three reasons: to remedy current discrimination, to redress past discrimination, and to achieve fair and visible representation in leadership position. Identity-conscious activities include targeting women (or other protected groups) for management development training, establishing a women's interest group in the workplace, and examining salary increases and bonuses for impact on equal pay.

In general, the identity-blind procedures are more common than identity-conscious activities. It is also the case that most people prefer gender-blind to gender-conscious activities, thinking them more fair. Many people misunderstand affirmative action. Identity-conscious activities strike some as preferential treatment that they generally consider unfair. Some consider identity-conscious activities as a form of "reverse discrimination," where the equal opportunity of men (at least White men) is violated.

In an analysis of identity-blind and identity-conscious human resource activities, Alison Konrad and Frank Linnehan found that the identity-blind activities have no noticeable impact on the progress of women (or minorities) in organizations. One reason why this may be so is that it is questionable whether it is possible to truly ignore the race or sex of a person once it is known. It is possible that identity-blind activities are subject to gender (and race) bias and stereotyping. On the other hand, identity-conscious activities were strongly associated with high levels of employment status for women and minorities. Thus, working environments that include activities targeted at women resulted in better outcomes for them.

There is a downside to affirmative action, though. Generally speaking, Americans respond negatively to the term even though they are much less negative about the activities that it entails. Having positive attitudes toward affirmative action is associated with a number of characteristics: being a member of a targeted group, holding antiracist attitudes, espousing liberal views, believing that race and sex discrimination occurs, and believing that affirmative action has desirable effects. Many types of discrimination are not all that easy to detect, so those who feel they have never experienced it find it is easy to believe that it does not exist in a society that claims to reward merit. Thus, women who work in environments where workers hold liberal values and there are other potential beneficiaries of affirmative action are likely to be and feel more supported than women who work in other environments.

Working in an environment where affirmative action is equated with preferential hiring and preferential treatment of women and minorities has negative consequences for women. In short, being viewed as having been selected on the basis of her sex hurts a woman in a variety of ways. Madeline Heilman and her colleagues have thoroughly explored this topic in a series of laboratory and field studies. Stated succinctly, preferential selection is associated with a stigma of incompetence. Women and minorities who are believed to have gotten an assignment or a job because of sex or race are evaluated as less competent than those who are believed to have gotten an assignment or job based on merit.

Besides affecting observers, sex-based preferential selection also affects the woman who believes she is selected on the basis of her sex rather than on her merits. In general, Heilman and her associates find that preferential selection based on sex affects women, but not men. Their studies showed that sex-based preferential selection procedures have detrimental effects on women's self-perceptions and self-evaluations, choice of a demanding versus easier task, and perceived level of stress. In addition, women express more interest in a job when they believed women were in that job because of their merits rather than as a "result of pressure from legal regulations." In contrast to women, preferential selection of men did not affect men's evaluations of their own abilities and it did not affect their behavior.

These sex differences may emerge because women have relatively less self-confidence, especially when it comes to male-typed tasks. But it may also be the case that women have become sensitized to concerns about affirmative action where some equate preferential selection of women and minorities with hiring or promoting people who lack appropriate qualifications. Where women are preferentially selected but were told they were indeed competent on the task prior to being selected, they responded no differently in self-evaluations or task choice than did women selected on the basis of merit.

These studies clearly show the extent to which selection on the basis of sex (or race) can be detrimental to those the preferential selection is intended to help. They also help to explain why some intended beneficiaries of affirmative action are opposed to it. They fear that others will assume they are incompetent and it leads them to question whether they were hired or promoted for their merits or because of their demographic features. It puts them in a position of "stereotype threat." Stereotype threat occurs when people are in a situation in which negative stereotypes apply. Under conditions of stereotype threat, people do tend to perform less well than they would otherwise. In a firm, if women are viewed as too passive to be effective senior managers, then a woman promoted to a senior management position must know that she was promoted on the basis of merit. If she thinks that she was promoted because of her sex, her performance is not likely to be as good as it would be if she believed she was promoted because

of her merits. She may, for example, overcompensate for concerns about being passive and in turn be judged "too aggressive" by her coworkers and supervisors. Furthermore, she is more likely to get more support from others if *they* think she was promoted because of merit, rather than because of her sex.

The data show quite clearly that identity-conscious tactics are more effective than identity-blind ones in increasing the numbers of women and minorities in areas where they were underrepresented. It would appear that to be maximally effective in increasing the representation of women and minorities in positions where they had previously been excluded, it is important to use identity-conscious activities, but to do them in a way that makes it clear to observers and those involved that merit is a strong consideration in activities involving affirmative action. It is important that the affirmative action employee knows that and that others do too. [*See* AFFIRMATIVE ACTION.]

IX. Conclusions

The environment in which they work is important to people. It influences their pay, opportunities for promotion, and how they feel about work. Overall, it influences whether or not women have equal opportunity at work. Most work is sex segregated, horizontally, by job and occupation, and vertically, by level in the hierarchy. In general, fewer jobs are classified as "women's jobs" than "men's jobs" in the sense that women traditionally have been crowded into a very small proportion of all the kinds of jobs that exist. They have furthermore been clustered at the lower-level jobs in organizations. The 1964 Civil Rights Act paved the way for greater integration of women into work environments from which they were previously excluded.

The women who are among the first women in their job or level of the hierarchy are tokens, subject to problematic token dynamics. Although many women leave nontraditional jobs when they change jobs, overall there has been a gradual increase in the proportion of women working in jobs previously held exclusively by men. Many of these jobs are attractive to women because the jobs are interesting, challenging, entail substantial responsibility and respect, pay well, and are paths to other interesting, challenging, responsible jobs that are even more remunerative. Many women encounter work environments that may be deemed "masculinist" and some are downright hostile to them. In the worst cases, the law provides recourse for women who work in hostile work environments. Nevertheless, as opportunities for women have increased, so, it appears, have their aspirations as their job preferences are quite similar to men's, especially among women who are pursuing nontraditional paths as managers or business owners or future managers or business owners.

In response to legal requirements, organizations have instituted a variety of human resource practices that affect working environments. Many of them are gender blind but some are gender conscious. Of the two types, the gender-conscious practices have had a more positive effect on women's opportunities at work. Unfortunately, many Americans oppose many of the gender-conscious strategies in the form of affirmative action. Being an "affirmative action" hire or otherwise being the benefit of what seems to be preferential treatment can, but does not need to, have negative effects on the intended beneficiaries.

SUGGESTED READING

Burn, S. (1996). *The Social Psychology of Gender*. McGraw-Hill, New York.

Cleveland, J. N., Stockdale, M., and Murphy, K. (2000). *Women and Men in Organizations: Sex and Gender Issues at Work*. Erlbaum, Mahwah, NJ.

Northcraft, G., and Gutek, B. A. (1993). Discrimination against women in management: Going, going, gone? or going, but never gone? *Women in Management: Trends, Issues, and Challenges in Managerial Diversity*, a volume in the series, Women and Work, (E. Fagenson, ed.), pp. 219–245. Sage, Newburg Park, CA.

Kanter, R. M. (1977). *Men and Women of the Corporation*. Basic Books, New York.

Konrad, A. M., Ritchie, J. E., Jr., Lieb, P., and Corrigall, E. (2000). Sex differences and similarities in job attribute preferences: A meta-analysis. *Psychological Bulletin* **126**(4), 593–641.

Powell, G. N. (ed.) (2000). *Handbook of Gender and Work*. Sage, Newbury Park, CA.

Tsui, A. S., and Gutek, B. A. (1999). *Demographic Differences in Organizations: Current Research and Future Directions*. Lexington Books, Lanham, MD.

Unger, R. K. (ed.) (2001). *Handbook of the Psychology of Women and Gender*. Wiley, New York.

CONTRIBUTORS

Alisha Ali
EMOTIONAL ABUSE OF WOMEN
University of Toronto and
Clarke Institute of Psychiatry
Toronto M5T 1R8, Canada

Adrienne Asch
DISABILITIES AND WOMEN: DECONSTRUCTING MYTHS AND
RECONSTRUCTING REALITIES
Wellesley College
Wellesley, Massachusetts 02481

Helen S. Astin
ACADEMIC ASPIRATIONS AND DEGREE ATTAINMENT
OF WOMEN
University of California, Los Angeles and
Higher Education Research Institute
Los Angeles, California 90095

Karen J. Bachar
RAPE
University of Arizona
Tucson, Arizona 85719

Nancy Lynn Baker
PREJUDICE
El Granada, California 94018

Rosalind Chait Barnett
WORK–FAMILY BALANCE
Brandeis University
Waltham, Massachusetts 02454

Susan A. Basow
ANDROCENTRISM
Lafayette College
Easton, Pennsylvania 18042

Kristin P. Beals
LESBIANS, GAY MEN, AND BISEXUALS IN RELATIONSHIPS
University of California, Los Angeles
Los Angeles, California 90095

Dana Becker
DIAGNOSIS OF PSYCHOLOGICAL DISORDERS:
DSM AND GENDER
Bryn Mawr Graduate School of Social Work
and Social Research
Bryn Mawr, Pennsylvania 19010

Janet K. Belsky
AGING
Middle Tennessee State University
Murfreesboro, Tennessee 37132

Eric A. Bermann
STRESS AND COPING
University of Michigan
Ann Arbor, Michigan 48109

Deborah Best
CROSS-CULTURAL GENDER ROLES
Wake Forest University
Winston-Salem, North Carolina 27109

Angela Bissada
CHILD ABUSE: PHYSICAL AND SEXUAL
University of Southern California/University Affiliated
Program and
Children's Hospital Los Angeles
Los Angeles, California 90027

Mary M. Brabeck
FEMINIST ETHICS AND MORAL PSYCHOLOGY
Boston College
Chestnut Hill, Massachusetts 02467

Judith S. Bridges
MIDLIFE TRANSITIONS
University of Connecticut at Hartford
West Hartford, Connecticut 06117

John Briere
CHILD ABUSE: PHYSICAL AND SEXUAL
University of Southern California
Los Angeles, California 90033

Phyllis Bronstein
PARENTING
University of Vermont
Burlington, Vermont 05405

Jeanne Brooks-Gunn
ADOLESCENT GENDER DEVELOPMENT
Teachers College, Columbia University
New York, New York 10027

Angela Browne
IMPRISONMENT IN THE UNITED STATES
Harvard School of Public Health and
Harvard Injury Control Research Center
Boston, Massachusetts 02115

Diane Burgermeister
SUBSTANCE ABUSE
Wayne State University
Detroit, Michigan 48202

Shawn P. Cahill
ANXIETY
University of Pennsylvania School of Medicine and
Center for the Treatment and Study of Anxiety
Philadelphia, Pennsylvania 19104

Joanne E. Callan
GENDER DEVELOPMENT: PSYCHOANALYTIC PERSPECTIVES
Alliant University and
San Diego Psychoanalytic Institute
La Jolla, California 92037

Paula J. Caplan
MOTHERHOOD: ITS CHANGING FACE
Brown University
Providence, Rhode Island 02906

Linda Carli
ASSERTIVENESS
Wellesley College
N. Grosvenordale, Connecticut 06255

Molly Carnes
HUMOR
University of Wisconsin
Madison, Wisconsin 53705

Allison Caruthers
MEDIA INFLUENCES
University of Michigan
Ann Arbor, Michigan 48109

Linda L. Collinsworth
SEXUAL HARASSMENT
University of Illinois at Urbana/Champaign
Champaign, Illinois 61820

Mary C. Crawford
METHODS FOR STUDYING GENDER
University of Connecticut
Storrs, Connecticut 06269

Faye Crosby
AFFIRMATIVE ACTION
University of California
Santa Cruz, California 95064

Judith Daniluk
SEXUALITY EDUCATION: WHAT IS IT, WHO GETS IT, AND
DOES IT WORK?
University of British Columbia
Vancouver V6T 1Z4, Canada

Henry P. David
ABORTION AND ITS HEALTH EFFECTS
Transnational Family Research Institute
Bethesda, Maryland 20817

Kay Deaux
SOCIAL IDENTITY
Graduate Center, City University of New York
New York, New York 10016

Anne P. DePrince
RECOVERED MEMORIES
University of Oregon
Eugene, Oregon 97403

Denise M. DeZolt
CLASSROOM AND SCHOOL CLIMATE
University at Albany, State University of New York
Albany, New York 12222

Lisa M. Diamond
SEXUALITY AND SEXUAL DESIRE
University of Utah
Salt Lake City, Utah 84112

Lisa Dinella
GENDER DEVELOPMENT: GENDER SCHEMA THEORY
Arizona State University
Tempe, Arizona 85287

Edward Donnerstein
MEDIA VIOLENCE
University of California
Santa Barbara, California 93106

Lauren E. Duncan
POLITICAL BEHAVIOR
Smith College and Clark Science Center
Northampton, Massachusetts 01063

Alice Eagly
SOCIAL ROLE THEORY OF SEX DIFFERENCES
AND SIMILARITIES
Northwestern University
Evanston, Ilinois 60208

Julie A. Eastin
STRESS AND COPING
University of Michigan
Ann Arbor, Michigan 48109

Jacquelynne S. Eccles
ACHIEVEMENT
University of Michigan
Ann Arbor, Michigan 48109

Carolyn Pope Edwards
PLAY PATTERNS AND GENDER
University of Nebraska-Lincoln
Lincoln, Nebraska 68588

Carolyn Zerbe Enns
FEMINIST THEORIES
Cornell College
Mt. Vernon, Iowa 52314

Jamie Epstein
AGORAPHOBIA, PANIC DISORDER, AND GENDER
New York University
New York, New York 10003

Kimberly M. Estep
EMPATHY AND EMOTIONAL EXPRESSIVITY
University of Houston-Clear Lake
Houston, Texas 77058

Claire A. Etaugh
MIDLIFE TRANSITIONS
Bradley University
Peoria, Illinois 61625

Kristen M. Eyssell
HISTORY OF THE STUDY OF GENDER PSYCHOLOGY
The Pennsylvania State University
University Park, Pennsylvania 16802

Melissa Farley
PROSTITUTION: THE BUSINESS OF SEXUAL EXPLOITATION
Prostitution Research and Education
San Francisco, California 94116

Ruth Fassinger
WOMEN IN NONTRADITIONAL WORK FIELDS
University of Maryland at College Park
College Park, Maryland 20742

Catherine Feuer
POSTTRAUMATIC STRESS DISORDER
Center for Trauma Recovery, University of Missouri,
St. Louis
St. Louis, Missouri 63108

Michelle Fine
DISABILITIES AND WOMEN: DECONSTRUCTING MYTHS
AND RECONSTRUCTING REALITIES
Graduate Center, City University of New York
New York, New York 10016

Louise Fitzgerald
SEXUAL HARASSMENT
University of Illinois at Urbana/Champaign
Champaign, Illinois 61820

Elizabeth H. Flanagan
LEADERSHIP
Auburn University
Auburn, Alabama 36849

Edna B. Foa
ANXIETY
University of Pennsylvania School of Medicine and
Center for the Treatment and Study of Anxiety
Philadelphia, Pennsylvania 19104

Iris Fodor
AGORAPHOBIA, PANIC DISORDER, AND GENDER
New York University
New York, New York 10003

Karen Franklin
HATE CRIMES
California School of Professional Psychology
El Cerrito, California 94530

Jennifer J. Freyd
RECOVERED MEMORIES
University of Oregon
Eugene, Oregon 97403

Cynthia Fuchs Epstein
SEX SEGREGATION IN EDUCATION
CUNY Graduate School and University Center
New York, New York 10036

Deborah Gambs
SEX SEGREGATION IN EDUCATION
CUNY Graduate School and University Center
New York, New York 10036

Pamela W. Garner
EMPATHY AND EMOTIONAL EXPRESSIVITY
University of Houston-Clear Lake
Houston, Texas 77058

Noni K. Gaylord
DIVORCE AND CHILD CUSTODY
University of Memphis
Memphis, Tennessee 38152

Mary Gergen
SOCIAL CONSTRUCTIONIST THEORY
Pennsylvania State University, Delaware County
Media, Pennsylvania 19063

Lucia Albino Gilbert
COUNSELING AND PSYCHOTHERAPY: GENDER, RACE/
ETHNICITY, AND SEXUALITY
University of Texas at Austin
Austin, Texas 78712

Diane L. Gill
SPORT AND ATHLETICS
University of North Carolina at Greensboro
Greensboro, North Carolina 27402

Thelma Jean Goodrich
FEMINIST FAMILY THERAPY
University of Texas-Houston Medical School
Houston, Texas 77030

Julia Graber
ADOLESCENT GENDER DEVELOPMENT
Teachers College, Columbia University
New York, New York 10027

Sandra Graham-Bermann
STRESS AND COPING
University of Michigan
Ann Arbor, Michigan 48109

Jessica L. Griffin
FRIENDSHIP STYLES
Virginia Consortium Program in Clinical Psychology
Virginia Beach, Virginia 23462

Barbara Gutek
WORKING ENVIRONMENTS
University of Arizona
Tucson, Arizona 85721

Diane Halpern
SEX DIFFERENCE RESEARCH: COGNITIVE ABILITIES
California State University, San Bernardino
San Bernardino, California 92407

Mykol C. Hamilton
SEX-RELATED DIFFERENCE RESEARCH: PERSONALITY
Centre College
Danville, Kentucky 40422

Melanie S. Harned
SEXUAL HARASSMENT
University of Illinois at Urbana/Champaign
Champaign, Illinois 61820

Michele Harway
MENTORING AND FEMINIST MENTORING
Phillips Graduate Institute
Encino, California 91316

Susan Hendrick
INTIMACY AND LOVE
Texas Tech University
Lubbock, Texas 79409

Candace Hill
CHILD CARE: OPTIONS AND OUTCOMES
Temple University
Philadelphia, Pennsylvania 19122

Kathy Hirsh-Pasek
CHILD CARE: OPTIONS AND OUTCOMES
Temple University
Philadelphia, Pennsylvania 19122

Patrick Hudgins
TRAUMA ACROSS DIVERSE SETTINGS
Old Dominion University
Norfolk, Virginia 23529

Stephen H. Hull
CLASSROOM AND SCHOOL CLIMATE
University at Albany, State University of New York
Albany, New York 12222

Aída Hurtado
MEDIA STEREOTYPES
University of California, Santa Cruz
Santa Cruz, California 95064

Janet Shibley Hyde
GENDER DIFFERENCE RESEARCH: ISSUES AND CRITIQUE
SELF-ESTEEM
University of Wisconsin-Madison
Madison, Wisconsin 53706

Dana Crowley Jack
ANGER
Western Washington University
Bellingham, Washington 98225

Rosemary Jadack
SEXUALLY TRANSMITTED INFECTIONS AND THEIR
CONSEQUENCES
University of Wisconsin-Eau Claire
Eau Claire, Wisconsin 54701

Deana Jefferson
POSTTRAUMATIC STRESS DISORDER
Center for Trauma Recovery, University of Missouri,
St. Louis
St. Louis, Missouri 63121

Dawn M. Johnson
FEMINIST APPROACHES TO PSYCHOTHERAPY
University of Kentucky
Lexington, Kentucky 40506

Anne S. Kahn
ENTITLEMENT
Derner Institute and Adelphi University
Garden City, New York 11530

Jeffrey A. Kelly
SAFER SEX BEHAVIORS
Medical College of Wisconsin
Milwaukee, Wisconsin 53202

Cathy Kessel
TEST BIAS
University of California, Berkeley
Berkeley, California 94720

M. Marlyne Kilbey
SUBSTANCE ABUSE
Wayne State University
Detroit, Michigan 48202

Ellen B. Kimmel
METHODS FOR STUDYING GENDER
University of South Florida
Tampa, Florida 33620

Mary Kite
GENDER STEREOTYPES
Ball State University
Muncie, Indiana 47306

Katherine M. Kitzmann
DIVORCE AND CHILD CUSTODY
University of Memphis
Memphis, Tennessee 38152

Kristen C. Kling
SELF-ESTEEM
St. Cloud State University
Rogers, Minnesota 55374

Elizabeth A. Klonoff
HEALTH AND HEALTH CARE: HOW GENDER
MAKES WOMEN SICK
San Diego State University
San Diego, California 92120

Lisa Knoche
PLAY PATTERNS AND GENDER
University of Nebraska-Lincoln
Lincoln, Nebraska 68588

Mary P. Koss
RAPE
University of Arizona
Tucson, Arizona 85719

Diane Kravetz
THE FEMINIST MOVEMENT
University of Wisconsin-Madison
Madison, Wisconsin 53706

Asiye Kumru
PLAY PATTERNS AND GENDER
University of Nebraska-Lincoln
Lincoln, Nebraska 68588

Hope Landrine
HEALTH AND HEALTH CARE: HOW GENDER
MAKES WOMEN SICK
San Diego State University
La Mesa, California 91941

Ellie Lee
ABORTION AND ITS HEALTH EFFECTS
University of Sussex
London NW8 OHP, United Kingdom

Ronald F. Levant
MEN AND MASCULINITY
Nova Southeastern University
Ft. Lauderdale, Florida 33314

Erika Lichter
IMPRISONMENT IN THE UNITED STATES
Harvard School of Public Health and
Harvard Injury Control Research Center
Boston, Massachusetts 02115

Jennifer A. Lindholm
ACADEMIC ASPIRATIONS AND DEGREE ATTAINMENT
OF WOMEN
University of California, Los Angeles and
Higher Education Research Institute
Los Angeles, California 90095

Marcia C. Linn
TEST BIAS
University of California, Berkeley
Berkeley, California 94720

Hilary M. Lips
POWER: SOCIAL AND INTERPERSONAL ASPECTS
Radford University
Blacksburg, Virginia 24060

Bernice Lott
GENDER DEVELOPMENT: SOCIAL LEARNING
University of Rhode Island
Kingston, Rhode Island 02881

M. Brinton Lykes
INDIVIDUALISM AND COLLECTIVISM
University of the Witwatersrand
Johannesburg, South Africa

Sonja Lyubomirsky
LIFE SATISFACTION
University of California, Riverside
Riverside, California 92521

Diane Maluso
GENDER DEVELOPMENT: SOCIAL LEARNING
Elmira College
Elmira, New York 14901

Jeanne Marecek
THE FEMINIST MOVEMENT
Swarthmore College
Swarthmore, Pennsylvania 19081

Carol Lynn Martin
GENDER DEVELOPMENT: GENDER SCHEMA THEORY
Arizona State University
Tempe, Arizona 85287

Vanessa L. McGann
ENTITLEMENT
Derner Institute and Adelphi University
Garden City, New York 11530

Kayce L. Meginnis-Payne
BEAUTY POLITICS AND PATRIARCHY: THE IMPACT ON
    WOMEN'S LIVES
Peace College
Raleigh, North Carolina 27608

Amy H. Mezulis
GENDER DIFFERENCE RESEARCH: ISSUES AND CRITIQUE
University of Wisconsin-Madison
Madison, Wisconsin 53706

Audrey Murrell
CAREER ACHIEVEMENT: OPPORTUNITIES AND BARRIERS
University of Pittsburgh and
Katz Graduate School of Business
Pittsburgh, Pennsylvania 15260

Virginia E. O'Leary
LEADERSHIP
Auburn University
Auburn, Alabama 36849

Lucia F. O'Sullivan
ADOLESCENT GENDER DEVELOPMENT
Columbia University
New York, New York 10032

Clifton Oyamot
SELF-FULFILLING PROPHESIES
University of Minnesota
Minneapolis, Minnesota 55455

Sandra Pacheco
MEDIA STEREOTYPES
California State University, Monterey Bay
Seaside, California 93955

Letitia Anne Peplau
LESBIANS, GAY MEN, AND BISEXUALS IN RELATIONSHIPS
University of California, Los Angeles
Los Angeles, California 90095

Tiffany Perkins
DISABILITIES AND WOMEN: DECONSTRUCTING MYTHS
    AND RECONSTRUCTING REALITIES
Graduate Center, City University of New York
New York, New York 10016

Niva Piran
EATING DISORDERS AND DISORDERED EATING
University of Toronto
Toronto M5S 1V6, Canada

Ken Pope
SEX BETWEEN THERAPISTS AND CLIENTS
TORTURE
Norwalk, Connecticut 06851

Dongxiao Qin
INDIVIDUALISM AND COLLECTIVISM
University of the Witwatersrand
Johannesburg, South Africa

Kathryn Quina
RECOVERED MEMORIES
University of Rhode Island
Kingston, Rhode Island 02881

Jill Rader
COUNSELING AND PSYCHOTHERAPY: GENDER, RACE/
    ETHNICITY, AND SEXUALITY
University of Texas at Austin
Austin, Texas 78712

Nancy Reame
MENSTRUATION
The University of Michigan
Ann Arbor, Michigan 48109

Pamela Trotman Reid
ACADEMIC ENVIRONMENTS: GENDER AND ETHNICITY IN
    U.S. HIGHER EDUCATION
University of Michigan
Ann Arbor, Michigan 48109

Carmen L. Regan
PREGNANCY
Hospital of the University of Pennsylvania
Philadelphia, Pennsylvania 19104

Patricia Resick
POSTTRAUMATIC STRESS DISORDER
Center for Trauma Recovery, University of Missouri,
    St. Louis
St. Louis, Missouri 63121

Tracey Revenson
CHRONIC ILLNESS ADJUSTMENT
The Graduate Center of the City University of New York
New York, New York 10012

Joy Rice
FAMILY ROLES AND PATTERNS, CONTEMPORARY TRENDS
University of Wisconsin, Madison
Madison, Wisconsin 53705

Karen Rook
SOCIAL SUPPORT
University of California, Irvine
Irvine, California 92697

Harilyn Rousso
DISABILITIES AND WOMEN: DECONSTRUCTING MYTHS AND RECONSTRUCTING REALITIES
Disabilities Unlimited Consulting Services
New York, New York 10003

Janis Sanchez-Hucles
TRAUMA ACROSS DIVERSE SETTINGS
Old Dominion University
Norfolk, Virginia 23529

Anmol Satiani
FEMINIST ETHICS AND MORAL PSYCHOLOGY
Boston College
Chestnut Hill, MA 02467

Diane Scott-Jones
REPRODUCTIVE TECHNOLOGIES
Boston College
Chestnut Hill, Massachusetts 02467

Stephanie A. Shields
HISTORY OF THE STUDY OF GENDER PSYCHOLOGY
The Pennsylvania State University
University Park, Pennsylvania 16802

Louise B. Silverstein
FEMINIST FAMILY THERAPY
Yeshiva University
Brooklyn, New York 11201

Ada Sinacore
FEMINIST THEORIES
McGill University
Montreal H3A 1Y2, Canada

Sirinda Sincharoen
AFFIRMATIVE ACTION
University of California, Santa Cruz
Santa Cruz, California 95062

Linda Smolak
BODY IMAGE CONCERNS
Kenyon College
Gambier, Ohio 43022

Mark Snyder
SELF-FULFILLING PROPHESIES
University of Minnesota
Minneapolis, Minnesota 55455

Barbara Sommer
MENOPAUSE
University of California, Davis
Davis, California 95616

Lorie A'lise Sousa
LIFE SATISFACTION
University of California, Riverside
Riverside, California 92521

Janice Steil
ENTITLEMENT
Derner Institute and Adelphi University
Garden City, New York 11530

Janice Steil
MARRIAGE: STILL "HIS" AND "HERS"?
Institute of Advanced Psychological Study and Adelphi University
Garden City, New York 11530

Linda R. Stoler
RECOVERED MEMORIES
University of Rhode Island
Kingston, Rhode Island 02881

Ruth Striegel-Moore
BODY IMAGE CONCERNS
Wesleyan University
Middletown, Connecticut 06459

Ethel Tobach
DEVELOPMENT OF SEX AND GENDER: BIOCHEMISTRY, PHYSIOLOGY, AND EXPERIENCE
American Museum of Natural History and The City University of New York
New York, New York 10024

Deborah L. Tolman
SEXUALITY AND SEXUAL DESIRE
Wellesley College Center for Research on Women
Wellesley, Massachusetts 02481

Brenda Toner
EMOTIONAL ABUSE OF WOMEN
University of Toronto and Clarke Institute of Psychiatry
Toronto M5T 1R8, Canada

Kristina Towill
SEXUALITY EDUCATION: WHAT IS IT, WHO GETS IT, AND DOES IT WORK?
University of British Columbia
Burnaby V5H 4R4, Canada

Cheryl Brown Travis
BEAUTY POLITICS AND PATRIARCHY: THE IMPACT ON
  WOMEN'S LIVES
GENDER DEVELOPMENT: EVOLUTIONARY PERSPECTIVES
  University of Tennessee
  Knoxville, Tennessee 37996

Lenore Walker
BATTERING IN ADULT RELATIONSHIPS
  Nova Southeastern University and
  Center for Psychological Studies
  Ft. Lauderdale, Florida 33314

L. Monique Ward
MEDIA INFLUENCES
  University of Michigan
  Ann Arbor, Michigan 48109

Marsha Weinraub
CHILD CARE: OPTIONS AND OUTCOMES
  Temple University
  Philadelphia, Pennsylvania 19122

Patricia Whelehan
CROSS-CULTURAL SEXUAL PRACTICES
  SUNY Potsdam
  Potsdam, New York 13676

Valerie Whiffen
DEPRESSION
  University of Ottawa
  Ottawa K1N 6N5, Canada

Jacquelyn W. White
AGGRESSION AND GENDER
  University of North Carolina at Greensboro
  Greensboro, North Carolina 27412

Barbara Winstead
FRIENDSHIP STYLES
  Old Dominion University
  Norfolk, Virginia 23529

Judith Worell
FEMINIST APPROACHES TO PSYCHOTHERAPY
  University of Kentucky
  Lexington, Kentucky 40506

Karen Fraser Wyche
POVERTY AND WOMEN IN THE UNITED STATES
  New York University
  New York, New York 10003

Janice D. Yoder
MILITARY WOMEN
  University of Akron
  Akron, Ohio 44325

Sue Rosenberg Zalk
ACADEMIC ENVIRONMENTS: GENDER AND ETHNICITY IN
  U.S. HIGHER EDUCATION
  Graduate Center, City University of New York
  New York, New York 10016

AUTHOR INDEX

A

Abel, G., 225, 231
Abraham, K., 881, 890
Abrams, D., 1067
Abrams, K., 113
Abramson, L. Y., 306, 314
Adams, J., 782
Adler, N. E., 10, 14
Adrian, J., 1127
Agarwal, K., 280
Aggleton, P., 302, 1031
Aida, Y., 852
Alberti, R. E., 158, 168
Alberts, B., 332
Alcoff, L., 474
Alexander, C. M., 277
Alexander, E. R., 1041
Ali, A., 145, 379, 390
Allen, M., 161, 691, 701
Allison, D., 787
Allport, G., 869
Allsworth, J., 123
Almeida, R., 453
Alpern, K. D., 931
Altabe, M., 210, 378
Altman, B., 348
Altmann, J., 501
Amato, P. R., 361, 367
Ambrose, S. A., 1180
Anda, R. F., 1121, 1126
Andersen, S., 950
Anderson, C., 450
Anderson, E. A., 939
Anderson, K. J., 808
Anderson, L. R., 1126
Anderson, M., 754
Andreski, P., 1126
Andrews, B., 307
Andrews, L., 833
Anthony, J. C., 1118, 1126

Antony, M. M., 156
Apfelbaum, E., 856
Aral, S. O., 1041
Araujo, K., 64
Arbreton, A., 53
Arcana, J., 784
Argyle, M., 676
Aries, E., 163, 484, 650, 656
Aristotle, 594
Armstrong, S., 592
Arneil, B., 480
Arnold, K. D., 53
Asch, A., 345, 352, 354
Astin, H. S., 15
Auerbach, C. F., 133, 135
Aukett, R., 483
Ault-Riche, M., 450
Austad, S., 107
Austin, J., 616
Averill, J., 138, 139, 140
Ayers, M., 487
Azar, B., 1111

B

Babey, S. H., 944
Bachar, K. J., 893, 903
Bacon, F., 674, 1047
Bacon, M., 285, 286, 806
Bailey, M. M., 650
Bailyn, L., 1189, 1190
Bakan, D., 1071
Baker, D., 1067
Baker, N. L., 865
Baldo, M., 1031
Baldwin, J., 1030
Baldwin, M. A., 888, 890
Balswick, J., 161
Banaji, M., 564

Banaji, M. R., 968, 971
Bandura, A., 27, 441, 538, 540, 541,
    547, 548, 549, 690, 694, 851
Bandyopadhyay, S., 890
Banjo, M. L., 950, 952
Banks, W. P., 917
Banyard, V. L., 844, 1111
Baral, I., 890
Barber, B., 47, 52
Bardari, K., 200
Barenbaum, N., 851
Barkan, H., 890
Barlow, D. H., 123
Barnard, M., 890, 891
Barnartt, S., 348
Barnett, O. W., 178, 181, 188
Barnett, R. C., 52, 276, 277, 652, 654,
    723, 1181, 1189
Barr, L., 944
Barreca, R., 604, 605, 609
Barrera, M., 1084
Barry, H., 285, 286, 806
Barry, K., 890, 890
Barth, R., 1031
Barton, A., 1162
Baruch, G. K., 52, 652
Basow, S. A., 125, 135, 570
Bates, C. M., 962
Baum, A., 254
Baumeister, R. F., 553, 554, 634, 643,
    944, 1075
Bausch, S., 845
Beale, F., 466
Beall, A. E., 570
Bealls, A., 605
Beals, K. P., 657
Beard, M. R., 605
Bearman, P., 66
Bebbington, P., 308, 310, 314
Bebeau, M. J., 446
Beck, A., 110, 118, 614

SUBJECT INDEX

E

Q

ISBN 0-12-227247-1